A History of Latin America

9/22

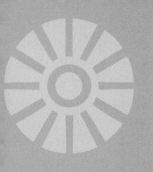

A History of Latin America

SEVENTH EDITION

Benjamin Keen

Keith Haynes

The College of Saint Rose

Houghton Mifflin Company   Boston   New York

Publisher: Charles Hartford
Editor in Chief: Jean L. Woy
Senior Sponsoring Editor: Sally Constable
Development Editor: Leah R. Strauss
Senior Project Editor: Christina M. Horn
Senior Production/Design Coordinator: Jodi O'Rourke
Senior Designer: Henry Rachlin
Senior Manufacturing Coordinator: Marie Barnes
Senior Marketing Manager: Sandra McGuire

Cover image: Frida Kahlo (1907–1954), *El Camión* (The Bus), 1929. Oil on canvas. Fundación Dolores Olmedo, Mexico City, D.F., Mexico. © Banco de México Trust/Schalkwijk/Art Resource, NY.

Text credits: On pages 73–74, approximately 200 words from a letter written by Lope de Aguirre to Philip II of Spain, translated by Thomas Holloway. Reprinted by permission.

Printed in the U.S.A.

Library of Congress Control Number: 2002109494

ISBN: 0-618-31851-8

7 8 9-FFG-10 09 08 07

CONTENTS

MAPS

PREFACE

THE SEVENTH EDITION of *A History of Latin America* has two major objectives. First, it seeks to make available to teachers and students of Latin American history a text based on the best recent scholarship, enriched with data and concepts drawn from the sister social sciences of economics, anthropology, and sociology. Because the book is a history of Latin American *civilization,* it devotes considerable space to the way of life adopted at each period of the region's history. To enable students to deepen their knowledge of Latin American history and culture on their own, it includes an updated bibliography, "Suggestions for Further Reading," limited to titles in English.

The second objective of this edition is to set Latin American history within a broad interpretive framework. This framework is the "dependency theory," the most influential theoretical model for social scientists concerned with understanding Latin America. Not all followers of the theory understand it in precisely the same way, but most probably agree with the definition of *dependency* offered by the Brazilian scholar Theotonio dos Santos: "A situation in which the economy of certain countries is conditioned by the development and expansion of another economy to which the former is subject."

Writers of the dependency school employ some standard terms that we use in this text: *neocolonialism, neoliberalism, center,* and *periphery.* *Neocolonialism* refers to the dependent condition of countries that enjoy formal political independence. *Neoliberalism* refers to the policies of privatization, austerity, and trade liberalization accepted willingly or unwillingly by the governments of dependent countries as a condition of approval of investment, loans, and debt relief by the International Monetary Fund and the World Bank. (The IMF and the World Bank prefer to give such policies the innocuous-sounding name of "structural adjustment programs.") The term *center* is applied to the dominant group of developed capitalist countries, and *periphery* to the underdeveloped or dependent countries.

Periodically, dependency theory has come under attack from scholars, mostly North American, who announce its "collapse." The most recent announcements of dependency theory's "collapse" have been linked to the seeming triumph of neoliberal ideology and its creation, the so-called global economy. Claiming that the neoliberal tide can lift all ships, including the countries of Latin America and the rest of the Third World, and pointing for proof in the case of Latin America to such macroeconomic indicators as increased exports (often based on intense exploitation of finite natural resources and subject to sudden changes in price and demand) and large inflows of foreign capital (often speculative and volatile), these critics argue that dependency theory was basically flawed and outmoded, that its analysis of Latin America's problems has lost all meaning in today's world.

Those who reject the dependency approach typically favor one of a number of alternative paradigms for explaining Latin America's historical struggle for development. Among these scholars, modernization theory informed and dominated discussions in the United States and Western Europe in the first decades following World War II.

Drawing upon their own postwar national experiences, these theorists typically assumed that "underdevelopment" and "economic backwardness" were conditions common to all societies at one time in their evolution. The key to unlocking the mystery of development, for these scholars, was to study conditions in the "developed countries" in contrast to those in "tropical" or undeveloped areas. This produced a prescription for social, political, cultural, and economic change that sought to bring the developmental benefits of modernity to all. As a result of their studies, the modernizationists concluded that the undeveloped world suffered from a lack of personal freedom, excessive government regulation, highly politicized states, weak civil societies, a shortage of "entrepreneurial values," and the survival of powerful "antimodern" cultural traditions that stressed cooperative communal, rather than competitive individualistic, values.

For the modernization theorists, then, Latin America's "failure" to develop was largely a consequence of its own internal problems and its reluctance to open itself to the forces of modernity that allegedly emanated from Western Europe and the United States. Some authors even suggested that this "failure" was the product of a "distinct tradition" in Latin America, informed by a historical legacy of militarism, local political bosses (*caudillaje*), indigenous communalism, and insular Iberic Catholic culture. To combat these alleged deficiencies in the developmental experiences of Latin America, the modernizationists prescribed a bitter medicine that largely mirrored what recently have come to be known as neoliberal imperatives: dismantle state bureaucracies, reduce budget deficits, cut spending on social services, deregulate private business, privatize national resources, provide incentives to foreign investors, promote free trade, encourage entrepreneurial education, and reduce the political power of "antimodern" social sectors.

But a rapid glance at the results of over a decade of application of neoliberal therapy to Latin America's problems suggests that in all essential respects, the area's economic and social crisis has worsened and its dependency on the core capitalist powers has deepened. We draw upon a critical synthesis of these two intellectual traditions and emphasize both internal and external factors that have shaped Latin America's historical struggle for development. We expose the developmentalist myths that all countries have been equally "underdeveloped" in their historical past and that the "developed countries" achieved modernity by promoting personal freedom, free trade, and unfettered foreign direct investment. On the contrary, the text unambiguously shows that European and U.S. modernity was built upon a five-century legacy of brutal conquest, enslavement, exploitation, and unequal trade enforced alternately by military and market coercion. Moreover, unlike classical dependency theorists, who emphasized transnational social forces and institutional structures of power that seemingly rendered inconsequential all forms of popular resistance, this text documents the powerful role that internal class, racial, gender, ethnic, and interest group struggles have played in shaping the region's development.

Unlike both classical dependency and modernizationist formulations, this text's "revised dependency" approach also draws upon recent feminist theorization that defines women as the "last colony," whose shared experiences, according to feminist scholars Christine Bose and Edna Acosta-Belén, include unwaged and low-wage labor, extreme poverty, and "structural subordination and dependency." But women, like colonial peoples more generally, have not been passive victims in the developmental process. They have been active in the spheres of both production and reproduction. As producers of material wealth in Latin America, women have played a significant, but largely neglected, historical role, working endless hours without pay in household activities that have been an essential source of private capital accumulation. For example, even an inefficient colonial workforce needed certain household services—shopping, cooking, cleaning, first aid, child-rearing, washing, elder care, and so on—in order to reproduce its labor on a daily basis. If poorly paid male workers in Latin America had had to purchase these services that women—wives and daughters—freely provided, they would have had to insist upon higher wages and employers would have had to pay these higher costs out of profits.

Historically, women were largely confined to the family household, where they were responsible for reproduction, rearing, nurturing, and educating the next generation of producers. Once "freed" from these constraints to seek employment in the marketplace, however, many working-class women became doubly exploited, first as poorly paid wage earners whose collective hard work outside the home produced great value that enriched their employers, and second as traditional unwaged household labor that sustained working-class families as the bedrock of classical capital accumulation. This text both highlights the transition of women's roles in Latin America and documents women's demand for state regulation of market activities to protect their developmental contributions in the vital areas of production and reproduction.

Like classical dependency writers who originally blamed global markets for Latin America's poverty and doubted the region's developmental potential in the absence of socialism, we conclude that market expansion has created economic growth at the expense of development. But unlike these classical dependency theorists, we stress the key role of popular social movements in taming markets, restraining inequities produced by their unregulated activities, and transforming them into agents of development. Contrary to modernizationists who argued that market expansion was key to development, this text shows that markets in and of themselves have been far less important than how they have been regulated. The specific nature of these regulations, in turn, has been shaped by historical struggles. In socialist Cuba, for example, the expansion of market activities since the collapse of the Soviet Union and its global trading partners has had a decidedly different developmental impact than it has had in neoliberal Argentina or Peru. Similarly, global markets have been regulated differently in Chile, Venezuela, and Brazil, with correspondingly different developmental impacts. Our text documents these conclusions in historical detail, but here we present a few telling facts that underline the general collapse of the neoliberal, modernizationist model and simultaneously reinforce the relevance of our revised dependency perspective.

First, since the early 1980s, when neoliberal orthodoxy emerged as the dominant paradigm for promoting development in Latin America, this region, in effect, has subsidized wealthy industrial nations. During this period, Latin American nations claimed smaller shares of the world's income as the U.S. share grew. According to the *Atlas of Global Inequality* compiled at the University of California at Santa Cruz, the national income of the United States as a percentage of the global mean average national income doubled between 1980 and 1999, while it declined for every single Latin American country, with two types of exceptions: those countries like Haiti and Honduras, whose national incomes in 1980 already ranked at the lowest level, and those like Panama, Colombia, and the Dominican Republic, whose rank remained unchanged. According to Mexican economic historian Carlos Marichal, since 1980 Mexico alone has paid almost $300 billion in foreign debt service on an original loan of $100 billion.

Second, poverty and inequality within each of the countries in the region either have remained stubbornly high or have grown. Recent estimates in 2002 suggest that more than 200 million Latin Americans live below the poverty line. Even the World Bank, a relentless and enthusiastic champion of neoliberalism, acknowledges that its prescription for national development has not solved the problem of poverty, which it conservatively estimated at affecting 159 million people in 1998, an increase over the 1987 figure of 148 million. Extreme poverty, according to the Economic Commission on Latin America, grew even more steadily from 36 million people in 1980 to 74.5 million in 1995. Even more significant than this decade-long growth in poverty was the stark inequality that the World Bank reported in its *World Development Indicators* for 2002: on average, the poorest 20 percent of the region's population received only 3.5 percent of their country's income, while the richest 10 percent claimed 40 percent of their nation's wealth.

Third, the region is more dependent on foreigners than ever before in its history. External debt in 1980 almost doubled from $257.3 billion to $475.4 billion in 1990, and then it grew by another 70 percent to $813.4 billion in 1999. During the same period, debt service as a percentage of revenues from exports increased dramatically from 34.4 to 41.8 percent, which meant that out of every $1 earned in export sales, Latin America sent 42¢ to foreign bankers. Foreign export trade dependency also grew. From 1980 to 1990, Latin American exports grew at 4.3 percent per year, but they rose to 15 percent per year in the decade ending in 2000. Moreover, the export-oriented nature of neoliberal development strategies reinforced the region's traditional reliance on a few largely agricultural and mineral raw materials. With the exception of Mexico, all Latin American nations depended on one or two products for 40 percent of their export revenues. Reliance on foreign imports also increased faster than export growth, rising from an average annual rate of 2.1 percent in the 1980s to 17.3 percent in the 1990s. The resulting trade imbalances, combined with other hidden costs of trade, produced dramatically larger deficits in Latin America's current account balance, which skyrocketed from $1.1 billion in 1990 to $46.8 billion in 2000.

Fourth, unemployment, underemployment, and precarious, low-income "informal sector" employment all increased steadily throughout the region, making it virtually impossible for working families to subsist on a single income. Even the World Bank's conservative official estimates show that regional unemployment grew each year from a low of 6 percent in 1990 to a high of 9.2 percent in 1999. Moreover, neoliberal policies that increased unemployment forced women to enter the wage force at significantly higher rates, to prevent their families from falling below the poverty line. By 1995 women constituted 44.5 percent of the paid labor force. Women who were not heads of households contributed from 25 to 35 percent of household income. But the number of female heads of households also rose by 2 to 5 percent throughout the 1990s, and these women, according to a 1995 ECLA report, "experience higher rates of unemployment, lower numbers of hours worked, lower salaries and greater difficulties in entering the market than do male heads of household."

Fifth, political violence and disillusionment with democracy have grown dramatically, along with popular disrespect for politicians who preach electoral populism and practice neoliberal governance. According to a respected Chilean public opinion pollster, Latinobarómetro, popular support for democracy over the past five years has declined in every country except Mexico. In Argentina, it fell from 71 percent in 2000 to 58 percent in 2001; in Venezuela, support declined only modestly from 61 to 57 percent, in part due to the popularity of Hugo Chávez, the populist paratrooper elected to the presidency in 1998. More people now trust the military (39 percent) than political parties (19 percent), parliament (22 percent), or the judiciary (26 percent). Even more striking, the percentage of people who feel trust in their fellow citizens has fallen steadily in every country except Mexico and Nicaragua.

Sixth and finally, these changes were not the result of economic recession but occurred in the context of substantial economic growth largely fueled by the region's close ties to U.S. markets, which experienced a decade of unprecedented prosperity. With the exception of significant declines in 1994 and 1997, Latin America benefited from a decade of generally strong global economic expansion. After a comparatively anemic increase of 43 percent from 1980 to 1990, the region's average gross national product nearly doubled from 1990 to 2000. Perhaps the most striking of these facts is this: dramatic economic growth in the 1990s bequeathed a legacy of social inequality and political disenchantment.

Meanwhile, the deepening Latin American dependency has assumed a more sinister form. The drug traffic to the United States and Europe has virtually become the life support system of the economies of Bolivia, Colombia, and Peru, and its influence, as recent revelations show, has reached into the highest levels of officialdom in countries like Colombia and Mexico. Another symptom of growing dependency, directly linked to the impact of neoliberal policies on the Mexican economy, is the swelling flood of illegal immigrants seeking to cross the U.S.-Mexican border and the violence inherent in U.S. policies designed to prevent this immigration, such as Operation Gatekeeper. According to a study by the University of Houston, "Death at the Border," from 1993 to 1996 nearly 1,200 immigrants died while attempting to cross the U.S.-Mexican border. In the light of these and other compelling facts, it appears that dependency theory continues to have a large relevance for Latin America. It remains, in the words of Professor Peter Evans, "one of the primary lenses through which both Latin American and North American scholars analyze the interaction of classes and the state in the context of an increasingly internationalized economy."

A number of events provides compelling evidence of a crisis of the "global economy" project and the neoliberal theory on which it rests. An economic storm, beginning in the Far East in 1997, left the economies of Indonesia, South Korea, and other "Asian tigers" in ruins, spread to Russia, and deeply affected Latin America. Countries such as Brazil, Argentina, Chile, Venezuela, Mexico, and Colombia, which had commercial ties with Asian markets, suffered sharp declines in the prices of their raw material exports. Michel Camdessus, the IMF's managing director, himself described the situation as "the crisis of a system." The famed financier George Soros proclaimed "the crisis of global capitalism." The board of directors of the International Forum on Globalization drew its own conclusion: "After more than 50 years of this experiment, it is breaking down. Rather than leading to economic benefits for all people, it has brought the planet to the brink of environmental and social catastrophe. The experiment has failed" (*New York Times*, Nov. 24, 1998).

In the early twenty-first century, a growing popular movement in the region appeared to share this assessment. Argentina's economy, which never really recovered from the 1997 global crisis, unceremoniously collapsed in 2001, unleashing wage reductions of more than 20 percent, unemployment rates that approached 25 percent, unprecedented poverty, rapidly rising prices, and a torrent of general strikes, urban riots, and looting that forced a succession of presidents to resign. To stem the hemorrhaging, a new interim president, Eduardo Duhalde, denounced his predecessors'

free-market policies and pledged to create a "new model" of development based on an "alliance between labor and domestic industries." Although less violent, Peruvians likewise protested the neoliberal reforms implemented by Alejandro Toledo, the nation's first president of indigenous descent, who received a Ph.D. in economics from Stanford University. General strikes and weekly protests against Toledo's efforts to privatize state companies led to rapidly deteriorating popular support, which, according to the Peruvian pollster *Apoyo*, plunged to less than 14 percent in 2003. Brazilians similarly endorsed a new strategy for development. The perennial candidate of the democratic socialist left, Lula da Silva, who had consistently resisted the neoliberal agenda during the 1990s, won a landslide victory in the 2002 presidential elections with 61 percent of the vote. In Ecuador in the same year, a coalition of workers, women, students, and indigenous peoples elected populist president Lucio Gutiérrez. In Venezuela, however, a popular movement joined forces with loyal soldiers to reverse a military coup organized and led by Pedro Carmona, wealthy businessman and president of the National Chamber of Commerce. Carmona had opposed the charismatic, democratically elected populist president, Hugo Chávez, whose efforts to redistribute national wealth alienated Venezuelan elites, international bankers, and the U.S. State Department alike.

A word about the organization of this text. In the book's planning, the decision was made to reject the approach that tries to cover the postindependence history of the twenty Latin American republics in detail, including mention of every general who ever passed through a presidential palace. Most teachers will agree that this approach discourages students by miring them in a bog of tedious facts. Accordingly, it was decided to limit coverage of the national period in the nineteenth century to Mexico, Argentina, Chile, and Brazil, whose history seemed to illustrate best the major issues and trends of the period. In addition to covering these four countries, the survey of the twentieth century broadened to include the central Andean area, with a special concentration on Peru, and Cuba, the scene of a socialist revolution with continental repercussions.

The Second Edition added a chapter on Central America, where a revolutionary storm, having toppled the U.S.-unsupported Somoza tyranny in Nicaragua, threatened the rickety structures of oligarchical and military rule in El Salvador and Guatemala. The Fourth Edition recognized the political and economic importance of the Bolivarian lands of Venezuela and Colombia by including a chapter on the modern history of those countries. The current Seventh Edition more fully integrates the discussion of the Andean and Central American regions, Cuba, and the Bolivian republics into the text's original layout. Chapters 9 and 10, for example, now examine these nations' nineteenth-century histories, along with those of Mexico, Argentina, Chile, and Peru. Because teachers rarely have time to cover all Latin American countries in their survey classes, this organization provides greater flexibility, without sacrificing historical continuity, as instructors select those nations upon which they wish their students to focus.

To accommodate alternative course configurations, *A History of Latin America* continues to be published in two volumes as well as in a complete version. Volume 1 includes Latin American history from ancient times to 1910, and Volume 2 covers Latin American history from independence to the present.

Last, the recent history of all the countries under discussion has been brought up to date, and the rest of the book has been thoroughly revised to reflect current scholarship, particularly the respective roles of race, class, and gender in the region's historical development. Special emphasis is placed on such topics as the impact of neoliberal economic policies and the gathering revolt against them, the effects of the North American Free Trade Agreement, the growing urgency of environmental issues, the heightened visibility of the women's movement, and the significance of popular culture.

The book has also benefited from the careful scrutiny of the Sixth Edition by colleagues who made valuable suggestions for revision:

Julia E. Rodriguez, University of New Hampshire
William Schell, Jr., Murray State University
Michael Snodgrass, Indiana University Purdue University–Indianapolis
Karen Sundwick, Southern Oregon University
Ernest S. Sweeney, Loyola Marymount University

Many but not all of these colleagues' suggestions were adopted; these individuals bear no responsibility for any remaining errors of fact or interpretation. We also want to acknowledge a special debt of gratitude to Professor Asunción Lavrín who graciously shared her photo archive on Latin American feminism. We wish to recall, too, the many students, graduate and undergraduate, who helped us to define our views on Latin American history through the give-and-take of classroom discussion and the reading and discussion of their papers and theses.

Benjamin Keen
Keith Haynes

INTRODUCTION

The Geographical Background of Latin American History

L ATIN AMERICA, a region of startling physical contrasts, stretches 7,000 miles southward from the Mexican-U.S. border to the tip of Tierra del Fuego on Cape Horn. The widest east-west point, across Peru and Brazil, spans 3,200 miles. This diverse geography has helped produce the distinctive development of each Latin American nation.

Latin America has two dominant physical characteristics: enormous mountains and vast river systems. The often snowcapped and sometimes volcanic mountain ranges—the three Sierra Madre ranges in Mexico and the 4,000-mile-long Andes in South America that make a western spine from Venezuela to Tierra del Fuego—form the backbone of the landmass. Nearly impassable for most of their length, these mountain ranges boast many peaks of over 22,000 feet. The mountains have presented a formidable barrier to trade and communications in Mexico and the nations of the southern continent. Not only do the mountain ranges separate nations from each other, but they divide regions within nations.

The enormous rivers most often lie in lightly populated areas. Three mammoth river systems (the Amazon, the Orinoco, and the Río de la Plata) spread over almost the entire South American continent east of the Andes. The size of the Amazon River Basin and the surrounding tropics—the largest such area in the world—has posed another impediment to the development of transportation and human settlement, although some rivers are navigable for long distances. Only with the advent of modern technology—

railroads, telegraph, telephones, automobiles, and airplanes—has geographical isolation been partly overcome, a condition that has helped create markets and forge independent states.

Latin America encompasses five climatological regions: high mountains, tropical jungles, deserts, temperate coastal plains, and temperate highlands. The first three are sparsely populated, while the latter two tend to be densely inhabited. With the exception of the Maya, all the great ancient civilizations arose in the highlands of the Andes and Mexico.

The varied climate and topography of South America, Mexico, and Central America have helped produce this highly uneven distribution of population. Three notable examples—the gargantuan Amazonian region of mostly steamy tropical forests and savannah, the vast desert of Patagonia in southern Argentina, and the northern wastelands of Mexico—support few inhabitants. In contrast to these inhospitable regions, a thin strip along Brazil's coast, the plain along the Río de la Plata estuary in Argentina, and the central plateau of Mexico contain most of the people in these countries. Thus these nations are overpopulated and underpopulated at the same time.

In western South America the heaviest concentration of people is found on the inland plateaus. None of the major cities—Santiago, Chile; Lima, Peru; Quito, Ecuador; and Bogotá and Medellín, Colombia—are ports; there are few good natural harbors on the west coast. In contrast, in eastern South America the major cities—Buenos

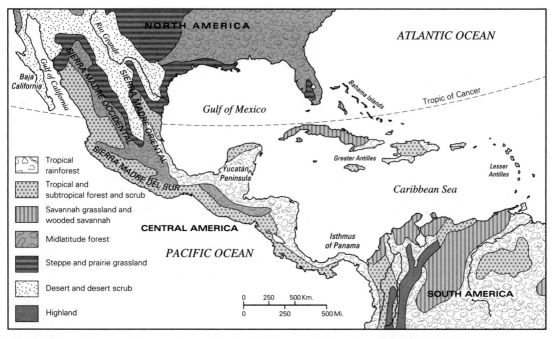

The maps on these two pages form an overall picture of the natural geographical features of Latin America: Middle America (*above*), composed of Mexico, Central America, and the Caribbean region; and South America (*next page*).

Aires, Argentina; Montevideo, Uruguay; and São Paulo–Santos, Rio de Janeiro, Bahia, and Recife, Brazil—are situated on the Atlantic coast. The majority of people in Argentina, Brazil, and Uruguay reside on the coastal plains. Mexico City, Guadalajara, and Monterrey, Mexico's largest cities, are inland. Almost all these cities have a population of over 1 million, with Mexico City, the largest, having over 20 million.

The number of waterways and the amount of rainfall vary greatly from region to region. Mexico has no rivers of importance, while Brazil contains the huge Amazon network. Lack of rain and rivers for irrigation in large areas makes farming impossible. Barely 10 percent of Mexico's land is fertile enough to farm; rainfall is so uncertain in some cultivable areas that drought strikes often and for years at a time. Mexico, with too little water, contrasts with Brazil, with too much. Much of Brazil's vast territory, however, is equally uncultivable, as its tropical soils have high acidity and have proved infertile and incapable of sustaining agricultural crops.

On the other hand, Latin America has enormous natural resources for economic development. Mexico and Venezuela rank among the world's largest oil producers. Mexico may have the biggest petroleum reserves of any nation other than Saudi Arabia. Bolivia, Ecuador, Colombia, and Peru also produce oil. Over the centuries, Latin American nations have been leading sources of copper (Mexico and Chile), nitrate (Chile), silver (Peru and Mexico), gold (Brazil), diamonds (Brazil), and tin (Bolivia). Much of the world's coffee is grown on the fertile highlands of Central America, Colombia, and Brazil. Much of the world's cattle have been raised on the plains of northern Mexico, southern Brazil, and central Argentina. Argentina's immense plains, the Pampas, are among the planet's most fertile areas, yielding not only cattle but sheep and wheat as well. Over the past five centuries, the coastal plains of Brazil have produced enormous amounts of sugar. In addition, human ingenuity has converted geographical obstacles into assets. Some extensive river systems

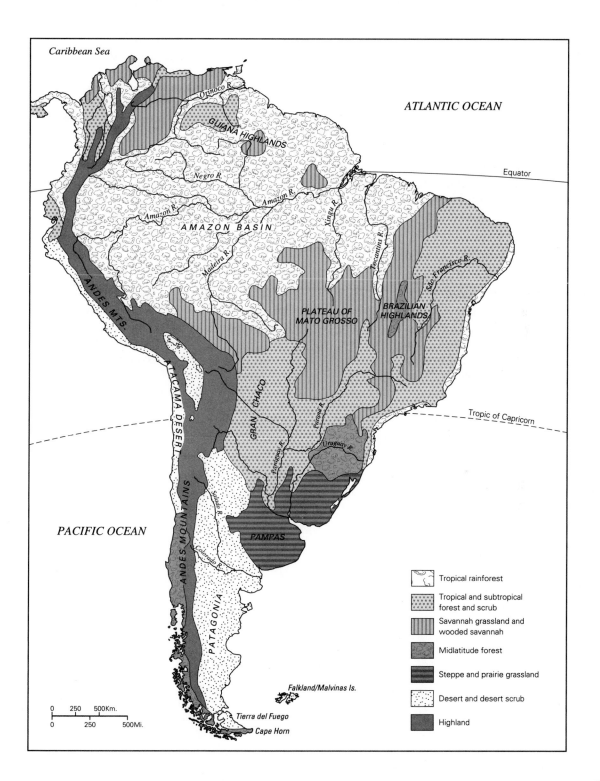

Caribbean Sea

ATLANTIC OCEAN

Orinoco R.

GUIANA HIGHLANDS

Equator

Negro R.

Amazon R.

Amazon R.

AMAZON BASIN

Xingu R.

Tocantins R.

São Francisco R.

Madeira R.

ANDES MTS.

PLATEAU OF
MATO GROSSO

BRAZILIAN
HIGHLANDS

ATACAMA DESERT

GRAN CHACO

Paraguay R.

Paraná R.

Uruguay R.

Tropic of Capricorn

PACIFIC OCEAN

ANDES MOUNTAINS

Salado R.

PAMPAS

Colorado R.

PATAGONIA

Falkland/Malvinas Is.

0   250   500Km.
0   250   500Mi.

Tierra del Fuego

Cape Horn

Tropical rainforest

Tropical and subtropical
forest and scrub

Savannah grassland and
wooded savannah

Midlatitude forest

Steppe and prairie grassland

Desert and desert scrub

Highland

have potential for hydroelectric power and provide water for irrigation as well, as has been done in Mexico's arid regions.

The historical record shows that the richness of Latin America's resources has had a significant impact on the economic and political development of Europe and North America. The gold and silver of its New World empire fueled Spain's wars and diplomacy in Europe for four hundred years. Many scholars trace the origins of the Industrial Revolution in such nations as Great Britain and the Netherlands to resources extracted from Latin America by its colonial masters, Spain and Portugal.

Latin America's resources have affected economic development elsewhere, but how these resources have been developed and by whom and in which ways has profoundly changed the history of the nations in this area. Geography has perhaps narrowed historical alternatives in Latin America, but the decisions of people determined its development. Going back to the colonization by Spain and Portugal, Latin America's history has been marked by exploitation of its peoples and its natural resources. Imperial Spain's policy to drain the lands it conquered of gold, silver, and other resources fixed the pattern for later exploiters. With European dominance came the decision to subjugate the indigenous peoples and often force them to labor under subhuman conditions in mines and on large estates, where many died. In the more recent era, there has been the decision to grow bananas on the coastal plains of Central America instead of corn or other staples of the local diet; this has made export profitable, usually for North American concerns, but this land use has left many, like the Guatemalans, without sufficient food. Meanwhile the uncontrolled expansion of capitalism in the area has led to an ecological crisis, reflected in massive deforestation, severe soil exhaustion, and growing agricultural and industrial pollution. These developments have contributed to rapid depletion of renewable resources, lack of clean water and air, and major epidemics of contagious diseases and other health problems.

The work that follows is a history of the development of Latin America's economy, politics, and society viewed primarily from the perspective of ordinary people, who were exploited and oppressed but who resisted and endured. It is the story of the events and forces that produced the alternatives from which Latin Americans created their world.

A History of
Latin America

PART ONE

The Colonial Heritage of Latin America

The Great City of Tenochtitlan (detail), 1945, by Diego Rivera. National Palace, Mexico City, D.F., Mexico. © Banco de Mexico Trust. Schalkwijk/Art Resource, NY.

OR MOST NORTH AMERICANS, perhaps, the colonial past is a remote, picturesque time that has little relevance to the way we live now. The situation is very different in Latin America. "Even the casual visitor to Latin America," says the historian Woodrow Borah, "is struck by the survival of institutions and features that are patently colonial." The inventory of colonial survivals includes many articles and practices of everyday life, systems of land use and labor, and a wealth of social relations and attitudes.

Characteristic of the Latin American scene is the coexistence and mingling of colonial and modern elements: the digging stick, the foot plow, and the handloom coexist with the tractor, the conveyor belt, and the computer. In Latin America the colonial past is not a nostalgic memory but a harsh reality. It signifies economic backwardness; political arbitrariness, corruption, and nepotism; a hierarchical social order and attitudes of condescension and contempt on the part of elites toward the masses.

We begin our survey of the colonial period of Latin American history with some account of Ancient America, the name of that long span of time during which indigenous Americans developed their cultures in virtual isolation from the Old World. This past profoundly influenced the character of the colonial era. By no accident, the chief capitals of the Spanish Empire in America arose in the old indigenous heartlands—the Mexican and Peruvian areas—the homes of millions of industrious natives accustomed to performing tribute labor for their ruling classes. These people, the Spaniards well knew, were the true wealth of the Indies. Territories with small indigenous populations remained marginal in the Spanish colonial scheme of things.

Equally decisive for the character of the colonial period was the Hispanic background. The conquistadors came from a Spain where seven centuries of struggle against Muslims had made warfare almost a way of life and had created a large *hidalgo* (noble) class that regarded manual labor with contempt. To some, like the Spanish chronicler Francisco López de Gómara, "The conquest of Indians began when the conquest of the Moors had ended, in order that Spaniards may always war against the infidels." Spain's economic backwardness and immense inequalities of wealth, which sharply limited opportunities for advancement or even a decent livelihood for most Spaniards, help explain both the desperate valor of the conquistadors and their harshness in dealing with others. It seems significant that many great captains of the Conquest—Cortés, Pizarro, Valdivia, Balboa—came from the bleak land of Estremadura, Spain's poorest province.

Another factor that may help to explain the peculiarly ferocious, predatory character of the Conquest is the climate of violence that existed in contemporary Spain, a clear legacy of the reconquest and its social conditions and values. In his *Spanish Character: Attitudes and Mentalities from the Sixteenth to the Nineteenth Century*, Bartolomé Bennassar notes that assassins proliferated, as did the ancient practice of issuing writs of pardon in return for the payment of blood money—usually a small amount—for the murder of individuals of humble social status. To concede that the historical background had created this climate of violence is not to ascribe to Spaniards a unique capacity for cruelty or deviltry. We know all too well that colonial, imperialist, and civil wars are replete with atrocities and horrors of every kind. Indeed, what distinguishes Spain among the colonial powers of history is the fact that it produced a minority of men who denounced in the face of the world the crimes of their own countrymen and did all in their power to stop what Bartolomé de Las Casas called "the destruction of the Indies."

Since the sixteenth century, defenders of Spain's colonial record have charged Las Casas and other accusers with bias and exaggeration, claiming that they created a "Black Legend" of Spanish cruelty and intolerance. In fact, every colonial power has its own Black Legend that is no legend but a dismal reality. The brutality of the Spanish Conquest is matched by that of the genocidal "Indian wars" waged by American folk heroes like General and President Andrew Jackson, who supervised the mutilation of some eight hundred Creek corpses, cutting off their noses to count and keep a record of the dead. The 1899–1902 Filipino revolt against U.S. colonialism was suppressed with massacres, use of "water torture" to elicit information, and incarceration of civilian populations in concentration camps. General J. Franklin Bell, who took part in that repression, estimated that in Luzon alone over 600,000 people had been killed or died from disease as a result of the war.

On the ruins of indigenous societies Spain laid the foundations of a new colonial order. Three aspects of that order need to be stressed. One is the predominantly feudal character of its economic structure, social organization, and ideology. This feudal character was most clearly expressed in Spain's "Indian" policy, which assigned to them the status of a hereditary servile class, obliged to pay tribute in goods, cash, and labor and to engage in unequal trade with their European masters. The same feudal principles assigned separate legal status to Europeans, *castas* (persons of mixed race), and blacks and regulated the conduct and lifestyle of each racial category. These feudal characteristics, admixed with some capitalist elements, formed part of Spain's (and Portugal's) legacy to independent Latin America and help explain the tenacious hold of some anachronistic institutions on the area today.

Second, the colonial economy, externally dependent on the export of precious metals and such staples as sugar, cacao, tobacco, and hides, became gradually integrated into the new capitalist order that arose in northern Europe in the seventeenth and eighteenth centuries. Spain, itself increasingly dependent economically on the capitalist North, was powerless to prevent the flow of colonial treasure and commodities to its rivals through smuggling, piracy, and foreign takeover of Spanish merchant houses. In the process of insertion into the European capitalist system, the feudal colonial economy acquired some capitalist features. Thus slavery, relatively patriarchal in Europe, acquired a peculiarly brutal character in the Caribbean colonies, with "the civilized horrors of overwork," in the words of Karl Marx, "grafted onto the barbaric horrors of slavery."

Third, Spain's colonial order was rooted in conflict between the crown and the conquistadors and their descendants. The crown feared the rise of a colonial seigneurial class and sought to rein in the colonists' ambitions; on the other hand, it relied on them for security against internal and external threats, and this disposed the crown to make major concessions to them. Against this background, there developed a continual struggle, sometimes open, sometimes muffled, between the Spanish crown and the conquistadors and their descendants for control of indigenous labor and tribute. In that struggle the colonists gradually gained the upper hand.

Spain's seventeenth-century decline contributed to this shift in the balance of power in favor of the colonists. The emergence of a hereditary colonial aristocracy rich in land and peons represented a defeat for the crown and for indigenous communities whose interests, however feebly, the crown defended. When in the late eighteenth century Spain's kings sought to tighten their control over the colonies, exclude creoles (American-born Spaniards) from high official posts, and institute reforms that sometimes clashed with creole vested interests, it was too late. These policies only alienated a powerful colonial elite whose members already felt a dawning sense of nationality and dreamed of the advantages of a free trade with the outside world.

A parallel development occurred during the same period in relations between Portugal and Brazil. Between 1810 and 1822, American elites, taking advantage of Spain's and Portugal's distresses, seized power in most of Spanish America and Brazil. These aristocratic rebels wanted no radical social changes or economic diversification; their interests as producers of staples for export to western Europe required the continuance of the system of large estates worked by peons or slaves. As a result, independent Latin America inherited almost intact the colonial legacy of a rigidly stratified society and an economy dependent on foreign countries for capital and finished goods.

Ancient America

A GREAT NUMBER OF INDIGENOUS GROUPS, speaking many different languages and having different ways of life, occupied America at the time of Columbus's arrival. For at least ten thousand years the New World had existed in virtual isolation from the Old. Sporadic and transient contacts between America and Asia no doubt occurred, and some transfer of cultural traits, mainly stylistic embellishments, probably took place through trans-Pacific diffusion. But there is no convincing evidence that people or ideas from China, India, or Africa significantly influenced the cultural development of indigenous America.

Environment and Culture in Ancient America

During its thousands of years of isolation, America was a unique social laboratory in which indigenous communities worked out their own destinies, adapting in various ways to their special environments. By 1492 this process had produced results that suggest that the patterns of early human cultural evolution are basically similar the world over. The first Europeans found native groups in much the same stages of cultural development through which parts of the Old World had once passed: Old Stone Age hunters and food gatherers, New Stone Age farmers, and empires as complex as those of Bronze-Age Egypt and Mesopotamia.

The inhabitants of Ancient America were blends of several Asiatic physical types. They had dark eyes, straight or wavy black hair, and yellowish or copper skin. Their remote ancestors had probably come from Asia across the Bering Strait in waves of migration that began perhaps as early as forty thousand years ago and continued until about 10,000 B.C. Much controversy, however, surrounds the problem of the approximate date of the first human habitation in America. Some archaeologists argue that no firm evidence exists to refute the traditional view, based on the dating of so-called Folsom stone projectile points found throughout North and South America, that such habitation began about twelve thousand years ago. Revisionists point to the discoveries made in recent decades, especially in Chile and Brazil, that suggest a much earlier occupation. Most recently, the arguments in favor of such an earlier occupation have been reinforced by linguistic evidence that takes account of the immense time span required for the formation of the many languages spoken in Ancient America.

Two waves of migrations appear to have taken place. The first brought extremely primitive groups who lived by gathering wild fruit, fishing, and hunting small game. A recent archaeological discovery suggests that these primitive hunters and gatherers passed through Peru about twenty-two thousand years ago. The second series of invasions brought big-game hunters who, like their predecessors, spread out through the continent. By 9000 B.C., these Asiatic invaders or their descendants had reached Patagonia, the southern tip of the continent.

This first colonization of America took place in the last part of the great geological epoch known as the Pleistocene, a period of great climatic changes. Glacial ages, during which blankets of ice covered extensive areas of the Old and New Worlds, alternated with periods of thaw, when temperatures rose to approximately present-day levels. Even in ice-free areas, precipitation often increased markedly during the glacial ages, creating lush growth of pastures and woodlands that supported many varieties of game. Consequently, large sections of America in this period were a hunter's paradise. Over its plains and through its forests roamed many large prehistoric beasts. The projectile points of prehistoric hunters have been found near the remains of such animals from one end of America to the other.

Around 9000 B.C., the retreat of the last great glaciation (the Wisconsin), accompanied by drastic climate changes, caused a crisis for the hunting economy. A warmer, drier climate settled over vast areas. Grasslands decreased, and the large animals that had pastured on them gradually died out. The improved techniques of late Pleistocene hunting also may have contributed to the disappearance of these animals. The hunting folk now had to adapt to their changing environment or vanish with the animals that had sustained them.

The southwestern United States, northern Mexico, and other areas offer archaeological evidence of a successful adjustment to the new conditions. Here, people increasingly turned for food to smaller animals, such as deer and jackrabbits, and to edible wild plants, especially seeds, which were ground into a palatable meal. This new way of life eventually led to the development of agriculture. At first, agriculture merely supplemented the older pursuits of hunting and food collecting; its use hardly constituted an "agricultural revolution." The shift from food gathering to food producing was more likely a gradual accumulation of more

and more domesticated plants that gradually replaced the wild edible plants. Over an immensely long period, time and energy formerly devoted to hunting and plant collecting were diverted to such agricultural activities as clearing, planting, weeding, gardening, picking, harvesting, and food preparation. But in the long run, agriculture, in the New World as in the Old, had revolutionary effects: people began to lead a more disciplined and sedentary life, the food supply increased, population grew, and division of labor became possible.

In caves in the Mexican highlands, archaeologists have found the wild plants that were gradually domesticated; among the more important are pumpkins, beans, and maize. Domestication of these plants probably occurred between 7000 and 2300 B.C. Among these achievements, none was more significant than the domestication of maize, the mainstay of the great cultures of Ancient America. Manioc (a starchy root cultivated in the tropics as a staple food) and the potato (in Peru) were added to the list of important domesticated plants between 5000 and 1000 B.C.

From its place or places of origin, agriculture swiftly spread over the American continents. By 1492 maize was under cultivation from the northern boundary of the present-day United States to Chile. But not all indigenous peoples adopted agriculture as a way of life. Some, like those who inhabited the bleak wastes of Tierra del Fuego at the far tip of South America, were forced by severe climatic conditions either to hunt and collect food or starve. Others, like the prosperous, sedentary peoples of the Pacific northwest coast, who lived by waters teeming with fish and forests filled with game, had no reason to abandon their good life in favor of agriculture.

Where agriculture became the principal economic activity, its yield depended on such natural factors as soil fertility and climate and on the farming techniques employed. Forest people usually employed the slash-and-burn method of cultivation. Trees and brush were cut down and burned, and maize or other staples were planted in the cleared area with a digging stick. Because this method soon exhausted the soil, the clearing had to be left fallow and a new one made. After this process had gone on long enough, the whole village had to move to a new site or adopt a dispersed pattern of settlement that would allow each family group sufficient land for its needs. Slash-and-burn agriculture thus had a structural weakness that usually sharply limited the cultural development of those who employed it. That a strong controlling authority could at least temporarily overcome the defects of this method is suggested by the success of the Maya: their brilliant civilization arose in a tropical forest environment on a base of slash-and-burn farming directed by a powerful priesthood, but there is now abundant evidence that from very early times this was supplemented by more intensive methods of agriculture.

A more productive agriculture developed in the rugged highlands of Middle America and the Andean altiplano and on the desert coast of Peru. In such arid or semiarid country, favored with a temperate climate and a naturally rich soil, the land could be tilled more easily and its fertility preserved longer with digging-stick methods. Most important, food production could be increased with the aid of irrigation, which led to larger populations and a greater division of labor. The need for cooperation and regulation on irrigation projects favored the rise of strong central governments and the extension of their authority over larger areas. The Aztec and Inca empires arose in natural settings of this kind.

Finally, the vast number of human groups inhabiting the American continents on the eve of the Spanish Conquest can be classified by their subsistence base and the complexity of their social organization into three levels or categories—tribe, chiefdom, and state. These categories correspond to stages in general cultural evolution. The simplest or most primitive, the *band* and *tribal* level, usually correlated with difficult environments (dense forests; plains; or extremely wet, dry, or frigid areas) that sharply limited productivity. It was characterized by small, egalitarian groups who relied on hunting, fishing, and collecting; on a shifting agriculture; or on a combination of these activities. Hunting and gathering groups were typically nomadic, migrating within a given territory in a cyclical pattern according to the seasonal availability of game and edible plants. Groups that supplemented hunting, fishing, and gathering with slash-and-burn agriculture were semisedentary. The often precarious nature of the subsistence base tended to keep band and tribal population densities low and hinder development of division of labor. The social unit on this level was an autonomous band or a village; a loose association of bands or villages, linked by ties of kinship, real or fictitious, formed a tribe. Social stratification was unknown; all members of the group had access to its hunting and fishing grounds and its land. Village and tribal leaders or chiefs owed their authority to their prowess in battle or other outstanding abilities; the exercise of their authority was limited to the duration of a hunt, a military operation, or some other communal activity.

Typical of these egalitarian societies were many Brazilian tribes of the Amazon basin. A frequent feature of their way of life was constant intertribal warfare whose purpose was to capture prisoners. After being kept for weeks or months, the captured warriors were ritually executed and their flesh was cooked and eaten by members of the tribe to gain spiritual strength and perpetuate the tribal feud. The sixteenth-century French philosopher Michel de Montaigne, who read about their customs in travel accounts and met some Brazilian Indians brought to France, was much impressed by their democratic spirit and freedom from the familiar European contrasts of extreme poverty and wealth. He used these impressions to draw an influential literary portrait of the noble savage, the innocent cannibal who represents a type of moral perfection free from the vices of civilization.

The *chiefdom,* the second category of indigenous social organization, represented an intermediate level. Most commonly the subsistence base of the chiefdom was intensive farming, which supported a dense population living in large villages. These villages had lost their autonomy and were ruled from an elite center by a paramount chief, who was aided by a hierarchy of subordinate chiefs. Ranking was an important element in chiefdom social organization, but it was defined in kinship terms. Persons were ranked according to their genealogical nearness to the paramount chief, who was often assigned a sacred character and attended by a large retinue of officials and servants. The paramount chief siphoned off the surplus production of the group by requiring tribute payment and forced donations; he used much of this surplus for selective redistribution to officials, retainers, and warriors, thereby enhancing his own power. Warfare between chiefdoms was very common and probably played a decisive role in their origin and expansion through the absorption of neighboring villages. Warfare, leading to the taking of captives who were enslaved and made to labor for their owners, also contributed to the growth of incipient social stratification.

Numerous chiefdoms existed in ancient America on the eve of the Spanish Conquest, with the largest number in the Circum-Caribbean area (including Panama, Costa Rica, northern Colombia, and Venezuela; and the islands of Hispaniola, Puerto Rico, Jamaica, and Cuba). The Cauca Valley of Colombia alone contained no less than eighty chiefdoms.

The complex, densely populated Chibcha or Muisca chiefdoms, located in the eastern highlands of Colombia, may serve to illustrate this level of social and political integration. They rested on a subsistence base of intensive agriculture and fishing, and hunting was an important supplementary activity. The agricultural techniques most likely included terracing and ridged planting beds (raised above wet basin floors to control moisture) as well as slash-and-burn methods. In addition to maize, these chiefdoms cultivated potatoes, *quinoa* (a hardy grain resembling buckwheat), and a wide variety of other plants. The crafts—pottery, weaving, and metallurgy—were highly developed. Their magnificent gold work ranks among the finest such work in ancient America.

At the time of the Spanish Conquest, most of the Muisca territory was dominated by two rival chiefdoms, centered at Bogotá and Tunja respectively; the population of the area has been estimated at about 1.5 million. The Muisca lived in large villages of several hundred to several thousand persons. Each village consisted of pole-and-thatch houses and was surrounded by a palisade. The society was divided into commoners and elites, and membership in both sectors entailed differential rights and obligations. Commoners owed tribute in goods and in labor for the support of the chiefs and nobles, who controlled the distribution and consumption of surplus production.

The chiefdom marks the transition to the next and highest stage of organization, sometimes called *civilization* or more simply the *state* level of social and political integration. The dividing line between the two stages, especially in the case of larger and more complex chiefdoms, is difficult to draw, since the state reflected an expansion and deepening of tendencies already present in the chiefdom. There was a growth of division of labor and specialization, indicated by the formation of artisan groups who no longer engaged in farming, the rise of a priesthood in charge of religious and intellectual activities, the rise of a distinct warrior class, and a bureaucracy entrusted with the administration of the state. These changes were accompanied by intensified social stratification and corresponding ideological changes. The kinship ties that in fact or in theory had united the paramount chief and the elite with the commoners became weakened or dissolved, and there arose a true class structure, with a ruling group claiming a separate origin from the commoners whose labor supported it. At the head of the state stood a priest-king or emperor who was sometimes endowed with divine attributes.

The state level of organization required a technological base of high productivity, usually an intensive agriculture that made large use of irrigation, terracing, and other advanced techniques. The state differed from the chiefdom in its larger size and population, the increased exchange of goods between regions, sometimes accompanied by the emergence of a professional merchant class, and the rise of true cities. In addition to being population, administrative, and industrial centers, these cities were cult centers often featured by a monumental architecture not found in chiefdoms. The Aztec, Maya, and Inca societies offer the best-known examples of the state level of organization.

What were the decisive factors in the qualitative leap from the chiefdom to the state in Ancient America? Some regard warfare leading to territorial conquest as the prime mover in this process; others believe that the state arose primarily as a coercive mechanism to resolve internal conflict between economically stratified classes. Others stress the importance of religious ideology in promoting centralized control by elites over populations and their resources. All these factors played a part in the process of state formation.

What appears certain is that, as we noted above, certain environmental conditions are more favorable than others for the formation of early states, especially of their highest form, empire. Indeed, it is more than doubtful that such states could have arisen in such natural settings as the grassy plains of North America, whose hard sod was impervious to digging sticks, or the Amazonian rain forests, usually thought to be unsuitable for farming other than transient slash-and-burn clearings.[1] Specialists often refer to the favored region that combined the necessary environmental conditions for the rise of states and empires as *Nuclear America.*

POPULATIONS IN 1492

As a result of researches by anthropologists and historians, information on Ancient America is growing at a rapid rate. Students are more impressed with the complexity of the civilizations of Ancient America and commonly compare them with such advanced Old World cultures as ancient Egypt and Mesopotamia. Recent studies of the population history of Ancient America have contributed to the rising respect for its cultural achievement. If we assume, as many social scientists do, that population density is correlated with a certain technological and cultural level, then a high estimate of the indigenous population in 1492 is in some measure a judgment of its social achievement and of the colonial societies that arose on its ruins.

---

[1]Archaeologists have recently found evidence at various sites along the shores of the Amazon of complex societies with elaborate pottery, raised fields, and large statues of chiefs. But none of these ancient Amazonian societies appear to have evolved beyond the chiefdom level, and questions remain regarding their origin and the size of their populations.

The subject of the pre-Conquest population of the Americas, however, has produced sharp, sometimes bitter debate. The first Spanish arrivals in the New World reported very dense populations. Some early estimates of the native population of Hispaniola (modern Haiti and the Dominican Republic) ranged as high as 2 and 4 million. The famous missionary known as Motolinía, who arrived in Mexico in 1524, offered no numbers but wrote that the inhabitants were as numerous as "the blades of grass in a field." Great densities were also reported for the Inca Empire and Central America. In the twentieth century scholars who assessed these early reports tended to divide into two groups. Some found them generally credible; in the 1920s the American archaeologist H. J. Spinden and the German archaeologist Karl Sapper, taking account of indigenous technology and resources, came up with the same overall totals of 40 to 50 million for the whole New World. Others, like the U.S. anthropologist A. L. Kroeber and the Argentine scholar Angel Rosenblat, concluded that this technology could not support the densities cited by the early sources and that the Spaniards had consciously or unconsciously exaggerated the number of people they found in order to enhance their own achievements as conquerors or missionaries. Kroeber produced a hemispheric estimate of 8,400,000; Rosenblat raised this figure to 13,385,000.

Beginning in the 1940s, three professors at the University of California, Woodrow Borah, Sherburne Cook, and Lesley B. Simpson, opened a new line of inquiry into the demographic history of Ancient America with a remarkable series of studies focusing on ancient Mexico. Using a variety of records and sophisticated statistical methods, the Berkeley school projected backward from a base established from Spanish counts for tribute purposes and arrived at a population figure of 25.3 million for central Mexico on the eve of the Conquest.

Later, Cook and Borah extended their inquiries into other areas. Particularly striking are their conclusions concerning the population of Hispaniola in 1492. Previous estimates of the island's population had ranged from a low of

600,000 to the 3 to 4 million proposed by the sixteenth-century Spanish friar Bartolomé de Las Casas, but those high figures had long been regarded as the exaggerations of a "Black Legend" enthusiast. After a careful study of a series of statements and estimates on the aboriginal population of Hispaniola made between 1492 and 1520, Cook and Borah not only confirmed the reliability of Las Casas's figures but offered even higher probable figures of from 7 to 8 million.

Aside from Borah's suggestion in 1964 that the population of America in 1492 may have been "upwards of 100 million," the Berkeley school did not attempt to estimate the pre-Columbian population of the continent as a whole. A systematic effort of this kind was made by the U.S. anthropologist Henry Dobyns. Assuming that the indigenous population was reduced by roughly 95 percent after contact with the Europeans, primarily as a result of new diseases to which they had no acquired immunity, he estimated a pre-Conquest population of between 90 and 112 million; of this figure he assigned 30 million each to central Mexico and Peru.

The findings and methods of the Berkeley school and Dobyns have provoked strong dissent; two notable dissenters from those high findings are William T. Sanders and David Henige. In general, however, the evidence of the last half-century of research in this field quite consistently points to larger populations than were accepted previously. One effort to generalize from this evidence, taking account both of the findings of the Berkeley school and its critics, is that of William T. Denevan, who postulates a total population of 57.3 million—a far cry from Kroeber's 1939 estimate of 8.4 million.

Scholars have also attempted to establish long-range population trends in Ancient America. There is general agreement that on the whole, in Woodrow Borah's words, "American Indians had relatively few diseases and, aside from natural disasters such as floods or droughts causing crop failures, seem to have enjoyed especially good health." Until 1492 their isolation protected them from the unified pool of diseases like smallpox, measles, and typhus that had formed in the Old World by the time of the Renaissance. What the long-range per-spective may have been, assuming no European contact, is problematical. In many areas indigenous peoples had developed a system that combined hunting-gathering and shifting slash-and-burn agriculture, often based on the corn-beans-squash triad, that was sustainable, inflicting little damage on the ecosystem. The Taino of the West Indies had developed a sophisticated form of agriculture based on permanent fields of knee-high mounds, called *conucos*, planted in cassava, the sweet potato, and various beans and squashes, that retarded erosion and "gave the highest returns of food in continuous supply by the simplest methods and modest labor." There is little evidence of population pressure on food resources in such areas. On the other hand, historical demographers have found evidence of approaching crisis in the Aztec Empire; Borah gloomily observes: "By the close of the fifteenth century the Indian population of central Mexico was doomed even had there been no European conquests." And scholars are now convinced that population pressure on scant resources may have played a major part in the collapse of the classic Maya civilization of Central America; the evidence includes signs of chronic malnutrition, high infant mortality, and a decline of population from perhaps 12 million to a remnant of about 1.8 million within 150 years. The crisis is linked to deforestation, loss of surface water, and overcultivated, worn-out soils, among other factors.

NUCLEAR AMERICA

Mexico and Peru were the centers of an extensive high culture area that included central and southern Mexico, Central America, and the Andean zone of South America. This is the heartland of Ancient America, the home of its first agricultural civilizations. Evidence of early village life and the basic techniques of civilization—agriculture, pottery, weaving—has been found in almost every part of this territory.

In recent decades, this region has been the scene of major archaeological discoveries. In the Valley of Mexico, in southern Mexico and on its gulf coast, on the high plateau of Bolivia, and in the desert sands of coastal Peru, excavations have uncovered the remains of splendid temples, mighty fortresses, large cities and towns, and pottery and textiles of exquisite artistry. Combining the testimony of the spade with that provided by historical accounts, specialists have attempted to reconstruct the history of Nuclear America. The framework for this effort is a sequence of stages based on the technology, social and political organization, religion, and art of a given period. To this sequence of stages specialists commonly assign the names Archaic, Formative or Preclassic, Classic, and Postclassic. This scheme is tentative in detail, with much chronological overlap between stages and considerable variation in the duration of some periods from area to area.

The *Archaic* stage began about nine thousand years ago when a gradual shift from food gathering and hunting to agriculture began in many parts of Nuclear America. This incipient agriculture, however, did not cause revolutionary changes in these societies. For thousands of years, people continued to live in much the same primitive fashion as before. Social groups were small and probably seminomadic. Weaving was unknown, but a simple pottery appeared in some areas toward the end of the period.

Between 2500 and 1500 B.C., a major cultural advance in various regions of Nuclear America opened the *Formative,* or *Preclassic,* period. Centuries of haphazard experimentation with plants led to the selection of improved, high-yield varieties. These advances ultimately produced an economy solidly based on agriculture and sedentary village life. Maize and other important domesticated plants were brought under careful cultivation; irrigation came into use in some areas; a few animals were domesticated. By the end of the period, pottery and weaving were highly developed. Increased food production enabled villagers to support a class of priests who acted as intermediaries between people and gods. More abundant food also released labor for the construction of ceremonial sites—mounds of earth topped by temples of wood or thatch.

The social unit of the Formative period was a village community composed of one or more kinship groups, but by the end of the period small chiefdoms uniting several villages had appeared. Since land and food were relatively plentiful and populations small, warfare must have been infrequent. Religion centered on the worship of water and fertility gods; human sacrifice was probably absent or rare.

The advances of the Formative period culminated in the *Classic* period, which began around the opening of the Christian era and lasted until approximately A.D. 1000. The term Classic refers to the flowering of material, intellectual, and artistic culture that marked this stage. There was no basic change in technology, but the extension of irrigation works in some areas caused increases in food production and freed manpower for construction and technical tasks. Population also increased, and in some regions genuine cities arose. Architecture, pottery, and weaving reached an impressive level of style. Metallurgy flourished in Peru, as did astronomy, mathematics, and writing in Mesoamerica (central and south Mexico and adjacent upper Central America). The earlier earth mounds gave way to huge stone-faced pyramids, elaborately ornamented and topped by great temples. The construction of palaces and other official buildings nearby made each ceremonial center the administrative capital of a state ruled by a priest-king. Social stratification was already well developed, with the priesthood the main ruling class. However, the growing incidence of warfare in the late Classic period (perhaps caused by population pressure, with greater competition for land and water) brought more recognition and rewards to successful warriors. Religion became an elaborate polytheism served by a large class of priests.

Typical cultures of the Classic period were the Teotihuacán civilization of central Mexico, the Monte Albán culture in southwestern Mexico, and the lowland Maya culture of southern Yucatán and northern Guatemala. The Olmec civilization of the Mexican gulf lowlands displays some Classic features but falls within the time span usually allotted to the Formative. In Peru the period is best represented by the brilliant Mochica and Nazca civilizations of the coast. The available evidence suggests that the Classic stage was limited to

Mesoamerica, the central Andean area (the highlands and coasts of Peru and Bolivia), and the Ecuadorian coast.

The Classic era ended abruptly in both the northern and southern ends of Nuclear America. Shortly before or after A.D. 1000, most of the great Classic centers in Mesoamerica and Peru were abandoned or destroyed by civil war or foreign invasion. Almost certainly, the fall of these civilizations came as the climax of a longer period of decline. Population pressure, soil erosion, and peasant revolts caused by excessive tribute demands are among the explanations that have been advanced for the collapse of the great Classic city-states and kingdoms.

A Time of Troubles, of obscure struggles and migrations of peoples, followed these disasters. Then new civilizations arose on the ruins of the old. The *Postclassic* stage, from about A.D. 1000 to 1500, seems to have repeated on a larger, more complex scale, the rise-and-fall pattern of the previous era. Chronic warfare, reflected in the number of fortifications and fortified communities, and an increased emphasis on urban living were distinguishing features of this stage. Another was the formation of empires through the subjugation of a number of states by one powerful state. The dominant state appropriated a portion of the production of the conquered people, primarily for the benefit of its ruling classes. The Aztec and Inca empires typify this era.

No important advances in technology occurred in the Postclassic period, but in some regions the net of irrigation works was extended. The continuous growth of warfare and the rise of commerce sharpened economic distinctions between nobles and commoners, between rich and poor. The warrior class replaced the priesthood as the main ruling class. Imperialism also influenced the character of religion, enhancing the importance of war gods and human sacrifice. The arts and crafts showed some decline from Classic achievements; there was a tendency toward standardization and mass production of textiles and pottery in some areas.

After reaching a peak of power, the empires displayed the same tendency toward disintegration as their Classic forerunners. The Tiahuanaco civilization and the Inca Empire in Peru may have rep-resented two cycles of empire growth, whereas the first true Mexican imperial cycle, that of the Aztec conquests, had not ended when the Spaniards conquered America.

Three high civilizations, the Maya of Central America, the Aztecs of Mexico, and the Incas of Peru, have held the center of attention to the virtual exclusion of the others. This partiality is understandable. We know more about these peoples and their ways of life. The Aztec and Inca civilizations still flourished at the coming of the Spaniards, and some conquistadors wrote vivid accounts of what they saw. The colorful story of the Conquest of Mexico and Peru and the unhappy fate of their emperors Moctezuma (Montezuma) and Atahualpa have also served to focus historical and literary attention on the Aztecs and the Incas. Unfortunately, the fame and glamour surrounding these peoples have obscured the achievements of their predecessors, who laid the cultural foundations on which the Maya, Aztecs, and Incas built.

EARLY AMERICAN CIVILIZATIONS

As early as 1000 B.C., the inhabitants of the Valley of Mexico lived in small villages set in the midst of their maize, bean, and squash fields. They cultivated the land with slash-and-burn methods, produced simple but well-made pottery, and turned out large numbers of small clay figures that suggest a belief in fertility goddesses. By the opening of the Old World's Christian era, small flat-topped mounds had appeared, evidence of a more formal religion and directing priesthood.

Much earlier (perhaps spanning the period 1500 to 400 B.C.) there arose the precocious and enigmatic Olmec civilization of the gulf coast lowlands, whose influence radiated widely into the central Mexican plateau and Central America. The origins, development, and disappearance of the Olmec culture remain a mystery.

Important elements of the Olmec civilization were its ceremonial centers, monumental stone carving and sculpture, hieroglyphic writing, and probably a calendrical system. The principal Olmec sites are La Venta and Tres Zapotes, in the modern state of Veracruz. Discovery of Olmec culture and

In the ceremonial center of the great city-state of Teotihuacán, the Avenue of the Dead linked the "Citadel," the royal palace compound, to the Pyramids of the Sun and Moon. With a population estimated between 125,000 and 200,000, it was the world's sixth-largest city in A.D. 600. [CORBIS/Richard A. Cooke]

evidence of the wide diffusion of its art style have made untenable the older view that Maya civilization was the first in Mesoamerica. It seems likely that Olmec culture was the mother civilization of Mesoamerica.

The technical, artistic, and scientific advances of the Formative period made possible the climactic cultural achievements of the Classic era. In Mexico's central highlands, the Classic period opened in splendor. About the beginning of the Christian era, at Teotihuacán, some twenty-eight miles from Mexico City, arose the mighty pyramids later given the names of the Sun and the Moon, which towered over clusters of imposing temples and other buildings. The stone sculpture used in the decoration of the temples, as well as the marvelous grace and finish of the cement work and the fresco painting, tes-

tify to the high development of the arts among the Teotihuacáns. The ancient water god, known to the Aztecs as Tlaloc, seems to have been the chief deity. But the feathered serpent with jaguar fangs, later known as Quetzalcóatl, is also identified with water and fertility and appears prominently in the greatest temple. There is little evidence of war or human sacrifice until a relatively late phase. Priests in benign poses and wearing the symbols of their gods dominate the mural paintings.

This great ceremonial center at Teotihuacán was sacred ground. Probably only the priestly nobility and their servants lived here. Farther out were the residential quarters inhabited by officials, artisans, and merchants. Teotihuacán is estimated to have had a population of at least 125,000. On the outskirts of the city, which covered an area of

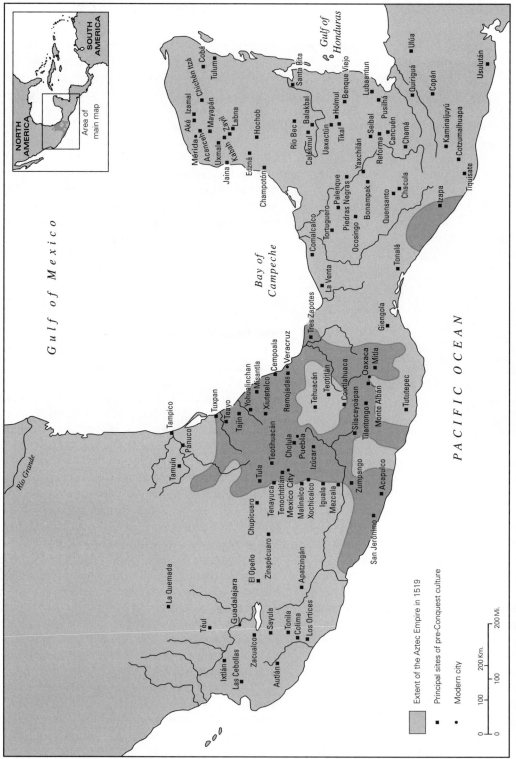

Principal Sites of Pre-Conquest Culture in Mesoamerica

Extent of the Aztec Empire in 1519

Principal sites of pre-Conquest culture

Modern city

NORTH AMERICA

SOUTH AMERICA

Area of main map

Gulf of Mexico

Bay of Campeche

Gulf of Honduras

PACIFIC OCEAN

Rio Grande

La Quemada

Teúl

Ixtlán

Las Cebollas

Zacualco

Guadalajara

Sayula

Tonila

Colima

Los Ortices

Autlán

Apatzingán

Zinapécuaro

El Opeño

Chupícuaro

Tamuín

Tamuín

Tampico

Pánuco

Tula

Tenayuca

Tenochtitlán

Mexico City

Malinalco

Xochicalco

Iguala

Mezcala

Zumpango

San Jerónimo

Acapulco

Tuxpan

Teayo

Tajín

Yohualinchan

Misantla

Xiutetelco

Cempoala

Veracruz

Remojadas

Teotihuacán

Cholula

Puebla

Izúcar

Tehuacán

Teotitlán

Coxtlahuaca

Oaxaca

Mitla

Monte Albán

Tututepec

Silacayoápan

Tilantongo

Tres Zapotes

Giengola

La Venta

Comalcalco

Tortuguero

Piedras Negras

Palenque

Ocosingo

Bonampak

Quensanto

Chacula

Tonalá

Izapa

Tiquisate

Cotzumalhuapa

Kaminaljuyú

 Usulután

Copán

Quiriguá

Ulúa

Pusilhá

Cancuén

Chamá

Reforma

Seibal

Yaxchilán

Uaxactún

Tikal

Holmul

Benque Viejo

Lubaantun

Balakbal

Calakmul

Río Bec

Champotón

Etzná

Hochob

Jaina

Mérida

Acanceh

Aké

Izamal

Mayapán

Chichén Itzá

Cobá

Tulum

Santa Rita

Uxmal

Kabáh

Zayil

Labna

200 Km.

200 Mi.

100

100

0

0

14

seven square miles, lived a large rural population that supplied the metropolis with its food. It is likely that an intensive agriculture using canal irrigation and terracing on hillslopes formed the economic foundation of the Teotihuacán civilization. Despite the predominantly peaceful aspect of its religion and art, Teotihuacán seems to have been not only a major trading center but also a military state that directly controlled regions as remote as highland Guatemala.

Contemporary with Teotihuacán, but overshadowed by that great city, were other centers of Classic culture in Mesoamerica. To the southwest, at Monte Albán in the rugged mountains of Oaxaca, the Zapotecs erected a great ceremonial center that was also a true city. One of their achievements, probably of Olmec origin, was a complicated system of hieroglyphic writing. In the same period, the Maya Classic civilization flowered in the Petén region of northern Guatemala.

The Maya of Central America

Among ancient American civilizations, the Maya were preeminent in cultural achievement. Certainly, no other group ever demonstrated such extraordinary abilities in architecture, sculpture, painting, mathematics, and astronomy.

The ancient Maya lived in a region comprising portions of modern-day southeastern Mexico, almost all of Guatemala, the western part of Honduras, all of Belize, and the western half of El Salvador. But the Maya civilization attained its highest development in the tropical forest lowland area whose core is the Petén region of Guatemala, at the base of the Yucatán Peninsula. This was the primary center of Maya Classic civilization from about A.D. 250 to 900.[2] The region was rich in wild game and building materials (limestone and fine

hardwoods). In almost every other respect, it offered immense obstacles to the establishment of a high culture. Clearing the dense forests for planting and controlling weeds were extremely difficult tasks with the primitive implements available. There was no metal, the water supply was uncertain, and communication facilities were poor. Yet it was here that the Maya built some of their largest ceremonial centers.

The contrast between the forbidding environment and the Maya achievement led some specialists to speculate that Maya culture was a transplant from some other, more favorable area. This view has been made obsolete by the discovery of long Preclassic sequences at lowland sites. There is, however, linguistic and archaeological evidence that the lowland Maya were descendants of groups who lived in or near the Olmec area before 1000 B.C. and who brought with them the essential elements of Mesoamerican civilization. In time they developed these elements into their own unique achievements in the sciences, art, and architecture.

Just as puzzling as the rise of the Maya lowland culture in such an inhospitable setting is the dramatic decline that led to a gradual cessation of building activity and eventual abandonment of the ceremonial centers after A.D. 800. Specialists have advanced various explanations for this decline. They include soil exhaustion as a result of slash-and-burn farming, invasion of cornfields by grasslands from the same cause, failure of the water supply, peasant revolts against the ruling priesthood, and the disruptive effects of the fall of Teotihuacán, which had close commercial and political ties with the Maya area. None of these explanations by itself, however, appears completely satisfactory.

Recently a more complex explanation of the Classic Maya collapse has emerged. According to this theory, the cessation of political and commercial contacts with Teotihuacán after about A.D. 550 led to a breakdown of centralized authority—perhaps previously exerted by Tikal, the largest and most important ceremonial center of the southern lowlands—and increased autonomy of local Maya elites. These elites expressed their pride and power by constructing ever more elaborate ceremonial centers, which added to the burdens of commoners.

[2]Recent archaeological discoveries, however, are revolutionizing the dates traditionally assigned to the Maya Classic period. The newly discovered city of Nakbé in the dense tropical forest of northern Guatemala, containing extensive stone monuments and temples, is dated from 600 to 400 B.C., pushing the Classic era back into the time span commonly assigned to the Formative or Preclassic period.

Growing population size and density strained food resources and forced the adoption of more intensive agricultural methods. These, in turn, increased competition for land, which was reflected in the growth of warfare and militarism. Improved agricultural production relieved population pressures for a time and made possible the late Classic flowering (A.D. 600 to 800), marked by a revival of ceremonial center construction, architecture, and the arts. But renewed population pressures, food shortages, and warfare between regional centers, perhaps aggravated by external attacks, led to a severe cultural and social decline in the last century of the Classic period. The build-up of pressure—so runs the theory—"resulted in a swift and catastrophic collapse accompanied by widespread depopulation through warfare, malnutrition, and disaster, until those who survived were again able to achieve a stable agricultural society at a much lower level of population density and social organization."

No such decline occurred in northern Yucatán, a low, limestone plain covered in most places with dense thickets of thorny scrub forest. This area had been occupied by the Maya fully as long as the south, although with less impressive cultural achievements. But here, too, there arose great ceremonial centers complete with steep pyramids, multistoried palaces, and large quadrangles. Into this area, in about 900, poured invaders from the central Mexican highlands, probably Toltec emigrants from strife-torn Tula. Toltec armies overran northern Yucatán and established their rule over the Maya, governing from the temple city of Chichén Itzá. The invaders introduced Toltec styles in art and architecture, including colonnaded halls, warrior columns, and the reclining stone figures called Chac Mools. Toltec influence was also reflected in an increased obsession with human sacrifice. After 1200, Maya cultural and political influence revived. Chichén Itzá was abandoned, and power passed to the city-state of Mayapan, a large, walled town from which Maya rulers dominated much of the peninsula, holding tribal chiefs and their families as hostages to exact tribute from surrounding provinces. But in the fifteenth century, virtually all centralized rule disappeared. A successful revolt overthrew the tyranny of Mayapan and destroyed the city itself in 1441. By this time, Maya civilization was in full decline. By the arrival of the Spaniards, all political unity or imperial organization in the area had disappeared.

Maya Economy and Society

Archaeological discoveries of the past three decades have radically revised our notions about the subsistence base of the ancient Maya. Until recently, the prevailing view assumed the primary role of maize in the diet and the almost exclusive reliance on the slash-and-burn (swidden) system of agriculture. Since this system excluded the possibility of such dense populations as were found at Teotihuacán and other Mesoamerican Classic or Postclassic centers, the traditional interpretation assumed a dispersed peasant population whose houses—typically one-room pole-and-thatch structures—were widely scattered or grouped in small hamlets across the countryside between the ceremonial and administrative centers. These centers, containing temples, pyramids, ritual ball courts, and other structures, were denied the character of true "cities"; it was believed that only the Maya elites—a few priests, nobles, and officials and their attendants—lived in them. The rural population, on the other hand, living out among their *milpas* (farm plots), only visited these centers for religious festivals and other special occasions.

This traditional view began to be seriously questioned in the late 1950s, when detailed mapping of the area around the Tikal ceremonial precinct revealed that dense suburbs spread out behind the center for several miles. Similar dense concentrations of house clusters were later found at other major and even minor centers of the Classic period. In the words of Norman Hammond, "the wide-open spaces between the Maya centers, with their scattered bucolic farmers, suddenly became filled with closely packed and hungry suburbanites."

These revelations of the size and density of Classic Maya settlements forced a reassessment of the economic system that supported them. It has now been clearly established that, in addition to slash-and-burn farming, the Maya practiced an intensive and permanent agriculture that included highly productive kitchen gardens with root crops as staples, arboriculture, terracing, and raised fields—artificial platforms of soil built up from low-lying areas.

The evidence of dense suburban populations around ceremonial centers like Tikal has also provoked a debate about the degree of urbanism present in the Maya lowlands. The traditional view that the Classic Maya centers were virtually deserted for most of the year has become untenable. There is, however, no agreement as to whether they were "cities" in the sense that Teotihuacán was clearly a city. Tikal, in the heart of the Petén, was certainly a metropolitan center with a population of perhaps fifty thousand and a countryside heavily populated over an area of some fifty square miles. There is also evidence of some genuine urbanization in northern Yucatán during the Postclassic period, possibly a result of Toltec influence and the tendency to develop the city or town as a fortified position. Chichén Itzá, an old Classic ceremonial center, was greatly enlarged under Toltec influence, while Mayapan, which succeeded Chichén Itzá as a political and military center, constituted a large urban zone encircled by a great wall.

Awareness of the large size and density of Classic Maya populations, the intensive character of much of their agriculture, and the strict social controls that such complex conditions require has also led to a reassessment of Maya social organization. The older view that the ruling class was a small theocratic elite that ruled over a dispersed peasant population from basically empty ceremonial centers has been abandoned. Increased ability to decipher glyphs on the stelae (carved monuments) periodically erected at Classic Maya centers has contributed to a better understanding of the Maya social order. It was once believed that the content of these inscriptions was exclusively religious and astronomical. In recent decades, however, evidence has accumulated that many of the glyphs carved on stelae, lintels, and other monuments record accessions, wars, and other milestones in the lives of secular rulers.

The new interpretation assumes a very complex social order with large distance between the classes.

At the apex of the social pyramid stood a hereditary ruler who combined the political, military, and religious leadership of the state. He was surrounded by an aristocracy or nobility, from which were drawn the administrative and executive bureaucracy. Intellectual specialists such as architects, priests, and scribes may have formed another social level. Below them were the numerous artisans required for ceremonial and civil construction—potters, sculptors, stoneworkers, painters, and the like. At the bottom of the social pyramid were the common laborers and peasant farmers who supplied the labor and food that supported this massive superstructure. The weight of their burdens must in time have become crushing, and their discontent may have ignited revolts that brought about the ultimate collapse of the lowland Maya civilization.

Archaeological investigations have thrown new light on Classic Maya family and settlement patterns. The fact that the residential platforms on which most Maya houses rested occur in groups of three or more suggests that the Maya family was extended rather than nuclear. It probably consisted of two or more nuclear families spanning two or more generations with a common ancestor. Male predominance is suggested by the richer furnishings of male graves and the preeminence of men in monumental art, leading to the conclusion that descent was patrilineal, from father to son. Maya dress and diet, like its housing, reflected class distinctions. Maya clothing was typically Mesoamerican: cotton loincloths, leather sandals, and sometimes a mantle knotted about the shoulder for men; and wrap-around skirts of cotton and blouses with holes for the head and arms for the women. The same articles of clothing, more ornately decorated, were worn by the upper classes.

MAYA RELIGION AND LEARNING

The great object of Maya religion, as the Spanish bishop Diego de Landa concisely put it, was "that they [the gods] should give them health, life, and sustenance." The principal Maya divinities represented those natural forces and objects that most directly affected the material welfare of the people. The supreme god in the Maya pantheon was Itzam

Na, a creator god who incorporated in himself the aspects of many other gods; not only creation, but fire, rain, crops, and earth were among his functions or provinces. Other important divinities were the sun god, the moon goddess, the rain god, the maize god, and the much-feared god of death. The Maya believed that a number of worlds had successively appeared and been destroyed; this present world, too, would end in catastrophe.

The Maya believed in an afterlife. They believed in an Upper World constituted of thirteen layers and an Under World of nine. Over each layer presided a certain god; over the lowest layer of the Under World presided the god of death, Ah Puch. In common with the Aztecs and other peoples of Middle America, the Maya worshiped and placated the gods with a variety of ritual practices that included fasting, penance by bloodletting, the burning of incense, and human sacrifice. Human sacrifice on a large scale already existed in the late Classic period, marked by growing political turbulence and strife among the lowland Maya states, but may have increased in the Postclassic period under Toltec influence.

The Maya priests were obsessed with time, to which they assigned an occult, or magical, content. They developed a calendar that was more accurate than ours in making adjustments in the exact length of the solar year. Maya theologians thought of time as burdens carried on the backs of the gods. At the end of a certain period one god laid down his burden for another god to pick up and continue on the journey of time. A given day or year was lucky or unlucky depending on whether the god-bearer was benevolent or malevolent. Thus, the Maya calendars were primarily divinatory in character; that is, they were used to predict conditions in a particular time period.

The Maya had two almanacs. One was a sacred round of 260 days, corresponding to the pattern of ceremonial life. This calendar was composed of two intermeshing and recurrent cycles of different length: one of thirteen days, recorded as numbers, and the second of twenty days, recorded as names. The name of the fourteenth day-name began with one again. A second cycle was the solar year of 365 days, divided into eighteen "months" of twenty

days each, plus a final period of five unlucky days during which all unnecessary activity was banned. Completion of these two cycles coincided every fifty-two years. Stelae bearing hieroglyphic texts indicating the date and other calendrical data, such as the state of the moon, the position of the planet Venus, and so on, were frequently erected at the end of the fifty-two-year cycle and at other intervals.

The Maya developed the science of mathematics further than any of their Middle American neighbors. Their units were ones, fives, and twenties, with ones designated by dots, fives by bars, and positions for twenty and multiples of twenty. Place-value numeration, based on a sign for zero, was perhaps the greatest intellectual development of Ancient America. In this system, the position of a number determined its value, making it possible for a limited quantity of symbols to express numbers of any size. Its simplicity made it far superior to the contemporary western European arithmetical system, which employed the cumbersome Roman numeration consisting of distinct symbols for each higher unit. It remained for the Arabs to bring their numeration concept to Europe from India, the only other place where it had been invented. Maya mathematics, however, appears to have been applied chiefly to calendrical and astronomical calculation; there is no record of Maya enumeration of people or objects.

Until recently it was believed that Maya hieroglyphic writing, like the mathematics, chiefly served religious and divinatory rather than utilitarian ends. We now have abundant evidence that many of the glyphs carved on the monuments are historical, recording milestones in the lives of Maya rulers. In addition to the inscriptions that appear on stone monuments, lintels, stairways, and other monumental remains, the Maya had great numbers of sacred books or codices, of which only three survive today. These books were painted on folding screens of native paper made of bark. Concerned above all with astronomy, divination, and other related topics, they reveal that Maya astronomers made observations and calculations of truly astounding complexity.

The Maya had no alphabet, properly speaking; that is, the majority of their characters represent ideas or objects rather than sounds. But Maya

Ancient murals uncovered at the Bonampak acropolis depict Mayan cultural rituals integrating history, music, and dance. Here, dancers dressed as lobsters, birds, and crocodiles accompany musicians playing drums, gourd-maracas, and trumpets in a celebration of the debut of a royal heir to the throne. [E.T. Archive, London]

writing had reached the stage of syllabic phonetics through the use of rebus writing, in which the sound of a word is represented by combining pictures or signs of things whose spoken names resemble sounds in the word to be formed. Thus, the Maya word for drought, *kintunyaabil,* was written with four characters, the signs of sun or day (*kin*), stone or 360-day unit of time (*tun*), solar year (*haab*), and the affix *il.* In the 1950s a Russian scholar advanced a theory that Maya writing was truly syllabic and hence could be deciphered by matching the most frequent sound elements in modern Maya to the most frequent signs in the ancient writing, using computers to speed the process of decipherment. The existence of purely phonetic glyphs in the Maya script is now generally accepted by scholars, but they seem to be relatively rare in the deciphered material.

Maya writing was not narrative used to record literature, but the Maya had a large body of myth, legends, poetry, and traditional history that was transmitted orally from generation to generation. Examples of such material are found in the *Popol Vuh,* the so-called Sacred Book of the Quiche Maya of Guatemala. This book deals, among other matters, with the adventures of the heroic twins Hunahpu and Xbalanque, who after many exploits ascended into heaven to become the sun and the moon. It was written in post-Conquest times in the Spanish alphabet by a native who drew on the oral traditions of his people.

In certain types of artistic activity the Maya surpassed all other Middle American peoples. The temples and pyramids at Teotihuacán and Tenochtitlán were often larger than their Maya counterparts but lacked their grace and subtlety. A distinctive feature of Maya architecture was the corbeled vault, or false arch. Other Middle American peoples used horizontal wooden beams to bridge entrances, producing a heavy and squarish impression. The Maya solved the same problem by having the stones on either side of the opening project farther and farther inward, bridging the two sides at the apex by a capstone. Other characteristics of the Maya architectural style were the great façades richly decorated with carved stone and high ornamental roof combs in temples and palaces. Inner walls were frequently covered with paintings, a few of which have survived. The most celebrated of these paintings are the frescoes discovered in 1946 at Bonampak, an isolated site in the tropical forests of the northeastern corner of the Mexican state of Chiapas. They date from about A.D. 800. These frescoes completely cover the inner walls of a small build-ing of three rooms. They tell a story that begins with a ritual dance, goes on to portray an expedi-tion to obtain sacrificial victims, which is fol-lowed by a battle scene, and ends with a human sacrifice, ceremonies, and dance. Despite the highly conventionalized and static style, the absence of perspective and shading, and obvious errors in the human figure, there is an effect of realism that is often missing from other Mesoamerican art.

Students of the Maya have frequently testified to the admirable personal qualities of the people who, with a very limited technology and in a most forbidding environment, created one of the great-est cultural traditions of all time. Bishop Diego de Landa, who burned twenty-seven Maya codices as "works of the devil," nevertheless observed that the Maya were very generous and hospitable. No one could enter their houses, he wrote, without being offered food and drink.

Maya Decline and Transformation of Mesoamerica

By A.D. 800 the Mesoamerican world had been shaken to its foundations by a crisis that seemed to spread from one Classic center to another. Teotihuacán, Rome of that world, itself perished at the hands of invaders, who burned down the city sometime between A.D. 650 and 800. Toward the latter date, the great ceremonial center at Monte Albán was abandoned. And by A.D. 800 the process of disintegration had reached the Classic Maya heartland of southern Yucatán and north-ern Guatemala, whose deserted or destroyed cen-ters reverted one by one to the bush.

From this Time of Troubles in Mesoamerica (approximately A.D. 700 to 1000) a new Postclassic order emerged, sometimes appropri-ately called Militarist. Whereas priests and benign nature gods may have sometimes presided over Mesoamerican societies of the Classic era, warriors and terrible war gods clearly dominated the states that arose on the ruins of the Classic world. In cen-tral Mexico the sway of Teotihuacán, probably based above all on cultural and economic supremacy, gave way to strife among new states that warred with one another for land, water, and tribute.

The most important of these, successor to the power of Teotihuacán, was the Toltec "empire," with its capital at Tula, about fifty miles from present-day Mexico City. Lying on the periphery of the Valley of Mexico, Tula may have once been an outpost of Teotihuacán, guarding its frontiers against the hunting tribes of the northern deserts. Following the collapse of Teotihuacán, one such tribe, the Toltecs, swept down from the north, entered the Valley of Mexico, and overwhelmed the pitiful survivors among the Teotihuacán people.

Toltec power and prosperity reached its peak under a ruler named Topiltzin, who moved his capital to Tula in about 980. Apparently renamed Quetzalcóatl in his capacity of high priest of the ancient god worshiped by the Teotihuacáns, Topiltzin-Quetzalcóatl reigned for nineteen years with such splendor that he and his city became legendary. The Song of Quetzalcóatl tells of the wonders of Tula, a true paradise on earth where cotton grew colored and the soil yielded fruit of such size that small ears of corn were used, not as food, but as fuel to heat steam baths. The legends of ancient Mexico celebrate the Toltec's superhu-man powers and talents; they were described as master artisans, as creators of culture. Over this Golden Age presided the great priest-king Quetzalcóatl, who thus revived the glories of Teotihuacán.

Toward the end of Quetzalcóatl's reign, Tula seems to have become the scene of an obscure struggle between two religious traditions. One was associated with the worship of Tezcatlipoca, a Toltec tribal god pictured as an all-powerful and capricious deity who demanded human sacrifice. The other was identified with the cult of the ancient god Quetzalcóatl, who had brought men and women maize, all learning, and the arts. In a version of the Quetzalcóatl legend that may reflect post-Conquest Christian influence, the god demanded of them only the peaceful sacrifice of jade, snakes, and butterflies. This struggle found fanciful expression in the native legend that tells how the black magic of the enchanter Tezcatlipoca caused the saintly priest-king Quetzalcóatl to fall from grace and drove him into exile from Tula.

Whatever its actual basis, the Quetzalcóatl legend, with its promise that a mystical Redeemer would someday return to reclaim his kingdom, profoundly impressed the people of ancient Mexico and played its part in the destruction of the Mesoamerican world. By a singular coincidence, the year in which Quetzalcóatl promised to return was the very year in which Cortés landed at Veracruz. Belief in the legend helped immobilize indigenous resistance, at least initially.

Topiltzin-Quetzalcóatl was succeeded by lesser kings, who vainly struggled to solve the growing problems of the Toltec state. The causes of this crisis are obscure: tremendous droughts may have caused crop failure and famines, perhaps aggravated by Toltec neglect of agriculture in favor of collection of tribute from conquered peoples. A series of revolutions reflected the Toltec economic and social difficulties. The last Toltec king, Huemac, apparently committed suicide about 1174, and the Toltec state disappeared with him. In the following year, a general dispersion or exodus of the Toltecs took place. Tula itself fell into the hands of barbarians in about 1224.

The fall of Tula, situated on the margins of the Valley of Mexico, opened the way for a general invasion of the valley by Nahuatl-speaking northern peoples. These newcomers, called Chichimecs, may be compared to the Germanic invaders who broke into the dying Roman Empire. Like them, the Chichimec leaders respected and tried to absorb the superior culture of the vanquished people. They were eager to intermarry with the surviving Toltec royalty and nobility.

These invaders founded a number of succession-states in the lake country at the bottom of the Valley of Mexico. Legitimately or not, their rulers all claimed the honor of Toltec descent. In artistic and industrial development, the Texcocan kingdom, organized in 1260, easily excelled its neighbors. Texcocan civilization reached its climactic moment two centuries later in the reign of King Nezahualcoyotl (1418–1472), distinguished poet, philosopher, and lawgiver, perhaps the most remarkable figure to emerge from the mists of Ancient America.

The Aztecs of Mexico

Among the last of the Chichimecs to arrive in the valley were the Aztecs, or Mexica, the name they gave themselves. The date of their departure from the north was probably about A.D. 1111. Led by four priests and a woman who carried a medicine bundle housing the spirit of their tribal god, Huitzilopochtli, they arrived in the Valley of Mexico in about 1218 after obscure wanderings. The traditional belief that they were basically a hunting and gathering people who were only "half civilized" but had some acquaintance with agriculture has been questioned by some scholars, who hold that by the time of their arrival the Aztecs were typically Mesoamerican in culture, religion, and economic and social organization. Finding the most desirable sites occupied by others, they had to take refuge on marshy lands around Lake Texcoco. Here in 1344 or 1345, they began to build the town of Tenochtitlán. At this time, the Aztec community was composed of a small number of kinship, landholding groups called *calpulli.*

The patches of solid ground that formed the Aztec territory were gradually built over with huts of cane and reeds. They were followed later by more ambitious structures of turf, adobe, and light stone. As the population increased, a larger cultivable area became necessary. For this purpose the Aztecs borrowed from their neighbors the technique of making *chinampas*—artificial garden beds formed of masses of earth and rich sediment dredged from the lake bed and held in place by wickerwork. Eventually the roots, striking downward, took firm hold in the lake bottom and created solid ground. On these chinampas the Aztecs grew maize, beans, and other products.

AZTEC IMPERIAL EXPANSION

For a long time, the Aztecs were subservient to their powerful neighbors in Azcapotzalco, the dominant power in the lake country in the late fourteenth and early fifteenth centuries. A turning point in Aztec history came in 1428. Led by their war chief Itzcoatl, the Aztecs joined the rebellious city-state of Texcoco and the smaller town of Tlacopan to destroy the tyranny of Azcapotzalco. Their joint victory (1430) led to the rise of a Triple Alliance for the conquest first of the valley, then of much of the Middle American world. Gradually the balance of power shifted to the aggressive Aztec state. Texcoco became a junior partner, and Tlacopan was reduced to a satellite. The strong position of their island fortification and a shrewd policy of forming alliances and sharing the spoils of conquest with strategic mainland towns, which they later came to dominate, help explain Aztec success in gaining control of the Valley of Mexico. In turn, conquest of the valley offered a key to the conquest of Middle America. The valley had the advantages of short internal lines of communication surrounded by easily defensible mountain barriers. Openings to the north, east, west, and south gave Aztec warriors easy access to adjacent valleys.

Conquest of Azcapotzalco gave the Aztecs their first beachhead on the lakeshore. Most of the conquered land and the peasantry living on it were assigned to warrior-nobles who had distinguished themselves in battle. Originally assigned for life, these lands tended to become fiefs held in permanent inheritance. Thus, warfare created new economic and social cleavages within Aztec society. In the process the original kinship basis of the calpulli was eroded and in the Valley of Mexico, at least, it lost most of its autonomy, becoming primarily a social and territorial administrative unit. Composed mostly of *macehualtin* (commoners) who owed tribute, labor, and military service to the Aztec state, the calpulli continued to be led by hereditary elite families who were completely subject to superior Aztec officials whose orders they carried out.

In the Valley of Mexico, and in other highly developed areas, the communal landownership formerly associated with the calpulli also suffered erosion as a result of growing population pressure, forcing some members to leave, internal economic differentiation, and the need to sell or rent communal land in time of famine or some other crisis. Calpulli of the original kinship, landowning type survived better in areas where the process of class stratification and state formation was less pronounced. Over much of central Mexico, however, by the time of the Spanish Conquest landlessness and tenant farming appear to have become very widespread, with serflike peasants (*mayeque*) forming perhaps the majority of the Aztec population. These unfree peasants enjoyed only the usufruct of the land and had to render tribute and service to the noble owner. The picture that emerges from recent studies is one of a society "like medieval European society, highly complicated and locally diverse." The growing cleavage between commoners and nobles found ideological reflection in the origin myth that claimed a separate divine origin (from the god Quetzalcóatl) for the Aztec nobility.

Other ideological changes included the elevation of the tribal god Huitzilopochtli to a position of equality with, or supremacy over, the great nature gods traditionally worshiped in the Valley of Mexico, the burning of the ancient picture writings because these books slighted the Aztecs, and the creation of a new history that recognized the Aztec grandeur. A new emphasis was placed on capturing prisoners of war to use as sacrifices on the altars of the Aztec gods in order to assure the continuance of the universe.[3]

The successors of Itzcoatl, sometimes individually, sometimes in alliance with Texcoco, extended

---

[3]Some social scientists have attempted to explain the Aztec practice of mass human sacrifice and its accompaniment of ritual cannibalism by the lack of protein in the Aztec diet. This theory is contradicted by the variety of animal foods available to the Aztecs and by the fact that neither Indian nor Spanish sources refer to the practice of cannibalism during the great famine that hastened the end of Aztec resistance to the Spanish conquest. For the rest, the sacramental feast, designed to let participants share the grace of the god to whom the prisoner was sacrificed, was simplicity itself, and the captor could not eat of his flesh because of an assumed mystical kinship relationship between the captor and his prisoner.

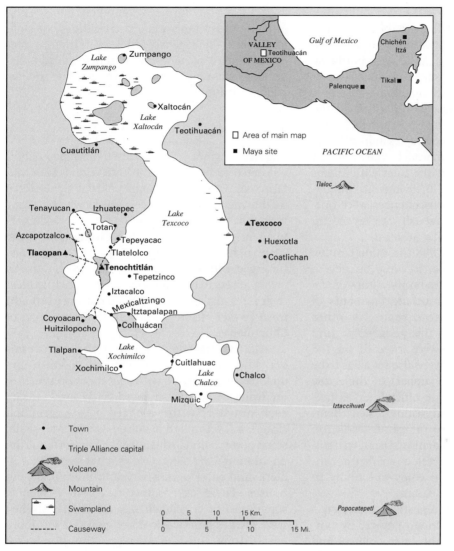

Map legend:

- • Town
- ▲ Triple Alliance capital
- Volcano
- Mountain
- Swampland
- - - - - Causeway

Inset legend:
- ▢ Area of main map
- ■ Maya site

Valley of Mexico

Aztec rule over and beyond the Valley of Mexico. By the time Moctezuma II became ruler in 1502, the Triple Alliance was levying tribute on scores of towns, large and small, from the fringes of the arid northern plateau to the lowlands of Tehuantepec, and from the Atlantic to the Pacific. Within this extensive area only a few states or kingdoms, like the fierce Tarascans' state or the city-state of Tlaxcala, retained complete independence. Others, like Cholula, were left at peace in return for their benevolent neutrality or cooperation with the Aztecs. According to some controversial modern estimates, the Aztecs and their allies ruled over a population of perhaps 25 million.

The Aztecs waged war with or without cause. Refusal by a group to pay tribute to the Aztec ruler was sufficient pretext for invasion by the Aztecs. Injuries to the far-ranging Aztec merchants by people of the region they visited sometimes served as motive for invasion. Aztec merchants also prepared the way for conquest by reporting on the resources and defenses of the areas in which they traded; sometimes they acted as spies in hostile territory. If they returned home safely, these valiant merchants were honored by the ruler with amber lip plugs and other gifts. If their enemies discovered them, however, the consequences were horrid. "They were slain in ambush and served up with chili sauce," says a native account.

Victory in war always had the same results: long lines of captives made the long journey to Tenochtitlán to be offered up on the altars of the gods. In addition, periodic tribute payments of maize, cotton mantles, cacao beans, or other products—depending on the geography and resources of the region—were imposed on the vanquished. Certain lands were also set aside to be cultivated by them for the support of the Aztec crown, priesthood, and state officials or as fiefs given to warriors who had distinguished themselves in battle. A steward or tribute collector, sometimes assisted by a resident garrison, was stationed in the town. For the rest, as a rule the conquered people continued to enjoy autonomy in government, culture, and customs.

Because of its nonintegrated character—reflected in the relative autonomy enjoyed by vanquished peoples and the light Aztec political and military presence in conquered territories—the Aztec Empire has traditionally been regarded as an inferior or deficient political organization in comparison with the Inca Empire, with its centralized administration, standing armies, massive transfers of populations, and other integrative policies. Recently, however, it has been argued that rather than being inferior, the Aztec imperial system represented an alternative—but no less efficient— approach to the problem of extracting surplus from tributary peoples at a minimal administrative and military cost. The Aztec army mobilized only for further conquests and the suppression of rebellions. By leaving the defeated regimes in place and avoiding direct territorial control, the Aztec state was spared the expense, inherent in a more integrated empire, of maintaining provincial administrations, standing armies, permanent garrisons, and fortifications.

AZTEC CULTURE AND SOCIETY

The Aztec capital of Tenochtitlán had a population estimated to be between 150,000 and 200,000. Like Venice, the city was an oval island connected to the mainland by three causeways that converged at the center of the city and served as its main arteries of traffic. There were few streets; their place was taken by numerous canals, thronged with canoes and bordered by footpaths giving access to the thousands of houses that lined their sides. An aqueduct in solid masonry brought fresh water from the mountain springs of Chapultepec.

On the outlying chinampas, the Aztec farmers, who paddled their produce to town in tiny dugouts, lived in huts with thatched roofs resting on walls of wattle smeared with mud. Inside each hut were a three-legged *metate* (grinding stone), a few mats that served as beds and seats, some pottery, and little more. The majority of the population—artisans, priests, civil servants, soldiers, and entertainers—lived in more imposing houses. These were sometimes built of adobe, sometimes of a reddish *tezontli* lava, but they were always lime-washed and painted. Far more pretentious than most were the houses of calpulli leaders, merchants, and nobles.

As in housing, Aztec clothing differed according to the individual's economic and social status. For men the essential garments were a loincloth with broad flaps at front and back, usually decorated with fringes and tassels as well as embroidery work, and a blanket about two yards by one in size. This blanket hung under the left arm and was knotted on the right shoulder. Commoners wore plain blankets of maguey fiber or coarse cotton; rich merchants and nobles displayed very elaborate cotton mantles adorned with symbolic designs. Women wore shifts, wraparound skirts of white cotton tied with a narrow belt, and loose, short-sleeved tunics. Both shifts and tunics were decorated with vivid embroidery. Men wore sandals of leather or woven maguey fiber; women went barefoot.

As with dress, so with food: wealth and social position determined its abundance and variety. The fare of the ordinary Aztec consisted of ground maize meal, beans, and vegetables cooked with chili. Meat was rarely seen on the commoner's table, but on festive occasions a dog might be served. It was otherwise with the nobility. A native account of the foods eaten by the lords includes many varieties of tortillas and tamales, roast turkey hen, roast quail, turkey with a sauce of small chilies, tomatoes, and ground squash seeds, venison sprinkled with seeds, many kinds of fish and fruits—and such delicacies as maguey grubs with a sauce of small chilies, winged ants with savory herbs, and rats with sauce. They finished their repast with chocolate, a divine beverage forbidden to commoners.

Education among the Aztecs was highly formal and served the dual purpose of preparing the child for his or her duties in the world and of indoctrinating him or her with the ideals of the tribe. Boys were sent to school at the age of ten or twelve. Sons of commoners, merchants, and artisans attended the *Telpochcalli* (House of Youth), where they received instruction in religion, good usage, and the art of war. The *Calmecac* (Priests' House), a school of higher learning, was reserved in principle for the sons of the nobility, but there is evidence that at least some children of merchants and commoners were admitted. Here, in addition to ordinary training, students received instruction that prepared them to be priests, public officials, and military leaders. The curriculum included what we would today call rhetoric, or a noble manner of speaking, study of religious and philosophical doctrines as revealed in the divine songs of the sacred books, the arts of chronology and astrology, and training in history through study of the *Xiuhamatl* (Books of the Years). The *tlamatinime* (sages) who taught in the Aztec schools were also concerned with the formation of "a true face and heart," the striking Nahuatl metaphor for personality. Self-restraint, moderation, devotion to duty, a stoic awareness that "life is short and filled with hardships, and all comes to an end," an impeccable civility, modesty: these were among the qualities and concepts that the Aztec sages instilled in their charges.

Girls had special schools where they were taught such temple duties as sweeping, offering incense three times during the night, and preparing food for the idols; weaving and other womanly tasks; and general preparation for marriage. Education for the men usually terminated at the age of twenty or twenty-two; for girls, at sixteen or seventeen. These were also the ages at which marriage was contracted. The development of Aztec militarism may have led to some decline in women's status, and the Aztec "speeches of the elders" warned the wife that "your obligation is to obey your husband. You are to make the beverage, the food for him, and his shirt, his cape, his breeches." The model wife was represented as a diligent housewife and a mother dedicated to the careful raising of her children. But in some respects the status of Aztec women was complementary to that of men, rather than subordinate. Childbirth, for example, was symbolically compared to warfare: successful delivery was equated with the taking of a prisoner, and death in childbirth was equivalent to being killed in battle. For the rest, Aztec women worked as doctors, artisans, merchants, and priests.

In a society with such a complex economic and social life, disputes and aggressions inevitably arose and necessitated the development of an elaborate legal code. A hierarchy of courts was topped by two high tribunals that met in the royal palace in Tenochtitlán. The punishments of the Aztecs were severe. Death was the penalty for murder, rebellion, wearing the clothes of the other sex, and adultery; theft was punished by slavery for the first offense, by hanging for the second.

Economic life in Aztec Mexico rested on a base of intensive and extensive agriculture. Intensive irrigation was practiced in areas with reliable water sources; its most notable form was that of the chinampas. Slash-and-burn cultivation, with field rotation, was the rule in other areas, but everywhere maize and beans were the principal crops. In the absence of large domesticated animals to produce manure, night soil was regularly used as fertilizer in chinampa agriculture in the Valley of Mexico. To prevent contamination of the valley's two freshwater lakes by flows of water from the saline ones that were harmful to chinampa agriculture, and to maintain the fairly constant water level that it required, the construction of an elaborate system of dikes, canals, and aqueducts was begun during the reign of King Itzcoatl. This led to the creation of large chinampa areas producing foodstuffs for Tenochtitlán. Productive as they were, however, it is estimated that they accounted for only 5 percent of the city's subsistence needs, and their expansion was limited by the salinity of the remaining lakes. For the balance of its food needs, therefore, Tenochtitlán had to rely on imports obtained by way of tribute and trade. An elaborate, state-controlled trade and transportation network based on regional and metropolitan markets, the *tlameme* (professional carrier) system of portage, and an efficient canoe traffic that linked the entire lake system of the Valley of Mexico funneled a vast quantity of foodstuffs and other bulk goods into Tenochtitlán. Manufactured goods were then exported from Tenochtitlán to its hinterlands, forming a core-periphery relationship.

The vast scale on which the exchange of goods and services was carried on in the great market of Tenochtitlán aroused the astonishment of the conquistador Cortés, who gave a detailed account of its immense activity. "Each kind of merchandise is sold in its respective street," he wrote, "and they do not mix their kinds of merchandise of any species; thus they preserve perfect order." The Aztecs lacked a unitary system of money, but cacao beans, cotton mantles, quills filled with gold dust, and small copper axes were assigned standardized values and supplemented a barter system of exchange. The Aztecs had no scales; goods were sold by count and measure. The market was patrolled by officials who checked on the fairness of transactions; a merchants' court sat to hear and settle disputes between buyers and sellers.

As the above account implies, by the time of the Conquest division of labor among the Aztecs had progressed to the point where a large class of artisans no longer engaged in agriculture. The artisan class included carpenters, potters, stonemasons, silversmiths, and featherworkers. In the same category belonged such specialists as fishermen, hunters, dancers, and musicians. All these specialists were organized in guilds, each with its guildhall and patron god; their professions were probably hereditary. The artist and the craftsman enjoyed a position of high honor and responsibility in Aztec society. Assigning the origin of all their arts and crafts to the Toltec period, the Aztecs applied the name Toltec to the true or master painter, singer, potter, or sculptor.

Advances in regional division of labor and the growth of the market for luxury goods also led to the emergence of a merchant class, which was organized in a very powerful guild. The wealth of this class and its important military and diplomatic services to the Aztec state made the merchants a third force in Aztec society, ranking only after the warrior nobility and the priesthood. The wealth of the merchants sometimes aroused the distrust and hostility of the Aztec rulers and nobility. Popular animosity toward the merchants is reflected in the words of a native account: "The merchants were those who had plenty, who prospered; the greedy, the well-fed man, the covetous, the niggardly, the miser, who controlled wealth and family . . . the mean, the stingy, the selfish."

The priesthood was the main integrating force in Aztec society. Through its possession of a sacred calendar that regulated the performance of agricultural tasks, it played a key role in the life of the people. The priesthood was also the repository of the accumulated lore and history of the Aztec tribe. By virtue of his special powers of intercession with the gods, his knowledge and wisdom, the priest was called on to intervene in every private or collective crisis of the Aztec. Celibate, austere, continually engaged in the penance of bloodletting, priests wielded an enormous influence over the Aztec people.

The priesthood shared authority and prestige with the nobility, a class that had gained power through war and political centralization. In addition to many warriors, this class consisted of a large bureaucracy made up of tribute collectors, judges, ambassadors, and the like. Such officeholders were rewarded for their services by the revenue from public lands assigned to support them. Their offices were not hereditary. They were, however, normally conferred on sons of fathers who had held the same positions.

The wealth of the warrior nobility consisted chiefly of landed estates. Originally granted for life, these lands eventually became private estates that were handed down from father to son and could be sold or exchanged. The formerly free peasants on these lands were probably transformed into mayeque, farm workers, or tenant farmers tied to the land. With the expansion of the Aztec Empire, the number of private estates steadily grew.

On the margins of Aztec society was a large class of slaves. Slavery was the punishment for a variety of offenses, including failure to pay debts. Slavery was sometimes assumed by poor people in return for food. Slave owners frequently brought their chattels to the great market at Azcapotzalco for sale to rich merchants or nobles for personal service or as sacrificial offerings to the gods.

The Aztec political system was a mixture of royal despotism and theocracy. Political power was concentrated in a ruling class of priests and nobles, over which presided an absolute ruler resembling an Oriental despot. Originally, the ruler had been chosen by the whole Aztec community, assembled for that purpose. Later he was chosen by a council or electoral college dominated by the most important priests, officials, and warriors, including close relatives of the king. The council, in consultation with the kings of Texcoco and Tlacopan, selected the monarch from among the sons, brothers, or nephews of the previous ruler. The new ruler was assisted by a council of four great nobles. At the time of the Conquest, the emperor was the luckless Moctezuma II, who succeeded his uncle Ahuitzotl.

Great splendor and intricate ceremonies prevailed in Moctezuma's court. The great nobles of the realm took off their rich ornaments of feather, jade, and gold before entering his presence; barefoot, eyes on the ground, they approached the basketry throne of their king. Moctezuma dined in solitary magnificence, separated by a wooden screen from his servitors and the four great lords with whom he conversed.

This wealth, luxury, and ceremony revealed the great social and economic changes that had taken place in the small, despised Aztec tribe that had come to live in the marshes of Lake Texcoco less than two centuries before. The Aztec Empire had reached a peak of pride and power. Yet the Aztec leaders lived in fear; the Aztec chronicles register a deep sense of insecurity. The mounting demands of the Aztec tribute collectors caused revolts on the part of tributary towns. Though repressed, they broke out afresh. The haunted Aztec imagination saw portents of evil on earth and in the troubled air. A child was born with two heads; the volcano Popocatepetl became unusually active; a comet streamed across the sky. The year 1519 approached, the year in which, according to Aztec lore, the god-king Quetzalcóatl might return to reclaim the realm from which he had been driven centuries before by the forces of evil.

The Incas of Peru

In the highlands of modern Peru in the mid-fourteenth century, a small tribe rose from obscurity to create by 1500 the mightiest empire of Ancient America. From the time of the discovery and conquest of Peru by Pizarro to the present, the Inca achievements in political and social organization have attracted intense interest. Soon after the Conquest a debate began on the nature of Inca society that has continued almost to the present day. For some it was a "socialist empire"; others viewed it as a forerunner of the "welfare state" of our own time; for still others the Inca realm anticipated the totalitarian tyrannies of the twentieth century. Only recently has more careful study of the evidence, especially the evidence of colonial provincial records of official economic and social inquiries, litigation, wills, and the like, provided a more correct picture of Inca society and banished the traditional labels.

The physical environment of the central Andean area offers a key to the remarkable cultural development of this region. In Peru high mountains rise steeply from the sea, leaving a narrow coastal plain that is a true desert. The Humboldt Current runs north along the coast from the Antarctic, making the ocean much colder than the land; hence the rains fall at sea. But lack of rainfall is compensated for by short rivers that make their precipitous way down from the high snowfields. These rivers create oases at intervals along the coast and provide water for systems of canal irrigation. The aridity of the climate preserves the great natural wealth of the soil, which in areas of heavy rainfall is leached away. The coastal waters of Peru are rich in fish, and its offshore islands, laden in Inca times with millions of tons of guano, made available an inexhaustible source of fertilizer for agriculture.

To be sure, the rugged highlands of modern Peru and Bolivia offer relatively little arable land. But the valleys are fertile and well watered and support a large variety of crops. Maize is grown at lower levels (up to about eleven thousand feet), potatoes and quinoa at higher altitudes. Above the agricultural zone, the *puna* (plateau) provides fodder for herds of llamas and alpacas, domesticated members of the camel family, which were important in Inca times as a source of meat and wool. Potentially, this environment offered a basis for large food production and a dense population.

ORIGINS OF INCA CULTURE

Like the Aztecs of ancient Mexico, the Incas of Peru were heirs to a cultural tradition of great antiquity. This tradition had its origin not in the highlands but on the coast. By 2500 B.C., a village life, based chiefly on fishing and food gathering and supplemented by the cultivation of squash, lima beans, and a few other plants, had arisen about the mouths of rivers in the coastal area. Maize, introduced into Peruvian agriculture about 1500 B.C., did not become important until many centuries later.

The transition from the Archaic to the Preclassic period seems to have come later and more suddenly in Peru than in Mesoamerica. After long centuries of the simple village life just described, a strong advance of culture began on the coast about 900 B.C. This advance seems to have been associated with progress in agriculture, especially greater use of maize, and with a movement up the river valleys from the littoral, possibly as a result of population pressure. Between 900 and 500 B.C., a distinctive style in building, art, ceramics, and weaving, known as Chavín (from the name of the site of a great ceremonial center discovered in 1946), spread along the coast and even into the highlands. The most distinctive feature of Chavín is its art style, which features a feline being, presumably a deity, whose cult spread over the area of Chavín influence.

The Classic or Florescent period that emerged in Peru at or shortly before the beginning of the Old World's Christian era reflected further progress in agriculture, notably in the use of irrigation and fertilization. The brilliant culture called Nazca displaced the Chavín along the coast and highlands of southern Peru at this time. Nazca pottery is distinguished by its use of color. Sometimes there are as many as eleven soft pastel shades on one pot. The lovely Nazca textiles display an enormous range of colors.

Even more remarkable was the Mochica culture of the northern Peruvian coast. The Mochica built pyramids and temples, roads and large irrigation canals, and evolved a complex, highly stratified society with a directing priesthood and a powerful priest-king. Metallurgy was well developed, as evidenced by the wide use of copper weapons and tools and the manufacture of alloys of gold, copper, and silver. But as craftsmen and artists the Mochica are best known for their red and black pottery, never surpassed in the perfection of its realistic modeling. The so-called portrait vases, apparently representing actual individuals, mark the acme of Mochica realism. The pottery was also frequently decorated with realistic paintings of the most varied kind, including erotic scenes, which today are collectors' items. The pottery frequently depicts war scenes, suggesting chronic struggles for limited arable land and sources of water. The aggressive Mochica were themselves finally conquered by invaders who ravaged their lands, and a time of turbulence and cultural decline came to northern Peru.

About A.D. 600, the focus of Andean civilization shifted from the coast to the highlands. At the site called Tiahuanaco, just south of Lake Titicaca on the high plateau of Bolivia, there arose a great ceremonial center famed for its megalithic architecture, which was constructed with great stone blocks perfectly fitted together, and for its monumental human statuary. Tiahuanaco seems to have been the capital of a military state that eventually controlled all of southern Peru from Arequipa south to highland Bolivia and Chile. Another people, the Huari, embarked on a career of conquest from their homeland near modern Ayacucho; their territory ultimately included both the coast and highlands as far north as Cajamarca and south to the Tiahuanaco frontier. After a few centuries of domination, the Huari Empire broke up about A.D. 1000. At about the same time the Tiahuanaco sway also came to an end. The disintegration of these empires was followed by a return to political and artistic regionalism in the southern Andean area.

By A.D. 1000, a number of Postclassic states, differing from their predecessors in their greater size, had established their control over large portions of the northern Peruvian coast. Their rise was accompanied by the growth of cities. Each river valley had its own urban center, and an expanded net of irrigation works made support of larger populations possible. The largest of these new states was the Chimu kingdom. Its capital, Chanchan, was an immense city spread over eight square miles, with houses made of great molded adobe bricks grouped into large units or compounds. The Chimu kingdom survived until its conquest by the Inca in the mid-fifteenth century.

INCA ECONOMY AND SOCIETY

In the highlands, meanwhile, where less settled conditions prevailed, a new power was emerging. The Incas (so called after their own name for the ruling lineage) made a modest appearance in history as one of a number of small tribes that inhabited the Cuzco region in the Andean highlands and struggled with each other for possession of land and water. A strong strategic situation in the Valley of Cuzco and some cultural superiority over their neighbors favored the Incas as they began their career of conquest. Previous empires—

This sculpted handle of the *tumi*, a ceremonial knife produced by the Chimu empire that dominated coastal Peru between the tenth and fifteenth centuries, was made of gold, inlaid with turquoise. It is a totemic representation of the divine power of the king, who wears the *orejones* (earplugs) typical of royal authority in the ancient Andean world. [The Art Archive/Museo del Oro Limo/Dagli Orti]

Huari, Tiahuanaco, and Chimu—no doubt provided the Incas with instructive precedents for conquest and the consolidation of conquest through a variety of political and socioeconomic techniques. Like other imperialist nations of antiquity, the Incas had a body of myth and legend that ascribed a divine origin to their rulers and gave their warriors a comforting assurance of supernatural favor and protection.

True imperial expansion seems to have begun in the second quarter of the fifteenth century, in the reign of Pachacuti Inca, who was crowned in 1438. Together with his son Topa Inca, also a great conqueror, Pachacuti obtained the submission of many

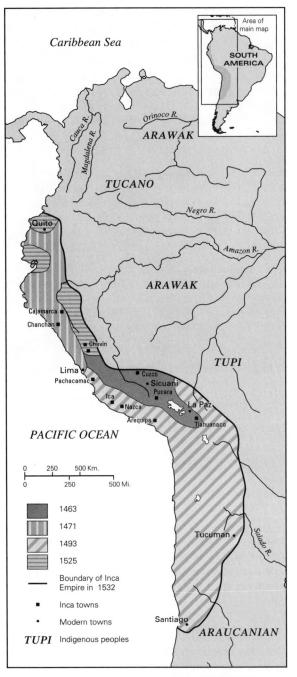

Growth of the Inca Empire, 1460–1532

Pachacuti is credited with many reforms and innovations, including the establishment of the territorial divisions and elaborate administrative bureaucracy that made the wheels of the Inca Empire go round. By 1527 the boundary markers of the Children of the Sun rested on the modern frontier between Ecuador and Colombia to the north and on the Maule River in Chile to the south. A population of perhaps 9 million people owed allegiance to the emperor. When the Spaniards arrived, the ruler was Atahualpa, who had just won the imperial mantle by defeating his half-brother Huascar.

The Incas maintained their authority with an arsenal of devices that included the spread of their Quechua language (still spoken by five-sixths of the indigenous peoples of the central Andean area) as the official language of the empire, the imposition of a unifying state religion, and a shrewd policy of incorporating chieftains of conquered regions into the central bureaucracy. An important factor in the Inca plan of unification was the policy of resettlement, or colonization. This consisted of deporting dissident populations and replacing them with loyal *mitimaes* (colonists) from older provinces of the empire. An excellent network of roads and footpaths linked administrative centers and made it possible to send armies and messengers quickly from one part of the empire to another. Some roads were paved; others were cut into solid rock. Where the land was marshy, the roads passed over causeways; suspension bridges spanned gorges, and pontoon bridges of buoyant reeds were used to cross rivers. The Incas had no system of writing, but they possessed a most efficient means of keeping records in a memory aid called the *quipu*, a stick or cord with a number of knotted strings tied to it. Strings of different colors represented different articles, people, or districts; knots tied in the strings ascended in units representing ones, tens, hundreds, thousands, and so on.

The economic basis of the Inca Empire was its intensive irrigation agriculture capable of supporting without serious strain not only the producers but the large Inca armies, a large administrative bureaucracy, and many other persons engaged in nonproductive activities. The Incas did not develop this agriculture. By the time of their rise, the original coastal irrigation systems had probably been

provinces by the skillful use of claims of divine aid, fair promises, threats, and naked force. Reputed to be a great organizer as well as a mighty warrior, extended over all suitable areas in coastal and highland Peru. But along with their political and religious institutions, the Incas introduced the advanced practices of irrigation, terracing, and fertilization among conquered peoples of more primitive culture. Terracing was widely used to extend the arable area and to prevent injury to fields and settlements in the narrow Andean valleys from runoff from the steep slopes during the rainy season. Irrigation ditches, sometimes mere trenches, sometimes elaborate stone channels, conducted water to the fields and pastures where it was needed.

Agricultural implements were few and simple. They consisted chiefly of a foot plow, used to break up the ground and dig holes for planting, and a hoe with a bronze blade for general cultivation. As previously noted, the potato and quinoa were staple crops in the higher valleys; maize was the principal crop at lower altitudes; and a wide variety of plants, including cotton, coca, and beans, was cultivated in the lower and hotter valleys. A major function of the Inca state was to regulate the exchange of the products of these multiple environments, primarily through the collection of tribute and its redistribution to various groups in Inca society. The Inca state also promoted self-sufficiency by allowing members of a given community to exploit the resources of different levels of the Andean "vertical" economy.

The basic unit of Inca social organization was the *ayllu*, a kinship group whose members claimed descent from a common ancestor and married within the group. The joining of two people in marriage linked the kin of each partner, who were "henceforth expected to behave toward one another as brothers and sisters." Not only brothers and sisters born of the same parents, but first, second, and third cousins (that is, all those who traced their ancestry back to the same great-grandfather) regarded one another as brothers and sisters, so marriage created a large extended kinship group. The members of this extended kinship group were expected to aid one another in tasks beyond the capacity of a single household.

A village community typically consisted of several ayllu. Each ayllu owned certain lands, which were assigned in lots to heads of families. Each family head had the right to use and pass on the land to descendants, but not to sell or otherwise dispose of it. Villagers frequently practiced mutual aid in agricultural tasks, in the construction of dwellings, and in other projects of a private or public nature. The Inca rulers took over this communal principle and utilized it for their own ends in the form of corvée, or unpaid forced labor. In the words of the anthropologist Nathan Wachtel, "the imperial Inca mode of production was based on the ancient communal mode of production which it left in place, while exploiting the principle of reciprocity to legitimate its rule."

Gender parallelism, beginning with parallel lines of descent, played a key role in ayllu kinship organization and ideology. Women regarded themselves as descendants through their mothers of a line of women; men viewed themselves as descending from their fathers in a line of men. "This organization of gender relations and kin ties through parallel descent," writes Irene Silverblatt in her remarkable study of gender relations in Andean society, *Sun, Moon, and Witches,* "was inherent in the ways Andean women and men created and re-created their social existence. The values and tone of gender parallelism were continuously reinforced in the practical activities through which they constructed and experienced their lives."

Parallel transmission ensured that women, through their mothers, enjoyed access to land, herds, water, and other resources. Gender parallelism also defined the division of labor in Andean society, some activities being regarded as most appropriate to men, others to women. Weaving and spinning were regarded as peculiarly women's tasks, plowing and bearing arms as the special tasks of men; but these activities were viewed as complementary, as having equal importance.

After the Inca conquest, however, notes Silverblatt, "the imperial ideal of Andean malehood became the norm." "Soldier" was the title given to a commoner man when, as a married adult, he was inscribed in the imperial census rolls; "soldier's wife" was the equivalent category for a woman. There is evidence that before the Inca conquest, women, inheriting rights from their mothers, sometimes held leadership positions on the ayllu level. However, the Inca imperial norm "attaching masculinity to political power and conquest skewed the balance of gender relations as the empire expanded, as men filled positions of authority in the Inca administration and military which were denied to women of an equivalent social station." But the Andean tradition of parallel descent allowed Inca noblewomen to claim access to their own resources, with rights to land in the Cuzco region passing down from noblewoman to noblewoman.

Before the Inca conquest, the ayllu were governed by *curacas* (hereditary chiefs) assisted by a council of elders, with a superior curaca or lord (*jatun curaca*) ruling over the whole people or state. Under Inca rule, the kinship basis of ayllu organization was weakened through the planned removal of some of its members and the settlement of strangers in its midst (the system of mitimaes). A varying amount of land was taken from the villages and vested in the Inca state and the state church. In addition to working their own lands and those of their curaca, ayllu members were required to till the Inca state and church lands. The Inca government also used the forced labor of villagers to create new arable land by leveling and terracing slopes. This new land was often turned over as private estates to curacas and Inca military leaders and nobles who had rendered conspicuous service to the Inca state. The Inca himself possessed private estates, and others were owned by the lineages of dead emperors and used to maintain the cult of these former rulers. These private estates were not worked by ayllu members but by a new servile class, the *yanacona*,[4] defined by Spanish sources as "permanent servants"; each ayllu had to contribute a number of such servants or retainers, who also worked in the Inca temples and palaces and performed personal service.

In addition to agricultural labor, ayllu members had to work on roads, irrigation channels, fortresses, and in the mines, in a system called the *mita*, later adopted by the Spaniards for their own purposes. Another requirement was that villages produce specified quantities of cloth for the state to use in clothing soldiers and retainers. All able-bodied commoners between certain ages were subject to military service.

There is no trace of socialism or a welfare state in these arrangements, which favored not the commoners but the Inca dynasty, nobility, priesthood, warriors, and officials. Many of the activities cited as reflecting the benevolence and foresight of the Inca state were actually traditional village and ayllu functions. One such activity was the maintenance of storehouses of grain and cloth by the community for times of crop failure. The Inca state merely took over this principle, as it had taken over the principle of cooperative labor for communal ends, and established storehouses containing the goods produced by the peasants' forced labor on state and church lands. The cloth and grain stored in these warehouses were used primarily to clothe and feed the army, the crown artisans, the conscript labor for public works, and the officials who lived in Cuzco and other towns.

The relations between the Inca and the peasantry were based on the principle of reciprocity, expressed in an elaborate system of gifts and countergifts. The peasantry cultivated the lands of the Inca, worked up his wool and cotton into cloth, and performed various other kinds of labor for him. The Inca, the divine, universal lord, in turn permitted them to cultivate their communal lands and in time of shortages released to the villages the surplus grain in his storehouses. Since the imperial gifts were the products of the peasants' own labor, this "reciprocity" amounted to intensive exploitation of the commoners by the Inca rulers and nobility. We must not underestimate, however, the hold of this ideology, buttressed by a religious world view that regarded the Inca as responsible for defending the order and very existence of the universe, on the Inca peasant mentality.

At the time of the Conquest, a vast gulf separated the regimented and laborious life of the commoners from the luxurious life of the Inca nobility. At the apex of the social pyramid were the Inca and his kinsmen, composed of twelve lineages. Members of these lineages had the privilege of piercing their ears and distending the lobes with

[4]A plural term in Quechua but treated by the Spaniards as singular.

large ornaments; hence the name *orejones* (big ears) assigned to the Inca kinsmen by the Spaniards. The orejones were exempt from tribute labor and military service; the same was true of the curacas, who had once been chieftains in their own right, and of a numerous class of specialists—servants, retainers, quipu keepers and other officials, and entertainers. Side by side with the Inca state, which drained off the peasants' surplus production, regulated the exchange of goods between the various regions, and directed vast public works, there arose the incipient feudalism of the Inca nobility and curacas. Their loyalty and services to the Inca were rewarded with rich gifts of land, llamas, and yanacona. Their growing resources enabled them to form their own local clienteles, achieve a certain relative independence of the crown, and play an important role in the disputes over the succession that sometimes followed the emperor's death.

Inca rule over the peasant masses was largely indirect, exercised through local chieftains. It probably did not seriously affect the round of daily life in the villages. The typical peasant house in the highlands was a small hut with walls of fieldstone or adobe and a gable roof thatched with grass. The scanty furniture consisted of a raised sleeping platform, a clay stove, and some clay pots and dishes. A man's clothing consisted of a breechcloth, a sleeveless tunic, and a large cloak over the shoulders with two corners tied in front; the fineness of the cloth used and the ornamentation varied according to social rank. A woman's dress was a wraparound cloth extending from beneath the arms to the ankles, with the top edges drawn over the shoulders and fastened with straight pins. An ornamented sash around the waist and a shoulder mantle completed the woman's apparel. Men adorned themselves with earplugs and bracelets; women wore necklaces and shawl pins.

On the eve of the Spanish Conquest, the Inca state appeared all-powerful. But, like the Aztec Empire, it was rent by deep contradictions. Frequent revolts by conquered peoples were put down with ferocious cruelty. Even the outwardly loyal curacas, former lords of independent states,

chafed at the vigilant Inca control and dreamed of regaining their lost freedom.

INCA RELIGION AND LEARNING

The Inca state religion existed side by side with the much older ancestor cults and the worship of innumerable *huacas* (local objects and places). Chief of the Inca gods was a nameless creator called Viracocha and Pachayachachic (lord and instructor of the world). His cult seems to have been a philosophical religion largely confined to the priesthood and nobility. First in importance after Viracocha was the sun god, claimed by the Inca royal family as its divine ancestor. Other notable divinities were the thunder god, who sent the life-giving rain, and the Moon, wife of the Sun, who played a vital role in the regulation of the Inca festival calendar. The Inca idols were housed in numerous temples attended by priests who directed and performed ceremonies that included prayer, sacrifice, confession, and the rite of divination. Another priestly function was the magical cure of disease. The priests were assisted in their religious duties by a class of *mamacuna* (holy women) who had taken vows of permanent chastity. Human sacrifice was performed on very momentous occasions, such as an important victory or some great natural calamity.

Inca art was marked by a high level of technical excellence. The architecture was solid and functional, characterized by massiveness rather than beauty. The stone sculpture, more frequent in the highlands than on the coast, has been described as ponderous and severe. But the tapestries of Inca weavers are among the world's textile masterpieces, so fine and intricate is the weaving. Inca metallurgy was also on a high technical and artistic plane. Cuzco, the Inca capital, abounded in gold objects: the imperial palace had gold friezes and panels of gold and silver, and the Temple of the Sun contained a garden with lifelike replicas of plants and animals, all made of hammered gold.

Although the Incas had no system of writing and hence no written literature, narrative poems, prayers, and tales were handed down orally from generation to generation. The Inca hymns and prayers that have been preserved are notable for their lofty thought and beauty of expression. Of the long narrative poems that dealt with Inca mythology, legends, and history, there remain only summaries in Spanish prose.

A melancholy and nostalgic spirit pervades many of the traditional Inca love songs, and the same plaintiveness characterizes the few examples of their music that have come down to us. Based on the five-toned, or pentatonic, scale, this music was performed with an assortment of instruments: flutes, trumpets, and whistles; gongs, bells, and rattles; and several kinds of skin drums and tambourines. The dances that accompanied the music sometimes represented an elementary form of drama.

Spanish conquistadors destroyed Inca political organization and dealt shattering blows to all aspects of Inca civilization, but elements of that culture survive everywhere in the central Andean area. These survivals, tangible and intangible, include the Quechua speech; the numerous indigenous communities, or ayllu, still partly based on cooperative principles; the widespread pagan beliefs and rites of the people; and of course the monumental ruins of Sacsahuaman, Ollantaytambo, Machu Picchu, Pisac, and Cuzco itself. Inca civilization also lives in the writings of Peruvian historians, novelists, and statesmen, who evoke the vanished Inca greatness and praise the ancient virtues of their people. For many Peruvians, the great technical achievements and social engineering of the Incas, ensuring a modest well-being for all, offer proof of the inherent capacity of their native peoples and a prospect of what the poverty-ridden, strife-torn Peru of today may yet become.

The Hispanic Background

CONQUEST WAS A MAJOR THEME of Spanish history from very remote times. The prehistoric inhabitants of the peninsula, whose unknown artists produced the marvelous cave paintings of Altamira, were overrun by tribes vaguely called Iberians and by the Celts, who are believed to have come from North Africa and central Europe, respectively, probably before 1000 B.C. New waves of invasion brought the Phoenicians, Greeks, and Carthaginians, commercial nations that established trading posts and cities on the coast but made no effort to dominate the interior. Still later, Spain became a stake of empire in the great struggle for commercial supremacy between Rome and Carthage that ended with the decisive defeat of the latter in 201 B.C. For six centuries thereafter, Rome was the dominant power in the peninsula.

Unlike earlier invaders, the Romans attempted to establish their authority throughout Spain (the name comes from the word *Hispania*, applied by the Romans to the whole peninsula) and to impose their language and institutions on the native peoples. From Latin, made the official language, sprang the various dialects and languages still spoken by the Hispanic peoples. Roman law replaced the customary law of the Celts, Iberians, and other native groups. Native tribal organization was destroyed through forced changes of residence, concentration in towns, and the planting of Roman colonies that served as agencies of pacification and assimilation. Agriculture, mining, and industry developed, and Roman Spain carried on an extensive trade in wheat, wine, and olive oil with Italy. Roman engineers constructed great public roads and aqueducts, some of which are still in use. Roman education and literary culture were brought to Spain, and a number of Spaniards by birth or residence (the satirical poet Martial, the epic poet Lucan, and the philosopher Seneca) made notable contributions to Latin literature.

Early in the fifth century A.D., as a result of the decline of Roman military power, a number of barbarian peoples of Germanic origin invaded Spain. By the last half of the century, one group of invaders, the Visigoths, had gained mastery over most of the peninsula. As a result of long contact with the empire, the Visigoths had already assimilated Roman culture, which continued in Spain through contact with the Hispano-Romans. The Visigothic kingdom was Christian; its speech became Latin with a small admixture of Germanic terms; in administration it followed the Roman model. But the succession to the kingship followed Germanic tradition in being elective, a frequent source of great internal strife.

Spain's Medieval Heritage

The divisions among the Goths caused by struggles over kingship played into the hands of the Moors, the new Muslim power in North Africa. In 711 the

35

Moors crossed the straits and decisively defeated Roderic, the last Gothic king. Within a few years, all of Spain, aside from the remote region north of the Cantabrian Mountains, had fallen into Muslim hands. But the Muslims' hold on the bleak uplands of Castile was never strong; they preferred the fertile plains and mild climate of southern Spain, which they called Al-Andalus, the land of Andalusia.

The Moors, heirs to the accumulated cultural wealth of the ancient Mediterranean and Eastern worlds, enriched this heritage with their own magnificent contributions to science, arts, and letters. In the tenth and eleventh centuries, Muslim Spain, with its capital at Córdoba, was an economic and intellectual showplace from which fresh knowledge and ideas flowed into Christian lands. Spanish agriculture gained by the introduction of new irrigation and water-lifting devices and new crops: sugar, saffron, cotton, silk, and citrus fruits. Industry was broadened through the introduction of such products as paper and glass, hitherto unknown to the West. Muslim metalwork, pottery, silk, and leatherwork were esteemed throughout Europe. Many Muslim rulers were patrons of literature and learning; the scholar-king Al-Haquem II built up a library said to have numbered four hundred thousand volumes.

As a rule, the Muslim conquerors did not insist on the conversion of the vanquished Christians, preferring to give them the option of accepting the Islamic faith or paying a special poll tax. The relatively tolerant Muslim rule was favorable to economic and cultural advance. The Jews, who had suffered severe persecution under the Visigoths, enjoyed official protection and made major contributions to medicine, philosophy, and Talmudic studies. The condition of the peasantry probably improved, for the conquerors distributed the vast estates of the Visigothic lords among the serfs, who paid a certain portion of the produce to the Muslim lords and kept the rest for themselves. But in later centuries, these trends were reversed; great landed estates again arose, taxation increased, and severe persecution of Jews and *Mozárabes* (Christians who had adopted Arab speech and customs) drove many to flee to Christian territory.

With the aid of Iberian Jews oppressed by Christian kings, Islamic forces conquered the peninsula in the eighth century and inaugurated a period of peaceful coexistence that, even after the Christian reconquest, left a lasting multicultural imprint on Spanish art, architecture, music, and literature. [*The Conversion of a Moor,* illustrations to Cantiga 46, from "Cantigas de Santa Maria" (13th century); Biblioteca Monasterio de Escorial, Madrid/Index/Bridgeman Art Library, London/New York]

Despite its noble achievements, Muslim civilization rested on insecure foundations. The Arab conquerors never fully threw off the tribal form of social organization under which they began their prodigious advance, and the Muslim world was torn by fierce political and religious feuds over control of the empire. In Spain these internal differences were complicated by conflicts between the Arabs and the North African Berbers, recent converts to Islam who were more fanatically devout than were their teachers. By the mid-eleventh century, the caliphate of Córdoba had broken into a large number of *taifas* (states) that constantly warred with each other. These discords enabled the petty Christian kingdoms that had arisen in the north to survive, grow strong, and eventually launch a general advance against the Muslims. In the west, Portugal, having achieved independence from Castile by the mid-twelfth century, attained its historic boundaries two centuries later. In the center, the joint realm of León and Castile pressed its advance; to the east, the kingdom of Aragon steadily expanded at the expense of the disunited Muslim states.

The Reconquest began as a struggle of Christian kings and nobles to regain their lost lands and serfs; only later did it assume the character of a crusade. Early in the ninth century, the tomb of St. James, supposedly found in northwest Spain, became the center of the famous pilgrimage of Santiago de Compostela and gave Spain a warrior patron saint who figured prominently in the Reconquest and the conquest of the New World. But the career of the famous Cid (Ruy Díaz de Vivar), to whom the Arabic title of "lord" was given by his Muslim soldiers, illustrates the absence of religious fanaticism in the first stage of the struggle. True to the ideals of his time, the Cid placed feudal above religious loyalties and, as a vassal of the Muslim kings of Saragossa and Valencia, fought Moorish and Christian foes alike. When he captured Valencia for himself in 1094, he allowed the Muslims to worship freely and retain their property, requiring only the payment of tributes authorized by the Koran.

The Muslims vainly sought to check the Christian advance by calling on newly converted, fanatically religious Berber tribes in North Africa to come to their aid. The Christian victory at Las Navas de Tolosa (1212) in Andalusia over a large Berber army marked a turning point in the Reconquest. Ferdinand III of Castile captured Córdoba, the jewel of Muslim Spain, in 1236; the surrender of Seville in 1248 gave him control of the mouth of the Guadalquivir River and communication with the sea. By the time of Ferdinand's death in 1252, the Muslim territory in Spain had been reduced to the small kingdom of Granada. The strength of its position, protected by steep mountains and impassable gorges, and the divisions that arose within the Christian camp gave Granada two and a half more centuries of independent life.

CASTILE

Castile, the largest and most powerful of the Spanish kingdoms, played the leading role in the Reconquest. The great movement left an enduring stamp on the Castilian character. Centuries of struggle against the Moor made war almost a Castilian way of life and created a large class of warrior-nobles who regarded manual labor with contempt. In the Castilian scale of values, the military virtues of courage, endurance, and honor took the first place. Not only the nobles but the commoners accepted these values. The lure of plunder, land, and other rewards drew many peasants and artisans into the armies of the Reconquest and diffused militarist and aristocratic ideals throughout Castilian society. To these ideals the crusading spirit of the Reconquest, especially in its later phase, added a strong sense of religious superiority and mission.

The Reconquest also helped to shape the character of the Castilian economy. As the Muslims fell back, vast tracts of land came into the possession of the crown. The kings assigned the lion's share of this land to the nobility, the church, and the three military orders of Calatrava, Alcántara, and Santiago. As a result, Castile, especially the area from Toledo south (New Castile), became a region of enormous estates and a very wealthy, powerful aristocracy.

The Reconquest also insured the supremacy of sheep raising over agriculture in Castile. In a time of constant warfare, of raids and counterraids, the mobile sheep was a more secure and valuable form of property than land. With the advance of the Christian frontier, much new territory—frequently too arid for easy agricultural use—was opened to the sheep industry. The introduction of the merino sheep into Spain from North Africa around 1300, coinciding with a sharply increased demand in northern Europe for Spanish wool, gave a marked stimulus to sheep raising. By the late thirteenth century, there had arisen a powerful organization of sheep raisers, the *Mesta*. In return for large subsidies to the crown, this organization received extensive privileges, including the right to move great flocks of sheep across Spain from summer pastures in the north to winter pastures in the south, with frequent injury to the farmlands and woods in their path. The great nobles dominated the sheep industry as well as agriculture. Their large rents and the profits from the sale of their wool gave them an economic, social, and military power that threatened the supremacy of the king.

The Castilian towns represented the only counterpoise to this power. The advance of the Reconquest and the need to consolidate its gains promoted municipal growth. To attract settlers to the newly conquered territory, the king gave generous *fueros* (charters of liberties) to the towns that sprang up one after another. These charters endowed the towns with administrative autonomy and vast areas of land that extended their jurisdiction into the surrounding countryside. The towns were governed by elected judicial officials known as *alcaldes* and by members of the town council, called *regidores*. The economic expansion of the thirteenth and fourteenth centuries and the growth of the wool trade, above all, made the Castilian towns bustling centers of industry and commerce. The wealth of the towns gave them a peculiar importance in the meetings of the consultative body, or parliament, known as the *Cortes*. Since the nobles and the clergy were exempt from taxes, the towns' deputies had to vote the money needed by the king. Their price for voting it became the redress of grievances presented in the form of petitions that royal approval transformed into laws.

The Castilian towns had their time of splendor, but in the last analysis the middle class remained small and weak; it was overshadowed by the enormous power of the great nobles. Aware of their weakness, the towns joined their forces in *hermandades*, military associations that resisted the aggressions of the nobles and sometimes of the king. But the posture of the towns was essentially defensive. Without the aid of the king, they could not hope to impose their will on the aristocracy.

As Muslim power waned, the great nobles turned from fighting the infidel to battling the king, the towns, and each other. In the course of the fourteenth and fifteenth centuries, the nobles gained the upper hand in their struggle with the king, usurping royal lands and revenues and often transforming the monarch into their pawn. The degradation of the crown reached its lowest point in the reign of Henry IV (1454–1474), when there was an almost total breakdown of central government and public order. Beneath this anarchy, however, the continued expansion of economic life inspired a growing demand for a strong monarchy capable of establishing peace and order.

ARAGON

The medieval history of the smaller, less populous kingdom of Aragon differed in important ways from that of Castile. The king of Aragon ruled over three states: Aragon, Valencia, and Catalonia, each regarded as a separate *reino* (kingdom), each having its own Cortes. The upland state of Aragon was the poorest, most backward of the three. Valencia was the home of a large Moorish peasant population subject to a Christian landowning nobility. The dominant role in the union was played by Catalonia and its great city of Barcelona, which had given Aragon its dynasty and most of its revenues. A thriving industry and powerful fleets had made Barcelona the center of a commercial empire based on the export of textiles. Catalan arms had also won Sardinia and Sicily for the crown of Aragon. In Aragon, therefore, the ruling class was not the landed nobility, which was relatively poor, but the commercial and industrial oligarchy of Barcelona. The constitutional system of Aragon reflected the supremacy of this class by giving legislative power to the Cortes of Catalonia and by providing special watchdog committees of the Cortes, which guarded against any infringement of the rights and liberties of the subjects.

In the fourteenth and fifteenth centuries, the prosperity of Barcelona was undermined by the ravages of the Black Death, agrarian unrest in the Catalan countryside, struggles between the merchant oligarchy and popular elements in Barcelona, and above all by the loss of traditional Catalan markets to Genoese competitors. This economic decline sharpened Catalan internal struggles, in which the crown joined on the side of the popular elements. The result was the civil war of 1462–1472, which ended in a qualified victory for the king, John II, but which completed the ruin of Catalonia. The weakness of Aragon on the eve of its union with Castile insured Castilian leadership of the coming new Spain.

Isabella and Ferdinand transformed Spain into one of the strongest European kingdoms of the fifteenth century. [Giraudon/Art Resource, NY]

The chain of events leading to Spanish unity began with the secret marriage in 1469 of Isabella, sister of Henry IV of Castile, and Ferdinand, son of John II of Aragon. This match was the fruit of complex intrigues in which the personal ambitions of the young couple, the hostility of many Castilian nobles to their king, and the desire of John II to add Castile to his son Ferdinand's heritage all played their part. On the death of Henry IV in 1474, Isabella proclaimed herself queen of Castile with the support of a powerful faction of Castilian nobles and towns that declared that Henry's daughter Juana was illegitimate. This claim led to a dynastic war in which Portugal supported Juana. By 1479 the struggle had ended in Isabella's favor. In the same year, John II died and Ferdinand succeeded to his dominions. Ferdinand and Isabella now became joint rulers of Aragon and Castile, but the terms of their marriage contract carefully subordinated Ferdinand to Isabella in the government of Castile and excluded Isabella from the administration of Aragon. The process of Spanish unification, however, had begun. Under the leadership of Castile, Spain embarked on a remarkable career of domestic progress and imperial expansion.

The Spain of Ferdinand and Isabella

RESTORATION OF ORDER

The young monarchs faced an urgent problem of restoring peace and order in their respective kingdoms. Catalonia was still troubled by struggles between feudal lords and serfs determined to end their legal servitude. Ferdinand intervened to bring about a solution relatively favorable to the peasantry. His ruling of Guadalupe (1486) ended serfdom in Catalonia and enabled fifty thousand peasants to become small landowners. But he made no effort to reform Aragon's archaic constitutional system, which set strict limits on the royal power. As a result, Castile and Aragon, despite their newfound unity, continued to move along divergent political courses.

The task of restoring order was greater in Castile. The age of anarchy under Henry IV had transformed cities into battlefields and parts of the countryside into a desert. To eradicate the evils of banditry and feudal violence, Isabella counted above all on the support of the towns and the middle classes. The Cortes of Madrigal (1476) forged a solid alliance between the crown and the towns for the suppression of disorder. Their instrument was the *Santa Hermandad*, a police force paid for and manned principally by the towns but under the direct control of the crown. The efficiency of this force and the severe and prompt punishments meted out by its tribunals gradually restored peace in Castile.

But Isabella's program went beyond this immediate goal. She proposed to bend to the royal will all the great institutions of medieval Castile: the nobility, the church, and the towns themselves. The Cortes of Toledo of 1480 reduced the power of the grandees (nobles of the first rank) in various ways. An Act of Resumption compelled them to return to the crown about half the revenues they had usurped since 1464. Another reform reorganized the Council of Castile, the central governing agency of the kingdom. This reform reduced the grandees who had dominated the old royal council to holders of empty dignities. It vested effective responsibility and power in *letrados* (officials usually possessed of legal training), who were drawn from the lower nobility, the middle class, and *conversos* (converted Jews). The same end of curbing aristocratic power was served by the establishment of a hierarchy of courts and magistrates that ascended from the *corregidor* (the royal officer who watched over the affairs of a municipality) through the *cancillerías* (the high law courts of Castile) up to the Council of Castile, the highest court as well as the supreme administrative body of the country. At all levels, the crown asserted its judicial primacy, including the right of intervention in the feudal jurisdiction of the nobility.

The vast wealth of the military orders made them veritable states within the Castilian state. The crown determined to weaken their power by securing for itself control of these orders. When the grand mastership of Santiago fell vacant in 1476, Isabella personally appeared before the dignitaries of the order to insist that they confer the headship on her husband; they meekly assented. When the grand masterships of Calatrava and Alcántara fell vacant, they too were duly conferred on Ferdinand. By these moves, the crown gained new sources of revenue and patronage.

The towns had served the crown well in the struggle against anarchy, but in the past two centuries their democratic traditions had declined, and many had fallen under the control of selfish oligarchies. Some, like Seville, had become battlefields of aristocratic factions. These disorders provided Isabella with pretexts for resuming the policy, initiated by some of her predecessors, of intervening in

municipal affairs by introducing corregidores into the towns. These officials combined administrative and judicial functions and steadily usurped the roles of the alcaldes and regidores. Ferdinand and Isabella also carried forward another practice begun by their predecessors. The offices of alcalde and regidor in towns with royal charters were made appointive by the crown instead of elective by the householders. *Villas de señorío* (towns under noble or ecclesiastical jurisdiction) were permitted to function under the traditional system, but with the right of royal intervention if necessary.

The taming of the towns was accompanied by a decline in the importance of the Cortes. An important factor in this decline was the large increase in revenues from royal taxes, such as the *alcabala* (sales tax), which freed the crown from excessive dependence on the grants of the Cortes. The increased supervision of the crown over the municipalities also decreased the likelihood of resistance by their deputies in the Cortes to royal demands. The sovereigns summoned the Castilian Cortes only when they needed money. When the treasury was full or when peace prevailed, they ignored them.

RELIGIOUS AND ECONOMIC REFORMS

In their march toward absolute power, the monarchs did not hesitate to challenge the church. Under their pressure, the weak popes of this period yielded to them the right of *patronato* (the right of appointment to all major ecclesiastical benefices in the Spanish realms). Although, unlike Henry VIII of England, Ferdinand and Isabella never despoiled the church of its vast landed possessions, they did drain off for themselves a part of the ecclesiastical wealth by taking one-third of all the tithes paid to the Castilian church and the proceeds from the sale of indulgences.

To ensure the loyalty of the church, to make it an effective instrument of royal policy, the sovereigns had to purge it of abuses that included plural benefices, absenteeism, and concubinage. The pious Isabella found a strong ally in the work of reform in a dissident faction of the regular clergy (those belonging to a monastic order or religious community). This group, who called themselves Observants, protested against the worldliness of their colleagues and demanded a return to the strict simplicity of the primitive church. The struggle for reform began within the Franciscan order under the leadership of the ascetic Francisco Jiménez de Cisneros, whom Isabella appointed archbishop of Toledo in 1495, and spread to the other orders. It grew so heated that four hundred Andalusian friars preferred moving to North Africa and becoming Muslims, rather than accept the new rule. The dispute ended in the complete victory of the Observants over their more easygoing brethren.

Isabella was less successful in efforts to reform the secular (or nonmonastic) clergy, but here too an improvement took place. The great ecclesiastical offices ceased to be a monopoly of the aristocracy. Isabella preferred to select prelates from the lower nobility and the middle class, taking account of the morals and learning of the candidates. The Isabelline religious reform had a special meaning for the New World: it insured that the Faith would be carried to the Indies by an elite force of clergy often distinguished for their zeal, humanity, and learning.

The sovereigns also gave attention to the need for economic reform. They attempted to promote Castilian industry and commerce by protectionist measures. They forbade the export of gold and silver, sporadically barred the import of cloth that competed with native products, and encouraged Italian and Flemish artisans to settle in Spain. They promulgated navigation acts that gave preference to domestic shipping and subsidies to domestic shipbuilding. They suppressed all the internal tolls that had been established in Castile since 1464 and made an effort to standardize weights and measures. Under Isabella's predecessors, a serious depreciation of the currency had taken place. To restore the credit of the coinage, Isabella suppressed all private mints and struck an excellent money that equaled foreign coins in value. All these measures contributed to an economic expansion and consequently to a rapid increase of crown revenues, from 885,000 *reales* in 1474 to 26,283,334 *reales* in 1504.

Despite their basically pragmatic outlook, the sovereigns had broad intellectual and artistic interests. To their court they summoned Italian humanists like Alessandro Geraldini, Lucio Marineo Siculo, and Peter Martyr de Anghera to tutor their children and the sons of the greatest houses of Spain. Enlightened prelates like Archbishop Jiménez de Cisneros founded new schools and universities to rival the famed University of Salamanca. Spain itself produced some distinguished practitioners of the new learning, such as Antonio de Nebrija, grammarian, historian, and lexicographer, who in 1492 published and presented to Isabella a Castilian grammar— the first grammar of any modern European language. The vitality of the Castilian language and life found expression in a realistic masterpiece, the novel *La Celestina* (1499) by Fernando de Rojas. Meanwhile, Spanish architecture and sculpture developed its own style, known as plateresque, an ornamental blend of Moorish arabesques, flowers, foliage, and Renaissance motifs.

FOREIGN POLICY

The restoration of domestic peace enabled the sovereigns to turn their attention to questions of foreign policy. For the Castilian Isabella, the conquest of Granada came first. Hardly had their authority been firmly restored when the sovereigns demanded of the Granadan ruler the tribute paid by his predecessors to Castile. Abdul Hassan replied that his mints now coined steel, not gold. The wealth of the Granadan kingdom and its mountainous terrain enabled the Moors to hold out for ten years. But the superior Spanish military power, especially the formidable new arm of artillery, finally broke the Muslim resistance. In January 1492, Granada surrendered to Ferdinand and Isabella, on whom Pope Alexander VI bestowed the title "The Catholic Sovereigns" in honor of their crusading piety.

Whereas Isabella's heart was set on the conquest of Granada, Ferdinand, heir to Aragon's Mediterranean empire and the traditional rivalry between France and Aragon, looked eastward to Aragon's borders with France and to Italy. He achieved most of his goals after Isabella's death in

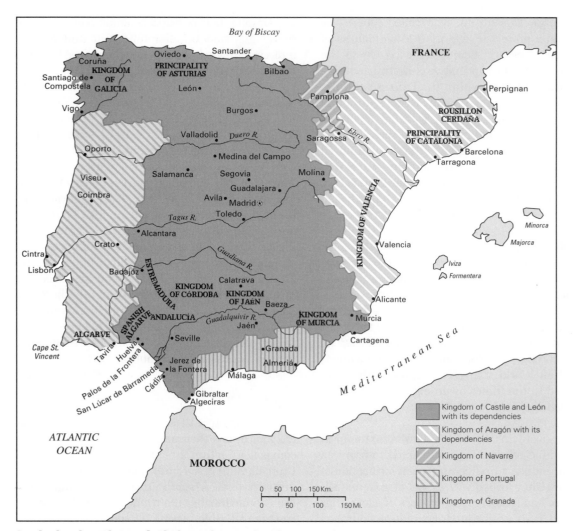

Spain in the Time of Christopher Columbus

1504. Employing an adroit blend of war and diplomacy, he obtained the return of two Aragonese provinces lost to France by previous rulers, the incorporation of the kingdom of Naples into the Aragonese empire, and the checkmating of French designs in Italy. In the course of Ferdinand's Italian wars, his commanders, especially the "Great Captain," Gonzalo de Córdoba, created a new-style Spanish army armed with great firepower and strong offensive and defensive weapons. The new system, first tested in Italy, established Spain's military supremacy in Europe. Before his death, Ferdinand rounded out his conquests with the acquisition of Navarre (1512), which gave Spain a strongly defensible frontier with France.

The Catholic Sovereigns rendered major services to the Spanish people. They tamed the arrogant nobility, defeated the Moors, and united the Spanish kingdoms in the pursuit of common goals. They encouraged the growth of trade and industry and showed themselves to be intelligent patrons of learning and the arts. Their prudent diplomacy gave Spain a place among the first powers of Europe. In the same period, America was discovered under Castilian auspices, the Caribbean became a Spanish lake, and Spanish explorers and adventurers, by the end of the reign, were at the approaches to the great Indian empires of Mexico and Peru. Small wonder that monarchs who presided over such victories became for succeeding generations of Spaniards the objects of a national cult and legend.

REAPPRAISAL OF FERDINAND AND ISABELLA'S POLICIES

For modern historians, the fame of the Catholic Sovereigns has lost some of its luster. These historians charge Ferdinand and Isabella with mistaken policies that nullified much of the sound part of their work. One of these errors was a definite bias in favor of the economic and social interests of the aristocracy. If the nobility lost most of its political power under Ferdinand and Isabella, nothing of the kind happened in the economic sphere. Concentration of land in noble hands actually increased during their reign. The Cortes of 1480, which forced the nobility to surrender about half the lands and revenues usurped from the crown since 1464, explicitly authorized the nobles to retain the vast holdings acquired prior to that date. A policy of assigning a lion's share of the territory reconquered from the Muslims to the grandees also favored the growth of land monopoly. After the War of Granada, moreover, the great nobles used their private armies and increased political influence to expand their territories and seigneurial control. This "aristocratic offensive" met with little resistance from the crown. As a result, about 2 or 3 percent of the population owned 95 percent of the land by 1500.

This land monopoly reduced the great majority of the Castilian peasants to the condition of tenants heavily burdened by rents, seigneurial dues, tithes, and taxes. True, serfdom in the strict sense had apparently disappeared from most parts of Castile by 1480; the Castilian peasant was legally free to leave his village and move elsewhere at will. But since the nobility owned virtually all the land, the peasant's liberty was, as the Spanish historian Jaime Vicens Vives puts it, the liberty "to die of hunger."

The royal policy of favoring sheep raising over agriculture was equally harmful to long-range Spanish economic interests. Like their predecessors, the Sovereigns were influenced by the taxes and export duties paid by the sheep farmers and by the inflow of gold in payment for Spanish wool. As a result, they granted extensive privileges to the sheep raisers' guild, the Mesta. The climax of these favors was a 1501 law that reserved in perpetuity for pasture all land on which the migrant flocks had ever pastured. This measure barred vast tracts of land in Andalusia and Estremadura from being used for agriculture. The privilege granted the shepherds to cut trees for fuel, fencing, or pasturage contributed heavily to deforestation and soil erosion. Moreover, the overflow of sheep from their legal passage caused much damage to crops and soil. In a time of growing population, these policies and conditions inevitably produced serious food deficits. Chronic shortages climaxed in a devastating food crisis in the early sixteenth century.

Modern historians also question the traditional view that Spanish industry made spectacular advances under the Catholic Sovereigns. These historians claim that the only true industries of the period were the iron industry of the Basque provinces and the cloth industry of the Castilian central zone, which received a strong stimulus from the discovery of America and the opening of American markets. The resulting industrial prosperity lasted until shortly after the middle of the sixteenth century. But the level of industrial production never reached that of England, the Low Countries, and Italy. The abject poverty of the peasantry, which composed 80 percent of the population, sharply limited the effective market for manufactured goods. Shortages of capital and skilled labor also acted as a brake on industrial expansion.

Other obstacles to industrial growth were the excessive costs of transport by mule train and oxcarts across the rugged peninsula and the customs barriers that continued to separate the Spanish kingdoms. Nor were the paternalistic measures of the Sovereigns invariably helpful to industry. Through Ferdinand's influence, a guild system modeled on the rigid Catalan model was introduced into the Castilian towns. In this the Sovereigns did Castilian industry no service, for they fastened the straitjacket of guild organization on it precisely at the time when the discovery and colonization of America, the influx of American gold and silver, and the resulting economic upsurge challenged Spanish industry to transform its techniques, lower costs, increase output and quality, and thereby establish Spanish economic as well as political supremacy in Europe.

No policy of the Sovereigns has come under harsher attack than their anti-Semitic measures. During the early Middle Ages, Jews formed an influential and prosperous group in Spanish society. Down to the close of the thirteenth century, a relatively tolerant spirit prevailed in Christian Spain. Relations among Jews, Christians, and Muslims were so close and neighborly as to provoke protests by the church. In the fourteenth century, these relations began to deteriorate. Efforts by the clergy to arouse hatred of Jews and popular resentment of such specialized Jewish economic activities as usury and tax collecting, which caused severe hardship for peasants and other groups, contributed to this process. The rise of anti-Semitism led to the adoption of repressive legislation by the crown and to a wave of attacks on Jewish communities. To save their lives, many Jews accepted baptism; they came to form a very numerous class of conversos.

The converts soon achieved a marked prosperity and influence as tax farmers, court physicians, counselors, and lawyers. Wealthy, unhampered by feudal traditions, intellectually curious, intensely ambitious, the conversos incurred the hostility not only of peasants but of the church and of many nobles and burghers. Whether heretics or not, they posed a threat to the feudal order based on landed wealth, hereditary status, and religious orthodoxy. The envy and hostility they aroused help to explain why the Sovereigns, who had sur-

Even as they continued secretly to observe their religious and cultural traditions, Jews publicly converted to Christianity to avoid the torture and burning depicted in this 1475 woodcut, which shows the Spanish Inquisition at work in Granada. [The Granger Collection, New York]

rounded themselves with Jewish and converso advisers, and one of whom (Ferdinand) had Jewish blood in his veins, established the inquisition and expelled the Jews from Spain. When the crown had tamed the nobility and the towns, when it had acquired large new sources of revenue, its dependence on the Jews and conversos was reduced; these groups became dispensable. The sacrifice of the Jews and conversos sealed the alliance between the absolute monarchy and the church and nobility.

The conversos first felt the blows of religious persecution with the establishment of the Spanish Inquisition in Castile in 1478. The task of this tribunal was to detect, try, and punish heresy, and its special target was the mass of conversos, many of whom were suspected of secretly adhering to Judaism. As a result of the Inquisition's activities, some two thousand conversos were burned at the stake; a hundred and twenty thousand fled abroad. As certain Spanish towns pointed out in memorials protesting the establishment of the Inquisition, the purge had a disastrous effect on the Spanish economy by causing this great flight of the conversos and their capital.

The Jews had a breathing space of twelve years during the costly War of Granada, for they were among the largest contributors to the royal finances. The surrender of Granada, however, brought near a decision on the fate of the Jews. The conquest of a rich territory and an industrious Moorish population, ending the drain of the war, meant that the Jews were no longer financially indispensable. After some hesitation, the Sovereigns yielded to anti-Semitic pressure and, on March 30, 1492, signed the edict giving the Jews the choice of conversion or expulsion.

The destruction or flight of many conversos and the expulsion of the Jews certainly contributed to the dreary picture presented by the Spanish economy at the close of the sixteenth century. The purge of the conversos eliminated from Spanish life its most vital merchant and artisan elements, the groups that in England and Holland were preparing the ground for the Industrial Revolution. The flight of converso artisans dealt Spanish industry a heavy blow and was directly responsible for royal edicts (1484) inviting foreign artisans to settle in Castile with exemption from taxes for ten years.

The anti-Semitic policies of the Sovereigns also harmed Spanish science and thought in general. The Inquisition helped to blight the spirit of free inquiry and discussion in Spain at a time when the Renaissance was giving an extraordinary impulse to the play of European intellect in all fields. The Sovereigns, who laid the foundations of Spain's greatness in so short a time, bear much of the responsibility for its premature decline. But the contradictions in their policies, the incorrect decisions that nullified much of the sound part of their work, resulted from more than personal errors of judgment; they reflected the structural weakness and backwardness of Spanish society as it emerged from seven centuries of struggle against the Moor.

The Hapsburg Era: Triumph and Tragedy

Isabella's death in 1504 placed all of the Iberian Peninsula except Portugal under the rule of Ferdinand. Isabella's will had named her daughter Juana as successor, with the provision that Ferdinand should govern in case Juana proved unable. Since Juana's growing mental instability made her unfit to govern, Ferdinand assumed the regency. Juana's husband, Philip the Handsome of Burgundy, supported by a number of Castilian nobles, challenged Ferdinand's right to rule Castile, but Philip's sudden death in 1506 left Ferdinand undisputed master of Spain. Ferdinand himself died in 1516. To the Spanish throne ascended his grandson Charles, eldest son of Juana and Philip. Through his maternal grandparents, Charles inherited Spain, Naples and Sicily, and the Spanish possessions in Africa and America. Through his paternal grandparents, Marie of Burgundy and the Holy Roman Emperor Maximilian, he inherited the territories of the house of Burgundy, which included the rich Netherlands and the German possessions of the house of Hapsburg.

THE REIGN OF CHARLES V

The Catholic Sovereigns, whatever their errors, had attempted to foster Spain's economic development and its partial unity; their prudent diplomacy set for itself limited goals. They had advanced toward absolute monarchy discreetly, respecting both the sensitivities of their peoples and those traditions that did not stand in the way of their designs.

A solemn youth with the characteristic jutting underjaw of the Hapsburgs, Charles (first of that name in Spain and fifth in the Holy Roman Empire) had been born and reared in Flanders and knew no

Spanish. Reared at the court of Burgundy in a spirit of royal absolutism, he had a different notion of kingship. On his arrival in Spain, he immediately alienated his subjects by his haughty manner and by the greed of his Flemish courtiers, whom he placed in all key positions. He aroused even greater resentment by attempting to make the Castilians pay the bill for his election as Holy Roman Emperor to succeed his grandfather Maximilian. Having achieved his ambition by expending immense sums of money, which placed him deeply in debt to the German banking house of Fugger, Charles hurried off to Germany.

For Castilians the election appeared to mean an absentee king and heavier tax burdens. Popular wrath burst forth in the revolt of the Castilian towns, or communes, in 1520–1521. The revolt of the *Comuneros* has been called the first bourgeois revolution in Europe, but it began as an essentially conservative movement: the rebels demanded that Charles return to Spain and make his residence there, that the drain of money abroad end, that no more foreigners be appointed to offices in Spain. Many nobles supported the rebellion at this stage, although the grandees remained neutral or hostile. But the leadership of the revolution soon fell into more radical hands. Simultaneously, there arose in Valencia a revolt of the artisans and middle classes against the great landowners. As a result of these developments, the Comunero movement lost almost all aristocratic support. In April 1521 the Comunero army suffered a total defeat, and the revolt began to fall apart. In July 1522, Charles returned to Spain with four thousand German troops at his side. The last effort of the Spanish people to turn the political clock back, to prevent the final success of the centralizing and absolutist policies initiated by the Catholic Sovereigns, had failed.

For a time, at least, the dazzling successes of Charles V in the New and the Old Worlds reconciled the Spanish people to the new course. Spaniards rejoiced over the conquests of Cortés and Pizarro and the victories of the invincible Spanish infantry in Europe. They set to dreaming of El Dorados, universal empires, and a universal church. The poet Hernando de Acuña gave voice to Spain's exalted mood:

One Fold, one Shepherd only on the earth . . .
One Monarch, one Empire, and one Sword.

War dominated Charles's reign: war against France, against the Protestant princes of Germany, against the Turks, even against the pope, whose holdings in central Italy were threatened by Spanish expansionism. Actually, only one of these wars vitally concerned Spain's national interests: the struggle with the Turkish Empire, whose growing naval power endangered Aragon's possessions in Italy and Sicily and even threatened Spain's coasts with attack. Yet Charles, absorbed in the Protestant problem and his rivalry with France, pursued this struggle against the infidel less consistently than the others; in the end, it declined to a mere holding operation.

The impressive victories of Spanish arms on land and sea had few tangible results, for Charles, embroiled in too many quarters, could not take full advantage of his successes. In 1556 Charles renounced the Spanish throne in favor of his son Philip. Charles had failed in all his major objectives. The Protestant heresy still flourished in the north; the Turks remained solidly entrenched in North Africa, and their piratical fleets prowled the Mediterranean. Charles's project of placing his son Philip on the imperial throne had broken on the opposition of German princes, Protestant and Catholic, and of Charles's own brother Ferdinand, who wished to make the title of Holy Roman Emperor hereditary in his own line. Charles's other dream of bringing England into the empire by marrying Philip to Mary Tudor collapsed when Mary died in 1558.

Meanwhile, Spaniards groaned under a crushing burden of debts and taxes, with Castile bearing the main part of the load. German and Italian merchant-princes and bankers, to whom an ever-increasing part of the royal revenue was pledged for loans, took over important segments of the Spanish economy. The Fuggers assumed the administration of the estates of the military orders and the exploitation of the mercury mines of Almadén. Their rivals, the Welsers, took over the Galician mines and received the American province of Venezuela as a fief whose inhabitants they barbarously exploited. To find money for his fantastically expensive foreign enterprises, Charles resorted to extraordinary measures: he extracted ever larger grants from the Cortes of Castile and Aragon; he multiplied royal taxes; he appropriated remittances of American treasure to private individuals, compensating the victims with *juros* (bonds). When his son Philip came to the throne in 1556, Spain was bankrupt.

THE REIGN OF PHILIP II
AND THE REMAINING HAPSBURGS

The reign of Philip (1556–1598) continued in all essential respects the policies of his father, with the same general results. Spain won brilliant military victories, which Philip failed to follow up from lack of funds or because some new crisis diverted his attention to another quarter. His hopes of dominating France by playing on the divisions between Huguenots and Catholics were frustrated when the Protestant Henry of Navarre entered the Catholic church, a move that united France behind Henry and forced Philip to sign a peace with him. The war against the Turks produced the great sea victory of Lepanto (1571), which broke the Turkish naval power, but when Philip's reign ended, the Turks remained in control of most of North Africa. In the prosperous Netherlands, the richest jewel in his imperial crown, Philip's policies of religious repression and absolutism provoked a great revolt that continued throughout his reign and imposed a terrible drain on the Spanish treasury. War with England flowed from the accession of the Protestant Elizabeth to the throne, from her unofficial support to the Dutch rebels, and from the encroachments of English corsairs and smugglers in American waters.

The crushing defeat of the Invincible Armada in 1588 dealt a heavy blow to Spain's self-confidence and virtually sealed the doom of Philip's crusade against the heretical north. Philip succeeded in another enterprise, the annexation of Portugal (1580), which gave Spain considerably more naval strength and a long Atlantic seaboard to use in a struggle against the Protestant north. But Philip failed to exploit these strategic opportu-

nities, and Portugal, whose colonies and ships now became fair game for Dutch and English seafarers, grew increasingly discontent with a union whose disadvantages exceeded its gains.

At his death in 1598, Philip II left a Spain in which the forces of disintegration were at work but which was still powerful enough militarily and territorially to be feared and respected. Under his successors, Spain entered a rapid decline. This decline first became visible in the area of diplomacy and war. The truce of 1609 with the Dutch, which tacitly recognized Dutch independence, was an early sign of waning Spanish power. The defeat of the famous Spanish infantry at the battle of Rocroi (1643) revealed the obsolescence of Spanish military organization and tactics and marked the end of Spanish military preponderance on the Continent. By the third quarter of the century, Spain, reduced to the defensive, had been compelled to sign a series of humiliating treaties by which it lost the Dutch Netherlands, part of Flanders, Luxembourg, and a string of lesser possessions.

The crisis existed at home as well as abroad. Efforts to make other Spanish kingdoms bear part of the burdens of the wars in which Castile had been so long engaged caused resentment and resistance. The able but imprudent favorite of Philip IV, Count Olivares, aroused a storm by his efforts to billet troops in Catalonia and otherwise make Catalonia contribute to the Castilian war effort at the expense of the ancient *fueros*, or privileges, of the principality. In 1640 a formidable revolt broke out; it continued for twelve years and shattered the economy of Catalonia. In the same year, Portugal, weary of a union that brought more losses than gains, successfully revolted against Spanish rule. Lesser insurrections took place in Biscay, Andalusia, Sicily, and Naples.

THE WANING ECONOMY AND SOCIETY

A decline in the quality of Spain's rulers no doubt contributed to its political decline, but this was guaranteed by the crumbling of the economic foundations on which the empire rested. By the 1590s, the Castilian economy had begun to crack under the strain of costly Hapsburg adventures in foreign policy. Philip II several times resorted to bankruptcy to evade payments of debts to foreign bankers. His successors, lacking Philip's resources, were driven to currency inflation, which caused a flight of gold and silver abroad, until the national currency consisted largely of copper. But the development that contributed most to the Spanish economic crisis was a drastic decline in the inflow of American treasure in the middle decades of the seventeenth century, from about 135 million pesos in the decade from 1591 to 1600 to 19 million pesos in the decade from 1651 to 1660 (the complex causes of this decline are discussed in Chapter 4).

By 1621 signs of economic decline were on every hand. Seville had only four hundred looms producing silk and wool, down from sixteen thousand a century earlier. Toledo had fifty woolen manufacturing establishments in the sixteenth century; it had thirteen in 1665. The plight of agriculture was shown by a chronic shortage of foodstuffs, sometimes approaching famine conditions, and by the exodus of peasants from the countryside. Castile became a land of deserted villages. In the period from 1600 to 1700, Spain also suffered an absolute loss of population, from about 8 million to 6 million. The ravages of epidemics, aggravated by near-famine conditions; the expulsion of the Moriscos, or converted Moors, between 1609 and 1614; and emigration to the Indies contributed to this heavy loss.

The economic decline caused a contraction of Spain's artisan and merchant class, strengthened the domination of aristocratic values, and fostered the growth of parasitism. In the seventeenth century, ambitious young Spaniards looked above all to the church and the court for an assured living. In 1626, Spain had nine thousand monasteries; at the end of the century, there were about 200,000 monks and priests in a population of 6 million. The nobility formed another very large unproductive class. At the end of the century, according to one calculation, Spain had four times as many nobles as France with its much larger population. The highest rung of the ladder of nobility was occupied by a small number of grandees—counts, dukes, marquis—who possessed enormous wealth and immense prerogatives; the lowest was occupied by

a great number of hidalgos, petty nobles whose sole capital often was their honor and the precious letters patent that attested to their rank and their superiority over base *pecheros* (taxpayers), peasants, artisans, and burghers. The noble contempt for labor infected all classes. The number of vagabonds steadily grew; meanwhile, agriculture lacked enough laborers to till the land.

LITERARY AND ARTISTIC DEVELOPMENTS

Spreading into all areas of Spanish life, the *decadencia* (decadence) inspired moods of pessimism, fatalism, and cynicism. Spanish society presented extreme contrasts: great wealth and abject poverty, displays of fanatical piety and scandalous manners, desperate efforts to revive the imperial glories of a past age by kings who sometimes lacked the cash to pay their servants and supply the royal table. The paradoxes of Spanish life, the contrast between the ideal and the real, stimulated the Spanish literary imagination. In this time, so sterile in other respects, Spain enjoyed a Golden Age of letters. As early as 1554, the unknown author of *Lazarillo de Tormes*, first of the picaresque novels, captured the seamy reality of a Spanish world teeming with rogues and vagabonds. Its hero relates his adventures under a succession of masters—a blind beggar, a stingy priest, a hungry hidalgo; he finally attains his highest hope, a sinecure as a town crier, secured for him by a priest whose mistress he had married.

The picaresque genre reached its climax in the *Guzmán de Alfarache* of Mateo de Alemán (1599), with its note of somber pessimism: "All steal, all lie. . . . You will not find a soul who is man unto man." The cleavage in the Spanish soul, the conflict between the ideal and the real, acquired a universal meaning and symbolism in the *Don Quijote* (1605) of Miguel Cervantes de Saavedra. The corrosive satires of Francisco Quevedo (1580–1645) gave voice to the despair of many seventeenth-century intellectuals. "There are many things here," wrote Quevedo, "that seem to exist and have their being, and yet they are nothing more than a name and an appearance."

Diego Velázquez's portrait *Las Meniñas (The Maids of Honor)* is a culminating work of the Spanish seventeenth-century school of painting. Note the utter detachment with which Velázquez treats the members of the Royal Family, the ladies-in-waiting, and the dwarf, making no effort to enhance the dignity or beauty of one at the expense of the other. [*Las Meniñas* (detail) by Diego Rodríguez Velázquez. Museo del Prado, Madrid/Alinari/Art Resource, NY]

By contrast, Spanish drama of the Golden Age only faintly reflected the national crisis. The plays of Lope de Vega (1562–1645) were rich in invention, sparkling dialogue, and melodious verse; his gallant hidalgos, courageous and clever heroines, and dignified peasants evoked the best traditions of Spain's past with a curious disregard for the dismal present. The dramas of Calderón de la Barca (1600–1681), however, suggested the defeatist temper of late seventeenth-century Spain by their tragic view of life and their stress on the illusory nature of reality: "*La vida es sueño, y los sueños sueño son*" ("Life is a dream, and our dreams are part of a dream").

Spanish painting of the Golden Age, like its literature, mirrored the transition from the confident and exalted mood of the early sixteenth century to the disillusioned spirit of the late sev-enteenth century. The great age of painting began with El Greco (1541–1616), whose work blends naturalism, deliberate distortion, and intense emotion to convey the somber religious passion of the Spain of Philip II. Yet some of El Greco's portraits were done with a magnificent realism. The mysticism of El Greco was completely absent from the canvases of Diego Velázquez (1599–1660). With a sovereign mastery of light, coloring, and movement, Velázquez captured for all time the palace life of two Spanish kings, presenting with the same detachment the princes and princesses and the dwarfs and buffoons of the court.

As we shall see in Chapter 5, the seventeenth-century Spanish *decadencia* profoundly influenced the relations between Spain and its American colonies. The loosening of economic and political ties between the mother country and the colonies, along with growing colonial self-sufficiency and self-consciousness, produced a shift in the balance of forces in favor of the colonists—a change that Spain's best efforts could not reverse.

The death of the wretched Charles II in 1700 brought the Hapsburg era to its end. Even before that symbolic death there had been some signs of a Spanish demographic and economic revival, notably in Catalonia, which by the 1670s had made a strong recovery from the depths of the great depression. Under a new foreign dynasty, the Bourbons, who were supported by all the progressive elements in Spanish society, Spain was about to begin a remarkable, many-sided effort at national reconstruction.

The Conquest of America

EUROPEAN CONTACT WITH AMERICA resulted from efforts to find a sea road to the East that would break the monopoly of Egypt and Venice over the lucrative trade in spices and other Asian products. The drain of their scanty stock of gold and silver into the pockets of Italian and Levantine middlemen had grown increasingly intolerable to the merchants and monarchs of western Europe. Portugal took a decisive lead in the race to find a waterway to the land of spices. It had important advantages over its rivals: a long Atlantic seaboard with excellent harbors, a large class of fishermen and sailors, and an aristocracy that early learned to supplement its meager revenue from the land with income from trade and shipbuilding. Earlier than any other European country, Portugal became a unified nation-state under an able dynasty, the house of Avis, which formed a firm alliance with the merchant class and took a personal interest in the expansion of commerce. This fact helps explain Portugal's head start in the work of discovery. The Portuguese victory of Aljubarrota (1385), gained with English support, ended for a time Castile's efforts to absorb its smaller neighbor and released Portuguese energies for an ambitious program of overseas expansion.

The Great Voyages

EXPLORATION UNDER PRINCE HENRY

The famous Prince Henry (1394–1460) initiated the Portuguese era of exploration and conquest. Henry, somewhat misleadingly known as "the Navigator" since he never sailed beyond sight of land, united a medieval crusading spirit with the more modern desire to penetrate the secrets of unknown lands and seas and reap the profits of expanded trade. In 1415, Henry participated in the capture of the Moroccan seaport of Ceuta, a great Muslim trading center from which caravans crossed the desert to Timbuktu, returning with ivory and gold obtained by barter from the blacks of the Niger basin. Possession of the African beachhead of Ceuta opened up large prospects for the Portuguese. By penetrating to the sources of Ceuta gold, they could relieve a serious Portuguese shortage of the precious metal; Henry also hoped to reach the land of the fabled Christian ruler Prester John. Prester John was already identified with the emperor of Abyssinia, but no one knew how far his empire extended. An alliance with this ruler, it was hoped, would encircle the Muslims in North Africa with a powerful league of Christian states.

Efforts to expand the Moroccan beachhead, however, made little progress. If the Portuguese could not penetrate the Muslim barrier that separated them from the southern sources of gold and the kingdom of Prester John, could they not reach these goals by sea? In 1419, Henry set up a headquarters at Sagres on Cape St. Vincent, the rocky tip of southwest Portugal. Here he assembled a group of expert seamen and scientists. At the nearby port of Lagos, he began the construction of stronger and larger ships, equipped with the compass and the improved astrolabe. Beginning in 1420, he sent ship after ship to explore the western coast of Africa. Each captain was required to enter in his log data concerning currents, winds, and calms and to sketch the coastline. An eminent converso mapmaker, Jehuda Crespes, used these data to produce ever more detailed and accurate charts.

The first decade of exploration resulted in the discovery of the Madeiras and the Azores. But progress southward was slow; the imaginary barriers of a flaming torrid zone and a green sea of darkness made sailors excessively cautious. Passage in 1434 around Cape Bojador, the first major landmark on the West African coast, proved these fears groundless. Before Henry's death in 1460, the Portuguese had pushed as far as the Gulf of Guinea and had begun a lucrative trade in gold dust and slaves captured in raids or bought from coastal chiefs. Henry's death brought a slackening in the pace of exploration. But the advance down the African coast continued, under private auspices and as an adjunct to the slave trade, the first bitter fruit of European overseas expansion. In 1469 a wealthy merchant, Fernão Gomes, secured a monopoly of the trade to Guinea (the name then given to the whole African coast), on condition that he explore farther south at the rate of a hundred miles a year. Complying with his pledge, Gomes sent his ships eastward along the Gold, Ivory, and Slave coasts and then southward almost to the mouth of the Congo.

The Sea Route to the East

Under the energetic John II, who came to the throne in 1481, the crown resumed control and direction of the African enterprise. At Mina, on the Gold Coast, John established a fort that became a center of trade in slaves, ivory, gold dust, and a coarse black pepper, as well as a base for further exploration. If Henry had dreamed of finding gold and Prester John, the project of reaching India by rounding Africa was now uppermost in John's mind. In 1483 an expedition commanded by Diogo Cão discovered the mouth of the Congo River and sailed partway up the mighty stream. On a second voyage in 1484, Cão pushed as far south as Cape Cross in southwest Africa. The Portuguese monarch sensed that victory was near. In 1487 a fleet headed by Bartholomeu Dias left Lisbon with orders to pass the farthest point reached by Cão and if possible sail round the tip of Africa. After he had cruised farther south than any captain before him, a providential gale blew Dias's ships in a wide sweep around the Cape of Good Hope and to landfall on the coast of East Africa. He had solved the problem of a sea road to the Indies and returned to Lisbon to report his success to King John.

The route to the East lay open. But domestic and foreign problems distracted John's attention from the Indian enterprise. He died in 1495 without having sent the expedition for which he had made elaborate preparations. His successor, Manuel I, known as the Fortunate, carried out John's plan. In 1497 a fleet of four ships, commanded by the tough, surly nobleman Vasco da Gama, sailed from Lisbon on a voyage that inaugurated the age of European colonialism in Asia. After rounding the Cape, da Gama sailed into the Indian Ocean and up the coast of East Africa. At Malinda, in modern Kenya, he took on an Arab pilot who guided the fleet to Calicut, the great spice trade center on the west coast of India. Received with hostility by the dominant Arab traders and with indifference by the local Indian potentate, who scorned his petty gifts, the persistent da Gama managed to load his holds with a cargo of pepper and cinnamon and returned to Lisbon in 1499 with two of the four ships with which he had begun his voyage. A new fleet, commanded by Pedro Álvares Cabral, was quickly outfitted and sent to India. Swinging far west in the south Atlantic, Cabral made landfall on the coast of Brazil in early 1500 and sent one ship back to Lisbon to report his discovery before continuing to India. He returned to Portugal with a cargo of spices and a story of severe fighting with Arab merchants determined to resist the Portuguese intruders.

The great soldier and administrator Afonso de Albuquerque, who set out in 1509, completed the work begun by da Gama. He understood that to squeeze out the Egyptian and Venetian competition and gain a total monopoly of the spice trade, he must conquer key points on the trade routes of the Indian Ocean. Capture of Malacca on the Malay Peninsula gave the Portuguese control of the strait through which East Indian spices entered the Indian Ocean. Capture of Muscat and Ormuz barred entrance to the Persian Gulf and closed that route to Europe to other nations' ships. The Portuguese strategy was not completely successful, but it diverted to Lisbon the greater part of the spice supply.

For a time, Portugal basked in the sun of an unprecedented prosperity. But the strain of maintaining its vast Eastern defense establishment was too great for Portugal's limited manpower and financial resources, and expenses began to outrun revenues. To make matters worse, under Spanish pressure King Manuel decreed the expulsion of all unbaptized Jews in 1496. As a result, Portugal lost the only native group financially capable of exploiting the investment opportunities offered by the Portuguese triumph in the East. Florentine and German bankers quickly moved in and diverted most of the profits of the Eastern spice trade abroad. Lisbon soon became a mere depot. Cargoes arriving there from the East were shipped almost at once to Antwerp or Amsterdam, better situated as centers of distribution to European customers. In time, Dutch and English rivals snatched most of the Asiatic colonies from Portugal's failing hands.

ADVANCE INTO THE ATLANTIC

Certain groups of islands lying in the eastern Atlantic—the Canaries, Madeiras, Azores, and Cape Verdes—early attracted the attention of Portugal and Spain. These islands played a strategic role in the colonization of America, providing steppingstones and staging areas for the Atlantic crossing. Moreover, their conquest and colonial economic organization set the pattern for Iberian policies in the New World.

The Madeira island group, colonized in 1425, became the most important Portuguese colony in the eastern Atlantic. Madeira's soil and climate were suitable for growing sugar, the most lucrative cash crop of the time, and with Genoese financial and technical aid sugar production was established in Madeira, using slaves from the Canary Islands and later Africa. By 1460, Madeira had its first sugar mill; by 1478 it was the largest sugar producer in the Western world. The Portuguese applied the same successful formula—the combination of sugar and African slave labor—in their colonization of Brazil.

The Canaries had been known to Europeans since the early fourteenth century, but their definitive conquest by Castile began in 1402. The islanders (Guanches), a herding and farming people organized in mutually hostile tribes, resisted fiercely, and the conquest was not complete until about 1497. Less than two centuries after the conquest of the Canaries began, the Guanches, who once may have numbered between 50,000 and 100,000, were extinct, chiefly as a result of mistreatment and disease. The conquest of the Canaries foretold similar developments in the Caribbean.

Like the Madeiras, the Canaries became a laboratory for testing political and economic institutions later transferred to the Americas. Although the lordship of the islands was vested in the crown, the monarchs made agreements (*capitulaciones*) with individual captains (*adelantados*) who were authorized to conquer specific regions and granted large governing powers and other privileges. These agreements resembled the contracts made with military leaders during the Reconquest and with Columbus, Francisco Pizarro, and other great captains during the conquest of America.

Like the Madeiras, too, the Canaries became a testing ground for a plantation system based on sugar and slave labor. By the early sixteenth century, there were twenty-nine sugar mills in operation. The character of the Canaries as a way station between Europe and America for sugar production is indicated by the fact that cuttings for the planting of sugar cane and sugar-processing techniques were transferred from the Canaries to the Caribbean soon after its conquest.

THE VOYAGES OF COLUMBUS

The search for a sea road to the Indies inspired more than one solution. If some believed that the route around Africa offered the answer to the Eastern riddle, others favored sailing due west across the Atlantic. This view had the support of an eminent authority, the Florentine scientist Paolo Toscanelli, who in 1474 advised the Portuguese to try the western route as "shorter than the one which you are pursuing by way of Guinea." His letter came to the attention of an obscure Italian seafarer, Christopher Columbus, who had been reflecting on the problem, and helped confirm his belief that such a passage from Europe to Cipangu (Japan) and Cathay (China) would be easy. This conception rested on a gross underestimate of the earth's circumference and an equal overestimate of the size and eastward extension of Asia. Since all educated Europeans believed the world was round, that question never entered into the dispute between Columbus and his opponents. The main issue was the extent of the ocean between Europe and Asia, and on this point the opposition was right.

For Columbus the idea of reaching the East by sailing west acquired all the force of an obsession. A figure of transition from the dying Middle Ages to the world of capitalism and science, a curious combination of mystic and practical man, Columbus became convinced that God Himself had revealed to him "that it was feasible to sail from here to the Indies, and placed in me a burning desire to carry out this plan."

About 1484, Columbus, who then resided in Lisbon, offered to make a western voyage of discovery for John II, but a committee of experts who listened to his proposal advised the king to turn it down. Undismayed by his rebuff, Columbus next turned to Castile. After eight years of discouraging delays and negotiation, Isabella—in a last-minute change of mind—agreed to support the "Enterprise of the Indies." The capitulación (contract) made by the queen with Columbus named him admiral, viceroy, and governor of the lands he should discover and promised him a generous share in the profits of the venture.

On August 3, 1492, Columbus sailed from Palos with three small ships, the *Pinta*, the *Santa María*, and the *Niña*, manned not by the jailbirds of legend but by experienced crews under competent officers. The voyage was remarkably prosperous, with fair winds the whole way out. But the great distance beyond sight of land began to worry some of the men, and by the end of September there was grumbling aboard the *Santa María*, Columbus's flagship. According to Columbus's son Ferdinand, some sailors proposed to heave the admiral overboard and return to Spain with the report that he had fallen in while watching the stars. Columbus managed to calm his men, and soon floating gulfweed and bosun birds gave signs of land. On October 12, they made landfall at an island in the Bahamas that Columbus named San Salvador.

Cruising southward through the Bahamas, Columbus came to the northeast coast of Cuba, which he took for part of Cathay. An embassy sent to find the Great Khan failed in its mission but returned with reports of a hospitable reception by natives who introduced the Spaniards to the use of "certain herbs the smoke of which they inhale," an early reference to tobacco. Next Columbus sailed eastward to explore the northern coast of an island (present-day Dominican Republic and Haiti) he named Española (Hispaniola). Here the Spaniards were cheered by the discovery of some alluvial gold and gold ornaments, which the natives bartered for Spanish trinkets.

From Hispaniola, on whose coast Columbus lost his flagship, he returned to Spain to report his supposed discovery of the Indies. The Sovereigns received him with signal honors and ordered him to prepare immediately a second expedition to follow up his discovery. In response to Portuguese charges of encroachment on an area in the Atlantic reserved to Portugal by a previous treaty with Castile, Ferdinand and Isabella appealed for help to Pope Alexander VI, himself a Spaniard. The pontiff complied by issuing a series of bulls in 1493 that assigned to Castile all lands discovered or to be discovered by Columbus and drew a line from north to south a hundred leagues west of the Azores and Cape Verdes; west of this line was to be a Spanish sphere of exploration. To John II this demarcation line seemed to threaten Portuguese interests in the south Atlantic and the promising route around Africa to the East. Yielding to Portuguese pressure, Ferdinand and Isabella signed in 1494 the Treaty of

Tordesillas, which established a boundary 270 leagues farther west. Portugal obtained exclusive rights of discovery and conquest east of this line; Castile gained the same rights to the west.

Columbus returned to Hispaniola at the end of 1493 with a fleet of seventeen ships carrying twelve hundred people, most of them artisans and peasants, with a sprinkling of "caballeros, hidalgos, and other men of worth, drawn by the fame of gold and the other wonders of that land." The settlers soon gave themselves up to gold hunting and preying on indigenous peoples. A foreigner of obscure origins, Columbus lacked the powers and personal qualities needed to control this turbulent mass of fortune hunters.

After founding the town of Isabella on the north coast of Hispaniola, Columbus sailed again in quest of Cathay. He coasted down the southern shore of Cuba almost to its western end. The great length of the island convinced him that he had reached the Asiatic mainland. To extinguish all doubts he made his officers and crews take a solemn oath, "on pain of a hundred lashes and having the tongue slit if they ever gainsaid the same," that Cuba was the mainland of Asia. In 1496 he returned to Spain to report his discoveries and answer charges sent by disgruntled settlers to the court. He left behind his brother Bartholomew, who removed the settlement from Isabella to a healthier site on the south shore, naming the new town Santo Domingo.

The first two voyages had not paid their way, but the Sovereigns still had faith in Columbus and outfitted a third fleet in 1498. On this voyage he landed at Trinidad and the mouths of the Orinoco. The mighty current of sweet water discharged by the great river made Columbus conclude that he was on the shores of a continent, but his crotchety mysticism also suggested that the Orinoco was one of the four rivers of Paradise and had its source in the Garden of Eden.

Columbus arrived in Hispaniola to find chaos. The intolerable demands of the greedy Castilian adventurers had provoked the peaceable Taino natives to the point of war. The Spaniards, disappointed in their hopes of quick wealth, blamed the Columbus brothers for their misfortunes and rose in revolt under a leader named Roldán. To appease the rebels Columbus issued pardons and granted land and native slaves. Meanwhile, acting on a stream of complaints against Columbus, the Sovereigns had sent out an agent, Francisco de Bobadilla, to supersede Columbus and investigate the charges against him. Arriving at the island, the irascible Bobadilla seized Columbus and his brother and sent them to Spain in chains. Although Isabella immediately disavowed Bobadilla's arbitrary actions, Columbus never again exercised the functions of viceroy and governor in the New World.

Still gripped by his great illusion, Columbus continued to dream of finding a western way to the land of spices. He was allowed to make one more voyage, the most difficult and disastrous of all. He was now convinced that between the mainland on which he had recently landed and the Malay Peninsula shown on ancient maps, there must be a strait that would lead into the Indian Ocean. In 1502 he sailed in search of this strait and a route to southern Asia. From Hispaniola, where he was not permitted to land, he crossed the Caribbean to the coast of Central America and followed it south to the Isthmus of Panama. Here he believed he was ten days' journey from the Ganges River. In Panama he found some gold, but the hoped-for strait continued to elude him. He finally departed for Hispaniola with his two remaining ships but was forced to beach the worm-riddled craft on Jamaica, where he and his men were marooned for a year awaiting the arrival of a relief ship. In November 1504 Columbus returned to Europe. Broken in health, convinced of the ingratitude of princes, he died in 1506 a rich but embittered man.

THE DISCOVERY OF AMERICA IN HISTORICAL PERSPECTIVE

The five-hundredth anniversary of Columbus's 1492 voyage to America produced an outpouring of writings seeking to throw new light on that momentous event. There has long been agreement that it had prodigious consequences, but also dispute as to whether they should cause jubilation or regret. The Spanish chronicler Francisco López de Gómara, filled with imperialist pride, had no doubts on that score. "The greatest event since the creation of the world (excluding the incarnation of Him

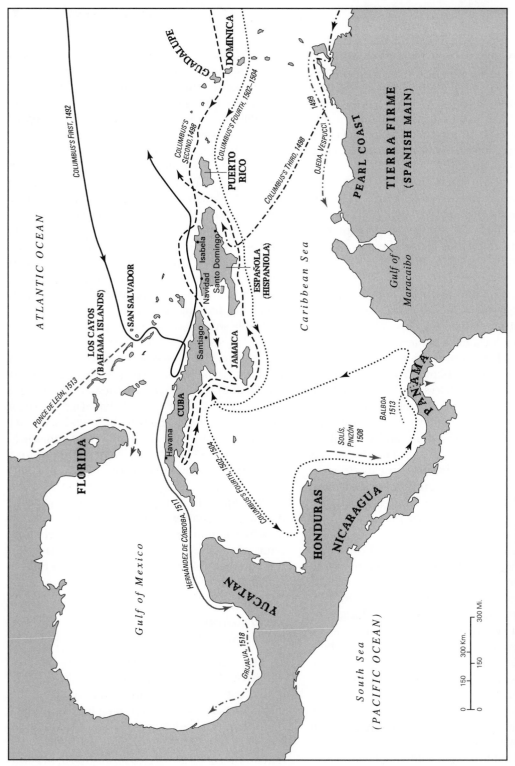

Early Spanish Voyages in the Caribbean

who created it)," he wrote in 1552, "is the discovery of the Indies." But the radical Italian philosopher Giordano Bruno, who was burned for heresy in 1600, strongly dissented, assailing Columbus as one of those "audacious navigators" who only "disturbed the peace of others . . . increased the vices of nations, spread fresh follies by violence, and . . . taught men a new art and means of tyranny and assassination among themselves."

Until recently, however, few Europeans and Americans questioned the splendor and value of Columbus's achievement. In the nineteenth century his voyages came to be viewed as a harbinger and cause of the great movement of Western economic expansion and global domination that was then under way. Celebrations of Columbus were especially exuberant in the United States, where a mystic link was seen between that event and the spectacular rise of the great republic of the West. In this period Columbus was transformed into an almost mythic hero, a larger-than-life figure who overcame all the obstacles placed in his path by prejudiced and ignorant adversaries in order to complete his providential task.

Until well into the twentieth century, this view of the "Discovery" as an event that should inspire unalloyed pride and satisfaction was rarely challenged. Only the immense political and economic changes caused by World War II and the anticolonial revolutions unleashed by the conflict led to a new way of looking at the "Discovery" and its repercussions. That new frame of reference is commonly known as "The Vision of the Vanquished," because it takes as its point of departure the impact of Columbus's voyages not on Europe but on the peoples and cultures of the Americas. Awareness of the ethnocentric, Eurocentric connotations of the term "discovery" has even led many scholars to replace it with the more neutral term "encounter" (*encuentro* in Spanish). America, after all, was not an empty continent when the first Europeans arrived; its true "discoverers" were the people who had crossed over from Asia by way of the Bering Strait many thousands of years before. But the word "encounter," with its suggestion of a peaceful meeting of peoples and cultures, hardly fits the grim reality of the European invasion of indigenous America, so we shall continue to use "discovery" for lack of a better word.

"The Vision of the Vanquished" initiated a more balanced assessment of the discovery of America and its consequences. For the native peoples of America, the Discovery and its sequel of the Conquest were an unmitigated disaster. The combination of new diseases to which they had no acquired immunity, their brutal exploitation, and the resulting social disorganization and loss of will to live led to perhaps the greatest demographic catastrophe in recorded history, with an estimated loss of between 90 and 95 percent of the native population between 1492 and 1575.

The Discovery and the Conquest also cut short the independent development of brilliant civilizations like the Aztec and Inca empires, which, many scholars believe, had not exhausted their possibilities for further cultural advance and flowering. Finally, the Discovery initiated a process of ecological devastation in the New World through the introduction of European animals, plants, and agricultural practices that transformed long-stable ecosystems. Columbus began the process on Hispaniola by introducing the extensive Spanish system of farming with plows and cattle ranching, producing rapid soil erosion and deforestation. The process begun by Columbus continues to this day, as evidenced by the rapid destruction of Latin America's rain forests. This too is part of the "Columbian legacy."

The impact of the Discovery on Europe and its long-term development was much more positive. That impact, as noted long ago by Adam Smith and Karl Marx, is clearest in the realm of economics. Historians may debate the impact of American precious metals on Europe's sixteenth-century "price revolution" or the contribution of the slave trade to the "primitive accumulation" of capital in Europe. It is beyond dispute, however, that the combination of these and other events flowing from the discovery of America gave an immense stimulus to Europe's economic modernization and the rise of capitalism, which in turn hastened and facilitated its domination of the rest of the globe.

The intellectual impact of the Discovery on Europe is more difficult to measure, but it seems indisputable that the expansion of geographic horizons produced by the discovery of America was accompanied by an expansion of mental horizons and the rise of new ways of viewing the world that significantly contributed to intellectual progress. One of the first casualties of the great geographic discoveries was the authority of the ancients and even of the church fathers. Thus the Spanish friar Bartolomé de Las Casas (1484–1566), writing on the traditional belief in uninhabitable zones, in one paragraph managed to demolish the authority of Saint Augustine and the ancients, who, "after all, did not know very much."

The discovery of America and its peoples also produced disputes about their origins and nature that led to the founding of anthropology. The desire to prove the essential humanity and equality of these indigenous Americans inspired some sixteenth-century Spanish missionaries to make profound investigations of their culture. One of the greatest of these friar-anthropologists was, again, Bartolomé de Las Casas, one of whose works is an immense accumulation of ethnographic data used to demonstrate that indigenous Americans fully met the requirements laid down by Aristotle for the good life. Las Casas, resting his case above all on experience and observation, offered an environmentalist explanation of cultural differences and regarded with scientific detachment such deviations from European standards as human sacrifices and ritual cannibalism.

Reflection on the apparent novelty and strangeness of some indigenous ways, and the effort of friar-anthropologists to understand and explain those ways, also led to the development of a cultural relativism that, like the rejection of authority, represented a sharp break with the past. Las Casas, for example, subjected the term "barbarian" to a careful semantic analysis that robbed it, as applied to advanced cultures like the Aztec or the Inca, of most of its sting. Michel de Montaigne, who avidly read accounts of indigenous American customs, observed in his famous essay on native Brazilians, "Of Cannibals": "I think there is nothing barbarous and savage in this nation, from what I have been told, except that each man calls barbarian whatever is not his own practice."

The discovery of America and its peoples also inspired some Europeans, troubled by the social injustices of Renaissance Europe, to propose radical new schemes of political and economic organization. In 1516, for example, Thomas More published *Utopia*, portraying a pagan, socialist society whose institutions were governed by justice and reason, so unlike the states of contemporary Europe, which More described as a "conspiracy of the rich" against the poor. More's narrator, who tells about the Utopians and their institutions, claims to be a sailor who made three voyages with Amerigo Vespucci. The principal source of More's ideas about the evils of private property and the benefits of popular government appears to be a key passage about indigenous customs and beliefs in Vespucci's *Second Letter:*

> Having no laws and no religious doctrine, they live according to nature. They understand nothing of the immortality of the soul. There is no possession of private property among them, for everything is in common. They have no king, nor do they obey anyone. Each is his own master. There is no administration of justice, which is unnecessary to them. . . .

But if the Discovery had a beneficial impact on European intellectual life, reflected in the new rejection of authority, the growth of cultural relativism, and the impulse it gave to unorthodox social and political thought, it also reinforced the negative European attitudes of racism and ethnocentrism. The great Flemish mapmaker Abraham Ortelius gave clear expression to these attitudes in his 1579 world atlas. To the map of Europe Ortelius attached a note proclaiming Europe's historic mission of world conquest, in process of fulfillment by Spain and Portugal, "who between them dominate the four parts of the globe." Ortelius declared that Europeans had always surpassed all other peoples in intelligence and physical dexterity, thus qualifying them to govern the other parts of the globe.

The broad vision of Las Casas, who proclaimed that "all mankind is one," and of Montaigne, who furiously denounced European savagery and proposed a "brotherly fellowship and understanding" as the proper relationship between Europeans and the peoples of the New World, was not typical of contemporary thinking on the subject. Colonial rivals might condemn Spanish behavior toward indigenous Americans, but they usually agreed in regarding them as tainted with vices, and as "poor barbarians."

The perspective of "The Vision of the Vanquished" and new approaches in historical research combine to give us a better understanding of the man Columbus and his dealings with the people he wrongly called "Indians." A curious blend of medieval mystic and modern entrepreneur, Columbus revealed the contradictions in his thought by his comment on gold: "O, most excellent gold! Who has gold has a treasure with which he gets what he wants, imposes his will on the world, and even helps souls to paradise." In *Conquest of America*, Tźvetan Todorov subjects the ideology of Columbus (which represented the ideology of the European invaders) to a careful and subtle dissection that reveals other contradictions. Sometimes Columbus viewed the "Indians" as "noble savages"; sometimes, according to the occasion, he saw them as "filthy dogs." Todorov explains that both myths rest on a common base: scorn for "Indians" and refusal to admit them as human beings with the same rights as himself. In the last analysis, Columbus regarded indigenous peoples not as human beings but as objects. This is well illustrated by a letter he wrote to the Spanish monarchs in September 1498:

> We can send from here in the name of the Holy Trinity, all the slaves and brazilwood that can be sold. If my information is correct, one could sell 4000 slaves that would bring at least twenty millions. . . . And I believe that my information is correct, for in Castile and Aragon and Italy and Sicily and the islands of Portugal and Aragon and the Canary Islands they use up many slaves, and the number of slaves coming from Guinea is diminishing. . . . And although the Indian slaves tend to die off now, this will not always be the case, for the same thing used to happen with the slaves from Africa and the Canary Islands.

In fact, Columbus early on conceived the idea of supplementing the search for a western route to the Indies and for gold with the enslavement of indigenous Americans and their sale in Castile. To make the idea more palatable to the Spanish monarchs, he proposed to limit the slave hunting to a supposed "cannibal" people, the Caribs. When the Tainos of Hispaniola rose in revolt against their intolerable treatment, it provided another legal justification for their enslavement. Between 1494 and 1500 Columbus sent some 2,000 "Indians" to the slave markets of Castile. Contrary to legend, Queen Isabella approved the majority of these shipments.

Columbus, of course, viewed this slavery from the background of a merchant adventurer who was very familiar with the conduct of Portugal's African slave trade, in which other Genoese merchants were deeply involved. He lived at a time when slavery, under certain conditions, was almost universally regarded as licit and proper. His callous lack of concern for the life and death of the enslaved did not make him a monster. If he ardently desired gold, it was not from vulgar greed alone. To be sure, as the Spanish scholar Juan Gil observes, he was "fascinated by the tinkle of maravedis."[1] He bargained hard with the Spanish monarchs for the highest possible share of profits from his discoveries, and despite his lamentation in his last years about his poverty and even the lack of a roof over his head, he died a millionaire. But there was another side to Columbus. He viewed gold as a means of promoting the universal triumph of Christianity, urged his royal masters to use the revenues from the Indies for a crusade to wrest the Holy Land from Muslim hands, and offered himself to head the crusader host. There was a constant tension in Columbus between the medieval mystic who believed the world would end in 155 years and the Renaissance man filled with a drive to achieve power, titles, wealth, and fame.

To assess the significance of Columbus's achievement properly, it must be understood that he was the instrument of historical forces of which he was unaware, forces of transition from the dying Middle Ages to the rising world of capitalism, whose success rested upon conquest and the creation of a global market. That process in turn required an ideological justification, a proud

---

[1]A Spanish coin.

conviction of the superiority of white Europeans over all other peoples and races. Columbus's work in the Caribbean represents the first tragic application of that ideology in the New World. If not the father of colonialism, he was at least one of its fathers, and he bears part of the responsibility for the devastating effects of that system of domination.

BALBOA AND MAGELLAN

Others followed in the wake of Columbus's ships and gradually made known the immense extent of the mainland coast of South America. In 1499 Alonso de Ojeda, accompanied by the pilot Juan de la Cosa and the Florentine Amerigo Vespucci, sailed to the mouths of the Orinoco and explored the coast of Venezuela. Vespucci took part in another voyage in 1501–1502 under the flag of Portugal. This expedition, sent to follow up the discovery of Brazil by Pedro Álvares Cabral in 1500, explored the Brazilian coast from Salvador da Bahia to Rio de Janeiro before turning back. Vespucci's letters to his patrons, Giovanni and Lorenzo de' Medici, reveal an urbane, cultivated Renaissance figure with a flair for lively and realistic description of the fauna, flora, and inhabitants of the New World. His letters were published and circulated widely in the early 1500s. One (whose authenticity is disputed) told of a nonexistent voyage in 1497 and gave him the fame of being the first European to set foot on the South American continent. A German geographer, Martin Waldseemuller, decided to honor Vespucci by assigning the name America to the area of Brazil in a map of the newly discovered lands. The name caught on and presently was applied to the whole of the New World.

A growing shortage of indigenous labor and the general lack of economic opportunities for new settlers on Hispaniola incited Spanish slave hunters and adventurers to conquer the remaining Greater Antilles. Puerto Rico, Jamaica, and Cuba were occupied between 1509 and 1511. In the same period, efforts to found colonies on the coast of northern Colombia and Panama failed disastrously, and the remnants of two expeditions were united under the energetic leadership of the conquistador Vasco Núñez de Balboa to form the new settlement of Darien on the Isthmus of Panama. Moved by local tales of a great sea, south of which lay a land overflowing with gold, Balboa led an expedition across the forests and mountains of Panama to the shores of the Pacific. He might have gone on to make contact with the Inca Empire of Peru if he had not aroused the jealousy of his terrible father-in-law, the "two-legged tiger," Pedrarias Dávila, sent out by Charles V in 1514 as governor of the isthmus. Charged with treason and desertion, Balboa was tried, condemned, and beheaded in 1519.

After Balboa had confirmed the existence of the Pacific Ocean, subsequent European voyages centered on the search for a waterway to the East through or around the American continent. Ferdinand Magellan, a Portuguese who had fought in India and the East Indies, was convinced that a short passage to the East existed south of Brazil. Failing to interest the Portuguese king in his project, Magellan turned to Spain, with greater success. The resulting voyage of circumnavigation of the globe, 1519–1522, the first in history, represented an immense navigational feat and greatly increased Europe's stock of geographic knowledge. But, aside from the acquisition of the Philippines for Spain, Magellan's exploit had little practical value, for his new route to the East was too long to have commercial significance. The net result was to enhance the value of America in Spanish eyes. Disillusioned with the dream of easy access to the riches of the East, Spain turned with concentrated energy to the task of extending its American conquests and to the exploitation of the human and natural resources of the New World.

The Conquest of Mexico

EARLY CONTACT WITH MOCTEZUMA

A disturbing report reached the Aztec capital of Tenochtitlán in 1518. Up from the coast of the Gulf of Mexico hurried the tribute collector Pinotl to inform King Moctezuma of the approach from the sea of winged towers bearing men with white faces and heavy beards. Pinotl had communicated with these men by signs and had exchanged gifts with their leader. Before departing, the mysterious visitors had promised (so Pinotl interpreted their gestures) to return soon and visit Moctezuma in his city in the mountains.

Aztec accounts agree that the news filled Moctezuma with dismay. Could the leader of these strangers be the redeemer-god Quetzalcóatl, returning to reclaim his lost kingdom? According to one Aztec source, Moctezuma exclaimed: "He has appeared! He has come back! He will come here, to the place of his throne and canopy, for that is what he promised when he departed!"

The "winged towers" were the ships of the Spanish captain Juan de Grijalva, sent by Governor Diego Velázquez of Cuba to explore the coasts whose existence the slave-hunting expedition of Francisco Hernández de Córdoba (1517) had already made known. Córdoba had landed at the peninsula of Yucatán, inhabited by Maya peoples whose cotton cloaks and brilliant plumes, stone pyramids, temples, and gold ornaments revealed a native culture far more advanced than any the Spaniards had hitherto encountered. Córdoba met with disastrous defeat at the hands of the Maya and returned to Cuba to die of his wounds. He brought back enough gold and other signs of wealth, however, to encourage Velázquez to outfit a new venture, which he entrusted to his kinsman Juan de Grijalva.

Grijalva sailed from Santiago in April 1518 and, following Córdoba's route, reached the limits of Moctezuma's empire, where he was greeted by natives waving white flags and inviting them by signs to draw near. Here Grijalva's flagship was boarded by the Aztec official Pinotl, whose report was to cause so much consternation in Tenochtitlán. A lively trade developed, with Aztecs bartering gold for Spanish green beads. Grijalva was now convinced that he had come to a wealthy kingdom filled with many large towns. Near the present port of Veracruz, Grijalva sent Pedro de Alvarado back to Cuba with the gold that had been gained by barter. Alvarado was to report to Velázquez what had been accomplished, request authority to found a colony, and seek reinforcements. Grijalva himself sailed on with three other ships, perhaps as far as the river Pánuco, which marked the northern limits of the Aztec Empire. Then he turned back and retraced his course, arriving in Cuba in November 1518.

CORTÉS-QUETZALCÓATL[2]

Velázquez was already planning a third expedition to conquer the Mexican mainland. He passed over Grijalva and chose as leader of the expedition the thirty-four-year-old Hernando Cortés, a native of Medellín in the Spanish province of Estremadura. Cortés was born in 1485 into an hidalgo family of modest means. At the age of fourteen he went to Salamanca, seat of a great Spanish university, to prepare for the study of law, but left some years later, determined on a military career. He had to choose between Italy, the great battlefield of Europe, where Spanish arms were winning fame under the great captain Gonzalo de Córdoba, and the Indies, land of gold, Amazons, and El Dorados. In 1504, at the age of nineteen, he embarked for Hispaniola.

Soon after arriving on the island, he participated in his first military exploit, the suppression of a revolt of Arawaks made desperate by Spanish mistreatment. His reward was an *encomienda* (a grant of indigenous tribute and labor). In 1511 he served under Velázquez in the easy conquest of Cuba. The following year he was appointed alcalde of the newly founded town of Santiago in Cuba. In

[2]In relating the conquest of Mexico, we have often given the Aztec version of events, with all its fantastic elements, as told in the *Florentine Codex*, compiled by the great missionary-scholar Bernardino de Sahagún, because it offers a remarkable insight into the Aztec mentality and reaction to the Conquest. In that version, the legend that foretold the return of the god-king Quetzalcóatl plays a prominent role; initially, at least, the conquistador Cortés appears to have been identified with the god himself or with his emissary. Recently, however, some skeptical scholars have suggested that the legend is a post-Conquest native rationalization of the Aztec defeat or a combined Spanish-Aztec creation, or even a pure invention of Cortés, who twice cites a version of the legend as told by Moctezuma. This skeptical point of view strikes us as ahistorical. History records numerous legends prophesying the return of redeemer-gods or -kings. If medieval Germans could believe in the return of the emperor Frederick Barbarossa, if Renaissance Portuguese could believe in the return of King Sebastian, why could not the Aztecs believe in the return of the god-king Quetzalcóatl?

1518 he persuaded Velázquez to give him command of the new expedition to the Mexican mainland. At the last moment the distrustful governor decided to recall him, but Cortés simply disregarded Velázquez's messages. In February 1519, he sailed from Cuba with a force of some six hundred men. Because Velázquez had not completed negotiations with the emperor Charles for an agreement authorizing the conquest and settlement of the mainland, Cortés's instructions permitted him only to trade and explore.

Cortés's fleet first touched land at the island of Cozumel, where they rescued a Spanish castaway, Jerónimo de Aguilar, who had lived among the Maya for eight years. In March 1519 Cortés landed on the coast of Tabasco, defeated local natives in a sharp skirmish, and secured from them along with pledges of friendship the Mexican girl Malinche,[3] who was to serve him as interpreter, adviser, and mistress. In April Cortés dropped anchor near the site of modern Veracruz. He had contrived a way to free himself from Velázquez's irksome authority. In apparent deference to the wishes of a majority of his followers, who claimed that conquest and settlement would serve the royal interest better than mere trade, Cortés founded the town of Villa Rica de la Vera Cruz and appointed its first officials, into whose hands he surrendered the authority he had received from Velázquez. These officials then conferred on Cortés the title of captain general with authority to conquer and colonize the newly discovered lands. Cortés thus drew on Spanish medieval traditions of municipal autonomy to vest his disobedience in a cloak of legality.

[3] After the achievement of Mexican independence, her conspicuous services to Cortés and the Conquest made her name a byword, a synonym for selling out to foreigners; for many Mexicans it continues to have that meaning today. In fairness to Malinche, it should be pointed out that in her time there was no Mexican nationality and no sense of unity among the various ethnic groups inhabiting Mesoamerica. A talented young woman who apparently possessed extraordinary linguistic skills, Malinche found herself thrown against her will into a very dangerous situation. Her best hope of survival, writes Frances Karttunen, was to serve Cortés, and she "served him unwaveringly. Rather than the embodiment of treachery, her consistency could be viewed as an exercise in total loyalty."

Some days later, Moctezuma's ambassadors appeared in the Spanish camp. The envoys brought precious gifts, the finery of the great gods Tlaloc, Tezcatlipoca, and Quetzalcóatl. Reverently, they arrayed Cortés in the finery of Quetzalcóatl. On his face they placed a serpent mask inlaid with turquoise, with a crossband of quetzal feathers and a golden earring hanging down on either side. On his breast they fastened a vest decorated with quetzal feathers; about his neck they hung a collar of precious stones with a gold disc in the center. In his hand they placed a shield with ornaments of gold and mother-of-pearl and a fringe and pendant of quetzal feathers. They also set before him sandals of fine, soft rubber, black as obsidian.

The Aztec account relates that the god was not satisfied. "Is this all?" Cortés is said to have asked. "Is this your gift of welcome? Is this how you greet people?" The stricken envoys departed and returned with gifts more to the god's liking, including a gold disc in the shape of the sun, as big as a cartwheel, an even larger disc of silver in the shape of the moon, and a helmet full of small grains of gold.

The envoys reported to Moctezuma what they had heard and seen, supplementing their accounts with painted pictures of the gods and their possessions. They described the firing of a cannon, done on Cortés's order to impress the Aztec emissaries:

> A thing like a ball of stone comes out of its entrails; it comes out shooting sparks and raining fire. The smoke that comes out with it has a pestilent odor, like that of rotten mud. . . . If the cannon is aimed against a mountain, the mountain splits and cracks open. If it is aimed against a tree, it shatters the tree into splinters.

Vividly, they described other weapons, the armor, and the mounts of the Spaniards.

Of the terrible war dogs of the Spaniards the envoys said:

> Their dogs are enormous, with flat ears and long dangling tongues. The color of their eyes is burning yellow; their eyes flash fire and shoot off sparks. Their bellies are hollow, their flanks long and narrow. They are tireless and very powerful. They bound here and there,

The famed Mexican muralist Diego Rivera depicted the horrors of slavery, oppression, and genocide that Hernan Cortés and the Spanish Conquest imposed on indigenous people to accumulate wealth and expand the Spanish Empire. [Schalkwijk/Art Resource, NY]

panting, with their tongues hanging out. And they are spotted like an ocelot.

Moctezuma's envoys assured Cortés that they would serve him in every way during his stay on the coast but pleaded with him not to seek a meeting with their king. This pleading was part of Moctezuma's pathetic strategy of plying Cortés-Quetzalcóatl with gifts in the hope that he would be dissuaded from advancing into the interior and reclaiming his lost throne. Suavely, Cortés informed the ambassadors that he had crossed many seas and journeyed from very distant lands to see and speak with Moctezuma and could not return without doing so.

THE MARCH TO TENOCHTITLÁN

Becoming aware of the bitter discontent of tributary towns with Aztec rule, Cortés began to play a double game. He encouraged the Totonacs of the coast to seize and imprison Moctezuma's tax collectors but promptly obtained their release and sent them to the king with expressions of his regard and friendship. He took two other steps before beginning the march on Tenochtitlán. To Spain he sent a ship with dispatches for the emperor Charles in which he sought to obtain approval for his actions by describing the great extent and value of his discoveries. To help in gaining the emperor's goodwill, Cortés persuaded his men to send Charles not only his *quinto* (royal fifth) but all the treasure received from Moctezuma. In order to stiffen the resolution of his followers by cutting off all avenues of escape, he scuttled and sank all his remaining ships on the pretext that they were not seaworthy. Then Cortés and his small army began the march on Mexico-Tenochtitlán.

Advancing into the sierra, Cortés entered the territory of the tough Tlaxcalans, traditional enemies of the Aztecs. The Spaniards had to prove in battle the superiority of their weapons and their fighting capacity before they obtained an alliance with this powerful nation. Then Cortés marched on Cholula, an ancient center of Classic cultural traditions and the cult of Quetzalcóatl. Here, claiming that the Cholulans were conspiring to attack him, Cortés staged a mass slaughter of the Cholulan nobility and warriors after they had assembled in a great courtyard. When news of this event reached Tenochtitlán, terror spread throughout the city.

The Spaniards continued their inexorable advance:

> They came in battle array, as conquerors, and the dust rose in whirlwinds on the roads. Their spears glinted in the sun, and their pennons fluttered like bats. They made a loud clamor as they marched, for their coats of mail and their weapons clashed and rattled. Some of them were dressed in glistening iron from head to foot; they terrified everyone who saw them.

Moctezuma's fears and doubts had by now reduced him to a hopelessly indecisive state of mind. He wavered between submission and resistance, between the conviction that the Spaniards were gods and half-formed suspicions that they were less than divine. He sent new envoys, who brought rich gifts to Cortés but urged him to abandon his plan of visiting the Aztec capital. Moctezuma's naive efforts to bribe or cajole the terrible strangers who "longed and lusted for gold," who "hungered like pigs for gold," in the bitter words of an Aztec account, proved vain. As Moctezuma's doom approached, his own gods turned against him. A group of sorcerers and soothsayers sent by the king to cast spells over the Spaniards were stopped by the young god Tezcatlipoca, who conjured up before their terrified eyes a vision of Mexico-Tenochtitlán burning to the

ground. His forces spent, Moctezuma ended by welcoming Cortés at the entrance to the capital as a rightful ruler returning to his throne. The Aztec king completed his degradation by allowing himself to be kidnaped from his palace by Cortés and a few comrades and taken to live as a hostage in the Spanish quarters.

The Aztec nation had not said its last word. In Cortés's absence from the city—he had set off for the coast to face an expedition sent by Governor Velázquez to arrest him—his lieutenant Pedro de Alvarado ordered an unprovoked massacre of the leading Aztec chiefs and warriors as they celebrated with song and dance a religious festival in honor of Huitzilopochtli. The result was a popular uprising that forced the Spaniards to retreat to their own quarters. This was the situation that Cortés, having won over most of the newcomers and defeated the rest, found when he returned to Tenochtitlán to rejoin his comrades. His efforts to pacify the Aztecs failed. The Aztec council deposed the captive Moctezuma and elected a new chief, who launched heavy attacks on the invaders. As the fighting raged, Moctezuma died, killed by stones cast by his own people as he appealed for peace, according to Spanish accounts; strangled by the Spaniards themselves, according to Aztec sources. Fearing a long siege and famine, Cortés evacuated Tenochtitlán at a heavy cost in lives. The surviving Spaniards and their indigenous allies at last reached friendly Tlaxcala.

Strengthened by the arrival of Spanish reinforcements from Cuba and by thousands of indigenous enemies of the Aztec Empire, Cortés again marched on Tenochtitlán in December 1520. A ferocious struggle began in late April 1521. On August 23, after a siege in which the Aztecs fought for four months with extraordinary bravery, their last king, Cuauhtémoc, surrendered amid the laments of his starving people. Cortés took possession of ruins that had been the city of Tenochtitlán.

THE AFTERMATH OF CONQUEST

From the Valley of Mexico the process of conquest was extended in all directions. Guatemala was conquered by Pedro de Alvarado, Honduras by Cortés himself. In 1527, Francisco de Montejo began the conquest of Yucatán, but as late as 1542 the Maya rose in a desperate revolt that was crushed with great slaughter. Meanwhile, expeditions from Darien subjugated indigenous Nicaraguans. Thus did the two streams of Spanish conquest, both originally starting from Hispaniola, come together again.

For a brief time, Cortés was undisputed master of the old Aztec Empire, renamed the Kingdom of New Spain. He made grants of encomienda to his soldiers, reserving for himself the tributes of the richest towns and provinces. The crown rewarded his services by granting him the title of marquis of the Valley of Oaxaca and the tributes of twenty-three thousand vassals; he lived in almost kingly style, dining "with minstrels and trumpets." But royal distrust of the great conquerors soon asserted itself. He was removed from his office of governor, his authority was vested in an *audiencia* (high court), pending the appointment of a viceroy, and all his actions came under close legal scrutiny. In 1539 he returned to Spain and served with distinction in the expedition against Algiers in the following year, but he was ignored and snubbed by the king. Filled with bitterness, he retired to live in seclusion in Seville. He died in 1547, leaving his title and estates to his eldest legitimate son, Martín Cortés.

The Conquest of Peru

The conquest of Mexico challenged other Spaniards to match the exploits of Cortés and his companions. The work of discovering a golden kingdom rumored to lie beyond the "South Sea" was begun by Balboa but cut short by his death at the hands of Pedrarias Dávila. In 1519 Dávila founded the town of Panama on the western side of the isthmus, and this town became a base for explorations along the Pacific coast. Three years later, Pascual de Andagoya crossed the Gulf of San Miguel and returned with more information concerning a land of gold called "Biru."

PIZARRO AND ATAHUALPA

Dávila entrusted direction of a southward voyage to Francisco Pizarro, an illiterate soldier of fortune little of whose early history is known. Pizarro recruited two partners for the Peruvian venture:

Atahualpa, last of the independent Incan emperors, grandly displayed his regal power with golden objects, including vestments, earrings, and headband. [Atahualpa, Peru, mid-18th century. Oil on canvas. 23¾ × 21⅝. Brooklyn Museum of Art, Museum Purchase]

Diego de Almagro, an adventurer of equally obscure origins, and Hernando de Luque, a priest who acted as financial agent for the trio. Two preliminary expeditions, fitted out from Panama in 1524 and 1526, yielded enough finds of gold and silver to confirm the existence of the elusive kingdom. Pizarro now left for Spain to obtain royal sanction for the enterprise of Peru. He returned to Panama with the titles of captain general and *adelantado* (commander), accompanied by his four brothers and other followers. Almagro, dissatisfied with the allotment of titles and other rewards in the royal contract, accused Pizarro of slighting his services to the king. The quarrel was patched up, but it contained the seeds of a deadly feud.

In December 1531, Pizarro again sailed from Panama for the south with a force of some two hundred men and landed several months later on the Peruvian coast. On arrival the Spaniards learned that civil war was raging in the Inca Empire. Atahualpa, son of the late emperor Huayna Capac by a secondary wife, had risen against another claimant of the throne, his half-brother, Huascar, defeated him in a war marked by great slaughter, and made him prisoner. Atahualpa was advancing toward the imperial capital of Cuzco when messengers brought him news of the arrival of white strangers. After an exchange of messages and gifts between the leaders, the two armies advanced to a meeting at the town of Cajamarca, high in the mountains.

Perhaps in direct imitation of Cortés, Pizarro proposed to win a quick and relatively bloodless victory by seizing the Inca Atahualpa, through whom he may have hoped to rule the country, much as Cortés had done with Moctezuma. In one important respect, however, the Peruvian story differs from that of Mexico. If Moctezuma's undoing was his passive acceptance of the divinity of the invaders, Atahualpa's mistake was to underestimate the massed striking power of the small Spanish force. He had been led to believe that the swords were no more dangerous than women's weaving battens, that the firearms were capable of firing only two shots, and that the horses were powerless at night. This last delusion apparently led to his delayed entry into Cajamarca at dusk, instead of noon, as Pizarro had been told to expect.

When Atahualpa and his escort appeared for the rendezvous in the square of Cajamarca, he found it deserted, for Pizarro had concealed his men in some large buildings opening on the square. Then the priest Vicente de Valverde came forward, accompanied by an interpreter, to harangue the bewildered Inca concerning his obligations to the Christian God and the Spanish king until the angry emperor threw down a Bible that Valverde had handed him. At a signal from Pizarro, his soldiers, supported by cavalry and artillery, rushed forward to kill hundreds and take the Inca prisoner. "It was a very wonderful thing," wrote a Spanish observer, "to see so great a lord, who came in such power, taken prisoner in so short a time."

Atahualpa vainly sought to gain his freedom by offering to fill his spacious cell higher than a man could reach with gold objects as the price of his ransom. Pizarro accepted the offer, and hundreds of llama-loads of gold arrived from all parts of the empire until the room had been filled to the stipulated height. But Pizarro had no intention of letting the emperor go; he remained in "protective custody," a puppet ruler who was to ensure popular acceptance of the new order. Soon, however, the Spaniards began to suspect that Atahualpa was becoming the focal point of a widespread conspiracy against them and decided that he must die. He was charged with treason and condemned to death by burning, a sentence commuted to strangling on his acceptance of baptism.

After the death of the Inca, the Spaniards marched on the Inca capital of Cuzco, which they captured and pillaged in November 1533. A major factor in the success of this and later Spanish campaigns was the military and other assistance given by the late Huascar's branch of the Inca royal family and by curacas who, seeing an opportunity to regain their lost independence and power, rallied to the Spanish side after the capture of Atahualpa. The gold and silver looted from Cuzco, together with Atahualpa's enormous ransom of gold, was melted down and divided among the soldiers. Hernando Pizarro, Francisco's brother, was sent to Spain with Emperor Charles's share of the plunder. Hernando's arrival with his load of gold and silver caused feverish excitement, and a new wave of Spanish fortune hunters sailed for the New World. Meanwhile, Francisco Pizarro had begun construction of an entirely new Spanish capital, Lima, the City of the Kings, conveniently near the coast for communication with Panama.

POST-CONQUEST TROUBLES

After Atahualpa's death, Pizarro, posing as the defender of the legitimate Inca line, proclaimed Huascar's brother Manco as the new Inca. But Manco was not content to play the role of a Spanish puppet. A formidable insurrection, organized and led by Manco himself, broke out in many parts of the empire. A large army laid siege to Cuzco for ten months but failed by a narrow margin to take the city. Defeated by superior Spanish weapons and tactics and by food shortages in his army, Manco retreated to a remote stronghold in the Andean mountains, where he and his successors maintained a kind of Inca government-in-exile until 1572, when a Spanish military expedition entered the mountains, broke up the imperial court, and captured the last Inca, Tupac Amaru, who was beheaded in a solemn ceremony at Cuzco.

The Inca siege of Cuzco had barely been broken when fighting began between a group of the conquerors headed by the Pizarro brothers and a group led by Diego de Almagro over possession of the city of Cuzco. Defeated in battle, Almagro suffered death by strangling but left behind him a son and a large group of supporters to brood over their poverty and supposed wrongs. Twelve of them, contemptuously dubbed by Pizarro's secretary "the knights of the cape" because they allegedly had only one cloak among them, planned and carried out the assassination of the conqueror of Peru in June 1541. But their triumph was of short duration. From Spain came a judge, Vaca de Castro, sent by Charles V to advise Pizarro concerning the government of his province. Assuring himself of the loyalty of Pizarro's principal captains, Vaca de Castro made war on Almagro's son, defeated his army on the "bloody plains of Chupas," and promptly had him tried and beheaded as a traitor to the king.

Presently, fresh troubles arose. Early in 1544 a new viceroy, Blasco Núñez Vela, arrived in Lima to proclaim the edicts known as the New Laws of the Indies. These laws regulated Indian tribute, freed indigenous slaves, and forbade forced labor. They evoked outraged cries and appeals for their suspension from the Spanish landowners in Peru. When these pleas were not heeded, the desperate conquistadors rose in revolt and found a leader in Gonzalo Pizarro, brother of the murdered Francisco.

The first phase of the great revolt in Peru ended auspiciously for Gonzalo Pizarro with the defeat and death of the viceroy Núñez Vela in a battle near Quito. Pizarro now became the uncrowned king of the country. The rebel leader owed much of his initial success to the resourcefulness and demoniac energy of his eighty-year-old field commander and principal adviser, Francisco de Carbajal. To these qualities Carbajal united an inhuman cruelty that became legendary in Peru.

After his victory over the viceroy, Carbajal and other advisers urged Pizarro to proclaim himself king of Peru. But Pizarro, a weaker man than his iron-willed lieutenant, hesitated to avow the revolutionary meaning of his actions. The arrival of a smooth-tongued envoy of the crown, Pedro de la Gasca, who announced suspension of the New Laws and offered pardons and rewards to all repentant rebels, caused a trickle of desertions from Pizarro's ranks that soon became a flood.

Finally, the rebellion collapsed almost without a struggle, and its leaders were executed. Before the civil wars in Peru had run their course, four of the Pizarro "brothers of doom" and the Almagros, father and son, had met violent deaths; a viceroy had been slain; and numberless others had lost their lives. Peace and order were not solidly established in the country until the administration of Viceroy Francisco de Toledo, who came out in 1569, a quarter-century after the beginning of the great civil wars.

How a Handful of Spaniards Won Two Empires

The fact of Spanish Conquest raises a question: How did small groups of Spaniards, initially numbering a few hundred men, conquer the Aztec and Inca empires, which had populations in the millions, large armies, and militarist traditions of their own? Here we have a paradox. With relative ease the Spaniards conquered the Aztecs and the Incas, peoples who were organized on the state level, lived a sedentary life based on intensive agriculture, and were ruled by emperors to whom they owed complete obedience. On the other hand, tribes of marginal culture such as the nomadic Chichimecs of the northern Mexican plains or the Araucanians of Chile, who practiced a simple shifting agriculture and herding, were indomitable; the Araucanians continued to battle white invaders for hundreds of years until 1883.

A sixteenth-century Spanish soldier and chronicler of uncommon intelligence, Pedro Cieza de León, reflecting on the contrast between the swift fall of the Inca Empire and the failure of the Spaniards to conquer the "uncivilized" tribes of the Colombian jungles, found an explanation in the simple social and economic organization of the tribes, which made it possible for the people to flee before a Spanish advance and soon to rebuild village life elsewhere. In

In this mural, *Cuauhtémoc contra el mito,* David Alfaro Siqueiros immortalizes
Cuauhtémoc, the last Aztec emperor to die resisting the Spanish conquest. For many
Mexicans, Cuauhtémoc became a symbol of rebellion and national resistance to for-
eign intervention and oppression. [*Cuauhtémoc Against the Myth,* 1944. Mural on Teepan Union
Housing Project, Tlateco, Mexico, © VAGA, NY. Schalkwijk, Art Resource, NY]

contrast, the mass of the Inca population, docile subjects, accepted their emperor's defeat as their own
and quickly submitted to the new Spanish masters.
For these people, flight from the fertile valleys of the
Inca to the deserts, bleak plateaus, and snowcapped
mountains that dominate the geography of the
region would have been unthinkable.

Cieza's comments are insightful but do not sat-
isfactorily explain the swift fall of these great
empires. At least four other factors contributed to
that outcome:

1. Spanish firearms and cannon, though
primitive by modern standards, gave the invaders
a decided superiority over Aztecs and Incas

armed with bows and arrows, wooden lances and
darts, slings, war clubs with stone or bronze
heads, and wooden swords tipped with obsidian
points. Even more decisive for the Spanish was
the horse, an animal unknown to both Aztecs
and Incas, who at least initially regarded it with
awe. The Spanish cavalryman, armed with lance
and sword, clad in armor and chain mail, had a
striking force comparable to that of the modern
tank. Time and time again, a small Spanish
squadron of cavalry routed a much larger number of Aztec and Inca warriors.

2. Diseases, notably smallpox, unwittingly
introduced by the invaders, became effective

Spanish allies. To give one instance, smallpox raged in Tenochtitlán during the Spanish siege of the city, killing King Cuitlahuac and many Aztec soldiers and civilians, and thereby contributed to its fall.

3. The Spaniards were Renaissance men with a basically secular outlook, whereas their adversaries represented a much more archaic worldview in which ritual and magic played a large role. Certainly the conquistadors were in part inspired by religious zeal. For the Spanish, however, war was basically a science or art based on centuries of European study and practice of military strategy and tactics. For the Aztecs and the Incas, war had a large religious component. The Aztec method of waging war, for example, emphasized capturing Spaniards and dragging them off to be sacrificed to their gods instead of killing them on the spot. Aztec and Inca warfare also included elaborate ceremonies and conventions that required giving proper notice to a people targeted for attack. The Spaniards did not limit themselves with such conventions.[4]

4. Internal division was a major factor in the swift collapse of these empires. Hatred of the Aztecs by tributary peoples or unvanquished peoples like the Tlaxcalans explains why they formed a majority of Cortés's forces during the last struggle for Tenochtitlán. In what is now Peru, the conflict between two claimants of the Inca throne and their followers played directly into Pizarro's hands. Also, the Inca Empire was a mosaic of states, some quite recently incorporated into the empire, and the former lords or curacas of these states, eager to regain their independence, rallied to the Spanish side. All too late, they discovered that they had exchanged one oppressor for a worse one.

Thus, these sophisticated, highly organized empires fell to the Spaniards because of the superior armament and decimating diseases brought by the latter, the differing worldviews of the two peoples, and the internal divisions within the empires themselves.

---

[4]One exception was the *Requerimiento*, or Requirement, a document designed to satisfy Spanish royal conscience. It contained Spanish demands that must be read before making war. For the farcical use of this document, see Chapter 4.

The Quest for El Dorado

FAILURES IN NORTH AMERICA

From its original base in the West Indies and from the two new centers of Mexico and Peru, the great movement of Spanish conquest radiated in all directions. While Spanish ships were launched on the waters of the Pacific to search for the Spice Islands, land expeditions roamed the interior of North and South America in quest of new golden kingdoms.

The North American mainland early attracted the attention of Spanish gold hunters and slave hunters based in the West Indies. In 1513, Ponce de León, governor of Puerto Rico, sailed west and claimed a subtropical land to which he gave the name La Florida. His subsequent efforts to colonize the region ended with his death. In the 1520s another expedition, ineptly led by Pánfilo de Narváez, met with disaster in the vast, indefinite expanse of La Florida. Only four survivors of the venture, among them its future chronicler, the honest and humane Alvar Núñez Cabeza de Vaca, reached Mexico safely after a great, circuitous trek over the plains of Texas.

Cabeza de Vaca's tales of adventure, with their hints of populous cities just beyond the horizon, inspired the conquistador Hernando de Soto, a veteran of the conquest of Peru, to try his fortune in La Florida. In 1542, after three years of unprofitable wanderings and struggles with peoples indigenous to the great area between modern-day South Carolina and Arkansas, de Soto died in the wilderness of a fever.

The strange tales told by Cabeza de Vaca and his three companions on their arrival in Mexico in 1536, and the even stranger story told by a certain Fray Marcos, who claimed to have seen in the far north one of the Seven Cities of the mythical golden realm of Cibola, persuaded Viceroy Antonio de Mendoza in 1540 to send an expedition northward commanded by Francisco Vásquez de Coronado. For two years, Spanish knights in armor pursued the elusive realm of gold through the future states of Arizona, New Mexico, Colorado, Oklahoma, Kansas, and possibly Nebraska. Disillusioned by the humble reality of the Zuñi pueblos of Arizona, the apparent source of the Cibola myth, Coronado pushed east in search of still another El Dorado, this time called Quivira. Intruders who left no trace of their passage, the Spaniards were repelled by the immensity of the Great Plains and returned home bitterly disappointed with their failure to find treasure.

FRUSTRATIONS IN SOUTH AMERICA

The golden will-o'-the-wisp that lured Spanish knights into the deserts of the Southwest also beckoned to them from South America's jungles and mountains. From the town of Santa Marta, founded in 1525 on the coast of modern Colombia, an expedition led by Gonzalo Jiménez de Quesada set out in 1536 on a difficult journey up the Magdalena River in search of gold and a passage to the Pacific. They suffered incredible hardships before they finally emerged onto the high plateau east of the Magdalena inhabited by the Chibcha. Primarily farmers, skillful in casting gold and copper ornaments, the Chibcha lived in palisaded towns and were ruled by a chieftain called the Zipa. After defeating them in battle, Jiménez de Quesada founded in 1538 the town of Santa Fé de Bogotá, future capital of the province of New Granada. The immense treasure in gold and emeralds looted from the Chibcha fired Spanish imaginations and inspired fantasies about yet other golden kingdoms. The most famous of these legends was that of El Dorado (the Golden Man).

The dream of spices also inspired the saga of Spanish conquest. Attracted by accounts of an eastern land where cinnamon trees grew in profusion, Gonzalo Pizarro led an expedition in 1539 from Quito in modern Ecuador across the Andes and down the forested eastern mountain slopes. Cinnamon was found, but in disappointingly small quantities. Lured on by local tall tales of rich kingdoms somewhere beyond the horizon, designed to trick the Spanish intruders into moving on, the treasure hunters plunged deep into the wilderness. Gonzalo's lieutenant, Francisco de Orellana, sent with a party down a certain stream in search of food, found the current too strong to return and went on to enter a great river whose course he followed in two makeshift boats for a distance of eighteen hundred leagues, eventually emerging from its mouth to reach Spanish settlements in

Venezuela. On the banks of the great river, Orellana fought natives whose women joined the battle. For this reason, he gave the river its Spanish name of Amazonas, an illustration of the myth-making process among the Spaniards of the Conquest.

In the southern reaches of the continent, which possessed little gold or silver, new agricultural and pastoral settlements arose. In 1537, Pizarro's comrade and rival, Diego de Almagro, made a fruitless march across the rugged Andean altiplano and the sun-baked Chilean desert in search of gold. He returned bitterly disappointed. Two years later, Pizarro authorized Pedro de Valdivia to undertake the conquest of the lands to the south of Peru. After crossing the desert of northern Chile, Valdivia reached the fertile Central Valley and founded there the town of Santiago. In constant struggle with Araucanians, Valdivia laid the foundations of an agricultural colony based on the servile labor of other, more pacific native peoples. He was captured and killed by the Araucanians during an expedition southward in 1553.

In the same period (1536), the town of Buenos Aires was founded on the estuary of the Rio de la Plata by the adelantado Pedro de Mendoza, who brought twenty-five hundred colonists in fourteen ships. But Buenos Aires was soon abandoned by its famished inhabitants, who moved almost a thousand miles upstream to the newly founded town of Asunción in Paraguay, where a genial climate, an abundance of food, and a multitude of docile Guarani people created more favorable conditions for Spanish settlement. Asunción became the capital of Paraguay and all the Spanish territory in southeastern South America.

THE CONQUISTADORS

What sort of men were the conquistadors? The conquest of America attracted a wide variety of types. There was a sprinkling of professional soldiers, some with backgrounds of service in the Italian wars and some with pasts they preferred to forget. The old conquistador Gonzalo Fernández de Oviedo had such men in mind when he warned the organizers of expeditions against "fine-feathered birds and great talkers" who "will either slay you or sell you or forsake you when they find that you promised them more in Spain than you can produce." In one of his *Exemplary Tales*, Cervantes describes the Americas as "the refuge and shelter of the desperate men of Spain, sanctuary of rebels, safe-conduct of homicides." No doubt men of this type contributed more than their share of the atrocities that stained the Spanish Conquest. But the background of the conquistadors was extremely varied, running the whole gamut of the Spanish social spectrum. The majority were commoners, but there were many marginal hidalgos, poor gentlemen who wished to improve their fortunes. Of the 168 men who captured Atahualpa at Cajamarca in 1532, 38 were hidalgos and 91 plebeians, with the background of the rest unknown or uncertain. According to James Lockhart, who has studied the men of Cajamarca, 51 members of the group were definitely literate and about 76 "almost certainly functioning literates." The group included 19 artisans, 12 notaries or clerks, and 13 "men of affairs."

Of the Spanish kingdoms, Castile provided the largest contingent, with natives of Andalusia predominating in the first, or Caribbean, phase of the Conquest; men from Estremadura, the poorest region of Spain, made up the largest single group in the second, or mainland, phase. Cortés, Pizarro, Almagro, Valdivia, Balboa, Orellana, and other famous conquistadors all came from Estremadura. Foreigners were not absent from the Conquest. Oviedo assures us that men had come "from all the other nations of Asia, Africa, and Europe."

By the 1520s an institution inherited from the Spanish Reconquest, the *compaña* (warrior band), whose members shared in the profits of conquest according to certain rules, had become the principal instrument of Spanish expansion in the New World. At its head stood a military leader who usually possessed a royal capitulación, which vested him with the title of adelantado and with the governorship of the territory to be conquered. Sometimes these men were wealthy in their own right and contributed large sums or incurred enormous debts to finance the expedition. Italian, German, and Spanish merchant capitalists and royal officials grown wealthy through the slave trade or other means provided much of the capital needed to fit out ships, acquire horses and slaves, and supply arms and food.

The warrior band was in principle a military democracy, with the distribution of spoils carried out by a committee elected from among the entire company. After subtracting the quinto and the common debts, the remaining booty was divided into equal shares. In the distribution of Atahualpa's treasure, there were 217 such shares, each worth 5,345 gold pesos, a tidy sum for that time. Distribution was made in accordance with the individual's rank and contribution to the enterprise. The norm was one share for a *peón* or foot soldier, two for a *caballero* or horseman (one for the rider, another for the horse), and more for a captain.

Despite its democratic aspect, the captains, large investors, and royal officials dominated the enterprise of conquest and took the lion's share for themselves. Some of the men were servants or slaves of the captains and investors, and their shares went entirely or in part to their employers or masters; in other cases, conquistadors had borrowed or bought on credit to outfit themselves, and the greater part of their earnings went to their creditors. Contemporary accounts complain of the predatory ways of some captains, who sold supplies to their men in time of need at profiteering prices. At a later stage of each conquest came the distribution of encomiendas. Craftsmen and other plebeians received encomiendas after the conquest of Mexico and Peru; later, however, only the leaders and hidalgo members of expeditions were rewarded with such grants.

Many conquistadors were hard, ruthless men, hard in dealing with each other and harder still with indigenous peoples. The conquistador and chronicler Gonzalo Fernández de Oviedo, an ardent imperialist, wrote that some conquistadors could more accurately be called "depopulators or destroyers of the new lands." The harshness of the conquistador reflected the conditions that formed his character: the climate of violence in Spain as it emerged from seven centuries of warfare against the Moor, the desperate struggle of most Spaniards to survive in a society divided by great inequalities of wealth, and the brutalizing effects of a colonial war.

It would be wrong, however, to conclude that all conquistadors fitted this negative pattern. Some were transformed by their experiences, were taught humility and respect for indigenous values, or even came to concede the moral superiority of the "Indian" over the Spaniard. This was the lesson that Alvar Núñez Cabeza de Vaca learned in the course of his immense eight-year trek from the gulf coast of Texas to Mexico. In his account of his adventures, the Spaniards are presented as savages and the "Indians" as humane and civilized. Another conquistador, Pedro Cieza de León, the "prince of chroniclers," had high praise for Inca civilization, criticized the cruelties of the Conquest, and clearly sympathized with the ideas of Las Casas. Yet another conquistador, Alonso de Ercilla, author of the finest Spanish epic poem of the sixteenth century, *La Araucana*, dealing with the struggle of the Araucanians of Chile against the Spaniards, praises and even glorifies the Araucanians, who appear throughout the poem as a heroic people determined to be free. Meanwhile the victorious Spaniards are portrayed as cowardly, greedy, and selfish.

Of the trinity of motives (God, Gold, and Glory) commonly assigned to the Spanish conquistador, the second was certainly uppermost in the minds of most. "Do not say that you are going to the Indies to serve the king and to employ your time as a brave man and an hidalgo should," observed Oviedo in an open letter to would-be conquerors, "for you know the truth is just the opposite: you are going solely because you want to have a larger fortune than your father and your neighbors." Pizarro put it even more plainly in his reply to a priest who urged the need for spreading the Faith. "I have not come for any such reasons. I have come to take away from them their gold." The conquistador and chronicler of the conquest of Mexico, Bernal Díaz del Castillo, ingenuously declared that the conquerors died "in the service of God and of His Majesty, and to give light to those who sat in darkness—and also to acquire that gold which most men covet."

Most conquistadors dreamed of eventually returning to Spain with enough money to found a family and live in a style that would earn them the respect and admiration of their neighbors. Only a minority, chiefly large merchants and *encomenderos*, acquired the capital needed to fulfill this ambition, and not all of them returned to Spain. The majority, lacking encomiendas or other sources of wealth, remained and often formed ties of dependency with more powerful Spaniards, usually encomenderos in whose service they entered as artisans, military retainers, or overseers of their encomiendas or other enterprises. After 1535 more and more would-be conquistadors came to the Americas while the opportunities for joining profitable conquests diminished. As a result, the problem of a large number of unemployed and turbulent Spaniards caused serious concern to royal officials and to the crown itself.

Most conquistadors and other early Spanish settlers in the Indies were single young males, with a sprinkling of married men who had left their wives at home while they sought their fortunes. Aside from an occasional mistress or camp follower, few Spanish women accompanied the expeditions. Once the fighting had stopped, however, a small stream of Spanish women began to cross the Atlantic. Some were wives coming to rejoin their husbands (there were laws, generally unenforced, requiring that a married man must have his wife come to live with him or be deported to Spain); others were mothers, sisters, or nieces of the settlers. Marriages with indigenous women were not uncommon; even hidalgos were happy at the opportunity to marry a wealthy noblewoman like Moctezuma's daughter, Tecuixpo (Isabel Moctezuma), who was wed to three Spanish husbands in turn. After mid-century, however, most Spaniards of all social levels tended to marry Spanish women, either immigrants or those born in the Indies. By the last quarter of the century, the Spanish family and household, based on strong clan and regional loyalties, had been reconstituted.

Of the thousands of bold captains and their followers who rode or marched under the banner of Castile to the conquest of America, few lived to enjoy in peace and prosperity the fruits of their valor, their sufferings, and their cruelties. "I do not like the title of adelantado," wrote Oviedo, "for actually that honor and title is an evil omen in the Indies, and many who bore it have come to an evil end." Of those who survived the battles and the marches, a few received the lion's share of spoils, land, and labor; the majority remained in modest or worse circumstances, and frequently in debt. The conflict between the haves and the have-nots among the conquerors contributed significantly to the explosive, tension-ridden state of affairs in the Indies in the decades following the Conquest.

LOPE DE AGUIRRE: AN UNDERDOG OF THE CONQUEST

That conflict was a major ingredient in the devil's brew of passions that produced three decades of murderous civil wars and revolts among the Spaniards in Peru following the fall of the Inca Empire. The defeat of the great revolt of Gonzalo Pizarro in 1548 brought no lasting peace to Peru, for it left seething with discontent the many adventurers who had flocked from all parts of the Indies to join the struggle against Pizarro. These men had hoped to be fittingly rewarded for their services to the crown. Instead, Pizarro's wily conqueror, La Gasca, added to the encomiendas of the rich and powerful friends who had abandoned Pizarro and come over to the royal side. The sense of betrayal felt by many rank-and-file conquistadors was expressed by Pero López, who charged that La Gasca had left "all His Majesty's servants poor, while he let many of His Majesty's foes keep all they had and even gave them much more."

The Viceroy Cañete clearly defined the economic essence of the problem in a letter that he wrote to Emperor Charles V in 1551; he reported that there were only 480 encomiendas in Peru, whereas the number of Spaniards was 8,000. Including the jobs that the colonial administration could provide, only 1,000 Spaniards could "have food to eat." Cañete's only solution to rid Peru of the plague of unemployed conquistadors was to send them off on new conquests, "for it is well known that they will not work or dig or plow, and they say that they did not come to these parts to do such things." The emperor agreed; permission for new conquests, he wrote the viceroy in December 1555, would serve "to rid and cleanse the country of the idle and licentious men who are there at present and who would leave to engage in that business. . . ." Accordingly, Charles revoked a decree of 1549, issued at the urging of Las Casas, which prohibited new conquests.

The career of the famous Lope de Aguirre, "the Wanderer," casts a vivid light on the psychology and mentality of the disinherited conquistador host. A veteran conquistador, Aguirre was fifty, lame in one leg as a result of wounds, and had spent a quarter-century in a fruitless search for fortune in the Indies when the rumor of a new El Dorado in the heart of the Amazon wilderness caused feverish excitement in Peru. Whether or not the legendary realm existed, it provided a convenient means of solving a potentially explosive social problem. In 1559, Viceroy Andrés Hurtado de Mendoza authorized Pedro de Ursúa to lead an expedition to search for the province of "Omagua and Dorado." Lope de Aguirre, accompanied by his young mestiza daughter, formed part of the expedition when it sailed down the Huallaga River, a tributary of the Amazon, in quest of the new golden realm. Ursúa proved to be a poor leader, and unrest, aggravated by intolerable heat, disease, and lack of food, soon grew into a mutiny whose ringleader was Lope de Aguirre. Ursúa was murdered and, although the rebels raised a Spanish noble named Fernando de Guzmán to be their figurehead "prince," Aguirre soon became the expedition's undisputed leader.

He had devised an audacious new plan that had nothing to do with the quest for El Dorado. It called for the conquest of Peru, removal of its present rulers, and rewards for old conquistadors like himself

> for the labors we have had in conquering and pacifying the native Indians of those kingdoms. For although we won those Indians with our persons and effort, spilling our blood, at our expense, we were not rewarded. . . . Instead the Viceroy exiled us with deception and falsehood, saying that we were coming to the best and most populous land in the world, when it is in fact bad and uninhabitable. . . .

Having constructed two large boats on the banks of the Amazon, the expedition sailed off down the great river, bound for the conquest of Peru. Aguirre's distrust of Guzmán soon led to the killing of the "lord and Prince of Peru" and his mistress and followers. By the time Aguirre and his men entered the Atlantic in July 1561, other killings had reduced the number of Spaniards from 370 to 230. Sailing past the shores of Guiana, they seized the island of Margarita and killed its governor. In September he landed on the coast of Venezuela, captured the town of Valencia, and proclaimed a "cruel war of fire and sword" against King Philip II of Spain. But by now the alarm had gone out in all directions and overwhelming royal forces were moving against him. His small army, already much diminished by his summary executions of suspected traitors, began to melt away as a result of growing desertions. On October 27, 1561, after a number of his most trusted followers had fled to the royalist camp, Aguirre ran his sixteen-year-old daughter through with his sword to save her, he said, from going through life as the daughter of a rebel. Shortly after he was killed by arquebus shots fired by two of his former soldiers.

Some weeks before his death, Aguirre had written King Philip a remarkable letter that offers a conquistador's vision of the Conquest and the world it created. In stark contrast to the heroic vision of the great captains like Cortés, however, Aguirre described the Conquest's underdogs, bitter over their betrayal by the great captains, the viceroys, cunning letrados (officials with legal training) or judges like La Gasca, and their king. Aguirre insisted that he was of Old Christian descent and of noble blood but admitted that he was born of "middling parents," an admission that he was probably one of the many poor hidalgos who came to the Indies in search of fame and fortune.

Aguirre recounted the services that he and his comrades had rendered to the crown and fiercely attacked the king's ingratitude:

> Consider, King and Lord, that you cannot justly take any profits from this land, where you risked nothing, until you have properly rewarded those who labored and sweated there in your service. . . . Few kings go to hell, because there are so few of you, but if there were many none would go to heaven. I hold it for certain that even in hell you would be worse than Lucifer, for your whole ambition is to quench your insatiable thirst for human blood.

Despite this blasphemously revolutionary sentiment, Aguirre expressed the horror that he and his comrades felt for the Lutheran heresy and assured the king that, sinners though they were, they accepted completely the teachings of the Holy Mother Church of Rome. But Aguirre denounced the scandalous dissolution and pride of the friars in the Indies. "Their whole way of life here is to acquire material goods and sell the sacraments of the church for a price. They are enemies of the poor—ambitious, gluttonous, and proud—so that even the meanest friar seeks to govern and rule these lands."

Aguirre was also harsh in his comments on the royal officials in Peru. He noted that each royal *oidor* (judge) received an annual salary of 4,000 pesos plus 8,000 pesos of expenses, yet at the end of three years of service each had saved 60,000 pesos and acquired estates and other possessions to boot. Moreover, they were so proud that "whenever we run into them they want us to drop on our knees and worship them like Nebuchadnezzar." Aguirre advised the king not to entrust the discharge of his royal conscience to these judges, for they spent all their time planning marriages for their children, and their common refrain was, "To the left and to the right, I claim all in my sight."

Aguirre closed his revealing letter by wishing King Philip good fortune in his struggle against the Turks and the French and all others "who wish to make war on you in those parts. In these, God grant that we may obtain with our arms the reward rightfully due us, but which you have denied." He signed himself, "son of your loyal Basque vassals and rebel till death against you for your ingratitude, Lope de Aguirre, the Wanderer."[5]

---

[5]Thanks to Professor Thomas Holloway of the University of California at San Diego for calling attention to the peculiar interest of the Aguirre episode and for allowing the use of his translation of Aguirre's letter to Philip II.

The Economic Foundations of Colonial Life

4

FROM THE FIRST DAYS of the Conquest, the Spanish government faced a problem of harmonizing the demand of the conquistadors for cheap labor, which they frequently employed in a wasteful and destructive manner, with the crown's interest in the preservation of a large, tribute-paying indigenous population. The first decades of colonial experience demonstrated that indigenous peoples, left to the tender mercies of the colonists, might either become extinct, as actually happened on the once densely populated island of Hispaniola, or rise in revolts threatening the very existence of the Spanish Empire in America. The crown naturally regarded these alternatives with distaste.

Equally distasteful, the crown feared that Spanish colonists' monopolistic control of indigenous lands and labor might lead to the rise of a class of feudal lords independent of royal authority, a development the Spanish kings were determined to prevent. The church also had a major interest in this problem. If the *indígenas* (indigenous peoples) died out as a result of Spanish mistreatment, the great task of saving pagan souls would remain incomplete and the good name of the church would suffer. Besides, who then would build churches and monasteries and support the servants of God in the Indies?

The dispute over indigenous policy immediately assumed the dramatic outward form of a struggle of ideas. For reasons deeply rooted in Spain's medieval past, Spanish thought of the sixteenth century had a strongly legalistic and scholastic character. At a time when scholasticism[1] was dying in other Western lands, it retained great vitality in Spain as a philosophic method and as an instrument for the solution of private and public problems. The need "to discharge the royal conscience," to make the royal actions conform to the natural and divine law, helps explain Spanish preoccupation with the doctrinal foundations of its policy. What was the nature of the *indígenas*? What was their cultural level? Were they the slaves by nature described by Aristotle, a race of subhumans who might properly be conquered and made to serve the Spaniards? What rights and obligations did the papal donation of America to the Spanish monarchs confer on them? Summoned by the monarchs to answer these and similar questions, jurists and theologians waged a battle of books in which they bombarded each other with citations from Aristotle, the church fathers, and medieval philosophers. Less frequently, they supported their positions with materials based on direct observation or written accounts of indigenous life.

[1]A system of theological and philosophical doctrine and inquiry that predominated in the Middle Ages. It was based chiefly on the authority of the church fathers and of Aristotle and his commentators.

Tribute and Labor in the Spanish Colonies

Behind the subtle disputations over Spain's obligations to the indígenas, however, went on a complex struggle over the question of who should control their labor and tribute, the foundations of the Spanish Empire in America. The main parties to this struggle were the crown, the church, and the colonists.

THE ENCOMIENDA AND SLAVERY

Hispaniola was the first testing ground of Spain's policy. The situation created on the island by the arrival of Columbus's second expedition has been aptly summed up by Samuel Eliot Morison in the phrase "Hell on Hispaniola." Eager to prove to the crown the value of his "discoveries," Columbus compelled the natives to bring in a daily tribute of gold dust. When the hard-pressed Arawaks revolted, they were hunted down, and hundreds were sent to Spain as slaves. Later, yielding to the demands of rebellious settlers, Columbus distributed Arawaks among them, with the grantees enjoying the right to use the forced labor of the natives.

This temporary arrangement, formalized in the administration of Governor Nicolás de Ovando and sanctioned by the crown, became the *encomienda*. This system had its origin in the Spanish medieval practice of granting to leading warriors jurisdiction over lands and people captured from the Moors. The encomienda assigned to a colonist responsibility for indigenous people who were to serve him with tribute and labor. He in turn assumed the obligation of protecting them, paying for the support of a parish priest, and helping defend the colony. In practice, the encomienda in the West Indies proved a hideous slavery. Basically as a result of this mistreatment, the indigenous population of Hispaniola dwindled from several million to 29,000 within two decades. This decline was not the result of epidemic disease, for there is no record of any epidemic in the Antilles before 1518.

The first voices raised against this state of affairs belonged to a company of Dominican friars who arrived in Hispaniola in 1510. Their leader was Father Antón Montesinos, who on Advent Sunday, 1511, ascended the church pulpit to threaten the island's Spaniards with damnation for their offenses against the natives. The angry colonists and the Dominicans soon carried their dispute to the court. King Ferdinand responded by approving the Laws of Burgos (1512–1513), which did little more than sanction and regularize the existing situation.

This agitation raised the larger question of the legality of Spain's claim to the Indies. To satisfy the royal conscience, a distinguished jurist, Dr. Juan López de Palacios Rubios, drew up a document, the *Requerimiento*, which the conquistadors were supposed to read before making war on indigenous peoples. This curious manifesto called on the natives to acknowledge the supremacy of the church and the pope and the sovereignty of the Spanish monarchs over their lands by virtue of the papal donation of 1493, on pain of suffering war and enslavement. Not until they had rejected those demands, which were to be made known to them by interpreters, could war be legally waged against them. Some conquistadors took the Requirement lightly, mumbling it into their beards before an attack or reading it to captured natives after a raid; the chronicler Oviedo relates that Palacios Rubios himself laughed heartily when told of the strange use these captains made of the document.

Bartolomé de Las Casas, the former encomendero who had repented of his ways and later turned friar, now joined the struggle against indigenous slavery and the doctrines of Palacios Rubios. Of the Requirement, Las Casas said that on reading it he could not decide whether to laugh or weep. Las Casas argued that the papal grant of America to the crown of Castile had been made solely for the purpose of conversion; it gave the Spanish crown no temporal power or possession in the Indies. The indígenas had rightful possession of their lands by natural law and the law of nations. All Spanish wars and conquests in the New World were illegal. Spain must bring Christianity to

In sharp contrast to Spanish art that depicted the heroic civilizing influence of conquest and colonization, this Mayan codex emphasized Spanish barbarism and the pivotal role of enslaved Mayan labor in the colonial economy. [Tozzer Library, Harvard University]

indigenous peoples by the only method "that is proper and natural to men . . . namely, love and gentleness and kindness."

Las Casas hoped for a peaceful colonization of the New World by Spanish farmers who would live side by side with the natives, teach them to farm and live in the European way, and gradually bring into being an ideal Christian community. A series of disillusioning experiences, including the destruction of an experimental colony on the coast of Venezuela (1521), turned Las Casas's mind toward more radical solutions. His final program called for the suppression of all encomiendas, liberation of the indígenas from all forms of servitude except a small voluntary tribute to the crown in recompense for its gift of Christianity, and the restoration of their ancient states and rulers, the rightful owners of those lands. Over these states the Spanish king would preside as "Emperor over many kings" in order to fulfill his sacred mission of bringing them to the Catholic faith and the Christian way of life. The instruments of that mis-

sion should be friars, who would enjoy special jurisdiction over indigenous peoples and protect them from the corrupting influence of lay Spaniards. Although Las Casas's proposals appeared radical, they in fact served the royal aim of curbing the power of the conquistadors and preventing the rise of a powerful colonial feudalism in the New World. Not humanitarianism but self-interest, above all, explains the partial official support that Las Casas's reform efforts received in the reign of Charles V (1516–1556).

This question became crucial with the conquest of the rich, populous empires of Mexico and Peru. The most elementary interests of the crown demanded that the West Indian catastrophe should not be repeated in the newly conquered lands. In 1523, Las Casas appeared to have won a major victory. King Charles sent Cortés an order forbidding the establishment of encomiendas in New Spain (the name given to the former Aztec Empire), because "God created the Indians free and not subject." Cortés, who had already assigned encomiendas to himself and his comrades, did not enforce the order. Backed by the strength and needs of his hard-bitten soldiers, he argued so persuasively for the encomienda system as necessary for the welfare and security of the colony that the royal order was revoked. Encomienda tribute and labor, supplemented by slaves captured in war, continued to be the main source of income for the colonists until the middle of the sixteenth century.

THE NEW LAWS OF THE INDIES AND THE ENCOMIENDA

Despite its retreat in the face of Cortés's disobedience, the crown renewed its efforts to bring indigenous tribute and labor under royal control. Cautiously, it moved to curb the power of the conquistadors. The second *audiencia* (high court) of New Spain was established in 1531–1532 after a stormy period of rule by the first "gangster" audiencia, which devoted itself to despoiling Cortés and mercilessly oppressing the natives. Taking the first steps in the regulation of tribute and labor, the second audiencia moderated the tribute paid by many indigenous towns, provided for registration of tribute assessments, and forbade, in principle, the use of natives as carriers without their consent. The climax of royal intervention came with proclamation of the New Laws of the Indies (1542). These laws appeared to doom the encomienda. They prohibited the enslavement of native peoples, ordered the release of slaves to whom legal title could not be proved, barred compulsory personal service by indígenas, regulated tribute, and declared that existing encomiendas were to lapse on the death of the holder.

In Peru the New Laws provoked a great revolt; in New Spain they caused a storm of protest by the encomenderos and a large part of the clergy. Under this pressure the crown again retreated. The laws forbidding indigenous slavery and forced labor were reaffirmed, but the right of inheritance by the heir of an encomendero was recognized and even extended by stages to a third, fourth, and sometimes even a fifth life. Thereafter, or earlier in the absence of an heir, the encomienda reverted to the crown. In the natural course of events, the number of encomiendas steadily diminished and that of crown towns increased.

By about 1560 the encomienda had been partially "tamed." Royal intervention had curbed the power of the encomenderos and partially stabilized the tribute and labor situation, at least in areas near the colonial capitals. Tribute was now assessed in most places by the audiencias, which made a continuing effort to adjust it to the fluctuations of population and harvests on appeal from indigenous villages. The institution of *visita* and *cuenta* was employed to make such adjustments. The visita (inspection of an indigenous town) yielded information concerning its resources or capacity to pay, which was needed to determine its per capita quota. The cuenta (count), made at the same time, gave the number of tribute payers. About 1560 the annual tribute paid to the king or to an encomendero by each married tributary in New Spain was usually one silver peso and four-fifths of a bushel of maize or its equivalent in other produce.

This mechanism of assessment and copious protective legislation did not bring significant or enduring relief to indigenous peoples. Padding of population counts and other abuses by encomenderos and other interested parties were common. More important, recounts and reassessments consistently lagged behind the rapidly shrinking number of tribute payers, with the result that the survivors had to bear the tribute burdens of those who had died or fled. Moreover, from the accession to the throne of Philip II (1556), the dominant motive of Spain's policy became the increase of royal revenues to relieve the crown's desperate financial crisis. Native groups hitherto exempt from tribute lost their favored status, and the tribute quota was progressively raised. As a result of these measures and the gradual reversion of encomiendas to the crown, the amount of royal tribute collected annually in New Spain rose from about 100,000 pesos to well over 1 million pesos between 1550 and the close of the eighteenth century. (These figures do not take into account the impact on the tribute's value of the considerable rise in prices during the same period.)

For the colonists, however, the encomienda steadily declined in economic value. They lost the right to demand labor from their tributaries (1549); they also lost their fight to make the encomienda perpetual. The heaviest blow of all to the encomendero class was the catastrophic decline of the native population in the second half of the sixteenth century. In central Mexico, it dropped from perhaps 25 million in 1519 to slightly over 1 million in 1605. On the central coast of Peru, the tributary population seems to have fallen by 1575 to 4 percent of what it had been before the Conquest. For reasons that remain unclear, the rates of population decline in both Mexico and Peru appear to have been considerably higher on the coast than in the highlands. Disease, especially diseases of European origin against which the natives had no acquired immunity, such as measles, smallpox, typhus, and malaria, was the major direct cause of this demographic disaster. But overwork, malnutrition, severe social disorganization, and the resulting loss of will to live underlay the terrible mortality associated with the great epidemics and even with epidemic-free years. In Peru the great civil wars and disorders of the period from 1535 to 1550 undoubtedly contributed materially to depopulation.

As the number of their tributaries fell, the encomenderos' income from tribute dropped proportionately, whereas their expenses, which included the maintenance of a steward to collect tribute, support of a parish priest, and heavy taxes, remained steady or even increased. As a result, many encomenderos, as well as other Spaniards without encomiendas, began to engage in the more lucrative pursuits of agriculture, stock raising, and mining. The decline of the indigenous population, sharply reducing the flow of foodstuffs and metals, stimulated a rapid growth of *haciendas* (Spanish estates) producing grain and meat.

Thus, in central Mexico by the 1570s, and in the northern and central Andean highlands by the end of the sixteenth century, the encomienda had lost its original character of an institution based on the use of native labor without payment. Its importance as a source of revenue to Spanish colonists had greatly diminished, and it had been placed in the way of extinction through the progressive reversion of individual encomiendas to the crown. These changes, however, did not take place everywhere. In areas that lacked precious metals or where agricultural productivity was low, and where consequently there was little danger of the colonists acquiring excessive power, the crown permitted encomenderos to continue exploiting the forced labor of the natives. This was the case in Chile, where the encomienda based on personal service continued until 1791; in Venezuela, where it survived until the 1680s; and in Paraguay, where it still existed in the early 1800s. The crown also allowed the encomienda as a labor system to continue in such areas of New Spain as Oaxaca and Yucatán.

In Paraguay the encomienda assumed a peculiar form that reflected the culture and social organization of its Guaraní people. After a failed attempt to colonize Argentina, the Spaniards who moved into the vicinity of the present-day city of Asunción found a population that lived in villages, each having four to eight communal buildings. Each building housed a patrilineal lineage composed of several families, which were frequently polygynous. There was no hereditary chiefly class; the chiefs' tenure depended above all on their personal qualities, and there was no political organization above the village level. The Spaniards won the friendship of the Guaraní by helping them defeat their warlike neighbors, the nomadic hunting groups of the Chaco desert, and were rewarded with presents of food and women. In effect, the Spaniards became a class of headmen in Guaraní society. Because women played a key role in Guaraní agriculture and social organization, the relatives of the women who became Spanish concubines were expected to provide the Spaniards with labor services as part of their kinship obligations. The lineage or household thus became the basis of the Paraguayan encomienda—the name with which the Spaniards formalized their control of the groups of concubines and their relatives who surrounded and served them. Because the Spaniards could increase their access to labor by adding to the number of their concubines, official efforts to stop the colonists from invading native villages to get them or from trading women for horses or dogs proved ineffective. Efforts to limit the number of days the Guaraní had to work for the Spaniards were equally ineffective.

This arrangement was the *encomienda originaria*, and it continued to the end of the colonial period. In 1556 a second encomienda, the *encomienda mitaya*, was established alongside the original one. Guaraní men living within a 139-mile radius of Asunción were allocated to Spaniards, with the number of tributaries varying according to the rank or merits of the grantee. In Paraguay, unlike in the central areas of the empire, there was no payment for labor or specified amounts of tribute in goods or money. By 1688, as a result of the ravages of disease, the effects of *mestizaje*, and flight, only 21,950 Guaraní were recorded as being held in encomienda. By 1778 the number had dwindled to hundreds. Consequently, the *mestizo* (mixed-race) descendants of Spanish fathers began to supplement the few surviving Guaraní with black slaves, paying for them with the proceeds from the export of yerba mate, the area's chief staple and the source of a tea still greatly prized in southern South America. By 1782 blacks outnumbered Guaraní in the area.

THE REPARTIMIENTO, YANACONAJE, AND FREE LABOR

In the key areas of central Mexico and the Andean highlands, however, a new system, the *repartimiento*, replaced forced labor under the encomienda after 1550. Under this system, all adult male indígenas had to give a certain amount of their time in rotation throughout the year to work in Spanish mines and workshops, on farms and ranches, and on public works. By this means, the crown sought to regulate the use of an ever-diminishing pool of native labor and give access to such labor to both encomenderos and the growing number of Spaniards without encomiendas. The indígenas received a token wage for their work, but the repartimiento, like the encomienda, was essentially disguised slavery. Those who avoided service and community leaders who failed to provide the required quotas were imprisoned, fined, and physically punished.

In Peru, where the condition of indigenous peoples seems to have been generally worse than in New Spain, the repartimiento (here known as the *mita*) produced especially disastrous effects. Under this system, developed by Viceroy Francisco de Toledo in the 1570s, all able-bodied native men in the provinces subject to the mita were required to work for six-month periods, one year in seven, at Potosí or other mining centers, or were assigned to other Spanish employers. The silver mines of Potosí and the Huancavelica mercury mine were notorious deathtraps for laborers under the mita. In Peru and Bolivia, the mita remained an important source of labor in mining and agriculture to the end of the colonial period.

In the Andean area, the repartimiento was supplemented by another institution taken over from Inca society—the system of *yanaconas*, which separated indígenas from their communities and forced them to serve Spaniards as personal servants. Like European serfs, the yanaconas were transferred from one landowner to another together with the estate. It is estimated that by the end of the sixteenth century the number of yanaconas on Spanish haciendas was almost equal to the number of natives who lived in their own communities.

Although the repartimiento offered a temporary solution for the critical labor problem, many Spanish employers found it unsatisfactory, for it did not provide a dependable and continuing supply of labor. From an early date, mine owners and *hacendados* in New Spain turned increasingly to the use of wage labor. The heavy weight of tribute and repartimiento obligations on a diminishing native population and Spanish usurpation of indigenous communal lands induced many to accept an hacendado's invitation to become farm laborers working for wages, mostly paid in kind. Some traveled back and forth to work from their communities; others became resident peons on the haciendas. Yet others were drawn to the northern silver mines by the lure of relatively high wages.

By 1630, when the crown abolished the agricultural repartimiento in central Mexico, the move provoked little or no protest, for most landowners relied on wage labor. The mining repartimiento continued longer in New Spain. It was still employed intermittently in the eighteenth century but had little importance, for the mines of New Spain operated mainly with contractual labor. In Peru and Bolivia, where the mita, supplemented by *yanaconaje*, was the dominant labor system, providing a mass of cheap workers for the high-cost silver mines, wage labor was less important. However, there were as many as forty thousand free indigenous miners (known as *mingas*) employed at the Potosí mines in the seventeenth century.[2]

From the first, this wage labor was often associated with debt servitude. The second half of the seventeenth century saw the growth of the system of *repartimiento* or *repartimiento de mercancías*,[3] the compulsory purchase by indigenous villages of goods from district governors (corregidores, alcaldes mayores). In combination with their other burdens, repartimiento was a powerful inducement for them to accept advances of cash and goods from Spanish hacendados; the tribute payment was usually included in the reckoning. A native so indebted had to work for his employer until the debt was paid. Despite its later evil reputation, peonage, whether or not enforced by debts, had definite advantages. It usually freed indígenas from the recurrent tribute and repartimiento burdens of their community and often gave some security in the form of a plot of land they could work for themselves and their families. But if the hacienda offered escape from intolerable conditions, it aggravated the difficulties of those who remained on their ancestral lands. The hacienda expanded by legal or illegal means at the expense of the indigenous pueblo, absorbing whole towns and leaving others without enough land for their people when the long population decline finally ended in the first half of the seventeenth century and a slow recovery began. The hacienda also lured laborers from the pueblo, making it difficult for indigenous towns to meet their tribute and repartimiento obligations. Between the two *repúblicas* (commonwealths), the *república de indios* and the *república de españoles,* as Spanish documents frequently called them, stretched a gulf of hostility and distrust.

The importance of debt servitude as a means of securing and holding labor seems to have varied according to the availability of wage labor. It was used extensively in northern Mexico, where such labor was scarce, but appears to have been less important in central Mexico, where it was more abundant. Some recent studies stress that debt peonage was "more of an inducement than a bond," with the size of advances reflecting the bargaining power of labor in dealing with employers, and that hacendados sometimes made no special effort to recover their peons who had fled without repayment of loans. But the evidence for such relative lack of concern about fugitive peons comes chiefly from late-eighteenth-century Mexico, when labor was increasingly abundant. For earlier, labor-scarce periods, there is much evidence of strenuous efforts to compel indígenas to remain on estates until their debts had been paid off. Indeed, hacendados and officials sometimes likened Mexican peons to European serfs who were bound to their estates, with the right to their services passing with the transfer of the land from one owner to another.

Widely used in agriculture and mining, debt servitude assumed its harshest form in the numerous *obrajes* (workshops) producing cloth and other goods that sprang up in many areas in the sixteenth and seventeenth centuries. Convict labor, assigned to employers by Spanish judges, was early supplemented by the "free" labor of natives ensnared by a variety of devices. They were often tempted into these workshops by an offer of liquor

[2]In the early seventeenth century the growing shortage of indigenous labor, due to the ravages of epidemic disease and the flight from communities subject to the mita, gave rise to a system whereby the delivery of mita labor was replaced by deliveries of silver collected from native communities and raised through the operation of economic enterprises supervised by the curacas. Mine owners used this silver to cover minga costs and to hire minga substitutes for mita labor (*mitayos*) not received in person.

[3]The term *repartimiento* was also applied to the periodic conscription of natives for labor useful to the Spanish community.

or a small sum of money and, once inside the gates, were never let out again. "In this way," wrote a seventeenth-century observer, "they have gathered in and duped many married Indians with families, who have passed into oblivion here for twenty years, or longer, or their whole lives, without their wives or children knowing anything about them; for even if they want to get out, they cannot, thanks to the great watchfulness with which the doormen guard the exits."

BLACK SLAVERY

Side by side with the disguised slavery of repartimiento and debt servitude existed black slavery. For a variety of reasons, including the fact that Spaniards and Portuguese were accustomed to the holding of black slaves, the tradition that blacks were descendants of the biblical Ham and bore his curse, and the belief that they were better able to support the hardships of plantation labor, Spanish defenders of the "Indian" did not display the same zeal on behalf of enslaved Africans.

In fact, the rapid development of sugar-cane agriculture in the West Indies in the early 1500s brought an insistent demand for black slave labor to replace the vanishing natives. There arose a lucrative slave trade, chiefly carried on by foreigners under a system of *asiento* (contract between an individual or company and the Spanish crown). The high cost of slaves tended to limit their use to the more profitable plantation cultures or to domestic service in the homes of the wealthy. Large numbers lived on the coasts of Venezuela and Colombia, where they were employed in the production of such crops as cacao, sugar, and tobacco, and in the coastal valleys of Peru, where they labored on sugar and cotton plantations, but smaller concentrations were found in every part of the Indies. In Chapter 5, we shall consider the much-disputed question of whether African slavery in Hispanic America was "milder" than in other European colonies.

In summary, all colonial labor systems rested in varying degrees on servitude and coercion. Although contractual labor gradually emerged as the theoretical norm, all the labor systems just described coexisted throughout the colonial period.

Indigenous slavery, for example, was legally abolished in 1542, but it continued in frontier areas on various pretexts into the eighteenth century. Which labor system dominated at a given time and place depended on such factors as the area's natural resources, the number of Europeans in the area and the character of their economic activities, the size and cultural level of its indigenous population, and the crown's economic and political interests. Finally, it should be noted that in the course of the sixteenth and seventeenth centuries, the labor pool was gradually expanded by the addition of mestizos, free blacks and mulattos, and poor whites. Since most of these people were exempt from encomienda and repartimiento obligations, they usually worked for wages and enjoyed freedom of movement, but like the indígenas, they were subject to control through debts. In Chapter 6, we shall discuss eighteenth-century changes in the labor system.

The Colonial Economy

The Conquest disrupted the traditional subsistence-and-tribute economy of indigenous communities. War and disease took a heavy toll of lives, to the detriment of production; in some areas the complex irrigation networks established and maintained by centralized native authorities were destroyed or fell into ruin. The Conquest also transformed the character and tempo of economic activity. When the frenzied scramble for treasure had ended with the exhaustion of the available gold and silver objects, the encomienda became the principal instrument for the extraction of wealth from the vanquished. The peoples of the Aztec and Inca empires were accustomed to paying tribute in labor and commodities to their rulers and nobility. But the tribute demands of the old ruling classes, although apparently increasing on the eve of the Conquest, had been limited by custom and by the capacity of their ruling groups to utilize tribute goods. The greater part of such tribute was destined for consumption or display, not for trade. The demands of the new Spanish masters, on the other hand, were unlimited. Gold and silver were the great objects; if these could not

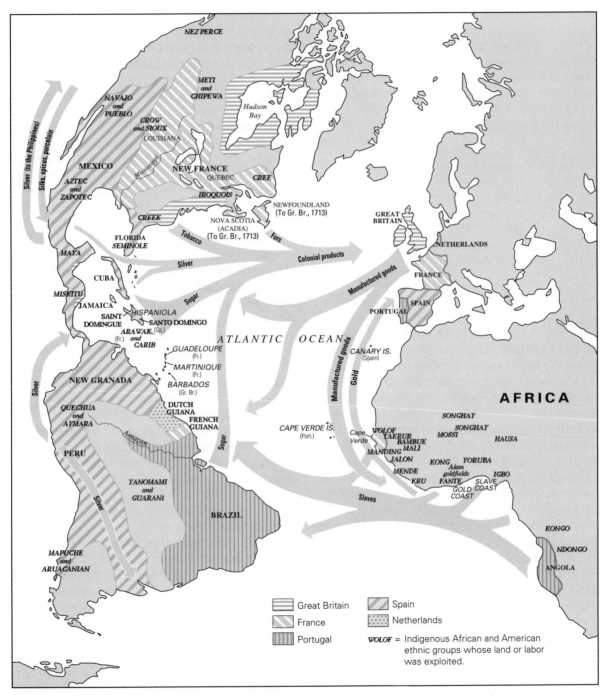

Colonial Conquest, Trade, and Enslavement in the Making of Latin America

be obtained directly, the encomenderos proposed to obtain them by sale in local or distant markets of their tribute goods. Driven by visions of infinite wealth, the Spaniards took no account of indigenous tribute traditions and exploited them mercilessly. A compassionate missionary, writing in 1554, complained that before the Conquest the native peoples in his part of Mexico

> never used to give such large loads of *mantas* [pieces of cotton cloth], nor had they ever heard of beds, fine cotton fabrics, wax, or a thousand other fripperies like bed sheets, tablecloths, shirts, and skirts. All they used to do was cultivate the fields of their lords, build their houses, repair the temples, and give of the produce of their fields when their lords asked for it.

Cortés as a Businessman

The business career of Hernando Cortés illustrates the large variety and scale of the economic activities of some encomenderos. By 1528, Cortés was already worth 500,000 gold pesos. Part of this wealth represented his share of the loot taken in Tenochtitlán and other places during and immediately after the Conquest. But his chief source of income was his encomienda holdings. To himself he assigned the richest tribute areas in the former Aztec Empire. At the time of his death in 1547, although many of his encomiendas had been drastically reduced and tribute assessments lowered, he was still receiving 30,000 gold pesos annually from this source. He received large quantities of gold dust, textiles, maize, poultry, and other products from encomienda towns. The pueblo of Cuernavaca (near Mexico City) alone gave as part of its annual tribute cloth worth 5,000 gold pesos. Cortés's agents sold the tribute cloth and other products to traders who retailed them in Mexico City and other Spanish towns. Cortés had his own extensive real estate holdings in Mexico City. On or near the central square he erected shops, some of which he used for his own trading interests, others of which he rented out.

Cortés was an empire builder in the economic as well as political sense of the word. He invested the capital he acquired from encomienda tribute and labor in many enterprises. Mining attracted his special attention. In the Oaxaca and Michoacán districts, he had gangs of indigenous slaves, more than a thousand in each, panning gold; many of these slaves died from hard labor and inadequate food. In 1529 these mining areas brought him 12,000 pesos in gold annually. In addition to his own mining properties, Cortés held others, such as silver mines in the Taxco area of Mexico, in partnerships. In such cases, his investment usually consisted of goods, livestock, encomienda, or black slave labor.

After encomienda tribute, agriculture and stock raising were Cortés's largest sources of income. He had large landholdings in various parts of Mexico, some acquired by royal grant, others usurped from native peoples. He employed encomienda labor to grow maize on his land. His fields in the vicinity of Oaxaca alone produced ten to fifteen thousand bushels a year. Part of this grain he sold in the Spanish towns and at the mines; part went to feed his gangs of slaves at the gold washings. Cortés also raised great numbers of cattle and hogs, which were butchered in his own slaughterhouses. Near Tehuantepec he had herds of more than ten thousand wild cattle, which supplied hides and tallow for export to Panama and Peru.

The restless Cortés also pioneered in the development of the Mexican sugar industry. By 1547 his plantations were producing more than three hundred thousand pounds of sugar annually, most of which was sold to agents of European merchants for export. If he was not the first to experiment with silk raising in New Spain, as he claimed, he certainly went into the business on a large scale, laying out thousands of mulberry trees with native labor paid in cash or cacao beans. In this venture, however, he suffered heavy losses. Nonetheless, the variety and extent of Cortés's business interests suggest how misleading is the familiar portrait of the conquistador as a purely feudal type devoted only to war and plunder, disdainful of all trade and industry.

THE GROWTH OF THE HACIENDAS

Among the first generation of colonists, large-scale enterprises such as those of Cortés were rare. The typical encomendero was content to occupy a relatively small land grant and draw tribute from natives, who continued to live and work in large numbers on their ancestral lands. The major shift from reliance on encomienda tribute to the development of Spanish commercial agriculture and stock raising came after 1550 in response to the massive indigenous population decline and the crown's restrictive legislation, which combined to deprive the encomienda of much of its economic value. Acute food shortages in the Spanish towns created new economic opportunities for Spanish farmers and ranchers. Simultaneously, this population decline left vacant large expanses of land, which Spanish colonists hastened to occupy for wheat raising or, more commonly, for sheep or cattle ranges.

By the end of the sixteenth century, the Spanish-owned hacienda was responsible for the bulk of agricultural commercial production and pressed ever more aggressively on the shrinking native sector of the colonial economy. Spanish colonists used various methods to "free" land from indigenous occupation: purchase, usurpation, and *congregación* (forced concentration of natives in new communities, ostensibly to facilitate control and Christianization). Although Spain's declared policy was to protect community land, the numerous laws forbidding encroachment on such land failed to halt the advance of the hacienda. The power of the hacendados, whose ranks included high royal officials, churchmen, and wealthy merchants, usually carried all before it.

In the seventeenth century, the crown, facing an acute, chronic economic crisis, actually encouraged usurpation of indigenous lands by adopting the device of *composición* (settlement), which legalized the defective title of the usurper through payment of a fee to the king. Not only native communities but communities of Spanish or mestizo small farmers saw their lands devoured by the advancing hacienda. A striking feature of this process was that land was sometimes primarily acquired not for use but to obtain day laborers and peons by depriving them of their fields or to eliminate competition by small producers. The establishment of a *mayorazgo* (entailed estate) assured the perpetuation of the consolidated property in the hands of the owner's descendants, but this feudal device required approval by the crown and payment of a large fee and benefited only a small number of very wealthy families.

A more common strategy for consolidation and preservation of holdings was marriage within the extended family, often between cousins. In the majority of cases, however, this and other strategies for ensuring the longevity of family estates were less than successful. Spanish inheritance laws requiring the equal division of estates among heirs, economic downturns, and lack of investment capital as a result of large expenditures for conspicuous consumption and donations to the church were some of the factors that made for an unstable landed elite and a high turnover rate in estate ownership. Historian Susan Ramírez studied the collective biography of colonial elite families who lived in north coastal Peru over a period of three hundred years. She found that, contrary to tradition, this elite was "unstable, open, and in constant flux," with most families lasting no more than two or three generations. The historian Lucas Alamán, himself a member of Mexico's former colonial elite, alluded to this instability at the top, citing the Mexican proverb that said, "The father a merchant, the son a gentleman, the grandson a beggar."

The tempo of land concentration varied from region to region according to its resources and proximity to markets. In the Valley of Mexico, for example, the bulk of the land was held by great haciendas by the end of the colonial period. Native commoners and chiefs, on the other hand, retained much of the land in the province of Oaxaca, which had limited markets for its crops. Recent studies of the colonial hacienda stress the large variations in hacienda size and productivity from one region to another. This variety in size and productivity reflects the great regional divergencies in productive potential—determined by proximity to water and quality of soil—and in access to labor and markets, among other variables, in the vast Spanish Empire in America.

Despite the long-term trend toward land concentration, there gradually arose a class of mostly mixed-blood small farmers of uncertain size. In Mexico such small farmers, typically mestizos, came to be known as *rancheros,* and they were interspersed among the native villages and commercial estates of the central and southern highlands. Some were former majordomos or foremen of large landowners from whom they rented or leased unused portions of their estates, generally raising products for sale in local markets. Their limited resources and dependence on large landowners made their situation precarious; in prosperous times of rising land values, their small properties were often swallowed up by their wealthy neighbors. Less frequently, successful rancheros might expand their holdings and themselves join the ranks of the landed elite.

SPANISH AGRICULTURE IN THE NEW WORLD

Spanish agriculture differed from indigenous land use in significant ways. First, it was extensive, cultivating large tracts with plows and draft animals, in contrast with the intensive native digging-stick agriculture. Second, Spanish agriculture was predominantly commercial, producing commodities for sale in local or distant markets, in contrast with the subsistence character of traditional agriculture. Through the need to pay tribute and other obligations in cash, the indigenous farmer came under increasing pressure to produce for the market. But, as a rule, the hacendado's superior resources made it difficult for him to compete except in times of abundant harvests, and he tended to fall back to the level of subsistence agriculture, whose meager yield he sometimes supplemented by labor for the local hacendado.

Spanish colonial agriculture early produced wheat on a large scale for sale in urban centers like Mexico City, Lima, Veracruz, and Cartagena; maize was also grown on haciendas for the sizable native consumers' market in Mexico City and Lima. Sugar, like wheat, was one of Europe's agricultural gifts to America. Spaniards brought it from the Canary Islands to Hispaniola, where it soon became the foundation of the island's prosperity.

By 1550 more than twenty sugar mills processed cane into sugar, which was shipped in great quantities to Spain. "The sugar industry is the principal industry of those islands," wrote José de Acosta at the end of the sixteenth century, "such a taste have men developed for sweets." From the West Indies sugar quickly spread to Mexico and Peru. Sugar refining, with its large capital outlays for equipment and black slaves, was, after silver mining, the largest-scale enterprise in the Indies.

In the irrigated coastal valleys of Peru, wine and olives, as well as sugar, were produced in quantity. The silk industry had a brief period of prosperity in Mexico but soon declined in the face of labor shortages and competition from Chinese silk brought in the Manila galleons from the Philippines to the port of Acapulco. Spain's sporadic efforts to discourage the production of wine, olives, and silk, regarded as interfering with Spanish exports of the same products, seem to have had little effect. Other products cultivated by the Spaniards on an extensive plantation basis included tobacco, cacao, and indigo. A unique Mexican and Central American export, highly valued by the European cloth industry, was cochineal, a blood-red dye made from the dried bodies of insects parasitic on the nopal cactus.

Spain made a major contribution to American economic life with the introduction of various domestic animals—chickens, mules, horses, cattle, pigs, and sheep. The mules and horses revolutionized transport, gradually eliminating the familiar spectacle of long lines of native carriers loaded down with burdens. Horses and mules became vital to the mining industry for hauling and for turning machinery. Cattle and smaller domesticated animals greatly enlarged the food resources of the continent. Meat was indispensable to the mining industry, for only a meat diet could sustain the hard work of the miners. "If the mines have been worked at all," wrote a Spanish judge in 1606, "it is thanks to the plentiful and cheap supply of livestock." In addition to meat, cattle provided hides for export to Spain and other European centers of leather manufacture, as well as hides and tallow (used for lighting) for the domestic market, especially in the mining areas. Sheep raisers found a large market for their wool in the textile workshops that arose in many parts of the colonies.

In a densely settled region like central Mexico, the explosive increase of Spanish cattle and sheep had catastrophic consequences. A horde of animals swarmed over the land, often invading not only the land vacated by the dwindling native population but the reserves of land needed by their system of field rotation. Cattle trampled the indigenous crops, causing untold damage; torrential rains caused massive erosion on valley slopes close-cropped by sheep. By the end of the sixteenth century, however, the Mexican cattle industry had become stabilized. Exhaustion of virgin pasturelands, mass slaughter of cattle for their hides and tallow, and official efforts to halt grazing on native harvest lands had produced a marked reduction in the herds. The problem further abated in the seventeenth century as a result of the cumulative transfer of these lands in the Central Valley to Spaniards who established haciendas producing pulque (a fermented drink very popular with the natives) and wheat. Gradually, the cattle ranches and sheep herds moved to new, permanent grazing grounds in the sparsely settled, semiarid north.

An equally rapid increase of horses, mules, and cattle took place in the vast, rich pampas (grasslands) of the Río de la Plata (modern Argentina). Their increase in this area of almost infinite pasturage soon outstripped potential demand and utilization, and herds of wild cattle became a common phenomenon in La Plata as in other parts of Spanish America. Barred by Spanish law from seaborne trade with the outside world, the inhabitants of this remote province, lacking precious metals or abundant native labor, relieved their poverty by illegal commerce with Dutch and other foreign traders, who carried their hides and tallow to Europe. In addition, they sent mules and horses, hides and tallow to the mining regions of Upper Peru (Bolivia).

Another center of the cattle industry was the West Indies. José de Acosta wrote in 1590 that

> the cattle have multiplied so greatly in Santo Domingo, and in other islands of that region that they wander by the thousands through the forests and fields, all masterless. They hunt these beasts only for their hides; whites and Negroes go out on horseback, equipped with a kind of hooked knife, to chase the cattle, and any animal that falls to their knives is theirs. They kill it and carry the hide home, leaving the flesh to rot; no one wants it, since meat is so plentiful.

COLONIAL MINING AND INDUSTRY

Mining, as the principal source of royal revenue in the form of the quinto, or royal fifth of all gold, silver, or other precious metals obtained in the Indies, received the special attention and protection of the crown. Silver, rather than gold, was the principal product of the American mines. Spain's proudest possession in the New World was the great silver mine of Potosí in Upper Peru, whose flow of treasure attained gigantic proportions between 1579 and 1635. Potosí was discovered in 1545; the rich Mexican silver mines of Zacatecas and Guanajuato were opened up in 1548 and 1558. In the same period, important gold placers (sand or gravel deposits containing eroded particles of the ore) were found in central Chile and in the interior of New Granada (Colombia).

At first silver was processed by the simple and inexpensive technique of smelting, in which the ore was broken up by the use of heavy iron hammers and stamping mills, then fired in furnaces using charcoal or other fuel. But smelting was labor-intensive and heavily dependent on adequate supplies of fuel, which created serious problems for an Andean mining center like Potosí, lying high above the timberline, or the Mexican center of Zacatecas, situated in a semiarid area far from the densely populated central zone from which it needed to draw its work force. Thus, in 1556 the introduction of the patio or amalgamation process, which used mercury to separate the silver from the ore, gave a great stimulus to silver mining. The chief source of mercury for Potosí silver was the Peruvian Huancavelica mine, whose health hazards and wretched working conditions made labor there "a thing of horror." Mexican silver was chiefly processed with mercury from the Almaden mine in Spain.

Lack of capital to finance technical improvements required by the gradual exhaustion of veins and increasing depth of mines, flooding, and other problems, combined with the high cost of mercury (a crown monopoly), caused a precipitous decline in silver production at Potosí after 1650. But this decline was at least partly offset by the rise of new Peruvian centers like Oruro and Cerro de Pasco. In Mexico production levels fluctuated, with output declining in some old centers like Zacatecas and rising in new ones like Parral, but here the long-range trend for the seventeenth century seems to have been upward. Notwithstanding earlier historians' claims that an acute labor shortage caused by the catastrophic fall of the native population was the root cause of a supposed decline in silver production in New Spain, it now appears that mine owners in general had no difficulty filling their labor needs. After 1650 in both Peru and Mexico, there was some shift of silver mining from large centers like Potosí and Zacatecas to small, dispersed, and mobile mining camps. In the same period many mine owners abandoned the amalgamation process, based on scarce and costly mercury, in favor of smelting. Because the quantity of mercury a mine owner purchased gave royal officials a fairly accurate measure of silver production, by using the smelting process the mine owner could cut his costs and also evade payment of all or a part of the quinto, the *alcabala* (sales tax), and other taxes, to the detriment of the royal treasury. Great quantities of such untaxed, illegal silver circulated at home or went to Europe or Asia to pay for smuggled goods. The loss of royal control over the quality and destination of a large part of silver production aggravated the chronic colonial problem of coin shortage and unreliability,[4] causing

increased resort to barter and substitute money on the local level and adding to the difficulty of long-distance trade.

The transformation of the silver mining industry in the seventeenth century had other consequences. One was the disruption of the commercial and agricultural networks that had arisen to provide the great mining centers with grain, hides, tallow, and work animals. The resulting contraction of commercial agriculture and stock raising gave rise in some areas, like northern New Spain, to a characteristic institution of the period, the self-sufficient great hacienda, housing an extended elite family led by a patriarch—monarch of all he surveyed, ruling his own little world with its work force, church, jail, workshops, storehouses, and private army.

Scholars continue to debate whether the seventeenth century was a time of crisis and depression for colonial Spanish America—the dominant view a few decades ago—or one of growing colonial autonomy, both economic and political—a view now favored by many students. An argument cited by the supporters of the thesis of a colonial economic crisis was the spectacular decline in silver remittances to Spain after 1630. Recent studies of the accounts of colonial treasuries, however, suggest that much of this decline was caused by the decision of Spanish officials to retain large quantities of silver in America to cover local administrative and defense needs. Another cause of the decline was a growing colonial self-sufficiency that, combined with a vast increase in smuggled goods, sharply reduced the demand for higher-priced Spanish goods. By the opening of the seventeenth century, Mexico, Peru, and Chile had become self-sufficient in grains and partly so in wine, olive oil, ironware, and furniture. The moribund state of Spanish industry in the seventeenth century contributed to its loss of American markets.

Then, in 1985, a French scholar, Michel Morineau, published a book that radically changed the terms of the debate regarding the colonial "economic crisis." Based on Dutch commercial journals that recorded the arrival of colonial precious metals and merchandise in European ports, he showed that the decline in remittances of pre-

---

[4] By way of example, in the mid-seventeenth century the *alcalde provincial* of Potosí, in collusion with officials and technicians of the Potosí mint, adulterated with copper the silver coins that went into circulation. The fraud, says Peruvian historian Luis Millones, had "enormous repercussions," causing a loss of 200,000 ducats to the royal treasury and an immediate steep rise in prices.

Theodore de Bry's 1590 engraving graphically depicts the exploitation of enslaved labor in the mines of Potosí, whose wealth provided an extraordinary stimulus to European economic development. [The Art Archive/Science Academy, Lisbon/Dagli Orti]

cious metals to Spanish ports was offset by contraband shipments of colonial silver and gold in the same period to northern European ports. If the sum of contraband shipments is added to that of the legal remittances to Spain, it becomes clear that there was no decline in the volume of colonial precious metals shipped to Europe in the seventeenth century, and the thesis of a colonial "economic crisis" based on that assumption falls of its own weight.

The debate continues, but the evidence regarding colonial economic trends is at best mixed and contradictory, making it difficult to determine how real the assumed seventeenth-century "depression" was. In New Spain, for example, proceeds from the alcabala, or sales tax, a significant indicator of the state of the economy, increased until 1638 and declined only slightly thereafter. If there was a seventeenth-century depression, its impact was uneven, with some regions and sectors of the economy rising and others falling. Thus, after the cacao industry of Central America collapsed, together with its native population, there arose a brisk trade in cacao between Venezuela and Mexico. In short, there is no evidence of a decline in overall levels of production and domestic trade. As regards foreign trade, Morineau's findings suggest the contrary is true.

The Spaniards had found a flourishing handicrafts industry in the advanced culture areas of Mexico, Central America, and Peru. Throughout the colonial period, the majority of the natives continued to supply most of their own needs for pottery, clothing, and household goods. In the Spanish towns, craft guilds modeled on those of Spain arose in response to the high prices for all Spanish imported goods. To avoid competition from indigenous, black, and mestizo artisans, who quickly learned the Spanish crafts, they were incorporated into the Spanish-controlled guilds but were barred from becoming masters. The chronic shortage of skilled labor, however, soon made all such racial restrictions a dead letter. These guilds attempted to maintain careful control over the quantity and quality of production in industries serving the needs of the colonial upper class.

The period up to about 1630 saw a steady growth of obrajes, many of which produced cheap cotton and woolen goods for popular consumption. Most of these enterprises were privately owned, but some were operated by indigenous communities to meet their tribute payments. A number of towns in New Spain (Mexico City, Puebla, and Tlaxcala, among others) were centers of this textile industry. Other primitive factories produced such articles as soap, chinaware, and leather. The population increase of the late seventeenth century may have also stimulated the growth of manufacturing. There is little evidence that sporadic Spanish legislative efforts to restrict the growth of colonial manufacturers achieved their purpose.

Commerce, Smuggling, and Piracy

THE COLONIAL COMMERCIAL SYSTEM

Spain's colonial commercial system was restrictive, exclusive, and regimented in character, in conformity with the mercantilist standards of that day. Control over all colonial trade, under the Royal Council of the Indies, was vested in the *Casa de Contratación* (House of Trade), established in 1503 in Seville. This agency licensed and supervised all ships, passengers, crews, and goods passing to and from the Indies. It also collected import and export duties and the royal share of all precious metals and stones brought from the Indies, licensed all pilots, and maintained a *padrón real* (standard chart) to which all charts issued to ships in the Indies trade had to conform. It even operated a school of navigation that trained the pilots and officers needed to sail the ships in the transatlantic trade.

Commerce with the colonies was restricted until the eighteenth century to the wealthier merchants of Seville and Cádiz, who were organized in a guild that exercised great influence in all matters relating to colonial trade. With the aim of preventing contraband trade and safeguarding the Seville monopoly, trade was concentrated in three American ports, Veracruz in New Spain, Cartagena in New Granada, and Nombre de Dios on the Isthmus of Panama. The Seville merchant oligarchy and corresponding merchant groups in the Indies, particularly the merchant guilds in Mexico City and Lima, deliberately kept the colonial markets understocked. In general they played into each other's hands at the expense of the colonists, who were forced to pay exorbitant prices for all European goods acquired through legal channels. Inevitably, the system generated colonial discontent and stimulated the growth of contraband trade.

With the object of enforcing the closed-port policy and protecting merchant vessels against foreign attack, a fleet system was developed and made obligatory in the sixteenth century. As perfected about the middle of the century, it called for the annual sailing under armed convoy of two fleets, each numbering fifty or more ships, one sailing in the spring for Veracruz and taking with it ships bound for Honduras and the West Indies, the other sailing in August for Panama and convoying ships for Cartagena and other ports on the northern coast of South America. Veracruz supplied Mexico and most of Central America; from Portobelo goods were carried across the isthmus and shipped to Lima, the distribution point for Spanish goods to places as distant as Chile and Buenos Aires. Having loaded their returns of silver and colonial produce, the fleets were to rendezvous at Havana and sail for Spain in the spring, before the onset of the hurricane season. In the seventeenth century, as a result of Spain's economic decadence and the growing volume of contraband trade, fleet sailings became increasingly irregular.

In the 1570s, Mexican merchants pioneered an immensely lucrative trade between Acapulco and Manila. The annual voyage of the Manila galleon exchanged Mexican silver, in great demand in China, for silks, porcelains, and spices. A foreign observer estimated that the Mexican merchants who dominated the trade doubled the money they spent on it every year. From Acapulco to Manila, the ship ran with the trade wind for a space of eight to ten weeks; but the return passage, in a region of light and variable winds and frequent typhoons, could take from four to seven months, and on the longer voyages the ravages of "hunger, thirst and scurvy cold reduce a ship to a floating cemetery." Spanish officials disliked the trade because it drained off bullion, most of which came from Peru, and because it flooded Peru with Chinese silks that reduced the demand for Spanish textiles. But the demand for silk was so insatiable and the supply so inadequate that considerable quantities went by pack train across Mexico to Veracruz and there were shipped again to Spain. As with the trans-Atlantic trade, Spain sought to regulate and limit trade with Asia, limiting the size of ships in 1593 to 300 tons and allowing only two ships to sail in any one year. The Manila galleon made its last voyage in 1811.

Danger and difficulty attended the long voyage to the Indies from the time a ship left Seville to thread its careful way down the shoal-ridden Guadalquivir to the Mediterranean. Hunger and thirst, seasickness and scurvy at sea, and yellow fever and malaria in tropical harbors like Veracruz and Portobelo were familiar afflictions. Storms at sea took a heavy toll of ships; foreign pirates and privateers posed a chronic threat. Gluts of goods in the colonial markets as a result of competition from foreign smugglers and frequent confiscation of silver by the crown, with tardy or inadequate compensation, often reduced merchants' profits to the vanishing point.

Spanish industry, handicapped by its guild organization and technical backwardness, could not supply the colonies with cheap and abundant manufactures in return for colonial foodstuffs and raw materials, as required by the implied terms of the mercantilist bargain. Indeed, it was not in the interest of the merchant monopolists of Seville and Cádiz, who throve on a regime of scarcity and high prices, to permit an abundant flow of manufactures to the colonies. Prices to the colonial consumer were also raised by a multitude of taxes: the *avería* (convoy tax), the *almojarifazgo* (import duty), and the alcabala. Inevitably, the manufacturers and merchants of the advanced industrial nations of northern Europe sought to enter by force or guile into the large and unsatisfied Spanish-American markets. The ambitious monarchs of those lands scoffed at Spain's claim of dominion over all the Western Hemisphere except that portion that belonged to Portugal; they defied Spanish edicts forbidding foreigners to navigate American waters or trade on American coasts on pain of destruction of ships and crews. The ironic query said to have been addressed by Francis I of France to the kings of Spain and Portugal summed up the foreign viewpoint: "Show me, I pray you, the will of our father Adam, that I may see if he has really made you his only universal heirs."

SIR FRANCIS DRAKE, PIRACY, AND FOREIGN PLUNDER

England soon emerged as the principal threat to Spain's empire in America. The accumulation of capital and development of manufacturing under the fostering care of the Tudor kings produced an explosion of English commercial energies in the reign of Queen Elizabeth I. The Old World did not provide sufficient outlets for these erupting energies, and England's merchant adventurers eagerly turned to America. The historic slave-trading voyage of John Hawkins to the West Indies in 1562 opened England's drive to break into the closed Spanish-American markets. Half honest trader, half corsair, Hawkins came to the Indies heavily armed and ready to compel the colonists to trade with him at cannon point, but he showed himself scrupulously honest in his business dealings with the Spaniards, even to the point of paying the royal license and customs dues. Hawkins owed the success of his first two American voyages to the needs of the Spanish settlers, who were ready to trade with a Lutheran heretic or the devil himself to satisfy their desperate need for slave labor and European wares. To cover up these violations of Spanish law, the venal local officials made a thin pretense of resistance. But by 1567 the pretense had worn too thin, the Spanish government had taken alarm, and angry orders went out to drive the English smugglers away. Stiffening Spanish resistance culminated in the near-destruction of Hawkins's trading fleet by a Spanish naval force at Veracruz in 1568.

Only two of the English ships managed to get away; one was commanded by Hawkins, the other by his cousin, Francis Drake. Four years later, Drake left England with four small ships, bound for the Isthmus of Panama. In actions marked by audacity and careful planning, he stormed and plundered the town of Nombre de Dios, escaping at dawn. Later, he made the most lucrative haul in the history of piracy by capturing the pack train carrying Peruvian silver from the Pacific side of the isthmus to Nombre de Dios. In 1577, Drake set sail again on an expedition that had the secret sponsorship and support of Queen Elizabeth. Its objects were to "singe the King of Spain's beard" by seizing his treasure ships and ravaging his colonial towns; to explore the whole Pacific coast of America, taking possession of the regions beyond the limits of Spanish occupation; and to display English maritime prowess by means of a second circumnavigation of the globe. The expedition of 1577 led by Francis Drake achieved these goals. In the 1580s, Drake made other voyages of reprisal against Cartagena, St. Augustine, and Santo Domingo. It is small wonder that the name of Drake became a word of fear to the inhabitants of colonial coastal towns.

But piracy entered on a decline following the signing of the Treaty of Madrid in 1670 between England and Spain, by which the British government agreed to aid in the suppression of the corsairs in return for Spanish recognition of its sovereignty over the British West Indian islands. French buccaneers, however, continued to be active until the sign-

ing of the Treaty of Ryswick in 1697, by which Spain formally recognized French possession of St. Domingue.

The injury inflicted on Spanish prosperity and prestige by pirates and privateers, great as it was, was dwarfed by the losses caused by the less spectacular operations of foreign smugglers. Contraband trade steadily increased in the course of the sixteenth and seventeenth centuries. European establishments in Jamaica, St. Domingue, and the Lesser Antilles became so many bases for contraband trade with the Spanish colonies. Buenos Aires was another funnel through which Dutch and other foreign traders poured immense quantities of goods that reached markets as distant as Peru. By the end of the seventeenth century, French companies operating behind the façades of Spanish merchant houses in Seville and Cádiz dominated even the legal trade with the Indies.

A shrewd Englishman, John Campbell, identified the major source of Spain's misfortunes: its economic weakness. The Spaniards, he remarked, were said to be stewards for the rest of Europe:

> Their galleons bring the silver into Spain, but neither wisdom nor power can keep it there; it runs out as fast as it comes in, nay, and faster. . . . At first sight this seems to be strange and incredible; but when we come to examine it, the mystery is by no means impenetrable. The silver and rich commodities which come from the Indies come not for nothing (the king's duties excepted) and very little of the goods or manufactures for which they come, belong to the subjects of the crown of Spain. It is evident, therefore, that the Spanish merchants are but factors, and that the greatest part of the returns from the West Indies belong to those foreigners for whom they negotiate.

Spanish economists of the seventeenth century understood the causes of Spain's plight. Their writings offered sound criticisms of the existing state of affairs and constructive proposals for reform. But their arguments were powerless to change the course of Spanish policy, dictated by small mercantile and aristocratic cliques whose special interests and privileges were wholly incompatible with the cause of reform.

THE FRAMEWORK OF THE COLONIAL ECONOMY

Was the colonial economy capitalist, feudal, or something in between? Scholars have hotly debated this issue. Some, who believe that production for the market is the defining feature of capitalism, argue that Latin America has been capitalist since 1492.[5] Others deny the relevance of the concepts of feudalism and capitalism, taken from a European context, to a unique colonial reality. Most students, however, will admit the presence of capitalist, feudal, and even more archaic elements, such as the pre-Columbian indigenous communities based on communal land tenure, in the colonial economy. Spain tried, though not consistently, to preserve and protect that ancient corporate landowning system because it gave the crown direct control over native labor and tribute, which it could then allocate to the colonial elite in accord with its own policies and interests. That collective landowning system suffered severe erosion in the course of the colonial period due to the expansion of the Spanish agricultural sector but at its close still maintained a large presence in many areas.

The feudal or semifeudal elements in the colonial economy included labor systems based in varying degrees on servitude and coercion, the nonmonetary character of many economic transactions,[6] and the technical backwardness of industry and agriculture, which reflected the very low level of investment in production and contrasted with the high levels of expenditure for conspicuous consumption, the church, and charity. Regulations, such as those that forbade indígenas to wear European clothes or own land privately, seriously hampered the development of a market economy and may also be called feudal.

This predominantly feudal character of the colonial economy reflected Spain's own backwardness. Indeed, in the course of the colonial period, Spain became in certain ways more feudal, more seigneurial. Part of the reason is that most of the wealth that flowed from the Indies to Spain went to pay for costly wars and diplomacy, support a parasitic nobility, and import goods from northern Europe, leaving little for development. Spain's dependence on colonial tribute and colonial trade monopoly inevitably strengthened the dominant aristocratic ideology and discouraged the rise of a dynamic entrepreneurial class. In fact, the passion for noble titles infected many members of the small middle class, who hastened to abandon their trades and invest their wealth in a *mayorazgo* (an entailed estate). If the nobility had lost their feudal power to the crown on the national level, they were compensated, says John Lynch, "by the extension of their economic power, a process in which the crown itself was a willing ally." They also retained their feudal powers in their own districts, where they levied feudal dues, appointed local officials, and meted out justice. Indeed, under the last, weak Hapsburg kings, the nobility regained much of their old political power. "By the late seventeenth century," writes Henry Kamen, "Spain was probably the only west European country to be completely and unquestionably under the control of the titled aristocracy." This aristocratic hegemony was a recipe for economic decay and collapse. We shall see that Spanish efforts in the eighteenth century to reverse these trends were too little and too late.

The colonial economy also contained some capitalist elements. Although based on such noncapitalist labor systems as slavery and debt peonage, the gold and silver mines and the haciendas, ranches, and plantations producing sugar, hides,

---

[5]A leading exponent of the "Latin America-has-been-capitalist-all-along" view is André Gunder Frank; see Frank's *Capitalism and Underdevelopment in Latin America* (1969). That view has come under heavy fire from scholars who define capitalism, first and foremost, as a mode of production based on wage labor that has lost its own means of production. See, for example, Colin Mooers, *The Making of Bourgeois Europe* (1991), pp. 5–17.

[6]As late as the mid-eighteenth century, according to historian John Coatsworth, perhaps 10 percent of New Spain's internal trade was carried on in silver coins, and storekeepers everywhere resorted to tokens in trading.

cochineal, indigo, and other commodities for external markets were fully integrated into the expanding world market. These enterprises reflected the price fluctuations and other vicissitudes of that market and promoted the accumulation of capital, not in Spain, but in England and other lands of rising capitalism. Some capitalist shoots appeared in the colonies as well, notably in the great mining centers, sugar mills, and workshops that were marked by some development of wage labor and division of labor.

But the development of colonial capitalism remained embryonic, stunted by the overwhelming weight of feudal relationships and attitudes and the continuous siphoning off of wealth to Spain, itself increasingly an economic satellite of the more advanced capitalist countries of northwest Europe. The double character of the colonial plantation—often self-sufficient and nonmonetary in its internal relations but oriented externally toward European markets—reflected the dualism of the colonial economy.

State, Church, and Society

THE POLITICAL ORGANIZATION of the Spanish Empire in America reflected the centralized, absolutist regime by which Spain itself was governed. By the time of the conquest of America, Castilian parliamentary institutions and municipal rights and exemptions had lost most of their former vitality. The process of centralization begun by the Catholic Sovereigns reached its climax under the first two Hapsburgs. In Castile there arose a ponderous administrative bureaucracy capped by a series of royal councils appointed by and directly responsible to the king. Aragon, which stubbornly resisted royal encroachments on its *fueros* (charters of liberties), retained a large measure of autonomy until the eighteenth century. Even in Castile, however, Hapsburg absolutism left largely intact the formal and informal power of the great lords over their peasantry. In Aragon, in whose soil feudal relations were more deeply rooted, the arrogant nobility claimed a broad seigneurial jurisdiction, including the right of life and death over its serfs, as late as the last decades of the seventeenth century. This contrast between the formal concentration of authority in the hands of royal officials and the actual exercise of supreme power on the local level by great landowners was to characterize the political structure of independent Spanish America as well.

Political Institutions of the Spanish Empire

FORMATION OF COLONIAL ADMINISTRATION

The pattern of Spain's administration of its colonies was formed in the critical period between 1492 and 1550. The final result reflected the steady growth of centralized rule in Spain itself and the application of a trial-and-error method to the problems of colonial government. To Columbus, Cortés, Pizarro, and other great expeditionary leaders, the Spanish kings granted sweeping political powers that made these men almost sovereign in the territories they had won or proposed to subdue. But once the importance of these conquests was revealed, royal jealousy of the great conquistadors was quick to show itself. Their authority was soon revoked or strictly limited, and the institutions that had been employed in Spain to achieve centralized political control were transferred to America for the same end. By the mid-sixteenth century, the political organization of the Indies had assumed the definitive form it was to retain, with slight variations, until late in the eighteenth century.

The Council of the Indies, originally a standing committee of the all-powerful Council of Castile but chartered in 1524 as a separate agency, stood at the head of the Spanish imperial administration almost to the end of the colonial period. Although great nobles and court favorites were appointed to the council, especially in the seventeenth century, its membership consisted predominantly of lawyers. Under the king, whose active participation in its work varied from monarch to monarch, it was the supreme legislative, judicial, and executive institution of government. One of its most important functions was the nomination to the king of all high colonial officials. It also framed a vast body of legislation for the Indies—the famous Laws of the Indies (1681)—which combined decrees of the most important kind with others of a very trivial character. Although the council was frequently staffed by conscientious and highly capable officials in the early Hapsburg period, the quality of its personnel tended to decline under the inept princes of the seventeenth century. Nonetheless, historians owe the council a particular debt for its initiative in seeking to obtain detailed information on the history, geography, resources, and population of all the colonies. The *relaciones* (reports) that incorporated this information represent a rich mine of materials for students of colonial Spanish America.

THE ROYAL AGENTS

The principal royal agents in the colonies were the viceroys, the captains general, and the audiencias. The viceroys and captains general had essentially the same functions, differing only in the greater importance and extent of the territory assigned to the jurisdiction of the former. Each was the supreme civil and military officer in his realm, having in his charge such vital matters as the maintenance and increase of the royal revenues, defense, indigenous welfare, and a multitude of other responsibilities. At the end of the Hapsburg era, in 1700, there were two great American viceroyalties. The viceroyalty of New Spain, with its capital at Mexico City, included all the Spanish possessions north of the Isthmus of Panama; that of Peru, with its capital at Lima, embraced all of Spanish South America except for the coast of Venezuela. Captains general, theoretically subordinate to the viceroys but in practice virtually independent of

them, governed large subdivisions of these vast territories. Other subdivisions, called *presidencias,* were governed by audiencias. Their judge-presidents acted as governors, but military authority was usually reserved to the viceroy. Overlapping and shifting of jurisdiction was common throughout the colonial period and formed the subject of frequent disputes among royal officials.

A colonial viceroy, regarded as the very image of his royal master, enjoyed an immense delegated authority, which was augmented by the distance that separated him from Spain and by the frequently spineless or venal nature of lesser officials. He might be a lawyer or even a priest by background but was most commonly a representative of one of the great noble and wealthy houses of Spain. A court modeled on that of Castile, a numerous retinue, and the constant display of pomp and circumstance bore witness to his exalted status. In theory, his freedom of action was limited by the laws and instructions issued by the Council of the Indies, but a sensible recognition of the need to adapt the laws to existing circumstances gave him a vast discretionary power. The viceroy employed the formula *obedezco pero no cumplo*—"I obey but do not carry out"—to set aside unrealistic or unenforceable legislation.

The sixteenth century saw some able and even distinguished viceroys in the New World. The viceroy Francisco de Toledo (1569–1581), the "supreme organizer of Peru," was certainly an energetic, hardworking administrator who consolidated Spanish rule and imposed royal authority in Peru. His resettlement program and his institution of *mita,* the system of forced labor in the mines, however, profoundly disrupted indigenous social organization and took a heavy toll of lives. In New Spain, such capable officials as Antonio de Mendoza (1530–1550) and his successor, Luis de Velasco (1550–1564), wrestled with the problems left by the Conquest. They strove to curb the power of the conquistadors and to promote economic advance; sometimes they also tried, to a limited degree, to protect the interests of indígenas. But the predatory spirit of the colonists, royal distrust of excessive initiative on the part of high colonial officials, and opposition from other sectors of the

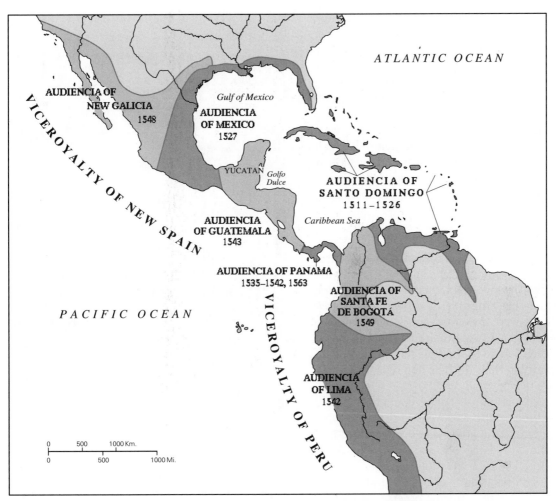

ATLANTIC OCEAN

AUDIENCIA OF NEW GALICIA 1548

Gulf of Mexico

AUDIENCIA OF MEXICO 1527

YUCATAN   Golfo Dulce

AUDIENCIA OF SANTO DOMINGO 1511–1526

AUDIENCIA OF GUATEMALA 1543

Caribbean Sea

AUDIENCIA OF PANAMA 1535–1542, 1563

AUDIENCIA OF SANTA FE DE BOGOTÁ 1549

PACIFIC OCEAN

AUDIENCIA OF LIMA 1542

VICEROYALTY OF NEW SPAIN

VICEROYALTY OF PERU

0   500   1000 Km.
0   500   1000 Mi.

Viceroyalties and Audiencias in Sixteenth-Century Spanish America

official bureaucracy largely thwarted their efforts. In the seventeenth century, in an atmosphere of growing financial crisis, corruption, and cynicism at the Spanish court, the quality of the viceroys inevitably declined. In 1695, by way of illustration, the viceroyships of Peru and Mexico were, in effect, sold to the highest bidders.

Each viceroy or captain general was assisted in the performance of his duties by an audiencia, which was the highest court of appeal in its district and also served as the viceroy's council of state. The joint decisions of viceroy and audiencia, taken in administrative sessions, had the force of law,

giving the audiencia a legislative character roughly comparable to that of the Council of the Indies in relation to the king. Although the viceroy had supreme executive and administrative power, he was not legally obliged to heed the advice of the audiencia. Still, its immense prestige and its right to correspond directly with the Council of the Indies made it a potential and actual check on viceregal authority. The crown, ever distrustful of its colonial officers, thus developed a system of checks and balances that assured ample deliberation and consultation on all important questions, but it also encouraged indecision and delay.

In addition to hearing appellate cases and holding consultative meetings with their viceroy or captain general, *oidores* were required to make regular tours of inspection of their respective provinces with the object of making a searching inquiry into economic and social conditions, treatment of the natives, and other matters of interest to the crown. Although viceroys and oidores were well paid by colonial standards, the style of life their positions demanded was expensive, and the viceroy or oidor who did not take advantage of his office to enrich himself could expect to return to Spain poor.

PROVINCIAL ADMINISTRATION

Provincial administration in the Indies was entrusted to royal officials who governed districts of varying size and importance from their chief towns and who usually held the title of *corregidor* or *alcalde mayor.* Some were appointed by the viceroy (from whom they often bought their jobs), others by the crown. They possessed supreme judicial and political authority in their districts and represented the royal interest in the *cabildos* (town councils). Certain civil and criminal cases could be appealed from the municipal magistrates to the corregidor, and from him to the audiencia. If not trained as a lawyer, the corregidor was assisted by an *asesor* (legal counsel) in the trial of judicial cases.

Corregidores were of two kinds. Some presided over Spanish towns; others, *corregidores de indios,* administered indigenous pueblos, or towns, which paid tribute to the crown. One of the principal duties of the corregidor de indios, who was usually appointed for three years, was to protect the natives from fraudulent or extortionate practices, but there is ample testimony that the corregidor was himself the worst offender in this respect. Native *caciques* (chiefs) often were his accomplices in these extortions. Perhaps the worst abuses of his authority arose in connection with the practice of repartimiento or repartimiento de mercancías, the requirement that indigenous peoples purchase goods from the corregidor. Ostensibly designed to protect the natives from the frauds of private Spanish traders, the corregidor's exclusive right to trade with indígenas became an

Scenes showing mistreatment of native peoples by a corregidor, from *La Nueva Crónica (The New Chronicle)* of the seventeenth-century indigenous noble Felipe Waman Puma de Ayala, illustrated by the author. [Waman Puma de Ayala, *La nueva crónica.* The Royal Library, Copenhagen]

instrument for his own speedy enrichment at the expense of the natives.

The crown employed an arsenal of regulations to ensure good and honest performance on the part of public officials. Viceroys and oidores were forbidden to engage in trade or hold land within their jurisdictions or to accept gifts or fees; even their social life was hedged about with many restrictions. All royal officials, from the viceroy down, faced a *residencia* (judicial review) of their conduct at the end of their term of office. This took the form of a public hearing at which all who chose could appear before the judge of residence to present charges or testify for or against the official in question. At the end of the process, the judge found the official guilty or innocent of part or all of the charges and handed down a sentence that could be appealed to the Council of the Indies. Another device, the *visita,* was an investigation of official conduct, usually made unannounced by a *visitador* specially appointed for this purpose by the crown or, in the case of lesser officials, by the viceroy in consultation with the audiencia. As a rule, the *visita* was no more effective than the residencia in preventing or punishing official misdeeds.

The only political institution in the Indies that satisfied to some degree local aspirations for self-rule was the town council, known as the cabildo or *ayuntamiento.* Any suggestion, however, that the cabildo had some kind of democratic character has no basis in fact. At an early date, the crown assumed the right to appoint the *regidores* (councilmen) and alcaldes. Under Philip II and his successors, it became the established practice for the king to sell these posts to the highest bidder, with a right of resale or bequest, on condition that a certain portion of the value be paid to the crown as a tax at each transfer. In some towns, however, cabildo members elected their successors.

Throughout the colonial period, the municipal councils were closed, self-perpetuating oligarchies of rich landowners, mine owners, and merchants, who "ran the council as an exclusive club." These men frequently received no salaries for their duties and used their positions to distribute municipal lands to themselves, assign themselves native labor, and in general serve the narrow interests of their class. Their official tasks included supervision of local markets, distribution of town lands, and local taxation. They also elected the alcaldes, who administered justice as courts of first instance. Vigilantly supervised by the provincial governor, or corregidor, who frequently intervened in its affairs, the cabildo soon lost such autonomy as it may have possessed in the early days. Yet despite its undemocratic character, inefficiency, and waning prestige and autonomy, the cabildo was not without potential significance. As the only political institution in which the creoles (American-born Spaniards) were largely represented, it was destined to play an important part in the coming of the nineteenth-century wars of independence.

The officials and agencies just described represented only a small part of the apparatus of colonial government. A large number of secretaries (*escribanos*) attended to the paperwork of the various departments. As a rule, they collected no salaries but were reimbursed by fees for their services. There was a multitude of police officers, collectors of the royal fifth, alcaldes with special jurisdiction, and the like. Under Charles V control of such offices often lay in the hands of high Spanish officials, who sold them to persons who proposed to go to the Indies to exploit their fee-earning possibilities. Beginning with Philip II, many of these offices were withdrawn from private patronage and sold directly by the crown, usually to the highest bidder. In the second half of the seventeenth century, the sale of offices by the crown or the viceroy spread from fee-earning positions to higher, salaried posts. As a rule, the beneficiaries of such transactions sought to return to Spain rich, having made the highest possible profit on their investment. Consequently, corruption in this period became structural in government. Colonial officials, high and low, abused their trusts in innumerable and ingenious ways.

If the royal authority was more or less supreme in the capitals and the surrounding countryside, the same was not true of more distant and isolated regions. In such areas, royal authority was very remote, and the power of the great landowners was virtually absolute. On their large, self-sufficient estates, they dispensed justice in the manner of feudal lords, holding court and imprisoning peons in their own jails; they raised and maintained their own private armies; and they generally acted as monarchs of all they surveyed. Sometimes these powerful individuals combined their de facto military and judicial power with an official title, which made them representatives of the crown in their vicinities. Spain's growing economic and political weakness in the late seventeenth century, which loosened the ties between the mother country and its colonies, favored this decentralization of power.

INEFFECTIVENESS OF MUCH SPANISH COLONIAL LAW

The frequent violation of Spanish colonial law was a fact of colonial political life. In considerable part, this situation reflected the dilemma of royal officials faced with the task of enforcing laws bitterly opposed by powerful colonial elites with whom they generally had close social and economic ties. This dilemma found its most acute expression in the clash between the crown's legislative desire to regulate indigenous labor—the real wealth of the Indies—and the drive of colonial elites for maximum profits. The result was that these protective laws were systematically flouted. The crown often closed its eyes to the violations, not only because it wished to avoid confrontation with powerful colonial elites but because those laws sometimes collided with the crown's own narrow, short-range interests (its need for revenue to finance wars and diplomacy and to support a parasitic nobility).

Hence the contradiction between that protective legislation, so often cited by defenders of Spain's work in America, and the reality of indigenous life and labor in the colonies. In a report to Philip II, Alonso de Zorita, a judge who retired to an honorable poverty in 1566 after nineteen years of administrative activity in the Indies, wrote:

> The wishes of Your Majesty and his Royal Council are well known and are made very plain in the laws that are issued every day in favor of the poor Indians and for their increase and preservation. But these laws are obeyed and not enforced, wherefore there is no end to the destruction of the Indians, nor does anyone care what Your Majesty decrees.

But not all colonial legislation was so laxly enforced. There was a considerable body of exploitative or discriminatory laws that was in general vigorously enforced, including laws requiring indígenas to pay tribute and perform forced labor for token wages, permitting the forced sale of goods to them at fixed prices, and limiting their landownership to a low maximum figure while allowing the indefinite growth of Spanish estates.

How can the longevity of Spanish rule over its American colonies, so distant from a European country that grew steadily weaker in the course of the seventeenth century, be explained? The answer does not lie in Spain's military power, because Spain maintained few troops in the Indies until the eighteenth century. Much of the durability of Spanish rule seems to lie in a royal policy of making the large concessions needed to gain and maintain the loyalty of colonial elites. The political apparatus of viceroys, audiencias, corregidores, and the like played a decisive role in implementing this royal program. The frequent failure to enforce protective legislation, the strict enforcement of the exploitative laws, the *composiciones* (settlements that legalized usurpation of native lands through payment of a fee to the king), and the toleration of great abuses by colonial oligarchs are illustrations of the policy. To be sure, alongside this unwritten pact between the crown and the colonial elite for sharing power and the fruits of exploitation of indigenous, black, and mixed-blood people in the Indies went a royal effort to restrain the colonists' power and ambitions. Until the eighteenth century, however, this effort did not go far enough to threaten the existing arrangements.

The Church in the Indies

The Spanish church emerged from the long centuries of struggle against the Muslims with immense wealth and an authority second only to that of the crown. The Catholic Sovereigns, Ferdinand and Isabella, particularly favored the clergy and the spread of its influence as a means of achieving national unity and royal absolutism. The Spanish Inquisition, which they founded, had political as well as religious uses, and under their great-grandson, Philip II, it became the strongest support of an omnipotent crown. While the Spanish towns sank into political and then into economic decadence, and the great nobles were reduced to the position of a courtier class aspiring for favors from the crown, the church steadily gained in wealth and influence. Under the last Hapsburgs, it threatened the supremacy of its royal master. It remained for the enlightened Bourbon kings of the eighteenth century to curb in some measure the excessive power of the church.

Royal control over ecclesiastical affairs, both in Spain and the Indies, was solidly founded on the institution of the *patronato real* (royal patronage). As applied to the colonies, this consisted of the absolute right of the Spanish kings to nominate all church officials, collect tithes, and found churches and monasteries in America. Under diplomatic pressure from King Ferdinand, Pope Julius II had accorded this extraordinary privilege to Spain's rulers in 1508, ostensibly to assist in converting New World heathen. The Spanish monarchs regarded the patronato as their most cherished privilege and reacted sharply to all encroachments on it.

THE SPIRITUAL CONQUEST OF AMERICA

Beginning with Columbus's second voyage, one or more clergymen accompanied every expedition that sailed for the Indies, and they came in swelling numbers to the conquered territories. The friars formed the spearhead of the second religious invasion that followed on the heels of the Conquest. The friars who came to America in the first decades after the Conquest were, on the whole, an elite group. They were products of one of the periodic revivals of asceticism and discipline in the medieval church, especially of the reform of the orders instituted in Spain by the Catholic Sovereigns and carried out with implacable energy by Cardinal Cisneros. This vanguard group of clergy frequently combined with missionary zeal a sensitive social conscience and a love of learning. The missionaries were frequently impressed by the admirable qualities of the indígenas, by their simplicity and freedom from the greed and ambitions of Europeans. Wrote Vasco de Quiroga, royal judge and later bishop of the province of Michoacán in Mexico:

> Anything may be done with these people, they are most docile, and, proceeding with due diligence, may easily be taught Christian doctrine. They possess innately the instincts of humility and obedience, and the Christian impulses of poverty, nakedness, and contempt for the things of this world, going barefoot and bareheaded with the hair long like apostles; in

fine, with very tractable minds void of error and ready for impression.

Millenarian[1] and utopian ideals strongly influenced many members of the reformed clergy who came to the Indies in the first decades after the Conquest. Inspired by the vision of a multitude of native souls waiting to be saved, they dreamed of a fruitful fusion of indigenous and Spanish cultures under the sign of a Christianity returned to its original purity. Such men as Juan de Zumárraga, first bishop and archbishop of Mexico, Vasco de Quiroga, and Bartolomé de Las Casas were profoundly influenced by the humanist, reformist ideas of Erasmus and by Thomas More's *Utopia.* Indeed, Quiroga proposed to the Spanish crown that indigenous cities be established and organized on the lines of More's ideal commonwealth, in which the natives' natural virtues would be preserved and perfected by training in the Christian religion and culture. When the crown ignored his proposals, Quiroga used his own resources to found the pueblos or refuges of Santa Fe in Michoacán. In these communities Quiroga established collective ownership of property, systematic alternation between agricultural and craft labor, the six-hour working day, work for women, the distribution of the fruits of collective labor according to need, and the shunning of luxuries and of all occupations that were not useful. Quiroga's dream of establishing islands of charity and cooperative life in a sea of exploitive encomiendas and haciendas was doomed to eventual failure, but to this day the indígenas of Michoacán revere the name and memory of "Tata Vasco."

These attitudes of reformist clergy inevitably placed them on a collision course with the encomenderos and other lay Spaniards who sought the unchecked exploitation of native peoples and commonly described them as "dogs" (*perros*). To be sure, not all the religious saw eye to eye on this

---

[1]Millenarianism is the medieval doctrine, based on a prophecy in the Book of Revelation and widely held by the reformed clergy, that Christ would return to earth to reign for a thousand years of peace and righteousness, to be followed by the Last Judgment at the end of the world.

Bartolomé de Las Casas condemned the racist attitudes of the conquistadors and defended indigenous culture against the scorn of Europeans. His teachings emphasized the dignity of all people. [Institut Amatller d'Art Hispànic, Barcelona]

issue. Some, like the famous Franciscan Toribio de Benavente (better known by his Nahuatl name of Motolinía), may be called "realists" or "moderates." These clergy believed that the encomienda, carefully regulated to safeguard indigenous welfare, was necessary for the prosperity and security of the Indies. Others, mostly Dominicans whose leader and spokesman was Bartolomé de Las Casas, believed that the encomienda was incompatible with the welfare of the natives and must be put in the way of extinction.

As we saw in Chapter 4, during the reign of Charles V—who feared the rise of a colonial feudalism based on the encomienda—the Lascasian wing of the clergy won certain victories, capped by the passage of the New Laws of the Indies (1542). By their militant efforts to secure the enforcement of these laws, Las Casas and his disciples incurred

the mortal enmity of the encomenderos. Las Casas was repeatedly threatened. The Dominican bishop Antonio de Valdivieso of Nicaragua, who had tried to enforce the abolition of indigenous slavery by the New Laws, was assassinated in 1550 by a group of men led by the governor's son. These and other courageous defenders of indígenas, like Bishop Juan del Valle in Colombia and Fray Domingo de Santo Tomás in Peru, may be regarded as forerunners of today's progressive current in the Catholic church. The ideology of Las Casas, with its demand that the Spaniards "cease to be *caballeros* by grace of the blood and sweat of the wretched and oppressed," seems to anticipate today's Latin American liberation theology and its "preferential option for the poor."

Despite the partial victories won by Las Casas during the reign of Charles V, this movement entered on a decline when Philip II took the throne in 1556. Denial of absolution to Spaniards who had violated these protective laws—an important weapon employed by Las Casas and his co-religionists— was forbidden by various royal decrees. The church was instructed to concern itself only with questions of worship and preaching, leaving problems in the economic and social relations between Spaniards and native peoples to the civil authorities. Since those authorities as a rule were ready to comply with the wishes of encomenderos, great landowners, and other ruling-class groups, the descendants of the conquistadors finally obtained the direct, unchallenged dominion over indígenas for which their forebears had struggled. The encomienda (although in decline), the repartimiento or mita, and even slavery (legalized on various pretexts) remained the basic institutions in colonial Spanish America. This new political climate was marked by a growing belief in the constitutional inferiority of indigenous peoples, based on the Aristotelian theory of natural slavery, a theory that Las Casas and virtually all other Spanish theologians had previously condemned.

The first missionaries in the Indies did not regard their defense of the natives against enslavement and exploitation as separate from their primary task of conversion; they reasoned that for conversion to be effective the prospective converts must survive the shock of Conquest, multiply, and live better under the new religion than the old one. Despite the clandestine opposition of surviving pagan priests and some native nobility, the friars converted prodigious numbers of natives, who, willingly or unwillingly, accepted the new and more powerful divinities of the invaders. In Mexico, the Franciscans claimed to have converted more than a million people by 1531; the energetic Motolinía asserted that he had converted more than fifteen hundred in one day! Where persuasion failed, pressures of various kinds, including force, were used to obtain conversions. Natives who had been baptized and relapsed into idolatry were charged with heresy and punished, some nobles being hanged or burned at the stake. In order to facilitate the missionary effort, the friars studied the native languages and wrote grammars and vocabularies that are still of value to scholars.

The religious, especially the Franciscans, also assigned a special importance to the establishment of schools in which indigenous upper-class youth might receive instruction in the humanities, including Latin, logic, and philosophy, as well as Christian doctrine. The most notable of these centers was the Franciscan Colegio de Santa Cruz in Mexico. Before it entered on a decline in the 1560s as a result of lay hostility or lack of interest and the waning fervor of the friars themselves, the school had produced a harvest of graduates who often combined enthusiasm for European culture with admiration for their own pagan past. These men were invaluable to the missionaries in their effort to reconstruct the history, religion, and social institutions of the ancient civilizations.

Although some of the early friars undertook to destroy all relics of the pagan past—idols, temples, picture writings—the second generation of missionaries became convinced that paganism could not be successfully combated without a thorough study and understanding of the old pre-Conquest way of life. In Mexico there arose a genuine school of ethnography devoted to making an inventory of the rich content of pre-Columbian cultures. If the primary and avowed motive of this effort was to arm the missionary with the knowledge he needed to discover the concealed presence

of pagan rites and practices, intellectual curiosity and delight in the discovery of the material, artistic, and social achievements of these vanished empires also played a part.

The work of conversion, by the subsequent admission of the missionaries themselves, was less than wholly successful. In Mexico, concludes historian Louise M. Burkhart, the Aztecs "were able to become just Christian enough to get by in the colonial social and political setting without compromising their basic ideological and moral orientation." Here the result of the missionary effort was generally a fusion of old and new religious ideas, in which the cult of the Virgin Mary sometimes merged with the worship of pagan divinities. Writing half a century after the conquest of Mexico, the Dominican Diego Durán saw a persistence of paganism in every aspect of indigenous life, "in their dances, in their markets, in their baths, in the songs which mourn the loss of their ancient gods." In the same period, the great scholar-missionary Sahagún complained that they continued to celebrate their ancient festivals, in which they sang songs and danced dances with concealed pagan meanings. In Peru the work of conversion was even less successful. "If the Indians admitted the existence of a Christian god," writes Nathan Wachtel, "they considered his influence to be limited to the Spanish world, and looked themselves for protection to their own gods." To this day, native peoples in lands like Guatemala and Peru perform ceremonies from the Maya and Inca period.

The friars also had to battle divisions within their own camp. Violent disputes arose among the orders over the degree of prebaptismal instruction required by indigenous converts, with the Dominicans and Augustinians demanding stiffer standards than the Franciscans. Other disputes arose as to which order should have jurisdiction over a particular area or pueblo. A more serious conflict arose between the secular and the regular clergy. The pastoral and sacramental duties performed by the regular clergy in America were normally entrusted only to parish priests. Special papal legislation (1522) had been required to grant these functions to the regulars, a concession made necessary by the small number of seculars who came to the Indies in the early years. But after mid-century their number increased, and the bishops increasingly sought to create new parishes staffed by seculars. These seculars were intended to replace the regulars in the spiritual direction of converts. The friars resisted by every means at their disposal, but they fought a losing battle.

Another source of division within the church was rivalry between American-born and peninsular clergy for control of the higher positions, especially in the orders. Threatened with loss of those positions in provincial elections by the growing creole majority in the seventeenth century, the peninsulars sought and obtained decrees making mandatory alternation of offices between themselves and creoles.

The Moral Decline of the Clergy and the Missionary Impulse

To the factors contributing to the decline of the intellectual and spiritual influence of the orders one must add the gradual loss of a sense of mission and of morale among the regular clergy. Apostolic fervor inevitably declined as the work of conversion in the central areas of the empire approached completion; many of the later arrivals among the clergy preferred a life of ease and profit to one of austerity and service. By the last decades of the sixteenth century, there were frequent complaints against the excessive number of monasteries and their wealth. The principal sources of this wealth were legacies and other gifts from rich donors: for a rich man not to provide for the church in his will was a matter of scandal. A common procedure used to endow churches, convents, or other religious institutions was to assume a mortgage (*censo*) on the landowner's estate for a fixed amount on which he or she agreed to pay the beneficiary an annual interest of 5 percent. This method of expressing piety was so widely used that in New Spain "at the end of the eighteenth century it was said that there was no hacienda which was not burdened with one or more censos." Another procedure, which served both the donor's piety and family interest, consisted in establishing a

chantry to celebrate in perpetuity memorial masses for his or her soul. By designating a family member as chaplain, the donor ensured that control of the income from the endowment would remain in the family. These procedures, continually draining money from the income of estates, writes Mexican historian Enrique Florescano, "helped to destabilize the already precarious haciendas and ranches . . . leaving the religious institutions, in effect, as the real landowners and beneficiaries of rural income."

The resources the church acquired became inalienable in the form of mortmain, or perpetual ownership. When invested in land and mortgages, this wealth brought in more wealth. The enormous economic power of the church gave it a marked advantage over competitors and enabled it to take advantage of weaker lay property owners, especially in time of recession. The last important order to arrive in Spanish America, the Society of Jesus (1572), was also the most fortunate in the number of rich benefactors and the most efficient in running its numerous enterprises, which were largely used to support its excellent system of *colegios* (secondary schools) and its missions.

Inevitably, this concern with the accumulation of material wealth weakened the ties between the clergy and the humble masses whose spiritual life they were supposed to direct. As early as the 1570s, there were many complaints of excessive ecclesiastical fees and clerical exploitation of native labor. A viceroy of New Spain, the Marqués de Monteclaros, assured King Philip III in 1607 that indigenous peoples suffered the heaviest oppression at the hands of the friars and that one native paid more tribute to his parish priest than twenty paid to His Majesty. Hand in hand with a growing materialism went an increasing laxity of morals. Concubinage became so common among the clergy of the later colonial period that it seems to have attracted little official notice or rebuke. By the last decades of the colonial period, the morals of the clergy had declined to a condition that the Mexican historian Lucas Alamán, himself a leader of the clerical party in the period of independence, could only describe as scandalous. From this charge one must in general exclude the Jesuits, noted for their high moral standards and strict discipline; and of course men of excellent character and social conscience were to be found among both the secular and regular clergy.

The missionary impulse of the first friars survived longest on the frontier, "the rim of Christendom." Franciscans first penetrated the great northern interior of New Spain, peopled by hostile Chichimecs, "wild Indians." Franciscans accompanied the Oñate expedition of 1598 into New Mexico and dominated the mission field there until the end of the colonial period; they were also found in such distant outposts of Spanish power as Florida and Georgia. After the expulsion of the Jesuits from the Indies in 1767, the Franciscans took their place directing missionary work in California.

The mission was one of three closely linked institutions—the other two being the *presidio* (garrison) and the civil settlement—designed to serve the ends of Spanish imperial expansion and defense on the northern frontier. The mission, it was hoped, would gather the native converts into self-contained religious communities, train them to till the land, herd cattle, and practice various crafts until they became fully Christianized and Hispanicized. The presidios would provide military protection for the neighboring missions and ensure a cooperative attitude on the part of indigenous novices. Finally, attracted by the lure of free land, Spaniards of modest means would throng into the area, forming civil settlements that would become bustling centers of life and trade. By all these means, the frontier would be pushed back, pacified, and maintained against foreign encroachment.

This three-pronged attack on the wilderness was not very successful. Certain tribes on the northern frontier, such as the powerful Apaches of Arizona, New Mexico, and Texas and the Comanches of Texas, were never reduced to mission life. The missionaries had greater success among such sedentary peoples as the Pueblo of New Mexico, the Pima and Opata of Sonora in northwest Mexico, and the Hasinai of east Texas. Even among these peaceful communities, however, revolts and desertions were frequent. In 1680 the supposedly Christianized Pueblos of New Mexico revolted, slaughtered the friars, and maintained a

long, tenacious resistance against Spanish efforts at reconquest. The rise of native leaders who proclaimed that the old gods and way of life were best often sparked wholesale desertions. Mistreatment by soldiers in nearby presidios and the terror inspired by Apache and Comanche raiding parties also provoked frequent flight from the missions.

The civil settlements proved no more successful. By the end of the colonial period, there were only a few scattered towns on the northern frontier, and the continuous raids made life and property so insecure that in New Mexico settlers who petitioned for permission to leave outnumbered recruits coming to the area. Ultimately, the whole task of defending Spanish claims fell on a chain of presidios stretching approximately along the present border between the United States and Mexico. Successive military defeats compelled Spanish troops to take refuge behind the security of the high presidio walls. In the end Spain was forced to adopt a policy of neutralizing the Apaches and Comanches by periodic distribution of gifts to them. When the outbreak of the wars of independence stopped the flow of gifts, however, they again took to the warpath, driving by the useless line of presidios into the interior of Mexico.

The most notable instance of successful missionary effort, at least from an economic point of view, was that of the Jesuit establishments in Paraguay, where, favored by a genial climate and fertile soil, the Jesuits established more than thirty missions; these formed the principal field of Jesuit activity in America. Strict discipline, centralized organization, and absolute control over the labor of thousands of docile Guaraní producing large surpluses enabled the Jesuits to turn their missions into a highly profitable business enterprise. Great quantities of such goods as cotton, tobacco, and hides were shipped down the Paraná River to Buenos Aires for export to Europe. Rather than "Christian socialism," the Jesuit mission system could more correctly be described as "theocratic capitalism."

Jesuit rule in Paraguay and Jesuit mission activity everywhere in the colonies ended when a royal decree expelled the order from the colonies in 1767. Among the motives for this action were the conflict between the nationalistic church policy of the Bourbons and Jesuit emphasis on papal supremacy, suspicions of Jesuit meddling in state affairs generally, and the belief that the Jesuit mission system constituted a state within a state. The expulsion of the Jesuits from Paraguay resulted in intensified exploitation of the Guaraní by Spanish officials and landowners. Within a generation the previously thriving Jesuit villages were in ruins.

The Inquisition in the New World

The Inquisition formally entered the Indies with the establishment by Philip II of tribunals of the Holy Office in Mexico and Lima in 1569. Prior to that time, its functions were performed by clergy who were vested with or assumed inquisitorial powers. Its great privileges, its independence of other courts, and the dread with which the charge of heresy was generally regarded by Spaniards made the Inquisition an effective check on "dangerous thoughts," whether religious, political, or philosophical. The great mass of cases tried by its tribunals, however, had to do with offenses against morality or minor deviations from orthodox religious conduct, such as blasphemy.

Spain's rulers, beginning with Queen Isabella, forbade Jews, Muslims, conversos (New Christians), and persons penanced by the Inquisition from going to the Indies. Many conversos, however, hoping to improve their fortunes and escape the climate of suspicion and hostility that surrounded them in Spain, managed to settle in the Indies, coming as seamen, as servants of licensed passengers, or sometimes even with licenses purchased from the crown. Some attained positions of wealth and authority. Toward the end of the sixteenth century, many conversos settled in New Spain and Peru. Many came from Portugal, where there was a strong revival of Inquisitorial activity following the country's annexation by Spain (1580). One who came to New Spain was Luis de Carvajal, who rose to be captain general and governor of the northern kingdom of New León. Carvajal was a sincere Catholic, but his son and other relatives were fervent practicing Jews, mystics who urged other members of the large converso community of New Spain to return to Judaism. They were denounced to the Inquisition, which tried and condemned them to death as relapsed heretics. The sentences were carried out at a great auto-da-fé (public sentencing) in Mexico City in 1595. In 1635 the Lima Inquisition struck at the converso community of the city. Some were sent to the stake; all suffered confiscation of goods. It suggests the wealth of the Lima conversos, mostly rich merchants, that the Lima office of the Inquisition, having confiscated their property, "emerged as the wealthiest in the world."

As in Spain, the Inquisition in the Indies relied largely on denunciations by informers and employed torture to secure confessions. As in Spain, the damage done by the Inquisition was not limited to the snuffing out of lives and the confiscation of property but included the creation of an atmosphere of fear, distrust, and rigid intellectual conformity. The great poetess Sor Juana Inés de la Cruz alludes to this repressive atmosphere when she mentions her difficulties with "a very saintly and guileless prelate who believed that study was a matter for the Inquisition." Indigenous peoples, originally subject to the jurisdiction of inquisitors, were later removed from their control as recent converts of limited mental capacity and hence not fully responsible for their deviations from the Faith, but were subject to trial and punishment by an episcopal inquisition.

The Structure of Class and Caste

The social order that arose in the Indies on the ruins of the old indigenous societies was based, like that of Spain, on aristocratic or feudal principles. Race, occupation, and religion were the formal criteria that determined an individual's social status. All mechanical labor was regarded as degrading, but large-scale trade (as opposed to retail trade) was compatible with nobility, at least in the Indies. Great emphasis was placed on *limpieza de sangre* (purity of blood), meaning above all descent from "Old Christians," without mixture of converso or Morisco (Muslim) blood. Proofs of such descent were jealously guarded and sometimes manufactured.

The various races and racial mixtures were carefully distinguished and graded in a kind of hierarchy of rank. A trace of black blood legally sufficed to deprive an individual of the right to hold public office or enter the professions, as well as depriving him of the other rights and privileges. The same taint attached to the great mass of mestizos. True, the Laws of the Indies assigned perfect legal equality to those of legitimate birth, but to the very end of the colonial period the charters of certain colonial guilds and schools excluded all mestizos, without distinction.

The lack of solid demographic information and major disagreements among historians regarding the size of pre-Conquest populations make estimates of Spanish America's population in 1650, and of the relative numerical strength of the racial groups composing that population, conjectural. It appears, however, that by that date, or even earlier, the long decline of the indigenous population had ended and a slow recovery had begun. It also appears that the European element in the population was growing more rapidly. But the groups growing most rapidly were the *castas*, mixed-race peoples, the great majority of whom were born out of wedlock.

As noted above, Spanish law and opinion ranked all these racial groups in a descending order of worth and privilege, with Europeans on top, followed by the castas, indígenas, and blacks. This formal ranking did not necessarily correspond to the actual standing of individuals of different racial makeup in society, but it provided the colonial ruling groups with an ideological justification for their rule. It also created a conflict society par excellence, pitting natives against blacks, caste against caste, and inflating poor Spaniards with a sense of their superiority over all other groups, which hindered forging the unity of the exploited masses and thus served to maintain an oppressive social order. The idea of "race" in Latin America, as elsewhere, was socially constructed to rationalize and preserve the power of a tiny elite.

THE RULING CLASS

In practice, racial lines were not very strictly drawn. In the Indies, a white skin was a symbol of social superiority, roughly the equivalent of *hidal-*

guía, a title of nobility in Spain, but it had no cash value. Not all whites belonged to the privileged economic group. Colonial records testify to the existence of a large class of "poor whites"—vagabonds, beggars, or worse—who disdained work and frequently preyed on the indígenas. A Spaniard of this group, compelled by poverty to choose his mate from the castas, generally doomed his descendants to an inferior economic and social status. But the mestizo or mulatto son of a wealthy Spanish landowner or merchant, if acknowledged and made his legal heir, could pass into the colonial aristocracy. If traces of indigenous or African descent were too strong, the father might reach an understanding with the parish priest, who had charge of baptismal certificates; it was also possible for a wealthy mestizo or mulatto to purchase from the crown a document establishing his legal whiteness. Wealth, not gentle birth or racial purity, was the distinguishing characteristic of the colonial aristocracy. Granted this fact, it remains true that the apex of the colonial pyramid was composed overwhelmingly of whites.

This white ruling class was itself divided by group jealousies and hostilities. The Spaniards brought to the New World their regional rivalries and feuds—between Old Castilians and Andalusians, between Castilians and Basques—and in the anarchic, heated atmosphere of the Indies, these rivalries often exploded into brawls or even pitched battles. But the most abiding cleavage within the upper class was the division between the Spaniards born in the colonies, called creoles, and the European-born Spaniards, called peninsulars or referred to by such disparaging nicknames as *gachupín* or *chapetón* (tenderfoot). Legally, creoles and peninsulars were equal; indeed Spanish law called for preference to be given in the filling of offices to the descendants of conquistadors and early settlers. In practice, the creoles suffered from a system of discrimination that during most of the colonial period virtually denied them employment in high church and government posts and large-scale commerce.

The preference shown for peninsulars over creoles sprang from various causes, among them the greater access of Spaniards to the court, the fountainhead of all favors, and royal distrust of the creoles. By the second half of the sixteenth century, the sons or grandsons of conquistadors were complaining of the partiality of the crown and its officials for unworthy newcomers from Spain. The creoles viewed with envenomed spite these Johnny-come-latelies, who often won out in the scramble for *corregimientos* and other government jobs. A Mexican poet, Francisco de Terrazas, expressed the creole complaint in rhyme:

> Spain: to us a harsh stepmother you have been,
> A mild and loving mother to the stranger,
> On him you lavish all your treasures dear,
> With us you only share your cares and
>   danger.[2]

The resulting cleavage in the colonial upper class grew wider with the passage of time. Both groups developed an arsenal of arguments to defend their positions. Peninsulars often justified their privileged status by reference to the alleged indolence, incapacity, and frivolity of the creoles, which they sometimes solemnly attributed to the American climate or other environmental conditions. The creoles responded in kind by describing the Europeans as mean and grasping parvenus. The growing wealth of the creoles from mines, plantations, and cattle ranches only sharpened their resentment at the discrimination from which they suffered.

THE MESTIZO: AN AMBIGUOUS STATUS

The mestizo arose from a process of racial mixture that began in the first days of the Conquest. In the post-Conquest period, when Spanish women were scarce, the crown and the church viewed marriages between indigenous peoples and Spaniards with some favor; mixed marriages were not uncommon in those years. But this attitude soon changed as the crown, for its own reasons, adopted a policy of systematic segregation. By the first

quarter of the seventeenth century, the authoritative writer on Spain's colonial legislation, Juan Solórzano Pereira, could write: "Few Spaniards of honorable position will marry Indian or Negro women." Consequently, the great mass of mestizos had their origin in irregular unions. The stigma of illegitimacy, unredeemed by wealth, doomed the majority to the social depths. Some became peons, resembling natives in their way of life; others swelled the numerous class of vagabonds; still others enrolled in the colonial militia. Mestizos also contributed to the formation of the rancheros (small farmers) and formed part of the lower middle class of artisans, overseers, and shopkeepers. Without roots in either indigenous or Spanish society, scorned and distrusted by both, small wonder that the lower-class mestizo acquired a reputation for violence and instability.

INDIGENOUS PEOPLES: A SEPARATE NATION

By contrast with the mestizo, no ambiguity marked the position of indígenas in Spanish law and practice. They constituted a separate nation, the república de indios, which also constituted a hereditary tribute-paying caste. The descendants of indigenous rulers and hereditary nobility, however, received special consideration, partly from Spanish respect for the concept of señor natural (the natural or legitimate lord), partly because they played a useful role as intermediaries between the Spanish rulers and native tribute payers. These nobles were allowed to retain all or part of their patrimonial estates and enjoyed such special privileges as the right to ride horses, wear European dress, and carry arms.

There is ample evidence that members of the indigenous aristocracy were among the worst exploiters of their own people. In Mexico, where in Aztec times there already existed a semifeudal order and serflike peasants formed a large part of the population, some Aztec lords took advantage of the fluid conditions created by the Conquest to usurp communal lands, impose excessive rents on their tenants, and force the commoners to work for them. In both Mexico and Peru, their new role as tribute-collectors and labor recruiters for the Spaniards

---

[2]Francisco de Terrazas, *Poesías*, ed. Antonio Castro Leal (Mexico, 1941), p. 87. From *The Aztec Image in Western Thought* by Benjamin Keen, p. 90. Copyright © 1971 by Rutgers University, the State University of New Jersey. Reprinted by permission of Rutgers University Press.

offered the native elites large opportunities for wheeling-and-dealing with corregidores, encomenderos, and priests at the expense of commoners. For example, chiefs and corregidores might falsify the tribute lists and share the resulting profits, or they might conceal the true number of workers available for mita or repartimiento labor and employ the hidden workers on their own estates. In Peru, where traditional bonds of kinship, ritual, and mutual dependence still powerfully linked kurakas, or headmen, to ayllu commoners, most kurakas probably at first sought to maintain a balance among complying with the new rulers' demands for labor and tribute, protecting their ayllus against excessive Spanish exactions, and defending their own interests. Gradually, however, adapting to the new commercial climate, they began to exploit commoners to feather their own nests.

Many kurakas became hacendados in their own right; by the end of the sixteenth century, says Peruvian historian Luis Millones, some kurakas controlled such large, complex enterprises, producing a variety of products for the Peruvian internal market, that they had to hire Spanish employees to assist them. Native peasant women, writes Irene Silverblatt, were primary targets of kuraka exploitation because they were especially vulnerable to loss of land and water rights. The seventeenth-century Inca chronicler Waman Puma de Ayala claimed that no matter how much colonial authorities and native elites robbed poor peasant men, "they robbed poor peasant women much more"; and he accused the kurakas of illegally exploiting the labor of women in their jurisdiction and abusing them sexually, just as Spanish officials, encomenderos, and priests did.

The result of these trends pitting kurakas against ayllu commoners, writes Steve Stern, was the creation of "a more strained, suspicious relationship in which conflict, coercion, and economic power acquired added importance." In 1737, for example, community members of San Pedro de Tacna brought suit against their kuraka for illegally expropriating communal lands; they claimed he was forcing them off communal property to facilitate creation of an *aji* (chili pepper)-producing estate. In their testimony, writes Silverblatt, "wit-

ness after witness remarked that the kuraka's primary targets were peasant women."

In part, at least, what Charles Gibson says about Mexico was no doubt also true of Peru: the inordinate demands and aggressions of Mexican caciques and Peruvian kurakas against the commoners represented "a response to strain, an effort to maintain position and security" in the face of Spanish encroachments on the lands and perquisites of the native nobility. By the late sixteenth century, however, a considerable portion of the native aristocracy, especially the minor nobility or *principales,* was in full decline, apparently more rapid and general in Mexico than in Peru. Many Aztec nobles lost their retainers through flight or as a result of Spanish legislation converting former servile classes (like the mayeques) into free tribute-payers; and in both Mexico and Peru Spanish refusal to recognize the noble status of many *principales* reduced them to the condition of tribute-payers. One cause of the nobility's ruin was Spanish invasion of their lands, to which they responded with costly but often futile litigation; another was their responsibility for the collection of tribute from the commoners. When the number of tribute-payers declined because of an epidemic or some other circumstance, the cacique or kuraka had to make up the arrears or go to jail. To make good the deficit, he might have to sell or mortgage his lands or risk the anger of commoners by imposing an extra tribute assessment.[3]

[3]A revealing example of the trouble that his responsibility for collection of tribute might cause an indigenous governor is cited by Robert Heskett in his very informative *Indigenous Rulers: An Ethnohistory of Town Government in Colonial Cuernavaca* (1991). In 1694 the governor of Cuernavaca, don Antonio de Hinojosa, sought sanctuary in the town's Franciscan monastery because he owed nearly 4,000 pesos (a staggeringly large sum for that time and place) in unpaid tribute assessments. Maneuvers by don Antonio and his family to prevent the sequestration and auction of his estate were unsuccessful, and since his tribute debt was not completely erased by the sale, later Cuernavaca governors inherited the debt. Don Antonio died in the monastery in 1697 or 1698. His final years, observes Heskett, "saw the destruction of an estate carefully built up by his ancestors through marriage, inheritance, purchase, and perhaps usurpation."

However, down to the close of the colonial period there existed a group of thoroughly Hispanicized cacique or kuraka families who, in addition to serving as intermediaries between Spanish elites and their native communities, managed to enrich themselves as landowners and entrepreneurs, ultimately becoming full members of the propertied class. In late eighteenth-century Mexico, for example, the cacique of Panohuayan in Amecameca owned "the hacienda of San Antonio Tlaxomulco and other properties producing wheat and maguey and yielding an income of thousands of pesos per year." According to Charles Gibson, "Like any Spanish hacendado, the cacique received payments from Indians who cut wood and grazed animals on his property. His great house was equipped with Spanish furniture, silver dining service, and rich tapestries. He possessed a private arsenal of guns, pistols, and steel and silver swords. His stables and storehouse and other possessions compared favorably with those of wealthy Spaniards."

In eighteenth-century Peru, this small class of wealthy indigenous or mestizo nobles was represented by the famous kuraka José Gabriel Condorcanqui (Tupac Amaru). Lilian Fisher writes that he lived like a Spanish nobleman, wearing "a long coat and knee-breeches of black velvet, a waistcoat of gold tissue worth seventy or eighty duros (dollars), embroidered linen, silk stockings, gold buckles at his knees and on his shoes, and a Spanish beaver hat valued at twenty-five duros. He kept his hair curled in ringlets that extended nearly down to his waist." His source of wealth included the ownership of three hundred mules, which he used to transport mercury and other goods to Potosí and other places, and a large cacao estate.

By contrast with the privileged treatment accorded to indigenous rulers, the great majority of commoners suffered under crushing burdens of tribute, labor, and ecclesiastical fees. Viewed as a constitutionally inferior race and hence as perpetual wards of the Spanish state, they repaid the Spanish tutelage with the obligation to pay tribute and give forced labor. *Gente sin razón* ("people of weak minds") was a phrase commonly applied to native peoples in colonial documents. Their juridi-

cal inferiority and status as wards found expression in laws (universally disregarded) forbidding them to make binding contracts or to contract debts in excess of five pesos and in efforts to minimize contact between them and other racial groups. These and many other restrictions on indigenous activity had an ostensibly protective character. But an enlightened Mexican prelate, Bishop Manuel Abad y Queipo, argued that these so-called privileges

> do them little good and in most respects injure them greatly. Shut up in a narrow space of six hundred rods, assigned by law to the Indian towns, they possess no individual property and are obliged to work the communal lands. . . . Forbidden by law to commingle with the other castes, they are deprived of the instruction and assistance that they should receive from contact with these and other people. They are isolated by their language, and by a useless, tyrannical form of government.

He concluded that these ostensible privileges were "an offensive weapon employed by the white class against the Indians, and never serve to defend the latter."

Native commoners, however, did not form a single undifferentiated mass of impoverished, exploited people, for there existed a small minority who found paths to successful careers in the new colonial order. These included the skilled crafts and transport, for which there was a high demand. Artisans quickly entered such "Hispanic" occupations as silversmith, masonry, stonecutting, carpentry, and the like. In late sixteenth-century Peru, says Steve Stern, "an independent Indian craftsman could earn a very respectable income. In two months, a stonecutter could fashion a stone wheel worth sixty pesos." *Arrieros* (muleteers) could earn some 80 to 160 pesos a year. Some accumulated enough wealth to acquire landholdings for commercial production of grains, vegetables, and other products. To protect themselves against expropriations (periodic official inspections of indigenous communal land could result in redistribution of "surplus" land to Spanish petitioners), these farmers acquired individual title under

Spanish law, which protected the owner from the legal confiscation to which communal land was subject. Commoners also successfully resisted Spanish exploitation by gaining exemption from heavy tribute and repartimiento obligations, which made it difficult to accumulate money needed for investment in land or other enterprise. In addition to recognized caciques and kurakas, the exempted classes included independent women heads of household, artisans, officials of indigenous cabildos, and lay assistants of Catholic priests.

These achievements of that small minority of successful commoners had their price. Writing about late sixteenth-century Peru, Steve Stern observes that "the tragedy of Indian success lay in the way it recruited dynamic, powerful, or fortunate individuals to adopt Hispanic styles and relationships, thereby buttressing colonial domination. The achievements of native individuals, in the midst of a society organized to exploit indigenous peoples, educated Indians to view the Hispanic as superior, the Andean as inferior."

Most indigenous people lived in their own towns, some of pre-Hispanic origin, others created by a process of resettlement of dispersed populations in new towns called "reductions" or "congregations." To serve the ends of Spanish control and tribute collection, these towns were reorganized on the peninsular model, with municipal governments patterned on those of Spanish towns. There were some differences between the organization of indigenous local government in New Spain and Peru. In New Spain the indigenous cabildo, which in the mid-sixteenth century gradually replaced the pre-Conquest system of government by hereditary native rulers, had its regidores or councilmen, its alcaldes who tried minor cases, and its *gobernador* (governor), who was responsible for the collection and delivery of tribute to the corregidor or the encomendero. Spanish colonial law required periodic election of these and other municipal officers, but voting was generally restricted to a small group of elite males, and candidates as a rule were drawn from an even smaller number of hereditary aristocratic families, with the selection of officers usually the result of discussion and consultation with an assembly of elders, leading to final consensus. Election disputes were not unknown, however, and generally reflected factional divisions within the elite. Women, although barred from voting or holding office, sometimes played an active part in these disputes, as illustrated by the case of Josefa María Francisca, who in the 1720s was a leader of one faction in the Mexican town of Tepoztlán. Josefa, who had already gained notoriety as a principal litigant in a stubborn effort to exempt Tepoztlán natives from the dreaded mining repartimiento, was accused by the rival faction of setting "a dangerous example by openly encouraging people to join her in 'endless lawsuits.'"

In Peru, Viceroy Francisco de Toledo imposed a structure of local government with two levels of authority. Here the key figure in the indigenous cabildo was the alcalde or mayor (there were one or two alcaldes, depending on the number of households), who had general charge of administration and was assisted by one or two regidores and other officials. All these officials were to be replaced yearly by election, and none could succeed himself. Regarded as creatures of the Spanish state, these officials commanded little respect from the local community, for "the new power structure imposed by the Spaniards," says Karen Spalding, "cut across the traditional Andean hierarchy based on age and inherited position." Toledo distrusted the traditional Andean elite, the kurakas, but could not dispense with them, and their status was finally codified as a provincial nobility, supported by salaries paid out of tribute money and the labor service of their communities. Kurakas held important posts in the new officialdom and often served as allies and agents of the all-powerful Spanish corregidores, priests, and encomenderos. But their personal liability for such community obligations as mita and tribute placed them at risk of having to sell their estates or losing their wealth through confiscation by corregidores.

The indigenous town typically was composed of one or more neighborhood or kinship groups (calpulli in Mexico, ayllu in the Andean region), each with its hereditary elders who represented their community in intergroup disputes, acted as intermediaries in arranging marriages, supervised the allotment of land to the group's members, and otherwise served their communities. A certain degree of Hispanicization of commoners took place, reflected above all in religion but also in the adoption of various tools and articles of dress and food. But the barriers erected by Spain between the two communities and the fixed hostility with which they regarded each other prevented any thoroughgoing acculturation. In response to the aggressions and injustices inflicted on it by Spaniards, the indigenous community drew into itself and fought stubbornly to preserve not only its land but also its cultural identity, speech, social organization, and traditional dances and songs. After the kinship group, the most important instrumentality for the maintenance of collective identity and security was the *cofradia* (religious brotherhood), whose members were responsible for the maintenance of certain cult activities.

The Conquest and its aftermath inflicted not only heavy material damage on indigenous society but serious psychological injury as well. Spanish accounts frequently cite the lament of native elders over the loss of the severe discipline, strong family ties, and high moral standards of the pre-Conquest regimes. The Spanish judge Zorita quoted approvingly the remark of one elder that with the coming of the Spaniards to Mexico "all was turned upside down . . . liars, perjurers, and adulterers are no longer punished as they once were because the *principales* (nobles) have lost the power to chastise delinquents. This, say the Indians, is the reason why there are so many lies, disorders, and sinful women."

BLACKS, MULATTOS, ZAMBOS: THE LOWEST CLASS

Blacks, mulattos, and *zambos* (African and indigenous peoples) occupied the bottom rungs of the colonial social ladder. By the end of the sixteenth century, some 75,000 African slaves had been introduced into the Spanish colonies under the system of asiento. The infamous Middle Passage (the journey of enslaved Africans across the Atlantic) was a thing of horror; the Jesuit Alonso de Sandoval, who had charge of conversion of slaves and who wrote a book on the subject, left

this harrowing description of the arrival of a cargo of slaves in the port of Cartagena in New Granada:

> They arrive looking like skeletons; they are led ashore, completely naked, and are shut up in a large court or enclosure . . . and it is a great pity to see so many sick and needy people, denied all care or assistance, for as a rule they are left to lie on the ground, naked and without shelter. . . . I recall that I once saw two of them, already dead, lying on the ground on their backs like animals, their mouths open and full of flies, their arms crossed as if making the sign of the cross . . . and I was astounded to see them dead as a result of such great inhumanity.

By the end of the eighteenth century, some 9.5 million slaves had been brought to the Americas. Especially dense concentrations were found in Brazil and in the Caribbean area, which were dominated by plantation economies. Historians have hotly disputed the relative mildness or severity of Latin American black slavery. Recent studies generally support the view that the tempo of economic activity was decisive in determining the intensity of slave exploitation and the harshness of plantation discipline. Certainly manumission of slaves was more frequent in the Hispanic than in the English, Dutch, or French colonies, but it is likely that the unprofitability of slavery under certain conditions contributed more than cultural traditions to this result. Whatever the reasons, by the close of the colonial period slaves formed a minority of the total black and mulatto population. Whatever their treatment, slaves retained the aspiration for freedom. Fear of slave revolts haunted the Spanish ruling class, and slaves frequently fled from their masters. Some of them formed independent communities in remote jungles or mountains that successfully resisted Spanish punitive expeditions.

This stubborn attachment of the black slaves to freedom, reflected in frequent revolts, flights, and other forms of resistance, suggests that the debate over the relative mildness or severity of black slavery in Latin America evades the main issue: the dehumanizing character of even the "mildest" slavery. Brought from Africa by force and violence, cut off from their kindred and peoples, the uprooted Africans were subjected in their new environment to severe deculturation. For reasons of security, slave owners preferred to purchase slaves of diverse tribal origins, language, and religious beliefs and deliberately promoted tribal disunity among them. The economic interest of the planters dictated that the great majority of the imported slaves should be young, between the ages of fifteen and twenty. This contributed to the process of deculturation, for very few aged blacks, the repositories of tribal lore and traditions in African societies, came in the slaveships.

The scarcity of women (the proportion of females in the slave population on Cuban plantations between 1746 and 1822 ranged between 9 and 15 percent) distorted the lives of the slaves, creating a climate of intense sexual repression and family instability. The church might insist on the right of the slave to proper Christian marriage and the sanctity of the marriage, but not until the nineteenth century was the separate sale of husbands, wives, and children forbidden in the Spanish colonies. The right of the master to sell or remove members of the slave's family and his free sexual access to slave women made difficult if not impossible a normal family life for slaves. The world of the slave plantation, resembling a prison rather than a society, left to independent Latin America a bitter heritage of racism, discrimination, and backwardness, problems that in most Latin American countries still await full solution.

Because of harsh treatment, poor living conditions, and the small number of women in the slave population, its rate of reproduction was very low. Miscegenation between white masters and slave women, on the other hand, produced a steady growth of the mulatto population. Free blacks and mulattos made important contributions to the colonial economy, both in agriculture and as artisans of all kinds. Free blacks and mulattos also were required to pay tribute.

LIFE IN THE CITY AND ON THE HACIENDA

In addition to indigenous communities, social life in the Spanish colonies had two major centers: the colonial city and the hacienda, or large landed estate. Unlike its European counterpart, the colonial city as a rule did not arise spontaneously as a center of trade or industry but developed in planned fashion to serve the ends of Spanish settlement and administration of the surrounding area. Sometimes it was founded on the ruins of an ancient capital, as in the case of Mexico City. More often it was founded on a site chosen for its strategic or other advantages, as in the case of Lima. By contrast with the usually anarchical layout of Spanish cities, the colonial town typically followed the gridiron plan, with a large central plaza flanked by the cathedral, the governor's *palacio*, and other public buildings. From this central square originated long, wide, and straight streets that intersected to produce uniform, rectangular blocks. This passion for regularity reflected both the influence of Renaissance neoclassical works on architecture and the regulatory zeal of the crown. In sharp contrast to the carefully planned nucleus of the colonial city was the disorderly layout of the surrounding native *barrios*, slum districts inhabited by a large native and mestizo population that provided the Spanish city with cheap labor and combustible material for the riots that shook the cities in times of famine or other troubles.

Into the capitals flowed most of the wealth produced by the mines, plantations, and cattle ranches of the surrounding area. In these cities, in houses whose size and proximity to the center reflected the relative wealth and social position of their owners, lived the rich mine owners and landowners of the colonies. They displayed their wealth by the magnificence of their homes, furnishings, dress, and carriages, and by the multitude of their servants and slaves. By the end of the sixteenth century, Mexico City had already acquired fame for the beauty of its women, horses, and streets; the riches of its shops; and the reckless spending, gaming, and generosity of its aristocracy. The poet Bernardo de Balbuena, in a long poem devoted to "La Grandeza Mexicana" ("The Grandeur of Mexico City"), wrote of

That lavish giving of every ilk,
Without a care how great the cost
Of pearls, of gold, of silver, and of silk.

This sixteenth-century portrait, painted by the indigenous artist Andres Sanchez Gallque, depicts Don Francisco de Arobe, the black ruler of an Ecuadorian province, who surrendered to Spanish forces in 1597. Within a decade, however, local rebellions continued to challenge Spanish rule. [Museo América, Madrid. *Primeros mulatos de Esmeraldas* by Adrián Sánchez Galque. Institut Amatller d'Art Hispànic, Barcelona]

By the close of the seventeenth century, Mexico City had a population estimated to number 200,000.

Lima, founded in 1534, proud capital of the viceroyalty of Peru, and Potosí, the great Peruvian mining center whose wealth became legendary, were two other major colonial cities. By 1650, when its wealth had already begun to decline, Potosí, with a population of 160,000 inhabitants, was the largest city in South America.

Before the eighteenth century, when changes in government and manners brought a greater stability, violence was prevalent in the colonial city. Duels, assassinations, even pitched battles between different Spanish factions were events frequently mentioned in official records and private diaries. From time to time, the misery of the masses in the native and mixed-blood wards exploded in terrifying upheavals. In 1624 the mobs of Mexico City, goaded by famine and a decree of excommunication issued by the archbishop against an unpopular viceroy, rose with cries of "Death to the evil government" and "Long live the church." They vented their wrath in widespread destruction and looting. In 1692 similar circumstances caused an even greater explosion, which ended in many deaths, the sacking of shops, and the virtual destruction of the viceroy's palace and other public buildings.

The hacienda constituted another great center of colonial social life. We must again stress the major variations in size, productive potential, labor systems, and other aspects of the colonial hacienda. Changing economic trends brought frequent changes in the size, products, and ownership of these enterprises, with large haciendas sometimes broken up into smaller units, and vice versa. The overall trend in the course of the colonial period was toward concentration of landownership in fewer hands, usually at the expense of small landowners. Because of the "polymorphic" nature of the colonial hacienda, however, the following description of its social life may be regarded as more characteristic of "traditional" haciendas found in certain areas of Mexico and Peru, and not of haciendas everywhere.

On the haciendas lived those creole aristocrats who could not support the expense of a city establishment or whose estates were in remote provinces or frontier areas. By the end of the seventeenth century, the hacienda in many areas had become a largely self-sufficient economic unit, combining arable land, grazing land for herds of sheep and cattle, timberland for fuel and construction, and even workshops for the manufacture and repair of the implements used on the hacienda. The hacienda was often also a self-contained social unit, with a church or chapel usually served by a resident priest, a store from which workers could obtain goods charged against their wages, and even a jail to house disobedient peons. In the hacendado's large, luxuriously appointed house often lived not only his immediate family but numerous relatives who laid claim to his protection and support.

The hacienda often contained one or more indigenous villages whose residents had once owned the land on which they now lived and worked as virtual serfs. They lived in one-room adobe or thatch huts whose only furniture often was some sleeping mats and a stone used for grinding maize (called *metate* in New Spain). Unlike the independent indigenous communities, which continued to resist the landowners' aggressions with strategies ranging from revolts to prolonged litigation, the resident peons had usually learned to make the appropriate responses of resigned servility to the master. The hacienda, with its characteristic economic and social organization, represented the most authentic expression of the feudal side of colonial society.

MARRIAGE, SEXUALITY, AND THE STATUS OF WOMEN

Marital and familial relationships in elite society were generally characterized by male domination, expressed in the customary right of fathers to arrange marriages for their daughters and in a double standard of sexual morality enjoining strict chastity or fidelity for wives and daughters without corresponding restrictions on husbands and sons. Both the church—the guardian of public morality—and the state—concerned with the eco-

nomic and political consequences of marriage— sought to supervise and control it. Throughout the sixteenth and seventeenth centuries, the church tended to support the right of children to select their marriage partners, while conceding the right of parents to have a say in the matter. In the second half of the eighteenth century, however, when large property interests grew in importance and influence, the state and then the church gradually adopted positions supporting parental objections to marriage between "unequal" partners as prejudicial to the family's "honor." Although the royal decree of 1778 on the subject sanctioned parental opposition to only one kind of "inequality"—that arising from interracial unions—the interpretation placed upon it by high colonial courts made clear that they regarded a wealthy mulatto family as the equal of a wealthy Spanish family. "A mulatto or a descendant of mulattoes," writes Patricia Seed, "was unequal to a Spaniard only if he was poor. The trend in decision making was that economic differences tied to racial differences, rather than racial disparity alone, constituted substantial social disparity." This issue of "inequality," of course, rarely arose on the top elite level, where marriage partners were almost invariably selected with an eye to conserving or strengthening the fortunes of the aristocratic families involved.

The concept of sexual honor also underwent some change in the same period. Previously, when a young woman lost her "honor" as a result of premarital sexual activity and sued for restitution of that honor through marriage or other compensation, the church tended to hold the man responsible and require him to marry her or compensate her for her loss. In the middle of the eighteenth century, however, aristocratic parents often argued that the girl's sexual activity made her—but not him— "unequal," thereby creating a bar to marriage. "This new concept of gender-related honor," says Patricia Seed, "framed an elaborate double standard that allowed young men to take the honor of young women without damage to their reputations or matrimonial consequences, but at the same time condemned women for the identical action."

Despite the emphasis placed by the Hispanic code of honor on virginity and marital fidelity, many colonial women, including members of the elite, disregarded conventional morality and church laws by engaging in premarital and extra-marital sex. Sexual relations between betrothed couples were common. Elite women who bore children out of wedlock had available a number of strategies to cover up their indiscretions and legitimate their offspring. The many lower-class women who transgressed in this way lacked the means and perhaps the will to recover their lost "honor." Illegitimacy appears to have been pervasive in colonial cities in the seventeenth and eighteenth centuries. Illegitimacy, signifying the lack of honor, could be a bar to holding public office and obstruct access to higher positions in the church, the military, and the civil service. The protection of wealthy relatives and access to education, however, could mitigate or remove the taint of illegitimacy. The chronicler Garcilaso de la Vega (1539–1616) took pride in being the natural son of a noble conquistador, and Sor Juana Inés de la Cruz (1651–1695) found her out-of-wedlock birth no obstacle to achieving a brilliant literary career.

The contrast between the formal code of sexual honor and the actual sexual conduct of colonial men and women was especially striking in a plantation area like Venezuela, where the large-scale existence of slavery and the enormous power of the great landowners tended to loosen the restraints of law and convention on such conduct. In 1770 Bishop Martí of Venezuela made a *visita* of his diocese. To evaluate the moral health of his subjects, he invited the people of each town he visited to speak to him in confidence about their own sins and those of their neighbors. Martí's detailed record of these reports and his own investigations and judgments give an impression of sexuality run rampant. "Over fifteen hundred individuals stood accused, primarily of sexual misdeeds," writes Kathy Waldron; "nearly ten percent of the clerics in the province came under attack; and even the governor of Maracaibo was denounced. The accusations included adultery, fornication, concubinage, incest, rape, bigamy, prostitution, lust, homosexuality, bestiality, abortion, and infanticide."

The economic, social, and physical subordination of colonial women to men (prevailing church

Talented girls like Isabel Flores de Oliva, later named Saint Rose of Lima, the first female saint in the Americas, sought artistic and intellectual independence in the convent. [St. Rose of Lima by Carlo Dolci; Palazzo Pitti Florence, Italy/Bridgeman Art Library, London/New York]

doctrine accepted a husband's right to beat disobedient or erring wives, but in moderation) is an undisputed fact. But male domination was to some extent limited by the Hispanic property law, which required equal division of estates among heirs and gave women the right to control their dowries and inheritances during and beyond marriage. Some colonial women operated as entrepreneurs independently of their husbands; women were often appointed executors of their husbands' wills and frequently managed a husband's business after his death. Two specialists in the field, Asunción Lavrín and Edith Couturier, concluded that colonial women enjoyed more economic independence than had been supposed, "that there was repression; but repression was not the whole reality, and that it did not wholly impair women's ability of expression."

Convent life provided an especially important means for achieving self-expression and freedom from male domination and sexual exploitation for elite and middle-class women. It was common for one or more daughters of an elite family to enter a convent; in the seventeenth century thirteen Lima convents held more than 20 percent of the city's women.[4] The convents were self-governing institutions that gave women an opportunity to display their capacity for leadership in administration, management of resources (like other church bodies, convents invested their wealth in mortgages on urban and rural properties), and sometimes in politicking, for convents could be the scenes of stormy factional struggle for control. "The convents," says Octavio Paz in his biography of the great poetess Sor Juana Inés de la Cruz, "experienced the rebellions, quarrels, intrigues, coalitions, and reprisals of political life." Nuns frequently complained to religious authorities about the tyranny of their abbesses, and violent encounters were not unknown. The convents were also the scenes of a busy social life—the nuns received their visitors unveiled, despite the rule forbidding them to uncover their faces in the presence of outsiders, and the rule requiring separation by wooden bars was not strictly observed. "These nuns excelled in exquisite confectionary arts," writes Paz, "and in the no less exquisite arts of martyring themselves and their sisters." Paz wonders that Sor Juana, a lucid intellect familiar with seventeenth-century European rationalist thought, kept her reason in that atmosphere of flagellations and mysticism. In her autobiographical letter to the bishop of Puebla, she confessed that convent life imposed obligations "most repugnant to my temperament" and referred to the "conventual bustle" that dis-

turbed "the restful quiet of my books." Somehow she managed to keep a distance between her intellect and that atmosphere, so foreign to her nature, but occasionally her self-control snapped under strain. Paz tells the story of a mother superior who complained to the archbishop of Sor Juana's haughtiness and accused her of having rudely said, "Quiet, Mother, you are a silly woman." The archbishop, a friend of Sor Juana, wrote on the margin of the complaint, "Prove the contrary, and I shall pass judgment."

Despite these drawbacks, the convent represented a heaven-sent opportunity for a young woman like Sor Juana, who was of a modest family background and who had no particular religious vocation. Her intellectual brilliance made it difficult for her to find a suitable marriage partner, and in any case she lacked the dowry to attract such a man. The convent, though, offered Sor Juana a way to escape the traps of sexual exploitation and cultivate her immense talents. A recent study of Hispanic women in colonial Peru by Luis Martín describes the Peruvian nunnery as "a fortress of women, a true island of women, where . . . women could protect themselves from the corroding and dehumanizing forces of Don Juanism." But a caveat is in order; the subjects of Martín's book are mostly upper-class Hispanic women who often scorned and sometimes abused the slaves and servants who surrounded them.

There is a growing body of information on the lives of indigenous women in colonial Spanish America. The evidence suggests that despite the damaging impact of Spanish patriarchal social relations, native women were far from being passive victims; they enjoyed economic importance as producers and traders of goods, owned property in their own right, litigated, countered male abuse with a variety of strategies ranging from mobilization of kin to witchcraft, and played leading roles in the organization of resistance to Spanish measures that threatened their communities. In his study of 142 native rebellions in colonial Mexico, William Taylor notes the highly visible role of women. "In at least one-fourth of the cases," he writes, "women were visibly more aggressive, insulting, and rebellious."

---

[4]The high cost of marriage dowries, frequently mentioned by colonial observers, continued to the influx of middle-class and elite women into convents. In a letter to the king, requesting the establishment of a convent, the cabildo of Buenos Aires noted that "in order to marry off a daughter with a modicum of decency one needs much more fortune than for two daughters to become nuns."

6

Colonial Brazil

BRAZIL'S EXISTENCE was unknown in Europe when the Treaty of Tordesillas (1494) between Spain and Portugal fixed the dividing line between their overseas possessions 370 leagues west of the Cape Verde Islands, assigning a large stretch of the coastline of South America to the Portuguese zone of exploration and settlement. In 1500, Pedro Alvares Cabral sailed with a large fleet to follow up Vasco da Gama's great voyage to India. He was, according to one explanation, driven by a storm farther west than he had intended and therefore made landfall on the Brazilian coast on April 22. Some historians speculate that he purposely changed course to investigate reports of land to the west or to verify a previous discovery. Whatever the reason for his westward course, Cabral promptly claimed the land for his country and sent a ship to report his discovery to the king.

The Beginning of Colonial Brazil

Portugal's limited resources, already committed to the exploitation of the wealth of Africa and the Far East, made it impossible to undertake a full-scale colonization of Brazil. But Portugal did not entirely neglect its new possession. Royal expeditions established the presence of a valuable dyewood, called brazilwood, that grew abundantly on the coast between the present states of Pernambuco and São Paulo. Merchant capitalists soon obtained conces-

sions to engage in the brazilwood trade and established a scattering of trading posts where European trinkets and other goods were exchanged with indígenas for brazil logs and other exotic commodities. A small trickle of settlers began—some castaways, others *degredados* (criminals exiled from Portugal to distant parts of the empire). These exiles were often well received by the local indígenas and lived to sire a large number of mixed-bloods who gave valuable assistance to Portuguese colonization. Meanwhile, French merchant ships, also drawn by the lure of brazilwood, began to appear on the Brazilian coast. Alarmed by the presence of these interlopers, King João III in 1530 sent an expedition under Martim Affonso de Sousa to drive away the intruders and to establish permanent settlements in Brazil. In 1532 the first Portuguese town in Brazil, named São Vicente, was founded near the present port of Santos.

THE CAPTAINCY SYSTEM

The limited resources of the Portuguese crown, combined with its heavy commitments in the spice-rich East, forced the king to assign to private individuals the major responsibility for the colonization of Brazil. This responsibility took the form of the captaincy system, already used by Portugal in Madeira, the Azores, and the Cape Verde Islands. The Brazilian coastline was divided into fifteen parallel strips extending inland to the uncer-

Colonial Brazil

tain line of Tordesillas. These strips were granted as hereditary captaincies to a dozen individuals, each of whom agreed to colonize, develop, and defend his captaincy or captaincies at his own expense. The captaincy system represented a curious fusion of feudal and commercial elements. The grantee or donatory was not only a vassal owing allegiance to his lord the king, but also a businessman who hoped to derive large profits from his own estates and from taxes obtained from the

colonists to whom he had given land. This fusion of feudal and commercial elements characterized the entire Portuguese colonial enterprise in Brazil from the first.

Few of the captaincies proved successful from either the economic or political point of view, because few donatories possessed the combination of investment capital and administrative ability required to attract settlers and defend their captaincies against indigenous attacks and foreign intruders. One of the most successful was Duarte Coelho, a veteran of the India enterprise who was granted the captaincy of Pernambuco. His heavy investment in the colony paid off so well that by 1575 his son was the richest man in Brazil, collecting large amounts in quitrents (rents paid in lieu of feudal services) from the fifty sugar mills of the province and himself exporting more than fifty shiploads of sugar a year.

By the mid-sixteenth century, sugar had replaced brazilwood as the foundation of the Brazilian economy. Favored by its soil and climate, the northeast (the provinces of Pernambuco and Bahia) became the seat of a sugar-cane civilization characterized by three features: the *fazenda* (large estate), monoculture, and slave labor. There soon arose a class of large landholders whose extensive plantations and wealth marked them off from their less affluent neighbors. Only the largest planters could afford to erect the *engenhos* (mills) needed to process the sugar before export. Small farmers had to bring their sugar to the millowner for grinding, paying one-fourth to one-third of the harvest for the privilege. Because Europe's apparently insatiable demand for sugar yielded quick and large profits, planters had no incentive to diversify crops, and food agriculture was largely limited to small farms.

Although the basic techniques of sugar making remained relatively unchanged from the late sixteenth to the late eighteenth centuries, the reputation of the Brazilian sugar industry for being traditional and backward appears unjustified. In the seventeenth century the Brazilian system was considered a model, and other powers sought to copy it. Not until the mid-eighteenth century, when declining demand and prices for Brazilian sugar produced a crisis and Brazil's Caribbean rivals developed some new techniques, did that reputation for backwardness arise, and even then, according to historian Stuart Schwartz, "the charge was undeserved."

PORTUGAL'S INDIGENOUS POLICY

The problem of labor was first met by raids on local villages, the raiders returning with trains of cap-

Soldiers of mixed racial background, like the mulatto soldier shown in this picture, played a large role in expeditions into the Brazilian interior in search of gold, indigenous slaves, and runaway black slaves. [Albert Eckhout, *A Mulatto Soldier,* 1640. © The National Museum of Denmark, Department of Ethnography. Photographer: Lennart Larsen]

tives who were sold to planters and other employers of labor. These aggressions were the primary cause of the chronic warfare between indigenous peoples and the Portuguese. But this labor was unsatisfactory from an economic point of view, because the natives lacked any tradition of organized work of the kind required by plantation agriculture, were especially susceptible to Old World diseases to which they had no acquired immunity, and offered many forms of resistance, ranging from attempts at escape to suicide. (In this last respect, of course, their response did not differ from that of the African slaves who gradually replaced them.)

As a result, after 1550, planters turned increasingly to the use of black slave labor imported from Africa. But the supply of black slaves was often cut off or sharply reduced by the activity of Dutch pirates and other foreign foes, and Brazilian slave hunters continued to find a market for their wares throughout the colonial period. The most celebrated slave hunters were the *bandeirantes* (from the word *bandeira*, meaning "banner" or "military company") from the upland settlement of São Paulo. Unable to compete in sugar production with the more favorably situated plantation areas of the northeast, these men, who were themselves mestiço in most cases, made slave raiding in the interior their principal occupation. The eternal hope of finding gold or silver in the mysterious interior gave added incentive to their expeditions. As indígenas near the coast dwindled in numbers or fled before the invaders, the bandeirantes pushed even deeper south and west, expanding the frontiers of Brazil in the process.

Indigenous peoples in Brazil did not accept the loss of land and liberty without a struggle, but their resistance was handicapped by the fatal tendency of tribes to war against each other, a situation the Portuguese utilized for their own advantage. Forced to retreat into the interior by the superior arms and organization of the Portuguese, the natives often returned to make destructive forays on isolated Portuguese communities. As late as the first part of the nineteenth century, stretches of the Brazilian shore were made uninhabitable by this unremitting warfare.

But the unequal struggle at last ended here, as in the Spanish colonies, in the total defeat of the natives. Overwork, loss of the will to live, and the ravages of European diseases caused very heavy loss of life among the enslaved indígenas. Punitive expeditions against tribes that resisted enslavement or gave some other pretext for sanctions also caused depopulation. The Jesuit father Antônio Vieira, whose denunciations of Portuguese cruelty recall the accusations of Las Casas about the Spanish, claimed that Portuguese mistreatment of natives had caused the loss of more than 2 million lives in Amazonia in forty years. A distinguished English historian, Charles R. Boxer, considers this claim exaggerated but concedes that the Portuguese "often exterminated whole tribes in a singularly barbarous way."

Almost the only voices raised in protest against the enslavement and mistreatment of native peoples were those of the Jesuit missionaries. The first fathers, led by Manoel da Nóbrega, came in 1549 with the captain general Tomé de Sousa. Four years later, another celebrated missionary, José de Anchieta, arrived in Brazil. Far to the south, on the plains of Piratininga, Nóbrega and Anchieta established a colegio or school for Portuguese, mixed-blood, and native children that became a model institution of its kind. Around this settlement gradually arose the town of São Paulo, an important point of departure into the interior for "adventurers in search of gold and missionaries in search of souls."

The Jesuits followed a program for the settlement of their native converts in *aldeias* (villages), where they lived under the care of the priests, completely segregated from the harmful influence of Portuguese colonists. This program provoked many clashes with the slave hunters and the planters, who had very different ends in view. In an angry protest to the *Mesa da Consciência*, a royal council entrusted with responsibility for the religious affairs of the colony, the planters sought to turn the tables on the Jesuits by claiming that residents in the Jesuit villages were "true slaves, who labored as such not only in the colegios but on the so-called Indian lands, which in the end became the estates and sugar mills of the Jesuit fathers."

The clash of interests between the planters and slave hunters and the Jesuit missionaries reached a climax about the middle of the seventeenth century, an era of great activity on the part of the bandeirantes of São Paulo. In various parts of Brazil, the landowners rose in revolt, expelled the Jesuits, and defied royal edicts proclaiming the freedom of native peoples. In 1653, Antônio Vieira, a priest of extraordinary oratorical and literary powers, arrived in Brazil with full authority from the king to settle these questions as he saw fit. During Lent, Vieira preached a famous sermon to the people of Maranhão in which he denounced indigenous slavery in terms comparable to those used by Father Montesinos on Santo Domingo in 1511. The force of Vieira's tremendous blast was weakened by his suggestion that slavery should be continued under certain conditions and by the well-known fact that the Jesuit order itself had both indigenous and black slaves. Yet there can be no doubt that the condition of natives in the Jesuit mission villages was superior to that of the slaves in the Portuguese towns and plantations. A stronger argument against Jesuit practices is the fact that the system of segregation, however benevolent in intent, represented an arbitrary and mechanical imposition of alien cultural patterns on the native population and hindered rather than facilitated true social integration.

The crown, generally sympathetic to the Jesuit position but under strong pressure from the planter class, pursued for two centuries a policy of compromise that satisfied neither Jesuits nor planters. A decisive turn came during the reform ministry of the marquis de Pombal (1750–1777), who expelled the Jesuits from Portugal and Brazil and secularized their missions. His legislation, forbidding enslavement, accepted the Jesuit thesis of indigenous rights; he also accepted the need for preparing the natives for civilized life and even the principle of concentrating them in communities under the care of administrators responsible for their education and welfare. But his policy did not segregate indígenas from the Portuguese community; it made them available for use as paid workers by the colonists and actually encouraged contact and mingling between the two races, including interracial marriage. Meanwhile, the growth of the African slave trade, also encouraged by Pombal, diminished the demand for native labor. Whether Pombal's reform legislation significantly improved the material condition of indigenous peoples is doubtful, but it contributed to their absorption into the colonial population and ultimately into the Brazilian nation. The decisive factor here was race mixture, which increased as a result of the passing of the Jesuit temporal power.

THE FRENCH AND DUTCH CHALLENGES

The dyewood, the sugar, and the tobacco of Brazil early attracted the attention of foreign powers. The French were the first to challenge Portuguese control of the colony. With the aid of indigenous allies, they made sporadic efforts to entrench themselves on the coast and in 1555 founded Rio de Janeiro as the capital of what they called Antarctic France. One cultural by-product of French contact with natives was the creation of a French image of them as "noble savages," immortalized by the sixteenth-century French philosopher Montaigne in his essay "On Cannibals." But the French offensive in Brazil was weakened by Catholic-Huguenot strife at home, and in 1567 the Portuguese commander Mem de São ousted the French and occupied the settlement of Rio de Janeiro.

A more serious threat to Portuguese sovereignty over Brazil was posed by the Dutch, whose West India Company seized and occupied for a quarter of a century (1630–1654) the richest sugar-growing portions of the Brazilian coast. Under the administration of Prince Maurice of Nassau (1637–1644), Dutch Brazil, with its capital at Recife, became the site of brilliant scientific and artistic activity. The Portuguese struggle against the Dutch became an incipient struggle for independence, uniting elements of all races from various parts of Brazil. These motley forces won victories over the Dutch at the first and second battles of Guararapes (1648–1649). Weakened by tenacious Brazilian resistance and a simultaneous war with England, the Dutch withdrew from Pernambuco in 1654. But they took with them the lessons they had learned in the production of sugar and tobacco, and reestablished themselves in the West Indies. Soon the plantations and refineries of Barbados and other Caribbean islands gave serious competition to Brazilian sugar in the world market, with a resulting fall of prices. By the last decade of the seventeenth century, the Brazilian sugar industry had entered a long period of stagnation.

THE MINERAL CYCLE, THE CATTLE INDUSTRY, AND THE COMMERCIAL SYSTEM

In this time of gloom, news of the discovery of gold in the southwestern region later known as Minas Gerais reached the coast in 1695. This discovery opened a new economic cycle, led to the first effective settlement of the interior, and initiated a major shift in Brazil's center of economic and political gravity from north to south. Large numbers of colonists from Bahia, Pernambuco, and Rio de Janeiro, accompanied by their slaves and servants, swarmed into the mining area. Their exodus from the older regions caused an acute shortage of field hands that continued until the gold boom had run its course by the middle of the eighteenth century. The crown tried to stem the exodus by legislation and by policing the trails that led to the mining area, but its efforts were in vain. For two decades (1700–1720), it had no success in asserting royal authority and collecting the royal fifth in the gold fields. Violence between rival groups, especially pioneers from São Paulo and European-born newcomers, reached the scale of civil war in 1708. The mutual weakening of the two sides as a result of these struggles finally enabled the crown to restore order.

In 1710 a new captaincy of "São Paulo and the Mines of Gold" was established; in 1720 it was divided into "São Paulo" and "Minas Gerais." In 1729 wild excitement was caused by the discovery that certain stones found in the area, hitherto thought to be crystals, were in reality diamonds; many adventurers with their slaves turned from gold to diamond washing. The great increase in the supply of diamonds to Europe upset the market, causing a serious fall in price. As a result, the Portuguese government instituted a regime of drastic control over the *Diamantina* (Diamond District) to limit mining and prevent smuggling and thus maintain prices; this regime effectively isolated the district from the outside world.

Like sugar production, the mineral cycle was marked by rapid and superficial exploitation of the new sources of wealth, followed by an equally swift decline. Mining revenue peaked about 1760, and thereafter both the river gold washings of Minas Gerais and the Diamond District suffered a progressive exhaustion of deposits. By 1809 the English traveler John Mawe could describe the gold-mining center of Villa Rica as a town that "scarcely retains a shadow of its former splendor."

Yet the mineral cycle left a permanent mark on the Brazilian landscape in the form of new centers of settlement in the southwest, not only in Minas Gerais but also in the future provinces of Goias and Matto Grosso, Brazil's Far West, which was penetrated by pioneers in search of gold. If the mining camps became deserted, the new towns survived, although with diminished vitality. The decline of the mining industry also spurred efforts to promote the agricultural and pastoral wealth of the region. The shift of the center of economic and political gravity southward from Pernambuco and Bahia to Minas Gerais and Rio de Janeiro was formally recognized in 1763, when Rio de Janeiro became the seat of the viceregal capital.

As the provinces of Minas Gerais and Goias sank into decay, the northeast experienced a partial revival based on increasing European demand for sugar, cotton, and other semitropical products. Between 1750 and 1800, Brazilian cotton production made significant progress but then declined as rapidly as a result of competition from the more efficient cotton growers of the United States. The beginnings of the coffee industry, future giant of the Brazilian economy, also date from the late colonial period.

Cattle raising also made its contribution to the advance of the Brazilian frontier and the growing importance of the south. The intensive agriculture of the coast and the concentration of population in coastal cities like Bahia and Pernambuco created a demand for fresh meat that gave an initial impulse to cattle raising. Since the expansion of plantation agriculture in the coastal zone did not leave enough land for grazing, the cattle industry inevitably had to move inland.

By the second half of the seventeenth century, the penetration of the distant São Francisco Valley from Bahia and Pernambuco was well under way. Powerful cattlemen, with their herds of cattle, their *vaqueiros* (cowboys), and their slaves, entered the *sertão* (backcountry), drove out the indigenous peoples, and established fortified ranches and villages for their retainers. Such occupation was legitimized before or after the fact by the official grant of a huge tract of land, a virtual feudal domain, to the cattle baron in question, whose word became law on his estate. The landowner's cattle provided meat for the coastal cities and mining camps, draft animals for the plantations, and hides for export to Europe.

The cattle industry later expanded into the extreme southern region of Rio Grande do Sul, which was colonized by the government in the interests of defense against Spanish expansionist designs. Here too vast land grants were made. The counterpart of the vaqueiro in the south was the *gaucho.* Like the vaqueiro, the gaucho was an expert horseman, but he reflected the blend of cultures in the Río de la Plata in his speech, a mixture of Portuguese, Spanish, and indigenous dialects; in his dress, the loose, baggy trousers of the Argentine cowboy; and in his chief implement, the *bolas,* balls of stone attached to a rawhide rope, a weapon used by the pampas natives to entangle and bring down animals.

Portugal, like Spain (with which it was loosely united, 1580–1640), pursued a mercantilist commercial policy, though not as consistently or rigorously. During this period, Brazil's commerce was firmly restricted to Portuguese nationals and ships. The Dutch, who had been the principal carriers of Brazilian sugar and tobacco to European markets, responded with extensive smuggling and a direct attack on the richest sugar-growing area of Brazil.

Following the successful Portuguese revolt against Spain, the Methuen treaty (1703) was made with England, Portugal's ally. By this treaty, British merchants were permitted to trade between Portuguese and Brazilian ports. But English ships frequently neglected the formality of touching at Lisbon and plied a direct contraband trade with the colony. Because Portuguese industry was incapable of supplying the colonists with the required quantity and quality of manufactured goods, a large proportion of the outward-bound cargoes consisted of foreign textiles and other products, of which England provided the lion's share. Thus, Portugal, master of Brazil, itself became a colony of Dutch and English merchants with offices in Lisbon.

In the eighteenth century, during the reign of Dom José I (1750–1777), his prime minister, the marquis de Pombal, an able representative of the ideology of enlightened despotism, launched an administrative and economic reform of the Portuguese Empire that bears comparison with the Bourbon reforms in Spain and Spanish America

that were taking place at the same time. Pombal's design was to nationalize Portuguese-Brazilian trade by creating a Portuguese merchant class with enough capital to compete with British merchants and a national industry whose production could dislodge English goods from the Brazilian market. The program required an active state intervention in the imperial economy through the creation of a Board of Trade, which subsidized merchant-financiers with lucrative concessions in Portugal and Brazil; the formation of companies that were granted monopolies over trade with particular regions of Brazil and were expected to develop the economies of those regions; and the institution of a policy of import substitution through state assistance to old and new industries. Despite mistakes, failures, and a partial retreat from Pombal's program after he was forced out of office in 1777, the Pombaline reform achieved at least partial success in its effort to reconquer Brazilian markets for Portugal. Between 1796 and 1802, 30 percent of all the goods shipped to Brazil consisted of Portuguese manufactures, especially cotton cloth. But the flight of the Portuguese royal family from Lisbon to Brazil in 1808 as a result of Napoleon's invasion of Portugal, followed two years later by the signing of a treaty with England that gave the British all the trade privileges they requested, effectively "dismantled the protective edifice so painfully put together since 1750." Britain once again enjoyed a virtual monopoly of trade with Brazil.

Government and Church

The donatory system of government first established in Brazil by the Portuguese crown soon proved unsatisfactory. There was a glaring contradiction between the vast powers granted to the donatories and the authority of the monarch; moreover, few donatories were able to cope with the tasks of defense and colonization for which they had been made responsible. The result was a governmental reform. In 1549, Tomé de Sousa was sent out as governor general to head a central colonial administration for Brazil. Bahia, situated about midway between the flourishing settlements of Pernambuco and São Vicente, became his capital. Gradually, the hereditary rights and privileges of the donatories were revoked, as they were replaced by governors appointed by the king. As the colony expanded, new captaincies were created. In 1763, as previously noted, the governor of Rio de Janeiro replaced his colleague at Bahia as head of the colonial administration, with the title of viceroy. In practice, however, his authority over the other governors was negligible.

THE ADMINISTRATORS AND THEIR DEFICIENCIES

The government of Portuguese Brazil broadly resembled that of the Spanish colonies in its spirit, structure, and vices. One notable difference, however, was the much smaller scale of the Portuguese administration. The differing economies of the two empires help to explain this divergence. The Spanish Indies had a relatively diversified economy that served local and regional, as well as overseas, markets and a large native population that was an important source of labor and royal tribute. Combined with a Spanish population that numbered 300,000 in 1600 (when only 30,000 Portuguese lived in Brazil), these conditions created an economic base for the rise of hundreds of towns and the need for a numerous officialdom charged with the regulation of labor, the collection of tribute, and many other fiscal and administrative duties. In Portuguese America, on the other hand, the establishment of an elaborate bureaucracy was rendered unnecessary by several factors: the overwhelming importance of exports, especially of sugar, which could be taxed when it was unloaded in Lisbon; the economic and social dominance of the plantation, which made for a weak development of urban life; and the minor role of the native population as a source of labor and royal revenue.

During the union of Portugal and Spain, the colonial policies of the two countries were aligned by the creation in 1604 of the *Conselho de India*, whose functions resembled those of the Spanish Council of the Indies. In 1736 the functions of the conselho were assumed by a newly created ministry of *Marinha e Ultramar* (Marine and Overseas). Under the king, this body framed laws for Brazil,

appointed governors, and supervised their conduct. The governor, captain general, or viceroy combined in himself military, administrative, and even some judicial duties. His power tended to be absolute but was tempered by certain factors: the constant intervention of the home government, which bound him with precise, strict, and detailed instructions; the counterweights of other authorities, especially the *relações* (high courts), which were both administrative and judicial bodies; and the existence of special administrative organs, such as the intendancies created in the gold and diamond districts, which were completely independent of the governor. Thus in Brazil, as in the Spanish colonies, there operated a system of checks and balances through overlapping functions and the oversight of some officials by others with similar or competing authority, a system that reflected above all the distrust felt by the home government for its agents. Other factors that tended to diminish the authority of the governor were the vastness of the country, the scattered population, the lack of social stability, and the existence of enormous landholdings in which the feudal power of the great planters and cattle barons was virtually unchallenged.

The most important institution of local government was the *Senado da Câmara* (municipal council). The influence of this body varied with the size of the city. Whether elected by a restricted property-owning electorate or chosen by the crown, its membership represented the ruling class of merchants, planters, and professional men. Elections were often marked by struggles for control by rival factions, planters and creoles on one side, merchants and peninsulars on the other. The authority of the câmara extended over its entire *comarca* (district), which often was very large. But its power was limited by the frequent intervention of the *ouvidor*, who usually combined his judicial functions with the administrative duties of corregedor. Generally speaking, the greater the size and wealth of the city, and the farther it was from the viceregal capital, the greater its powers.

Both the crown and the municipal councils levied numerous taxes, whose collection was usually farmed out to private collectors. In return for making a fixed payment to the treasury, these men collected the taxes for the crown and could keep the surplus once the set quota had been met. The system, of course, encouraged fraud and extortion of every kind. Another crippling burden on the population was tithes, which came to 10 percent of the total product, originally payable in kind but later only in cash. Tithes, writes the Brazilian historian Caio Prado Júnior, "ran neck and neck with conscription as one of the great scourges inflicted on the population by the colonial administration."

The besetting vices of Spanish colonial administration—inefficiency, bureaucratic attitudes, slowness, and corruption—were equally prominent in the Portuguese colonial system. Justice was not only costly but incredibly slow and complicated. Cases brought before lower courts ascended the ladder of the higher tribunals: ouvidor, relação, and on up to the crown Board of Appeals, taking as long as ten to fifteen years for resolution.

Over vast areas of the colony, however, administration and courts were virtually nonexistent. Away from the few large towns, local government often meant the rule of great landowners, who joined to their personal influence the authority of office, for it was from their ranks that the royal governors invariably appointed the *capitães móres* (district militia officers). Armed with unlimited power to enlist, command, arrest, and punish, the capitão mór became a popular symbol of despotism and oppression. Sometimes these men used the local militia as feudal levies for war against a rival family; boundary questions and questions of honor were often settled by duels or pitched battles between retainers of rival clans.

Corruption pervaded the administrative apparatus from top to bottom. The miserably paid officials prostituted their trusts in innumerable ways: embezzlement, graft, and bribery were well-nigh universal. Some improvement, at least on the higher levels of administration, took place under the auspices of the extremely able and energetic marquis de Pombal. The same tendency toward centralization that characterized Bourbon colonial policy appeared in Portuguese policy in this period. Pombal abolished the remaining hereditary captaincies, restricted the special privileges of the municipalities, and increased the power of the viceroy.

In a mercantilist spirit, Pombaline reforms sought to promote the economic advance of Brazil with a view to promoting the reconstruction of Portugal, whose condition was truly forlorn. Typical of these enlightened viceroys was the marquis de Lavradio (1769–1779), whose achievements included the transfer of coffee from Pará into São Paulo, in whose fertile red soil it was to flourish mightily. How little changed the administration of Brazil was by the Pombaline reform, however, is suggested by Lavradio's letter of instructions to his successor, in which he gloomily observed that

> as the salaries of these magistrates [the judges] are small . . . they seek to multiply their emoluments by litigation and discord, which they foment, and not only keep the people unquiet, but put them to heavy expenses, and divert them from their occupations, with the end of promoting their own vile interest and that of their subalterns, who are the principal concocters of these disorders.

During the twelve years he had governed in Brazil, wrote the viceroy, he had never found one useful establishment instituted by any of these magistrates.

THE CHURCH AND THE STATE

In Brazil, as in the Spanish colonies, church and state were intimately united. By comparison with the Spanish monarchs, however, the Portuguese kings seemed almost niggardly in their dealings with the church. But their control over its affairs, exercised through the *padroado*—the ecclesiastical patronage granted by the pope to the Portuguese king in his realm and overseas possessions—was as absolute. The king exercised his power through a special board, the *Mesa da Consciência e Ordens* (Board of Conscience and Orders). Rome, however, long maintained a strong indirect influence through the agency of the Jesuits, who were very influential in the Portuguese court until they were expelled from Portugal and Brazil in 1759.

With some honorable exceptions, notably that of the entire Jesuit order, the tone of clerical morality and conduct in Brazil was deplorably low. The clergy were often criticized for their extortionate fees and for the negligence they displayed in the performance of their spiritual duties. Occasionally, priests combined those duties with more mundane activities. Many were planters; others carried on a variety of businesses. One high-ranking crown official summed up his impressions of the clergy in the statement "All they want is money, and they care not a jot for their good name."

Yet the church and the clergy made their own contributions to the life of colonial Brazil. The clergy provided such educational and humanitarian establishments as existed in the colony. From its ranks—which were open to talent and even admitted individuals of mixed blood despite the formal requirement of a special dispensation—came most of the few distinguished names in Brazilian colonial science, learning, and literature. Among them, Jesuit writers again occupy a prominent place. But the cultural poverty of colonial Brazil is suggested by the fact that throughout the colonial period there was not a single university or even a printing press.

Masters and Slaves

Race mixture played a decisive role in the formation of the Brazilian people. The scarcity of Portuguese women in the colony, the absence of puritanical attitudes, and the despotic power of the great planters over their indigenous and black slave women all gave impetus to miscegenation. Of the three possible race combinations—white-black, white-native, black-native—the first was the most common. The immense majority of these unions were outside wedlock. In 1755 the marquis de Pombal, pursuing the goals of population growth and strengthening Brazil's borders, issued an order encouraging marriages between Portuguese men and native women and proclaiming the descendants of such unions eligible to positions of honor and dignity. This favor was not extended to other interracial unions, however.

COLOR, CLASS, AND SLAVERY

In principle, color lines were strictly drawn. A "pure" white wife or husband, for example, was indispensable to a member of the upper class. But the enormous number of mixed unions outside wedlock and the resulting large progeny, some of whom, at least, were regarded with affection by Portuguese fathers and provided with some education and property, inevitably led to the blurring of color lines and the fairly frequent phenomenon of "passing." There was a tendency to classify individuals racially, if their color was not too dark, on the basis of social and economic position rather than on their physical appearance. The English traveler Henry Koster alludes to this "polite fiction" in his anecdote concerning a certain great personage, a capitão mór, whom Koster suspected of being a mulatto. In response to his question, his servant replied, "He was, but is not now." Asked to explain, the servant continued, "Can a capitão mór be a mulatto man?"

Slavery played as important a role in the social organization of Brazil as race mixture did in its ethnic makeup. The social consequences of the system were entirely negative. Slavery brutalized enslaved Africans, corrupted both master and slave, fostered harmful attitudes with respect to the dignity of labor, and distorted the economic development of Brazil. The tendency to identify labor with slavery sharply limited the number of socially acceptable occupations in which Portuguese or free mixed-bloods could engage. This gave rise to a populous class of vagrants, beggars, "poor whites," and other degraded or disorderly elements who would not or could not compete with slaves in agriculture and industry. Inevitably, given the almost total absence of incentive to work on the part of the slave, the level of efficiency and productivity of his or her labor was very low.

Much older historical writing fostered the idea that Brazilian slavery was mild by comparison with slavery in other colonies. In part, this tradition owed its popularity to the writings of the Brazilian sociologist Gilberto Freyre, who emphasized the patriarchal relations existing between masters and slaves in the sugar plantation society

A scene of Brazilian slavery. New arrivals from Africa wait in a slave dealer's establishment while the seated proprietor negotiates the sale of a child to a prospective customer. [Jean-Baptiste Debret, *Voyage Pittoresque et Historique au Bresil*. By permission of The British Library]

of the northeast. But the slaves described by Freyre were usually house slaves who occupied a privileged position. Their situation was very different from that of the great majority of slaves, who worked on the sugar and tobacco plantations of Bahia and Pernambuco. During harvest time and when the mills were grinding the cane, says Charles Boxer, the slaves sometimes worked round the clock and often at least from dawn to dusk. In the off-season, the hours were not so long. But "discipline was maintained with a severity that often degenerated into sadistic cruelty where the infliction of corporal punishment was concerned." A royal dispatch of 1700 denounced the barbarity with which owners of both sexes treated their slaves and singled out for special condemnation

the practice of women owners who forced their female slaves to engage in prostitution.

The harsh labor discipline on the plantation reflected calculations of cost and profit. "Slaveowners," says Stuart Schwartz, "estimated that a slave could produce on the average about three-quarters of a ton of sugar a year. At the prices of the period, this meant in effect that a slave would produce in two or three years an amount of sugar equal to the slave's original purchase price and the cost of maintenance. Thus if the slave lived only five or six years, the investment of the planter would be doubled, and a new and vigorous replacement could be bought." This way of reasoning provided little incentive for improving work conditions or fostering a higher birthrate among slaves, since children would have to be supported for twelve or fourteen years before they became productive. The basic theory of slave management, concludes Schwartz, seems to have been: "Work them hard, make a profit, buy another."

Obviously, the treatment of slaves varied considerably with the temperament of the individual slave owner. Although the crown provided slaves with legal means of redress, there is little evidence that these were effective in relieving their plight. The church, represented on the plantation by a chaplain paid and housed by the landowner, probably exerted little influence on the problem. A very low rate of reproduction among slaves and frequent suicides speak volumes concerning their condition. Many slaves ran away and formed *quilombos* (settlements of fugitive slaves in the bush). The most famous of these was the so-called republic of Palmares, founded in 1603 in the interior of the northeastern captaincy of Alagoas. A self-sufficient African kingdom with several thousand inhabitants who lived in ten villages spread over a 90-mile territory, Palmares was exceptional among quilombos in its size, complex organization, and ability to survive repeated expeditions sent against it by colonial authorities. Not until 1694 did a Paulista army destroy it after a two-year siege. But the quilombos continued to alarm planters and authorities; as late as 1760 they complained of the threat posed by quilombos around Bahia.

Manumission was another way that slaves achieved freedom. Slaveowners frequently freed favored slaves or children (sometimes their own) who were reared in the *Casa Grande* (Big House), in wills or baptisms. In other cases slaves bought their freedom, sometimes combining the resources of family and friends. The grant of freedom might be conditional on assurance of further service of one kind or another. Thus, in a variety of ways, combining economic, cultural, and religious motives, a class of freedmen and their descendants arose and by the eighteenth century had achieved a certain importance in the economic and social life of colonial Brazil.

Slavery played a decisive role in the economic life of colonial Brazil and placed its stamp on all social relations. In addition to masters and slaves,

however, there existed a large free peasant population of varied racial makeup who lived on estates and in villages and hamlets scattered throughout the Brazilian countryside. Some were small landowners, often possessing a few slaves of their own, who brought their sugar cane for processing or sale to the *senhor de engenho* (sugar-mill owner). Their economic inferiority made their independence precarious, and their land and slaves tended to pass into the hands of the great planters in a process of concentration of landownership and growing social stratification. The majority, however, were *lavradores, moradores,* or *foreiros* (tenant farmers or sharecroppers) who owed labor and allegiance to a great landowner in return for the privilege of farming a parcel of land. Other free peasants were squatters who in the seventeenth and eighteenth centuries pushed out of the coastal zone to settle in the backcountry where they were regarded as intruders by the cattle barons and other great landowners who laid claim to those lands.

Other free commoners were the artisans, including many black or mulatto freedmen, who served the needs of the urban population. An important group of salaried workers—overseers, mechanics, coopers, and the like—supplied the special skills required by the sugar industry.

LARGE ESTATES AND COLONIAL TOWNS

The nucleus of Brazilian social as well as economic organization was the large estate, or fazenda, which usually rested on a base of black slavery. The large estate centered about the Casa Grande and constituted a patriarchal community that included the owner and his family, his chaplain and overseers, his slaves, his *obrigados* (sharecroppers), and his *agregados* (retainers), free men of low social status who received the landowner's protection and assistance in return for a variety of services.

In this self-contained world, an intricate web of relations arose between the master and his slaves and white or mixed-blood subordinates. No doubt, long contact sometimes tended to mellow and humanize these relationships and added to mere commercial relationships a variety of emotional ties. The protective role of the master found expression in the relationship of *compadrio* (godfathership), in which the master became sponsor or godfather of a baptized child or a bridal pair whose marriage he witnessed. The system implied relations of mutual aid and a paternalistic interest in the welfare of the landowner's people. But it by no means excluded intense exploitation of those people or the display of the most ferocious cruelty if they should cross him or dispute his absolute power.

In the sugar-growing northeast, the great planters became a distinct aristocratic class, possessed of family traditions and pride in their name and blood. In the cattle-raising regions of the sertão and the south, the small number of slaves, the self-reliant character of the vaqueiro or gaucho, and the greater freedom of movement of workers gave society a somewhat more democratic tone. Everywhere, however, says the Brazilian historian Caio Prado Júnior, "the existence of pronounced social distinctions and the absolute and patriarchal domination of the owner and master were elements invariably associated with all the colony's large landed estates."

By contrast with the decisive importance of the fazenda, most colonial towns were mere appendages of the countryside, dominated politically and socially by the rural magnates. Even in the few large cities like Bahia and Rio de Janeiro, the dominant social group was composed of *fazendeiros* and sugar-mill owners. These men often left the supervision of their estates to majordomos and overseers, preferring the pleasures and bustle of the cities to the dreary routines of the countryside. But in the city lived other social groups that disputed or shared power with the great landowners: high officials of the colonial administration; dignitaries of the church; wealthy professional men, especially lawyers; and the large merchants, almost exclusively peninsulars, who monopolized the export-import trade and financed the industry of the planters.

The social position of the merchant was not very high, because of the medieval prejudice against commerce brought over from Portugal (a prejudice that did not prevent the highest officials from engaging in trade, albeit discreetly), but nothing barred the merchants from membership on the municipal councils. The conflict between native-born landowners and European-born merchants, aggravated by nationalistic resentment against upstart immigrants, sometimes broke out into armed struggle. An illustration is the petty War of the Mascates (1710–1711) between Olinda, provincial capital of Pernambuco, which was dominated by the sugar planters, and its neighboring seaport of Recife, which was controlled by the merchants.

This struggle between *mazombos* (Brazilian-born whites) and *reinóis* (peninsulars) foreshadowed the later rise of a broader Brazilian nationalism and the first projects of Brazilian independence. In the late eighteenth century, Minas Gerais, the most urbanized Brazilian region, had the most diversified economy. It became a seat of much unrest as a result of official efforts to reinforce the area's dependency on Portuguese exporters, collect large amounts of delinquent taxes, and impose a new head tax. A conspiracy to revolt and establish a republic on the North American model was hatched in 1788–1789 by a group of dissidents, most of whom were highly placed members of the colonial elite. The only leading conspirator who was not a member of the aristocracy was José da Silva Xavier, a military officer of low rank who practiced the part-time profession of "toothpuller," whence the name of *Tiradentes* by which he is known in Brazilian history. An enthusiast for the American Revolution, Silva Xavier apparently possessed copies of the Declaration of Independence and American state constitutions. When the conspiracy was discovered, all the principal conspirators were condemned to death, but the sentences were commuted to exile for all but the plebeian Silva Xavier. His barbarous execution, which he faced with great courage, made him a martyr as well as a precursor of Brazilian independence.

The Bourbon Reforms and Spanish America

7

HE DEATH OF the sickly Charles II in November 1700 marked the end of an era in Spanish history and the beginning of a new and better day, although the signs under which the new day began were far from hopeful. On his deathbed the unhappy Charles, more kingly in his dying than he had ever been before, fought desperately to prevent the triumph of an intrigue for the partition of the Spanish dominions among three claimants of that inheritance, the prince of Bavaria, the archduke Charles of Austria, and Louis XIV's grandson, Philip of Anjou. In one of his last acts, Charles signed a will naming the French Philip, who became Philip V, successor to all his dominions.

English fears at the prospect of a union of France and Spain under a single ruler precipitated the War of the Spanish Succession (1702–1713). The war ended with the Treaty of Utrecht (1713), which granted to Great Britain Gibraltar and Minorca, major trade concessions in the Spanish Indies, and a guarantee against a union of the French and Spanish thrones under Philip. Another peace treaty, concluded the following year, gave the Spanish Netherlands and Spain's Italian possessions to Austria.

Reform and Recovery

Spain's humiliating losses deepened the prevailing sense of pessimism and defeatism, but there were compensations: the shock of defeat in the succession war drove home the need for sweeping reform of Spanish institutions; the loss of the Netherlands and the Italian possessions left Spain with a more manageable, more truly Spanish empire, consisting of the kingdoms of Castile and Aragon and the Indies.

THE BOURBON REFORMS

The return of peace permitted the new dynasty to turn its attention to implementing a program of reform inspired by the French model. The reform and ensuing revival of Spain are associated with three princes of the House of Bourbon: Philip V (1700–1746) and his two sons, Ferdinand VI (1746–1759) and Charles III (1759–1788). Under the aegis of "enlightened despotism," the Bourbon kings attempted nothing less than a total overhaul of existing political and economic structures, a total renovation of the national life. Only such sweeping reform could close the gap that separated Spain from the foremost European powers and arm the country with the weapons—a powerful industry, a prosperous agriculture, a strong middle class—it needed to prevent its defeat by England and England's allies in the struggle for empire that dominated the eighteenth century.

The movement for reform, although carried out within the framework of royal absolutism and Catholic orthodoxy, inevitably provoked the hostility

131

of reactionary elements within the church and the nobility. As a result, the Bourbons, although supported by such liberal grandees as the count of Floridablanca and the count of Aranda, recruited many of their principal ministers and officials from the ranks of the lesser nobility and the small middle class. These men were strongly influenced by the rationalist spirit of the French Encyclopedists,[1] although they rejected French anticlericalism and deism. They were characteristic of the Spanish Enlightenment in their rigid orthodoxy in religion and politics combined with enthusiastic pursuit of useful knowledge, criticism of defects in the church and clergy, and belief in the power of informed reason to improve society by reorganizing it along more rational lines.

The work of national reconstruction began under Philip V but reached its climax under Charles III. This great reformer-king attempted to revive Spanish industry by removing the stigma attached to manual labor, establishing state-owned textile factories, inviting foreign technical experts into Spain, and encouraging technical education. He aided agriculture by curbing the privileges of the Mesta, or stockbreeders' corporation, and by settling colonies of Spanish and foreign peasants in abandoned regions of the peninsula. He continued and expanded the efforts of his predecessors to encourage shipbuilding and foster trade and communication by the building of roads and canals. Clerical influence declined as a result of the expulsion of the Jesuits in 1767 and of decrees restricting the authority of the Inquisition. Under the cleansing influence of able and honest ministers, a new spirit of austerity and service began to appear among public officials.

But the extent of the changes that took place in Spanish economic and social life under the Bourbons must not be exaggerated. The crown, linked by a thousand bonds to the feudal nobility and church, never touched the foundation of the old order, the land monopoly of the nobility, with its corollaries of mass poverty and archaic agricul-

tural methods. As a result of these weaknesses, as well as the lack of capital for industrial development and the debility of the Spanish middle class, Spain, despite marked advances in population and production, remained at the close of the era a second- or third-class power by comparison with Great Britain, France, or Holland.

The outbreak of the French Revolution, which followed by a few months the death of Charles III in December 1788, brought the reform era effectively to a halt. Frightened by the overthrow of the French monarchy and the execution of his royal kinsman, Charles IV and his ministers turned sharply to the right. The leading reformers were banished or imprisoned, and the importation of French rationalist and revolutionary literature was forbidden. Yet the clock could not be and was not entirely turned back, either in Spain or in the colonies. It was under the corrupt government of Charles IV, for example, that the expedition of Francisco Xavier Balmis sailed from Spain (1803) to carry the procedure of vaccination to the Spanish dominions in America and Asia, an act that probably saved innumerable lives.

In the field of colonial reform, the Bourbons moved slowly and cautiously, as was natural in view of the powerful vested interests identified with the old order of things. There was never any thought of giving a greater measure of self-government to the colonists or of permitting them to trade more freely with the non-Spanish world. On the contrary, the Bourbons centralized colonial administration still further, with a view to making it more efficient. In addition, their commercial reforms were designed to diminish smuggling and strengthen the exclusive commercial ties between Spain and its colonies, to "reconquer" the colonies economically for Spain.

REVIVAL OF COLONIAL COMMERCE AND BREAKDOWN OF TRADING MONOPOLY

The first Bourbon, Philip V, concentrated his efforts on an attempt to reduce smuggling and to revive the fleet system, which had fallen into decay in the late seventeenth century. With the Treaty of Utrecht, the English merchant class had scored an

---

[1]Writers of the famous *Encyclopédie* (1751–1780), who were identified with the Enlightenment and advocated deism and a rationalist world outlook.

impressive victory in the shape of the asiento; the South Sea Company was granted the exclusive right to supply slaves to Spanish America, with the additional right of sending a shipload of merchandise to Portobelo every year. It was well known that the slaveships carried contraband merchandise, as did the provision ships that accompanied the annual ship and reloaded it with goods. Buenos Aires, where the South Sea Company maintained a trading post, was another funnel through which English traders poured large quantities of contraband goods that penetrated as far as Peru.

The Spanish government sought to check smuggling in the Caribbean by commissioning *guardacostas* (private warships), which prowled the main lanes of trade in search of ships loaded with contraband. It also tried to end the monopoly of the Cádiz *consulado* (merchant guild), whose members alone could load Spanish merchant vessels. The first breach in the wall of this monopoly came in the 1720s, with the organization of the Caracas Company, which was founded with the aid of capitalists in the Biscay region. In return for the privilege of trade with Venezuela, this company undertook to police the coast against smugglers and develop the resources of the region. Despite the company's claims of success in achieving these objectives, it failed to stop a lively contraband trade with the nearby Dutch colony of Curaçao or to overcome the bitter hostility of Venezuelan planters and merchants, who accused the company of paying too little for cocoa, taking too little tobacco and other products, and charging excessive prices for Spanish goods.

Biscayan and Catalan capital organized similar companies for trade with Havana, Hispaniola, and other places the old system of colonial trade had left undeveloped. These enterprises, however, were financial failures, in part because of inadequate capital, in part because of poor management. These breaches of the Cádiz monopoly brought no benefits to creole merchants, who continued to be almost completely excluded from the legal trade between Spain and its colonies.

The first Bourbons made few changes in the administrative structure of colonial government, contenting themselves with efforts to improve the quality of administration by more careful selection of officeholders. One major reorganization was the separation of the northern Andean region (present-day Ecuador, Colombia, and Venezuela) from the viceroyalty of Peru. In 1739 it became a viceroyalty, named New Granada, with its capital at Santa Fe (modern Bogotá). This change had strategic significance, reflecting a desire to provide better protection for the Caribbean coast, especially the fortress of Cartagena. It also reflected the rapid growth of population in the central highlands of Colombia. Within the new viceroyalty, Venezuela was named a captaincy general, with its capital at Caracas, and became virtually independent of Santa Fe.

The movement for colonial reform, like the program of domestic reform, reached a climax in the reign of Charles III. Part of this reform had been foreshadowed in the writings of a remarkable Spanish economist and minister of finance and war under Ferdinand VI, José Campillo. Shortly before his death in 1743, Campillo wrote a memorial on colonial affairs that advocated the abolition of the Cádiz monopoly, a reduction of duties on goods bound for America, the organization of a frequent mail service to America, the encouragement of trade between the colonies, and the development of colonial agriculture and other economic activities that did not compete with Spanish manufacturers. Most of these recommendations were incorporated in a report made to Charles III by a royal commission in 1765. The shock of Spain's defeat in the Seven Years' War, which cost it the loss of Florida and almost the loss of Cuba, provided impetus for a program of imperial reorganization and reform.

In this period, the trading monopoly of Cádiz was gradually eliminated. In 1765 commerce with the West Indies was thrown open to seven other ports besides Cádiz and Seville; this reform, coming at a time when Cuban sugar production was beginning to expand, gave a sharp stimulus to the island's economy. This privilege was gradually extended to other regions until, by the famous decree of free trade of 1778, commerce was permitted between all qualified Spanish ports and all the American provinces except Mexico and

Venezuela. In 1789, New Spain and Venezuela were thrown open to trade on the same terms.[2] The burdensome duties levied on this trade were also replaced by simple ad valorem duties of 6 or 7 percent. Restrictions on intercolonial trade were also progressively lifted, but this trade was largely limited to non-European products. A major beneficiary of this change was the Río de la Plata area, which in 1776 was opened for trade with the rest of the Indies. Meanwhile, the Casa de Contratación, symbol of the old order, steadily declined in importance until it closed its doors in 1789. A similar fate overtook the venerable Council of the Indies. As a consultative body it lasted on into the nineteenth century, but most of its duties were entrusted to a colonial minister appointed by the king.

The success of the "free-trade" policy was reflected in a spectacular increase in the value of Spain's commerce with Spanish America, an increase said to have amounted to about 700 percent between 1778 and 1788. The entrance of new trading centers and merchant groups into the Indies trade, the reduction of duties, and the removal of irksome restrictions had the effect of increasing the volume of business, reducing prices, and perhaps diminishing contraband (although one cannot speak with certainty here, for the easing of restrictions inevitably facilitated the activity of smugglers).

But the achievements of the Bourbon commercial reform must not be overestimated. The reform ultimately failed in its aim of reconquering colonial markets for Spain for two basic reasons: first, Spain's industrial weakness, which the best efforts of the Bourbons were unable to overcome, and second, Spain's closely related inability to keep its sea-lanes to America open in time of war with England, when foreign traders again swarmed into

Spanish-American ports. Indeed, the Spanish government openly confessed its inability to supply the colonies with needed goods in time of war by lifting the ban against foreign vessels of neutral origin (which meant United States ships, above all) during the years from 1797 to 1799 and again in the years from 1805 to 1809. This permission to trade with neutrals gave rise to spirited commerce between the United States and the Caribbean area and the Río de la Plata.

INCREASED ECONOMIC ACTIVITY

Perhaps the most significant result of the Bourbon commercial reform was the stimulus it gave to economic activity in Spanish America. To what extent this increased economic activity should be ascribed to the beneficial effects of the Bourbon reform; to what degree it resulted from the general economic upsurge in western Europe in the eighteenth century cannot be stated with certainty. What is certain is that the latter part of the century saw a rising level of agricultural, pastoral, and mining production in Spanish America. Stimulated by the Bourbon reform and by the growing European demand for sugar, tobacco, hides, and other staples, production of these products rose sharply in this period. There developed a marked trend toward regional specialization and monoculture in the production of cash crops. After 1770 coffee, grown in Venezuela and Cuba, joined cacao and sugar as a major export crop of the Caribbean area. The gradual increase in population also stimulated the production of food crops for local markets, notably wheat, preferred over maize by the European population. Tithe collections offer an index of agricultural growth: in the decade from 1779 to 1789, tithe collections in the principal agricultural areas were 40 percent greater than in the previous decade.

It appears, however, that agricultural prosperity was largely limited to areas producing export crops or with easy access to domestic markets. David Brading paints a gloomy picture of the financial condition of the Mexican haciendas in the eighteenth century. Except in the Valley of

---

[2]It must be stressed, however, that these reforms did not seriously weaken the dominant role of the Cádiz monopolists and their American agents in colonial trade. As late as 1790, more than 85 percent of the trade moved through Cádiz, thanks to its superior facilities for shipping, insurance, warehousing, and communication.

Mexico, the Bajío,[3] and the Guadalajara region, markets were too small to yield satisfactory returns. Great distances, poor roads, and high freight costs prevented haciendas from developing their productive capacity beyond the requirements of the local market. Private estates were worse off than church haciendas, because they had to pay tithes and sales taxes and bore the double burden of absentee landowners and resident administrators. Great landed families who possessed numerous estates in different regions, producing varied products for multiple markets, were more fortunate; their profits averaged from 6 to 9 percent of capital value in the late eighteenth century. Thanks to cheap labor, however, even a low productivity yielded large revenues, which enabled hacendados to maintain a lavish, seigneurial style of life. Many haciendas were heavily indebted to ecclesiastical institutions, the principal bankers of the time.

The increase in agricultural production, it should be noted, resulted from more extensive use of land and labor rather than from the use of improved implements or techniques. The inefficient *latifundio* (great estate), which used poorly paid peon labor, and the slave plantation accounted for the bulk of commercial agricultural production. The Prussian traveler Alexander von Humboldt, commenting on the semifeudal land tenure system of Mexico, observed that "the property of New Spain, like that of Old Spain, is in a great measure in the hands of a few powerful families, who have gradually absorbed the smaller estates. In America, as well as in Europe, large commons are condemned to the pasturage of cattle and to perpetual sterility."

The increasing concentration of landownership in Mexico and the central Andes in the second half of the eighteenth century reflected the desire of hacendados to eliminate the competition of small producers in restricted markets and to maintain prices at a high level. To help achieve this end, great landowners hoarded their harvests in their granaries and sent grain to market at that time of the year when it was scarcest and prices were at their highest. Given the low productivity of colonial agriculture, however, such natural disasters as drought, premature frosts, or excessive rains easily upset the precarious balance between food supplies and population, producing frightful famines like that of 1785–1787 in central Mexico. Thousands died of hunger or diseases induced by that famine.

What sugar, cacao, and coffee were for the Caribbean area, hides were for the Río de la Plata. The rising European demand for leather for footwear and industrial purposes and the permission given in 1735 for direct trade with Spain in register ships sparked an economic upsurge in the Plata area. The unregulated hunting of wild cattle on the open pampa soon gave way to the herding of cattle on established *estancias* (cattle ranches). By the end of the century, these were often of huge size—15 to 20 square leagues—with as many as eighty or a hundred thousand head of cattle. By 1790, Buenos Aires was exporting nearly a million and a half hides annually. The meat of the animal, hitherto almost worthless except for the small quantity that could be consumed immediately, now gained in value as a result of the demand for salt beef, processed in large-scale *saladeros* (salting plants). Markets for salt beef were found above all in the Caribbean area, especially Cuba, where it was chiefly used for feeding the slave population. The growth of cattle raising in La Plata, however, was attended by the concentration of land in ever fewer hands and took place at the expense of agriculture, which remained in a very depressed state.

The eighteenth century also saw a marked revival of silver mining in the Spanish colonies. Peru and Mexico shared in this advance, but the Mexican mines forged far ahead of their Peruvian rivals in the Bourbon era. The mine owners included creoles and peninsulars, but the Spanish merchants who financed the mining operations received most of the profits. As in the case of agriculture, the increase in silver production was not due primarily to improved technique; it resulted from the opening of many new as well as old mines

[3]A relatively urbanized area with a diversified economy (agriculture, mining, manufacturing) lying within the modern Mexican states of Guanajuato and Querétaro.

and the growth of the labor force. The crown, however, especially under Charles III, contributed materially to the revival by offering new incentives to entrepreneurs and by its efforts to overcome the backwardness of the mining industry. The incentives included reductions in taxes and in the cost of mercury, a government monopoly.

In New Spain the crown promoted the establishment of a mining guild (1777) whose activities included the operation of a bank to finance development. Under this guild's auspices was founded the first school of mines in America (1792). Staffed by able professors and provided with modern equipment, it offered excellent theoretical and practical instruction and represented an important source of Enlightenment thought in Mexico. Foreign and Spanish experts, accompanied by teams of technicians, came to Mexico and Peru to show the mine owners the advantages of new machinery and techniques. These praiseworthy efforts were largely frustrated by the traditionalism of the mine owners, by lack of capital to finance changes, and by mismanagement. Yet the production of silver steadily increased. Supplemented by the gold of Brazil, it helped spark the Industrial Revolution in northern Europe and stimulate commercial activity on a worldwide scale. In addition, American silver helped the Bourbons meet the enormous expenses of their chronic wars.

In 1774, José Antonio Areche, the reformist *fiscal* (attorney) to Viceroy Antonio María Bucareli y Ursua of Spain, prepared a report on the state of the Mexican economy. He described it as a backward economic system, marked by practices and ideas that offered insuperable obstacles to modernization. People were deserting the countryside for the city, filling the cities with the unemployed and unemployable. A major cause of this flight was an inefficient agriculture whose low productivity and unprofitability were due to primitive tilling methods, heavily indebted estates, and poor working conditions. Areche complained of landowners who paid wages in goods rather than in cash, treated their workers badly, and preferred to concentrate on production of a few basic commodities rather than experiment with new products and seek new markets. Retail trade lagged because of the practice of paying workers in goods rather than cash and because too few coins were in circulation. Areche also criticized merchants who preferred to engage in the forced sale of goods to indigenous villages (*repartimiento de mercancías*), failing to see that these communities were potential vast markets for a wide variety of consumer goods. But Areche failed to see that Spain's use of Mexico as an "extraction machine," in the words of John Coatsworth, that funneled off a substantial part of the colony's silver output (some 500 to 600 million pesos in the last half-century of Spanish rule) contributed to Mexico's lack of capital formation and structural economic backwardness.

Areche's report makes it clear that increased economic activity in the Bourbon era was not accompanied by significant qualitative changes in the colonial economy; the phrase "growth without development," often applied to Latin America's economic performance in modern times, applies equally to the colonial economy in the Bourbon era.

Colonial manufacturing, after a long and fairly consistent growth, began to decline in the last part of the eighteenth century, principally because of the influx of cheap foreign wares with which the domestic products could not compete. The textile and wine industries of western Argentina fell into decay as they lost their markets in Buenos Aires and Montevideo to lower-priced foreign wines and cloth. The textile producers of the province of Quito in Ecuador complained of injury from the same cause. In the Mexican manufacturing center of Puebla, production of chinaware slumped catastrophically between 1793 and 1802. Puebla and Querétaro, however, continued to be important centers of textile manufacturing.

Although Spain adopted mercantilist legislation designed to restrict colonial manufacturing—especially of fine textiles—this legislation seems to have been only a small deterrent to the growth of large-scale manufacturing. More important deterrents were lack of investment capital, the characteristic preference of Spaniards for land and mining as fields of investment, and a semiservile system of labor that was equally harmful to the workers and to productivity. Humboldt, who visited the woolen workshops of Querétaro in 1803, was disagreeably impressed

> not only with the great imperfection of the technical process in the preparation for dyeing, but in a particular manner also with the unhealthiness of the situation, and the bad treatment to which the workers are exposed. Free men, Indians, and people of color are confounded with the criminals distributed by justice among the manufactories, in order to be compelled to work. All appear half naked, covered with rags, meager, and deformed. Every workshop resembles a dark prison. The doors, which are double, remain constantly shut, and the workmen are not permitted to quit the house. Those who are married are only allowed to see their families on Sunday. All are unmercifully flogged, if they commit the smallest trespass on the order established in the manufactory.

One of the few large-scale lines of industry was the manufacture of cigars and cigarettes. In the same town of Querétaro, Humboldt visited a tobacco factory that employed three thousand workers, including nineteen hundred women.

LABOR SYSTEMS IN THE EIGHTEENTH CENTURY

Humboldt's comments testify to the persistence of servitude and coercion as essential elements of the labor system from the beginning to the end of the colonial period. Despite the Bourbons' theoretical dislike of forced labor, they sought to tighten legal enforcement of debt peonage in the Indies. Concerned with more efficient collection of tribute, José de Gálvez, the reforming minister of Charles III, tried to attach the natives more firmly to their pueblos and haciendas. In 1769 he introduced in New Spain the system of clearance certificates, documents that certified that peons had no outstanding debts and could seek employment with other landowners. The mobility of peons who lacked these papers could be restricted. Debt peonage was authorized by the Mining Ordinances of New Spain and was also practiced in the gold and silver mines of Chile, where a system of clearance

certificates like that used in Mexico was employed. A recent study by James D. Riley notes a trend in Bourbon policy to make debts "considerably less coercive" in Mexico after 1785, but also notes that there was little official reluctance to pursue debtors and force them to pay up or work. On Jesuit farms in eighteenth-century Quito (Ecuador), says Nicholas Cushner, "the debt was a mechanism for maintaining a stable work force" whose wages were pitifully low. "It was an Indian analogue of black slavery," adds Cushner.

In practice, as previously noted, the importance of debt peonage and the severity of its enforcement depended on the availability of labor. In New Spain, by the late eighteenth century, the growth of the labor force through population increase and the elimination of small producers had sharply reduced the importance of debt as a means of securing and holding laborers. Eric Van Young, for example, has documented a reduction of the per capita indebtedness of resident peons in the Guadalajara area, suggesting their decreased bargaining power in dealing with employers. The new situation enabled hacendados to retain or discharge workers in line with changing levels of production. Thus in late eighteenth-century Mexico, landowners simply dismissed workers when crop failures occurred in order to save on their rations. These changes were accompanied by a tendency for real wages and rural living standards to decline.

In the Andean area, the mita—in provinces subject to it—continued to play an important role in the provision of mining and agricultural labor almost to the end of the colonial period. In other provinces, agricultural labor was theoretically free, but heavy tribute demands and the operations of the repartimiento de mercancías created a need for cash that compelled many natives to seek employment on Spanish haciendas. These yanaconas included a large number of so-called *forasteros* ("outsiders") who had fled their native pueblos to escape the dreaded mita service and tribute burdens. In addition to working the hacendado's land, these laborers or sharecroppers and their families had to render personal service in the master's household. Theoretically free, their dependent status must have sharply limited their mobility.

EARLY LABOR STRUGGLES

Our knowledge of labor struggles in colonial Spanish America is fragmentary, in part because historians took little interest in the subject until recently. The first labor conflicts of a relatively modern type seem to have taken place in late eighteenth-century Mexico, the colony with the most developed and diversified economy. Strikes sometimes took place in artisan shops; in 1784, for example, the workers in the bakery of Basilio Badamler went on strike to protest "horrible working conditions." More commonly, they occurred in a few industries having large concentrations of workers or a division of labor that promoted workers' cooperation and solidarity. One large-scale industry was the manufacture of cigars and cigarettes by the royal tobacco monopoly, whose founding was accompanied by a ruthless suppression (1773–1776) of artisan production of these goods. The immense factory operated by the monopoly in Mexico City employed about 7,000 workers of both sexes. The workers, who included natives, mestizos, and some Spaniards, were paid in cash, and the annual payroll in the 1780s and 1790s came to about 750,000 pesos. The militancy of these workers was displayed in strikes and protests and worried the authorities. In 1788 the consulado of Mexico City declared that this large assembly of workers presented a threat to public order, citing a march on the viceroy's palace caused by a "small increase" in the length of the workday. The workers, heedless of the guards, swarmed into the palace and occupied the patios, stairs, and corridors. The viceroy, having heard their complaint, "prudently gave them a note ordering the factory's administrator to rescind that change, and so with God's help that tumult ended, the multitude left, bearing that note as if in triumph, and the viceroy decided to overlook that turbulent action, so likely to cause sedition." In 1794 the workers again marched on the viceregal palace to protest a change in the contractual arrangement that permitted them to take part of their work home to prepare for the next day's tasks.

A more dramatic labor struggle broke out in the 1780s in the Mexican silver mining industry. The scene of the conflict was the mines of Real del Monte in northern Mexico. Here, as in all other Mexican silver mines, the majority of the work force was free, but a minority of the workers were conscripted from the surrounding indigenous villages through a repartimiento, or labor draft. Press gangs also picked up men charged with "idleness" or "vagrancy" to relieve the chronic shortage of labor. It was the grievances of the free skilled workers, however, that caused a series of confrontations and ultimately a work stoppage with an arrogant, unyielding employer. The extreme division of labor in the silver mining industry—to get the ore out of the vein below and load it on mules above required some thirty different specialized tasks—tended to develop a sense of shared interests and cooperation among the workers.

Work in the mines was dangerous, daily exposing the miners to loss of life and limb through accidents and even more to debilitating or fatal diseases. According to Francisco de Gamboa, the leading Mexican mining expert of the time, the miners worked "in terror of ladders giving way, rocks sliding, heavy loads breaking their backs, dripping icy waters, diseases, and the damp, hot, suffocating heat." Humboldt, who visited Mexico in the last years of the colony, claimed that Mexican miners seldom lived past the age of thirty-five. But the pay was good by colonial standards: workers who went below received four reales (fifty cents) for each twelve-hour shift (one real would buy a pound of wool or five pounds of beef or veal), more than double the pay of agricultural workers. This customary pay was supplemented by the *partido*, the skilled worker's right to a certain share of his day's haul of silver ore over an assigned quota.

Attempts by mine owner Romero de Terreros to lower wage rates of *peones* (ore carriers) from four to three reales, increase quotas, and gradually eliminate partidos provoked a series of crises culminating in the strike. A sympathetic parish priest advised the workers on legal ways to achieve their objectives and sought to mediate their dispute with the employer. (The priest was later expelled from the pueblo for his activism.) Eventually, the state intervened, aware of the critical importance of silver production to the royal treasury and of the workers' strong bargaining position because of the chronic labor shortage. Francisco de Gamboa, the leading expert on mining and mining law, was sent to arbitrate the conflict. His arbitration satisfied virtually all the workers' demands: abusive bosses were fired, the pay cuts revoked, and the right to partidos confirmed in writing.[4]

Doris Ladd has written a brilliant, sensitive reconstruction of these events. She interprets the struggle at Real del Monte as a class struggle prior to the existence of a working class—reflecting an emerging class consciousness—and describes the workers' ideas as "radical" and "revolutionary." She cites the strikers' insistence on social and economic justice, expressed in the words of their lawyer: "It is a precept in all systems of divine, natural, and secular law that there should be a just proportion between labor and profit." But this appeal for justice had a limited scope and significance. It applied to a group of relatively privileged, skilled free workers, but did not call into question the forced labor of natives dragged by press gangs from their homes to the mines. Thanks to a set of favorable conditions, the strikers won a victory, meaning a return to the situation that had prevailed before the dispute broke out. But that victory left the conscripted indigenous workers in the same intolerable conditions as before. One wonders whether ideas that accepted such servitude as normal can be described as truly "radical" or "revolutionary."

POLITICAL REFORMS

Under Charles III, the work of territorial reorganization of the sprawling empire continued. The viceroyalty of Peru, already diminished by the creation of New Granada, was further curtailed by the creation in 1776 of the viceroyalty of the

Río de la Plata, with its capital at Buenos Aires. This act reflected official Spanish concern over the large volume of contraband in the estuary. It also reflected fear of a possible foreign attack on the area by the British, who had recently entrenched themselves in the nearby Malvinas, or Falkland, Islands, or by the Portuguese who, advancing southward from Brazil, had established the settlement of Sacramento on the banks of the estuary, a base from which they threatened shipping and the town of Montevideo. To put an end to this danger, the Spanish government mounted a major military expedition designed to establish full control of both banks of the river. The commander Pedro de Cevallos came out with the temporary title of viceroy of Buenos Aires. In 1778 the viceroyalty was made permanent with the appointment of the viceroy Juan José de Vértiz y Salcedo, whose rule of over a decade saw a remarkable growth in the prosperity of the area. This prosperity owed much to the decree of "free trade" of 1778, which authorized direct trade between Buenos Aires and Spain and permitted intercolonial trade. In 1783 the establishment of a royal audiencia at Buenos Aires completed the liberation of the Río de la Plata provinces from the distant rule of Lima. The inclusion of Upper Peru in the new viceroyalty, with the resulting redirection of the flow of Potosí silver from Lima to Buenos Aires, signified a stunning victory for the landowners and merchants of Buenos Aires over their mercantile rivals in Lima.

The trend toward decentralization in the administration of Spanish America, combined with a greater stress on supervision and control from Madrid, reflected not only the struggle against foreign military and commercial penetration but an enlightened awareness of the problems of communication and government posed by the great distances between the various provinces, an awareness spurred by advances in cartography and knowledge of the geography of the continent in general. Two indications of this tendency were the greater autonomy enjoyed by the captaincies general in the eighteenth century and the increase in their number. Thus Venezuela and Chile were raised to the status of a captaincy general. The

---

[4]But the workers' victory at the Real del Monte was not the usual outcome of labor conflicts in the mining areas of New Spain in this period. In the late Bourbon era, Mexican mine owners displayed a more aggressive attitude toward their workers. Supported by military and paramilitary forces, they often succeeded in eliminating or reducing the partidos that workers were permitted to keep and in reducing wages.

Viceroyalties in Latin America in 1780

increased autonomy enjoyed by the captains general enabled an enlightened ruler like Ambrosio O'Higgins in Chile to attempt major economic reforms, stimulate mining and manufacturing, introduce new crops, and in general try to promote not only the interests of the Spanish crown but the welfare of the Chilean people.

The creation of new viceroyalties and captaincies general went hand in hand with another major political reform, the transfer to the colonies between 1782 and 1790 of the intendant system, already introduced to Spain by France. This reform was made in the interests of greater administrative efficiency and in the hope of increasing royal revenues from the colonies. The intendants, provincial governors who ruled from the capitals of their provinces, were expected to relieve the overburdened viceroys of many of their duties, especially in financial matters. Among their other duties, the intendants were expected to further the economic development of their districts by promoting the cultivation of new crops, the improvement of mining, the building of roads and bridges, and the establishment of consulados and economic societies. Under their prodding, the lethargic cabildos or town councils were in some cases stirred to greater activity. The Ordinance of Intendants also abolished the offices of corregidor and alcalde mayor, notorious vehicles for the oppression of the natives. These officials were replaced as governors of indigenous towns by men called *subdelegados*, who were nominated by the intendants and confirmed by the viceroys.

Many of the intendants at the height of the reform era were capable and cultivated men who not only achieved the objectives of increased economic activity and revenue collection but promoted education and cultural progress generally. But the same could not be said of the majority of their subordinates, the subdelegados, who, like their predecessors, soon became notorious for their oppressive practices. A common complaint was that they continued to compel the natives to trade with them, although the repartimiento had been forbidden by the Ordinance of Intendants. The great popular revolts of the 1780s were fueled in large part by the failure of the indigenous and

In the early seventeenth century, Felipe Guaman Poma de Ayala, a self-educated indigenous writer, chronicled the corruption and impunity of corregidores, who "feared neither justice nor God" and used their power to amass private fortunes by exploiting impoverished indigenous people, torturing their *caciques*, and stealing the wealth that indigenous communities produced. [Waman Puma de Ayala, *La nueva crónica*. The Royal Library, Copenhagen]

mixed-blood populations to share in the fruits of the eighteenth-century economic advance, whose principal beneficiaries were Spanish and creole landowners, mine owners, and merchants.

STRENGTHENING THE DEFENSES

Increased revenue was a major objective of the Bourbon commercial and political reforms. A major purpose to which that revenue was applied was the strengthening of the sea and land defenses of the empire. Before the eighteenth century, primary dependence for defense had been placed on naval power: convoy escorts and cruiser squadrons. Before the middle of the eighteenth century, standing armed forces in the colonies were negligible, and authorities relied on local forces raised for particular emergencies. The disasters of the Seven Years' War and the loss of Havana and Manila (1762) to the English, in particular, resulted in a decision to correct the shortcomings in the defense system of the colonies. Fortifications of important American ports were strengthened and colonial armies were created. These included regular units, which were stationed permanently in the colonies or rotated between peninsular and overseas service, and colonial militia whose ranks were filled by volunteers or drafted recruits.

To make military service attractive to the creole upper class, which provided the officer corps of the new force, the crown granted extensive privileges and exemptions to creole youths who accepted commissions. To the lure of prestige and honors, the grant of the *fuero militar* added protection from civil legal jurisdiction and liability, except for certain specified offenses. The special legal and social position thus accorded to the colonial officer class helped form a tradition that has survived to the present in Latin America—the armed forces as a special caste with its own set of interests, not subject to the civil power, that acts as the arbiter of political life, usually in the interests of conservative ruling classes. Under the Bourbons, however, the power of the colonial military was held in check by such competing groups as the church and the civil bureaucracy.

Although the expansion of the colonial military establishment under the Bourbons offered some opportunities and advantages to upper-class creole youth, it did nothing to allay the long-standing resentment creoles felt about their virtual exclusion from the higher offices of state and church and from large-scale commerce. Bourbon policy in regard to the problem went through two phases. In the first half of the eighteenth century, wealthy creoles could sometimes purchase high official posts, and for a time they dominated the prestigious audiencias of Mexico City and Lima. But in the second half of the century, an anticreole reaction took place. José de Gálvez, Charles III's colonial minister, was the very embodiment of the spirit of enlightened despotism that characterized his reign. Gálvez distrusted creole capacity and integrity and removed high-ranking creoles from positions in the imperial administration. The new upper bureaucracy, such as the intendants who took over much of the authority of viceroys and governors, was in the great majority Spanish-born.

Other Bourbon policies injured creole vested interests or wounded their sensibilities and traditions. In 1804 the Spanish crown enacted an emergency revenue measure—the *Consolidación de Vales Reales*—that ordered church institutions in the colonies to call in all their outstanding capital, the liens and mortgages whose interest supported the charitable and pious works of the church. The proceeds were to be loaned to the crown, which would pay annual interest to the church to fund its ecclesiastical activities. Although the primary motive of the Consolidation was to relieve the crown's urgent financial needs, it had the secondary reformist aim of freeing the colonial economy from the burden of mortmain and thus promoting a greater circulation of property.

The measure, however, struck hard at two bulwarks of the colonial order, the church and the propertied elite—the numerous hacendados, merchants, and mine owners who had borrowed large sums from church institutions and now had to repay those sums in full or face loss of property or bankruptcy. Many elite families had also assigned part of the value of their estates to the church to found a chaplaincy, paying annual interest to provide the stipend of the chaplain, often a family member. Although the church had not loaned this capital, officials in charge of the Consolidation demanded that the families involved immediately turn over the value of these endowments, in cash. Many small and medium landowners and other middle-class borrowers from the church were also threatened by the Consolidation decree.

The measure caused a storm of protest, and its application was gradually softened by willingness on the part of the officials in charge to negotiate the amounts and other terms of payment. So strong was the opposition of debtors, both creoles and peninsulars, to the decree that little effort was made to implement it outside of New Spain, which provided more than two-thirds of the 15 million pesos collected before it was canceled in 1808 following Napoleon's invasion of Spain. The Consolidation left a heritage of bitterness, especially among individuals like Father Miguel Hidalgo, future torchbearer of the Mexican War for Independence, whose hacienda was embargoed for several years for failure to pay his debts to the Consolidation.

Thus, despite and partly because of the reformist spirit of the Bourbon kings, the creoles became progressively alienated from the Spanish crown. Their alienation intensified an incipient creole nationalism that, denied direct political outlets, found its chief expression in culture and religion.

Colonial Culture and the Enlightenment

At least until the eighteenth century, a neomedieval climate of opinion, enforced by the authority of church and state, sharply restricted the play of the colonial intellect and imagination. Colonial culture thus suffered from all the infirmities of its parent but inevitably lacked the breadth and vitality of Spanish literature and art, the product of a much older and more mature civilization. Despite these and other difficulties, such as the limited market for books, colonial culture left a remarkably large and valuable heritage.

THE CHURCH AND EDUCATION

The church enjoyed a virtual monopoly of colonial education at all levels. The primary and secondary schools maintained by the clergy, with few exceptions, were open only to children of the Spanish upper class and the indigenous nobility. Poverty condemned the overwhelming majority of the natives and mixed castes to illiteracy. Admission to the universities, which numbered about twenty-five at the end of the colonial era,

was even more restricted to youths of ample means and "pure" blood.

The universities of Lima and Mexico City, both chartered by the crown in 1551, were the first permanent institutions of higher learning. Patterned on similar institutions in Spain, the colonial university faithfully reproduced their medieval organization, curricula, and methods of instruction. Indifference to practical or scientific studies, slavish respect for the authority of the Bible, Aristotle, the church fathers, and certain medieval schoolmen, and a passion for hairsplitting debate of fine points of theological or metaphysical doctrine were among the features of colonial academic life. Theology and law were the chief disciplines; until the eighteenth century, science was a branch of philosophy, taught from the *Physics* of Aristotle.

A strict censorship of books (no book could be published in either Spain or the colonies without the approval of the Royal Council) limited the spread of new doctrines in colonial society. In recent decades it has been shown that the laws prohibiting the entry of works of fiction into the Spanish colonies were completely ineffective, but this tolerance did not extend to heretical or subversive writings. The records of the colonial Inquisition reveal many tragic cases of imprisonment, torture, and even death for individuals who were charged with the possession and reading of such writings. At least until the eighteenth century, when the intellectual iron curtain surrounding Spanish America began to lift, the people of the colonies were effectively shielded from literature of an unorthodox religious or political tendency.

Yet, within the limits imposed by official censorship and their own backgrounds, colonial scholars were able to make impressive contributions, especially in the fields of indigenous history, anthropology, linguistics, and natural history. The sixteenth century was the Golden Age of these studies in Spanish America. In Mexico a large group of missionaries, especially members of the Franciscan order, carried out long, patient investigations of the native languages, religion, and history. With the aid of native informants, Friar Bernardino de Sahagún compiled a monumental *General History of the Things of New*

Spain, a veritable encyclopedia of information on all aspects of Aztec culture; scholars have only begun to mine the extraordinary wealth of ethnographic materials in Sahagún's work. Another Franciscan, usually known by his native name of Motolinía (Friar Toribio de Benavente), wrote a *History of the Indians of New Spain* that is an invaluable guide to native life before and after the Conquest. Basing his work on Aztec picture writings and a chronicle, now lost, written by an Aztec noble in his own language, Father Diego Durán wrote a history of ancient Mexico that preserves both the content and spirit of Aztec epics and legends. The Jesuit José de Acosta sought to satisfy Spanish curiosity about the natural productions of the New World and the history of the Aztecs and Incas in his *Natural and Moral History of the Indies.* His book, simply and pleasantly written, displays a critical spirit rare for its time; it achieved an immediate popularity in Spain and was quickly translated into all the major languages of western Europe.

Not a few historical works were written by indigenous or mestizo nobles actuated by a variety of motives: interest and pride in their native heritage joined to a desire to prove the important services rendered by their forebears to the Conquest and the validity of their claims to noble titles and land. Products of convent schools or colegios, they usually combined Christian piety with nostalgic regard for the departed glories of their ancestors. A descendant of the kings of Texcoco, Fernando de Alva Ixtlilxochitl, wrote a number of historical works that show a mastery of European historical method. These works combine a great amount of valuable information with a highly idealized picture of Texcocan civilization.

Another writer of the early seventeenth century, the mestizo Garcilaso de la Vega, son of a Spanish conquistador and an Inca princess, gives in his *Royal Commentaries of the Incas,* together with much valuable information on Inca material culture and history, an idyllic picture of Peruvian life under the benevolent rule of the Inca kings. His book, written in a graceful, fluent Spanish, is more than a history; it is a first-class work of art. No other Spanish history was as popular in Europe as Garcilaso's *Royal Commentaries;* its favorable image

of Inca civilization continues to influence our view of ancient Peru down to the present.

A precious work, richly informative about social conditions in Peru before and after the Conquest, and illustrated with the author's own delightfully naive drawings, is the *New Chronicle* by the seventeenth-century Aymara noble Felipe Waman Puma de Ayala, whose manuscript did not come to light until the early twentieth century. Waman Puma tells that he left his home "to know the needs of, and to redeem the poor Indians, for whom there is no justice in this kingdom," and that he hoped that his work would be read by Philip III. Waman Puma's painful effort to express himself in the unfamiliar Castilian tongue, the passionate rush of words interspersed with Quechua terms, and the melancholy and disillusioned tone of the work testify to the author's sincerity and the reality of the abuses that he denounces.

SCIENCE, LITERATURE, AND THE ARTS

The second half of the seventeenth century saw a decline in the quantity and quality of colonial scholarly production. This was the age of the baroque style in literature, a style that stressed word play, cleverness, and pedantry, that subordinated content to form, meaning to ornate expression. Yet two remarkable men of this period, Carlos Sigüenza y Góngora in Mexico and Pedro de Peralta Barnuevo in Peru, foreshadowed the eighteenth-century Enlightenment by the universality of their interests and their concern with the practical uses of science. Sigüenza—mathematician, archaeologist, and historian—attacked the ancient but still dominant superstition of astrology in his polemic with the Jesuit priest Kino over the nature of comets; he also defied prejudice by providing in his will for the dissection of his body in the interests of science.

Peralta Barnuevo, cosmographer and mathematician, made astronomical observations that were published in Paris in the *Proceedings* of the French Royal Academy of Sciences, of which he was elected corresponding member; he also superintended the construction of fortifications in Lima.

Yet this able and insatiably curious man of science also sought refuge in a baroque mysticism, and in one of his last works he concluded that true wisdom, the knowledge of God, was not "subject to human comprehension."

Colonial literature, with some notable exceptions, was a pallid reflection of prevailing literary trends in the mother country. The isolation from foreign influences, the strict censorship of all reading matter, and the limited audience for writing of every kind made literary creation difficult. "A narrow and dwarfed world," the discouraged Mexican poet Bernardo de Balbuena called the province of New Spain. To make matters worse, colonial literature in the seventeenth century succumbed to the Spanish literary fad of *Gongorismo* (so called after the poet Luis de Góngora), the cult of an obscure, involved, and artificial style.

Amid a flock of "jangling magpies," as one literary historian describes the Gongorist versifiers of the seventeenth century, appeared the incomparable songbird, known to her admiring contemporaries as "the tenth muse"—Sor Juana Inés de la Cruz, the remarkable nun and poet who assembled in her convent one of the finest mathematical libraries of the time. But Sor Juana could not escape the pressures of her environment. Rebuked by the bishop of Puebla for her worldly interests, she ultimately gave up her books and scientific interests and devoted the remainder of her brief life to religious devotion and charitable works.

Because of her brilliant defense of the rights of women to education and intellectual activity and her attacks on the prevailing irrationality with regard to the sexual conduct of men and women ("foolish men," she asks in one of her sonnets, "why do you want them [women] to be good when you incite them to be bad?"), Sor Juana's work belongs to what has been called "colonial subversive discourse," discourse that challenged the official ideology and idealized vision of colonial life propounded by church and state. Satire and mockery, often carried to extremes of grotesque distortion, were the weapons used by colonial critics to expose the hollowness of the ruling ideology, the gap between the idealized vision and the seamy reality of colonial life. They drew much of their inspiration from the rich

Sor Juana Inés de la Cruz, sometimes called the greatest Spanish American poet of the colonial period, entered a convent when she was eighteen years old and died at the age of forty-four. Sor Juana wrote both secular and religious poetry, but it is her love poems for which she was most admired. [Bradley Smith Collection/Laurie Platt Winfrey, Inc.]

traditions of the Spanish picaresque novel and satirical poetry that subjected the follies and frailties of Spanish society to pungent criticism. Naturally, because of the strict censorship of published works, colonial satire circulated principally in manuscript form, and the satirists often took measures to conceal their identities.

The first known Spanish-American writer of satire was the peninsular-born Mateo Rosas de Oquendo, whose "Satire About the Things That Happened in Peru in 1598" was devoted to exposing Lima's social ills, the wealth that flaunted itself in the colonial capital, and the "sea of misery" that was the life of the mass of ordinary people. In another poem, a mock epic describing a viceroy's handling of the defense of the viceroyalty against English pirates, Rosas reduced a celebration of the victory of the Spanish fleet over a single English ship to "a lot of cackling over a single egg." His conclusion, sums up Julie Greer Johnson, was that the ruling aristocracy shared "the same basic attributes of ugliness, corruption, and hypocrisy" of the lower classes, differing only in their manifestations. "Anarchy and fraud prevail at court just as they do on the street, and money again controls lives, this time by buying power and influence."

In the same satirical tradition is the work *El Carnero* (the meaning of the word has not been firmly established), a history of the first century of Spanish colonization in New Granada begun late in life by Juan Rodríguez Freile, an impoverished creole landowner, and not completed until 1638. The ironic tone of the work, says Greer Johnson, reflects "the creole resentment and frustration of being considered a second-class Spaniard, the result of his American birth, and of being treated more like the colonized than the colonizers." Reversing the approach of official chroniclers of the Conquest and Spain's work in America, Rodríguez Freile questioned the "justification for the Conquest, the effectiveness of colonization, and even the character of the conquering Spaniard." Government officials appear as bumbling fools who "literally tripped over one another in the performance of their duties." Rodríguez Freile appears as the "omniscient narrator" who passes judgment on a long succession of crimes and follies but is capable of laughing at himself, even admitting to "having pursued the Golden Alligator like the conquerors who sought the illusive El Dorado."

Juan del Valle y Caviedes, who arrived in Peru from Spain between 1645 and 1648, is commonly considered the best colonial satirist and second only to Sor Juana Inés de la Cruz as a poet. Evidently because of his unfortunate experience as a patient, Lima's physicians became the principal targets of his savage mockery, but he also subjected Lima's women, nobility, and other social types to ferocious verbal attack. In his collection of poems, *Diente del Parnaso* (*Tooth of Parnassus*), incompetent medical practice is presented as a full-scale conspiracy against patients by members of the profession, regarded as troops led by their general, Death. By equating seventeenth-century Peruvian doctors with sixteenth-century conquerors and then with modern pirates—a growing threat to the colony—Caviedes gave a subversive tinge to his irony, placing "conquerors, doctors, and pirates on the same plane for their part in causing death and destruction in the Western Hemisphere." Still more audaciously, he actually named some of Lima's best-known "malpractitioners," who are introduced by Death during a roll call of his troops. One was Francisco Bermejo y Roldán, the *protomedicato*, or chief physician, of Peru; Caviedes mocked the title, calling him the *protoverdugo*, or chief executioner, and charged that he took advantage of his female patients by prescribing "injections that were administered in the front."

Colonial art drew its principal inspiration from Spanish sources, but, especially in the sixteenth century, indigenous influence was sometimes visible in design and ornamentation. Quito in Ecuador and Mexico City were among the chief centers of artistic activity. The first school of fine arts in the New World was established in Mexico City in 1779 under royal auspices. As might be expected, religious motifs dominated painting and sculpture. In architecture the colonies followed Spanish examples, with the severe classical style of the sixteenth century giving way in the seventeenth to the highly ornamented baroque and in the eighteenth to a style that was even more ornate.

The intellectual atmosphere of the Spanish colonies was not conducive to scientific inquiry or achievement. As late as 1773, the Colombian botanist Mutis was charged with heresy for giving lectures in Bogotá on the Copernican system. The prosecutor of the Inquisition asserted that Mutis was "perhaps the only man in Latin America to uphold Copernicus." In the last decades of the eighteenth century, however, the growing volume of economic and intellectual contacts with Europe and the patronage and protection of enlightened governors created more favorable conditions for scientific activity. Science made its greatest strides in the wealthy province of New Spain, where the expansion of the mining industry stimulated interest in geology, chemistry, mathematics, and metallurgy. In Mexico City there arose a school of mines, a botanical garden, and an academy of fine arts. The Mexican scientific renaissance produced a galaxy of brilliant figures that included Antonio de León y Gama, Antonio de Alzate, and Joaquín Velázquez Cárdenas y León. These men combined Enlightenment enthusiasm for rationalism, empiricism, and progress with a strict Catholic orthodoxy; Alzate, for example, vehemently denounced the "infidelity" and skepticism of Europe's philosophes.

Spain itself, now under the rule of the enlightened Bourbon kings, contributed to the intellectual renovation of the colonies. A major liberalizing influence, in both Spain and its colonies, was exerted by the early eighteenth-century friar Benito Feijóo, whose numerous essays waged war on folly and superstition of every kind. Feijóo helped to naturalize the Enlightenment in the Spanish-speaking world by his lucid exposition of the ideas of Bacon, Newton, and Descartes. Spanish and foreign scientific expeditions to Spanish America, authorized and sometimes financed by the crown, also stimulated the growth of scientific thought and introduced the colonists to such distinguished representatives of European science as the Frenchman Charles Marie de La Condamine and the German Alexander von Humboldt.

Among the clergy, the Jesuits were most skillful and resourceful in the effort to reconcile church dogma with the ideas of the Enlightenment, in bridging the old and the new. In Mexico, Jesuit writers like Andrés de Guevara, Pedro José Marquez, and Francisco Javier Clavigero praised and taught the doctrines of Bacon, Descartes, and Newton. These Jesuits exalted physics above metaphysics and the experimental method over abstract reasoning and speculation, but all of them combined these beliefs with undeviating loyalty to the teachings of the church. Thus the expulsion of the Jesuits from

Spanish America removed from the scene the ablest, most subtle defenders of the traditional Catholic worldview. In their Italian exile—for it was in Italy that most of the Jesuit exiles settled—some of them occupied their leisure time writing books designed to make known to the world the history and geography of their American homelands. The most important of these works by Jesuit exiles was the *History of Ancient Mexico* (1780–1781) of Francisco Clavigero, the best work of its kind written to date and an excellent illustration of the characteristic Jesuit blend of Catholic orthodoxy with the critical, rationalist approach of the Enlightenment.

Despite their frequent and sincere professions of loyalty to the crown, the writings of colonial intellectuals revealed a sensitivity to social and political abuses, a discontent with economic backwardness, and a dawning sense of nationality that contained potential dangers for the Spanish regime. Colonial newspapers and journals played a significant part in the development of a critical and reformist spirit among the educated creoles of Spanish America. Subjected to an oppressive censorship by church and state and beset by chronic financial difficulties, they generally had short and precarious lives.

The circulation and influence of forbidden books among educated colonials steadily increased in the closing decades of the eighteenth century and the first years of the nineteenth. It would nevertheless be incorrect to conclude, as some writers have done, that the Inquisition became a toothless tiger in the eighteenth century and that radical ideas could be advocated with almost total impunity. It is true that the influence of the Inquisition weakened under the Bourbons, especially Charles III, because of the growth of French influence. But the censorship was never totally relaxed, the Inquisition continued to be vigilant, and with every turn of the diplomatic wheel that drew Spain and France apart the inquisitorial screws were tightened. Thus, the outbreak of the French Revolution brought a wave of repression against advocates of radical ideas in Mexico, culminating in a major *auto-da-fé* in Mexico City at which long prison sentences and other severe penalties were handed out. How powerless these repressions were to check the movement of new thought is illustrated by the writings of the fathers of Spanish-American independence. Their works reveal a thorough knowledge of the ideas of Locke, Montesquieu, Raynal, and other important figures of the Enlightenment.

Creole Nationalism

The incipient creole nationalism, however, built on other foundations than the ideas of the European Enlightenment, which were alien and suspect to the masses. Increasingly conscious of themselves as a class and of their respective provinces as their *patrias* (fatherlands), creole intellectuals of the eighteenth century assembled an imposing body of data designed to refute the attacks of such eminent European writers as Comte Georges de Buffon and Cornelius de Pauw, who proclaimed the inherent inferiority of the New World and its inhabitants.

In the largest sense, the creole patria was all America. As early as 1696, the Mexican Franciscan Agustín de Vetancurt claimed that the New World was superior to the Old in natural beauty and resources. New Spain and Peru, he wrote in florid prose, were two breasts from which the whole world drew sustenance, drinking blood changed into the milk of gold and silver. In a change of imagery, he compared America to a beautiful woman adorned with pearls, emeralds, sapphires, chrysolites, and topazes, drawn from the jewel boxes of her rich mines.

In the prologue to his *History of Ancient Mexico*, Clavigero stated that his aim was "to restore the truth to its splendor, truth obscured by an incredible multitude of writers on America." The epic, heroic character that Clavigero gave the history of ancient Mexico reflected the creole search for origins, for a classical antiquity other than the European, to which the peninsulars could lay better claim. The annals of the Toltecs and the Aztecs, he insisted, offered as many examples of valor, patriotism, wisdom, and virtue as the histories of Greece and Rome. Mexican antiquity displayed such models of just and benevolent rule as the wise Chichimec king Xolotl and philosopher-

The myth of the Virgin of Guadalupe, appropriated by creole nationalists to advance their nineteenth-century struggle for independence and cultural hegemony, later served lower-class indigenous and mestizo peasants in their fight for social justice. [The Granger Collection]

kings such as Nezahualcoyotl and Nezahualpilli. In this way, Clavigero provided the nascent Mexican nationality with a suitably dignified and heroic past. The Chilean Jesuit Juan Ignacio Molina developed similar themes in his *History of Chile* (1782).

The creole effort to develop a collective self-consciousness also found expression in religious thought and symbolism. In his *Quetzalcoatl and Guadalupe: The Formation of Mexican National Consciousness* (1976), Jacques Lafaye has shown how creole intellectuals exploited two powerful myths in the attempt to achieve Mexican spiritual autonomy and even superiority vis-à-vis Spain. One was the myth that the Virgin Mary appeared in 1531 on the hill of Tepeyac, near Mexico City, to an indígena from Cuauhtitlan named Juan Diego and through him commanded the bishop of Mexico to build a church there. The proof demanded by the bishop came in the form of winter roses from Tepeyac, enfolded in Juan Diego's cloak, which was miraculously painted with the image of the Virgin. From the seventeenth century, the *indita*, the brown-faced Virgin (as opposed to the Virgin of Los Remedios, who had allegedly aided Cortés) was venerated throughout Mexico as the Virgin of Guadalupe. Under her banner, in fact, Miguel Hidalgo in 1810 was to lead the indigenous and mestizo masses in a great revolt against Spanish rule.

The other great myth was that of Quetzalcóatl, the Toltec redeemer-king and god. Successive colonial writers had suggested that Quetzalcóatl was none other than the Christian apostle St. Thomas. On December 12, 1794, the creole Dominican Servando Teresa de Mier arose in his pulpit in the town of Guadalupe to proclaim that Quetzalcóatl was in fact St. Thomas, who long centuries before had come with four disciples to preach the Gospel in the New World. In this the apostle had succeeded, and at the time of the Conquest, Christianity—somewhat altered, to be sure—had reigned in Mexico. If Mier was right, America owed nothing to Spain, not even Christianity. Spanish officials, quickly recognizing the revolutionary implications of Mier's sermon, arrested him and exiled him to Spain.

The episode illustrates the devious channels through which creole nationalism moved to achieve its ends. One of those ends was creole hegemony over the indigenous and mixed-blood masses, based on their awareness of their common patria and their collective adherence to such national cults as that of the Virgin of Guadalupe in Mexico. In the 1780s, however, the accumu-

lated wrath of those people broke out in a series of explosions that threatened the very existence of the colonial social and political order. In this crisis the creole upper class showed that their aristocratic patria did not really include indígenas, mestizos, and blacks among its sons, that their rhetorical sympathy for the dead of Moctezuma's and Atahualpa's time did not extend to their descendants.

Colonial Society in Transition, 1750–1810: An Overview

An estimate by the late historian Charles Gibson put the population of Spanish America toward the end of the colonial period at about 17 million people. Gibson supposed that of this total some 7,500,000 were indígenas; about 3,200,000, Europeans; perhaps 750,000, blacks; and the remaining 5,500,000, castas. Those figures point to a continuing steady revival of the native population from the low point of its decline in the early seventeenth century, a more rapid increase of the European population, and an even faster increase of the castas.

In the late colonial period, the racial categories used to describe and rank the groups composing the colonial population in terms of their "honor" or lack of "honor" became increasingly ambiguous. One reason was the growing mobility of the colonial population, resulting in a more rapid pace of Hispanicization and racial mixture. The laws forbidding indígenas to reside in Spanish towns and whites and mixed-bloods to live in native towns were now generally disregarded. Large numbers of indígenas seeking escape from tribute and repartimiento burdens migrated to the Spanish cities and mining camps, where they learned to speak Spanish, wore European clothes, and adopted other Spanish ways. Those who lived in villages remote from the main areas of Spanish economic activity were less likely to be influenced by the presence of Spaniards and mestizos and therefore remained more "indigenous." For a variety of reasons connected with the area's history, geography, and economic patterns, the native communities in the viceroyalty of Peru seem to have resisted acculturation more tenaciously than those of New Spain. But the process of political and social change gradually transformed the Peruvian ayllu as well. Its kinship basis was weakened in time by the influx of *forasteros* ("outsiders"), peasant squatters fleeing from distant provinces subject to the mining mita. It was also attacked by late eighteenth-century Bourbon policy, which defined it by its geographic location, periodically redistributed its lands on the basis of its population, and sold any "excess" land in auctions for the benefit of the royal exchequer.

In the late eighteenth century those who left their native pueblos and became assimilated to the Spanish population in dress and language and who achieved even a modest level of prosperity increasingly came to be legally regarded as Spaniards, that is, creoles. The same was true of Hispanicized mestizos and, less frequently, perhaps, of blacks and mulattos. An individual's race, in short, now tended to be defined not by skin color but by such traits as occupation, dress, speech, and self-perception.

The economic advance of the late Bourbon era, marked by the rapid growth of commercial agriculture, mining, and domestic and foreign trade, created opportunities for some fortunate lower-class individuals and contributed to the declining significance of racial labels. A growing number of wealthy mestizo and mulatto families sought to rise in the social scale by marrying their sons and daughters to children of the Spanish elite. Charles III's policy on interracial marriage reflected the dilemmas of this reformer-king, who wished to promote the rise of a progressive middle class but feared to undermine the foundations of the old aristocratic order. Charles, who removed the stigma attached to artisan labor by decreeing that it was no bar to nobility, also issued decrees that empowered colonial parents to refuse consent to interracial marriages of their children that threatened the family's "honor." As interpreted by high colonial courts, however, these decrees as a rule only sanctioned such parental refusal when the parties to a proposed marriage were unequal in wealth, meaning, as previously noted, that a wealthy mulatto was a suitable marriage partner for a member of the Spanish elite. The last Bourbon kings also promoted social mobility by permitting *pardos* (free mulattos), despised for their slave origin, to buy legal whiteness through the purchase of dispensations (*cédulas de gracias al sacar*) that freed them from the status of "infamous."

It would be an error to suppose that these concessions to a small number of wealthy mixed-bloods reflected a crumbling of the caste system and the ideology on which it was based. The very eagerness of mulattos and mestizos to achieve whiteness by purchase of the dispensations mentioned above, the protest of elite groups like the cabildo of Caracas against the more liberal Bourbon racial policy as promoting "the amalgamation of whites and pardos," and the readiness of some parents to litigate against their children to prevent their marriage to dark-skinned individuals testify to the continuing hold of racial prejudice and stereotypes on the colonial mentality.

The partial penetration of elite society, even on its highest levels, by individuals having some traces of indigenous or African blood did not alter the rigidity of the class structure, the sharp class distinctions, or the vast gulf separating the rich and the poor. Humboldt spoke of "that monstrous inequality of rights and wealth" that characterized late colonial Mexico. But the late colonial period saw some change in the economic base of the elite and some shifts in the relative weight of its various sectors. If the seventeenth century was the golden age of the large landowners, the eighteenth century, especially its last decades, saw their ascendancy challenged by the growing wealth and political and social influence of the export-import merchant class, most of the members of which were of Spanish immigrant origin. The merchants provided the capital needed by the mining industry and absorbed much of its profits. They also financed the purchase of the posts of corregidors, officials who monopolized trade with indigenous communities in collusion with the merchants. To provide a hedge against commercial losses—not just to secure the prestige identified with landownership—wealthy merchants acquired estates, establishing hacienda complexes that produced a variety of crops and were situated to supply the major markets. They further diversified by acquiring flour mills or obrajes and by establishing themselves as major retailers, not only in the cities but also in the countryside. The wealthiest married into rich and powerful creole extended families, forming an Establishment whose offspring had preference in appointments to important and prestigious positions in the colonial government and church.

The second half of the eighteenth century saw a new wave of immigration from the peninsula. The presence of these newcomers, often of humble origins, who competed with the American-born Spaniards for limited employment opportunities, sharpened the traditional creole resentment of gachupines or chapetones (tenderfoots). Although, according to Humboldt, "the lowest, least educated and uncultivated European believes himself superior to the white born in the New World," most of the new arrivals failed to find the high-status and well-paid employments they had expected. The 1753 and 1811 census reports for Mexico City listed some Spaniards working as unskilled laborers and house servants and still others as jobless. The *Diario de México* often carried advertisements by jobless Spanish immigrants willing to accept any kind of low-level supervisory post. Two observant Spanish officials, Jorge Juan and Antonio de Ulloa, who visited the city of Cartagena in New Granada about 1750, found that there creoles and Europeans disdained any trade below that of commerce. "But it being impossible for all to succeed, great numbers not being able to secure sufficient credit, they become poor and miserable from their aversion to the trades they follow in Europe, and instead of the riches which they flattered themselves with possessing in the Indies, they experience the most complicated wretchedness."

The Revolt of the Masses

A traditional view portrayed indigenous peoples as the more or less passive object of Spanish rule or of an acculturation process. In recent decades, deeper, more careful study of their response to Spanish rule has revealed that they were not mere "passive victims of Spanish colonization" but activists who from the first resisted Spanish rule with a variety of strategies and thereby were able in some degree to modify the colonial environment and shape their own lives and futures. These strategies included revolts, flight, riots, sabotage, and sometimes even using their masters' legal codes for purposes of defense and offense.

Flight, under conditions of intense Spanish competition for indigenous labor, effectively evaded Spanish pressures. Historian Jeffrey Cole points out, for example, that natives' abandonment of pueblos subject to the mita in order to work as yanaconas on farms, ranches, and other enterprises in exempted areas "was their most effective means of opposing the mita, the demands of their curacas and corregidores, and other obligations." Indigenous peoples also skillfully used Spanish legal codes for purposes of "defense, redress, and even offense." Historian Steve Stern's recent study of the Peruvian province of Huamanga shows that they lightened the burdens of the mita through the defensive strategy of "engaging in aggressive, persistent, often shrewd use of Spanish juridical institutions to lower legal quotas, delay delivery of specific corvées and tributes, disrupt production, and the like." In Mexico there were countless riots—*tumultos*—in the eighteenth century. Indígenas let Spanish authority know that it could not take them for granted and must heed their complaints.

The recent stress in historical writing on native peoples as agents who were able in some degree to shape their own lives and futures by using Spanish juridical institutions, disruption of production, and similar relatively peaceful strategies is salutary, but it can be carried too far. Such efforts were by no means always successful and sometimes resulted in severe reprisals. A recent study of eighteenth-century Quito (in modern Ecuador) by historian Martin Minchom reports that when indígenas complained of a powerful Spanish nobleman's encroachment on their communal lands, local officials responded to their "temerity" in bringing him before the law-courts by burning down seventy-one indigenous houses in the area. Another recent case study by Mexican historian Hildeberto Martínez of indigenous efforts to halt alienation of their lands in two former native domains in sixteenth- and seventeenth-century Mexico (in the modern state of Puebla) suggests that their resort to lawsuits and other peaceful tactics proved completely futile. Spanish methods of spoliation included outright violence, fraudulent manipulation of sales and rental agreements, theft of title documents, and the unleashing of livestock on lands they coveted, in addition to more subtle maneuvers. Between 1521 and 1644 these methods resulted in the loss of more than 137,000 hectares of land by the two native communities.

Revolt was the most dramatic form of resistance to Spanish rule by oppressed groups. Numerous indigenous and black slave revolts punctuated the colonial period of Spanish-American history. Before Spanish rule had been firmly established, indígenas rose against their new masters in many regions. In Mexico the Mixton war raged from 1540 to 1542. The Maya of Yucatán staged a great uprising in 1546. A descendant of the Inca kings, Manco II, led a nationwide revolt in 1536 against the Spanish conquerors of Peru. In Chile the indomitable Araucanians began a struggle for independence that continued into the late nineteenth century. In the jungles and mountains of the West Indies, Central America, and northern South America, groups of runaway black slaves established communities that successfully resisted Spanish efforts to destroy them. The revolutionary wave subsided in the seventeenth century but peaked again in the eighteenth when new burdens were imposed on the common people.

The Bourbon reforms helped enrich colonial landowners, merchants, and mine owners, beautified their cities, and broadened the intellectual horizons of upper-class youths, but the multitude did not share in these benefits. On the contrary, Bourbon efforts to increase the royal revenues by the creation of governmental monopolies and privileged companies and the imposition of new taxes actually made more acute the misery of the lower classes. This circumstance helps explain the popular character of the revolts of 1780–1781, as distinct from the creole wars of independence of the

next generation. With rare exceptions, the privileged creole group either supported the Spaniards against the native uprisings or joined the revolutionary movements under pressure, only to desert them at a later time.

Most eighteenth-century revolts had a predominantly native peasant character. A significant exception was the Quito insurrection of 1765; in his study of this revolt, Anthony McFarlane calls it "the longest, largest, and most formidable urban insurrection of eighteenth-century Spanish America." Against a backdrop of economic depression caused by the decline of Quito's textile industry as a result of competition from Spanish and foreign contraband imports, sections of the elite joined artisans and shopkeepers in protest against threatened new taxes and changes in the aguardiente (rum) monopoly that endangered vested interests. Despite the large size of the ensuing riots and the strong hostility displayed toward Spanish merchants, the insurrection never challenged Spanish sovereignty. Mexico City had a series of riots in the eighteenth century, sparked by efforts of Bourbon administrators to suppress begging, regulate the use of liquor, and change working conditions in the tobacco factory. Silvia Arróm finds it significant that in Mexico City, as in Quito, the urban poor successfully resisted Bourbon efforts to regulate their lives. "Thus, the popular classes contested the state for control of their daily lives, and they often won."

REVOLT IN PERU

In the eighteenth century, Spanish pressures and demands on the Peruvian indígenas increased considerably. A major mechanism for the extraction of surplus from the natives was the previously mentioned repartimiento de mercancías. The system functioned as follows: a Lima merchant advanced the sum of money needed by a corregidor to buy his post from the crown. The merchant also outfitted the corregidor with the stock of goods that he would "distribute," that is, force indigenous residents of his district to buy, sometimes for six or eight times their fair market price. In the Cuzco region typical repartimiento goods were mules and textiles, but sometimes these goods included items for which the natives had no possible use. They had to pay for their purchases within an allotted time or else go to prison, forcing many to leave their villages to obtain the needed cash by working in mines, obrajes, and haciendas. The system thus served to erode the traditional peasant economy and promoted two objectives of the state, the merchants, and other ruling-class groups: the expansion of the internal market for goods and the enlargement of the labor market.

The repartimiento de mercancías was among the most hateful of the exactions to which indigenous people were subjected. A recent study finds that it figured as a cause in the great majority of revolts in Peru in the eighteenth century.

In the same period the burdens imposed by the mining mita increased. Determined to return the output of Potosí silver to its former high levels, the crown and the mine owners made innovations that greatly intensified the exploitation of native labor. The ore quotas that the *mitayos* (drafted workers) were required to produce were doubled between 1740 and 1790 from about fifteen loads per day to thirty, forcing the mitayos to work longer for the same wages and compelling their wives and children to assist them in meeting the quotas. In the same period the wages of both mitayos and mingas (free workers) were reduced. These innovations produced the desired revival of Potosí, with a doubling of silver production, but they were gained at a heavy price in native health and living standards.

Coupled with increases in alcabalas (sales taxes), the continuing abuses of the repartimiento de mercancías and the mita caused intense discontent. A critical point was reached when visitador José de Areche, sent out by Charles III in 1777 to reform conditions in the colony, tightened up the collection of tribute and sales taxes and broadened the tributary category to include all mestizos. As a result the contribution of indígenas was increased by 1 million pesos annually. These measures not only caused great hardships to the commoners, but they also created greater difficulties for the native curacas, or chiefs, who were responsible for meeting tribute quotas. Areche himself foretold the storm to come when he wrote: "The lack of righteous judges, the mita of the Indians, and provincial commerce have made a corpse of this America. Corregidores are interested only in themselves. . . . How near everything is to ruin if these terrible abuses are not corrected, for they have been going on a long time."

The discontent of the masses with their intolerable conditions inspired messianic dreams and expectations of a speedy return of the Inca and the Inca Empire. The popular imagination transformed this Inca Empire into an ideal state, free from hunger and injustice, and free from the presence of oppressive colonial officials and exploitative mines, haciendas, and obrajes. This utopian vision of a restored Inca Empire played a part in causing the great revolt of 1780–1781 and determining its direction.

That revolt had its forerunners; between 1730 and 1780 there were 128 rebellions, large and small, in the Andean area. From 1742 to 1755, a native leader called Juan Santos, "the invincible," waged partisan warfare against the Spaniards from his base in the eastern slopes of the Andes. The memory of his exploits was still alive when the revolt of José Gabriel Condorcanqui began. A well-educated, wealthy mestizo descendant of the Inca kings who was strongly influenced by accounts of Inca splendor in the *Royal Commentaries* of Garcilaso de la Vega, he had made repeated, fruitless efforts to obtain relief for his people through legal channels. In November 1780 he raised the standard of revolt by ambushing the hated corregidor Antonio de Arriaga near the town of Tinta and putting him to death after a summary trial. At this time he also took the name of the last head of the neo-Inca state and became Tupac Amaru II. His actions were preceded by an uprising led by the Catari brothers in the territory of present-day Bolivia. By the first months of 1781, the southern highlands of the viceroyalty of Peru were aflame with revolt. Although the various revolutionary movements lacked a unified direction, the rebel leaders generally recognized Tupac Amaru as their chief and continued to invoke his name even after his death.

A descendant of the last great Inca, José Gabriel Condorcanqui assumed the name Tupac Amaru II, and in 1780 he and his wife, Micaela Bastidas, led a broad-based rebellion against the corruption of the corregidores. The revolt became a precursor of the independence wars that spread across the continent a few decades later. [The Art Archive/Coll Abric de Vivero Lima/Mireille Vautier]

In the first stage of the revolt, Tupac Amaru did not make his objectives entirely clear. In some public statements he proclaimed his loyalty to the Spanish king and church, limiting his demands to the abolition of the mita, the repartimiento, the alcabala, and other taxes; the suppression of the corregidors; and the appointment of indigenous governors for the provinces. But it is difficult to believe that the well-educated Tupac Amaru, who had had years of experience in dealing with Spanish officialdom, seriously believed that he could obtain sweeping reforms from the crown by negotiation, especially after his execution of the corregidor Arriaga. His protestations of

loyalty were soon contradicted by certain documents in which he styled himself king of Peru, by the war of fire and blood that he urged against peninsular Spaniards (excepting only the clergy), and by the government he established for the territory under his control.

More plausible is the view that his professions of loyalty to Spain represented a mask by which he could utilize the still strong faith of many in the mythical benevolence of the Spanish king, attract creole supporters of reform to his cause, and perhaps soften his punishment in case of defeat.

For Tupac Amaru, who had been educated in a Spanish colegio and had thoroughly absorbed the values of Spanish culture, the objective of the revolt was the establishment of an independent Peruvian state that would be essentially European in its political and social organization. His program called for complete independence from Spain, expulsion of peninsular Spaniards, and the abolition of the offices of viceroy, audiencia, and corregidor. The Inca Empire would be restored, with himself as king, assisted by a nobility formed from other descendants of the Cuzco noble clans. Caste distinctions would disappear, and creoles, on whose support Tupac Amaru heavily counted, would live in harmony with native peoples, blacks, and mestizos. The Catholic church would remain the state church and be supported by tithes. Tupac Amaru's economic program called for suppression of the mita, the repartimiento de mercancías, customshouses, and sales taxes, and for elimination of great estates and servitude, but would permit small and medium-sized landholdings and encourage trade. Tupac Amaru's plan, in short, called for an anticolonial, national revolution that would create a unified people and a modern state of European type that could promote economic development.

But the native peasantry who responded to his call for revolt had a different conception of its meaning and goal. In an atmosphere of messianic excitement, they came to view it as a *pachacuti*, a great cataclysm or "overthrow" that would bring a total inversion of the existing social order and a return to an idealized Inca Empire where the humble *runa* or peasant would not be last but first. In their desire to avenge the cruelties of the Conquest and two and a half centuries of brutal exploitation, they sacked haciendas and killed their owners without troubling to ascertain whether they were creoles or Europeans; a Spaniard was one who had a white skin and wore European dress. As the revolt spread, the old pagan religion emerged from the underground where it had hidden and flourished for centuries. Tupac Amaru, who sought to maintain good relations with the Catholic church, always went about accompanied by two priests and hoped for support by Bishop Moscoso of Cuzco. But his peasant followers sacked the vestments and ornaments of churches and attacked and killed priests, hanging a number of friars during the siege of Cuzco. In December 1780, Tupac Amaru entered one village and summoned its inhabitants, who greeted him with the words: "You are our God and we ask that there be no priests to pester us." He replied that he could not allow this, for it would mean that there would be no one to attend them "in the moment of death."

These opposed conceptions of the meaning and objectives of the revolt held by Tupac Amaru and his peasant followers spelled defeat for Tupac Amaru's strategy of forming a common pro-independence front of all social and racial groups except the peninsular Spaniards. The spontaneous, uncontrollable violence of the peasant rebels ended what little chance existed of attracting the support of the creoles, reformist clergy like Bishop Moscoso, and many indigenous nobles. At least twenty of these caciques, jealous of Tupac Amaru or fearful of losing their privileged status, led their subjects into the Spanish camp. A prominent loyalist figure was Diego Choquehanca, head of the wealthiest and most powerful kuraka family in Peru. His sixteenth-century ancestor of the same name had been declared a hidalgo and granted the title of marquis de Salinas by the Spanish crown; by 1780 the Choquehancas owned eleven estancias (estates) in the province of Azangaro. "Not surprisingly," says Nils Jacobsen, "the Choquehanca family remained firmly loyal during the Tupac Amaru crisis."

Although the principal base of the revolt was the ayllus (free peasant communities), it also attracted a number of mestizos and a few creoles, mostly of middle-class status (artisans, shopkeep-

ers, clerks, urban wage earners), some of whom formed part of the rebel command. Starting in the corregimiento of Tinta, near the southeastern rim of the strategic Cuzco valley system, the rebellion exploded into the Lake Titicaca basin, the scene of the longest and most intensive fighting. Encouraged by his initial victories, Tupac Amaru moved south with a rebel army in the thousands and in a short time took control of the whole altiplano south of Puno. But he failed to take advantage of those initial successes. Tactical errors contributing to his defeat included failure to attack Cuzco early, as strongly urged by his wife Micaela, a heroine of the revolt and his principal adviser, who had wanted to capitalize on the political and psychological significance of the ancient Inca capital before the arrival of Spanish reinforcements. In addition, communications among the rebel forces were poor, and the royalist armies possessed vastly superior arms and organization. The Spaniards also mobilized large numbers of yanaconas, who helped break the siege of Cuzco and suppress the revolt. Despite some initial successes, the rebel leader soon suffered a complete rout. Tupac Amaru, members of his family, and his leading captains were captured and put to death, some with ferocious cruelty. In the territory of present-day Bolivia the insurrection continued two years longer, reaching its high point in two prolonged sieges of La Paz (between March and October of 1781).

The last Inca revolt moved the crown to enact a series of reforms that included the replacement of the hated corregidores by the system of intendants and subdelegados and the establishment of an audiencia or high court in Cuzco, another of Tupac Amaru's goals before the revolt. But these and other reforms proved to be changes in form rather than substance. The miserably paid subdelegados, many of whom were former corregidores, continued the exploitative practices of their predecessors, including the repartimiento de mercancías, which was forbidden by the Ordinance of Intendants, but less regularly and on a smaller scale. Meanwhile the death or flight of some Hispanic landowners, clergy, and loyal kurakas as a result of the revolt had led to the occupation of their estates by peasant squatters. "In the last decades before independence," writes

Nils Jacobsen, "a sense of uncertainty permeated social and property relations in the altiplano. To say that the peasants lost the Tupac Amaru Rebellion is only half true."

INSURRECTION IN NEW GRANADA (1781)

The revolt of the Comuneros in New Granada, like that in Peru, had its origin in intolerable economic conditions. Unlike the Peruvian upheaval, however, it was more clearly limited in its aims to the redress of grievances. Increases in the alcabala and a whole series of new taxes, including one on tobacco and a poll tax, provoked an uprising in Socorro, an important agricultural and manufacturing center in the north. The disturbances soon spread to other communities. The reformist spirit of the revolt was reflected in the insurgent slogan: *Viva el rey y muera el mal gobierno!* (Long live the king, down with the evil government!).

In view of its organization and its effort to form a common front of all colonial groups with grievances against Spanish authority (excepting the black slaves), the revolt of the Comuneros marked an advance over the rather chaotic course of events to the south. A *común* (central committee), elected in the town of Socorro by thousands of peasants and artisans from adjacent towns, directed the insurrection. Each of the towns in revolt also had its común and a captain chosen by popular election.

Under the command of hesitant or unwilling creole leaders, a multitude of indigenous and mestizo peasants and artisans marched on the capital of Bogotá, capturing or putting to flight the small forces sent from the capital. Playing for time until reinforcements could arrive from the coast, the royal audiencia dispatched a commission headed by the archbishop to negotiate with the Comuneros. The popular character of the movement and the unity of oppressed groups that it represented were reflected in the terms that the rebel delegates presented to the Spanish commissioners and that the latter signed and later repudiated; these terms included reduction of indigenous and mestizo tribute and sales taxes, return of usurped land, abolition of the new tax on tobacco, and preference for creoles over Europeans in the filling of official posts.

An agreement reached on June 4, 1781, satisfied virtually all the demands of the rebels and was sanctified by the archbishop in a special religious service. Secretly, however, the Spanish commissioners signed another document declaring the agreement void because it was obtained by force. The jubilant insurgents scattered and returned to their homes. Only José Antonio Galán, a young mestizo peasant leader, maintained his small force intact and sought to keep the revolt alive.

Having achieved their objective of disbanding the rebel army, the Spanish officials prepared to crush the insurrection completely. The viceroy Manuel Antonio Flores openly repudiated the agreement with the Comuneros. Following a pastoral visit to the disaffected region by the archbishop, who combined seductive promises of reform with threats of eternal damnation for confirmed rebels, Spanish troops brought up from the coast moved into the region and took large numbers of prisoners. The creole leaders of the revolt hastened to atone for their political sins by collaborating with the royalists. Galán, who had vainly urged a new march on Bogotá, was seized by a renegade leader and handed over to the Spaniards, who put him to death by hanging on January 30, 1782. The revolt of the Comuneros had ended.

The Independence of Latin America

8

THE BOURBON REFORMS, combined with the upsurge of the European economy in the eighteenth century, brought material prosperity and less tangible benefits to many upper-class creoles of Spanish America. Enlightened viceroys and intendants introduced improvements and refinements that made life in colonial cities more healthful and attractive. Educational reforms, the influx of new books and ideas, and increased opportunities to travel and study in Europe widened the intellectual horizons of creole youth.

These gains, however, did not strengthen creole feelings of loyalty to the mother country. Instead, they enlarged their aspirations and sharpened their sense of grievance. The growing wealth of some sections of the creole elite made more galling its virtual exclusion from important posts in administration and the church. Meanwhile, the swelling production of creole haciendas, plantations, and ranches pressed against the trade barriers maintained by Spanish mercantilism. The intendant of Caracas, José Abalos, warned that "if His Majesty does not grant them [the creoles] the freedom of trade which they desire, then he cannot count on their loyalty." At the same time, Bourbon policy denied American manufacturers the protection they needed against crippling European competition.

Background of the Wars of Independence

CREOLES AND PENINSULAR SPANIARDS

The conflict of interest between Spain and its colonies was most sharply expressed in the cleavage between the creoles and the peninsular Spaniards. This quarrel was constantly renewed by the arrival of more Spaniards. In the late eighteenth century, a typical immigrant was a poor but hardworking and thrifty Basque or Navarrese who became an apprentice to a peninsular merchant, often a relative. In the course of time, as his merits won recognition, the immigrant might receive a daughter of the house in marriage and eventually succeed to the ownership of the business. One of the merchant's own creole sons might be given a landed estate; other creole sons might enter the church or the law, both overcrowded professions.

Thus, although there was some elite creole presence in both foreign and domestic trade, peninsular Spaniards continued to dominate the lucrative export-import trade and provincial trade. Spanish-born merchants, organized in powerful consulados, or merchant guilds, also played a key role in financing mining and the repartimiento business carried on among the natives by Spanish officials. Not unnaturally,

157

some upper-class creoles, excluded from mercantile activity and responsible posts in the government and church, developed the aristocratic manners and idle, spendthrift ways with which the peninsulars reproached them. Many other creoles of the middling sort, vegetating in ill-paid indigenous curacies and minor government jobs, bitterly resented the institutionalized discrimination that barred their way to advancement.

As a result, although some wealthy and powerful creoles maintained excellent relations with their peninsular counterparts, fusing their economic interests through marriage and forming a single colonial Establishment, creoles and peninsulars tended to become mutually hostile castes. The peninsulars sometimes justified their privileged position by charging the creoles with innate indolence and incapacity, qualities that some Spanish writers attributed to the noxious effects of the American climate and soil; the creoles retorted by describing the Europeans as mean and grasping parvenus. So intense was the hatred between many members of these groups that a Spanish bishop in New Spain protested against the feeling of some young creoles that "if they could empty their veins of the Spanish part of their blood, they would gladly do so." This inevitably fostered the growth of creole nationalism; Humboldt, who traveled in Spanish America in the twilight years of the colony, reports a common saying: "I am not a Spaniard, I am an American."

The entrance of Enlightenment ideas into Latin America certainly contributed to the growth of creole discontent, but the relative weight of various influences is uncertain. Bourbon Spain itself contributed to the creole awakening by the many-sided effort of reforming officials to improve the quality of colonial life. Typical of this group was the intendant Juan Antonio Riaño, who introduced to the Mexican city of Guanajuato, the capital of his province, a taste for the French language and literature; he was also responsible "for the development of interest in drawing and music, and for the cultivation of mathematics, physics, and chemistry in the school that had been formerly maintained by the Jesuits."

Many educated creoles read the forbidden writings of Raynal, Montesquieu, Voltaire, Rousseau, and other radical philosophes, but another, innocuous-seeming agency for the spread of Enlightenment ideas in Latin America consisted of scientific texts, based on the theories of Descartes, Leibnitz, and Newton, which circulated freely in the colonies. By 1800 the creole elite had become familiar with the most advanced thought of contemporary Europe.

The American Revolution contributed to the growth of "dangerous ideas" in the colonies. Spain was well aware of the ideological as well as political threat the United States posed to its empire. Spain had reluctantly joined its ally France in war against England during the American Revolution, but it kept the rebels at arm's length, refused to recognize American independence, and in the peace negotiations tried unsuccessfully to coop up the United States within the Allegheny Mountains. After 1783 a growing number of United States ships touched legally or illegally at Spanish-American ports. Together with "Yankee notions," these vessels sometimes introduced such subversive documents as the writings of Thomas Paine and Thomas Jefferson.

The French Revolution probably exerted an even greater influence on the creole mind. Recalled the Argentine revolutionary Manuel Belgrano,

> Since I was in Spain in 1789, and the French
> Revolution was then causing a change in
> ideas, especially among the men of letters
> with whom I associated, the ideals of liberty,
> equality, security, and property took a firm
> hold on me, and I saw only tyrants in those
> who would restrain a man, wherever he might
> be, from enjoying the rights with which God
> and Nature had endowed him.

Another cultivated creole, the Colombian Antonio Nariño, incurred Spanish wrath in 1794 by translating and printing on his own press the French Declaration of the Rights of Man of 1789. Sentenced to prison in Africa for ten years, Nariño lived to become leader and patriarch of the independence movement in Colombia and to witness its triumph.

Inspired by a long-standing tradition of local resistance to European enslavement, Toussaint L'Ouverture seized upon the political chaos and ideological appeal of the French Revolution to lead the Haitian Revolution in its demand for political autonomy, abolition of slavery, and social justice for all Haitians. [The Menil Collection, Houston. Photo by A. Mewbourn]

But the French Revolution soon took a radical turn, and the creole aristocracy became disenchanted with it as a model. Scattered conspiracies in some Spanish colonies and Brazil owed their inspiration to the French example, but they were invariably the work of a few radicals, drawing their support almost exclusively from lower-class elements. The most important result directly attributable to the French Revolution was the slave revolt in the French part of Haiti under talented black and mulatto leaders: Toussaint L'Ouverture, Jean Jacques Dessalines, Henri Christophe, and Alexandre Pétion. In 1804, Toussaint's lieutenant, General Dessalines, proclaimed the independence of the new state of Haiti. Black revolutionaries had established the first liberated territory in Latin America. But their achievement dampened rather

than aroused support for independence among the creole elite of other colonies. Thus, fear that secession from Spain might touch off a slave revolt helped keep the planter class of neighboring Cuba loyal to Spain during and after the Latin American wars of independence.

Despite the existence of small conspiratorial groups, organized in secret societies, with correspondents in Europe as well as America, the movement for independence might have long remained puny and ineffectual. As late as 1806, when the precursor of revolution, Francisco de Miranda, landed on the coast of his native Venezuela with a force of some two hundred foreign volunteers, his call for revolution evoked no response, and he had to make a hasty retreat. Creole timidity and political inexperience and the apathy of the people might have long postponed the coming of independence if external developments had not hastened its arrival. The revolution Miranda and other forerunners could not set in motion came as a result of decisions by European powers with very different ends in view.

THE CAUSES OF REVOLUTION

Among the causes of the revolutionary crisis that matured from 1808 to 1810, the decline of Spain under the inept Charles IV was certainly a major one. The European wars unleashed by the French Revolution glaringly revealed the failure of the Bourbon reforms to correct the structural defects in Spanish economic and social life. In 1793, Spain joined a coalition of England and other states in war against the French republic. The struggle went badly for Spain, and in 1795 the royal favorite and chief minister, Manuel de Godoy, signed the Peace of Basel. The next year, Spain became France's ally. English sea power promptly drove Spanish shipping from the Atlantic, virtually cutting off communication between Spain and its colonies. Hard necessity compelled Spain to permit neutral ships, sailing from Spanish for foreign ports, to trade with its overseas subjects. United States merchants and shipowners were the principal beneficiaries of this departure from the old, restrictive system.

Godoy's disastrous policy of war with England had other results. An English naval officer, Sir

Home Popham, undertook on his own initiative to make an attack on Buenos Aires. His fleet sailed from the Cape of Good Hope for La Plata in April 1806 with a regiment of soldiers on board. In its wake followed a great number of English merchant ships eager to pour a mass of goods through a breach in the Spanish colonial system. A swift victory followed the landing of the British troops. The English soldiers entered Buenos Aires, meeting only token resistance. Hoping to obtain the support of the population, the English commander issued a proclamation guaranteeing the right of private property, free trade, and freedom of religion. But creoles and peninsulars joined to expel their unwanted liberators. A volunteer army, secretly organized, attacked and routed the occupation troops, capturing the English general and twelve hundred of his men. To an English officer who tempted him with ideas of independence under a British protectorate, the creole Manuel Belgrano replied: "Either our old master or none at all."

The British government, meanwhile, had sent strong reinforcements to La Plata. This second invasion force was met with a murderous hail of fire as it tried to advance through the narrow streets of Buenos Aires and was beaten back with heavy losses. Impressed by the tenacity of the defense, the British commander gave up the struggle and agreed to evacuate Buenos Aires and the previously captured town of Montevideo. This defeat of a veteran British army by a people's militia spearheaded by the legion of *patricios* (creoles) was a large step down the road toward Argentine independence. The creoles of Buenos Aires, having tasted power, would not willingly relinquish it again.

In Europe, Spain's distresses now reached a climax. Napoleon, at the helm of France, gradually reduced Spain to a helpless satellite. In 1807, angered by Portugal's refusal to cooperate with his Continental System by closing its ports to English shipping, Napoleon obtained from Charles IV permission to invade Portugal through Spain. French troops swept across the peninsula; as they approached Lisbon, the Portuguese royal family and court escaped to Brazil in a fleet under British convoy. A hundred thousand French troops continued to occupy Spanish towns. Popular resentment

at their presence, and at the pro-French policies of the royal favorite Godoy, broke out in stormy riots that compelled Charles IV to abdicate in favor of his son Ferdinand. Napoleon now intervened and offered his services as a mediator in the dispute between father and son. Foolishly, the trusting pair accepted Napoleon's invitation to confer with him in the French city of Bayonne. There Napoleon forced both to abdicate in favor of his brother Joseph, his candidate for the Spanish throne. Napoleon then summoned a congress of Spanish grandees, which meekly approved his dictate.

The Spanish people had yet to say their word. On May 2, 1808, an insurrection against French occupation troops began in Madrid and spread like wildfire throughout the country. The insurgents established local governing juntas in the regions under their control. Later, a central junta assumed direction of the resistance movement in the name of the captive Ferdinand VII. This junta promptly made peace with England. When the Spanish armies fought the superbly trained French troops in conventional battles in the field, they usually suffered defeat, but guerrilla warfare pinned down large French forces and made Napoleon's control of conquered territory extremely precarious.

By early 1810, however, French victory seemed inevitable, for French armies had overrun Andalusia and were threatening Cádiz, the last city in Spanish hands. The central junta now dissolved itself and appointed a regency to rule Spain; this body in turn yielded its power to a national Cortes, or parliament, which met in Cádiz from 1810 to 1814 under the protection of English naval guns. Because most of the delegates came from Cádiz, whose liberal, cosmopolitan atmosphere was hardly typical of Spain, their views were much more liberal than those of the Spanish people as a whole. The constitution the Cortes approved in 1812 provided for a limited monarchy, promised freedom of speech and assembly, and abolished the Inquisition. But the Cortes made few concessions to Spain's American colonies. It invited Spanish-American delegates to join its deliberations but made clear that the system of peninsular domination and commercial monopoly would remain essentially intact.

In Spanish America, creole leaders, anticipating the imminent collapse of Spain, considered how they might turn this dramatic rush of events to their own advantage. Those events had transformed the idea of self-rule or total independence, until lately a remote prospect, into a realistic goal. Confident that the armies of the invincible Napoleon would crush all opposition, some creole leaders prepared to take power into their hands with the pretext of loyalty to the "beloved Ferdinand." They could justify their action by the example of the Spanish regional juntas formed to govern in the name of the captive king. The confusion caused among Spanish officials by the coming of rival emissaries who proclaimed both Ferdinand and Joseph Bonaparte the legitimate king of Spain also played into creole hands.

In the spring of 1810, with the fall of Cádiz apparently imminent, the creole leaders moved into action. Charging viceroys and other royal officials with doubtful loyalty to Ferdinand, they organized popular demonstrations in Caracas, Buenos Aires, Santiago, and Bogotá that compelled those authorities to surrender control to local juntas dominated by creoles. But creole hopes of a peaceful transition to independence were doomed to failure. Their claims of loyalty did not deceive the groups truly loyal to Spain, and fighting broke out between patriots and royalists.

The Liberation of South America

The Latin American struggle for independence suggests comparison with the American Revolution. Some obvious parallels exist between the two upheavals. Both sought to throw off the rule of a mother country whose mercantilist system hindered the further development of a rapidly growing colonial economy. Both were led by well-educated elites who drew their slogans and ideas from the ideological arsenal of the Enlightenment. Both were civil wars in which large elements of the population sided with the mother country. Both owed their final success in part to foreign assistance (although the North American rebels received far more help from their French ally than came to Latin America from outside sources).

The differences between the two revolutions are no less impressive, however. Unlike the American Revolution, the Latin American struggle for independence did not have a unified direction or strategy, due not only to vast distances and other geographical obstacles to unity but to the economic and cultural isolation of the various Latin American regions from each other. Moreover, the Latin American movement for independence lacked the strong popular base provided by the more democratic and fluid society of the English colonies. The creole elite, itself part of an exploitative white minority, feared the oppressed natives, blacks, and half-castes, and as a rule sought to keep their intervention in the struggle to a minimum. This lack of unity of regions and classes helps explain why Latin America had to struggle so long against a power like Spain, weak and beset by many internal and external problems.

The struggle for independence had four main centers. In Spanish South America there were two principal theaters of military operations, one in the north, another in the south. One stream of liberation flowed southward from Venezuela; another ran northward from Argentina. In Peru, the last Spanish bastion on the continent, these two currents joined. Brazil achieved its own swift and relatively peaceful separation from Portugal. Finally, Mexico had to travel a very difficult, circuitous road before gaining its independence.

SIMÓN BOLÍVAR, THE LIBERATOR

Simón Bolívar is the symbol and hero of the liberation struggle in northern South America. Born in Caracas, Venezuela, in 1783, he came from an aristocratic creole family rich in land, slaves, and mines. His intellectual formation was greatly influenced by his reading of the rationalist, materialist classics of the Enlightenment. Travel in various European countries between 1803 and 1807 further widened his intellectual horizons. He returned to Caracas and soon became involved in conspiratorial activity directed at the overthrow of the Spanish regime.

A portrait of the liberator, Simón Bolívar, by José Gil de Castro. His appearance conforms closely to descriptions of Bolívar in contemporary accounts. [José Gil de Castro, *Portrait of Simón Bolívar in Lima* (detail), 1825, oil on canvas, Salón Elíptico del Congreso Nacional. The Granger Collection, New York]

In April 1810 the creole party in Caracas organized a demonstration that forced the abdication of the captain general. A creole-dominated junta that pledged to defend the rights of the captive Ferdinand took power, but its assurances of loyalty deceived neither local Spaniards nor the Regency Council in Cádiz. A considerable number of wealthy creoles of the planter class also opposed independence, and when it triumphed many emigrated to Cuba or Puerto Rico. The patriots were also divided over what policy to follow; some, like Bolívar, favored an immediate declaration of independence, while others preferred to postpone the issue.

Perhaps to get Bolívar out of the way, the junta sent him to England to solicit British aid. He had no success in this mission but convinced the veteran revolutionary Francisco de Miranda to return to Venezuela and take command of the patriot army.

In 1811 a Venezuelan congress proclaimed the country's independence and framed a republican constitution that abolished special privileges (fueros) and native tribute but retained black slavery, made Catholicism the state religion, and limited the rights of full citizenship to property owners. This last provision excluded the free pardo (mulatto) population.

Fighting had already broken out between patriots and royalists. In addition to peninsulars, the troops sent from Puerto Rico by the Regency Council, and a section of the creole aristocracy, the royalist cause had the support of some free blacks and mulattos, angered by the republic's denial of full citizenship to them. In many areas the black slaves took advantage of the chaotic situation to rise in revolt, impartially killing creole and peninsular Spanish hacendados. But the majority of the population remained neutral, fleeing from their villages at the approach of royal or republican conscription officers; if conscripted, they often deserted when they could or changed sides if prospects seemed better.

On the patriot side differences arose between the commander in chief, Miranda, and his young officers, especially Bolívar, who were angered by Miranda's military conservatism and indecisiveness. Amid these disputes came the earthquake of March 26, 1812, which caused great loss of life and property in Caracas and other patriot territories but spared the regions under Spanish control. The royalist clergy proclaimed this disaster a divine retribution against the rebels. A series of military defeats completed the discomfiture of the revolutionary cause.

With his forces disintegrating, Miranda attempted to negotiate a treaty with the royalist commander and then tried to flee the country, taking with him part of the republic's treasury. He may have intended to continue working for independence, but the circumstances made it appear as if he wished to save his own skin. Bolívar and some of his comrades, regarding Miranda's act as a form of treachery, seized him before he could embark and turned him over to the Spaniards. He died in a Spanish prison four years later. Bolívar, saved from the Spanish reaction by the influence of a friend of his family, received a safe conduct to leave the country.

Bolívar departed for New Granada (present-day Colombia), which was still partially under patriot control. Here, as in Venezuela, creole leaders squabbled over forms of government. Two months after his arrival, Bolívar issued a Manifesto to the Citizens of New Granada in which he called for unity, condemned the federalist system as impractical under war conditions, and urged the liberation of Venezuela as necessary for Colombian security. Given command of a small detachment of troops to clear the Magdalena River of enemy troops, he employed a strategy that featured swift movement, aggressive tactics, and the advancement of soldiers for merit without regard to social background or color.

A victory at Cúcuta gained Bolívar the rank of general in the Colombian army and approval of his plan for the liberation of Venezuela. In a forced march of three months, he led five hundred men through Venezuela's Andean region toward Caracas. In Venezuela the Spaniards had unleashed a campaign of terror against all patriots. At Trujillo, midway in his advance on Caracas, Bolívar proclaimed a counterterror, a war to the death against all Spaniards. As Bolívar approached the capital, the Spanish forces withdrew. He entered Caracas in triumph and received from the city council the title of liberator; soon afterward the grateful congress of the restored republic voted to grant him dictatorial powers.

Bolívar's success was short-lived, for developments abroad and at home worked against him. The fall of Napoleon in 1814 brought Ferdinand VII to the Spanish throne, released Spanish troops for use in Spanish America, and gave an important lift to the royal cause. Meanwhile, the republic's policies alienated large sectors of the lower classes. The creole aristocrats stubbornly refused to grant freedom to their slaves. As a result, the slaves continued their struggle, independent of Spaniards and creoles, and republican forces had to be diverted for punitive expeditions into areas of slave revolt.

The *llaneros* (cowboys) of the Venezuelan *llanos* (plains) also turned against the republic as a result of agrarian edicts that attempted to end the hunting or rounding up of cattle in the llanos without written permission from the owner of the land in question. These edicts also sought to transform the llaneros into semiservile peons by forcing them to carry an identity card and belong to a ranch. These attacks on their customary rights and freedom angered the llaneros. Under the leadership of the formidable José Tomás Boves, a mass of cowboys, armed with the dreaded lance, invaded the highlands and swept down on Caracas, crushing all resistance. In July 1814 Bolívar hastily abandoned the city and retreated toward Colombia with the remains of his army. Although Boves died in battle in late 1814, he had destroyed the Venezuelan "second republic."

Bolívar reached Cartagena in September to find that Colombia was on the verge of chaos. Despite the imminent threat of a Spanish invasion, the provinces quarreled with each other and defied the authority of the weak central government. Having determined that the situation was hopeless, Bolívar left in May 1815 for the British island of Jamaica. Meanwhile, a strong Spanish army under General Pablo Morillo had landed in Venezuela, completed the reconquest of the colony, and then sailed to lay siege to Cartagena. Cut off by land and sea, the city surrendered in December, and the rest of Colombia was pacified within a few months. Of all the provinces of Spanish America, only Argentina remained in revolt. Had Ferdinand made the concession of granting legal equality with whites to the mixed-bloods who supported his cause, the Spanish Empire in America might have survived much longer. But the reactionary Ferdinand would make no concessions.

Bolívar still had an unshakable faith in the inevitable triumph of independence. From Jamaica he sent a famous letter in which he affirmed that faith and offered a remarkable analysis of the situation and prospects of Spanish America. He scoffed at the ability of Spain, that "aged serpent," to maintain Spanish America forever in subjection. Bolívar also looked into the political future of the continent. Monarchy, he argued, was foreign to the genius of Latin America; only a republican regime would be accepted by its peoples. A single government for the region was impracticable, divided as it was by "climatic differences, geographic diversity, conflicting interests, and dissimilar characteristics." Bolívar boldly forecast the destiny of the different regions, taking account of their economic and social structures. Chile, for example, seemed to him to have a democratic future; Peru, on the other hand, was fated to suffer dictatorship because it contained "two factors that clash with every just and liberal principle: gold and slaves."

From Jamaica, Bolívar went to Haiti, where he received a sympathetic hearing and the offer of some material support from the mulatto president Alexandre Pétion, who asked in return for the freedom of the slaves in the territory that Bolívar should liberate. In March 1816, Bolívar and a small band of followers landed on the island of Margarita off the Venezuelan coast. Two attempts to gain a foothold on the mainland were easily beaten back, and soon Bolívar was back in the West Indies. Reflecting on his failures, he concluded that the effort to invade the well-fortified western coast of Venezuela was a mistake and decided to establish a base in the Orinoco River valley, distant from the centers of Spanish power. Roving patriot bands still operated in this region, and Bolívar hoped to win the allegiance of the llaneros, who were becoming disillusioned with their Spanish allies. In September 1816, Bolívar sailed from Haiti for the Orinoco River delta, which he ascended until he reached the small town of Angostura (modern Ciudad Bolívar), which he made his headquarters.

The tide of war now began to flow in his favor. The patriot guerrilla bands accepted his leadership; even more important, he gained the support of the principal llanero chieftain, José Antonio Páez. European developments also favored Bolívar. The end of the Napoleonic wars idled a large number of British soldiers; many of these veterans came to Venezuela, forming a British Legion that distinguished itself in battle by its valor. English merchants made loans enabling Bolívar to secure men and arms for the coming campaign. Helpful too was the mulish attitude of Ferdinand VII, whose refusal to consider making any concessions

to the colonists caused the English government to lose patience and regard with more friendly eyes the prospect of Spanish-American independence.

On the eve of the decisive campaign of 1819, Bolívar summoned to Angostura a makeshift congress that vested him with dictatorial powers. To this congress he presented a project for a constitution for Venezuela in which he urged the abolition of slavery and the distribution of land to revolutionary soldiers. But the proposed constitution also had some nondemocratic features. They included a president with virtually royal powers, a hereditary senate, and restriction of the suffrage and officeholding to the propertied and educated elite. The congress disregarded Bolívar's reform proposals but elected him president of the republic and adopted a constitution embodying many of his ideas.

The war, however, still had to be won. Bolívar's bold strategy for the liberation of Venezuela and Colombia envisaged striking a heavy blow at Spanish forces from a completely unexpected direction. While llanero cavalry under Páez distracted and pinned down the main body of Spanish troops in northern Venezuela with swift raids, Bolívar advanced with an army of some twenty-five hundred men along the winding Orinoco and Arauco rivers, across the plains, and then up the towering Colombian Andes until he reached the plateau where lay Bogotá, capital of New Granada. On the field of Boyacá the patriot army surprised and defeated the royalists in a short, sharp battle that netted sixteen hundred prisoners and considerable supplies. Bogotá lay defenseless, and Bolívar entered the capital to the cheers of its people, who had suffered greatly under Spanish rule.

Leaving his aide, Francisco Santander, to organize a government, Bolívar hurried off to Angostura to prepare the liberation of Venezuela. Then thrilling news arrived from Spain; on January 1, 1820, a regiment awaiting embarkation for South America had mutinied, starting a revolt that forced Ferdinand to restore the liberal constitution of 1812 and give up his plans for the reconquest of the colonies. This news caused joy among the patriots, gloom and desertions among the Venezuelan royalists. In July 1821 the troops of

Bolívar and Páez crushed the last important Spanish force in Venezuela at Carabobo. Save for some coastal towns and forts still held by beleaguered royalists, Venezuela was free.

Bolívar had already turned his attention southward. The independence of Spanish America remained precarious as long as the Spaniards held the immense mountain bastion of the central Andes. While Bolívar prepared a major offensive from Bogotá against Quito, he sent his able young lieutenant, Antonio José Sucre, by sea from Colombia's Pacific coast to seize the port of Guayaquil. Before Sucre even arrived, the creole party in Guayaquil revolted, proclaimed independence, and placed the port under Bolívar's protection. With his forces swelled by reinforcements sent by the Argentine general José de San Martín, Sucre advanced into the Ecuadoran highlands and defeated a Spanish army on the slopes of Mount Pichincha, near Quito. Bolívar, meanwhile, advancing southward from Bogotá along the Cauca River valley, encountered stiff royalist resistance, but this crumbled on news of Sucre's victory at Pichincha. The provinces composing the former viceroyalty of New Granada—the future republics of Venezuela, Colombia, Ecuador, and Panama—were now free from Spanish control. They were temporarily united into a large state named Colombia or Gran Colombia, established, at the initiative of Bolívar, by the union of New Granada and Venezuela in 1821.

THE SOUTHERN LIBERATION MOVEMENT AND SAN MARTÍN

The time had come for the movement of liberation led by Bolívar to merge with that flowing northward from Argentina. Ever since the defeat of the British invasions of 1806–1807, the creole party, although nominally loyal to Spain, had effectively controlled Buenos Aires. The hero of the invasions and the temporary viceroy, Santiago Liniers, cooperated fully with the creole leaders. A new viceroy, sent by the Seville junta to replace Liniers, joined with the viceroy at Lima to crush abortive creole revolts in Upper Peru (Bolivia). But in Buenos Aires he walked softly, for he recognized the superior power of the creoles. Under their pressure he issued a decree permitting free trade with allied and neutral nations, a measure bitterly opposed by representatives of the Cádiz monopoly. But this concession could not save the Spanish regime. Revolution was in the air, and the creole leaders waited only, in the words of one of their number, for the figs to be ripe.

In May 1810, when word came that French troops had entered Seville and threatened Cádiz, the secret patriot society organized a demonstration that forced the viceroy to summon an open town meeting to decide the future government of the colony. This first Argentine congress voted to depose the viceroy and establish a junta to govern in the name of Ferdinand. The junta promptly attempted to consolidate its control of the vast viceroyalty. The interior provinces were subdued after sharp fighting. Montevideo, across the Río de la Plata on the eastern shore (modern Uruguay), remained in Spanish hands until 1814, when it fell to an Argentine siege. The junta met even more tenacious resistance from the gauchos of the Uruguayan pampa, led by José Gervasio Artigas, who demanded Uruguayan autonomy in a loose federal connection with Buenos Aires. The *porteños* (inhabitants of Buenos Aires) would have nothing to do with Artigas's gaucho democracy, and a new struggle began. It ended when Artigas, caught between the fire of Buenos Aires and that of Portuguese forces claiming Uruguay for Brazil, had to flee to Paraguay. Uruguay did not achieve independence until 1828.

The creole aristocracy in another portion of the old viceroyalty of La Plata, Paraguay, also suspected the designs of the Buenos Aires junta and defeated a porteño force sent to liberate Asunción. This done, the creole party in Asunción rose up, deposed Spanish officials, and proclaimed the independence of Paraguay. A key figure in this uprising was the remarkable Dr. José Rodríguez de Francia, soon to become his country's first president and dictator.

Efforts by the Buenos Aires junta to liberate the mountainous northern province of Upper Peru also failed. Two thrusts by a patriot army into this area were defeated and the invaders rolled back.

The steep terrain, long lines of communication, and the apathy of Bolivian indigenous peoples contributed to these defeats.

The Buenos Aires government also had serious internal problems. A dispute broke out between liberal supporters of the fiery Mariano Moreno, secretary of the junta and champion of social reform, and a conservative faction led by the great landowner Cornelio Saavedra. This dispute foreshadowed the liberal-conservative cleavage that dominated the first decades of Argentine history after independence. In 1813 a national assembly gave the country the name of the United Provinces of La Plata and enacted such reforms as the abolition of mita, encomienda, titles of nobility, and the Inquisition. A declaration of independence, however, was delayed until 1816.

Also 1816 was the year in which the military genius of José de San Martín broke the long-standing military stalemate. San Martín, born in what is now northeastern Argentina, was a colonel in the Spanish army with twenty years of service behind him when revolution broke out in Buenos Aires. He promptly sailed for La Plata to offer his sword to the patriot junta. He was soon raised to the command of the army of Upper Peru, which was recuperating in Tucumán after a sound defeat at royalist hands. Perceiving that a frontal attack on the Spanish position in Upper Peru was doomed to failure, San Martín offered a plan for total victory that gained the support of the director of the United Provinces, Juan Martín de Pueyrredón. San Martín proposed a march over the Andes to liberate Chile, where a Spanish reaction had toppled the revolutionary regime established by Bernardo O'Higgins and other patriot leaders in 1810. This done, the united forces of La Plata and Chile would descend on Peru from the sea.

To mask his plans from Spanish eyes and gain time for a large organizational effort, San Martín obtained an appointment as governor of the province of Cuyo, whose capital, Mendoza, lay at the eastern end of a strategic pass leading across the Andes to Chile. He spent two years recruiting, training, and equipping his Army of the Andes. Like Bolívar, he used the promise of freedom to secure black and mulatto volunteers, and later

declared they were his best soldiers. Chilean refugees fleeing the Spanish reaction in their country also joined his forces.

San Martín, methodical and thorough, demanded of the Buenos Aires government arms, munitions, food, and equipment of every kind. In January 1817 the army began the crossing of the Andes. Its march over the frozen Andean passes equaled in difficulty Bolívar's scaling of the Colombian sierra. Twenty-one days later, the army issued onto Chilean soil. A decisive defeat of the Spanish army at Chacabuco in February opened the gates of Santiago to San Martín. He won another victory at Maipú (1818), in a battle that ended the threat to Chile's independence. Rejecting Chilean invitations to become supreme ruler of the republic, a post assumed by O'Higgins, San Martín began to prepare the attack by sea on Lima, fifteen hundred miles away.

The execution of his plan required the creation of a navy. He secured a number of ships in England and the United States and engaged a competent though eccentric naval officer, Thomas, Lord Cochrane, to organize the patriot navy. In August 1820, the expedition sailed for Peru in a fleet made up of seven ships of war and eighteen transports. San Martín landed his army about a hundred miles south of Lima but delayed moving on the Peruvian capital. He hoped to obtain its surrender by economic blockade, propaganda, and direct negotiation with the Spanish officials. The desire of the Lima aristocracy, creole and peninsular, to avoid an armed struggle that might unleash an indigenous and slave revolt worked in favor of San Martín's strategy. In June 1821 the Spanish army evacuated Lima and retreated toward the Andes. San Martín entered the capital and in a festive atmosphere proclaimed the independence of Peru.

But his victory was far from complete. He had to deal with counterrevolutionary plots and the resistance of Lima's corrupt elite to his program of social reform, which included the end of indigenous tribute and the grant of freedom to the children of slaves. San Martín's assumption of supreme military and civil power in August 1821 added to the factional opposition. Meanwhile, a large Spanish army maneuvered in front of Lima, challenging San Martín to a battle he dared not join with his much smaller force. Disheartened by the atmosphere of intrigue and hostility that surrounded him, San Martín became convinced that only monarchy could bring stability to Spanish America and sent a secret mission to Europe to search for a prince for the throne of Peru.

Such was the background of San Martín's departure for Guayaquil, where he met in conference with Bolívar on July 26 and 27, 1822. The agenda of the meeting included several points. One concerned the future of Guayaquil. San Martín claimed the port city for Peru; Bolívar, however, had already annexed it to Gran Colombia, confronting San Martín with a fait accompli. Another topic was the political future of all Spanish America. San Martín favored monarchy as the solution for the emergent chaos of the new states; Bolívar believed in a governmental system that would be republican in form, oligarchical in content. But the critical question before the two men was how to complete the liberation of the continent by defeating the Spanish forces in Peru.

San Martín's abrupt retirement from public life after the conference, the reluctance of the two liberators to discuss what was said there, and the meager authentic documentary record of the proceedings have surrounded the meeting with an atmosphere of mystery and produced two opposed and partisan interpretations. A view favored by Argentine historians holds that San Martín came to Guayaquil in search of military aid but was rebuffed by Bolívar, who was unwilling to share with a rival the glory of bringing the struggle for independence to an end; San Martín then magnanimously decided to leave Peru and allow Bolívar to complete the work he had begun. Venezuelan historians, on the other hand, argue that San Martín came to Guayaquil primarily to recover Guayaquil for Peru. The historians deny that San Martín asked Bolívar for more troops and insist that he left Peru for personal reasons having nothing to do with the conference.

Both interpretations tend to diminish the stature and sense of realism of the two liberators. San Martín was no martyr, nor was Bolívar an ambitious schemer who sacrificed San Martín to

his passion for power and glory. San Martín must have understood that Bolívar alone combined the military, political, and psychological assets needed to liquidate the factional hornets' nest in Peru and gain final victory over the powerful Spanish army in the sierra. Given the situation in Lima, San Martín's presence there could only hinder the performance of those tasks. In this light, the decision of Bolívar to assume sole direction of the war and of San Martín to withdraw reflected a realistic appraisal of the Peruvian problem and the solution it required.

San Martín returned to Lima to find that in his absence his enemies had rallied and struck at him by driving his reforming chief minister, Bernardo Monteagudo, out of the country. San Martín made no effort to reassert his power. In September 1822, before the first Peruvian congress, he announced his resignation as protector and his impending departure. He returned to Buenos Aires by way of Chile, where the government of his friend O'Higgins was on the verge of collapse. In Buenos Aires the people seemed to have forgotten his existence. Accompanied by his daughter, he sailed for Europe at the end of 1823. He died in France in 1850 in virtual obscurity. His transfiguration into an Argentine national hero began a quarter-century later.

San Martín's departure left Lima and the territory under its control in serious danger of reconquest by the strong Spanish army in the sierra. Bolívar made no move to rescue the squabbling factions in Lima from their predicament; he allowed the situation to deteriorate until May 1823, when the Peruvian congress called on him for help. Then he sent Sucre with only a few thousand men, for he wanted to bring the Lima politicians to their knees. The scare produced by a brief reoccupation of the capital by the Spanish army prepared the creole leaders to accept Bolívar's absolute rule.

Bolívar arrived in Peru in September 1823. He required almost a year to achieve political stability and to weld the army he brought with him and the different national units under his command into a united force. After a month of difficult ascent of the sierra, in an altitude so high that Bolívar and most of his men suffered from mountain sickness, cavalry elements of the patriot and royalist armies clashed near the lake of Junín, and the Spaniards suffered defeat (August 6, 1824). The royalist commander, José de Canterac, retreated toward Cuzco. Leaving Sucre in command, Bolívar returned to Lima to gather reinforcements. To Sucre fell the glory of defeating the Spanish army in the last major engagement of the war, at Ayacucho (December 9, 1824). Only scattered resistance at some points in the highlands and on the coast remained to be mopped up. The work of continental liberation was achieved.

THE ACHIEVEMENT OF BRAZILIAN INDEPENDENCE

In contrast to the political anarchy, economic dislocation, and military destruction in Spanish America, Brazil's drive toward independence proceeded as a relatively bloodless transition between 1808 and 1822. The idea of Brazilian independence first arose in the late eighteenth century as a Brazilian reaction to the Portuguese policy of tightening political and economic control over the colony in the interests of the mother country. The first significant conspiracy against Portuguese rule was organized in 1788–1789 in Minas Gerais, where rigid governmental control over the production and prices of gold and diamonds, as well as heavy taxes, caused much discontent, and where there existed a group of intellectuals educated in Europe and familiar with the ideas of the Enlightenment. But this conspiracy never went beyond the stage of discussion and was easily discovered and crushed. Other conspiracies in Rio de Janeiro (1794), Bahia (1798), and Pernambuco (1801), as well as a brief revolt in Pernambuco (1817), reflected the influence of republican ideas over sections of the elite and even the lower strata of urban society. All proved abortive or were soon crushed. The stagnation of Brazilian life and the fear of slave owners that resistance to Portugal might spark slave insurrections effectively inhibited the spirit of revolt. Were it not for an accident of European history, the independence of Brazil might have long been delayed.

The French invasion of Portugal (1807), followed by the flight of the Portuguese court to Rio de Janeiro, brought large benefits to Brazil. Indeed, the transfer of the court in effect signified achievement of Brazilian independence. The Portuguese prince regent João opened Brazil's ports to the trade of friendly nations, permitted the rise of local industries, and founded a Bank of Brazil. In 1815 he elevated Brazil to the legal status of a kingdom co-equal with Portugal. In one sense, however, Brazil's new status signified the substitution of one dependence for another. Freed from Portuguese control, Brazil came under the economic domination of England, which obtained major tariff concessions and other privileges by the Strangford Treaty of 1810. One result was an influx of cheap machine-made goods that swamped the handicrafts industry of the country.

Brazilian elites took satisfaction in Brazil's new role and the growth of educational, cultural, and economic opportunities for their class. But this feeling was mixed with resentment at the thousands of Portuguese courtiers and hangers-on who came with the court and who competed with Brazilians for jobs and favors. Portuguese merchants in Brazil, for their part, were bitter over the passing of the Lisbon monopoly. Thus, the change in the status of Brazil sharpened the conflict between mazombos (Portuguese elites born in Brazil) and reinóis (elites born in Portugal and loyal to the Portuguese crown).

The event that precipitated the break with the mother country was the revolution of 1820 in Portugal. The Portuguese revolutionists framed a liberal constitution for the kingdom, but they were conservative or reactionary in relation to Brazil. They demanded the immediate return of Dom João to Lisbon, an end to the system of dual monarchy that he had devised, and the restoration of the Portuguese commercial monopoly. Timid and vacillating, Dom João did not know which way to turn. Under the pressure of his courtiers, who hungered to return to Portugal and their lost estates, he finally approved the new constitution and sailed for Portugal. He left behind him, however, his son and heir, Dom Pedro, as regent of Brazil, and in a private letter advised him, in the event the Brazilians should demand independence, to assume leadership of the movement and set the crown of Brazil on his head. Pedro received the same advice from José Bonifácio de Andrada, a Brazilian scientist whose stay in Portugal had completely disillusioned him about the Portuguese capacity for colonial reform.

Soon it became clear that the Portuguese Côrtes intended to set the clock back by abrogating all the liberties and concessions won by Brazil since 1808. One of its decrees insisted on the immediate return of Dom Pedro from Brazil in order that he might complete his political education. The pace of events moved more rapidly in 1822. On January 9, Dom Pedro, urged on by José Bonifácio de Andrada and other Brazilian advisers who perceived a golden opportunity to make an orderly transition to independence without the intervention of the masses, refused an order from the Côrtes to return to Portugal and issued his famous *fico* ("I remain"). On September 7, regarded by all Brazilians as Independence Day, he issued the even more celebrated Cry of Ipiranga, "Independence or Death!" In December 1822, having overcome slight resistance by Portuguese troops, Dom Pedro was formally proclaimed constitutional emperor of Brazil.

Mexico's Road to Independence

In New Spain, as in other colonies, the crisis of the Bourbon monarchy in 1808–1810 encouraged some creole leaders to strike a blow for self-rule or total independence under "the mask of Ferdinand." But in Mexico the movement for independence took an unexpected turn. Here the masses, instead of remaining aloof, joined the struggle and for a time managed to convert it from a private quarrel between two elites into an incipient social revolution.

In July 1808 news of Napoleon's capture of Charles IV and Ferdinand VII and his invasion of Spain reached Mexico City and provoked intense debates and maneuvers among Mexican elites to take advantage of these dramatic events. Faced with the prospect of an imminent collapse of Spain, creoles and peninsulars alike prepared to seize power and ensure that their group would control New Spain, whatever the outcome of the Spanish crisis. The creoles moved first. The Mexico City cabildo, a creole stronghold, called on the viceroy to summon an assembly to be chosen by the creole-dominated cabildos. This assembly, composed of representatives of various elite groups, would govern Mexico until Ferdinand VII, whose forced abdication was null and void, regained his throne. The viceroy, José de Iturrigaray, supported such a call, noting that Spain was in "a state of anarchy."

The conservative landed elite that sponsored the movement for a colonial assembly, it must be stressed, desired free trade and autonomy or home rule within the Spanish empire, not independence. They had no intention of taking up arms in a struggle that might bring a dangerous intervention of the exploited classes and thus endanger their own personal and economic survival. The reforms that the chief creole ideologist, Fray Melchor de Talamantes, recommended to the proposed assembly suggested the limits of creole elite ambitions: abolition of the Inquisition and the ecclesiastical fuero (the clergy's privilege of exemption from civil courts); free trade; and measures to promote the reform of mining, agriculture, and industry.

The creole movement for home rule and free trade, however, posed a threat to the peninsular merchants, whose prosperity depended on the continuance of the existing closed commercial system with Seville as its center. On the night of September 15, 1808, the merchants struck back. The wealthy peninsular merchant Gabriel de Yermo led the consulado's militia in a preemptive coup, ousting Viceroy Iturrigaray and arresting leading creole supporters of autonomy. A series of transient, peninsular-dominated regimes then held power until a new viceroy, Francisco Javier de Venegas, arrived from Spain in September 1810.

The leaders of the creole aristocracy, mindful of its large property interests, did not respond to the peninsular counteroffensive. The leadership of the movement for creole control of Mexico's destiny now passed to a group consisting predominantly of "marginal elites"—upper-class individuals of relatively modest economic and social standing—in the Bajío, a geographic region roughly corresponding to the intendency of Querétaro.

The special economic and social conditions of this region help explain its decisive role in the first stage of the Mexican struggle for independence. It was the most modern of Mexican regions in its agrarian and industrial structure. There were few indigenous communities of the traditional type; the bulk of its population consisted of partially Europeanized urban workers, miners, and peons or tenants of various types. Agriculture was dominated by large commercial irrigated estates producing wheat and other products for the upper classes; maize, the diet of the masses, was chiefly grown on marginal land by impoverished tenants. There was an important textile industry that had experienced a shift from large obrajes using slaves and other coerced labor to a putting-out system in which merchant-financiers provided artisan families with cotton and wool, which they turned into cloth on their own looms, "forcing growing numbers of artisan families to exploit themselves by working long hours for little compensation." Mining was the most profitable and capital-intensive industry of the region; in some good years the largest mine at Guanajuato, the Valenciana, netted its owners over 1 million pesos in profits.

The quasi-capitalist structure of the Bajío's economy, based largely on free wage labor, promoted a growth of workers' class consciousness and militancy. The mineworkers at Guanajuato, for example, resisted attempts to end their partidos (shares of the ores they mined over a given quota) by methods that included a production slowdown; the employers responded by calling in the militia to force resumption of full production. The Bajío's labor force experienced a decline of wage and living standards and employment opportunities in the last decades of the eighteenth century. These losses were a result of conditions over which they had no control: rapid population growth that enabled landowners to drive down wages or replace permanent workers by seasonal laborers; competition for domestic textiles from cheap, industrially produced imports; and the rising cost of aging mines. These factors caused deep insecurity and resentment. Then in 1808 and 1809, drought and famine again struck the Bajío, aggravating all the existing tensions and grievances. As in the earlier drought and famine in 1785, the great landowners profited from the misery of the poor by holding their reserves of grain off the market until prices reached their peak. It was against this background of profound social unrest and a grave subsistence crisis that the struggle for Mexican independence began. The Bajío was its storm center, and the Bajío's peasantry and working class formed its spearhead.

In 1810 a creole plot for revolt was taking shape in the important political and industrial center of Querétaro. Only two of the conspirators belonged to the highest circle of the creole regional elite, and efforts to draw other prominent creoles into the scheme were rebuffed. The majority were "marginal elites"—struggling landowners, a grocer, an estate administrator, a parish priest. From the first the conspirators seem to have planned to mobilize the indigenous and mixed-blood proletariat, probably because they doubted their ability to win over the majority of their own class. If the motive of most of the plotters was the hope of raising troops, Miguel Hidalgo y Costilla, a priest in the town of Dolores and one-time rector of the colegio of San Nicolás at Valladolid, was inspired by a genuine sympathy with the natives. The scholarly Hidalgo had already called the attention of Spanish authorities to himself by his freethinking ideas; he was also known for his scientific interests and his efforts to develop new industries in his parish.

Informed that their plot had been denounced to Spanish officials, the conspirators held an urgent council and decided to launch their revolt although arrangements were not complete. On Sunday, September 16, 1810, Hidalgo called on the people of his parish, assembled for Mass, to rise against their Spanish rulers. Here, as elsewhere in Spanish America, the "mask of Ferdinand" came into play; Hidalgo claimed to be leading an insurrection in support of a beloved king treacherously captured and deposed by godless Frenchmen. In less than two weeks the insurgent leaders had assembled thousands of rebels and begun a march on the industrial and mining center of Guanajuato. On the march Hidalgo secured a banner bearing the image of the Virgin of Guadalupe

This sympathetic portrait of the Mexican liberator Miguel Hidalgo well conveys Hidalgo's warm character. [Culver Pictures, Inc.]

the basic objective of Hidalgo and his allies—creole domination of an autonomous or independent Mexico—and the thirst for revenge and social justice of their lower-class followers. Learning of the events at Guanajuato, the great majority of the creole elite recoiled in horror before the elemental violence of a movement that Hidalgo was unable to control.

After his first victories, Hidalgo issued decrees abolishing slavery and tribute, the yearly head tax paid by indígenas and mulattos. Three months later, from his headquarters at Guadalajara, in his first and only reference to the land problem, he ordered that indigenous communal lands in the vicinity of the city that had been rented to Spaniards be returned to the pueblos; it was his wish that "only the Indians in their respective pueblos should enjoy the use of those lands." Moderate though they were, these reforms gave the Mexican struggle a popular character absent from the movement for independence in South America but further alienated many creoles who may have desired autonomy or independence, but not social revolution. On the other hand, these reforms did not go far enough to redress the fundamental grievances of Hidalgo's peasant and working-class followers in regions like the Bajío and Jalisco: landlessness, starvation wages and high rents, lack of tenant security, and the monopoly of grain by profiteering landowners. In the absence of a clearly defined program of structural social and economic reform, Hidalgo's followers vented their rage at an intolerable situation by killing Spaniards and plundering the properties of creoles and peninsulars alike.

Hidalgo proved unable to weld his rebel horde into a disciplined army or to capitalize on his early victories. Having defeated a royalist army near Mexico City, he camped outside the city for three days and then, after his demand for its surrender was rejected, inexplicably withdrew from the almost defenseless capital without attacking. It has been suggested that he feared a repetition of the atrocities that followed earlier victories or that he believed that he could not hold the great city without the support of the local population, which, according to historian Eric Van Young, doomed

and proclaimed her the patron of his movement, thus appealing to the religious devotion of his followers. All along the route the established elites held back from joining the revolt. They watched with dismay as the rebels looted stores and took the crops provided by the bountiful harvest of 1810, after two years of drought and famine. The capture of Guanajuato on September 28 was accomplished with the aid of several thousand mineworkers, who joined in storming the massive municipal granary in which Spanish officials, militia, and local elites attempted to hold out. It was followed by the killing of hundreds of Spaniards in the granary and the city. The massacre and sack of Guanajuato was a turning point in the rebellion, for it brought into the open the conflict between

Hidalgo's movement to defeat. But the peasantry of the central highlands, who still possessed communal lands that satisfied their minimal needs and supplemented their meager crops by wage labor on large haciendas, also did not rally to Hidalgo's cause. With his army melting away through desertions, Hidalgo retreated toward the Bajío. Driven out of Guanajuato by royalist forces, Hidalgo and other rebel leaders fled northward, hoping to establish new bases for their movement in Coahuila and Texas. Less than one year after his revolt had begun, Hidalgo was captured as he fled toward the United States border, condemned as a heretic and subversive by an inquisitorial court, and executed by a firing squad.

The defeat and death of Hidalgo did not end the insurrection he had begun. The fires of revolt continued to smolder over vast areas of Mexico. New leaders arose who learned from the failure of Hidalgo's tactics. Many, abandoning the effort to defeat the royalist forces with their superior arms and training in conventional warfare, developed a flexible and mobile guerrilla style of fighting. The Spaniards themselves had effectively employed guerrilla warfare—a war of swift movement by small units that strike and flee—in their struggle against Napoleon, taking advantage of a familiar terrain and the support of rural populations to foil pursuit and repression. The new Mexican rebel strategy was not to win a quick victory but to exhaust the enemy and undermine his social and economic base by pillaging the stores and haciendas of his elite allies, disrupting trade, and creating war weariness and hostility toward an increasingly arbitrary colonial regime.

Following Hidalgo's death, a mestizo priest, José María Morelos, assumed supreme command of the revolutionary movement. Morelos had ministered to poor congregations in the hot, humid Pacific lowlands of Michoacán before offering his services to Hidalgo, who asked him to organize insurrection in that area. Economic and social conditions in the coastal lowlands region bore some resemblance to those of the Bajío; its principal industries, sugar, cotton, and indigo, were in decline as a result of competition from regions closer to highland markets and from imported cloth. As a result, the position of estate tenants and laborers had become increasingly dependent and insecure. The material conditions of indigenous villagers had also deteriorated as a result of the renting of community lands by village leaders to outsiders, a practice that left many families without the minimal land needed for subsistence.

The discontent generated by these conditions provided Morelos and his insurgent movement with a mass base in the coastal lowlands. Morelos was sensitive to the problems and needs of the area's rural folk. Like Hidalgo, he ordered an end to slavery and tribute. He also ended the rental of indigenous community lands and abolished the community treasuries (*cajas de comunidad*), whose funds were often misused by village notables or drained off by royal officials; henceforth, the villagers were to keep the proceeds of their labor. Morelos also extended Hidalgo's program of social reform by prohibiting all forced labor and forbidding the use of all racial terms except *gachupines*, applied to the hated peninsular Spaniards. There seems little doubt that in principle Morelos favored a radical land reform. In a "plan" found among his papers, he proposed the division of all haciendas greater than two leagues into smaller plots, denounced a situation in which "a single individual owns vast extents of uncultivated land and enslaves thousands of people who must work the land as *gañanes* [peons] or slaves," and proclaimed the social benefits of the small landholding. But Morelos's freedom of action was restrained by his links with the creole landowning elite, some of whom were his lieutenants and whose property he promised to respect.

A brilliant guerrilla leader who substituted strict discipline, training, and centralized direction for the loose methods of Hidalgo, Morelos, having established a firm base in the Pacific lowlands, advanced toward the strategic central highlands and the capital. His thrust into the rich sugar-producing area (modern Morelos) just south of Mexico City failed to gain sufficient support from the local indigenous communities, which retained substantial landholdings, and he was forced to retreat southward into the rugged mountainous region of Oaxaca. His military efforts were hampered by differences with fractious civilian allies and by his decision to establish a representative government at a time when his military situation was turning precarious. In the fall of 1813, a congress he had convened at Chilpancingo declared Mexico's independence, enacted Morelos's social reforms, and vested him with supreme military and executive power. But in the months that followed, the tide of war turned against the insurgent cause, in part because of tactical mistakes by Morelos that involved abandonment of fluid guerrilla warfare in favor of fixed-position warfare, illustrated by his prolonged siege of the fortress of Acapulco. In late 1813 Morelos suffered several defeats at the hands of royalist forces directed by the able and aggressive viceroy Felix Calleja.

The defeat of Napoleon and the return of the ferociously reactionary Ferdinand VII to the throne of Spain in 1814 released thousands of soldiers who could be sent overseas to suppress the Spanish-American revolts. The congress of Chilpancingo, put to flight, became a wandering body whose squabbling and need for protection diverted Morelos's attention from the all-important military problem. Hoping to revitalize the rebel cause and gain creole elite support by offering an alternative to Ferdinand's brutal despotism, the congress met at Apatzingan and drafted a liberal constitution (October 1814) that provided for a republican frame of government and included an article proclaiming the equality of citizens before the law and freedom of speech and the press. In the course of the year 1815, unrelenting royalist pressure forced the congress to flee from place to place. In November, fighting a rear-guard action that enabled the congress to escape, Morelos was captured by a royalist force and brought to the capital. Like Hidalgo, he was found guilty by an Inquisition court of heresy and treason; he was shot by a firing squad on December 22, 1815.

The great guerrilla leader had died, but the revolutionary movement, although fragmented, continued. Indeed, the struggle between numerous insurgent bands and the Spanish counterinsurgency reached new heights of virulence between 1815 and 1820. Avoiding the mistakes of Hidalgo and even Morelos, the rebel leaders shunned

pitched battles and made no effort to capture large population centers. Instead, they conducted a fluid warfare in which small units sacked and destroyed loyalist haciendas, disrupted or levied tolls on trade, severed communications, and controlled large stretches of the countryside. They fled when pursued by counterinsurgent forces and reappeared when the overextended Spanish troops had departed. The destructive effects of a hopeless war on the economy, the heavy taxes imposed on all inhabitants by regional commanders and local juntas for the support of that war, and the harsh treatment meted out not only to insurgents but also to high-ranking creoles who favored compromise and autonomy alienated even the most loyal elements of the creole elite.

These elements, as well as many conservative Spaniards, sought a way out of the impasse that would avoid radical social change under a republican regime of the kind Morelos had proposed. A way out seemed to appear in 1820 when a liberal revolt in Spain forced Ferdinand VII to accept the constitution of 1812. Mexican deputies elected to the Spanish Cortes, or parliament, proposed a solution that would have retained ties with Spain but granted New Spain and the other American "kingdoms" autonomy within the empire. The Spanish majority in the Cortes rejected the proposal and sealed the doom of the empire.

The radical reforms the Cortes adopted in 1820, including the abolition of the ecclesiastical and military fueros, antagonized conservative landlords, clergy, army officers, and merchants, whether creole or peninsular. Fearing the loss of privileges, they schemed to separate Mexico from the mother country and to establish independence under conservative auspices. Their instrument was the creole officer Agustín de Iturbide, who had waged implacable war against the insurgents. Iturbide offered peace and reconciliation to the principal rebel leader, Vicente Guerrero. His plan combined independence, monarchy, the supremacy of the Roman Catholic church, and the civil equality of creoles and peninsulars. Guerrero was a sincere liberal and republican, Iturbide an unprincipled opportunist who dreamed of placing a crown on his own head. But for the moment

Iturbide's program offered advantages to both sides, and Guerrero reluctantly accepted it. The united forces of Iturbide and Guerrero swiftly overcame scattered loyalist resistance. On September 28, 1821, Iturbide proclaimed Mexican independence, and eight months later an elected congress summoned by Iturbide confirmed him as Agustín I, emperor of Mexico.

Despite its tinsel splendor, Iturbide's empire had no popular base. Within a few months, Agustín I had to abdicate, with a warning never to return. Hoping for a comeback, Iturbide returned from England in 1824 and landed on the coast with a small party. He was promptly captured by troops of the new republican regime and shot.

The liberation of Mexico brought the struggle for Latin American independence to a successful conclusion. The story of that struggle would not be complete without mention of the contribution made by Latin American women to its outcome. A Mexican heroine is Doña Josefa Ortiz de Domínguez, wife of the creole corregidor of Querétaro, the courageous woman who warned Miguel Hidalgo and other conspirators of their impending arrest by Spanish authorities and thereby saved the revolution from destruction before it had even begun. The lands freed under Simón Bolívar's leadership remember his bright and saucy mistress, Manuela Saenz, who left her prosy British husband to join the Liberator and saved him from death at the hands of assassins. "That she shared his thoughts, consoled him, and encouraged him to fight for his beliefs cannot be denied," writes Harold Bierck. "In many respects she was, as many called her, *La Libertadora.*"

In every part of Latin America, women, often drawn from the middle and lower classes, took part in the armed struggle. Bolívar praised the "Amazons" of Gran Colombia; they included the heroic Policarpa Salvarrieta, who was only twenty-three when the Spaniards executed her for aiding the revolution. In Brazil, María Quiteira de Jesus, born on a small cattle and cotton-raising ranch in the province of Bahia, disguised herself as a young man to join the revolutionary army. Her valor won her a decoration in 1823 from Dom Pedro, the first

The illegitimate daughter of a Spanish aristocrat, Manuela Saenz was expelled from a Catholic convent and later became a fierce proponent of political independence and women's rights. During the struggle for independence, she met and fell in love with Simón Bolívar, whose life she saved in 1828. [Photo courtesy of Gregory Kauffman, author of *Manuela*, published by RLN & Company, Seattle]

ruler of independent Brazil. In the struggle for the independence of Haiti, says Francesca Miller, women were "omnipresent," and some commanded troops.

In the aftermath of the struggle for independence, some women drew the logical consequences of their participation in that cause: If women fought and died for independence, why did they not have the right to vote and be elected? This was the message of a petition submitted in 1824 to the government of the Mexican state of Zacatecas: "Women also wish to have the title of citizen . . . to see themselves counted in the census as 'la ciudadana H . . . la ciudadana N.' " But it would take another one and a half centuries for that wish to be realized for all the women of Latin America.

Latin American Independence: A Reckoning

After more than a decade of war, accompanied by immense loss of life and property, most of Latin America had won its political independence. The revolutions were accompanied or quickly followed by a number of social changes. Independence brought the death of the Inquisition, the end of legal discrimination on the basis of race, and the abolition of titles of nobility in most lands. It also gave an impetus to the abolition of slavery, to the founding of public schools, and to similar reforms. All these changes, however, were marginal; independence left intact the existing economic and social structures. This was natural, for the creole elite that headed the movement had no intention of transforming the existing order. They sought to replace the peninsulars in the seats of power and open their ports to the commerce of the world but desired no change of labor and land systems. Indeed, their interests as producers of raw materials and foodstuffs for sale in the markets of Europe and North America required the maintenance of the system of great estates worked by a semiservile native proletariat. No agrarian reform accompanied independence. The haciendas abandoned by or confiscated from loyalists usually fell into the hands of the creole aristocracy. Some land also passed into the possession of mestizo or mulatto officers, who were assimilated into the creole elite and as a rule promptly forgot the groups from which they had come.

Instead of broadening the base of landownership in Latin America, the revolutions actually helped narrow it. The liberal, individualist ideology of the revolutionary governments undermined indigenous communal land tenure in some cases by requiring the division of community lands among its members. This process facilitated the usurpation of these communal lands by creole landlords and hastened the transformation of the native peasantry into a class of peons or serfs on Spanish haciendas (see Chapters 9 and 10). Because no structural economic change took place, aristocratic values continued to dominate Latin American society, despite an elaborate façade of republican constitutions and law codes.

PART TWO

Latin America in the Nineteenth Century

Coffee Plantation, 1935, by Candido Portinari/Museo Nacional Bellas Artes, Rio de Janeiro, Brazil/Index/Bridgeman Art Library, London/New York.

A FTER WINNING THEIR INDEPENDENCE, the new Latin American states began a long, uphill struggle to achieve economic and political stability. They faced immense obstacles, for independence, as previously noted, was not accompanied by economic and social changes that could spur rapid progress—for example, no redistribution of land and income in favor of the lower classes took place. The large estate, generally operated using primitive methods and slave or peon labor, continued to dominate economic life. Far from diminishing, the influence of the landed aristocracy actually increased as a result of the leading military role it had played in the wars of independence and the passing of Spanish authority.

Economic life stagnated, for the anticipated large-scale influx of foreign capital did not materialize and the European demand for Latin American staples remained far below expectations. Free trade brought increased commercial activity to the coasts, but this increase was offset by the near destruction of some local craft industries by cheap, factory-made European goods. The sluggish pace of economic activity and the relative absence of interregional trade and true national markets encouraged local self-sufficiency, isolation, political instability, and even chaos.

As a result of these adverse factors, the period from about 1820 to about 1870 was for many Latin American countries an age of violence and of alternate dictatorship and revolution. Its symbol was the *caudillo* (strongman), whose power was always based on force, no matter what kind of constitution the country had. Usually the caudillo ruled with the aid of a coalition of lesser caudillos, each supreme in his region. Whatever their methods, the caudillos generally displayed some regard for republican ideology and institutions. Political parties, bearing such labels as "conservative" and "liberal," "unitarian" and "federalist," were active in most of the new states. Conservatism drew most of its support from the great landowners and their urban allies. Liberalism typically attracted provincial landowners, professional men, and other groups that had enjoyed little power in the past and were dissatisfied with the existing order. As a rule, conservatives sought to retain many of the social arrangements of the colonial era and favored a highly centralized government. Liberals, often inspired by the example of the United States, usually advocated a federal form of government, guarantees of individual rights, lay control of education, and an end to special privileges for the clergy and military. Neither party displayed much interest in the problems of the native peasantry and other lower-class groups.

Beginning in about 1870, the accelerating tempo of the Industrial Revolution in Europe stimulated more rapid change in the Latin American economy and politics. European capital flowed into the area and was used to create the facilities needed to expand and modernize production and trade. The pace and degree of economic progress of the various countries were very uneven and depended largely on their geographic position and natural resources.

Extreme one-sidedness was a feature of the new economic order. One or two products became the basis of each country's prosperity, making these commodities highly vulnerable to fluctuations in world demand and price. Meanwhile, other sectors of the economy remained stagnant or even declined through diversion of labor and land to other industries.

The late nineteenth-century expansion had two other characteristics: in the main, it took place within the framework of the hacienda system of land tenure and labor, and it was accompanied by a steady growth of foreign control over the natural and human-made resources of the region. Thus, by 1900 a new structure of dependency, or colonialism, had arisen, called neocolonialism, with Great Britain and later the United States replacing Spain and Portugal as the dominant powers in the area.

The new economic order demanded peace and continuity in government, and after 1870 political conditions in Latin America did, in fact, grow more stable. Old party lines dissolved as conservatives adopted the positivist dogma of science and progress, while liberals abandoned their concern with constitutional methods and civil liberties in favor of an interest in material prosperity. A new type of "progressive" caudillo—Porfirio Díaz in Mexico, Rafael Núñez in Colombia, Antonio Guzmán Blanco in Venezuela—symbolized the politics of acquisition. The cycle of dictatorship and revolution continued in many lands, but the revolutions became less frequent and less devastating.

These major trends in the political and economic history of Latin America in the period extending from about 1820 to 1900 were accompanied by other changes in the Latin American way of life and culture, notably the development of a powerful literature that often sought not only to mirror Latin American society but to change it. In Part Two, we present short histories of Mexico, Argentina, Chile, Brazil, Peru, Cuba, the United Provinces of Central America, and Gran Colombia in the nineteenth century. All these histories contain themes and problems common to Latin America in that period, but each displays variations that reflect the specific backgrounds of the different states.

9 Dictators and Revolutions

INDEPENDENCE DID NOT bring Latin America the ordered freedom and prosperity the liberators had hoped for. In most of the new states, decades of civil strife followed the passing of Spanish and Portuguese rule. Bolívar reflected the disillusionment of many patriot leaders when he wrote in 1829: "There is no good faith in America, nor among the nations of America. Treaties are scraps of paper; constitutions, printed matter; elections, battles; freedom, anarchy; and life, a torment." The contrast between Latin American stagnation and disorder and the meteoric advance of the former English colonies—the United States—intensified the pessimism and self-doubt of some Latin American leaders and intellectuals.

The Fruits of Independence

Frustration of the great hopes with which the struggle for liberation began was inevitable, for independence was not accompanied by economic and social changes that could shatter the colonial mold. Aside from the passing of the Spanish and Portuguese trade monopolies, the colonial economic and social structures remained intact. The hacienda, fazenda, or estancia, employing archaic techniques and a labor force of peons or slaves, continued to dominate agriculture; no significant

class of small farmers arose to challenge the economic and political might of the great landowners. Indeed, the revolutions strengthened the power of the landed aristocracy by removing the agencies of Spanish rule—viceroys, audiencias, intendants—and by weakening among the landowners the ingrained habits of obedience to a central authority. In contrast, all other colonial elites—the merchant class, weakened by the expulsion or emigration of many loyalist merchants; the mine owners, ruined by wartime destruction or confiscation of their properties; and the church hierarchy, often in disgrace for having sided with Spain—emerged from the conflict with diminished weight.

To their other sources of influence, members of the landed aristocracy added the prestige of a military elite crowned with the laurels of victory, for many revolutionary officers had arisen from its ranks. The militarization of the new states as a result of years of destructive warfare and postwar instability assured a large political role for this officer group. Standing armies that often consumed more than half of the national budgets arose. Not content with the role of guardians of order and national security, military officers became the arbiter of political disputes, as a rule intervening in favor of the conservative landowning interests and the urban elites with whom the great landowners were closely linked.

ECONOMIC STAGNATION

Revolutionary leaders had expected that a vast expansion of foreign trade would follow the passing of Spanish commercial monopoly and aid economic recovery. In fact, some countries, favored by their natural resources or geographic position, soon recovered from the revolutionary crisis and scored modest to large economic advances; these included Brazil (coffee and sugar), Argentina (hides), and Chile (metals and hides). But others, such as Mexico, Bolivia, and Peru, whose mining economies had suffered shattering blows, failed to recover colonial levels of production.

Several factors accounted for the economic stagnation that plagued many of the new states in the first half of the nineteenth century. Independence was not accompanied by a redistribution of land and income that might have stimulated a growth of internal markets and productive forces. The anticipated large-scale influx of foreign capital did not materialize, either, partly because political disorder discouraged foreign investment, partly because Europe and the United States, then financing their own industrial revolutions, had as yet little capital to export. Exports of Latin American staples remained below expectations, for Europe still viewed Latin America primarily as an outlet for manufactured goods, especially English textiles. The resulting flood of cheap, factory-made European products damaged local craft industries and drained the new states of their stocks of gold and silver, creating a chronic balance-of-trade problem. The British conquest of the Latin American markets further weakened the local merchant class, which was unable to compete with its English rivals. By mid-century the wealthiest and most prestigious merchant houses, from Mexico City to Buenos Aires and Valparaíso, bore English names. Iberian merchants, however, continued to dominate the urban and provincial retail trade in many areas.

Taken together, these developments retarded the development of native capitalism and capitalist relations and reinforced the dominant role of the hacienda in the economic and political life of the new states. The deepening stagnation of the interior of these nations, aggravated by the lack of roads and by natural obstacles to communication (such as jungles and mountains), intensified tendencies toward regionalism and the domination of regions by caudillos great and small, who were usually local large landowners.[1] The sluggish tempo of economic activity encouraged these caudillos to employ their private followings of peons and retainers as pawns in the game of politics and revolution on a national scale. Indeed, politics and revolution became in some countries a form of economic activity that compensated for the lack of other opportunities, because the victors, having gained control of the all-important customhouse (which collected duties on imports and exports) and other official sources of revenue, could reward themselves and their followers with government jobs, contracts, grants of public land, and other favors. This reliance by members of the elite on political and military activity as a career and on the customhouse as a source of government revenue had two negative results. One was the rise of bloated military and bureaucratic establishments that diverted resources from economic development; the other was a stress on foreign trade that intensified the trend toward dependency.

POLITICS: THE CONSERVATIVE AND LIBERAL PROGRAMS

The political systems of the new states made large formal concessions to the liberal ideology of the nineteenth century. With the exception of Brazil,

---

[1]The term *caudillo* is commonly applied to politico-military leaders who held power on the national and regional level in Latin America before more or less stable parliamentary government became the norm in the area beginning about 1870. Military ability and charisma are qualities often associated with caudillos, who came in many guises, but not all possessed the same qualities. Because the semifeudal conditions that gave rise to the caudillo still survive in parts of Latin America, it can be said that caudillos and *caudillismo* still exist.

all the new states adopted the republican form of government (Mexico had two brief intervals of imperial rule) and paid their respects to the formulas of parliamentary and representative government. Their constitutions provided for presidents, congresses, and courts; often they contained elaborate safeguards of individual rights.

These façades of modernity, however, poorly concealed the dictatorial or oligarchical reality behind them. Typically, the chief executive was a caudillo whose power rested on force, no matter what the constitutional form; usually, he ruled with the support of a coalition of lesser caudillos, each more or less supreme in his own domain. The supposed independence of the judicial and legislative branches was a fiction. As a rule, elections were exercises in futility. Because the party in power generally counted the votes, the opposition had no alternative but revolt.

Literacy and property qualifications disfranchised most natives and mixed-bloods; where they had the right to vote, the *patrón* (master) often herded them to the polls to vote for him or his candidates. The lack of the secret ballot (voting was usually open, with colored ballots) made coercion of voters easy. Whether liberal or conservative, all sections of the ruling class agreed on keeping the peasantry, gauchos, and other "lower orders" on the margins of political life, on preventing their emergence as groups with collective philosophies and goals. The very privileges that the new creole constitutions and law codes granted indigenous peoples—equality before the law, the "right" to divide and dispose of their communal lands—weakened their solidarity and their ability to resist the creole world's competitive individualism. But especially gifted, ambitious, and fortunate members of these marginal groups were sometimes coopted into the creole elite and provided some of its most distinguished leaders; two examples are the Zapotec Benito Juárez in Mexico and the mestizo president Andrés Santa Cruz in Bolivia.

At first glance, the political history of Latin America in the first half-century after independence, with its dreary alternation of dictatorship and revolt, seems pointless and trivial. But the political struggles of this period were more than disputes over spoils between sections of a small upper class. Genuine social and ideological cleavages helped produce those struggles and the bitterness with which they were fought. Such labels as "conservative" and "liberal," "unitarian" and "federalist," assigned by the various parties to themselves or each other, were more than masks in a pageant, although opportunism contributed to the ease with which some leaders assumed and discarded these labels.

Generally speaking, conservatism reflected the interests of the traditional holders of power and privilege, men who had a stake in maintaining the existing order. Hence, the great landowners, the upper clergy, the higher ranks of the military and the civil bureaucracy, and monopolistic merchant groups tended to be conservatives. Liberalism, in contrast, appealed to those groups that in colonial times had had little or no access to the main structures of economic and political power and were naturally eager to alter the existing order. Thus, liberalism drew much support from provincial landowners, lawyers and other professionals (the groups most receptive to new ideas), shopkeepers, and artisans; it also appealed to ambitious, aspiring indígenas and mixed-bloods. But regional conflicts and clan or family loyalties often cut across the lines of social and occupational cleavage, complicating the political picture.

Liberals wanted to break up the hierarchical social structure inherited from the colonial period. They had a vision of their countries remade into dynamic middle-class states on the model of the United States or England. Inspired by the success of the United States, they usually favored a federal form of government, guarantees of individual rights, lay control of education, and an end to a special legal status for the clergy and military. In their modernizing zeal, liberals sometimes called for the abolition of entails (which restricted the right to inherit property to a particular descendant or descendants of the owner), dissolution of convents, confiscation of church wealth, and abolition of slavery. The federalism of the liberals had a special appeal for secondary regions of the new states, eager to develop their resources and free themselves from domination by capitals and wealthy primary regions.

Conservatives typically upheld a strong centralized government, the religious and educational monopoly of the Roman Catholic church, and the special privileges of the clergy and military. They distrusted such radical novelties as freedom of speech and the press and religious toleration. Conservatives, in short, sought to salvage as much of the colonial social order as was compatible with the new republican system. Indeed, some conservative leaders ultimately despaired of that system and dreamed of implanting monarchy in their countries.

Neither conservatives nor liberals displayed much interest in the problems of the indigenous, black, and mixed-blood masses that formed the majority of the population in most Latin American countries. Liberals, impatient with the supposed backwardness of indigenous peoples, regarded their communalism as an impediment to the development of a capitalist spirit of enterprise and initiated legislation providing for the division of communal lands—a policy that favored land grabbing at the expense of indigenous villages. Despite their theoretical preference for small landholdings and a rural middle class, liberals recoiled from any program of radical land reform. Conservatives correctly regarded the great estate as the very foundation of their power. As traditionalists, however, the conservatives sometimes claimed to continue the Spanish paternalist policy toward indigenous communities and often enjoyed their support.

This summary of the conservative and liberal programs for Latin America in the first half-century after independence inevitably overlooks variations from the theoretical liberal and conservative norms, variations that reflected the specific conditions and problems of the different states. A brief examination of the history of Mexico, Argentina, Chile, Brazil, Peru, Cuba, the United Provinces of Central America, and Gran Colombia reveals not only certain common themes but also a rich diversity of political experience.

Mexico

The struggle for Mexican independence, begun by the radical priests Hidalgo and Morelos, was completed by Agustín de Iturbide, who headed a coalition of creole and peninsular conservatives terrified at the prospect of being governed by the liberal Spanish constitution of 1812, which was reestablished in 1820. Independence, achieved under such conservative auspices, meant that Mexico's economic and social patterns underwent little change. To be sure, recent scholarship has shown that the popular insurgency begun by Hidalgo had at least a short-term impact on the social, economic, and political patterns of Mexican development. John Tutino, for example, has shown that in the Bajío the insurgency destroyed commercial hacienda production, which generated profit by storing maize until prices peaked with scarcity, and forced a shift to tenant ranchero production, which maximized maize production, bringing "real and enduring benefits to both rural producers and urban consumers of maize across the Bajío during the first half-century of national life." Similarly, Florencia Mallon and Peter Guardino stress the revolutionary participation of popular urban and rural groups in Mexican nineteenth-century political struggles, revealing their long-term impact on Mexican state formation and peasant consciousness. Nonetheless, the great hacienda continued to dominate the countryside in many areas. Although indigenous villages managed to retain substantial community lands until after mid-century and even improved their economic and political position somewhat with the passing of Spanish centralized authority, the trend toward usurpation of indigenous lands grew stronger as a result of the lapse of Spanish protective legislation. Peons and tenants on the haciendas often suffered from debt servitude, miserable wages, oppressive rents, and excessive religious fees. At the constitutional convention of 1856–1857, the liberal Ponciano Arriaga declared:

> With some honorable exceptions, the rich landowners of Mexico . . . resemble the feudal lords of the Middle Ages. On his seigneurial lands, with more or less formalities, the landowner makes and executes laws, administers justice and exercises civil power, imposes taxes and fines, has his own jails and irons, metes out punishments and tortures,

ATLANTIC OCEAN

MEXICO
1821

San
Antonio

Gulf of Mexico

Mexico City • • Veracruz

Guatemala •

BR. HONDURAS

UNITED PROVINCES OF
CENTRAL AMERICA
1823–1839

Panama •

Caribbean Sea

CUBA
(Sp.)

BAHAMA IS.
(Br.)

PUERTO RICO
(Sp.)

HAITI
1804

TRINIDAD
(Br.)

Caracas •

BR. GUIANA
DUTCH GUIANA
FR. GUIANA

Bogotá •

GRAN COLOMBIA
1819–1830

Galapagos Is.

Quito •

PERU
1821

Indefinite Boundary

EMPIRE OF BRAZIL
1822

PACIFIC OCEAN

Lima •

BOLIVIA
1825

Sucre •

• Bahia

PARAGUAY
1813

• Rio de Janeiro

UNITED
PROVINCES
OF LA PLATA
1816

Asunción •

Santiago •

CHILE
1817

URUGUAY
1828

Buenos Aires •

Montevideo

0   500   1000 Km.

0   500   1000 Mi.

Latin America in 1830

monopolizes commerce, and forbids the conduct without his permission of any business but that of the estate.

The church continued to wield diminished but still considerable economic and spiritual power. An anonymous contemporary writer reflected the disillusion of the lower classes with the fruits of independence: "Independence is only a name. Previously they ruled us from Spain, now from here. It is always the same priest on a different mule. But as for work, food, and clothing, there is no difference."

The Mexican Economy

The ravages of war had left mineshafts flooded, haciendas deserted, the economy stagnant. The end of the Spanish commercial monopoly, however, brought a large increase in the volume of foreign trade; the number of ships entering Mexican ports jumped from 148 in 1823 to 639 in 1826. But exports did not keep pace with imports, leaving a trade deficit that had to be covered by exporting precious metals. The drain of gold and silver aggravated the problems of the new government, which had inherited a bankrupt treasury and had to support a swollen bureaucracy and an officer class ready to revolt against any government that suggested a cut in their numbers or pay. The exodus of Spanish merchants and their capital added to the economic problems of the new state. Complicating those problems was the disorder that was a legacy of the war; bands of robbers made travel on the roads so unsafe that "whether coming or going from Puebla or Veracruz, the Mexico City traveler expected to be robbed."

Foreign loans appeared to be the only way out of the crisis. In 1824–1825, English bankers made loans to Mexico amounting to 32 million pesos, guaranteed by Mexican customs revenues. Of this amount the Mexicans received only a little more than 11 million pesos, as the bankers went bankrupt before all the money due to Mexico from the loan proceeds was paid. By 1843 unpaid interest and principal had raised the nation's foreign debt to more than 54 million pesos. This mounting foreign debt not only created crushing interest burdens, but it also threatened Mexico's independence and territorial integrity, for behind foreign capitalists stood governments that might threaten intervention in case of default.

Foreign investments, however, mainly from Britain, made possible a partial recovery of the decisive mining sector. Old mines, abandoned and flooded during the wars, were reopened, but the available capital proved inadequate, the technical problems of reconstruction were greater than anticipated, and production remained on a relatively low level.

An ambitious effort to revive and modernize Mexican industry also got under way, spurred by the founding in 1830 of the *Banco de Avío*, which provided governmental assistance to industry. Manufacturing, paced by textiles, made some limited progress in the three decades after independence. Leading industrial centers included Mexico City, Puebla, Guadalajara, Durango, and Veracruz. But shortages of capital, lack of a consistent policy of protection for domestic industry, and a socioeconomic structure that sharply limited the internal market hampered the growth of Mexican factory capitalism. By 1843 the Banco de Avío had to close its doors for lack of funds. The Mexican economy, therefore, continued to be based on mining and agriculture. Mexico's principal exports were precious metals, especially silver, and such agricultural products as tobacco, coffee, vanilla, cochineal, and henequen (a plant fiber used in rope and twine). Imports consisted primarily of manufactured goods that Mexican industry could not supply.

Politics: Liberals Versus Conservatives

A liberal-conservative cleavage dominated Mexican political life in the half-century after independence. That conflict was latent from the moment that the "liberator" Iturbide, the former scourge of insurgents, rode into Mexico City on September 27, 1821, flanked on either side by two insurgent generals, Vicente Guerrero and Guadalupe Victoria, firm republicans and liberals. The fall of Iturbide in 1823 cleared the way for the establishment of a republic. But it soon became apparent that the republicans were divided into liberals and conservatives, federalists and centralists.

The constitution of 1824 represented a compromise between liberal and conservative interests. It appeased regional economic interests, which were fearful of a too-powerful central government, by creating nineteen states that possessed taxing power; their legislatures, each casting one vote, chose the president and vice president for four-year terms. The national legislature was made bicameral, with an upper house (Senate) and a lower house (Chamber of Deputies). By assuring the creation of local civil bureaucracies, the federalist structure also satisfied the demand of the provincial middle classes for greater access to political activity and office. But the constitution had a conservative tinge as well: although the church lost its monopoly on education, Catholicism was proclaimed the official religion, and the fueros of the church and the army were specifically confirmed.

A hero of the war of independence, the liberal general Guadalupe Victoria, was elected first president under the new constitution. Anxious to preserve unity, Victoria brought the conservative Lucas Alamán into his cabinet. But this era of good feeling was very short-lived; by 1825, Alamán was forced out of the government. The liberal-conservative cleavage now assumed the form of a rivalry that reflected the Anglo-American competition for economic and political influence in Mexico. Founded by the American minister Joel Roberts Poinsett, the York Rite Masonic lodge favored liberals and federalists, who regarded the United States as a model for their own reform program. Its rival, the Scottish Rite lodge, sponsored by the British chargé d'affaires Henry Ward, appealed to the Conservative Party, which represented the old landed and mining aristocracy, the clerical and military hierarchy, monopolistic merchants, and some manufacturers. Its intellectual spokesman and organizer was Lucas Alamán, statesman, champion of industry, and author of a brilliant history of Mexico from the conservative point of view.

The Liberal Party represented a creole and mestizo middle class—provincial landowners, professional men, artisans, the lower ranks of the clergy and military—determined to end special privileges and the concentration of political and economic power in the upper class. A priest-economist, José María Luis Mora, presented the liberal position with great force and lucidity. But the Liberal Party was divided: its right wing, the *moderados*, wanted to proceed slowly and sometimes joined the conservatives; its left wing, the *puros*, advocated sweeping antifeudal, anticlerical reforms.

During the first decade after independence, none of these factions could consolidate its control over the nation, but the year 1833 was a high-water mark of liberal achievement. Aided by Mora, his minister of education, the puro President Valentín Gómez Farías pushed through Congress a series of radical reforms: abolition of the special privileges and immunities of the army and church (meaning that officers and priests would now be subject to the jurisdiction of civil courts), abolition of tithes, secularization of the clerical University of Mexico, creation of a department of public instruction, reduction of the army, and creation of a civilian militia. These measures were accompanied by a program of internal improvements designed to increase the prosperity of the interior by linking it to the capital and the coasts. In their use of the central government to promote education and national economic development, the liberals showed that they were not doctrinaire adherents of laissez faire.

This liberal program inevitably provoked clerical and conservative resistance. Army officers began to organize revolts; priests proclaimed from their pulpits that the great cholera epidemic of 1833 was a sign of divine displeasure with the works of the impious liberals. Meanwhile, General Antonio López de Santa Anna, a classic caudillo who earlier had supported liberal movements, now placed himself at the head of the conservative rebellion, occupied the capital, and sent Gómez Farías and Mora into exile. Assuming the presidency, he summoned a hand-picked reactionary congress that repealed the reform laws of 1833 and suspended the constitution of 1824. Under the new conservative constitution of 1836, the states were reduced to departments completely dominated by the central government, upper-class control of politics was assured through high property and income qualifications for holding office, and the fueros of the church and army were restored.

Santa Anna and the conservatives ruled Mexico for the greater part of two decades, 1834 to 1854. Politically and economically, the conservative rule subordinated the interests of the regions and the country as a whole to a wealthy, densely populated central core linking Mexico City, Puebla, and Veracruz. Its centralist trend was reflected in the Tariff Act of 1837, which restored the alcabala, or sales tax system, inland customhouses, and the government tobacco monopoly, ensuring the continuous flow of revenues to Mexico City.

Thereafter, conservative neglect and abuse of outlying or border areas like northern Mexico and Yucatán contributed to the loss of Texas in 1836 and almost led to the loss of Yucatán. Santa Anna's destruction of provincial autonomy enabled American colonists in Texas, led by Sam Houston, to pose as patriotic federalists in revolt against Santa Anna's tyranny. In Yucatán, the Caste or Social War of 1839 combined elements of a regional war against conservative centralism and an indigenous war against feudal landlords. For almost a decade, Yucatán remained outside Mexico.

After the United States annexed Texas in 1845, the North American Invasion or Mexican War (1846–1848) marked another conservative disaster. Its immediate cause was a dispute between Mexico and the United States over the boundary of Texas, but the decisive factor was the determination of the Polk administration to acquire not only Texas but California and New Mexico as well. The war ended in catastrophic Mexican defeat, basically due to U.S. superiority in resources, military training, and leadership, but the irresponsible, selfish attitudes of the Mexican aristocracy and church contributed to the debacle. Most particularly, conservatives, dreading the mobilization of peasant armies in a prolonged guerrilla war against the U.S. invasion, concluded a hasty surrender.

Naturally, puro leaders, including Benito Juárez, Melchor Ocampo, and Ponciano Arriaga, urged continued resistance. "Give the people arms," said Ocampo, "and they will defend themselves." In some regions of the country, peasant revolts broke out that combined demands for division of large haciendas among the peasantry and other reforms with calls for a continued resistance to the invaders. But the aristocratic creoles—some of whom favored a total takeover of Mexico by the United States—and their clerical allies feared the consequences of partisan warfare to their wealth and privileges and hastened to make peace. "The Mexican government," says Mexican historian Leticia Reina, "preferred coming to terms with the United States rather than endanger the interests of the ruling class." By the treaty of Guadalupe Hidalgo (1848), Mexico gave up half the country, ceding Texas, California, and New Mexico to the United States; in return, Mexico received $15 million and the cancellation of certain claims against it.

Even after the signing of the treaty, a vocal opposition in and outside the Mexican congress argued against ratification and urged continuing the war. In his "Observations on the Treaty of Guadalupe Hidalgo," the liberal Manuel Rejón predicted that the treaty would mean the inevitable economic conquest of Mexico by the United States. He foresaw that the new boundary, bringing American commerce closer to the Mexican heartland, would lead to the americanization of Mexico; he argued that "we will never be able to compete in our own markets with the American imports. . . . The treaty is our sentence of death." Finally, in view of the intense American racism, he questioned whether Mexican citizens in the ceded territories would be protected in their civil and property rights as promised by the treaty.

Rejón's fears concerning the treatment of Mexican citizens in the newly annexed territories were soon justified. The gold rush in California caused a wave of attacks by Anglo-American miners against native Californians. In his reminiscences, Antonio Coronel, from Los Angeles, described "stabbings, extortions, and lynchings as commonplace American reactions to native Californios, whom they regarded as interlopers." Even worse was the fate of indigenous Californians, who were considered full Mexican citizens under the constitution of 1824. Denied the protection specified in the treaty of Guadalupe Hidalgo, they "became the victims of murder, slavery, land theft, and starvation." In two decades the indigenous population of the state declined by more than one hundred thousand. "Genocide," writes Richard Griswold del Castillo, "is not too strong a word to use in describing what happened to the California Indians during that period." In New Mexico, which became a territory rather than a state, Hispanic inhabitants did not gain citizenship status until New Mexico achieved statehood in 1912, and its native peoples were denied the vote until 1953.

Violation of their land rights, the protection of which was promised by the treaty of Guadalupe Hidalgo, was and remains a major grievance of many Mexican Americans. Claiming that the great majority of Mexican land grants in the ceded territory were "imperfect," American courts ruled that the U.S. government had inherited the right to complete the process of land confirmation. In California and New Mexico, this process, creating for Mexican American landowners an immense expense of litigation and legal fees, aggravated by usurious interest rates and falling cattle prices, resulted in the loss of their land by most rancheros. Even the few who survived the confirmation process came under great pressure from squatters, mostly wealthy and influential Anglo-Americans, to surrender their land. In New Mexico, a fraternity of predatory lawyers and politicians, the so-called Santa Fe Ring, "used the long legal battles over land grants to acquire empires extending over millions of acres." Here, the struggle of Mexican Americans to regain the lost lands of their ancestors, based on the claim that the United States violated the articles of the treaty of Guadalupe Hidalgo that guaranteed the citizenship and property rights of Mexicans, continues to this day.

LA REFORMA, CIVIL WAR, AND THE FRENCH INTERVENTION

The disasters suffered by Mexico under conservative rule had created widespread revulsion against conservative policies and stimulated a revival of puro liberalism. In 1846, during the war, liberal administrations came to power in the states of Oaxaca and Michoacán. In Michoacán the new governor was Melchor Ocampo, a scholar and scientist profoundly influenced by Rousseau and French utopian socialist thought. In Oaxaca a Zapotec lawyer, Benito Juárez, became governor and earned a reputation for honesty, efficiency, and democratic simplicity.

Ocampo and Juárez were two leaders of a renovated liberalism that ushered in the movement called *La Reforma.* Like the older liberalism of the 1830s, the Reforma sought to destroy feudal vestiges and implant capitalism in Mexico. Its ideology, however, was more spirited than the aristocratic, intellectual liberalism of Mora; and its puro left wing included a small number of figures, such as Ponciano Arriaga and Ignacio Ramírez, who transcended liberal ideology with their attacks on the latifundio, defense of labor and women's rights, and other advanced ideas.

This revived liberal ferment inspired alarm among the reactionary forces led by Alamán and Santa Ana, who in 1853 had proclaimed himself perpetual dictator, with the title of His Most Supreme Highness.

Santa Anna's return to power, accompanied by a terrorist campaign against all dissenters, spurred a gathering of opposition forces, including many disgruntled moderados and conservatives. In early 1854 the old liberal caudillo from the state of Guerrero, Juan Alvarez, and the moderado general Ignacio Comonfort issued a call for revolt, the Plan of Ayutla, demanding the end of the dictatorship and the election of a convention to draft a new constitution. Within a year, Santa Anna's regime began to disintegrate, and in August 1855, seeing the handwriting on the wall, he went into exile for the last time. Some days later, a puro-dominated provisional government took office in Mexico City. The seventy-five-year-old Juan Alvarez was named provisional president; to his cabinet he named Benito Juárez as minister of justice and Miguel Lerdo de Tejada as treasury minister.

One of Juárez's first official acts was to issue a decree, the *Ley Juárez,* proclaiming the right of the state to limit the clerical and military fueros to matters of internal discipline. The *Ley Lerdo* (Lerdo Law) of 1856, drafted by Miguel Lerdo de Tejada, also struck a heavy blow at the material base of the church's power, its landed wealth. The law barred

Mexico's famous muralist, José Clemente Orozco, celebrated Mexican national resistance to French colonialism and the heroic leadership of Benito Juárez in this painting entitled *The Triumph of Juarez*. It depicts ordinary Mexican citizens rising to assist outgunned and overmatched Mexican regular army soldiers in a great victory over the French Legion at the Battle of Puebla on May 5, 1862. [Archivo Iconografico, S.A./Corbis]

the church from holding land not used for religious purposes and compelled the sale of all such property to tenants, with the rent considered to be 6 percent of the sale value of the property. Real estate not being rented was to be auctioned to the highest bidder, with payment of a large sales tax to the government.

The law's intent was to create a rural middle class, but because it made no provision for division of the church estates, the bulk of the land passed into the hands of great landowners, merchants, and capitalists, both Mexican and foreign. Worse, the law barred indigenous villages from owning land and ordered that such land be sold in the same manner as church property, excepting only land and buildings designed exclusively for the "public use" of the inhabitants and for communal pastures (*ejidos*). As a result, land-grabbers descended on the native villages, "denounced" their land to the local courts, and proceeded to buy it at auction for paltry sums. The law provided that the native owners should have the first opportunity to buy, but few could pay the minimum purchase price. When they responded with protests and revolts, Lerdo explained in a circular that the intent of his law was that their community lands should be divided among the natives, not sold to others. But he insisted that "the continued existence of the Indian communities ought not to be tolerated . . . , and this is exactly one of the goals of the law." He was also adamant on the right of those who rented indigenous lands to buy them if they chose to do so. So, during the summer and fall of 1856 many pueblos lost crop and pasturelands from which they had derived revenues vitally needed to defray the cost of their religious ceremonies and other communal expenses. Indigenous resistance and the liberals' need to attract popular support during their struggle with the conservative counterrevolution and French interventionists in the decade 1857–1867 seem to have slowed enforcement of the Lerdo Law as it applied to native villages, but the long-range tendency of liberal agrarian policy was to compel division of communal lands, facilitating their acquisition by hacendados and even small and middle-sized farmers. The result was a simultaneous strengthening of the latifundio and some increase in the size of the rural middle class.

While the provisional government was causing consternation among conservatives with the Ley Juárez and the Ley Lerdo, a constitutional convention dominated by moderate liberals had been completing its work. The constitution of 1857 proclaimed freedom of speech, press, and assembly; limited fueros; forbade ecclesiastical and civil corporations to own land; and proclaimed the sanctity of private property. It restored the federalist structure of 1824, with the same division of Mexico into states, but replaced the bicameral national legislature with a single house and eliminated the office of vice president.

A few voices were raised against the land monopoly, peonage, and immense inequalities of wealth. "We proclaim ideas and forget realities," complained the radical delegate Ponciano Arriaga. "How can a hungry, naked, miserable people practice popular government? How can we condemn slavery in words, while the lot of most of our fellow citizens is more grievous than that of the black slaves of Cuba or the United States?" Despite his caustic attack on the land monopoly, Arriaga

offered a relatively moderate solution: the state should seize and auction off large uncultivated estates. The conservative opposition promptly branded Arriaga's project "communist"; the moderate majority in the convention passed over it in silence.

Because the new constitution incorporated the Lerdo Law and the Juárez Law, the church now openly entered the political struggle by excommunicating all public officials who took the required oath of loyalty. Counterrevolution had been gathering its forces for months, and the Three Years' War soon erupted in 1857. In regional terms, the war pitted the rich central area, dominated by the conservatives, against the liberal south, north, and Veracruz. Controlling extensive regions and enjoying the support of a clear majority of the population, the liberals, relying on largely undisciplined guerrilla forces, nevertheless suffered serious defeats in the first stage of the war.

As the struggle progressed, both sides found themselves in serious financial difficulties. The conservatives, however, had the advantage of generous support from the church. In July 1859, Juárez struck back at the clergy with reform laws that nationalized without compensation all ecclesiastical property except church buildings; the laws also suppressed all monasteries, established freedom of religion, and separated church and state. The reform laws were designed to encourage peasant proprietorship by dividing church estates into small farms, but this goal proved illusory; thanks to the Ley Lerdo, wealthy purchasers had already acquired much of the church land.

By the middle of 1860, although conservative bands in the provinces continued to make devastating raids, the tide of war had turned in favor of the liberals and Juárez reentered the capital in 1861. The war was effectively over, but diehard reactionaries now looked for help abroad. The conservative governments of England, France, and Spain had no love for the Mexican liberals and Juárez. Moreover, there were ample pretexts for intervention, for both sides had seized or destroyed foreign property without compensation, and foreign bondholders were clamoring for payments from an empty Mexican treasury. The three European powers demanded compensation for damages to their nationals and payment of just debts. Noting the dubious nature of some of the claims, Juárez vainly pleaded poverty, but the three powers nonetheless invaded and occupied Veracruz in 1862. England and Spain, having received assurances of future satisfaction of their claims, soon withdrew, but the French government rejected all Mexican offers, and its troops remained.

But Napoleon III wanted more than payment of debts. A group of Mexican conservative exiles had convinced the ambitious emperor that the Mexican people would welcome a French army of liberation and the establishment of a monarchy. Napoleon had visions of a French-protected Mexican Empire that would yield him great political and economic advantages. It remained only to find a suitable unemployed prince, and one was found in the person of Archduke Ferdinand Maximilian of Hapsburg, brother of Austrian emperor Franz Josef.

To prepare the ground for the arrival of the new ruler of Mexico, the French army advanced from Veracruz into the interior toward Puebla. At Puebla, instead of being received as liberators, the interventionists met determined resistance from a poorly armed Mexican garrison and were thrown back with heavy losses. The date—Cinco de Mayo de 1862—is still celebrated as a Mexican national holiday. On June 10, however, French reinforcements finally entered the city to the rejoicing of the clergy; by the end of the year the interventionists had occupied Querétaro, Monterrey, San Luis Potosí, and Saltillo. But the invaders had secure control only of the cities; republican guerrilla detachments controlled most of the national territory.

Meanwhile, a delegation of conservative exiles called on Maximilian to offer him a Mexican crown, which he and his wife Carlota gratefully accepted in 1864. The conservative conspirators had counted on Maximilian to help them recover their lost wealth and privileges, but the emperor, mindful of realities, would not consent to their demands; the purchase of church lands by native and foreign landlords and capitalists had created new interests that Maximilian refused to antagonize. Confident of conservative support, Maximilian even wooed moderate liberals and won the support of notable intellectuals like historians José Fernando Ramírez and Manuel Orozco y Berra, who were impressed by Maximilian's goodwill and cherished the illusion of a stable, prosperous Mexico ruled by an enlightened monarch.

But the hopes of both conservatives and misguided liberals were built on quicksand. The victories of Maximilian's generals could not destroy the fluid and elusive liberal resistance, firmly grounded in popular hatred for the invaders and aided by Mexico's rugged terrain. A turning point in the war came in the spring of 1865, with the Union triumph over the Confederacy in the U.S. Civil War. U.S. demands that the French evacuate Mexico, a region regarded by Secretary of State William Seward as a U.S. zone of economic and political influence, grew more insistent, and U.S. troops were massed along the Rio Grande. Facing serious domestic and diplomatic problems at home, Napoleon decided to cut his losses and liquidate the Mexican adventure.

Captured on May 14, 1867 and tried by court-martial, Maximilian and his leading generals, Miguel Miramón and Tomás Mejía, were found guilty of treason, sentenced to death, and executed by a *Juarista* firing squad.

POSTWAR ATTEMPTS AT RECONSTRUCTION AND THE DEATH OF *LA REFORMA*

Juárez, symbol of Mexican resistance to a foreign usurper, assumed the presidency in August 1867. His government inherited a devastated country. Agriculture and industry were in ruins; as late as 1873, the value of Mexican exports was below the level of 1810. To reduce the state's financial burdens and end the danger of military control, Juárez dismissed two-thirds of the army, an act that produced discontent and uprisings that his generals managed to suppress. He also devoted the state's limited resources to the development of a public school system, especially on the elementary level; by 1874 there were about eight thousand schools with some three hundred and fifty thousand pupils.

However, his agrarian policy continued the liberal program that aimed to implant capitalism in the countryside, at the expense not of the haciendas but of indigenous communities. Indeed, the period of the "Restored Republic" (1868–1876) saw an intensified effort by the federal government to implement the Lerdo Law by compelling dissolution and partition of indigenous communal lands, opening the way for a new wave of fraud and seizures by neighboring hacendados and other land-grabbers. The result was a series of nationwide peasant revolts, the most serious occurring in the state of Hidalgo (1869–1870). Proclaiming the rebels to be "communists," the hacendados, aided by state and federal authorities, restored order by the traditional violent methods. A few liberals raised their voices in protest, but they were ignored; one was Ignacio Ramírez, who condemned the usurpations and fraud practiced by the hacendados with the complicity of corrupt judges and officials and called for suspension of the law.

Reelected president in 1871, Juárez put down a revolt by a hero of the wars of the Reforma, General Porfirio Díaz, who charged Juárez with attempting to become a dictator. But Juárez died the next year of a heart attack and was succeeded as acting president by the chief justice of the Supreme Court, Sebastían Lerdo de Tejada, who governed until 1876 when Díaz, aided by a group of Texas capitalists with strong links to New York banks, successfully overthrew him.

Díaz had seized power in the name of the ideals of the Reforma. In fact, however, the year 1876 marked the death of the Reforma and the libertarian creed to which Juárez subscribed, no matter how often he deviated from it. Thereafter, a new, profoundly anti-revolutionary ideology of positivism, which ranked order and progress above freedom, dominated Mexico.

The Reforma had paved the way for this change by transforming the Mexican bourgeoisie from a revolutionary class into a ruling class that was more predatory and acquisitive than the old creole aristocracy. The remnants of that aristocracy speedily adapted to the ways of the new ruling class and merged with it. The interests of the old and the new rich required political stability, a docile labor force, internal improvements, and a political and economic climate favorable to foreign investments. The mission of the "honorable tyranny" of Porfirio Díaz was to achieve those ends.

Argentina

In 1816 delegates to the congress of Tucumán proclaimed the independence of the United Provinces of the Río de la Plata. "Disunited," however, would have better described the political condition of the La Plata area, for the creole seizure of power in Buenos Aires in 1810 brought in its train a dissolution of the vast viceroyalty of the Río de la Plata.

THE LIBERATION OF PARAGUAY, URUGUAY, AND UPPER PERU

Paraguay was first to repel the Buenos Aires junta's efforts to "liberate" it, and, under the dictatorial rule of the creole lawyer José Gaspar Rodríguez de Francia, it declared its own independence. Thereafter, Francia effectively sealed it off from its neighbors to avoid submission and payment of tribute to Buenos Aires, which controlled Paraguay's river outlets to the sea. Francia did permit a limited licensed trade with the outside world by way of Brazil, chiefly to satisfy military needs.

Francia's state-controlled economy brought certain benefits: the planned diversification of agriculture, which reduced production of such export crops as yerba maté, tobacco, and sugar, ensured a plentiful supply of foodstuffs and the well-being of the indigenous and mestizo masses. An interesting feature of Francia's system was the establishment of state farms or ranches—called *estancias de la patria*—that successfully specialized in the raising of livestock and ended Paraguay's dependence on livestock imports from the Argentine province of Entre Ríos. Those who suffered most under Francia's dictatorship were Spaniards, many of whom he expelled or penalized in various ways, and creole aristocrats, who were kept under perpetual surveillance and subjected to severe repression.

The gaucho chieftain José Artigas also resisted the efforts of the Buenos Aires junta to dominate the area and led Uruguay, then known as the Banda Oriental, toward independence. In 1815 the junta abandoned these efforts, evacuated Montevideo, and turned it over to Artigas. No ordinary caudillo, Artigas not only defended Uruguayan nationality but sought to achieve social reform. In 1815 he issued a plan for distributing royalist lands to the landless, with preference shown to blacks, indigenous peoples, zambos, and poor whites. But he was not given the opportunity to implement this radical program. In 1817 a powerful Brazilian army invaded Uruguay and soon had a secure grip on the Banda Oriental. Artigas had to flee across the Paraná River into Paraguay. He received asylum from Francia but was never allowed to leave again; he died in Paraguay thirty years later.

Meanwhile, Uruguay was occupied by foreign armies until 1828, when Great Britain, unwilling to see it fall under the control of either Brazil or Argentina, intervened to negotiate its independence.

Upper Peru, the mountainous northern corner of the old viceroyalty of La Plata, also escaped the grasp of Buenos Aires after 1810. Three expeditions were sent into the high country, won initial victories, then were rolled back by Spanish counteroffensives. Logistical problems, the apathy of the native population, and the hostility of the creole aristocracy, which remained loyal to Spain until it became clear that the royalist cause was doomed, contributed to the patriot defeats. Not until 1825 did General Antonio José de Sucre, Bolívar's lieutenant, finally liberate Peru. Renamed Bolivia in honor of the liberator, it began its independent life the next year under a complicated, totally impractical constitution drafted by Bolívar himself.

THE STRUGGLE FOR PROGRESS AND NATIONAL UNITY

Even among the provinces that had joined at Tucumán to form the United Provinces of La Plata, discord grew and threatened the dissolution of the new state. The efforts of the wealthy port and province of Buenos Aires to impose its hegemony over the interior met with tenacious resistance. The end of the Spanish trade monopoly brought large gains to Buenos Aires and lesser gains to the littoral provinces of Santa Fe, Entre Ríos, and Corrientes; their exports of meat and hides increased, and the value of their lands rose. But the wine and textile industries of the interior, which had been protected by the colonial monopoly, suffered from the competition of cheaper and superior European wares imported through the port of Buenos Aires.

The interests of the interior provinces required a measure of autonomy or even independence to protect their primitive industries, but Buenos Aires preferred a single free-trade zone under a government dominated by the port city. This was one cause of the conflict between Argentine *federales* (federalists) and *unitarios* (unitarians). By 1820 the federalist solution had triumphed: the United Provinces had in effect dissolved into a number of independent republics, with the interior provinces ruled by caudillos, each representing the local ruling class and having a gaucho army behind him.

A new start toward unity came in 1821 when Bernardino Rivadavia, an ardent liberal strongly influenced by the English philosopher Jeremy Bentham, launched an ambitious program of educational, social, and economic reform. He promoted primary education, founded the University of Buenos Aires, abolished the ecclesiastical fuero and the tithe, and suppressed some monasteries. Rivadavia envisioned a balanced development of industry and agriculture, with a large role assigned to British investment and colonization. But the obstacles in the way of industrialization proved too great, and little came of efforts in this direction. The greatest progress was made in cattle raising, which expanded rapidly southward into territory formerly claimed by native peoples. To control the large floating population of gauchos, Rivadavia enacted vagrancy laws requiring them to have passports for travel and to have written permission from the *estanciero* to leave his ranch.

In 1822, hoping to raise revenue and increase production, Rivadavia introduced the system of emphyteusis, a program that distributed public lands to leaseholders at fixed rentals. Some writers have seen in this system an effort at agrarian reform, but there were no limits on the size of

GENERAL ROSAS.

Although he cultivated the populist image of a *gaucho*, Juan Manuel Rosas was a wealthy *estanciero* and military *caudillo*, whose policies inevitably defended the interests of Argentina's landed aristocracy. [Culver Pictures, Inc.]

grants, and the measure actually contributed to the growth of latifundia. The lure of large profits in livestock raising induced many native and foreign merchants, politicians, and members of the military to join the rush for land. The net result was the creation not of a small-farmer class but of a new and more powerful estanciero class that was the enemy of Rivadavia's progressive ideals.

Rivadavia's planning went beyond the province of Buenos Aires; he had a vision of a unified Argentina under a strong central government that would promote the rounded economic development of the whole national territory. In 1825 a constituent congress met in Buenos Aires at Rivadavia's call to draft a constitution for the United Provinces of the Río de la Plata. Rivadavia, who was elected president of the new state, made a dramatic proposal to federalize the city and port of Buenos Aires. The former capital of the province would henceforth belong to the whole nation, with the revenues of its customhouse used to advance the general welfare.

Rivadavia's proposal reflected his nationalism and the need to mobilize national resources for a war with Brazil (1825–1828) over Uruguay. Congress approved Rivadavia's project, but the federalist caudillos of the interior, fearing that the rise of a strong national government would mean the end of their power, refused to ratify the constitution and even withdrew their delegates from the congress. In Buenos Aires a similar stand was taken by the powerful estancieros, who had no intention of surrendering the privileges of their province and regarded Rivadavia's program of social and economic reform as a costly folly. Defeated on the issue of the constitution, Rivadavia resigned the presidency in 1827 and went into exile. The liberal program for achieving national unity had failed.

After an interval of factional struggles, the federalism espoused by the landed oligarchy of Buenos Aires triumphed in the person of Juan Manuel Rosas, who became governor of the province in 1829. He forged (in 1831) a federal pact under which Buenos Aires assumed representation for the other provinces in foreign affairs but left them free to run their own affairs in all other respects. Federalism, as defined by Rosas, meant that Buenos Aires retained the revenues of its customhouse for its exclusive use and controlled trade on the Río de la Plata system for the benefit of its merchants. A network of personal alliances between Rosas and provincial caudillos, backed by use of force against recalcitrant leaders, ensured for him a large measure of control over the interior.

Rosas's long reign saw a reversal of Rivadavia's policies. For Rosas and the ruling class of estancieros, virtually the only economic concern was the export of hides and salted meat and the import of foreign goods. The dictator also showed some favor to wheat farming and artisan industry, which he protected by the Tariff Act of 1835, but the competition for land and later from livestock raising and the primitive character of artisan industry prevented both from taking much advantage of the act. Rosas himself was a great estanciero and owner of a *saladero* (salting plant) for the curing of meat and hides. He vigorously pressed the conquest of indigenous territory, bringing much new land under the control of the province of Buenos Aires; this land was sold for low prices to estancieros, and Rivadavia's policy of retaining ownership of land by the state was abandoned.

Although he professed to favor the gauchos, Rosas enforced the vagrancy laws against them even more rigorously, seeking to convert so-called idlers into ranch hands or soldiers for his army. The notion propagated by some historians that Rosas represented the rural masses against the urban aristocracy is contradicted by his own words. Fearing the masses, he cultivated gauchos and urban blacks to control them. "As you know," he wrote in a letter, "the dispossessed are always inclined to rise against the rich and the powerful. So . . . I thought it very important to gain a decisive influence over this class in order to control and direct it." But Rosas's "populism," his cultivation of gaucho manners and dress, did nothing to improve their condition. Under Rosas discipline on the estancias was enforced by punishments inherited from the colonial past that included torture, the lash, the stocks, and staking delinquent peons out "like hides in the sun." His government, observes John Lynch, was a seigneurial regime based on an informal alliance of estancieros and militia commanders, often the same people.

By degrees the press and all other potential dissidents were cowed or destroyed. To enforce the dictator's will there arose a secret organization known as the *Mazorca* (ear of corn—a reference to the close unity of its members). In collaboration with the police, this terrorist organization beat up or even murdered Rosas's opponents. The masthead of the official journal and all official papers carried the slogan "Death to the savage, filthy unitarians!" Even horses had to display the red ribbon that was the federalist symbol. Those opponents who did not knuckle under to escape death fled by the thousands to Montevideo, Chile, Brazil, or other places of refuge.

Under Rosas, the merchants of the city and the estancieros of the province of Buenos Aires enjoyed a measure of prosperity. But this prosperity bore no proportion to the possibilities of economic growth; technical backwardness marked all aspects of livestock raising and agriculture, and port facilities were totally inadequate.

Meanwhile, the littoral provinces, which had experienced some advance of livestock raising and agriculture, became increasingly aware that Rosas's brand of federalism was harmful to their interests and that free navigation of the river system of La Plata was necessary to assure their prosperity. In 1852 the anti-Rosas forces formed a coalition that united liberal émigrés with the caudillo Justo José de Urquiza of Entre Ríos, who together defeated Rosas's army and sent him fleeing to an English exile.

Victory over Rosas did not end the dispute between Buenos Aires and the other provinces, between federalism and unitarianism. Only the slower process of economic change would forge the desired unity. A rift soon arose between the liberal exiles who assumed leadership in Buenos Aires and the caudillo Urquiza of Entre Ríos, who still sported the red ribbon of federalism. A sincere convert to the gospel of modernity and progress, he had proposed a loose union of the provinces, with all of them sharing the revenues of the Buenos Aires customhouse. But the leaders of Buenos Aires feared the loss of their economic and political predominance to Urquiza, whom they wrongly considered a caudillo of the Rosas type.

After Urquiza had attempted unsuccessfully to make Buenos Aires accept unification by armed force, the two sides agreed to a peaceful separation. As a result, delegates from Buenos Aires were absent from the constitutional convention that met at Santa Fe in Entre Ríos in 1852.

The constitution of 1853 reflected the influence of the ideas of the journalist Juan Bautista Alberdi on the delegates. His forcefully written pamphlet, *Bases and Points of Departure for the Political Organization of the Argentine Republic*, offered the United States as a model for Argentina. The new constitution strongly resembled that of the United States in certain respects. The former United Provinces became a federal republic, presided over by a president with significant power who served a six-year term without the possibility of immediate reelection. Legislative functions were vested in a bicameral legislature, a senate and a house of representatives. The Catholic religion was proclaimed the official religion of the nation, but freedom of worship for non-Catholics was assured. The states were empowered to elect governors and legislatures and frame their own constitutions, but the federal government had the right of intervention—including armed intervention—to ensure respect for the provisions of the constitution. General Urquiza was elected the first president of the Argentine Republic.

The liberal leaders of Buenos Aires, joined by the conservative estancieros who had been Rosas's firmest supporters, refused to accept the constitution of 1853, for they feared the creation of a state they did not control. As a result, two Argentinas arose: the Argentine Confederation, headed by Urquiza, and the province of Buenos Aires. For five years, the two states maintained their separate existences. In Paraná, capital of the confederation, Urquiza struggled to repress gaucho revolts, stimulate economic development, and foster education and immigration. Modest advances were made, but the tempo of growth lagged far behind that of the wealthy city and province of Buenos Aires, which prospered on the base of a steadily increasing trade with Europe in hides, tallow, salted beef, and wool.

Hoping to increase the confederation's scanty revenues, Urquiza began a tariff war with Buenos Aires, levying surcharges on goods landed at the Paraná River port of Rosario if duties had been paid on them at Buenos Aires. Buenos Aires responded with sanctions against ships sailing to Rosario and threatened to close commerce on the Paraná altogether. In 1859 war between the two Argentine states broke out and the forces of Bartolomé Mitre, governor of Buenos Aires, emerged victorious.

The military and economic superiority of Buenos Aires, the need of the other provinces to use its port, and an awareness on all sides of the urgent need to achieve national unity dictated a compromise. At an 1862 congress representing all the provinces, it finally was agreed that the city should be the provisional capital of both the Argentine Republic and the province and that the Buenos Aires customhouse should be nationalized, with the proviso that for a period of five years the revenues of the province would not fall below the 1859 level. Bartolomé Mitre—distinguished historian, poet, soldier, and statesman—was elected the first president of a united Argentina.

Mitre promoted economic progress and consolidated national unity. The customhouse was nationalized, as had been promised, and plans were made for the federalization of the capital. The construction of railways and telegraph lines that would forge closer links between Buenos Aires and the interior had begun, and European immigrants arrived in growing numbers. Some advances were made in the establishment of a public school system. But great problems remained, the most difficult of which was the long, exhausting Paraguayan War (1865–1870).

THE PARAGUAYAN WAR

On the death of the dictator Francia in 1840, power in Paraguay was assumed by a triumvirate in which Carlos Antonio López soon emerged as the dominant figure. In essence, López continued Francia's dictatorial system but gave it a thin disguise of constitutional, representative government. Since he had inherited a stable, prosperous state, López could afford to rule in a less repressive fashion than his predecessor. More flexible than Francia, too, with a better understanding of the outside world, López made a successful effort to end Paraguay's diplomatic and commercial isolation. After the fall of Rosas, a stubborn enemy of Paraguayan independence, López obtained Argentine recognition of his country's independence, and the Paraná was at last opened to Paraguayan trade. López also established diplomatic relations with a series of countries, including England, France, and the United States.

The end of the policy of isolation was accompanied by a major expansion of the Paraguayan economy. Although agriculture (especially the production of such export crops as tobacco and yerba maté) continued to be the principal economic activity, López assigned great importance to the development of industry. One of his proudest achievements in this field was the construction of an iron foundry, the most modern enterprise of its type in Latin America. Transportation was improved with the building of roads and canals, the creation of a fleet of merchant ships, and the construction of a short railroad line.

Continuing Francia's policy, López enlarged the role of the state sector in the national economy. In 1848 he transferred to state ownership forest lands producing yerba maté and other commercial wood products and much arable land. The lucrative export trade in yerba maté and some other products became a government monopoly, and the number of state-owned ranches rose to sixty-four. López promoted education as well as economic growth; by the time of his death, Paraguay had 435 elementary schools, with some 25,000 pupils, and a larger proportion of literate inhabitants than any other Latin American country.

At the same time, López took advantage of his position to concentrate ownership of land and various commercial enterprises in his own hands and those of his children, relatives, and associates; thus, there arose a bourgeoisie that profited by its close connection with the state apparatus, which enabled it to promote its own interests. The number of large private estates, however, was small; the private agricultural sector was dominated by small or medium-sized farms cultivated by owners or tenants, sometimes aided by a few hired laborers. In contrast with the situation in other Latin American countries, peonage and debt servitude were rare and slavery was gradually abolished by an 1842 manumission law. The relative absence of peonage and other feudal survivals contributed to a rapid growth of Paraguayan capitalism and the well-being of its predominantly indigenous and mestizo population. When López died in 1862, Paraguay was one of the most progressive and prosperous states in South America.

His son, Francisco Solano, succeeded him as dictator. The younger López inherited a tradition of border disputes with Brazil that erupted into open war when Brazil sent an army into Uruguay in 1864 to ensure the victory of a pro-Brazilian faction in that country's civil strife. López could not be indifferent to this action, which threatened the delicate balance of power in the basin of La Plata. López also feared that Brazilian control of Uruguay would end unrestricted Paraguayan access to the port of Montevideo, which would make Paraguayan trade dependent entirely on the good will of Buenos Aires.

When the Brazilian government disregarded his protests, López declared war and Brazil quickly concluded a Triple Alliance with Argentina and Uruguay; a separate secret treaty between Brazil and Argentina provided for the partition of more than half of Paraguay's territory between them. Paraguay thus faced a coalition that included the two largest states in South America, with an immense superiority in manpower and other resources.

Yet the war dragged on for five years, for at its outset Paraguay possessed an army of some 70,000 well-armed and disciplined soldiers that outnumbered the combined forces of its foes. By 1870, however, the Triple Alliance had depleted Paraguay's economic strength and defeated its military forces. Perhaps as much as 20 percent of Paraguay's prewar population of some 300,000 perished as a result of military action, famine, disease, and a devastating Brazilian occupation. The peace treaty assigned much Paraguayan territory to the victors and burdened Paraguay with extremely heavy reparations. Brazil, the occupying power, installed a puppet regime that radically reconstructed the Paraguayan economy and state.

The essence of the new policy was to liquidate the progressive changes made under the Francia and López regimes. Most of the state-owned lands were sold to land speculators and foreign businessmen at bargain prices, with no restriction on the size of holdings. Tenants who could not present the necessary documents were ejected even though they and their forebears had cultivated the land for decades. By the early 1890s, the state-owned lands were almost gone. Foreign penetration of the economy through loans, concessions, and land purchases soon deprived Paraguay of its economic as well as its political independence.

PROGRESS AND DEVELOPMENT UNDER SARMIENTO

The Paraguayan War also changed Argentina, which obtained its share of Paraguayan reparations and territorial concessions (Formosa, Chaco, and Misiones). Politically, it ushered in a transfer of power to Domingo Faustino Sarmiento (1868–1874), a gifted essayist, sociologist, and statesman, who worked for Argentine unity and economic and social progress.

Even more importantly, however, a flood of technological change began to sweep over Argentina. Railways penetrated the interior, extending the stock-raising and farming area. The gradual introduction of barbed-wire fencing and alfalfa ranges made possible a dramatic improvement in the quality of livestock. In 1876 the arrival of an experimental shipload of chilled carcasses from France prepared the way for the triumph of frozen over salted meat, which led to a vast expansion of European demand for Argentine beef. Labor was needed to exploit the rapidly expanding pasturelands and farmlands, so Sarmiento's administration promoted immigration; some three hundred thousand immigrants poured into the country. Sarmiento, believing it necessary to educate the citizens of a democratic republic, expanded the public school system and introduced to Argentina teacher-training institutions of the kind his friend Horace Mann had founded in the United States. But there also was a darker side to Sarmiento's policies. Regarding native peoples and gauchos as obstacles to the advance of "civilization," he waged a war of extermination against the indígenas and used vagrancy laws, press gangs, and other repressive measures to control the gauchos.

When Sarmiento left office, Argentina presented the appearance of a rapidly developing, prosperous state. But there were clouds in the generally bright Argentine sky. The growth of exports and the rise in land values did not benefit the forlorn gauchos, aliens in a land over which they had once freely roamed, or the majority of European immigrants. Little was done to provide newcomers with homesteads. Immigrants who wished to farm usually found the price of land out of reach; as a result, many preferred to remain in Buenos Aires or other cities of the littoral, where they began to form an urban middle class largely devoted to trade. Meanwhile, foreign economic influence grew as a result of increasing dependence on foreign—chiefly British—capital to finance the construction of railways, telegraph lines, gasworks, and other needed facilities. The growing concentration of landownership reinforced a colonial land tenure pattern; the tightening British control of markets and the country's economic infrastructure reinforced a colonial pattern—dependence on a foreign metropolis, with London replacing Seville as commercial center. But Mitre, Sarmiento, and other builders of the new Argentina were dazzled by their successes in nation-building and by a climate of prosperity they believed permanent. These men did not suspect the extent of the problems in the making, nor did they anticipate the nature of the problems future generations of Argentines would face.

Chile

The victories of José de San Martín's Army of the Andes over royalist forces at Chacabuco and Maipú in 1817 and 1818 gave Chile its definitive independence. From 1818 until 1823, Bernardo O'Higgins, a hero of the struggle for Chilean liberation and a true son of the Enlightenment, ruled the country with the title of supreme director. O'Higgins energetically pushed a program of reform designed to weaken the landed aristocracy and the church and promote rapid development of the Chilean economy along capitalist lines. His abolition of titles of nobility and entails angered the great landowners of the fertile Central Valley between the Andes and the Pacific; his expulsion of the royalist bishop of Santiago and his restrictions on the number of religious processions and the veneration of images infuriated the church. Dissident liberals who resented his sometimes heavy-handed rule joined the opposition to O'Higgins. In 1823, O'Higgins resigned and went into exile in Lima. There followed seven turbulent years, with presidents and constitutions rising and falling.

PORTALES AND ECONOMIC GROWTH

In Chile, as in other Latin American countries, the political and armed struggle gradually assumed the form of a conflict between conservatives, who usually were also centralists, and liberals, who were generally federalists. The conservative-centralists were the party of the great landowners of the Central Valley and the wealthy merchants of Santiago; the liberal-federalists spoke for the landowners, merchants, and artisans of the northern and southern provinces, who were resentful of political and economic domination by the wealthy central area. By 1830 the conservatives emerged victorious under the leadership of Joaquín Prieto and his cabinet minister Diego Portales.

Until 1837, Portales, who never held an elective office, indelibly stamped his ideas on Chilean politics and society. A businessman of aristocratic origins, owner of a successful import house, he faithfully served the interests of an oligarchy of great landlords and merchants that dominated the Chilean scene for decades. Although Portales expressed atheist views in private, he supported the authority of the church as an instrument for keeping the lower classes in order. He understood the importance of trade, industry, and mining and promoted their interests by removing remaining obstacles to internal trade. He introduced income and property taxes to increase the state's revenues and trimmed government spending by dismissing unnecessary employees. Agriculture was protected by high tariffs on agricultural imports. Port facilities were improved, measures were taken to strengthen the Chilean merchant marine, and in 1835 a steamship line began to connect Chilean ports. Under the fostering care of the conservative regime and in response to a growing European demand for Chilean silver, copper, and hides, the national economy made steady progress in the 1830s.

Measures designed to stimulate economic growth were accompanied by others that fortified the social and political power of the oligarchy. Portales restored the privileges the church had lost under liberal rule and normalized the troubled relations between Chile and the papacy.

In 1833 a conservative-dominated assembly adopted a constitution that further consolidated the power of the oligarchy. Elections were made indirect, with the suffrage limited to men of twenty-five years or over who could satisfy literacy and property qualifications. Still higher property qualifications were required of members of the lower and upper houses. The constitution restored entails, ensuring perpetuation of the latifundio. Catholicism was declared the state religion, and the church was given control over marriage. The president enjoyed an absolute veto over congressional legislation, appointed all high officials, and could proclaim a state of siege. The process of amending the constitution was made so difficult as to be virtually impossible. Since the president controlled the electoral machinery, the outcome of elections was a foregone conclusion.

ECONOMIC EXPANSION UNDER BULNES

In 1841, General Manuel Bulnes succeeded Prieto to the presidency; he was reelected to a second five-year term in 1846. Victorious at home and abroad, the conservative leadership decided it could relax the strict discipline of the Portales period. Chile's economic life began a renewed advance. Commerce, mining, and agriculture prospered as never before. The Crimean War and the gold rushes to California and Australia of the 1850s created large new markets for Chilean wheat, stimulating a considerable expansion of the cultivated area. In 1840 a North American, William Wheelright, established a steamship line to operate on the Chilean coast, using coal from newly developed hard coal mines. Wheelright also founded a company that in 1852 completed Chile's first railroad line, providing an outlet to the sea for the production of the mining district of Copiapó. The major Santiago-Valparaíso line, begun in 1852, was not completed until 1863. Foreign—especially British—capital began to penetrate the Chilean economy; Britain dominated foreign trade and had a large interest in mining and railroads, but Chilean capitalists constituted an important, vigorous group and displayed much initiative in the formation of joint stock companies and banks.

The great landowners were the principal beneficiaries of this economic upsurge; their lands appreciated in value without any effort on their part. Some great landowners invested their money in railroads, mining, and trade. But the essential conservatism of the landed aristocracy and the urge to preserve a semifeudal control over its peons discouraged the transformation of the great landowners into capitalist farmers. A pattern of small landholdings arose in southern Chile, to which German as well as Chilean colonists came in increasing numbers in the 1840s and 1850s. The rich Central Valley, still dominated by the latifundio, reflected inefficient techniques and reliance on the labor of *inquilinos*—tenants who also had to work the master's fields. Thus, alongside an emerging capitalist sector based on mining, trade, banking, intensive agriculture, and some industry, there existed a semifeudal sector based on the latifundio, peonage, and an aristocracy that hindered the development of Chilean capitalism.

Although Chile appeared more progressive than most other Latin American states, militants like José Victorino Lastarria—historian, sociologist, and a deputy of the Liberal Party—were dissatisfied with the new conservatives' modest concessions to modernity. They wanted to accelerate the rate of change and demanded both a radical revision of the constitution of 1833 and an end to oligarchical rule.

To the left of Lastarria stood the firebrand Francisco Bilbao, author of a scorching attack on the church and Hispanic heritage, "The Nature of Chilean Society" (1844). Later, he spent several years in France and was profoundly influenced by utopian socialist and radical republican thought. He returned to Chile in 1850 to found, with Santiago Arcos, the Society of Equality, uniting radical intellectuals and artisans, which advocated these advanced ideas. The society carried on an intensive antigovernmental campaign and within a few months had a membership of four thousand.

MONTT'S MODERATE REFORMS

The Society of Equality was founded on the eve of the election of 1850, for which President Bulnes had designated Manuel Montt his heir. Despite Montt's progressive educational policies and patronship of the arts and letters, liberals identified him with the repressive system of Portales and the constitution of 1833. Liberals like Lastarria and radical democrats like Bilbao proclaimed the impending election a fraud and demanded constitutional reforms. The government responded by proclaiming a state of siege and suppressing the Society of Equality. Regarding these acts as a prelude to an attempt to liquidate the opposition, groups of liberals in Santiago and La Serena rose in revolts that were quickly crushed. Lastarria was exiled; Bilbao and Arcos fled to Argentina. Montt became president and immediately crushed another liberal revolt, but thereafter took steps to resolve future crises by granting amnesty to the insurgents and abolishing both entails and the tithe.

The abolition of entails, which was designed to encourage the breakup of landed estates among the children of the great landowners, affected a dwindling number of great aristocratic clans. Its effects were less drastic than the anguished cries of the affected parties suggested, for the divided estates were almost invariably acquired by other latifundists, and the condition of the *inquilinos* who worked the land remained the same. The elimination of the tithe, and Montt's refusal to allow the return of the Jesuits, greatly angered the reactionary clergy. Responding to their attacks, Montt promulgated a new civil code in 1857 that placed education under state control, gave the state jurisdiction over the clergy, and granted non-Catholics the right of civil marriage.

The abolition of entails and the tithe represented a compromise between liberals and conservatives, between the new bourgeoisie and the great landowners. In the process, the bourgeoisie gained little, and the landowners lost almost nothing; the chief loser was the church. Although Montt's reforms alienated the most reactionary elements of the Conservative Party, they gained him the support of moderate liberals who joined with moderate conservatives to form a new coalition, the National Party. Its motto was the typically positivist slogan "Freedom in Order."

In the last years of his second term, President Montt faced severe economic and political problems. The 1857 depression caused a sharp fall in the price of copper and reduced Australian and Californian demand for Chilean wheat. The economic decline fed the fires of political discontent, and another large-scale revolt erupted in January 1859. The rebels included radical intellectuals, northern mining capitalists and their workers, artisans, and small farmers, all groups with grievances against the dominant Central Valley alliance of great merchants and landowners. Their demands included a democratic republic, state support for mining and industry, the splitting up of the great estates, and abolition of the semifeudal *inquilinaje* system of peonage as incompatible with democratic principles. Before the revolt was crushed, it had taken five thousand lives. Some of the bourgeois leaders of the revolt were imprisoned, others were deported, and others fled into exile, but a large number of miners, artisans, and peasants were executed. Maurice Zeitlin regards it as a crucial turning point in Chilean history: "Defeat of the revolutionary bourgeoisie amounted to virtual suppression of an alternative and independent path of capitalist development for Chile—a realm of objective historical possibilities unfulfilled because of the failure of the bourgeois revolution."

By 1861 the depression had lifted and another boom began, creating new fortunes and bringing large shifts of regional influence. A growing stream of settlers, including many Germans, flowed into southern Chile, founding cities and transforming woodlands into farms.

But Chile's true center of economic gravity became the desert north, rich in copper, nitrates, and guano; the last two, in particular, were objects of Europe's insatiable demand for fertilizers. The major nitrate deposits, however, lay in the Bolivian province of Antofagasta and the Peruvian province of Tarapacá. Chilean capital, supplemented by English and German capital, began to pour into these regions and soon dominated the Peruvian and Bolivian nitrate industries. In the north there arose an aggressive mining capitalist class that demanded a place in the sun for itself and its region. A rich mine owner, Pedro León Gallo, abandoned the liberals to form a new middle-class party, called Radical, that fought more militantly than the liberals for limited constitutional changes, religious toleration, and an end to repressive policies.

LIBERAL CONTROL

The transition of Chile's political life to liberal control, begun under Montt, was completed in 1871 with the election of the first liberal president, Federico Errázuriz Zañartú. Between 1873 and 1875 a coalition of liberals and radicals pushed through the congress a series of constitutional reforms: reduction of senatorial terms from nine to six years; direct election of senators; and freedom of speech, press, and assembly. These victories for enlightenment also represented a victory of new capitalist groups over the old merchant-landowner oligarchy that traced its beginnings back to colonial times. By 1880, of the fifty-nine Chilean personal fortunes of over 1 million pesos, only twenty-four were of colonial origin and only twenty had made their fortunes in agriculture; the rest belonged to coal, nitrate, copper, and silver interests or to merchants whose wealth had been formed only in the nineteenth century. Arnold Bauer has observed that the more interesting point is "not that only twenty made their fortune in agriculture, but that the remaining thirty-nine—designated as miners, bankers, and capitalists— subsequently invested their earnings in rural estates. This would be comparable to Andrew Carnegie sinking his steel income into Scarlett O'Hara's plantation." Bauer's comment points to the "powerful social model" that the Chilean agrarian oligarchy continued to exert. For the rest, the victories of the new bourgeoisie brought no relief to the Chilean masses, the migrant laborers and tenant farmers on the haciendas, and the young working class in Chile's mines and factories.

Brazil

Brazil took its first major step toward independence in 1808, when the Portuguese crown and court, fleeing before a French invasion of Portugal, arrived in Rio de Janeiro to make it the new capital of the Portuguese Empire. Formal national independence came in 1822 when Dom Pedro, who ruled Brazil as regent for his father, João VI, rejected a demand that he return to Portugal and issued the famous Cry of Ipiranga: "Independence or Death!"

DOM PEDRO, EMPEROR

Dom Pedro acted with the advice and support of the Brazilian aristocracy, which was determined to preserve the autonomy Brazil had enjoyed since 1808. It was equally determined to make a transition to independence without the violence that marked the Spanish-American movement of liberation elsewhere. The Brazilian aristocracy had its wish; Brazil made a transition to independence with comparatively little disruption and bloodshed. But separation from Portugal with a minimum of internal dislocation meant that independent Brazil retained not only monarchy and slavery but also the large landed estate and monoculture; a wasteful, inefficient agricultural system; a highly stratified society; and a free population that was 90 percent illiterate and prejudiced against manual labor.

Dom Pedro had promised to give his subjects a constitution, but the constituent assembly he summoned in 1823 drafted a document that seemed to the emperor to place excessive limits on his power. He responded by dissolving the assembly and assigning to a hand-picked commission the task of making a new constitution, which he approved and promulgated by imperial proclamation. This constitution, under which Brazil was governed until the fall of the monarchy in 1889, concentrated great power in the hands of the monarch. In addition to a Council of State, it provided for a two-chamber parliament—a lifetime Senate, the members of which were chosen by the emperor, and a Chamber of Deputies elected by voters who met property and income requirements. The emperor had the right to appoint and dismiss ministers and summon or dissolve parliament at will. He also appointed the provincial governors or presidents.

Resentment over Dom Pedro's highhanded dissolution of the constituent assembly and the highly centralist character of the constitution of 1824 was particularly strong in Pernambuco, a center of republican and federalist ferment. Here in 1824 a group of rebels, led by the merchant Manoel de Carvalho, proclaimed the creation of a Confederation of the Equator that would unite the six northern provinces under a republican government. A few leaders voiced antislavery sentiments, but nothing was done to abolish slavery, which deprived the movement of the potential support of a large slave population. Within a year imperial troops had smashed the revolt and executed fifteen of its leaders.

Dom Pedro had won a victory, but resentment of his autocratic tendencies continued to smolder, and his popularity steadily waned. The emperor's foreign policies contributed to this growing discontent. In 1826, in return for recognition of Brazilian independence and a trade agreement, Dom Pedro signed a treaty with Great Britain that obligated Brazil to end the slave traffic by 1830. Despite this ban and the efforts of British warships to intercept and seize the slaveships, the trade continued with the full knowledge and approval of the Brazilian government. But British policing practices caused the price of slaves to rise sharply. The prospering coffee growers of Rio de Janeiro, São Paulo, and Minas Gerais could afford to pay high prices for slaves, but the cotton and sugar growers of the depressed north could not compete with them for workers and blamed Dom Pedro for their difficulties.

News of the July Revolution of 1830 in France, a revolution that toppled an unpopular, autocratic king, produced rejoicing and violent demonstrations in Brazilian cities. *Exaltados* (radical liberals) placed themselves at the head of the movement of revolt and called for the abolition of the monarchy and the establishment of a federal republic. In the face of the growing crisis, Dom Pedro abdicated in favor of his five-year-old son Pedro, and two weeks later he sailed for Portugal, never to return. These developments, eliminating the dominant influence of Portuguese merchants and Portuguese-born courtiers under Emperor Pedro I, completed the transition to full Brazilian independence.

REGENCY, REVOLT, AND A BOY EMPEROR

The revolution had been the work of radical liberals, who viewed Dom Pedro's downfall as the first step toward the establishment of a federal republic, but its fruits were garnered by the moderates. In effect, the radicals had played the game of the monarchist liberals, who had guided the movement of secession from Portugal and later lost influence at court as a result of Dom Pedro's shift to the right. Dom Pedro's departure was a victory for these moderates, who hastened to restore their ascendancy over the central government and prevent the revolution from getting out of hand.

As a first step, parliament appointed a three-man regency composed of moderate liberals to govern for the child emperor until he reached the age of eighteen. Another measure created a national guard, recruited from the propertied classes, to repress urban mobs and slave revolts. Simultaneously, the new government began work on a project of constitutional reform designed to appease the strong federalist sentiment. After a three-year debate, parliament approved the Additional Act of 1834, which gave the provinces elective legislative assemblies with broad powers, including control over local budgets and taxes. This provision assured the great landowners a large measure of control over their regions. The Council of State, identified with Dom Pedro's reactionary rule, was abolished. But centralism was not abandoned, for the national government continued to appoint provincial governors with a partial veto over the acts of the provincial assemblies.

Almost immediately, the regency government struggled against a rash of revolts, most numerous in the northern provinces, where the economy suffered from a loss of markets for their staple crops, sugar and cotton. None occurred in the central southern zone (the provinces of Rio de Janeiro, São Paulo, and Minas Gerais), whose coffee economy prospered and whose planter aristocracy had secure control of the central government. These revolts had a variety of local causes. Some were elemental, popular revolts; such was the so-called *cabanagem* (from the word *cabana*, "cabin") of Pará, which originated in the grievances of small tradesmen, farmers, and lower-class elements against the rich Portuguese merchants who monopolized local trade. Others, like the republican and separatist revolt in Bahia (1837–1838), reflected the frustrations of the planter aristocracy of this once-prosperous area over its loss of economic and political power.

Most serious of all was the revolt that broke out in 1835 in the province of Rio Grande do Sul. Although it was dubbed the *Revolução Farroupilha* (Revolution of the Ragamuffins) in contemptuous reference to its supposed lower-class origins, the movement was led by cattle barons who maintained a more or less patriarchal sway over the gauchos who formed the rank-and-file of the rebel armies. An intense regionalism, resentment over taxes and unpopular governors imposed by the central government, and the strength of republican sentiment all induced the revolt that established the independent republic of Rio Grande in 1836. The presence of considerable numbers of Italian exiles such as Giuseppe Garibaldi, ardent republicans opposed to slavery, gave a special radical tinge to the revolt. For almost a decade, two states—one a republic, the other an empire—existed on Brazilian territory.

The secession of Rio Grande and the inability of imperial troops to quell the revolt further weakened the regency government. Soon the political struggle began to assume an organized form, with the emergence of a Liberal Party composed chiefly of moderate liberals who favored concessions to federalism, and a Conservative Party, which preferred to strengthen the central government. However, on such essential issues as the monarchy, slavery, and the maintenance of the status quo in general, liberals and conservatives saw eye to eye.

They also agreed on the need to suppress the Rio Grande rebellion and other regional revolts in the north. The Rio Grande experiment in republican government and its offer of freedom to all slaves who joined the republic's armed forces posed an especially serious threat to monarchy and slavery. To strengthen the central government in its war against these subversive and separatist movements, liberals and conservatives decided to call the young Pedro to rule before his legal majority. In 1840 the two legislative chambers orchestrated a parliamentary coup d'état and proclaimed the fourteen-year-old Dom Pedro emperor. He empowered a conservative government that dismantled the federalist reforms in the Additional Act of 1834, sharply curtailed the powers of provincial assemblies, and stripped locally elected judges of their judicial and police powers.

The liberals of São Paulo and Minas Gerais responded with a revolt (1842) that had little popular support, for it was dictated solely by the desire for the spoils of office. Conservative troops swiftly crushed the uprising, but the emperor treated the vanquished rebels leniently and, a short time later, he called on the liberals to form a new ministry. Once returned to power, the liberals made no effort to repeal the conservative revisions of the constitution and made use of the broad police powers vested in the central government for their own ends.

With the unity of the ruling class restored, the government undertook to settle scores with the rebels of Rio Grande. As a result of internal squabbles and the cessation of aid from friendly Uruguay after Argentina invaded it in February 1843, the situation of the republic became extremely difficult. Facing the prospect of military defeat, the republican leaders accepted an offer from Rio de Janeiro to negotiate a peace, which was signed in February 1845. The peace treaty extended amnesty to all rebels but annulled all laws of the republican regime. The cattle barons won certain concessions, including the right to nominate their candidate for provincial governor and retain their military titles.

The last large-scale revolt in the series that shook Brazil in the 1830s and 1840s was the uprising of 1848 in Pernambuco. Centered in the city of Recife, its causes included hostility toward the Portuguese merchants who monopolized local trade, the appointment of an unpopular governor by the conservative government, and hatred for the greatest landowners of the region, the powerful Cavalcanti family. The rebel program called for the removal from Recife of all Portuguese merchants, expansion of provincial autonomy, work for the unemployed, and division of the Cavalcanti lands. Even this radical program, however, contained no reference to the abolition of slavery. The movement collapsed after the capture of Recife by imperial troops in 1849. Many captured leaders were condemned to prison for life, but all were amnestied in 1852.

Underlying these rebellions and armed conflicts of the 1830s and 1840s was economic stagnation caused by the weakness of foreign markets for Brazil's traditional exports. The expansion in the center-south of coffee, already important in the 1830s but flourishing after 1850, strengthened the hand of the central government with increased revenues and laid the basis for a new era of cooperation between regional elites and the national government. The new coffee prosperity, confirming the apparent viability and rationality of the neocolonial emphasis on export agriculture, also discouraged any thought of taking the more durable but difficult path of Brazilian autonomous development.

THE GAME OF POLITICS AND THE CRISIS OF SLAVERY

By 1850, Brazil was at peace. The emperor presided over a pseudoparliamentary regime, exercising his power in the interests of a tiny ruling class. He paid his respects to parliamentary forms by alternately appointing conservative and liberal prime ministers at will; if the new ministry did not command a majority in parliament, one was obtained by holding rigged elections. Because the ruling class was united on essential issues, the only thing at stake in party struggles was patronage, the spoils of office. An admirer of Dom Pedro, Joaquim Nabuco, described the operation of the system in his book *O abolicionismo*:

> The representative system, then, is a graft of parliamentary forms on a patriarchal government, and senators and deputies only take their roles seriously in this parody of democracy because of the personal advantage they derive therefrom. Suppress the subsidies, force them to stop using their positions for personal and family ends, and no one who had anything else to do would waste his time in such shadow boxing.

The surface stability of Brazilian political life in the decades after 1850 rested on the prosperity of the coffee-growing zone of Rio de Janeiro, São Paulo, and Minas Gerais, itself the product of growing demand and good prices for Brazilian coffee. But the sugar-growing northeast and its plantation society continued to decline because of exhausted soil, archaic techniques, and competition from foreign sugars.

The crisis of the northeast grew more acute as a result of English pressure on Brazil to enforce the Anglo-Brazilian treaty banning the importation of slaves into Brazil after November 7, 1831. Before 1850 this treaty was never effectively enforced; more than fifty thousand slaves a year were brought to Brazil during the 1840s. In 1849 and 1850, however, the British government pressured Brazil to pass the Queiroz anti–slave-trade law and instructed its warships to enter Brazilian territorial waters if necessary to destroy Brazilian slave ships. By the middle 1850s, the importation of slaves had virtually ended.

Abolition of the slave trade had major consequences. Because of the high mortality among slaves due to poor food, harsh working conditions, and other negative factors, the slave population could not be maintained by natural reproduction, and the eventual doom of the slave system was assured. The end of the slave trade created a serious labor shortage, with a large flow of slaves from the north to the south because of the coffee planters' greater capacity to compete for slave labor. This movement aggravated the imbalance between the declining north and the prosperous south-central zone, where Brazil's first telegraph lines were established in 1852 and the first railroad line was begun in 1854. In these years, a pioneer of Brazilian capitalism, Irineu Evangelista de Sousa, later the Baron Mauá, laid the foundations of a veritable industrial and banking empire.

By the 1860s, a growing number of Brazilians had become convinced that slavery brought serious discredit to Brazil and must be ended. The abolition of slavery in the United States as a result of the Civil War, which left Brazil and the Spanish colonies of Cuba and Puerto Rico the only slave-holding areas in the Western Hemisphere, sharpened sensitivity to the problem. The Paraguayan War also promoted the cause of emancipation. In an effort to fill the gaps caused by heavy losses at the front, a decree was issued granting freedom to government-owned slaves who agreed to join the army, and some private slave owners followed the official example. Criticism of slavery was increasingly joined with criticism of the emperor, censured for his cautious posture on slavery.

Alongside the antislavery movement there arose a nascent republican movement. In 1869 the Reform Club, a group of militant Liberals, issued a manifesto demanding restrictions on the powers of the emperor and the grant of freedom to the new-born children of slaves. The crisis of slavery was fast becoming a crisis of the Brazilian Empire.

Peru

The liberation of Peru from Spanish rule had come from without, for the creole aristocracy, whose wealth was derived from the forced labor of indigenous peoples and enslaved Africans in mines, workshops, and haciendas, rightly feared that revolution might set fire to this combustible social material. The liberators, General José de San Martín and Simón Bolívar, had attempted to reform the social and economic institutions of the newly created Peruvian state. Before he left to meet Bolívar in Guayaquil, San Martín had decreed a ban on slave importation, the automatic emancipation of all children born of slaves in Peru, and the abolition of native tribute as well as the mita and all other kinds of indigenous forced labor; he also proclaimed that all inhabitants of Peru, whether native or creole, were Peruvians.

Because these reforms did not conform to the interests of the creole elite, however, they were never implemented after San Martín left Lima to meet Bolívar in Guayaquil. When Bolívar assumed power in Peru in 1823, he enacted reforms reflecting the same liberal ideology. Wishing to create a class of independent small-holders, he decreed the dissolution of indigenous communities and ordered the division of communal lands into individual parcels; each family was to hold its plot as private property, with the surplus to become part of the public domain. While attacking communal property, Bolívar left alone feudal property, the great haciendas serviced by *yanaconas* or *colonos* (native sharecroppers or serfs) who had to pay their landlords a rent that amounted to as much as 50 to 90 percent of the value of their crops, in addition to *pongueaje* (free personal service).

The well-intentioned Bolivarian land reform played into the hands of hacendados, public officials, and merchants, who used it to build up vast estates at the expense of indigenous communal lands; the process began slowly but gathered momentum as the century advanced. Bolívar's efforts to abolish native tribute had no greater success. After he left Peru in 1826, Peru's creole government reinstituted the tribute for *serranos* under the name *contribución de indígenas,* and for good measure it also reintroduced the *contribución de castas* for the mestizo population of the coast.

The new government's heavy dependence on such tribute as a source of revenue reflected the stagnant condition of the Peruvian economy. The revolution completed the ruin of the mining industry and coastal plantation agriculture, both of which had been declining since the close of the eighteenth century, and the scanty volume of exports could not pay for the much greater volume of imports of manufactured goods from Britain. As a result, the new state, already burdened with large wartime debts to English capitalists, developed a massive trade deficit with Great Britain, its largest trading partner. There was some growth of wool exports after 1836, and in 1840 a new economic era opened on the coast with the exploitation of guano, but in its first stage the guano cycle failed to provide the capital accumulation needed to revive coastal agriculture.

Cuba

Because of its distinctive colonial past, Cuba's nineteenth-century development differed markedly from that of most other Latin American countries. For three centuries after Christopher Columbus landed in 1492, the island served primarily as a strategic stopover for the Spanish treasure fleet. Largely isolated from expanding transatlantic markets and without precious metals or a large indigenous population to exploit, Cuba remained a neglected, sparsely populated outpost of the empire. The island's inhabitants engaged, for the most part, in small-scale farming for domestic consumption. Unlike the sugar-producing islands of the Caribbean, at the end of the seventeenth century Cuba had few slaves (its population of African descendents numbered 40,000, only one-

tenth that of Haiti), many of whom worked in nonagricultural occupations, often as skilled craftsmen.

ECONOMIC AND SOCIAL CHANGE: THE BITTER HARVEST OF KING SUGAR

The second half of the eighteenth century, however, had brought profound economic and social change as Cuba was transformed into a classic case of monoculture—an area dependent on the production and export of a single crop for its economic livelihood. Spurred by the short-lived British occupation of Havana in 1762 and further stimulated by the growing U.S. market produced by independence in 1783, the island experienced a commercial awakening. Most important, Cuba developed into a major sugar producer and slave importer in the aftermath of the Haitian Revolution of the 1790s, which ruined that island as a sugar producer (until then, it had been the world's leader). During the next half-century, sugar production in Cuba skyrocketed, and nearly 600,000 enslaved Africans arrived on its shores. From 1774 to 1861, the island's population leaped from 171,620 to 1,396,530, 30 percent of whom were of African descent. Havana and Santiago de Cuba became large, busy urban centers and ports, and no fewer than eight other cities attained populations exceeding 10,000.

Initially, the transfer to sugar did not stimulate the creation of the latifundio—first, because much of the land converted to sugar was the underused acreage of large cattle haciendas, and second, because many farmers did not change over to sugar, preferring instead to produce coffee and tobacco, which then enjoyed high prices resulting from the abolition of the royal monopoly on these commodities. Furthermore, the sugar mills themselves stimulated demand for livestock (to turn the mills) and food crops for the slaves. During the first decades of the nineteenth century, the number of farm proprietors increased markedly, and from their ranks came the leaders of Cuban society for the next century.

The boom that followed the destruction of Haitian sugar production ended by the turn of the century because other Caribbean islands expanded and initiated production in response to the same stimuli, thereby creating an enormous glut on the market. Just as the industry recovered from this setback, diplomatic maneuvering during the Napoleonic wars closed U.S. ports. Shortly thereafter, two new challenges to the Cuban economy arose: the introduction of beet sugar in Europe and the British campaign to end the slave trade. (England forced Spain to end the trade in 1821.) Further impediments resulted from the restrictions imposed by Spanish hegemony: high tariffs, scarce and expensive credit, and the disruptions brought on by the Spanish-American wars of independence.

By 1820 the first of a series of technological innovations began to transform the character of the sugar industry in Cuba. Mill owners had to invest heavily in steam-operated machinery to compete with beet sugar. Modern machinery allowed the mills to expand in size, but they could do so only gradually because of limited transportation facilities. Because railroads were enormously expensive, and in any case there was not sufficient capital on the island or in Spain for large projects of this type, they did not become important until much later.[2] The mills also carried a huge overhead because they were largely unused during the off-season. Slaves and livestock had to be fed and sheltered even when the harvest was completed. The problem of fuel for the mills also slowed their expansion. The forests close to the mills were quickly consumed, and transport of wood to the mills proved prohibitively costly. As a result, sugar production was expanded in the first half of the century through an increase in the number of mills. In 1827 there were 1,000 mills, by 1846 there were 1,442, and by 1860 there were 2,000.

The expansion of trade and the introduction of large-scale sugar production created a fantastic economic boom and delayed the development of the spirit of rebellion against Spanish rule that swept the rest of Spanish America. Cuba stayed loyal to Spain during the Spanish-American wars of independence, for its creole leaders saw no reason to tamper with their newfound prosperity.

Discontent grew among slaves and free blacks, however, as a result of the rise of an increasingly harsh plantation system; in addition to everyday acts of resistance, such as work slowdowns, feigned illness, equipment sabotage, and abortion, African men and women periodically punctuated their protests against enslavement with major slave rebellions, led by free blacks, in 1810, 1812, and 1844.

But during the last half of the nineteenth century, wealthy creoles became increasingly resentful of the arbitrary ways of corrupt Spanish officialdom, which was determined to enforce continued obedience from Spain's last and richest colony in the New World. The colony grew increasingly dissatisfied with repressive Spanish rule and less dependent economically on the mother country. As Cuba turned increasingly toward the United States as a market for its products and a source of needed imports, schemes for the annexation of Cuba to the United States emerged both on the island and in some North American circles. In Cuba, conservative creole planters saw in annexation an insurance policy against the abolition of slavery; in the United States, some pro-slavery groups regarded annexation as a means of gaining a vast new area for the expansion of plantation slavery. Some of these groups even dreamed of carving Cuba up into three or five states that would give the South increased power in the national government. The U.S. Civil War put an end to these projects.

Meanwhile, large plantations developed in Cuba in response to the necessity of building bigger and bigger mills (*centrales*). Sugar technology was continually improving, and Cuban mills had to expend huge sums to remain competitive. The larger the mill, the more sugar it could process, the more fuel it consumed, and the more employees it needed. Smaller and less efficient mills were at a severe competitive disadvantage.

Sugar production traditionally had been set up in one of two ways: the land was cultivated by resident or temporary labor, or the land was parceled out to farmers, known as *colonos*, who worked the land for a salary or a share of the crop. The landowners, in either situation, might or might

---

[2] The first railroad in Cuba was built in 1836.

not also be the millowners. As the number of mills grew smaller, the colonos became the main suppliers of sugar to the mills. They planted and harvested the cane and brought it to the mill to be processed. They paid for the processing in sugar. By the 1860s production was specialized into these components, colonos and centrales. The number of large plantations did not increase; instead, the number of colonos gradually rose.

During the 1860s creole discontent grew and was heightened by a developing national and class consciousness. The creole elite rejected various reform proposals offered by a weak Spanish government that was battered by internal dissension and economic difficulties. It became increasingly clear to the creoles that Spanish economic and political policies were severely restricting Cuban development—a feeling sharpened by a serious economic downturn. On October 10, 1868, in the small town of Yara in Oriente Province, a group of landowners proclaimed Cuban independence and initiated a struggle that was to continue for ten years.

THE TEN YEARS' WAR

The Ten Years' War, a long, bitter, devastating guerrilla struggle, ended in 1878 when the Cubans accepted a peace that granted them some concessions but withheld independence. The Pact of Zanjón ended hostilities, but some rebel leaders, like the black revolutionary Antonio Maceo, the "Bronze Titan," rejected the settlement because it did not achieve the main goals of the revolution—independence and the abolition of slavery. Ironically, the Spanish government, hoping to win the loyalty of the black population, abolished slavery in 1880, with provision for an eight-year *patronato*, or period of apprenticeship, for the liberated slaves. The abolition of slavery removed the last major factor tending to keep creole planters loyal to Spain. Thereafter, the prospect of independence, offering free, unlimited trade with the United States, became increasingly attractive.

The Ten Years' War had a far-reaching impact on the development of Cuban society. It decimated the creole landowning class, hindering the formation of a traditional Latin American landed elite

on the island. Moreover, the shakeout of mills during the war, the financial crisis of 1885–1890, and the expansion of the island's railroad network combined to stimulate the spread of the latifundio. As they grew, the mills required more cane, which came from a wider geographic area than previously. At the same time, the introduction of cheap rails spurred railroad construction in Cuba (and all over the world). In their quest for more cane, owners of centrales began to lay their own track, and competition among centrales for cane, a condition previously unknown because of transportation limitations, resulted.

The owners of centrales confronted the necessity of guaranteeing enough cane at the lowest possible prices for the *zafra* (harvest). They could do this either by reducing the independence of the colonos or by acquiring their own cane land. The first method transformed the once-free farmers into satellites of the giant mills. The second led to the creation of latifundia. Small- and medium-sized growers fell by the wayside, to be replaced by tenants or day labor. The colonos managed to hold their own until independence, after which time the massive influx of foreign capital into the sugar mills overwhelmed them. With their lesser financial resources, they were doomed.

Entrepreneurs from the United States filled the vacuum created by the ruin of the creole aristocracy and the bankruptcy of Spanish interests by the war. Thousands of North Americans accompanied their investment dollars to the island to run the sugar mills and merchant houses. The McKinley Tariff Act of 1890, which abolished import duties on raw sugar and molasses, greatly increased American trade with and economic influence in Cuba; by 1896, U.S. interests had invested $50 million in Cuba and controlled the sugar industry. The United States purchased 87 percent of Cuba's exports. The growth of U.S. investment in Cuba also brought about an increasing concentration of sugar production, a trend signaled by the entry of the "Sugar Trust" (the American Sugar Refining Company of Henry Q. Havemeyer) into the island in 1888.

Although the Ten Years' War had transformed Cuba into a haven for North Americans, it had done nothing to eliminate racial segregation and discrimination, even after emancipation. Elite Spanish and creole white supremacists dominated late nineteenth-century Cuba and routinely blamed Afro-Cubans for all manner of Cuban social ills, denied them access to education and adequate health care, engaged in employment discrimination, and created obstacles to full citizenship. Interracial marriage, prohibited by law until 1881, remained socially stigmatized thereafter.

This racial apartheid created two Cubas—one steeped in Spanish cultural traditions and ritual practices like Catholicism and Freemasonry, and the other centered in African *santería*, a syncretic popular religion, and *ñáñigos*, secret mutual aid societies. According to historian Aline Helg, Afro-Cubans, frustrated by limits imposed on their ability to rise in Spanish society, increasingly relied on their African heritage to protect themselves and to organize social protest movements that demanded their "rightful share."

United Provinces of Central America

On the eve of independence, the five republics—Guatemala, El Salvador, Honduras, Nicaragua, and Costa Rica[3]—were provinces of the captaincy general of Guatemala, with its capital at Guatemala City. Under the captain general and his *audiencia*, a small group of wealthy creole merchants, organized in a powerful *consulado*, had dominated the economic, social, and political life of the colony. But Spain's hold over its American colonies had weakened after 1800 as a result of its involvement in European wars, the resulting disruption of trade, and growing political turmoil at home. Central America drifted toward independence. When Mexico proclaimed its independence in 1821, Central America followed suit. City after city declared its independence, not only from Spain, but from Guatemala and rival cities and towns. The captaincy general dissolved into a mul-

titude of autonomous *cabildo* (municipal) governments. The transition to independence was complicated by the efforts of Agustín de Iturbide to incorporate Central America into his Mexican empire, efforts supported by Central American conservatives and opposed by many liberals. In 1822 a majority of cabildos voted in favor of union with Mexico, but Iturbide's overthrow the next year permanently ended the Mexican connection.

INDEPENDENCE AND THE FAILURE OF UNION, 1810–1865

Despite provincial rivalries and resentment against Guatemalan domination, a tradition of Central American unity remained and attempts were made to strengthen that unity. In 1823 a constituent assembly met and created the federal republic of Central America out of the five former provinces: Guatemala, Honduras, Nicaragua, Costa Rica, and El Salvador. The constitution provided for a federal government with free and independent state governments and had a strong liberal tinge: it abolished slavery and the special privileges of the clergy and established the principles of laissez faire, free trade, and free contract of labor. The next year a Salvadoran liberal, Manuel José Arce, was elected as the first president of the republic. Meanwhile, the states were forming their own governments. On the state as on the federal level, conservatives and liberals struggled for power: conservatism—the ideology of the old monopolistic merchant clique, many great landowners, and the church—had its base in Guatemala; liberalism was the dominant doctrine among many large and small landowners of the other states and the small middle class of artisans, professionals, and intellectuals. Behind the façade of elections and universal male suffrage, power throughout the area was held by great landowning and mercantile families, who often mobilized their private armies of retainers and tenants in a struggle for control of regions and states.

The superficial unity of Central America soon dissolved as it became clear that the states were neither willing nor able to finance both their own governments and the federal government in Guatemala

---

[3]Although, for descriptive convenience, Belize and Panama are usually included in Central America, the former was a British colony and the latter a province of Colombia. Neither, therefore, was linked historically to the region.

City. Efforts by Arce's federal government to assert its prerogatives by the establishment of a strong army and the collection of taxes led him to abandon liberalism, which ignited a destructive civil war between 1826 and 1829. The struggle ended with the defeat of the national government and its conservative leadership by liberal forces headed by Francisco Morazán and the reorganization of the union on a basis of liberal hegemony.

Morazán, elected president of the federal republic and commander of its armed forces, both based in San Salvador, defended it against conservative plots and attacks. At the same time, a former conservative turned liberal, Mariano Gálvez, governor of Guatemala, launched a program for the economic and social reconstruction of his state. The program included the establishment of civil marriage and divorce and secular schools on all levels, anticlerical measures that allowed nuns to leave their orders and reduced the number of church holidays, large land concessions to British companies that were to colonize the land with foreign immigrants and provide it with an infrastructure, and even an agrarian reform that allowed squatters to buy land for half its value and permitted natives to settle on vacant land. Gálvez also sought to reform Guatemala's judicial system by basing it on the Livingston Code,[4] which provided for trial by jury and *habeas corpus* and vested power to appoint all judges in the governor of the state. This last feature alienated powerful landed interests who often served as *jefes políticos*, local officials who combined judicial and administrative functions and were permitted to keep a share of tax collections.

The loss of the support of local landed interests combined with the ravages of a cholera epidemic that spread over Central America in 1837 to bring down the Gálvez regime and its ambitious reform program. Stirred up by local clergy who proclaimed the epidemic to be divine retribution for the heresies of civil marriage and divorce, the native and mixed-blood masses rose in revolt against Gálvez's radical innovations in law and taxation, attacks on their landholdings by creole landowners, and sanitary measures instituted to prevent the spread of disease. The principal revolt in February 1838 was led by the mestizo Rafael Carrera, whose army of indígenas and castas cried, "Long live religion and death to all foreigners!"

Carrera took Guatemala City, defeated Morazán in 1842, and ended the federal republic. He then established a conservative regime in Guatemala, which he controlled until his death in 1865. In 1854, dispensing with the formality of elections, he had Congress name him president for life and implemented a reactionary program that revived the authority of the church, returned church and indigenous communal properties to their original owners, brought back native forced labor, and even changed the title of local officials from jefe político to the old colonial title of corregidor. But what had begun as a lower-class protest against radical innovations and the spoliation of communal lands was soon taken over by the conservative merchant oligarchy, who provided the taxes Carrera needed to pay his army and foreign loans. Conservative ministers drawn from the elite surrounded the dictator. Alongside the traditional labor arrangements, there existed free labor and a money economy, with landless natives and mestizos working, sometimes under debt peonage, on the plantations.

Similar trends prevailed throughout Central America in the age of Carrera, although labor was freer in most of the area than it was in Guatemala. By the 1850s, a rising world demand for coffee stimulated expansion of the crop, which had been grown on a large scale in Costa Rica since the 1830s, and spurred attacks on indigenous communal lands. Coffee in Costa Rica and indigo and coffee in El Salvador made for relative political stability in those countries. In the more backward republics of Nicaragua and Honduras, where cattle barons warred with each other, little centralized authority existed.

The discovery of gold in California gave a new importance to Central America as a transoceanic transit route and sharpened the rivalry of the United States and Great Britain in the area. The threat to the sovereignty and territorial integrity of the Central American republics grew acute as a

---

[4] An influential code of legal and penal reform completed by U.S. lawyer and statesman Edward Livingston in 1824.

result of the folly of Nicaraguan liberals, who in 1855 invited William Walker, an adventurer from the United States, to help them overthrow a conservative regime. Having brought the liberals to power, Walker, supported by a band of some three hundred countrymen, staged a coup, proclaimed himself president, legalized slavery, and made English the official language. By mid-1856, in a rare display of unity, Nicaraguan liberals and conservatives, joined by all the other Central American republics, had combined in the National War against the Yankee intruders, but the Central American army opposing Walker was essentially a conservative army. Defeated in 1857, Walker returned to the United States. He nevertheless made two other attempts to conquer Central America, the last ending in his death before a Honduran firing squad in 1860.

The National War revived the moribund movement for Central American unity. The liberal Salvadoran president Gerardo Barrios was a leading advocate of federation. His efforts to realize Morazán's dream provoked Carrera, who was determined to maintain conservative domination over Central America, to send troops into El Salvador and its ally Honduras. The war ended with Barrios's defeat and exile; there were now conservative regimes in every Central American republic. In 1865 Barrios attempted to make a comeback, but he was captured and executed by his enemies. Carrera died in the same year. With his death the violence-filled formative period of Central American history came to an end.

Gran Colombia

The early history of Venezuela and Colombia is inseparably linked to the name of the liberator Simón Bolívar. Venezuela was his homeland; Colombia (then called New Granada) and Venezuela, the theaters of his first decisive victories in the war for Latin American independence. Bolívar sought to unite Venezuela and New Granada into a single large and powerful state and looked toward the creation of a vast federation of all the Spanish-American republics, extending from Mexico to Cape Horn. In 1819 the Congress of Angostura (in Venezuela) approved the formation of the state of Colombia (later called Gran Colombia, or Greater Colombia) that would combine Venezuela, New Granada, and Ecuador (then still in Spanish hands). In 1821, at Cúcuta on the Venezuelan-Colombian border, the union was formalized with the adoption of a centralized constitution drafted according to Bolívar's wishes, and he was elected provisional president of the new state. But he soon went off to launch a campaign for the liberation of Peru and Bolivia and entrusted the administration of the new state, with its capital at Bogotá, to his vice president, Francisco de Paula Santander, a veteran revolutionary leader whose policies in general conformed to Bolívar's.

Santander presided over the implementation of a liberal reform program that included the gradual abolition of slavery, the abolition of native tribute, the division of indigenous communal lands into private parcels (a "reform" that opened the door to land-grabbing), the suppression of smaller male convents and the seizure of their property for the support of public secondary education, and a general expansion of education.

The major threat to Gran Colombia's survival came from its geographic, economic, and social realities. Immense distances separated its component parts, and a mountainous terrain made communication very difficult; it took about a month for a letter to reach Bogotá from Caracas. These conditions also hindered the development of economic ties between Venezuela and New Granada, and also Ecuador; Caracas and other Venezuelan coastal cities communicated more easily with Europe than overland via the Andes with Bogotá. Finally, the Venezuelan elite of cacao planters and merchants, joined by a new elite of military leaders or caudillos, had little sympathy for Bolívar's idea of fusing several independent Spanish-American republics into one and even less for his vision of a confederation that would unite all the Spanish-American states.

The latent conflict broke out into the open in 1826, when José Antonio Páez, the principal Venezuelan military commander, refused to appear before Congress in Bogotá to answer charges that he had violated the rights of citizens by sending soldiers to round them up for militia service. Supported by his army of llaneros and other caudillos, Páez proclaimed a revolt against the Bogotá government. Bolívar finally returned to deal with Páez's rebellion and the growing unrest. But Bolívar's efforts to keep the union alive were in vain. In 1829 in Venezuela, "popular assemblies," carefully organized by the caudillos, voted overwhelmingly in favor of independence, for Páez against Bolívar. In mid-1830, Ecuador followed the example of Venezuela and seceded from the union. Gran Colombia was dead. Months before, Bolívar, filled with despair and terminally ill with tuberculosis, had resigned from office. Attended by a retinue of faithful officers and soldiers, he left Bogotá and made his way to the coast, planning to go into self-imposed exile in Europe. But he died near Santa Marta in 1830.

Páez, the Conservative-Liberal Split, and the Federal War in Venezuela, 1830–1863

On May 6, 1830, a congress assembled in Valencia to provide the independent state of Venezuela with a constitution, the third in the country's short history. The document limited suffrage to males who were twenty-one, literate, and had a high income. These requirements excluded most of the population, numbering under 900,000, from participation in political life. Of that number some 60 percent were descended from Africans. Another 15 percent were natives and a quarter identified themselves as white. A tiny minority of these, about ten thousand, composed the ruling class of wealthy merchants, great landowners, and high officeholders and military officers, who usually were also landowners. The members of this class, often linked through family networks, dominated politics.

Military hero, longtime champion of Venezuelan independence, and former ranch hand José Antonio Páez was elected president, a post he combined with that of supreme army commander. His rise illustrates the renewal of the old colonial ruling class through the admission of a new elite of military caudillos, frequently of very humble origins. The Venezuelan society and economy over which

Páez presided essentially resembled the colonial social and economic order. The latifundio continued as the basic unit of economic activity; concentration of landownership increased after independence because of the rapid acquisition of royalist estates and public lands by a small group of military caudillos. A decree of October 15, 1830, compelling the sale of so-called uncultivated indigenous lands, gave the latifundists more opportunities to expand their landholdings. Labor relations in the countryside continued to be based on slavery, peonage, and various forms of tenancy, including sharecropping and obligatory personal service. Slavery in Venezuela, as in other parts of Latin America, had long been in decline. Enslaved Africans' defiant opposition to enslavement, either through passive forms of resistance, rebellions, or escape to *cumbes* (runaway slave settlements), had made slavery socially destabilizing and less economically efficient. So the Constituent Congress of 1830 adopted a manumission law freeing the children of slaves but requiring them to work for their masters until the age of twenty-one. Continuing a tendency that began in the late colonial period, however, many slave owners found it more profitable to free their slaves voluntarily, because they generally remained on their former masters' land as tenants or peons bound by debts and other obligations. By 1841, 14,000 had been freed in this manner and only 150 because they had reached the age of manumission.

The long revolutionary war had caused immense material damage and loss of life—the population had been reduced by 262,000—and destroyed the fragile economic links between the country's different regions. By the time Páez became president, however, a partial recovery had taken place, leading to a boom based on the switch from cacao to coffee as Venezuela's principal export and the country's integration into the capitalist world market, which henceforth absorbed about 80 percent of Venezuela's exports of coffee, cacao, indigo, tobacco, and hides.

The high coffee prices that accompanied the 1830s boom made planters hungry for credit to expand production by obtaining new land. Foreign merchant capitalists, the Venezuelan export-import merchants who were their agents, and native moneylenders obliged, using coffee crops and the planters' estates as security, but colonial legislation that regulated interest rates and punished usury posed an obstacle. The Venezuelan congress removed this impediment by passing a credit law in 1834 that abolished all traditional Spanish controls on contracts; the state then enforced legally executed contracts, no matter how exorbitant the interest rates. By the late 1830s, with the world price of coffee in decline, the Venezuelan economy was in serious trouble. Creditors refused to refinance their debtors, and by the 1840s Venezuela was in a severe depression.

The economic crisis caused a rift in the elite, with the emergence of factions that turned into political parties in the 1840s. One called itself Conservative, but opponents dubbed its members *godos* (Goths), to identify them with the unpopular Spanish colonial rule. Páez was its acknowledged leader, and it represented the views and interests of the export-import merchants and their foreign partners, the moneylenders, the high civil and military bureaucracy, and some great landowners. The Liberal Party was led by Antonio Leocadio Guzmán and was a loose coalition of debt-ridden planters, the urban middle class, artisans, intellectuals seeking reform, and disaffected caudillos resentful of Páez's long reign.

Guzmán's rhetorical press attacks on Conservative economic policies and on the elections of 1842 and 1846 as fraudulent contributed to the growing social tension. A series of popular uprisings, which Páez described as open warfare against private property, terrified the Conservatives, who raised the specter of a general social race war, waged by pardos and slaves, which they blamed on Guzmán's inflammatory propaganda. In fact, Guzmán and most Liberals feared social revolution as much as their opponents and had no links to the popular revolts of 1846–1847. But the government determined to crush these revolts at their supposed source, brought Guzmán to trial, found him guilty of instigating the revolutionary movements, and sentenced him to death.

In 1848 war hero General José Tadeo Monagas, an eastern caudillo, became the Conservative president through the customary controlled election. If Páez had expected to find a pliant executor of Conservative policies, he was disappointed. Monagas, determined to free himself from Páez's control and establish his own dynasty, favored moderate Liberals for posts in his cabinet and other government positions. His commutation of Guzmán's death sentence to exile was a virtual declaration of independence from Páez and the Conservatives. But those Liberals who expected substantial social and political reforms from Monagas were also disillusioned. He paid his political debt to his planter allies by supporting congressional passage of several laws designed to give relief to distressed planters. Under his brother José Gregorio, slavery was abolished in Venezuela (March 23, 1854), with compensation to the slave owners. Slavery had been increasingly unprofitable as a result of falling coffee prices; even as Congress was discussing emancipation, some planters were voluntarily freeing their slaves to avoid paying their support.

Emancipation brought little change in the lives of most freedmen. In the absence of a modern factory system to provide alternative employment or any program for distributing land to them, most were doomed to remain on their former owners' estates as tenants burdened with heavy obligations or peons whose scanty wages were paid in *vales* (tokens) redeemable only for goods purchased in the estate store (*tienda de raya*) at inflated monopoly prices.

Hard times continued in the late 1850s: depressed coffee prices; the unwillingness of foreign capitalists to invest in Venezuela because of the debt-relief legislation, which increased the risk of investment; elite fears of a social explosion; and general resentment of the greed and nepotism of the Monagas dynasty persuaded Conservatives and Liberals to join forces in March 1858 in a revolution that overthrew the hated regime. The coalition soon fell apart, however, when a group of extreme Conservatives seized power and installed a government even more repressive than the Monagas regime, imprisoning or deporting many Liberals, who responded with an uprising that began the Federal War (1858–1863).

The term "federal" here had different meanings for the Liberal elite and its rank-and-file followers, most of whom were pardos or blacks who rallied to the federalist battle cry: "Death to the whites." But whereas Conservatives denounced the Liberal elite for fomenting a "race war," the "colored population" saw it as a war of the poor majority against the wealthy, propertied elite. After their victory, Liberal leaders gave the country a new constitution (1864) with many reforms, including universal male suffrage and increased autonomy for the twenty states. But without substantive social reform, these rights were virtually meaningless. "Federalism" under these conditions simply meant the continued supremacy of the local caudillo, who often was a great landowner as well, and whose arbitrary rule was tolerated by the Caracas government as long as he remained its loyal proconsul.

For the peasants and artisans who rose in spontaneous revolt against the reactionary Conservative regime and rallied to the Liberal leadership's slogan of federalism, the term had a different meaning. Their vague hopes were expressed in a manifesto by Ezequiel Zamora, the veteran guerrilla fighter who had been freed by the revolution of 1858 and then exiled by the Conservative regime, and who returned to Venezuela in February 1859 to open another front of a rapidly expanding peasant war. The advance of Zamora's troops was accompanied by the occupation of large estates by their former peons and tenants, the creation of federal states, and the election of local governments by the citizenry. Zamora's death by an assassin's bullet in 1860 cut short the life of a leader who represented a genuinely democratic, social revolutionary tendency in the Federal War.

Conservatives rejoiced, moderate Liberals heaved sighs of relief, and both, fearing the growing power of peasant revolutionists, agreed to a negotiated peace. The 1863 Treaty of Coche, negotiated by Antonio Guzmán Blanco, son of the famous Liberal caudillo, ended the war. It had cost some fifty thousand lives and inflicted immense damage on the economy. Many haciendas had been destroyed, and the cattle herds of the llanos had virtually disappeared as a result of wartime depredations and neglect. Like the War of Independence, the Federal War produced limited social changes. The old Conservative oligarchy disintegrated and victorious Liberal military officers, some of plebeian background, occupied their estates. But for the revolutionary rank-and-file, the war's end forced them to surrender the parcels of land they had occupied and return as peons to the great estates.

SANTANDER AND THE BIRTH OF A TWO-PARTY SYSTEM IN COLOMBIA, 1830–1850

Following the secession of Venezuela and Ecuador from Gran Colombia in 1830, the remaining territory went its separate way under the name of the Republic of New Granada (present-day Colombia plus Panama). Struggles for control of the governmental apparatus in Bogotá between followers of Bolívar and those of Santander ended in the latter's victory. He became the first president of an independent New Granada under a constitution that provided for a president elected for four years, a bicameral Congress, and provincial legislatures. The constitution granted suffrage to all free males who were married or aged twenty-one and were not domestic servants or day laborers. In practice, political life was dominated by a small aristocratic ruling class.

The geographic, economic, and social conditions of the new state posed even greater obstacles to the creation of a true national society than those facing Venezuela. The country's difficult geography, dominated by the towering Andean cordillera, whose ranges, valleys, and plateaus were the home of the overwhelming majority of a population numbering less than one and a half million, offered formidable barriers to communication and transport; as late as the end of the nineteenth century, it was cheaper to transport goods from Liverpool to Medellín than from Medellín to Bogotá. This geography contributed to the formation of an economic structure called an "economic archipelago," consisting of a number of isolated regions having little contact with each other. The economy of some of these regions was characterized by traditional haciendas mainly dedicated to growing wheat, barley, potatoes, and raising cattle.

Their labor force usually consisted of mestizo peons or tenants who paid rent in labor or in kind for the privilege of cultivating their own small parcels of land; their freedom of movement could be restricted by debts, and sometimes they owed personal service to their patrón.

Alongside these haciendas and on marginal lands and mountain slopes lived other peasants whose precarious independence came from subsistence farming and supplying food to nearby towns. The northwest region of Antioquia, with its rugged terrain and low population, had few haciendas and numerous small- and medium-size landholdings; a more independent peasantry had also arisen in neighboring Santander. The Spanish had enslaved thousands of Africans and their descendants to labor on plantations and in gold-mining districts in the western states and on the Caribbean coast, but the institution, greatly weakened by the revolutionary wars, slave resistance, and legislation providing for the freedom of the children of slaves, was in decline. In fact, by the nineteenth century, many Africans had escaped enslavement and established *palenques*, free villages that had negotiated with the crown for rights to communal lands and political autonomy. Although the 1821 Congress of Cúcuta had ordered the division of *resguardos* (native communal lands) to conform with the prevailing liberal ideology, indigenous peoples had resisted. The dissolution of the resguardos was implemented in 1839. A large part of remaining indigenous lands was acquired for low prices by white landowners and merchants. Some of the former owners became peons or tenants on haciendas; others became *minifundio* farmers, peasant proprietors of small plots.

New Granadan industry in 1830, like agriculture, displayed many precapitalist features. Most industrial activity (weaving and spinning, pottery making, shoeware) was done in the home, chiefly by women. The 1830s saw numerous state-sponsored efforts to establish factories making soap, glassware, textiles, and iron in Bogotá, but most ended in failure. By the 1840s sizable artisan groups had arisen in larger towns like Bogotá, Medellín, and Cali, but despite moderate tariff protections for local industries, they had difficulty competing with imported foreign goods. The backwardness of economic life was most apparent in transportation; in parts of the country porters and pack mules were used for transport well into the twentieth century. Even after steamboat navigation became regular on the Magdalena River in the 1840s, it took between four and six weeks to make the voyage from Atlantic ports to Bogotá. The limited development of productive forces and the sluggish tempo of economic activity were reflected in the modest wealth of even the upper classes. In the first half of the nineteenth century, the income of Bogotá's upper class came to about $5,000 per capita and the number of persons whose capital exceeded $100,000 could be counted on one hand.

The lack of a dynamic export base to stimulate the economy and provide resources for a strong nation-state was a major factor in Colombia's economic and political difficulties in its first half-century. Efforts to replace gold production—which had been in decline even before independence—with tobacco, cotton, cinchona bark, and other products as export staples produced a series of short booms that quickly collapsed because of declining markets and prices, competition from foreign producers whose prices or quality Colombia could not match, or exhaustion of resources. The absence of an export base and a nationally dominant elite helps explain the "economic archipelago" or regional isolation and self-sufficiency that developed. A corollary of this economic autarchy was political autarchy, an almost permanent instability punctuated by frequent civil wars or threats of war and even secession by hacendado-generals, who could mobilize private armies of peons to settle scores with rival caudillos or the weak central government.

Under Santander's successor, José Ignacio de Márquez (1837–1841), whose policies continued Santander's brand of moderate liberalism, the political climate turned stormy. Responding to a measure of Congress that closed some small convents in the fervently Catholic province of Pasto in the far South, the population rose up in arms. By 1841 the revolt had been defeated, but it had one lasting effect: its contribution to the formation of the classic Colombian two-party system—Liberals versus Conservatives. Until the late 1840s the difference between the ideologies and programs of the two groups was far from absolute. Actually both had more in common with the moderate liberalism of Santander than with Bolívar's late conservatism. Both represented upper-class interests but accepted the formal democracy of representative, republican government; both had faith in social and technological progress, believed in the freedoms of speech and of the press as well as other civil liberties, and in economic policy accepted laissez-faire and liberal economics. Neither party cared about the agrarian problem or other problems of the rural and urban masses. The only genuine issue separating them was the relation between church and state and the church's role in education. The emergent Liberal party was distinctly anticlerical, regarding the church as hostile to progress; they did, however, favor freedom of worship and separation of church and state. The nascent Conservative party endorsed religious toleration but favored cooperation between church and state, believing that religion promoted morality and social peace.

In 1849 the ideological gap between Liberals and Conservatives widened and three new political factions emerged: *Gólgotas*, urban artisans, and *Draconianos*, military from the lower officer ranks, who would later align themselves with the artisans. Shaped by the rapid expansion of tobacco cultivation, the beginnings of the coffee cycle, internal improvements of the Conservative administrations, and a resulting growth of foreign and domestic trade, the Gólgotas were the sons of a merchant class whose population increased to 2,000,000 in 1850. Well educated and influenced by French romanticism, utopian socialism, and the Revolution of 1848 in France, they developed a peculiar sentimental brand of liberalism based on a romantic interpretation of Christianity in which Christ, described as the "Martyr of Golgotha," appeared as a forerunner of nineteenth-century secular reformism. This ideology's practical essence was its demand for the abolition of slavery, the ecclesiastical and military fuero, compulsory tithing, and all restraints on free enterprise.

The third element in the Liberal coalition was the urban artisan group, whose numbers also had increased in the preceding decade. Competition with foreign imported manufactures had caused serious unemployment among these artisans, who attributed their distress to lower tariffs; perhaps an equally important cause was the then-recent establishment of permanent steam navigation on the Magdalena River, which ended the protective isolation of their markets from the outside world. These artisans created a network of "Democratic Societies," beginning with the Democratic Society of Bogotá (1847), which had almost four thousand members. These clubs were mutual-aid societies and carried on educational and philanthropic activities, but they also served as important political vehicles for the Liberal leadership that triumphed in 1849, enabling the new merchant elite, with large support from regional landed oligarchies, to seek the triumph of laissez faire and modernity. This noisy revolution, although full of drama, produced little change in the basic structures of Colombian economy and society.

The Triumph of Neocolonialism

BEGINNING ABOUT 1870, the quickening tempo of the Industrial Revolution in Europe stimulated a more rapid pace of change in the Latin American economy and politics. Responding to a mounting demand for raw materials and foodstuffs, Latin American producers increased their output of those commodities. The growing trade with Europe helped stabilize political conditions in Latin America, for the new economic system demanded peace and continuity in government.

Encouraged by the increased stability, European capital flowed into Latin America, creating railroads, docks, processing plants, and other facilities needed to expand and modernize production and trade. Latin America became integrated into an international economic system in which it exchanged raw materials and foodstuffs for the factory-made goods of Europe and North America. Gradual adoption of free-trade policies by many Latin American countries, which marked the abandonment of efforts to create a native factory capitalism, hastened the area's integration into this international division of labor.

The New Colonialism

The new economic system fastened a new dependency on Latin America, with Great Britain and later the United States replacing Spain and Portugal in the dominant role; it may, therefore, be called "neocolonial." Despite its built-in flaws and local breakdowns, the neocolonial order displayed a certain stability until 1914. By disrupting the markets for Latin America's exports and making it difficult to import the manufactured goods that Latin America required, World War I marked the beginning of a general crisis the area has not yet overcome.

Although the period from 1870 to 1914 saw rapid overall growth of the Latin American economy, the pace and degree of progress were uneven, with some countries (like Bolivia and Paraguay) joining the advance much later than others. A marked feature of the neocolonial order was its one-sidedness (monoculture). One or a few primary products became the basis of prosperity for each country, making it highly vulnerable to fluctuations in the world demand and price of these products. Argentina and Uruguay depended on wheat and meat; Brazil on coffee, sugar, and briefly rubber; Chile on copper and nitrates; Honduras on bananas; Cuba on sugar.

In each country, the modern export sector became an enclave largely isolated from the rest of the economy; this enclave actually accentuated the backwardness of other sectors by draining off their labor and capital. The export-oriented nature of the modern sector was reflected in the pattern of the national railway systems, which as a rule were not designed to integrate each country's regions but to satisfy the traffic needs of the export industries. In addition, the modern export sector often rested on extremely precarious foundations. Rapid, feverish growth, punctuated by slumps that sometimes ended in a total collapse, formed part of the neocolonial pattern; such meteoric rise and fall is the story of Peruvian guano, Chilean nitrates, and Brazilian rubber.

The triumph of neocolonialism in Latin America in the late nineteenth century was not inevitable or predetermined by Europe's economic "head start" or the area's past history of dependency. The leap from a feudal or semifeudal economy and society to an autonomous capitalist system, although difficult, is not impossible, as the case of Japan makes clear. Following independence, the new states had to choose between the alternatives of autonomy or dependency, or in the words of historian Florencia Mallon, "between focusing on internal production and capital formation, on the one hand, and relying increasingly on export production, foreign markets, and ultimately foreign capital, on the other." Given Latin America's history, however, the formation of the dynamic entrepreneurial class and the large internal market required by autonomous capitalism could not be achieved without such sweeping reforms as the breakup of great estates, the abolition of peonage and other coercive labor systems, and the adoption of a consistent policy of supporting native industry, reforms that most sections of the elite found too costly and threatening. Most Latin American elites, therefore, chose the easier road of continued dependency, with first Great Britain and later the United States replacing Spain as the metropolis.

Latin America in the nineteenth century, however, produced some serious efforts to break with the pattern of dependence. We have already described two such efforts. A remarkable and temporarily successful project for autonomous development was launched in Paraguay under the rule of Dr. Francia and the Lópezes, father and son. Their state-directed program of agrarian reform and industrial diversification transformed Paraguay from a backward country into a rela-

tively prosperous and advanced state, but the disastrous Paraguayan War interrupted this progress and returned Paraguay to backwardness and dependency. In Chile, in the 1850s, an alliance of mining capitalists, small farmers, and artisans attempted to overthrow the landed and mercantile oligarchy and implement a radical program of political and social reform; their "frustrated bourgeois revolution" was drowned in blood. In the present chapter we describe a second Chilean effort to achieve autonomous development under the slogan "Chile for the Chileans"; it too ended in defeat and in the death of the president who led it.

EXPANSION OF THE HACIENDA SYSTEM

The neocolonial order evolved within the framework of the traditional system of land tenure and labor relations. Indeed, it led to an expansion of the hacienda system on a scale far greater than the colonial period had known. As the growing European demand for Latin American products and the growth of national markets raised the value of land, the great landowners in country after country launched assaults on the surviving indigenous community lands. In part at least, this drive reflected an effort to eliminate indigenous competition in the emerging market economy. In Mexico the Reforma laid the legal basis for this attack in the 1850s and 1860s; it reached its climax in the era of Porfirio Díaz. In the Andean region similar legislation turned all communal property into individual holdings, leading to a cycle of indigenous revolt and bloody governmental repressions. Not all native peoples opposed the nineteenth-century drive to dissolve the ancient communal landholding system, however. In both Mexico and the Andean regions, where market relations had induced significant socioeconomic differentiation within villages, indigenous leaders often willingly accepted privatization of communal lands, viewing it as a road to personal enrichment.

Seizure of church lands by liberal governments also contributed to the growth of the latifundio. Mexico again offered a model, with its Lerdo Law and the Juárez anticlerical decrees.

Following the Mexican example, Colombian liberal governments confiscated church lands in the 1860s, the liberal dictator Antonio Guzmán Blanco seized many church estates in Venezuela in the 1870s, and Ecuadoran liberals expropriated church lands in 1895.

Expansion of the public domain through railway construction and wars also contributed to the growth of great landed estates. Lands taken from the church or wrested from indigenous communities were usually sold to buyers in vast tracts at nominal prices. Concentration of land, reducing the cultivable area available to native and mestizo small landowners, was accompanied by a parallel growth of the *minifundio*, an uneconomical small plot worked with primitive techniques.

The seizure of indigenous community lands, to use immediately or to hold for a speculative rise in value, provided great landowners with another advantage by giving them control of the local labor force at a time of increasing demand for labor. Expropriated natives rarely became true wage earners paid wholly in cash, for such workers were too expensive and independent in spirit. A more widespread labor system was debt peonage, in which workers were paid wholly or in part with vouchers redeemable at the *tienda de raya* (company store), whose inflated prices and often devious bookkeeping created a debt that was passed on from one generation to the next. The courts enforced the obligation of peons to remain on the estate until they had liquidated their debts. Peons who protested low wages or the more intensive style of work demanded by the new order were brought to their senses by landowners' armed retainers or by local police or military authorities.

In some countries, the period saw a revival of the colonial repartimiento system of draft labor for indigenous peoples. In Guatemala, this system required able-bodied natives to work for a specified number of days on haciendas. It was the liberal president Justo Rufino Barrios who issued instructions to local magistrates to see to it "that any Indian who seeks to evade his duty is punished to the full extent of the law, that the farmers are fully protected and that each Indian is forced to do a full day's work while in service."

Slavery survived in some places well beyond mid-century—for example, in Peru until 1855, in Cuba until 1886, in Brazil until 1888. Closely akin to slavery was the system of bondage, under which some ninety thousand Chinese coolies were imported into Peru between 1849 and 1875 to work on the guano islands and in railway construction. The term *slavery* also applies to the system under which political deportees and captured native rebels were sent by Mexican authorities to labor in unspeakable conditions on the coffee, tobacco, and henequen plantations of southern Mexico.

More modern systems of agricultural labor and farm tenantry arose only in such regions as southern Brazil and Argentina, whose critical labor shortage required the offer of greater incentives to the millions of European immigrants who poured into those countries between 1870 and 1910.

Labor conditions were little better in the mining industry and in the factories that arose in some countries after 1890. Typical conditions were a workday of twelve to fourteen hours, miserable wages frequently paid in vouchers redeemable only at the company store, and arbitrary, abusive treatment by employers and foremen. Latin American law codes usually prohibited strikes and other organized efforts to improve working conditions, and police and the armed forces were commonly employed to break strikes, sometimes with heavy loss of life.

FOREIGN CONTROL OF RESOURCES

The rise of the neocolonial order was accompanied by a steady growth of foreign corporate control over the natural and human-made resources of the continent. The process went through stages. In 1870 foreign investment was still largely concentrated in trade, shipping, railways, public utilities, and government loans; at that date, British capital enjoyed an undisputed hegemony in the Latin American investment field. By 1914 foreign corporate ownership had expanded to include most of the mining industry and had deeply penetrated real estate, ranching, plantation agriculture, and manufacturing; by that date, Great Britain's rivals had effectively challenged its domination in Latin America. Of these rivals, the most spectacular advance was made by the United States, whose Latin American investments had risen from a negligible amount in 1870 to over $1.6 billion by the end of 1914 (still well below the nearly $5 billion investment of Great Britain).

Foreign economic penetration went hand in hand with a growth of political influence and even armed intervention. The youthful U.S. imperialism proved to be the most aggressive of all. In the years after 1898, a combination of "dollar diplomacy" and armed intervention transformed the Caribbean into an "American lake" and reduced Cuba, the Dominican Republic, and several Central American states to the status of dependencies and protectorates of the United States.

THE POLITICS OF ACQUISITION

The new economy demanded new politics. Conser-vatives and liberals, fascinated by the atmosphere of prosperity created by the export boom, the rise in land values, the flood of foreign loans, and the growth of government revenues, put aside their ideological differences and joined in the pursuit of wealth. The positivist slogan "Order and Progress" now became the watchword of Latin America's ruling classes. The social Darwinist idea of the struggle for survival of the fittest and Herbert Spencer's doctrine of "inferior races," frequently used to support claims of the inherent inferiority of the native, mestizo, and mulatto masses, also entered the upper-class ideological arsenal.

The growing domination of national economies by the export sectors and the development of a consensus between the old landed aristocracy and more capitalist-oriented groups caused political issues like the federalist-centralist conflict and the liberal-conservative cleavage to lose much of their meaning; in some countries, the old party lines dissolved or became extremely tenuous. A new type of "progressive" caudillo—Porfirio Díaz in Mexico, Rafael Núñez in Colombia, Justo Rufino Barrios in Guatemala, Antonio Guzmán Blanco in Venezuela—symbolized the politics of acquisition.

As the century drew to a close, dissatisfied urban middle-class, immigrant, and entrepreneurial groups in some countries combined to form parties, called Radical or Democratic, that challenged the traditional domination of politics by the creole landed aristocracy. They demanded political, social, and educational reforms that would give more weight to the new middle sectors. But these middle sectors—manufacturers, shopkeepers, professionals, and the like—were in large part a creation of the neocolonial order and depended on it for their livelihood; therefore, as a rule they did not question its viability. The small socialist, anarchist, and syndicalist groups that arose in various Latin American countries in the 1890s challenged both capitalism and neocolonialism, but the full significance of these movements lay in the future.

The trends just described lend a certain unity to the history of Mexico, Argentina, Chile, Brazil, Central America, Venezuela, and Colombia in the period from 1870 to 1914. Each presents significant variations on the common theme, however—variations that reflect distinctive historical backgrounds and conditions.

Mexican Politics and Economy

DICTATORSHIP UNDER DÍAZ

General Porfirio Díaz seized power in 1876 with the support of disgruntled regional caudillos and military personnel, liberals angered by the old regime's patronage politics, and indigenous and mestizo small landholders who believed that Díaz would protect them. He also owed his success to the open support of American capitalists, army commanders, and great Texas landowners who, regarding his predecessor as "anti-American," supplied Díaz with arms and cash. Having installed himself as president, Díaz paid his respects to the principle of no reelection by allowing a trusted crony, General Manuel González, to succeed him in 1880. However, he returned to the presidential palace in 1884 and continued to occupy it through successive reelections until his resignation and flight from Mexico in 1911. Thus, Díaz, who had seized power in the name of republican

Beginning in the 1920s, with considerable support from the state, there arose in Mexico a school of socially conscious artists who sought to enlighten the masses about their bitter past and the promise of the revolutionary present. One of the greatest of these artists was David Alfaro Siqueiros, whose painting depicts with satire the former President Porfirio Díaz, who tramples on the constitution of 1857 as he diverts his wealthy followers with dancing girls. [Fresco of Mexican president Porfirio Díaz, by David Alfaro Siqueiros. © Estate of David Alfaro Siqueiros/SOMAAP, Mexico/VAGA, New York. Photo from Artes e Historia México.]

legality, erected the *Porfiriato*, one of the longest personal dictatorships in Latin American history.

But the construction of the dictatorship was a gradual process. During his first presidential term, Congress and the judiciary enjoyed a certain independence, and the press, including a vocal radical labor press, was free. The outlines of Díaz's economic and social policies, however, soon became clear. Confronted with an empty treasury, facing pressures from above and below, Díaz decided in favor of the great landowners, moneylenders, and foreign capitalists, whose assistance could ensure his political survival. In return, he assured these groups of protection for their property and other interests. Díaz, who had once proclaimed that in the age-old struggle between the people and the haciendas he was on the side of the people, now sent troops to suppress peasant resistance to land seizures. And although before taking power, he had denounced generous concessions to British capitalists, by 1880 Díaz had granted even more lavish subsidies for railway construction to North American companies. Economic development had become for Díaz the great object, the key to the solution of his own problems and those of the nation.

Economic development required political stability; accordingly, Díaz promoted a policy of conciliation, described by the formula *pan o palo* (bread or the club). This consisted of offering an olive branch and a share of spoils to all influential opponents, no matter what their political past or persuasion. A dog with a bone in its mouth, Díaz cynically observed, neither kills nor steals. In effect, Díaz invited all sections of the upper class and some members of the middle class, including prominent intellectuals and journalists, to join the great Mexican barbecue, from which only the poor and humble were barred. Opponents who refused Díaz's bribes—political offices, monopolies, and the like—suffered swift reprisal. Dissidents were beaten up, murdered, or arrested and sent to the damp underground dungeons of San Juan de Ulúa or the grim Belén prison, a sort of Mexican Bastille. An important instrument of this policy was a force of mounted police, the *rurales,* originally composed of former bandits and vagrants who later were gradually replaced by artisan and peasant recruits dislocated by the large social changes that took place during the *Porfiriato.* Aside from chasing unrepentant bandits, the major function of the rurales was to suppress peasant unrest and break strikes.

By such means, Díaz virtually eliminated all effective opposition at the end of his second term (1884–1888). The constitution of 1857 and the liberties it guaranteed existed only on paper. Elections to Congress, in theory the highest organ of government, were a farce; Díaz simply circulated a list of his candidates to local officials, who certified their election. The dictator contemptuously called Congress his *caballada,* his stable of horses. The state governors were appointed by Díaz, usually from the ranks of local great landlords or his generals. In return for their loyalty, he gave them a free hand to enrich themselves and terrorize the local population. Under them were district heads called *jefes políticos,* petty tyrants appointed by the governors with the approval of Díaz; below them were municipal presidents who ran the local administrative units. One feature of the Díaz era was a mushrooming of the administrative and coercive apparatus; government costs during this period soared by 900 percent.

The army, as indispensable to Díaz as it had been to Santa Anna, naturally enjoyed special favor. Higher officers were well paid and enjoyed many opportunities for enrichment at the expense of the regions in which they were quartered. But the Díaz army was pathetically inadequate for pur-

poses of national defense. Generals and other high officers were appointed not for their ability but for their loyalty to the dictator. Discipline, morale, and training were extremely poor. A considerable part of the rank-and-file were recruited from the dregs of society; the remainder were young native conscripts. These soldiers, often used for brutal repression of strikes and agrarian unrest, were themselves harshly treated and miserably paid: the wage of ranks below sergeant was fifty cents a month.

The church became another pillar of the dictatorship. Early in his second term, Díaz reached an accommodation with the hierarchy. The church agreed to support Díaz; in return he allowed the anticlerical Reforma laws to fall into disuse. In disregard of those laws, monasteries and nunneries were restored, church schools were established, and wealth again began to accumulate in the hands of the church. Faithful to its bargain, the church turned a deaf ear to the complaints of the lower classes and taught complete submission to the authorities. As in colonial times, many priests were utterly venal and corrupt. Only in the closing years of the dictatorship did the church, sensing the coming storm, begin to advocate modest social reforms.

The Díaz policy of conciliation was directed at prominent intellectuals as well as more wealthy and powerful figures. A group of such intellectuals, professional men, and businessmen made up a closely knit clique of Díaz's advisers. Known as *Científicos,* they got their name from their insistence on "scientific" administration of the state and were especially influential after 1892. About fifteen men made up the controlling nucleus of the group. Their leader was Díaz's all-powerful father-in-law, Manuel Romero Rubio, and after his death in 1895, the new minister of finance, José Yves Limantour.

For the Científicos, the economic movement was everything. Most Científicos accepted the thesis of the inherent inferiority of the native and mestizo population and the consequent necessity for relying on the native white elite and on foreigners and their capital to lead Mexico out of its backwardness. In the words of the journalist Francisco

G. Cosmes, "the Indian has only the passive force of inferior races, is incapable of actively pursuing the goal of civilization."

Thanks to the devoted efforts of educators like Justo Sierra, Díaz secured modest advances in public education, such as a federal law making primary education obligatory. Despite the law, however, on average only one out of three children between the ages of six and twelve were enrolled, the vast majority of whom probably completed only the first year and remained functionally illiterate. The principal beneficiaries of educational progress under Díaz were the sons of the rich: for every student enrolled in the primary schools in 1910, the state spent about seven pesos; for every student in the college preparatory schools, it spent nearly a hundred pesos.

In the last analysis, however, supporters of the dictatorship rested their case on the "economic miracle" that Díaz had allegedly worked in Mexico. A survey of the Mexican economy in 1910 reveals how modest that miracle was.

CONCENTRATION OF LANDOWNERSHIP

At the opening of the twentieth century, Mexico was still predominantly an agrarian country; 77 percent of its population of 15,000,000 still lived on the land. The laws of the Reforma had already promoted the concentration of landownership, and under Díaz this trend was greatly accelerated. There is some evidence of a link between the rapid advance of railway construction, which increased the possibilities of production for export and therefore stimulated a rise in land values, and the growth of land-grabbing in the Díaz period.

A major piece of land legislation was a law of 1883 that provided for the survey of so-called vacant public lands, *tierras baldías*. The law authorized real estate companies to survey such lands and retain one-third of the surveyed area; the remainder was sold for low fixed prices in vast tracts, usually to Díaz's favorites and their foreign associates. The 1883 law opened the way for vast territorial acquisitions. One individual alone obtained nearly 12,000,000 acres in Baja California and other northern states. But the land companies were not satisfied with the acquisition of true vacant lands. Another law, in 1894, declared that a parcel of land to which a legal title could not be produced could be declared vacant land, opening the door to expropriation of land from indigenous villages and other small landholders whose forebears had tilled their lands from times immemorial but who could not produce the required titles. If the victims offered armed resistance, troops were sent against them, and the vanquished rebels were sold like slaves to labor on henequen plantations in Yucatán or sugar plantations in Cuba. This was the fate of the Yaquis of the northwest, defeated after a long, valiant struggle.

Another instrument of land seizure was an 1890 law designed to give effect to older Reforma laws requiring the distribution of indigenous village lands among the villagers. The law created enormous confusion. In many cases, land speculators and hacendados cajoled the illiterate villagers into selling their titles for paltry sums. Hacendados also used other means, such as cutting off a village's water supply or simply brute force, to achieve their predatory ends. By 1910 the process of land expropriation was largely complete. More than 90 percent of the indigenous villages of the central plateau, the most densely populated region of the country, had lost their communal lands. Only the most tenacious resistance enabled villages that still held their lands to survive the assault of the great landowners. Landless peons and their families made up 9,500,000 of a rural population of 12,000,000.

As a rule, the new owners did not use the land seized from indigenous villages or small landholders more efficiently. Hacendados let much of the usurped land lie idle. They waited for a speculative rise in value or for an American buyer. By keeping land out of production, they helped keep the price of maize and other staples artificially high. The technical level of hacienda agriculture was generally extremely low, with little use of irrigation, machinery, and commercial fertilizer, although some new landowning groups—northern cattle raisers and cotton growers, the coffee and rubber growers of Chiapas, and the henequen producers of Yucatán—employed more modern equipment and techniques.

The production of foodstuffs stagnated, barely keeping pace during most of the period with the growth of population, and per capita production of such basic staples as maize and beans actually declined toward the end of the century. This decline culminated in three years of bad harvests, 1907 to 1910, due principally to drought. As a result, the importation of maize and other foodstuffs from the United States steadily increased in the last years of the Díaz regime. Despite the growth of pastoral industry, per capita consumption of milk and cheese barely kept pace with the growth of population, for a considerable proportion of the cattle sold was destined for the export market.

The only food products for which the increase exceeded the growth of population were alcoholic beverages. Some idea of the increase in their consumption is given by the fact that the number of bars in Mexico City rose from 51 in 1864 to 1,400 in 1900. At the end of the century, the Mexican death rate from alcoholism—a common response to intolerable conditions of life and labor—was estimated to be six times that of France. Meanwhile, inflation, rampant during the last part of the Díaz regime, greatly raised the cost of the staples on which the mass of the population depended. Without a corresponding increase in wages, the situation of agricultural and industrial laborers deteriorated sharply.

The Economic Advance

Whereas food production for the domestic market declined, production of food and industrial raw materials for the foreign market experienced a vigorous growth. By 1910, Mexico had become the largest producer of henequen, a source of fiber in great demand in the world market. Mexican export production became increasingly geared to the needs of the United States, which was the principal market for sugar, bananas, rubber, and tobacco produced on plantations that were largely foreign owned. U.S. companies dominated the mining industry, whose output of copper, gold, lead, and zinc rose sharply after 1890. The oil industry, controlled by U.S. and British interests, developed spec-

tacularly, and by 1911, Mexico was third among the world's oil producers. French and Spanish capitalists virtually monopolized the textile and other consumer-goods industries, which had a relatively rapid growth after 1890.

Foreign control of key sectors of the economy and the fawning attitude of the Díaz regime toward foreigners gave rise to a popular saying: "Mexico, mother of foreigners and stepmother of Mexicans." The ruling clique of Científicos justified this favoritism by citing the need for a rapid development of Mexico's natural resources and the creation of a strong country capable of defending its political independence and territorial integrity. Thanks to an influx of foreign capital, some quickening and modernization of economic life did take place under Díaz. The volume of foreign trade greatly increased, a modern banking system arose, and the country acquired a relatively dense network of railways. But these successes were achieved at a very heavy price: a brutal dictatorship, the pauperization of the mass of the population, the stagnation of food agriculture, the strengthening of the inefficient latifundio, and the survival of many feudal or semifeudal vestiges in Mexican economic and social life.

Labor, Agrarian, and Middle-Class Unrest

The survival of feudal vestiges was especially glaring in the area of labor relations. There was some variation in labor conditions from region to region. In 1910 forced labor and outright slavery, as well as older forms of debt peonage, were characteristic of the southern states of Yucatán, Tabasco, Chiapas, and parts of Oaxaca and Veracruz. The rubber, coffee, tobacco, henequen, and sugar plantations of this region depended heavily on the forced labor of political deportees, captured indigenous rebels, and contract workers kidnapped or lured to work in the tropics by a variety of devices.

In central Mexico, where a massive expropriation of village lands had created a large landless native proletariat, tenantry, sharecropping, and the use of migratory labor had increased and living standards had declined. The large labor surplus of this area diminished the need for hacendados to

Striking workers at the Rio Blanco textile works in Mexico in 1909; the business was controlled by French capital. Troops broke up the strike and much blood was shed.
[Brown Brothers]

tie their workers to their estates with debt peonage. In the north the proximity of the United States, with its higher wage scales, and the competition of hacendados with mine owners for labor made wages and sharecropping arrangements somewhat more favorable and weakened debt peonage. In all parts of the country, however, the life of agricultural workers was filled with hardships and abuses of every kind.

Labor conditions in mines and factories were little better than in the countryside. Workers in textile mills labored twelve to fifteen hours daily for a wage ranging from eleven cents for unskilled women and children to seventy-five cents for highly skilled workers. Employers found ways of reducing even these meager wages. Wages were discounted for alleged "carelessness" in the use of tools or machines or for "defective goods"; workers were usually paid wholly or in part with vouchers good only in company stores, the prices of which were higher than in other stores. Federal and state laws banned trade unions and strikes. Scores of workers, both men and women, were shot down by troops who broke the great textile strike in the Orizaba (Veracruz) area in 1909, and scores were killed or wounded in putting down the strike at the U.S.-owned Consolidated Copper Company mine at Cananea (Sonora) in 1906. Despite such repressions, the trade union movement continued to grow in the last years of the Díaz era, and socialist, anarchist, and syndicalist ideas began to influence the still-small urban working class.

The growing wave of strikes and agrarian unrest in the last, decadent phase of the Díaz era indicated an increasingly rebellious mood among even broader sections of the Mexican people. Alienation spread among teachers, lawyers, journalists, and other professionals, whose opportunities for advancement were sharply limited by the monolithic control of economic, political, and social life by the Científicos, their foreign allies, and regional oligarchies. In the United States in 1905 a group of middle-class intellectuals, headed by the Flores Magón brothers, organized the Liberal Party, which called for the overthrow of Díaz and advanced a platform whose economic and social provisions anticipated many articles of the constitution of 1917.

Even members of the ruling class began to join the chorus of criticism. These upper-class dissidents included liberal reformers, like the wealthy hacendado and businessman Francisco Madero, and national capitalists who resented the competitive advantages enjoyed by foreign companies in Mexico. They also feared that the static, reactionary Díaz policies could provoke the masses to overthrow the capitalist system itself. Fearing revolution, these upper-class critics urged Díaz to end his personal rule, shake up the regime, and institute modest reforms needed to placate popular protest and preserve the existing economic and social order. When their appeals fell on deaf ears, some of these bourgeois reformers reluctantly prepared to take the road of revolution.

The simultaneous advent of an economic recession and a food crisis sharpened this growing discontent. The depression of 1906–1907, which spread from the United States to Mexico, caused a wave of bankruptcies, layoffs, and wage cuts. At the same time the crop failures of 1907–1910 provoked a dramatic rise in the price of staples like maize and beans. By 1910, Mexico's internal conflicts had reached an explosive stage. The workers' strikes, the agrarian unrest, the agitation of middle-class reformers, and the disaffection of some great landowners and capitalists all reflected the disintegration of the dictatorship's social base. Despite its superficial stability and posh splendor, the house of Díaz was rotten from top to bottom. Only a slight push was needed to send it toppling to the ground.

Argentine Politics and Economy

Although the principal source of conflict in Argentina remained rivalry between provincial caudillos and Buenos Aires, Nicolás Avellaneda, a lawyer from Tucumán and his protégé, a fellow Tucumano, Julio Roca, dominated late nineteenth-century Argentine politics and shared Sarmiento's interest in unifying the nation. Avellaneda promoted education, immigration, and domestic tranquility. In 1876 he inaugurated railroad service between Buenos Aires and his native city of Tucumán. The new line forged stronger economic and political links between the port city and the remote northwest, contributing to the end of the long quarrel between Buenos Aires and the interior.

CONSOLIDATION OF THE STATE

Julio Roca, Avellaneda's presidential successor, institutionalized this new unification by carrying out a long-standing pledge to federalize the city of Buenos Aires, which now became the capital of the nation, while La Plata became the new capital of Buenos Aires province. The interior seemed to have triumphed over Buenos Aires, but that apparent victory was an illusion; the provincial lawyers and politicians who carried the day in 1880 had absorbed the commercial and cultural values of the great city and wished not to diminish but to share in its power. Far from losing influence, Buenos Aires steadily gained in wealth and power until it achieved an overwhelming ascendancy over the rest of the country.

The federalization of Buenos Aires completed the consolidation of the Argentine state, the new leaders of which were closely identified with and often recruited from the ruling class of great landowners and wealthy merchants. The "generation of 1880," or the oligarchy, as it was called, shared a faith in economic development and the value of the North American and European models, but it was also deeply tinged with cynicism, egotism, and a profound distrust for the popular classes. These autocratic liberals prized order and progress above freedom. They regarded the gauchos, indigenous peoples, and the mass of illiterate

European immigrants flooding Argentina as unfit to exercise civic functions. Asked to define universal suffrage, a leading oligarch, Eduardo Wilde, replied, "It is the triumph of universal ignorance."

The new rulers identified the national interest with the interest of the great landowners, wealthy merchants, and foreign capitalists. Regarding the apparatus of state as their personal property or as the property of their class, they used their official connections to enrich themselves. Although they maintained the forms of parliamentary government, they were determined not to let power slip from their hands and organized what came to be called the *unicato* (one-party rule), exercised by the National Autonomist Party, which they formed. Extreme concentration of power in the executive branch and systematic use of fraud, violence, and bribery were basic features of the system.

ECONOMIC BOOM AND INFLATION

The ominous new trends of the oligarchy emerged in the administration of President Julio Roca (1880–1886) and flowered exuberantly under his political heir and brother-in-law, Miguel Juárez Celman (1886–1890). Roca presided over the beginnings of a great boom that appeared to justify all the optimism of the oligarchy. As secretary of war under Avellaneda, Roca had led a military expedition—the so-called Conquest of the Desert—southward against native peoples of the pampa in 1879–1880. This conquest added vast new areas to the province of Buenos Aires and to the national public domain. The campaign created a last opportunity for implementing a democratic land policy directed toward the creation of an Argentine small-farmer class. Instead, the Roca administration sold off the area in huge tracts for nominal prices to army officers, politicians, and foreign capitalists. The aging Sarmiento, who had seen the defeat of his own effort to acquire and distribute to settlers public land suitable for farming, lamented: "Soon there will not remain a palm of land for distribution to our immigrants."

Coming at a time of steadily mounting European demand for Argentine meat and wheat, the Conquest of the Desert triggered an orgy of land speculation that drove land prices ever higher and caused a prodigious expansion of cattle raising and agriculture. This expansion took place under the sign of the latifundio. Few of the millions of Italian and Spanish immigrants who entered Argentina in this period realized the common dream of becoming independent small landowners. Although some immigrant agricultural colonies were founded in the provinces of Santa Fe and Entre Ríos in the 1870s and 1880s, by the mid-1890s, with wheat prices now declining, there was a shift from small-scale farming to extensive tenant farming. The traditional unwillingness of the estancieros to sell land forced the majority of would-be independent farmers to become ranch hands or tenant farmers, whose hold on the land was very precarious; because leases were usually limited to a few years, these immigrants broke the virgin soil, replaced the tough pampa grass with the alfalfa pasturage needed to fatten cattle, and produced the first wheat harvests but then had to move on, leaving the landowner in possession of all improvements.

As a result, the great majority of new arrivals settled in Buenos Aires, where the rise of meat-salting and meat-packing plants, railroads, public utilities, and many small factories created a growing demand for labor. True, the immigrant workers received very low wages, worked long hours, and crowded with their families into one-room apartments in wretched slums. But in the city barrio they lived among their own people, free from the loneliness of the pampa and the arbitrary rule of great landowners, and had some opportunity of rising in the economic and social scale. As a result, the population of Buenos Aires shot up from 500,000 in 1889 to 1,244,000 in 1909. The great city, which held the greater portion of the nation's wealth, population, and culture, grew at the expense of the interior—particularly the northwest—which was impoverished, stagnant, and thinly peopled. Argentina, to use a familiar metaphor, became a giant head set on a dwarf body.

Foreign capital and management played a decisive role in the expansion of the Argentine economy in this period. The creole elite obtained vast profits from the rise in the price of their land

and the increasing volume of exports but showed little interest in plowing those gains into industry or the construction of the infrastructure required by the export economy, preferring a lavish and leisurely lifestyle over entrepreneurial activity. Just as they left to English and Irish managers the task of tending their estates, so they left to English capital the financing of meat-packing plants, railroads, public utilities, and docks and other facilities. As a result, most of these resources remained in British hands. Typical of the oligarchy's policy of surrender to foreign interests was the decision of Congress in 1889 to sell the state-owned Ferrocarril Oeste, the most profitable and best-run railroad in Argentina, to a British company. Service on a growing foreign debt claimed an ever larger portion of the government's receipts.

Meanwhile, imports of iron, coal, machinery, and consumer goods grew much faster than exports. Combined with the unfavorable price ratio of raw materials to finished goods, the result was an unfavorable balance of trade and a steady drain of gold. New loans with burdensome terms brought temporary relief but aggravated the long-range problem. Under President Miguel Juárez Celman, the disappearance of gold and the government's determination to keep the boom going at all costs led to the issue of great quantities of unbacked paper currency and a massive inflation.

The great landowners did not mind, for they were paid for their exports in French francs and English pounds, which they could convert into cheap Argentine pesos for the payment of local costs; besides, inflation caused the price of their lands to rise. The sacrificial victims of the inflation were the urban middle class and the workers, whose income declined in real value.

THE FORMATION OF THE RADICAL PARTY

In 1889–1890, just as the boom was turning into a depression, the accumulated resentment of the urban middle class and some alienated sectors of the elite over the catastrophic inflation, one-party rule, and official corruption produced a protest movement that took the name *Unión Cívica* (Civic

Union). Although the new organization had a middle-class base, its leadership united such disparate elements as disgruntled urban politicians like Leandro Além, its first president; new landowners and descendants of old aristocratic families denied access to patronage; and Catholics outraged by the government's anticlerical legislation. Aside from the demand for effective suffrage, the only thing uniting these heterogeneous elements was a common determination to overthrow the government.

The birth of the new party in 1890 coincided with a financial storm: the stock market collapsed, bankruptcies multiplied, and in April the cabinet resigned. Encouraged by this last development, and counting on support from the army, the leaders of the Unión Cívica planned a revolt against Juárez Celman that ended in defeat for the rebels.

The oligarchy now showed its ability to maneuver and divide its enemies. Carlos Pellegrini (1890–1892) replaced Juárez Celman, appeased disgruntled elements of the elite by revising the system of state patronage, and took steps to improve economic conditions by a policy of retrenchment that reduced inflation, stabilized the peso, and revived Argentine credit abroad. Thanks to these measures and a gradual recovery from the depression, popular discontent began to subside.

These reforms isolated Leandro Além and other dissidents, who now formed a new party committed to a "radical" democracy—the *Unión Cívica Radical*. The party named Bernardo de Yrigoyen as its presidential candidate in 1892 but, knowing that rigged elections made his victory impossible, they also prepared for another revolt—a move that Pellegrini effectively squelched by deporting Além and other Radical leaders until after the election of Luis Sáenz Peña (1892–1895).

On his return from exile, Além organized a new revolt in July 1893. The rebels briefly seized Santa Fe and some other towns, but after two and a half months of fighting, the revolt collapsed for lack of significant popular support. Depressed by his failures and the intrigues of his nephew, Hipólito Yrigoyen, to seize control of the Radical Party, Além committed suicide in 1896. Until 1910, the Radical Party, now led by Yrigoyen, proved unable to achieve political reform by peaceful or revolutionary means, as the reunited oligarchy consolidated its power.

In Yrigoyen, however, the Radicals possessed a charismatic personality and a masterful organizer who refused to admit defeat. Yrigoyen, a one-time police superintendent in Buenos Aires, was formerly a minor politician who used his official party connections to acquire considerable wealth, which he invested in land and cattle. As a Radical caudillo, Yrigoyen was the architect of a program whose vagueness was dictated by the party's need to appeal to very diverse elements and by its wholehearted acceptance of the economic status quo. "Abstention," refusal to participate in rigged elections, and "revolutionary intransigence," the determination to resort to revolution until free elections were achieved, were the party's basic slogans.

The Radical Party represented the bourgeoisie, but it was a dependent bourgeoisie that did not champion industrialization, economic diversification, or nationalization of foreign-owned industries. Far from attacking the neocolonial order, the Radical Party proposed to strengthen it by promoting cooperation between the landed aristocracy and the urban sectors, which were challenging the creole elite's monopoly of political power. In all respects, it was much more conservative than the contemporaneous reformist movement of José Batlle y Ordóñez in Uruguay.[1]

---

[1] Under the leadership of José Batlle y Ordóñez (1856–1929), president of Uruguay from 1903 to 1907 and again from 1911 to 1915, Uruguay adopted an advanced program of social reform that made it "the chief laboratory for social experimentation in the Americas and a focal point of world interest." The program included the establishment of the eight-hour day, old-age pensions, minimum wages, and accident insurance; abolition of capital punishment; separation of church and state; education for women; recognition of divorce; and a system of state capitalism that gradually brought under public ownership banks, railroads, electric systems, telephone and telegraph companies, street railways, and meat-packing plants. Batlle supported labor in its strikes against foreign-owned enterprises. But he did not challenge the land monopoly of the great estancieros and refused to apply his social legislation to their peons.

The Radical Party went into eclipse after the debacles of 1890 and 1893 but gradually revived after 1900, due in part to Yrigoyen's charismatic personality and organizing talent. The most important factor, however, was the steady growth of an urban and rural middle class largely composed of sons of immigrants. The domination of the export sector, which limited the growth of industry and opportunities for entrepreneurial activity, focused middle-class ambitions more and more on government employment and the professions, two fields dominated by the creole elite. Signs of growing unrest and frustration in the middle class included a series of student strikes in the universities, caused by efforts of creole governing boards to restrict enrollment of students of immigrant descent.

ELECTORAL REFORM AND THE GROWTH OF THE LABOR MOVEMENT

Meanwhile, a section of the oligarchy, headed by Carlos Pellegrini, had begun to advocate electoral reform. These aristocratic reformers argued that the existing situation created a permanent state of tension and instability; they feared that sooner or later the Radical efforts at revolution would succeed. It would be much better, they believed, to make the concessions demanded by the Radicals, open up the political system, and thereby gain for the ruling party—now generally called Conservative—the popular support and legitimacy it needed to remain in power. Moreover, the conservative reformers were aware of a new threat from the left—from the labor movement and especially its vanguard, the socialists, anarchists, and syndicalists—and hoped to make an alliance with the bourgeoisie against the revolutionary working class. They therefore supported a series of measures known collectively as the Sáenz Peña Law (1912). The new law established universal and secret male suffrage for citizens when they reached the age of eighteen. This law, which historian David Rock calls "an act of calculated retreat by the ruling class," opened the way for a dependent bourgeoisie to share power and the spoils of office with the landed aristocracy.

The principal political vehicle for working-class aspirations was the Socialist Party, founded in 1894 as a split-off from the Unión Cívica Radical by the Buenos Aires physician and intellectual Juan B. Justo, who led the party until his death in 1928. Despite its professed Marxism, the party's socialism was of the parliamentary reformist kind, appealing chiefly to highly skilled, native-born workers and the lower-middle class. The majority of workers, foreign-born noncitizens who still dreamed of returning someday to their homelands, remained aloof from electoral politics but readily joined trade unions that valiantly resisted deteriorating wages and working conditions; a series of great strikes was broken by the government with brutal repression and the deportation of so-called foreign agitators. Despite these defeats, the labor movement continued to grow and struggle, winning such initial victories as the ten-hour workday and the establishment of Sunday as a compulsory day of rest.

Chilean Politics and Economy

NITRATES AND WAR

In 1876 the Liberal president Aníbal Pinto inherited a severe economic crisis (1874–1879). Wheat and copper prices dropped, exports declined, and unemployment grew. The principal offset to these unfavorable developments was the continued growth of nitrate exports from the Atacama Desert as a result of a doubling of nitrate production between 1865 and 1875. But nitrates, the foundation of Chilean material progress, also became the cause of a major war with dramatic consequences for Chile and its two foes, Bolivia and Peru.

The nitrate deposits exploited by the Anglo-Chilean companies lay in territories belonging to Bolivia (the province of Antofagasta) and Peru (the province of Tarapacá). In 1866 a treaty between Chile and Bolivia defined their boundary in the Atacama Desert as the twenty-fourth parallel, gave Chilean and Bolivian interests equal rights to exploit the territory between the twenty-third and twenty-fifth parallels, and guaranteed each government half of the tax revenues obtained from the export of minerals from the whole area. Anglo-Chilean capital soon poured into the region, developing a highly efficient mining-industrial complex. By a second treaty of 1874, Chile's northern border with Bolivia was left at the twenty-fourth parallel. Chile relinquished its rights to a share of the taxes from exports north of that boundary but received in return a twenty-five-year guarantee against increase of taxes on Chilean enterprises operating in the Bolivian province of Antofagasta.

Chile had no boundary dispute with Peru, but aggressive Chilean mining interests, aided by British capital, soon extended their operations from Antofagasta into the Peruvian province of Tarapacá. By 1875, Chilean enterprises in Peruvian nitrate fields employed more than ten thousand workers, engineers, and supervisory personnel. At this point, the Peruvian government, on the brink of bankruptcy as a result of a very expensive program of public works, huge European loans, and the depletion of the guano deposits on which it had counted to service those loans, decided to expropriate the foreign companies in Tarapacá and establish a state monopoly over the production and sale of nitrates. Meanwhile, Peru and Bolivia had negotiated a secret treaty in 1874 providing for a military alliance in the event either power went to war with Chile.

Ejected from Tarapacá, the Anglo-Chilean capitalists intensified their exploitation of the nitrate deposits in Antofagasta. In 1878, Bolivia, counting on its military alliance with Peru, challenged Chile by imposing higher taxes on nitrate exports from Antofagasta, in violation of the treaty of 1874. When the Chilean companies operating in Antofagasta refused to pay the new taxes, the Bolivian government threatened them with confiscation. The agreement of 1874 provided for arbitration of disputes, but the Bolivians twice rejected Chilean offers to submit the dispute to arbitration.

In February 1879, despite Chilean warnings that expropriation of Chilean enterprises would void the treaty of 1874, the Bolivian government ordered the confiscation carried out. On February 14, the day set for the seizure and sale of the

Chilean properties, Chilean troops occupied the port of Antofagasta, encountering no resistance, and proceeded to extend Chilean control over the whole province. Totally unprepared for war, Peru made a vain effort to mediate between Chile and Bolivia. Chile, however, having learned of the secret Peruvian-Bolivian alliance, charged Peru with intolerable duplicity and declared war on both Peru and Bolivia on April 5, 1879.

In this war, called the War of the Pacific, Chile faced enemies whose combined population was more than twice its own; one of these powers, Peru, also possessed a respectable naval force. But Chile enjoyed major advantages. By contrast with its neighbors, it possessed a stable central government, a people with a strong sense of national identity, and a disciplined, well-trained army and navy. Chile also enjoyed the advantage of being closer to the theater of operations, because Bolivian troops had to come over the Andes and the Peruvian army had to cross the Atacama Desert.

All three powers had serious economic problems, but Chile's situation was not as catastrophic as that of its foes. Equally important, Chile had the support of powerful English capitalist interests, who knew that the future of the massive English investment in Chile depended in large part on the outcome of the war. The prospect of Chilean acquisition of the valuable nitrate areas of Antofagasta and Tarapacá naturally pleased the British capitalists. British capital was also invested in Bolivia and Peru, but whereas the Chilean government had maintained service on its debt, Bolivia and Peru had suspended payment on their English loans. Besides, the Peruvian nationalization of the nitrate industry in Tarapacá had seriously injured British interests.

With British assistance, Chile won the war in 1883 and imposed its terms. By the Treaty of Ancón (October 20, 1883), Peru ceded the province of Tarapacá to Chile in perpetuity. The provinces of Tacna and Arica would be Chilean for ten years, after which a plebiscite would decide their ultimate fate. But the plebiscite was never held, and Chile continued to administer the two territories until 1929, when Peru recovered Tacna

and Arica went to Chile. An armistice signed in April 1884 by Bolivia and Chile assigned the former Bolivian province of Antofagasta to Chile, but for many years no Bolivian government would sign a formal treaty acknowledging that loss. Finally, in 1904, Bolivia signed a treaty in which Chile agreed to pay an indemnity and to build a railroad connecting the Bolivian capital of La Paz with the port of Arica. That railroad was completed in 1913.

AFTERMATH OF THE WAR OF THE PACIFIC

Chile took advantage of the continued mobilization of its armed forces during the negotiations with Peru to settle scores with the Araucanians, whose struggle in defense of their land against encroaching whites had continued since colonial times. After two years of resistance against very unequal odds, the Araucanians were forced to admit defeat and sign a treaty (1883) that resettled them on reservations but retained their tribal government and laws. The Araucanian campaign of 1880–1882, which extended the Chilean southern frontier into a region of mountain and forest, sparked a brisk movement of land speculation and colonization in that area.

From the War of the Pacific, which shattered Peru economically and psychologically and left Bolivia more isolated than before from the outside world, Chile emerged the strongest nation on the west coast, in control of vast deposits of nitrates and copper, the mainstays of its economy. But the greater part of these riches would soon pass into foreign hands. In 1881 the Chilean government made an important decision: it decided to return the nitrate properties of Tarapacá to private ownership; that is, to the holders of the certificates issued by the Peruvian government as compensation for the nationalized properties.

During the war, uncertainty as to how Chile would dispose of those properties had caused the Peruvian certificates to depreciate until they fell to a fraction of their face value. Speculators, mostly British, had bought up large quantities of these depreciated certificates. In 1878 British capital controlled some 13 percent of the nitrate industry of Tarapacá; by 1890 its share had risen to at least

70 percent. British penetration of the nitrate areas proceeded not only through formation of companies for direct exploitation of nitrate deposits, but also through the establishment of banks that financed entrepreneurial activity in the nitrate area and the creation of railways and other companies more or less closely linked to the central nitrate industry. An English railway company with a monopoly of transport in Tarapacá, the Nitrate Railways Company, controlled by John Thomas North, paid dividends of up to 20 and 25 percent, compared with earnings of from 7 to 14 percent for other railway companies in South America.

The Chilean national bourgeoisie, which had pioneered the establishment of the mining-industrial-railway complex in the Atacama, offered little resistance to the foreign takeover. Lack of strong support from the state, the relative financial weakness of the Chilean bourgeoisie, and the cozy and profitable relationships maintained throughout the nineteenth century between the Chilean elite and British interests facilitated the rapid transfer of Chilean nitrate and railway properties into British hands and the transformation of Chilean mine owners into a dependent bourgeoisie content with a share of the profits of British companies.

But elsewhere in Chile, the war had energized the national economy and mobilized local manufacturers and workers, who pressed for electoral reform; in 1884 the property qualification for voting was replaced with a literacy test. Because the great majority of Chilean males were illiterate *rotos* (seasonal farm workers) and inquilinos, this change did not materially add to the number of voters; as late as 1915, out of a population of about 3.5 million, only 150,000 persons voted. But it did secure the 1886 victory of liberal president José Manuel Balmaceda, who took office with a well-defined program of state-directed economic modernization. By the 1880s factory capitalism had taken root in Chile. In addition to consumer goods industries—flour mills, breweries, leather factories, furniture factories, and the like—there existed foundries and metalworking enterprises that served the mining industry, railways, and agriculture. Balmaceda proposed to consolidate and expand this native industrial capitalism.

BALMACEDA'S NATIONALISTIC POLICIES

Balmaceda came to office when government revenues were at an all-time high (they had risen from about 15 million pesos a year before the War of the Pacific to about 45 million pesos in 1887). The chief source of this government income was the export duty on nitrates. Knowing that the proceeds from this source would taper off as the nitrate deposits diminished, Balmaceda wisely planned to employ those funds for the development of an economic infrastructure that would remain when the nitrate was gone. Hence, public works figured prominently in his program. In 1887 he created a new ministry of industry and public works, which expended large sums on extending and improving the telegraphic and railway systems and on the construction of bridges, roads, and docks. Balmaceda also generously endowed public education, needed to provide skilled workers for Chilean industry. During his presidency the total enrollment in Chilean schools rose in four years from some 79,000 in 1886 to over 150,000 in 1890. He also favored raising the wages of workers but was inconsistent in his labor policy; yielding to strong pressure from foreign and domestic employers, he sent troops to crush a number of strikes.

Central to Balmaceda's program was his determination to "Chileanize" the nitrate industry. In his inaugural address to Congress, he declared that his government would consider what measures it should take "to nationalize industries which are, at present, chiefly of benefit to foreigners," a clear reference to the nitrate industry. Later, Balmaceda's strategy shifted; he encouraged the entrance of Chilean private capital into nitrate production and exportation to prevent the formation of a foreign-dominated nitrate cartel whose interest in restricting output clashed with the government's interest in maintaining a high level of production to collect more export taxes. In November 1888 he scolded the Chilean elite for their lack of entrepreneurial spirit:

> Why does the credit and the capital which are brought into play in all kinds of speculations in our great cities hold back and leave the foreigner to establish banks at Iquique and aban-

don to strangers the exploiting of the nitrate works of Tarapacá? . . . The foreigner exploits these riches and takes the profit of native wealth to give to other lands and unknown people the treasures of our soil, our own property and the riches we require.

Balmaceda waged a determined struggle to end the monopoly of the British-owned Nitrate Railways Company, whose prohibitive freight charges reduced production and export of nitrates. His nationalistic policies inevitably provoked the hostility of English nitrate "kings" like North, who had close links with the Chilean elite and employed prominent liberal politicians as their legal advisers.

But Balmaceda had many domestic as well as foreign foes. The clericals opposed his plans to further curb the powers of the church. The landed aristocracy resented his public works program because it drew labor from agriculture and pushed up rural wages. The banks, which had profited from an uncontrolled emission of notes that fed inflation and benefited mortgaged landlords and exporters, were angered by his proposal to establish a national bank with a monopoly of note issue. The entire oligarchy, liberals as well as conservatives, opposed his use of the central government as an instrument of progressive economic and social change.

Meanwhile, the government's economic problems multiplied, adding to Balmaceda's political difficulties by narrowing his popular base. By 1890 foreign demand for copper and nitrates had weakened. Prices in an overstocked world market fell, and English nitrate interests responded to the crisis by forming a cartel to reduce production. Reduced production and export of nitrates and copper sharply diminished the flow of export duties into the treasury and caused growing unemployment and wage cuts even as inflation cut into the value of wages. The result was a series of great strikes in Valparaíso and the nitrate zone in 1890. Despite his sympathy with the workers' demands and unwillingness to use force against them, Balmaceda, under pressure from domestic and foreign employers, sent troops to crush the strikes. These repressive measures ensured much working-class apathy

or even hostility toward the president in the eventual confrontation with his foes.

Indeed, Balmaceda had few firm allies at his side when that crisis came. The industrial capitalist group whose growth he had ardently promoted was still weak. The mining interests, increasingly integrated with or dominated by English capital, joined the bankers, the clericals, and the landed aristocracy in opposition to his nationalist program of economic development and independence. The opposition mobilized its forces in parliament, where Balmaceda lacked a reliable congressional majority, forcing him to abolish the system of parliamentary government and return to the traditional system of presidential rule established by the constitution of 1833. His rash act, made without any serious effort to mobilize popular forces, played into the hands of his enemies, who were already preparing for civil war.

On January 7, 1891, congressional leaders proclaimed a revolt against the president in the name of legality and the constitution. The navy, then as now led by officers of aristocratic descent, promptly supported the rebels, who seized the ports and customhouses in the north and established their capital at Iquique, the chief port of Tarapacá.

English-owned enterprises also actively aided the rebels. Indeed, by the admission of the British minister at Santiago, "our naval officers and the British community of Valparaíso and all along the coast rendered material assistance to the opposition and committed many breaches of neutrality." Many nitrate workers, alienated by Balmaceda's repression of their strike, remained neutral or even joined the rebel army, organized by a German army officer, General Emil Korner. Politically isolated and militarily defeated, Balmaceda sought refuge in the Argentine embassy and, on September 19, 1891, the day on which his legal term of office came to an end, Balmaceda put a bullet through his head.

The death of Chile's first anti-imperialist president restored the reign of the oligarchy, a coalition of landowners, bankers, merchants, and mining interests closely linked to English capital. A new era began, the era of the so-called Parliamentary

Republic. Taught by experience, the oligarchy now preferred to rule through a congress divided into various factions rather than through a strong executive. Such decentralization of government favored the interests of the rural aristocracy and its allies. A new law of 1892, vesting local governments with the right to supervise elections both for local and national offices, reinforced the power of the landowners, priests, and political bosses who had fought Balmaceda's progressive policies.

THE PARLIAMENTARY REPUBLIC, FOREIGN ECONOMIC DOMINATION, AND THE GROWTH OF THE WORKING CLASS

The era of the Parliamentary Republic was accompanied by a growing subordination of the Chilean economy to foreign capital, which was reflected in a steady increase in the foreign debt and foreign ownership of the nation's resources. English investments in Chile amounted to 24 million pounds in 1890; they rose to 64 million pounds in 1913. Of this total, 34.6 million pounds formed part of the Chilean public debt. In the same period, North American and German capital began to challenge the British hegemony in Chile. England continued to be Chile's principal trade partner, but U.S. and German trade with Chile grew at a faster rate. German instructors also acquired a strong influence in the Chilean army, and the flow of German immigrants into southern Chile continued, resulting in the formation of compact colonies dominated by a Pan-German ideology. The revival of the Chilean economy from the depression of the early 1890s brought an increase of nitrate, copper, and agricultural exports and further enriched the ruling classes, but it left inquilinos, miners, and factory workers as desperately poor as before. Meanwhile, the working class grew from 120,000 to 250,000 between 1890 and 1900, and the doctrines of trade unionism, socialism, and anarchism achieved growing popularity in its ranks.

Luis Emilio Recabarren (1876–1924), the father of Chilean socialism and communism, played a decisive role in the social and political awakening of the Chilean proletariat. In 1906 Recabarren was elected to Congress from a mining area but was not allowed to take his seat because he refused to take his oath of office on the Bible. In 1909, he organized the Workers Federation of Chile, the first national trade union movement. Three years later, he founded the Socialist Party, a revolutionary Marxist movement, and became its first secretary.

The growing self-consciousness and militancy of the Chilean working class found expression in a mounting wave of strikes. Between 1911 and 1920, almost three hundred strikes, involving more than 300,000 workers, took place. Many were crushed with traditional brutal methods that left thousands of workers dead.

Brazilian Politics and Economy

THE ANTISLAVERY MOVEMENT

From the close of the Paraguayan War (1870), the slavery question surged forward, becoming the dominant issue in Brazilian political life. Dom Pedro, personally opposed to slavery, was caught in a crossfire between a growing number of liberal leaders, intellectuals, and urban middle-class groups who demanded emancipation and slave owners determined to postpone the inevitable as long as possible. In 1870 Spain freed all the newborn and aged slaves of Cuba and Puerto Rico, leaving Brazil the only nation in the Americas to retain slavery in its original colonial form. Yielding to pressure, a conservative ministry pushed the Rio Branco Law through parliament in 1871. This measure freed all newborn children of slaves but obligated the masters to care for them until they reached the age of eight. At that time, owners could either release the children to the government in return for an indemnity or retain them as laborers until they reached the age of twenty-one. The law also freed all slaves belonging to the state or crown and created a fund to be used for the manumission of slaves.

The Rio Branco Law was a tactical retreat designed to put off a final solution of the slavery problem. As late as 1884, when Brazil still had over 1 million slaves, only 113 had been freed by this means.

Slaves drying coffee on a plantation in Terreiros, in the state of Rio de Janeiro, about 1882. [Courtesy of Hack Hoffenburg]

Abolitionist leaders denounced the law as a sham and illusion and advanced ever more vigorously the demand for total and immediate emancipation. From 1880 on, the antislavery movement developed great momentum. Concentrated in the cities, it drew strength from the process of economic, social, and intellectual modernization under way there. To the new urban groups, slavery was an anachronism, glaringly incompatible with modernization.

Among the slave owners themselves, divisions of opinion appeared. In the north, where slavery had become economically inefficient, a growing number of planters shifted to wage labor, drawing on the pool of freedmen made available by the Rio Branco Law and the *sertanejos* (inhabitants of the interior), poor whites and mixed-bloods who lived on the fringes of the plantation economy. Another factor in the decline of the slave population in the northeast was the great drought of 1877–1879, which caused many of the region's wealthier folk to sell their slaves or abandon the area, taking their slaves with them. States like Amazonas and Ceará, where black slaves were few and most of the work was done by natives and mixed-bloods, abolished slavery within their borders in 1884. By contrast, the coffee planters of Rio de Janeiro, São Paulo, and Minas Gerais, joined by northern planters who trafficked in slaves, selling them to the coffee zone, offered the most tenacious resistance to the advance of abolition.

The abolitionist movement produced leaders of remarkable intellectual and moral stature. One was Joaquim Nabuco, son of a distinguished liberal statesman of the empire, whose eloquent dissection and indictment of slavery, *O abolicionismo*, had a profound impact on its readers. Another was a mulatto journalist, José de Patrocinio, a master propagandist noted for his fiery, biting style. Another mulatto, André Rebouças, an engineer and teacher whose intellectual gifts won him the respect and friendship of the emperor, was a leading organizer of the movement. For Nabuco and his comrades-in-arms, the antislavery struggle was the major front in a larger struggle for the transformation of Brazilian society. Abolition, they hoped, would pave the way for the attainment of other goals: land reform, public education, and political democracy.

Yielding to mounting pressure, parliament adopted another measure on September 28, 1885, that liberated all slaves when they reached the age of sixty but required them to continue to serve their masters for three years and forbade them to leave their place of residence for five years. These conditions, added to the fact that few slaves lived beyond the age of sixty-five, implied little change in the status of the vast majority of slaves. The imperial government also promised to purchase the freedom of the remaining slaves in fourteen years—a promise that few took seriously, in the light of experience with the Rio Branco Law. Convinced that the new law was another tactical maneuver, the abolitionists spurned all compromise solutions and demanded immediate, unconditional emancipation. By the middle 1880s, the antislavery movement had assumed massive proportions and a more militant character. Large numbers of slaves began to vote for freedom with their feet; they were aided by abolitionists who organized an underground railway that ran from São Paulo to Ceará, where slavery had ended. Efforts to secure the return of fugitive slaves encountered growing resistance. Army officers, organized in a *Club Militar*, protested against the use of the army for the pursuit of fugitive slaves.

In February 1887, São Paulo liberated all slaves in the city with funds raised by popular subscription. Many slave owners, seeing the handwriting on the wall, liberated their slaves on condition that they remain at work for some time longer. By the end of 1887 even the die-hard coffee planters of São Paulo were ready to adjust to new conditions by offering to pay wages to their slaves and improve their working and living conditions; they also increased efforts to induce European immigrants to come to São Paulo. These efforts were highly successful; the flow of immigrants into São Paulo rose from 6,600 in 1885 to over 32,000 in 1887 and to 90,000 in 1888. As a result, coffee production reached record levels. With its labor problem solved, São Paulo was ready to abandon its resistance to abolition and even join the abolitionist crusade.

On May 13, 1888, Brazil finally abolished slavery, but contrary to a traditional interpretation, this decision was not the climax of a gradual process of slavery's decline and slave owners' peaceful acceptance of the inevitable. The total slave population dropped sharply only after 1885, as a result of abolitionist agitation, mass flights of slaves, armed clashes, and other upheavals that appeared to threaten anarchy. In effect, abolition had come not through reform but by revolution.

The aftermath of abolition refuted the dire predictions of its foes. Freed from the burdens of slavery and aided by the continuance of very high world coffee prices (until about 1896), Brazil made more economic progress in a few years than it had during the almost seven decades of imperial rule. For the former slaves, however, little had changed. The abolitionist demand for the grant of land to the freedmen was forgotten. Relationships between former masters and slaves in many places remained largely unchanged; racist traditions and the economic and political power of the fazendeiros gave them almost absolute control over their former slaves. Denied land and education, freedmen were now compelled by the "whip of hunger" to labor at the hardest, most poorly paid jobs. Fazendeiros replaced freedmen with immigrants on the coffee plantations; in the cities, black artisans lost their jobs to immigrants.

THE FALL OF THE MONARCHY

But abolition did sabotage slavery's sister institution, the monarchy, which had long rested on the support of the planter class, especially the northern planters, who saw in it a guarantee of slavery's

Allegory of the Departure of Dom Pedro II for Europe After the Declaration of the Republic. This romantic painting suggests the respect and affection many Brazilians, including supporters of the republic, felt for the ousted emperor. [Anonymous, 1890, oil on canvas. Fundaçao Maria Luisa e Oscar Americano, São Paolo]

survival. Before 1888 the Republican Party had its principal base among the coffee interests, who resented the favor shown by the imperial government to the sugar planters and wished to achieve political power that corresponded to their economic power. Now, angered by abolition and embittered by the failure of the crown to indemnify them for their lost slaves, those planters who had opposed abolition now joined the Republican movement. The monarchy that had served the interest of regional elites for the previous sixty-seven years had lost its reason for existence.

Republicanism and a closely allied ideology, positivism, also made many converts in the officer class, disgruntled by the imperial government's neglect and mistreatment. Many of the younger officers came from the new urban middle class or, if of aristocratic descent, were discontented with the ways of their fathers. Positivism, it has been said, became "the gospel of the military academy," where it was brilliantly expounded by a popular young professor of mathematics, Benjamin Constant Botelho de Magalhães, a devoted disciple of Auguste Comte, the doctrine's founder. The positivist doctrine, with its stress on science, its ideal of a dictatorial republic, and its distrust of the masses, fit the needs of urban middle-class groups, progressive officers, and businessmen-fazendeiros who wanted modernization but without drastic changes in land tenure and class relations. On

November 15, 1889, a military revolt led by Benjamin Constant and Marshal Floriano Peixoto overthrew the government, proclaimed a republic with Marshal Deodoro da Fonseca as provisional chief of state, and sent Pedro II into exile in France.

Like the revolution that gave Brazil its independence, the republican revolution came from above; the coup d'état encountered little resistance but also inspired little popular enthusiasm. Power was firmly held by representatives of the business, landed, and military elites.

The new rulers promptly promulgated a series of reforms, including a decree that ended corporal punishment in the army, a literacy test that replaced property qualifications for voting (because property and literacy usually went together, this measure did not significantly enlarge the electorate), and successive decrees that established a secular state and civil marriage.

THE NEW REPUBLIC

Two years after the revolt, a constituent assembly met in Rio de Janeiro to draft a constitution for the new republic. It provided for a federal, presidential form of government with the customary three branches—legislative, executive, and judicial. The principal debate was between the partisans of greater autonomy for the states and those who feared the divisive results of an extreme federalism. The coffee interests, which dominated the wealthy south-central region, sought to strengthen their position at the expense of the central power. The urban business groups, represented in the convention chiefly by lawyers, favored a strong central government that could promote industry, aid the creation of a national market, and offer protection from British competition.

The result was a compromise tilted in favor of federalism. The twenty provinces in effect became self-governing states with popularly elected governors, the exclusive right to tax exports (a profitable privilege for wealthy states like São Paulo and Minas Gerais), and the right to maintain militias. The national government was given control over the tariffs and the income from import duties, whereas the president obtained very large powers:

he designated his cabinet ministers and other high officers, he could declare a state of siege, and he could intervene in the states with the federal armed forces in the event of a threat to their political institutions. The constitution proclaimed the sanctity of private property and guaranteed freedom of the press, speech, and assembly.

If these freedoms had some relevance in the cities and hinterlands touched by the movement of modernization, they lacked meaning over the greater part of the national territory. The fazendeiros, former slave owners, virtually monopolized the nation's chief wealth, its land. The land monopoly gave them absolute control over the rural population. Feudal and semifeudal forms of land tenure, accompanied by the obligation of personal and military service on the part of tenants, survived in the backlands, especially in the northeast. Powerful *coronéis* maintained armies of *jagunços* (full-time private soldiers) and waged war against each other.[2]

In this medieval atmosphere of constant insecurity and social disintegration, there arose messianic movements that reflected the aspirations of the oppressed sertanejos for peace and justice. One of the most important of such movements arose in the interior of Bahia, where the principal activity was cattle raising. Here, Antônio Conselheiro (Anthony the Counselor) established a settlement at the abandoned cattle ranch of Canudos. Rejecting private property, Antônio required all who joined his sacred company to give up their goods, but he promised a future of prosperity in his messianic kingdom through the sharing of the treasure of the "lost Sebastian" (the Portuguese king who had disappeared in Africa in 1478 but would return as a redeemer) or through division of the property of hostile landowners.

Despite its religious coloration, the existence of such a focus of social and political unrest was intolerable to the fazendeiros and the state authorities. When the sertanejos easily defeated state forces

---

[2]The title *coronel* (Portuguese for "colonel"; *coronéis* is the plural) was often honorary and did not necessarily indicate a military command or landownership; especially after 1870, a coronel might be simply a political boss, a merchant, or even an influential lawyer or priest.

sent against them in 1896, the governor called on the federal government for aid. Four campaigns were required to break the epic resistance of the men, women, and children of Canudos, nearly all of whom were killed in the final assault by the national army. A Brazilian literary masterpiece, *Os sertões (Rebellion in the Backlands)* by Euclides da Cunha (1856–1909), immortalized the heroism of the defenders and the crimes of the victors. It also revealed to the urban elite another and unfamiliar side of Brazilian reality.

THE ECONOMIC REVOLUTION

An enormous historical gulf separated the bleak sertão—in which the tragedy of Canudos was played out—from the cities, the scene of a mushrooming growth of banks, stock exchanges, and corporations. In Rio de Janeiro, writes Pedro Calmon, there was "a multitude of millionaires of recent vintage—commercial agents, bustling lawyers, promoters of all kinds, politicians of the new generation, the men of the day." Even the physical appearance of some of Brazil's great urban centers changed. These changes were most marked in the federal capital of Rio de Janeiro, which was made into a beautiful and healthful city between 1902 and 1906 when Prefect Pereira Passos mercilessly demolished narrow old streets to permit the construction of broad, modern avenues, and the distinguished scientist Oswaldo Cruz waged a victorious struggle to conquer mosquito-borne disease by filling in swamps and installing adequate water and sewage systems.

The economic policies of the new republican regime reflected pressures from different quarters: the planter class, urban capitalists, the military. Many planters, left in a difficult position by the abolition of slavery, demanded subsidies and credits to enable them to convert to the new wage system. The emerging industrial bourgeoisie, convinced that Brazil must develop an industrial base to emerge from backwardness, asked for protective tariffs, the construction of an economic infrastructure, and policies favorable to capital formation. Within the provisional government, these aspirations had a fervent supporter in the minister of finance, Ruy Barbosa, who believed that the factory was the crucible in which an "intelligent and independent democracy" would be forged in Brazil. Finally, the army, whose decisive role in the establishment of the republic had given it great prestige and influence, called for increased appropriations for the armed services. These various demands far exceeded the revenue available to the federal and state governments.

The federal government solved this problem by resorting to the printing press and allowing private banks to issue notes backed by little more than faith in the future of Brazil. In two years, the volume of paper money in circulation doubled, and the foreign-exchange value of the Brazilian monetary unit, the *milréis,* plummeted disastrously. Because objective economic conditions (the small internal market and the lack of an adequate technological base, among other factors) limited the real potential for Brazilian growth, much of the new capital was used for highly speculative purposes, including the creation of fictitious companies.

The resulting economic collapse brought ruin to many investors, unemployment and lower wages to workers, and a military coup that replaced President da Fonseca with his vice president, Marshal Floriano Peixoto.

The urban middle-class sector briefly gained greater influence in the Peixoto government, and inflation continued unchecked. The rise in the cost of many imported items to almost prohibitive levels stimulated the growth of Brazilian manufactures: the number of such enterprises almost doubled between 1890 and 1895.

But the suppression of a new revolt with strong aristocratic and monarchical overtones increased Peixoto's reliance on the financial and military support of the state of São Paulo, whose coffee oligarchy resolved to use its clout to end the ascendancy of the urban middle classes. The oligarchy distrusted their policies of rapid industrialization and blamed them for the financial instability that had plagued the first years of the republic. In 1893 the old planter oligarchies, whose divisions had temporarily enabled the middle classes to gain the upper hand in coalition with the military, reunited to form the Federal Republican Party, with a program of support for federalism and fiscal responsibility. Because they controlled the electoral machinery, they easily elected Prudente de Morais president in 1894, and his administration again institutionalized the domination of the coffee interests, relegating urban capitalist groups to a secondary role in political life.

Morais's successor, Manuel Ferraz de Campos Sales (1898–1902), continued and expanded his program of giving primacy to agriculture. Campos Sales fully endorsed the system of the international economic division of labor as it applied to Brazil. "It is time," he proclaimed, "that we take the correct road; to that end we must strive to export all that we can produce better than other countries, and import all that other countries can produce better than we." This formula confirmed the continuity of neocolonialism from the empire through the early republic. Determined to halt inflation, Campos Sales drastically reduced expenditures on public works, increased taxes, and made every effort to redeem the paper money to improve Brazil's international credit and secure new loans to cover shortfalls in government revenues.

Coffee was king. Whereas Brazil produced 56 percent of the world's coffee output from 1880 to 1889, it accounted for 76 percent from 1900 to 1904. Its closest competitor, rubber, supplied only 28 percent of Brazil's exports in 1901. Sugar, once the ruler of the Brazilian economy, now accounted for barely 5 percent of the nation's exports. Minas Gerais and especially São Paulo became the primary coffee regions, and Rio de Janeiro declined in importance. Enjoying immense advantages—the famous rich, porous *terra roxa* (red soil), an abundance of immigrant labor, and closeness to the major port of Santos—the *Paulistas* harvested 60 percent of the national coffee production.

The coffee boom from the late 1880s through the mid-1890s soon led to overproduction, falling prices, and the accumulation of unsold stocks after 1896. Because coffee trees came into production only four years after planting, the effects of expansion into the western frontier of São Paulo continued to be felt even after prices fell; between 1896

and 1900 the number of producing trees in São Paulo alone went from 150 million to 570 million. Large international coffee-trading firms controlled the world market, and they added to planters' difficulties by paying depressed prices during the height of each season and selling off their reserves in periods of relative shortage when prices edged up.

Responding to the planters' clamor for help, the São Paulo government took the first step for the "defense" of coffee in 1902, forbidding new coffee plantings for five years. Other steps soon proved necessary. Faced with a bumper crop in 1906, São Paulo launched a coffee price-support scheme to protect the state's economic lifeblood. With financing from British, French, German, and U.S. banks and the eventual collaboration of the federal government, São Paulo purchased several million bags of coffee and held them off the market in an effort to maintain profitable price levels. Purchases continued into 1907; from that date until World War I, the stocks were gradually sold off with little market disruption. The operation's principal gainers were the foreign merchants and bankers who, because they controlled the Coffee Commission formed to liquidate the purchased stocks, gradually disposed of them with a large margin of profit. The problem, temporarily exorcised, was presently to return in an even more acute form.

The valorization scheme, which favored the coffee-raising states at the expense of the rest, reflected the coffee planters' political domination. Under President Campos Sales, this ascendancy was institutionalized by the so-called *política dos governadores* (politics of the governors). Its essence was a formula that gave the two richest and most populous states (São Paulo and Minas Gerais) a virtual monopoly of federal politics and the choice of presidents. Thus, the first three civilian presidents from 1894 to 1906 came from São Paulo; the next two, from 1906 to 1910, came from Minas Gerais and Rio de Janeiro, respectively.

In return, the oligarchies of the other states were given almost total freedom of action within their jurisdictions, the central government intervening as a rule only when it suited the local oligarchy's interest. Informal discussions among the state governors determined the choice of president, whose election was a foregone conclusion since less than two percent of the population was eligible to vote. No official candidate for president lost an election before 1930. Similar reciprocal arrangements existed on the state level between the governors and the coronéis, urban or rural bosses who rounded up the local vote to elect the governors and were rewarded with a free hand in their respective domains.

Despite the official bias in favor of agriculture, industry continued to grow in the period from 1904 to 1914. By 1908, Brazil could boast of more than three thousand industrial enterprises. Foreign firms dominated the fields of banking, public works, utilities, transportation, and the export and import trade. Manufacturing, on the other hand, was carried on almost exclusively by native Brazilians and permanent immigrants. This national industry was concentrated in the four states of São Paulo, Minas Gervais, Rio de Janeiro, and Rio Grande do Sul. Heavy industry did not exist; over half of the enterprises were textile mills and food-processing plants. Many of these "enterprises" were small workshops employing a few artisans or operated with archaic technology, and Brazilians in the market economy continued to import most quality products. The quantitative and qualitative development of industry was hampered by the semifeudal conditions prevailing in the countryside; by the extreme poverty of the masses, which sharply limited the internal market; by the lack of a skilled, literate labor force; and by the hostility of most fazendeiros and foreign interests to industry.

Together with industry there arose a working class destined to play a significant role in the life of the country. The Brazilian proletariat was partly recruited from sharecroppers and minifundio peasants fleeing to the cities to escape dismal poverty and the tyranny of coronéis, but above all it was composed of the flood of European immigrants, who arrived at a rate of 100,000 to 150,000 each year. Working and living conditions of the working class were often intolerable. Child labor was common, for children could be legally employed from the age of twelve. The workday ranged from nine hours for some skilled workers to more than sixteen hours for various categories of unskilled workers. Wages were pitifully low and often paid in vouchers redeemable at the company store. There was a total absence of legislation to protect workers against the hazards of unemployment, old age, or industrial accidents.

Among the European immigrants were many militants with socialist, syndicalist, or social-democratic backgrounds who helped organize the Brazilian labor movement and gave it a radical political orientation. National and religious divisions among workers, widespread illiteracy, and quarrels between socialists and anarcho-syndicalists hampered the rise of a trade union movement and a labor party.

But trade unions grew rapidly after 1900, and the first national labor congress, representing the majority of the country's trade unions, met in 1906 to struggle for the eight-hour workday. One result of the congress was the formation of the first national trade union organization, the Brazilian Labor Confederation, which organized a number of strikes that authorities and employers tried to suppress by arresting labor leaders, deporting immigrants, and sending dissidents to forced labor on a railroad under construction in distant Mato Grosso. The phrase "the social question is a question for the police" was often used to sum up the labor policy of the Brazilian state.

Peruvian Politics and Economy

Peru's backward, stagnant economy, the profound cleavage between the sierra and the coast, and the absence of a governing class (such as arose in Chile) capable of giving firm and intelligent leadership to the state produced chronic political turbulence and civil wars.

Under these conditions, military caudillos, sometimes men of plebeian origin who had risen in the ranks during the wars of independence, came to play a decisive role in the political life of the new state. Some were more than selfish careerists or instruments of aristocratic creole cliques. The ablest and most enlightened of the military caudillos was the mestizo general Ramón Castilla, who served as president of Peru from 1845 to 1851 and again from 1855 to 1862. Castilla presided over an advance of the Peruvian economy based on the rapid growth of guano exports. This export trade was dominated by British capitalists, who obtained the right to sell guano to specified regions of the world in return for loans to the Peruvian government (secured by guano shipments). Exorbitant interest and commission rates swelled their profits. Although Castilla gave some thought to direct government exploitation of some guano deposits, to setting controls over the amount and price of guano to be sold, and to plowing guano revenues into development projects, he did nothing to implement these ideas. The guano boom, however, stimulated some growth of native Peruvian commerce and banking and created the nucleus of a national capitalist class. Guano prosperity also financed the beginnings of a modern infrastructure; thus, in 1851 the first railway line began to operate between Lima and its port of Callao.

The rise of guano revenues enabled Castilla to carry out a series of social reforms that also contributed to the process of modernization. In 1854 he abolished slavery and indigenous tribute, relieving natives of a heavy fiscal burden and freeing enslaved Africans, who numbered some twenty thousand. Abolition had an initial disruptive effect on coastal agriculture, but in the long run it was very advantageous to the planter aristocracy, who received compensation of up to 40 percent of their slaves' value. With these indemnities, planters could buy seeds, plants, and Chinese coolies brought to Peru on a contract basis that made them virtual slaves. Meanwhile, the freed blacks often became sharecroppers who lived on the margins of the hacienda and supplied a convenient unpaid labor force and a source of rent. Stimulated by these developments, cotton, sugar cane, and grain production expanded on the coast. Highland economic life also quickened, though on a smaller scale, with the rise of extensive cattle breeding for the export of wool and leather through Arequipa and Lima.

The general upward movement of the Peruvian economy after 1850 was aided by such favorable factors as the temporary dislocation of the cotton industry of the southern United States

and large inflows of foreign capital. As a result, exports of cotton and sugar increased sharply. The coastal latifundia continued to expand at the expense of indigenous communities, sharecroppers, and tenants, all of whom were expelled from their lands. This process was accompanied by the modernization of coastal agriculture through the introduction of cotton gins, boilers, refinery equipment for sugar, and steam-driven tractors.

Although profits from the agricultural sector enabled the commercial and landed aristocracy of Lima to live in luxury, the Peruvian state sank even deeper into debt. The guano deposits, Peru's collateral for its foreign borrowings, were being depleted at an ever-accelerating rate, and the bulk of the proceeds from these loans went to pay interest on old and new debts. In 1868, during the administration of the military caudillo José Balta, his minister of the treasury, Nicolás de Piérola, devised a plan for extricating Peru from its difficulties and providing funds for development. The project eliminated the numerous consignees to whom guano had been sold and awarded a monopoly of guano sales in Europe to the French firm of Dreyfus and Company. In return, the Dreyfus firm agreed to service its foreign debt and to make Peru a loan that would tide it over immediate difficulties. The contract initiated a new flow of loans that helped create a boundless euphoria, an invincible optimism, about the country's future.

U.S. adventurer and entrepreneur Henry Meiggs, who had made a reputation as a railway builder in Chile, easily convinced Balta and Piérola that they should support the construction of a railway system to tap the mineral wealth of the sierra. As a result, much of the money obtained under the Dreyfus contract, and a large part of the proceeds of the dwindling guano reserves, were poured into railway projects that could not show a profit in the foreseeable future.

PARDO AND THE CIVILIANIST PARTY

The good fortune of Dreyfus and Company displeased the native commercial and banking bourgeoisie that had arisen in Lima. A group of these men—including former guano consignees who had been eliminated by the Dreyfus contracts—headed by the millionaire businessman Manuel Pardo, challenged the legality of the contract before the Supreme Court, arguing that assignment of guano sales to a corporation of native consignees that they proposed to form would be more beneficial to Peru's economic development. The native bourgeoisie suffered defeat, but in 1871 they organized the *Civilista*, or Civilianist Party (in reference to their opposition to military caudillos), which ran Pardo as its candidate for president. An amalgam of "an old aristocracy and a newly emerging capitalist class," the Civilianist Party opposed clerical and military influence in politics and advocated a large directing role for the state in economic development. Pardo won handily over two rivals and took office in 1872.

Pardo presided over a continuing agricultural boom, with exports reaching a peak in 1876. Foreign capital poured into the country. In those years, an Irish immigrant, W. R. Grace, began to establish an industrial empire that included textile mills, a shipping line, vast sugar estates, and Peru's first large-scale sugar-refining plants. Whereas private industry prospered, the government sank ever deeper into a quagmire of debts and deficits. The guano cycle was nearing its end, with revenues steadily declining as a result of falling prices, depletion of guano beds, and competition from an important new source of fertilizer: nitrates exploited by Anglo-Chilean capitalists in the southern Peruvian province of Tarapacá. In 1875, wishing to control the nitrate industry and make it a dependable source of government income, Pardo expropriated the foreign companies in Tarapacá and established a state monopoly over the production and sale of nitrates. This measure angered the Anglo-Chilean entrepreneurs, whose holdings had been nationalized and who were indemnified with bonds of dubious value. Meanwhile, due to unsatisfactory market conditions in Europe, the nationalization measure failed to yield the anticipated economic benefits.

In 1876, Peru felt the full force of a worldwide economic storm. In a few months, all the banks of Lima had to close; by the following year, the government had to suspend payments on its foreign debt and issue unbacked paper money. The economic collapse was followed by a military disaster: the War of the Pacific. Despite heroic resistance, Peru suffered a crushing defeat at the hands of a Chilean state that enjoyed more advanced economic organization, political stability, and the support of British capitalists. The war completed the work of economic ruin begun by the depression. The Chileans occupied and ravaged the economically advanced coastal area: they levied taxes on the hacendados; dismantled equipment from the haciendas and sent it to Chile; and sent troops into the sierra to exact payment from hacendados, towns, and villages. Their extortions infuriated the native peasantry. Led by General Andrés Cáceres, they began to wage an effective guerrilla war of attrition against the Chilean occupiers. The war was finally ended by the 1883 Treaty of Ancón.

Central American Politics and Economy

In the last third of the nineteenth century, the three Central American countries selected for special study—Guatemala, Nicaragua, and El Salvador—underwent major economic changes in response to growing world demand for two products the area was ideally fitted to produce: coffee and bananas. The changes included a "liberal" reform that sought to modernize economic and social structures but left intact existing class and property relations; the rise of a new dependency based on the export of one or two products and foreign control of key natural resources and infrastructure; and acceptance of U.S. political hegemony. Everywhere, these changes were accompanied by concentration of landownership, intensified exploitation of labor, and a growing gulf between the rich and the poor.

GUATEMALA, 1865–1898

Rafael Carrera's death in 1865 was followed by six years of continuous liberal political and military challenge to conservative rule in Guatemala. The liberals responded to changes in the world economy, in particular to the mounting foreign demand for coffee and the adjustments this required in Guatemala's economic and social structures. In 1871 they seized power, and two years later the energetic Justo Rufino Barrios became president. Although a hard, dictatorial man, Barrios had a genuine passion for reform and was an apostle of Central American unity; he died in battle in 1885 trying to unify Central America by force. His successors grew increasingly cynical, corrupt, and repressive in their efforts to consolidate state power, subjugate relatively autonomous indigenous communities, and create a unified national market for land, labor, and commodities.

The liberal reform program included major economic, social, and ideological changes. The ideological reform introduced doctrines of white supremacy then current in Europe and the United States to justify racist immigration policies designed to "whiten" the population. It also rejected clerical and metaphysical doctrine in favor of a firm faith in science and material progress. This called for the secularization and expansion of education. The shortage of public funds, however, greatly limited public education; as late as 1921 the Guatemalan illiteracy rate was over 86 percent. Seeking to reduce the power and authority of the church, the liberal governments nationalized its lands, ended its special privileges, and established freedom of religion and civil marriage.

The economic transformation encompassed three major areas: land tenure, labor, and infrastructure. A change in land tenure was necessary for the creation of the new economic order. The old staples of Guatemalan agriculture, indigo and cochineal, had been grown by thousands of small- and medium-sized producers; coffee, however, required large expanses of land concentrated in relatively few hands. Under Barrios, there began an "agrarian reform" designed to make such land available to the coffee growers. Church and monastery lands, confiscated by Barrios, were the first target. Next came uncultivated state holdings, which were divided and sold cheaply or granted to private interests, and indigenous communal lands. Legislation requiring titles to private property provided the legal basis for this expropriation. The principal native beneficiaries of this process were

small- and medium-sized coffee growers who could purchase or otherwise obtain land from the government. But foreign immigrants, warmly welcomed by the liberal regimes, also benefited from the new legislation. By 1914 foreign-owned (chiefly German) lands produced almost half of Guatemala's coffee. By 1926 concentration of landownership had reached a point where only 7.3 percent of the population owned land.

The land reform helped achieve another objective of the liberal program—the supply of a mass of cheap labor to the new group of native and foreign coffee growers. Many highland natives who had lost their land migrated to the emerging coffee-growing areas near the coast. The most common labor system was debt peonage—legal under Guatemalan law—in which indígenas were tied to the *fincas* (plantations) by hereditary debts. This was supplemented by the recruitment of native peoples who came down from the mountains to work as seasonal laborers on haciendas and plantations to add to their meager income from their own tiny landholdings. Barrios also revived the colonial system of mandamientos, under which indígenas were required to accept offers of work from planters. The registers of native peoples maintained by local officials for this purpose were also used to conscript them for military service and public works. Those who could not pay the two-peso head tax—the great majority—were required to work (two weeks a year) on road construction.

Constituting 70 percent of the nation's 1,000,000 people in the late nineteenth century, indigenous peoples naturally resisted this liberal onslaught, occasionally through overt acts of localized rebellion. But in the face of a ruthless military state prepared to obliterate them, they more commonly survived by deploying "weapons of the weak," modes of resistance designed to limit the risk of annihilation. In rural Guatemala, these indigenous communities relied on *guachibales*, independent religious brotherhoods rooted in colonial Catholic traditions, to maintain their cultural identities, defend their autonomy, and preserve communal customs, ancestral languages, and religious rituals against the homogenizing power of liberalism's unfettered market forces.

NICARAGUA, 1870–1909

The history of Nicaragua for two decades after the collapse of the Central American federation in 1838 also was dominated by a struggle between liberals and conservatives. Their responsibility for inviting William Walker to assist them, followed by Walker's attempt to establish his personal empire in Central America, so discredited the liberals that the conservatives were able to rule Nicaragua with very little opposition for more than three decades (1857–1893).

Although coffee was grown commercially as early as 1848, the principal economic activities in Nicaragua until about 1870 were cattle ranching and subsistence agriculture. Indigenous communities still owned much land, there existed a class of independent small farmers who lived on public land, and peonage was rare. On the Atlantic coast, however, the autonomous Kingdom of Mosquitia, controlled by the British since 1678, was inhabited by traditional Miskitos, Sumus, and Afro-creoles, who labored at low wages on thriving British- and U.S.-owned banana plantations, timber lands, gold mines, and commercial port facilities. But the sudden growth of the world market for coffee created a nationalist demand by some members of the Nicaraguan elite for land suitable for coffee growing and for a supply of cheap labor.

Beginning in 1877 a series of laws required these villages to sell their communal lands and effectively drove the indigenous and mestizo peasants off their land, gradually transforming them into a class of dependent peons or sharecroppers. The passage of vagrancy laws and laws permitting the conscription of native peoples for agricultural and public labor also ensured the supply of cheap labor needed by the coffee growers. These laws provoked a major indigenous revolt, the War of the Comuneros (1881), which ended in defeat for the indígenas and was followed by a ferocious repression that took five thousand lives.

The new class, made up of coffee planters, was impatient with the traditional ways of the conservative cattle raisers who had held power in Nicaragua since 1857. In 1893 the planters staged a revolt that brought the liberal José Santos Zelaya to the presidency. A modernizer, Zelaya ruled for the next seventeen years as dictator-president. He undertook to provide the infrastructure needed by the new economic order through the construction of roads, railroads, port facilities, and telegraphic communications. He reorganized the military, separated church and state, and promoted public education. Like other Latin American liberal leaders of his time, he believed that foreign investment was necessary for rapid economic progress and granted large concessions to foreign capitalists, especially U.S. firms. By 1909, North Americans controlled much of the production of coffee, gold, lumber, and bananas—the principal sources of Nicaragua's wealth.

EL SALVADOR, 1876–1911

By the mid-nineteenth century, El Salvador had already passed through two economic cycles. The first was dominated by cacao, the prosperity of which collapsed in the seventeenth century; the second by indigo, which entered a sharp decline in the latter half of the nineteenth century, first as a result of competition from other producing areas and then as a result of the development of synthetic dyes. The search for a new export crop led to the enthronement of coffee. Coffee cultivation began at about the time of independence, but it did not expand rapidly until the 1860s. As elsewhere in Central America, the rise of coffee was marked by expropriation and usurpation of native lands—carried out in the name of private property and material progress—because most of the land best suited to coffee cultivation was held by indigenous communities.

Unlike indigo, which was planted and harvested every year, coffee trees did not produce for three years. Producers, therefore, had to have capital or credit, and the people with capital or access to credit were the hacendados who had prospered from the growing of indigo. To help these hacendados in their search for land and labor, a government decree of 1856 declared that if two-thirds of a pueblo's communal lands were not planted in coffee, ownership would pass into the hands of the state. Later, the liberal president and military strongman, Rafael Zaldívar, directly attacked native landholdings with passage of an 1881 law that ordered all communal lands to be divided among the co-owners (which opened the way for their acquisition by legal or illegal means by the expanding coffee growers); thirteen months later he decreed the abolition of all communal land tenure. The new legislation harmed not only these communities but *ladino* (mestizo) small farmers as well. These farmers often relied on municipal *tierras comunes* (the free pasture and woodlot where they could graze their stock) for an important part of their subsistence. In 1879, 60 percent of the people depended upon communal properties, which composed 40 percent of arable lands.

The result of this new legislation was a rapid concentration of landownership in the hands of a landed oligarchy often referred to as "the fourteen families." The number, though not an exact figure, expresses symbolically the reality of the tiny elite that dominated the Salvadoran economy and state. Throughout most of the nineteenth century, the great landowners used their own private armies to deal with the problem of recalcitrant peasants. Governmental decrees of 1884 and 1889 made these private armed forces the basis of the public Rural Police, later renamed the National Police. In 1912 the *Guardia Nacional* (National Guard), modeled after the Spanish National Guard, was established. Like the National Police, the National Guard patrolled the countryside and offered police protection to haciendas. The national army, created in the 1850s, did not become an instrument of repression until the late twentieth century.

For the rural poor, the social consequences of the coffee boom were disastrous. A few of the dispossessed peasants were permitted to remain on the fincas, or new estates, as colonos—peons who were given a place to live and a milpa, or garden plot, where they could raise subsistence crops. Unlike the old indigo or sugar latifundia, however, which required a large permanent labor force, the need for labor on the coffee plantations was seasonal, so for the most part planters relied on hired hands. This circumstance determined the pattern of life of most Salvadoran campesinos. They might farm a small plot as squatters or as colonos on a plantation, but their tiny plots did not as a rule provide subsistence for their families. They would therefore tend to follow the harvests, working on coffee fincas during the harvest season, moving on to cut sugar cane or harvest cotton during August and September, and finally returning to their milpas, hopeful that the maize had ripened. This unstable migratory pattern created many social problems.

Venezuelan Politics and Economy

Turmoil in the aftermath of the Federal War ended in 1870 when Antonio Guzmán Blanco, the ablest of Venezuela's nineteenth-century rulers, seized power. Like his father, Guzmán Blanco was a master of demagogic rhetoric. He was a self-proclaimed liberal and foe of the oligarchy, an anticlerical and devout believer in the positivist creed of science and progress whose ambition was to create a "practical republic" of "civilized people." To secure this vision, he forged pacts with the conservative merchant class of Caracas, which viewed him with suspicion when he came to power; with the regional caudillos, traditionally identified with the principle of local autonomy; and with foreign economic interests, whose support he needed for his ambitious program to construct roads, railroads, and telegraph systems. In the end Guzmán Blanco's dream of a developed capitalist Venezuela proved to be a mirage; after two decades of his rule, Venezuela remained rural, monocultural, and dependent, a country in which caudillos again ran rampant as they struggled for power.

His system has been called "a national alliance of caudillos," but over this alliance "the illustrious American," as he came to be called by his sycophantic Congress and press, presided as the supreme caudillo. The constitution of 1864 was periodically replaced by new constitutions that reinforced the centralization of power. Although Guzmán's dictatorship was mild by comparison with some others in Venezuelan history, he did not hesitate to use repressive measures against his foes.

By his pact with the caudillos, Guzmán secured a relatively stable peace (though there were several large-scale revolts against him between 1870 and 1888 and local uprisings were common throughout the period). Soon after coming to power he established a *compañía de crédito* with a powerful group of Caracas merchants. This gave him the resources needed to initiate a program of public works designed to improve transportation and communication. Between 1870 and 1874 fifty-one road-building projects were begun. But local funding did not suffice; Guzmán needed the cooperation of foreign capital, hesitant to invest in a country whose recent history had been marked by recurrent episodes of civil war. In 1879 he secured his first foreign contract, with a group of British investors for the construction of a railroad connecting Caracas with its major port, La Guaira. By the time he left office, Venezuela had eleven railroad lines completed or under construction, all designed to serve the export-import trade by connecting Caracas and the major agricultural and mining areas with the ports. Given Venezuela's unfavorable terms of trade—the long-term tendency for the prices of its exports to decline and those of its manufactured imports to rise—the net result was to reinforce Venezuela's economic dependency, promote decapitalization, and leave the country a legacy of large unpaid foreign debt that in time posed a threat of foreign intervention and loss of sovereignty.

Guzmán Blanco's anticlerical policies led to a further weakening of the church. Tithing had already been abolished as "an excessive tax burden" on the citizenry. Under Guzmán Blanco the priestly fuero was ended, civil marriage and civil registration of birth and deaths established, and convents and seminaries closed. The church was also forbidden to inherit real estate, and many church estates were seized by the government. Guzmán Blanco also tried to prohibit black and Asian immigration, even as he enticed Europeans with generous subsidies. Ultimately this failed, and Venezuela remained a society in which a small, self-proclaimed "white" wealthy minority ruled a "black" majority.

For the rest, Guzmán Blanco's development programs caused little change in the country's economic and social structures. In 1894 the population, numbering some 2,500,000, was overwhelmingly rural; only three cities had a population of more than 10,000. Most of the working population was employed in agriculture; what little modern industry existed was limited to light industry such as food processing and textiles. Artisan shops, employing some 50,000 workers, were economically much more important.

In 1888 "the illustrious American," whose interest in modernizing Venezuela appeared to flag, departed for Europe, leaving a hand-picked successor in charge. After a chaotic decade during which governments rose and fell, in 1899 Cipriano Castro, an energetic young caudillo from the Andean state of Táchira, seized power with his *compadre* (buddy) Juan Vicente Gómez, a prosperous cattle raiser and coffee grower. Castro's seizure of power reflected the growing economic importance of the Andean coffee-growing region. Announcing a program of "new men, new ideals, new methods," Castro formed a provisional government of national unity that included all political factions. In 1901 a constituent assembly elected him president and framed a constitution that extended the executive's term of office to six years.

Castro continued Guzmán Blanco's policy of centralization, appointing or confirming local officials and state governors, and sought to establish a strong national armed force that would replace the old-time personal armies and state militias. His program of military reform was handicapped by declining coffee prices that reduced state revenues, a series of caudillo revolts repressed at heavy cost, and a major conflict with foreign powers whose blockade of Venezuelan ports deprived the government of a vital source of income, custom duties.

Castro presided over a country in ruin due to devastating civil wars and a prolonged depression. Hard-pressed for funds, in December 1900 he demanded that Manuel Antonio Matos, Guzmán Blanco's brother-in-law and the country's wealthiest man, and his fellow financiers loan the government money. When they refused, he paraded them through the streets of Caracas on the way to jail. The loan was made, but Matos took his revenge, organizing a large-scale revolt that brought together Caracas financiers, foreign investors, and regional caudillos. This *Revolución Libertadora* received considerable aid from foreign firms. Despite this assistance and Matos's own resources, Castro, leading the government forces in person, inflicted a decisive defeat on the rebels at La Victoria in November 1902.

The German and British governments chose this time to demand immediate settlement of their nationals' claims for unpaid debts and damages suffered in various civil wars. The government, having thrown all its resources into the struggle against the Matos revolt, could not pay these claims. In December 1902, despite Castro's offer to negotiate, the two powers sent an Anglo-German squadron of twelve warships into Venezuelan waters with orders to seize or destroy Venezuela's tiny fleet and blockade its ports. The powerful guns of the Anglo-German squadron soon silenced the answering fire of Venezuelan coastal batteries, and the aggressors occupied several Venezuelan ports. The unequal nature of the struggle, the catastrophic economic impact of the Anglo-German blockade, and the continuing Matos revolt in some areas of the country made a settlement necessary. Accordingly, Castro asked the U.S. ambassador to serve as mediator in negotiating a settlement. The terms required Venezuela to allocate 30 percent of its customs duties to the payment of claims and provided for an end to the blockade and reestablishment of diplomatic relations between the parties but denied Venezuela the right to demand compensation for its losses.

Castro's last years in power were troubled by new clashes with foreign states—France, Holland, the United States—usually caused by his insistence that foreign nationals were subject to Venezuelan courts and laws. As Castro's health declined, Juan Vicente Gómez conspired to take power. The regime divided into two bands—one supporting Castro, the other Gómez. Gómez also had the support of foreign powers, notably the United States, which was eager to get rid of Castro. On November 24, 1908, on the advice of his physicians, Castro left for Europe to seek medical aid. Gómez, assuming the duties of president, staged a coup d'état. Castro attempted to return but was blocked by U.S. warships off the Venezuelan coast and by French authorities on Martinique, who put him on board a ship sailing for Europe. He spent the rest of his life in exile, dying in Puerto Rico in 1924.

Colombian Politics and Economy

Dominating the presidency and Congress, the Liberals in Colombia began to establish a reign of liberty and reason in New Granada. The new constitution of 1853 provided for universal male suffrage, a provision that troubled some Liberals, who knew that illiterate proclerical peasants were most likely to vote Conservative. As a matter of fact, because in most areas voters continued to vote the wishes of the local *gamonales*, or bosses, the new electoral law did not significantly change anything.

In economics the Liberals sought a decisive break with the colonial tradition of restriction and monopoly. The abolition of the state tobacco monopoly finally took effect in 1850. An 1850 law ceded to the provinces revenues from tithes (hitherto collected by the state but used for support of the church), the *quinto* tax on gold and other precious metals, and other traditional sources of state revenue. The provinces were also empowered to abolish these taxes. To compensate for the resulting loss of state revenues, Congress adopted a tax on individuals.

Slavery was completely abolished in 1851, and slave owners were compensated. The measure, freeing about twenty-five thousand individuals, had its most severe impact on gold-mining areas, which generally relied heavily on slave labor. Some of the freedmen became peons on haciendas; others turned to subsistence farming.

But the Liberals always equated emancipation with *mestizaje*, a belief in "one God, one race, one tongue" that required the sacrifice of African and indigenous ethnic identities and the invention of a unified national Hispanic culture. This naturally led to the sacrifice of indigenous and African communal lands and their autonomous political traditions. Thereafter, the Liberals intensified the attack on resguardos, and land "liberated" by forced division often passed into the hands of neighboring hacendados by legal or illegal means. Natives made landless by such means often became peons serving the hacendados. Vagrancy laws similarly coerced the labor of "free" blacks.

Having achieved their ends with artisan support, the Liberal elite now ignored their allies' demands for tariff protection. This triggered a new political crisis in 1854 when a coup, supported by artisans who formed workers' battalions to defend the revolution, briefly installed General José María Melo. But Liberal and Conservative generals, putting aside their differences, raised private armies and defeated Melo in a short campaign. His artisan allies were imprisoned and three hundred were deported to Panama. The economic, political, and military rout of the artisans was complete.

In 1860, Liberals carried their religious and political reforms to their extreme and logical conclusions. Compulsory tithes and ecclesiastical fueros were abolished. All religious orders were suppressed, all convents and monasteries were closed, and all church wealth was seized by the government and sold. The transfer of massive amounts of church land into private hands produced little or no change in the land tenure system; clerical latifundia simply became lay latifundia, contributing to a further concentration of landownership. The principal buyers were Liberal merchants, landowners, and politicians, but Conservatives also participated in the plunder of church land.

In 1863, Liberal political reform reached its climax when a new constitution carried the principle of federalism to great lengths. The nine sovereign states became, in effect, independent nations, each with its own armed forces, possessing all the legislative powers not explicitly granted to the central government, which was made as weak as possible. The Liberals remained in power until 1885 in a political climate that approximated institutionalized anarchy, as the central government was powerless to intervene against the local revolutions that toppled and set up state governments.

The economic movement and its quest for the export base that could firmly integrate Colombia into the capitalist world economy continued. By the 1870s tobacco exports were down sharply, but this decline was made up by exporting coffee, qui-

nine, and other products. Coffee was emerging as the country's major export product, but its development lagged behind that of Brazil, which relied increasingly on European immigrant free labor. In Colombia coffee production in its principal centers of Santander and Cundinamarca was based on traditional haciendas worked by peons and tenants who lived and labored under oppressive conditions. A more satisfactory situation existed in Antioquia and Caldas, characterized by a mix of haciendas with more enlightened forms of sharecropping and small holdings, operations marked by high productivity. It was in these states that the twentieth-century takeoff of the Colombian coffee industry occurred.

The development of coffee as the major export, the growing ties between foreign and domestic merchants and coffee planters, and the stimulus given to trade and speculation by the expropriation of church lands created economic interests that required a new political model—a strong state capable of imposing order and creating the railroads and the financial infrastructure needed for the expansion of the coffee industry. The Liberal reform had removed many obstacles to capitalist development but had created others by its federalist excesses. By the early 1880s not only Conservatives but many moderate Liberals were convinced that political and social stability required making peace with the church and restoring its traditional role. The unlikely instrument for the creation of this new conservative, unitary order was the poet and intellectual Rafael Núñez, whom his party elected president in 1879.

RAFAEL NÚÑEZ, THE "REGENERATION," AND THE WAR OF A THOUSAND DAYS, 1880–1903

Núñez began political life as a radical Liberal and had spent thirteen years in the consular service in Europe. He returned home in 1875 and was elected president in 1879, governing with a coalition of right-leaning elements from both the Liberal and Conservative Parties. Elected again in 1884 he swiftly crushed a radical Liberal revolt and announced that the 1863 constitution had "ceased to exist." In 1886 he presented the country with a new constitution that replaced the sovereign states with departments headed by governors appointed by the president, extended the presidential term to six years, established literacy and property qualifications for voting for representatives, and provided for indirect election of senators. Under that constitution, personally or through surrogates, Núñez ruled Colombia until his death in 1894.

Like another religious skeptic, Bolívar, Núñez believed the authority of religion and the church was the foundation of the social order and must be fully supported by the state. The 1886 constitution made Catholicism the official religion and entrusted education to the clergy. The other foundations of Núñez's authoritarian republic were a strong standing army and a national police force. The Liberal regimes had virtually dismantled the regular army; the revolts and civil wars of the federal period had been fought by private armies formed by the great landowners with their tenants and peons. The existence of these regional private armies and militias was incompatible with Núñez's unitary project. The 1886 constitution created a permanent army and reserved to the central government the right to possess arms and ammunition. The national police, organized in 1891, kept under vigilance political suspects and disrupted most plots against the government.

Núñez is credited with two major economic innovations. Claiming that the Liberal policy of free trade or low tariffs was the cause of economic decadence and poverty, which had caused the civil war, he proposed to use tariff protection to stimulate the growth of certain industries. He believed this would create a new middle class that would form a buffer between the governing social class and the unlettered multitude. But his implementation of this program was timid and inconsistent. The new policy succeeded, however, in providing a modest level of protection for domestic industry.

Núñez's other innovation was the creation in 1881 of a national bank designed to relieve the financial distress of a government always on the verge of bankruptcy. The bank had the exclusive right to issue money; this monopoly enabled the state to provide for its needs and was managed pru-

dently until 1890. Then its uncontrolled emissions of paper money caused a galloping inflation. An expensive civil war in 1899 provoked the emission of paper money on such a scale that the printers could not keep up with the demand, and the country was flooded with millions of pesos of depreciated currency.

The "Regeneration," as the Núñez era is known, represented an effort to achieve national unification from above under reactionary auspices; it has been compared with Bismarck's project for German national unification, a compound of feudal and capitalist elements. Under Núñez the conditions for the rise of a modern, capitalist state began. An important step in this direction was his creation of a permanent army and the assumption of a monopoly of the use of force by the state. His removal of internal barriers to trade and his policy of tariff protection, however modest, contributed to the formation of an internal market; his national bank, despite its later scandalous mismanagement, represented an initial effort to create a national system of credit; and he gave impulse to the construction of internal improvements, especially railroads. Finally, he sought to give private enterprise access to frontier lands by formally denying the existence of ethnic Afro-Colombian and indigenous communities, voiding their proprietary claims. These policies, combined with the coffee boom, created national markets in land, labor, and commodities and contributed to a growth of capitalism in Colombia.

When he died, Núñez's leadership was assumed by Conservative politicians who lacked his intelligence and iron will. Their corruption, flagrant rigging of elections, and division over freedom of the press and electoral reform collided with Liberal anger at their long exclusion from power and an economic slump caused by a sharp decline of coffee prices. The result was a political crisis followed by a resort to arms. Confident of victory over a thoroughly unpopular government, the Liberals launched a revolt in 1899 that ushered in the disastrous War of a Thousand Days. It raged for three years, caused an estimated loss of 100,000 lives, and created immense material damage. It ended in a government victory.

Society and Culture in the Nineteenth Century

INDEPENDENCE LEFT MUCH of the colonial social structure intact. This fact was very apparent to liberal leaders of the postindependence era. "The war against Spain," declared the Colombian liberal Ramón Mercado in 1853, "was not a revolution. . . . Independence only scratched the surface of the social problem, without changing its essential nature." A modern historian, Charles C. Griffin, comes to much the same conclusion. "Only the beginnings of a basic transformation took place," he writes, "and there were many ways in which colonial attitudes and institutions carried over into the life of republican Spanish America."

How New Was the New Society?

We should not minimize, however, the extent and importance of the changes that did take place. Independence produced, if not a major social upheaval, at least a minor one. It opened wide fissures within the elite, dividing aristocratic supporters of the old social order from modernizers who wanted a more democratic, bourgeois order. Their struggle is an integral aspect of the first half-century after the end of Spanish and Portuguese rule. Independence also enabled such formerly submerged groups as artisans and gauchos to enter the political arena, although in subordinate roles, and even allowed a few to climb into the ranks of the elite. The opening of Latin American ports to foreign goods also established a relatively free market in ideas, at least in the capitals and other cities. With almost no time lag, such new European doctrines as utopian socialism, romanticism, and positivism entered Latin America and were applied to the solution of the continent's problems. These new winds of doctrine, blowing through what had lately been dusty colonial corridors, contributed to the area's intellectual renovation and promoted further social change.

The Passing of the Society of Castes

Verbally, at least, the new republican constitutions established the equality of all before the law, destroying the legal foundations of colonial caste society. Because little change in property relations took place, however, the ethnic and social lines of division remained essentially the same. Wealth, power, and prestige continued to be concentrated in the hands of a ruling class that reproduced colonial racial structures and identified itself with whiteness, although in some countries, such as Venezuela, it became more or less heavily tinged with individuals of darker skin who had managed to climb the social ladder through their prowess in war or politics.

INDIGENOUS PEOPLES

Of all the groups composing the old society of castes, the status of indígenas changed least of all. Mexican historian Carlos María Bustamante was one of the few creole leaders who recognized that independence had not freed them from their yoke. "They still drag the same chains," he wrote, "although they are flattered with the name of freemen." Even native tribute and forced labor, abolished during or after the wars of independence, soon reappeared in many countries under other names. What was worse, indigenous communal landholding, social organization, and culture, which Spanish law and policy had to some extent protected in colonial times, came under increasing attack, especially from liberals who believed that these communal traditions constituted as much of an obstacle to progress as the Spanish system of castes and special privileges did.

Until about 1870, however, large, compact indigenous populations continued to live under the traditional communal landholding system in Mexico, Central America, and the Andean region. Then, the rapid growth of the export economy, the coming of the railroads, and the resulting rise in land values and demand for labor caused "white" and mestizo landowners and landowner-dominated governments to launch a massive assault on native lands. The expropriation of these lands was accompanied, as noted in Chapter 10, by a growth of peonage and tenantry. Employers used a variety of devices, ranging from debt servitude to outright coercion, to attach laborers to their estates. In some areas, there arose a type of indigenous serfdom that closely resembled the classic European model. In the Andean region, for example, Aymara tenants, in addition to working their masters' land, had to render personal service in their households, sometimes at the hacienda, sometimes in the city. During their term of domestic service, these serfs could be given or sold to their masters' friends. This and other forms of serfdom survived well into the twentieth century.

The master class, aided by the clergy and local magistrates, sought to reinforce the economic subjection of indigenous peoples with psychological domination. There evolved a pattern of relations and role-playing that assigned to the *patrones* the role of benevolent figures who assured their peons or tenants of a livelihood and protected them in all emergencies in return for their absolute obedience. In countries with large indigenous populations, the relations between masters and peons often included an elaborate ritual that required natives to request permission to speak to *patrones*, to appear before them with head uncovered and bowed, and to seek their approval for all major personal decisions, including marriage.

But these relationships and attitudes of submission and servility, more characteristic of resident peons, were not accepted by all indigenous peoples. In the Andean area, Mexico, and elsewhere during the second half of the nineteenth century, the surviving native landowning communities fought stubbornly to prevent the absorption of their lands by advancing haciendas and to halt the process by which they became landless laborers. They fought with all the means at their disposal, including armed revolts as a last resort. Such revolts occurred in Mexico in the 1860s and 1870s and were called "communist" by the landowners and government officials, who crushed them with superior military force.

The greater freedom of movement that came with independence, the progressive disappearance of indigenous communities, and the growth of the hacienda, in which natives mingled with mestizos, strengthened a trend toward acculturation that had begun in the late colonial period. This acculturation was reflected in a growth of bilingualism: indigenous peoples increasingly used Spanish in dealing with whites, reserving their native languages for use among themselves. To the limited extent that public schools entered their regions, they contributed to the adoption of Spanish as a second language or sometimes led to total abandonment of their native tongues. Mexican historian Eduardo Ruiz recalled that as a child he spoke only Tarascan but had forgotten it during his twelve years of study at the colegio. "I did not want to remember, I must confess, because I was ashamed of being thought to be an Indian." Some acculturation also occurred in dress, with frequent abandonment of regional fashions in favor of a quasi-European style, sometimes enforced by legislation and fines. Over much of Mexico, for example, the white trousers and shirt of coarse cotton cloth and the broad-brimmed hat became almost a native "uniform."

Yet pressures toward indigenous acculturation or assimilation failed to achieve integration into "white" society that well-meaning liberals had hoped to secure through education and employment in the modern world of industry and trade. At the end of the nineteenth century, the processes of acculturation had not significantly reduced the size of the indigenous sector in the five countries with the largest native populations: Mexico, Guatemala, Ecuador, Peru, and Bolivia. There were various reasons for this. The economic stagnation and political troubles of the first postrevolutionary decades tended to reinforce the isolation and cultural separateness of their communities. When the Latin American economies revived as a result of the expansion of the export sector, this revival was achieved largely at the expense of indigenous peoples and served mainly to accentuate their poverty and backwardness. Their economic marginality; their almost total exclusion from the political process; the intense exploitation to which they were subjected by white and mestizo landowners, priests, and officials; and the barriers of distrust and hatred that separated them from the white world prevented any thoroughgoing acculturation, much less integration.

Indigenous communities made such concessions to the pressures for assimilation as were necessary but preserved their traditional housing, diet, social organization, and religion, which combined pagan and Christian features. In some regions, the pre-Conquest cults and rituals, including occasional human sacrifice, survived. The existence in a number of countries of large native populations, intensely exploited and branded as inferior by the ruling social Darwinist ideology, constituted a major obstacle to the formation of a national consciousness in those lands. With good reason, pioneer Mexican anthropologist Manuel Gamio wrote

in 1916 that Mexico did not constitute a nation in the European sense but was composed of numerous small nations, differing in speech, economy, social organization, and psychology.

A QUESTION OF COLOR

The wars for independence, by throwing "careers open to talent," enabled a few natives and a larger number of mestizos of humble origins to rise high on the military, political, and social scale. The liberal caudillos Vicente Guerrero and Juan Alvarez in Mexico and such talented leaders as Juan José Flores of Ecuador, Andrés Santa Cruz of Bolivia, and Ramón Castilla of Peru illustrate the ascent of mixed-race people.

The rise of these mestizo or mulatto leaders inspired fears in some members of the creole elite, beginning with Bolívar, who gloomily predicted a race war that would also be a struggle between haves and have-nots. Bolívar revealed his obsessive race prejudice in his description of the valiant and generous Mexican patriot Vicente Guerrero as the "vile abortion of a savage Indian and a fierce African." These fears proved groundless; although some mixed-race leaders, like Guerrero and Alvarez, remained to one degree or another loyal to the humble masses from which they had sprung, the majority were soon co-opted by the creole aristocracy and firmly defended its interests.

On the other hand, creole politicians of the postrevolutionary era had to take account of the new political weight of the mixed-race middle and lower classes, especially the artisan groups. They were exploited politically by white elites who promised to satisfy the aspirations of the masses, promises they failed to fulfill. This happened in Bogotá, where Colombian liberals courted the artisans in their struggle against conservatives, and in Buenos Aires, where Rosas demagogically identified himself with the mixed-race gauchos and urban artisans against the aristocratic liberal *unitarios*.

After mid-century, the growing influence of European racist ideologies, especially Spencerian biological determinism, led to a heightened sensitivity to color. From Mexico to Chile, members of the so-called white elite and even the middle class claimed to be superior to natives and mestizos. Dark skin increasingly became an obstacle to social advancement. Typical of the rampant pseudoscientific racism by the turn of the century was the remark of the Argentine Carlos Bunge, son of a German immigrant, that mestizos and mulattos were "impure, atavistically anti-Christian; they are like the two heads of a fabulous hydra that surrounds, constricts, and strangles with its giant spiral a beautiful, pale virgin, Spanish America."

As a rule, neither liberals nor conservatives were free from the pervasive racism of the time. Carried away by his enthusiasm for "civilization," which he identified with the European bourgeois order and white supremacy, the Argentine liberal Sarmiento proclaimed: "It may appear unjust to exterminate savages, destroy nascent civilizations, conquer peoples who occupy land that is rightly theirs, but thanks to this injustice America, instead of being abandoned to savages who are incapable of progress, is today occupied by the Caucasian race, the most perfect, intelligent, beautiful, and progressive of all the races that inhabit the earth." A handful of Latin American intellectuals dissented from such a view. One was the Chilean Bilbao, who condemned "the great hypocrisy of covering up every crime and outrage with the word *civilization*" and pointedly referred to Sarmiento's war against native peoples and gauchos. Another was the Cuban José Martí, who denounced "the pretext that 'civilization,' the name commonly given to the present state of Europe, has the natural right to seize the land of 'barbarians,' the name given by those who hunger for other people's land to everyone who is not European or of European descent."

Even before the revolutions, black slavery had declined in various parts of Latin America. This occurred in part because of economic developments that made slavery unprofitable and favored manumission or commutation of slavery to tenantry. An even more significant reason, perhaps, was the frequent flight of slaves to remote jungles and mountains, where they formed self-governing communities. In Venezuela, in about 1800, it was

estimated that alongside some eighty-seven thousand slaves there were twenty-four thousand fugitive slaves.

The wars of independence gave a major stimulus to emancipation. Patriot commanders like Bolívar and San Martín and royalist officers often offered slaves freedom in return for military service, and black slaves sometimes formed a majority of the fighting forces on both sides. About a third of San Martín's army in the campaign of the Andes was black. Moreover, the confusion and disorder produced by the fighting often led to a collapse of plantation discipline, easing the flight of slaves and making their recovery difficult if not impossible.

After independence, slavery further declined, partly because of its patent incompatibility with the libertarian ideals proclaimed by the new states but even more as a result of the hostile attitude of Great Britain, which had abolished the slave trade in all its possessions in 1807 and henceforth brought pressure for similar action by all countries still trading in slaves: we have seen that British pressure on Brazil contributed to the crisis of Brazilian slavery and its ultimate demise.

Emancipation came most easily and quickly in countries where slaves were a negligible element in the labor force; thus, Chile, Mexico, and the Federation of Central America (1823–1839) abolished slavery between 1823 and 1829. In other countries, the slave owners fought a tenacious rear-guard action. In Venezuela a very gradual manumission law was adopted in 1821, but not until 1854 was slavery finally abolished. Slavery was abolished in Peru in 1855 by Ramón Castilla. The Spanish Cortes decreed the end of slavery in Puerto Rico in 1873 and in Cuba in 1880, but in Cuba the institution continued in a disguised form (the *patronato*) until 1886, when it was finally abolished.

The record of Latin American slavery in the nineteenth century, it should be noted, does not support the thesis of some historians that cultural and religious factors made Hispanic slavery inherently milder than the North American variety. In its two main centers of Cuba and Brazil, under conditions of mounting demand for Brazilian coffee and Cuban sugar and a critical labor shortage, there is ample evidence of systematic brutality with use of the lash to make slaves work longer and harder. The slaves responded with a resistance that varied from slowdowns to flight to open rebellion—a resistance that contributed to the final demise of the institution.

The Process of Modernization

THE LANDOWNERS

Patriarchal family organization, highly ceremonial conduct, and leisurely lifestyle continued to characterize the landed aristocracy and Latin American elites after independence. The kinship network of the large extended family ruled by a patriarch was further extended by the institution of *compadrazgo*, which established a relationship of patronage and protection on the part of an upper-class godparent toward a lower-status godchild and his or her parents. The lower-class family members in turn were expected to form part of the godparent's following and to be devoted to the godparent's interests.

As in colonial times, great landowners generally resided most of the time in the cities, leaving their estates in the charge of administrators (but it must not be assumed that they neglected to scrutinize account books or were indifferent to considerations of profit and loss). From the same upper class came a small minority of would-be entrepreneurs who challenged the traditional agrarian bias of their society and, in the words of Richard Graham, were "caught up by the idea of capitalism, by the belief in industrialization, and by a faith in work and practicality." Typical of this group was the Brazilian Viscount Mauá, who created a banking and industrial empire between 1850 and 1875 against the opposition of traditionalists. Mauá's empire collapsed, however, partly because the objective conditions for capitalist development in Brazil had not fully matured, partly because of official apathy and even disfavor. The day of the entrepreneur had not yet come; the economic history of Latin America in the nineteenth century is strewn with the wrecks of abortive industrial projects. These fiascos also represented defeats for the capitalist mentality and values.

After mid-century, with the gradual rise of a neocolonial order based on the integration of the Latin American economy into the international capitalist system, the ruling class, although retaining certain precapitalist traits, became more receptive to bourgeois values and ideals. An Argentine writer of the 1880s noted that "the latifundist no longer has that semibarbarous, semifeudal air; he has become a scientific administrator, who alternates between his home on the estate, his Buenos Aires mansion, and his house in Paris." In fact, few estancieros or hacendados became "scientific administrators." They preferred to leave the task of managing their estates to others, but the writer accurately pointed to a process of modernization or Europeanization of elites under way throughout the continent.

The process began right after independence but greatly accelerated after mid-century. Within a decade after independence, marked changes in manners and consumption patterns had occurred. "Fashions alter," wrote Fanny Calderón de la Barca, Scottish-born wife of the Spanish minister to Mexico, who described Mexican upper-class society in the age of Santa Anna in a series of sprightly letters. "The graceful mantilla gradually gives place to the ungraceful bonnet. The old painted coach, moving slowly like a caravan, with Guido's Aurora painted on its gaudy panels, is dismissed for the London-built carriage."

The old yielded much more slowly and grudgingly to the new in drowsy colonial cities like Quito, capital of Ecuador, but yield it did, at least in externals. The U.S. minister to Ecuador in the 1860s, Friedrich Hassaurek, who was harshly critical of Quitonian society and manners, noted that "in spite of the difficulty of transportation, there are about one hundred and twenty pianos in Quito, very indifferently tuned." Another U.S. visitor to Quito in this period, Professor James Orton, observed that "the upper class follow *la mode de*

These fine sketches of Colombian mestizo farmers and upper-class figures effectively make the point that in nineteenth-century Latin America, clothes still made the man. [Carmelo Fernandez, *Mestizo Farmers of Anis, Ocana Province, Colombia*, 1850–59, watercolor, Biblioteca Nacional de Colombia, Bogotá]

Paris, gentlemen adding the classic cloak of Old Spain." He added sourly that "this modern toga fits an Ecuadoran admirably, preventing the arms from doing anything, and covers a multitude of sins, especially pride and poverty."

Under the republic, as in colonial times, dress was an important index of social status. According to Orton, "no gentleman will be seen walking in the streets of Quito under a poncho. Hence citizens are divided into men with ponchos and gentlemen with cloaks." Dress even served to distinguish followers of different political factions or parties. In Buenos Aires under Rosas, the artisans who formed part of

the dictator's mass base were called *gente de chaqueta* (wearers of jackets), as opposed to the aristocratic unitarian liberals, who wore dress coats. In the army of Urquiza, Rosas's conqueror, a gaucho army like that of Rosas, the only Argentine officer dressed as a European was Sarmiento, a strange sight in his frock coat and kepi (a French military cap) among the gauchos with their lances and ponchos. For Sarmiento, writes John Lynch, "it was a matter of principle, a protest against barbarism, against Rosas and the caudillos. . . . 'As long as we do not change the dress of the Argentine soldier,' said Sarmiento, 'we are bound to have caudillos.'"

By the close of the century, European styles of dress had triumphed in such great cities as Mexico City and Buenos Aires and among all except native peoples. Attitudes toward clothes continued to reflect aristocratic values, especially scorn for manual labor; dress still made the man. In Buenos Aires, for example, at the turn of the century, a worker's blouse would bar the entrance of its wearer to a bank or the halls of Congress. As a result, according to James Scobie, "everyone sought to hide the link with manual labor," and even workingmen preferred to wear the traditional coat and tie.

THE IMMIGRANTS

After 1880 there was a massive influx of European immigrants into Argentina, Uruguay, and Brazil and of lesser numbers into such countries as Chile and Mexico. Combined with growing urbanization and continued expansion of the export sector, this helped accelerate the rate of social change. These developments helped create a small, modern industrial working class and swelled the ranks of blue-collar and middle-class white-collar workers.

But aside from that minority of the working class that adopted socialist, anarchist, or syndicalist doctrines, the immigrants posed no threat to the existing social structure or the prevailing aristocratic ideology; instead, many were conquered by that ideology. The foreigners who entered the upper class as a rule already belonged to the educated or managerial class. Movement from the middle class of immigrant origin to the upper class was extremely difficult and rare; for the lower-class immigrant it was almost impossible. A few immigrants made their fortunes by commerce or speculation. Their children or grandchildren took care to camouflage the origins of their wealth and to make it respectable by investing it in land. These nouveaux riches regarded natives and workers with the same contempt as their aristocratic associates.

WOMEN

Independence did not better the status of women. Indeed, their civil status probably worsened as a result of new bourgeois-style law codes that strengthened husbands' control over their wives' property. More than ever, women were relegated to the four walls of their houses and household duties. Church and parents taught women to be submissive, sweetly clinging, to have no wills of their own. Typical of the patriarchal attitudes that prevailed with regard to relations between the sexes was the advice that the Colombian Mariano Ospina Rodríguez gave in an 1864 letter to his daughter Maria on the eve of her marriage to José Mariano Roma y Batres. "Your happiness depends . . . on the sincere and constant practice of these modest virtues: humility, patience, resignation, abnegation, and . . . the proper conduct of the domestic relations that depend on those same Christian virtues." Mariano Ospina went on to caution his daughter: "One of your first cares must be to study your husband's inclinations, habits, and tastes, so that you never contradict them. Never seek to impose your will or make him give up his habits or tastes, no matter how insignificant they may seem; on the contrary, act in such a manner that he may continue them without disturbance. . . . Frequently you will find that you have different tastes and habits; never hesitate for a moment to sacrifice your own tastes and habits in favor of his." The double standard of sexual conduct prevailed; women were taught to deny their sexuality and believe that procreation was the sole end of sexual intercourse. But women's actual conduct did not necessarily conform to the law and ideology. Silvia Arróm has shown, for example, that the restrictions did not deter women in early nineteenth-century Mexico from engaging in extramarital affairs.

Few Latin American women of the elite class, however, strayed so far beyond the bounds of propriety as did Flora Tristán (1803–1844), pioneer feminist and socialist. Daughter of an aristocratic Peruvian landowner and a French mother, she spent most of her life in France, but Peruvian feminists and socialists regard her as one of their own. A woman of striking beauty, she separated early from her husband and became active in French feminist and socialist circles. In 1835 she published a novel, *Méphis*, which proposed the transformation of society on socialist and feminist principles, and in 1840 *Promenades in London*, a description of the monstrous contrasts between wealth and poverty in the English metropolis. In her last book, *The Workers' Union* (1844), she called on "the working men and women of the world" to unite, anticipating by four years Marx's appeal in *The Communist Manifesto*. Tristán clearly identified the gendered layers of exploitation. " The most oppressed male can oppress another human being who is his own wife," she wrote. "Woman is the proletariat of the proletariat." She also presaged theoretical formulations of twentieth-century feminists by arguing that "the liberation of women is the necessary condition for the liberation of men."

The democratic, liberal movements of the first half-century after independence stimulated some developments in favor of women. In Argentina, Sarmiento wrote that "the level of civilization of a people can be judged by the social position of its women"; his educational program envisaged a major role for women as primary-school teachers. In Mexico, the triumph of the Reforma was followed by promulgation of a new school law that called for the establishment of secondary schools for girls and normal schools for the training of women primary-school teachers. In both countries after 1870 there arose small feminist movements, largely composed of schoolteachers, that formed societies, edited journals, and worked for the cultural, economic, and social improvement of women.

Even in a backward slave society like Brazil, there arose a women's rights press, pioneered by Joana Paula Manso de Noronha, who stated in the introductory editorial to *O Jornal das Senhoras* (1852) her intention to work for "social betterment and the moral emancipation of women." In the last decades of the century, with the development of industry, women in increasing numbers entered factories and sweatshops, where they often were paid half of what male workers earned, becoming a source of superprofits for capitalist employers. By 1887, according to the census of Buenos Aires, 39 percent of the paid work force of that city was composed of women.

THE CHURCH

The church, which in some countries had suffered discredit because of the royalist posture of many clergy during the wars of independence, experienced a further decline in influence as a result of increasing contacts with the outside world and a new and relatively tolerant climate of opinion. In country after country, liberals pressed with varying success for restrictions on the church's monopoly over education, marriage, burials, and the like. Because the church invariably aligned itself with the conservative opposition, liberal victories brought reprisals in the form of heavy attacks on its accumulated wealth and privileges.

The colonial principle of monolithic religious unity was early shattered by the need to allow freedom of worship to the prestigious and powerful British merchants. It was, in fact, the reactionary Rosas, who disliked foreigners and brought the Jesuits back to Argentina, who donated the land on which the first Anglican church in Buenos Aires was built. Despite the efforts of some fanatical clergy to incite the populace against foreign heretics, there gradually evolved a system of peaceful coexistence between Catholics and dissenters, based on reciprocal goodwill and tact.

The Inquisition, whose excesses had made it odious even to the faithful, disappeared during the wars of independence. In many countries, however, the civil authorities assumed its right to censor or ban subversive or heretical writings. Occasionally, governments exercised this right. In the 1820s clerical and conservative opposition forced the liberal vice president of Gran Colombia, Francisco de Paula Santander, to authorize the dropping of a textbook by the materialist Jeremy Bentham from law school courses. In Buenos Aires, under Rosas, subversive books and other materials were publicly burned. According to Tulio Halperín-Donghi, however, a reading of the press advertisements of Buenos Aires booksellers suggests that this repression was singularly ineffective. In Santiago in the 1840s, Francisco Bilbao's fiery polemic against Spain and Catholicism was burned by the public hangman. According to Sarmiento, however, it was not the content of

Bilbao's book but its violent, strident tone that caused this reaction; Bilbao, he added, had been justly punished for his clumsiness.

After mid-century, with the enthronement of positivism, which glorified science and rejected theology as an approach to truth, efforts to suppress heretical or anticlerical writings diminished or ended completely in many countries. In general, during the last half of the nineteenth century, there existed in Latin America a relatively free market in ideas—free, that is, as long as these ideas were couched in theoretical terms or referred primarily to other parts of the world and were not directed against an incumbent regime. Governments were often quick to suppress and confiscate newspapers and pamphlets whose contents they considered dangerous to their security, but they remained indifferent to the circulation of books containing the most audacious social theories. By way of example, the Díaz dictatorship in Mexico struck at opposition journalists and newspapers but permitted the free sale and distribution of the writings of Marx and anarchist theoretician Peter Kropotkin.

As a result of the ascendancy of positivism, the church suffered a further decline in influence and power. Conservative victories over liberalism sometimes produced a strong pro-clerical reaction, typified by Gabriel García Moreno, who ruled Ecuador from 1860 to 1875 and carried his fanaticism to the point of dedicating the republic to the Sacred Heart of Jesus. Rafael Núñez, dictator of Colombia from 1880 to 1894, drafted a concordat with the Vatican that restored to the church most of the rights it had enjoyed in colonial times. But such victories failed to arrest the general decline of the church's social and intellectual influence among the literate classes. Anticlericalism became an integral part of the ideology of most Latin American intellectuals and a large proportion of other upper-class and middle-class males, including many who were faithful churchgoers and observed the outward forms and rituals of the church. But church influence continued to be strong among women of all classes, indigenous peoples, and the submerged groups generally.

The Romantic Revolt

The achievement of political independence did not end Latin American cultural dependence on Spain and Portugal. The effort of Latin American writers to find their own means of self-expression, to create national literatures, fused with the larger effort to liquidate the Hispanic colonial heritage in politics, economics, and social life. Thus, Latin American literature was from the first a literature of struggle; the concept of art for art's sake had little meaning for the writers of the first half-century after independence. Many writers were also statesmen and even warriors, alternately using pen and sword in the struggle against tyranny and backwardness. This unity of art and politics is expressed by the famous comment of Ecuadoran essayist and polemicist Juan Montalvo when he learned that the dictator García Moreno had been assassinated; *"Mi pluma lo mató"* ("My pen killed him"). That unity found its most perfect embodiment in the Cuban José Martí, who devoted himself almost from childhood to the struggle against Spanish rule in Cuba and died in 1895 in action against Spanish troops. He also blazed new trails in Latin American poetry and prose.

Latin American writers took the first step toward literary independence by breaking with Hispanic classic traditions and adopting as their models the great French and English poets and novelists of the romantic school. Romanticism, which Sarmiento once defined as "a true literary insurrection, like the political uprising that preceded it," seemed peculiarly appropriate for the achievement of the tasks the revolutionary young writers of Latin America had set themselves.

Victory over classicism, however, did not come without a struggle. In 1842 a famous debate took place in Chile between the Venezuelan Andrés Bello, conservative arbiter of literary taste, and the Argentine Domingo Sarmiento, who upheld a democratic freedom of expression and the superiority of contemporary French literature over all others. Their opposition was by no means absolute, for Bello was not a true reactionary in politics or literature. A distinguished poet, scholar, and educator, he had made major contributions to the development of Hispanic culture. His Spanish grammar, published in 1857, ended the domination of Latin grammatical rules and forms over the language and won acceptance by the Spanish Academy. His poem "The Agriculture of the Torrid Zone," despite its classic form, stimulated the rise of literary Americanism.

But Bello had a conservative's love for order and decorum and regarded himself as a guardian of the purity of the Castilian language. He was shocked when Sarmiento, in a review of a recently published grammar, wrote that "teachers of grammar are useless, for people learn by practical example and general discussion . . . the people are the real creators of a language, while grammarians are only the maintainers of tradition and compilers of dictionaries." Writing in a conservative journal, Bello retorted with praise of linguistic purity and academic standards; it would make as little sense, he wrote, to allow the people to make their own laws as to permit them to dictate the forms of their language. Sarmiento countered with an ardent defense of democracy in language and style. Bello, who disliked polemics, soon withdrew from the fray, but his disciples continued the debate.

Before the controversy ended, Sarmiento had silenced his opponents and converted Bello's chief disciple, José Victorino Lastarria, to his own beliefs. Romanticism soon triumphed everywhere, but Latin American romanticism was not a simple carbon copy of the European original; it bore its own vigorous stamp, displayed its own distinctive character.

ROMANTICISM IN ARGENTINE WRITING

By no coincidence, Esteban Echeverría, the founder of Argentine romanticism, gave the name *Dogma socialista (Socialist Teaching)* to his first important writing, in which *socialism* stood for a nebulous concept of the primacy of the general interest of society over individual interests. "Association, progress, liberty, equality, fraternity: these sum up the great social and humanitarian synthesis; these are the divine symbols of the happy future of nations and of humanity." By the time *Dogma socialista* was published in 1839,

Echeverría had been forced by the Rosas terror to flee from Buenos Aires to Montevideo, where a group of young exiles combined literary activity with plots to overthrow the Rosas regime.

In his short prose masterpiece *The Slaughterhouse* (published posthumously but probably written about 1840), Echeverría rejects one element of European romanticism: its idealized view of the common people. With unsparing realism, he describes the repellent sights and smells of a slaughterhouse that is also a gathering place of the Mazorca, the band of thugs who terrorize Rosas's enemies. The story is also a political allegory: the slaughterhouse, with its butchers in gaucho dress and the black and mulatto women who carry away entrails, empty stomachs and bladders, and wade in blood, is a symbol of Rosas's Argentina, in which barbarous lower-class elements are given a free hand to torture and kill. The climax of the story comes when the butchers intercept a passing unitarian, a young man who wears stylish European dress and has his beard cut in the shape of a U. They tie him up, taunt him, and prepare to beat him. He scornfully replies to their taunts, breaks loose with a supreme effort, and dies from a hemorrhage before their very eyes. In the words of Arturo Torres-Rioseco, "the whole story is a sombre and terrible vignette, against a background of howling curs, bedraggled Negresses, circling vultures— a slaughterhouse that represents the real *matadero* [slaughterhouse] tyranny of Rosas."

A few years after Echeverría's death in 1851, another Argentine émigré, José Marmol, began to publish in serial form in Montevideo the first Argentine novel, *Amalia*. Again, as in *The Slaughterhouse*, literature and political attack fuse. The young unitarian Eduardo Belgrano tries to escape from his federalist pursuers; he takes refuge in the house of the widowed Amalia, and the two fall deeply in love. But the dictator's secret police discover Eduardo's hiding place and kill the lovers. Despite a stilted style and the artificiality of some of the characters, its intensity of feeling and the vivid descriptions of various social types and life in Buenos Aires lend portions of the book a genuine power.

Another exile from Rosas's Argentina, Domingo Sarmiento, illustrated his artistic theories in his formless masterpiece, *Life of Juan Facundo Quiroga: Civilization and Barbarism* (1845). Sarmiento offers a geographical and sociological interpretation of Argentine history, showing how the pampa had molded the character and lifestyle of the gauchos, the mass base of the Rosas dictatorship and the petty caudillos who ruled under him. From this tough, self-reliant breed of men springs the "hero" of Sarmiento's book, the provincial caudillo Facundo. Facundo was master of the Argentine western provinces and Rosas's lieutenant until the greater tyrant, who brooked no rival, had him ambushed and killed.

The ambiguity of Sarmiento's posture toward the gaucho—condemnation tempered by recognition of his admirable qualities—gave way to total defense and vindication of the gaucho and his values in the climactic work of gaucho literature, the epic poem *The Gaucho Martín Fierro* (1872) of José Hernández. Written some thirty years after Sarmiento's *Facundo*, its poignant, nostalgic mood reflects the uprooting of the old patriarchal estancia, the unfenced pampa, and the freedom of the gaucho's life by triumphant bourgeois "civilization" championed by Sarmiento. Hernández, a federalist who opposed Mitre and Sarmiento, supported the revolt of the last untamed gaucho chieftain, General López Jordán, and believed the city, the seat of the central government, was exploiting and strangling the countryside. He portrayed the gaucho as a victim of the forces of "civilization"—judges, recruiting officers, corrupt police. The poem is strongly influenced by the folk songs of the gaucho *payador* (minstrel) and makes restrained but effective use of gaucho dialect.

MEXICAN NATIONAL LITERATURE

The beginnings of a Mexican national literature are linked to the founding in 1836 of the Academy of Letrán, an informal literary circle whose members met to talk of literature or listen to readings of poetry and prose. Here, according to Mexican literary historian González Peña, "was incubated the generation which later filled half a century of the history of Mexican literature." One of its founders, Guillermo Prieto, wrote that "the great and transcendent significance of the Academy was its decided tendency to 'Mexicanize' our literature, emancipating it from all other literatures and giving it a specific character." Prieto also noted that the academy "democratized literary studies, recognizing merit without regard to social position, wealth, or any other considerations." The effort to create a Mexican literature was closely linked to the struggle for political and social reform. Most major Mexican literary figures of the first half-century after independence—such men as Guillermo Prieto, Ignacio Altamirano, and Ignacio Ramírez—took an active part in that struggle.

The most serious effort to create a national Mexican literature was made by Ignacio Altamirano, like his comrade-in-arms Benito Juárez, born of indigenous parents. Believing that Mexican poetry and literature should be as completely original as "are our soil, our mountains, our generation," Altamirano rejected the imitation of foreign models. He attempted to offer an example of such originality in his novel *Clemencia* (1869), set in the period of the French intervention. More successful, because of its fresh, unpretentious descriptions of life in a small Mexican village, was his *Christmas in the Mountains* (1870).

From the Academy of Letrán also issued a school of romantic poetry whose most remarkable creation was the "Prophecy of Cuauhtemoc" (1839) by Ignacio Rodríguez Galván. The poem sounds some major themes of Mexican romanticism: nationalism, anti-Spanish sentiment, and the glorification of pre-Cortesian Mexico. The magnificent coloring of the poem, its authentic romantic agony, the restless alternation in the poet's mind between thoughts of his personal sorrow and the woes of his people, make it, in the words of Menéndez y Pelayo, "the masterpiece of Mexican romanticism."

CHILEAN WRITERS

Chile lagged behind some of the other republics in the development of a national literature, perhaps—as Sarmiento suggested in his duel with Bello—

The Chilean writer Francisco Bilbao was an activist intellectual and radical democrat whose literary works denounced equally slavery, the Catholic church, U.S. expansionism, and racist assaults on indigenous peoples. [Frontispiece for *Obras Completas*, 1897]

because the absolute sway of Bello's classicist doctrines had created inertia, or perhaps because the relative stability of Chilean politics and the upward movement of the Chilean economy deprived its writers of the spur that the more dramatic contrasts of Argentine and Mexican life gave to creative literary activity. But if Chile lacked a Sarmiento or an Echeverría, it produced, in José Victorino Lastarria and Francisco Bilbao, two major writers on sociological topics who in their own way promoted the ideal of Chilean cultural emancipation.

Francisco Bilbao threw a bombshell into staid Santiago society with his essay "The Nature of Chilean Society" (1844), in which he declared: "Slavery, degradation: that is the past. . . . Our past is Spain. Spain is the Middle Ages. The Middle Ages are composed, body and soul, of Catholicism and feudalism." Later (1856), in *America in Danger*, Bilbao issued a powerful cry of warning to Latin America to unite under a regime of freedom and democracy. He sounded a special alarm against the expansionist designs of the United States in Latin America. In *The American Gospel* (1864), he offered much the same message: Latin America must throw off its Hispanic heritage of repression and obscurantism, and it must adopt rationalism rather than Catholicism as its guide if the Disunited States of Latin America were to achieve the place the United States had gained among the nations of the earth.

Lastarria, more moderate and scholarly than Bilbao, caused a lesser stir with his address, "Investigations of the Social Influence of the Conquest and the Colonial System of the Spaniards in Chile" (1844). Despite an occasional factual error, it remains an effective summary of the liberal case against the Spanish colonial regime. Andrés Bello undertook to review it. Conceding the general correctness of Lastarria's criticism of Spanish policy and work in Latin America, he offered a partial defense that stressed the mildness of Spanish rule and its civilizing mission in the New World. Whereas Bilbao was profoundly influenced by French left-wing republican and utopian socialist ideas, Lastarria's thought reflected the more conservative positivist teachings of the French philosopher Auguste Comte. Like Bilbao, however, Lastarria waged a consistent struggle against the backwardness he identified with Spanish civilization, which he felt was "the principal cause of our political and social disasters. . . . We cannot remedy these disasters except by reacting frankly, openly, and energetically against that civilization, in order to free our minds and adapt our country to the new form, democracy."

BRAZILIAN ROMANTIC LITERATURE

A strong nationalism characterized the Brazilian romantic literature of the first decades after independence. In contrast with the Argentine writers of the same period, Brazilian writers expressed their nationalism in glorification of the indigenous past. This reflected differences in the historical experience of the two countries: Brazilian natives had long ceased to pose a serious threat to white society, and mixed-race peoples were common in Brazilian society. The celebration of its indigenous past, moreover, represented an effort to find roots for Brazilian nationalism, roots that could not be found in Portugal or Europe generally.

The greatest romantic poet of the first generation was Antônio Gonçalves Dias, whose ancestry included Portugal, Africa, and indigenous Brazil. Basing himself on a careful study of native languages and culture, Gonçalves Dias conjured up the image of indigenous defeat with extraordinary emotive power in his *American Poems* (1846) and in the narrative poem "The Timbiras" (1857). He also celebrated the beauty of the Brazilian landscape in poems like the nostalgic "Song of Exile" (1846), which opens with the line: "My land has palm trees where the sabiá sings."

This identification with native traditions also found expression in the novels of José de Alencar, whose two most popular novels, *Iracema* (1865) and *The Guarani* (1856), deal with the theme of love between native and Portuguese. Despite the improbable plots and the sentimentality and artificiality of the dialogue and characters, Alencar's limpid, poetic style successfully evokes, somewhat in the manner of James Fenimore Cooper, the drama of the clash of indigenous and European cultures and the grandeur of the Brazilian wilderness, with its majestic rivers, dense forests, and great waterfalls.

After the optimistic nationalism of the first generation of Brazilian romantic poets came the introspection, pessimism, and escapism of the second generation, which perhaps were a reaction to the defeat of the republican revolts of the 1830s and 1840s. In sharp contrast to these second-generation poets, who appeared to be sensitive to their own sufferings and misfortunes only, Antônio de Castro Alves devoted his poetic talent above all to the struggle against slavery. Because of his lofty, impassioned style, he is known as the founder of the *condoreira*, or condor school of poetry. Castro Alves's verses, read at countless abolitionist meetings and frequently published in the abolitionist press, gave a major stimulus to the growth of the abolitionist and republican movements in Brazil.

In 1867, Latin American romanticism, already in decline, produced its finest prose flower, the delicate love story *María* by the Colombian Jorge Isaacs. The story is set in a patriarchal country estate in the Cauca River Valley. Told in a simple, elegiac style, pervaded by a mood of gentle nostalgia, it relates the unfolding of an idyllic romance between a landowner's son and his cousin María. The story ends tragically when María dies during her lover's absence in London.

THE HISTORICAL NOVEL

The romantic movement yielded an abundant harvest of historical novels, most of which dealt with episodes from the Spanish Conquest and the colonial era. Often their authors seemed chiefly concerned with exposing Spanish cruelty and the horrors of the Inquisition. Whether or not faithful to the historical facts, they generally lacked originality, talent, and psychological realism.

In 1872, however, Ricardo Palma began to publish his ironic and sparkling evocations of colonial Lima, *The Peruvian Traditions* (1872–1906). With these "traditions," Palma created a new genre: "a short sketch that was not history, anecdote, or satire, but a distillation of all three." Drawing on his immense knowledge of the colonial period (he was director of the National Library of Peru during the latter part of his life), Palma applied his own formula for the traditions: "a little bit, and quite a little bit of lying, a dose of the truth be it ever so infinitesimal, and a great deal of nicety and gloss in the style." From these elements Palma spun a long succession of cheerfully malicious tales that played on the follies and frailties of viceroys, priests, and highborn ladies as well as lesser folk. Palma's "traditions" evoked the past far more successfully than the typical historical novel of this period.

Literature and Social Change, 1880–1910

By 1880 the romantic movement in Latin American literature had almost completed its tasks and exhausted its creative possibilities. As a result of the economic and political changes that we have surveyed, a new social reality had arisen. The growth of industry, immigration, and urbanization gave a new face to Latin American society. The ruling classes were increasingly acquisitive, arrogant, and philistine; the condition of the masses had not improved and may even have deteriorated. Latin America had become more European; in the process, it had failed to solve some old problems and had acquired some new ones.

In conformity with the specific conditions of their countries and their own backgrounds, writers responded to the new environment in a variety of ways. Generally speaking, romanticism survived as a vital force only in those countries where the old problems had not been solved. (Examples are Ecuador, the scene of a bitter struggle between liberals and conservatives, and Cuba, whose struggle for independence did not reach its climax until the 1890s.)

POETRY AND MODERNISM

In poetry, the most important new phenomenon was the movement called modernism. Because the movement comprises an immense variety of stylistic and ideological tendencies, it is difficult to define. The common feature of modernist poets, however, was their search for new expressive means, for new stylistic forms, in reaction against the outworn language and forms of romanticism. The artistic creed of many modernist poets included rejection of literature as an instrument of social and political struggle. Turning their backs on "a world they never made," the world of shoddy and unstable prosperity ruled, in Rubén Darío's

words, by *el rey burgués* (the bourgeois king), these escapists sought refuge in the ivory tower of art.

Most escapist of all was the prodigiously gifted Nicaraguan Rubén Darío (1867–1916), who defined modernism as the rejection of any explicit message in art; stress on beauty as the highest value (in Darío's poems, the swan is the recurrent symbol of beauty as an end in itself); and the determination to free verse from the tyranny of traditional forms. Not unexpectedly, in view of their conception of the artist as an outcast from bourgeois society, bohemianism, alcohol, and drugs were elements in the lifestyle of many escapist poets, and not a few came to tragically early ends.

In their effort to achieve a renovation of poetry (and prose as well), the modernists drew on a variety of foreign sources (French Parnassianism, impressionism, symbolism; Whitman and Poe; Spain's medieval ballads). But they did not imitate; they appropriated these foreign methods for the creation of poetry and prose that were "entirely new, new in form and vocabulary and subject matter and feeling."

Escapism was a major current of modernism but not the only one. Indeed, before the movement had run its course, some of the leading escapist poets had risen to a new awareness of the continent's social and political problems and the writer's responsibility to the people. Darío himself exemplifies this evolution. If in the first, escapist phase of his poetic career he peopled his verses with satyrs, nymphs, centaurs, peacocks, and swans, in its second phase he gave voice to a powerful public poetry that reflected his new Americanism and concern with political and social themes. Darío's Americanism led him to a search for symbols in both the Spanish and the indigenous past, regarded as the sources of a Latin American culture threatened by the aggressive expansionism of the United States.

Literary critics dispute whether the Cuban José Martí was a precursor of modernism or one of its major figures and creators. Certainly, his spirit was alien to the escapist tendency of many modernist poets. Far from seeking refuge in an ivory tower, he dedicated his life to the struggle for

Cuban independence; Cubans of all political faiths still call him "the Apostle." Martí's faith in humanity and progress reflected his links to Enlightenment thought, to romanticism, and to the optimistic evolutionism of the late nineteenth century. "I have faith," he wrote in the preface to his first book of verse (1882), "in the improvement of man, in the life of the future, in the utility of virtue." In a time of rampant racism, he denounced race prejudice of every kind.

From 1881 to 1895, Martí lived in exile in New York. As a correspondent for various Latin American newspapers, he wrote a vast number of articles in which he subjected political, economic, and cultural developments in the United States to searching analysis. Martí fervently admired Lincoln, Emerson, Mark Twain, and the abolitionist Wendell Phillips but expressed growing concern over the rise of monopolistic and imperialist tendencies. He especially feared and disliked the Republican leader James G. Blaine, whom he regarded as the chief exponent of North American imperialist designs on Latin America. In 1895 he left the United States to launch the Cuban Revolution. On the day before his death on May 19, 1895, while fighting Spanish troops, he set down his fears concerning U.S. policy toward Cuba: "I know the monster because I have lived in its lair, and my sling is that of David."

Martí's artistic ideas reflected his belief in the organic links between art and society, in the social responsibility of the artist. Art should reflect the joys and sorrows of the masses; in that sense it is a collective product. "Poetry is durable when it is the work of all. Those who understand it are as much its authors as those who make it." Simplicity and directness characterize his poems, but he was capable of using vivid, concrete imagery of great symbolic power. The very simplicity of his verse makes it difficult to render into English. In prose he achieved a genuine stylistic revolution. "The style he achieved," writes Pedro Henríquez-Ureña, "was entirely new to the language. He follows no single rhythmical pattern, but constantly varies it . . . he combines words—and meanings—in many unfamiliar ways. The effect is a constantly varied inter-play of light and color. In style, as well as in what lies beyond style and becomes expression, his power of invention was inexhaustible." Darío said of Martí: "He writes more brilliantly than anyone in Spain or America."

The Romantic Revolt Continued: Ecuador and Peru

The fires of romantic revolt continued to burn in two Andean republics where small groups of intellectuals battled the rule of reactionary landowners, generals, and the church. In Ecuador, the writer Juan Montalvo, exiled by the fanatical dictator Gabriel García Moreno, leveled polemical attacks against him and claimed credit for García Moreno's assassination. Unhappy with the new rulers of Ecuador, Montalvo spent much of his life in exile from his native country. His *Seven Essays* (1882), reflecting a somewhat old-fashioned liberalism, propose the regeneration of Latin America through the formation of a model elite. His curious *Chapters That Cervantes Forgot*, a continuation of *Don Quijote*, published posthumously, displays Montalvo's virtuosity in the use of sixteenth-century Castilian and expresses his ideas on a wide variety of topics.

The Peruvian writer Manuel González Prada advanced more radical ideas. A member of that generation of Peruvian youth that witnessed with feelings of profound humiliation the swift defeat of their country in the War of the Pacific, he initiated a new era of social unrest and intellectual ferment in Peru. He launched his "prose thunderbolts" against all that was sacrosanct in Peruvian society: the army, the church, the state, the creole aristocracy. In 1886 he founded a *círculo literario* (literary circle) with the declared aim of creating a nationalistic literature of "propaganda and attack." He proclaimed that "the people must be shown the horror of their degradation and misery; a good autopsy was never made without dissecting the body, and no society can be thoroughly known until its skeleton is laid bare."

González Prada made good his promise of dissecting the Peruvian organism by the ferocity of his attacks. Peru, he wrote, was a great boil: "press down anywhere and the pus comes out." He described the Peruvian Congress as a sewer where all the filth of the country had come together. He called for the creation of a vigorous new literature that would deal with national problems; this required writers to reject tradition and forge a new language: "Archaism implies backwardness: show me an archaic writer and I show you a reactionary thinker."

A woman writer who formed part of González Prada's literary circle and shared many of his progressive ideas, Clorinda Matto de Turner (1854–1909), wrote the first protest novel, *Birds Without a Nest* (1889). Set in an indigenous village of the sierra, the novel denounces the abuses committed against natives by the exploitive trinity of judge, priest, and governor. However, its lesson is that the well-being of Peru's indigenous peoples must depend upon the charity and benevolence of well-disposed upper-class whites. With all its weaknesses, however, *Birds Without a Nest* was the forerunner of a genre.

PART THREE

Latin America Since 1900

Los explotatores, 1926–1927, by Diego Rivera. Mural Universidad Autonoma de Chapingo Chapel, Mexico. Schalkwijk/Art Resource, NY.

U NDERSTANDING THE COMPLEXITY of Latin America's evolution in the twentieth century requires particular attention to the social, political, economic, and cultural histories of each nation and its integration into the international economic order. Throughout this text, we consistently have emphasized both internal and external factors that have shaped and constrained Latin American development. These have included domestic class conflicts; gender, racial, and ethnic struggles; strategic rivalries among the United States and certain European powers; and the shifting demands of international markets.

Internally, the struggle of Latin America's peoples to eliminate neocolonialism and *latifundismo*, the chief obstacles to the achievement of a more just economic and social order, gives meaning and direction to the turbulent flow of modern Latin American history. Viewed in the large, that history, with all its contradictory aspects, its gains and setbacks, appears to form a sequence of stages, each representing a higher level of effort to achieve complete economic and political emancipation. Such an overview inevitably ignores the great differences between the Latin American countries, but it helps make clear the general unity of problems and the common direction of movement of all the Latin American states.

The single most significant external factor in Latin America's twentieth-century development was the emergence of the United States as first a hemispheric and then a global hegemonic power. Its recurrent military, economic, and diplomatic interventions in the region established the international context within which local events unfolded. Changes in the global economy also impacted greatly on Latin America, giving rise to three distinct periods.

1900–1930

From 1900 to 1930, a fierce competition among industrially developed capitalist countries for overseas markets led to recurrent imperialist interventions, chiefly by the United States. U.S. and European statesmen and corporate businessmen continued their competition for privileged access to Latin American markets for strategic raw materials, cheap labor, and direct investment. This typically required alliances with traditional latifundistas and the oligarchical or dictatorial governments that protected their interests. It also reinforced late nineteenth-century trends toward urbanization, the decline of independent peasantries and relatively autonomous indigenous communities, and the parallel growth of new national bourgeoisies and a wage-earning working class in which women would play an increasingly decisive role. Throughout the region, market forces steadily eroded traditional barriers between public and private life and doubly exploited women—as menial, poorly paid wage earners and as unpaid labor in the patriarchal household. Simultaneously, these same market forces assaulted the rural, relatively isolated, provincial hinterland and drove a steady stream of migrant workers first to urban slums in search of industrial employment and then as immigrants to new lands.

Not surprisingly, these new social actors sought out political alliances and often joined social protest movements that challenged the power of traditional oligarchs like Porfirio Díaz in Mexico, Cipriano Castro and Juan Vicente Gómez in Venezuela, and Gerardo Machado in Cuba. By the end of this period, these opposition groups, which formed the core constituency of an emerging regional "populism," had taken advantage of the political space created by intra-elite conflicts and international rivalries to demand the creation of a more modern nation-state that would regulate private sector relations in a way that would promote greater economic independence, social justice, and political stability.

The Mexican Revolution of 1910 and the start of World War I offer two points of departure for this period. The revolution swiftly developed into the first major effort in Latin American history to uproot the system of great estates and peonage and curb foreign control of the area's natural resources. The famous constitution of 1917 spelled out this social content of the revolution. In the leadership struggle between agrarian and bourgeois revolutionaries, the latter emerged victorious and adopted a program that subordinated the interests of peasants and workers to the goals of rapid capitalist development. Nonetheless, the determined struggles of Mexico's lower classes made lasting contributions to the construction of a new, modern state that incorporated popular demands for reform and political participation. Moreover, despite discrepancies between its professed social ideals and its practical political-economic achievements, the revolution also unleashed creative energies in art, literature, and the social sciences that gave Mexico a leading role in the cultural life of Latin America.

World War I seriously disrupted the markets for Latin America's goods and placed difficulties in the way of importing needed manufactured products. As a result, some local capital and labor were diverted from agriculture to manufacturing in an effort to supply these goods. Although the postwar period saw some revival of the export economy, declines in the price levels of Latin America's exports encouraged a further growth of manufacturing. But at the end of this period, industrialization was still almost completely limited to light consumer goods industries.

The United States, which emerged from World War I as the world's principal industrial and financial power, soon replaced Great Britain as the major source of foreign investments in Latin America. Continuing the "big stick" and "dollar diplomacy" policies of their predecessors, Democratic and Republican administrations used armed intervention and economic pressure to expand U.S. control over the Caribbean area. By the end of the period, deep Latin American resentment of these strong-arm tactics had forced Republican policy makers to consider a change in dealing with Latin America.

1930–1970

In rapid succession, the devastation of the Great Depression and World War II brought substantial changes to the nations of Latin America, the world economic order, and the international balance of power. With the emergence of the United States as a global hegemonic power and the absorption of Japanese and European capitalists in the herculean postwar task of national reconstruction, international competition for access to and control over foreign markets in Latin America diminished, at least temporarily. This left traditional latifundista oligarchies vulnerable to the political challenges of popular movements from below and often required military dictatorships to preserve their interests. As an alternative to these dictatorships, newly emerging national industrial bourgeoisies were forced to join with, or even help mobilize, alienated peasants, militant workers, indigenous peoples, racial minorities, and women's groups to create a new national corporative state committed to an ambiguous notion of collective social justice, the specific elements of which each constituent faction defined differently.

Ultimately, in virtually every Latin American country, these struggles produced a populist state dominated by a new national bourgeoisie. This new state, in turn, typically subsumed a plethora of local class, ethnic, racial, and clientelist identities to fashion a single new national identity, the foundation of which was national private sector industrial and agricultural development that would benefit, however unequally, all domestic social sectors. To secure this objective, these populists typically pursued programs that included limited agrarian reform, greater social welfare expenditures, nationalistic and state-centered economic policies like import substitution and export-led industrialization, and an expansion of citizenship rights among workers, women, and racial minorities.

Naturally, from country to country, the scope and intensity of these populist reforms varied proportionately with the level of internal popular political mobilization and its success in shaping the ideology and practice of the new bourgeoisies that occupied the corridors of power. Nonetheless, without substantial foreign competition, these new rulers could afford to raise wages, pay higher taxes, and submit to otherwise expensive state regulations by passing these higher costs on to consumers through a protected price system. Despite the obvious tensions and contradictions that divided the social constituents of Latin American populism, these developmental strategies often produced dynamic economies that expanded the local working class, simultaneously fortified the power of a sometimes fiercely nationalistic bourgeoisie, and consolidated populist political alliances—even as they reinforced the region's capitalist social structures and long-term dependency on external markets.

The Great Depression dramatically exposed the vulnerability of a neocolonial, monocultural economy: the area's foreign markets collapsed, and the prices of its raw materials and foodstuffs fell much more sharply than those of the manufactured goods it had to import. Latin America's unfavorable balance of trade made necessary exchange controls and other trade restrictions that encouraged the growth of industries to produce goods formerly supplied through importation. World War II, which caused a virtual suspension of imports of manufactured goods, gave further stimulus to the movement for Latin American industrialization.

The nationalist temper of the times also found expression in the formation of state enterprises in such fields as oil exploitation and in efforts to nationalize some foreign-owned utilities and natural resources. The most dramatic example of this trend was the seizure of foreign oil properties in Mexico by President Lázaro Cárdenas in 1938. The new nationalist regimes also made concessions to labor in the form of social legislation but maintained tight control over working-class organizations.

By 1945 the movement for Latin American industrialization could point to some successes. Consumer-goods industries had arisen in all the Latin American republics, and some countries had laid the foundations of heavy industry. Industrial development, however, was everywhere hampered by shortages of capital, lack of advanced technology, and the extremely low purchasing power of the masses. Latin American economists often related these deficiencies to such background conditions as latifundismo and its corollary of wretchedly small farms (minifundismo), widespread disease and illiteracy, and absorption of a large part of the area's economic surplus by foreign investors in the form of dividends, interest, and the like. Meanwhile, aside from the massive assault of Lázaro Cárdenas on the Mexican latifundio, little or nothing was done in the way of agrarian reform.

In the same period, the United States, reacting to the diplomatic and economic losses caused by the old-style imperialism and a wave of "anti-Yanqui" feeling throughout the continent, adopted the Good Neighbor Policy, which proclaimed the principle of nonintervention by one American state in the affairs of another. But the policy represented more of a change in form than in content. Washington's friendly, cooperative relations with such tyrannies as those of Anastasio Somoza in Nicaragua, Rafael Trujillo in the Dominican Republic, and Fulgencio Batista in Cuba ensured a continuance of North American hegemony in the Caribbean. For the rest, the immense economic power of the United States in Latin America, exercised through investments and its role as the area's main trading partner, usually sufficed to obtain approval of its policies in most parts of the continent.

In the new postwar era, the Latin American drive to industrialize continued, but after 1950, with the gradual restoration of competition among the industrially developed capitalist countries, the pace of Latin America's advance slowed and the industrialization process underwent a certain deformation. Perceiving the changes taking place in the Latin American society and economy as a result of industrialization and the growth of urban markets, foreign firms began to shift the bulk of their new investments from agricultural and mining activities to manufacturing. This shift allowed them to leap over tariff walls and penetrate the Latin American market. The immensely superior resources of foreign firms and their advanced technology gave them a great advantage over national companies. The result was that many small and middle-sized national companies failed or were swallowed up by subsidiaries of foreign firms.

A favorite device of foreign economic penetration was the mixed company, dominated by foreign capital, with native capitalists reduced to the role of junior partners or directors. The huge sums exported annually by foreign companies in profits, dividends, and other types of income led to a process of "decapitalization" that slowed down the rate of Latin American capital accumulation and industrial growth.

The failure to reform archaic agrarian structures and improve income distribution also held back industrialization. Indeed, the experience of those countries that had the largest growth of capitalism, such as Brazil and Argentina, suggested that the new industrial and financial oligarchies were as fearful of social change, as prone to come to terms with foreign economic interests, as the old landed aristocracy had been. During the 1950s and 1960s ruling elites in various Central and South American countries increasingly abandoned the populistic, more or less democratic, state-centered, nationalistic strategies of industrialization that earlier had achieved considerable success in modernizing the region.

A similar rightward swing took place in Mexico, where the conservative successors of President Lázaro Cárdenas pursued policies favorable to big business and large landowners but neglected the peasantry. As a result, a new corporate hacienda arose and soon dominated Mexican agriculture. By the end of the 1960s, the once-fashionable hope that a dynamic entrepreneurial class could lead Latin America out of dependence and underdevelopment had largely faded.

Meanwhile, the discontent of the masses, sharpened by the "revolution of rising expectations," continued to erupt in revolts: in 1944, a revolution in Guatemala had established a standard of democracy and social justice against which later popular movements there and throughout Latin America would measure themselves; a spontaneous rising of Bolivian peasants and miners in 1952 similarly demanded political and economic democracy; a 1964 democratic upheaval in Brazil forced a moderate president, João Goulart, to radicalize his policies with a call for nationalization of oil and wholesale land reform; popular mobilizations in Peru led to a reformist military coup in 1968; in the same year, the Latin American Bishops' Conference, announcing its intent to exercise "a preferential option for the poor," introduced the idea of Liberation Theology and, in Mexico, a general protest against authoritarian politics led to the massacre of university students and workers in Tlatelolco Square; urban uprisings, led by Montoneros and Tupamaros, spread throughout the industrial cities of Argentina and Uruguay; and in 1970 a popular coalition of Chilean industrial workers, peasants, women, and students freely elected the first avowedly Marxist president in the hemisphere. But the single most important popular mobilization in the region was the armed struggle begun by Fidel Castro and his comrades against the Cuban dictator Batista in July 1953. Their long guerrilla war ended with the victorious entry of the rebel army into Havana on January 1, 1959.

The victory of the Cuban Revolution, soon transformed into a socialist revolution, marked a turning point in Latin American history. The swift, thoroughgoing Cuban agrarian reform and nationalization of foreign enterprises and the revolution's successes in raising living standards offered Latin America a radical alternative to development along capitalist lines.

Washington responded to the Cuban threat to the old order in Latin America with a variety of tactics. In 1961, President John F. Kennedy proclaimed the establishment of the Alliance for Progress, designed to show that Latin America's social revolution, with U.S. help, could be achieved peacefully within the framework of capitalism. But within a few years, the failure of the corruption-ridden program to achieve structural change was apparent.

Simultaneously, the U.S. government sought to undermine and destroy the Castro regime, first by economic blockade and political isolation and then by a CIA-sponsored effort by Cuban exiles to invade Cuba (1961), an effort that met with a swift and humiliating defeat. The Soviet Union stepped up its flow of arms to Cuba, which led to the Cuban missile crisis (1962). For ten days, a jittery world lived under the threat of nuclear war between the United States and the Soviet Union. The crisis ended with a pledge on the part of the United States not to invade Cuba in return for the withdrawal of Soviet missiles from the island.

Forced to retreat in Cuba, the United States, supported by the old and new Latin American elites fearful of radical social change, redoubled its efforts to prevent a spread of the Cuban "contagion" to other parts of the hemisphere. In 1964 a coalition of reactionary Brazilian military, great landowners, and large capitalists overthrew the mildly progressive government of President João Goulart, whose heresies included a modest program of agrarian and electoral reform. It was succeeded by a heavy-handed military dictatorship that offered large incentives to foreign investors and proclaimed its unswerving loyalty to the United States, which responded with generous financial assistance.

But the movement for structural social change and economic independence proved irrepressible. Nationalist military officers sometimes played a leading role in these upheavals, disproving the common assumption that the Latin American officer class is one reactionary group. Thus, the military takeover in Peru in 1968 was quickly followed by nationalization of key foreign-owned industries and land reform that transferred many large estates to peasants and workers, organized into cooperatives. The Peruvian Revolution—a revolution from above, without significant participation by the masses—soon faltered, however, primarily because of its failure to break with the traditional strategy of development based on foreign loans and export expansion.

The struggle against neocolonialism scored a temporary major victory with the triumph of the Marxist presidential candidate Salvador Allende and his Popular Unity coalition in Chile in 1970. In three years, it carried out the nationalization of copper mines and banks and a massive agrarian reform and made significant advances in housing, health, and education. But the Allende government also made serious errors. Most serious was its failure to take preventive action against a coup by reactionary military. In September 1973, military plotters overthrew the Allende government. Published evidence has since confirmed the complicity of the United States in a "destabilization" of his government that prepared the way for the coup.

1970–2003

By the 1970s the global marketplace once again had shifted dramatically. The system of international capitalism would no longer tolerate the relatively modest nationalist constraints imposed on foreign corporations in Latin America by populist governments, much less those of democratically elected socialists like Allende. Japanese and European capitalists, with the assistance of the United States and, ironically, a host of local statist protections, had fully reconstructed their war-ravaged economies and once again looked to overseas markets to acquire strategically valuable raw materials, sell surplus products, invest surplus capital, and exploit cheap labor. Meanwhile, the United States itself had experienced a serious economic decline and international competitive crisis, largely the product of its expensive investment in a military establishment designed to police the postwar new world order.

Peaceful resolution of these resurgent international capitalist rivalries seemed to require that the core capitalist countries have freer access to the world's resources; transnational corporate capitalist elites, through their control of national governments and private organizations like the Trilateral Commission, thereafter sought to promote a neoliberal strategy of economic development that emphasized free trade, an open door for foreign investment, state deregulation of business, privatization, free convertibility of local currencies, tax and spending cuts beneficial to investors and disastrous to workers, balanced federal budgets, currency devaluation, and liquidation of public sector debt. These new "reforms" attacked the material foundation of the old populist political alliances that had supported the region's state-led industrialization during the previous forty years.

Latin America's established industrial, commercial, agricultural, and financial elites, all of whom had profited handsomely from the nationalistic policies promoted by populists, now found themselves squeezed between resurgent, aggressive foreign interests and growing domestic popular mobilizations that continued to demand expansion of social programs that redistributed power and wealth. Always suspicious of the goals and methods of these popular social movements, these elites also were increasingly attracted to the relatively low-cost loans and lucrative business partnerships that transnational corporations and core capitalist governments promised.

Populist redistributive policies, whose success had always depended on a dynamic economic expansion, increasingly came to rely on foreign loans. However, under President Ronald Reagan, the Federal Reserve Board raised the prime rate from 9 percent in 1979 to 21.5 percent in January 1981, "the highest interest rate since the birth of Jesus Christ," according to West German chancellor Helmut Schmidt. Trapped by these high floating interest rates, in just three years (1981–1983) Latin America had to pay out $94.8 billion in interest payments, twice the outlay on interest for the whole of the 1970s. Despite the negative impact of the skyrocketing external debt on redistributive policies and state-sponsored economic growth, Latin American elites quickly became enthusiastic champions of foreign-inspired neoliberal strategies. These appeared first in Brazil in 1964, when General Humberto de Alencar Castelo Branco overthrew the democratically elected government of João Goulart. But they reached their fullest expression in the policies of General Augusto Pinochet, who ousted Allende in 1973. His new, openly terrorist military junta, in league with the most reactionary elements of Chile's ruling class and its foreign allies, not only reversed the progressive policies of the Allende regime but transformed Chile into a concentration camp, torturing and killing thousands of opponents. Its economic policies reduced the living standards of the masses to near-starvation levels.

The destruction of Chilean democracy was part of a general counteroffensive by Latin American cities and their foreign allies to halt and roll back the movement for structural economic and social change. By mid-1976 a block of authoritarian states—Brazil, Chile, Bolivia, Uruguay, and Paraguay—had taken shape. Following the overthrow of the government of President Isabel Perón by a right-wing military in early 1976, they were soon joined by Argentina.

But these regimes, whose policies included the systematic use of torture and assassination against political opponents and the abandonment of the effort to achieve economic independence, offered no solutions for the deep-seated problems of their countries. Their most shining success, the "Brazilian miracle" of steady economic growth since 1964, was made possible by reducing wages to the subsistence level, an annual inflation rate of about 20 percent, and massive foreign investments that hastened the foreign conquest of Brazilian industry. By the mid-1970s the Brazilian miracle was running down; by 1980 Brazil was in a deep recession, with factories closing, unemployment rising, and a balance of payments problem growing steadily worse.

Other military regimes, such as Argentina and Chile, faced similarly grave economic problems. But the crisis was not one of dictatorships alone; it confronted all the countries of the region, whatever their political systems, that pursued a strategy of dependent development based on foreign loans and investments.

At the heart of the continuing debt problem lay the unequal exchange between advanced capitalist countries, such as the United States, and Latin America. A major factor in Latin America's balance of payments deficit is the imbalance between the low prices of Latin American export commodities and the high prices of the manufactured goods and oil that most of the countries in the area must buy. In recent decades falling commodity prices, themselves the product of growing global competition, have greatly aggravated the problem. These unfavorable terms of trade help to explain Latin America's mountainous debt.

Certain changes in the Latin American industrialization programs contributed to the growing gap between its exports and imports. Since about 1955, countries like Brazil and Mexico increasingly stressed production of consumer durables and capital goods that required the importation of expensive machinery, equipment, and technical licenses from countries like the United States. The result was a growing surplus of imports over exports. The transnational companies' takeover of much of the Latin American manufacturing sector contributed to the same result. In the 1970s, for every dollar invested in Latin America, transnationals repatriated approximately $2.20 to their home countries. To cover the deficits in their balance of payments, Latin American countries had to borrow from Western bankers at interest rates that reached double digit figures by 1980.

By 1982, with their national treasuries almost empty of foreign exchange, a number of major Latin American countries faced the prospect of immediate default. This posed immense dangers to the international banking system, for defaults by Mexico and Brazil alone could have wiped out 95 percent of the capital of the nine largest U.S. banks. Defaults were averted by emergency aid packages provided by Western governments and bankers in return for agreements by the recipient governments to carry out "austerity" programs that further reduced the living standards of their workers and peasants. Nevertheless, the problem had been postponed, not resolved. There was no prospect that even a portion of the huge Latin American debt could be repaid without large write-offs and long delays in payment. Meanwhile the flow of new loans by commercial banks sharply declined.

In the later 1980s, despite populist rhetoric about resisting the tyranny of the International Monetary Fund and the World Bank, which monitored debtor countries' compliance with the "structural adjustment programs"—privatization of state companies, an end to subsidies, opening their economies to foreign investment—imposed as a condition for new loans, Latin American governments did little more than demand reschedulings and lower interest payments. Efforts by Latin American governments to reduce their debt burdens under the Brady Plan proposed by the United States included debt-bond swaps, in which foreign debt was exchanged at a discount for new government bonds, and debt-equity swaps, in which foreign debt was exchanged for equity, that is, shares in local companies. None of this made a serious dent in the region's foreign debt, which grew between 1990 and 2000 from $439 billion to $774 billion, an increase of 76 percent. In the same period exports grew from $147 billion to $359 billion. The debt problem was complicated by the fact that Latin America's imports grew more rapidly than its exports, with the area's balance of payments deficit rising from $6.171 billion in 1990 to $45.5 billion in 2001. By 1996, despite paying back $648 billion, the area's foreign debt had risen to $611 billion. Four years later, despite devoting 38.7 percent of its export earnings to service the external debt, Latin America's foreign debt rose to $774 billion. Without an expansion of exports, a new debt crisis was likely to arise. Meanwhile, major Western banks reduced their Latin American exposure by selling parts of the debt at a discount, by setting aside huge reserves to cover possible losses on loans to developing countries, and by the debt-bond swaps and debt-equity swaps mentioned above.

The United States, under successive Presidents Reagan, Bush, and Clinton, used debt as a weapon of coercion and played a leading role in imposing the neoliberal or "structural adjustment" system. The logical next step was the incorporation of Latin America into a U.S.-dominated Western Hemisphere common market that would aid the United States in its competition with Japan and the European Community. A major move toward that goal was approval of the North American Free Trade Agreement with Mexico (1993). By eliminating remaining tariff restrictions and restrictions on investment, the pact ensured that Mexico would become a cheap-labor preserve for U.S industry, with a loss of better-paying jobs in the United States. The opening of Mexico to U.S. low-cost agricultural products, especially corn, had a devastating effect on less efficient and less productive Mexican small farmers. Similar pacts were planned with other Latin American countries, beginning with Chile.

Now, after more than a decade of experience with neoliberal policies that promised to produce economic growth, reduce poverty, and promote development in Latin America, the people of the region appear to have become increasingly disillusioned with it. According to polling by Latinobarómetro, by the end of the 1990s almost half the population described the current economic situation as either bad or very bad; 60 percent said that their parents lived better, more than 20 percent described unemployment as the most important problem in their country, and 40 percent described their economic situation as unstable. Even more important, almost 80 percent complained that income distribution was either unfair or very unfair. Even José Manuel Salazar-Xirinachs, a neoliberal trade adviser to the Organization of American States, reluctantly acknowledged that "liberalization was not the miracle or the magic formula that many expected."

The chapters that follow document in detail the staggering economic and social costs of the neoliberal or structural adjustment program for Latin America. Here we offer a few social indicators of Latin American "underdevelopment": between 1980 and 1990 the number of poor people in the region increased by 66 million and a decade later, despite a slight decline in that rate, a record 211 million people remained mired in poverty. Morever, of these, some 89 million lived in extreme poverty, meaning they did not have the means to acquire a basic family food basket.

To emerge from underdevelopment, Latin American countries will have to learn from the historical successes and failures of reforms undertaken from the 1930s to the 1970s when the region, largely left alone to pursue developmental strategies consistent with its internal social, political, and cultural needs, experienced substantial growth and a significant reduction of social inequality. This will require the reinvigoration of "positive government" and its collaboration with nongovernmental organizations to formulate more autonomous, inward-directed strategies of development based on more rational exploitation of human and natural resources. But such strategies cannot be implemented without profound changes in the relations between Latin America and the developed countries and in Latin America's economic and social structures, particularly in land tenure and use, ownership of industry, and income distribution. Nor can such strategies be implemented without powerful, well-organized social movements that can spearhead a democratic revitalization of Latin American political life that would allow popular interests and wishes to influence the direction of economic and social policy.

In the early 1980s, in fact, it appeared that a democratic revival had begun as the reactionary tide of the 1970s began to recede and in country after country—Argentina, Brazil, Bolivia, Uruguay—discredited military regimes gave way to popularly elected governments. By 1990 the last military or personal dictatorships, in Chile and Paraguay, had fallen. In part because of the long repression of left-wing parties and trade union movements, the emerging democratic movements of the 1980s and 1990s as a rule had a centrist or conservative complexion. Often they cultivated accommodation with the former military rulers, granting pardons or amnesties for their crimes, and thus perpetuated a climate of impunity for human rights abuses. Sometimes, too, the new democratic regimes displayed a broad authoritarian streak, resorting to free use of rule by decree to bypass Congress and other arbitrary measures. Peruvian President Alberto Fujimori's seizure of power by a "self-coup" (*autogolpe*) (1992), the overthrow of populist President Jean-Bertrand Aristide by Haiti's military leaders (1991), the collapse of the Argentine economy and the elected government of Fernando de la Rua, and the aborted coup against Venezuela's populist President Hugo Chávez all revealed the fragility of the recent democratic revival.

None of the new democracies made a clean break with the failed economic policies of the past. This was reflected in their usual acquiescence in payment of the immense foreign debt and their acceptance of the harsh neoliberal remedies prescribed by the International Monetary Fund and the World Bank. In particular, the acceptance by Latin America's old and new democracies of privatization and tariff-reduction policies represented a virtual abandonment of half a century of struggle to achieve independent capitalist development. To date, in countries like Mexico, Brazil, Argentina, Peru, and Bolivia, these policies have resulted in increases in unemployment and declines in living standards, relieved in Peru and Bolivia by a thriving informal or underground economy based on the production of coca and cocaine. The reliance by Peru, Colombia, and Bolivia on the demand for cocaine in the United States and Europe represents a grotesque new kind of Latin American "dependency" on the advanced countries.

But as the new millennium opened, neoliberalism, which demolished Latin America's statist institutions and the old populist, corporative consensus that underwrote them, was unable to fashion a cohesive new social order. In this age of neoliberalism, the fruits of an unregulated marketplace proved incompatible with basic human needs; everywhere the signs of discontent proliferated as the insistent political-economic demands of foreign bankers and Latin America's "new billionaires" conflicted with popular democratic political aspirations. In the Mexican state of Chiapas, the dramatic 1994 revolt led by the self-styled Zapatista Army of National Liberation was called an "armed critique" of Mexico's neoliberal policies.

Electoral opposition to neoliberalism also continued to grow. Brazil's Lula (Luis Inaçio da Silva) of the Socialist Workers' Party won the 2002 presidential elections with the support of women, blacks, and diverse social movements like the Landless People's Movement (MST). In Ecuador, Paraguay, and Bolivia, indigenous people, trade union activists, women's organizations, and student groups mobilized to resist neoliberal austerity programs.

Environmentalists, indigenous groups, and trade union organizations in Venezuela similarly organized to support the election of President Hugo Chávez, running on a populist platform opposed to neoliberalism. He inaugurated new policies that reinforced state control of the Venezuelan oil industry to promote the public interest.

In Argentina, the neoliberalism of Carlos Menem, another politician who betrayed his electoral promises, produced high rates of unemployment and provoked massive street demonstrations. More recently, Argentina's problems spiraled out of control, forcing the nation to close its banks and default on its foreign debt payments. Spreading poverty, popular political protest, and food riots quickly swept Fernando de la Rua, Menem's elected successor, from the presidency in 2001. Everywhere angry Argentines blamed the wealthy bankers and industrialists who had benefited from a decade of neoliberal policies. "We're somewhat less popular than serial killers," one banker candidly confessed to *The Economist.*

In 1997 hundreds of thousands of Haitians participated in a series of national strikes to protest the economic hardships imposed by the IMF, the World Bank, and the U.S. government, which had successfully engineered both a restoration of formal democratic rule and the power of a Haitian elite committed to the principles of neoliberalism. By 2000, however, the impoverished majority managed to mobilize its resources in support of the Family Lavalas Party, which won control of the Haitian Senate, and a year later it reelected former president Jean Bertrand Aristide, a populist priest whose radical ambition was to promote economic growth and an equitable distribution of its fruits in a nation that throughout the twentieth century had suffered from dictatorship, crushing poverty, and brutal political violence.

In Central America, the popular struggle against market deregulation and the sale of state companies to private corporations occurred in the midst of a transition from armed insurrection to peacetime political struggle. A formidable guerrilla offensive in El Salvador forced the right-wing government to the bargaining table, and by 1992 the two sides had reached a U.N.-sponsored agreement that provided for a sweeping reduction and cleansing of the armed forces and full integration of the insurgents into the country's political life. But twelve long years of revolution and counterrevolution had rendered the government utterly dependent on the United States, devastated the nation's economy, and left it vulnerable to foreign pressure to adopt neoliberal policies. The leftist coalition that had championed the armed struggle now had to monitor implementation of the peace accords and simultaneously resist the privatization of the national patrimony. Proclaiming its commitment to a "social market economy" that promised to expand public accessibility to potable water, subsidize the poor, and "make public services accessible to the people," the FMLN triumphed in the March 2000 legislative elections, took control of the National Assembly, and won 77 mayoral races, retaining its control of San Salvador. According to former Guatemalan guerrilla leader Jorge Monsanto, the FMLN's victory portended dramatic changes for the rest of the region because it was "an answer to the neoliberal-style policies applied by [other Central American] governments, which only drag the people down into deeper poverty than they already suffered."

Meanwhile, Guatemala's insurgent forces tried a slightly different tactic. In exchange for an agreement to end the thirty-six-year-old civil war and demobilize guerrilla armies, they negotiated peace accords in 1996 that required popular input into government plans to reconstruct civil society in a way that, in the words of long-time revolutionary activist Alfonso Bauer Paiz, offered "some resistance to current trends of economic globalization and neoliberalism." This agreement, for example, identified poverty as a problem that government policies must address, and it further required a tax system that was "fair, equitable, and on the whole, progressive, in keeping with the constitutional principle of ability to pay"; the agreement also provided a legal basis for indigenous people, who constituted 60 percent of the nation's population, to make claims against the state. Of course, the extent to which these accords were actually enforced would determine the success or failure of this strategy; but this, as elsewhere in Latin America, would depend on popular political mobilization and struggle.

By 2002 the neoliberal model, for over a decade the dominant policy prescription for Latin American development, ceased to offer credible solutions to the region's many social, economic, and political problems. Its patent failure to promote genuine development, raise living standards, and reduce the gigantic Latin American foreign debt gave new life to broad regional and national social and political movements, uniting trade unions, activist women, peasant cooperatives, church groups, and community organizations intent on securing social justice and democratic models of development. Even stalwart neoliberals like Joseph Stiglitz, the World Bank's chief economist, appeared to have lost faith in the developmental potential of the "free movement of capital." As the new millennium opened, Latin America appeared to be perched on the precipice of a new era in its historic struggle for development and social justice.

12

The Mexican Revolution— and After

Democracy

O N THE EVE of the presidential election of 1910, signs of unrest multiplied in Mexico. Peasant risings and workers' strikes became more frequent, and the Mexican Liberal Party (PLM), founded and led by the exiled revolutionary journalist Ricardo Flores Magón, intensified its conspiratorial activities. Drawn by the PLM's programmatic commitment to "equality between the sexes" and repelled by miserably low wages, abusive working conditions, and legal discrimination, women like Juana Gutiérrez de Mendoza and Dolores Jiménez became influential activists, organizers, and propagandists in this growing opposition to Porfirio Díaz's dictatorial regime. Divisions soon appeared within the oligarchy. Bernardo Reyes, a foe of the Científicos and the powerful governor of Nuevo León whose rule combined iron-fisted repression with reformist rhetoric, announced his candidacy for the post of vice president. Reyes saw this office as a stepping-stone to the presidency when Díaz, who was eighty years old in 1910, died or retired.

In an unusual atmosphere of political ferment and debate, there appeared a tract for the times, *The Great National Problems* (1909) by the lawyer Andrés Molina Enríquez. Financed by Reyes, the book combined the customary eulogies of Díaz with incisive criticism of his political system and especially of his agrarian policy. Its denunciation of the latifundio and appeal for land reform anticipated the radical slogans of the coming revolution.

Díaz had contributed to this ferment by announcing in 1908 that Mexico was now ready for democracy and that he would welcome the emergence of an opposition party. Francisco Madero, a Coahuila hacendado whose extensive family interests included cattle ranches, wheat farms, vineyards, textile factories, and mines, took Díaz at his word. A member of the elite, Madero was no revolutionary, but he feared that continuance of the existing political order would inevitably breed social revolution. Madero made clear, however, that by democracy he meant control by an elite. "The ignorant public," he wrote, "should take no direct part in determining who should be the candidate for public office."

Madero criticized Díaz's social policies—his genocidal Indian wars and violent repression of strikes—as counterproductive; in place of those brutal tactics, he proposed a policy of modest concessions to peasants and workers that would reduce mounting tensions and check the growth of radical ideas. Madero regarded democracy as an instrument of social control that would promote the acceptance of capitalism through the grant of limited political and social reforms, with a large stress on education.

In December 1909, Madero began to tour the country, making speeches in which he explained his reform program. In April 1910 an opposition anti-reelectionist party was formed and announced Madero as its candidate for president.

282

Díaz at first refused to take Madero seriously but soon became alarmed by his growing popularity. In early June he had Madero arrested and charged with preparing an armed insurrection; arrests of many of his supporters followed. On June 21 the election was held, and it was announced that Díaz and his hand-picked vice-presidential candidate, Ramón Corral, had been elected by an almost unanimous vote.

After the election, Díaz no longer considered Madero dangerous and allowed him to be released on bail. Convinced that the dictator could not be removed by peaceful means, Madero also feared the demands of radical women, peasants, and workers; in September 1910, for example, Dolores Jiménez, a working-class leader of the feminist Daughters of Cuauhtémoc, advocated women's empowerment in their "economic, physical, intellectual, and moral struggles." Caught between the Scylla of reaction and the Charybdis of lower-class revolution, Madero opted for armed struggle.

On October 7 he fled across the border to Texas and from there announced the Plan of San Luis Potosí. Declaring the recent elections null and void, Madero assumed the title of provisional president of Mexico but promised to hold free elections as soon as conditions permitted. The plan made a vague reference to the return of usurped peasant lands, but most of its articles dealt with political reforms. That Madero was allowed to organize the revolution on U.S. soil with little interference by the authorities suggests the U.S. government's displeasure with Díaz. Fearing that North American domination of investments in Mexico threatened Mexican economic and political independence, the dictator had recently favored British over North American capitalists in the grant of concessions and had given other indications of an anti-U.S. attitude. The administration of President Taft evidently hoped that Madero would display a more positive attitude toward U.S. interests.

The Great Revolution, 1910–1920

The revolution got off to a shaky start when Madero, having crossed back into Mexico, found only twenty-five supporters waiting for him and hurriedly returned to Texas. But it soon gathered momentum as two major movements of peasant revolt responded to his call. In the huge northern border state of Chihuahua, where peons and small farmers suffered under the iron rule of the Terrazas-Creel clan, masters of a vast landed empire, the rising began under the leadership of Pascual Orozco, a mule driver, and Pancho Villa, a bandit with a reputation for taking from the rich to give to the poor. By the end of 1910, guerrilla armies had seized control of most of the state from federal troops.

Another seat of rebellion was the mountainous southern state of Morelos, where Indian communities had long waged a losing struggle against encroaching sugar haciendas. Here the mestizo insurgent leader Emiliano Zapata, attracted by the promise of land reform in the Plan of San Luis Potosí, proclaimed his loyalty to Madero.

Meanwhile, in March 1911, former PLM leaders Camilo Arriaga and Dolores Jiménez, now *maderistas*, organized Mexico City's Complot de Tacubaya, an urban revolt against Díaz that advocated a revolutionary social agenda including protection of indigenous rights, agrarian reform, an eight-hour workday, equal pay for equal work, and equal access to education. In the political context of a countryside in arms, the Tacubaya uprising, though prematurely betrayed and suppressed, nonetheless successfully undermined Díaz's confidence in his ability to rule and led directly to a decision to seek compromise with Madero a month later.

In May 1911, moreover, the Zapatistas won two decisive victories. Rather than face an invasion of the poorly defended capital by Zapata's dreaded agrarian rebels, Díaz and his advisers decided to reach an agreement with Madero. Disregarding urgent warnings by the left wing of the revolutionary movement against compromises with the Díaz regime, Madero signed the Treaty of Ciudad Juárez on May 21, which provided for the removal of Díaz but left intact all existing institutions. It was completely silent on the subject of social change. On May 25 the aged dictator resigned the presidency; a few days later he left for Europe. Francisco León de la Barra, the Mexican ambassador to the United States, assumed the interim presidency.

The *soldaderas*, women who joined their lovers or husbands and often fought at their side, made their own contribution to the victory of the Mexican Revolution. [Library of Congress]

On June 7, 1911, Madero entered Mexico City in triumph, but the rejoicing of the crowds who thronged into the streets to greet the "apostle of democracy" was premature. The provisional president was closely tied to the old regime and had no sympathy with the revolution. The *Porfirista* aristocracy and its allies had not given up hope of regaining power; they regarded the compromise that made León de la Barra provisional president a tactical retreat, a means of gaining time to allow the revolutionary wave to subside so they could prepare a counterblow. Under the interim president, the huge Díaz bureaucracy remained largely intact. The reactionary officer corps remained in command of the federal army and burned for revenge over the revolutionary peasant armies that had defeated it.

Social conditions throughout the country remained largely unchanged, and the provisional government sought a total restoration of the status quo. Efforts were made to disband the revolutionary troops, and León de la Barra sent federal forces into Morelos to initiate hostilities against the Zapatistas, who had begun to confiscate large estates and distribute land to the villages. Madero's ineffective efforts to halt the fighting and mediate between Zapata and León de la Barra only deepened the reactionaries' hatred for the visionary meddler who had unleashed anarchy in Mexico. But the revolutionary wave was still running strong, and reaction had to bide its time. In October 1911, Madero and his running mate, José María Pino Suárez, were elected president and vice president by overwhelming majorities. Despite numerous public protests and petitions, led by leaders like Juana Gutiérrez de Mendoza and her *Amigas del Pueblo* (AP), feminists failed to secure voting rights, but their political agitation in support of the "apostle of democracy" was undiminished.

MADERO'S PRESIDENCY: INADEQUACY AND REVOLT

It soon became evident that the "apostle" had no fundamental solutions for Mexico's grave social and economic problems. Even on the political plane, Madero's thought was far from advanced. His conception of democracy was a formal democracy that would give the masses the illusion of power and participation in political life but would vest all decision making in the hands of an elite.

In regard to economic and social democracy, his vision was even more limited. Madero allowed workers to organize trade unions and to strike and permitted a national workers' center, the *Casa del Obrero Mundial*, to be formed in Mexico City. But his answer to the agrarian problem was a totally inadequate program of purchase of land from large landowners and recovery of national land for distribution among landless peasants. In fact, Madero, who believed that only large landholdings would permit Mexican agriculture to modernize, was totally opposed to land reform at the expense of the haciendas. Madero's retreat on the land issue led to a break with his most faithful ally, Emiliano Zapata. Zapata urged Madero to carry out the agrarian provisions of the Plan of San Luis Potosí. Madero refused, arguing that the treaties that set up the interim government of León de la Barra obliged him to accept the legality of the legal and administrative decisions of the Díaz regime. Madero also demanded the total surrender and disarmament of Zapata's peasant troops.

Convinced that Madero did not intend to carry out his pledges to restore land to the villages, Zapata announced his own program on November 28, 1911. The Plan of Ayala proclaimed that "the lands, woods, and waters usurped by the hacendados, Científicos, or caciques through tyranny and venal justice" would be returned to their owners, and Zapata began to put the plan into effect. The Zapatista movement soon spread to other states in central and southern Mexico. Historian John Womack paints a vivid portrait of these peasant armies,

one of which, composed of "the widows, wives, daughters, and sisters of rebels," was commanded by a woman warrior known as "La China." Clad "in rags, some in plundered finery, wearing silk stockings and dresses, sandals, straw hats, and gun belts," these women so terrorized federales and hacendados in the region that even veteran Zapatista commanders "treated La China with respect." Madero sent a series of generals against Zapata and his allies but failed to crush the revolt.

Madero's failure to carry out a genuine agrarian reform lost him the trust and support of the revolutionary peasantry without mollifying the reactionaries, who resented his modest concessions to labor and his efforts to transform Mexico into a bourgeois democracy with freedom of speech and press and the rule of law. They also feared that under pressure from the peasantry and under the influence of urban middle-class reformers like Luis Cabrera, a strong advocate of land reform, Madero might move farther to the left.

The aristocracy, its possessions and influence almost intact, dreamed of restoring the lost paradise of Don Porfirio, when peasants, workers, and natives knew their place. Almost from the day that Madero took office in November 1911, therefore, counterrevolutionary revolts sprouted in various parts of Mexico. Most serious was a revolt in the north led by Pascual Orozco, who was encouraged and bribed by conservative elements in Chihuahua, especially the Terrazas-Creel clan. Federal troops under General Victoriano Huerta crushed the Orozco revolt in a series of battles, but Huerta's victory, joined with the alienation of Zapata and other of Madero's old revolutionary allies, increased Madero's dependence on an officer corps whose loyalty to his cause was highly dubious.

Abortive revolts followed one after another throughout the rest of 1912. The danger to Madero increased as it became clear that he had lost the support of the United States. Although Madero had made it clear that he favored foreign investments and guaranteed their security, he refused to show special favors to U.S. capitalists and warned foreign investors that the crony system that had operated under Díaz was dead. This

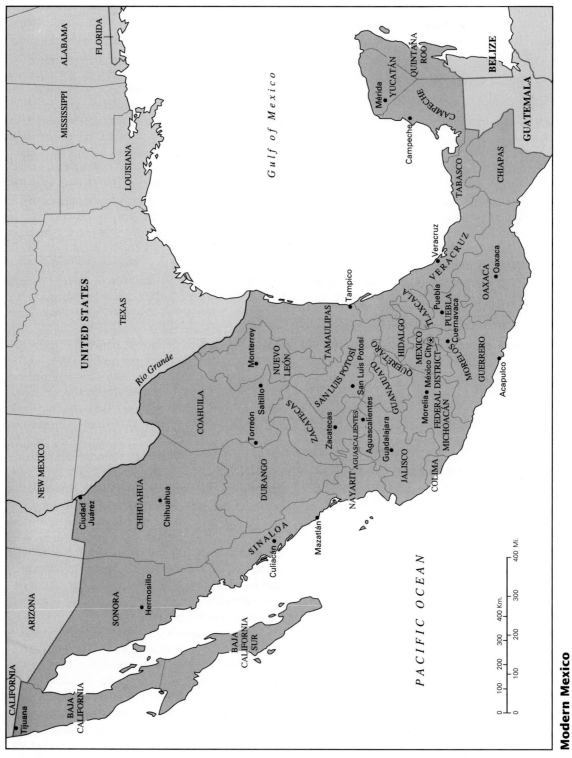

Modern Mexico

independent spirit, plus Madero's legalization of trade unions and strikes and his inability to cope with the peasant revolution and establish stability, alienated the United States, whose foreign policy, originally favorable to Madero, turned against him.

U.S. Ambassador Henry Lane Wilson became increasingly hostile to Madero. In February 1912 a hundred thousand U.S. troops were stationed along the border, and throughout the year Wilson made vehement threats of intervention if the Madero government failed to protect U.S. lives and property.

Meanwhile, preparations for a coup d'état were under way in the capital. Implicated in the conspiracy were General Huerta, the recent conqueror of Orozco; General Miguel Mondragón, former chief of artillery under Díaz; Bernardo and Rodolfo Reyes, father and son; and Félix Díaz, nephew of the old dictator.

The blow fell on February 9, 1913, when the military garrison at Tacubaya "pronounced" against Madero and marched on the National Palace. Meanwhile, the U.S. ambassador, in complete sympathy with the counterrevolutionary revolt, was secretly negotiating with Huerta and Díaz. On February 12, Wilson sent Madero a sharp protest against the conduct of military operations in Mexico City because they threatened U.S. life and property. At his urging, the British, German, and Spanish representatives sent similar demands. As the crisis moved toward a climax, Wilson became feverishly active. On February 14 he demanded that the Mexican government begin negotiations with the other warring parties; otherwise, U.S. marines would be landed in Mexican ports. The same day, Wilson invited other foreign diplomats to a conference at which it was agreed to force Madero to resign. A message to that effect was sent to Madero from the diplomatic corps. Madero firmly rejected the demand. He would rather die, he said, than allow foreign intervention.

HUERTA'S DICTATORSHIP

Ambassador Wilson's activities were clearly coordinated with those of the conspirators and encouraged Huerta to arrest the president and other members of his government. A dispute between Huerta and Díaz over who should head the new regime was settled through Wilson's mediation. At a meeting at the U.S. embassy, agreement was reached that Huerta should head a provisional government, with Díaz to succeed him as soon as an election could be held. Wilson then called a meeting of foreign diplomats to whom he introduced Huerta as the "savior of Mexico."

To give some semblance of legality to his usurpation, Huerta obtained the "voluntary" resignations of Madero and Pino Suárez in return for the promise that they would then be free to leave Mexico. An intimidated Congress accepted the resignations and recognized Huerta as provisional president, almost without dissent. There remained the question of what should be done with Madero. Asked by Huerta for his advice, the U.S. ambassador replied that he should do "what was best for the country." Despite urgent requests by other members of the diplomatic corps and Madero's wife that he intercede to save Madero's life, Wilson refused. On the evening of February 22, Madero and Pino Suárez were murdered as they were being transferred from the National Palace to the penitentiary; the official explanation was that they had been killed during an attempt by armed men to release them. The two assassins, officers of the rurales, were quickly advanced in rank, one being made a general.

Huerta's seizure of power, which was greeted with rejoicing by the landed aristocracy, the big capitalists, and the church, was an effort to set the Mexican clock back, to restore the Díaz system of personal dictatorship. The promise to Félix Díaz that he would succeed Huerta as president was soon broken, and Díaz was shunted aside by sending him off on a diplomatic mission to Japan.

Hoping to broaden the social base of his dictatorship and conceal its reactionary character as long as possible, Huerta for a time continued Madero's labor policies, but as the terrorist nature of the regime became more apparent and labor more and more allied itself with the anti-Huerta movement, he proceeded to arrest its leaders and eventually closed down the Casa del Obrero Mundial.

THE OPPOSITION: ZAPATA, VILLA, CARRANZA, AND OBREGÓN

Huerta had counted on a quick victory over the peasant revolutionaries of the south and favorable reception of his coup d'état by conservative economic and political interests in the north. However, the revolutionary wave, still running strong, rose even higher in reaction to Madero's brutal murder and the imposition of Huerta's terrorist regime. Zapata intensified his struggle against local great landowners, Huerta's allies, and federal troops. In the northern border states of Sonora, Chihuahua, and Coahuila, meanwhile, an anti-Huerta coalition of disparate social groups—liberal hacendados, middle classes, miners, industrial workers, vaqueros, and peasants—began to take form.

By forcing Huerta to commit a considerable part of his troops to the campaign in the south, Zapata assured the success of the revolutionary movement that sprang up anew in the north. Pancho Villa assumed leadership of the Constitutionalists, as Huerta's northern opponents called themselves. Enjoying an immense popularity among the state's vaqueros, he soon recruited an army of three thousand men who soon controlled almost all Chihuahua, including Ciudad Juárez and Chihuahua City.

Master of Chihuahua, Villa imposed a revolutionary new order on the state. He employed his soldiers as a civil militia and administrative staff to restore normal life. Villa ordered a reduction of meat prices and distributed money, clothing, and other goods to the poor. Education was a passion with the almost illiterate Villa; according to the U.S. correspondent John Reed, who accompanied him, Villa established some fifty new schools in Chihuahua City.

Clearly, Villa's social policies were more radical than those implemented by the Constitutionalist leaders in the neighboring states of Sonora and Coahuila. In December 1913 he announced the expropriation without compensation of the holdings of the pro-Huerta oligarchy in Chihuahua. His agrarian program, however, differed in significant ways from that of Zapata. Whereas in the area ruled by Zapata confiscated estates were promptly distributed among the peasants, Villa's decree provided that they should remain under state control until the victory of the revolution. The revenues from these estates would be used to finance the revolutionary struggle and support the widows and orphans of the revolutionary soldiers. Once victory had been achieved, they were to be used to pay pensions to such widows and orphans, to compensate veterans of the revolution, to restore village lands that had been usurped by the hacendados, and to pay taxes left unpaid by the hacendados.

Meanwhile Villa turned control of some confiscated haciendas over to his lieutenants; the rest were administered by the state. Cattle were sold in the United States to secure arms and ammunition for Villa's army, and meat was distributed on a large scale to the urban unemployed, to public institutions like orphanages and children's homes, and for sale in the markets. The differences between the agrarian programs of Villa and Zapata may be explained in part by the fact that the economy of the north was based not on agriculture but on cattle raising, which required large economic units. These units had to be administered by the state or on a cooperative basis. In addition, the percentage of peasants in the population was much smaller in the north, and the problem of land hunger much less acute.

In the neighboring state of Coahuila, meanwhile, the elderly Venustiano Carranza, a great landowner who had once served Díaz but joined Madero in 1911 and was appointed by him governor of the state, raised the standard of revolt against Huerta. On March 26, 1913, he announced his Plan of Guadalupe, which called for the overthrow of the dictator and the restoration of constitutional government but did not mention social reforms. Carranza assumed the title of first chief of the Constitutionalist Army. By April he commanded some forty thousand men. He was soon joined by Villa, who placed himself under Carranza's command but retained much autonomy in Chihuahua; Villa's troops were renamed the Northern Division. Carranza gained another important recruit in the young ranchero Álvaro Obregón, who led the anti-Huerta forces in the state of Sonora. Named commander of the Army of the Northwest, he soon proved his large military gifts by driving the federal troops out of almost all Sonora; in April the state legislature recognized Carranza as first chief of the revolution.

Meanwhile, within Mexico City, Huerta also faced clandestine opposition, led by prominent intellectuals like José Vasconcelos and Martín Luís Guzmán. Just as troublesome, however, was the public resistance of the feminist Loyalty Club, headed by María Árias Bernal, which protested the regime's brutality and organized a public demonstration at the site of Madero's tomb.

INTERVENTION BY THE UNITED STATES

By the beginning of 1914, the Constitutionalist revolt had assumed significant proportions and Huerta's fall appeared inevitable. Meanwhile, in March 1913, Woodrow Wilson had succeeded Taft as president of the United States. Alone among the great powers, Wilson's government refused to recognize the Huerta regime, although it continued to embargo revolutionary arms purchases while permitting U.S. arms sales to Huerta to consolidate his rule. Wilson justified his nonrecognition policy with moralistic rhetoric, refusing to recognize a government that had come to power illegally. More important, he was convinced that Huerta could not provide the stable political climate U.S. interests required in Mexico. Noting Huerta's strong support among European governments, Wilson also suspected that Huerta had cut a deal to grant British and German investors privileged access to Mexican markets at the expense of U.S. business. In the first six months of his regime, Huerta clearly favored British interests, thereby solidifying his support in London and further alienating Washington.

Wilson's concern with a suitable political climate for U.S. investments emerged from a note sent to British officials in November 1913, in which he assured those officials that his U.S. government "intends not merely to force Huerta from power, but also to exert every influence it can exert to secure Mexico a better government under which all contracts and business concessions will be safer than they have been."

Shortly thereafter, growing tensions between England and Germany, ultimately leading to World War I, dramatically affected the Huerta regime's security and international backing. Both nations now openly courted the United States and began to distance themselves from Huerta. By yielding to a British request for uniform rates on all goods shipped through the nearly completed Panama Canal, Wilson obtained an end of British support for Huerta in early 1914. As a result, Huerta's financial position became increasingly difficult. Seeking to avert a catastrophe, he suspended payment on the interest on the national debt for six months, but that extraordinary measure only increased Huerta's difficulties. Foreign creditors began to demand the seizure of Mexican customhouses, and some even clamored for immediate intervention. By February 1914, Wilson decided force must be used. After receiving assurances from Carranza's agent in Washington that the Constitutionalists would respect foreign property rights, including "just and equitable concessions," Wilson lifted the existing embargo on arms shipments to the Carranza forces.

Wilson found a pretext for intervention when a party of U.S. sailors from the cruiser *Dolphin* landed in a restricted area of Tampico and were arrested. They were almost immediately released with an apology, but the commander of the *Dolphin*, under orders from Washington, demanded a formal disavowal of the action, severe punishment for the responsible Mexican officer, and a twenty-one-gun salute to the U.S. flag. For Huerta to grant these demands might have meant political suicide, and he refused.

President Wilson now sent a fleet into the Gulf of Mexico, and on April 21, 1914, learning that a German merchant ship was bound for Veracruz with munitions, he ordered the seizure of the city. When Mexican batteries at the fortress of San Juan de Ulua attempted to prevent a landing, they were silenced by answering fire from the U.S. ships. Huerta's forces evacuated Veracruz the same day, but the local population and cadets of the naval academy continued a courageous resistance until April 27, when U.S. troops occupied Veracruz, setting off a wave of anti-Yankee sentiment in Mexico and a number of Latin American countries. Meanwhile Carranza, whom Wilson had hoped to control, bitterly denounced the U.S. action and demanded the immediate evacuation of Veracruz.

The rising storm of Mexican anger and Carranza's defiant stand placed Wilson in a quandary. He sought a way out of his difficult situation by obtaining an offer from Argentina, Brazil, and Chile to mediate the dispute between the United States and Mexico. A conference was convened at Niagara Falls, Canada, in May 1914. Wilson hoped to do more than reduce tensions; he intended to use the mediation as a means of eliminating Huerta and establishing a new provisional Mexican government that he could control. The U.S. candidate to head this provisional government was the moderate Carranza, because the revolutionary peasant leaders Zapata and Villa were obviously unacceptable. But Carranza would not rise to Wilson's bait. The conservative but fiercely nationalist first chief sent representatives to the Niagara Falls conference but did not give them official status and refused the conference's mediation. Mexico, his representatives informed the U.S. delegates, would settle its own problems without interference from foreign sources.

By this time the fall of the Huerta regime was imminent. With the northern tier of states securely in Constitutionalist hands, Pancho Villa's Northern Division drove south to Zacatecas. Meanwhile, Obregón's Army of the Northwest seized the important railroad and industrial center of Guadalajara. Recognizing that his situation had become hopeless, Huerta took flight for Europe on July 15. On August 15, Obregón's troops entered Mexico City.

Huerta's fall deprived the United States of any pretext for continuing its armed intervention, but Wilson delayed the evacuation of Veracruz as long as possible in the hope of securing commitments from Carranza that would have effectively prevented any basic changes in Mexico's social and economic structure. Despite hints that "fatal consequences" might follow, Carranza resolutely rejected these demands and continued to insist on the end of the military intervention. U.S. troops finally evacuated Veracruz on November 23, 1914.

FIGHTING AMONG THE VICTORS

As the day of complete victory drew near, differences emerged within the Constitutionalist camp, especially between Carranza and Villa. There were personal factors, such as Carranza's jealousy of Villa as a potential rival, but more important was Carranza's failure to define his position on such fundamental issues as the agrarian question, the role of the church, and the new political order. Villa proposed to incorporate in an agreement a clause drawn up by one of his intellectuals that defined "the present conflict as a struggle of the poor against the abuses of the powerful" and committed the Constitutionalists "to implant a democratic regime . . . to secure the well-being of the workers; to emancipate the peasants economically, making an equitable distribution of lands or whatever else is needed to solve the agrarian problem." Under pressure from his generals, who recognized the potential dangers of an open break with Villa, Carranza permitted his representatives to sign the agreement containing this radical clause, which he personally found unacceptable. Villa, however, continued to distrust Carranza, and his distrust was confirmed by various of Carranza's actions, notably his unilateral occupation of the capital.

Relations also deteriorated between Carranza and Zapata, who had waged war against Huerta independently and refused to recognize Carranza's leadership; a Zapatista manifesto proclaimed that the Plan of Ayala must prevail and all adherents of the old regime must be removed.

In October 1914 a convention of revolutionary leaders and their delegates met at Aguascalientes to settle the conflict between Carranza and Villa. At the insistence of the *Villistas*, Zapata was invited to attend, and presently a delegation from "the Liberating Army of the South" arrived. The convention endorsed the Plan of Ayala, assumed supreme authority, called for the resignation of Carranza as first chief, and appointed General Eulalio Gutiérrez provisional president of the nation. Gutiérrez was a compromise candidate pushed by delegates equally opposed to Carranza and Villa. Because Aguascalientes swarmed with Villa's troops, Gutiérrez had no choice but to name

In early December 1914, Pancho Villa (*on throne*) met with Emiliano Zapata (*center right, with sombrero*) in Mexico City, where both attended the installation of a new president. Earlier, Villa and Zapata had reached agreement on a course of action for the revolution, but the arrangement soon fell apart. [Culver Pictures, Inc.]

Villa commander in chief of the Conventionist Army, as the Northern Division now came to be called.

But Carranza refused to accept the decisions of the Aguascalientes convention, claiming it had no authority to depose him. When he failed to meet the deadline for his resignation, November 10, the armies of Zapata and Villa advanced on the capital and occupied it. Carranza retreated with his depleted forces to Veracruz, which had been evacuated by the Americans shortly before. According to historian John Hart, although the United States remained suspicious of Carranza's nationalism, its decision to withdraw from Veracruz in favor of the Constitutionalists reflected U.S. fears of the revolutionary convention's radical threat to U.S. eco-

nomic interests, especially investments in Mexican oil production. Veracruz became a safehouse for *Carrancista* forces led by Obregón, who had remained loyal to Carranza and rebuilt his army with the aid of arms and munitions stockpiled in Veracruz during the U.S. occupation.

On December 4, Villa and Zapata held their first meeting and came to full agreement. But although the peasant revolutionaries controlled the capital and much of the country, they could not consolidate their successes. Unskilled in politics, they entrusted state power to the unreliable provisional president, Gutiérrez, a former general in Carranza's army, who sabotaged the Conventionist war effort and opened secret negotiations with Obregón. Meanwhile a conservative wing in the convention strongly opposed land reform, expropriation of foreign properties, and other radical social changes. Villa's sympathies on land reform were with the radicals, but he avoided taking sides in the dispute, probably because he believed that unity was necessary to gain both a rapid military victory and recognition by the United States, which he also regarded as essential to his final triumph. For these and other reasons the convention proved unable to forge a clear national program of socioeconomic reforms that could unite the interests of the peasantry, industrial workers, and the middle class. His later attempts to broaden his program to attract labor, the middle class, and even national capitalists were too little and too late.

The Constitutionalists did not make the same mistake. At the insistence of Obregón and intellectuals like Luis Cabrera, who were aware of the need for broadening the social base of the Constitutionalist movement, the conservative Carranza adopted a program of social reforms designed to win the support of peasants and workers. In December 1914, during the darkest days of the Constitutionalist cause, Carranza issued his "Adiciones" to the Plan of Guadalupe, promising agrarian reform and improved conditions for industrial workers. Other decrees followed: on January 6, 1915, he restored lands usurped from the villages and expropriated additional needed land from haciendas. (Simultaneously, Carranza secretly promised the hacendados that he would return the haciendas that had been confiscated by revolutionary authorities—promises that in the end he would keep.) Carranza's agrarian decrees gained him a certain base among the peasantry. Carranza courted labor support by the promise of a minimum-wage law applying to all branches of industry and by affirming the right of workers to form trade unions and to strike. He also appealed for women's support, and thousands flocked to his ranks from diverse social classes. According to historian Shirlene Soto, working-class radicals like Artemisa Sénz Royo, a labor organizer who later served in the "red battalions," joined with middle-class feminists such as Hermila Galindo de Topete, Carranza's private secretary, to demand "women's complete equality, including sexual equality."

After Obregón's troops reoccupied Mexico City in January 1915, an alliance was formed between the Carranza government and the Casa del Obrero Mundial, which was restored after the fall of Huerta. Members of the Casa agreed to join "the struggle against reaction," meaning above all the revolutionary peasantry. Six "red battalions" of workers were formed and made an important contribution to the offensive launched by Obregón against Villa and Zapata in January 1915. Inadequate understanding on the part of the peasant and working-class leaders of their common interests and the skillful opportunism of the middle-class politicians in Carranza's camp contributed to this disastrous division between labor and the peasantry.

With growing support from a diverse, cross-class political constituency and emboldened by financial and arms transfusions from the United States, the Constitutionalists benefited from a dramatic shift in the balance of forces in Mexico. Under pressure from Carranza's troops, Villa was forced on January 19 to evacuate Mexico City, which Obregón soon occupied. In April 1915, Obregón advanced toward the important railroad center of Celaya, occupied it, and awaited Villa's attack. Obregón had studied accounts of the great war in progress in Europe and had learned that trenches and barbed wire could stop mass attacks. His army received Villa's furious infantry and cavalry assault with a withering fire from machine-gun emplacements and entrenched infantry. For the first time in his military career, Villa suffered a disastrous defeat, with thousands of men killed or taken prisoner. By the end of 1915, the Constitutionalists had destroyed Villa, whom they regarded as the primary danger.

There remained the Zapatistas, who threatened the capital and who had temporarily occupied it in July. But Zapata's battered forces could not check the advance of General Pablo González's army. In August the Constitutionalists returned to Mexico City to stay, while González, one of Carranza's ablest generals, pursued the Zapatistas into Morelos in a campaign of devastation and plunder.

In October 1915, after unsuccessful efforts to play off the revolutionary chiefs against each other or to achieve a coalition under U.S. leadership, President Wilson acknowledged Carranza's ascendancy and extended de facto recognition of his regime; equally important, he placed an arms embargo on Carranza's opponents. But the United States had not abandoned its efforts to influence the course of the Mexican Revolution. A memorandum to Carranza dictated the conditions he must meet before he could obtain *de jure* recognition. They amounted to a claim to determine Mexican policy not only in the area of foreign economic rights but in such internal matters as the role of the church, elections, and the like. These demands were as unacceptable to Carranza in October 1915 as they had been a year before.

In early 1916 relations between the United States and Mexico deteriorated sharply. In part, this resulted from initial efforts by Mexican federal and state authorities to regulate the operations of foreign oil companies. A crisis arose in March when Villa, angered by the arms embargo and wrongly convinced that Carranza had bought U.S. recognition by agreeing to a plan to convert Mexico into a U.S. protectorate, raided Columbus, New Mexico, in an apparent effort to force Carranza to show his hand. The Wilson administration responded by ordering General John Pershing to pursue Villa into Mexico. The United States counted on the enmity between Villa and Carranza to secure the latter's neutrality. But Carranza denounced the invasion, demanded the immediate withdrawal of U.S. forces, and began to prepare for war. In a note to other Latin American nations, the Mexican government declared its belief that the basic reason for U.S. intervention was its opposition to the Mexican policy of eliminating privileged treatment of foreign capital and affirmed that the "foreign invasion" must be repelled and Mexican sovereignty respected.

The United States had anticipated an easy victory, but Pershing's hot pursuit of the elusive Villa proved a fiasco, and Wilson accepted Carranza's offer to negotiate a settlement. Wilson was unsuccessful in his efforts to link the evacuation of U.S. forces with acceptance of the U.S. formula for Mexican domestic policy. In January 1917, influenced by the troubled international scene and his

conviction that a war with Mexico would involve at least half a million men, Wilson decided to liquidate the Mexican venture. Mexican nationalism had won a major victory over yet another effort by the United States to impose its hegemony.

THE CONSTITUTION OF 1917

In the fall of 1916, Carranza issued a call for the election of deputies to a convention that was to frame a new constitution and prepare the way for his election as president. The convention opened in Querétaro on December 1, 1916. Because the call effectively excluded women and those who had not sworn loyalty to his 1913 Plan of Guadalupe, it seemed likely that the constitution would be what Carranza wanted. The draft did not contemplate a radical agrarian reform; for labor, it limited itself to proclaiming the "right to work" and the right of workers to form organizations for "lawful purposes" and to hold "peaceful" assemblies.

These abstract proposals were unsatisfactory to a majority of the deputies, who formed the radical wing of the convention. The principal spokesman for this left wing was Francisco J. Múgica, a young general who helped make the first land distribution of the revolution. The radicals obtained majority approval to create a commission to revise Carranza's project. Múgica himself was largely responsible for Article 3, which struck a heavy blow at church control of education by specifically forbidding "religious corporations" and "ministers of any cult" to establish or conduct schools.

Hermila Galindo and other women revolutionaries were very interested in Articles 34 and 35, which dealt with citizenship and voting rights. Addressing the convention, Galindo appealed to the delegates' "sense of justice as popular representatives" and argued that women should have an equal right to vote and hold office precisely because working women paid taxes, obeyed the same laws as men, and participated fully in the revolutionary struggle for social justice. But others, especially the more radical delegates like Luís Monzón and Inés Malváez, early supporters of the PLM and principled proponents of gender equality, opposed women's suffrage for practical political reasons: they feared that the vast majority of women, sheltered from the harsh realities of the working world (less than 20 percent worked for wages in 1917) and seduced by a conservative Catholic church, would use the franchise to restrain the revolution's radical anticapitalist, anticlerical tendencies. Fear triumphed over principle and women were denied citizenship and political rights.

But wage-earning women did win important protections in Article 123, dealing with the rights of labor. Carranza had asked only that the federal government be empowered to enact labor legislation. The convention went much further. The finished article, a true labor code, provided for the eight-hour day; secured childbirth benefits for women, including paid prenatal and postnatal maternity leaves; required companies employing more than fifty women to provide on-site childcare; abolished the tienda de raya, or company store, and debt servitude; guaranteed the right of workers to organize, bargain collectively, and strike; and granted many other rights and privileges, making it the most advanced labor code in the contemporary world.

Article 27, dealing with property rights, had an equally advanced character. It proclaimed the nation the original owner of all lands, waters, and the subsoil; the state could expropriate them, with compensation to the owners. National ownership of water and the subsoil was inalienable, but individuals and companies could obtain concessions for their exploitation. Foreigners to whom that privilege was granted must agree that they would not invoke the protection of their governments in regard to such concessions. Of prime importance were the same article's agrarian provisions. It declared that all measures passed since 1856 alienating ejidos (communal lands) were null and void; if the pueblos needed more land, they could acquire it by expropriation from neighboring haciendas.

These and other provisions of the constitution of 1917 made it the most progressive law code of its time. It laid legal foundations for a massive assault on the latifundio, for weakening the power of the church, and for regulating the operations of foreign capital in Mexico. But the constitution was not anticapitalist. It sanctioned and protected private property; it sought to control rather than eliminate foreign enterprises, creating more favorable conditions for the development of national capitalism.

Nonetheless, Carranza expressed reservations about the new constitution but promised to uphold it. Shortly after its promulgation on February 5, 1917, Carranza became the first legally elected president since Madero. On inauguration day, Obregón, his secretary of war, resigned and retired to private life. Obregón, who had been moving to the left, distrusted many of the men around Carranza as reactionaries of Porfirista stamp.

CARRANZA'S PRESIDENCY

The three remaining years of the Carranza regime were marked by a sharp swing to the right. Carranza soon made it clear that he did not intend to implement the reform articles of the constitution. Only a trifling amount of land was distributed to the villages. Carranza returned many confiscated haciendas to their former owners; others he turned over to his favorite generals. Official corruption existed on a massive scale. The working class suffered severe repression. Carranza shut down the Casa del Obrero Mundial. The constitution's promise of free education was ignored. Only in Carranza's foreign policy, marked by a genuine revolutionary nationalism, did the spirit of the constitution live. Carranza staunchly resisted U.S. pressure to give guarantees that Article 27 of the constitution would not be implemented against foreign interests. He kept Mexico neutral in World War I and insisted on an independent Mexican diplomatic position in the hemisphere, postures that the United States regarded as unfriendly.

Carranza also appealed to upper- and middle-class women with decrees that legalized civil divorce, established alimony rights, and authorized women to own and manage property. On April 9, 1917, he signed the Law of Family Relations, which guaranteed women equal rights to exercise guardianship and child custody, file lawsuits, and sign contracts. But cultural taboos against divorce and other legal inequities institutionalized what historian Shirlene Soto calls a "sexual double standard" in Mexico.

Meanwhile, Carranza continued to battle the tenacious Zapatista movement in the south and Villa in the north. Against the Zapatistas, Carranza's favorite general, Pablo González, launched campaign after campaign. Zapata's forces diminished and the territory under his control shrank to the vanishing point, but he remained unconquerable, supported by the affection and loyalty of the peasantry. His fall came through treachery. Invited to confer with a Carrancista officer who claimed to have gone over to his side, Zapata was ambushed and slain on April 10, 1919. But his people continued their struggle for *tierra y libertad* (land and liberty).

Carranza's legal term was due to end in 1920, but the president had no intention of relinquishing power. Barred from running again by the constitutional rule of no reelection, he nonetheless tried to extend his power by imposing a weak puppet president. But Obregón, supported by a Labor Party formed to further his interests, rejected both Carranza and his surrogate. In May 1920, Carranza fled from the capital toward Veracruz, taking with him 5 million pesos in gold and silver from the national treasury. He was slain on May 21.

On May 24, Adolfo de la Huerta, a loyal Obregón ally, became interim president and sought to reconcile with Zapatistas by implementing agrarian reform. Villa, who also aided the anti-Carranza movement, was rewarded with a hacienda, and other lands were given to his men. Villa did not long enjoy his newfound peace and prosperity; he was assassinated in the summer of 1923 under obscure circumstances.

In November 1920, Obregón assumed the presidency. Peace had come to Mexico, and the work of reconstruction could begin. It would not be an easy task. The great wind that swept through Mexico had left a devastated land, with hundreds of thousands dead or missing; the Mexican population had actually declined by 1 million since 1910. The constitution of 1917 offered a blueprint for a new and better social order, but major obsta-

cles to change remained. Not the least were the hundreds of generals thrown up by the great upheaval, men of humble origins who once had nothing and now had an incurable itch for wealth and power. With his characteristic wry humor, Obregón summed up the problem when he said that the days of revolutionary banditry had ended because he had brought all the bandits with him to the capital to keep them out of trouble.

Reconstructing the State: Rule of the Millionaire Socialists

OBREGÓN AND REFORM

With Obregón there came to power a group of northern generals and politicians who began the work of economic and social reconstruction that Madero, Huerta, and Carranza were unable or unwilling to achieve. Obregón and his successor, Calles, were of middle-class or even lower-class origins—Obregón had been a mechanic and farmer, Calles, a schoolteacher. They both were products of a border region where U.S. cultural influence was strong and where capitalism and capitalist relations were more highly developed than in any other part of Mexico. Obregón and Calles thus possessed a pragmatic business mentality as far removed from the revolutionary agrarian ideology of Zapata as it was from the aristocratic reformism of Carranza. These men deliberately set out to lay the economic, political, and ideological foundations of a Mexican national capitalism.

Aware that the revolution had radicalized the masses, aware of the appeal of socialism and anti-imperialism to the workers on whose support they counted, Obregón and Calles employed a revolutionary rhetoric designed to mobilize popular support and conceal how modest were the social changes that actually took place. In practice, Obregón's program was revolutionary only by contrast with the reactionary trend that characterized the last years of Carranza's rule. Far from promoting socialism, Obregón sought accommodation with all elements of Mexican society except the most reactionary clergy and landlords. He allowed exiles of the most varied political tendency to return to Mexico, and radical intellectuals rubbed shoulders with former Científicos in his government. Power was held by a ruling class of wealthy generals, capitalists, and landlords. Labor and the peasantry were the government's obedient clienteles.

Regarding agrarian reform as a useful safety valve for peasant discontent, Obregón distributed some land to the pueblos. But the process proceeded slowly, haltingly, against the intense opposition of the hacendados and the church, which condemned the agrarian reform because it did not take account of the "just rights of the landlords." Litigation by landlords, their use of armed force to resist occupation of expropriated land, and the opposition of the clergy slowed down the pace of the land reform.

Even after a village had received land, its prospect for success was poor, for the government failed to provide the peasants with seeds, implements, and adequate credit facilities or modern agricultural training. Such credit assistance as they received usually came from government rural banks, which exercised close control over land use, intensifying the client status of the peasantry, or from rural loan sharks. The Obregón land reform was neither swift nor thoroughgoing; by the end of his presidency, only some 3 million acres had been distributed among 624 villages, whereas 320 million acres remained in private hands.

Obregón also encouraged labor to organize, for he regarded trade unions as useful for stabilizing labor-capitalist relations and as an important bulwark of his regime. The principal trade union organization was the *Confederación Regional Obrera Mexicana* (CROM), formed in 1918. Despite the rhetoric of its leaders about "class struggle" and freedom from the "tyranny of capitalism," CROM was about as radical as the American Federation of Labor, with which it maintained close ties. Its perpetual boss was Luis Morones, known for his flashy dress, diamonds, and limousines. As the only labor organization sponsored and protected by the government, CROM had virtually official status. Despite this official protection, Morones's method of personal negotiation with employers yielded

scanty benefits to labor; wages barely kept pace with the rising cost of living.

Perhaps the most solid achievements of the Obregón regime were in the areas of education and culture. The creation of a native Mexican capitalism demanded the development of a national consciousness, which meant the integration of indigenous peoples—still made up of so many small nations—into the national market and the new society. From this point of view, they were the key problem of Mexican reconstruction. Because incorporating them into the modern world required a thorough understanding of their past and present conditions of life, the revolutionary regimes encouraged scientific study of the indigenous peoples.

An integral part of *indigenismo* was a reassessment of indigenous cultural heritage. To insist on the greatness of the old native arts was one way of asserting the value of one's own, of revolting against the tyranny of the pallid, lifeless French and Spanish academicism over Mexican art during the last decades of the Díaz era.

From Europe returned two future giants of the Mexican artistic renaissance, Diego Rivera and David Alfaro Siqueiros, to join another gifted artist, José Clemente Orozco, in creating a militant new art that drew much of its inspiration from the indigenous peoples and their ancient art. Believing that "a heroic art could fortify the will to reconstruction," Obregón's brilliant young secretary of education, José Vasconcelos, offered the walls of public buildings for the painting of murals that glorified the natives, past and present.

The "Indianist" cult had great political significance. The foes of the revolution, unregenerate Porfiristas, clericals, and reactionaries of all stripes, looked back to Spain as the sole source of enduring values in Mexican life and regarded Cortés as the creator of Mexican nationality; partisans of the revolution tended to idealize Aztec Mexico (sometimes beyond recognition) and elevated the last Aztec warrior-king, Cuauhtémoc, to the status of a demigod.

Convinced that the school was the most important instrument for unifying the nation, that "to educate was to redeem," Vasconcelos, with ample budgetary support from Obregón, launched an imaginative program of cultural missions designed to bring literacy and health to indigenous villages. Professor Elena Torres, a founding member of the Mexican National Council of Women and a fiery socialist feminist, supervised the training of more than 4,000 rural teachers, the majority of whom were women, commissioned to bring the gospel of sanitation and literacy to remote pueblos. Torres acquired practical experience in this field during her collaboration with Yucatán state governor Felipe Carrillo Puerto, whose progressive reform agenda included "socialist education," state-supported birth control, women's suffrage, and civil equality.

Vasconcelos also founded teacher-training colleges, agricultural schools, and other specialized schools. An achievement in which he took special pride was the publication of hundreds of classic works in cheap editions for free distribution in the schools. Although these state education programs aimed to promote capitalist land and labor relations by building a patriarchal solidarity with peasants otherwise hostile to this goal, the result was much more ambiguous; according to historian Mary Kay Vaughan, the rural literacy crusades "injected new notions of women's work and personhood" into traditional rural images of women, thereby empowering *campesinas* and their local communities in ways unanticipated by national leaders. These villagers soon took advantage of the growing institutional rivalry between church and state to expand their autonomy.

The new secular, nationalist school provoked clerical anger, for it threatened to supplant the priest with the teacher as the guiding force of the rural community and to replace the religious world outlook taught by the Catholic church with a scientific world outlook. The church fought back with all the means at its disposal. Some priests denounced secular education from their pulpits and threatened parents who sent their children to state schools with excommunication. As a result of this campaign, many teachers were attacked and some killed by fanatical villagers. Despite this campaign, Obregón made no effort to implement Article 3 of the constitution, which banned religious primary schools, for he believed that in the absence of enough resources on the part of the state it was better that Mexican children receive instruction from priests than remain illiterate.

The Catholic issue joined with other issues to cause Obregón difficulties in his relations with the United States. For three years, the U.S. government withheld diplomatic recognition from Obregón in an effort to force him to recognize that Article 27 of the constitution should not apply to mineral concessions obtained by foreigners before 1917. Like Carranza, Obregón was willing to respect the principle of nonretroactivity but refused to formalize it in a treaty as a condition of U.S. diplomatic recognition, which he considered humiliating and politically destabilizing.

Obregón's practical policies, however, confirmed his interest in securing the rights of private property essential to foreign investment and capitalist growth. He signed agreements that renewed Mexico's foreign debt service payments, returned the National Railways to private ownership, and resolved various indemnity claims; he also secured Supreme Court rulings that declared unconstitutional any attempt to apply Article 27 retroactively. Faced with Obregón's uncompromising demand for unconditional U.S. recognition and a growing counterrevolutionary insurgency that threatened once again to destabilize Mexico, thereby undermining these agreements, the United States formally recognized the Mexican government in August 1923. When the expected revolt broke out in December, the United States allowed Obregón to procure large quantities of war materiel. Together with the help of the organized labor and peasant movements, this aid enabled Obregón to crush the uprising, which was supported by reactionary landowners, clergy, and military. On November 30, 1924, Obregón's hand-picked successor, Plutarco Elías Calles assumed the presidency of Mexico.

CALLES'S REGIME

In and out of office, as legal president or de facto dictator, Calles dominated the next decade of Mexican politics. Building on the foundations Obregón had laid, he continued his work with much the same methods. His radical phraseology tended to conceal the pragmatic essence of his policy, which was to promote the rapid growth of Mexican national capitalism, whose infrastructure he helped to establish. To strengthen the fiscal and monetary system, he created the Bank of Mexico, the only bank permitted to issue money. A national road commission was organized, and a national electricity code was enacted to aid the electric power industry. These measures stimulated the growth of construction and consumer goods industries, in which members of Calles's official family—or the "revolutionary family," as the ruling elite came to be called—were heavily involved. Protective tariffs, subsidies, and other forms of aid were generously extended to industry, both foreign and domestic. In 1925 an assembly plant of the Ford Motor Company began operations in Mexico after Calles and the company negotiated an agreement providing for numerous concessions.

Calles showed more enthusiasm for land reform than Obregón, and the tempo of land distribution increased sharply during his presidency. Like Obregón, Calles regarded land reform as a safety valve for peasant unrest. During the four years of his term, Calles distributed about twice as much land as Obregón had.

But less than one-fourth of that amount consisted of arable land, for Calles did not require the hacendados to surrender productive land, and most of the land given up came from pasture or forest lands, or even land that was completely barren. Nor did Calles make a serious effort to provide the peasantry with irrigation, fertilizer, implements, or seed. He established a government bank that was supposed to lend money to the ejidos, promote modern farming techniques, and act as agents for the sale of their produce. But four-fifths of the bank's resources were loaned not to ejidos but to hacendados with much superior credit ratings, and many of the bank's agents took advantage of their position to enrich themselves at the expense of the peasants.

Under these conditions, it is no wonder that the land reform soon appeared to be a failure. By 1930 grain production had fallen below the levels of 1910, and Calles, concluding that peasant

proprietorship was economically undesirable, announced the abandonment of land distribution. Meanwhile, on his own large estates Calles introduced machinery and other modern agricultural techniques and advised other large landowners to do the same.

Like Obregón, Calles regarded labor unions as desirable because they helped stabilize labor-capitalist relations and avert radical social change. But by the end of the *Callista* decade, Mexican labor, disillusioned with a corrupt leadership that kept wages at or below the subsistence level, had begun to break away from CROM and form independent unions.

Although Calles had announced his rhetorical support for women's rights, he did little to advance them, prompting women to organize themselves to secure their political, social, and economic liberation. Socialist Elvia Carrillo Puerto, sister of the Yucatecan *caudillo*, and communist María "Cuca" García organized women government employees; Elena Torres joined García to establish the Mexican Feminist Council, and the Mexican Feminist League appeared a few years later. At successive national and international conferences, however, these women inevitably clashed over issues of class. For example, when a middle-class delegate argued for prohibitions on begging, García objected: "How can one prevent begging when there is no work, when salaries are so meager, and you have the poor in complete helplessness?" Carrillo Puerto concluded the ensuing debate, scorning "the people of class" as "parasites that suck the lifeblood from the country."

Calles continued the Carranza and Obregón policies of asserting Mexico's right to regulate the conditions under which foreign capital could exploit its natural resources, but he was far from hostile to foreign capital. Indeed, he gave assurances that "the government will do everything in its power to safeguard the interests of foreign capitalists who invest money in Mexico."

But a serious dispute with the United States arose in 1925 when the Mexican Congress passed laws to implement Article 27. The most important of these measures required owners of oil leases to exchange their titles for fifty-year concessions dating from the time of acquisition, to be followed, if necessary, by a thirty-year renewal, with the possibility of yet another extension if needed. No Mexican oil well had ever lasted more than eighty years. Far from injuring the foreign oil companies, the law eliminated the vagueness of their status under Article 27, gave them firm titles emanating from the government, and served to quiet more radical demands for outright nationalization. However, a number of U.S. oil companies denounced the law as confiscatory and threatened to continue drilling operations without confirmatory concessions.

The U.S. State Department vigorously protested the restrictive legislation, and the U.S. ambassador, James R. Sheffield, pursued a hardline, uncompromising policy. By late 1926 the United States appeared to be moving toward war with Mexico.

Fortunately, the interventionist policy came under severe attack from progressive Republican senators, the press, church groups, and the academic world. President Calvin Coolidge and Secretary of State Kellogg, realizing that war with Mexico would have little national support, sought a way out of the impasse and were aided by U.S. international bankers, who had a firmer grasp of Mexican policies and intentions. The appointment of Dwight Morrow, a partner in the financial firm of J. P. Morgan, as ambassador to Mexico in September 1927 marked a turning point in the crisis. Morrow managed to persuade Calles that portions of the oil law had the potential for injuring foreign property rights, with the result that the Mexican Supreme Court found unconstitutional that portion of the law setting a time period on concessions. But as rewritten the law still provided for confirmatory concessions and reaffirmed national ownership of the subsoil.

In addition, a serious domestic dispute arose as a result of the government's alienation of peasant communities disadvantaged by its market reforms and the growing opposition of the church to the whole modernizing thrust of the revolution. Under Calles this opposition assumed the proportions of a civil war. In January 1926 the church hierarchy signed a letter declaring that the constitution of 1917 "wounds the most sacred rights of the Catholic Church" and disavowed the document. Calles responded by enforcing the anticlerical clauses of the constitution, which had lain dormant. The Calles Law, as it was called, ordered the registration of priests with the civil authorities and the closing of religious primary schools. The church struck back by suspending church services throughout Mexico, a powerful weapon in a country so overwhelmingly Catholic.

But neither this strike nor the boycott organized by the church, which urged the faithful to buy no goods or services except absolute necessities, brought the government to its knees. By the end of 1926, militant Catholics, in frequent alliance with local hacendados, had taken up arms. Guerrilla groups were formed, with the mountainous backcountry of Jalisco the main focus of their activity. Government schools and young teachers sent into remote areas were frequent objects of clerical fury; many teachers were tortured and killed. The total number of Catholic guerrillas, known as *Cristeros* from their slogan, *Viva Cristo Rey* (Long Live Christ the King), was small, but federal commanders helped keep the insurrection alive by the brutality of their repressions. By the summer of 1927, however, the revolt had largely burned itself out.

In 1928, fearing the divisiveness historically associated with Mexico's democratic electoral transitions, Obregón and Calles sought a constitutional amendment to extend the presidential term to six years and allow former presidents to seek reelection after one term out of office. Although this was designed to rotate the presidency between Obregón and Calles, Obregón's assassination by a fanatical *Cristero* in July spawned a new political crisis.

With the passing of the formidable Obregón, Calles became the *jefe máximo*, the maximum chief of the revolution. The presidents who successively held office during what was to have been Obregón's six-year term—Emilio Portes Gil, Pascual Ortiz Rubio, and Abelardo Rodríguez— were Calles's stooges and obediently resigned when they incurred his displeasure. In 1929, after crushing a rebellion that proved to be almost the last hurrah of the regional military caudillos, Calles organized the National Revolutionary Party

(PNR) as an instrument for pacifying the country and institutionalizing the rule of the "revolutionary family," the military leaders and politicians who had ruled the country since 1920. Under different names and with leaderships of differing composition, the party formed by Calles remained the ruling party of Mexico for six decades. The official party's candidates for president did not lose an election until 2000.

As the "revolutionary family" consolidated its power and its wealth increased, its members became even more corrupt and predatory than the old Porfirista aristocracy. As large landowners, they were naturally hostile to agrarian reform; as owners of construction firms and factories, they were hostile to strikes and unions.

Calles and his cronies had never been committed to a radical reconstruction of Mexican society, but after 1928, they retreated from their own modest reform program. To camouflage this shift of emphasis and validate their revolutionary credentials they indulged freely in anticlerical demagoguery and excesses. Their acts blew new life into the dying Cristero movement, causing a brief but bitter new conflict that took many lives.

This change in the Callista regime coincided with the beginning in 1929 of the Great Depression, which exposed the bankruptcy of capitalist economics and added to the misery of Mexican peasants and workers. Their growing unrest created fears of a new revolutionary explosion. Rumblings of protest were heard even within the ruling party. A new generation of young, middle-class reformers demanded vigorous implementation of the constitution of 1917. Some were intellectuals influenced by Marxism and the success of the Soviet example, especially by its concept of economic planning, but their basic message was the need to resume the struggle against the latifundio, peonage, and economic and cultural backwardness; that is, to resume the advance of the bourgeois revolution, stalled by the corruption and cynicism of the Callistas.

This message was loudly trumpeted at successive meetings of the National Congress of Women Workers and Peasants in the early 1930s. Here, "Cuca" García, for example, accused the Callistas of murdering campesinos and denounced their neglect of poor peasant women: "the agrarian legislation," she thundered, "condemns them always to live in their father's, husband's, or brother's poverty," denying them the "economic independence [that] is the foundation of women's political independence." García was promptly arrested but was later released when thousands of women rallied to her defense at the jail. Despite rancorous debate, these meetings typically pressed for more progressive state action to expand indigenous rights, protect women workers, raise the minimum wage, increase land reform, and promote women's suffrage.

By 1933 the influence of the progressive wing within the PNR had grown. Its acknowledged leader was General Lázaro Cárdenas, governor of Michoacán, who had established an enviable record for honesty, compassion, and concern for commoners. He had spent almost 50 percent of his budget on education, doubling the number of schools in the state. Despite his progressive ideas, he was close to the inner circle of the "revolutionary family," and the jefe máximo supported Cárdenas for president in 1933. Although there was no doubt that he would be elected, Cárdenas campaigned vigorously, visiting the most remote areas of the country, patiently explaining to workers and peasants his Six-Year Plan to strengthen the ejidos, build modern schools, and develop workers' cooperatives. Although Calles remained confident that the loyal Cárdenas would carry out his orders as the puppet presidents who preceded him had done, Cárdenas had established his political independence.

Cárdenas and the Populist Interlude

Under Cárdenas, the Mexican Revolution resumed its advance. Land distribution to the villages on a massive scale was accompanied by a many-sided effort to raise agricultural productivity and improve the quality of rural life. Labor was encouraged to replace the old, corrupt leadership with militant leaders and to struggle for improved conditions. A spirit of service began to pervade at least a part of the governmental bureaucracy. Cárdenas set an example to subordinates by the democratic simplicity of his manners, by cutting his own salary in half, and by making himself available to the delegations of peasants and workers who thronged the waiting rooms of the National Palace.

These and other policies of the new president—such as the closing down of illegal gambling houses, most of which were owned by wealthy Callistas—angered the jefe máximo. In 1935, Calles denounced the labor movement and its alleged radicalism and threatened to depose Cárdenas, who responded by forming a new cabinet dominated by the left wing but representing a broad coalition of anti-Callista elements. By the end of 1935, Cárdenas was the undisputed master of Mexico, and he ordered Calles's immediate deportation to the United States in 1936.

LAND REFORM

Having consolidated his political control, Cárdenas proceeded to implement his reform program. He regarded land distribution as of prime importance. Land was distributed to the peasantry in a variety of ways, according to the climatic and soil conditions of the different regions. The principal form was the ejido, the communal landholding system under which land could not be mortgaged or alienated (except under very special conditions), with each *ejidatario* entitled to use a parcel of community land. The ejido was the focal point of the agrarian reform. But Cárdenas also distributed land in the form of the *rancho*, the individual small holding widely prevalent in the northern Mexican states. Finally, in regions where natural conditions favored large-scale cultivation of such commercial crops as sugar, cotton, coffee, rice, and henequen, large cooperative farms (collective ejidos) were organized on a profit-sharing basis. The government generously endowed these enterprises with seeds, machinery, and credit from the *Banco de Crédito Ejidal*.

During the Cárdenas years, some 45 million acres of land were distributed to almost twelve thousand villages. The Cárdenas distribution program struck a heavy blow at the traditional, semi-feudal hacienda and peonage, satisfied the land hunger of the Mexican peasantry for the time being, and promoted a general modernization of Mexican life and society. By 1940, thanks to the land reform and supplemented by the provision of villages with schools, medical care, roads, and other facilities, the standard of living of the peasantry had risen, if only modestly. These progressive changes in turn contributed to the growth of the internal market and therefore of Mexican industry. The land reform also justified itself in terms of productivity; average agricultural production during the three-year period from 1939 to 1941 was higher than it had been at any time since the beginning of the revolution.

Granted these benefits and Cárdenas's excellent intentions, the fact remains that the land reform suffered from the first from certain structural defects. To begin with, it was basically conceived as a means of satisfying land hunger by the grant or restitution of land to the villages, and it overlooked the need to establish agricultural units that would be viable from an economic point of view. In many cases, the *ejidal* parcel, especially in areas of very dense population, was so small as to form a minifundio. Much of the distributed land was of poor quality (the agrarian law always allowed the landowner to retain a portion of his estate, and naturally landowners kept the best portions for themselves), and aid in the form of seeds, technical assistance, and credit was frequently inadequate.

In addition, peasants received their land from the government, which controlled their activities through the operations of the *Departamento Agrario*, the Banco de Crédito Ejidal, and officially organized peasant leagues; thus, they were increasingly dependent on public authorities. Under Cárdenas, officials of these agencies often worked in a spirit of disinterested service and sought to develop peasant collective initiative and democracy; under his successors in the presidency, they tended to become corrupt and self-seeking, to enmesh the peasantry and its organizations in a bureaucratic network that manipulated them to satisfy its own interests. After 1940, Mexican governments increasingly favored large private property and neglected the ejido. In concert with the structural defects of the land reform, this produced a gradual decline of the ejido system and a parallel growth of large landed property, leading to the emergence of a new latifundio.

LABOR REFORM

Under Cárdenas the labor movement was revitalized. Aware of the sympathetic attitude of the new regime, workers struck in unprecedented numbers for higher wages and better working conditions; in 1935 there were 642 strikes, more than twice the number in the preceding six years. In 1936 the young radical intellectual Vicente Lombardo Toledano organized a new labor federation, the *Confederación de Trabajadores Mexicanos* (CTM), to replace the dying and discredited CROM. Labor supported and in turn was supported by Cárdenas.

Labor, the peasantry, and the army became the three main pillars of the official party, reorganized in 1938 and renamed the Party of the Mexican Revolution (PRM). The power of the generals was weakened by a policy of raising wages and improving the morale of the rank-and-file and by the distribution of weapons to the peasantry, formed into a militia.

Like the land reform, the labor reform had structural flaws that created serious problems for the future. In return for concessions from a paternal government, labor, like the peasantry, was invited to incorporate itself into the official apparatus and to give automatic and obligatory support to a government that in the last analysis represented the interests of the national bourgeoisie. In the domestic and international situation of the 1930s, which was dominated by a struggle between profascist and antifascist forces, the interests of that bourgeoisie and Mexican labor largely coincided, but in the changed conditions after 1940, labor's loss of independence and the meshing of its organizations with the official apparatus led to a revival of corruption and reactionary control of the trade unions.

ECONOMIC REFORM

Although Cárdenas was sympathetic to labor's demands for better conditions, he was no foe of private enterprise, despite efforts by his foes to link him to socialism and communism. In fact, industrial capitalism made significant strides under Cárdenas. If Cárdenas supported labor's efforts to raise wages where the financial condition of an enterprise warranted it, he also favored Mexican industry with government loans and protective tariffs that insured the creation of a captive market for high-priced consumer goods. In 1934 his government established the *Nacional Financiera*, a government bank and investment corporation that used funds supplied by the federal government and domestic investors to make industrial loans, finance public welfare projects, and issue its own securities. The coming of World War II, which sharply reduced the availability of imports, greatly stimulated the movement toward industrialization and import substitution.

Mexico's struggle for economic sovereignty reached a high point under Cárdenas. In 1937 a dispute between North American and British oil companies and the unions erupted into a strike, followed by legal battles between the contending parties. When the oil companies refused to accept a much-scaled-down arbitration-tribunal wage finding in favor of the workers, Cárdenas intervened. On March 18, 1938—a date celebrated by Mexicans as marking their declaration of economic independence—the president announced in a radio speech that the properties of the oil companies had been expropriated in the public interest. With support from virtually all strata of the population, Cárdenas was able to ride out the storm caused by economic sanctions against Mexico on the part of the United States, England, and the oil companies. The oil nationalization was a major victory for Mexican nationalism. It provided cheap, plentiful fuel for Mexican industry, and the needs of the nationalized oil industries further stimulated industrialization. But the oil nationalization did not set a precedent; some 90 percent of Mexico's mining industry remained in foreign hands.

WOMEN'S RIGHTS

Pressured by a well-organized, increasingly cohesive women's movement, Cárdenas supported constitutional reform "to grant equal rights" and pledged to create a women's section of the PNR to guarantee that "working women have the right to participate in electoral struggles." Meanwhile, women consolidated their organizational efforts in the United Front for Women's Rights, under the leadership of veteran feminist "Cuca" García and other socialist and communist women. The Front, incorporating some eight hundred women's groups with more than fifty thousand members, demanded women's right to vote and hold office, civil equality, protective legislation for women workers, social integration of indigenous women, and women's centers for cultural education and vocational training.

In 1937, even though the law forbade women to hold elective office and the PNR refused to slate her, the Front supported García's successful primary race for a seat in the Chamber of Deputies. It also secured congressional and state legislative approval of a constitutional amendment permitting woman suffrage beginning in 1939, but thereafter the PNR-dominated Congress, split by fractious party infighting and fearful of a resurgent Catholic conservatism that might have benefited politically from women's enfranchisement, neglected to pass the necessary enabling legislation. Woman suffrage would have to wait until 1953, when a more conservative ruling party had reached a *modus vivendi* with the Catholic church.

CÁRDENAS'S GROWING MODERATION AND THE ELECTION OF 1940

Education, especially the rural school system, made considerable progress under Cárdenas. Of Tarascan origin, Cárdenas displayed much concern for indigenous welfare. He created a *Departamento de Asuntos Indígenas* to serve and protect their interests and encouraged the study of their culture, past and present, by founding the *Instituto Nacional de Antropología de México*.

But in the last years of his presidency, in apparent deference to clerical and conservative opposition, Cárdenas abandoned many reforms and soft-pedaled the so-called socialist character of Mexican education. He also slowed down the pace of land distribution and displayed a conciliatory attitude toward the entrepreneurial class, assuring its members that he regarded them as part of the *fuerzas vivas* (vital forces) of the country and that they need not fear for the safety of their investments.

On the eve of the presidential election of 1940, Cárdenas and the official party, an amalgam of social forces including increasingly conservative and influential industrialists, nominated General Manuel Ávila Camacho, a Cárdenas loyalist, a devout Catholic, and a man of generally conservative views. Ávila Camacho was elected with almost 99 percent of the vote and soon began to reassure foreign and domestic capital. He dissociated himself from the radical leadership of the unions, expressed a flexible attitude toward the question of whether the ejido or small private property was the best form of agrarian organization, and assured the Catholics that he was a *creyente* (believer).

The Big Bourgeoisie in Power, 1940–1976: Erosion of Reform

The Cárdenas era was the high-water mark of the struggle to achieve the social goals of the revolution. Under his successors, there began an erosion of the social conquests of the Cárdenas years. During those years the material and cultural condition of the masses had improved, if only modestly; peasants and workers managed to secure a somewhat larger share of the total national income. After 1940 these trends were reversed. The new rulers of Mexico favored a development strategy that sharply restricted trade union activity, slowed the tempo of agrarian reform, and reduced the relative share of total income of the bottom two-thirds of the Mexican population.

Ávila Camacho presided over the first phase (1940–1946) of this policy reversal. Regarding unlimited private profit as the driving force of economic progress, he proposed to create a favorable climate for private enterprise. In practice, this meant the freezing of wages, the repression of strikes, and the use of a new weapon against dissidents, a vaguely worded law dealing with the "crime of social dissolution."

Meanwhile, World War II stimulated both the export of Mexican raw materials and import substitution through industrialization. Significant advances were made in food processing, textiles, and other consumer goods industries, and the capital goods industry, centered in the north, was considerably expanded. Steel production increased, with Monterrey Steel and other companies producing structural and rolled steel for buildings, hotels, highways, and steel hardware. The Nacional Financiera played a leading role in this process of growth through loans to industry for plant construction and expansion. In view of this spontaneous economic growth, the concept of planning was forgotten; the second Six-Year Plan remained on paper. No effort was made to produce a balanced development of the Mexican regions; most of the development took place in the Federal District and the surrounding area. Meanwhile, land distribution was sharply reduced.

In 1946 the official party changed its name to the PRI (*Partido Revolucionario Institucional*), and Ávila Camacho was succeeded as president by the lawyer Miguel Alemán (1946–1952), who continued the policies of his predecessor. Alemán made every effort to encourage private investment through tariff protection, import licensing, subsidies, and government loans. This favorable economic climate attracted domestic and foreign investors looking for outlets for their surplus capital after World War II. A characteristic of the new foreign capital investment was that it flowed primarily into manufacturing rather than the traditional extractive industries.

Under Alemán and his successor, Adolfo Ruiz Cortines (1952–1958), land distribution and efforts to increase the productivity of the ejidos were neglected in favor of the large private landholding. To provide an incentive to capitalist entrepreneurs, Alemán had Article 27 of the constitution amended. This "reform" consisted in the grant of certificates of "inaffectibility" to landowners, which exempted them from further expropriation for holdings up to 100 hectares of irrigated land or 200 hectares of land with seasonal rainfall. For the production of certain specified crops, the size of inaffectible holdings was made even larger.

A massive program of irrigation contributed to the explosion of capitalist agriculture that began in this period. The irrigation projects were concentrated in northern and northwestern Mexico, where much of the land was owned directly or indirectly by prominent Mexican politicians, their friends, and relatives. Alemán presided over a great boom in public works construction, accompanied by an orgy of plunder of the public treasury by entrepreneurs and officials; his was probably the most corrupt administration in modern Mexican history.

There arose a new hacienda, technically efficient and often arrayed in modern corporate guise, that soon accounted for the bulk of Mexico's commercial agricultural production and shared its profits with processing plants that were usually subsidiaries of foreign firms. By 1961, fifty years after the revolution began, less than 1 percent of all farms possessed 50 percent of all agricultural land. Increasing numbers of small landholders meanwhile, starved for credit and lacking machinery, had to abandon their parcels of land and become peons on the new haciendas or emigrate to the cities in search of work in the new factories.

Industry continued to grow but was increasingly penetrated and dominated by foreign capital. A favorite device for foreign penetration of Mexican industry was the mixed, or joint, company, which had a number of advantages. It satisfied the requirement of Mexican law that Mexican nationals hold 51 percent of most companies operating in Mexico; it camouflaged actual domination of such enterprises by the foreign partners through control of patents, licensing agreements, and other sources of technological and financial dependence; and it formed strong ties between foreign capitalists and the native industrial and financial bourgeoisie.

The economic and social policies of Presidents Adolfo López Mateos (1958–1964) and Gustavo Díaz Ordaz (1964–1970), did not differ significantly from those of their predecessors. Under Díaz Ordaz discontent among workers mounted as their real income shrank as a result of chronic inflation, a virtual freeze on wages, and official control of trade union organizations, known as *charrismo*. Demetrio Vallejo of the independent railway workers epitomized this growing instability and led a series of strikes that quickly spread to other workers. The teachers' strike was especially disturbing to the PRI's authoritarian state and its proponents, such as the newspaper *Excelsior*, which promptly lamented the lack of respect for "authority" that this inculcated among students who consequently were not taught about "the inviolable and absolute respect for private property."

The 1957 death of Pedro Infante also gave voice to this growing social alienation. Arguably Mexico's premier entertainer, Infante, born to poverty, became famous for his good looks, quick wit, anarchic lifestyle, enormously popular films, and *ranchera* songs that proclaimed "it's better to die while dreaming than to live in reality." According to cultural historian Anne Rubenstein, his funeral and the riots that it occasioned among his mostly working-class fans represented this same social turmoil and growing popular resistance to Mexico's authoritarian state. Angered at his untimely death in an airplane crash, Infante's working-class fans empathized with their hero, whom they saw as a victim of the same forces of modernization that daily assaulted their lives, and lashed out at Mexico City's police, the most visible and proximate representatives of an authoritarian state that had relentlessly promoted modernization in the postwar world.

Popular resistance to modernization also was reflected in the experience of Mexican workers at the General Motors plant in Mexico City, which further illustrated the impact of global market changes in the 1960s. For many years, General Motors had been the symbol par excellence of postwar modernity, the populist state's import-substitution industrialization strategy, and paternalistic transnational corporate managerial relations with workers. The company, according to historian Steven Bachelor, traditionally had prided itself on creating a family environment with which Mexican workers would readily identify. This included relatively high wages; paid vacations; educational scholarships for workers' children; and company-sponsored baseball, soc-

cer, and bowling leagues. These collaborative relationships began to deteriorate, however, as international markets for automobile production became increasingly competitive and domestic demand grew in response to the 1962 Integration Decree, which required domestic production of all cars sold in Mexico. Thereafter, GM's corporate management forcibly retired older workers, hired younger replacements at half the wages, restricted their bathroom breaks, and dramatically increased the speed of assembly line operations to maximize productivity and profits. One worker, unable to endure the relentless pressure of the accelerated assembly line, broke down in tears. Others naturally resisted these pressures through open acts of defiance: one, whose boss refused to authorize a bathroom break, simply urinated on the spot; others, like Clemente Zaldívar, sabotaged the assembly line. By 1965 these tensions exploded into a month-long strike against General Motors that won some considerable wage benefits but failed to achieve the workers' goal of greater control over production decisions.

Student unrest also grew. Historian Eric Zolov argues that this was, at least in part, the consequence of the invasion of British and U.S. rock and roll music in the late 1950s and 1960s. Initially embraced by the López Mateos's government as a symbol of Mexico's newly achieved modernity, Mexico's cultural industries celebrated rock and roll, along with other musical imports like *cha-cha-chá* and *mambo* from Cuba and *cumbia* from Colombia. Epitomized by the lyrics, facial expressions, and body movements of Elvis Presley, however, upper- and middle-class Mexican youth seemed more interested in rock's sneering contempt for traditional values, associated in Mexico with *buenas costumbres* or "good behavior." Because this threatened the stability of the nation's patriarchal, authoritarian power, it was quickly denounced in the press as *"rebeldismo sin causa"* (rebellion without a cause), and an effort to discredit foreign rock shortly ensued. For example, rumors soon circulated that Presley had said he would "rather kiss three black girls than a Mexican," and an advertising campaign entitled "Die Elvis Presley" was soon initiated.

But this did not dampen the enthusiasm of Mexican middle-class youth for rock-and-roll music. On the contrary, it became more popular than ever; Mexican bands like Los Loud Jets, Los Rebeldes del Rock, and Los Teen Tops became national icons, at least in part as a result of nationalistic laws that placed high tariffs on foreign imports and required radio stations to feature play lists, 25 percent of the artists of which were Mexican. Ironically, the popularity of these Mexican bands was a reflection of their skill at producing accurate English-language covers (*refritos*) of British and U.S. rock songs by bands like The Doors, The Beatles, The Rolling Stones, Jimi Hendrix, and Janis Joplin, whose music increasingly celebrated freedom, rebellion, and disrespect of tradition. By the end of the 1960s, the rock music that flourished in Mexico City's *cafes cantantes* (musical coffeehouses) unleashed *La Onda* (The Wave), which became Mexico's counterculture, championing alike the cultural contributions of Che Guevara, Allen Ginsberg, and Mick Jagger. Denouncing these coffeehouses as "centers of perversion" influenced by decadent foreigners, the authorities organized a campaign to close them down in 1965 and instructed border officials to deny visas to "dirty, long-haired North American youth."

This was the cultural background against which the student protest movement of 1968 unfolded. Many of those who rallied in support of student demands for an end to state repression were initially attracted to the movement by its association with the rock-and-roll subculture that had developed over the previous decade. Zolov interviewed one student who confessed that in his early teens he had known little about the movement except that it was composed of students from the national university who "listened to rock." Others recalled that the student movement recruited supporters for its opposition to an authoritarian patriarchal social order by invoking state and parental repression of rock music: "Isn't it true they don't let you listen to rock?"

This student movement denounced police brutality against student protesters and violations of the constitutional autonomy of the national university. The student protest broadened into a nationwide movement demanding democratiza-

tion of Mexican economic and political life. The government responded with a savage assault by army troops on a peaceful assembly of students and others in the Plaza of Three Cultures in Mexico City (October 2, 1968), leaving a toll of dead and wounded running into the hundreds.

This massacre of students at Tlatelolco Square ignited a fierce repression of popular resistance that forced political opposition underground and channeled it into cultural forms. The student movement fractured into two groups: political radicals and *jipitecas*, who joined foreign "hippies" in their common search for psychedelic mushrooms and an escape from the modern world into the "pristine poverty" of indigenous Mexico. During the next decade, Mexico's angry young urban working class laid its claim to the rebellious rock-and-roll culture that middle- and upper-class youth increasingly abandoned after 1968. Nurtured in the *hoyos fonquis* or "funky holes," bands like Los Dug-Dugs, with their "dirty and disheveled look" and "insolent gestures that offend," used these urban "raves" to reflect and represent their youthful working-class protest. This protest found its ultimate outlet at the Avándaro music festival in 1971. Here, Mexican rock bands attracted an audience of 200,000 that included *fresas* (wealthy, privileged elites), middle-class *onderos*, and a large number of *nacos*, lower-class youth from the "proletarian neighborhoods of the Federal District." Critics on the left and right alike denounced the cultural anarchy unleashed at Avándaro, but the participants themselves more closely identified with one of the featured bands, who insisted that "Rock isn't about peace and love; rock is about revolution." Although the rock subculture was self-consciously—even aggressively—antipolitical, it gave voice to anti-authoritarian popular protest and provided a potentially powerful instrument of political organization that seemingly transcended class barriers. "Avándaro," according to Zolov, "had revealed the political dangers of rock." Not surprisingly, the PRI thereafter tried to close it down.

The economic strategy of the Díaz Ordaz administration centered on providing the greatest possible incentives to private investment, foreign

Rock-and-roll music offered alienated Mexican youth a forum for their collective protest against cultural conformity, social inequality, and political repression. Organized in the aftermath of the Mexican government's slaughter of rebellious students at Tlatelolco Square, the 1971 Avándaro Music Festival provided some 250,000 young people an opportunity to express their enthusiasm for a music that defied Mexico's established traditions. [Alberto Cruz Molina]

and domestic. The foreign debt grew alarmingly, with the volume of foreign loans reaching a figure four times that of the Ruiz Cortines era. This heavy influx of loans increased the dependent character of the Mexican economy.

The official presidential candidate, Luis Echeverría, took office in 1970 amid deepening political, social, and economic storm clouds. Echeverría signaled a tactical shift when he released a large number of students and intellectuals imprisoned after the 1968 student disturbances, promised to struggle against colonialism and corruption, and condemned the unjust distribution of land and income in Mexico. However, recent publication of archival materials, memoirs, and other testimony removed any doubt about Echeverría's leading role in the Tlatelolco mas-

sacre and the *guerra sucia* (dirty war) thereafter waged by PRI regimes against leftist opposition.

But conservative Mexican capitalists, closely linked with foreign capital, struck back by withholding investment funds from the market, setting off a serious recession. Under intense pressure from the right, Echeverría retreated. During his last three years in office he reverted to traditional policies and methods, poorly concealed by a populist rhetoric. He publicly denounced colonialism and multinational corporations, but his government did its utmost to attract foreign investments, especially from the United States. With the investments came growing foreign penetration and domination of Mexican industry, especially of its most strategic sectors. By the mid-seventies, 70 percent of earnings from the capital goods industry went to foreign capital, leaving 20 percent for public firms and 10 percent for national private companies.

As the investments increased, so did Mexico's indebtedness and the drain of its capital in the form of dividends, interest, and other returns on foreign investment. By June 1976, Mexico's foreign debt had reached $25 billion. Mexico and Brazil shared the distinction of having the highest foreign debts among Third World countries. By September of that year the growing trade deficit had forced the government to order a 60 percent devaluation of the peso, causing a sharp rise in inflation and greater hardship for the masses. The problem of landlessness or inadequate land and rural unemployment and underemployment remained as stubborn as ever. Some 6 million peasants were landless.

Prospects for the solution of Mexico's urgent problems through the electoral process appeared dim because the PRI, dominated by the industrial and financial oligarchy, had an unshakable grip on power. That power rested in the last analysis on a system of institutionalized coercion and fraud. But other methods included the co-optation of dissidents into the state apparatus; the provision of greater access to medical services, schools, low-cost housing, and other benefits to such strategic groups as state employees, professionals, and organized workers; the paternalistic distribution of goods and services to the urban poor; and a populist rhetoric that identified the ruling party with the great ideals of the Revolution. These policies slightly reduced mass poverty and income inequalities in Mexican society, but they reinforced a precarious popular base and legitimacy for the PRI's monopoly of political power. By the 1970s, however, both were threatened by rampant inflation and a stagnant economy.

Deconstructing the State: Neoliberalism and the Second Conquest of Mexico, 1977–2003

José López Portillo assumed the presidency on December 1, 1976, and continued the long-

established policy of favoring the country's elites, making it clear that he was opposed to further large-scale land distribution and would not touch efficiently run large estates even if their size exceeded legal limits. In the words of one Mexican weekly, "the constitution is to protect peasants wearing collars and ties, and not those wearing rope sandals." Amid growing optimism over Mexico's economic prospects, López Portillo announced the discovery of vast new oil and gas deposits on Mexico's east coast. Figures for the country's estimated and proven oil reserves steadily rose; by 1980 they were put at 200 billion barrels, and Mexico ranked among the world's major oil producers. With oil prices increasing steeply due to the Arab oil embargo, government planners counted on the oil and gas bonanza to alleviate Mexico's balance-of-payments problem and to finance the purchase of the goods needed for further development and the creation of new jobs. The resulting expansion of production, however, was largely concentrated in capital-intensive industries—petrochemical factories, steel mills, and the like—that generated relatively few jobs and required expensive imports of capital equipment. In agriculture, too, the main growth was in capital-intensive, export-oriented agribusiness operations that created little employment and diverted labor and acreage from staple food production, which actually declined during the 1970s; by 1980 one-third of the maize consumed in Mexico came from the United States.

The cost of imported equipment and technology required to expand oil production came very high and had to be covered by new loans. Despite increasing revenues from oil and gas exports, Mexico's trade deficit steadily rose from $1.4 billion in 1977 to $3 billion in 1979. Inflation again moved upward; Mexican workers lost 20 percent of their purchasing power between 1977 and 1979. Despite these troubling signs, the international bankers appeared eager to lend more, advancing Mexico $10 billion in 1980. Who could question the credit of a country that seemed to float on a sea of oil?

The oil boom and the massive infusions of foreign loans gave a new dimension to the familiar problem of corruption in Mexican political life.[1] One of its signs was a wave of monumental private construction. But "the dance of the billions" was drawing to a close. In the first months of 1981, responding to weakening demand and a developing world oil glut, oil prices fell sharply. Mexico's projected earnings in 1982 from oil and gas exports, the source of 75 percent of Mexico's foreign exchange, fell from $27 billion to under $14 billion. Many wealthy Mexicans, losing confidence in their currency, hurried to buy dollars and deposit them in U.S. banks. In February 1982, with the government's foreign-exchange reserves dwindling at an alarming rate, López Portillo allowed the peso to fall by 60 percent. Fear of further devaluations provoked another flight of dollars. The growing shortage of dollars, vitally needed fuel for Mexican industry, caused a widening recession and unemployment.

DEBT CRISIS, THE IMF, AND NAFTA

Bankruptcies and closings multiplied as more and more businesses lacked the dollars needed to obtain imported parts and raw materials or to pay debts contracted in dollars. With the Banco de México almost drained of reserves, López Portillo announced the nationalization of all private (but not foreign) banks and the establishment of stringent exchange controls. The bank nationalization, the most radical measure taken by a Mexican president since the "Mexicanization" of the oil industry by Cárdenas in 1938, was greeted with cries of protest from the private banking sector and great demonstrations of support by the PRI and its client organizations, the trade unions, and the parties of the left.

In Washington, usually so allergic to all measures smacking of collectivism or socialism, the bank nationalization did not arouse the hostility that might have been expected, probably because even conservative U.S. officials regarded it as a necessary step, given the circumstances. The prime

concern of the Reagan administration was to save Mexico, the third largest trading partner of the United States, from a default that could wreck the international banking system and bring down the great U.S. banks to which Mexico owed $25.8 billion, almost a third of its foreign debt. Consequently, Mexican and U.S. officials negotiated a rescue operation that provided for U.S. aid of $2.9 billion for Mexico's current-accounts problem; a seven-month freeze on the repayment of principal due to foreign bankers; and an eventual IMF (International Monetary Fund) loan of $3.9 billion, which could initiate a new cycle of commercial bank loans to Mexico. The IMF loan was, of course, subject to the usual conditions: Mexico must accept certain austerity measures—reduction of subsidies, restraints on wage increases, and other economies that were bound to hit Mexico's poor the hardest.

Even before he took office, the PRI's designated successor, Harvard-trained economist Miguel De la Madrid had indicated his approval of the strong financial medicine prescribed by the IMF. These politically unpalatable steps included price increases of 100 percent and 50 percent on gasoline and natural gas, respectively, and the lifting of price controls and subsidies for consumer items ranging from shoes to television sets. Another measure was a new devaluation of the peso that was expected to stimulate exports. It would, however, also make imports more costly, increase the burden of foreign debt service, and reduce real wages.

The solution for the Mexican crisis consisted, in essence, of adding new debts to old ones, without the slightest prospect that the huge foreign debt of some $85 billion could ever be paid or even significantly reduced without a large write-off, and of imposing heavy new burdens on already impoverished groups of the Mexican population. Four years after the rescue operation, the debt problem was more intractable than ever. By the fall of 1986, Mexico's foreign debt had risen to more than $100 billion.

The economic crisis was intertwined with a growing crisis in U.S.-Mexican relations. The Reagan administration, fanatically devoted to a "free market" economy and committed to the

[1]One Mexican news magazine, *Proceso*, estimated that officials of López Portillo's administration had misused or stolen $3 billion of public funds.

overthrow of the Sandinist government in Nicaragua, sought to use negotiations with Mexico over its foreign debt as a means of reshaping Mexico's economic structures and even its foreign policy. The U.S. economic demands included the opening up of Mexican industry to foreign investments, selling off state-owned enterprises, liberalizing foreign trade, and abandoning regulation of direct foreign investment. Despite the many concessions made by the De la Madrid government in economic policy, the Reagan administration demanded more.

Thus Mexico faced a profound, many-sided crisis. In essence, it was a crisis of the import-substitution model of development institutionalized by Cárdenas and continued by his successors. That model was based on state ownership of key industries, protection and subsidies for private industry, and such redistributive policies as the provision of social services, subsidized food prices, and land reform. It also called for the alternate use of co-optation and repression by the one-party state to keep restive labor, peasants, and intellectuals in line. By the early 1980s, however, that model, encumbered by a suffocating foreign debt, had exhausted its possibilities for growth.

Confronted with this crisis, a dominant section of the Mexican elite opted for a new, neoliberal model of development that abandoned the internal market in favor of exports of manufactured goods and integration with the world economy, especially with the United States. The economic program of President De la Madrid marked the formal transition to the new economic order. Two important steps in that direction were Mexico's signing in 1986 of the General Agreement on Tariffs and Trade, designed to lower tariffs and eliminate quotas and other restrictions on trade, and the liberalization under U.S. and Japanese pressure of foreign investment laws. The full implementation of the neoliberal project, however, had to await the outcome of the historic election of 1988, which pitted the PRI candidate, another Harvard-trained economist, Carlos Salinas de Gortari, against Cuauhtémoc Cárdenas, son of former president and national hero Lázaro Cárdenas. Cárdenas's program called for an end to political corruption and electoral fraud, suspension of foreign debt payments and renegotiation of the debt with creditor banks and governments, a mixed economy, and state assistance to the ejido farming sector. His candidacy inspired a wave of popular enthusiasm and mobilization unknown since the election of 1934 that had brought his own father to power.

Most political observers believe that Cárdenas actually won the general election, but because the PRI counted the votes, Salinas was declared the winner with 50.1 percent of the 19 million ballots cast. Despite mass protests, including a march of thousands on Mexico City, Salinas assumed office and immediately slated for privatization almost all of Mexico's remaining 770 state-owned enterprises, presiding over a fire sale of some of Mexico's choicest properties, including mines, sugar mills, a five-star hotel chain, and the national insurance company. Two government airlines, state-owned steel companies, 70 percent of the petrochemical industry, and the Teléfonos de México were sold, many well below their market value, and only some were operating inefficiently at a loss. The process was accompanied by widespread layoffs and wage cuts and growing foreign conquest of Mexican industry, aided by repeal of the law that restricted foreign control to 49 percent ownership of Mexican businesses. Observers noted that the state companies were being sold to the same small group of people and their foreign partners who already controlled most of Mexico's economy, with no effort to promote "popular capitalism" through stock offerings in the open market. "Crony capitalism," ran one comment, "seems to be the current government's style."

The denationalization of Mexican industry through privatization was accompanied by the demise of many small and medium-sized domestic businesses as a result of the removal of most tariff barriers. These developments reflected a general tendency on the part of Mexico's recent rulers to abandon the struggle for economic independence that had been a major goal of the Mexican Revolution, of Lázaro Cárdenas, and even of the conservative but nationalistic presidents who followed him. The foreign conquest of the Mexican consumer goods market since 1986 was very evident: "Everything from Italian pasta and Diet Coke to European cookies and Italian loafers is now available. . . . In many cases local manufacturers have closed down because imports are cheaper and better made."

The decision to abandon the struggle for economic independence was reflected in the Mexican government's encouragement of the program that permitted U.S. companies to establish plants (called *maquiladoras* or *maquilas*) for production of parts and their assembly on the Mexican side of the border. The program allowed duty-free entry of parts and machinery into Mexico and total U.S. ownership of the plants. U.S. customs regulations permitted the finished products to enter the United States with duty paid only on the value of the labor, not on that of the goods themselves. The lure of low wages (averaging between $3.75 and $4.50 per day) caused an explosive growth of maquiladora plants, whose number grew from some 455 with 130,000 workers in 1982 to over 2,000 with more than 600,000 workers, two-thirds of them women, in 1998. In these plants workers assembled television sets, radios, computer hardware, and the like for the American market.

Many of these plants were unorganized; in others the workers were represented by government-controlled unions that usually offered employers "protection contracts" that kept wages low and did not meet the labor standards mandated by the Mexican Federal Labor Law. For example, the predominantly male supervisors in these U.S. companies routinely subjected a mostly poor, uneducated female labor force to sexual violence, harassment, and discrimination. To avoid the expense of complying with Mexican laws that mandated paid pre- and post-partum maternity leaves, these companies, according to a 1998 U.S. Labor Department report, often screened out pregnant job applicants, forced women employees to take birth control pills, checked their monthly menstruation flows, required them to submit to regular urine tests, and arbitrarily fired pregnant women or reassigned them to physically challenging tasks designed to induce voluntary resignations or miscarriages. Moreover, according to University of Chicago sociologist Leslie Salzinger,

this "sexualization of factory life," symbolized by annual industrywide "Señorita Maquiladora" beauty contests, discouraged worker solidarity and contributed directly to skyrocketing rates of violent crime against women.

Nonetheless, Mexican officials defended the program by arguing that it relieved high Mexican unemployment. But because many of the plants were true sweatshops, with health and safety problems widespread among the workers, it tended to institutionalize poverty on both sides of the border, for the program inevitably tended to depress wages in the U.S. border zone. In the United States, unions were concerned about the loss of thousands of jobs and the prospect of more to come. Environmentalists and health workers were alarmed by the shockingly poor environmental and health record of the maquiladoras, which freely released various toxins into the air and water and routinely neglected to treat hazardous wastes. The American Medical Association declared that the maquiladora program had created "a virtual cesspool" on the border.

The neoliberal assault on state regulation especially affected women. Privatization eliminated relatively high-paying jobs for men and thereby placed additional burdens on women to supplement family income by working outside the home, often as salaried employees but more commonly as self-employed street vendors in the "informal sector." The maquiladoras especially sought out women workers, largely because management viewed them as more docile and likely to accept lower wages. Consequently, between 1970 and 1993, women's waged employment almost doubled from 17.6 to 33 percent of the total work force. But, according to a recent study, 40 percent of women workers were paid less than the minimum wage and 60 percent received no additional benefits; moreover, 44 percent worked part time (less than thirty-five hours per week), and more than 54 percent were self-employed, working in microenterprises or on the streets.

All these economic, social, and environmental problems were exacerbated by the North American Free Trade Agreement, which was approved in November 1993 by the U.S. Congress after a bitter debate. In Mexico the treaty was denounced by independent labor, peasant unions, and Cuauhtémoc Cárdenas, all of whom called for a new trade agreement, providing workers in the three countries (Mexico, Canada, and the United States) with the same workplace conditions, collective bargaining rights, and occupational safety and health standards. But Mexico's PRI-dominated Senate swiftly brushed aside all objections and ratified the treaty on November 22.

NAFTA eliminated tariffs between Canada, the United States, and Mexico over fifteen years and permitted the free flow of investment capital across borders. To meet the concerns of labor unions and conservationists, negotiators from Canada, the United States, and Mexico worked out side agreements dealing with labor and the environment. But the commissions created by the accords were simply "watchdog" bodies, with no enforcement powers or minimum standards to enforce. Moreover, the Mexican government routinely manipulated or juggled workplace information.

U.S. labor unions had good reason to fear that free trade with Mexico, where wages were only one-tenth of those in the U.S.,[2] would result in the loss of many thousands of jobs. Estimates of the probable job losses in the United States as a result of the implementation of NAFTA ranged from 150,000 by President George H. W. Bush's Secretary of Labor Lynn Martin to the forecast of 550,000 jobs lost over ten years by Jeff Faux, president of the Economic Policy Institute. Aside from the actual job loss, NAFTA pressured U.S. labor to make wage and other concessions to employers. President Clinton and his Secretary of Labor Robert Reich argued that the United States would lose low-paid, unskilled jobs to Mexico but retain high-tech, high-paid jobs. In fact, three-quarters of the new manufacturing jobs created by U.S. com-

panies in Mexico were precisely in the high-tech, capital-intensive fields of automobiles and electronics, and the productivity of Mexican labor was rising rapidly. The claim that job creation through increased exports to Mexico would more than compensate for any job losses in the United States was equally dubious. The primary targets of NAFTA were the United States and Canada, not the impoverished Mexican market. Over 50 percent of the Mexican population lived below poverty levels set by the United Nations. Only one-third of the population had sufficient income to constitute an effective market for more than basic necessities.

Meanwhile the De la Madrid and Salinas policies created an unprecedented crisis for the ejido sector of Mexican agriculture. Even before the passage of NAFTA, Mexican small farmers faced increasing competition from foreign agricultural imports as a result of Mexico's entry into the General Agreement on Tariffs and Trade (GATT) and steadily reduced import restrictions. NAFTA, allowing the free entrance of U.S. corn into Mexico, dealt a death blow to Mexican maize producers, since maize costs about two or three times as much to produce per ton in Mexico as in the United States. Moreover, U.S. farmers still benefited from various government subsidies that enabled them to undersell their Mexican competitors. According to one estimate, as a result of NAFTA the number of maize farmers in Mexico would decline from about 2.8 million to 420,000 in a few years.

The very existence of the ejido system was threatened by a February 1992 reform of Article 27 of the constitution. This constitutional reform allowed the division of the ejidos into individual lots and their rental, sale, or joint cultivation with domestic or foreign partners. The provision for rental of ejido land legalized a previously existing practice, but it was predicted that the lure of cash would induce many impoverished ejidatarios to sell their land. Others lost their land through foreclosure by banks. Increasingly, companies with easier access to credit and capital bought the most productive areas of the Mexican countryside.

Where did the hundreds of thousands of farmers who abandoned the land as a result of NAFTA

---

[2]In October 1993 the Economic Research Institute of Vienna issued a report showing just how low average wages were in Mexico: about $2.35 per hour, compared with $17.02 in the United States, $16.16 in Japan, and $25.94 in Germany. They were even lower than those of the "Asian Tigers": $3.89 in Hong Kong, $4.93 in South Korea, and $5.19 in Taiwan.

and the agrarian reform go? Many left for the overcrowded cities, swelling the numbers of unemployed or underemployed Mexicans; others found low-wage jobs in the border maquiladoras or on farms producing fruit or vegetables for the U.S. market. Many headed for the United States to join the pool of Mexican undocumented workers, numbering in the millions and growing between 200,000 and 300,000 a year, who worked in agriculture, domestic service, small industry, and food service. The existence of this pool of low-paid, vulnerable workers—vulnerable precisely because they were undocumented, subject to deportation—represented a source of superprofits to employers and contributed to the weakness of organized labor. In general, U.S. unions did little to incorporate the migrants into their ranks or protest their abuse by police and border guards. A wave of anti-Mexican, anti-immigrant sentiment, with strong racist overtones, swept through the United States and heightened tension on both sides of the border. This sentiment was reflected in California's 1994 passage of Proposition 187, which denied social services to illegal immigrants.

NEOLIBERAL CRISIS AND POPULAR RESISTANCE

Despite widespread poverty, repression, and discontent, there appeared to be little effective opposition in 1993 to the PRI's monolithic control of Mexican politics and its neoliberal economic program. In late November the PRI held the traditional *destape* or "unveiling" of the party's presidential candidate, Luis Donaldo Colosio, who had managed the fraud-riddled 1988 election.

Then a succession of dramatic events shattered Mexico's surface calm and raised serious doubts about the ruling party's secure grip on power and its internal unity. On New Year's Day 1994, a revolt led by a self-styled "Zapatista Army of National Liberation" (EZLN), believed to number several thousand members, broke out in the southern state of Chiapas, one of the poorest regions of Mexico, with a largely Mayan population. The rebels proclaimed NAFTA and its free trade program "a death certificate" for the native peoples of Mexico and demanded sweeping political and economic reforms, including self-rule for Mexico's indigenous communities, repeal of the reforms to Article 27, and fraud-free elections. The rebels seized and briefly held the highland city of San Cristóbal de las Casas and three other towns before melting back into the Lacandon rain forest after a savage counteroffensive by fourteen thousand Mexican army troops, accompanied by bombing of villages, summary executions, torture of suspects, and other repressive measures.

With some specific features that reflected its tragic history, Chiapas's problems epitomized those of rural Mexico. The Mexican Revolution of 1910 never really reached Chiapas, with the result that no agrarian reform took place there. The great landowners still owned about 40 percent of the land, while 63 percent of the campesinos owned plots of less than 2.5 acres. Emboldened by the crisis and the standoff with the government, land-hungry campesinos, not waiting for the government to act, occupied nearly 100,000 acres of farmland, resulting in armed clashes with paramilitary groups organized by the great landowners.

The problems of the campesinos were aggravated by severely eroded soils, cutbacks in credits and subsidies by the Salinas administration since 1988, and the collapse of world coffee prices. According to economist José Luis Calva, the "time bomb" that exploded in Chiapas resulted from the government's structural adjustment plan and the official free trade policy, which resulted in a greatly increased importation of cheap corn from the United States. In his view, the reforms to Article 27 of the constitution, threatening what remained of the communal ejido system, "detonated" the crisis.

The Chiapas crisis deeply wounded the PRI and the Salinas regime, exposing sharp disagreements that widened appreciably with the shocking assassination of Colosio. Although Salinas quickly named another U.S.-trained economist, Ernesto Zedillo Ponce de León, as the PRI's new presidential candidate, a large majority of the Mexican public did not expect honest elections. So widespread skepticism greeted the government's announcement that Zedillo's margin of victory topped 50.08 percent, the "magic number" needed to retain control of the Congress and ensure a presidential mandate. Charging "colossal fraud," Cárdenas's opposition party discovered more than six thousand polling places in which more votes were cast than the number of voters on the voting list. An unknown number of persons was erased from the voting rolls; the independent observer group Civic Alliance (AC) found that 65 percent of the nation's polling stations featured shaved registries.

In the midst of the regime's crisis of delegitimacy, the Zapatistas of Chiapas convened a National Democratic Convention in the Lacandon forest to which it invited all sectors of "civil society," including all political parties except PRI, "the common enemy to us all." The convention, modeled on the 1914 revolutionary convention summoned by Zapata and Villa, reflected the Zapatista decision to broaden the scope of their movement—to develop electoral activity as an adjunct to armed struggle, leading to the drafting of a new constitution.

Consequently Zedillo faced a sea of troubles. In Chiapas the military standoff continued, but there was widespread and growing disorder. Meanwhile, indigenous and mestizo farmers established four autonomous zones in different regions of Chiapas. They blocked roads, refused to pay taxes and electricity bills to federal and state authorities, and ejected local PRI officials. The Zapatista leadership proclaimed these areas "zones of rebellion." A wave of land takeovers continued, producing the unfamiliar spectacle of over one hundred wealthy landowners staging a hunger strike in Mexico City to call attention to their plight. Zedillo was forced to choose between coming to terms with the rebels or crushing them with armed force. From the PRI's point of view, both options could have had dangerous consequences.

Mexican public opinion, as expressed in polls and demonstrations, favored a peaceful solution that took into account the just grievances of the Chiapas peasants. But PRI hardliners, the right-wing PAN, and foreign investors demanded a military solution of the problem. A January 1995 memorandum written by Chase Manhattan Bank advisor Riordan Roett and leaked to an investigative newsletter warned that "the government will need to eliminate the Zapatistas to demonstrate [to the investment community] their effective control of the national territory and of security policy." In addition to calling for the Zapatistas' liquidation, the memo warned the Zedillo administration "to consider carefully whether or not to allow opposition victories if fairly won at the ballot box," because "a failure to retain PRI controls runs the risk of splitting the government party."

Facing these rival pressures, Zedillo initially sought compromise. But on February 9, 1995, on the pretext that Zapatista arms caches had been found in Mexico City and Veracruz, Zedillo sent thousands of troops, backed by tanks and heavy artillery, into the rebel-held territory, with orders to arrest the Zapatista leadership. The rebels, along with thousands of their supporters, fled into the jungle area near the Guatemalan border. The government's action provoked angry protests, including a march of almost a hundred thousand people in Mexico City, that forced Zedillo to halt the military operation.

A more immediate threat to the regime was the prospect of an economic collapse. NAFTA, which was supposed to bring prosperity to Mexico, instead had deepened the recessive tendencies of the Mexican economy. The removal of trade barriers had ruined many small farmers who found themselves unable to compete with the influx of cheaper U.S. grain, milk, and other agricultural products. Mexican national industries like the shoe and textile industries were threatened with destruction by competition from more technologically advanced U.S. and Canadian producers. An overvalued peso—deliberately overvalued to promote confidence in the Mexican economy, ensure the passage of NAFTA, and attract foreign investment—contributed to the flood of imports. This in turn caused a chain of events: a growing trade deficit, a decline in the value of the peso against the dollar, and the flight of domestic and foreign capital out of the country.

Mexico had long financed its account deficits with foreign loans; its total foreign debt was about $174 billion, which cost more than $25 billion in interest and principal in 1997. Of the $80 billion borrowed in recent years, only some $15 billion

Thousands of supporters crowded into Mexico City's main square in March 2001 to greet a caravan of Zapatista commanders who had traveled from the southern state of Chiapas to press their claims for indigenous rights, popular democracy, and an end to neoliberal policies. [Gamma]

was invested in plant and equipment, and the rest was used to service previous loans and restore Mexico's exhausted currency reserves. In December 1994, with $20 billion in short-term loans coming due in a few months, the peso free-falling, and capital flight accelerating, Mexico faced a replay of the 1982 debacle of inflation and looming default. Mexican stocks fell sharply, sending shock waves through the hemisphere's money markets.

Once again foreign governments, led by the United States, and international lending agencies came to Mexico's rescue with a bailout package of loans and loan guarantees amounting to some $50 billion to pay or renegotiate the huge loans coming due and to stem the peso's collapse. But the price of the February 1995 bailout was high. In return for $20 billion from the United States in loan guarantees, Mexico had to put up $7 billion a

year in oil-export revenues as collateral, to be deposited at the New York Federal Reserve. Another $27.5 billion came from the IMF and the Bank for International Settlements, with the usual conditions: Mexico must cut social spending, restrain wage increases, and expand the privatization program to include PEMEX, the nation's prized petrochemical industry. Many Mexicans viewed the deal not as a bailout but as a sellout. "The gringos have us by the throat again," commented one Mexico City taxi driver.

The cost for ordinary Mexicans was more austerity and more hardships. With the peso down 55 percent since 1994 and inflation expected to top 15 percent in 1998, the real minimum wage, according to an economics writer for the national daily *La Jornada*, dropped from $4.00 a day to $2.82. These sacrifices did not restore the Mexican economy's health. The bailout, filling the pockets of bankers and multinationals, did nothing to promote economic development. "The immediate consequence of the $47.5 billion package," concluded a report in *The Nation*, "is to allow resumption of the speculative merry-go-round, with investment banks swiftly resuming their lucrative practice of underwriting and trading Mexican securities."

But, by the decade's end, recurrent economic troubles, combined with the regime's growing vacillation, had produced a crisis of state legitimacy, fractured elite consensus, and fueled widespread popular discontent. In 1996, the government signed the San Andrés Accords, halting troop movements in Chiapas and recognizing indigenous rights to create "autonomous municipalities." A grassroots coalition of human rights groups in neighboring oil-rich Tabasco state promptly mobilized 10,000 Chontal natives, declared local petroleum reserves "an autonomous region," and blocked access to sixty wells; meanwhile, the powerful oil workers' union successfully lobbied the PRI leadership to condemn Zedillo's plans to privatize PEMEX. The Chiapas revolt continued to seethe, even as its rebellious message spread.

Still another guerrilla group, the Popular Revolutionary Army (EPR), emerged in Guerrero and coordinated an armed campaign in six southern states that included seizure of radio stations, raids on police stations, and assaults on army posts. Although government leaders scoffed at the EPR's popularity and dismissed its threat to regime stability. Father Máximo Gómez, a local parish priest, concluded that "90 percent of the people here support the guerrillas in their hearts."

Popular opposition to the PRI and its neoliberal program, although clearly centered in the impoverished south, also continued to grow in central Mexico. *El Barzón*, a debtors' group initially composed of middle-class farmers and ejidatarios damaged by free trade and high interest rates, filed some 350,000 lawsuits to block mortgage foreclosures; organized mass protests to obstruct the nation's commercial highways; and staged sit-ins in government buildings, banks, courtrooms, and factories to demand debt relief. Under the leadership of leftist Juan José Quirino, the *barzonistas* expanded and became more politically partisan.

With an estimated membership of half a million to a million, the Barzón demanded that the banks return to ejidos over a million acres of land illegally foreclosed during the debt crisis and announced an alliance with the Zapatistas to establish a democratic front to resist neoliberalism.

But the most convincing evidence of massive popular resistance to the PRI and its neoliberal agenda were successive electoral repudiations in 1997 and 2000. This first secured a majority for opposition parties in the Chamber of Deputies that denied the PRI its traditional veto-proof Senate, thereby undermining the presidency's nearly unlimited de facto power, and gave Cuauhtémoc Cárdenas control of metropolitan Mexico City, home to a quarter of the nation's people. The second shattered the PRI's historic monopoly of presidential power, which dated to its founding in 1929, and elected Vicente Fox Quesada, the candidate of the National Action Party (PAN), to the presidency. Fox, a wealthy former Coca-Cola business executive, had campaigned on populist themes and was a founding member of "Latin American Alternatives," a group that denounced neoliberalism for its failure "to generate growth and development, and particularly to meet the challenge of achieving a more equitable distribution of income and wealth." He promised to support indigenous rights and negotiate a peaceful resolution of the Chiapas crisis; dismantle the structure of political authoritarianism; promote economic growth; protect the state-owned oil company, PEMEX, from privatization; reduce poverty and inequality throughout Mexico; and double state funding of education.

Once in office, however, Fox seemed to abandon his populist promises and surrounded himself with neoliberal advisors from the Mexican and transnational corporate business community: the World Bank, Union Carbide, DuPont-Mexico, Procter and Gamble, and Avantel, a subsidiary of WorldCom. His Minister of the Interior, Santiago Creel, was heir to an agricultural, mining, and timber fortune whose origins lay in the nineteenth-century world of Porfirio Díaz. Given their social backgrounds, it was no surprise that these men supported policies that favored investors, not social justice. During its first year in office, the Fox administration sought to cut subsidies to small farmers, open Mexico's energy and telecommunications industry to privatization, eliminate legal protections for workers, facilitate debt collection, and secure passage of a regressive 15 percent, value-added tax on food and medicine, which, opponents insisted, would fall disproportionately on 40 million poor people, 17 million of whom were desperately poor. Largely because he lacked a congressional majority, however, Fox failed to win legislative support for these proposals. His own party helped defeat a presidential initiative that would have protected indigenous rights, while other legislative coalitions blocked the president's remaining agenda. Fox himself even failed to win congressional authorization to leave the country to meet with Microsoft CEO Bill Gates! By December 2001 polls showed that his popularity had declined to 50 percent from an historical high of 75; moreover, according to another poll published by the Mexico City newspaper *El Universal*, only 37 percent said they would vote for Fox again.

Meanwhile, the economy, which grew at an annual average rate of 5.5 percent between 1997 and 2000, nonetheless produced slightly higher rates of poverty. After two decades of neoliberal policies and steady economic growth (averaging 2.8 percent), punctuated by major declines in 1982 and 1994, the share of poor Mexicans, according to conservative estimates of the InterAmerican Development Bank, had grown from 32 percent in 1977 to 36 percent in 1994 and to 38 percent in 1998. Using different standards and methods, Julio Bolvitnik, an economics professor at the Colegio de México and an advisor to the Fox government, reported in March 2001 that some 70 million Mexicans were poor, 27 million of whom earned less than was necessary to purchase their basic nutritional requirements. Moreover, the World Bank, a champion of neoliberalism, reported that in 1998, after two decades of neoliberal policies, income inequality in Mexico was greater than ever: the poorest 10 percent of the population earned 1.3 percent of national income, while the wealthiest 10 percent received 41.7 percent. This growing inequality was largely a function of unregulated

markets that empowered investors rather than workers. But fewer than 2 percent of Mexican households relied upon investment income, while 72 percent depended upon waged labor. Since 1993 about a million manufacturing jobs were created, but half of these were created in the *maquila* industry and the other half in the informal sector, both of which were renowned for low wages and part-time, insecure employment. In 1990, 40 percent of the Mexican work force was self-employed in these "microenterprises," but this rose to more than 50 percent in 2001. Between 1994 and 2000 average wages declined 21 percent.

By 2002, Mexico was utterly dependent on foreign export and investment-capital markets. Since 1990 its external debt rose steadily from $104 billion to $152 billion, it relied on the United States for 80 percent of its export sales, and it paid foreign bankers $1 of every $3 that it earned. Ominously, however, Mexico's economic boomlet recently began to wither, as the U.S. market contracted: export prices fell, export income dropped, economic output declined, and unemployment grew. Yet another economic crisis loomed, based on whether the U.S. economy rebounded strongly in 2003 and whether new foreign capital investment followed these declining economic indicators. Because the previous five years of growth had failed to reduce income inequality and poverty, even a normal cyclical economic downturn, compounded by an ineffective government response, threatened to produce a social catastrophe.

Whatever the outcome, at the heart of Mexico's continuing economic, political, and social crisis was the debt problem and the system of dependent capitalism that produced it. North American scholar Peter Evans had presciently written in 1979:

> Like Brazil, Mexico has found that dependent development requires a mass of imported outputs even larger than the exports it generates, and that even when the multinationals cooperate in the promotion of local accumulation they still ship more capital back to the center than they bring in. . . . Dependent development does not correct the imbalances in semiperipheral relations with the center; it replaces old imbalances with new ones.

13 Argentina: The Failure of Democracy

A FTER THIRTY YEARS of explosive economic growth and sustained political stability, Argentina seemed ready to take a place among the developed nations by the first decade of the twentieth century. Argentines could proudly point out that their nation was the world's greatest exporter of grain and one of the most important exporters of meat; they could boast of a railroad network unsurpassed outside western Europe and the United States and of a capital, Buenos Aires, that ranked among the world's most beautiful and cultured cities. Argentines were seemingly prosperous, relatively well educated, and increasingly urban. The burgeoning population (nearly 8 million in 1910) and transportation system promised to create an internal market that would stimulate the rise of native manufacturing and elevate Argentina to the position of one of the world's modern industrialized countries.

The full flowering of democracy, too, seemed close at hand. The landed oligarchy, known as *estancieros*, historically had monopolized Argentine politics by relying on military force and restricting the vote to propertied males, most of whom traditionally resided on rural estates. By the early twentieth century, however, Argentina had become a much more urban society and a propertied middle class consisting of shopkeepers, artisans, manufacturers, and government bureaucrats emerged. New political organizations like the Radical Party soon developed and began to compete effectively for this new constituency. Moreover, with the gradual professionalization of the army, the social composition of the officer corps also changed. Middle-class men, mostly the sons of immigrants, replaced the old officer groups and the oligarchy gradually lost its predominance. These developments and a series of unsuccessful Radical coups apparently convinced the estancieros that the time had come for electoral reform. Consequently, in the hope of attracting a significant share of newly enfranchised voters, they embraced the Saenz Peña Law, which provided for universal male suffrage and a secret ballot.

The appearance of prosperity and emerging democracy, however, proved illusory. Stagnation, interspersed with periods of depression and runaway inflation, marked the Argentine economy during succeeding decades. Military coups, disorder, and brutal repression afflicted the nation's politics. At the base of these problems lay Argentina's structural dependence on foreign markets and capital, a dependence that placed the country's economy at the mercy of foreign events and decisions made abroad. This helped perpetuate a deformed social and political system.

318

The Export Economy

Argentina's dynamic economic development during the last quarter of the nineteenth century and the early twentieth century was due to three factors: the appearance of a large market in Europe for its products—wool, mutton, beef, and wheat; the inflow of millions of immigrants, who provided cheap labor for the expanding agricultural sector; and the influx of large quantities of foreign investment capital, which went to construct railroads, put more land under cultivation, and establish food (mainly meat) processing plants. The nation's prosperity depended on its ability to export huge amounts of agricultural commodities, to import the manufactured goods it required, and to attract a steady stream of large-scale foreign investment.

Consequently, Argentina was critically vulnerable to fluctuations in international market and finance conditions. Any reduction in overseas trade reverberated disastrously throughout the economy. Because Argentines usually imported more than they exported—a tendency made worse by the fact that the market price for raw materials remained steady or declined while the prices of manufactured goods rose—the country suffered from chronic trade deficits that habitually depleted the national economy of circulating coin and restricted local market development. To attract new sources of wealth, successive Argentine governments had opened Argentina to foreign capital.

Foreign investment reached enormous proportions in the first decades of the twentieth century. During the years 1900 to 1929, foreigners came to control between 30 and 40 percent of the nation's fixed investments. Argentina absorbed nearly 10 percent of all foreign investment carried out by capital-exporting nations, one-third of all the foreign investment in Latin America, and more than 40 percent of the total foreign investment of Great Britain, the world's leading capitalist power. Investment was concentrated in railroads and government bonds, the proceeds from which subsidized the construction of railroads and public works.

Although foreign investment unquestionably helped fuel economic growth, it simultaneously created immense economic difficulties. Huge interest payments on foreign debts and the profit remittances of foreign-owned companies, often representing between 30 and 50 percent of the value of Argentina's exports, produced serious balance-of-payments problems. Because government bodies owed much of the foreign debt, a substantial portion of government revenue went to service payments. Rigid interest rates and repayment schedules meant that the burden remained the same, even when state revenues declined because of adverse economic conditions, and that revenues earmarked for debt service could not be diverted to other areas.

Every sector of the Argentine economy depended on exports. Agriculture and livestock raising employed 35 percent of the work force. The nation's greatest agricultural area, the pampas, exported 70 percent of its production. Argentine industry centered on food processing, mainly meat packing. As late as 1935 food-stuff processing accounted for 47 percent of all industrial production, and textiles for another 20 percent. The transportation industry—railroads and coastal shipping—handled mostly export commodities.

Rich and poor alike relied on the export economy for their livelihood. The ruling elite was composed of large landowners, who produced almost entirely for the export trade. Their income and their political power rested squarely on the export economy. In addition to large numbers of farm laborers, many urban and industrial workers depended on exports for their jobs. The major trade and industrial unions in Argentina arose in those industries—coastal shipping, railroads, dock work, and packinghouses—whose workers owed their well-being to overseas trade. Because the government relied on revenues derived from import taxes, significant numbers of white-collar workers and professionals employed by the government also were intimately tied to the export economy.

Foreign control and influence permeated the economy. Most of the large merchant houses, which carried on the all-important export-import trade, were either owned by or closely affiliated with foreign houses. The major shipping lines (both intercoastal and interoceanic), the railroads, and the *frigoríficos* (meat-packing plants) were owned and operated by British or U.S. companies.

The export economy brought indisputable benefits to Argentina, but those benefits were unequally distributed. There were, for example, sharp differences in economic development among regions. Whereas the pampas and Buenos Aires boomed, most of the interior provinces stagnated. Mendoza and Tucumán with their wine and sugar made some headway, but all the other central and northwestern provinces—Jujuy, La Rioja, Santiago del Estero, and Salta—experienced social and economic decline.

The inequalities of property and income between the various classes were equally glaring. The rich were very rich and growing richer; the poor grew poorer. In the countryside, the estancieros, masters of thousands of acres of rich land, built palaces, while the majority of foreign-born immigrant sharecroppers eked out a miserable living. In Buenos Aires, wealthy landowners, merchants, and lawyers gathered at the sumptuous Jockey Club, while laborers struggled to make ends meet as inflation eroded their already insufficient paychecks.

The expansion of market forces also dissolved traditional barriers between private and public spheres, forcing women into low-paid, menial positions in urban factories and sweatshops without releasing them from their unpaid responsibilities in the home. According to a late nineteenth-century Buenos Aires census, women composed 39 percent of the paid work force, and a 1904 report by Dr. Juan Bialet Masse confirmed that, in an industrial environment generally characterized by intolerable working conditions and low wages, Argentine women "suffered the most intense discrimination and exploitation." Apparently male employers preferred women workers because they were cheaper, more reliable, more efficient, and more docile than men. A 1913 report for the National Labor Department revealed that, on average, children employed in industry received half the wages of women, whose income, in turn, was half that of men.

Argentina's greatest treasure was its land, but only a few Argentines owned sizable portions of it.

In 1914 farm units larger than 2,500 acres accounted for only 8.2 percent of the total number of farms but held 80 percent of the nation's farm area. Over 40 percent of farms were worked by tenants, most on terms that were less than favorable. In 1937 a mere 1 percent of the active rural population controlled over 70 percent of Argentina's farmland, much of which they left idle. Yet the land was fertile and suitable for intensive agriculture. Thousands of immigrants came to Argentina in search of land only to discover that virtually all had long since been monopolized by the estanciero oligarchy.

Income distribution followed the same pattern. Less than 5 percent of the active population garnered 70 percent of the gross income derived from agriculture. Not only did workers and rural laborers receive little benefit from the export system, but the operation of the system's finances and taxation eroded what little return they did receive for their labor. Faced with chronic deficits in the balance of payments and unwilling or unable to tax the land or income of the landed elite, the government had no alternative but to resort to the printing press to finance its costs. The result was inflation. Exporters also demanded a fluctuating currency-exchange rate, which had an adverse effect on wage earners. Finally, the tax structure burdened the mass of consumers with high sales taxes that discouraged internal market expansion.

Argentine Society

Argentine society divided roughly into three classes—upper, middle, and lower. The upper class acquired its wealth and prestige through its virtual monopoly of landownership. These large landholders used the late nineteenth-century export boom to solidify and enhance their power. Cattle fatteners, who supplied beef for both the domestic and foreign markets, constituted the most powerful faction within this elite. This inner circle was composed of approximately four hundred families who were closely allied through social clubs and business associations. Geographically, most of the wealth was located in the cattle and cereal regions of the pampas near Buenos Aires. From 1880 to

Modern South America

1912 this landed oligarchy also controlled national politics. It used its control over the government to promote meat and grain exports, guarantee easy credit for members, and provide more favorable taxation and currency policies. The other great institutions of Argentine society, the military and the church, also reflected the views of the elite.

Late nineteenth-century economic growth stimulated urbanization, which transformed the nation's class structure. An urban middle class arose. This middle class, heavily concentrated in the bureaucracy and professions, depended on the export economy and attached itself to the Radical Party.

The lower class divided into two groups: urban marginals and workers. Urban marginals were a racially and ethnically diverse group, composed largely of immigrant foreigners, including Eastern European Jews, against whom regular employers routinely discriminated. Not surprisingly, according to historian Donna Guy, women constituted a large share of this underclass, a considerable number of whom became involved in prostitution, which the Argentine government had legalized in 1875. For elites, legalized prostitution—which required prostitutes to undergo regular medical examinations and restricted their activities to particular urban zones—aimed to stabilize the patriarchal family by providing a safe, secure outlet for the release of men's sexual frustrations; it also enabled elites to collect revenues from, and establish control over, a population considered "dangerous." But for the prostitutes and pimps, these licensed bordellos became a means of survival and, ironically, gave birth to a cultural form—the tango—that eventually defined Argentina's national identity.

The tango, first as dance and later as song, had emerged in the early nineteenth century among the nation's lower classes, especially its black population, which composed 25 percent of Buenos Aires. According to historian John Charles Chasteen, the dance originally was performed by enslaved Africans to celebrate their individual black kings and distinguish their African national identities. Later, it evolved into *candombe*, a dance style typical of the Argentine black community, and by the middle of the nineteenth century, it was

adopted by Argentine elites to mock Afro-Argentine culture. By the early twentieth century, however, the tango or *milonga* had become, according to the *Dictionary of Argentine Expressions*, "a dance found only among people of the lower orders." It was featured routinely in the brothels, nightclubs, and *academios* (dancehalls) of Buenos Aires, where poor women mixed with men of all social classes. Its songs typically addressed themes about life in the tenements (*conventillos*), criminals, slum dwellers, and the relentless intrusion of poverty on the dreams of young girls.

By contrast, most members of the working class labored in small factories, where Argentina's industrial expansion was concentrated until 1914. (The primary exception to the predominance of small industries were the frigoríficos.) A considerable number of workers were employed by the shipping industry, railroads, and urban tramways in the Port of Buenos Aires, where organizations like *La Fraternidad*, the railroad workers' union, and the Maritime Workers' Federation were especially strong. Numerous strikes occurred after the turn of the century and throughout the first Radical regime (1916–1922). The labor movement, however, was weakened by diverse viewpoints on political activity and by internecine rivalries among Socialists, anarchists, and syndicalists.

The Radical Era, 1916–1930

THE RISE OF THE RADICAL PARTY

Naturally, increasing social inequality produced growing unrest among the urban middle class, university students, women, workers, ethnic minorities, and small groups of junior military officers. The Radicals drew upon this discontent in their efforts to overthrow the oligarchy by force in 1905. Despite their failure, the Radicals attracted growing popular support in the decade that followed.

Radical Party strength rested on twin pillars: its local urban organization, which acted to meet the needs of the middle class, and its leader, Hipólito Yrigoyen, who played a dual role as the titular head of the Radical Party. First, he was the great mediator who managed to reconcile the

Carolina Muzzilli and Alicia Moreau were militant Argentine feminists who agitated for civil and political equality, social justice, and international solidarity in the early twentieth century. [From the cover of *Nuestra Causa,* a feminist newspaper published in Argentina. Biblioteca Juan B. Justo, Buenos Aires. Photograph courtesy of Asunción Lavrín]

often conflicting interests of the middle class and large landowners who made up his political coalition. Second, although inarticulate and a recluse, Yrigoyen managed to project an austere democratic image that made him the party's charismatic leader. This clever deal maker and manipulator symbolized for the middle class the Radical dedication to democracy. Despite a checkered past that included shady business deals, he furnished the party with much of its moral appeal.

The Radical propaganda effectively presented an image of a national party, transcending the narrow regional and class interests that had previously governed Argentine politics. The Radical program was purposely vague. It straddled the line between its two major constituencies, the middle class and the landed elite. The Radicals therefore never challenged the basic premises of the export

economy and its dependence on foreign capital. The party advocated neither land reform nor industrialization.

During the Radical era, Argentine women, who historically had been treated like children or, worse, the legal property of men (*patria potestad*), continued to organize and agitate for equality both within and outside the formal structure of political parties. Cecelia Grierson, Argentina's first female doctor, formed the National Women's Council to lobby for women's greater access to education and professional employment. These women's groups, like others in Latin America, typically sought to protect and conserve the primary power of women within the family. Although some viewed this as an implicitly "conservative" role, in the context of a traditional society battered by unfettered market forces, the communal maternal values of family life quickly translated into civic actions, which Francesca Miller calls "social motherhood."

This meant that, irrespective of class, ethnic, racial, or regional identity, women activists came to expect the state to intervene to monitor, regulate, protect, and harmonize the interests of all members of the Argentine national family, especially when these were threatened by outsiders. "The aristocratic women and the proletarian women are equally victims," thundered Carolina Muzzilli, a prominent feminist. "It is time that the Argentine woman recognizes that she is not inferior to men and, even if she has a different mission, her civil and natural rights must be restored."

In practice, however, class interests often distinguished the activities of various women's organizations. For example, feminist leaders like Alicia Moreau de Justo, founder of the Socialist Feminist Center in 1900, pressured her husband, Juan Bautista Justo, the nation's premier Socialist, and his male colleagues to sponsor Law 5291, which attempted to regulate working conditions for women and children, providing them special legal protections against the ravages of unfettered market forces.

By 1910 these and other women's organizations had coalesced to sponsor Argentina's first International Feminist Congress, which attracted women's groups throughout Latin America to its agenda for civil equality, better working conditions for women, equal pay for equal work, school reform, and revision of divorce laws to allow divorced mothers custody of themselves, their children, and their property. Not content merely with equality of opportunity, delegates from the Socialist Women's Center argued that this would only reinforce the existing inequality of social condition between men and women; they consequently called on male leaders in government, business, and education to institute affirmative action in support of women's issues. They demanded special treatment that would consider women's historical responsibilities in both public and private realms; for example, they wanted a special commercial school for women and legal provisions that would give wage-earning women thirty-four days of paid leave before and after giving birth.

European ethnic immigrant groups also protested against the elite's discriminatory laws designed to "ghettoize," stigmatize, and limit the civil rights of the non-native-born, who also—not coincidentally—happened to be either prosperous small farmers, urban petty proprietors, or "organized proletarians." Ironically, the late nineteenth-century white supremacist oligarchy had encouraged their arrival in Argentina in order to "whiten" the nation's population and provide relatively cheap labor on the great estates and in export-oriented urban industry. But continuous harassment greeted those immigrants who either resisted acculturation, demanded worker rights, or successfully competed against the creole estancieros. Swiss and German immigrant farmers, for example, organized a revolt in the province of Santa Fe to denounce the oligarchy's discriminatory policies. Similarly, Jewish schools, especially in the province of Entre Ríos, had been the target of racist violence in 1910, which prompted Jewish organizations to protest. Finally, a coalition of immigrant groups including Italians, Germans, and Russian Jews, many of whom were sympathetic to socialist, anarchist, and trade unionist ideas, challenged the Social Defense Law of 1910, which authorized the expulsion of foreign "agitators" and defined some immigrant groups as "undesirable elements."

THE FIRST RADICAL GOVERNMENT: YRIGOYEN, 1916–1922

With a finely tuned grassroots political organization, a well-known presidential candidate, and a vague program promoting "class harmony," the Radicals won the 1916 presidential elections. But they were limited by their tenuous bond with the conservative landowner elite. The elite controlled the military and the major agricultural lobbying groups and had close contacts with powerful foreign business interests. Yrigoyen continually walked an unsteady tightrope between the middle class, which wanted a piece of the governmental pie, and the oligarchy, which was still wary of the party that had rebelled three times in three decades and that had won an election campaigning against the selfish interests of that oligarchy. He could not push too hard too fast or the oligarchy would surely overthrow him.

The Radical government's program combined a conservative fiscal policy and moderate social reforms designed to secure political stability, in return for which the oligarchy was to allow the middle class wider access to the governmental bureaucracy and the professions. There were inherent contradictions in this strategy. First, expansion of access to government employment meant that government expenditures necessarily had to increase. But this violated the tenet of fiscal conservatism, unless the economy continued to expand at a rapid rate. Second, Yrigoyen had to maintain the fragile alliance of landowners and members of the middle class within his own party. In sum, the key to the Radicals' staying in power was Yrigoyen's ability to distribute the fruits of Argentine economic development to the middle class without antagonizing the oligarchy.

There was growing discontent on the part of the middle class, too, because the decline in government revenues from imports meant fewer government jobs for its members. Yrigoyen's balancing act became even more difficult with the emergence of labor agitation for improved wages and working conditions. Wartime demand for Argentine exports had brought on inflation, and as a result, the purchasing power of wages was seriously eroded. Yrigoyen had to move cautiously in attempting to alleviate labor's plight, for the oligarchy might look upon such moves as interference in their economic domain. The problem was complicated by the fact that much of the labor agitation was directed against foreign-owned companies with close ties to the elite. Facing bitter opposition from the ruling elite, Yrigoyen abandoned his modest efforts to incorporate labor into his coalition.

Consequently, from 1916 to 1919, Yrigoyen's policy toward workers' struggles was clearly determined by expediency and, in the last analysis, by the degree of pressure exerted by the landed elite. Major strikes occurred against foreign-owned companies engaged in export-related enterprises. Because Argentine governments often sent in the police and armed forces to break strikes, the attitude of the Yrigoyen regime was decisive. The Maritime Workers' Federation struck twice, in 1916 and 1917, for higher wages. The first strike was timed to coincide with harvest shipments. In both instances the union gained access to Yrigoyen, the government kept out of the dispute, and the union won. But in late 1917, the government abandoned the unions when a general strike began to jeopardize export interests. With the strike threatening the entire harvest, the British government and the elite brought joint pressure on Yrigoyen to intervene, and troops were used. The strike collapsed. The frigorífico strike of 1917–1918 met the same fate when the government sent in marines to subdue the strikers.

The climactic episode came in January 1919 and is known in Argentine history as the *Semana Trágica* (Tragic Week), in reference to the heavy loss of life that followed when Yrigoyen, apparently fearing intervention by the army to topple his government, abandoned his original conciliatory position and sent police and armed forces to break a general strike that had grown out of a strike in a metal works. This violence was accompanied by a wave of brutal pogroms against Russian Jewish immigrants by members of the elite and the middle class, organized in an Argentine Patriotic League. Instead of denouncing the anti-"communist" witch hunt, the Radical government added its voice to the right-wing cry that the strike was a revolutionary conspiracy and even encouraged party members to join the vigilante bands. Thereafter, Yrigoyen concentrated on catering to his middle-class constituency through the use of patronage and on strengthening his popular electoral base.

The Radicals also faced growing opposition among women, who, according to the 1914 national census, composed 22 percent of the total work force. These women activists continued to press the government for greater access to the professions and government jobs, equal pay, the right to vote and hold office, and a variety of regulations designed to protect women from the brutality of unfettered market forces. In 1919, Elvira Rawson de Dellepiane, a veteran feminist leader, organized the Women's Rights Association (ADF) to rally women, regardless of political affiliation, around this progressive platform. Within a relatively short time, the ADF claimed some eleven thousand members and worked closely with other feminist organizations like the Women's Union and Labor Group to pressure the Yrigoyen administration. The last three years of Yrigoyen's term were a struggle merely to survive.

The Argentine university reform of 1918, which had continental reverberations, reflected Yrigoyen's desire to cater to his middle-class constituency. The series of events leading to this famous reform began with a student strike at the University of Córdoba; the students demanded, among other changes, simplification of the entrance requirements and secularization of the curriculum. When the strike deteriorated into violence, Yrigoyen intervened and acceded to the student demands. But he went further, establishing a series of new universities that increased middle-class access to the professions and the government jobs for which so many middle-class aspirants hungered. This especially benefited Argentine women.

The Radicals also sought to strengthen their electoral position by expanding the patronage system and removing provincial governors on the pretext that they had violated the federal constitution.

By 1921 the boom unleashed by World War I had ended, and depression followed. The union movement disintegrated. Layoffs eroded union membership, and internal bickering rendered the unions ineffective. The Radicals actually experienced some success in recruiting among workers during the Depression, because their local committees were able to provide charitable services.

THE SECOND RADICAL GOVERNMENT: ALVEAR, 1922–1928

Despite adverse economic conditions, Marcelo de Alvear, Yrigoyen's hand-picked successor, became president. Immediately, however, the party began to come apart. Although couched in personal terms— Alvear against Yrigoyen—the division more accurately reflected the growing split between the middle-class and elite sectors of the party.

Alvear cut the payroll to trim expenses and hiked tariff rates to increase revenue. The tariff increase was also aimed at reducing imports and alleviating the balance-of-payments problem, thereby satisfying the middle class. A balanced budget, however, appealed to estancieros but directly contradicted middle-class demands for even more government employment opportunities. In 1924 the Radicals split into two factions, with the Anti-Personalist wing under Alvear's leadership.

Meanwhile, although largely excluded from these debates, subordinate social sectors nonetheless sought to organize popular movements to take advantage of the political discord within the Radical Party and between propertied elites and the middle class. Although workers, women's rights organizations, and ethnic minorities were themselves often internally divided, the devastating impact of external market forces on their daily lives helped to mobilize a common agenda that occasionally managed to intrude on the national political discourse. In 1924, for example, a coalition of trade unions and women's groups, including the Socialist Feminist Center and the Women's Rights Association, successfully secured the passage of Law 11.317, which established an eight-hour workday for women, limited a woman's workweek to forty-eight hours, and prohibited night work.

The law also required large, typically foreign-owned, companies to obey special rules for pregnant workers, including a stipulation that factories hiring at least fifty women should provide facilities for nursing mothers. Two years later, women's groups pressured Argentina's patriarchal political parties to pass another law, this time empowering adult married women to sign contractual agreements and pursue personal, educational, and career goals without their husbands' permission. Naturally, none of this legislation protected women employed in agriculture or domestic service, nor did it address the gender wage gap. But these victories, no matter how seemingly modest, laid the foundation for future state intervention on behalf of women and other historically oppressed people disadvantaged by an unregulated market.

The decade also pioneered the expansion of radio, a new technology that assisted the Radicals in their efforts to fashion a unified national culture. Although "decent" women historically had been precluded from participation in Argentina's rich cultural night life, the radio brought the tango from the dancehalls and brothels into middle-class homes, where women thrilled to its raunchy disrespect for an established social order that confined them to their kitchens and bedrooms. Moreover, the tango had been widely acclaimed in Paris, which lent it still greater credibility as a national cultural expression acceptable to Francophile elites and the middle-class folk who simultaneously envied and mimicked their lifestyle. From this moment onward, the tango became the new symbol of Argentine modernity and national identity.

YRIGOYEN'S SECOND TERM, 1928–1930

Yrigoyen made a smashing comeback in 1928, winning his second presidential term with an overwhelming 57 percent of the vote. But in October 1929 the Great Depression hit Argentina. The Radicals, whose strength had been increasing, suffered a mortal blow. Exports dropped 40 percent; foreign investment stopped. Unemployment was widespread. Government efforts to spark a recovery served only to induce inflation. The decline in imports severely undermined the government's fiscal position, since it relied on import duties for most of its revenue.

The government incurred a huge deficit, which it tried to cover by borrowing. As a result, it found itself in the position of competing for increasingly scarce credit resources with the landed elite, which desperately needed money to ride out the decline in the export market. Yrigoyen's policy threatened the interests of the landed elite, and he became expendable. Further, his meddling with the military had seriously undercut his standing with that powerful institution. Finally, the Depression destroyed his personal popularity among the middle class, his main base.

Yrigoyen became the scapegoat. His enemies pictured him as senile and corrupt, incapable of ruling the nation in a time of crisis. The Depression ruined the party apparatus, for there was no patronage to dispense. The political situation continued to disintegrate, and violence increased. Yrigoyen was overthrown by the military on September 6, 1930.

The "Infamous Decade," 1930–1943: The Conservative Restoration

The coup marked the end of Argentina's short experiment with democracy and the entry of the military into the nation's politics; it ushered in a period of harsh repression and corruption, which came to be known as the "Infamous Decade." Lieutenant General José F. Uriburu, who had led the group of conspirators that overthrew Yrigoyen, became the head of a coalition of widely diverse elements, including traditional conservatives, right-wing nationalist-fascists, and such center and left parties as the Progressive Democrats, Independent Socialists, and Socialists. These strange bedfellows had agreed on the elimination of Yrigoyen, but little else. Consequently, the loosely built alliance soon fell apart.

Following the coup, Uriburu conducted a campaign of brutal repression against opponents of his provisional government. He especially targeted prostitutes, whose defiance of established law had spread venereal disease and undermined the patriarchal family. Their scandalous behavior threatened public authority and led the military to abolish prostitution in 1934. Fearful that the abrupt abolition of the sex industry would create a new wave of unemployed in the midst of a global depression, however, the military government passed the Law of Social Prophylaxis, which offered former prostitutes state-sponsored medical care and employment opportunities in the public and private sector. The military also strictly controlled radio, decreeing the Dry Law, which censored electronic broadcasts that featured tango music, soap operas, and other lewd activities that corrupted public morality.

With its political and social opposition dispersed and defenseless, the military sought to reorganize Argentina's civilian political institutions and created a new coalition, the *Concordancia*, which united conservative aristocrats, dissident Radicals, the Catholic church, and the military. With the help of fraud, the intimidation tactics of goon squads and gangsters, and the general apathy of an embittered and cynical electorate, the Concordancia won control of the national government.

The Great Depression, the first modern crisis of the international capitalist system, powerfully proclaimed the fragility of the nation's economically dependent, externally oriented national development policies and ushered in a new era of internal sociopolitical struggle that dramatically transformed Argentine society. The global economic collapse bankrupted Argentina's largest companies and inundated the nation with a tidal wave of unemployment, which, not surprisingly, disproportionately afflicted women, who lost jobs at a much higher rate than men.

It also precipitated a pronounced demographic shift in the social origins of the national labor force: before 1930, urban industrial and rural agricultural employers alike had relied upon more than 6 million European immigrants, half of whom had arrived after 1880; in the ensuing decades, expansion of Argentine industry and agriculture would have to depend on internal migration from rural to urban areas.

Naturally, women constituted an increasingly important segment of this population; during the Depression and World War II, twice as many women as men migrated to Buenos Aires and other cities. This reflected both the destructive impact of market forces on rural life and the patriarchal nature of Argentine families. Unable to make a living in rural areas, men who lost their jobs or small agricultural plots often abandoned their families as well; under the circumstances, single female heads of households could not sustain their families' subsistence in the low-paying jobs traditionally available to women in agriculture, where wages were one-fourth those of urban industry. Not surprisingly, women's employment nationwide increased 27.4 percent from 1935 to 1939. In the textile, tobacco, and clothing industries, women composed a majority of the labor force by the end of the decade.

Although the military's intrusion into Argentine politics during the 1930s effectively reduced opportunities for democratic popular participation, trade union leaders still organized and agitated in defense of male workers' rights and for state regulation of the market. Here, they were joined by women's groups, which, reflecting their increased visibility in the public sector, also demanded an activist national government that would recognize their political rights and protect their socioeconomic interests. That is why the Argentine Association for Women's Suffrage, founded by Carmela Horne de Burmeister in 1932 and claiming a membership of eighty thousand, campaigned vigorously both for women's right to vote and for state-subsidized subsistence, maternity leave and health care benefits, and child care for working mothers. Argentina's conservative Concordancia faced one inescapable conclusion: an enduring social stability could not be imposed militarily; it would require an expanding economic pie, which the unfettered international market forces of a dependent capitalism could no longer guarantee.

Abandoning the free-trade, laissez-faire economic doctrines on which the prewar export economy was based, Conservative economic policy of the 1930s established state intervention as a decisive factor in the economy. The basic aim of their policy was to protect the nation from the effects of the cyclical nature of the world capitalist economy. To accomplish this, they sought to protect their main foreign market, Great Britain, limit production of farm commodities, and restrict imports through indirect methods, such as the establishment of a currency-exchange system that discriminated against non-British imports. They also sought to establish new import-substitution industries primarily through foreign investment.

In this period, finding that they could not export manufactured goods to Argentina on a competitive basis because of high tariffs and the discriminatory exchange system, U.S. manufacturers established plants in Argentina. As a result, foreign capital played an increasingly important role in the economy during the 1930s, accounting for 50 percent of the total capital invested in

Argentine industry. Foreign companies virtually monopolized the meat-packing, electric power, cement, automobile, rubber, petroleum, pharmaceutical, and several other industries.

The British market for beef and grain was critical for the Argentine export economy. During the late 1920s and early 1930s, the British government was under constant pressure to reduce Argentine imports, to protect producers within the empire. The result of Argentine efforts to secure the British market was the controversial Roca-Runciman Treaty of 1933. By this treaty, Britain guaranteed Argentina a fixed, though somewhat reduced, share of the chilled beef market. It also promised to eliminate tariffs on cereals. Argentina, in return, lowered or eliminated tariffs on British manufactures. It also agreed to spend its earnings from the British market on British goods to be imported into Argentina.

The economy improved after 1934, and by 1936 the crisis had passed. Cereal prices rose gradually on the world market until 1937, when they again dropped. Meat prices rose until 1936 and then remained steady. Industrial investment reached pre-Depression levels. Although real wages declined, unemployment fell sharply as a result of public works and industrial investment. In general, Argentines were relatively well off during the 1930s. Consumption of consumer goods and food rose considerably.

The process of industrialization was accompanied by a growth of the native industrialist class and a parallel increase in the size of the working class and its organizations. In 1930 the General Confederation of Labor (CGT) arose from the merger of two large unions. By 1943 the membership of the trade union movement was estimated to be between three hundred and three hundred and fifty thousand.

The growth of the Argentine industrial bourgeoisie, a class profoundly dissatisfied with the economic policies of the landed oligarchy, and of the working class, still relatively small and unorganized but gaining in self-consciousness and developing new social and political aspirations, heightened the tensions within Argentine society. These ultimately exploded in 1943 when a coup d'état, organized by a secret officers' lodge known as the Group of United Officers (GOU), overthrew the Concordancia government and established a ruling military junta headed successively by Generals Arturo Rawson, Pedro P. Ramírez, and Edelmiro Farrell, who ruled from 1944 until the elections of 1946.

The Perón Era, 1943–1955

PERÓN'S RISE TO POWER

The 1943 military coup had deep and tangled roots. The fraud and corruption that tainted both conservative and Radical politics in the "Infamous Decade" no doubt offended military sensibilities. During the 1930s, the officer corps of the Argentine armed forces, predominantly middle class in its social origins, had developed an ardent nationalism that saw the solution for Argentina's problems in industrialization and all-around technical modernization. The interest of the military in industrialization also was closely linked to its desire to create a powerful war machine capable of creating a Greater Argentina that could exercise hegemony in a new South American bloc. To industrialize it was necessary to end Argentina's neocolonial status, to free it from dependence on foreign markets. The pro-German attitude of many officers stemmed in part from the German military instruction that they had received and from their admiration for the supposed successes of the Nazi New Order, but even more, perhaps, from the conviction that England and the United States had conspired to keep Argentina a rural economic colony. Their pro-German attitude was not translated into a desire to enter the war on Germany's side but rather into the wish to keep Argentina neutral in the great conflict.

World War II had a lasting impact on the ideology and practical political-economic needs of Argentina's military leaders. First, absorbed with waging global war, neither the United States, Great Britain, France, Germany, nor Japan could intervene effectively in Argentina's internal affairs. Second, with the war's disruption of international commercial trade and the conversion of the great powers' industrial production to military needs, an externally dependent Argentina lacked the essential inputs—capital equipment, technology, replacement parts, and private sector investment—necessary to sustain economic expansion and social stability. In the absence of any organized and effective foreign opposition and pressed by domestic popular movements for a social justice based on economic growth, these military leaders had no alternative except to expand the state-centered, import-substitution industrialization policies inaugurated during the 1930s.

Consequently, the military proposed a massive government investment in industrialization and technical modernization, even though it feared the social changes and forces that such transformations might unleash. In particular, it feared the revolutionary potential of the working class. In effect, the military proposed to build Argentine industrial capitalism with a thoroughly cowed, docile working class.

As a result, one of the first acts of the military regime was to launch an offensive against organized labor. The government took over the unions, suppressed newspapers, and jailed opposition leaders. It also sought to silence women's public voice and force them to return to their gendered lives as mothers, wives, and daughters—to be the familial anchor of a revitalized Catholic morality within their private households. Here, gender discrimination aimed to undermine class solidarity by blaming male workers' economic difficulties on women's highly visible presence in the workplace. This policy of direct confrontation and collision with labor and women had disastrous results and threatened to wreck the industrialization program. The military was saved from itself by an astute young colonel, Juan Domingo Perón, who took over the Department of Labor in October 1943, promptly raised it to the status of the Ministry of Labor and Welfare, and opened a new bureau, the Women's Division of Labor and Assistance. As he noted in his inaugural speech, Perón wanted officially to recognize that "more than 900,000 Argentine women are part of the paid work force."

Born in 1895, the son of immigrant and creole parents of somewhat marginal economic status (his father was a farmer), Perón entered the military college at sixteen and very slowly rose in rank to captain in 1930. During the next decade, he spent several years in Europe, where he was much impressed by the German and Italian dictatorships. In 1941, Perón joined the Group of United Officers; although only a junior colonel, he quickly rose to its leadership ranks.

His genius lay in his recognition of the potential of women, ethnic minorities, and the working class and the need to broaden the social base of the nationalist revolution. He became the patron of the urban proletariat and, under considerable pressure from a well-organized and vocal women's rights movement, immediately courted its support by endorsing woman suffrage. Within a year, such legislation was submitted to the Congress and approved in 1947. Perón secured the enactment of protective legislation designed to increase women's access to education and improve their wages and working conditions. Not surprisingly, from 1941 to 1950, the number of women admitted to universities more than doubled.

As Minister of Labor in 1944, Perón established a minimum wage for piecework produced in the home, largely by women; naturally, this raised the issue of a broader minimum wage, and workers in the food industry, mostly women, received this protection the following year. By 1949 women constituted 45 percent of the industrial workers in Buenos Aires. In this year, again pressed by women's groups and apparently recognizing the potential divisiveness of a gendered wage gap between men and women workers, Perón supported legislation to require equal pay for equal work in Argentina's flourishing textile industry. As a result, by 1959 the differential wage between men and women ranged between 7 and 15 percent, which historian Nancy Caro Hollander characterizes as "one of the lowest in the non-Socialist world."

Perón also cultivated a political constituency among Argentina's male work force. Workers were not only encouraged to organize but favored in bargaining negotiations, in which his department participated. As a result, workers' wages not only rose in absolute terms, but their share of the national income also grew. This, of course, increased mass purchasing power and thereby promoted the process of industrialization. Perón also created a state system of pensions and health benefits, with the result that employers' contributions for pensions, insurance, and other benefits rose steadily until the year of Perón's fall (1955). In return for these real gains, however, the unions lost their independence and became part of a state-controlled apparatus in Perón's hands.

Naturally, Perón's progressive social policies created considerable opposition both within certain factions of the military and among the landed oligarchy. In October 1945 these groups staged a coup that led to Perón's imprisonment. But the organizers of the coup were divided and unclear about their objectives, and Perón's followers mobilized rapidly. Loyal labor leaders organized the Buenos Aires working class for massive street demonstrations to protest Perón's jailing. The workers virtually took over the city, without opposition from the armed forces. The bewildered conspirators released Perón from prison. Thereupon, he resigned from his various government posts, retired from the army, and began his campaign for the presidency in the 1946 elections.

In preparation for those elections, Perón, taking due account of the defeat of fascism in Europe, cast himself in the role of a democrat. He created a Labor Party to mobilize the working class, the principal component in a class alliance whose other major elements were the national industrial bourgeoisie and the army. Perón's chief opponent was a heterogeneous coalition of conservative landed elite, middle-class Radicals, and even the Socialists and Communists. Perón, who was greatly assisted by the blundering foreign policy of the United States, won easily.

Once in office, Perón turned to confront a new cultural threat. Since the Great Depression and the advent of movie theaters had bankrupted many small cabarets frequented by middle- and working-class men, Argentina's national obsession with the tango had been displaced by *fútbol* (soccer). Whereas the tango had celebrated unbridled heterosexual passion, soccer had emerged as an all-male sport in its appeal to participants and spectators alike. According to historian Donna

Guy, the Peronistas increasingly feared what appeared to be an increase in homosexual relationships and their open representation in national artistic and cultural expression; they therefore determined to use state power to revive the tango and legal prostitution in the hope that this would stimulate more interest in heterosexuality. According to historian Donald Castro, Perón understood the tango's popular appeal and fostered its reemergence for his own political ends. During his administration, the state-owned movie company produced *La historia del tango* and three films that celebrated the life of Argentina's most famous tango artist, Carlos Gardel.

POSTWAR ECONOMICS

After the war, the United States bestrode the emerging new world order like a colossus, but its extraordinary economic output found ample demand in wartorn Europe, Asia, and Africa, where domestic policies focused on internal socioeconomic reconstruction. Consequently, Argentine industrialists and landed oligarches alike faced relatively little postwar competition as they sought to develop internal markets and expand agricultural raw materials exports. International prices remained high, profits were secure, and domestic tariff protection meant that local companies could afford to pay higher wages and benefits to workers without jeopardizing their control over production.

The postwar boom enabled Perón to keep his coalition together. The export sector produced large surpluses in the balance of payments, making available funds for industrialization, mainly in labor-intensive manufactures. Perón also nationalized railroads and public utilities and created powerful state-owned companies that dominated local shipping, steel, and banking industries. Between 1945 and 1948 real wages for industrial workers rose 20 percent. Personal consumption also rose. Because there was only a slight decline in the share of the national income that went to profits, the redistribution of income to the working class did not come at the expense of any other segment of the alliance. Industrialists kept profits up and benefited from increased domestic consumption,

Juan and Evita Perón, 1952. [Bettmann/Corbis]

which provided a growing market for their products. The only sector of the economy that was slighted was agriculture.

Perón managed to win over a considerable sector of the dependent middle class through his use of government patronage, just as Yrigoyen had done before. He kept the military happy by his commitment to industrialization, which was an important aspect of the military's desire for national self-sufficiency, and by providing it with generous salaries and the latest equipment for modern warfare.

One of Perón's greatest allies was his beautiful and stylish wife Eva Duarte de Perón, known affectionately by Argentines as "Evita" (little Eva), who relished her role as his liaison to the working class.

"The people can be sure," she triumphantly announced to admiring throngs at Perón's presidential inaugural, "that between them and their government, there could never be a separation, because in this case, in order to divorce himself from his people, the President would have to first divorce his wife!" Shortly after the enfranchisement of women in 1947, Evita joined with other feminists to create the Peronist Feminist Party, an organization to mobilize women in support of the Peronist political platform. She also formed the Eva Perón Foundation, a charitable institution that distributed large sums of money to neighborhood groups; financed various women's centers to link impoverished women to vital social, medical, and legal services; and built a large patronage army for Peronism.

Although her role as a feminist in Argentina's history is controversial, one thing is indisputable: Eva Perón's activism showed women and her working-class supporters, the adoring *descamisados* (shirtless ones), that they should not rely on the beneficence of any politician to defend their rights. "Just as only workers could wage their own struggle for liberation," she insisted, "so too could only women be the salvation of women." In the presidential election of 1951, this was a lesson that was not lost on women or the working class; 90 percent of registered women, eligible to vote for the first time, went to the polls and some 65 percent cast their votes for Perón, but they also elected seven women senators and twenty-four women deputies, the largest female delegation of government representatives in the Americas. Evita's vision of a government and people linked by her marriage to Perón seemed prophetic, but a year later death, not divorce, intervened; Evita's tragic demise in 1952 at the age of thirty-two dramatically weakened the populist caudillo's attachment to Argentine workers and women.

Perhaps more significant, the global economy had begun to shift, as did Perón's policies. Except for a short-lived recovery during the Korean war, Argentina entered a period of severe recession, which included several drought-induced bad harvests. The late 1940s brought the first signs that Argentina would face serious long-term economic difficulties. Its export commodities began to confront increased competition from the United States and from revitalized Western European agriculture. Later, the advent of the Common Market worsened Argentina's position. Balance-of-payments deficits replaced the large surpluses that had financed the nation's import-substitution industrialization. Industrial production fell, as did per capita income. Real wages dropped 20 percent from the 1949 level in 1952–1953. It was in this decline that Perón's political failure was rooted.

PERÓN'S DOWNFALL

After his reelection in 1952 and in response to the economic crisis of the early 1950s, Perón formulated a new plan (the Second Five-Year Plan, 1953–1957) that to a great extent reversed his previous strategy. He tried to expand agricultural production by paying higher prices to farmers for their produce and by buying capital equipment for this sector (tractors and reapers). He sought to increase the agricultural production available for export by means of a wage freeze, which he hoped would restrict domestic consumption. Although real wages declined, workers did not suffer proportionately more than other groups. But the industrial bourgeoisie was unhappy, for labor productivity declined while the regime's prolabor policies propped up wages. The industrialists, supported by a considerable portion of the army, wanted deregulation of the economy so they could push down wages. But the major problem of the industrial sector was lack of capital, since the agricultural sector no longer generated a large surplus.

To solve the capital shortage, Perón abandoned his previously ultranationalistic stand and actively solicited foreign investment. In 1953 the government reached an agreement with a North American company, the Standard Oil Company of California, for exploration, drilling, refining, and distribution rights in Argentina. Perón hoped thereby to reduce the adverse effect of oil purchases abroad on the balance of payments. Foreign capital, however, used the most modern technology and machines, which required fewer workers and tended to create unemployment in the affected industrial sectors.

To maintain government expenditures and a bloated bureaucracy in the face of declining revenues, Perón printed more money. The amount in circulation increased from 6 to 45 billion pesos during his two terms. By 1954 he had had some success in stabilizing the economy; he achieved a balance-of-payments surplus, and capital accumulation showed an upward curve. But his new economic strategy had alienated key elements of his coalition of workers, industrialists, and the armed forces. Perón then sought to divert attention from economic issues—with disastrous results.

Perón adopted two new strategies. First, he attempted to enhance his moral and ideological appeal. Second, he began to employ greater coercion to suppress a growing opposition. The vehicle for his ideological and moral appeal was *justicialismo*, Perón's ideal of justice for all—a third route to development that was neither communist nor capitalist.

Perón's strategy included attacking the church. Starting in 1951 the regime grew more repressive. The government suppressed and took over Argentina's most famous newspaper, *La Prensa* (1951). Further, Perón used his National Liberating Alliance, a private army of thugs, and the thirty-five-thousand-man federal police force to intimidate the political opposition. Torture, imprisonment, censorship, purges, and exile became the order of the day. After 1954 even the General Confederation of Labor became a coercive force, whose prime function seemed to be to suppress opposition within the labor movement.

Perón's reluctance to go along with the industrialists' desire to push down wages and increase productivity alienated that group; the industrial bourgeoisie then joined forces with the agrarian interests, which had long and bitterly opposed Perón. This desertion ended Perón's once highly successful coalition. Inevitably, Perón's hold on the working class loosened as the wage freeze and inflation reduced the value of their wages.

Despite economic adversity, Perón could not have been overthrown had not the military abandoned him. For the better part of a decade, he had masterfully balanced, divided, and bribed the military. Most of the senior officers owed him both their rank and their prosperity. The army was heavily involved in industrial production, and this provided an excellent means to become rich. In addition, to win its allegiance, Perón had showered the military with expensive military hardware and excellent wages. However, his relations with the armed forces began to disintegrate when he altered his economic policy to lessen emphasis on industrialization and self-sufficiency. On this score, his concession to Standard Oil in 1953 was the last straw for the nationalist military.

Thus, in struggling to extricate the nation from an economic quagmire, Perón undermined the multiclass coalition that had brought him to power and sustained him there. When the final successful revolt took place in 1955, enough of the working class was alienated to assure the military's success. Perón briefly threatened to arm the descamisados but instead fled into exile.

Although there is considerable scholarly debate about Perón and his populist policies, the fact remains that he solved none of the country's major economic problems. The main roadblocks remained. Transportation continued to be inadequate and obsolete, and a scarcity of electric power stood in the way of industrial modernization. Argentina did not produce enough fuel to meet domestic needs, and this created an enormous drain on the balance of payments. The nation's industry remained limited for the most part to import-substitution light industry. Despite his anti-imperialist rhetoric, Perón did not nationalize such key foreign-owned industries as meat packing and sugar refining. Most serious of all, Perón did nothing to break the hold of the latifundio on the land. As a result, agriculture was marked by inefficient land use, which impeded long-range development.

The Shadow of Perón, 1955–1973

ECONOMIC STAGNATION

The gradual restoration of global economic competition among the leading capitalist countries led to chronic, sometimes violent, economic fluctuations during this period. At the base of these difficulties lay continuous balance-of-payments deficits, which were caused by the decline in agricultural prices. The nation could not earn enough from its exports to pay for the large expenditures necessary to fuel domestic industry. Periods of rapid economic growth were invariably followed by acute depressions, which wiped out all previous gains. Runaway inflation accompanied these cyclical conditions.

The governments of this period, whether military or civilian, tended to promote the inflow of foreign investment as a development strategy. Arturo Frondizi (1958–1962), for example, was elected on a political platform of "Peronismo Without Perón," that is, nationalism and state regulation of market forces. Nonetheless, he quickly bowed to pressure from the U.S. State Department and the International Monetary Fund (IMF), a multilateral institution created after World War II to manage the postwar global economy. These agencies promised low-interest loans to ease the economic pain produced by mounting trade deficits, but in return they insisted that Frondizi break his political promises to the Argentine people and slash social welfare spending, deregulate private sector business, and expand investment opportunities for foreign capital.

But this development strategy had severe drawbacks. Foreign companies tended to monopolize credit opportunities, certain key industries became concentrated in foreign hands, and profits earned by foreign subsidiaries and remitted to the home company added to the balance-of-payments deficits. Moreover, since the IMF's principal concern was inflation, its stabilization programs invariably increased the cost of credit, deepened economic recessions, and contributed to growing business failures. Finally, foreign investment was usually technologically intensive and therefore created unemployment. It was during the post-Perón era of development spurred by foreign capital that Argentina saw the emergence of large numbers of underemployed and unemployed urban workers.

This economic insecurity was politically untenable for working men and women who recurrently joined with students, small businesspersons, and other disadvantaged groups in publicly protesting these intolerable policies that disproportionately benefited wealthy foreigners and Argentine elites. The resulting political disorder inevitably led to a cycle of political violence and periodic military coups d'état against Frondizi in 1962 and his civilian successor, Arturo Illia, in 1966.

THE MILITARY IN POLITICS

In the past, military interventions had been brief, largely designed to destroy popular political opposition, intimidate the lower classes, and reconstruct civil society so that civilian governments favorable to the ruling elites could be elected. However, General Juan Carlos Onganía, who replaced Illia, was determined to govern longer.

Consequently, he suspended the constitution; dismissed all civilian government entities, including the Congress, the Supreme Court, and provincial governors; abolished all political parties; and purged the universities of moderates and leftists, reserving a special hatred for Jewish intellectuals.

As minister of the economy, Onganía sought foreign investment by removing all restrictions on profit remittances; he also stimulated the process of industrial denationalization by devaluating the peso by 40 percent. This meant that many local companies could no longer afford expensive capital imports and royalty payments to owners of foreign technology. These local companies disappeared, leaving their share of the market to foreign firms. In this way, Coca-Cola and Pepsi gained control of 75 percent of the soft-drink market. Between 1963 and 1971, foreign interests bought out fifty-three Argentine companies representing almost every industrial sector, particularly the automotive, chemical, petrochemical, metallurgical, and tobacco industries. Meanwhile, wages were frozen although prices continued their steady rise.

Growing outrage on the part of workers and students over the government's economic program, especially its policy of industrial denationalization and the wage freeze, erupted into violence in the interior in the spring of 1969. Major riots took place in Rosario, Corrientes, and Córdoba, the most industrialized city of Argentina. There, workers and students rose in the famous Cordobaza revolt, occupying major sectors of the city until they were ousted by troops. At the same time, there was an upsurge of urban guerrilla activity by groups like the Montoneros, who represented the left wing of the Peronist movement. Their tactics included raids on police stations, assassinations, and robberies.

Onganía's failure to cope with the mounting wave of guerrilla activity precipitated the 1970 military coup, which installed General Roberto M. Levingston as president. An expert in military intelligence and counterinsurgency, Levingston decreed the death penalty for terrorist acts and kidnappings, but his repressive decrees failed to establish a permanent social peace that would restore investors' confidence and reverse Argentina's 1970–1971 economic decline.

THE RETURN OF PERÓN

Displeased with a resurgence of labor unrest, the military ousted Levingston in March 1971. His replacement, General Alejandro Lanusse, carried out a dual policy combining brutal repression of leftist guerrillas with a general liberalization of the political climate. In effect admitting the military's failure to renovate Argentine politics, Lanusse undertook negotiations that led to the restoration of political activity and the return of the Peronists to full electoral participation for the first time since 1955.

The military briefly held out hope that the moderate political parties would unite to stand against the Peronists, but the latter's superior organization and their leader's unchallenged popularity assured their victory. At the heart of the Peronist program were formal agreements with labor (*Pacto Social*) and industry (*Acto Compromiso del Campo*) that pledged compliance with a wage and price freeze. This cooperation lasted for about a year, while the Argentine economy, buoyed by high world-market prices for beef and grain, boomed. The agreements disintegrated in mid-1974 with the onset of renewed inflation brought on by a huge increase in international oil prices.

Even before these economic arrangements ended, the Peronist movement had begun to disintegrate, divided between left and right wings. By the time Perón died in July 1974, the level of violence had increased. In 1975 left- and right-wing thugs reportedly killed eleven hundred people. In the face of this escalating violence and economic chaos, the military stepped in again and installed General Jorge Rafael Videla as president.

Military Dictatorship, 1974–1983

In the ensuing years, the military unleashed a reign of terror unprecedented in the nation's history and imposed an equally harsh neoliberal economic policy that decimated Argentine society. By the summer of 1982, the annual rate of inflation shot up to a catastrophic 500 percent, the highest in the world. Economic growth fluctuated wildly.

Worst of all, the free market policies of finance minister José Alfredo Martínez de Hoz led to record numbers of bankruptcies and bank failures. By eliminating tariffs on imported industrial goods and reducing government involvement in the economy, Martínez de Hoz presided over the destruction of many of Argentina's largest corporations. The real wages of Argentine workers plummeted 40 percent between 1976 and 1979, before recovering in 1980 and falling again in the severe crisis of 1982.

Between 1975 and 1990, Argentina experienced a prolonged period of economic stagnation: low or erratic growth coupled with high inflation, declining manufacturing production, and sharply rising unemployment that contributed to falling real wages, increasing income inequality, and the dramatic growth of an "informal sector" comprised mostly of impoverished urban female street vendors. Misery spread as the share of households earning income below the poverty line steadily expanded from 2.6 percent in 1974 to 7.5 percent in 1980 to an all-time high of 38.3 percent in 1989.

Naturally, this economic devastation contributed to political discontent and social turmoil. To defend its power, Videla's military junta banned all normal political activity and embarked on a "dirty war" against the left. Under military rule, perhaps as many as thirty thousand Argentines disappeared, many victims of illegal rightist death squads. Argentines came to fear the knock on the door at midnight, after which unknown kidnappers would take family and friends who were never to be heard from again.

Opposition to the military's barbaric cruelty grew steadily, if clandestinely. Direct political action was replaced by popular movements among human rights advocates, labor, youth, community groups, and women. Human rights organizations, with a longer history of social activism, were most influential and included veteran groups like the Communist party–affiliated Argentine League for Human Rights, established in 1937, and the Permanent Assembly for Human Rights, co-founded in 1977 by Raul Alfonsín, who parlayed his prestige into a convincing presidential electoral victory in 1983.

Labor, on the other hand, long the most powerful organized social group in Argentina, suffered dramatic declines because it was a special target of the military's political and economic violence. Determined to eradicate all vestiges of working-class resistance and heroic struggle, military officials attacked the gender identities of union leaders by subjecting them to what Jean Franco calls the "feminization" of torture: systematic assaults on the reproductive organs of men and women. Economically, union membership fell as privatization, government budget cuts, and foreign competition combined to increase unemployment. Under these conditions, important sectors of the labor movement, especially the leadership of the General Labor Confederation (CGT), collaborated with the military government. Some even testified years later that they "did not remember" the massive disappearance of workers and shop stewards during the dictatorship.

Young people also resisted the military's invasion of their schools, disruption of home life, and wholesale assault on youth culture. With traditional vehicles for expressing youth activism closed, their outrage found new channels of discontent, the most influential of which was "national rock." Outdoor concerts during the dictatorship regularly drew as many as sixty thousand youth who routinely defied the authorities with collective chants of *"Se va a acabar"* ("the dictatorship will soon end") and thrilled to the subversive lyrics of Argentine rock stars like Fito Paez, León Gieco, and Charley García. For example, García's *"Los dinosaurios"* ("The Dinosaurs"), lampoons the military as witless prehistoric beasts destined to extinction, and Paez's *"Tiempos difíciles"* ("Hard Times") envisions the fires of hell emerging from the nation's cemeteries to avenge the youthful disappeared.

Community organizations offered a similar outlet to adults threatened by the military's economic and political war against citizens. With the moral, logistical, and financial support of local parish priests, squatters—impoverished, homeless, and unemployed families—organized to reclaim vacant lands in urban centers. The first such group, the Neighbor's Commission, organized some twenty thousand people for a land invasion in San Francisco Solano, a working-class neighborhood in Buenos Aires. Thereafter, these neighborhood groups spread rapidly, protesting higher taxes, skyrocketing food prices, decreased social services, the lack of affordable housing, and inadequate schools and health clinics.

Drawing on a rich historical legacy of "social motherhood," Argentine women, in the words of Jean Franco, "subverted the boundaries between public and private and challenged the assumption that mothering belonged only to the private sphere." The best-known of these women's groups, the Mothers and Grandmothers of the Plaza de Mayo, became the country's moral conscience; they refused to be intimidated by the military's daily death threats and routinely marched in the Plaza de Mayo, the nation's "symbolic center," demanding the return of their "disappeared" children and calling for the end of a dictatorship whose political and economic policies destroyed family life.

Women also campaigned for the abolition of compulsory military service, joint child custody, reproductive rights, sex education, and legal rights for children born to unmarried mothers. An organization known as Housewives of the Country denounced the high cost of living, sponsored shopping boycotts, and coordinated voluntary blackouts to protest the regime's neoliberal economic policies. Collectively, these popular protest movements weakened the military dictatorship and laid the organizational foundation for a return to democratic civilian government in 1983.

THE MALVINAS WAR

Facing growing domestic opposition and international pressure, the military sought to divert the nation from the government's program of economic and political violence by manipulating traditional *peronista* populist themes of nationalism and anti-imperialism. Suddenly, Argentine soldiers, who earlier had been ordered to root out domestic opposition to the dictatorship's sale of the national patrimony, were now sent to defend Argentina's national dignity against British colonialism by capturing the Malvinas Islands (also known as the Falklands) in the south Atlantic, three hundred miles off the coast.

The invasion was the culmination of a series of colossal miscalculations by the Argentine military. First, it had not expected Britain to fight to retain the islands. The British, however, sensitive to their position as a declining world power, chose to fight as a matter of national honor. The Argentines also misjudged the position of the United States. They believed that the United States, which had recently made a number of friendly overtures, would remain neutral in the conflict. Instead, after an initial period during which it tried to mediate a peaceful agreement, the United States actively supported the British.

The war was a disaster for Argentina. Thoroughly humiliated and discredited, the military faced an unprecedented political and economic crisis. Inevitably, the generals had to yield power to a civilian government.

Return to Democracy and the Death of Peronismo

Argentina ended nine years of nightmarish military rule in the fall of 1983 with the landslide victory of Raul Alfonsín, whose visibility in the human rights movement had earned him popular support. Alfonsín thus became the first democratically elected majority president since Perón in 1946.

Alfonsín first attacked inflation, which soared to 1,200 percent in 1985, by instituting the "austral plan." This established wage and price controls, replaced the peso with a new currency, the *austral*, and reduced government spending. Almost overnight currency stabilized. Inflation fell to 25 percent. Though the immediate crisis ended, the nation's economic problems remained manifold and profound. Argentina's industrial base was technologically backward, its foreign debt exceeded $50 billion by the late 1980s, and it was still dependent on primary export markets plagued by low prices. Unemployment in 1985 was the highest it had been in twenty years.

Alfonsín faced the difficult problem of the trials of the military accused of atrocities during the so-called dirty war of the 1970s and failures during the war with Great Britain. When the military refused to try officers in its own courts, the president transferred the cases to civilian jurisdiction and appointed a commission to investigate military terrorism. The commission found the armed forces responsible for 8,971 disappearances; it documented torture, kidnapping, and other crimes, and labeled the acts as "the greatest and most savage tragedy in our history." In the trials that followed, several generals were convicted and given long prison sentences. But in 1987, against overwhelming public opposition, Alfonsín ended prosecutions of lower-rank military for human rights abuses on the grounds that they had simply carried out orders.

Alfonsín also faced an economic crisis of unprecedented proportions in 1989 when Argentina's per capita gross product fell more than 15 percent. To cope with the crisis he resorted to neoliberal remedies, seeking to push exports and enacting the austerity measures—cuts in government services and wage restraints—demanded by the IMF as a condition for new foreign loans to keep the Argentine economy afloat. By spring 1989 the foreign debt stood at about $60 billion. Payment on the debt took some $6 billion a year, but the country's earnings in 1988 were below $3 billion. The deficit had to be made up by new loans, which only increased the country's dependency. The policy of austerity and faithful service of the foreign debt meant that little capital was available for development. The economic program contributed to a deterioration of the infrastructure, with long daily blackouts and energy rationing.

The situation sparked a week of food riots that spread across the country, with desperate thousands of people taking over supermarkets, cleaning out the shelves but usually leaving the cash in the registers. The government responded by declaring a nationwide state of emergency and banning all demonstrations and strikes.

Against this background of economic collapse, Alfonsín lost to the Peronist candidate Carlos Saúl Menem, governor of La Rioja province, who had campaigned against the Radical Party's liquidation of the national patrimony. Menem's follow-

Mothers of the Plaza de Mayo wear white kerchiefs in silent protest against the disappearance of their loved ones and distribute newspapers that report the trials of those held responsible for the "dirty war." [Owen Franklin/Corbis]

ers, including the powerful Peronist-controlled unions, naturally expected him to repudiate the policies that had led to an unprecedented economic and social crisis. What followed was a stunning surprise. Convinced that an even more powerful dose of those policies offered the only solution for the crisis, Menem, who professed his admiration for Ronald Reagan, Margaret Thatcher, and Augusto Pinochet, abandoned his party's traditional economic and political positions in favor of a thoroughgoing neoliberal program.

Contrary to all expectations, therefore, Menem included in his cabinet many conservatives, including representatives of big business like the great firm of Bunge and Born, representing one of the most powerful multinational groups, with links to the agricultural oligarchy that Peronists had traditionally distrusted, and announced a program of privatization of state-owned companies, the dismissal of thousands of state employees, and cuts of billions in government spending over the next year. The program represented a deepening of the policies attempted without much success by the brutal military governments between 1976 and 1983 and by the Alfonsín regime, with equal lack of success.

The process of privatization was carried out with frenzied haste and clearly favored large economic groups. Typical of the process was the "fire-sale" aspect of the privatization of two profitable state firms, Entel (the telephone company) and Aerolineas Argentinas (the national airline). The *Wall Street Journal* commented that these two privatizations "more resemble corporate raids than stockholders' sales. Both Aerolineas Argentinas and Entel are being sold for a fraction of their net worth." In July 1993 bidding began for the jewel of the state properties, the state oil company, Yacimientos Petrolíferos Fiscales, a profitable company with assets calculated at $7.4 billion and projected revenues of $5 billion. Among Latin America's oil producers, Argentina alone sold off its oil state monopoly, usually regarded as a "strategic" asset.

Menem's "shock therapy" on his way to the goal of a free market economy provoked resistance. The Peronist trade union movement, once his ardent supporter, split into pro- and anti-Menem wings, followed by a series of strikes to which Menem responded by firing strike leaders and seeking to curtail the right to strike by law or decree. The generally ineffective resistance of the once powerful labor movement to Menem's policies reflected a number of factors: the decline in size of the blue-collar labor force; the increase in the number of unemployed and underemployed, creating a substantial reserve labor force that weakened militancy; labor's traditional loyalty to the Peronist party; and the opportunism and greed of Peronist labor bosses, who were accustomed to live off state money and collaborate with the party, whatever its policies. To these factors one should add the weakness of the Argentine left, divided and decimated by state terrorism during the years of military rule.

To combat inflation, Menem's finance minister, Domingo Cavallo, unveiled the "ultimate anti-inflation shock," a plan making the Argentine currency convertible in relation to the dollar and forbidding the Central Bank to print money that was not backed by gold or foreign currency. To ensure wage and price stabilization Cavallo pledged government budget cuts of $6 billion, largely at the expense of public sector jobs. The policy entailed extensive budget cuts in health, education, welfare, and pensions. From the government's point of view, the Cavallo plan was a great success. Prices plummeted, the stock market exploded, and the Buenos Aires financial district hailed the start of the "Argentine miracle." The United States and the IMF rewarded Menem's fiscal orthodoxy by approving a Brady Plan that refinanced $21 billion of Argentina's foreign debt over thirty-five years.

This latest round of neoliberal orthodoxy deepened national income inequality, especially damaging women workers. During the next few years, unemployment soared from 13.1 percent in 1993 to 17.4 percent in 1995; the share of households that fell below the poverty line similarly increased from 13 percent in 1993 to 20 percent in 1996. During Menem's administration, women were forced to compensate for the decline in family income caused by higher male unemployment and falling real wages by entering the job market at much lower wage levels than men. In 1992, 45.9 percent of women were employed in waged work, but only three years later almost 52 percent worked for wages. Even as more women were forced to enter the job market, however, unemployment among women grew, from 6.3 percent in 1992 to more than 20 percent in 1995.

These neoliberal policies had a significant impact on family relations. The number of families with a primary male breadwinner declined steadily from 73 percent in 1980 to 65 percent in 1994, with these trends intensifying between 1992 and 1994, when the number of families with primary female breadwinners increased by 62 percent. The resulting double burden on women both within the household and in the public sector undermined the traditional family; divorce rates rose markedly and, since 1980, the number of single-mother households increased by 93 percent while the number of nontraditional families tripled between 1992 and 1994. What's more, under the relentless pressure of global market forces, the working conditions of wage-earning women deteriorated: sociologist Rosa Geldstein concludes that, under the neoliberal regime, women suffered greater gender discrimination in the workplace and were required to work faster, with shorter and less frequent breaks, longer and less flexible hours, for lower wages.

Another legacy of Menem's neoliberalism was the appearance of a class of "new poor," including many members of Argentina's once substantial middle class. It was estimated that nearly 30 percent of Argentina's population over age sixty fell into this category. An agricultural crisis, itself the result of low international prices, declining local markets, and the high cost of credit contributed to this state of affairs. Moreover, the removal of tariff protections, which caused a flood of cheap textiles and other imports, forced many small businesses to close. Lastly, there were savage budget cuts for education and other social welfare programs, all of which prompted the Argentine social scientist Atilio Borón to disparage "democracy that demonstrates by its deeds that it has no obligation to the poor and weak and has no concern for their fate, a democracy that manipulates injustice to protect the powerful and its favorites while it imposes the law of the jungle on the shantytowns." More to the point, he wondered, "Can a democracy of this kind consolidate itself through successive endorsements at the polls?"

With the utter collapse of the economy in 1999, however, growing popular discontent removed all doubt about this possibility. If poverty and social inequality grew ominously even during Argentina's "miraculous" growth in the early 1990s, they skyrocketed thereafter when Menem's economic house of cards, battered by low export prices, high debt, and the flight of foreign investment, came crashing down. Between 1999 and 2002 the economy shrank 3 percent per year, unemployment increased from 15 to 25 percent, and Argentina's capital account fell from a surplus of $16.8 billion to a deficit of $4.1 billion. Poverty, which rose during Argentina's prosperous years from 7 percent in 1987 to 19 percent in 1996, swelled to half the population in 2002. It was not uncommon to see families scouring garbage piles, competing with flies and maggots in their search for scraps of food to eat. One such man, cooking a small pot of fetid potatoes retrieved from a local dumpster, reflected simultaneously the anger and resiliency of a proud people victimized by foreign bankers and Argentina's elite: "Tell Mr. Bush we still want to pay back the debt, but give us more time," he laughed derisively.

Indeed, as the new millennium opened, Argentina found itself mired in a virtually unpayable foreign debt that, since 1990, had grown steadily to $155 billion. To service this debt between 1990 and 1996, Argentina had paid foreign bankers $3 of every $10 that it earned in export sales, but thereafter this rose precipitously to an average of $6. Nonetheless, to be eligible for low-interest loans that might have prevented national bankruptcy, the IMF insisted that the national government ignore the urgent cry of its own citizens and implement a domestic austerity program that balanced its budget on the backs of the Argentine people, whom it expected to pay the costs of these economic hard times. Not surprisingly, "capitalism in Argentina," according to an investment banker at Salomon Smith Barney, "has become a dirty word; profit has become a dirty word." Another banker put the issue much more starkly: "We're somewhat less popular than serial killers."

It did not take long for this simmering contempt for the inequities produced by unregulated markets to boil over in open revolt, as unemployed *piqueteros* (picketers) blockaded roads and middle-class youth burned cars, smashed windows, and looted stores; in the process, this popular wrath ignited a political tempest that led to the resignations of President Fernando de la Rua, only recently elected in 1999 on a populist platform, and Alejandro Rodríguez Saa, his interim successor. To combat the economic mess bequeathed by

Menem and generate the revenues necessary to appease the foreign bankers, de la Rua had deserted his own constituents and slashed pension benefits, cut state workers' wages 13 percent, reduced public expenditures 20 percent, and raised taxes. This apparent surrender to wealthy foreign interests again reinforced a growing popular disdain for politicians and the political process. In the last elections, 40 percent of voters registered their protest by casting blank or defaced ballots. More recently, at weekly demonstrations throughout the nation, protesters ritualistically abused politicians, sometimes physically, chanting "*Que se vayan todos!*" ("Throw the bums out!").

By early 2002, Eduardo Duhalde, a Peronist and frequent critic of Argentina's decade-long neoliberal experiment, assumed the presidency with a popular mandate to defy the foreign bankers and rescue the nation from this devastating crisis. He immediately defaulted on the external debt; abandoned the dollar as Argentina's monetary standard; and devalued the peso to make Argentine exports more affordable, raise the cost of imports, and create more jobs. He regulated the largely foreign-owned utilities industries to lower electricity, gas, and telephone rates; imposed new energy taxes that mostly affected foreign companies; developed contingency plans for price controls; continued to limit the amounts that bank depositors could withdraw; regulated currency convertibility; expanded an emergency relief program that paid $42 per month to over a million families; and allowed Argentines to use devalued pesos to repay credit card debt at par. Although foreign bankers expressed skepticism about these reforms, workers, farmers, and small business owners clearly approved. In 2003 they elected as president Néstor Kirchner, Duhalde's populist political ally, who pledged not to be "a prisoner of the big corporations." After a decade of neoliberal addiction unregulated foreign markets and privatization, however, it remained unclear whether or not this modest methadone prescription would be sufficient to ease the nation's cold turkey convulsions of withdrawal, much less induce an independent recovery.

The Chilean Way

Chilean exports
— outline
— strengths/weakness

FOR A CENTURY and a half, Chile set a relatively high standard of political behavior on a continent notorious for its turmoil and dictatorships. Compared to its neighbors, Peru, Bolivia, and Argentina, Chile was a model of domestic tranquility. Chilean democracy appeared so firmly rooted that it permitted the election and installation of a Marxist head of state, President Salvador Allende Gossens, in 1970. Only three years later, however, amid growing economic and political chaos, military rebels overthrew Chile's legitimate government and established a right-wing dictatorship whose rule was characterized by brutal oppression.

How could Chile maintain its parliamentary democracy so long when the rest of Latin America could not? Why, after almost a hundred and fifty years of respect for parliamentary democracy, did it crumble so swiftly? In retrospect, the bounds of Chilean democracy were narrowly drawn; the elite never allowed political freedom and the practice of politics to endanger its basic interests. Instead of seeking to solve the nation's desperate economic and social problems, successive governments merely evaded them. When, finally, a coalition government headed by Chile's working-class parties came to power in 1970 and inaugurated structural reforms that threatened oligarchical privilege, the elite responded by calling in the army, abolishing parliamentary democracy, and establishing a reactionary dictatorship.

Foreign Dependency and the Parliamentary Republic, 1891–1920

The defeat and suicide of President José Manuel Balmaceda during the civil war of 1891 ushered in an era of unrestrained foreign investment and export-dependent trade, presided over by the so-called Parliamentary Republic, dominated by the Liberal and Conservative political parties, which represented the great landowners of the Central Valley.

A third major party, the Radicals, founded in 1861 by dissident Liberals, enjoyed the support of low-level professionals, bureaucrats, teachers, artisans, and other middle-class groups, as well as that of large landowners on the southern frontier around Concepción, northern mine owners from the Copiapó region, and businessmen from Santiago, the capital. A fourth party, the Democrats, had some base in the lower-middle class and among workers.

The only issue separating the major parties was the role of the church in education. The chief concerns of the parties appeared to be the preservation of the status quo and the distribution of the spoils of office. Corruption and inefficiency pervaded the political life of the era.

ECONOMIC GROWTH AND THE EXPORT SECTOR

While politics stagnated in an atmosphere of fraud and apathy, Chilean society underwent a profound transformation. The export sector played a crucial and basically detrimental role in this transformation. Raw material exports generated enormous profits, but relatively few benefits flowed to the nation as a whole. Like the "banana republics" of Central America and the sugar islands of the Caribbean, Chile relied for its revenues on one export commodity, first nitrate and then copper, making it extremely vulnerable to cyclical world market demands for its products. Moreover, the copper industry, which produced the nation's major export in the twentieth century, was operated as an enclave, almost totally isolated from the rest of the economy. Finally, and most important, the presence of an export sector that produced sufficient revenue to operate the government and provide employment for a growing middle class enabled the Chilean oligarchy to retain political power and maintain an obsolete system of land tenure and use; these conditions severely hampered the growth of democracy and economic development.

Nonetheless, the nation grew increasingly urbanized and industrialized, and new classes emerged from these processes. An industrial working class rose in the mining regions of the north, first in the nitrate fields and then in the copper mines. Although their wages were higher than elsewhere in the country, the miners suffered from low pay, inadequate housing, the tyranny of company stores, and unsafe working conditions. In the cities, where wages were even lower, workers lived in wretched slums and were periodically battered by epidemic disease.

After the turn of the century, workers struggled against these dismal conditions. The first major strike broke out in Iquique in the northern mining region in 1901 and lasted for two months. In 1907 the nitrate workers of Iquique again struck against inhuman living and working conditions; the government responded by sending in troops who slaughtered two thousand workers. The wave of strikes continued, with a notable upsurge during World War I. After the war, a cheaper synthetic product displaced Chilean nitrates in world markets and the industry collapsed, leaving thousands of miners unemployed and plunging the entire country into a severe depression. In 1919, faced with growing unrest, the government declared a state of siege (suspending civil liberties) in the mining areas.

Copper soon became Chile's leading export. Initially small-scale, low-technology operations had mined most of Chile's copper, but shortly after 1900 a downturn in copper prices had forced many of these producers to close. At the same time, the introduction of improved methods for the extraction of low-grade ore and the lower transportation costs promised by the opening of the Panama Canal attracted large North American companies, which dominated the industry after World War I. The Guggenheim interests and Anaconda Copper Co. now accounted for more than 80 percent of the nation's copper production. Foreigners also controlled Chile's other mineral exports: Bethlehem Steel monopolized iron ore and Guggenheim's *Compañía de Salitres de Chile* (COSACH) held 70 percent of the nitrate industry.

Labor had meantime begun to organize in the effort to achieve better conditions. Luis Emilio Recabarren played a leading part in establishing the Workers' Federation of Chile (*Federación de Obreros de Chile*, or *FOCH*) in 1909. Three years later he founded the first workers' party, the Socialist, or Socialist Labor, Party. In 1922 it became the Communist Party and joined the Third (Communist) International. By contrast with the Argentine Socialist Party, with its large middle-class base, Chile's first working-class party grew directly out of the labor movement.

In the same period, the middle class became larger and more diverse. The growth of industry and commerce and the expansion of the state created many new white-collar jobs. This growing middle class displayed few of the entrepreneurial traits commonly associated with the North American and European middle classes. The domination of decisive sectors of the economy by large-scale enterprise effectively barred small- and medium-size entrepreneurs from playing an important role in economic life. Aristocratic control of choice government jobs through clientele and kinship ties also restricted the sphere of middle-class activity. As the twentieth century opened, the middle class began to agitate for a place in the sun.

Meanwhile, the composition of the oligarchy was also changing, for it began to incorporate new elements from among industrialists and businessmen. More completely than elsewhere in Latin America, the Chilean landed elite fused with the new urban upper and upper-middle classes. They intermarried, and the urban rich acquired land, adopting the values of the traditional elite. This was a serious impediment to reform. Missing in Chile, too, were the large number of immigrants that in some measure had challenged the values and hegemony of the elite in Argentina.

WOMEN AND THE WORKPLACE

The lack of immigrants also meant there was only a limited supply of native-born Chilean workers to satisfy growing industrial and agricultural needs. But market demand for cheap labor quickly broke down the gendered walls of work and family; in addition to their unpaid labor in the household, women played an increasingly important role as wage-earning workers in the Chilean economy. By 1913, 21 percent of the labor force was women, almost all of whom were native-born and employed in blue-collar occupations; three years later, this figure rose rapidly to 26 percent. Most women worked in *"trabajo a domicilio,"* sweatshops in which they performed household chores like sewing and weaving for piece-rate wages. In a report on working conditions in the industry, Elena Caffarena showed that these workshops were "neither hygienic nor safe" and paid miserably low wages. This also inevitably damaged women's reproductive capacity; not surprisingly, child mortality rose from an average of 273 infant deaths per thousand in 1871 to 325 in 1908. To remedy this, Caffarena and other feminists advocated "strong government regulation" to abolish the sweatshop system and "female exploitation."

Ironically, they drew on traditional gendered ideals of womanhood and the family to lay the foundation for Chile's modern feminist movement. Needleworker and feminist leader Esther Valdés de Díaz, for example, denounced the "wolves" who waited to seduce women, made vulnerable by long hours of work and constant verbal abuse on the shop floor, and she argued the need for a paternalistic state to protect them. Like many working-class feminists, she stressed the class oppression of capitalism rather than the gendered tyranny of patriarchy. "Women who work in factories, pushed by the need to earn their daily bread, not only are not in their place, but, without knowing it, are competing with men and, in so doing, becoming victims of capitalism." Women, she believed, unconsciously and unavoidably contributed to the "devaluation of men's work."

But for these feminists, this lamentable state of affairs could be remedied only by an aggressive, activist state that defended women and workers against the predatory interests of capitalists. So they mobilized to pressure Chile's political leadership to regulate sweatshops; enforce minimum-wage protections for women and children; establish the legal right to equal pay for equal work; restrict women's workweek to six eight-hour days; prohibit work by children under fourteen years of age; abolish night work for women; require companies to provide partially paid pre- and post-partum leaves for pregnant women; compel industries employing more than twenty women to provide on-site child-care facilities; and allow nursing mothers periodic breaks to feed their children.

Alessandri and the Rise of Populism, 1920–1970

By 1920 even sections of the oligarchy were aware that they could no longer ignore the needs of the rest of Chilean society. Foreign interests like the Braden Copper Company actively contributed to this expanded social consciousness. According to Braden, a sturdy nuclear family could stabilize labor turnover; decrease such antisocial behavior as gambling, drinking, and fighting; deter absenteeism and the celebration of *"San Lunes"* (Saint Monday), the unofficial international workers' holiday; and discourage militant trade unionism that frequently led to strikes, industrial sabotage, and worker slowdowns—all of which reduced labor productivity. Braden therefore had developed a comprehensive private social welfare program to encourage family life, but workers typically opposed these paternalistic policies, which were transparently designed to control their labor; for example, they scorned the company's *Departamento de Bienestar* (Welfare Department) as the *Departamento de Bienfregar* (Molest Well Department).

However, state welfare programs enjoyed a social legitimacy that a company's private plan did not. Moreover, public welfare was an effective means of socializing private costs and thus increasing the competitive advantage of large companies over smaller businesses that routinely ignored workers' welfare. Finally, these state-sponsored programs also appealed to middle-class progressives who sought to "moralize" working-class culture and to radicals who sought to cultivate a "proletarian morality" that discouraged workers' fractious individualism and encouraged a politically disciplined, class-based solidarity. The stage was set for a populist reform program that would appeal to diverse political constituencies, and Arturo Allessandri, nicknamed the "Lion of Tarapacá," became its agent.

A former corporation lawyer turned populist politician, Alessandri appealed to the lower and middle classes with promises to reform the constitution and relieve the bleakness of working-class life. He promised a social security system, a labor code, cheap housing, educational reform, women's rights, and state control of banks and insurance companies. With considerable support from sections of the oligarchy, which hoped that he could placate the restless masses with a minimum of effective social change, Alessandri became president in 1920.

During the first four years of Alessandri's term, he proved unable to make good his campaign pledges. Congress, representing entrenched oligarchical interests, stood squarely in the way of any meaningful social and political reforms. Accordingly, Alessandri urged the passage of laws that would restore the balance of power between Congress and the executive branch, a balance destroyed after the civil war of 1891. He also sought such social reforms as a shorter workday,

labor laws to protect women and children, the right of workers to strike, and health insurance. These modest proposals certainly did not threaten the status quo, but they would require money. In view of the catastrophic decline of the nitrate industry, this money could be raised only by taxing the oligarchy's land and income, a solution the elite found unthinkable. As a result of the parliamentary deadlock, the Chilean government could not cope with the mounting economic and social crisis.

The Chilean military, predominantly of middle-class origins, had observed the unfolding crisis with growing impatience and resentment. Many junior and middle-grade officers favored the enactment of Alessandri's social and political reform program; they also felt that Congress had neglected the needs of the armed forces. A succession of military coups, the last of which was led by reformist officers Carlos Ibáñez del Campo and Marmaduke Grove, ultimately enabled Alessandri to accomplish the political reforms for which he had campaigned. The result was the constitution of 1925, which ended the Parliamentary Republic and restored the balance of power between Congress and the president. It provided that the president would be elected by direct vote, serve a six-year term, be ineligible for immediate reelection, and have control over his cabinet and government finance. The constitution proclaimed the inviolable right of private property but stated that this right could be limited in the interest of social needs. Other measures included a new and extensive labor code, the grant of the vote to literate males over twenty-one, the establishment of an electoral registry to reduce electoral fraud, a nominal income tax on income over ten thousand pesos a year, and the establishment of a central bank.

IBÁÑEZ AND THE GREAT DEPRESSION

But Ibáñez and the military remained powerful, and they initially sought an alliance with the working and middle classes for the achievement of structural reforms, but this ended in the military dictatorship of 1927 to 1931.

To implement his program and secure the position of state employees, which was necessary to maintain political stability, Ibáñez needed substantial amounts of money; his populist program of welfare, public works, and modernization was based above all on huge loans from foreign bankers. The armed forces were a special beneficiary of government largesse, obtaining generous promotions and salary increases. Most of the protective legislation for which women had lobbied during the previous decade was enacted. Meanwhile, all opposition was suppressed, political foes were jailed or deported, and efforts were made to split the Communist-led labor movement by the sponsorship of government-backed unions.

Aided by a temporary revival of copper and nitrate sales and massive foreign loans, the Chilean economy prospered for the first two years of Ibáñez's rule. But the Wall Street crash of 1929 unmasked Chile's dependency on external markets. It cut off the all-important flow of capital and loans, and by the following year the nitrate and copper markets had both collapsed. Because the government relied heavily on copper taxes for revenue, the Depression forced it to curtail daily operations severely and default on its large foreign debt. In 1932 the United States, Chile's main market for copper, adopted a high tariff on copper imports, which caused mine closings and severe unemployment. The Depression also accentuated gender-based wage inequities and unleashed a backlash against women in the work force. Conservatives called for women's return to the home to stabilize the family and reduce job competition among men, thereby increasing male wages and employment. Although the political left advocated elimination of gendered wage inequalities so that all workers could unite against capitalists on the basis of their shared class interest, they nonetheless agreed to identify certain industries, like copper and teaching, as exclusively male and female. In a vain effort to find a solution for the economic crisis, the government tried to limit nitrate sales to push up prices. Ibáñez trimmed social services and his public works program and hiked taxes, but the financial situation grew increasingly desperate.

In July 1931, confronted by a general strike that involved not only workers but professionals, white-collar employees, women, and students and faced with growing doubts about the army's loyalty to him, Ibáñez resigned and went into exile in Argentina. The next seventeen months brought a succession of military coups. One such coup, led by Marmaduke Grove, commander of the air force, led to the proclamation of a Socialist Republic of Chile, which lasted barely twelve days before it was overthrown by a new military revolt. Ironically, the program of the socialist republic was not socialist; it proposed, rather, to create jobs through public works financed by the issue of paper money.

Finally, in September 1932 a new coup installed a caretaker regime that presided over new elections, which returned Arturo Alessandri to the presidency.

THE RETURN OF ALESSANDRI

Alessandri began his second term in the depths of the Depression, with one hundred and sixty thousand people unemployed in Santiago alone, while a typhoid epidemic ravaged the country. Income from nitrates was one-twentieth the 1927 figure; public employees, including soldiers and policemen, had not been paid for months. In the succeeding five years, 1932 to 1937, the president and his finance minister, Gustavo Ross, presided over an economic recovery that reflected a partial revival and stabilization of the world market. Copper prices recovered in 1935, and by 1937 copper production exceeded pre-Depression levels. As the economy revived, government revenues generated from copper taxes enabled the government to avoid taxing large landholdings. Without the spur of equitable taxes, latifundists continued to leave vast tracts of fertile land uncultivated or underutilized. Although it had the potential to feed its own people, Chile had to import foodstuffs—a policy that drained the nation of foreign exchange that would have been better used to purchase capital goods for industrialization or to build roads and harbors.

With its coffers swelled by revenue from the export sector, the Chilean government expanded its role in the economy. A large bureaucracy developed, staffed by an emerging middle class. As the government became the major employer of the middle class and the nation's most important

In the 1930s, Chile's Women's Liberation Movement (MEMCH) mobilized thousands of women and influenced populist policies with a demand that the state guarantee women's right to equality in the home, in the workplace, and in politics. [Photograph courtesy of Asunción Lavrín]

venture capitalist, Chile grew ever more dependent for its economic development on factors beyond its control.

But Alessandri had no greater success in solving Chile's structural problems in the 1930s than he had in the 1920s. Foreign capital controlled the lucrative mining sector of the economy, and the inefficient latifundio continued to dominate Chilean agriculture. Workers' strikes for better wages and living conditions were often brutally suppressed.

Middle-class critics of the regime fared little better. Following the example of Ibáñez, Alessandri closed down hostile newspapers, exiled political critics, and dealt highhandedly with

Congress. These conditions produced a major new effort to mobilize workers, peasants, and the urban middle sector to defend democracy and promote social progress. This effort was called the Chilean Popular Front.

WOMEN AND THE RISE OF THE POPULAR FRONT

The Chilean left had its roots in the Communist Party during the 1920s. The Communists won considerable support among organized labor, particularly the railroad workers' union and the Confederation of Chilean Workers (FOCH), which claimed two hundred thousand members. Although they had had a part in framing the constitution of 1925, Communist leaders were imprisoned and exiled during the Ibáñez regime. After the fall of Ibáñez in 1931, however, the party revived under the leadership of Carlos Contreras Labarca and gained considerable popularity among workers and intellectuals.

Chile in the 1930s was fertile ground for the growth of left-wing parties and ideologies, many of which coalesced to form the Chilean Popular Front. Composed of Socialists, Communists, and Radicals, the Front's candidate, Radical Pedro Aguirre Cerda, won the presidency in 1938. The Popular Front's electoral platform called for the restoration of constitutional rule and civil liberties and basic social reforms, summed up in the slogan *pan, techo, y abrigo* (bread, clothing, and a roof).

The short, stormy life of the Popular Front yielded some achievements. In 1938 the State Development Agency, CORFO, was formed to foster industrialization. Aided by relatively high wartime copper prices, a virtual cessation of imports as a result of World War II, and by governmental subsidies, low taxes, and protective tariffs on imported consumer goods, native manufacturing made steady progress between 1940 and 1945.

The policy of state-supported industrialization also promoted the growth of the Chilean industrial working class; between 1940 and 1952, the number of workers employed in manufacturing rose from 15 percent of the work force to 19 percent. The industrialization process was accompanied, at least until 1945, by improvement in workers' real purchasing power—up 20 percent between 1940 and 1945—while that of white-collar workers increased 25 percent. After 1945, as Radical administrations moved to the right and the basis of the Popular Front strategy disintegrated, the working class's relative share of the national income declined.

Women also were active both as workers and mothers, but increasingly they insisted that they would need more than the "aura of dignity and respect, but should also receive the aid of the state when economic conditions demand it." For many women in the 1930s, this meant state protections against exploitation, prenatal health care, and subsidies for child care. But feminists like Clara de la Luz also wanted support for family planning. She defended "scientific procreation"—that is, birth control—and called on women to organize a "strike of the wombs" to liberate themselves from unwanted family responsibilities that increased the supply of new workers for industry and agriculture, lowered workers' wages, and reduced their freedom to resist capitalist exploitation. Others criticized the moral and legal double standard that gave "men impunity and women responsibility" in reproductive matters.

Although Chile's Catholic traditions made abortion illegal, it was widely practiced by midwives and amateurs. In 1936 five hospitals identified 10,514 cases of botched abortions that required medical attention; the following year, the Ministry of Health reported that 24 percent (13,351) of women in public maternity hospitals were there to be treated for complications from bungled abortions. Growing numbers of women, especially poor working-class women, viewed abortion, contraception, and family planning as one way to escape what the leftist Women's Liberation Movement (MEMCH) called "compulsory motherhood" and the "slavery of unwanted children."

Women also won basic political and civil rights. Conservatives, influenced by upper-class women's groups like the Club de Señoras, historically had supported enfranchisement of literate women because they believed that, as guardians of home, church, and family life, they were a natural conservative constituency necessary to counter the political advantages accruing to Socialist, Communist, and Radical Parties from the enfranchisement of illiterate men. Meanwhile, MEMCH insisted on the "integral emancipation of women, especially the economic, juridical, biological, and political emancipation." All pressed for civil equality and the right to vote, a campaign that achieved partial success in 1934 with the granting of municipal voting rights to literate women.

Local leftist parties failed to offer women candidates for municipal posts, preferring to emphasize class struggle while ignoring gender difference. This created an electoral void that conservatives filled by offering women candidates like Elena Doll de Díaz, whose populist campaign defended the moral center of family life and called for an aggressive program of state intervention to protect it against the injustice of market forces: workers' welfare, equal wages, sanitation, "popular restaurants" to feed the hungry, and electric trolleys to provide workers with cheap transportation. Not surprisingly, by 1941 two-thirds of the women registered to vote identified themselves as Conservatives; thereafter, the Popular Front coalition fractured and party leaders abandoned interest in woman suffrage.

World War II decisively reinforced the politics of the Popular Front and reignited the campaign for women's right to vote in national elections. Wartime alliances with the Soviet Union, a growing democratic discourse, and the decline of anti-imperialist rhetoric within the Chilean left contributed to the emergence of a cross-class, gender-based movement in support of women's suffrage. The Chilean Federation of Feminine Institutions (FECHIF), for example, which represented 213 women's organizations, mobilized massive street demonstrations that attracted thousands of women to its militant calls for "social democracy."

Although freed from traditional external constraints during the war, the Popular Front era produced no structural changes in the Chilean economy or society because the members of the governing coalition had irreconcilable differences over domestic and foreign policy. In the 1946 election, the Socialists, reflecting historic factional disputes within the party, abandoned the Popular Front, but Radical Gabriel González Videla (1946–1952) won with the support of the Communist Party. Soon, responding to the pressures of the cold war, González Videla moved to the right, ousted the Communist members of his cabinet, broke a strike of Communist-led coal miners, and passed the *Ley Maldita* (the Accursed Law), which outlawed the Communist Party and eliminated Communists from Congress. González Videla also established a concentration camp for Communist Party members and other left-wing militants in an abandoned mining camp in the northern desert.

With the repression and disenfranchisement of Communists like Elena Caffarena, who had written the women's suffrage legislation and organized on behalf of women's rights for decades, González Videla finally signed into law a 1949 bill to give literate women the vote in national elections. Thereafter, he tried to consolidate his political support among working-class women by organizing Women's Centers to provide education, training, and career services.

But massive discontent with skyrocketing inflation, the freezing of workers' wages, and González Videla's repressive policies paved the way for a comeback by the old ex-dictator Carlos Ibáñez del Campo in 1952. Ibáñez promised repeal of the Ley Maldita, a minimum salary, a family allowance for workers, and a sympathetic hearing for just wage demands. But the decline in Chilean copper revenues following the end of the Korean war made it impossible for Ibáñez to make good on his populist promises. To stabilize the economy he sought loans from North American banks and the International Monetary Fund; meanwhile, he sought to force the working class to absorb inflation through cuts in real wages. Threatened with labor unrest, Ibáñez embarked on a course of harsh repression. By the end of his term, he had alienated all sectors of the Chilean people.

NEW ALIGNMENTS: THE EMERGENCE OF CHRISTIAN DEMOCRACY

Between 1953 and the presidential election year of 1958, the parties of the left restored their unity by forming the *Frente de Acción Popular* (Popular Action Front, or FRAP), which included the Socialist Party and the Communists. Simultaneously, a new Christian Democratic Party emerged, led by Eduardo Frei; it appealed to Catholic workers, especially white-collar sectors, with a vague ideology that claimed to be neither capitalist nor socialist. In its first try for office in 1958, this party demonstrated its electoral force.

Four major candidates contested the presidency in 1958. They were the Conservative Jorge Alessandri, a son of the former president and a leading industrialist; Eduardo Frei, a Christian Democrat; Salvador Allende, of FRAP; and Luis Bossay, a Radical. Surprisingly, Alessandri beat Allende by a threadbare margin of only 33,500 votes. Allende would probably have won if an obscure minor-party candidate had not drawn away some slum and rural poor votes.

Despite booming copper prices, however, Alessandri had no more success than his predecessors in coping with Chile's problems of inflation and economic stagnation. His formula for recovery was to restore the free market, reduce state intervention in the economy, and employ foreign loans and investment as the basis for economic development.

Although depression and war had slowed the inflow, foreign capital now surged into Chile in the postwar period, not only into the extractive sector but into manufacturing and commerce as well. From 1954 to 1970, foreigners invested $1.67 billion in Chile. U.S. companies continued to dominate copper, nitrate, and iodine production. Foreign companies conducted approximately half the nation's wholesale trade, monopolized the telephone and telegraph industries, and had important stakes in electric utilities and banking. Even the major advertising agencies were foreign subsidiaries or affiliates.

In 1960 the three great mines of the Gran Minería, all owned by the foreign giants Anaconda and Kennecott, accounted for 11 percent of the country's gross national product, 50 percent of its exports, and 20 percent of government revenues. But the millions of dollars in sales, profits, and tax revenues generated by copper mining provided little stimulus for Chilean commerce and industry. Their huge profits, which they remitted to their parent corporations in the United States, added to the outflow of capital from the country.

Chile depended not only on direct investment from abroad but on loans as well. Payment of interest and amortization on the national debt consumed an increasing share of its revenue from the export sector. Because most foreign investment, like the copper enclave, was capital-intensive, it provided little employment and few linkages to the rest of the economy. Employment in the mines declined steadily in the post–World War II era, and the surplus of miners made it possible for the companies to pay the largely unskilled labor force relatively low wages. Until the 1950s, machinery, equipment, and technical skills were imported entirely from abroad. The benefits to Chile's long-range economic development were minimal. Without a doubt, Chile was not the master of its own economic fate.

Politics in Chile during the early 1960s was profoundly affected by changes in United States policy in response to the Cuban Revolution (1959). The United States sought to bolster reform movements throughout Latin America as an alternative to social revolution. As part of this policy, it covertly financed the Christian Democrats. Combined with the backing of the conservative parties, which were badly scared by Allende's near-election six years earlier, U.S. support enabled Frei to win the 1964 election with 56 percent of the vote.

Eduardo Frei came to the presidency with promises of a "revolution in freedom" that would correct the extreme inequities of Chilean society without a violent class struggle. He especially appealed to women to preserve the sanctity of the Catholic family against Allende's "godless communist revolution" and opened 6,000 Women's Centers. The problems he faced were familiar ones: inflation and stagnation, a domestic market too narrow to support an efficient mass industry, an extractive industry dominated by foreign ownership, and an agriculture incapable of supplying the basic needs of the population. To create the market needed for a modern mass industry, Frei proposed agrarian reform, tax reform, and other measures to redistribute income to the lower classes.

When Frei took office, there was an extreme concentration of landownership, the condition of rural laborers was wretched, and the inefficient great landed estates were clearly incapable of providing enough food to feed Chile's growing urban centers. By contrast with the situation in most underdeveloped nations, Chile's agricultural sector played only a small role in the economy. The inability of agriculture to provide employment, on the one hand, and sufficient food, on the other, resulted in an overurbanized, underemployed, and undernourished population.

The statistics of landholding indicate that there was little change in these patterns between 1930 and 1970. In 1930 holdings of over 2,500 acres composed only 2 percent of the total number of farms but constituted 78 percent of the cultivable land. Eighty-two percent of all farms were under 125 acres but held only 4 percent of the land. By the 1960s, 11,000 units, accounting for 4.2 percent of the farms, composed 79 percent of the land. Farms under 100 acres—77 percent of all farms—held 10.6 percent of the land. Over 700,000 people, the majority of the rural labor force, had no land at all. The living and working conditions of agricultural laborers were appalling—and getting worse. Agricultural wages had consistently declined since the 1940s, falling 23 percent from 1953 to 1964.

Government credit and tax policies before 1964 assured that the maldistribution of land and agricultural income would continue. Small landholders, having no access to bank or government loans, had to rely on moneylenders or store owners, who charged outrageous interest. Smallholders and agricultural laborers also bore a disproportionate burden of taxes. Taxes on land, capital, income, and inheritance, on the other hand, were light. The large estates, especially those that were not farmed, went virtually untaxed.

Frei's program of agrarian reform had mixed results. He began by attempting to improve conditions in rural areas by increasing wages, establishing peasant unions, and instituting a more equitable system of taxation; he also redistributed some land to the peasants, but inflation eroded wage gains and land redistribution fell far short of what was promised. As a gradualist, Frei shied away from precipitous or widespread expropriations. Peasants who received land faced a difficult time, for the government did not provide them with credit needed to start off as independent farmers.

Frei's plan for the Chileanization of the copper industry was designed both to appease widespread nationalist sentiment and to obtain new government revenue through increased copper production. The plan required the government to buy 51 percent of the shares in the foreign-owned mines. In return for a promise to increase production and refine more ore in Chile, the foreign companies retained control of management and obtained new concessions with respect to taxation and repatriation of profits. But the plan failed to expand production significantly or to increase government revenues.

Other sectors of the Chilean economy also were concentrated. A few powerful clans controlled a wide variety of industrial and financial enterprises and thus exerted a decisive influence on the national economy as a whole. In 1967, 12 companies out of 2,600 transacted nearly half the total wholesale business in the country. One bank, Banco de Chile, furnished 32 percent of the nation's private bank credit; the five largest banks furnished 57.4 percent.

These facts, however, tell only part of the story, for control of the economy was even more concentrated. Fifteen large economic groups controlled the Chilean economy. The most powerful of the clans, the Edwards family, controlled one commercial bank, seven financial and investment corporations, five insurance companies, thirteen industries, and two publishing houses and was closely associated with North American companies active in the country. The family's newspaper chain accounted for over half the circulation of daily newspapers in Chile; together with another publishing house, it virtually controlled the entire market for periodicals. As early as 1965, the president had decided to abandon his campaign promise to redistribute income and instead he implemented an economic policy that would attract foreign and domestic investors. During 1966 the government froze wages and reacted

harshly to strikes in the copper mines, at one point sending in troops. Increased worker militancy made Socialist and Communist union leadership more influential.

The need to appease his political constituency and the economic decline after 1966 defeated Frei's efforts at reform. Upper-class Catholic intellectuals had founded and provided the leadership of the Christian Democratic party. Its membership was overwhelmingly middle class, including urban professionals, white-collar workers—especially from the public sector—skilled workers, and managers, all groups that had emerged during the preceding two decades as the Chilean economy diversified. The party did well in the larger towns, among urban slum dwellers, and among women. In 1964 Frei got considerable support from industrialists and bankers who feared the election of Allende. These were hardly the elements of a revolutionary party. Frei's program of reform depended entirely on a healthy, expanding economy that would enable the government to distribute benefits to the lower class without injuring the middle class or altering the basic economic and social structures.

When Frei came to office in 1964, the economy was expanding rapidly, for the Vietnam War kept copper prices high. Frei's moderate reform goals insured good relations with the United States and a resulting flow of loans and private investment. Even Chile's chronic inflation slowed. Two good years, however, were followed by four bad ones. After 1967 the economy stagnated while inflation surged again. Income inequalities increased, and living standards declined sharply. Frei's rhetoric brought hope to Chileans, but he fulfilled few of his promises. During his term, the working class grew increasingly restive. Groups like *pobladores* (urban slum dwellers) and rural workers organized for the first time. As the Christian Democrats proved less and less capable of dealing with Chile's economic woes, these newly organized groups and the trade unions moved further to the left.

This transformation of Chilean politics was both reflected in and shaped by powerful cultural changes, the most significant of which was the birth of *Nueva Canción*, the New Song movement. First developed in Peronist Argentina, the New Song movement utilized indigenous musical instruments and typically explored folkloric lyrical themes. But in Chile and elsewhere throughout Latin America in the 1960s, it quickly became associated with revolution and the democratic struggle against poverty, social injustice, and tyranny. Violeta Parra, the daughter of a schoolteacher and seamstress in Chile's rural south, had pioneered the study of the nation's folkloric art and music in the 1950s. Her ballads, like her paintings and colorful *arpilleras* (tapestries), typically commemorated the struggles of poor folk and condemned the wealthy *pitucos* who profited from their exploitation.

Parra's work made an indelible impression on a young Víctor Jara, arguably Chile's most famous New Song musician. Born to a poor peasant family, Jara, whose songs celebrated the lives of ordinary Chileans, often combined traditional Catholic rituals with lyrics that reflected his leftist social conscience. Perhaps the most famous of these was his *"La plegaria del labrador"* ("Farmworkers' Prayer"), modeled on the Lord's Prayer. But Jara, giving voice to Chile's impoverished peasants, did not ask to be saved from some abstract evil; on the contrary, accompanied by his searing *charango*, an indigenous guitar made from an armadillo shell, he raised his powerful voice to demand: "Deliver us from the master who keeps us in misery, thy kingdom of justice and equality come."

In 1969, after Frei's police savagely attacked a group of peasants who illegally had occupied vacant lands in Puerto Montt, Jara wrote a stirring new song that became the battle cry of a generation. *"Preguntas por Puerto Montt"* ("Questions about Puerto Montt") denounced the barbaric murderers and declared that "All the rains in the south (of Chile) will not be enough to wash your hands clean." But Jara was not only interested in politics. He believed that the role of artists was to be cultural rebels. "An artist must be an authentic creator," he once said, "and in essence a revolutionary . . . a man as dangerous as a guerrilla because of his great power of communication." Artists became revolutionaries by celebrating a popular culture that all too often was ignored or scorned by a mass media monopolized by the wealthy. "We should ascend to the people, not feel that we are lowering ourselves to them," Jara once wrote. "Our job is to give them what belongs to them— their cultural roots." Jara and others later collaborated on a popular new musical, *"La Cantata de Santa María,"* which commemorated the 1907 slaughter of 3,000 striking nitrate miners, a massacre that sparked the development of Chile's modern trade union movement.

This leftward move also was reflected within the Christian Democratic Party itself. In 1969 disillusioned progressives split off to form the Movement for United Popular Action (MAPU), which later joined the Popular Unity Coalition. This break left Frei the leader of the right wing of the party and Radomiro Tomic the head of what remained of the left wing. Because Frei was ineligible to run again under the constitution and the party could not risk further erosion of its social base by running a hard-liner, it advanced Tomic as its presidential candidate in 1970. He ran on a platform almost indistinguishable from that of Allende, the candidate of the left coalition, Popular Unity (UP), whose main elements were the Socialist, Communist, and Radical Parties.

The right backed ex-President Jorge Alessandri of the National Party. The right, already alienated by Frei's agrarian reform, found Tomic totally unacceptable and refused to join forces with the Christian Democrats as it had in 1964. Allende won the election with 36 percent of the vote, whereas Alessandri got 35 percent and Tomic 28 percent. Preferring to stress class solidarity, Allende had not targeted the women's vote, but his share of it grew by 13 percent from 1958 and doubtlessly provided his razor-thin margin of victory. Because Allende failed to receive a majority, the election went to Congress which, after much-publicized maneuvering, approved Allende as president.

The Chilean Road to Socialism, 1970–1973

THE OPPOSITION

When Allende took office in 1970, domestic political conditions appeared favorable to his program for the achievement of socialism in Chile within a

Salvador Allende, president of Chile, died during the military coup of September 1973. [Bruno Barbey/Magnum Photos]

framework of legality and nonviolence. The assassination in October 1970 of General René Schneider, the commander in chief of the army, who had kept the army neutral during the period after the election just before Allende assumed the presidency, had discredited the right. Prospects were excellent that the Popular Unity would receive the cooperation of the left wing of the Christian Democratic Party in Congress. For the time being, the UP coalition remained united behind a program that called for expropriation of all landholdings over 80 hectares, and the progressive takeover of large foreign companies and monopolies.

Nonetheless, the forces against the UP were formidable. It did not have a majority in Congress. Both the judiciary and the *Controlaría General* (the government's fiscal arm) opposed Allende's policies. The entire domestic economic establishment, foreign interests, much of the officer corps of the military and national police, and the Catholic church were also aligned against the UP. The anti-UP political coalition, the *Confederación Democrática* (Democratic Confederation) controlled virtually all of the nation's media—two of the three television stations, 95 percent of the radio stations, 90 percent of the newspaper circulation, and all of the weekly magazines.

Even more significantly, however, substantial shifts were occurring in global markets. The European and Japanese economies had fully recovered from their wartime collapse and had emerged as vigorous competitors with the United States, whose economic and technological strength had been sapped by the Vietnam War and a host of other Third World military interventions. By the early 1970s, the leading capitalist countries were on the verge of an international trade war, looking to industrially developing, "semiperipheral" countries like Chile to earn profits otherwise unavailable to them in their own markets.

But this meant that foreign interests would no longer tolerate nationalistic, statist restrictions on their activities, no matter how popular these might be with local democratic electoral constituencies. Consequently, when the democratically elected UP coalition of Socialists and Communists sought to implement their campaign promises, U.S. government leaders like Henry Kissinger, President Richard Nixon's National Security Council adviser, imperiously intervened. "I don't see why we have to let a country go Marxist," Kissinger arrogantly insisted, "just because its people are irresponsible." Nixon immediately ordered the Central Intelligence Agency (CIA) to orchestrate a coup to overthrow Allende before the Congress could validate his election, but, even after this failed, he advised U.S. operatives to "make the economy scream." The ensuing economic chaos, according to Nixon, would undermine Allende's legitimacy and force his government to reopen Chile to foreign control.

But a lack of internal cohesion also hindered the UP. The old problem of how to satisfy the claims of both the working-class—even more militant than during the Popular Front days—and the middle-class sectors—who worried that their interests were being threatened by the structural reforms undertaken by the UP—was never fully resolved.

This competition between middle- and working-class constituents also had been reflected in cultural conflict among the nation's youth. During the tumultuous 1960s, the folk music of Parra and Jara, with its social conscience, political protest, and identification with Chile's popular classes, had starkly contrasted with a Chilean rock music that self-consciously emulated British and U.S. (counter)culture. Jara himself had campaigned for the UP, and he wrote *"Venceremos"* ("We Shall Overcome"), which quickly became the campaign's theme song.

On the other hand, rock musicians like *Los Macs* identified more with foreign cultures they defined as modern; they especially appealed to alienated upper- and middle-class youth who, like the later supporters of Pinochet's bloody dictatorship, rebelled against Chilean popular traditions they associated with backwardness. Chilean rockers typically sang their songs, even original compositions, in English and were greatly influenced by Elvis Presley, The Beatles, The Kinks, and The Byrds. So disgusted were these bands with Chilean popular cultural traditions and the nation's stormy politics that some rock musicians, like Juan Mateo O'Brien of *Los Vidrios Quebrados* (Broken Glass), "thought only about leaving Chile" and declined invitations to return to play for a Chilean audience. Others, like Willy Morales of *Los Macs*, specifically cited Allende's democratic socialist revolution, "the social and political events between 1970 and 1973," for his disinterest in returning to Chile.

Ironically, countercultural *gringos* who visited Chile to help build a peaceful, democratic socialist alternative to western capitalism often discovered to their amazement that the young Chilean rockers, who dressed like them, wore long hair, smoked marihuana, and listened to Jimi Hendrix, increasingly were politically more sympathetic to Richard Nixon. Middle- and upper-class countercultural Chilean rockers defined the dominant culture against which they rebelled as primitive, uneducated, undeveloped, and working class; in 1970, Salvador Allende had become its political symbol. But the countercultural *gringos* and folk enthusiasts like Víctor Jara defined the dominant culture against which they rebelled as modern, capitalistic, socially unjust, and foreign dominated; its political symbols were Richard Nixon and Jorge Alessandri, upon whom the Nixon administration had lavished covert financial support in the 1970 presidential elections.

THE FIRST YEAR, 1971

The UP's immediate goal was to improve the living standard of the working class and get the economy moving. The government accomplished this by increasing purchasing power, which in turn stimulated demand, industrial production, and employment. During the first year of Allende's term, worker income rose a startling 50 percent. The government instituted a massive program of public spending, especially for labor-intensive projects such as housing, education, sanitation, and health. At the same time, the government expanded its appeal to women. It developed a Ministry of the Family, created community daycare centers, organized low-income milk distribution programs, financed *Almacenes del Pueblo* (People's Grocery Cooperatives), and established price controls, which were monitored by local, housewife-operated price and supply committees. The rate of inflation fell to 22.1 percent in 1971 from 34.9 percent in 1970, and as a result, real income rose 30 percent. The Organization of American States independently confirmed that Allende's program had produced "high growth levels" during its first year.

For the first year, middle-class businessmen, industrialists, and peasants fared very well and cooperated with the Allende regime. There were scattered cases of larger owners sabotaging their own property but, for the most part, business was not hostile. The government also employed coercion to gain cooperation from industry, threatening companies with intervention if they did not agree to increase production. Coercion and increased demand combined to bring about an expansion of industrial production and employment.

The short-term policies of the UP government increased popular support for the minority regime, a success reflected in the municipal elections of April 1971, in which the Popular Unity won over 50 percent of the vote. In the long run, however, the depletion of stocks, the outflow of foreign exchange to pay for the import of consumer goods, and the fall of profits in what was still basically a market economy proved very damaging to the government's economic program.

Allende's first problems arose when the United States in effect declared economic war on Chile's fragile democratic socialist experiment. The United States covertly embargoed Chilean loans, imports, and exports, especially copper, whose price declined sharply, leading to an imbalance in terms of trade and the depletion of foreign-exchange reserves. In addition, the expropriation of the Gran Minería in July 1971 virtually halted the flow of private investment capital from the United States. The resulting economic difficulties led Allende to stop servicing the national debt, but he eventually managed to reach satisfactory agreements with all of Chile's creditors except the United States.

THE LEFT'S OLD DILEMMA: CAUGHT IN THE MIDDLE, 1972–1973

The first year's gains gave way to economic stagnation and a resurgence of inflation. Although Allende's popularity remained high in 1971, he struggled unsuccessfully to reach a delicate balance between the needed structural reform demanded by the working class and the special interests of the middle class. The government's policy of expropriating large enterprises alienated owners of small- and medium-size businesses, who employed 80 percent of the working population. Workers began occupying and operating factories. State enterprises were badly mismanaged.

The socialist government was also unable to solve the agricultural crisis. Chile's inefficiently managed agricultural production was perhaps the biggest economic roadblock, for it neither raised enough to feed the country's inhabitants nor provided employment for the large pool of rural labor. A hostile Congress forced Allende to operate with reform laws inherited from the Frei administration; nonetheless, by the end of 1972, Allende had effectively liquidated the latifundio system. Expropriation and redistribution proceeded, but with considerable cost to production. The amount of land under cultivation decreased by 20 percent, and the harvest of 1972–1973 was poor.

The Allende administration faced a full-fledged economic and political crisis by the fall of 1972. The inevitable disruptions that accompany revolutionary conditions were aggravated by mistakes and shortcomings of the UP government and conflicts within the coalition. Moreover, the Chilean oligarchy and its North American allies were formidable, unrelenting opponents. The United States was deeply involved in Chilean politics. According to its director, William Colby, the CIA spent $11 million between 1962 and 1970 to help prevent Allende from being elected president. Thereafter the CIA, with authorization from President Richard Nixon and Secretary of State Henry Kissinger, spent $8 million between 1970 and 1973 to "destabilize" the Chilean economy. Nixon told the U.S. ambassador to Chile that he would "smash that son-of-a-bitch Allende."

The Chilean upper class, although it had lost much of its economic base due to the nationalization of large industries and expropriation of large landholdings, retained control over much of the mass media, the judiciary, a majority in Congress, and the armed forces.

The struggle hinged, finally, on the middle sectors. Soaring inflation eroded their economic position. All of Allende's efforts to reassure and win over the middle class failed to overcome its traditional hostility toward socialism and its association with the bourgeoisie. This middle class provided the mass base for the coup that overthrew the Popular Unity.

Allende's opponents took advantage of the growing economic crisis to embark on a program of sabotage and direct action that included the mobilization of middle-class women in "empty pots" protest marches and a strike of truck drivers (subsidized by the CIA), which developed into a full-scale lockout by a majority of Chilean capitalists. The strike ended when Allende made major concessions to his opponents, guaranteeing the security of small- and medium-size industries. He also agreed to the inclusion of generals in his cabinet to ensure law and order and to supervise the congressional election scheduled for March 1973.

Relying on long established electoral trends, which saw the party in power lose congressional seats, the opposition expected to gain a sweeping victory in the election; it hoped to have the two-thirds majority needed to impeach Allende and legally oust his government. Instead, the UP vote rose from 36 percent (in 1970) to 44 percent, proof that its socialist policies had substantially increased its support among the working class and peasantry. Once again women now known as "hacedoras de presidentes" (makers of presidents)

provided Allende his margin of victory. The UP coalition received 41 percent of the women's vote, a 14 percent increase since the last congressional elections in 1969 and an 11 percent improvement over the 1970 presidential election totals. Allende also benefited from 1971 electoral reforms that enfranchised younger voters and eliminated literacy restrictions, all of which boosted women's participation from 47 percent of the electorate in 1970 to 56 percent in 1973.

But the opposition still commanded a majority in Congress and it redoubled efforts to create economic and political chaos by disruptive strikes, the organization of terrorist bands, and calls on the armed forces to intervene. The Chilean military, itself internally divided over the Allende government, was greatly influenced by the United States. Many Chilean officers had had counterinsurgency training either in the United States or in the Panama Canal Zone. Throughout the Allende presidency, even after the United States economically embargoed Chile, U.S. military aid continued. The United States even doubled its usual contribution in 1973.

By the spring of 1973, the balance of forces within the military had shifted in favor of conservatives. On June 29 a premature coup was put down by loyal troops under the direction of General Carlos Prats. Following the defeat of the coup, workers called for occupation of the factories and distribution of arms among them. Instead, Allende renewed his efforts to achieve a compromise with the Christian Democrats, foolishly relying on the armed forces, who raided factories in search of illegal weapons while making no effort to disarm rightist paramilitary groups. Control of many localities effectively passed from the UP administration to the armed forces. On September 10, 1973, a military coup led by General Augusto Pinochet toppled Allende and inaugurated a brutal dictatorship.

Neoliberalism and Democratic Constraints, 1973–2003

PINOCHET, STATE TERRORISM, AND FREE MARKETS

After the coup, Chileans endured a brutal and large-scale repression. The four-man military

During the 1980s, as the popular mobilization against the Pinochet dictatorship grew in numbers and audacity, the walls once used to divide and control neighborhoods became a national canvas upon which cultural resistance to oppression was graphically inscribed. This mural in Santiago celebrates the art of Violeta Parra and Víctor Jara (see page 352), two martyred champions of social justice and popular democracy. [Art by Alberto Díaz Parra, in Santiago, Chile, August 1989. Published in *Muralismo: Art in the Popular Chilean Culture*, © 1990 Committee of Defense of the Chilean Culture]

junta headed by General Pinochet set about to "regenerate" Chilean society. To this end they abolished all political parties, suppressed civil liberties, dissolved the Congress, banned union activities, prohibited strikes and collective bargaining, and erased the Allende administration's agrarian and economic reforms. The junta jailed, tortured, and put to death thousands of Chileans, including Víctor Jara, who had reportedly defied military authorities by singing "Venceremos." The dreaded secret police, DINA (*Dirección de Inteligencia Nacional*)—with guidance from Colonel Walter Rauff, a former Nazi who had supervised the extermination of Jews at Auschwitz—spread its network of terror throughout Chile and carried out assassinations abroad. The junta also set up at least six concentration camps. It is estimated that one of every one hundred Chileans was arrested at least once under the military regime.

Meanwhile, Pinochet worked to legitimize his brutal regime and, under cover of The Feminine Power (EPF), an organization of aristocratic and middle-class women who had opposed Allende, he sought to cultivate a female constituency committed to "traditional family values," self-sacrifice, and loyalty to the motherland. He established a National Ministry of Women and his wife, Lucía Hiriart, rejuvenated the Mothers' Centers, eventually organizing 10,000 groups that claimed 230,000 members. But the family was an early victim of the regime's political terror, and its economic policies also alienated working-class women.

Pinochet, influenced by a group of economists known as the Chicago Boys because many had studied at the University of Chicago under Milton

Friedman, implemented his neoliberal, free-market doctrines. Public spending was cut drastically, almost all state companies privatized, the peso devalued, and import duties sharply reduced. The social consequences of the "shock treatment" soon became apparent. Gross domestic product fell 16.6 percent in 1975. Manufacturing suffered particular injury, with some industries, like the textile industry, devastated by foreign imports. Wages had fallen by 1975 to 47.9 percent of their 1970 level. Unemployment stood at 20 percent, or 28 percent if the people working in government emergency programs were included.

A recovery partly based on export products—minerals, timber, and fish—but above all on a speculative spree of immense proportions began in 1977 and turned into a boom that lasted until 1980, with annual growth rates averaging 8 percent. The Chilean "economic miracle," however, was superficial and short-lived. Hoping to attract heavy foreign investment that would turn Chile into a South Korea or Taiwan, the Chicago Boys deliberately kept interest rates high. Foreign capital poured in, but almost all of it came in the form of loans to Chilean banks, which profited enormously by borrowing abroad at 12 percent and lending at 35 to 40 percent. The borrowing companies, subsidiaries of a few huge conglomerates, did not invest in production, which the high interest rates made unprofitable, but used the loans for speculation in real estate or to buy up at fire-sale prices the state companies sold under the privatization program. The bubble burst in 1980. By the end of 1981 the government, in violation of its own free-market principles, was forced to take over the nation's largest banks in order to forestall economic calamity. Bankruptcies multiplied. Production declined sharply. Between 1982 and 1986 unemployment rose to more than 30 percent and real wages fell by as much as 20 percent. An earthquake in 1985 added to the country's economic woes. By the late 1980s the economy was heavily dependent on foreign loans. With a population of 12.5 million, Chile's foreign debt in 1991 stood at $17 billion, in per capita terms one of the heaviest debt burdens in the world. In its last years the Pinochet regime pursued a policy of swapping debt for ownership of Chilean industries and natural resources, with a resulting growth of foreign control of the economy.

Great landowners who controlled the production, commercialization, and export of agricultural products profited handsomely. Exports of fruit and agricultural products sharply increased in these years. But the modernization and expansion of Chilean agriculture did not benefit the mass of the rural population, who lost most of the land and other gains made during the Allende years, suffered police repression, and endured chronic unemployment. Farm workers, prevented from forming labor unions and denied welfare benefits, worked no more than three or four months at a time and often lived in intolerable conditions.

The situation was even worse in urban areas, whose high levels of unemployment and underemployment forced workers to live with their families in squalid, overcrowded shantytowns. Even the middle class suffered a sharp decline in its standard of living. Between 1978 and 1988 the wealthiest 20 percent of the population increased their share of the national income from 51 to 60 percent. The next 60 percent, which includes Chile's large middle class, suffered a substantial drop in income, their share falling from 44 to 35 percent. And the poorest 20 percent continued to receive a meager 4 percent.

WOMEN AND RESISTANCE TO DICTATORSHIP

During the dictatorship's first decade, the opposition to Pinochet was fragmented. Nonetheless, Pinochet's harsh repression and unsuccessful economic policies soon gave rise to mass opposition. Although the Catholic church had initially supported the *Pinochetazo*, the Vicariate of Solidarity organized community support networks to provide legal aid, health care, and employment in craft workshops to working-class communities devastated by the dictatorship's political terror and economic war against the poor. Within a few months after the coup, the Vicariate served 700,000 people, many of whom were women who became involved in what political anthropologist James Scott calls "infrapolitics," a dissident political cul-

Mass opposition to the economic policies and repressive tactics of President Augusto Pinochet erupted in 1983 and 1984. Here thousands of Chilean youths march through Santiago calling for democracy and jobs for unemployed copper workers. [Carlos Carrión/Sygma]

ture largely hidden from the powerful but actively engaged in everyday forms of resistance. For example, these women hid people fleeing Pinochet's terror, baked and distributed bread containing secret messages about clandestine opposition activities, circulated information about the "disappeared," and created *arpilleras*, a folk art that used burlap and other common materials to fashion powerful political indictments of the dictatorship. These *arpilleristas* later participated in hunger strikes and *encadenamientos* (chain-ins), chaining themselves to the Supreme Court building, Pinochet's house, and various other government buildings to protest against the dictatorship.

The dictatorship especially damaged women's social position in Chilean society. It restored the *potestad marital*, authorizing a husband's legal control over his wife and her property, eliminated women's protective labor legislation, restricted women's access to unemployment compensation, disqualified women for legislative positions, and reduced women's median income to 36 percent of men's—a decline from a pre-coup high of 68 percent. These reverses in women's wage rates, coupled with skyrocketing male unemployment, created greater market demand for women's labor and the female work force grew 4.5 percent by 1985 even as the proportion of female heads of households increased 4 percent.

Women therefore played an active role in the political opposition; for example, to commemorate International Women's Day on March 8, 1978, the Women's Department (DF), a women's trade union group, organized the first public demonstration against Pinochet. But women's antidictatorial struggles also became increasingly antipatriarchal as well, and a decade later, at the Days of Protest demonstrations, women's groups like the Feminist Movement (MF) called for "Democracy in the Nation and in the Home," that is, a comprehensive democratic agenda to end the dictatorship, reform the constitution, eliminate misogynistic civil, criminal, and labor legislation, create a ministerial office for women's issues, revise educational curricula, and establish a government affirmative action goal of 30 percent female employment.

Under growing pressure from this swelling democratic movement, Pinochet made limited concessions to the demands for liberalization and amnesty for political prisoners and exiles, even as the repression sometimes intensified. Maneuvering to remain in power, Pinochet called a plebiscite for October 1988, in which Chileans voted by a resounding 54.6 percent to 43 percent to deny Pinochet a new term as president. But the old dictator had fallback positions. By the terms of an undemocratic constitution imposed on the country in 1980, even if defeated, Pinochet was to remain in power for one more year until new elections determined his successor. But Pinochet would still preside over a military council with broad powers, be able to appoint one-third of the new Senate, and himself become a senator for life. The civilian opposition's fatal decision to cut a deal with Pinochet, to accept his imposed constitution instead of obeying the thousands of Chileans whose jubilant street celebrations after the plebiscite demanded the general's resignation from the army, meant the continuing reign of Pinochet's economic model, his power to veto any significant political or social change, and an abiding impunity for the military killers and torturers protected by the dictatorship's self-serving amnesty law.

Nonetheless, pro-democratic forces, despite their differences, coalesced around Patricio Aylwin, who won the 1989 elections.

POPULAR STRUGGLE FOR DEMOCRACY AND SOCIAL JUSTICE, 1990–2003

The new president assumed office on March 11, 1990, with a cabinet dominated by Christian Democrats and Socialists. The first democratically elected government since 1970 faced enormous problems. First, Pinochet's power remained solidly entrenched in the state apparatus, especially the judiciary and security forces.

His 1980 constitution, which made it a crime even to think Marxist thoughts, also severely limited the new government's democratic options. Nonetheless, popular movements pressed for the release of all political prisoners, dissolution of the security forces, abolition of torture and other human rights abuses, and punishment of officials who had committed such abuses. Here a major obstacle was the amnesty decreed by Pinochet for acts committed during the so-called internal war between 1973 and 1978, but that amnesty did not cover the many brutal murders committed after that date. The discovery early in 1990 of secret cemeteries, generally located near armed forces bases, containing the remains of numerous victims who had frequently been tortured before being murdered, brought home to all Chileans the full horror of the regime under which they had suffered for seventeen years. One year later, a "Commission of Truth and Reconciliation," documented the horrific record of human rights violations committed under the Pinochet dictatorship; it identified 2,279 known deaths and disappearances, assigned direct responsibility for these crimes to the armed forces, and charged the courts with negligence for failing to respond properly to such violations of human rights.

But the process of settling accounts with the military murderers and torturers proceeded with excruciating slowness, due in part to the grim resistance offered by Pinochet and the army and in part to the government's anxiety to achieve compromise and "reconciliation" with the military. This led the president to support a "gentle accommodation" with them and to abandon efforts to make Pinochet step down as commander in chief, which angered organizations of relatives of the "disappeared" and many other Chileans who claimed that Aylwin's policies tended to institutionalize impunity.

Another major problem facing the new democratic government was the need to define its attitude toward the economic and social policies of the old regime, which benefited foreign transnationals and their domestic allies at the expense of long-range national interests and the welfare of Chilean workers. Aylwin had promised to make no major changes in the old regime's free-market policies but also committed himself to improve the living and working conditions of the Chilean masses. In fact, under Aylwin the government considerably increased spending for health care, education, and social services. This resulted in a significant reduction in poverty. Overall poverty fell from 40 percent of the population in 1990 to 28 percent in late 1994, and absolute poverty (defined as insufficient income to buy a basic food basket) fell from 14 percent to 9 percent.

But the decline in Chile's poverty rate did not reverse historic patterns of income inequality. After almost a decade of democratic reforms, the wealthiest 10 percent of the Chilean population still received almost 50 percent of national income while the poorest 40 percent, who had received only 10.5 percent in 1989, watched their share fall steadily during the 1990s.

This growing inequality was largely the product of the government's neoliberal economic model, which privileged employers' rights at the expense of labor. "Over the past twenty years," writes Orlando Caputo, a prominent Chilean economist, "$60 billion has been transferred from salaries to profits." Like its predecessor, the Aylwin government prohibited farm workers' strikes during harvest season, which effectively undermined their collective bargaining power. It also disguised unemployment rates by "privatizing" unemployment, that is, by forcing the unemployed into the "informal sector" of low-income, self-employed peddlers who composed 50 percent of the work force. Real wage and salary income, which was still 18 percent lower than it was during the Allende period, declined 10 percent since 1986. By the late 1990s, a third of the nation earned less than $30 a week.

Aylwin continued to stress such export products as seafood, lumber, fruit, and agricultural products, with production and commercialization dominated by agribusiness companies, many of them foreign-owned. Typical is the case of wood exports. There was a veritable explosion of Chilean lumbering, which increased by 57 percent and grew 6.4 percent per year in the 1990s. In south-central Chile the new tree farms replaced such traditional crops as wheat, corn, and rice. Environmentalists charged that the new forests were damaging the soil, drying up water sources, and causing a rapid decrease of many species of plants and animals. Chile's export-based economic strategy also had serious health costs. A study carried out in the large fruit-growing region around the city of Rancagua, south of the capital of Santiago, revealed an alarming increase in children born with physical deformities to parents whose work exposed them to dangerous pesticides.

The explosive growth of raw-material exports was accompanied by the collapse of large-scale industry in such areas as textiles and construction. This was reflected in the decline in the number of unionized workers, who by 1996 composed only 12 percent of the total labor force, compared with 41 percent in 1972. Meanwhile the number of Chileans who worked alone or owned firms with fewer than four employees (the so-called *microempresas*) greatly increased; these "microenterprises" employed more than 45 percent of the labor force in 1992. Typically, they contracted out to or serviced in a variety of ways the large conglomerates called AFPs (*Asociaciones de Fondos Provisionales*) or Mutual Funds, controlled by the ten richest families in Chile. "Workers in *microempresas*," writes Cathy Schneider, "are paid salaries barely above subsistence, without fringe benefits or job security. Irregular hours, unstable employment, and low caloric intake have increased levels of physical and mental exhaustion."

The AFPs also managed Chile's privatized pension system, to which all workers (but no employers) had to make contributions. This system empowered employers to withhold employees' contributions from their paychecks, but there were no mechanisms to ensure that the employers promptly deposited those sums into AFPs, leading to frequent complaints about delays of months or even years in so doing. Moreover, because so many Chileans were marginally employed in the "informal sector," almost half the enrolees did not keep their contributions up to date and consequently accumulated less than a $1,000 balance, clearly insufficient to support retirement. Finally, because the return on pensions depended on the value of the stocks in which contributions were invested, a prolonged decline in the Chilean stock market could have had a catastrophic effect on the system's health.

In December 1993 Chilean voters elected Eduardo Frei of the ruling center-left coalition, son of the reformist president of the same name. Frei's populist program pledged to eradicate extreme poverty by the year 2000, reform the labor laws and the public health system, and regain civilian control of the military, but he also declared his support for free markets. This meant that Chile's prosperity and democratic institutions, already severely compromised by civil society's Faustian bargain with the military, would depend on increasing exports, attracting new foreign investment, and expanding domestic consumer credit, all of which could easily collapse as the world market fluctuated. The 1997 Asian economic crisis, which briefly panicked the Chilean stock market, alerted many Chileans to the fragility of their government's developmental model.

As a result, there were significant indicators of growing popular resistance. First, labor unions became more defiant. The Teachers' Guild (*Colegio de Profesores*), led by Jorge Pávez, a long-time Communist party militant, organized a successful strike in 1996 and continued to coalesce with youth groups, environmentalists, women, and indigenous organizations like those of the Mapuches and Aymaras, all of whom had been damaged by the expansion of unregulated market forces.

Second, disenchanted with the political options available to them, none of which seemed to challenge the neoliberal orthodoxy, Chileans increasingly abandoned the political process altogether. In the December 1997 congressional election, 41 percent of eligible voters either failed to register, abstained from voting, or defaced the ballot. Young people especially lost interest in politics and increasingly associated all political parties with corruption; during the last decade, the percentage of 18- and 19-year-olds registered to vote declined from 5 percent of the electorate to less than 1 percent. Even more startlingly, the share of voters between 20 and 24 plummeted from 15.6 to 4.8 percent.

Third, there emerged greater public support for bringing to justice those accused of brutal crimes during the fifteen-year Pinochet dictatorship. A particularly courageous judge, Juan Guzmán Tapia, successively indicted Pinochet himself on murder and kidnapping charges, authorized a criminal investigation into the murders of two U.S. citizens, Charles Horman and Frank Teruggi, who had supported Allende's Socialist government thirty years ago, and declared former U.S. Consul General Fred Purdy *inculpado* (a suspect) in the crime. Intimating that he formally would seek their extradition to Chile if voluntary arrangements could not be made, Guzmán also respectfully asked the United States to make available to his investigation some sixteen other former U.S. government officials, including then U.S. Ambassador Nathaniel Davis and National Security Adviser Henry Kissinger. A recently declassified U.S. State Department document seemed to confirm the wisdom of Guzmán's inquiry into the activities of these U.S. government officials: "There is some circumstantial evidence," it reported, "to suggest U.S. intelligence may have played an unfortunate part in Horman's death."

Finally, Chileans elected Ricardo Lagos, presidential candidate of the ruling *Concertación* coalition and a lifelong member of the Socialist Party. Although Lagos's political platform was not remotely similar to that of Salvador Allende, the Socialist president who had died defending democracy against a vicious military coup, the martyred president was clearly on the minds of the massive crowd that wildly celebrated Lagos's election with electrifying cries of *"¡Se siente! ¡Se siente! ¡Allende está presente!"* ("I feel it! I feel it! Allende is here among us!"). However, Lagos found himself in an awkward political position.

He had campaigned on social themes, promising to sustain Chile's economic expansion, reduce unemployment, eliminate extreme poverty, promote equality for women and indigenous peoples, and guarantee workers' rights. But, thanks to undemocratic constitutional provisions imposed by the Pinochet dictatorship, his political opponents still controlled the Senate and blocked most of his legislative agenda, including a national heath care initiative, a dramatic increase in the minimum wage, and greater spending on education. Meanwhile, as global markets began to contract, unemployment continued to grow from 5.3 percent in 1997 to almost 10 percent in 2002; before the Asian economic crisis flattened Chile, its gross domestic product had peaked at 6.6 percent, but it averaged a meager 2.9 percent during the first two years of the Lagos presidency. Equally disheartening was the steady growth of Chile's external debt and the steady rise in the share of export revenues diverted to repay it.

Nonetheless, Lagos could point to some modest successes. He reformed the nation's labor laws to defend workers' rights, make workplace discrimination illegal, and strengthen trade unions. This legislation extended state protection to some 400,000 women, annually hired as temporary workers by *enganchadores* to harvest fruit in Chile's booming export industry. His government cut the military budget by severing its historical connection to copper exports and reallocated the resulting savings to social programs. During the Pinochet dictatorship, the military had been allocated $225 million or 10 percent of all export revenues earned by the state-owned copper company, CODELCO, whichever was higher. Even though world copper prices generally rose during the 1990s, successive Christian Democratic presidents, still fearful of the military's power, had continued this practice, paying as much as $341 million to the military account in 1995.

Finally, he worked to reduce Chilean poverty, which had rocketed to 40 percent by the end of the Pinochet dictatorship, the "glory days" of the "free market." Steady economic growth and increasing state social programs since 1990 had produced a gradual decline in poverty rates to 20 percent in 1996, but Lagos sought to reduce these numbers still further and to eliminate extreme poverty by the end of his presidential term in 2006. Declaring that "the poor cannot wait and these poor families will no longer have to wait," Lagos pledged to pay a monthly "protection bonus" of $16 to indigent families earning a dollar per day or less.

No matter how well-intentioned the current government was, however, it remained clear that history would judge Chile by its performance. But this judgment ultimately depended upon two factors: popular struggle to overcome the considerable institutional constraints imposed by almost two decades of dictatorship and a growing global economy upon which thirty years of neoliberal policies had rendered the nation utterly dependent. As the new millennium opened, progress on the former seemed assured even as the latter appeared increasingly uncertain; the fate of Chile's peculiar democracy thus continued to be clouded by its troubled past.

15

Republican Brazil

O N THE EVE of World War I, Brazil's economic, political, and social structures showed growing strain and instability. Between 1910 and 1914 the Amazonian rubber boom began to fade as a result of competition from the new and more efficient plantations of the Far East. The approaching end of the rubber cycle revealed the vulnerability of Brazil's monocultural economy to external factors beyond its control and heightened its dependence on coffee. The coffee industry was itself plagued by recurrent crises of overproduction that required periodic resort to valorization—governmental intervention to maintain coffee prices by withholding stocks from the market or restricting plantings.

Violence was endemic over large areas of the country. In the backcountry, feudal coronéis with private armies recruited from dependents and jagunços (hired gunmen) maintained a patriarchal but frequently tyrannical rule over the peasantry. Over large areas of the country, peasants lived in feudal bondage, obligated to give one or more days per week of free labor as homage to the landowners. Lacking written contracts, they could be evicted at any moment and could find work elsewhere only on the same conditions. The interior was also the scene of mystical or messianic movements that sometimes assumed the character of peasant revolts. Banditry, especially widespread in the northeast, was another response to the tyranny of rural coronéis and the impotence of

officials. A few cangaceiros (outlaws) took the part of the peasantry against their oppressors; most, however, served as mercenaries in the coronéis's private wars.

Violence was not confined to the countryside. Even in the growing cities, proud of their European culture and appearance, popular anger at the arbitrary rule of local oligarchies, or divisions within those oligarchies, sometimes flared up into civil war. Intervention by the federal government in these armed struggles on the side of its local allies greatly enlarged the scale of violence.

Decline and Fall of the Old Republic, 1914–1930

ECONOMIC IMPACT OF WORLD WAR I

The outbreak of World War I in August 1914 had a negative initial impact on Brazil. Exports of coffee, a nonessential product, declined, and in 1917 the government came to the rescue of the planters with a new valorization (price maintenance) program. However, the growing demand of the Allies for sugar, beans, and other staples had by 1915 sparked a revival that turned into a boom.

The war accelerated some changes under way in Brazilian economic life. It weakened British capitalism and therefore strengthened the North American challenge to British financial and commercial preeminence in Brazil. The virtual cessation of imports of manufactured goods also gave a strong stimulus to Brazilian industrialization. Profits derived from coffee, an industry protected by the state, provided a large part of the resources needed for industrialization. Favored by its wealth, large immigrant population, and rich natural resources, the state of São Paulo led the movement, replacing Rio de Janeiro as the foremost industrial region. Brazil doubled its industrial production during the war, and the number of enterprises (which stood at about 3,000 in 1908) grew by 5,940 between 1915 and 1918. But these increases were concentrated in light industry, especially food processing and textiles, and most of the new enterprises were small shops.

The advance of industry and urbanization enlarged and strengthened both the industrial bourgeoisie and the working class, which became racially, sexually, and ethnically more diverse. After emancipation, Brazil's late nineteenth-century white supremacist policies, drawing on foreign ideologies and elite fears of Afro-Brazilian power, had discriminated against blacks and encouraged European immigration to "whiten" the country's labor force and undermine the black majority's ability to negotiate favorable wages and working conditions. Thus immigrant women, especially from Italy, played a central role in the early development of Brazil's industrial working class and dominated employment in the rapidly expanding textile industry. Of the nine thousand workers hired in thirty-one representative textile mills in São Paulo in 1912, almost seven thousand were women.

In response to wartime inflation that eroded the value of workers' wages, the trade union movement grew, and strikes became more frequent. In 1917 a general strike—the first in Brazilian history—gripped the city and state of São Paulo. The strike was organized and initiated by women weavers whose paid and unpaid work responsibilities in the factory and in the home made them especially aware of the negative impact of wartime inflation on workers' wages. They therefore demanded a 20 percent wage increase, "more respect" from male supervisors, improvement of working conditions, and a promise that "in every-

thing there should be reason and justice." These women's grievances rapidly spread to other factories, mobilized thousands of strikers who won significant concessions from the city's industrialists, and energized the national labor movement. Although the strike wave of 1917 to 1920 forced many employers to grant higher wages, the living conditions of most workers did not permanently improve. The labor movement, composed largely of foreign-born workers, remained small and weak, without ties with the peasantry, who formed the overwhelming majority of the Brazilian people.

The economic expansion associated with the war also had a dramatic impact on the development of Brazilian culture. Displaced from their homelands and lured by new economic opportunities in Brazil, new immigrants from Japan and the Ottoman Empire joined with migrants of African descent from the nation's hinterland, especially the drought-ridden Northeast, in search of high-paying jobs that never seemed to materialize. Together they gathered in the urban centers of Rio de Janeiro and São Paulo in the sprawling slums known as *favelas* or *morros* and gave birth to the *samba*, a song and dance that drew heavily on Angolan and Congolese cultural traditions. The samba was closely associated with the ritualistic celebration of *carnival*, a popular street festival that preceded the Lenten season of self-sacrifice and created a safe public space for the lower classes to challenge established social hierarchies, to mock the customs, attitudes, dress, and beliefs of their social rivals; in fact, in its early days, the Brazilian aristocracy, which greatly feared the unruliness of its exploited work force, was scandalized by the wanton sexuality and the wild, irrepressible, and defiant behavior associated with carnival.

Samba lyrics similarly raised serious social and political issues, often using clever word play, double entendre, and the juxtaposition of contrasting images to scorn the arrogant power of the upper classes. In 1917, for example, one of Brazil's greatest samba artists, Ernesto dos Santos, better known as Dongo, recorded the first samba, "*Pelo Telefone*," which simultaneously celebrated the new technology and lamented its use by police officials to harass a poor man. During the postwar period, the radio broadened the popular appeal of the samba, repeatedly broadcasting the songs produced by competing *escolas da samba* ("samba schools"), the neighborhood clubs that organized community participation in carnival. Suddenly, the precise meaning of what it meant to be Brazilian had ceased to be as clear as the traditional light-skinned, Eurocentric plantation elites had imagined it. Change was in the air.

POSTWAR INDUSTRY AND LABOR

Industrialization and urbanization further weakened the foundations of the neocolonial order, which was based on the primacy of agriculture and dependence on foreign markets and loans, but it emerged from the war essentially intact, although its stabilization proved temporary and precarious. A chronically adverse balance of trade and a declining rate of exchange against foreign currencies gave Brazilian industry a competitive advantage in goods of popular consumption. It continued to grow, but it had little support from a central government dominated by the coffee interests. Bitter debates between the friends and foes of tariff protection for industry marked the political life of the 1920s.

As that decade opened, Brazil remained an overwhelmingly rural country. A few export products—coffee, sugar, cotton—dominated Brazilian agriculture; food production was so neglected that the country had to import four-fifths of its grain. There was an extreme concentration of landownership: 461 great landowners held more than 27 million hectares of land, while 464,000 small- and medium-sized farms occupied only 15.7 million hectares. Archaic techniques prevailed in agriculture: the hoe was still the principal farming instrument and the wasteful slash-and-burn method the favored way of clearing the land. Even relatively progressive coffee planters gave little attention to care of the soil, selection of varieties, and other improvements. As a result, the productivity of plantations rapidly declined, even in regions of superior soil.

In the cities, most workers toiled and lived under conditions that recalled those of the early Industrial Revolution in Europe. In 1920 the average industrial worker in São Paulo earned about four milréis (sixty cents) a day; for this wage he or she worked ten to twelve hours, six days a week. Women earned only 60 percent of men's wages and suffered from abusive patriarchal power in the workplace. Historian Joel Wolfe documents the case of one such woman, Ambrosina Pioli, who was beaten savagely when she complained about her foreman's threats to fire her to make room for his lover.

Malnutrition, parasitic diseases, and lack of medical facilities limited Brazilians' average life span in 1920 to twenty-eight years. In the same year, more than 64 percent of the population over the age of fifteen was illiterate. Since literacy was a requirement for voting, the general lack of schools kept the people not only ignorant but politically powerless. As expanding market forces dissolved traditional rural patron-client social relations, the impoverished peasantry often sought refuge in a culture of resistance that focused on daily survival strategies. Although periodically engaged in overt acts of sedition like the Contestado Rebellion of 1912–1916, peasants typically did not organize to transform Brazilian society.

CULTURAL CRISIS AND POLITICAL UNREST

The task of transforming society fell to the rapidly growing urban bourgeois groups, and especially to the middle class, which began to voice ever more strongly its discontent with the rule of corrupt rural oligarchies. In the early 1920s, there arose a many-faceted movement for the renovation of Brazilian society and culture. Intellectuals, artists, junior military officers, professional men, and a small minority of radical workers participated in this movement. But they had no common program and did not comprehend the convergence of their aims and work.

Three seemingly unrelated events of 1922 illustrate the diverse forms that the ferment of the times assumed. First, in February São Paulo intellectuals organized a Modern Art Week to commemorate the centenary of Brazilian independence. Influenced by rebellious European artists, these young poets, painters, and composers

One of the original organizers of Brazil's famous "Modern Art Week" in 1922 and a pioneer of Brazilian modernism was Emiliano di Cavalcanti. His *Samba* (1925) broke with artistic traditions that stressed the nation's European origins and instead celebrated Brazil's African and indigenous cultural roots. [Collection of Genevieve and Jean Boghici]

rejected the staid traditions of naturalism that had dominated the late nineteenth century Brazilian art world, declared their independence from old forms and content, and insisted upon the need to develop indigenous Brazilian culture. Among the young intellectuals gathered there were Heitor Villa-Lobos, who became the nation's premier samba artist, and Oswaldo de Andrade, who later shocked Brazilian audiences by proclaiming the need to become "cultural cannibals"; that is, to consume foreign artistic ideas, mix them with Brazil's digestive enzymes, and thereby produce an authentically Brazilian national cultural identity that was neither xenophobic nor nativist.

Then in March 1922, after the appearance of Marxist groups in a number of cities, the Brazilian Communist Party was founded at a congress in Rio de Janeiro and began a struggle against the anarcho-syndicalist doctrines that still dominated much of the small labor movement.

Last, in July *tenentes* (junior officers) at the Copacabana garrison in Rio de Janeiro rose to prevent the seating of Artur da Silva Bernardes, who had been elected president according to the agreement between the two dominant states of São Paulo and Minas Gerais. The rebel program denounced the rule of the coffee oligarchy, political corruption, and electoral fraud. Government forces easily crushed the revolt, but it left a legend when a handful of insurgents refused to surrender and fought to the death against overwhelming odds.

The officers' revolt signaled the beginning of a struggle by the Brazilian bourgeoisie to seize power from the rural oligarchy. Given the closed political system, it inevitably assumed the character of an armed struggle; that is why its spearhead was the nationalist young officer group, mostly of middle-class origins, which called for democratic elections, equal justice, and similar political reforms.

President Bernardes (1922–1926) took office amid growing economic and political turmoil. As a result of a massive increase in coffee plantings between 1918 and 1924, the industry again suffered from overproduction and falling prices. In 1924 another military revolt, organized by junior officers, broke out in São Paulo. The city's large working class was sympathetic to the revolt, but its conservative leaders rejected the workers' request for arms.

Meanwhile, the revolt had spread to other states. Another group of rebels in Rio Grande do Sul, led by Captain Luís Carlos Prestes, moved north to join the insurgents from São Paulo, and their combined forces, known in history as the Prestes column, began a prodigious fourteen-thousand-mile march through the interior. The tenentes hoped to enlist the peasantry in their struggle against Bernardes. But they knew little of the peasants' problems and offered no program of agrarian reform. The peasants, for their part, had no interest in fighting the "tyrant" Bernardes in distant Rio de Janeiro.

The long march had much educational value for the officers who took part in it. For the first time in their lives, many of these young men came face to face with the reality of rural Brazil and began to reflect on its problems. As a result, the tenente reform program acquired an economic and social content. It began to speak of the need for economic development and social legislation, including agrarian reform as well as minimum wages and maximum working hours.

Naturally, these conflicts provided additional political space for lower-class mobilization in the 1920s. Black Brazilians in Salvador da Bahia and elsewhere joined Marcus Garvey's black power movement, prompting the government to solicit the covert assistance of the FBI in the United States to monitor and disrupt their activities. Meanwhile, others flocked to the practice of *candomble*, a popular religion that evoked consciousness of the African past and created a spiritual community of resistance to white supremacist policies.

Brazilian women likewise mobilized in the militant tradition of nineteenth-century feminist Motta Diniz, who had declared that "in all the world, barbarous or civilized, woman is a slave." In 1922 women's rights activist Berta Lutz organized the Brazilian Federation for the Advancement of Women (FBPF). Largely composed of middle-class professionals, it nonetheless advocated state intervention against market forces and called on the Bernardes government to protect "female labor, which has been subject to inhuman exploitation, reducing women to an inferior position in the competition for industrial and agricultural salaries."

Although Bernardes survived this political opposition, he continued to be plagued by economic problems, with the coffee problem paramount. Bernardes applied the now orthodox remedy of valorization, but gave it a decentralized form. The central government turned over the supervision of the scheme to the individual coffee-producing states. The state of São Paulo established an agency, the Coffee Institute, which undertook to control the export trade in coffee by regulating market offerings to maintain a balance between supply and demand. This was done by withdrawing unlimited stocks of coffee, storing them in warehouses, and releasing them according to the needs of the export trade. The plan required financing the producers whose coffee was withheld from the market. The program appeared to work, for prices rose and remained stable until

1929. But the burdens of valorization steadily grew, for high prices stimulated production, requiring new withdrawals and new loans to finance the unsold output. To make matters worse, Brazil's competitors—especially Colombia—were attracted by the high coffee prices and expanded their own output.

ECONOMIC CRISIS

In 1926 Bernardes turned over the presidency to the Paulista Washington Luís de Sousa Pereira (1926–1930). During his administration, a series of new loans was made to support the valorization program. This especially alienated the nation's industrial bourgeoisie, whose interests and power had continued to expand. The coffee oligarchs and their foreign bankers siphoned off financial and labor resources needed by industry. High, state-sponsored coffee prices created greater demand for labor, which led to high turnover rates and increased costs in urban industry. By 1930 foreign loans had produced an external debt of $1,181 million, and Brazil was required to pay $200 million annually—one-third of the national budget—to service the debt. Squeezed between the conflicting demands of coffee planters and militant workers, these industrialists relied on local repression and privately funded social welfare programs to co-opt and control their labor force, even as they increasingly pressured the state to regulate economic activity in their interests.

By 1930, U.S. investment in Brazil had reached $400 million, considerably larger than the British total, and the United States had supplanted England as Brazil's chief trading partner. But Brazil's heavy dependence on foreign markets and loans made it extremely vulnerable to the crisis that shook the capitalist world after the New York stock market collapsed in October 1929. Coffee prices fell from 22.5 to 8 cents a pound between 1929 and 1931, and immense stocks of coffee piled up in the warehouses. By the end of 1930, Brazil's gold reserves had disappeared and the exchange rate plummeted to a new low. As foreign credit dried up, it became impossible to con-

tinue to finance the valorization program, which collapsed, leaving behind a mountain of debt.

The presidential campaign and election of 1930 took place against a background of economic crisis the principal burdens of which—unemployment, wage cuts, and inflation—fell chiefly on the working classes. But the crisis sharpened all class and regional antagonisms, especially the conflict between the coffee oligarchy and the urban bourgeois groups, who regarded the Depression as proof of the bankruptcy of the old order. A rift even appeared within the coffee oligarchy, and the traditional alliance of São Paulo and Minas Gerais fell apart. This emboldened a new coalition, the Liberal Alliance, that linked urban groups, great landowners—like the ranchers of Rio Grande do Sul—who resented São Paulo's dominant position, and disaffected politicians from Minas Gerais and other states. It named Getúlio Vargas, a wealthy rancher and politician from Rio Grande do Sul, as its candidate.

The working class was not a participant in the Liberal Alliance, but many workers sympathized with its program and openly pressured Vargas to improve working conditions, establish a minimum wage and mandatory vacations, organize consumer cooperatives, and regulate labor relations. Women's groups, in search of freedom from the tyranny of market forces, also lobbied the anti-oligarchical movement. Berta Lutz and the FBPF announced their "Thirteen Principles," which advocated women's suffrage, civil equality, equal pay for equal work, paid maternity leave for working women, affirmative action in government employment, a minimum wage, the eight-hour day, paid vacations, and medical, disability, and retirement insurance. All these provisions would eventually be incorporated into the 1934 constitution.

The most ardent supporters of Vargas were the veterans of the 1924 Tenentes revolt, but their former leader, Luís Carlos Prestes, an exile in Buenos Aires, would not endorse Vargas or his program. Instead Prestes, now a Marxist, proclaimed that the chief task before the Brazilian people was to struggle against the latifundio and Anglo-American imperialism. A few years later, he would join the Communist Party and become its leader.

During the 1930 campaign, Vargas, although careful not to give offense to his latifundist supporters, spoke of the need to develop industry, including heavy industry, advocated high tariffs to protect Brazilian industry using local raw materials, and called on Brazilians to "perfect our manufactures to the point where it will become unpatriotic to feed or clothe ourselves with imported goods." Reflecting the influence of the tenentes, he advanced a program of social welfare legislation and political, judicial, and educational reform. He even made a cautious pledge of "action with a view to the progressive extinction of the latifundio, without violence, and support for the organization of small landed property through the transfer of small parcels of land to agricultural laborers."

When the coffee oligarchs sought to deny Vargas the presidency, he overthrew the Washington Luís government. The successful revolt meant that the Old Republic, born in 1889 and dominated since 1894 by the coffee oligarchy, was dead. A new era had begun that may with fair accuracy be called the era of the bourgeois revolution. The political career of its chieftain, Getúlio Vargas, faithfully mirrored its advances, retreats, and ultimate defeat.

Vargas and the Bourgeois Revolution, 1930–1954

The liberal revolution of 1930 represented a victory for the urban bourgeois groups who favored industrialization and the modernization of Brazil's economic, political, and social structures. But the bourgeoisie had gained that victory with the aid of allies whose interests had to be taken into account. Getúlio Vargas presided over a heterogeneous coalition that included conservative fazendeiros—who had joined the revolution from jealousy of the overweening Paulista power but feared radical social change—and intellectuals and tenentes who called for agrarian reform, the formation of cooperatives, and the nationalization of mines. Women's groups and others disadvantaged by oligarchical rule and market forces pressured Vargas to endorse their campaign for liberation. The

Brazilian Black Front (FNB), established in 1931, organized massive protests against racial discrimination, advocated laws to require racial integration of all public places, educated Afro-Brazilians about Pan-Africanist political movements, and sought black representation in the national Congress. Of course, the working class, vital to the development of Brazilian capitalism, remained a potential threat to its very existence. Finally, Vargas had to take account of foreign capital interests, temporarily weakened but capable of applying great pressure on the Brazilian economy when the capitalist world emerged from the depths of the Great Depression. Vargas's strategy of attempting to balance and reconcile these conflicting interests helps to explain the contradictions and abrupt shifts of course that marked his career.

VARGAS'S ECONOMIC AND POLITICAL MEASURES

The most pressing problem facing the new government was to find some way out of the economic crisis. Vargas did not abandon the coffee industry, the base of his political enemies, to its fate; he attempted to revive it by such classic valorization measures as the restriction of plantings, the purchase of surplus stocks, and the more drastic expedient of burning excess coffee. But the level of coffee exports and prices remained low throughout the 1930s. The government had more success with efforts to diversify agriculture. Production of cotton, in particular, grew with the aid of capital and labor released by the depressed coffee industry, and cotton exports rose steadily until 1940, when the outbreak of war interrupted their advance. But diversification of agriculture could not compensate for the steep decline in Brazil's import capacity. The key to recovery was found in import substitution through industrialization.

The Great Depression did not create Brazilian industrialization, but it created the conditions for a new advance. Beginning as a spontaneous response to the loss of import capacity that resulted from the catastrophic decline of exports and a falling rate of exchange, industrialization received a fresh impetus from Vargas, who encouraged industry through exchange controls, import quotas, tax

During a long and complex political career, Getúlio Vargas struggled to create an autonomous Brazilian capitalist state. Here the populist president is surrounded by military officers after the 1930 revolution briefly united a broad coalition of disparate political interests and swept him to power. [Bettmann/Corbis]

incentives, lowered duties on imported machinery and raw materials, and long-term loans at low interest rates. Thanks to the combination of favorable background conditions and the Vargas policy of state intervention, Brazilian industrialization, based entirely on production for the home market, made notable strides in a few years: industrial production doubled between 1931 and 1936. As early as 1933, when the United States was still deep in the Depression, Brazil's national income had begun to increase, which indicated that for the moment, at least, the economy no longer depended on external factors but on internal ones.

Meanwhile, Vargas sought to centralize political power by making strategic concessions to his coalition allies. He appeased the political elite of

São Paulo with conservative ministerial appointments. He also tried to conciliate São Paulo's workers, who, again sparked by the women weavers in the textile industry, openly rebelled against industrialists in May 1932, demanding an eight-hour day, 20 percent wage increases, night-work bonuses, equal pay for equal work, prohibition of forced overtime, and recognition of their local bargaining units called "factory commissions." Tens of thousands joined the general strike, and Vargas was forced to intervene, co-opting the workers' movement by agreeing to most of their demands but requiring that future disagreements over working conditions be negotiated peacefully by tripartite "conciliation commissions" composed of workers, employers, and government appointees.

In February 1932 Vargas had promulgated an electoral code that established the secret ballot, lowered the voting age from twenty-one to eighteen, and extended the vote to working women, but the code still denied the vote to illiterates. Although these electoral reforms still left 95 percent of Brazilians ineligible to vote, they expanded suffrage sufficiently to allow women to get elected in eighteen of twenty state legislatures. Moreover, reflecting women's new political muscle, the state government of Rio de Janeiro appointed women to the cabinet portfolios of Labor and Education. The constituent assembly elected under this code also drafted a new constitution, which was promulgated on July 16, 1934. This document retained the federal system but considerably strengthened the powers of the executive. The assembly, constituting itself the first Chamber of Deputies, elected Vargas president for a term extending to January 1938.

The section of the constitution on "economic and social order" stressed the government's responsibility for economic development. Article 119 declared that "the law will regulate the progressive nationalization of mines, mineral deposits, and waterfalls or other sources of energy, as well as of the industries considered as basic or essential to the economic and military defense of the country."

The section on the rights and duties of labor revealed the importance Vargas attached to the imposition of a tutelage over the working class, a class to be courted through concessions but denied independence of action. The constitution of 1934 established a labor tribunal system, gave the government power to fix minimum wages, and guaranteed the right to strike. Subsequent decrees set the working day at eight hours in commerce and industry, fixed minimum wages throughout the country, and created an elaborate social security system that provided for pensions, paid vacations, safety and health standards, and employment security.

In exchange for these gains, the working class lost its freedom of action. The trade unions, formerly subject to harsh repression, but militant and jealous of their autonomy, became official agencies controlled by the Ministry of Labor. The workers had no voice in the drafting of labor legislation. Police and security agencies brutally repressed strikes not approved by the government.

The labor and social legislation, moreover, was unevenly enforced, and employers frequently evaded the law. The legislation did not apply to the great majority of agricultural workers, who comprised 85 percent of the labor force. Determined to maintain his alliance with the fazendeiro wing of his coalition, Vargas left intact the system of patrimonial servitude that governed labor relations in the countryside, just as he left intact the latifundio. The promises of agrarian reform made during the campaign of 1930 were forgotten.

Vargas's rightward shift grew more pronounced in 1934 and alienated liberal tenentes, intellectuals, radical workers, and the Communist Party, founded in 1922 by Luís Carlos Prestes. As honorary president of the *Aliança Nacional Libertadora* (National Liberation Alliance, or ANL), a popular front movement that attracted middle-class as well as working-class support, Prestes advocated the liquidation of the latifundio, nationalization of large foreign companies, and cancellation of imperialist debts.

Meanwhile, Vargas harassed the leftist opposition as "subversive." In 1935 after Prestes attacked Vargas's failure to implement the tenente ideals and called for the creation of a truly "revolutionary and anti-imperialist government," Vargas responded by banning the ANL and ordering the arrest of many leftist leaders.

With the legal avenues of opposition for the left disappearing, the ANL and one wing of the Communist Party began an armed uprising in November. Despite some initial successes, it was quickly crushed by government forces and followed by a savage repression. There were fifteen thousand arrests, and prisoners were tortured, some to death. Prestes and other leaders of the revolt were captured, tried, and sentenced to many years in prison. The Communist Party was banned and went underground for a decade.

VARGAS AS DICTATOR

The repression of the left paved the way for the establishment of Vargas's personal dictatorship.

On November 10 he canceled the 1938 presidential elections, dissolved Congress as an "inadequate and costly apparatus," and assumed dictatorial power under a new constitution patterned on European fascist models. On December 2, all political parties were abolished.

The new regime, baptized the *Estado Novo* (New State), copied not only the constitutional forms of the fascist regimes but also their repressive tactics. Strict press censorship was established, and prisons filled with workers, teachers, military officers, and others suspected of subversion. The apparatus of repression included a special police force for hunting down and torturing dissidents. The Estado Novo also dealt women workers a decided setback in their struggle for freedom and equality by actively soliciting their return to the private patriarchal province of home and family. The tax code penalized single women and childless families, while other laws provided special protections to mothers and children and actively discouraged women from working outside the home or joining trade unions. Yet there was little organized resistance to the regime. Labor, its most likely opponent, was neutralized by a paternalist social legislation and doped by populist rhetoric, and it remained passive or even supportive of Vargas.

By decade's end, Brazil's growing trade and increasingly friendly relations with Germany and Italy led to fears that the country was moving into the fascist orbit. Between 1933 and 1938, Germany became the chief market for Brazilian cotton and the second largest buyer of its coffee and cacao. German penetration of the Brazilian economy also increased, and the German Bank for South America established three hundred branches in Brazil.

But Brazil's economic rapprochement with Germany and Italy did not reflect sympathy with the expansionist goals of the fascist bloc; Vargas, the great realist, sought only to open up new markets for Brazil and to strengthen his hand in bargaining with the United States. Despite its authoritarian, repressive aspects, the Estado Novo continued the struggle against neocolonialism in its effort to achieve economic independence and modernization.

Indeed, under the new regime the state intervened more actively than before to encourage the growth of industry and provide it with the necessary economic infrastructure. Rejecting laissez faire, the Estado Novo pursued a policy of planning and direct investment for the creation of important industrial complexes in the basic sectors of mining, oil, steel, electric power, and chemicals. In 1940 the government announced a Five-Year Plan whose goals included the expansion of heavy industry, the creation of new sources of hydroelectric power, and the expansion of the railway network. In 1942 the government established the *Companhia Vale do Rio Doce* to exploit the rich iron-ore deposits of Itabira; in 1944 it created a company for the production of materials needed by the chemical industry; and in 1946 the National Motor Company began the production of trucks. In the same year, Vargas saw the realization of one of his cherished dreams: the National Steel Company began production at the Volta Redonda plant between Rio de Janeiro and São Paulo. Aware of the need of modern industry for abundant sources of power, Vargas created the National Petroleum Company in 1938 to press the search for oil.

By 1941, Brazil had 44,100 plants employing 944,000 workers; the comparable figure for 1920 was 13,336 plants with about 300,000 workers. Aside from some export of textiles, the manufacturing industries served the domestic market almost exclusively. State and mixed public-private companies dominated the heavy and infrastructural industries and private Brazilian capital predominated in manufacturing, but the 1930s also saw a significant growth of direct foreign investment as foreign corporations sought to enlarge their share of the internal market and overcome tariff barriers and exchange problems by establishing branch plants in Brazil. By 1940 foreign capital represented 44 percent of the total investment in Brazilian stock companies. Vargas made no effort to check the influx of foreign capital, perhaps because he believed that the growth of Brazilian state and private capitalism would keep the foreign sector in a subordinate status.

The Estado Novo banned strikes and lockouts but retained and even expanded the body of protective social and labor legislation. In 1942 the labor laws were consolidated into a labor code, regarded as one of the most advanced in the world. But it was unevenly enforced and brought no benefits to the great mass of agricultural workers. Moreover, spiraling inflation created a growing gap between wages and prices; prices rose 86 percent between 1940 and 1944, whereas between 1929 and 1939 they had risen only 31 percent. In effect, inflation, by transferring income from wages to capitalists, provided much of the financing for the rapid economic growth of the 1940s.

World War II accelerated that growth through the new stimulus it gave to industrialization. Brazil exported vast quantities of foodstuffs and raw materials, but the industrialized countries, whose economies were geared to war, could not pay for their purchases with machinery or consumer goods. As a result, Brazil built up large foreign-exchange reserves, $707 million in 1945. Most of the economic advance of the war years was due to expansion and more intensive exploitation of existing plants or the technical contributions of Brazilian engineers and scientists.

However, Vargas adroitly exploited Great Power rivalries to secure financial and technical assistance from the United States for the construction of the huge state-owned integrated iron and steel plant at Volta Redonda. U.S. companies and government agencies were notably cool to requests for aid for establishing heavy industry in Latin America. But Vargas's hints that he might have to turn for help to Germany removed all obstacles. Volta Redonda was a great victory for the Vargas policies of economic nationalism and state intervention in economic life. In return for its assistance, Vargas allowed the United States to lease air bases in northern Brazil even before it entered the war against the Axis.

The paradox of Brazil's participation in an antifascist war under an authoritarian regime was not lost on Brazilians; the demands for an end to the Estado Novo grew stronger as the defeat of the Axis drew near. Although the dictatorship and war had limited the political agenda of women's rights groups, their organizational strength continued to grow under the auspices of the Women's Division

of the League for National Defense, whose members staffed neighborhood committees to monitor food prices and demand social justice. This led to the creation of the Woman's Committee for Amnesty, which by war's end had built a broad coalition to restore civil liberties and secure political liberalization. During the war the struggle for Afro-Brazilian rights also took refuge in cultural organizations like the Black Experimental Theater (TEN), which rooted "antiracist civil and human rights demands" in the cultivation of African consciousness among blacks.

Likewise, a simmering worker discontent, blunted by repression and wartime co-optation of union leadership, could express itself only in popular protest sambas, clandestine factory commissions, spreading absenteeism, and personal appeals to Vargas for justice. But in February 1945 this dissatisfaction boiled over in a riot involving hundreds of protestors. In the summer, women textile workers in São Paulo again led a strike movement that mobilized thousands, destabilized Brazilian industrial society, and threatened Vargas's regime. Ever sensitive to changes in the political climate and the balance of forces, Vargas announced an amnesty for political prisoners, promulgated a law allowing political parties to function openly, and set December 2 as the date for presidential and congressional elections.

A MILITARY COUP

Vargas announced that he would not run for president but set the stage for a well-organized campaign by his supporters, called *queremistas* (from the Portuguese verb *querer*, "to want"), who wanted Vargas to declare himself a candidate in the forthcoming election. Soon after issuing the decrees restoring political freedom, Vargas, proclaiming himself the "father of the poor," authorized the expropriation of any organization whose practices were harmful to the national interest.

The authorization decree, which was aimed at keeping down the cost of living, inspired alarm in conservative foreign and domestic circles. Senior military officers regarded Vargas's leftward move with growing uneasiness. The wartime alliance with the United States had accentuated their inherent conservatism and made them ready to accept the gospel of free enterprise and U.S. leadership in the cold war against the Soviet Union and world communism.

On October 29, 1945, Generals Goes Monteiro and Eurico Dutra staged a coup, forced Vargas to resign, promptly repealed Vargas's authorization decree, and suppressed the Communist Party. They refused to expand the vote to illiterates and organized elections that guaranteed the victory of President Eurico Dutra (1946–1951), under whom neocolonial interests regained much of the influence they had lost under Vargas. In his foreign and domestic policies, Dutra displayed a blind loyalty to the anticommunist creed propounded by Washington.

In the 1945 elections, the Communist Party (PCB) had polled over half a million votes, and two years later the Brazilian Women's Federation, the country's leading feminist organization, joined the Communist-sponsored Women's International Democratic Federation. Alarmed by the growing influence of the Communist Party, Dutra outlawed it, and Congress followed by expelling the party's elected representatives. Dutra exploited the resulting witch-hunt to smash the independent, left-led labor movement; the Workers' Federation, organized in 1946, was declared illegal; and the government intervened in a large number of unions to eliminate "extremist elements." The imposition of a wage freeze and the failure to raise the officially decreed minimum wage caused the real income of workers to drop sharply.

With respect to economic development, Dutra pursued a laissez-faire policy that meant the virtual abandonment of the Vargas strategy of a state-directed movement toward economic independence. Dutra removed all import and exchange controls and allowed the large foreign exchange reserves accumulated during the war—reserves that Vargas had proposed to use for re-equipping Brazilian industry—to be dissipated on imported consumer goods, luxury goods in large part.

Attracted by the new economic climate, foreign capital flowed into Brazil. Meanwhile, seeking to curb inflation according to the prescription of U.S. advisers, the government pursued a restrictive credit policy harmful to Brazilian entrepreneurs and industrial growth.

Despite these setbacks, popular movements continued to organize and agitate for progressive reform. Afro-Brazilians, for example, created the National Black Convention and the Black Women's National Congress to expose the hypocrisy of the government's claim that Brazil was a "racial democracy." After years of public pressure—culminating in 1950 with a well-publicized incident in which a São Paulo hotel refused to accommodate the famous African American choreographer Katherine Dunham but reserved a room for her white secretary—the Dutra regime finally adopted a relatively timid, but nonetheless significant, antidiscrimination law, the Afonso Arinos Act.

VARGAS'S RETURN TO POWER

In 1950, having assured himself of the neutrality of the armed forces, Vargas drew upon *this* popular dissatisfaction and ran for president with the support of a broad coalition of workers, industrialists, and members of the urban middle class. His campaign concentrated on the need to accelerate industrialization and expand and strengthen social welfare legislation. Riding a wave of discontent with the economic and social policies of the Dutra regime, Vargas easily defeated his two opponents.

Vargas inherited a difficult economic situation. After a brief boom in coffee exports and prices in 1949–1951, the balance of trade again turned unfavorable and the inflation rate increased. In the absence of other major sources of financing for his developmental program, Vargas had to rely largely on a massive increase in the money supply, with all its inevitable social consequences. Meanwhile, his national program of state-directed industrialization, using state corporations as its major instrument, encountered increasing hostility from neocolonial interests at home and abroad. In the United States, the Eisenhower administration decided that the Vargas government had not created the proper climate for private investment and terminated the Joint United States–Brazilian Economic Commission. Within Brazil, Vargas's program faced sabotage at the hands of the rural forces that continued to dominate the majority of state governments and Congress. This hardening of attitudes signified that Vargas's options and his capacity for maneuvering between different social groups were greatly reduced.

Nonetheless, Vargas pursued his populist program. He created a mixed public-private petroleum corporation, called *Petrobrás*, which would give the state a monopoly on the drilling of oil and new refineries. Petrobrás illustrated Vargas's belief that the state must own the commanding heights of the economy and represented an attempt to reduce the balance-of-payments deficit by substituting domestic sources of oil for imported oil. Vargas sought to appease domestic and foreign opponents by leaving the distribution of oil in private hands and allowing existing refineries to remain privately owned. Vargas also proposed to create a similar agency for electric power, to be called *Electrobras*.

Vargas's labor policy became another political battleground. Under Vargas, labor regained much of the freedom of action it had lost during the Dutra years. In December 1951, under pressure from militant workers, the government decreed a new minimum wage that compensated for the most recent price rises. In 1953 three hundred thousand workers went on strike for higher wages and other benefits. In June of that year, Vargas appointed a young protégé, João Goulart, minister of labor. Goulart, a populist in the Vargas tradition, was sympathetic with labor's demands. In January 1954, Goulart recommended a doubling of the minimum wage.

The battle lines between Vargas and his foes were being drawn ever more sharply. In speeches to Congress, Vargas attacked foreign investors for aggravating Brazil's balance-of-payments problem by their massive remittances of profits and claimed that invoicing frauds had cost Brazil at least $250 million over an eighteen-month period. Meanwhile, attacks on him by conservatives grew even more bitter. On August 24, the military ordered him to resign or be deposed. Isolated and betrayed, the seventy-two-year-old Vargas found the way out of his dilemma by suicide. But he left a message that was also his political testament. It ended with the words:

I fought against the looting of Brazil. I fought against the looting of the people. I have fought bare-breasted. Hatred, infamy, and calumny did not beat down my spirit. I gave you my life. Now I offer my death. Nothing remains. Serenely I take the first step on the road to eternity and I leave life to enter history.

As in life, so also in death, Vargas remained a controversial figure. But a woman textile worker, Odette Pasquini, offered perhaps the most astute epitaph for Vargas and his populist programs. "Vargas," she opined, "oh he was the 'father of the poor,' as they used to say on the radio, but of course he was truly the mother of the rich!"

Reform and Reaction, 1954–1964

The death of Vargas foreshadowed the demise of the nationalist, populist model of independent capitalist development over which he had presided for the better part of a quarter century. That model, based on a strategy of maneuver and compromise, of reconciling the clashing interests of the national bourgeoisie, fazendeiros, foreign capitalists, and the working class, of avoiding such structural changes as agrarian reform, had about exhausted its possibilities.

Two options remained. One was for Vargas's political heirs to mobilize the working class and the peasantry for the realization of a program of structural changes, including agrarian reform, that could impart a new dynamic to Brazilian national capitalism. The alternative was for Vargas's political enemies to impose a streamlined neocolonial model based on the denationalization and modernization of Brazilian industry, on its transformation into an extension of the industrial park of the great capitalist powers, accompanied by a shift in emphasis from the export of raw materials to the export of manufactured goods. Because such a course entailed immense sacrifices for the Brazilian people, it also required the imposition of a dictatorship of the most repressive kind. The balance of forces in 1954 already favored the second option. For a decade, however, Brazil would sway uncertainly between the two alternatives.

THE KUBITSCHEK ERA

The presidential election of 1955 took place under the watchful gaze of the military. Juscelino Kubitschek, governor of Minas Gerais, with João Goulart as his running mate, stressed the defense of democracy and the acceleration of economic growth. Kubitschek was not an economic nationalist in the Vargas mold, but the nationalist and reformist groups, knowing the limits of military tolerance, gave him their support. As the campaign progressed, there grew a clamor on the right for a coup to prevent the victory of Kubitschek and Goulart. However, they won the election in October, with the popular Goulart polling more votes than the president-elect.

Kubitschek took office in January 1956 with a promise of "fifty years of progress in five." But this progress was to be achieved with the aid of massive foreign investments, to which Kubitschek offered most generous incentives. Foreign capital flowed into Brazil; the total inflow between 1955 and 1961 amounted to $2.3 billion. The bulk came from the United States, whose investments in Brazil reached $1.5 billion in 1960.

This influx of capital, which benefited from advantages denied to Brazilian enterprises, promoted a rapid foreign conquest of Brazilian national industry. In the process, the native entrepreneurs were frequently transformed into directors or partners of the foreign-controlled firms. The takeover concentrated on the most modern and fastest-growing industries (chemical, metallurgy, electrical, communications, and automotive). In 1960 foreign investment accounted for 70 percent of the capital invested in the 34 largest companies and more than 30 percent in the 650 corporations with capital of a million dollars or more.

The Kubitschek era was a heady time of unprecedented economic growth that averaged 7 percent per year between 1957 and 1961. By 1960, Brazil had been transformed from an agrarian country into an agrarian-industrial country with a base of heavy industry, for it could boast that it produced half its heavy-industry needs. Construction of a series of great dams provided much of the power needed by Brazil's growing industry. Kubitschek's decision to build a new capital, Brasilia, in the frontier state of Goias reflected his exuberant optimism about Brazil's future. Completed in three years, the new capital was inaugurated on April 21, 1960. A network of "highways of national unity" was constructed to link Brasilia with the rest of the country but failed to solve the many difficulties—housing and resettlement problems, cultural isolation, and the like—that faced its inhabitants.

These triumphs of development had to be paid for, and their cost was high. A major source of financing was foreign loans, which swelled Brazil's already large foreign debt from $1.6 billion in 1954 to $2.7 billion in 1961. Service of the foreign debt took an ever-increasing share of the national budget, rising from $180 million to $515 million (more than half the value of Brazil's exports) in the same period. This source of financing had its limits; by 1959 the International Monetary Fund (IMF) threatened to withhold loans if Brazil did not adopt a stabilization program and live within its means. Kubitschek responded by breaking off negotiations with the IMF and increasing the money supply. The result was an unprecedented inflation rate and a catastrophic decline in the value of the cruzeiro. This in turn greatly diminished the value of Brazil's exports. Inflation, like foreign loans, appeared to have reached its limits as a source of financing Brazilian development.

This economic growth, the resulting expansion of Brazil's middle class, and the ideology of modernity that accompanied both also affected Brazilian culture. *Bossa nova* (literally, the new beat), which emerged from fashionable cabarets in middle- and upper-class communities, sought to rescue Brazilian national music from the wild, seemingly uncontrollable, undulating rhythms of the samba, traditionally associated with mixed-race popular classes; instead it redefined Brazil's cultural identity in a way that emphasized modernity, personal freedom, and the pursuit of individual pleasure. Like the country's modernization during the 1950s, bossa nova relied heavily on imports from the United States, in this case syncopated jazz rhythms that artists like Antonio Carlos

(Tom) Jobim, João Gilberto, and Nara Leão fused with a samba drumbeat. Lyrically, bossa nova music like the internationally renowned "Girl from Ipanema," written by Brazilian beat poet extraordinaire Vinicius de Moraes, celebrated the bohemian lifestyles of young middle-class men who were more interested in the beach, beautiful girls, and drinking whiskey than the daily struggles of Brazil's popular classes, which samba songs traditionally memorialized.

THE QUADROS REGIME

The election of 1960 took place amid growing social unrest and intense debate over domestic and foreign policy. Women actively participated in this national dialogue, demanding civil equality and organizing a massive protest demonstration to commemorate the tenth anniversary of the Brazilian Women's Federation, which Kubitschek had outlawed in 1956. Workers also agitated for an end to inflation, corruption, and foreign control of the economy. Brazilian popular culture reflected and reinforced this social turmoil. According to cultural historian Eduardo Carrasco Pirard, bossa nova songs, which earlier had eschewed controversial subjects like exploitation, inequality, and oppression now increasingly discussed "social themes which presented a rather idealized and paternalistic vision of the black *favela*-dweller and the worker from the fringe areas of the big cities." Songs like "The Farmworker's Funeral," by Chico Buarque de Holanda, sarcastically lamented the misfortunes of a peasant who finally won in death that which in vain he had sought in life: a plot of latifundio land ("large enough for a grave, not too big, not too deep!").

The campaign oratory and programs of all the principal candidates reflected the ascendancy that the nationalist, populist ideology had gained over public opinion. Even conservatives supported the presidential candidacy of the flamboyant Jânio da Silva Quadros, former governor of São Paulo, whose populist campaign denounced "foreign exploiters" and promised to "sweep out of the government the corrupt elements, the thieves and exploiters of the people."

Without breaking with the traditional dependence on the capitalist countries for markets and loans, Quadros sought to reduce that dependence by developing new trade and diplomatic relations with the socialist countries and the Third World. Accordingly, he initiated negotiations for the resumption of diplomatic relations with the Soviet Union, sent a trade mission to the People's Republic of China, and denounced the CIA-backed Bay of Pigs invasion of Cuba in April 1961. Although he stressed the need for foreign investments and guaranteed their security, Quadros opposed foreign investment in Brazilian oil and proposed to modify the "laws and regulations which place the Brazilian company in an inferior position." He also restricted the remittance of profits abroad.

However moderate, Quadros's policies aroused the hostility of military and civilian conservatives. Quadros's problems were compounded by an increasingly recalcitrant Congress dominated by conservative fazendeiros. Determined to break the legislative deadlock by some dramatic act, Quadros submitted his resignation on August 25, 1961, after only seven months of rule. His resignation message claimed that hostile foreign forces had obstructed his program of Brazil for the Brazilians. Convinced that the military would not permit the prolabor vice president Goulart to succeed him, Quadros evidently believed that public clamor for his return would bring him back to office with the powers he needed to govern.

But he had miscalculated. Led by war minister Odílio Denys, military officers took control of the government and declared that, for reasons of "national security," Goulart, whom they distrusted as a dangerous radical, should not return from his trade mission to China. Naturally, this ignited a national popular uprising that caused a split within the military; in Goulart's home state of Rio Grande do Sul, the commander of the Third Army announced his support for Goulart, and the governor of the state rallied the population to defend the constitution and ensure Goulart's elevation to the presidency. The threat of civil war loomed, but the military ministers, facing divisions within the armed forces and feeling the pressure of public opinion, agreed to a compromise. Goulart took office, but a constitutional amendment restrained the power of democracy and required the president to share power with a parliamentary council drawn from the conservative legislature.

GOULART'S PRESIDENCY

Taking office in September 1961, Goulart steered a cautious course designed to allay conservative suspicions at home and abroad. In April 1962 he paid a visit to Washington. Addressing a joint session of Congress, he promised reasonable treatment of foreign-owned utilities in Brazil. The United States provided $131 million in aid for Brazil's depressed northeast, but the IMF, whose approval was a condition for the cooperation of private bankers, remained skeptical of Goulart's intentions.

The first year and a half of Goulart's rule under the parliamentary system saw few major legislative achievements. One was the passage of a Brazilian civil code that, under pressure from women's rights groups, prohibited gender discrimination in employment and gave married women legal control over their earnings and shared ownership of commonly acquired property. Another law established Electrobras, the national agency proposed by Vargas for the control of the production and distribution of electric power. Still another required foreign capital to be registered with the Brazilian government and barred profit remittances abroad in excess of 10 percent of invested capital, certainly not a radical measure. Yet it produced a sharp drop in foreign investments, from $91 million in 1961 to $18 million in 1962. Lacking other sources for financing development, Goulart had to resort to the Kubitschek formula of a massive increase of the money supply. The new inflationary spiral brought the collapse of the cruzeiro and a wave of strikes and food riots, as well as a growing radicalization of labor and sections of the peasantry. But the economic slowdown apparent since 1961 continued. Import substitution as a stimulus to industrialization appeared to have reached its limits, and further advance was blocked by the small domestic market, the inequities of Brazilian income distribution, and the drain of capital through debt repayment and profit remittances (amounting to $564 million, or 45 percent of the value of Brazil's exports, in 1962).

With the advice of the brilliant young economist Celso Furtado, who had directed an ambitious effort to develop Brazil's backward, poverty-ridden northeast, Goulart drafted a program of structural reforms that aimed to expand Brazil's democracy and impart a new dynamism to its faltering economy. Reform of the archaic land tenure system would expand the domestic market and increase agricultural production. Tax reform would reduce the inequities of income distribution and provide funds needed for public education and other social welfare purposes. The grant of votes to illiterates would, it was hoped, drastically reduce the power of the rural oligarchy in the national and state legislatures.

To implement these changes, however, the legislative deadlock in Congress had to be broken, so in mid-1962 Goulart launched a campaign for a plebiscite to let the people choose between presidential and parliamentary government. Under great public pressure, Congress agreed to the plebiscite, and on January 1, 1963, more than 12 million voters decided by a three to one majority to restore to Goulart his full presidential powers under the constitution of 1946.

But Goulart's victory only deepened a growing polarization of opinion in the country, with the bourgeoisie and the middle class joining the landed oligarchy in opposition to Goulart's domestic program. Goulart's moderate reform proposals in reality favored the industrial bourgeoisie and should have enjoyed its support. But the dynamic industrialist class that had arisen and thrived under Getúlio Vargas was now much weaker. The progressive foreign conquest of Brazilian industry had greatly reduced that class's influence as more and more national entrepreneurs gave up an unequal struggle and solved their personal problems by becoming directors or associates of foreign-owned firms. This dependent bourgeoisie shared the fears of social change of its foreign and rural allies. But even the more militant nationalists within the ranks of the progressive industrial bourgeoisie— industrialists long affiliated with organizations like the Industrial Social Service (SESI) and the National Service for Industrial Training (SENAI), which had collaborated with *getulista* populism— feared a growing radicalism of Brazil's peasant and urban industrial working class. As historian Barbara Weinstein argues, by the late 1950s and early 1960s, workers had become a more significant political force: they had expanded their autonomy from state controls, they increasingly relied on strikes and uncompromising demands for wage hikes to secure their interests, and they tended to elect leftist union leaders less inclined to collaborate with industrialists or the state.

The industrialists' apprehension increased as a result of the spread of radicalism to the country-side. Under the leadership of the lawyer Francisco Julião, peasants in the bleak northeast, afflicted by drought, famine, and oppressive land tenure and labor systems, joined Peasant Leagues and invaded fazendas. Their activities endangered the latifundio, which was also threatened by Goulart's proposal to give the vote to illiterates and enact agrarian reform.

By the end of 1963, the forces on the right— the fazendeiros, the big bourgeoisie, the military, and their foreign allies—had begun to mobilize against the threat from the left. Industrialists had long cultivated support among army officers, inviting generals like Humberto Castelo Branco, the future dictator, to speak at their Forum Roberto Simonsen, a regular meeting sponsored by the São Paulo Federation of Industrialists. But in early 1962 they began plotting in earnest and by March of 1964, according to Weinstein, the industrialists "had collected more than 1.5 billion cruzeiros equal to more than a million dollars, to aid the armed forces in the seizure of power."

Meanwhile, under strong pressure from impatient radicals, Goulart moved to the left. Appearing at a mass rally in Rio de Janeiro in March 1964, he signed two decrees. One nationalized all private oil refineries. The other made liable to expropriation all large and "underutilized" estates close to federal highways or railways and lands of over seventy acres near federal dams, irrigation works, or drainage projects. At the same meeting, Goulart announced that he would shortly issue a decree on

rent control. He asked Congress to pass reforms that included tax reform, the vote for illiterates and enlisted men, an amendment to the constitution providing for land expropriation without immediate compensation, and legalization of the Communist Party.

By the middle of March, the military-civilian conspiracy for Goulart's overthrow was well advanced. The governors of a number of important states met with a view to transferring the Congress to São Paulo, where a "legalist government" would be installed. An emissary returned from the United States with assurances from the State Department that the United States would immediately recognize the new government. Then, if it became necessary, the legalist government would solicit aid from the United States, and the dispatch of U.S. troops would not constitute intervention but a response to a legitimate government's request for aid to suppress communism and subversion.

On March 31 army units in Minas Gerais and São Paulo began to march on Rio de Janeiro. The U.S. ambassador to Brazil, Lincoln Gordon, was well informed of the conspiracy; five days before the coup he cabled Secretary of State Dean Rusk naming General Humberto de Alencar Castelo Branco as the probable head of the new military junta. Published documents also show that the United States was prepared to give military aid, if needed, to the rebels. But Operation Uncle Sam (its code name) proved unnecessary; the Goulart regime fell almost without a struggle on April 1, and the president fled into exile in Uruguay.

As the new military regime consolidated its power, it became clear that the generals had come to install the alternative to the nationalist economic model, a neocolonial model based on the thorough integration of a dependent Brazilian economy into the international capitalist economy and the rapid modernization of Brazilian industry and agriculture without regard to its social consequences. Because of the regime's combination of brutally repressive policies with primary economic and political dependence on the United States, the Brazilian scholar Hélio Jaguaribe has aptly called it "colonial fascism."

Brazil's "Colonial Fascism"

The first acts of the military leaders of the self-proclaimed "democratic revolution" on April 1964 revealed their long-range intentions. On April 9 the Supreme Revolutionary Command issued the First Institutional Act, permitting the president to rule by decree, declare a state of siege, and deprive any citizen of civil rights for a period of ten years. A docile Congress approved the military's choice for president, General Humberto de Alencar Castelo Branco. Like many of his colleagues, Castelo Branco was a product of the *Escola Superior de Guerra* (School of Higher Military Studies), dominated in recent years by advocates of a *linha dura* (hard line), whose main tenets were fanatical anti-communism, favorable treatment of foreign capital, and acceptance of the leadership of the United States in foreign affairs.

ENCOURAGEMENT OF FOREIGN CAPITAL AND REPRESSION OF LABOR

It was in the area of economic policy that the new government most clearly defined its character and long-range aims. Roberto Campos, minister of planning, worked out a program for stimulating the entry of foreign capital by incentives that included the free export of profits, reduced taxes on the income of foreign firms, and a special type of exchange for the payment of external financing in case of devaluation. At the same time, internal credit was severely reduced in compliance with the anti-inflationary prescriptions of the IMF, while the level of consumption of the domestic market fell as a result of a wage freeze and the decline in the real value of wages. These policies, placing Brazilian-owned companies in an unfavorable position, caused many to go under; 440 went bankrupt in 1966, 550 in 1967.

The new government's economic policies accelerated the foreign takeover of Brazilian industry. By 1968 foreign capital controlled 40 percent of the capital market of Brazil, 62 percent of its foreign trade, 82 percent of its maritime transport, 77 percent of its overseas air transport, 100 percent of its motor vehicle production, 100 percent of its tire production, more than 80 percent of its pharmaceutical industry, and 90 percent of its cement industry. The United States led, with about half of the total foreign investment, followed by Germany, Britain, France, and Switzerland.

To ensure foreign and domestic capital of an abundant supply of cheap labor, the government froze wages and banned strikes, with the result that workers' living standards fell sharply. In 1968 the minister of labor estimated that the real value of wages had fallen between 15 and 30 percent in the preceding four years. Labor was further shackled by the appointment of military intervenors to oversee more than two thousand of the country's leading industrial unions.

Further, the government suppressed dissent in all areas of Brazilian life and suspended the political rights of thousands of so-called extremists. Thousands of federal employees were fired, and hundreds of nationalist military officers were arbitrarily retired or dismissed. The government shut down the Brazilian Institute of Higher Studies, a major center of nationalist economic theory, suppressed the National Student Union, and outlawed the Peasant Leagues.

In 1965, Castelo Branco issued the Second Institutional Act, which dissolved all political parties and instituted indirect elections of the president and vice president. The Third Institutional Act (February 1966) ended the popular election of governors of states and mayors of state capitals. Yet Brazil's military rulers chose to maintain a façade of democracy and representative government. They established an official party and a legal opposition party, whose ranks were carefully screened to exclude "subversives." Its elected representatives had little or no impact on policy and legislation.

With electoral politics closed to serious democratic debate, opposition to the military dictatorship was increasingly reflected in popular youth culture, where lyrical metaphors and a driving musical beat initially avoided dictatorial censorship and substituted for political manifestos. Born in urban musical theaters that sponsored socially conscious plays like *Roda Viva* ("Commotion"), this new Brazilian popular music (MPB) soon provided a catalyst for youthful protest against the dictatorship. It quickly reached a mass audience because television, radio, and record companies, to attract a younger generation of consumers, sponsored competitions among musicians who were eager to play at music festivals originally held in large theaters and later in outdoor stadiums. Six months before each festival and following the carnival tradition, songs were played repeatedly on the radio and the most popular artists were invited to perform at the festival. Among them were the musicians like Geraldo Vandré and Chico Buarque who used love songs and traditional ballads to thinly disguise lyrics that railed against social injustice and oppression. Vandré's *"Disparada"* ("Stampede"), for example, tells the story of a cowboy from Brazil's arid and poverty-stricken Northeast who, tired of having the fazendeiro treat him worse than the cattle, violently rebels.

But perhaps the most popular song was *"Caminhando"* ("Walking"), which became a national anthem of youthful social protest, even after the dictatorship, citing its "subversive lyrics, its offensiveness to the armed forces, and its use as a slogan for student demonstrations," banned its publication and dissemination. It called upon workers, peasants, students, and intellectuals to unite and mobilize against dictatorship in defense of song, a metaphor for freedom and democracy: "Walking and singing and following the song/ We're all equal, arms linked or not/ In the schools, in the streets, fields, and construction sites/ Walking and singing and following the song." More ominously still for Brazil's military leaders, "Caminhando" insisted that "Those who know, take action now and don't wait for it to happen."

Costa e Silva and a New Constitution

In March 1967, Castelo Branco turned over the presidency to his hand-picked successor Marshal Artur da Costa e Silva. His first act was to give Brazil a new constitution, the sixth in its history, which incorporated the successive institutional acts. In general, Costa e Silva continued the policies of his predecessor but allowed a certain thaw in the climate of repression; this encouraged a revival of opposition activity and demands for changes in policy. Nationalists inside and outside the armed forces called for a return to the nationalist model of economic development, workers for an end to the wage freeze, intellectuals and students for an end to censorship and a return to academic freedom. A portion of the clergy, headed by the courageous archbishop of Recife and Olinda, Helder Câmara, added their voices to the general cry for social, political, and economic reforms.

During this period, a new musical force appeared that made a dramatic impact on Brazilian popular culture and the struggle against dictatorship. Known as *tropicalía*, this new genre criticized the bossa nova and another musical style, *a jovem guarda* (new guard), as hopelessly romantic, fundamentally "bourgeois," and insufficiently willing to confront the brutality of the repressive military dictatorship; it called not only for the ouster of the military regime, but also for a revolution of Brazilian culture and national identity.

Ironically, tropicalía music alienated both the military regime and traditional left-wing political opponents, because it self-consciously fused Brazilian and foreign instruments and musical styles to create a "universal sound." This contradicted the interests of the dictatorship, which sought to maintain social control by celebrating Brazil's national cultural traditions, but it also undermined the left's critique of foreign domination and cultural imperialism. Led by artists like Caetano Veloso and Gilberto Gil, the *tropicalistas* were greatly influenced by The Beatles' *"Sergeant Pepper's Lonely Hearts Club Band"* and drew heavily on Oswaldo de Andrade's concept of "cultural cannibalism" to shock their audiences with raucous, electric guitars and lyrics that juxtaposed contradictory images of modernity and repression. At the International Music Festival, Veloso and his band, *Os Mutantes* (The Mutants), dressed like futuristic automatons, initially were booed off the stage when they performed "To Prohibit Is Prohibited." Veloso, in an angry rage, chastised his audience for seeking "to police Brazilian music" in the same way that the dictatorship sought to police Brazil; by contrast, he and his tropicalía comrades aimed "to abolish the imbecility that rules Brazil." Indeed,

Gilberto Gil, Caetano Veloso, Tom Ze, and Os Mutantes shocked Brazilians with their new sound, which combined traditional Brazilian rhythms with the electrified guitar sounds of Jimi Hendrix. Before their arrest and exile in 1968, their psychedelic music scorned middle-class Brazilian consumerism and the military dictatorship that protected it. [© Universal Music Group. Photo from University of North Carolina Press]

Veloso, Gil, and their comrades equally savaged the dictatorship and its agenda of capitalist modernization. According to cultural historian Christopher Dunn, in the title song of his first album in 1968, "Tropicalía," Veloso contrasted the bossa nova, cultural symbol of Brazilian modernity in the late 1950s with *palhoça*, "the ubiquitous mud huts of the Brazilian backlands." Although this seemed harmless enough, the song concluded with still more disturbing images, ultimately describing a modern metaphorical Brasilia inhabited by a "smiling, ugly dead child" begging for coins.

The tropicalistas' sophisticated allegories confused the military censors and even secured their approval for a time. In fact, the military dictators were unsure how to classify the political meaning of the tropicalía movement, especially because it was also the target of their left-wing opponents. By late 1968, however, the dictatorship, according to

Veloso, was convinced that their music "represented anarchy, violence, and a threat to families, relations between generations, respect, and religion." According to Gilberto Gil, the military viewed tropicalía as "a threat, something new, something that can't quite be understood, something that doesn't fit into any of the well-defined compartments of existing cultural practices." The military government consequently incarcerated them and later exiled them to Europe because they were "sort of illegible, and that won't do, that is dangerous."

Heartened by this show of popular resistance to the dictatorship, Congress and the Supreme Court reasserted their independence. The Supreme Court defied the military by granting a writ of habeas corpus for three student leaders who had been imprisoned for three months. Congress protected the immunity of a deputy who had bitterly criticized the military for its brutal treatment of political prisoners and student dissenters.

These acts of defiance precipitated a governmental crisis that exposed a struggle within the regime between adherents of the hard line and a group of military officers who proposed to reduce foreign economic influence, pursue a more independent foreign policy, and make some concessions to the clamor for social and political reform. The hard-liners won out; under their pressure, Costa e Silva issued a Fifth Institutional Act in 1968 that dissolved Congress, imposed censorship, suspended the constitution, and granted the president dictatorial powers.

This "coup within a coup" escalated the use of terrorist tactics by a variety of police forces, local and national. The official security forces were joined by vigilante groups, operating with the covert approval of the government. The systematic use of torture by special units of the military police and the "death squads" reached a level without precedent in Brazilian history. The victims included intellectuals, students, workers, and even priests and nuns, as well as common criminals. Increasingly, Brazilians could express their opposition only in the allegorical style by now made famous by Brazilian popular music and the tropicalistas. On December 14, 1968, *Jornal do Brasil* published such a weather report that forecast "black weather, suffocating temperature, unbreathable air, and a country beset by strong winds." It could not have been more accurate.

The intensified campaign of repression convinced some elements of the Brazilian left that there was no alternative to armed struggle against the dictatorship. There arose some half-dozen guerrilla groups, but they never achieved a mass character. The slaying in 1969 by members of a death squad of the most prominent guerrilla leader, Carlos Marighella, dealt a heavy blow to the movement, which soon ceased to pose a serious problem for the regime. Brazil remained a police state.

THE ECONOMY AND DENATIONALIZATION

This vicious assault on Brazilian democracy and civil liberties aimed to preserve the military's power and to protect its neoliberal economic policies, which favored foreign investment and export production but attacked the living standards of Brazil's impoverished majority. By 1970 the denationalization of key sectors of Brazilian industry was almost complete. One or a few giant multinational firms dominated each major industry. The automotive industry, which was dominated by three firms—Volkswagen, General Motors, and Ford—typified the concentration of industrial ownership and production. The military champions of free enterprise did not dismantle the state sector, however, as one might expect. Instead they assigned to it the function of providing cheap steel, power, and raw materials to the profitable foreign-owned enterprises.

A counterpart of the concentration of production was the concentration of income. Brazil's gross national product grew at an average annual rate of 8 percent, one of the highest in the world, but there was no parallel growth of mass capacity to consume.

The contradiction between a highly productive, technologically advanced industrial plant and an extremely small domestic market had to be resolved somehow. The regime's economic planners found the answer by programming a vast increase in Brazil's exports. Primary products continued to dominate the export trade, but exports of manufactured goods increased at a rate of about 12 percent between 1968 and 1972. Most Brazilians lacked shoes and were poorly clad, but Brazil became a major exporter of shoes and textiles. Increasingly, however, primacy was placed on the export of durable consumer and capital goods, such as cars, electrical products, and machine tools.

Government planners hoped that exports would help solve the problem of the balance of payments, a problem that grew ever more acute. But even as the volume of exports increased, so did the annual trade deficit. Meanwhile, the foreign debt, which stood at $12.5 billion in 1973, climbed to $17.6 billion in 1974 and stood at about $30 billion by the end of 1976. Service on this foreign debt, an important component of which was the increased cost of imported oil, amounted to nearly the total value of Brazil's exports in 1977. The problem was compounded by the heavy drain of interest and dividends in amounts considerably greater than the foreign investments that generated them. The deficits in the balance of payments contributed to a steep fall in the exchange value of the cruzeiro and an inflationary spiral that reached a rate of about 46 percent in 1976.

The recession that spread throughout the capitalist world in 1973–1974, combined with much higher oil prices, added to Brazil's economic difficulties. The passage of "antidumping" laws[1] in various countries, including the United States, cut into Brazil's exports of manufactured goods, creating overproduction and unemployment in various industries. By the mid-1970s, the bloom was off Brazil's "economic miracle."

The government's own figures documented the devastating effect of the "economic miracle" on the general welfare. By 1974 the minimum wage was only half the minimum income required to buy food for subsistence. When the costs of rent, clothing, and transportation were added, a worker needed four times the minimum wage. Official data revealed an intolerable situation with respect to public health. Nearly half the population over the

---

[1]These laws imposed duties designed to prevent the sale of goods in international trade at below-market prices.

age of twenty suffered from tuberculosis and about 150,000 people died every year from the disease; about 42 million suffered from parasitic diseases that caused general debility and reduced working capacity. The great majority of Brazilian houses lacked running water and sanitary facilities, a condition that contributed to the prevalence of parasitic disease. According to the president of the National Institute of Nutrition, 12 million preschool children—70 percent of all children in that category—suffered from malnutrition in 1973.

The government's agrarian reform was primarily directed at prodding and assisting semifeudal great landowners to transform their estates into agribusinesses at the expense of their tenants. It threatened to expropriate latifundia that had not been exploited for four years. But the stress on "voluntary" adherence gave landowners time for delay and circumvention of the law by dividing the land among relatives or forming it into commercial enterprises exempt from the law's provisions. Thus, its principal result was to stimulate the development of capitalist large-scale agriculture, accelerating a process that had been under way since the 1930s. Sociologists warned that the "agrarian reform" was spurring a new wave of rural emigration, throwing a new mass of cheap labor on an overstocked urban labor market.

THE OPPOSITION AND THE STRUGGLE FOR RIGHTS

Ruled by a brutal military dictatorship, the Brazilian people expressed their dissent and discontent through the few available channels. Brazilian music quickly reemerged as an effective means through which popular discontent with the military dictatorship, especially among the nation's youth, was expressed. Strongly influenced by a decade of rigid internal military censorship of Brazilian artists and the regime's free-market exposure to the innovative electric sounds of foreign music (especially jazz), a new generation of Brazilian youth grew up less interested in a song's words, but very much aware of the liberating power of its sound. Milton Nascimento, perhaps the best known of these young artists, reflected this awareness in his *"Milagre dos Peixes"* ("Miracle

of the Fishes"), a popular song sung without lyrics to protest military censorship. To overcome the limitations imposed by television and radio censors, these musicians increasingly relied upon massive outdoor music festivals to communicate their ideas to the public; these became important sites for the organization of popular opposition to dictatorship.

Urban theater was another form of popular culture through which opposition to the military was expressed. Professional theater battled the dictatorship, using metaphor and historical narrative to escape the censors' disapproval. Chico Buarque's *"Calabar: O Elogio da Traição"* ("Calabar: In Praise of Treason"), for example, used a famous story of betrayal in the seventeenth-century Portuguese-Dutch colonial wars to celebrate Brazilian independence from Portuguese tyranny, an all too obvious metaphor that, after three months, ultimately failed to survive the regime's censorship. Largely because of the military's omnipresent censors, there was a dramatic expansion of local, decentralized amateur theater. These dramas likewise challenged the power of the military and sought to avoid individual recriminations by collectivizing all production decisions. They used narratives of well-known historical events to communicate themes of popular rebellion and resistance to oppression that resonated with contemporary antidictatorial struggles. *Teatro da rua* (street theater) also flourished during this dark period. It used the techniques of mime and clowning to scorn dictatorship and helped galvanize popular resistance in the nation's favelas, whose residents could not afford the price of a theater ticket. By the mid-1970s there was a thriving national subculture of popular protest and rebellion that belied the surface calm imposed by the military regime's brutal repression.

Influenced by liberation theology and its "preferential option for the poor," Christian Base Communities also emerged to play a key role in this struggle. Under church protection, women organized community and neighborhood groups that initially limited themselves to "feminine" demands for clean water, better housing, and lower food prices but increasingly became more overtly "political," agitating for the release of political prisoners, a restoration of democracy, and the "reconquest of lost equality." By decade's end, this had spawned a feminist movement, whose media voice, *Brasil Mulher,* claiming a circulation of ten thousand readers, concluded that "capitalism is the origin of numerous forms of the oppression of women."

Afro-Brazilians also created cultural organizations like the Center for Black Culture and Art, which advocated the abolition of racial discrimination and cultivated racial pride associated with a Pan-African consciousness. By 1978, however, these organizations had begun to coalesce in the Unified Black Movement (MNU), which organized *centros de luta* (struggle centers) to protest against racism, "the inevitable consequence of capitalist development." Likewise, a substantial minority of the Catholic church hierarchy, led by Archbishop Helder Câmara, openly began to oppose capitalism and neocolonialism.

Meanwhile, workers, whose average wages under the military regime's neoliberal economic program had fallen to two-thirds of their 1964 levels and one-half of their 1957 high, had become more vocal. A "new unionism" emerged to challenge the military government's policies and led directly to the formation of the Workers' Party (PT), which participated in the social struggle demanding an end to dictatorship, respect for human rights, and economic justice.

Finally, congressional elections in 1978 reflected Brazilians' immense discontent with the economic and social results of dictatorial rule and the growing strength of an opposition that united ever wider sections of the population.

THE DICTATORSHIP IN CRISIS, 1978–1983

There were three major developments on the Brazilian scene between 1978 and 1983. First, a weak recovery from the recession of 1974–1975 soon gave way to an even more severe recession, culminating in a balance-of-payments crisis that brought Brazil to the verge of national bankruptcy. Second, the living standards of the masses continued to decline as a result of mounting unemployment, skyrocketing inflation, and the government's austerity measures, causing increased discontent and resistance on the part of the working class and the peasantry. At the same time, opposition to the military regime grew among the middle class and sections of the capitalist class. Third, in an effort to defuse the growing opposition, the regime applied the policy of *abertura,* or "opening toward democracy." This policy of limited political concessions aimed to preserve the military's power.

The economic crisis resulted from the interplay of domestic and external factors. An important cause was the inability of the domestic market to absorb the growing output of Brazilian industry. For almost two decades, the dictatorship had pursued a policy of promoting the growth of profits and capital by keeping wage increases below the cost of living; this policy sharply limited the purchasing power of the people. The economic downturn of the 1970s and the 1980s, however, also reduced the purchasing power of the middle classes, who provided a major part of the market for cars, television sets, and other durable consumer goods.

The most direct cause of the crisis was an unmanageable balance of payments and debt service problem. By 1980, Brazil had a foreign debt of $55 billion, largest in the Third World, and service of the debt absorbed 40 percent of the nation's export earnings. Even Brazil's president complained that because of the drain of interest, Brazil had "nothing left over for development." The high interest rates caused by the monetarist tight money policies of the Reagan administration added to Brazil's debt service burden. The export of a considerable part of the profits made by multinational companies in Brazil also increased Brazil's payments deficit. By 1980 these companies controlled 40 percent of the major industrial and mining enterprises of the country and were sending home 55 percent of their profits.

By 1982 the balance-of-payments problem had reached a critical point. Brazil had almost run out of the foreign exchange it needed to meet its financial obligations. The foreign debt stood at about $89 billion, and many of the approximately 1,400 banks that had lent money to Brazil, grown suddenly nervous, were refusing to renew outstanding loans to Brazilian entities. A Brazilian default, however, would have sent shock waves through the world financial system. Once more, as in the similar Mexican emergency, the self-interest of the Western financial community dictated a rescue operation. The plan, organized by the IMF with strong support from the U.S. government, provided for rollover loans that allowed Brazil to continue paying the interest on its debt, thus maintaining the profits of the international banks. At the same time, austerity measures imposed by the agreement meant that the mass of impoverished Brazilians, already hard-pressed, suffered further. The new loans gave Brazil a breathing space, but the balance-of-payments problem remained as intractable as ever, and the financial juggling act of 1982 could not be indefinitely repeated.

The austerity program imposed by the IMF was a new blow at popular living standards, which had sharply declined since the establishment of the military dictatorship in 1964. In mid-1978 one study concluded that at least 70 percent of the population lived below the officially calculated economic survival level. In 1982 the minimum monthly wage was 23,000 cruzeiros, about $95. According to Brazilian sociologists, however, a family of five needed three times that amount to survive. The superexploitation of Brazilian workers took its heaviest toll on the weakest group of the population—its children. A partial census taken in 1982 indicated that half of all Brazilian children over ten worked.

These abysmal social conditions led to rural conflict that was intensified by an explosion of land concentration and land-grabbing. In part this process of land concentration reflected the expansion of capitalist, mechanized agriculture, producing such crops as soya beans or sugar cane,[2] primarily into marginal and frontier land that had not been cultivated previously. In part it was due to the pattern of occupation of the new lands opened up for settlement in the Amazon by the construction of the Trans-Amazonian Highway and other

roads. Instead of settling thousands of landless peasant families on the new agricultural frontier, the Amazon Development Agency gave big companies large sums of money to set up vast cattle ranches. As a result, some 95 percent of the new landholdings in the Amazon were of 10,000 hectares or more. Unlike coffee plantations, the large new soya bean and sugar-cane farms and cattle estates employed little labor. Many of the dispossessed or discharged tenants and rural laborers migrated to the cities, swelling the ranks of the unemployed and underemployed and aggravating all the urban social problems.

Thousands of others drifted to the Amazon frontier, becoming *posseiros* (squatters) who raised subsistence crops of rice, cassava, and maize on their small plots. They enjoyed considerable rights under Brazilian law, but these rights had little value on the violent frontier. The posseiros were (and are) frequently threatened with eviction by powerful land-grabbers, who arrived with their gunmen and sometimes enjoyed the open or covert support of the local military or other officials. The posseiros responded by organizing rural unions and defending their land by all the means at their disposal; they found allies in courageous Catholic clergy who on occasion were arrested, tortured, and even murdered for their humanitarian activities.

Discredited and isolated on account of its failed economic policies and corruption, the military regime sought a way out of its impasse by a strategy of détente with the opposition. This policy of abertura included the lifting of most censorship; an amnesty that permitted the return of political exiles and the restoration of their political rights; and an overhaul of the political system that allowed the formation of new parties in addition to the official government and opposition parties.

These concessions were certainly not without significance, but their limited, calculated character must be understood. They were hedged about by constitutional amendments designed to ensure the continuation of military rule. Although the opposition made large gains in the 1982 elections under the constitution imposed by the military, the all-powerful president controlled both the federal budget and the operating funds of the states. It still

---

[2] A major factor in the expansion of sugar-cane cultivation was the success of Brazil's program for developing alcohol as a fuel.

seemed certain that a military man or a nominee of the military would be the next president of Brazil.

The Transition to Democracy, 1983–2003: "The New Republic"

The march of events upset the calculations of the military rulers. The dictatorship had counted on an easy win over opposition candidate Tancredo Neves, but popular mobilization against the military swept Neves to victory. On the eve of his inauguration, however, Neves died, leaving his vice president, José Sarney, to carry out Neves's program of structural reforms, which included land reform and the grant of a larger voice in government to workers and unions. But Sarney took office without Neves's mandate and with little popular support.

THE MILITARY AND EXTERNAL CONSTRAINTS ON DEMOCRACY

The transition to democracy and civilian rule, made under the watchful eyes of the military, was a gradual process. Behind the scenes, the military continued to influence the decision-making process on all major issues. Consequently, the Sarney administration made little progress in solving Brazil's great social and economic problems, the chief of which was land reform. This was not simply a question of redistributive justice; it was a prerequisite for the creation of a modern national capitalism based on a large domestic market. In 1985, for example, Sarney signed into law an agrarian reform bill that provided for the distribution of 88 million acres of land to 1.4 million families through 1989. But a 1986 decree limited the land available for distribution and expropriation to state-owned lands and to private holdings whose production was below the land-use standards set by government agronomists.

So sluggish was the program's implementation that Minister of Agrarian Reform and Development Nelson Ribeiro resigned in protest. The major obstacle to land reform was the fierce resistance of the landowners. Organized under the Rural Democratic Union (UDR) and the Brazilian Society for the Defense of Tradition, Family, and Property, the landowners hired thousands of former military personnel to staff private militias, paying, it was reported, salaries three times higher than those of the army.

If land reform was the most acute, violence-ridden issue of the "New Republic," Brazil's greatest external problem remained the immense foreign debt, which in 1990 stood at about $120 billion. The continuous drain of foreign exchange had a profoundly negative impact on Brazil's efforts to achieve social reform and economic growth. To many Brazilians, it appeared that the nation must choose between paying the interest and supporting social and economic development.

Sarney defined his position on the debt in a 1985 speech to the United Nations General Assembly: "Brazil will not pay its foreign debt with recession nor with unemployment, nor with hunger . . . a debt paid for with poverty is an account paid with democracy." These were brave words, in sharp contrast to the docility with which military governments had accepted the debt status quo. But this revolt by a timid president did not last long. Under pressure from foreign bankers and right-wing domestic groups, Sarney lifted the debt moratorium and in 1988 began negotiations with the banks for a conventional rescheduling.

On taking office the Sarney administration found the economy in recession, racked by galloping inflation and high unemployment. To combat this economic crisis, he announced a stabilization program, *Plan Cruzado*, which established a freeze on wages, prices, and rents, and replaced Brazil's monetary unit, the cruzeiro, with a new and strong monetary unit, the *cruzado*. He also announced a series of devaluations designed to maintain export effectiveness; the immediate closing or merger of fifteen state companies and of thirty-two more in the coming months; and, most painful of all, large increases in postal rates, the cost of utilities, fuel, and sugar, and 100 percent increases in taxes on cigarettes and alcoholic beverages.

An explosion of popular wrath followed these announcements. Brazilian wage earners' purchasing power, already slashed 30 percent since 1986, faced another decline of 29 percent. Consequently, the two labor federations, the leftist *Central Unica dos Trabalhadores* (CUT) and its rival, the more conservative *Central Geral dos Trabalhadores* (CGT), joined in a general strike designed to bring about the total repeal of the austerity program; organizers claimed that the strike brought 70 percent of the nation to a standstill. By mid-1987 Sarney's popularity had declined to the vanishing point. The U.S. banker David Rockefeller astutely noted the source of this decline: "In all my visits to Brazil, I have never before come across such desperate poverty."

In 1988 the national Congress, acting as a constituent assembly and influenced by this massive popular mobilization, gave the country a new democratic constitution that represented a sweeping rejection of all the late military regime had stood for. It provided for popular election of the president and mandated that Brazilians should vote in 1993 to choose between the presidential and parliamentary systems. Presidential rule by decree, so often used by the military regime, was abolished. The basic civil rights of freedom of assembly, speech, and the press were guaranteed, workers were given the right to strike and engage in collective bargaining, and the workweek was reduced from forty-eight to forty-four hours. Another provision nationalized oil- and mineral-mining rights.

The constitution promised protection of indigenous rights but contained no concrete measures to prevent the destruction of their culture and habitat, the Amazon rain forest. With the approval and financial support of the military regimes and their civilian successors, big ranchers and mine companies, both Brazilian and foreign, cut down or burned vast stretches of forest to graze cattle or strip-mine, threatening the livelihoods and very survival of the indigenous peoples and *seringueiros* (rubber tappers), who depended on the forests for their existence. Those who protested the exploitive practices of the ranchers and mine owners were often murdered by hired gunmen protected by corrupt and racist government officials.

Sarney's administration received a stunning rebuff from Brazilian voters in the November 1988 municipal elections. In a sharp swing to the left, labor and socialist parties captured control of the major Brazilian cities and a majority of state capitals, and there was a rapid growth of left-wing parties, especially the Workers' Party, led by the militant trade union leader Luís Inaçio da Silva (Lula), whose membership grew into millions.

NEOLIBERAL WINE IN POPULIST BOTTLES

The election results and a general strike in March 1989, which mobilized 20 million workers, sounded an alarm bell to Brazil's elites and their political managers, preparing for the first popular presidential election in nearly thirty years, to be held in 1989. The new democratic environment required the right to present a populist, charismatic presidential candidate who could convince the Brazilian people to swallow the ill-tasting free-market prescription of austerity and privatization, something Sarney had been unable to do.

Such a candidate was found in the person of Fernando Collor de Mello, a dapper sportsman and athlete from a wealthy family. Sharply critical of official state corruption and inefficiency, his campaign focused on promises to reduce the bloated bureaucracy, attract foreign capital, and institute a free-market economy.

Although he combined populist initiatives with policies that reflected his hard-line free-market principles, the basic thrust of Collor's program conformed to the most traditional IMF recipes for economic solvency. Reduction of government spending and services, a halt to wage indexation (adjustment of wages to changing price levels), an end to collective bargaining except on the firm level, and wholesale privatization of state enterprises became the order of the day. A freeze of savings and banking deposits, designed to check inflation, helped produce the desired effect but had major recessive results; by 1990 industrial production had plummeted 25 percent and layoffs nationwide were well over 300,000. Caught between the scissors of declining sales and interest rates of 6 percent a month, many companies filed for bankruptcy; almost a million workers were unemployed in Rio de Janeiro, São Paulo, and four

Chico Mendes with his family, shortly before his death in 1988. The murder of Mendes, a leader of the crusade to save the Brazilian rain forest, shocked environmentalists around the world. [Denise Zmekhol]

other state capitals (this figure did not include workers in the so-called informal sector). Meanwhile, talks with foreign commercial banks that held much of Brazil's $121 billion foreign debt had bogged down, the banks rejecting Brazil's proposal to tie debt service payments to its future "capacity to pay."

Meanwhile, Brazil's land problem remained without solution. Amazonia continued to be the scene of violent clashes between great landowners who frequently acquired their land illegally and small farmers whose tiny plots would not support their families. Peasants who resisted usurpation and exploitation faced threats, harassment, and murder. Rent-a-killer agencies (*agências de pistolagem*) operated in many areas; they offered a sliding scale ranging from $600 for a peasant to $4,000 for an elected official. In southern Pará

state 172 rural activists were killed. A judge in Rio Maria (Pará state) expressed surprise about the excitement caused by such killings; "they were only peasants," he said. The Collor government did little to protect peasant leaders or punish their assassins. Arrests were rare and prosecutions rarer still. The conviction in December 1990 of a cattle rancher and his son for the murder of the celebrated Chico Mendes, an organizer of the rubber tappers and defender of the rain forest, was largely driven by international attention and pressure.

Responding to the devastating effects of the Collor program on wages, employment, and living standards, many unions went on strike and in some cases wrung concessions from employers and government. Collor's declining popularity was reflected in growing congressional and judicial resistance to his decrees. Left-of-center parties now held 246 votes in the new Congress, forming a strong opposition to President Collor.

Then, in a series of dramatic events in 1992, President Collor's administration collapsed amid accusations of personal corruption on a large scale. Congressional investigations established that Collor and his associates had accumulated at least $32 million in public funds and payoffs, but that amount was considered only a fraction of the total involved. After months of investigations, revelations, and legal maneuvering, Collor, who had campaigned on an anticorruption platform, resigned just before Congress would have voted to subject him to an impeachment trial.

ELECTORAL ENGANOS AND POPULAR PROTEST

Following Collor's resignation, his vice president, Itamar Franco, was named acting president. Franco, who was known for his nationalistic stands, had opposed Collor's neoliberal market reforms, including the privatization of state companies. On assuming the presidency, however, the unpredictable Franco announced that he would continue Collor's privatization program and honor Brazil's debt commitments but would assign priority to a campaign against hunger and poverty; he claimed the income of Brazil's poorest citizens had fallen 30 percent as a result of Collor's "false modernization program." Governing elites now understood clearly that the unadulterated neoliberal reforms so enthusiastically championed by the IMF, foreign investors, and Brazil's bourgeoisie were widely unpopular with the lower classes and therefore impossible to realize within the context of democracy, however carefully circumscribed.

This realization shaped a new debate between two groups within Franco's coalition cabinet: advocates of social reform who argued that growth to relieve hunger and poverty should take first place in a country where millions were destitute, where a "social time bomb" was ticking; and advocates of neoliberal economic reform who put first the need to achieve fiscal stability (the monthly inflation rate in late 1993 was over 30 percent) through reduced government spending, the sale of state companies, and improved tax collection. The conflict between

the cabinet's "social sector" and its "economic sector" and Franco's own unpredictability sometimes made it difficult to know in which direction the government was moving, but in general the neoliberal tendency had the better of it. To head his economic reform team Franco appointed as finance minister his former foreign minister, the major political figure and prominent sociologist Fernando Henrique Cardoso. Cardoso's program centered on deficit reduction through budget cuts and on securing the constitutional and fiscal changes needed to achieve tax reform, privatize state companies in such sensitive areas as oil, mining, and telecommunications, and promote foreign investment. But the program encountered strong resistance from left-wing parties who opposed the austerity and privatization plans, from state governments dismayed by demands that they pay their large debts to the federal government, and from members of congress who had their eyes fixed on the 1994 general election and feared the impact of unpopular measures like tax increases on their own fortunes.

That election would be the most sweeping in Brazilian history, with the president, two-thirds of the Senate, the Chamber of Deputies, the governors of all twenty-seven states, and deputies in the state assemblies all coming up for election. It also promised to be the most important election in Brazil's history, with voters likely to be offered a choice between the neoliberal profit-driven model of economic growth, based on exports and foreign investment, and a more statist, autonomous model of development, oriented toward the internal market and the solution of the country's great social problems. Workers' Party leader Lula, himself an automobile worker and trade unionist who had opposed the military dictatorship, championed the latter and campaigned tirelessly throughout the country, repeating his pledge to implement agrarian reform, fight unemployment, increase agricultural production, and improve health and education.

But Lula's chief rival was Cardoso, a distinguished academic who even described himself as representing the "viable left" (in contrast to Lula's "utopian left"). This reflected the increasingly leftward leanings of the Brazilian electorate. Cardoso's trump card was a new economic stabilization plan, the "Real Plan" (*Plan Real*), named after the new currency that was introduced on July 1. Under this tight-money plan, the monthly inflation rate fell from 50 percent in June to 6.1 percent in July 1994. Cardoso counted on the support of workers, whose salaries had been readjusted every two months but quickly lost their value as a result of uncontrollable price increases. Cardoso's plan, combined with promises of sweeping social reform and the right's fear of a leftist victory, led moderates and conservatives to unify behind Cardoso, who won decisively.

Cardoso faced staggering problems when he took office in 1995. True, the Brazilian economy grew strongly, with exports for the first five months of the year reaching $15.5 billion, an all-time record. But these exports consisted mainly of raw materials like soya products, coffee beans, iron ore, and some manufactured goods like footwear and auto parts that were extremely vulnerable to fluctuations in market demand. Moreover, the growth of these exports, produced mostly by highly mechanized agribusinesses and plants, had little or no multiplier effect. This was reflected in continuing high unemployment figures and the rapid growth of the informal sector of the economically active population, believed to range between 30 and 60 percent of the total. Cardoso's program of a balanced budget and the Real Plan tamed the monster of inflation, but other economic and social problems still loomed large.

Revealing once again Brazil's extraordinary vulnerability to global economic changes, the Asian financial crisis in the fall of 1997 panicked the Brazilian stock market and unleashed a speculative assault on its currency, the real. To defend the real against devaluation and still attract the foreign capital on which it depended to finance the nation's fiscal deficit (then 6 percent of gross domestic product, or GDP), Cardoso doubled interest rates to 40 percent and announced an austerity package of spending cuts and tax increases designed to save $17.7 billion, or 2.5 percent of GDP. Although Cardoso, facing reelection in the fall of 1998, sought to immunize social spending

from these draconian budget cuts, they plunged Brazil into a severe recession. Industrial production and unemployment rates continued to climb; in São Paulo, the country's industrial heartland, even official estimates of unemployment rose to 17 percent in 1997.

Another major social problem was the grossly inequitable distribution of land. Less than 3 percent of the population owned almost 60 percent of Brazil's arable land, 62 percent of which lay uncultivated and unoccupied. Meanwhile, 5 million rural families were landless and lacked the means to earn an income with which to purchase their survival. Although Cardoso acknowledged that "we need agrarian reform," his government was slow to enforce a 1993 law permitting the government to expropriate (with adequate compensation) lands that were 75 percent idle. Consequently, under the auspices of the Catholic Church, some 42,000 landless families joined together to form the Landless People's Movement (MST), which organized a campaign of direct action to invade uncultivated lands and establish "squatter" communities that gave more than 140,000 families access to land and pressured the Cardoso government to promise land to an additional 280,000 families.

But these popular victories often came with a heavy price. Jorge Neri, an indigenous leader and MST activist whose own family lost their communal lands during the construction of the Trans-Amazonian Highway, participated in more than sixty-seven land invasions, many of which ended in violence, but none so graphic as the wholesale slaughter of nineteen squatters by policemen and hired thugs in full view of television cameras. Despite international protests, however, no one was ever arrested, much less tried and convicted. For his part, although he deplored the violence, President Cardoso also chastised the MST as a "threat to democracy," thereby revealing the extraordinary shadow that historical memories of military dictatorship still cast over Brazil's "free institutions." Lest Cardoso's subtle allusion be lost, the local president of a landowners' organization was characteristically more blunt: if the government failed to curb the MST's activities, he boldly announced, "we could have a repeat of the coup d'état."

The Landless People's Movement (MST) demanded a more equitable distribution of land, occupied uncultivated lands, and galvanized a popular resistance that effectively forced President Cardoso to moderate his government's neoliberal policies. [Wide World Photos]

Widespread poverty was yet another problem that successive neoliberal policies only seemed to aggravate. According to government figures, the number of people living in poverty increased steadily from 50.9 million in 1979 to 61.03 million in 1987 to 64.7 million in 1989 and jumped 10 percent in 1990 to 69.8 million, almost half the entire population. Moreover, 32 million people, 21 percent of all Brazilians, lived in extreme poverty.

Sixty percent of this indigent population lived in the Northeast, racked by recurrent droughts that wiped out crops and jobs and produced a water shortage that threatened the area with a large-scale spread of cholera. Anthropologist Nancy Scheper-Hughes, with many years of work and residence in the region, noted that throughout the 1980s diseases like typhoid, tuberculosis, leprosy, and bubonic plague, once thought to be under control, resurfaced in Brazil, especially in the Northeast. Calling them diseases of "disorderly development," she traced their roots to the "social relations that produce rural to urban migration, unemployment, *favelas* [shantytowns], illiteracy, and malnutrition." She described an area that was still "in a transitional stage of state formation that contained many traditional and semifeudal structures, including its legacy of local political bosses (coroneis) spawned by an agrarian *latifundista* class of powerful plantation estate masters and their many dependents." And she quoted the words of a woman factory worker, disillusioned with civilian and military governments: "We need a government that will take care of the people, but I have begun to think that this doesn't exist; that it is another *engano* [deceit]."

The Northeast and the Amazon may provide the most extreme illustrations of the "disorderly development" that characterized contemporary Brazil, but the crisis pervaded every part of the country and most dramatically affected urban women, who were forced to shoulder increasing burdens in the workplace, working for low wages, even as their unpaid familial responsibilities in the home grew proportionately with the decline of public services in health care, education, and daycare. This crisis actually sharpened under the civilian, democratically elected regimes in power since 1985, regimes that embraced even more ardently than the discredited military rulers their neoliberal economic policies and their model of dependent capitalist development. Official figures told the story. According to the World Bank, in the 1980s the percentage of Brazilians surviving on less than $2 a day rose from 34 percent to 41 percent. At the same time the income gap between the rich and poor widened. According to Brazil's 1991 census, the poorest 10 percent of the population had less than 1 percent of the nation's wealth. The richest 10 percent, on the other hand, held 49 percent of the nation's wealth.

But this "disorderly development" could have created still more problems were it not for the determined opposition of diverse nationalist groups, including trade unions like the Central Federation of Workers, environmental clubs, social protest organizations like the Landless People's

Movement, various political parties, and certain loyal coroneis—all of whom defended popular interests against the worst excesses of neoliberalism. Senator Benedita da Silva, the nation's first elected *favelada* (slum dweller) and most prominent Afro-Brazilian woman activist, proudly claimed that "Brazil is perhaps the country in Latin America that has most resisted the neoliberal model, and our unions are on the forefront of this resistance."

Although politically divided, this social opposition nonetheless influenced the contours of Brazilian political debate. Even Cardoso, defending his leftist, nationalist credentials, sought to identify his policies with these popular interests, insisting that his privatization of government services never sought to eliminate the role of the state in Brazil's national development but merely to transform its function from a "producer state" to a "regulatory state." State social programs, he conceded, "are necessary because we cannot expect the market to solve the problem of poverty." This blend of neoliberal, market-centered policies and state-supported social services made Cardoso an elusive target for his political enemies, enabling him to win reelection in fall 1998 with slightly more than 50 percent of the votes.

For almost a decade, Cardoso worked to integrate the nation's economy into the global marketplace, adopting neoliberal reforms endorsed by the IMF and relying on a steady expansion of exports, foreign investment, privatization, and overseas loans to finance modest social programs and produce economic growth that averaged 2 percent since 1997. As a result, debt service as a share of export income rose steadily from 26 percent in 1993 to an improbable 122 percent in 1999. More distressingly, however, income inequality remained the highest in Latin America and poverty likewise stayed stubbornly high, falling only slightly from

46 to 45 percent between 1990 and 2001. This record ordinarily would not be expected to win considerable public support, but Cardoso's populist rhetoric and a divided political opposition ensured repeated electoral success.

Cardoso was unable to pass his good fortune to his successor, however. By 2002 the collapse of neighboring Argentina's economy, growing uncertainties in U.S. money markets, and a generalized global market contraction reduced foreign investment and external demand for Brazilian exports. With a stalled economy and few state resources left to sell, it was unclear how Brazil would pay its oppressive $245 billion public debt, stimulate renewed growth, and satisfy popular demands for greater equality. In the October 2002 presidential elections, the Brazilian people offered their authoritative answer and overwhelmingly elected veteran presidential candidate and leader of the leftist Workers' Party, Lula da Silva, who promised to "break with the current economic model" and "suspend or reevaluate the privatization program." Lula's platform sought to unite a broader coalition of leftist parties, ranging from Liberals to Communists. Presenting himself as a more mature, sophisticated candidate, Lula also went out of his way to reassure nervous investors that his government would honor its legitimate obligations, but he also promised to "negotiate new ones with an eye to protecting national interests and without accepting impositions."

Barring a repeat of the electoral enganos that had plagued the nation's past, it seemed as if the future augured a change for Brazil's developmental model. No wonder the George W. Bush administration made clear its displeasure with Brazil's democratic politics and Goldman, Sachs and Co., an influential stock brokerage firm, urged its clients to shift their investments to Mexico!

Storm over the Andes: The Struggle for Land and Development

16

I N THE SECOND HALF of the twentieth century, reform came at last to three countries whose economic and social structures were among the most archaic in Latin America: the Andean republics of Peru, Bolivia, and Ecuador. Here, as elsewhere on the continent, the movement for reconstruction fused the effort to modernize with the struggle for greater social justice for the masses: economic sovereignty, industrialization, and land reform were the main slogans of the Andean revolutions. But the presence of large, compact indigenous groups, ranging from some 70 percent of the population of Bolivia to about 40 percent of the populations of Peru and Ecuador, gave a distinctive character to the nationalist, reformist movements in these countries.

Three Andean Revolutions

BOLIVIA, 1952–2003

Landlocked Bolivia, with the largest indigenous population of the three lands, was the scene of the first true Andean social revolution. This revolution unfolded within the historical context of racial, class, and gender conflicts unleashed by foreign investment, transatlantic market growth, and dependent capitalist development. During the late nineteenth century, highland indigenous commu-

nities had agreed to pay tribute and provide seasonal labor services to Hispanic hacendados in exchange for their recognition of indigenous communal land rights, but the lure of larger profits produced by a growing market demand for exports led them to expand their haciendas at the expense of the indígenas.

In the early twentieth century, the *caciques apoderados*, an armed indigenous movement that spread throughout the Andean highlands, defended their community lands and cultural traditions in violent uprisings like the 1921 Aymara Rebellion, led by Jesús de Machaqa, and the Chayanta Rebellion of 1927, which together mobilized thousands of peasants. This rural ferment, further complicated by growing worker unrest in the mines, factories, and urban centers, where a nascent women's movement also became active, led to greater collaboration among the army, landed oligarchs, and their foreign allies. Against this background, the disastrous results of the Chaco War (1932–1935), economic depression, and the growing domination of foreign mining companies inspired by wartime demand for strategic mineral raw materials all combined to alienate middle-class support for successive military dictatorships that had dominated Bolivian politics before 1940.

The last straw was the army's 1942 Cataví massacre of unarmed striking miners and their

395

families. Fearing greater social unrest, the mobilization of popular sectors, and its implications for their own power and property, middle-class activists organized the National Revolutionary Movement (MNR) and led a massive protest that brought the reformist government of Gualberto Villaroel to power the following year. But Villaroel was assassinated three years later. Thereafter, during a six-year struggle, the MNR mobilized the countryside and urban centers. Women especially played a significant role: the Women Workers' Federation (FOF) and the Barzolas, the MNR's infamous female "secret police" (named for María Barzola, a woman miner who died in the Cataví massacre), organized street demonstrations, hunger strikes, and other political protests.

By 1952 the MNR, led by Victor Paz Estenssoro, finally overthrew the rule of the great landlords and tin barons with the support of armed miners and peasants. The Bolivian land reform, begun by the spontaneous rising of the peasantry and legitimized by the revolutionary government of President Paz Estenssoro, broke the back of the latifundio system in Bolivia. Like the Mexican land reform, however, the Bolivian reform created some new problems even as it solved some old ones. The former latifundia were usually parceled out into very small farms—true minifundia—and the new peasant proprietors received little aid from the government in the form of credit and technical assistance. Yet despite its shortcomings, the Bolivian land reform brought indisputable benefits: some expansion of the internal market, some rise in peasant living standards, and, in the words of Richard W. Patch, "the transformation of a dependent and passive population into an independent and active population."

Women, workers, and indigenous communities became politically energized. Women joined private charitable associations and international organizations like the Inter-American Women's Commission (CIM) to agitate for the right to vote, civil equality, indigenous rights, and greater access to education. Lydia Gueiler Tejada, for example, advocated "the free association of women in legitimate defense of her interests, without distinction of class, race, creed, or even political ideas."

Mineworkers, led by Juan Lechín, demanded nationalization of the tin mines and *control obrero*, workers' control in the management of state-owned mines. Indigenous communities called for immediate, wholesale land reform and greater cultural freedom.

In response, the new government nationalized the principal tin mines, most of which were controlled by three large companies, and recognized its debt to the armed miners by placing the mines under joint labor-government management. It also abolished the literacy and gender restrictions on voting and thus enfranchised women and the indigenous masses. But the new regime inherited a costly, rundown tin industry, while the initial disruptive effect of the agrarian reform on food production added to its economic problems.

Increasingly fearful of the lower classes' revolutionary demands for equality and social justice, and under strong pressure from the United States, which made vitally needed economic aid to the revolutionary government conditional on the adoption of conservative policies, the MNR leadership gradually moved to the right. The government of Paz Estenssoro offered generous compensation to the former owners of expropriated mines, invited new foreign investment on favorable terms, ended labor participation in the management of the government tin company, and reduced welfare benefits to the miners.

Likewise, Paz abandoned any particular interest in women's rights or their social agenda and, instead, cynically manipulated the party's historic support for women's enfranchisement to secure their votes. According to Domitila Barrios de Chungara, a militant activist in the mineworkers' Committee of Housewives (CAC), Paz, who excluded women from leadership positions in the government, nonetheless used the Barzolas women to disrupt radical working-class protests: "the Barzolas would jump in front of them, brandishing razors, penknives, and whips, attacking the demonstrators." But the largely middle-class male movement's patriarchal prejudices clearly limited the political ascendancy of women revolutionaries like Gueiler Tejada, a militant feminist and one-time commander of MNR militias, whose political influence dissipated after she was assigned to a distant diplomatic post in Germany.

Paz also ignored the needs of Bolivia's indigenous peoples, which caused Laureano Machaka, an Aymara peasant leader opposed to the government's policies, to organize a short-lived independent Aymara Republic in 1956. Equally important, Paz agreed to the restoration of a powerful U.S.-trained national army to offset the strength of peasant and worker militias. These retreats broke up the worker–middle class alliance formed during the revolution and facilitated the seizure of power in 1964 by right-wing generals.

In the violent ebb and flow of Bolivian politics since 1964, governments rose and fell, but a persistent theme was the conflict between radical workers, women, students, and nationalist military on the one side and a coalition of elite businessmen, politicians grown wealthy through U.S. aid, and conservative military on the other. The indigenous peasantry, neutralized by the land reform that satisfied its land hunger, initially remained passive or even sided with the government in its struggles with labor, but later unrest began to grow as a result of deteriorating economic conditions.

Major factors in Bolivia's continuing political and economic crisis since 1964 were the collapse in the price of tin, the country's major traditional export, compensated for by the meteoric rise of cocaine as its chief dollar earner; heavy pressure on Bolivia by international lending agencies to adopt neoliberal policies of austerity and privatization; and equally heavy pressure by the United States on Bolivia to take part in a "war on drugs."

The overall rightward direction of Bolivian politics since 1964 was reflected in the important election of July 1985, in which neither former dictator, General Hugo Banzer Suárez, nor Paz Estenssoro, the 78-year-old leader of the 1952 revolution, commanded more than 50 percent of the vote. Disillusioned with politics, two-thirds of the electorate stayed away from the polls.

Although Congress, with the support of leftist deputies, eventually elected Paz president, pressure from Banzer and the International Monetary Fund (IMF), which demanded a severe austerity program as a condition for badly needed new loans, forced him to the right. Accepting the IMF's terms, he slashed government subsidies for basic services and food, froze wages, devalued the currency over 1,000 percent, removed all restrictions on foreign imports and investments, and resumed payments on Bolivia's foreign debt.

In alliance with Banzer, Paz announced a neoliberal plan designed to end hyperinflation and stabilize the economy. The plan, drafted by Harvard economist Jeffrey Sachs, called for closing down as many as eleven unprofitable state-owned mines, laying off thousands of workers, selling other state enterprises to the private sector, making deep cuts in public services, and increasing taxes. Paz's decision to close down Bolivia's largest tin mine in August brought the conflict between the government and the labor movement to a head. The miners' union called a general strike and thousands began a march on the capital of La Paz. The government imposed a state of siege, arresting hundreds of labor and community leaders, and sending troops, tanks, and planes to patrol the mining regions.

The mining crisis added to the tension caused by a 1986 decision to invite U.S. troops to join with the Bolivian military in "Operation Blast Furnace," a campaign to eradicate the country's cocaine laboratories. Ironically, the cocaine trade was the most dynamic sector of Bolivia's economy— despite these well-publicized anti-narcotic raids, this chief source of dollars was compensating for the sharp decline in the country's export earnings. Sale of coca paste generated $600 million annually, one-third more than the nation's legal export earnings of $400 million.

The conflict between the miners and the government took a dramatic turn when some one thousand miners protested government mine-closing plans, the state of siege, and other repressive measures by occupying mine shafts and launching a hunger strike. The miners' plight and the stubborn refusal of the government to negotiate a solution to the conflict caused growing public sympathy and demonstrations of support for the miners. In a momentous show of solidarity, the Bolivian National Federation of Peasant Women led national sympathy strikes and blockades to protest the government's neoliberal policies.

Aware of the unpopularity of its position, the Paz government accepted the offer of church mediation in its dispute with the miners. Eleven days of talks produced an agreement providing for the release of a hundred labor, peasant, and community leaders, a halt to government efforts to close mines, new jobs or compensation for miners who lost jobs, a lifting of the blockade on the flow of supplies to the mining regions, and consultations with the union on further decisions regarding mines.

The miners, the backbone of the *Central Obrera Boliviana* (COB), historically Latin America's strongest labor movement, had beaten off government efforts to destroy their union. But there was no indication of a change in the government's overall economic policy, a neoliberal, free-market policy that sought to eliminate or sell off state-owned industries, remove tariff barriers to foreign imports, and lift all restrictions on foreign investment. The fruits of that policy were apparent in the decline of traditional industries, a drop in consuming power of some 40 percent in 1985–1986, and an unemployment rate of 30 percent.

Paz and Sachs celebrated their program's successful conquest of inflation. However, the resulting high unemployment contradicted their free-market theory that assumed the tens of thousands of displaced miners would find work in the private sector. But the only expanding private-sector economic activity in Bolivia was coca and cocaine production. Thousands of miners, finding no alternative employment, invested the indemnification money they received from the government in land and began to grow coca. Bolivian coca-leaf production increased 60 percent—from 50,000 metric tons before the Sachs plan to 80,000 afterward—making Bolivia the second largest producer of coca. It was also the second largest producer of cocaine. An estimated 500,000 Bolivians were now dependent on the coca economy, which made cocaine "like a cushion that is preventing a social explosion."

The neoliberal policies that made Bolivia dependent on coca cultivation also increased its dependence on U.S. military and financial aid, which ironically was conditioned by an agreement to mobilize the Bolivian army, as an instrument of the U.S. war on drugs, to eradicate coca plantings. Joint U.S.-Bolivian sorties were soon regularly occurring in the Chaparé region, where most of Bolivia's coca was cultivated. But there was no evidence that the sorties, the destruction of access roads, and other military measures won the Bolivian war on drugs. Increasing or declining supplies of coca from the Chaparé region seemed above all to reflect the movement of peasants into and out of coca cultivation according to fluctuations in coca-leaf prices.

Recognition by the Clinton administration that the highly militarized Andean "drug war" approach—after an expenditure of nearly $1 billion—had not achieved its goals, resulted in a sharp reduction in drug war allotments to Bolivia, Colombia, and Peru. Meanwhile, indigenous peasant communities, whose livelihoods increasingly depended on coca-leaf cultivation, fiercely resisted all Bolivian and U.S. military efforts to eradicate it. Under their relentless pressure, the Bolivian government in 1992 sought to decriminalize the coca leaf, as opposed to cocaine. This "coca diplomacy" stressed the coca leaf's alleged medical benefits. Coca had been used for centuries in Bolivia and other Andean countries to alleviate hunger and counter the debilitating effects of living at high altitudes. However, U.S. drug policy sternly opposed any proposal to end the illegal status of the coca leaf.

During the 1990s successive presidential elections provided a forum for populist campaign promises that invariably disguised neoliberal policies. Gonzalo Sánchez de Lozada, a millionaire businessman, won a comfortable victory in 1993, with 36 percent of the vote in a field of four candidates. At his inauguration, attended by Fidel Castro, to whom the new president granted his first formal audience, and by Rigoberta Menchú, the Guatemalan Nobel Peace Prize winner, Sánchez proclaimed his commitment to the country's poor and promised to redistribute income.

But the core of his economic program was the privatization of state enterprises and state restructuring demanded by the IMF and the World Bank

Evo Morales, a leader of Bolivia's indigenous rights movement and defender of peasant coca farmers, emerged as a powerful political force in that nation's 2002 presidential elections. As this poster shows, his campaign, which asked voters to choose between U.S. Ambassador Manuel Rocha and "the voice of the people," focused on the U.S. intervention in Bolivia's internal affairs. [Reuters NewMedia Inc./Corbis]

as the condition for continued economic aid to Bolivia. One month after the inauguration he fired ten thousand state workers, sparking a wave of strikes and demonstrations, led by the Bolivian Workers' Central (COB), that paralyzed the country for weeks.

The crisis over state restructuring, combined with a renewed crisis in the tin-mining industry, itself the result of falling world market prices, led to the closing of hundreds of small mining cooperatives employing thirty-five thousand workers, and to accumulating losses by the much diminished state-owned Corporación Minera de Bolivia (Comibol). Because tin accounted for almost 49 percent of Bolivia's total exports, the fall in its price had a disastrous impact on the country's trade balance.

By the end of Sánchez's term, Bolivian society remained desperately poor; despite moderately high annual economic growth rates, population increases produced an annual per capita income of only $800—next to Haiti, the lowest in the hemisphere. But even this figure understated the social crisis, because real wealth in Bolivia was so unequally distributed: 78 percent of urban households lived below the poverty line, and of these, 40 percent were classified as "indigent," meaning that their income did not cover their most basic needs.

Moreover, poverty there as elsewhere had a distinctively feminine cast: 10 percent of women were single heads of households, 67 percent of whom were raising one or more children. Two-thirds of rural women were illiterate and therefore limited to extremely low-wage jobs. Thirty-three percent of all children were chronically malnourished. Even Sánchez conceded that "while the economy is going well, what is going poorly are the social problems of the country."

The decade ended with neoliberalism firmly entrenched in the policies of the new president and former dictator Hugo Banzer, who soon resigned for health reasons in favor of Jorge Quiroga. This produced a stable, even impressive, economic growth rate averaging 4 percent annually, as elsewhere in the region largely financed by high interest rates to attract foreign capital, which expanded external debt from $385 to $494 million by 1999. But it also left over 5 million people—60 percent of the nation's population—impoverished, with the second-highest infant mortality rate (57 of 1000) in the hemisphere and the third-lowest life expectancy (64). Underemployment was widespread and unemployment rates hovered around 12 percent. Bolivian women, workers, trade unions, indigenous rights activists, and debtors' organizations increasingly joined together to protest neoliberalism's negative social consequences; they often won modest victories—for example, reversing the privatization of parts of the state-owned Bolivian Mining Company (COMIBOL) in 2002.

As the new millennium opened, it was clear that more than a decade of neoliberalism had brought Bolivia no closer to prosperity or balanced development. Even the *Economist*, the conservative English tribune of free trade, had to acknowledge that Bolivia's experience had sorely tested faith in market forces: "Market economics, whatever its promise for the future, has not brought prosperity to the poor."

This apparently also was a conclusion reached by the declining share of politically active Bolivians. In the 2002 elections, none of the presidential candidates sang the praises of privatization and unfettered markets. Former president and millionaire mine owner Gonzalo Sánchez de Lozada, who won a narrow plurality (22 percent) of the vote, promised to improve the free market by using state revenues to create jobs. But all the others severely criticized neoliberalism and called for its rejection or reform. The candidate of the Movement Toward Socialism (MAS), Evo Morales, a defiant leader of indigenous coca growers, shocked all observers by finishing second in the balloting with 20.94 percent. He advocated indigenous rights, suspension of foreign debt service, renationalization of industries privatized over the previous two decades, and state regulation of the economy to reduce poverty and promote greater social equality. Because no candidate received 50 percent of the vote, the new Congress selected Sánchez. Nonetheless, two things seemed certain: indigenous peoples, whose congressional representation increased from 10 to 30 percent, would play a more influential role in the nation's future, and there would be a change in the reigning neoliberal development model. According to Bolivian political analyst Carlos Toranzo, Evo Morales and Bolivia's newly mobilized indigenous rights movement represented "ideas that are in style all over the world—antiglobalization, antineoliberalism, anti-imperialism."

ECUADOR, 1972–2003

Ecuador, the smallest of the Andean republics, experienced the faint beginnings of a social revolution in 1972, when a group of nationalist military headed by General Guillermo Rodríguez Lara ousted the aging, demagogic President José María Velasco Ibarra, who had dominated Ecuadorian politics for the previous four decades. Velasco Ibarra had favored a dependent industrialization, shaped by the Alliance for Progress and based on massive importation of foreign capital and goods. This rapid modernization rested on the 1964 Agrarian Reform Act, which abolished the *huasipungo*, the country's serf-like labor system, expropriated church lands and inefficient haciendas, but also promoted colonization of so-called *tierras baldías*, untitled lands most of which had been occupied historically by self-sufficient indigenous communities. The discovery of oil in lowland territories in the late 1960s accelerated incursions into indigenous lands and cultural autonomy, even as petroleum production threatened the environment by contaminating surface and underground water supplies. By the early 1970s, foreign interests controlled some 35 percent of all industrial enterprises, nearly 60 percent of all commercial enterprises, and half of all banking assets in Ecuador.

The new nationalistic military junta promised social reform, including radical land reform, and offered a program of rapid economic development that stressed industrialization and the modernization of agriculture. It also promised to reverse previous official policy that surrendered the country's rich oil resources in the Amazonian lowlands to foreign companies. The new government counted on revenue from oil to finance the planned reforms and program of economic development.

Five years later, however, the advance of the Ecuadorian Revolution appeared to be stalled. Opposition from the still-powerful hacendado class had almost completely paralyzed agrarian and tax reform. Some land had been distributed to the peasants, but big landowners controlled 80 percent of the cultivated area. The military government appeared virtually to have abandoned land redistribution in favor of cooperating with the hacendados to increase production and revenues by mechanization, greater concentration of landownership, and the ouster of peasants from the land. The result was growing peasant agitation for true land reform, accompanied by invasions of estates and clashes between peasants and security forces.

Finally, under pressure from foreign oil companies for lower taxes and wider profit margins—a pressure exerted through a boycott on oil exports—the military regime also retreated from its insistence on tight control over prices, profits, and the volume and rate of oil production. These concessions represented a defeat for the nationalist left wing of the military junta and sharpened the divisions within it.

In Ecuador, as in other Latin American countries under military control, the late 1970s saw a growing popular movement for social justice and a return to civilian rule. But unlike other countries in the region, groups like the Indigenous People's Organization of Pastaza (OPIP), founded in 1979, increasingly played an influential role in these movements, joining with women's rights activists and trade unionists. In addition to a return to democracy, indigenous leaders demanded that the government recognize their communal land titles, cultural identities, and political autonomy.

Aware of its economic failures and especially its failure to relieve the dismal poverty of the Ecuadorian masses—official figures showed that the wage earners' share of the national income had declined from 53 percent in 1960 to less than 46 percent in 1973 and that 7 percent of the population received more than 50 percent of the national income—the military appeared quite willing to abandon the burden of governing the country. In July 1978, Jaime Roldós, a populist candidate, handily won the ensuing presidential election. During the campaign, the young, energetic Roldós promised to revive agrarian reform and end foreign economic control.

Central to this program was the use of large amounts of Ecuador's oil earnings to modernize agriculture, promote industrialization, and construct a network of roads to expand the internal market. Roldós's five-year plan called for investment of $800 million in rural development that would bring some 3 million acres of coastal, highland, and Amazonian farmland into new production. The pace of agrarian reform was to be accelerated, with almost 2 million acres to be distributed to landless peasants by 1984. Roldós's foreign policy stressed greater independence from the United States, reflected in his maintenance of friendly relations with Cuba, expansion of diplomatic and commercial ties with socialist countries, and support for Central American revolutionary movements. But Roldós's ambitious reform and development program had hardly begun when he was killed in a plane crash in May 1981.

His successor inherited deteriorating economic conditions as a result of a developing recession and declining prices for Ecuadorian oil. The economic slump sharpened the social problems created by advances in industrialization and the modernization of agriculture. From 1970 to 1980 the proportion of peasants in the population had fallen from 68 percent to 52 percent. The agrarian reform, stressing mechanization and concentration of landownership rather than distribution of land to the landless, had ended semiservile relations in the countryside but aggravated the problem of landlessness and rural unemployment. The result was to swell the number of rural people fleeing to the cities in search of work that only few found. By the early 1980s the great port city of Guayaquil had a population of 1,000,000; an estimated two-thirds of its inhabitants were unemployed or underemployed and lacked adequate shelter, food, or medical care. Thus, in an atmosphere of economic and political crisis, social problems and tension accumulated with little prospect that solutions would soon be found.

In the mid-1980s, Ecuador, like Bolivia, became the scene of a determined effort to implement the free-market, neoliberal policies for which the United States under the Reagan administration provided a model. In 1984 León Febres Cordero was elected president and signed an agreement with the IMF to defer payment on Ecuador's foreign debt, which stood at about $7 billion and consumed more than 30 percent of Ecuador's export earnings to pay interest. The price exacted was that usually demanded of Third World countries by the IMF: Ecuador must take steps to encourage foreign investment and restrict domestic consumption, lower tariffs on foreign imports, and modify the monetary exchange system in favor of exporters. In this and in other ways, Febres justified the tribute paid to him by President Reagan when he visited Washington in January 1986: Febres, declared Reagan, was "an articulate champion of free enterprise."

A balance sheet of the impact of Febres Cordero's economic and social policies on Ecuadorian living standards made dismal reading. A study by Ecuador's Catholic University disclosed that foreign corporations took three dollars out of the country for every dollar they invested. Between 1981 and 1984 workers' share of national income fell from 32 to 20 percent and employers' profits rose from 60 to 70 percent. Ninety percent of schoolchildren suffered from parasitic diseases, and the infant mortality rate according to various estimates stood at between 150 and 250 per thousand.

In the 1988 general elections, Ecuadorians voiced their displeasure with neoliberalism. The country's trade unions mobilized behind a program calling for the nationalization of the oil industry, the rescinding of price hikes, and a 100 percent increase in the country's $80-per-month minimum wage. They helped elect Rodrigo Borja Cevallos, whose campaign stressed social needs over debt interest payments to foreign banks. But Borja faced what he called "the worst economic crisis" in Ecuador's history. In the last four years food prices had jumped 240 percent and half the labor force was unemployed or underemployed. The crisis sharply limited Borja's options in economic and social policy. A moderate leftist in the social democratic mold, Borja assured businessmen that his government would carry out no nationalizations but would seek to regulate the economy and support the private sector.

His efforts to achieve debt payment relief met with resistance from the foreign banks: Ecuador was forced to accept IMF demands for a devaluation of its currency, a commitment to raise fuel prices, and other austerity measures as a condition for starting debt rescheduling talks with creditor banks. As a result, the Borja regime faced growing opposition both on the right and among its former supporters on the left. Denouncing Borja's economic policies as unjust and dictated by the IMF, the socialist parties joined conservatives in voting censure of the ministers responsible for the austerity measures.

The growing militancy of Ecuadorian labor, reflected in a 1991 general strike, was matched by that of indigenous peoples, who made up more than 40 percent of the country's population. In 1990 organizations like OPIP and the Ecuadorian Confederation of Indigenous Nationalities (CONAIE) spearheaded the Inti Raymi uprising, which mobilized hundreds of thousands of supporters from eight provinces in the sierra and several in the Amazon. The indigenous demands included land redistribution and a constitutional declaration that Ecuador was a multiethnic country. Although the government agreed to dialogue with indigenous leaders, pressure from the great planters and ranchers resulted in the government's abandoning its promises. The new militancy of indigenous peoples, traditionally reputed to be peaceful and docile, caused alarm among the country's landed elite.

By 1992, Ecuadorians had come to distrust Borja's promises and opted instead for the populist pledges of Sixto Durán-Ballén, who campaigned on a program of state reconstruction and privatization. But his plan for the "modernization of the state" called for the dismissal of up to 120,000 employees out of a total state sector of 400,000 over the following four years and the privatization of 160 state companies. Durán-Ballén also announced a structural adjustment package that included a 35 percent devaluation of the national currency, fuel price increases of more than 125 percent, rises in electricity rates of up to 90 percent, and a 190 percent increase in cooking-gas prices.

Received with enthusiasm by international financial institutions, this plan caused an immediate drastic decline in Durán-Ballén's popularity at home. The major trade union, the United Workers' Front (FUT) and CONAIE both opposed him. Two months into his four-year term, a poll showed that half of those who had voted for him would not do so again and 75 percent disapproved of his policies. In mid-1993 the unions claimed that living standards had fallen by 50 percent since Durán-Ballén had taken office. The minimum wage was about

$30 a month, but unofficial estimates put the cost of a shopping basket of basic goods at about $250.

In 1993 this opposition mounted a successful "guerrilla campaign" of strikes and demonstrations to limit the government's neoliberal "modernization" program. Peremptory dismissals of state employees were abandoned, and the privatization of state companies in areas regarded as "strategic," such as oil, telecommunications, and electric power, would require the passage of special laws by Congress.

A nationwide teachers' strike, the longest such strike in Ecuador's history, grew into a major battle in the war between the president and labor. It was provoked when Durán-Ballén pushed through Congress changes in the code governing teachers' salary scales and school administration. The strike became a battle of wills; it ended after Congress passed a new package of changes that restored the status quo and assured the National Educators' Union's participation in school policy-making. The union declared that the strike was a turning point in the grassroots struggle against "the IMF-dictated policies that [the government] is implementing."

Another front in Ecuador's social wars opened when indigenous Huaoranis, who live deep in the Ecuadorian Amazon, traveled to Quito in 1993 to protest the intrusion of oil companies into their territory. The protest was aimed at halting the construction of a highway by the Dallas-based company Maxus that would run through the heart of the Huaorani reserves. The Huaorani complained that the road would bring in thousands of settlers and land speculators, leading to deforestation, loss of animal and plant species, and destruction of the indigenous economy and way of life.

Although President Durán-Ballén met with the Huaorani, he made no promises. But even the state oil company (Petroecuador) admitted that since 1972, when Ecuador began oil production in large quantities, pipeline failures had dumped 450,000 barrels of oil into the Amazon forest. According to a 1993 "Letter from the Amazon" in *The New Yorker*, "a spill filled the Napo [River] with a slick that stretched from bank to bank for forty miles." The Huaorani, wrote reporter Joe Kane,

"were trapped in the path of an American juggernaut, their fate bound up with a culture whose thirst for oil was second to none." "It is likely," Kane noted sardonically, "that the Huaorani will be wiped out for the sake of enough oil to meet United States energy needs for thirteen days."

The Huaorani promised to use force if necessary to prevent construction of the highway. In 1993 other Ecuadorian indigenous groups filed a billion-dollar class action suit in New York against the Texaco oil conglomerate over massive environmental devastation of the Oriente rain forest. According to the suit, Texaco knowingly dumped millions of gallons of crude oil into open pits and lakes in the region at the rate of 3,000 gallons a day for twenty years. A Harvard University study confirmed that most residents of the area suffered severe health problems as a result of the dumping.

By the 1996 presidential elections, Durán-Ballén's popularity had declined from more than 70 percent to less than 10 percent because of his neoliberal economic policies. Simultaneously, indigenous peoples joined with Afro-Ecuadorians, women, students, trade unions, and peasant organizations to form the Movement of National Pluricultural Unity Pachakutik, a political coalition that won many state offices and successfully lobbied for the creation of CONPLADEIN, an independent state agency, to represent the autonomous cultural and economic interests of black and indigenous Ecuadorians. Pachakutik, though a successful and growing political party, still functioned as a powerful social movement that mobilized "pluricultural" opposition to the newly elected President Abdala Bucaram, a wealthy businessman who also violated his 1996 populist presidential campaign promises by privatizing state assets and cutting state spending on social services. By February 1997, outrage over this violation of campaign promises, fueled also by charges of widespread corruption, led directly to Bucaram's ouster, an ensuing political crisis, and economic chaos, exacerbated by devastating El Niño–inspired floods that wiped out whole villages and destroyed basic infrastructure.

In 1998, after campaigning on a populist platform, new president Jamil Mahuad, a Harvard

In 2000, indigenous rights protesters joined with disgruntled army officers and various social movements to denounce the neoliberal polices of Ecuador's President Jamil Mahuad. His subsequent resignation unleashed a national political instability that recently culminated in the 2002 presidential election of Lucio Gutiérrez, a military officer who had supported the populist rebellion. [AFP/Corbis]

graduate, faced an economic crisis aggravated by a steep decline in global oil prices and sought relief by implementing a neoliberal austerity program in exchange for an $800 million IMF loan. His government promptly declared a state of emergency, abolished income taxes, bailed out the nation's private banks, doubled gasoline prices, and reduced spending on social services for the 60 percent of the nation's population classified as poor. Strikes and massive, angry protest marches proliferated. Unemployment grew to more than 50 percent and

Mahuad's popularity fell to 16 percent, prompting even his congressional allies to abandon him.

In January 2000 the United Workers' Front and CONAIE, representing indigenous peoples, together organized massive protests against Mahuad's neoliberal privatization plans and his dramatic increase of the price of bus transportation and cooking gas, all of which targeted the nation's poor majority and curried favor with wealthy Ecuadorian business leaders and foreign bankers. Angered by military budget cuts, elements of Ecuador's army later joined the opposition and effectively forced Mahuad to resign. Fearing the radicalism of this popular rising, especially its indigenous complexion, military officers in this racially and class-stratified nation organized a countercoup to restore Mahuad's vice president, Gustavo Noboa, to power.

Although he initially made concessions, Noboa soon confronted an economic crisis in which inflation surpassed 90 percent, unemployment exceeded 10 percent, and external debt almost equaled the total value of the nation's GDP. To tame inflation and generate revenues to repay foreign bankers, Noboa adopted the U.S. dollar as the nation's currency, slashed social spending, and sought to privatize an array of state resources, prompting domestic business elites to celebrate and popular forces to renew their resistance. Now joined by university students, CONAIE and the popular coalition launched yet another massive demonstration to "combat the neoliberal economic model." But this time, with thousands of indigenous peoples camped out in Quito, they also pressed the Noboa government to end its cooperation with U.S. and Colombian forces seeking to militarize the border and use Ecuadorian military bases to support Plan Colombia, a U.S. proposal for a military solution to neighboring Colombia's decades-long conflict.

Negotiations to end the protest ultimately reinforced the social movement's power and its grassroots democratic structure; the protestors won various concessions, including increased spending on national indigenous health, education, and development projects and a pledge to end "the regionalization of Plan Colombia, and the involvement of Ecuador in foreign conflicts." Emboldened by these gains, the protesters mobilized in support of the 2002 presidential candidacy of Lucio Gutiérrez, a retired colonel who had joined the 2000 rebellion of workers and indigenous people. Gutiérrez promised to reduce poverty, create jobs, and stimulate national production. He pledged to root out business corruption, reform tariffs, and allocate 15 percent of the budget to public works projects.

Notwithstanding these important victories for the popular opposition, the contest over Ecuador's future was far from over. A traditional propertied elite preserved its privileged positions and, dependent upon a foreign debt whose repayment annually consumed 25 percent of export income, Ecuador remained vulnerable to external pressure to ignore the democratic voice of its own citizens in favor of a developmental model that they unambiguously rejected. In fact, "dollarization" of the economy effectively limited the capacity of domestic democratic politics to affect national economic policy and also reinforced the nation's economic dependency on the United States, because it now had to pay for the importation of its circulating currency. Augusto de la Torre, director of the World Bank's Ecuador office, candidly admitted that "politics are now less relevant in Ecuador. If you talk to entrepreneurs now, they look at politics like they look at soap operas." As the importance of electoral politics receded, it was clear that, in the words of a Pachacutik representative, "the struggle will continue in other forms."

PERU'S "AMBIGUOUS REVOLUTION"

A revolution of a unique kind began in Peru in October 1968. Developments in that country between 1968 and 1975 exposed the fallacy of the common assumption that the Latin American military constitutes one reactionary mass. Moving with greater speed and vigor than any civilian reformist regime in Latin American history, a military junta headed by General Juan Velasco Alvarado decreed nationalization of key industries and natural resources, land reform that transferred great estates to peasant and worker cooperatives, and creation of novel new forms of economic organization that should be "neither capitalist nor communist." In 1975 the Peruvian Revolution halted its advance and began a retreat that threatened even its major conquests—the agrarian reform and the great nationalizations— with erosion and even destruction. Yet it must rank among the more serious recent Latin American efforts to achieve a breakthrough in the struggle against backwardness and dependency. Despite its mistakes and failures, it made an indelible mark on Peruvian society. The study of those mistakes and failures should help Peruvians as they search for new approaches to the solution of their country's great national problems.

Peru's "ambiguous revolution" poses some intriguing questions. Why should a group of military officers, a class commonly regarded as the staunchest defenders of the old order in Latin America, launch a major attack on that order in Peru? What economic and social interests did the Peruvian military reformers represent? In the last analysis, was the Peruvian Revolution a "bourgeois revolution" designed to promote the rise of an autonomous native capitalism? If the military reformers failed to make a clean break with the past, with the model of dependent development and the problems it generates, what were the reasons for that failure? An attempt to answer these questions requires an examination not only of the revolution itself but of its late nineteenth century origins.

Neocolonial Peru: The English and North American Connections, 1883–1968

The War of the Pacific left a heritage of political and social turbulence as well as economic ruin. Military and civilian leaders disputed one another's claims to be the legitimate president and mobilized *montoneros* (bands of guerrillas and outlaws) for their armed struggles. In some areas, the indigenous peasantry, having acquired arms during the war with Chile, rose in revolt against oppressive hacendados and local officials. Banditry was rife in parts of the sierra; on the coast, factions armed by landowners or their agents fought among themselves for control of irrigation canals or over property boundaries.

From the struggle for power the militarists once again emerged victorious: in 1884 Andrés Cáceres battled his way into Lima and seized the National Palace. Two years later, he was elected president for a four-year term. Under Cáceres, a slow, painful process of economic recovery began. His first concern was the huge foreign debt. In 1886 the Peruvian government negotiated the so-

called Grace Contract with British bondholders. This agreement created a Peruvian Corporation, controlled by the British bondholders, that assumed the servicing of Peru's foreign debt and received in exchange Peru's railways for a period of sixty-six years. The agreement confirmed British financial domination of Peru but also initiated a new flow of investments that hastened the country's economic recovery. Particularly important was the resulting rehabilitation of the railways and their extension to important mining centers, especially into La Oroya, whose rich silver, zinc, and lead mines began to contribute to the economic revival.

Economic recovery strengthened the political hand of the planter aristocracy and the commercial bourgeoisie, who were increasingly impatient with the arbitrary ways of the military caudillos. In 1895 their leader was the flamboyant Nicolás Piérola, who sought to bring the military under civilian control and led a successful revolt against Cáceres. Piérola presided over four years of rapid economic recovery. On the coast, the sugar plantations expanded at the expense of small landholders and indigenous communities and underwent intensive modernization. In the Andes, the economic revival spurred a renewed drive by hacendados to acquire indigenous communal lands, a drive extended to regions hitherto free from land-grabbing. An 1893 law that in effect reenacted Bolívar's decree concerning the division and distribution of communal lands facilitated the process of land acquisition. In this period there also arose a new contract labor system, the *enganche*, designed to solve the labor problem of coastal landlords now that Chinese contract labor was no longer easily available. By this system, indígenas from the sierra were recruited for prolonged periods to labor on coastal haciendas, sometimes under conditions of virtual serfdom.

INDIGENOUS RESISTANCE

Yet the postwar period also saw the birth of a new sensitivity to the social struggle of indigenous peoples. The rise of this *indigenismo* among intellectuals was closely connected with the crisis of conscience caused by the disastrous War of the Pacific. By exposing the incompetence and irresponsibility of a creole elite that had totally failed to prepare Peru materially and morally for its greatest ordeal, the war led many intellectuals to turn to the indigenous peasantry as a possible source of national regeneration. At the University of San Marcos in Lima there arose a generation of teachers who rejected the traditional positivist tendency to brand Indians as inherently inferior. The alleged apathy, inertia, and alcoholism of indigenous peoples, these scholars claimed, resulted from the narrow, dwarfed world in which they were forced to live. But as a rule these bourgeois reformers ignored the economic conditions of indigenous peoples and focused on a program of education and uplift that would teach them ways to enter the new capitalist society.

The great iconoclast Manuel González Prada (1848–1918) rejected this gradual, reformist approach to the problem. "The Indian question is an economic and social question rather than one of pedagogy," he wrote. Schools and well-intentioned laws could not change a feudal reality based on the economic and political power of the *gamonales* (great landowners), lords of all they surveyed. Elimination of the hacienda system, therefore, was needed to rescue indigenous people. But that change would never come through the benevolence of the ruling class: "The Indian must achieve his redemption through his own efforts, not through the humanity of his oppressors." And González Prada advised them to spend on rifles and cartridges the money they now wasted on drink and fiestas. His powerful indictment of the oppressors of indigenous peoples, his faith in their creative capacity, and his rebellious spirit, expressed in prose that flowed like molten lava, profoundly influenced the next generation of intellectuals.

For their part, indigenous highland communities, whose passive resistance to the gamonales' encroachment on their lands and autonomy the intellectuals had mistaken for laziness and apathy, now openly rebelled. Sparked by indigenous leaders like Teodomiro Gutiérrez Cuevas, the Rumi Maqui movement, a millenarian insurrection that swept like wildfire through southern Peru and the central sierra between 1915 and 1930, proclaimed the restoration of Tawantinsuyu, the fabled empire of the great Inca kings.

THE RETURN OF PARDO

Integration of indigenous peoples was Peru's gravest social problem, but the rapid economic advance that began under Piérola produced the emergence of a working class whose demands also threatened the peace and security of the ruling class. By 1904 an organized labor movement had arisen, and strikes broke out in Lima's textile mills and other factories. In 1918, during World War I, miners, port workers, and textile workers, responding to a catastrophic inflation of food prices, went on strike. Armed clashes took place between the strikers and the troops sent out to disperse them, and many strikers were arrested. News of the success of the Russian Revolution contributed to the workers' militancy. This movement culminated in a three-day general strike in January 1919; the workers demanded the implementation of currently unenforced social legislation, the reduction of food prices, and the imposition of the eight-hour workday. Under pressure from the workers, President Manuel Pardo granted part of their demands, including the eight-hour day for the manufacturing and extractive industries. The labor struggles of that stormy year merged with the struggle of university students for the reform of an archaic system of higher education that made the university the preserve of a privileged few and denied students any voice in determining policies and faculty appointments.

But sections of the oligarchy were convinced that this new and unstable political and social atmosphere required a different way of ruling. An astute businessman and politician, Augusto B. Leguía, who had served as minister of finance in the early 1900s and as president from 1908 to 1912, offered a new political model that could be called Caesarist: it combined unswerving fidelity to the dominant domestic and foreign interests with severe repression of dissidents and a demagogic program of nationalism and social reform designed to disarm the workers and achieve class peace. In July 1919 he seized power, sent Pardo into exile, and established a personal dictatorship that lasted eleven years (1919–1930).

THE LEGUÍA REGIME: NORTH AMERICAN INVESTMENT AND PERUVIAN DISILLUSIONMENT

Leguía encouraged by every means at his disposal the influx of foreign—especially North American—capital. This was the cornerstone of his economic policies. Oil and copper were major fields of North American investment in Peru in this period. The fruits of Leguía's policy of opening the doors wide to foreign capital soon became evident; in 1927 a vice president of the First National City Bank wrote that "Peru's principal sources of wealth, the mines and oil-wells, are nearly all foreign-owned, and excepting for wages and taxes, no part of the value of their production remains in the country." Perhaps the most scandalous example of Leguía's policy of giving away Peru's natural resources was his cession of the oil-rich La Brea–Pariñas fields near the northern coastal town of Talara to the International Petroleum Company (IPC), a subsidiary of Standard Oil of New Jersey, in return for a minimal tax of about 71 cents a ton. This cession and a 1922 arbitral award confirming the dubious claims to the area in question of an English oil company, whose rights had passed to the IPC, became an abiding source of Peruvian nationalist resentment.

Peru under Leguía received a plentiful infusion of North American loans, amounting to about $130 million. The bankers were aware of the risks involved, but the prospects of extremely large profits made these transactions very attractive. A trail of corruption, involving Leguía's own family, followed these deals; Leguía's son Juan, acting as agent for Peru, received more than half a million dollars in commissions.

Leguía used the proceeds of these loans and the taxes on foreign trade and foreign investment operations for a massive public works program (including a large road-building program carried out with forced indigenous labor) that contributed to the boom of the 1920s. During those years, Lima was largely rebuilt, provided with modern drinking water and sanitation facilities, and embellished with new parks, avenues, bank buildings, a racetrack, and a military casino. But these amenities did not improve the living conditions of Andean peoples or dwellers in the wretched *barriadas* (shantytowns) that began to ring Lima.

Convinced that the threat of communism required some concessions to the masses, however, Leguía did make some gestures in the direction of reform. The constitution of 1920 had some striking resemblances to the Mexican constitution of 1917. It declared the right of the state to limit property rights in the interest of the nation, vested ownership of natural resources in the state, and committed the state to the construction of hospitals, asylums, and clinics. It empowered the government to set the hours of labor and to insure adequate compensation and safe and sanitary conditions of work. It also offered corporate recognition of indigenous communities, proclaimed their right to land, and promised primary education to their children. But these and other provisions of the constitution were, in the words of Fredrick Pike, a "model for the Peru that never was."

That same contrast between promises and performance marked Leguía's labor policy. During his campaign for the presidency, he denounced "reactionaries" and made lavish promises to the workers. Indeed, on seizing power in July 1919 he immediately freed the labor leaders imprisoned under Pardo. He also permitted a congress of workers to meet in Lima in 1921 and form a Federation of Workers of Lima and Callao. But when the labor movement began to display excessive independence, he intervened to crush it. Workers were forced to accept token reforms and a program of government- and church-sponsored paternalism, crumbs from the well-laden table of the wealthy.

Leguía's performance was especially disillusioning to the university students. Impressed by his promises of educational reform, they had proclaimed him "Mentor of the Youth" and supported his presidential campaign in 1919. But once in power, he sought to drive a wedge between students and workers, jailing student leaders and outlawing the Popular University of González Prada, organized by the students to provide workers with political education. Frequent jailings and deportations of dissident journalists and professors brought Leguía into chronic confrontation with students and faculty, who often went on strike, while the University of San Marcos was repeatedly closed down by the government.

The fledgling women's rights movement also fragmented during the Leguía dictatorship. In 1914, María Jesús Alvarado Rivera had created *Evolución Feminina*, a journal devoted to the cultivation of cross-class, interracial alliances in pursuit of women's liberation and social justice. But patrician women refused to join these mixed-race organizations. According to Carrie Chapman Catt, the U.S. feminist and president of the Pan-American Women's Suffrage Alliance, "the pure castillian woman would die before she moved equally herself with those of color." As a result, an aristocratic Peruvian National Women's Council supported Leguía, resisted broader social reforms, and largely favored enfranchisement of literate women because it would strengthen their conservative cause. Radicals like Alvarado and Magda Portal soon abandoned this feminism dominated by *"damas patrióticas civilistas"* and joined the class struggle against Leguía.

INDIGENISMO AND SOCIALISM

The traditional oligarchical parties' surrender to the dictator and the weakness of the young Peruvian working class meant that the leadership of the opposition to Leguía fell to middle- and lower-middle-class intellectuals who sought to mobilize the peasantry and the workers for the achievement of their revolutionary aims. Socialism, anti-imperialism, and indigenismo provided the ideological content of the movement that issued from the struggles of the turbulent year of 1919, but indigenismo was the most important ingredient.

Influenced by the revered González Prada, these intellectuals believed that the revolution necessary to regenerate Peru must come from the sierra, from the Andean indigenous peoples, who would destroy age-old systems of oppression and

unify Peru again, restoring the grandeur that had been the Inca Empire. Common to most of the indigenistas was the belief that the Inca Empire had been a model of primitive socialist organization (a thesis rejected by modern scholars) and that the indigenous community had been and still was the "indestructible backbone of Peruvian collectivity" (in fact, by the 1920s almost all land in Peru was individually owned and worked). The mission of the intellectuals, they believed, was to blow life into the coals of indigenous rebellion and link it to the urban revolution of students and workers.

An influential indigenista of this period was Luis E. Valcarcel, author of the widely read *Tempest in the Andes* (1927). In ecstatic prose, Valcarcel hailed indigenous revolts of the sierra as portents of the coming purifying revolution. A more important and systematic thinker, José Carlos Mariátegui (1895–1930), attempted the task of wedding indigenismo to the scientific socialism of Marx and Engels. His major work was the *Seven Interpretive Essays on Peruvian Reality* (1928). Basing his theory on indigenous communal practices and traditions, on the revolutionary experience of other lands, and on his study of history and economics, Mariátegui concluded that socialism offered the only true solution for the indigenous problems.

Like other indigenistas of his time, Mariátegui idealized the Inca Empire, which he regarded as the "most advanced primitive communist organization which history records." But he opposed a "romantic and anti-historical tendency of reconstruction or re-creation of Inca socialism," for only its habits of cooperation and corporate life should be retained by modern scientific socialism. Moreover, he stressed that the coming revolution must be led by the urban proletariat. Before his untimely death, Mariátegui in 1929 founded the Peruvian Communist Party, which affiliated the next year with the Communist International.

Indigenismo was a major plank in the program of the *Alianza Popular Revolucionaria Americana* (APRA), a party founded in Mexico in May 1924 by Victor Raúl Haya de la Torre and Magda Portal, student leaders who had been exiled by Leguía. Haya de la Torre proclaimed that APRA's mission was to lead the indigenous and proletarian masses of Peru and all "Indo-America" in the coming socialist, anti-imperialist revolution. Despite the high-sounding rhetoric of *Aprista* propaganda, the party's first concern was and remained Peru's middle sectors—artisans, small landowners, professionals, and small capitalists. These groups' opportunities for development diminished as a result of the growing concentration of economic power in Peru by foreign firms and a dependent big bourgeoisie.

In a revealing statement in the mid-1920s, Haya de la Torre declared that the Peruvian working class, whether rural or urban, lacked the class consciousness and maturity needed to qualify it for the leadership of the coming revolution. He assigned that role to the middle class. To this opinion he joined a belief in the mission of the great man (himself) who "interprets, intuits, and directs the vague and imprecise aspirations of the multitude." Portal's view of Peruvian women was equally condescending; without APRA's guidance, she insisted, they could not be entrusted with the vote because of their low "cultural level" and "unquestioning dependence on masculine influence."

Haya de la Torre early assumed an ambiguous position on imperialism. Standing on its head Lenin's theory that imperialism was the last stage of capitalism, he argued that in weak, underdeveloped countries like Peru, imperialism was not the last but the first stage of capitalism, for there it provided the capital needed to create industry, a powerful working class, and the middle class that would lead the nation in a socialist revolution. From this to the position that imperialism must be encouraged and defended was an easy step, one that Haya de la Torre eventually took. Mariátegui, who was associated with Haya de la Torre in the student and labor struggles of the early 1920s, soon perceived the inconsistencies and ambiguities of his position and assailed APRA for its "bluff and lies" and its personalism. Despite or precisely because of its opportunism and the vagueness of its ideology, APRA managed to win over an important section of the Peruvian middle class, especially the students, during the three decades after 1920 and to gain great influence over groups of

peasantry and urban workers, whom it organized into unions that were its main political base.

APRA VERSUS THE MILITARY

The onset of a world economic crisis in 1929, which caused a serious decline of Peruvian exports and dried up the influx of loans, brought the collapse of the Leguía dictatorship. But neither the small Communist party nor the stronger APRA movement was able to take political advantage of Leguía's downfall. An army officer of *cholo* (indigenous) background, Luis Sánchez Cerro, seized power and became the dominant figure in a ruling military junta. In 1931, Sánchez Cerro won the presidency campaigning on a populist platform that proclaimed the primacy of the indigenous problem, the need for agrarian reform through expropriation of uncultivated lands, and the aim of regulating foreign investments in the national interest. In effect, Sánchez Cerro had stolen much of APRA's thunder, to the annoyance of Haya de la Torre.

But the Apristas refused to accept the election results and launched an unsuccessful revolt in 1932 that led to mass executions and the assassination of Sánchez Cerro. This created a vendetta between the army and APRA that helps explain the long, stubborn opposition of the Peruvian armed forces to APRA's assumption of power, whether by force or peaceful means. More important, it enabled the financial and landed oligarchy to consolidate their power. Thereafter, they courted foreign investors like the U.S.-based International Petroleum Company, promoted export production, and presided over a stagnant economy due to low prices for the country's chief exports (copper, cotton, lead, and wool), a situation only temporarily relieved by growing demand and high prices during World War II (1939–1945) and the Korean war (1950–1953).

In the wars' aftermath, however, Peru, despite modest development of its extractive mineral industry, remained a largely agricultural, export-dependent country with a wealthy, powerful landed oligarchy, a weak and fragmented middle class, a marginalized indigenous peasant majority, and a largely unorganized and undeveloped urban working class. Nonetheless, APRA militants continued to agitate for policies designed to restore popular democracy, renew anti-imperialist struggle, and promote social justice. Largely influenced by the *comandos femeninos*, these policies included land reform; civil and political equality irrespective of race, class, or gender; and state regulation of foreign investment. In 1955, at the end of General Manuel Odría's dictatorial rule, Peruvian women finally won the right to vote, but little more. APRA's male leadership, fearful of a growing lower-class power, increasingly abandoned women and their social justice issues to curry favor with conservative elites.

Meanwhile the inequities of Peru's income distribution continued to increase, as did collisions between large landowners and increasingly militant and well-organized indigenous peasants. In some cases, peasants were revolting against precapitalist labor systems (like the yanacona system, which often required personal service); in others, violence arose as a result of the efforts of landowners to evict their tenants and sheep in favor of wage labor and cash rent systems. These evictions increased landlessness and population pressure in indigenous communities and accelerated the flow of highland emigrants to the coast, swelling the population of city slums and shantytowns.

This first generation of indigenous highland migrants, known as *provincianos*, now found themselves in a foreign environment, surrounded by hostile urban elites who ridiculed their rural lifestyles, scorned their racial origins, and limited their social, economic, and political opportunities. For hundreds of years, Peru's *criollo* elite had preserved its cultural authority and political power by institutionalizing a rigid race-based social hierarchy that defined criollos as "white," civilized, and superior; it likewise identified indigenous peoples, mestizos, and blacks as inferior, barbaric, ignorant, and uncivilized. Not surprisingly, the new migrants sought to assimilate into their strange surroundings by publicly emulating criollo culture even as they privately celebrated their various highland traditions. They settled together in *barriadas* (slums) or *pueblos jovenes* (squatter communities) and often supported their families by opening small businesses in the informal sector, selling a broad range of commodities on street corners or working as domestic servants. By the early 1960s, however, this postwar demographic shift had transformed them into a potentially useful political constituency that successive criollo politicians sought to exploit.

BELAÚNDE: BROKEN PROMISES

In 1963, Peruvians elected President Fernando Belaúnde Terry, whose campaign had a decided indigenista tinge. Visiting the remotest Andean villages, Belaúnde extolled the Inca grandeur, called on the natives to emulate the energy and hard work of their ancestors, and proclaimed the right of the landless peasantry to land. But his performance in the field of agrarian reform did not match his promises. The agrarian law that issued from Congress the following year stressed technical improvement rather than expropriation and division of latifundia, with the hope that hacendados would adopt modern methods to improve production. As amended in Congress by a coalition of Apristas and rightists, the law exempted from expropriation the highly productive coastal estates, whose workers had been unionized by APRA, reserving for land distribution the archaic haciendas of the sierra. But the loopholes or exceptions were so numerous that the results of the law were very modest.

Meanwhile, Belaúnde's lavish promises had given great impetus to peasant land invasions. By October 1963 invasions had multiplied in the central highlands and were spreading to the whole southern part of the sierra. The land-invasion movement also changed its character; whereas before the peasants had seized only uncultivated lands, they now occupied cultivated land, arguing that they had paid for it with their unpaid or poorly paid labor of several generations. Militant peasant unions under radical leadership appeared, and a guerrilla movement arose in parts of the sierra. Meanwhile, a wave of strikes broke out in the cities, and workers occupied a number of enterprises in Lima and Callao.

These outbreaks took the Belaúnde administration by surprise. The extreme right, supported by APRA, demanded the use of the armed forces to repress the peasant movement. Indeed, APRA—once so "revolutionary"—called for the harshest treatment of the rebellious peasants. At the end of 1963, after some vacillation, the Belaúnde government decided to crush the peasant movement by force, a task the armed forces apparently assumed with reluctance, preferring "civic action" programs of a reformist type. By 1966 the peasant and guerrilla movements had been suppressed, at least for the moment. According to one estimate, the repression left 8,000 peasants dead and 3,500 imprisoned, 14,000 hectares of land burned with fire and napalm, and 19,000 peasants forced to abandon their homes.

Belaúnde had failed to solve the agrarian problem. He also failed to keep his promise to settle the old controversy between Peru and the International Petroleum Company over the La Brea–Pariñas oil fields, claimed by Peru to have been illegally exploited for some forty years. Finally, under strong pressure from U.S. interests, who delayed large planned investments in Peru, Belaúnde's government signed the Pact of Talara, which represented a massive surrender to the IPC. Peru regained the now almost exhausted oil fields, but in return agreed to the cancellation of claims for back taxes and illegal profits amounting to almost $700 million. IPC also received a new concession to exploit a vast area in the Amazon region and was allowed to retain the refinery of Talara, to which the government agreed to sell all the oil produced from the wells it had regained at a fixed price. A scandal rocked the country when the government, forced to publish the document, claimed to have "lost" the page setting the price that the IPC must pay the state oil company for its crude oil. As public indignation grew, the armed forces, opposition parties, and even the Catholic church denounced the agreement.

For Peru's military leaders, this was the last straw. For some years, they had engaged in intense soul-searching over the past and future of their country; now they were convinced that Belaúnde's government and the social forces that supported it had sold out the national interest and were incapable of solving Peru's problems. In October 1968 the armed forces seized the presidential palace, sent Belaúnde into exile, and established a military governing junta that began a swift transformation of Peru's economic and social structures.

The Rise and Fall of the Peruvian Revolution, 1968–2003

THE MILITARY ABOUT-FACE

Initially, the military seizure of power appeared to be another in the long series of military coups that punctuate the history of Peru and other Latin American countries—coups that change the occupant of the presidential palace but leave the existing order intact. The error of this opinion became evident as the self-proclaimed "Revolutionary Government of the Armed Forces," under the leadership of General and President Juan Velasco Alvarado, decreed the nationalization of oil, a sweeping agrarian reform law, and a law providing for workers' participation in the ownership and management of industrial concerns.

Observers found these events as startling, in the words of Fidel Castro, "as if a fire had started in the firehouse," for the Latin American military had traditionally been regarded as loyal servants of the area's oligarchies. But in Peru a social and ideological gulf had been developing between the military and civilian elites for decades. Most army officers came from a military family or from the lower-middle class. These officers, fearing the rise of an autonomous, indigenous peasant and working-class radicalism, sought to protect and promote national capitalist development in Peru by shifting power from landed oligarchs, foreign investors, and their government representatives to a socially responsible state controlled by a nationalistic new bourgeoisie.

Within a week, the Velasco junta had nationalized the IPC's oil fields and its refinery at Talara, and soon after it seized all its other assets. Having settled the IPC question, the junta went on to tackle the country's most burning economic and social questions.

LAND REFORM AND NATIONALIZATION OF RESOURCES

Land reform was the key problem: Peru could not achieve economic independence, modernization, and greater social democracy without liquidating the inefficient, semifeudal latifundio system, the gamonal political system that was its corollary, and the coastal enclaves of foreign oligarchical power. Major specific objectives were to expand agricultural production and to generate capital for investment in the industrial sector; thus landowners were to be compensated for expropriated lands with bonds that could be used as investment capital in industry or mining. On June 24, 1969, President Velasco announced an agrarian reform designed to end the "unjust social and economic structures" of the past. The program deviated from orthodox Latin American reform policies in two respects: first, it did not retain the homestead or family-sized farm as its ideal; second, it did not exempt large estates from expropriation on account of their efficiency and productivity. Indeed, the first lands to be expropriated were the big coastal sugar plantations, largely foreign-owned and constituting highly mechanized agro-industrial complexes. These enterprises were transferred to cooperatives of farm laborers and refinery workers.

Next came the turn of the haciendas of the sierra. The reform applied to most highland estates above 35 to 55 hectares and initially aimed to encourage division of estates into small- or medium-sized commercial farms, but this would have reduced the number of potential beneficiaries. Under pressure from militant, unionized peasants, who were demanding employment and the formation of cooperatives, the junta moved from parcellation toward cooperative forms of organization. Eventually fully 76 percent of the expropriated lands were organized into cooperatives, with the remainder distributed in individual plots.

The agrarian reform produced some undeniable immediate and long-range benefits. To begin with, it ended the various forms of serfdom that still survived in the sierra in 1968. Second, food production increased, though not substantially or to the level required by Peru's growing population. Third, according to a 1982 field study of the agrar-

ian reform, it "proved a major economic and political benefit to a significant sector of the peasantry," at least in the case of cooperatives with an adequate capital endowment. "In such cooperatives, members' wages and quality of life improved, often dramatically."

But these gains were offset by the failure of the agrarian reform to raise the general material and political level of the Peruvian peasantry—a failure stemming from incorrect planning and methods on the part of the well-meaning military reformers.

First, the reform was neither as swift nor as thorough as the dimensions of the problem required. Delays in implementing the program and the ruses employed by landowners to evade it meant that a considerable amount of land escaped expropriation. As a result, the reform made only a slight impact on the problem of landlessness and rural unemployment and underemployment, especially in the sierra.

Second, the military reformers lacked a coherent strategy for the general modernization of the agricultural sector within an overall plan of balanced, inwardly directed national development. Basically, the agricultural sector was viewed as a means of pumping out food and capital to promote development in the urban-industrial area. This was reflected in the military government's food-pricing policy, which was to keep food prices low to check inflation and keep the urban working class and middle class content. In the absence of compensating subsidies for small farmers, this policy "served to perpetuate the long-run unfavorable trend of the rural-urban terms of trade." Within the agricultural sector, the allocation of resources and credit was skewed in favor of the already well endowed and efficient coastal estates producing for export, with the bulk of agricultural investment going into large-scale irrigation projects. The needs of highland small farmers for small-scale irrigation works, fertilizer, and technical assistance were neglected. As a result, the coastal sugar, cotton, and coffee cooperatives tended to become "islands of relative privilege in a sea of peasant poverty and unemployment."

The same lack of a coherent strategy for the development of the agricultural sector as a whole was reflected in the method of distributing hacienda lands. The land was generally transferred to the workers who had been employed full time on the estates. They alone were eligible to be members of the new cooperatives. This left out the temporary laborers and the neighboring peasant villagers who eked out subsistence livings from tiny plots and small herds of sheep. This often led to serious tension and conflict, with the cooperatives defending their privileges and land against invasions by the *comuneros* (peasant villagers). Combined with the failure to distribute all the land subject to expropriation, this pattern of distribution contributed to the continuing flight of campesinos to the coastal cities, where they swelled the ranks of a large unemployed or underemployed population.

Finally, a major flaw of the agrarian reform was that it was a "revolution from above," with little input from below. Despite lip service to participatory ideology, the military technocrats made the final decisions with respect to work conditions, income policy, crop selection, and the like. Because the government's economic policy tended to subordinate peasant interests to the drive for rapid industrial growth, many peasants became disillusioned with the cooperative model. In some cases, particularly after 1975, when the nationalist reformist Velasco wing of the military was ousted from power by a conservative group stressing private enterprise and a free market, the disillusionment led to peasant demands for dismantling the cooperatives and parceling out the land.

After land reform, the nationalization of key foreign-owned natural resources and enterprises and of domestic monopolies that the military regarded as obstacles to development was the most important objective of the junta's program. When the revolution began, foreign firms controlled the commanding heights of the Peruvian economy. Eight years later, state enterprises had taken over most of these firms. The process began with the nationalization of the IPC, whose assets passed into the control of *Petroperu*, the state-owned oil company. Later, the national telephone system, the railroads (the Peruvian Corporation), and Peru's international airline came under state ownership.

The cement, chemical, and paper industries, defined as basic and reserved to the state, were taken over. The important fishmeal industry, in which large amounts of foreign capital were invested, was nationalized. The sugar industry, in large part controlled by the Grace interests, and the cotton industry, dominated by the U.S. firm of Anderson, Clayton, were seized under the agrarian reform law. Nationalization of the giant U.S.-owned mining complex of Cerro de Pasco in 1974 gave the state ownership of four thousand concessions and vested control of the bulk of mining and refining of copper, lead, and zinc in two state companies, *Minoperu* and *Centrominperu;* nationalization of Marcona Mining in 1975 gave the state control of iron ore and steel. In addition to the takeover of these primarily extractive and manufacturing firms, state companies obtained marketing monopolies of all major commodity exports and most food distribution. Through stock purchases, the government nationalized most of the banking and insurance industries. Thus the state came to control decisive sectors of the Peruvian economy.

The original intent of the military reformers was not to substitute the state for local private capital but to promote its formation by removing such impediments as the latifundio and foreign monopolistic firms and by the creation of an industrial infrastructure to be financed through the export of minerals and agricultural exports. But the radical rhetoric of the nationalistic military only frightened the local bourgeoisie, who were generally satisfied with their technological and financial dependence on foreign capital, and they failed to respond to the incentives for industrial investment. As a result, the government itself had to assume the role of the economy's main investor and by 1972 accounted for more than half the total investment in the economy.

But the cost of this investment, added to the large sums expended for compensation for expropriated estates and foreign enterprises, came very high. Tax reform offered one possibility of mobilizing considerable amounts of previously untouched wealth. Such a move, however, would have antagonized the local bourgeoisie, whom the military was wooing, and the middle class, which formed its principal mass base. Because of disputes over expropriation, Peru could not apply for loans to the United States and the multinational agencies it controlled. Accordingly, Peru had to turn to foreign private banks. Encouraged by the high price of copper and other Peruvian exports and by the prospect of rich oil strikes in the Amazon Basin, the banks willingly complied with Peru's requests for loans. They lent $147 million in 1972 and $734 million in 1973, making Peru the largest borrower among Third World countries in the latter year.

Although women's rights issues clearly were not a priority for the military regime, a new women's movement, led by Virginia Vargas, founder of the Flora Tristán Peruvian Women's Center, nonetheless emerged. These women were very active in grassroots neighborhood organizations, unions, teachers' associations, and social work agencies, which provided experience with collective action and heightened their consciousness of gender-based inequality. Under pressure from this women's movement, the military adopted the eighteenth-century Inca revolutionary leaders, Micaela Bastidas and her husband, Tupac Amaru, as the symbols of their 1974 Plan Inca, which demanded civil and political equality for women, laws against discrimination, affirmative action in public employment, and rural education programs.

The military likewise had not intended to unleash a cultural revolution, but its nationalist ideology mobilized popular political participation and reinforced artistic explorations of the country's indigenous and African roots. This led to a dramatic expansion of popular theater and folk music that challenged criollo cultural hegemony and decisively shaped a radically new multiracial Peruvian national identity. In the early 1970s, for example, Yuyachkani, a politically committed theater group that took its name from a Quechua word meaning "thoughts and memories," sought to organize indigenous workers by touring highland mining communities and performing *Fist of Copper*. This was a play that drew on Spanish and European theatrical traditions to extol the virtues of popular resistance to violent police repression of a miners' strike. During post-performance discussions, the young urban actors, who aimed to raise the consciousness of their indigenous audiences, instead learned about the long tradition of indigenous Andean theater, which integrated dance, music, puppets, masks, and colorful costumes. These elements were later incorporated into plays that shared with highland peoples the "good news" about the 1969 land reform that gave them the legal authority to fight for their land against the landowners and their hired thugs. They also became very popular in the universities, urban slums, and squatter settlements, where provincianos had migrated in search of jobs.

By early 1975, a new cyclical crisis had begun to ravage the capitalist world. Rising prices for oil and imported equipment and technology, combined with falling prices for Peru's raw material exports, undermined the fragile prosperity that had made President Velasco's reforms possible. These circumstances created unmanageable balance-of-trade and debt service problems. The model of development based on export expansion and foreign borrowing had again revealed its inherent contradictions.

The experience of the Peruvian Revolution shows the difficulty of escaping from dependent development without radical structural changes in class and property relationships and income distribution. Like the Mexican Revolution, Peru's experience suggests that the revolution that does not advance risks stagnation and loss of whatever gains have been made.

THE REVOLUTION UNDER ATTACK, 1975–1983

The economic crisis of 1975 provoked a sharp struggle within the military between radical nationalists, who proposed to extend the social and economic reforms, and those who called for measures that would win the confidence of native and foreign capitalists, thereby making possible a revival of private investments. In August 1975 a peaceful coup replaced President Velasco with his conservative prime minister, Francisco Morales Bermúdez; this was followed by a gradual purge of radical nationalists from the government and the forced resignation of leftist officers from the armed forces.

The so-called First Phase of the revolution had ended. To appease foreign and domestic capitalists, the new government introduced a package of severe austerity measures that called for sharp reductions in government investments in state enterprises, steep increases in consumer prices, and a 44 percent devaluation of the currency, only partly offset by wage increases of from 10 to 14 percent. The government next announced the end of agrarian reform, although only about one-third of the land subject to expropriation had been distributed. In early 1978, after long negotiations, Morales Bermúdez capitulated to the IMF and accepted its conditions for a new loan, including privatization of state enterprises, heavy cuts in budgets and subsidies, large price increases, and severe restraints on wage increases. These measures provoked widespread strikes and rioting, which were crushed by the government with a full-scale military operation.

For the thoroughly discredited military junta, the prime concern was how to make a smooth transfer of power to a civilian regime that could be trusted to continue its conservative policies. A new constitution, remarkably similar to the 1933 document, served this function. It established a bicameral Congress, both elected, like the president, for five years. It contained language ensuring that the foundations of the Peruvian economy would be the free market and the primacy of the private sector. The constitution guaranteed the right to strike and collective bargaining, but those rights were subject to parliamentary regulation. The biggest novelty was the grant of the right to vote to illiterates.

Predictably, Fernando Belaúnde Terry, a master of populist rhetoric who enjoyed an aura of martyrdom thanks to his ouster by the military in 1968, won the 1980 elections. It soon became clear that he intended to continue and extend the "counterreformation" begun by the Morales Bermúdez government. Export expansion and debt repayment were the great priorities, to be achieved with the familiar arsenal of austerity measures and devaluation, combined with wage freezes.

The Belaúnde government also dismantled the major reforms of the Velasco era. A principal objective was to restore a free market in agricultural land by dissolving the cooperative system. A new agricultural promotion and development law gave the government the power to divide cooperative land into small individual plots and turn them over to cooperative members. The plots could then be bought, sold, or mortgaged, which fostered the reconcentration of land in a few hands.

Other legislation empowered the government to sell off state-owned companies and increase private participation in publicly owned firms through stock issues and other programs. The government proposed to ban general and sympathy strikes, and drastically reduce public works spending, and phase out subsidies on basic foods and fuel. These proposals caused bitter wrangling in parliament between the government and the opposition parties, but they caused unprecedented popular protest; for the first time in Peruvian history, all the major labor groups joined in a general strike.

Thus, fifteen years after the military seized power in Peru, the nation again faced a crisis of unprecedented proportions. Its population had doubled between 1960 and 1980, from 10 to 20 million, and its distribution between town and country had changed dramatically. In 1960, 60 percent of the people were rural, but in 1980, 60 percent were urban. Unemployment climbed to new heights; strikes succeeded each other in industry, the railroads, and the banks; and the rural exodus continued to swell the population of the barriadas that ringed Lima.

POPULAR CULTURE AND RESISTANCE

Second-generation provincianos had played a role in many of the urban protests that helped inaugurate the 1968 Peruvian revolution, and they likewise joined this new popular movement to defend its achievements. Unlike their parents, however, they had become more economically independent of criollo society. They had created their own self-help migrant community associations, usually based upon their region of origin (e.g., Punenos from Puno and Ayacuchanos from Ayacucho),

During the 1980s, migrants from highland communities adapted indigenous musical instruments and folk rhythms to reflect a new urban experience of modernity that they found simultaneously exciting and disturbing. [Alison Wright/Corbis]

joined trade unions, and participated in other grassroots social movements that strengthened their public embrace of indigenous identities. This growing independence of thought and action was clearly reflected in the birth of a new cultural form, a popular urban musical style variously called *cumbia andina* or *chicha*, for the corn beer that was the preferred beverage in highland Andean indigenous communities. No longer interested in assimilating criollo values, these sons and daughters of highland migrants increasingly challenged established social hierarchies based on race, ethnicity, and class power.

Chicha music drew on three radically different sources for its creative inspiration: Colombian cumbia rhythms, whose origins lay in Afro-Colombian cultural traditions; folk melodies indige-nous to the Andean highlands; and the electric instruments commonly associated with U.S. and British rock and roll. Chicha songs typically explored the everyday lives of poor, hard-working urban provincianos. According to ethnomusicologist Thomas Tutino, one of the earliest chicha bands, Los demonios del Mantaro (Mantaro Devils), sold 200,000 copies of "La Chichera," a song that celebrated the life of a street peddler who sold Andean corn beer. Established criollo critics understandably disparaged chicha as crude, amateurish, "mindless" music, and leftist intellectuals either dismissed its lyrical interest in unrequited love as politically disengaged or criticized it for "internalizing criollo values" by promoting upward mobility.

But young provincianos, often feeling unloved, socially marginalized, out of place, and lacking a clear sense of their own identity, thrilled to its "modern" beat and identified with its lyrical lament about their real life experiences. In one very popular song, "Ambulante Soy" ("I Am a Street Vendor"), the lead singer of Los Shapis, perhaps the most famous of the chicha bands, bemoaned "How sad is life, how sad it is to dream" and then proudly announced that "I am a street vendor, I am a proletarian." Similarly, Grupo Alegría's "Pequeño Luchador" ("Little Fighter") described the daily survival struggles of "a small child/Who runs through the city/Hawking advertisements that will sell" and then celebrated the heroism of this "Little boy with dirty face/Little fighter/Your hands now know/What it means to work." Even songs like Los Shapis's "Somos Estudiantes" ("We Are Students"), which some have criticized for its alleged identification with criollo concerns about "occupational status" and social mobility, clearly stressed the value of professional positions as a means of promoting the development of their communities, not their own personal self-aggrandizement. "We are teachers/For our children," Los Shapis sang, "Doctors we will be/For the orphans. We are lawyers/Of the poor."

Chicha music soon outsold all its competitors in Peruvian markets, including internationally renowned artists like Julio Iglesias and Michael Jackson. Initially performed on street corners and in vacant lots in the pueblos jovenes (squatter communities), chicha artists later regularly played to large crowds in "chichadromes" and provided musical entertainment at community religious festivals, weddings, birthday parties, and other social events. Supported by the progressive indigenista policies of Velasco's revolutionary nationalist regime, which had made Quechua an official national language and required radio stations to promote authentic local music, they soon dominated national radio broadcasts, claiming almost 40 percent of airtime by the early 1980s. Chicha music also expanded its popularity from the urban centers of its birth to rural highland communities. As the reformist Velasco dictatorship crumbled and more conservative forces seized control of the nation, chicha artists and their concerts provided young provincianos with useful meeting places to organize popular resistance and promote a return to democracy. Thereafter, they would lend their voice to support reformist state social programs proposed by Aprista and other populist politicians who sought to curry political favor with urban and rural provincianos alike.

APRA IN POWER, 1985–1990

The Aprista candidate who most benefited from Belaúnde's failure was thirty-six-year-old Alán García Pérez, a disciple of the late Haya de la Torre. García campaigned on a populist, reformist program in 1985, promising to defend the agrarian and industrial reforms of the Velasco era and to reject Belaúnde's free-market policies.

In his inaugural address, García proclaimed that henceforth Peru would not deal with the IMF but directly with the creditor banks. He also announced that he would limit interest payments on Peru's foreign debt of about $14 billion to 10 percent of Peru's export earnings—about $400 million. "Peru," García declared, "has one overwhelming creditor, its own people." Other parts of his economic program included measures to halt capital exports, freeze the price of necessities, and raise the minimum wage by 50 percent—all measures opposed by the IMF and the foreign financial community.

García's restrictions on foreign debt payments and his measures to prevent the flight of capital, prevent luxury imports, and raise wages formed part of a coherent program to revive the sluggish Peruvian economy. The long-term goal was promoting the development of an autonomous Peruvian capitalism based on expanded import-substitution industrialization and reduced dependence on imported raw materials. The restriction on debt repayments and the controls on foreign trade were designed to make capital available for development; the substantial wage increases were expected to expand purchasing power and demand for Peruvian-made goods. In a speech marking the anniversary of his first year in office, he took care to reassure businessmen, declaring that even as he rejected devaluation and new indebtedness as a regression to "the colonial recipes of the IMF," so he rejected nationalization. His path, he said, led to "a strong state redirecting the structure of Peruvian industry toward less import-dependent options."

But economic problems remained. Business's resistance to the price freeze produced shortages of consumer items and forced the government to relax price controls, allowing some prices to rise. Moreover, there was a growing gap between the costs of the recovery program and government income from all sources, including export earnings and the savings obtained by limiting debt payments. García had few options. He could try by tax reform to tap the large wealth of Peruvian elites, left untouched by the military reformers, but this was an unacceptable solution given the moderate nature of his program. Printing money or a slowdown in economic growth was equally unacceptable. There remained the option of going to foreign banks for loans, but García had ruled out "new indebtedness" as a colonial recipe of the IMF, which had in any case declared him ineligible for new credits.

A major obstacle to the sound, balanced economic growth envisaged by García was the continuing cleavage between the sierra and the coast; the contrast between the poverty of the highlands (largely populated by Quechua- and Aymara-speaking peasants) and the relative prosperity of the coast. Landlessness and unemployment or underemployment continued to be the burning problems of the sierra. The result was that the highlands became the scene of a struggle between the landless peasantry and the giant cooperatives, often controlled by elite groups of managers, engineers, and bureaucrats.

Into this struggle over land, with all its potential for violence, entered the Maoist *Sendero Luminoso* (Shining Path). This group was repudiated by other left-wing movements, which viewed it as terrorist and mistaken in its effort to polarize Peruvian society into militarists and *senderistas*. For the most part led by radicalized students and other middle-class individuals, the Sendero Luminoso emerged in May 1980 with a program of terrorist activity against all who supported the existing bourgeois order; it also encouraged peasants to invade, occupy, and loot cooperatives. The García government responded to this threat by continuing Belaúnde's counterinsurgency campaign, which had placed nineteen of Peru's twenty-three provinces under a state of emergency with the military in overall control and suspended most civil rights. García justified this action, claiming that thousands of officials, police, members of other security forces, and uncooperative peasants had been killed by the Sendero Luminoso, but church authorities and other independent observers asserted that the security forces had themselves committed many repressive acts and that many killings of peasants ascribed to the guerrillas were the work of these forces.

As his term of office drew to an end, a balance sheet of García's record in power could point to some positive initiatives and accomplishments, including his decision to limit debt interest payments to a certain proportion of export proceeds, thereby making more funds available for development purposes. García's debt strategy marked an advance over that of the military reformers, but it was not enough. Peru needed a program of structural economic and social change: the creation of a self-sufficient industrial base that would lessen dependency on foreign imports and capital; a more thoroughgoing agrarian reform that would attack the age-old problem of Andean poverty and backwardness, overcome the need for food imports, and expand the domestic market; and a reduction of the immense inequities in income distribution.

But these changes were not made. As a result, by 1987 García's project for creating an autonomous Peruvian capitalism was running out of steam; the country had a serious trade deficit, its foreign reserves were declining, and the business class, despite generous incentives from the government, was not increasing its level of investment. From 1988 to 1989 the per capita gross economic product declined by 20 percent, the biggest decline in the region. As if the economic crisis were not enough, the war with the Maoist Sendero Luminoso movement grew more intense. Moreover, the indigenous struggle to reclaim ancestral lands led to a wave of *tomas de tierras* (land invasions) that produced a new militance among peasant leaders and fueled the rural rebellion.

Amid the economic gloom, the only light and cheer was provided by Peru's illicit coca trade. In Peru, as in Bolivia, the jobs and dollars generated by the coca boom cushioned the impact of a devastating economic crisis. With opportunities for employment in the legal economy shrinking, thousands of migrants joined the "white gold rush" to the Upper Huallaga Valley, the heart of Peru's coca empire. The coca, processed into a white paste, was sold to Colombian dealers, who pocketed most of the profits. But Peru's share came to about $1.2 billion annually, roughly 30 percent of the value of all Peru's legal exports. Without these illicit dollars, according to one Peruvian economist, the exchange rate would have nearly doubled, making vitally needed imports much more expensive. Like Paz in Bolivia, García liberalized Central Bank rules to permit the purchase of coca dollars, no questions asked.

With APRA in total disgrace as a result of García's economic fiasco and failure to end the civil war, the 1990 presidential elections became the site of a new contest between neoliberal free-market philosophy and the populism of an obscure agronomist, Alberto Fujimori, the son of poor Japanese immigrants, who insisted that people's basic needs must be met before any economic adjustment was begun. Surprising most political pundits, Fujimori's populist crusade solidified his base and attracted leftist support, thereby ensuring his electoral triumph.

BACK TO THE PAST, 1990–2003

Following his election, Fujimori caused consternation among his followers by enacting severe austerity measures akin to those that they had soundly rejected at the polls. "Fujishock," as the program was immediately dubbed, included the removal of customer subsidies. The result was soaring price increases, with the price of such staple foods as milk and bread nearly tripling. The program provoked widespread rioting and looting in Peru's shantytowns. In contradiction of the pledge that he would not privatize major public enterprises,

EL FISGÓN

FUJIMORI: A MAN WHO SUITS ALL OCCASIONS.

Peru's President Fujimori quickly learned how to manage democratic capitalism's potentially fatal contradiction: to serve the powerful minority of international bankers and local elites who supported neoliberalism, successful politicians had to deceive their lower-class constituents with populist rhetoric and election-year patronage. [El Fisgón/NACLA]

Fujimori, hoping to attract foreign capital, offered to sell 232 state-owned companies, including the controlling shares of the state copper mines. Despite their many problems, these firms provided one-half of Peru's foreign exchange earnings.

Fujimori confronted a comatose economy kept alive only with large injections of coca dollars, a fanatical guerrilla movement rampaging in the countryside and gaining ground in the cities, and a Congress that was becoming increasingly restive over his use of the special decree powers it had granted him. Fujimori used those powers to promote his extreme neoliberal program and to give the military absolute control over the counterinsurgency. When Congress finally reacted to his abuse of the decree powers by overturning or amending some of the most offensive decrees in a special session, Fujimori aggressively attacked Congress and the judiciary for their alleged inefficiency and corruption. Then, on April 5, 1992, he carried out his famous *autogolpe* ("self-coup"), closing Congress and the judiciary, suspending the 1979 constitution, and proclaiming a "Government of Emergency and National Reconstruction."

Public support for this coup, revealed in polls that showed approval rates of between 70 and 90 percent, reflected widespread fear of the Shining Path, which played into Fujimori's hands by its merciless killing of popular community leaders who organized communal soup kitchens and glass-of-milk programs. As a result, the public applauded government victories in its fight against the Shining Path and the smaller Tupac Amaru Revolutionary Movement (MRTA), capped in September 1992 by the capture of Shining Path leader Abimael Guzmán.

This terrorism provided a convenient pretext for the security forces' equally indiscriminate repression of those who opposed Fujimori's insidious neoliberal program: popular organizations, leftist parties, and journalists, a number of whom were arrested on charges of promoting terrorism. Fujimori apparently had come to the same conclusion as Carlos Menem in Argentina: neoliberalism worked more efficiently in the context of an authoritarian political system.

In an effort to remove the taint of dictatorship and gain international respectability for his regime, in 1992 Fujimori drafted a new constitution that fully conformed to his authoritarian temper and neoliberal economic views. It concentrated all power in the president by allowing him to dissolve Congress at will, veto laws, and promulgate laws by decree; and it permitted his reelection in 1995. The document provided for a laissez-faire economy with the private sector assigned the dominant role, and for privatization of state enterprises. State activity in education would be reduced, with less support for free education. The constitution established a strongly centralized government, eliminating regional governments, subordinating the provinces to the executive branch, and denying provinces the right to keep a portion of the profits generated by the exploitation of nat-

ural resources in their territory. Finally, the document adopted the death penalty for terrorism.

In 1995, Fujimori sought to lower inflation, expand consumption, and guarantee his reelection by opening Peru to a flood of cheap foreign imports. Although this produced short-term benefits, it also doubled the trade deficit, increased the nation's balance-of-payments deficit by 80 percent, and, over time, drove small- and medium-sized industrial manufacturers and agricultural producers into bankruptcy. He also borrowed heavily from foreign bankers to pay for dramatically higher expenditures on poverty relief in poor communities devastated by his neoliberal structural adjustments. External debt grew by 72 percent from 1993 to 1995, and interest payments on that accumulated debt skyrocketed to 31 percent of export revenues.

In addition, the crafty president, dressed in indigenous garb, traveled daily to the *pueblos jovenes* (squatter cities), composed of indigent highland migrants forced off their lands or fleeing the grinding poverty of the countryside, and directly dispensed presidential patronage, agreeing to build schools, roads, or public infrastructure. Government allocations to poverty relief increased by nearly 60 percent in 1994 and another 90 percent in 1995. Social spending more than doubled from 3 percent of gross domestic product (GDP) in 1993 to 7.8 percent in 1995; whereas Fujimori had spent only $12 on the social welfare of each Peruvian in 1990, he paid out $176 in 1995. Despite the long-term risks for national development, the strategy worked and Fujimori captured 60 percent of the vote in the 1995 elections; moreover, according to political scientist Kenneth Roberts, "Fujimori's support in 1995 was highest in Peru's poorest departments, especially in the southern and central Andean highlands, where opposition to the constitution had been strongest in 1993."

However, although backing for Fujimori's economic policies was solid among foreign investors, the IMF, and domestic elites, it remained highly volatile among the impoverished masses. If every year were a presidential election year, the poor majority might be convinced to vote for Fujimori and poverty rates might even be expected to decline from their historic highs in 1993, when 53.6 percent of Peruvians lived in poverty and 21 percent lived in "extreme" poverty. His 1995 reelection effort alone reduced poverty by almost 10 percent, but recent statistics suggest a somewhat darker future.

Despite the dramatic increase in 1995 GDP and Fujimori's effective anti-inflation program, the nation's economy did not expand sufficiently during his tenure to justify the sacrifices that his neoliberal policies imposed on Peru. Growth rates averaged 4.7 percent per year since 1991, but unemployment, averaging almost 9 percent a year, remained stubbornly high and the poorly paid "informal sector," composed of part-time and self-employed street vendors, experienced the most sustained growth. As a result, despite a decade of growth, in 2002, 54 percent of Peruvians were anchored in poverty. External debt, trade deficits, and net outflows of wealth all increased steadily since Fujimori took over in 1991. In 2000, the external debt was a whopping $28 billion, almost twice as large as when he took office; the trade deficit averaged almost $1 billion per year during his administration, almost three times higher than the annual average $500 million surplus accumulated in the two economically depressed years before Fujimori took office; finally, the payments deficit, the measure of wealth which flowed *out* of the nation, also grew, to $3 billion in 1997, and averaged $2.5 billion per year since 1990, double the annual average rate in the last years of García's presidency.

But this economic picture of growing poverty and increased external dependency tells only part of the story. Fujimori's government continued to rely on authoritarian methods to preserve his power and implement his neoliberal agenda. But this weakened his standing among both political elites and popular sectors. After a constitutional tribunal ruled unconstitutional his bid to run for reelection in 2000, he promptly fired the justices. Next, reports surfaced that he had authorized his security forces to tap the telephones of 167 political opponents, including the former secretary-general of the United Nations, Javier Perez de Cuellar. Fujimori's military then virtually declared war on the opposition press, engaging in beating, kidnapping, and torture. When a television reporter criticized the $600,000 salary of the president's intelligence chief, Fujimori revoked the station owner's citizenship and transferred ownership to minority shareholders.

Determined to remain in power, no matter the cost, Fujimori pressed his National Intelligence Service (SIN), the equivalent of the United States's CIA, to intervene boldly in the electoral process to guarantee it. Emboldened by popular opposition to these high-handed, overtly authoritarian tactics, Alejandro Toledo, born to poor indigenous parents, denounced the impending fraud and withdrew from the elections. International observers quickly followed suit and even the U.S. State Department, which had supported Fujimori's neoliberal economic policies, described the 2000 election as "invalid." Popular grassroots movements quickly organized a general strike, and a wave of social protests, some of which became violent, swept the countryside. Suddenly, the issue that galvanized all Peruvians, regardless of their other disagreements, was Fujimori. Toledo, an economist educated in the United States, seized upon this popular mobilization to energize his own presidential ambitions; he now denounced Fujimori's authoritarianism, his "antipopular economic measures," corruption, and failure to reduce poverty among the 55 percent of the nation that earned less than $2 per day. The resulting tumult forced the Congress to dismiss Fujimori, who sought exile in Japan.

Ironically, this messy transition dramatically increased Toledo's popularity, but without requiring him to spell out his vision of a post-Fujimori Peru. Although he supported free trade, his populist campaign called for a review of Fujimori's privatization program, specifically promised not to sell off the state's public utilities, and pledged to reduce unemployment and poverty. As a result, when he assumed the presidency in 2001, public expectations were understandably high. The popular sectors that had supported his candidacy had one agenda, but the Peruvian business elite and foreign bankers urged another. Toledo quickly made clear which program would shape his presidential administration. After meeting with officials of the IMF, he agreed to raise $700 million in 2002 and almost $1 billion in 2003 by selling off state assets, but this required him to break his campaign pledge to the people who had elected him. Thereafter, he announced the privatization of two profitable state-owned electric companies, Egasa (which earned $14 million on sales of $50 million in 2001) and Egesur, to be sold to a Belgian company, Tractebel, for $167 million, one-half their declared value.

This naturally ignited a storm of violent popular protests that led to the declaration of a state of emergency and produced two deaths, hundreds of arrests, and $100 million in damages. Pressed by this "democracy in the streets," Toledo, whose popularity already had plunged from a historic high of 60 percent to 16 percent, was forced, at least temporarily, to abandon his privatization plans and apologize publicly for having violated his campaign promises. But Toledo also had failed to make good on a promise to create 2 million jobs, restore workers' rights usurped by Fujimori, and reduce unemployment and poverty, both of which rose as a result of his neoliberal policies. Greatly weakened by a growing popular clamor to "pay the poor, not the foreign debt," Francisco Toledo's future, like Peru's, seemed especially uncertain. Like the rest of the region, Peru appeared poised to abandon its decade-long experiment with unfettered free enterprise in search of a more socially productive mix of state regulations and market forces.

17 The Cuban Revolution

L IKE THE OTHER Latin American nations we have examined, Cuba has suffered from the cyclical nature of world market demand for its products. Moreover, Cuba suffered the additional burden of almost total economic domination by the United States. But in 1959, Cuba—an island ninety miles from Key West and ruled by one of the region's most firmly entrenched dictatorships—became the scene of perhaps the first and certainly the most successful social revolution in Latin America during the twentieth century. Under the banner of Marxism and with the military, economic, and political support of the Soviet Union, until recently the government led by Fidel Castro made great progress toward the elimination of such problems as illiteracy, mass unemployment, and unequal distribution of income and wealth. But the collapse of the Soviet Union and Cuba's other trading partners in the socialist bloc, combined with an intensified effort by the United States to bring about its downfall, produced the most serious crisis in socialist Cuba's history, a crisis it is now struggling to overcome.

Independence and the Spanish-Cuban-American War

JOSÉ MARTÍ AND THE REVOLUTIONARY MOVEMENT

By the early 1890s a global economic crisis, compounded by high U.S. tariffs on Cuban sugar imports, reduced external demand for sugar, destroyed sugar planters' profits, swelled unemployment, and inflamed long-simmering class, racial, and gender animosities. Afro-Cubans, workers, women, colonos, creole elites, and U.S. investors in Cuba increasingly identified Spanish imperial authority as the principal source of this injustice and therefore revived the movement for independence.

The spiritual, intellectual, and organizational leader of the revolutionary movement was José Martí (1853–1895). As a lad of sixteen, Martí was arrested on a charge of supporting the 1868 revolt and sentenced to six years in prison at hard labor; but in 1871 he was sent into exile. In 1880, Martí came to New York, his home for the next fourteen years. In the United States, he earned his living in brilliant journalistic and literary activity that won him fame throughout Latin America.

Meanwhile, Martí worked tirelessly to establish and unite Cuban émigré revolutionary groups. In 1892 he founded *El Partido Revolucionario Cubano* (the Cuban Revolutionary Party), which proposed to obtain, "with the united effort of all men of good will, the absolute independence of the island of Cuba, and to foment and aid that of Puerto Rico." He then set about recruiting such military veterans of 1868 as Máximo Gómez and Antonio Maceo, in preparation for an invasion of the island. In April 1895, Martí himself landed on a Cuban beach with a group of insurgents; a little

José Martí (*left*), a brilliant writer and thinker, became a towering figure in Latin American history when he joined with Antonio Maceo (*right*), the Bronze Titan, to lead the revolutionary movement for Cuban independence. [Bettmann/Corbis]

more than a month later, he was killed in a skirmish with a Spanish patrol.

Despite the loss of its charismatic leader, the revolution spread and the National Liberation Army achieved major successes with the aid of time-proven guerrilla tactics. Afro-Cubans played particularly prominent roles in the armed struggle. In every rebellious province except Camaguey, Afro-Cubans constituted a majority of the soldiers, known as *mambises*, and they fought in integrated battalions, often under the command of black officers like Maceo, his brother José, and Agustín Cebrerco. This prompted some Afro-Cubans to conclude that in the army, where "nobody cares about the color of a man," the *Cuba Libre* movement was "putting the principles of democracy into practice." This wartime experience reaffirmed Afro-Cubans' long-standing commitment to equality and social justice.

Women also shaped the independence struggle in decisive ways. Some, like university graduate Adela Azcuy, distinguished themselves in battle, whereas peasant women, despite Spanish attempts to enclose them in concentration camps, continued to provide food and intelligence information to the liberation army. This "women's war" shaped the consciousness of the revolutionary generation and led to a political demand for women's suffrage, public employment, and educational opportunity.

At the beginning of 1896 a new Spanish commander, General Valeriano Weyler, instituted counterinsurgency measures of the type that

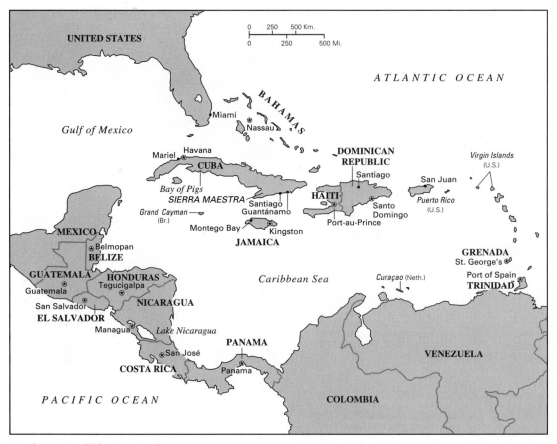

Modern Caribbean Nations

would later be employed against twentieth-century rebels in the Philippines, Algeria, and Vietnam. He set up population concentration centers and free-fire zones, which resulted in enormous hardships and losses to the peasantry. But his successes were transient and counterproductive, serving mostly to intensify popular hatred for Spanish rule, and whole provinces remained under the absolute control of the liberating army. The failure of Weyler's military policies and growing pressure from the United States led Spain to promise autonomy to Cuba in late 1897.

INVOLVEMENT BY THE UNITED STATES

As the rebellion spread over Cuba, it became an increasingly volatile issue in the United States.

Inevitably, property was destroyed or damaged in the fighting, and this brought complaints from powerful U.S. businessmen and financiers with interests in Cuba. These leaders, white supremacists themselves, also feared the possibility that Cuba's "race war," as Spanish propagandists depicted it, might transform the island into another Haiti and simultaneously inflame the African community in the United States. But the Cuban struggle for independence struck a sympathetic chord with some Americans, particularly among the working class. William Randolph Hearst and Joseph Pulitzer, then engaged in a newspaper circulation war in New York City, helped keep popular interest high by running lurid stories of Spanish brutality.

Meanwhile, within the McKinley administration as well as among enthusiastic expansionists like Theodore Roosevelt, there was a growing feeling that the Cuban situation was getting out of control, that the autonomy proposal sponsored by the United States was failing, and that if the United States did not intervene, an unmanageable Cuban revolutionary government might take over from the collapsing Spanish regime. In the midst of this ferment, the USS *Maine* blew up in Havana Harbor on February 15, 1898, with heavy loss of life. This incident helped spur McKinley to a more belligerent stance; he demanded that Spain terminate the concentration camp policy, offer an armistice to the rebels, and accept the United States as a final arbiter between the parties. There was no mention of Cuban independence. When Spain delayed its response to U.S. demands, McKinley sent a message to Congress asking it to authorize military intervention by the United States in Cuba. Congress, after considerable debate, adopted a joint resolution to that effect.

But Cubans did not rejoice: almost every major revolutionary figure—Martí, Maceo, Gómez—opposed U.S. entry into the war, fearing it would result in direct or indirect U.S. political and economic control of Cuba. "The Cuban war," Martí wrote in 1895, "has broken out in America in time to prevent . . . the annexation of Cuba to the United States." All they sought from the United States was recognition of Cuban belligerency and the right to purchase arms in the United States. McKinley, of course, had worked feverishly to defeat the Turpie-Foraker Amendment, recognizing Cuban belligerency, and had unsuccessfully opposed the 1898 Teller Amendment, which prohibited U.S. annexation of Cuba.

The ensuing war was short and nasty. U.S. commanders ignored their Cuban counterparts, excluding Cuban generals from decision making and relegating Cuban soldiers to sentry and cleanup duties. Incompetence was the key feature of both Spanish and U.S. war efforts. U.S. military actions were ill prepared and badly led. Thus, in a bizarre little war, the United States Army— wretchedly led, scandalously provisioned, and ravaged by tropical disease—swiftly defeated a demoralized, dispirited Spanish army and snatched the fruits of victory from the mambises,

who had fought gallantly in a struggle of three years' duration. The exclusion of Cuban leaders from both war councils and peace negotiations foreshadowed the course of U.S.-Cuban relations for the next sixty years.

THE FIRST U.S. OCCUPATION, 1899–1902

The United States Army occupied Cuba from January 1899 to May 1902. The occupation had three basic goals. First, the United States sought to make Cuba into a self-governing colony, an arrangement designed to achieve political stability without the administrative burdens and costs of an outright colonial occupation. To this end, the U.S. military sought to pacify the island without serious conflict with the Cuban army, which was still intact and in control of much of rural Cuba. The revolutionary army, however, did not resist the U.S. takeover, as did Emilio Aguinaldo and his insurgent forces in the Philippines at the same time. Cuban passivity in part reflected the fact that the years of struggle had taken their toll—the leading Cuban generals, such as Calixto García and Máximo Gómez, were tired old men, and many of the younger men who could have led a resistance movement had died in battle.

In addition, U.S. authorities bought off the army by offering to purchase its arms, an offer that hungry, unemployed soldiers found difficult to refuse. They also offered key rebel leaders well-paid positions and ably manipulated the volatile issue of race to divide and conquer Cuba Libre. At the same time, the occupation government established a Rural Guard, largely devoid of Afro-Cubans, most of whom could not meet eligibility requirements, which included literacy, a recommendation from propertied elites, and sufficient wealth to purchase a uniform, equipment, and horse. The Guard's primary purpose was to eradicate banditry and protect foreign property—in the words of General Leonard Wood, to put down the "agitators who began to grow restive at the presence of the Americans."

After political stability, necessary to attract U.S. capital, the second major goal was to repair the destruction wrought by the war and provide the services needed to sustain the U.S. occupation and promote economic recovery. General Leonard Wood, appointed governor general in 1899, launched a program of public works and sanitation that led to a major achievement of the occupation—the conquest of yellow fever. Taking its lead from a Cuban doctor, Carlos Finlay, whose theory correctly attributed the transmission of the dread disease to the mosquito, the American Sanitary Commission succeeded in eliminating it. Another major accomplishment of the Wood administration was the creation of a Cuban national education system, vastly superior to what had existed under Spain but designed to inculcate U.S. principles; even the textbooks were translations of U.S. textbooks. All these programs and reforms, as well as the expenses of the U.S. troops, were paid for from the Cuban treasury.

Ruling with arbitrary methods and largely ignoring the former revolutionaries, especially the Afro-Cubans, in favor of Spaniards and conservative planters who had opposed independence, Wood imposed a new electoral law that empowered the "better class" by restricting the franchise to literate adult males with property worth $250. Elihu Root, McKinley's secretary of war, especially celebrated the law's impact on Afro-Cubans: "Limited suffrage," he wrote, effectively excluded "so great a proportion of the elements which have brought ruin to Haiti and San Domingo." Elections for a constitutional convention, not surprisingly, produced a conservative assembly which, after several months of bitter debate, adopted a document that, under intense U.S. pressure, included the so-called Platt Amendment. This amendment limited the ability of independent Cuba to conduct foreign policy and to borrow money abroad, gave the United States the right to maintain a naval base at Guantánamo Bay, and most important, gave the United States the right to intervene in Cuba for the "preservation of Cuban independence" and for the "maintenance of a government adequate for the protection of life, property, and individual liberty."

The third goal of the occupation was to absorb Cuba into the United States's economic sphere of influence. Because the Platt Amendment assured U.S. businessmen of protection and a generally favorable investment climate on the island, capital poured into sugar and railroad construction. A reciprocal trade agreement signed by the two nations in 1903 was the final step in bringing Cuba under U.S. hegemony. This treaty cut by 20 percent the tariff on Cuban sugar exported to the United States; in return, Cuba reduced the duties on imported U.S. goods.

The end of Spanish rule and the U.S. occupation also transformed Cuban society by removing the final obstacle to the development of the latifundio in Cuba. Two processes worked hand in hand in the following decades: the concentration of land and mills and the proletarianization of the sugar workers. The two wars of independence had devastated small mills: the total number fell from two thousand in 1860 to one thousand in 1877 to only two hundred in 1899. The rapid and huge influx of foreign—mostly U.S.—investment into sugar enabled the larger mills to buy up surrounding cane land. The colono was reduced to circumstances close to slavery. Ramiro Guerra y Sánchez has estimated that the great mills owned perhaps 20 percent of the island's area in 1927.

The expansion of the latifundio impoverished the rural masses of the island. The colonos were kept at subsistence levels, deeply indebted to the mill and in constant fear of eviction. The wages of rural workers were kept low because the mills imported cheap labor from other Caribbean islands. As a result, a considerable reserve pool of labor was available; even those lucky enough to get work worked only four months of the year during the harvest period. Displaced farmers had two choices. They could remain and work for small wages on a seasonal basis for the sugar mills (*centrales*), or they could emigrate to the cities, where jobs also were scarce. Small independent growers were at a severe disadvantage, for the mills squeezed the price paid for their cane to a minimum. In addition, the mills controlled the transportation network.

The ruin of the small mills and farmers and the low wages paid rural labor, which reduced the purchasing power of the masses, sharply limited the domestic market for manufactured goods and commercial services. There was thus little Cuban industrialization. Sugar companies monopolized the railroads and operated them solely for their own benefit, often without regard to the public interest. Although Cuba's railroad network exceeded that of most Latin American nations, it was inadequate to develop an internal market.

U.S. companies, which had poured money into Cuban sugar during the first occupation, had invested $200 million by 1913, predominantly in sugar. This accounted for nearly one-fifth the total U.S. investment in all of Latin America.

Dependent Development and Popular Struggle, 1902–1953

INTERVENTION, CORRUPTION, AND POPULAR RESISTANCE, 1902–1924

Cuba's political life, afflicted by its status as a U.S. protectorate and suffering from interventions, had a weak and stunted growth. Its first president, Tomás Estrada Palma, the aging former head of the government-in-exile during the Ten Years' War, had not even lived in Cuba for twenty-five years and consequently relied heavily on U.S. support to secure his election in 1901. Without a loyal Cuban constituency even among the "better class," Estrada set an enduring pattern in twentieth-century Cuban politics by implementing U.S.-sponsored policies and currying favor among local elites through patronage, graft, fraud, corruption, and intimidation.

Although these tactics served Estrada well in his 1905 reelection bid, they also alienated propertied elites excluded from the public dole; meanwhile, lower-class Cubans—peasant *guajiros*, workers, and Afro-Cubans—seethed at the government's neglect of the national liberation struggle's original goals: independence, equality, and social justice. The combination of elite and popular discontent, always a volatile mix, produced a series of revolts (in 1906, 1912, 1917, and 1921) that caused weak Cuban governments to invite U.S. military intervention.

In 1906 President William Howard Taft responded by sending in the Marines, and shortly afterward appointed Charles Magoon, a judge from Minnesota, to preside over a U.S. provisional government. Magoon's solution for the problem of factional violence was to divide patronage more equitably among contending Cuban groups. During the second occupation, elite resistance to U.S. domination virtually disappeared, due in large part to this new system of institutionalized corruption, which united all sections of the elite in the eager pursuit of U.S. favor and protection.

Magoon's provisional government also reformed the Cuban Army and reinvigorated the decade-old racist immigration policy of "whitening," which prohibited "races of color" but encouraged Spanish immigrants with travel subsidies and promises of public employment. According to the 1907 census, this had significantly reduced the proportion of Afro-Cubans to less than 30 percent of the total population. Magoon also attacked *brujería, ñáñiguismo,* and *santería,* the cultural centers of Afro-Cuban resistance, purged political partisans from the Rural Guard, reorganized the Cuban Army as a political counterweight to it, and developed both as institutions designed to protect private property and elite rule in Cuba.

Nonetheless, the lower classes remained restive. Workers, irrespective of race and gender, continued to organize trade unions and press their agenda for social justice. Meanwhile, Afro-Cuban mambises like José Isabel Herrera complained that U.S. investors, Spanish immigrants, and loyalist elites "took over the businesses, factories, and public jobs that we had just brought to independence." The case of Quintín Banderas was instructive: an Afro-Cuban who fought for thirty years against Spanish colonialism and rose to the rank of general, he died penniless and propertyless, unable even to secure a janitorial job with the government of independent Cuba.

In 1908, under the leadership of Evaristo Estenoz, a veteran of Cuba Libre, Afro-Cubans organized the Independent Party of Color (PIC) to defend the interests of black Cubans, to promote integration and racial democracy, and to protest against monopolization of the material rewards of independence by white elites and foreigners. The PIC denounced white supremacy

This 1912 cartoon, entitled "Today's Trendy Sport," depicts a U.S. Marine and a white Cuban soldier playing soccer with the heads of Evaristo Estenoz and Pedro Ivonnet, leaders of the Afro-Cuban insurrection in Oriente province. The caption reads, "Is this how 'football' will be played in Oriente?" [Biblioteca Nacional José Martí]

and demanded an end to racial discrimination, expansion of public employment and education programs, establishment of the eight-hour day, agrarian reform, and "Cuba for the Cubans." Despite official efforts to disrupt its activities, the PIC continued to expand until 1912, when, fearing imminent threats to capitalist labor and property relations, U.S. Marines joined the Cuban Army in what historian Aline Helg calls a "racist massacre" that left thousands of blacks dead and thereafter forced Afro-Cubans to pursue social justice through class and anti-imperialist struggles.

WORLD WAR I AND THE DANCE OF THE MILLIONS

Cuba's greatest sugar boom and bust occurred as a consequence of World War I. The fighting in Europe, which disrupted sugar production on the continent, from the first caused large price increases: prices nearly doubled in the first two months alone. Eventually, the Allies became totally dependent on Cuban sugar production, because they were fighting their major former supplier, Austria-Hungary. This demand spurred further expansion of Cuban sugar production, with planters moving into previously uncultivated land. The last great surge of mill construction also

Cutting sugar cane, Cuba, 1920. The end of Spanish rule in 1898 and the onset of U.S. occupation hastened the transformation of the island into a "large sugar planta-tion producing sugar for the benefit of foreign customers." [Bettmann/Corbis]

occurred. As production spread into virgin land, centrales were built and new towns sprang up.

The Allies attempted to keep commodity prices from skyrocketing by establishing purchasing committees to handle the acquisition of raw materials and food. Nonetheless, Cuban production rose in 1916 to 3 million tons at an average price of 4¢ a pound. Expansion created a severe labor shortage on the island, and laborers were imported from Jamaica and other Caribbean islands to fill the void. The colonos staged a comeback, and a few actually prospered.

The war accelerated the trend toward the concentration of the industry in U.S. hands. By 1919 approximately half the island's mills were owned by U.S. companies, and these controlled more than half the total production. The boom also led to the integration of sugar mills and plantations with distributors and companies that were large sugar users. Giants such as Coca-Cola, Hershey (chocolate), and Hires (root beer) bought up producers to guarantee their supplies. Producers in turn purchased distributors and refiners.

The postwar years of 1918 to 1920 brought unprecedented prosperity to Cuba as sugar prices soared and Eastern European sugar-producing areas were slow to recover from the war. After the Allied purchasing committees deregulated prices in 1920, they began an incredible upward spiral called the "Dance of the Millions." In February 1920 the price of sugar stood at 9.125¢ per pound. By mid-May the price had climbed to 22.5¢. But soon prices collapsed as a result of a worldwide depression and Europe's agricultural recovery; by December, Cubans were getting 3.75¢ per pound—the prewar price level.

The precipitous rise and equally sudden collapse of sugar prices caused chaos in the Cuban economy. Mills had contracts to buy large quantities of sugar at high prices, prices that were now far higher than the world market. Producers and processors had taken out loans to expand—loans based on anticipated high prices. Banks began to call in these loans. In April 1921 the island's largest bank, the *Banco Nacional*, closed, and others throughout the country followed suit. Simultaneously, the United States raised its tariff on sugar by 1¢, thereby inflicting another blow on the already devastated industry. In 1921 the First National City Bank of New York—long heavily involved with U.S. sugar interests in Cuba—took over nearly sixty bankrupt mills. The harvest reached 4 million tons in 1922, but prices stayed low. The following year, prices rose to 5¢ a pound as a result of the crisis over the French invasion of the Rhineland. Prices were not to reach that level again for three decades.

In 1920, Alfredo Zayas, a former liberal who had participated in an unsuccessful revolt in 1917, won the presidency with conservative support. Troubled over the crash of sugar prices in the second half of 1920 and the resulting political unrest in Cuba, President Warren Harding sent General Enoch Crowder to Cuba in January 1921 as his special representative. In effect, Crowder ruled Cuba from his headquarters on board the battleship *Minnesota* until 1923, when he became U.S. ambassador.

In the last two years of the Zayas administration, Cuban nationalism revived. Crowder's blatant meddling in Cuban politics and the postwar collapse of Cuban sugar revealed the disastrous consequences of foreign domination and monoculture. Searching for solutions to these problems, Cuban university students, one-quarter of whom were women, entered the political arena in the postwar period. Believing that to change society they must change the university, they directed their first attacks against inept and corrupt professors and administrators; in 1922 students at the University of Havana demonstrated for reforms along the lines of the recent university reform in Argentina. Students would henceforth play an important role in Cuban politics until the fall of Batista in 1959.

Women also played increasingly influential roles in Cuba. Economic growth, especially in household services, textiles, and the tobacco and sugar-refining industries, created greater employment for women outside the home. But as they moved "from the house to the streets," in the words of historian Lynn Stoner, women brought to their public activities a communal consciousness forged in family life. Even the Women's Club, organized in 1917 and composed primarily of upper- and middle-class women, insisted that the state, the *pater familias* of Cuban society, should regulate domestic social relations consistent with the common welfare. It therefore supported women's suffrage, equal pay for equal work, greater access to education, and civil equality.

But for Cuban elites and U.S. policymakers, the growing political activism of students and women was not their greatest concern. In the 1920s there emerged a much larger cultural struggle over Cuban national identity that could have had grave implications for the future security of property rights and U.S. hegemony. Historically, Spanish and criollo elites alike had sought to identify the island's culture with Spain and racist doctrines of white supremacy. The various U.S. military occupations, reflecting their own racial and class prejudices, thereafter reinforced these efforts and joined criollo elites in fashioning an image of Cuba as a white Spanish woman menaced by its black population. This image of whiteness was reinforced by a "national music" identified with Spain and the *danzón*, a rigidly structured dance favored by Cuba's upper class, whose origins lay in the French *contredanse*. But popular sectors in Cuba, especially in Oriente province, long a stronghold of Afro-Cuban culture, had contested this elite vision of Cuba's national identity and preferred the multicultural sound of *son*, a musical style that joined traditional Spanish melodies with African rhythms to reimagine a racially diverse Cuban national culture.

Initially denounced by criollo elites like composer Luis Casas Romero as a "true disgrace," and suppressed by the Cuban government, postwar working-class Cubans defiantly resisted the elite's cultural hegemony and thrilled to the pulsating beat of *son* and the *rumba*, the dance it inspired. Together, son and the rumba, which pantomimed sexual intercourse, gave voice to a popular culture that sought to liberate Afro-Cubans and the lower classes from social controls imposed by the dominant class. During the 1920s the development of radio and recording industries soon created a new audience for this music and dance that, according to historian Louis Pérez, previously had been confined to "working class bars, waterfront cafés, and dancehalls." Boaz Long, the U.S. Minister to Cuba, perhaps best expressed elite fears of this spreading cultural rebellion in a 1920 letter that scorned Cubans' growing affection for the "syncopated music of Africa" and specifically deplored the social dangers of the rumba, which "often become indecent" and "have the effect of developing a mob spirit." More to the point, however, Long was especially concerned that "in the case of the negro they may arouse a sense of racial solidarity."

MACHADO, 1925–1933

Taking advantage of growing nationalistic sentiment and appealing for women's support with promises of enfranchisement, Gerardo Machado y Morales won the 1924 presidential election. Despite his nationalistic declarations, however, Machado had very close links to U.S. economic interests, for he had been until his election vice president of a U.S.-owned utility in Havana. Even before he took office, Machado visited the United States to assure President Calvin Coolidge of his government's good intentions. Likewise, Machado neglected his promise of suffrage for women, although he authorized breaks for working mothers to nurse their children and established some female hiring quotas.

Machado began his term auspiciously. He embarked on an ambitious program of public works and attempted to institute a system of controls for sugar production designed to protect small- and medium-sized producers against severe price declines. Thanks to these and similar efforts, Machado enjoyed unparalleled popularity and faced virtually no opposition for two years.

Already, however, there were disturbing signs of tyranny and economic instability. The number of political assassinations increased alarmingly. A wave of strikes during 1925 was broken by police shooting down strikers. The nation's most prominent Communist leader, Julio Antonio Mella, was murdered in his Mexican exile by a Machado gunman in 1929. Machado's secret police routinely eliminated his opponents by throwing them to the sharks in Havana Harbor.

Meanwhile, the sugar industry entered a long period of stagnation and decline. It became clear that the Cuban economy was painfully vulnerable not only to world-market fluctuations but also to U.S. political conditions. During this decade, Cuba lost much of its U.S. market because it encountered the powerful interests of sugar-beet farmers in the western United States. To make matters worse, sugar consumption stayed constant as international competition increased supply.

Consequently, the 1926 Cuban harvest reached nearly 5 million tons but brought an average of only 2.2¢ per pound. For the rest of the decade, the price of sugar stayed below 3.0¢, and after the U.S. Congress passed the Hawley-Smoot Tariff Act, Cuba's share of the U.S. market shrank steadily, from 49.4 percent in 1930 to 25.3 percent in 1933. By 1932 the price for sugar fell below a penny per pound. Mills closed, and people were thrown out of work all over the island.

Given this growing economic instability, Machado outlawed the party of his main rival, Carlos Mendieta, to secure his reelection in 1928. Until the onset of the world Depression in 1930, Machado maintained an iron grip on Cuba, despite mounting opposition from university students, women, Communists, labor unions, Afro-Cuban "negristas" like Nicolás Guillén, and many old-line politicians led by Mendieta. Because of Cuba's heavy reliance on exports, the Great Depression had particularly catastrophic consequences, fueling greater political unrest, to which Machado responded with increasingly harsh repression that included tightened censorship and stepped-up terror tactics on the part of his secret police, the *Porra*.

By 1933 the U.S. government had become seriously concerned about the spreading violence, which appeared to threaten U.S. economic interests. In April incoming President Franklin Roosevelt dispatched Sumner Welles in an unsuccessful attempt to negotiate agreement between Machado and the "responsible" opposition, which effectively excluded popular organizations like the

Student Directory and the National Confederation of Cuban Workers (CNOC). Then in the summer, a bus drivers' strike in Havana mushroomed into a general strike that nearly paralyzed the city. After the police massacred several demonstrators in August, Machado's position seriously deteriorated, for he had lost the support of Welles and the army, both of whom lacked confidence in his ability to contain the revolutionary storm. On August 12, Machado resigned and fled into exile.

THE REVOLUTION OF 1933

For the next three weeks, a provisional government headed by Carlos Manuel de Céspedes struggled unsuccessfully to end the escalating violence. But in August two hundred thousand sugar workers, led by Afro-Cuban Communist León Álvarez, joined student protests and seized a sugar mill in Camaguey province, sparking similar actions throughout Cuba; within a month fully 30 percent of Cuban sugar production was controlled by workers organized into rural soviets. With the old regime rapidly unraveling, a group of army sergeants, led by Fulgencio Batista, overthrew the government. The Student Directory immediately allied itself with the sergeants, and together they formed a revolutionary junta.

The new junta had no organized political backing, and its two main components, the noncommissioned officers and the Student Directory, had sharply divergent aims. The sergeants were concerned only with defending their newly won dominant position against any challenge, whereas the students sought genuine reforms but were unsure just how to achieve them. Within a week, the junta turned over the reins of government to Dr. Ramón Grau San Martín, a well-known physician and long-time opponent of Machado. Grau, Antonio Guiteras Holmes, a leader of the Student Directory, and Batista were dominant figures in the new alignment.

The first move of the new government was to abrogate the onerous Platt Amendment. A flurry of decrees produced more social legislation than in all the previous history of independent Cuba: an eight-hour day for labor, a labor department,

an end to the importation of cheap labor from other islands in the Caribbean, and greater access for children from lower-income groups to the university. There were also measures to redistribute land to peasants, eliminate usury, and give women the vote. Thus empowered, seven newly elected women congressional representatives helped expand the revolution's social achievements by legislating protections for working mothers, including a twelve-week maternity leave, mandatory employer-provided child care for infants, and prohibitions against firing women for getting married.

Ultimately, however, the revolutionary coalition soon disintegrated, leaving the Grau government caught in the classic bind of the reformer: the left, which included the Student Directory and Communists, was dissatisfied because the reforms were not sufficiently radical; moderates like the ABC, a group of middle-class intellectuals, opposed Grau because his program had become "too radical"; and the right opposed all reform. Grau also alienated U.S. financial and agricultural interests when he suspended repayment of several loans owed to the Chase National Bank of New York and seized two mills of the Cuban-American Sugar Company. The U.S. government adamantly refused to recognize the Grau government.

The behavior of Sumner Welles throughout the Grau interregnum was extraordinarily similar to the conduct of U.S. Ambassador Henry Lane Wilson in Mexico during the Madero administration. Welles persistently falsified reports and misrepresented the Cuban government to Secretary of State Cordell Hull and President Roosevelt. As Wilson had befriended Huerta and helped him to power, so Welles allied himself with Batista. Eventually (in November 1933), Welles was recalled, but he had seriously undermined the Grau government. As the economic and political situation worsened, Welles's successor, Jefferson Caffery, maneuvered with Batista to form a new government acceptable to the United States. In January 1934, Grau, unable to rule effectively in the face of U.S. opposition, went into exile and was replaced by Carlos Mendieta, but Batista ruled from the shadows.

POPULIST INTERLUDE, 1938–1952

Fulgencio Batista y Zaldívar, the sergeant-stenographer mulatto son of a sugar worker, dominated Cuban politics for the next decade, ruling the island through puppet presidents from 1934 to 1940 and as elected president from 1940 to 1944. Although Batista alienated many of the "respectable" elements of the middle and upper classes, he was extremely popular among the masses. During the first two years after his successful coup, he endorsed a mild reform program with some effort at land redistribution. In 1937, in preparation for a presidential candidacy, he distanced himself from the United States and moved leftward, openly courting the support of labor unions and the Communists.

In the same year, the world's sugar-producing nations met in London to try to reach an agreement that would divide up the market, limit production, and stabilize prices. They formed an International Sugar Council, which allotted Cuba 29 percent of the U.S. market, half its share in 1929. Moreover, the bulk of the profits generated by Cuba's sugar economy continued to flow out of the country, because foreign companies accounted for 80 percent of Cuban production (U.S. companies controlled 56 percent), whereas Cubans owned barely 20 percent.

At the end of 1939, Batista permitted the election of a constituent assembly to draft the constitution of 1940. Grau and his *Auténtico* Party (founded in 1934) and other moderates won the election to the assembly and produced a liberal document with provisions that protected labor, guaranteed women equal rights, and limited the right of property when it conflicted with the public good. Batista, however, won the presidential election.

World War II brought on another economic boom. In 1944 production reached its highest level since the Depression. In 1946, as part of its efforts to aid European recovery, the United States agreed to purchase the entire sugar harvest for 3.7¢ a pound. During the Korean war, the price of sugar soared to 5.0¢. Inevitably, however, Cuba's competitors, especially the Philippines, expanded production. The market soon became glutted with sugar, and prices fell. But wartime prosperity, while deepening Cuba's trade dependence on sugar and U.S. markets (sugar exports accounted for 80 percent of all Cuban export earnings, 69 percent of which came from U.S. sales), also swelled company profits and government tax receipts, creating a fund to support intra-elite corruption and populist social programs without unduly burdening business, foreign or domestic. These modest reform programs typically aimed to stabilize capitalist labor and property relations.

Grau, elected president in 1944, continued this tradition. A symbol of Cuban regeneration and democracy, he offered hope to Cuban workers, peasants, women, and fledgling industrialists. He especially acknowledged his political debt to Cuban women voters, declaring that "my government is a government of women." But Grau did little to make good on his promises; instead he presided over an unparalleled reign of corruption. True, the Grau government initiated some reforms, the most significant of which was encouragement of trade-union organizing. By the end of his presidential term, 30 to 50 percent of the work force was unionized and represented the key industries of sugar, tobacco, textiles, transportation, and light manufacturing. These workers used their collective bargaining power and the favorable market conditions to demand higher wages and better working conditions. But Grau made no attack on such key problems as agrarian reform and monoculture.

In 1947 a charismatic populist leader, Eddie Chibás, launched a new campaign against government oppression and corruption. A former ardent supporter of the Auténticos, Chibás had become disillusioned and formed the *Ortodoxo* Party, which featured a mild program of social reform and clean politics. Extremely popular, he posed a serious threat to the Auténticos, whose 1948 presidential candidate, Carlos Prío Socorrás, former leader of the Student Directory, nonetheless won easily because he controlled the election machinery. Prío became another in a long line of Cuban country-club presidents who spent much of his time serving his guests daiquiris at his opulent farm in the suburbs of Havana. There was no letup in the corruption, gangsterism, and spoils system characteristic of his predecessor's regime. As under Grau, the prosperity brought on by high sugar prices concealed Prío's mismanagement.

But a dramatic postwar contraction of overseas sugar markets and collapse of international sugar prices, intensified by U.S. laws that reduced the Cuban sugar quota to protect domestic sugar producers, spread economic depression throughout Cuba. This produced growing unrest among the lower class and increasing opposition among foreign and Cuban businesses that could no longer afford to finance the Auténticos' insatiable corruption or expensive populist reforms. Foreign investors especially insisted that the Auténticos rein in militant workers; an executive at the Cuban subsidiary of Bethlehem Steel, for example, noted with obvious displeasure that "the problem during the Grau and Prío Governments was labor strikes."

Still worse, the unorthodox populist Eddie Chibás, a leading candidate for the presidency in 1952, anticipated that either a military coup or fraud would prevent his election. Seeking to ignite a popular uprising against corruption and foreign influence, he killed himself during a nationwide radio broadcast, plunging the nation into political pandemonium. Six months later, Fulgencio Batista, with tacit U.S. support, overthrew the Prío government, outlawed the Cuban Communist Party, violently suppressed labor strikes, abolished recalcitrant unions, and eliminated most earlier populist restrictions on business freedom.

THE RETURN OF BATISTA AS DICTATOR, 1952–1959

Batista's new minister of labor, Dr. Carlos Saladrigas, seeking to reassure Cuban business elites and U.S. investors, immediately announced that the coup's goal was to "bring about a radical change in labor-employer relations and remove obstacles for investment of national and foreign capital." A week later, the U.S. government officially recognized the Batista regime, and corporate leaders praised his policies: "When Batista took over there were no more strikes," a Bethlehem Steel executive told historian Morris Morley. "I found economic conditions under Batista more

stable." A Merrill-Lynch executive likewise praised Batista for permitting "business, the competitive system, the free enterprise system to operate."

While the policies protected by Batista's political terrorism found much favor among business elites, they remained highly unpopular with most Cubans. Moreover, like his contemporaries, Carlos Ibáñez in Chile, Getúlio Vargas in Brazil, and Juan Perón in Argentina, Batista soon discovered that ruling a second time would prove more difficult than the first. A new generation of revolutionaries rose to replace the discredited leaders of 1933. Unlike Grau or Prío, they would not be bought off or collaborate with the dictator. Several groups opposed Batista, including the Federation of University Students (FEU) and the Auténticos, who plotted from their havens in Florida; the 26th of July Movement, led by Fidel Castro, unsuccessfully tried to overthrow the government in 1953 by assaulting the Moncada army barracks. Despite the activities of the students and Castro's guerrilla group, the dictator seemed to be firmly entrenched, but his greatest vulnerability remained the structural weakness of the economy, produced by reliance on a single crop, sugar.

Meanwhile, Cuba's sugar industry had stagnated, and the resulting malaise had spread throughout the economy. Agriculture had not become diversified because the land was concentrated in a very few hands—twenty-two companies held one-fifth of the island's farmland. Much of the land was kept idle in case sugar prices should ever boom. Industry was almost nonexistent, for a series of reciprocal trade agreements with the United States—which guaranteed Cuba's sugar market—made it impossible to compete with U.S. imports. These same treaties also stunted agriculture by permitting a flow of agricultural products from the United States, the low prices of which barred potential Cuban competition. Because of its stagnant economy and the peculiar nature of the sugar industry, Cuba suffered from structural unemployment and underemployment. Most sugar workers were needed only during the harvest; even if well paid during this four-month period, they went jobless and often hungry during the other eight months. These structural deficiencies and the economic injustices created by them helped lay the foundation for the Cuban Revolution.

The Revolution: The Odyssey of Fidel Castro

The Cuban Revolution was deeply rooted in the history of the island, for the movement headed by Fidel Castro continued the revolutionary traditions of 1868, 1898, and 1933. By no coincidence, both before and after gaining power, Castro often cited the ideals of José Martí and the principles of the liberal constitution of 1940. Yet profound disillusionment accompanied those traditions, for Cuba's past revolutions had invariably failed—either its leaders had succumbed to the temptations of great wealth, or the United States had intervened to thwart their programs. In large part, the complex development of the Cuban Revolution reflected a combination of loyalty to those revolutionary traditions and a fear of falling into their errors. Castro desperately sought to avoid past mistakes.

Fidel Castro Ruz, the son of a wealthy Spanish farmer in northwest Cuba, was born in 1927. He attended the famous Jesuit school of Belén in Havana and acquired a reputation as a fine athlete. In 1945 he went off to the University of Havana, where he soon became involved in the frequently violent politics that then plagued the university. In 1947 he participated in an ill-fated invasion of the Dominican Republic, sponsored by student political groups that sought to overthrow dictator Rafael Trujillo. Later he became a follower of Eddie Chibás, to whose Ortodoxo Party he belonged from 1947 to 1952.

On July 26, 1953, Castro, in hopes of sparking a rebellion against the Batista dictatorship, led a small band of lower-middle-class and working-class rebels that attacked the Moncada army barracks near Santiago de Cuba. Their program called for a return to the constitution of 1940, land reform, educational reform, and an end to the vast waste caused by government corruption and large weapons expenditures. Although the assault failed, with heavy casualties, and Castro was captured, the drastic acts of repression the government carried out in its wake and Castro's eloquent defense speech at his trial ("History Will Absolve Me") made him a national hero.

Castro spent the next nineteen months in prison on the Isle of Pines. During this period, the leadership of the 26th of July Movement fell largely to women compatriots like Haydée Santamaría, a founding member of the 1952 anti-Batista resistance, and Melba Hernández, the intrepid lawyer who had defended Castro at trial. They forged political alliances with other anti-Batista groups like the Association of United Cuban Women, led by Gloria Cuadras, and the Women's Martí Civic Front, organized by Carmen Castro Porta, whose antidictatorial activities were rooted in struggles against the Machado regime in the 1920s.

Together, they built a network of urban and rural women who served the revolution as lawyers, interpreters, medical aides, grassroots organizers, educators, spies, messengers, and armed combatants. In addition to Celia Sánchez, perhaps Cuba's best-known woman guerrilla, the revolution also spawned a female combat unit known as the Mariana Grajales Brigade, in honor of the "heroic mother" of the Afro-Cuban independence fighter, Antonio Maceo.

By 1955 these women had produced and distributed some ten thousand copies of Castro's *History Will Absolve Me*, which enhanced his reputation. Batista's general amnesty freed him in 1955, and shortly thereafter he went to Mexico to organize a new attack on the dictatorship. While in Mexico, Castro's group received support from ex-president Prío and Venezuelan exile Rómulo Betancourt (later president of Venezuela). Late in 1955, Castro met Ernesto (Che) Guevara, who was to become the revolution's second-in-command and its greatest martyr.

Castro was determined to return to the island to renew the struggle. In 1956 he and his band departed from Mexico aboard a small yacht, the *Granma*, with eighty-two persons aboard. Originally, Castro had planned to coordinate the landing in Oriente Province with an uprising in Santiago. As happened with the Moncada attack, however, the landing encountered logistical and scheduling problems, and Castro and his followers were betrayed. He and a small group of survivors barely escaped to the Sierra Maestra. From these mountains, the rebels carried out guerrilla raids and beat off attacks by vastly superior forces.

In February 1957, with Vilma Espín, wealthy daughter of a Bacardí rum company executive, acting as interpreter, Castro granted an interview in his mountain hide-out to Herbert Matthews, a well-known reporter for the *New York Times.* The resulting articles enhanced Castro's credibility in the United States and also gave notice to the Cuban people that he was still alive, despite government claims to the contrary. The articles overstated the numerical strength and success of the movement and thereby helped win adherents to the rebel cause all over the island. The guerrillas continued to conduct raids throughout the spring of 1957, picking up recruits and gaining increased sympathy and support from the peasants of Oriente, who rendered invaluable assistance in the form of supplies and intelligence information about government forces.

By mid-1957 violence, especially in Havana, had become endemic as various groups, most unaffiliated with Castro's 26th of July Movement, attacked the regime and met with brutal retaliation. Even women revolutionaries, insulated from earlier repression by the regime's sexism, began to experience wholesale arrests, torture, and imprisonment. But they maintained a sense of humor; when their lawyer, Margo Aniceto Rodríguez, was also imprisoned for denouncing Batista's terrorism, other jailed rebels joked that "Margo is such a good lawyer that, if she cannot free us, she at least comes to stay with us in prison."

Life in Santiago and Oriente Province was completely disrupted by terrorism and strikes. Cuba was increasingly gripped by civil war. In the fall there was an abortive uprising of junior naval officers at Cienfuegos. Batista used bombers and other military equipment to crush the revolt; this alienated some of his U.S. support, as the terms of Cuba's military assistance agreement with the United States expressly forbade using this equipment for domestic purposes.

After the new year, the trend of events turned decisively against Batista. The United States suspended arms shipments to the Cuban government in March 1958. The middle class abandoned the dictator. In May, Batista launched a major effort to dislodge Castro from his base in the Sierra Maestra, and the resulting defeat doomed his regime. Rebel forces inflicted heavy losses on the government troops. Withered by corruption and led by incompetent cronies of Batista, the army was no match for the guerrillas.

As Batista's plight grew desperate, frantic negotiations involving the U.S. embassy began with a view to staving off Castro's victory by the creation, through a coup or fraudulent elections, of a new government, which the U.S. government would recognize and assist militarily. Batista actually held presidential elections, printing up filled-in ballots in advance, and readied a president to take office in February. But the strong drive of the rebel forces frustrated these maneuvers; by the end of December 1958 the *barbudos* (bearded revolutionaries) were on the outskirts of Havana. On January 1, 1959, abandoned by his U.S. allies, Batista and his closest aides fled to Miami.

Thus, a rebel band, numbering fewer than three hundred until mid-1958 and scarcely three thousand when the old regime fell, won a great victory because they were persistent and disciplined and gained the sympathy of all the people—peasants, workers, and the middle class. But they also faced an army wracked by favoritism and incompetence. Batista's army, when put to the test, proved able to terrorize unarmed citizens but disintegrated when confronted with a formidable insurgency.

The Revolution in Power, 1959–2003

During its first four years (1959–1962), the revolution consolidated its domestic political position, began the socialization of the economy, and established a new pattern of foreign relations. In 1959 the revolutionary leaders made a series of decisions that determined the course of the revolution for the next decade. First, they concluded that parliamentary democracy was inappropriate for Cuba at that time. The Fundamental Law of the Republic, decreed in February 1959, concentrated legislative power in the executive. As prime minister and later as first secretary of the Communist Party, Castro held the decisive posts in the government and the ruling party of the Cuban state. Within eighteen months, the revolutionary regime had suppressed the right of free press and the centuries-old autonomy of the University of Havana. The revolutionaries conducted public trials of former *Batistianos*, and a large number of Batista's henchmen were executed.

Second, Castro moved the revolution leftward to consolidate its political support and accomplish its economic goals—land reform, income redistribution, agricultural diversification, and economic independence from the United States. The radicalism of this economic program and the concentration of political power in the hands of the close-knit 26th of July Movement alienated middle-class supporters like Major Huber Matos and President Manuel Urrutía, who resigned in July 1959. In October, Matos, one of the revolution's foremost military leaders and a violent anticommunist, was charged with treason and imprisoned. At the same time, the revolutionaries allied with the Popular Socialist (Communist) Party, seeking its help in administering the country.

In January 1960 moderate elements were purged from the leadership of Cuban labor unions and the Soviet Union was cultivated as an ally to diversify the nation's economic dependence and protect the revolution from U.S. intervention. Soviet deputy premier Anastas Mikoyan agreed that the Soviets would purchase 425,000 tons of Cuban sugar in 1960 and 1,000,000 tons the next year. In May, Cuba resumed diplomatic relations with the Soviet Union.

UNITED STATES–CUBAN RELATIONS

Meanwhile, Cuban relations with the United States, already suffering from the unfavorable publicity brought by the trials and the expropriation of large estates, reached a crisis in May 1960. The Cuban government requested that the major petroleum refineries, owned by Texaco, Standard Oil, and Royal Dutch Shell, process Soviet crude oil, which the Cubans had obtained at a lower price than the three companies charged for their oil. At the urging of the U.S. State Department, the companies refused, forcing Cuba to expropriate the refineries. The United States retaliated by abolishing the Cuban sugar quota, and Cuba in turn expropriated numerous U.S.-owned properties.[1] In October all U.S. exports to Cuba were banned—an embargo that has not yet been lifted. This action set off a new wave of expropriations of U.S. property, including that of Sears, Roebuck, Coca-Cola, and the enormous U.S. government–owned nickel deposits at Moa Bay.

As relations between the two nations deteriorated, the Central Intelligence Agency (CIA) funneled money to various exile groups for arms and set up a training camp in Guatemala to prepare an invasion force. On January 3, 1961, the outgoing Eisenhower administration severed diplomatic relations with Cuba, and three months later, President John F. Kennedy authorized the exile invasion at the Bay of Pigs on April 15. But the revolutionary army swiftly crushed the attack, which had been poorly planned and executed. Based on the false assumption that the Cuban people would revolt in support of the exile invasion, the Bay of Pigs fiasco immeasurably increased Castro's prestige and gave new impetus for radical reconstruction of the Cuban economy and society.

What had begun as a program of social and political reform within a framework of constitutional democracy and capitalism evolved into a Marxist revolution. One month after the Bay of Pigs, Castro proclaimed allegiance to socialism, and the Soviet Union, pledging to defend Cuba in the event of another U.S. attack, stepped up its flow of arms to the island.

These included missile emplacements and aircraft capable of delivering atomic weapons throughout most of North and South America. Although Cuba and the Soviet Union argued that

---

[1]The government had previously taken over only the operation of these properties.

the missiles had a defensive, deterrent character, the United States claimed that they were offensive weapons, ordered a naval quarantine of Cuba, and demanded the dismantling of the missile sites. For a time it appeared as if Kennedy was losing control of his military, which was pressing to use force against Cuba. After several days, during which the world came close to nuclear war, the two superpowers reached a compromise by which the Soviet Union agreed to remove its missiles from Cuba in return for a pledge from the United States not to invade Cuba and to remove its own missiles from Turkey. However, the United States continued to subvert and harass the Cuban Revolution with the aid of counterrevolutionary Cuban exiles; this included CIA-sponsored raids against refineries and ports, infiltration of enemy agents, and even some bizarre attempts to assassinate Castro.

REVOLUTIONARY ECONOMICS

The Cuban Revolution benefited from advantages few other socialist revolutions have enjoyed. The guerrilla war (in contrast to that of China or Vietnam) was relatively short and caused little destruction of human life or property. Moreover, Cuba had well-developed communications and transportation systems, including an extensive railroad network and excellent primary roads. The character of Cuba's rural population promised to make the process of socialist land reform easier than it had been in Russia, for example. Because the sugar industry had proletarianized much of the agricultural work force, farm workers did not demand their own land but sought improved working conditions and wages. Cuba also had considerable unused land and industrial capacity, which could be quickly employed to raise living standards and increase productivity. Finally, by 1959 there existed a number of developed socialist states that could offer Cuba substantial assistance, thus offsetting the severe negative effects of the U.S. embargo on exports.

But the revolution also faced serious problems. To begin with, the revolutionaries, inexperienced in economic affairs, made mistakes. The socialist reorientation of the economy inevitably caused disruptions, and the U.S. embargo caused crippling shortages of parts and other difficulties, which the development of new patterns of trade with countries in the socialist camp (and with some capitalist countries) only gradually overcame. Also, many of Cuba's ablest technicians joined the first wave of refugees that fled to the United States. Finally, revolutionary leaders initially spurned material incentives, endorsed by more traditional Marxists as the best spur to production, in favor of moral incentives, which would give rise to the "new socialist man." Application of this theory caused considerable economic damage before it was replaced in 1969 by a more pragmatic mix of material and moral incentives.

The first goal of the revolutionary government was to redistribute income to the rural and urban working class. During the first three years, it met with considerable success, raising wages 40 percent and overall purchasing power 20 percent. Unemployment was virtually wiped out. These benefits accrued predominantly to areas outside Havana, for the revolutionaries were determined to reverse the trend toward the superurbanization characteristic of most of Latin America.[2]

Castro decreed the first Law of Agrarian Reform in May 1959. This law restricted the size of landholdings and gave the government the right to expropriate private holdings in excess of stated limits; the owners would be indemnified depending on the assessed value of the property for tax purposes. The estates of Batistiano government officials were taken over immediately, followed by seizure of the great cattle estates when their owners resisted. The government distributed the expropriated land in small plots or established cooperatives, which the Institute of Agrarian Reform (INRA) administered. Much of the land redistribution took place in Oriente Province, where the peasants had provided early and crucial support for the 26th of July Movement. Eighty-five percent of all Cuban farms fell under the jurisdiction of the reform law because landownership had been so highly concentrated under the old regime.

---

[2]"Superurbanization" is used to describe the vast expansion through internal migration and concentrated industrialization of one city, usually the capital.

During the first year of its rule, the Cuban government experimented with various types of agrarian holdings. Eventually, all became *granjas del pueblo* (state farms). Administered by INRA, they usually employed the same workers who had toiled on them before the revolution, but workers were paid better wages and offered improved working conditions.

The redistribution of income to workers and peasants resulted in some long-range problems. With more money to spend, Cubans demanded more food, especially meat, the consumption of which rose 100 percent. This rising demand led to the overkilling of cattle, which seriously damaged the ability of the government to supply meat in later years. The government lowered rents and utility rates and supplied many services free of charge, which increased disposable income even more. Inevitably, shortages arose because Cuba no longer imported consumer goods and foodstuffs. Rather than limit consumption inequitably by raising prices, the government began rationing in March 1962. The revolutionaries also poured large sums into rural housing, roads, and other improvements, but poor planning wasted scarce resources.

Two other important programs had mixed success during the first three years: agricultural diversification and industrialization. The revolutionary government sought to become more self-sufficient by transferring cane land and idle fields to the production of cotton, vegetable oils, rice, soybeans, and peanuts, which would save badly needed foreign exchange on these previously imported commodities. Industrial reforms began slowly; the government at first took over the management of just one major foreign company, the extremely unpopular telephone company. But U.S. efforts to sabotage the revolution ultimately led to sweeping expropriations of U.S.-owned refineries, factories, utilities, and sugar mills. Next, the government took over the banking system and most urban housing. Finally, the revolutionary regime began to expropriate native-owned businesses. But more ambitious industrial development plans proved too difficult, and the program was officially put off in 1963.

The revolutionaries encountered serious problems in agriculture after 1961 because of their inability to organize, plan, and administer the economy. Although Castro set up a central planning agency, JUCEPLAN, in February 1961, more often than not he ignored or circumvented it with his personal "special" plans. For a long time, the government also ignored the private agricultural sector, a critical oversight because more than half the farmland remained in private hands. In early 1961, in an effort to overcome this neglect, the government established the National Association of Small Farmers (ANAP), which tried to coordinate the production of small farms with national goals. It also furnished credit, set up stores, and organized various associations.

THE RETURN TO SUGAR, 1963–1970: THE TEN-MILLION-TON HARVEST

Experience had shown that Cuba lacked the resources and the administrative and technical expertise to industrialize. As a consequence, Cubans decided in 1963 to reemphasize agriculture and return to intensive sugar production, while continuing the diversification program. Increased agricultural production, it was hoped, would generate large earnings and eventually underwrite future industrialization.

Unfortunately, agriculture, especially sugar, had suffered enormously from well-intentioned but short-sighted policies. The sugar harvests of 1960 and 1961 had been extraordinarily successful because they benefited from very favorable weather and because the island's cane was at the age of peak yield. Also, for the first time in a decade, the entire crop was harvested. But the sugar harvest of 1962 was the worst since 1955, and subsequent harvests continued to be disappointing. The essential problem was that the revolutionaries, in their fervor to diversify, had ripped up some of the best cane land. They had not replanted cane in two years, and as a result most Cuban cane was well past its peak yield. Moreover, equipment and manpower were badly administered. Transportation and distribution were in chaos. Sugar mills were damaged and left unrepaired for years. As a result, from 1962 to 1969, agricultural production fell 7 percent.

Nonetheless, the government made considerable efforts to correct the situation. The regime decreed the second Law of Agrarian Reform in October 1963; under this law, it expropriated thousands of medium-sized farms. State farms became the dominant form of agriculture, controlling 70 percent of the land and taking responsibility for all the major export crops. The government also forced those small farmers who remained to sell it their crops at low cost. Cuba put a remarkable portion of its gross national product into investment, but that achievement was largely wasted through inefficient administration and poor planning. Many projects were abandoned unfinished, and those that were completed were often improperly maintained and rendered useless.

Thereafter, Cuba launched a new campaign of socialization that centralized the administration of the economy. The most visible symbol of this policy change was the ill-fated, ten-million-ton sugar harvest of 1970. Designed to model the effectiveness of a socialist developmental strategy that stressed "moral" over "material" incentives for workers, it also aimed to produce the largest sugar harvest in Cuba's history and to use the anticipated foreign exchange bonanza to invest in the nation's independent industrial development. Confronted with the reality of a severely damaged and underdeveloped agricultural infrastructure capable of producing at best six million tons of sugar, however, the effort was doomed to fail. Ironically, even revolutionary successes contributed to its failure: the revolution had created considerable employment opportunities outside the sugar industry, but this left it with one-fifth the former number of professional cane cutters in 1959 and required a mobilization of nonagricultural labor that seriously depleted resources and destabilized the national economy.

FAILURE, REASSESSMENT, AND INSTITUTIONALIZED REVOLUTION, 1970–1990

The ballyhooed "ten-million-ton harvest" of 1970 failed to reach its acclaimed goal and in the process did extensive damage to the Cuban economy as a whole. To get the 8.5 million tons they did eventually harvest, the revolutionaries virtually ruined the sugar industry, and subsequent harvests generally were poor. Resources and labor were siphoned off from other sectors, causing disruption and turmoil.

Even more significantly, however, these disastrous economic policies—and the centralized authoritarian state whose administration they seemed to require—began to separate the revolutionary leadership from its base of popular support. No matter how much U.S.-sponsored counterrevolutionary terrorism may have justified it in these years, the regime's blatant disregard for civil liberties and its authoritarian manner would remain a permanent stain on an otherwise laudable revolutionary record. Many Cubans, especially young people excited by the revolution's democratic promise, refused to accept these practical constraints on their liberty. Slowly, a new popular anti-authoritarian cultural movement emerged around the *canción de protesta* (protest song). This movement attracted youth who believed in the revolution's goal of social justice but increasingly opposed the hierarchical nature of state decision making, especially its personalist association with Fidel Castro. Ironically, it was greatly influenced by African and Asian anticolonial struggles, the celebration of indigenous folk cultures in Chile and Argentina, and especially Brazilian popular resistance to military dictatorship—all of which the Cuban revolutionary regime also promoted.

Protest songs marked a distinctive development in Cuban music and culture. In the early 1960s folk artists like Carlos Puebla and Los Compadres (The Godfathers) had combined *son* and traditional Cuban country music (*música guajira*) with lyrics that sang the praises of the revolution and its guerrilla heroes. Los Compadres's popular song *"Se acabarán los bohíos"* ("The Shacks Will Disappear"), for example, celebrated the revolution's promise of "a living wage, an apartment for every family, hard work," and the eradication of bohíos, except those that "remain as museum pieces." The protest singers of the late 1960s, however, identified with the revolution's idealistic and humanitarian goals but criticized its failures, especially its authoritarianism and restraint of artistic freedom.

Silvio Rodríguez, one of the movement's principal voices, captured this sense of revolutionary patriotism and youthful alienation when he denounced state bureaucrats as "bosses who said one thing and did another, squares, those who didn't trust the young, guys with all the perks, enemies of culture, the establishment cowards who were ruining the revolution that I carried inside of me." For Rodríguez and thousands of other young Cubans, it was hypocritical for the revolutionary leadership to encourage Latin American, Asian, and African peoples to rebel against tradition but simultaneously to restrain youthful Cuban rebels, who expressed their dissatisfaction by wearing long hair, hippie clothing, and tattoos.

Some within the revolutionary state agreed. Haydée Santamaría, a veteran of the Sierra Maestra and the 1953 attack on Moncada, refused to surrender to bureaucratic pressures and sought to protect these young protest artists. As the head of the Casa de las Américas, a revolutionary state institution that coordinated cultural exchanges with the rest of Latin America, she organized a series of international music festivals that gave voice to protest songs and, for a time, secured their access to state radio and television programming. But in general, as sugar harvests failed and protest singers were jailed, these were bleak years for the revolutionary economy, cultural expression, and political freedoms.

The great failure of the 1970 sugar harvest, however, prompted a searching self-criticism and dramatic rethinking of revolutionary policies and process. Castro himself admitted his personal responsibility for this failure and vowed to make changes that would advance the revolution. This led to greater political openness and popular political participation. It also enabled the revolutionary leadership once again to embrace its rebellious youth culture. According to ethnomusicologist Robin Moore, "In the space of only a few years, protest song moved from the margin into the mainstream of socialist music making." Changes in revolutionary state policy, not the surrender of young artists' independence, clearly facilitated this rapid rapprochement.

The Cuban government now increasingly supported this new music, known as *nueva trova* (new ballad), and encouraged its young musicians to represent Cuba at international music festivals organized in Latin America, Spain, and Eastern Europe. It also created the National Movement of the Ballad (MNT), a state organization designed to encourage musical careers and fund the creative arts. Performance centers were established in every province. Although the MNT refused to support particular songs like Pablo Milanés's "La vida no vale nada" ("Life Is Worthless"), the lyrical content of which was deemed to be antisocial, it dramatically expanded the resources available to aspiring young musicians, introduced them to new instruments and electronic technologies like the synthesizer, increased their access to studio time, and helped them distribute their recordings.

During the next five years, Castro depersonalized the government and institutionalized the revolution. He delegated authority to a new executive committee of the Council of Ministers and gave the bureaucracy wider scope of action and more influence. President Osvaldo Dorticós and Carlos Rafael Rodríguez, a veteran Communist who had fought with Castro in the Sierra Maestra, took charge of Cuba's economic development. Castro reorganized the government to draw clear lines of separation between the armed forces, the bureaucracy, and the Communist Party. The militia was disbanded and merged into the army. The military was restructured along traditional hierarchical lines, and Cuba's first revolutionary generals were named. The judicial system was revamped. In addition, an attempt was made to broaden the popular base of the regime and to strengthen the Communist Party. The labor movement was revitalized; a larger role was assigned to the trade unions and the workers' tribunals that saw to the enforcement of labor laws and workers' rights. Steps were taken to involve workers more actively in the formulation of production goals and plans.

The Cuban leadership also drastically overhauled the revolution's policy of economic development. It introduced sophisticated computerized planning techniques and inaugurated a system of material incentives for workers and managers. A work quota system was implemented between 1971 and 1973, resulting in a 20 percent increase in productivity in just one year (1972). The government also began to differentiate between jobs for pay purposes. No longer were people paid according to their need but rather according to the productivity and complexity of their job. These and other economic reforms led to a dramatic rise in productivity. From 1971 to 1975 the gross national product grew at an annual rate of more than 10 percent, compared with an annual growth rate of 3.9 percent for the period from 1966 to 1970.

The first Communist Party congress in December 1975 completed the formal institutionalization of the revolution. The congress adopted Cuba's first socialist constitution, approved by nationwide referendum in February 1976. The constitution, an attempt to make government more responsive to the people, provided for a pyramid of elected bodies. At the bottom were popularly elected members of municipal assemblies, who elected delegates to provincial assemblies and to the National Assembly of People's Power. Most of these representatives were Communist Party members. Castro remained entrenched at the top as first secretary of the Communist Party, head of government, and president of the Council of State (elected from the National Assembly).

Political institutionalization was accompanied by efforts to reorganize and rationalize the economy, whose performance had slowed in the last half of the decade. Still heavily dependent on sugar for its economic well-being, Cuba's economy grew a disappointing 4 percent a year from 1976 to 1980. At the root of the problem was the lack of professional management, quality control, and labor discipline, all of which contributed to poorly manufactured goods, ranging from shoes to televisions.

Persistent economic problems and political disaffection led to a massive emigration of Cubans, primarily to the United States, from April to September 1980. More than 125,000 Cubans left, mostly through the port of Mariel, many aboard dangerously overcrowded, leaky boats. Nonetheless, Cuba's outmigration (a rate of less than 2 percent in 1980) compared favorably to that in the rest of the Caribbean, where émigrés constituted about 20 percent of the population.

Great political and social upheavals historically have caused similar flights of disaffected people; after the American Revolution, 10 percent of the population left for Canada or England rather than live under the new republican rule.

Between 1981 and 1985, Cuba seriously attacked its chronic economic problems, and there was a significant quantitative and qualitative improvement in the economy. The average annual growth rate for the period was 7.6 percent. Export diversification grew, with reexports of Soviet oil accounting for over 40 percent of Cuba's hard-currency earnings in 1985; but in 1988 this share fell to 17 percent because of lower prices on the world market. Despite Cuba's many economic problems, economists Claus Brundenius and Andrew Zimbalist have concluded that Cuba's economic growth between 1960 and 1985 was the second highest in Latin America. Moreover, the distribution of income generated by this growth was far and away the most equitable, both within and outside the region.

CUBA AND THE WORLD

From its early years, the Cuban revolutionary government sent military aid to other Third World countries. It helped the Algerian independence movement and guerrilla groups in Zaire, the Portuguese African colonies, and Tanzania during the 1960s. In the same period, facing the bitter hostility of most Latin American governments, Castro virtually declared war on them (with the exception of Mexico) in the Second Declaration of Havana (1962), vowing to turn the Andes into the Sierra Maestra of South America.

With the murder of Che Guevara and the economic disasters of the late 1960s, Cuba changed course and sought to reestablish normal diplomatic and trade relations with the other governments of the hemisphere. During the 1970s, as the danger of U.S. invasion diminished and the economy improved, Cuba again took an important role in Africa. Eleven thousand Cuban troops assisted Ethiopia in repelling Somalia's 1978 invasion of the Ogaden region, and fifty thousand Cuban soldiers helped Angolan forces in their fourteen-year

This witty cartoon reminds Americans, who still lack universal health care, that social-ist Cuba, against all odds, has transformed itself into a world-class health-care provider. [©1994 Dan Wasserman, *Boston Globe.* Distributed by Tribune Media Services]

struggle against counterrevolutionary rebels sup-ported by the United States and South Africa and in thwarting a South African invasion of Angola across its southern border. At Cuito Cuanavale, in one of the decisive battles of modern African his-tory, a joint Cuban-Angolan army inflicted a crushing defeat on the South African invaders, which led to the signing of an agreement in 1988 between Angola, Cuba, and South Africa for the mutual withdrawal of Cuban and South African troops and for the independence of Namibia.

Cuba sponsored what the *New York Times* called "perhaps the largest Peace Corps–style pro-gram of civilian aid in the world," with some 16,000 doctors, teachers, construction engineers, agronomists, economists, and other specialists serving in twenty-two Third World countries. The Cuban international aid program included free education in Cuba. In addition to the motive of "international solidarity," Cuban international aid had the objective of providing the country with much-needed hard currency. Fees were charged on the basis of ability to pay, and poor countries received aid free. Cuba's foreign construction proj-ects were a major income producer.

ACHIEVEMENTS

Despite its mixed economic record, the revolution's achievements in the areas of employment, equi-table distribution of income, public health, and education were remarkable. Until the onset of the

1990 economic crisis, which caused many factories to shut down due to lack of fuel, Cuba had the lowest rate of joblessness in Latin America. But workers who were laid off because of plant closings continued to receive 60 percent of their wages. Inequalities in the standard of living were dramatically reduced from the days of Batista. The working classes in particular benefited from government policies; rents were controlled, limited to no more than 10 percent of income, as were rationed food prices (but the government tolerated an open market in farm products). Eighty percent of Cubans owned their own homes. Agricultural workers on state farms and cooperatives got furnished houses with televisions and community recreational centers. Cuban city streets had virtually no beggars and sidewalk vendors, which set them apart from those in other Latin American countries. Education and health care were free and equally accessible to all.

The revolution had always promised equality and social justice, but these were special goals of the Cuban Women's Federation (FMC), organized in 1960 under Vilma Espín's leadership. The FMC played a crucial role early in the development of revolutionary social services: literacy crusades reduced illiteracy from 24 to 4 percent; a national child-care system freed women, irrespective of class, to pursue their own careers; an innovative rural education program taught vocational skills and provided peasant women with modern health-care information; and schools for maids and prostitutes discouraged exploitation of women and retrained them as professionals in socially productive activities.

Since then, the FMC, Latin America's largest women's organization with a membership of 3 million, has continued to influence Cuban policy regarding health care, education, women's employment, daycare, sexual discrimination, and family life. For example, it secured passage of the 1975 Family Code, which recognized the equal right of both spouses to education and career, required them to share in household duties and child care, and established divorce as a legal remedy for any spouse whose mate refused to comply. Although a 1988 survey showed that men worked

only 4.52 hours per week at home whereas women worked 22.28 hours, it also revealed the law's potential: most respondents acknowledged that this inequity was diminishing steadily.

Women gained enormously from the revolution. In 1953, 20 percent of women were illiterate, without hope of either education or rewarding employment; but by the early 1960s the revolution had eradicated illiteracy and established equal access to a free education. After the revolution, higher education, long the redoubt of elite women, who had composed 45 percent of a small university student population in 1956–1957, also opened its doors to women of every class; by 1990 women represented 57 percent of a university population that was ten times larger.

Before the revolution, women composed 13 percent of the work force, one-third of them employed as domestic servants. By 1990, however, women represented 38.6 percent of Cuba's workers and constituted 58 percent of technical, 85 percent of administrative, and 63 percent of service workers. Yet the percentage of women managers, Communist Party leaders, National Assembly members, and People's Power delegates was 27, 16, 33, and 17, respectively. Distressing as these figures might be, they resembled the gender inequality typical of developed countries and represented a vast improvement on the records of Cuba's Latin American and Caribbean neighbors. Nonetheless, Castro, clearly disturbed by this inequality, called for increased women's representation commensurate with "their participation and their important contribution to the building of socialism."

Children were special objects of the government's solicitude. Children aged seven and under and pregnant women received a daily distribution of milk and enjoyed the best medical care in Latin America. With the region's lowest doctor-to-patient ratio, according to a 1990 study in the *Latin American Research Review*, Cuba had "transformed itself into a world-class health-care provider, an extraordinary achievement." Sophisticated medical procedures performed in Cuba included heart transplants, heart-lung transplants, and microsurgery. The educational budget amounted to 7 percent of the nation's GNP, the highest in Latin America. The population had an average ninth-grade education, and illiteracy was wiped out.

For nearly thirty years, the Cuban Revolution's success had derived from a searching self-criticism, careful attention to its mass political base, and an enduring socialist pragmatism. The ongoing effort to correct past mistakes, known as *rectificación*, was renewed in the mid-1980s, even before the dramatic changes in Eastern Europe created economic difficulties for Cuba. In particular, Castro spoke of the need to improve economic efficiency and incorporate more blacks, women, and youth in revolutionary leadership positions.

Castro himself, by calling on Cubans in 1959 "to end racial discrimination at the workplace" and in "cultural centers," raised a public voice against Cuban racism that had long been silenced by the 1912 massacre of Afro-Cubans and white republican elites' insistence thereafter that Cuba was a racial democracy. The structural transformation of Cuban society since 1959 led most scholars to conclude that "the revolution has achieved racial equality" even as a "racist mentality" endured within Cuban culture. This was reflected in a demographic shift of blacks and mulattos from 26.9 percent of the population in 1953 to more than 60 percent recently, and it was confirmed by improvements in such social indices as literacy, employment, fertility, interracial marriage, and mortality rates.

Yet Afro-Cubans, who undeniably have benefited from the revolution and currently hold prestigious positions throughout Cuban society, still remained statistically underrepresented in higher education, professional employment, and leadership positions in both the government and mass organizations; they were also overrepresented in vocational schools, blue-collar jobs, and *solares* (substandard tenement houses). More disturbingly, they made up 58 percent of the *jóvenes desvinculados*, alienated youth who neither work nor study.

Undoubtedly, most Cubans benefited from the revolution, which explains their extraordinary support for it, almost forty years later in the midst of its deepest economic crisis. According to an independent 1994 poll commissioned by the Miami *Herald* and conducted by a Costa Rican affiliate of the Gallup Organization, 69 percent of Cubans identified themselves as revolutionaries, socialists, or communists and 58 percent believed the revolution had produced more achievements than failures.

RECTIFICACIÓN AND THE "SPECIAL PERIOD," 1990–2003

During the early 1990s, however, the socialist collapse in Europe threatened Cuba's progress in streamlining its economy and creating greater equality. As they transitioned toward a market economy, Cuba's Eastern European trading partners were forced to trade on international prices, conducted in hard currency. But Cuba also needed its limited stock of hard currency to pay interest on its foreign debt and purchase certain vital products from the West. Anticipating increased difficulties with some of its former socialist trading partners, Cuba diversified its trade links, doubling its trade with China and increasing its trade with Latin America by 20 percent.

Nonetheless, the Soviet collapse dealt a devastating blow to the Cuban economy, resulting in a national income decline of approximately 45 percent between 1989 and 1992. Before 1990, Cuba had received 13 million tons of oil annually from the Soviet Union, but this fell sharply to 1.8 million tons in 1992 (from Russia). In addition to routine blackouts and factory shutdowns, the resulting energy crunch led to a revival of horse-drawn carriages, the use of oxen-drawn tractors, and wholesale replacement of cars in transport by bicycles—good for the environment and health, but economically inefficient and uncomfortable. The shortfall in oil dealt a heavy blow to another of Cuba's major hard-currency earners, the nickel industry. Cuba had the world's third-largest nickel reserves, but the Soviet collapse caused production to fall 36 percent, from 46,600 metric tons in 1989 to 29,900 in 1994. To make matters worse, world-market prices for nickel, which had peaked at over $6 per pound in 1989, plummeted more than 50 percent during the next five years to $2.87. Foreign-exchange earnings therefore declined disastrously.

The economic crisis also temporarily reversed the trend of steadily improving social conditions and produced a decline in living standards. During the early years of this "special period," most Cubans lived on a drab diet of white rice and red beans, supplemented by some vegetables and fruit, an occasional chicken, and what they could purchase on the open market. The food rationing system, however, prevented the emergence of the massive hunger and malnutrition so common in the rest of Latin America.

This crisis was aggravated by the United States's intensified effort to strangle socialist Cuba through passage of the 1992 Torricelli Act, which extended the U.S. trade embargo against Cuba to U.S. subsidiaries in third countries and barred any ship docked in Cuba from entering a U.S. port for 180 days. The Helms-Burton Act of 1996 tightened the noose by allowing U.S. citizens to sue foreign corporations whose trade or investment profits derived from properties expropriated more than forty years ago. These laws drew angry protests from Canada and the European Community, which felt the United States had no right to apply its laws extraterritorially. Each year since 1992 the U.N. General Assembly has voted by overwhelming majorities (157 to 2 in 1998) to condemn the embargo, and in July 1993 a summit of the leaders of Latin America, Spain, and Portugal unanimously called for an end to the embargo against Cuba. Pope John Paul II, during a much-celebrated visit to Cuba in 1998, added his voice to those protesting the embargo, as did Nobel laureate and former president Jimmy Carter in 2002.

In the midst of crisis, the socialist government showed its revolutionary pragmatism. In 1992 the National Assembly adopted sweeping changes in the constitution and electoral law, including enhanced constitutional protections for all religious faiths; authorization of 100 percent foreign-owned companies and joint-venture enterprises with foreign capital; and provisions for direct, secret election by voters of deputies of the National Assembly and provincial assemblies. The first direct, competitive

elections for deputies of the National Assembly resulted in a lowering of their average age to forty-three—a reflection of the generational change of guard taking place in Cuba. In another sign of the new political atmosphere, candidates for office no longer needed approval by the Communist Party, and other reforms aimed to make the National Assembly "a more independent and effective body for legislation, governmental monitoring and oversight, and economic planning."

According to Cuban Vice President Carlos Lage, the revolutionary government during this "special period" also sought economic reform "without altering its socialist essence." In fact, unlike all the other Latin American countries pressed by their domestic business classes and the IMF to combat economic problems in the 1990s by slashing state social spending to reduce budget deficits, the Cuban government's investment in social services actually increased from an average 17 percent of GDP during the 1980s to 24 percent in 1993, the depth of the national crisis.

The government monitored foreign investment, closely regulated its relations with Cuban labor, and scrutinized its impact on the environment. Ironically, Cuba's socialist infrastructure of national planning, free universal health care, and education may be the most attractive feature to foreign investors, who grudgingly endure inevitable state interventions in exchange for the benefit of a healthy, disciplined, productive, highly educated work force; relative labor peace; and freedom from the extraordinary expense of unemployment and medical insurance payments. In effect, they gain access to scarce resources and First World workers at Third World costs. "It's one of the advantages of a centralized economy," a Cuban economist explained. "We can actually make a company's investment more secure than it would be in an unregulated economy."

As a result, foreign firms were eager to engage in joint ventures in fields ranging from a new overseas telephone system to tourism. In June 1994 a Mexican company signed a $1.5 billion deal to rehabilitate Cuba's telephone system. New hotels built by joint ventures with Spanish companies were rapidly springing up on Cuban beachfronts, with the number of foreign tourists topping 500,000 in 1993 and rising to 1,000,000 annually thereafter. In 2000 tourism earned $1.9 billion in reserves, Cuba's largest source of hard currency. More than three hundred joint ventures with some fifty-seven countries in forty different sectors of the economy attracted investments in excess of $5 billion; domestic investment also increased, rising to 9 percent in 1997. Cuba still depended greatly on sugar, but the economy also had diversified. Income from manufacturing netted $415 million, tobacco and cigars brought in $100 million, a relatively new biotechnology industry earned $100 million, and nickel production grossed $90.8 million. Moreover, the government invested heavily in modernizing the sugar industry. Most cane was harvested by machine and many new mills were built.

After five years of declines, Cuba's gross domestic product (GDP) rose steadily after 1993, averaging 3.3 percent per year between 1994 and 2000. Trade also rose consistently, although it failed to achieve its 1989 levels: the annual average increase in the value of exports and imports since 1993 was almost 20 percent. As a percentage of GDP, budget deficits had grown astronomically to 40 percent in 1993 but thereafter declined to 4 percent in 1996, producing dramatic improvement in consumer confidence and strengthening the Cuban peso by 40 percent. More important, these macroeconomic indices of national recovery were reflected in the experiences of everyday life in Cuba. Ascribing this apparent renaissance to Cuba's "entrepreneurial socialism," one recent visitor concluded that "in Havana some of the new wealth is clearly starting to be felt in the population generally. On almost every block, it seems, is a freshly painted house. The discos are jammed every night with both Cubans and foreigners."

Cuba hoped to overcome its energy crisis through the discovery of large oil reserves off its shoreline. In June 1994 two Canadian firms announced that they had found commercial quantities of oil at wells offshore in Matanzas Province. Utterly dependent on frequently expensive oil imports since its independence, Cuba produced more than 1 million metric tons of oil annually since 1993, an increase of 400 percent during the decade. This reduced the nation's import bill, lowered its energy costs, improved industrial efficiency, and contributed to greater economic independence.

In addition to promoting such traditional exports as sugar and nickel and expanding tourism, the Castro government made the development of biotechnology and medical exports an essential part of its economic survival strategy. In the 1980s, Havana's center for genetic engineering produced interferon, an important drug in the treatment of cancer. Since then Cuba invested more than $1 billion in biotech research, organized thirty-eight biotech centers, and developed four hundred patents on products ranging from fetal monitors to vaccines against hepatitis B and meningitis B. Ironically, in 2002, Cuba contracted with Glaxo SmithKline, a multinational pharmaceutical company, to market this meningitis B vaccine around the world, including the United States, where annually three thousand cases of meningitis claimed three hundred lives, mostly in impoverished, high-risk areas. But the U.S. government, which usually opposed restraints on private trade and investment, nonetheless prohibited the use of this life-saving vaccine unless Glaxo agreed to pay Cuba its royalties in kind—for example, through the export of medicines—rather than in cash. If Cuba can find sufficient markets for its biotechnological and medical products, the exports could be worth $1 billion a year.

In response to the continuing economic crisis, in 1993 the Cuban government instituted additional reforms. Most important, a reorganization of agriculture replaced large state farms with autonomous cooperatives in land "ceded for an indefinite period by the state." These "Basic Units of Cooperative Production (UBPC)" operated on a profit-sharing basis and administered their own resources. They received from the state credits for purchasing farm equipment, seeds, and other inputs in exchange for a commitment to sell a fixed amount of their harvest to the government; any surplus crops could be sold at prevailing prices in the open market. By 1998 over 1,500 UBPCs controlled 3 million hectares of land and employed almost 122,000 workers, 114,000 of whom were co-op members. This decentralization of agriculture, appealing to the workers' self-interest, led to more efficient use of resources and contributed to a 17.3 percent growth of agricultural production in 1996.

Cuba also launched a vast technological experiment in agriculture that aimed to end dependence on costly foreign agricultural inputs by converting from conventional modern agriculture to large-scale organic farming. The "alternative model," as the Cubans call it, sought "to promote ecologically sustainable production by replacing the dependence on heavy farm machinery and chemical inputs with animal traction, crop and pasture rotations, soil conservation, organic soil inputs, and what the Cubans call biofertilizers and biopesticides—microbial pesticides and fertilizers that are nontoxic to humans." Two agricultural scientists who have studied the program, Peter Rosset and Shea Cunningham, stress its "potentially enormous implications for other countries suffering from the declining sustainability of conventional agricultural production."

A second general reform authorized self-employment in a long list of trades and occupations. In reality these new rules simply legalized long-existing activities, but they also generated tax revenues and provided regulatory controls, inspections, and licenses. This "informal sector" expanded rapidly, averaging between 10,000 and 15,000 self-employed Cubans in 1993 and mushrooming to 180,000 by decade's end. Cuba's informal sector, however, contrasted sharply with the poverty and economic insecurity of its counterparts in the rest of Latin America. Because socialism guaranteed them inexpensive housing, basic subsistence, free health care, and education, self-employed Cubans typically spent their income on discretionary consumer goods; in a 1997 article in *The Atlantic Monthly,* Joy Gordon reports the example of a woman with a *paladar* (private home restaurant), serving dinners for four dollars, who could afford a Sony stereo system, a VCR, and new color television. "Yet," Gordon concludes, "this is possible in Cuba only because and insofar as it has remained socialist."

Finally, in an obvious move to encourage the inflow of dollars through family remittances from the United States, the government announced in July 1993 that it would no longer penalize the holding of foreign currencies and would authorize Cubans to spend U.S. dollars in a network of government stores. These measures eased the government's cash crisis and put a dent in the flourishing black market, but they created a privileged class of people with access to U.S. currency and increased inequality: according to one Cuban economist, "The 4:1 income gap between best-paid and worst-paid has widened in ten years to 25:1." But this still leaves Cuba the most egalitarian society in the hemisphere.

As a result of these reforms and Cuba's growing insertion into the world economy, the new millennium opened with Cuban officials expressing quiet confidence that Cuba had turned the corner, that the worst was over. Some professional economists agreed that, in defiance of neoliberal orthodoxy, this "Cuban miracle" had "confounded its critics," but many problems remained unsolved. Largely due to the U.S. economic blockade, which increased the cost of Cuban imports and limited income from exports, Cuba suffered from massive trade deficits that also increased its reliance on short-term foreign loans at high interest rates. By 2001 its foreign debt was $13 billion.

During the late 1990s the nation had relied upon dollar remittances and a rapidly growing $1.5 billion a year tourism industry to cushion the impact of its trade deficit. An important consequence of the September 11 terrorist attacks on the World Trade Center, however, was a dramatic decline in worldwide tourist travel, which threatened to reduce national revenues. Finally, the rising cost of oil and the fall of sugar prices damaged Cuban prospects for a full economic recovery. Although Cuban socialism guaranteed every citizen free access to health care, education, and a basic subsistence diet, Cubans interested in resurrecting pre-1990 living standards had to access private markets; but this required dollars that could be secured only in the tourist industry or through family remittances from abroad. Naturally, this tended to undermine the revolution's long-standing commitment to social and economic equality.

As a result, it was not surprising that a new debate about racism, civil rights, and equal opportunity emerged among Cuban intellectuals and in popular culture. Historian Alejandro de la Fuentes suggested that a recent proliferation of Cuban scholarly studies of race in its historical and contemporary context reflected concerns about rising inequality in Cuba. To be sure, dollarization immediately privileged families with relatives living in self-imposed exile in the United States, and these overwhelmingly tended to be light-skinned Cubans of Spanish ancestry. But more disconcerting was the virtual invisibility of Afro-Cubans in the tourism industry, the only other source of dollars. In 2000, Castro himself admitted that Cuba was not "a perfect model of equality and justice" and acknowledged that, although "we established the fullest equality before the law and complete intolerance for . . . sexual discrimination in the case of women, or racial discrimination," these racial, gender, and class prejudices persisted.

These prejudices, growing social inequality, and their collective impact on Afro-Cuban identity also became lyrical themes in the rapid emergence of a new hip-hop culture in Cuba. Initially influenced by rap music broadcast by Miami commercial radio stations, young, mostly black males fused hip-hop styles with traditional Afro-Cuban rhythms to deplore injustices associated with the "special period": racism, class inequality, prostitution, and selfishness. According to an official of a Cuban state organization that promoted rap artists, "Cuban rap is criticizing the deficiencies that exist in society, but in a constructive way, educating youth and opening spaces to create a better society." Indeed, Cuban rappers increasingly recognized the nation's enduring cultural identification with "whiteness" as the historical source of its lingering racism; this was reflected in the response of a hip-hop producer to a Cuban reporter's question about whether or not there were any "white" rappers: "Well, let's say there are lighter-skinned rappers," he replied, "because no one in Cuba is white."

Despite all these problems, however, it was still true in 2002 that, in the face of the collapse of its major trading partners a decade earlier and forty years of unremitting, implacable opposition from the United States, including a trade blockade that openly violated international law, Cuba had made a remarkably quick recovery. It ranked fifty-fifth in the United Nation's Human Development Index of 180 countries and fifth in Latin America behind Argentina, Chile, Uruguay, and Costa Rica.[3] Cuba's doctor-patient ratio ranked second in the world, with 530 physicians per 100,000 people. Among eighty-eight developing countries, Cuba had the fourth-lowest poverty index. Its infant mortality rate, at 7 per 1,000 live births, was the lowest in Latin America and equaled that of the United States. Its literacy rate for youth was the highest in Latin America (99.8%) and the second highest for adults (96.7%). It had the largest number of scientists and engineers per capita of any Latin American nation (1,611 per 1,000,000 people), twice that of second-place Argentina. During the 1990s, Cuba's 3.7 percent average annual per capita economic growth rate placed it second only to Chile among Latin American nations. Despite growing inequality, it still had the most egalitarian income distribution in the region, perhaps in the world. With understandable pride, in June 2000, Cuban president Fidel Castro surveyed the devastation wreaked by the early 1990s economic Armageddon and remarked: "In spite of this we did not close down a single health care centre, a single school or daycare center, a single university, or a single sports facility. . . . What little was available we distributed as equitably as possible." No other nation in the region could make a similar claim.

Further Cuban development would of course be greatly facilitated and hastened by a change in U.S. policy that would result in economic advantages for both countries. Unfortunately, the United States continued to harbor cold-war prejudices and illusions about Cuba that it abandoned long ago about a much more powerful communist state,

---

[3]Cuba's ranking in Latin America likely would have been higher if the calculations had been based upon 2002 data instead of information from 2000, before the Argentine economy collapsed and Uruguay staggered.

the People's Republic of China. The collapse of socialism in a number of Eastern European states, the success of the U.S. invasion of Panama in December 1989, and the victory of the U.S.-supported opposition in the Nicaraguan elections of February 1990 produced gloating in Washington and predictions that Cuba, whose economic collapse was considered imminent, was next.

But reports of the early demise of the Cuban Revolution were greatly exaggerated. Short of a massive U.S. invasion, there was very little prospect that Cuba's socialist regime would be overthrown from within or without. In Cuba, unlike in Eastern Europe, socialism did not arrive in the wake of a victorious Red Army; it was created by an indigenous popular revolution that linked the ideals of socialism and independence, and it still enjoys overwhelming popular support: 98 percent of eligible voters participated in the 1998 National Assembly and People's Power elections and less than 4 percent protested by defacing their ballots. Despite many economic problems, the Cuban Revolution had a record of social achievement without parallel in Latin American history and presented a vivid contrast to the economic and social crises gripping most of the capitalist societies of Latin America.

Until 2003, the process of "rectification" included efforts to democratize still further Cuba's political and economic structures, widening popular participation in decision making and increasing tolerance for expressions of dissidence. This process seemed to culminate with the release of most "prisoners of conscience" in 1998, Pope John Paul's historic January 1998 visit, and the 2002 arrival of former U.S. president Jimmy Carter, who condemned the forty-year U.S. blockade and openly promoted the Cuban dissidents associated with the Varela Project.

But despite this new openness and the Cuban government's agreement to allow Cubans who wish to leave to do so, U.S. government hostility to Cuba remained relentless, in the process violating its own sacred rhetorical commitments to the free movement of people, trade, and investment. The United States denied travel visas to internationally renowned intellectuals like Gabriel García

Márquez; prevented, under terms of the Helms-Burton Act, Canadian, Mexican, and European business executives with Cuban investments from entering the United States; and refused to allow U.S. citizens to travel freely to Cuba.

Moreover, the 1978 Cuban Adjustment Act, which granted immediate legal status to all Cubans arriving in the United States, effectively encouraged Cubans to emigrate illegally aboard dangerous, leaky, makeshift boats and rafts or to hijack planes and ferries, without fear of serious punishment in the United States. Meanwhile, the United States approved fewer than three thousand legal immigration applications per year, even though a 1984 immigration accord permitted annual legal immigration of twenty thousand Cubans and three thousand political prisoners. President Castro accordingly chastised the U.S. government for needlessly endangering Cuban lives through its cynical manipulation of the immigration issue to destabilize Cuba and subvert the revolution. U.S. radio broadcasts routinely urged Cubans to protest and commit terrorist acts of sabotage against their government, reinforcing this lawlessness by refusing to prosecute Cubans who hijacked boats or planes en route to the United States. By contrast, in the 1960s, when several planes were hijacked to Cuba, the Cuban government arrested and convicted the hijackers for their crimes; more recently, it executed Cubans found guilty of hijacking a ferry.

As the new millennium opened, however, Cuba's economic renewal had created additional pressure on the U.S. government to lift its economic blockade. Influential newspapers called for rolling back the embargo. The *New York Times* complained that U.S. policy toward Cuba remained frozen in the past and appeared to be dictated by the most radical factions of the anti-Castro Cuban exile community. Fearing the impact of Asia's economic crisis on U.S. trade and investment, "an exponential increase" of U.S. companies became interested in Cuban markets, according to the May 1998 testimony of the United States–Cuba Trade and Economic Council, a business group that supported a gradual dismantling of the embargo. Eager to claim a share of Cuba's health care market, worth $500 million to $1 billion, and its bulk-food commodity imports, valued at $800 million, influential corporate executives like Dwayne Andreas of Archer Daniels Midland Company, Ted Turner of Time Warner, and Donald Fites of Caterpillar also opposed the embargo. Because removal of the embargo would produce an estimated $3 billion to $7 billion of trade, at least $2 billion worth of exports, and some forty thousand new jobs, doing so clearly would bring substantial economic benefits to both the United States and Cuba, and would undoubtedly contribute to the further liberalization of Cuban life that the Bush administration claimed to desire.

Doubtlessly, this explains why a bipartisan majority in the House of Representatives overcame the truculent opposition of Republican leaders to pass a 2002 bill that foreshadowed the demise of the U.S. embargo by lifting U.S. restrictions on travel, trade, and monetary remittances to Cuba. According to Cuba expert Wayne Smith, "This vote reflects the growing momentum in favor of getting rid of the embargo against Cuba altogether." But before this could occur, there were still powerful obstacles that would have to be overcome, not least of which was the opposition of President Bush, whose election in 2000 had depended upon the votes of a rabidly anti-Castro, antirevolutionary Cuban exile community in Florida. In 2003, perhaps flushed with confidence from his apparent victory in another "splendid little war," this time in Iraq, President Bush once again appeared to ratchet up the political pressure on Cuba. James Cason, head of the United States Interest Section in Cuba, opened a more extensive and aggressive campaign to encourage, organize, and coordinate dissident, anti-Castro groups in Cuba, prompting the Cuban government to respond by arresting, summarily convicting, and sentencing some seventy-five alleged dissidents to long prison sentences. As the United States vainly sought another U.N. resolution condemning Cuba for its alleged human rights abuses and the international community joined Cuba in its annual denunciation of the U.S. trade embargo, the island nation's future remained uncertain, but seemed likely to mirror its turbulent past.

18

Revolution and Counterrevolution in Central America: Twilight of the Tyrants?

HE JULY 1979 VICTORY of the Sandinista Front for National Liberation (FSLN) over one of Latin America's oldest tyrannies—the Somoza family dynasty of Nicaragua—was an extraordinary event that reverberated throughout Latin America and the United States. Like the Cuban Revolution of 1959, this anti-imperialist social revolution challenged U.S. power in a part of the world that for almost a century had been its own secure preserve. In Washington, the Sandinista triumph caused gloom and disarray as to how to deal with the new Nicaragua and prevent the spread of the revolutionary virus to its Central American neighbors. It heartened Latin American revolutionaries, their supporters, and all the democratic forces of the region, ending the discouragement caused by a long series of defeats for radical and progressive causes—from the Brazilian counterrevolution of 1964 to the destruction of Chilean democracy in 1973. Some unique aspects of the Nicaraguan revolution—its blend of Marxism and progressive Catholic thought, its effort to maintain a mix of state and private enterprise—excited the imaginations of those committed to social change in Latin America.

In El Salvador, meanwhile, guerrilla activities against a repressive military-civilian junta had developed into a full-scale civil war by the spring of 1980. The guerrillas had created a revolutionary

government (the *Frente Democrático Revolucionario*) with its own army, the *Frente Farabundo Martí de Liberación Nacional* (FMLN). Ten years later, despite massive infusions of U.S. military and economic aid (over $4.5 billion) to the government, rebel forces held much of the country and showed themselves capable of disrupting its economic life and launching powerful offensives at will. By the spring of 1990 popular discontent with the U.S.-supported government, revulsion in the United States at the atrocities committed by the Salvadoran military, and the demonstrated strength of the guerrillas had forced the government to accept rebel proposals for U.N.-sponsored peace talks without preconditions. The resulting peace accords provided for demilitarization and democratic elections in which the FMLN would take part. Less than completely "free and fair," those elections (March–April 1994) gave victory to the entrenched right-wing parties, but the FMLN obtained a strong presence in the national legislature and prepared for a long struggle for the political and social transformation of El Salvador.

Guerrilla movements had risen and waned in Guatemala since 1954, when a counterrevolutionary coup organized and armed by the CIA overthrew a reformist regime and the social changes it had instituted. The guerrilla struggle gained in intensity and popular support in the late 1970s, even as the level of violence on the part of government security forces and death squads reached new heights. After the Guatemalan military government adopted a scorched-earth policy, accompanied by massacres of indigenous villagers thought to have supported the guerrillas, the rebels faded into the mountains and jungles. The roots of revolution—massive poverty, injustice, and repression—remained, however, even after the civilian government of Vinicio Cerezo took office in 1986. By the spring of 1990 the guerrilla war had revived and rebel units maintained a presence only thirty miles from the capital, Guatemala City. Here too, peace talks made slow progress against the bitter resistance of the dominant military, but they finally produced the Peace Accords of 1996.

Why should Central America, a region so richly endowed by nature—where U.S. economic, political, and cultural influence has been so strong—be such a violent land and present such immense contrasts of wealth and poverty? The answer to this question requires a more detailed survey of the twentieth-century history of three countries, Guatemala, Nicaragua, and El Salvador, where revolutionary movements shaped the contours of modern life.

Guatemala

In Guatemala, the historical sources of political violence and late twentieth century revolution could be found in the nation's growing external dependence, its domination by foreign monopoly, and the collaboration of a rapacious landed oligarchy that supported a series of military dictatorships between 1898 and 1944. The first of these was led by Manuel Estrada Cabrera, a tyrant famous for his cruelty, who ruled ruthlessly for two decades before his own previously obedient Congress declared him insane and sought his removal. During his presidency, Estrada Cabrera began to invest in the national infrastructure, particularly road and port facilities for transporting and shipping coffee.

Although initially funded with Guatemalan resources, the financing and construction contracts for this infrastructure soon passed into the hands of foreign, predominantly U.S., companies.

A U.S. firm, International Railways of Central America (IRCA), which was linked to the United Fruit Company (UFCO) through interlocking directors, acquired monopolistic control over land transport in Guatemala and virtual ownership of the major Atlantic port of Puerto Barrios. The UFCO secured a contract in 1901 to carry Guatemalan mail from Puerto Barrios to the United States in its "Great White Fleet" and to carry bananas, obtained from producers at fixed prices, to the North American market. In time the company acquired vast banana holdings of its own on very favorable terms from the Guatemalan government.

The enormous U.S. economic influence, based on direct investments, loans, and control over Guatemala's chief foreign market, was translated into a growing U.S. tutelage over Guatemala. After World War I, the U.S. embassy became in effect a branch of the Guatemalan government; U.S. ambassadors were approached for favors in return for cooperation with U.S. corporations.

By the end of Estrada Cabrera's brutal regime, Guatemala's economy was utterly dependent upon the export of bananas and its land was concentrated in the hands of a few, but unlike Nicaragua and El Salvador, much of this was owned by a single foreign company, UFCO. During the next decade coffee oligarchs battled each other, sought to renegotiate the state's relationship with UFCO, pursued constitutional limitations on the military, and simultaneously worked to preserve their control over natives, peasants, and workers. The resulting instability provided fertile ground for the emergence of a new military strongman, Jorge Ubico, who seized power in 1930 and dominated Guatemala until a 1944 revolution overthrew him.

During his reign, Ubico consistently supported UFCO and IRCA, but he also cultivated close relations with the nation's coffee oligarchy, whose interests were threatened by the Great Depression. During the 1930s coffee prices declined to less than half the 1929 level. By cutting off European markets, World War II deepened dependence on the U.S. market and further depressed coffee prices. The crisis in foreign trade led to rising unemployment, wage cuts, and business failure for many small producers. The Guatemalan planter oligarchy and associated export-import interests, closely linked to U.S. enterprises, made the masses pay for the Depression through wage cuts, intensified exploitation, and reduced government expenditures. In the 1930s the level of official repression rose; in 1933 alone the government executed some one hundred labor leaders, students, and political dissidents.

Ubico was determined to guarantee the planter class a reliable, cheap source of labor. In 1934 he abolished debt peonage, replacing it with a vagrancy law that required all persons owning less than a stipulated amount of land to carry cards (*libretas*) to show that they had worked at least 150 days a year on the haciendas. Those who failed to comply with this obligation to do "useful work" were jailed. Fearing popular uprisings and peasant land invasions, Ubico also legalized murder for landlords seeking to protect their properties.

The fall of the detested Ubico regime came as a result of popular democratic opposition movements, fostered by the antifascist climate of opinion created by U.S. and Latin American participation in the war against the Axis powers. Although Guatemala, under U.S. pressure, had declared war on the Axis in December 1941, Ubico's profascist views and the ties of many of his close advisers and ministers to German interests were well known. In June 1944 a general strike and antigovernment demonstrations forced Ubico to resign. A triumvirate of two army officers and a civilian took over and organized congressional and presidential elections to be held in December 1944. The overwhelming victory of Juan José Arévalo, a prominent educator and scholar who had spent many years in exile, confirmed the demand of the Guatemalan people for the establishment of a government pledged to democracy and social progress.

REVOLUTION AND COUNTERREVOLUTION, 1944–1983

The Guatemalan democratic revolution of 1944 was largely the work of a coalition of urban middle-class groups and discontented junior military, with the small working class as junior partner and the indigenous peasantry in a marginal role. The revolutionary leadership favored a capitalist course of development and was friendly to the United States. The program of the Arévalo administration (1945–1951) reflected its desire for a capitalist modernization. An ambitious social welfare program was launched that stressed construction of schools, hospitals, and housing as well as a national literacy campaign.

The 1945 constitution abolished all forms of forced labor, enfranchised literate women, prohibited press censorship, limited presidential power, criminalized racial discrimination, required equal pay for equal work, and established civil equality for men and women. The 1947 labor code guaranteed to workers the right to decent working conditions, social security coverage, and collective bargaining through trade unions of their own choosing; it also provided for compulsory labor-management contracts and mandatory paid maternity leaves. These reforms spurred a rapid organizing drive among urban, banana, and railroad workers, who made a number of limited gains.

Following the example of many Latin American governments in this period, Arévalo began a program of industrial development and diversification, employing the newly created state bank and other agencies for this purpose. As for the existing foreign economic enclaves (chiefly UFCO and IRCA), Arévalo's policy was not to nationalize but to regulate their operations in the national interest. The government insisted, for example, that UFCO submit wage disputes to arbitration. New laws stipulated that in the future the state or predominantly national companies should exploit natural resources; in industry, foreign investors could operate on the same terms as nationals.

Arévalo's agrarian program was equally moderate. Government programs offered state support to cooperatives and provided agricultural credit and technical assistance. A new law protected tenants from arbitrary ouster by landlords, who were required to rent uncultivated lands to landless peasants, but the latifundia remained intact, although the constitution of 1945 permitted expropriation of private property.

Urban, middle-class *ladina* women played an influential role in the Arévalo government. The Democratic Union of Women (UMD), organized in 1946, included former students at the University of San Carlos who had mobilized against Ubico. They agitated for women's rights, participated as teachers in the literacy crusade, and hosted a 1947 Inter-American Women's Conference that advocated greater democracy, human rights, and national industrial development. The Guatemalan Women's Alliance (AFG), founded in 1947 and closely associated with the clandestine Communist Party, championed working-class interests, agrarian reform, and indigenous rights. Its most famous member arguably was María Vilanova de Arbenz, whose husband became Guatemala's president in 1950.

The pace of reform quickened with the election of Major Jacobo Arbenz, who sought to convert Guatemala from a dependent nation with a semicolonial economy into an economically independent country. His major strategy to achieve this objective was import-substitution industrialization, to be accomplished by private enterprise. But the creation of a modern capitalist economy was impossible without an expansion of the internal market—that is, of mass purchasing power—through agrarian reform.

Prompted by indigenous peasant uprisings, the phenomenal growth of the Guatemalan National Peasant Confederation (CNCG), claiming more than 200,000 members, and a 1950 census report showing that 2 percent of Guatemalans controlled 74 percent of the arable land, Arbenz supported a 1952 agrarian reform law. It provided for the expropriation of holdings over 223 acres and their distribution to the landless, with compensation made through twenty-five-year bonds. By June 1954 approximately 100,000 peasant families had received land, together with credit and technical assistance from new state agencies.

The agrarian reform inevitably affected UFCO. No more than 15 percent of its holdings of over 550,000 acres were cultivated; the company claimed that it needed these large reserves against the day when its producing lands were worn out or ruined by banana diseases. The land expropriation, coming on top of a series of clashes between the government and UFCO over its labor and wage policies, brought their relations to the breaking point.

Meanwhile, in its struggle with the landed oligarchy, a weak middle class needed allies, and workers used this situation to expand their demands. They organized independent trade unions like the Guatemalan Confederation of Labor (CTG) and the Guatemalan Syndicalist Federation (FSG) and pressed for higher wages and greater worker autonomy. Their success, reflected in the establishment of the General Confederation of Guatemalan Workers (CGTG), with more than 100,000 members, coupled with the growing politicization of indigenous peasants organized in the CNCG, moved Arbenz to the left, but it frightened his supporters in the agro-industrial middle class, inducing them to seek a modus vivendi with the planter aristocracy and its U.S. associates.

The moderate Arévalo had already been attacked in the U.S. media as being procommunist. Arbenz's deepening of the revolution, threatening the profits and properties of UFCO, evoked a much angrier reaction in the United States and caused UFCO's friends in high places to prepare for direct action against Guatemala. By 1953, President Dwight D. Eisenhower had approved "Operation Success," a CIA–State Department plan to remove Arbenz and replace him with Colonel Carlos Castillo Armas. Deeply involved in the conspiracy against Guatemala were Secretary of State John Foster Dulles and his brother, CIA director Allen Dulles (both former partners in UFCO's legal counsel), United Nations Ambassador Henry Cabot Lodge, and Assistant Secretary of State for Latin America John Moors Cabot, both UFCO stockholders. Headquartered in Miami, a CIA official served as field commander for the operation and funneled guns and ammunition to Castillo Armas's army. The man in charge of psychological warfare was E. Howard Hunt, later of Watergate fame.

Because the United States had imposed an arms embargo against Guatemala, Arbenz purchased a shipment of Czech arms, whose arrival in May 1954 provided a pretext for implementing "Operation Success." In June, Castillo Armas advanced six miles from the Honduras border into Guatemala and waited for his U.S. allies to do the rest. While U.S. pilots in CIA planes dropped propaganda leaflets and incendiary bombs on the capital, Guatemalan army officers refused to arm workers and peasants who wanted to defend the revolution. Instead, they pressured Arbenz to resign, turning over the government to a three-man junta. But the United States insisted on the installation of Castillo Armas, the CIA candidate, as president. On July 3 he arrived in the capital in a U.S. embassy plane and promptly launched a campaign of terror against supporters of the revolution. According to one estimate, eight thousand persons were executed. The land reform of 1952 was revoked, UFCO and other landowners regained holdings that had been expropriated, and Castillo Armas surrounded himself with an entourage that has been described as a gang of "grafters and cutthroats."

The counterrevolution returned power and property to the landed oligarchy, its foreign allies, and their new middle-class partners. The process of land reform was reversed; after 1954 the size of the average peasant landholding decreased, whereas the percentage of land devoted to commercial farming increased. But the Guatemalan economy did not stand still. The new ruling coalition promoted the growth of a small dependent industry and some major shifts in the composition of agricultural exports.

Despite a modest advance of industry, mostly of the maquiladora type controlled by foreigners, Guatemala remained basically a producer of foodstuffs and raw materials. The composition of its exports changed considerably as a result of declining coffee prices. Coffee was still the leading export in 1980, but cotton, sugar, and cardamom ranked second, third, and fourth in value. While commercial agriculture gained, basic grains (wheat and maize) had to be imported from the United States. This reflected the continuing concentration of the best lands in the hands of latifundistas, often by usurpation of the plots of mestizo and indigenous smallholders, with army and security forces present to suppress armed resistance. Because peasant unions were forbidden by law and the minimum-wage laws were ignored, extremely low wages were the rule.

The narrow social base of the post-1954 regimes and the fact that they owed their existence to a flagrant foreign intervention explain their militaristic, repressive character. In the thirty-four years after 1954, there was only one civilian president—Mario Méndez Montenegro, elected in 1966—and he escalated the repression, directing counterinsurgency operations as much against peasants as guerrillas. Aided by U.S. military advisers, an estimated fifteen thousand people were slaughtered in the department of Zacapa alone between 1966 and 1968.

Despite the crushing blows inflicted by this and subsequent counterinsurgency campaigns, the guerrilla movements survived and reached a new height of activity in the mid-1970s with the formation of the Guerrilla Army of the Poor (EGP). The resurgence was marked by growing cooperation among guerrilla movements, trade unions, and peasant organizations. Another significant development was a cleavage in the church between the conservative Archbishop Mario Casariego, firmly loyal to the regime, and some bishops sympathetic to liberation theology and many working clergy active in the Catholic *comunidades de base* (grassroots communities). Their involvement in the daily struggles of the poor brought charges of subversion and attacks by government and paramilitary forces against them; in 1981 alone, twelve priests were killed and many others, including some bishops, were threatened with death.

The guerrilla struggle achieved a high point of organizational unity in 1981 following the decision of the three major guerrilla organizations and the Guatemalan Communist Party to form a unified command to coordinate their military operations. By the end of 1981 they had scored considerable successes. The widespread violence and the growing power of the guerrillas intensified the flight of capital, adding to the economic gloom brought on by low commodity prices and declining industrial activity.

The guerrilla advances produced discord among the military. One group of officers favored a more defensive strategy, controlling what was feasible; others favored an aggressive policy, including "scorched earth" tactics against the areas that were supposed to support the guerrillas. This group gained the upper hand in March 1982 and installed General Efraín Ríos Montt as head of a new three-man junta, whose policy, according to the *Latin America Weekly Report*, was to eradicate the mainly indigenous population: "Troops and militias move into the villages, shoot, burn, or behead the inhabitants they catch; the survivors are machine-gunned from helicopters as they flee. Any survivors are later rounded up and taken to special camps where Church and aid agencies cope as best they can."

These conditions did not deter the Reagan administration from certifying to Congress that the human rights situation in Guatemala had improved, thereby renewing military aid and arms sales to its government. But the United States, carefully avoiding the subversive term *reform*, also continued to pressure the military government to build a broader domestic political constituency by implementing periodic programs of "agrarian transformation." This typically meant that landless indigenous peasants were relocated on inaccessible, uncultivated, relatively infertile, state-owned jungle lands and received minimal credit and technical assistance, all of which increased their dependence on markets and eroded traditional autonomy.

RETURN TO DEMOCRACY, GUATEMALAN STYLE, 1983–2003

In August 1983 a military coup toppled Ríos Montt. The desperate state of the economy, the country's international isolation, and growing internal opposition from social movements that overcame traditional racial, ethnic, gender, and class divisions all persuaded the military to withdraw in favor of civilian elites. The domestic opposition particularly frustrated the army. Despite savage repression, hundreds of thousands of indigenous peoples, Catholic activists, homeless people, urban workers, and housewives bravely resisted the government by joining organizations like the Committee of Peasant Unity (CUC), Catholic Action, the National Movement of Shantytown Dwellers (MONAP), the National Committee of Union Solidarity (CNUS), and the Consumers' Defense Committee (CDC). Together these groups organized the Democratic Front Against Repression (FDCR), to demand democracy and social justice. But the return to democracy was hedged with conditions. It was well understood that no future civilian government could hope to survive if it interfered with the military's conduct of the ongoing counterinsurgency war or attacked the oppressive land system.

The first step in the transition to this curious democracy was the election of a constituent assembly. Notable for its repressive atmosphere, a "reactionary pluralism" that severely limited political debate, and the resulting abstention of 57 percent of eligible voters, this constituent assembly enabled basically conservative parties to schedule elections in 1985 and write a new constitution that ignored social problems, institutionalized the military repression, and sanctified the rights of private property.

Despite constitutional provisions that criminalized voter abstention, fewer than 50 percent of eligible Guatemalans voted in successive elections that empowered Vinicio Cerezo Arévalo and José Serrano Elías, both of whom promised to honor the military's autonomy, curb inflation, create jobs, respect human rights, and expand democracy. Although the military distrusted these civilian leaders, it understood that their governments, with connections to powerful sister parties in Europe and patrons in Washington, had the best chance of securing urgently needed foreign aid and overseeing the "recomposition" of the state and civil society.

Under Cerezo and Serrano, the military retained effective control of rural Guatemala, scene of a prolonged counterinsurgency war that transformed 38 percent of urban women and 56 percent of rural wives into widows, and caused an immense flow of indigenous refugees, an estimated 10 percent of the population. In Phase One of the process, the army burned down Maya villages, laid waste fields, and killed over 30,000 villagers, according to estimates. Phase Two, designed to turn the indígenas against the guerrillas, created "model villages" (reservations) in which to resettle surviving indígenas and those who had returned home after fleeing and living like hunted animals in the mountains.

The military also reorganized indigenous society, forcing hundreds of thousands of Mayans to participate in a civil defense patrol program. Israel, a major supplier of arms to Guatemala, provided it with a wide range of sophisticated hardware and also furnished advisers on counterinsurgency.

Meanwhile the guerrilla struggle, after suffering severe defeats that drove the partisans into remote parts of the mountains and jungles, revived. Many model villages were surrounded by guerrilla territory; the guerrilla presence was particularly strong in three zones: the Petén, Quiché and Huehuetenango, and Solola. Despite the increase in guerrilla activities, the *Unidad Revolucionaria Nacional Guatemalteca* (URNG), which led and coordinated the guerrilla movement, sent Cerezo an open letter expressing willingness to discuss peace talks. In April 1989 preliminary talks were held between a reconciliation commission approved by the government and rebel leaders, and the talks continued under Serrano.

Nor were Cerezo and Serrano able to deliver on their economic promises. An economic austerity program reflecting the dominant influence of landowning and business elites kept both unemployment and inflation high. Economic aid from the United States and European countries fell below expectations. The economy continued to stagnate, and poverty skyrocketed. Between 1980 and 1987, according to the United Nations, the proportion of poor people rose from 79 to 87 percent; the percentage of people in "extreme poverty" grew from 52 to 67 percent. Guatemala's historically high income inequality also worsened substantially. Naturally, this led to dramatic declines in the "physical quality of life," measured by infant mortality, literacy, and life expectancy. Still worse, this crushing poverty was disproportionately concentrated among women and indigenous people.

But popular sectors took advantage of greater political freedoms to create a powerful opposition. Guided by the United Guatemalan Workers (UNSITRAGUA), a new independent labor confederation, students, teachers, workers, shantytown dwellers, human rights activists, peasants, women's groups, and indigenous rights organizations joined together to form a cross-class coalition that called for nationwide general strikes to protest neoliberal policies that produced greater unemployment and higher prices for bread, milk, and urban transportation. Although they succeeded in winning some important concessions, these popular social movements still lacked the power of the army, international bankers, and Guatemala's propertied elites; but they functioned effectively, consciously or not, as a civilian front for the rural guerrilla insurgency.

Although Cerezo and Serrano pledged to work for peace and end human rights abuses, their promises were contradicted by a wave of assassinations. The U.S.-based Council on Hemispheric Affairs found that Guatemala, closely followed by El Salvador, was the worst human rights violator in Latin America in 1990. In that year, according to one human rights organization, there were 773 killings, including the murders of dozens of street children, mostly at the hands of the military, the national police, and right-wing civilian death squads.

By 1993 a number of factors combined to produce a crisis for the Serrano regime. One was the public anger caused by a series of drastic electricity rate increases. A second shock was the 1992 award of the Nobel Peace Prize to the Maya activist Rigoberta Menchú, which provided the indigenous masses of Guatemala with an internationally recognized leader in their struggle for political and social rights. Against a background of mounting unrest and popular demonstrations, Serrano announced the dissolution of Congress and the Supreme Court and took all power into his own hands. The move, reminiscent of Fujimori's power grab in Peru, was quickly dubbed the *autogolpe*, or self-coup.

By a certain irony, the United States—which in 1954 had plotted the ouster of the democratic nationalist government of Jacobo Arbenz—now suspended economic assistance to Guatemala in protest against the coup, producing consternation in business circles and wavering within the military, which finally withdrew its support from Serrano. The coup promptly collapsed, and Serrano fled to Panama.

There followed prolonged negotiations among the military, political, and business elite, which searched for a presidential candidate acceptable to them and the United States but hostile to Serrano. They selected Ramiro de León Carpio, a lawyer and human rights critic who also opposed the guerrillas and supported the neoliberal economic policies sponsored by the International Monetary Fund (IMF) and the World Bank.

The military undoubtedly saw in him a figure who could give Guatemala a respectable image but with whom they could live, a judgment that his first presidential acts served to confirm. After firing some members of the military high command who allegedly backed the coup, he promptly replaced them with very similar individuals. Against the advice of human rights groups, León Carpio decided to keep the Presidential Guard, a group implicated in numerous human rights violations, including the assassination of anthropologist/ activist Myrna Mack. He reopened negotiations with the guerrillas, but the talks proceeded slowly and haltingly, largely because León Carpio insisted on separating the negotiations for a cease-fire from discussion of the social and economic issues—land, labor, and political reform—that were at the base of the war.

In general, despite his populist rhetoric, León Carpio showed little interest in the problems of the 90 percent of the population who lived in poverty. Even by the low Latin American standards, the dimensions of those problems were staggering: the share of national income received by the poorest 10 percent of the population dropped from 2.4 percent in 1980 to 0.5 percent in 1991. The problems were especially acute for indigenous people (55 to 60 percent of the population). According to official statistics, the indigenous infant mortality rate was 134 per 1,000 live births, twice that of the nonindigenous population. Only 10 percent of the indigenous population was literate; three out of four indigenous children suffered to some degree from malnutrition; and the average life expectancy

of forty-five years represented a sixteen-year gap separating them from other Guatemalans. The root cause of indigenous poverty was lack of access to land. According to a U.S. Agency for International Development (AID) study, 2 percent of the country's farms held two-thirds of the farmland, whereas 70 percent of the farms possessed 17 percent of the land. Government efforts to promote highland production of winter vegetables for export replaced grain production for local consumption, promoted concentration of landownership, and spurred the flight of the indigenous population to the cities.

Many indigenous (and nonindigenous) people found employment in the free-trade zone factories or *maquilas*, the fastest-growing sector of the Guatemalan economy. A 1984 law exempted these factories from import duties and (for ten years) from taxes. The majority were owned by Koreans. The maquilas accounted for 36 percent of Guatemala's exports to the United States. Seventy percent of the workers were women, and they earned about $2.50 a day. "I work from 7:30 in the morning to 10:00 o'clock at night," said one machine operator, "and what I earn doesn't cover what I need to eat." But employers successfully resisted demands for higher wages, shorter hours, and better working conditions.

The repression continued, but it met with growing resistance from thousands of Guatemalan refugees returning from exile in Mexico and from thousands of indigenous people who had lived for a decade in the so-called communities in resistance, refugees in their own country. The award of the Nobel Peace Prize to Rigoberta Menchú gave indigenous people new hope and courage. In November 1993 thousands of indigenous Guatemalans held a protest march in the capital to demand total abolition of the civil defense patrols imposed by the army. The social ferment was accompanied by a renaissance of Maya culture, which included the formation of centers for the study of Maya culture, an association of Maya writers, and a publishing house devoted to the publication of books in the Maya languages.

Álvaro Arzu Irygoyen, whose campaign had stressed a negotiated peace with the guerrillas, won the 1995 election, but even more significant was the surprising success of a newly formed, poorly financed political party, the New Guatemala Democratic Front (FDNG), which won almost 8 percent of the presidential vote and elected six congressional deputies, three of them women: Nineth Montenegro, head of a national organization of women widowed by army violence; Rosalina Tuyuc, a Maya founder of the Guatemalan Widows' Confederation (CONAVIGUA); and Manuela Alvarado, a Maya indigenous rights activist.

Arzu seemed to appreciate the significance of these elections and seized upon his "mandate" to sign peace accords with the URNG that required United Nations verification of compliance with its provisions. These included demobilization of guerrilla forces; promotion of indigenous rights; legislative, judicial, and electoral reforms; state decentralization and public administration reform; increased social spending; rural development; and the restructuring of public security and national defense.

But there remained powerful opposition to the accords within the military, its oligarchical allies, and the international community. First, contrary to the Accord on Socioeconomic and Agrarian Issues, elites supported neoliberal policies designed to secure international loans, encourage foreign private-sector investment, and expand export trade by discouraging business regulation, higher taxes, social spending, and higher wages—none of which benefited the poor majority. Also, foreign financiers made it clear that Guatemala's access to international credit depended on its compliance with IMF prescriptions, not the 1996 peace accords.

Moreover, privatization of public utilities and other neoliberal policies did little to stimulate growth or stem the nation's mushrooming poverty. Per capita gross domestic product (GDP) had grown an anemic 1.3 percent since 1988 but averaged only 0.8 percent since 1996. Although tax revenues in the 1990s grew modestly from 7 to 9 percent of GDP (well below the peace accord's target of 12 percent), government spending fell steadily, even as capital expenditures doubled.

Trade and payments deficits, though alarmingly high, had begun to decline slightly until 1996, when both rose sharply. In Guatemala neoliberalism produced economic stagnation and aggravated social decline, the very situation that earlier had precipitated years of violent civil war.

Second, the elected Congress, notoriously unrepresentative of the nation's politically excluded indigenous majority, was dominated by wealthy propertied elites. Declaring their opposition to the accords, supporters of ex-dictator Efraín Ríos Montt, the second largest political bloc in Congress, defiantly refused to cooperate. In 1997 they used their power to create a new civilian police force, in clear violation of the demilitarization accord.

Last, the military and paramilitary death squads associated with Guatemala's landed oligarchy, shielded by a 1996 amnesty law and a corrupt judicial system, continued to operate with impunity. This was the unmistakable message delivered on April 26, 1998, when Bishop Monsignor Juan Gerardi, a veteran champion of indigenous and human rights, was assassinated, allegedly by the right-wing *Jaguar Justiciero* (Righteous Jaguar). His exhaustive report on human rights abuses had just concluded that the army and its allies were responsible for 90 percent of the two hundred thousand civilians who were killed or "disappeared" during the civil war.

In 2000, Guatemalans elected Alfonso Portillo, a rightist whose presidential campaign had endorsed populist measures like salary increases for workers and an investigation of the Arzu administration's sale of the state-owned telephone company. Although many critics doubted his commitment to reform, he deserved credit for securing convictions of three high-ranking military officers accused of murdering Bishop Gerardi. But an atmosphere of terror and impunity continued to reign in Guatemala. Between November 2000 and February 2002, six judges and lawyers were assassinated, an accountant for the Rigoberta Menchú Foundation was murdered, a prosecutor and ten judges in the Gerardi case were forced into exile, and six Gerardi witnesses were killed.

This menacing atmosphere had become a potent weapon in the Guatemalan oligarchy's struggle to maintain its power in a changing world. In November 2000, the head of a coffee workers' union received a message, signed by "The Gladiators," advising him "to leave the country if you don't want to die." Threats of this kind helped explain the weakness of Guatemalan labor; as of 1997, only 2.9 percent of Guatemalan workers were unionized. But this weakness reflected more than "a history of intense anti-union repression, including firings, threats, kidnappings, and murders of union activists." The cards were stacked against workers in every possible way. They could not legally unionize until they had worked continuously for the same employer for three months, after which they became eligible for social security programs like retirement and disability benefits. To avoid this requirement, plantation owners rarely hired workers for more than ninety consecutive days.

Moreover, conditions in the coffee industry, which employed 2.2 million workers out of the total Guatemalan population of 11 million, had fundamentally changed. Historically most coffee workers had lived full-time on the plantations where they worked. In recent decades, however, owners, seeking to cut costs, replaced these workers with temporary labor. According to a United Nations report, in 1992, 87.5 percent of rural workers had temporary or migratory jobs. This contributed to an appalling rate of poverty: 76 percent of rural Guatemalans lived on an income of less than $2 a day, and 49 percent of this number lived in extreme poverty (defined as income of less than $1 a day).

In addition, racism and prejudice reinforced rural poverty and also prevented the multiethnic masses of Guatemala from uniting in a common struggle for their economic and social liberation. Until the mass of ordinary Guatemalans—Maya, ladinos, former guerrillas, trade unionists, peasants, and the middle class—united to oppose the power of the propertied elite and its foreign allies, Guatemala would remain a savage mix of the sixteenth-century conquistador's brutality and the maquilized society created by modern neoliberalism.

Nicaragua

MODERNIZATION, U.S. INTERVENTION, AND SANDINO, 1894–1934

Like Guatemala, Nicaragua's twentieth-century history was shaped by foreign economic dependency and gross inequality in the distribution of land; but unlike its northern neighbor, it also suffered from recurrent U.S. military intervention that weakened progressive local elites and decisively undermined national sovereignty. José Santos Zelaya, the late-nineteenth-century Nicaraguan dictator who had opened his nation to foreign investment and trade, nonetheless had been an ardent nationalist: he successfully asserted Nicaragua's claim to sovereignty over the Atlantic Mosquitia coast in 1894; he was a champion of Central American federation; and he angered the United States by turning down its canal treaty proposal and negotiating with other countries for construction of a Nicaraguan canal that would have competed with the United States–controlled route in Panama. Like Porfirio Díaz in Mexico in the same period, Zelaya had become alarmed over the extent of U.S. economic influence in his country; he sought to reduce that influence by granting concessions to nationals of other countries.

These signs of independence convinced the United States, where imperialist attitudes and policies had flowered since 1898, that Zelaya must go. With U.S. encouragement, a conservative revolt broke out in 1909. The U.S. Marines landed at Bluefields on the Atlantic coast and protected the conservative forces there against government attack. Under military and diplomatic pressure from the United States, Zelaya resigned, and in 1910 the conservatives came to power. Their triumph represented a victory for the traditional landed oligarchy and a defeat for its progressive wing, which sought a capitalist modernization.

The conservatives installed Adolfo Díaz, an obscure bookkeeper in a U.S. mining firm in eastern Nicaragua, as president of a puppet regime that hastened to satisfy all the U.S. demands. A U.S. banking firm made loans to the Nicaraguan government, receiving as security a controlling interest in the national bank and state railways and the revenues from the customhouse.

The servility and unpopularity of Díaz and his puppet regime provoked a liberal revolt in 1912, led by the young liberal Benjamín Zeledón. The rebels were on the brink of victory when U.S. Marines were again sent in at the request of the conservative government. Ordered by U.S. officials to end his revolt, Zeledón fought on, warning the U.S. commander that he and his country would bear "a tremendous responsibility and eternal infamy before history . . . for having employed your arms against the weak who have been struggling to reconquer the sacred rights of their fatherland." Zeledón, fighting to the last, suffered defeat and was executed by the conservatives with the apparent approval of the United States. There followed the first U.S. occupation of Nicaragua, with the United States ruling the country through a series of puppet presidents from 1912 to 1925. In return for U.S. protection, the conservative regimes made a number of important concessions, notably the Bryan-Chamorro treaty of 1916, which gave the United States the exclusive right to construct an interoceanic canal across Nicaragua (because the Panama Canal already existed, its real purpose was to prevent any other country from doing the same).

In August 1925, convinced that the conservatives could maintain themselves in power without U.S. assistance, the United States withdrew the Marines. Two months later fighting again broke out, and in 1926 the Marines returned, ostensibly to protect U.S. and other foreign property. This time they stayed until 1933. The new U.S. strategy was to arrange a peace settlement between cooperative conservative and liberal politicians that would give the latter an opportunity to share in the political spoils. With Henry L. Stimson (President Coolidge's personal representative) as mediator, such a settlement was reached in 1927. Under U.S. supervision, presidential elections held in 1928 and 1932 gave victory to the liberals. But real power remained in the hands of the United States.

Only one liberal officer, Augusto César Sandino, refused to accept the U.S.-sponsored peace treaty of 1927. The mestizo son of a moderately well-to-do, ardently liberal landowner and an indigenous servant girl, Sandino had worked as a mechanic and had lived in postrevolutionary Mexico between 1923 and 1926. There he was exposed to radical nationalist and social revolutionary ideas. He returned to Nicaragua in 1926 to join the liberal struggle against a conservative puppet regime. He met with a cool reception from José María Moncada, the head of the liberal army, who later claimed that he immediately distrusted Sandino because he heard him speak of "the necessity for the workers to struggle against the rich and other things that are the principles of communism." Although no Marxist, Sandino was a revolutionary leader who had profound sympathy with all the disinherited and planned to make far-reaching social and economic changes after achieving his primary goal, the departure of U.S. troops.

Unable to convince the liberal leaders that he should be given an independent command, Sandino organized his own force, consisting mainly of miners, peasants, workers, and indígenas. "I decided," he wrote, "to fight, understanding that I was the one called to protest the betrayal of the Fatherland." For seven years (1927–1933), Sandino's guerrilla army waged war against the U.S. Marines and the U.S.-sponsored Nicaraguan National Guard. Learning from early defeats and heavy losses when he attempted to meet the enemy in frontal combat, Sandino developed a new kind of warfare based on hit-and-run attacks, ambushes, temporary occupation of localities and, most important of all, close ties with the peasantry, who provided a supply base for the guerrillas and gave them accurate information about enemy movements and other assistance.

In the United States, meanwhile, the war was growing increasingly unpopular, and eventually Congress cut off all funding for it. The new Hoover administration decided to extricate itself from the Nicaraguan quagmire, but without loss of control. The instrument of that control would be a powerful National Guard, created by the Marines in 1927 and trained and equipped by them. In February 1932, Secretary of State Stimson announced the withdrawal of one thousand

General Sandino (*second from left*) and his staff. Third from left is Salvadoran Agustín Farabundo Martí. (The soldiers at left and right are unidentified.) [Corbis]

Marines in Nicaragua, the rest of whom were to be recalled after the U.S.-supervised presidential election in November.

The conservative Adolfo Díaz, widely regarded as a U.S. puppet, was pitted against Juan B. Sacasa, generally regarded as a more independent and genuine liberal than his predecessor Moncada. The election results gave Sacasa a substantial majority, and on January 1, 1933, he was sworn in as president. Meanwhile, the U.S. minister to Nicaragua had picked a new director of the National Guard, Anastasio Somoza García, a liberal general who had links to the prominent Moncada and Sacasa clans and who had served as foreign minister under Moncada. After his election, Sacasa wrote Sandino, proposing a peace conference. The election and postelection developments created a

dilemma for Sandino. He had promised to lay down his arms after the Marines left on January 2, 1934. But he profoundly mistrusted Sacasa's entourage, especially Somoza, who demanded that Sacasa order the total disarmament of the Sandinistas. In February 1934, Sacasa invited Sandino to Managua for negotiations, giving assurances for his security. In these negotiations Sandino demanded that the National Guard be disbanded— a demand that angered Somoza—but as the talks ended, the president and Sandino appeared to be moving toward agreement. On February 21 the president held a farewell dinner, but as Sandino, his brother, and two Sandinist officers were leaving, they were arrested by Somoza's officers, taken to the airfield, and shot. Questioned by Sacasa, Somoza protested his innocence; he later assumed full responsibility for the murders. It was his first step toward the establishment of a tyranny that would oppress the Nicaraguan people for well over four decades.

THE SOMOZA ERA, 1934–1979

Following the assassination of Sandino, Somoza gradually consolidated his political power, more and more openly defying President Sacasa. With the aid of a fascist-type paramilitary force known as the Blue Shirts, Somoza easily secured election to the presidency as the liberal candidate in 1936, taking care to combine the post with that of director of the National Guard. With the Guard at his disposal, Somoza had no difficulty extending his term of office indefinitely, ruling directly as president or indirectly through puppet presidents until 1956, when he was assassinated, or *ajusticiado* (brought to justice) as Nicaraguans saw it, by the young poet Rigoberto López Pérez.

Thoroughly cynical and self-seeking, Somoza represented the total degeneration of the liberal ideology that had inspired the progressive acts of a Barrios or Zelaya. Always obsequiously pro-U.S., he abandoned his admiration for Hitler and Mussolini when the United States moved toward war with the Axis powers in the 1930s. Thereafter, President Franklin D. Roosevelt professed admiration for Somoza's democratic and progressive ideas, which unfortunately were not reflected in Nicaragua's political system. The saying ascribed to Roosevelt, "Somoza is an S.O.B. but he is our S.O.B." may be apocryphal, but it accurately sums up the U.S. official posture toward the Nicaraguan despot. U.S. friendship for Somoza brought him loans and assistance in establishing a military academy to turn out officers for the National Guard. Graduates of the school usually spent their senior year at the School of the Americas, the U.S. military training center in Panama.

Following Somoza's assassination in 1956, his elder legitimate son and vice president, Luis Somoza Debayle, took over. Somoza's younger son, Anastasio Somoza, Jr., a West Point graduate, became director of the National Guard. Luis was president from 1956 to 1963; he then allowed puppet presidents to rule from 1963 to 1967, when he died. In that year, Anastasio Somoza, Jr., had himself elected president for a term that was to have lasted until 1971. Once in office, however, he amended the constitution to allow himself another year, then retired for two years while a puppet junta presided over the writing of a constitution that permitted him to be reelected for another term, which was supposed to run until 1981.

Differences between the Somozas' ruling styles reflected their adaptations to the changing phases of U.S.–Latin American policy. The relative mildness of Luis's rule appeared to reflect the reformist and developmentalist stress of the Alliance for Progress of the 1960s. In fact, all three dictators ruled Nicaragua as a personal estate for their benefit and that of their domestic and foreign allies. By 1970 the Somoza family controlled about 25 percent of the agricultural production of the country and a large proportion of its industry; the total wealth of the family was estimated to be $500 million. U.S. firms also enjoyed profitable investment opportunities in the food-processing industry and mining. Both foreign and domestic employers benefited from the repressive labor policies of the regime, but Nicaraguan capitalists grew increasingly unhappy with the monopolistic propensities of the Somoza family. The church, originally aligned with the Conservative Party, shifted its support to the first Somoza and generally remained loyal to the family until the 1960s, when it joined the Christian Democratic Party in opposition to Anastasio Jr.'s plans for his perpetual reelection. From first to last, however, the ultimate foundation of the family's power was the National Guard, whose top command always remained in the hands of a Somoza.

While the dynasty and its allies prospered, the economic and social condition of the Nicaraguan people steadily worsened as a result of the unchecked exploitation of rural and urban labor and the developmental programs of the Somoza era. Responding to growing world demand for new products, especially cotton, the Somozas opened up new lands to the planter class. Once again, as during the coffee boom a century earlier, many peasant families were driven from the land and into the cities. Nicaragua under the Somozas had one of the most extreme disparities in income distribution in Latin America; in 1978 the lower 50 percent of the population had an annual per capita income of $256.

Resistance to the Somoza dictatorship had begun in the 1950s, with a series of unsuccessful revolts led by the irrepressible Pedro Joaquín Chamorro, publisher of the highly respected *La Prensa* and son of parents from two of the most powerful conservative clans—a fact that explains why he was pardoned and allowed to return to Managua after each revolt. A more serious threat to the dictatorship arose with the formation in 1961 of the Sandinista Front for National Liberation (FSLN) founded by Carlos Fonseca, Silvio Mayorga, and Tomás Borge and composed largely of students. Its initial efforts to organize guerrilla warfare in the mountains met with defeat, but the rebels gradually improved their tactics and organization, attracting a growing number of recruits, especially among students.

A turning point in Nicaragua's recent history was the devastating earthquake in 1972, which killed ten thousand Nicaraguans and reduced the entire center of Managua to rubble, wiping out almost all businesses. There was immense public indignation over the shameless behavior of the Somozas, who diverted large amounts of foreign international aid into their own pockets and those of the National Guard. The center of Managua remained "an unreconstructed moonscape," for Somoza and his cronies had bought large parcels of land on the periphery of the city where they built new houses and shops, profiting from the disaster.

In January 1978 the Somozas committed an act of folly that largely contributed to their downfall. Stung by a series of articles in *La Prensa* about the commercial blood-plasma operation through which Somoza sold the blood of his people in the United States, the family or one of its supporters ordered Pedro Joaquín Chamorro's liquidation. The murder of a much-loved and courageous journalist provoked an effective general strike that ended only after considerable violence and repression by the National Guard, but its repercussions continued. The crime alienated from the regime

sections of the elite who could tolerate the murder, jailing, and torture of peasants and Sandinistas, but who were shocked at the killing of a member of an old privileged family like Chamorro.

The Chamorro affair, the general strike, and a brutal National Guard attack on an indigenous community that was commemorating the forty-fourth anniversary of Sandino's assassination with a Catholic celebration strengthened the FSLN and contributed to a general broadening of the resistance movement. In August 1978 the Sandinistas launched their most audacious operation to date. Invading the National Palace, twenty-five guerrillas seized as hostages most of the members of the Chamber of Deputies and some two thousand public employees. After frantic negotiations, Somoza agreed to most of the Sandinista demands: the release of fifty-nine Sandinista prisoners, a huge ransom, and a safe flight for the guerrillas and released prisoners to Panama. This development was soon followed by another prolonged general strike and a spontaneous uprising in the city of Matagalpa by *muchachos* (youngsters) who forced the National Guard to retreat to their barracks and hold out for two weeks. On September 8 the FSLN launched uprisings in five cities. With their headquarters surrounded by civilian and FSLN combatants, the Guard called in Somoza's air force for a ferocious bombing of the cities before government ground forces retook the cities one at a time. This was followed by a house-to-house search in a genocidal "Operation Cleanup," with a death toll of some five thousand persons.

Alarmed by the September uprisings, the United States attempted to mediate a compromise between Somoza and his traditional elite opponents through a committee of the Organization of American States (OAS). The U.S. initiative was frustrated by Somoza's obstinate refusal to resign and the withdrawal of liberal factions from the mediation process, charging that the OAS commission wanted "*Somocismo* without Somoza." Meanwhile the FSLN, overcoming the differences over insurrectionary tactics of three groups within it, created a nine-man directorate.

The September uprisings were followed by a mobilization of both sides for a final struggle.

Somoza prepared for the worst by liquidating his vast assets and shipping his capital abroad. Meanwhile the FSLN, aided by the Social Democratic Parties of Western Europe and governments as diverse as those of Costa Rica, Panama, Venezuela, and Cuba, restocked its arms supply with weapons purchased on the international arms market. The regular FSLN army expanded from a few hundred to several thousand. Throughout the country the network of neighborhood defense committees established after the September revolts worked feverishly to prepare for the coming struggle by stockpiling food and medical supplies. Comunidades de base (Catholic grassroots organizations) took an active part in these preparations.

In June 1979 the FSLN announced a general strike and launched a final offensive, infiltrating Managua and occupying barrios on both sides of the central zone. Somoza, retreating into his recently constructed bunker in the fortress of La Loma, ordered a counterattack that included a massive air and artillery bombardment of the city.

By July 5 the Sandinistas had encircled the capital, leaving only one way out via the airport six miles east of the city. The Sandinistas could have taken it at will but allowed it to remain in the government's hands, perhaps to give the Somozas and their entourage an opportunity to leave the capital and thus avoid another bombardment and battle. With victory in sight, the Sandinista directorate named a provisional government—a five-member junta that included three Sandinistas; Alfonso Robelo, the leader of the business opposition to Somoza; and Violeta Chamorro, the widow of the martyred Pedro Joaquín Chamorro.

Meanwhile the United States made last-minute efforts to prevent the coming to power of a radical revolutionary regime. It called on the OAS to send a "peacekeeping" force to Managua but was unanimously rebuffed. Then it sent a special representative to Nicaragua to try to persuade the FSLN to broaden the base of the new junta. But the Sandinistas pointed out that they had already made a large concession by including the conservative Robelo and the moderate Violeta Chamorro in the junta; inclusion of the persons nominated by the United States—one being a general of the National Guard and the other a personal friend of Somoza—would ensure the preservation of "Somocismo without Somoza."

Under intense pressure from Archbishop Miguel Obando y Bravo and people in other influential quarters to accept his inevitable defeat and to spare the capital a new assault, Somoza agreed on July 16, 1979, to go into exile in Florida. The next day he drove to the airport and left Nicaragua forever. Two days later the FSLN and its government entered Managua.

THE SANDINISTAS IN POWER, 1979–1990

The cost of the Sandinista victory in lives and material destruction was enormous. Estimates of the dead ranged up to fifty thousand, or a loss of 2 percent of Nicaragua's population. The material damage was estimated at $1.3 billion; the national debt, a large part of which represented sums that Somoza had diverted into his foreign bank accounts, stood at $1.6 billion.

The government that presided over the immense task of national reconstruction consisted of four parts. The official government included the five-member junta; its cabinet or ministries of state; and the council of state, a legislative and consultative assembly in which a broad variety of mass and economic organizations were represented. The composition of these bodies reflected the sincere desire of the Sandinista leaders to maintain a pluralistic system and approach to the solution of the country's problems. In the first cabinet, in addition to Marxists like Tomás Borge, minister of the interior, and Jaime Wheelock Román, minister of agriculture, sat two bankers and two Catholic priests, the Maryknoll Father Miguel D'Escoto and the Trappist monk Ernesto Cardenal, "making Nicaragua probably the only country in the world with Catholic priests in the cabinet." From the first, however, it was understood that these formal organs of government were responsible to the nine-member directorate of the FSLN that had created them. The directorate had direct control of the Sandinista armed forces and police. Elections had been promised, but the state of war in which Nicaragua soon found itself as a result of CIA-organized efforts to destabilize and overthrow the Sandinista regime delayed elections until 1984.

Economic problems dominated the agenda of the new government. One immediate problem was that of repairing the ravages of war and the earthquake of 1972, a task mainly entrusted to the municipalities and the Sandinist Defense Committees. It was completed with such speed that visitors to Nicaragua in the fall of 1979 marveled at the relatively normal appearance of the country. Food shortages were another serious problem and required the importation of great quantities of foodstuffs, mostly financed with foreign donations. Meanwhile emergency food crops were sown so that domestic supplies of food would be available by the middle of 1980. The work of repair was combined with food-for-work schemes to provide a temporary solution for the vast unemployment that was a legacy of the war.

What to do about the national debt was a vexing question for the new government, for it knew well that many of the more recent loans had served only to swell the bank accounts of Somoza and his cronies. But it decided to agree to pay all the loans, even the corrupt ones, for both economic and political reasons. The Sandinistas wanted to retain access to Western loans and technology; they also wished to disprove the charge that the new Nicaragua was a Soviet or Cuban "puppet," solely dependent on the socialist bloc for economic and political support. The socialist countries, particularly the Soviet Union and Cuba, in fact did give considerable aid in the form of food shipments and other supplies. Cuba also sent large numbers of teachers and doctors to assist in the work of reconstruction.

The international lending agencies and Western governments hoped financial aid to Nicaragua would enable the private sector of the country to survive and keep the economy pluralistic. The principal difficulty in renegotiation arose with the United States. The Carter administration agreed to make a new loan of $75 million, chiefly for aid to the private sector. When Ronald Reagan came to the presidency, however, he froze the remaining $15 million of the loan, alleging without evidence that Nicaragua was sending arms to the rebels in El Salvador. Thereafter Nicaragua had to rely for aid on the socialist countries, friendly social democratic governments of Western Europe, and Third World countries, including Brazil.

Although some Sandinista leaders viewed socialism as a more or less distant goal, the regime pursued a mixed-economy strategy of national development and recognized that private enterprise had a vital role to play in the reconstruction of the national economy. The state, however, became the most decisive and the most dynamic element in the economy and in the provision of social services, particularly health, education, and housing. The strengthening of the state sector was a direct result of the takeover of the enormous properties of the Somoza dynasty and its allies. These properties became the basis of the People's Property Area, including half the large farms over 500 hectares, a quarter of all industry, large construction firms, hotels, real estate, an airline, a fishing fleet, and more. The expropriation of the holdings of Somoza and his supporters placed approximately 40 percent of the gross national product in the hands of the state. The banking system and foreign trade were completely nationalized.

These expropriations, however, left 60 percent of the gross national product (GNP) in the hands of the Nicaraguan capitalist class, which continued to control 80 percent of agricultural production and 75 percent of manufacturing. Thus, the country remained capitalist, with the state sector no larger than that of France, Mexico, and Peru in the 1970s. The policy of the Sandinista government was to avoid radical changes that might cause a rupture with the "patriotic bourgeoisie," the results of which would be disastrous for the economy. Accordingly, it courted and maintained an alliance with some of the country's largest entrepreneurs. At the same time the government insisted on safeguards with respect to working conditions, wages, hours, and the like that would at least modestly improve the life of Nicaraguan workers. It also encouraged the trade unions to watch over the proper functioning of factories to prevent decapitalization, slowdowns in production, and other sabotage by capitalists hostile to the revolution. The result was a built-in tension between the government and a section of the business class. Partly because of this tension and partly because of objective conditions—lack of foreign exchange to buy inputs, obsolete machinery, and other problems—private businessmen began dropping out of manufacturing or failing to invest.

The growth of the public sector was most marked in agriculture. Land reform was placed under the *Instituto de Reforma Agraria* (INRA), which by the end of 1979 had confiscated without compensation over one-fifth of Nicaragua's cultivable land that belonged to persons or corporations affiliated with the Somoza regime, land that "was almost universally held to be little more than stolen property." The government proposed to maintain these estates as productive units rather than to divide them into small parcels. Most of these lands were large farms that had been operated as capital-intensive enterprises, so parcelization would have resulted in heavy production losses. Consequently, many of these estates were converted into state farms. Others were organized as production cooperatives, called Sandinist agricultural communes. In late 1980 there were about 1,327 of these cooperatives. INRA simultaneously tried to improve the living conditions of state-sector workers through the establishment of clinics, schools, and housing projects. In 1980 more than fifty thousand workers worked full time in the state sector.

Although the government favored state farms and production cooperatives as basic agricultural units, small independent farmers were not neglected. Agricultural credit for small producers was greatly expanded, and they were encouraged to form credit and service cooperatives. In 1979–1980 there were 1,200 of these co-ops organized; they received over 50 percent of the agricultural credit extended by the government in the same period.

Even after the confiscation of Somocista estates, large commercial farms producing such crops as cotton, coffee, cattle, and sugar still held 66.5 percent of Nicaragua's cultivable land. The relationship between this private agricultural sector and the revolutionary government was an uneasy one. Most of the large landowners despised the Somozas, resented their hoggish propensities, and welcomed their overthrow. But the rules of the game had changed, and the new rules were not always to their liking. Landowners could no longer mistreat their workers; they had to comply with reform legislation defining the rights of tenants and workers.

Despite the government's assurances that it wanted to preserve a private sector, large landowners were understandably nervous about their future. The commercial farmers and cattle ranchers defended their interests through their own associations, which negotiated with the government over prices, acreage quotas, and the like. The commercial farmers had access to credit at low interest rates, and a coffee stabilization fund was established to protect growers against fluctuations in the world market. The economic importance of this sector is evident from the fact that in 1979–1980 it accounted for 62 percent of the production of cotton and 55 percent of the production of coffee.

The difficulties of Nicaraguan agriculture were not due primarily to inadequate volume of production but stemmed above all from falling world prices for its major export crops. Sugar, which sold for 24¢ a pound in 1981, sold for 9¢ in 1983. Natural disasters also hurt production of staple foods in 1982. In May flooding destroyed twenty thousand acres of just-planted basic grain crops, destroyed $3.6 million in stored grains, and caused $350 million in damage to the national economic infrastructure, according to a United Nations survey. A drought in July and August caused estimated losses of $47 million. Finally, the greatly increased scale of CIA-organized counterrevolutionary activity that began in 1981, diverting manpower and resources to military purposes, caused serious damage to Nicaraguan agriculture and to the economy in general—a major aim of the U.S. destabilization program.

The implacable pressure of the Reagan administration on Nicaragua represented a threat not only to its economy but to the existence of the revolutionary government. Although the Carter administration's policy was "more than a little schizophrenic," once the FSLN was firmly in power it made a serious effort to come to terms with the revolution, hoping thereby to enable capitalism to survive in Nicaragua. With the election of Reagan, the U.S. attitude changed drastically.

Reagan authorized formation of a paramilitary force of ex-National Guardsmen, with an acknowledged budget of $19 million. In a move recalling the 1954 coup against Guatemala, Honduras was converted into a staging area for Nicaraguan operations. Beginning in 1981, Argentine and U.S. advisers trained the Somocistas (familiarly called the *contras* by both sides) and assisted them in making terrorist raids into Nicaragua, killing hundreds of Nicaraguan soldiers and civilians and destroying bridges and construction equipment.

The "secret war" against Nicaragua quickened its pace when Ambassador John Negroponte arrived in Honduras in 1982 to mastermind the operation. The CIA station in Honduras grew to an admitted fifty employees, plus a large number of secret agents, including many Vietnam veterans who were now mercenaries under contract to the CIA. To secure the Honduran military's cooperation in this "secret war," U.S. military aid to Honduras, under $2 million in 1980, grew to $10 million in 1981, and may have reached as high as $144 million in 1982–1983, with some of it coming from a hidden budget.

In March 1983 the operation moved into high gear when several thousand Somocistas and other mercenaries, supported by Honduran troops, invaded Nicaragua at several points on its northern border with Honduras. Simultaneously, in a gesture of "gunboat diplomacy" several U.S. warships were sent to Nicaragua's Pacific coast, ostensibly to monitor suspected movements of arms from Nicaragua to rebels in El Salvador. By the end of March, despite claims of victory from the invaders' radio, the Nicaraguan armed forces and militia had crushed the counterrevolutionary attacks, although the contras continued to make raids, mostly of the hit-and-run variety.

Under the hardest conditions, Nicaragua's Sandinista leadership continued its difficult struggle to stabilize the economy, expand social reforms, replace the revolutionary government with a parliamentary democracy, and solve long-standing problems like the demand for autonomy from the Miskito and Sumo peoples of Nicaragua's Atlantic coast. In the same period the United States intensified its "covert" war against Nicaragua, provided the contras with supplies and logistical support, mined Nicaraguan harbors, and even issued a manual for use within Nicaragua instructing the contras in terrorist methods—including the liquidation of government officials and progovernment activists. The "covert" war flouted U.S. laws, treaty obligations, and international law. In June 1986 the World Court, acting on a complaint by Nicaragua, ordered the United States to halt all its military and paramilitary actions against Nicaragua, but the Reagan administration, refusing to accept the jurisdiction of the court, disregarded the order.

Despite hundreds of millions of dollars' worth of U.S. financial and military aid to the contras, in early 1986 Nicaraguan President Daniel Ortega celebrated the rebels' "strategic defeat." A major factor in this "victory," despite stepped-up U.S. aid, was growing Sandinista military effectiveness and superior morale.

But the Reagan administration had not sought a contra military victory. The administration's support for the contras aimed to sustain a "low-intensity conflict" designed to wear down the Nicaraguan government, disrupt its economy, create hardships and war weariness to undermine popular support for the regime, force the Sandinistas to divert precious resources from social programs to its army, and thereby eventually to produce an internal collapse.

The war contributed to a sharp decline in the Nicaraguan economy between 1983 and 1990. The GDP fell by 30 percent in 1985 alone and continued to fall until the "covert war" ended; inflation reached an annual rate of 10,000 percent in 1988; and severe shortages of goods of every kind prevailed. But the war was not the sole factor responsible for the economic decline. Other causes included deterioration in the terms of trade for Nicaragua's exports; the U.S. trade embargo of May 1985, which isolated Nicaragua from its traditional export market and from a source of goods and technology difficult to replace; and the unwillingness of some private sector interests to invest in maintaining and expanding Nicaragua's production.

The Nicaraguan government responded to the economic crisis with measures to stimulate production by increasing prices paid for basic grains and other staples, while protecting the real value of salaries and wages by periodic adjustments to compensate for inflation; by expanding trade with the European Economic Community and the socialist bloc to compensate for the loss of the U.S. market; and by redesigning the agrarian reform to make more land available to individual peasants as a means of stimulating production of basic grains.

The Sandinistas had promised in 1979 that elections would be held by 1985, but the need to refute U.S. charges that their regime was undemocratic and illegitimate led to a decision to accelerate the timetable for elections. In November 1984, Nicaraguans went to the polls to vote for a president, a vice president, and a ninety-member national assembly that would frame a constitution for the country. Opposition poll watchers and a large number of foreign observers, including a task force of the Latin American Studies Association (LASA), the major organization of teachers and students of Latin American affairs in the United States, found no evidence of irregularities in the voting or the vote-counting process. The Sandinista Front received 67 percent of the vote, the rest going to opposition parties. In January 1985 Daniel Ortega Saavedra and Sergio Ramírez Mercado took office as president and vice president, respectively.

The new constitution, adopted after intense democratic discussion and debate at mass meetings throughout the country and in the national assembly, established political pluralism, a mixed economy, and nonalignment as its guiding principles, and divided power among the executive, legislative, judicial, and electoral branches. It guaranteed individual and social rights, including the rights to a job, education, and health care; free expression of opinion and association; the right to strike; and the right to a fair trial. The constitution

also sought a definitive solution for the troubled relations between the central government and the indigenous peoples of the Atlantic coast.

SELF-DETERMINATION FOR THE PEOPLES OF THE ATLANTIC COAST

The Sandinistas inherited a long history of state neglect of coastal peoples, who consequently distrusted government. The Sandinistas acknowledged that they had made serious errors in their effort to integrate indigenous peoples into the revolution because the government failed to take account of their unique culture and traditions. The problem was complicated by the fact that the United States and the contras sought to exploit those errors and misunderstandings and draw the Atlantic coast peoples to the side of counterrevolution.

In 1981 the Nicaraguan government, to prevent their use as a contra military base, forcibly evacuated thousands of Miskitos and Sumos from ancestral lands along the Coco River, destroyed their villages, and resettled the refugees in camps away from the threatened coastal area. Although the camps provided improved health care, food subsidies, education, and improved housing and electricity, the indígenas, who were strongly attached to their villages and lands, viewed the camps as prisons. As a result, several antigovernment native-based guerrilla groups arose on the Atlantic coast. However, U.S. efforts to pressure the Miskitos into an alliance with the major contra groups, as a condition of military and financial aid, also produced splits that the Sandinistas exploited to negotiate cease-fire agreements with individual indigenous commanders.

Two major Nicaraguan government initiatives paved the way for a solution of the Atlantic coast problem. First, in 1984 the government created a commission to define an autonomous status for the Atlantic coast peoples under the new constitution. The ensuing dialogue led to a compromise that recognized the right of the Atlantic coast peoples to autonomy and guaranteed the preservation of their languages, religions, cultures, and social organization. They would elect their own representatives to the national Congress and use their resources to satisfy their own needs, as determined by a regional assembly. Second, in 1985 Interior Minister Tomás Borge announced that the Miskitos living in relocation camps would be allowed to return to the Coco River area.

WOMEN AND THE REVOLUTION

Women also gained appreciably from the revolution, in which they had played a large role militarily, economically, and politically. Making up one-third of all combatants, many women had been integrated into the guerrilla army; others had organized all-women battalions like the Juana Elena Mendoza Infantry Company; and some, like Doris Tijerino and Dora María Téllez, had become respected field commanders. Although their participation in the regular army after 1979 declined to about 20 percent, women were especially active both in local civil defense committees and the popular militias, where they made up 60 percent of urban contingents.

Most women had always worked both inside and outside the home, but before the revolution, their waged labor (estimated at 48 percent of the labor force) had tended to be relatively invisible and greatly undervalued, concentrated in the informal sector and domestic service. After the revolution, labor legislation guaranteed equal pay for equal work, paid maternity leave, and legal protections against the dismissal of pregnant women. Of course, private employers frequently ignored these laws, and the revolutionary government, due to the contra war, often lacked the necessary financial resources to enforce them. But these laws, instead of providing traditional protections to employers, now placed the state on the side of women, their trade unions, and mass organizations like the Nicaraguan Women's Association (AMNLAE).

Moreover, as the state sector of the economy grew and an escalating contra war absorbed more men, women's waged employment expanded: in 1985 women comprised 50 percent of state employees, 70 percent of coffee harvesters, and 70 percent of textile workers. This naturally raised the issue of the inequitable "double workday," wherein women, in addition to laboring eight hours in the factory or field, worked nine to twelve hours at home whereas their husbands worked less than an hour at household chores. To remedy this injustice, the Sandinistas encouraged men to assume their fair share of domestic responsibilities and by 1988 also funded daycare centers—182 at urban workplaces and 69 on state farms. But once again wartime fiscal demands sabotaged this initiative.

Women made up nearly two-thirds of the *brigadistas* who participated in the Sandinista literacy crusade that between 1979 and 1980 reduced illiteracy from 50 to 12 percent. Thereafter, Popular Education Collectives (CEPs) allowed mostly rural people to select local teachers whose instruction would further develop literacy skills; 95 percent of these teachers were women. Free, universal education for adults and children six to twelve years of age was the Sandinista revolution's commitment; before 1985 nearly four thousand new classrooms were built and the number of primary school teachers, again mostly women, tripled. Here again, however, the contra war intervened; by the late 1980s fewer resources were available for education, and illiteracy rates climbed to 23 percent.

Politically, the revolution facilitated women's participation in the leadership of the FSLN Party, the national government, and grassroots organizations. In the 1984 and 1990 parliamentary elections, women comprised almost 20 percent of the FSLN candidates and almost 22 percent of those Sandinistas elected to the legislature. In 1994 the party decided to allot 30 percent of leadership positions to women, who also made up 34 and 43 percent, respectively, of their department and national legislative candidates in the 1996 elections. By decade's end almost one-third of FSLN legislators were women.

THE QUEST FOR PEACE AND THE NEOLIBERAL DEBATE, 1990–2003

By the end of 1986 external opposition to the revolution had begun to fragment. The U.S. congressional elections had handed a heavy defeat to President Reagan, and his administration suffered another blow due to the revelation that part of the proceeds of an arms sale to Iran, in a supposed swap for U.S. hostages in Lebanon, had been illegally diverted to the contras through the use of secret Swiss bank accounts. The scandal—with new revelations of CIA involvement in drug smuggling—increased opposition to the additional contra aid that President Reagan requested. By the end of the Reagan presidency, Congress had rejected an administration request for military aid and voted to limit funding to so-called humanitarian aid.

The Iran-contra scandal and its repercussions created a favorable atmosphere for new peace negotiations. An earlier peace initiative by the Contadora group of Latin American nations had produced a draft regional peace treaty, which Nicaragua in September 1984 offered to sign immediately without further modifications. But U.S. pressure on its Central American allies caused them to reject it. The new peace process was initiated by Costa Rica and Guatemala, whose governments had no love for the Sandinistas but feared that the Nicaraguan conflict might provoke a direct U.S. intervention, with unforeseeable consequences for the entire region. In August 1987 all five Central American presidents signed a set of agreements that barred outside assistance to insurgent forces, provided for the release of political prisoners, and called for steps toward democratization and the holding of honest elections in all countries, with particular reference to Nicaragua.

Thanks to the Sandinista government's desire for peace and its full compliance with conditions set by the 1987 agreements, elections were held on schedule in February 1990. The FSLN faced the National Opposition Union (UNO), an unlikely coalition of fourteen small parties, ranging from the far right to the Communist Party (PC de N). The overwhelming majority of foreign observers found that the elections were free and fair, but some noted that they took place "within a climate of U.S.-generated military and economic pressure." For example, on election eve, largely due to the decade-long U.S.-sponsored contra war, the national economy teetered on the verge of collapse: purchasing power had declined 90 percent since 1980; per capita GDP had fallen almost 20

percent since 1988; basic food shortages were epidemic; inflation raged at over 5,000 percent; foreign debt service payments consumed 62 percent of export income; and unemployment had reached a postrevolution high. The Sandinista government reluctantly acceded to a modest program of "structural adjustment," or *compactación*, which meant still more pain for Nicaragua's impoverished majority. As if the deck were not sufficiently stacked against the FSLN, the Bush administration also intervened directly in the election, plowing millions of dollars into the campaign of the UNO presidential candidate Violeta Chamorro, who triumphed with 55 percent of the vote.

What factors caused the UNO victory? Most observers agreed that the election results did not represent a popular repudiation of the Sandinista program of social reforms. There was general agreement that the key factors in the Sandinista defeat were the war and the disastrous state of the economy. In a country of less than 4 million people, the war had left sixty thousand dead, twenty-eight thousand wounded, and thousands of others kidnapped. For years, more than half the national budget had been directed to military needs. UNO campaign literature had concentrated on the war-weariness and opposition to the draft, omitting mention that the contra war was the cause of the draft. UNO campaign rhetoric also blamed the Sandinista government alone for the economic crisis.

Washington's strategy of bringing Nicaragua to its knees by a combination of economic blockade and low-intensity warfare had finally achieved its goal. But the aftermath of the election produced new surprises. In a stinging defeat for the extreme right wing in the UNO coalition, Chamorro announced that General Humberto Ortega, chief of the Sandinista army and brother of the outgoing president, would remain. Moreover, Chamorro loyalists next joined FSLN deputies in electing a slate of National Assembly officers that included two Sandinista deputies. Chamorro's temporary alliance with the FSLN was sealed by her appointment of three Sandinistas to cabinet positions, including the strategic position of agrarian reform. "In a strange twist of events," commented

Latinamerica Press, the "coalition that Chamorro led to victory in 1990 has switched places with the Sandinistas and now considers itself the opposition." Chamorro's moderation also irritated Bush administration officials, who warned that $300 million in U.S. aid would be endangered if she made appointments that did not meet with Washington's approval.

But the spirit of amity soon vanished as the Chamorro government began to implement a harsh neoliberal economic austerity program, including periodic devaluations that weakened the earning power of workers, an end to subsidized prices for staple products, massive layoffs of government workers, and efforts to dismantle the agrarian reform and other social conquests of the Sandinista revolution. Although designed to achieve "stabilization," this policy produced political and social conflicts that threatened to end in civil war.

The first major confrontation between the Chamorro government and the Sandinista unions ended in victory for the latter. A ten-day general strike was settled on July 10, 1990, on terms that were very favorable to the strikers, including wage increases and major political concessions like union consultation on economic policies, assurances there would be no large-scale layoffs of government workers, and the abandonment of a program for returning confiscated land to its former owners. The agreement proved to be only a truce in a continuing struggle between the Chamorro government, which sought to dismantle most of the Sandinista reforms, and the unions, which sought to preserve their social and economic gains. But it gave the government a breathing space at least to seek relief from its desperate economic crisis through foreign loans and U.S. aid. Chamorro officials admitted that they needed "the Sandinistas to keep the country from exploding."

Sandinista supporters of this temporary alliance could point to other victories as well as some defeats. If the Sandinistas could not prevent the return of many large properties to their former owners, with Chamorro's support they succeeded in defeating UNO's plan to totally undo the Sandinista agrarian reform. If they could not pre-vent the privatization of almost all the state enterprises, they succeeded in including a provision for the workers' right to own 25 percent of the privatized firms and in some cases acquire total ownership of such firms.

Meanwhile the Chamorro government had expected Washington and the international financial community to reward its free-market policies of austerity and privatization with the aid and loans it needed to rebuild a shattered economy. But U.S. aid was slow in coming and limited in amount, largely due to the opposition of right-wing Republican Senator Jesse Helms, who contended that the Sandinistas were still in power. Combined foreign aid and loans were clearly insufficient. Between April 1990 and January 1993 the country received about $715 million in donations and about $997 million in new loans, but in the same period the government paid over $1,210 million in debt payments on its foreign debt of more than $11 billion to remain qualified for loans and another $456 million for oil. The country's exports in 1992 were valued at a little more than $250 million, but it imported goods valued at more than $850 million. The resulting deficit left nothing for development.

Internal disputes, the FSLN's temporary collaboration with Doña Violeta, and declining voter turnout weakened the party in the 1996 presidential elections, which Arnoldo Alemán, a wealthy Somocista coffee planter, won decisively with 51 percent of the vote. Assured of solid support from traditional conservative Nicaraguan oligarchs and foreign bankers, Alemán's populist campaign, promising economic growth, lower prices, and more jobs, reached out to middle-income and poor people crushed by years of neoliberal reforms sponsored by Chamorro and reluctant Sandinistas.

Once elected, however, Alemán ignored his promises and embraced the neoliberal faith, fully aware of its devastating impact on the poor majority. "We know that to move forward and confront the future," he arrogantly announced, "we have to take bitter medicine." Thereafter, his regime privatized state-owned industries and banks, fired state workers, reduced protective tariffs, raised interest rates, restricted credit, cut

In 2001, outgoing millionaire President Arnoldo Alemán greatly assisted the election of his successor, Enrique Bolaños, another wealthy businessman, but Bolaños quickly abandoned his mentor, who faced devastating corruption charges in 2002. This cartoon depicts the historical links that bound Bolaños to the portly Alemán, pictured here wallowing in the tar pits, grasping the slimy tail of the Bolaños salamander, and shouting, "Come back here little buddy. We started out together, let's finish together." [From *Vision Sandinista*, October 2002]

taxes and social spending, created "free-trade zones" to encourage foreign investment by exempting companies from all taxes, and subsidized sugar production on big commercial estates while denying peasants access to alternative credit programs. To secure open access to U.S. markets, Asian *maquilas*—foreign companies that used low-cost Nicaraguan labor to assemble imported raw materials for overseas export markets—eagerly took advantage of these benefits and Central America's lowest average hourly wage of 41¢ to fatten corporate profits.

Alemán's "bitter medicine" kept inflation low and, largely stimulated by foreign loans, increased average per capita GDP by an anemic 2 percent. This left a 1997 external debt three times greater than Nicaragua's national income, and debt service payments consumed 40 percent of foreign-exchange earnings, five times the rate paid in 1988 when the Sandinistas were in power. The largest single component of national income, $300 million, almost equal to total export earnings, came from family remittances paid by Nicaraguans living abroad! High interest rates, designed to lure foreign investment, drove peasants in search of rural survival to mountainside cultivation and forest destruction, decisive factors in the devastation wreaked by Hurricane Mitch (1998), which killed more than three thousand people in Nicaragua. Alemán's government contributed to the scale of the disaster by what can only be called criminal neglect. Three days after Mitch assumed hurricane strength, "Alemán played meteorologist in front of television cameras, assuring everyone that the little drizzle would soon pass."

Still worse, social indicators declined dramatically. Because the Chamorro government had dismantled the literacy program in 1990, illiteracy, reduced to 12 percent in 1980, exceeded 34 percent in 2000. Nicaragua's infant mortality also remained high, vying with Guatemala for the unenviable distinction of having the highest rate in Central America. Ranked eighty-ninth on the U.N. Human Development Index in 1990, Nicaragua plummeted to one hundred eighteenth in 2001, making it the third-poorest country in Latin America after Guatemala and Haiti. Seventy percent of Nicaraguans were unemployed or underemployed, 80 percent were mired in poverty, and half lived on less than $1 a day—one-fifth of the $150 per month that the government conservatively estimated to be the price of a family's basic survival. Health care and education, free and universally available during the revolution, were plagued by material shortages and limited to the wealthy few who could afford the rising fees. "It's very bad now," complained Dr. Manuela Rodríguez of Bluefields' Hospital. "There are often no medications, no analgesia, no sheets. People are dying because they can't afford to pay." According to the Catholic Church, sixty thousand children had abandoned school for the streets, where they begged for coins or sold worthless trinkets to survive. A *Washington Post* correspondent captured the heart-rending scenes that marked the Alemán administration's indifference toward the sea of misery that surrounded it. "In a soccer field in the town of Matagalpa," he wrote in 2001, "100 hungry children begged for some rice or milk—anything. Some just whimpered, unable to muster more of a protest on hollow stomachs."

Nonetheless, a majority of Nicaraguans voted for Alemán's ally, Enrique Bolaños, in the 2001 presidential election. The Bolaños campaign benefited greatly from a massive U.S. intervention that included money, provision of food aid for Bolaños to distribute at rallies, and pressure on other conservative candidates to withdraw from the race. But perhaps most decisive was the full-page ad in *La Prensa* featuring Jeb Bush, the president's brother, denouncing Bolaños' opponent, Daniel Ortega, as "an enemy of everything the United States represents" and "a friend of our enemies." In the aftermath of the September 11 terrorist attacks and the Bush warning that "every nation in every region now has a decision to make: either you are with us or you are with the terrorists," the ad suggested to Nicaraguans that the United States would again make war on Nicaragua if its people elected Ortega, who "has a relationship of more than 30 years with states and individuals who shelter and condone international terrorism." As bad as life was under the neoliberal regimes of the 1990s, many Nicaraguans seemed to be saying that it was better than a nation at war with itself and the United States.

El Salvador

The history of El Salvador, the smallest and most densely populated country in Central America, presents in exaggerated form all the economic and social problems of the area: an extreme dependence on a single crop, making the economy very vulnerable to fluctuations in price and the demand of outside markets; a marked concentration of land and wealth in a few hands; and intolerable exploitation of the peasantry, accompanied by ferocious repression of all attempts at protest or revolt.

Ironically, however, the early twentieth century bore witness to considerably more political freedoms, at least among the landed aristocracy. Although nineteenth-century liberal reforms had promoted a concentration of land ownership in El Salvador, the coffee oligarchs, largely orchestrated by the Meléndez and Quiñónez families, had developed a political consensus that allowed them to deploy various weapons of social control. Moreover, before World War I, the demand for coffee had not appreciably affected the nation's labor markets and *finqueros* still relied upon a healthy supply of migrant and resident workers. Consequently, in addition to the usual repressive violence of the National Guard and the Casa Salvadoreña, the Salvadoran elite also created mass-based political organizations like the Liga Roja to co-opt and contain urban-middle-class-peasant, and working-class challenges to its power.

Driven by a postwar international market expansion, however, coffee markets expanded by 50 percent during the 1920s. The coffee oligarchs hastened to respond, both by dedicating more acreage to coffee and by securing new supplies of labor. As a result of these changes, more peasants were deprived of their traditional *milpas*, the subsistence plots that were the bedrock of peasant survival. This transformed them into full-fledged proletarians, propertyless people whose survival depended exclusively upon the sale of their labor.

The economic and social problems generated by the coffee monoculture became more acute with the advent of the Great Depression in 1929. Campesinos who made 50¢ a day before the Depression had their wages reduced to 20¢ a day. The price of coffee was cut in half between July 1929 and the end of the year, ruining many small producers and forcing them to sell their lands. High unemployment and below-subsistence-level wages added to the discontent caused by harsh treatment by overseers and frauds practiced by company stores.

Even before the Depression, there had been scattered peasant revolts in the twentieth century; they were always put down by the National Guard. In the 1920s urban workers and some of the peasantry began to form unions. In 1925 a small Communist Party began to operate underground; its leader was Agustín Farabundo Martí, who had been introduced to Marxism at the national university. Expelled from El Salvador in 1927 for his radical activities, Martí joined Augusto César Sandino, who was fighting the U.S. Marines in Nicaragua. Martí returned to El Salvador in 1930 and again plunged into political activity. Aided by a small group of youths, mostly university students, he carried out propaganda and organizational activity among peasants in the central and western parts of the country. He was soon jailed but was released after going on a hunger strike.

Against this background of depression and growing left-wing agitation, perhaps the first free presidential election in Salvadoran history was held. The winner was the wealthy landowner and civil engineer Arturo Araujo, whose admiration for the British Labour Party led him to conclude that an enduring social peace required class harmony and modest reforms, like improving education, defending the rights of women and workers, and promoting limited land redistribution. His election caused much disquiet among the coffee planters and the military. The new president immediately ran into storms: teachers and other public servants clamored for back pay and peasants demanded land and other reforms, while the coffee oligarchy and the military pressed him to make no concessions.

On December 21, 1931, a military coup ousted Araujo and installed his vice president, General Maximiliano Hernández Martínez, as president. The coup signified the end of direct rule by the oligarchy and the beginning of a long era of military domination. The fall of the liberal Araujo and the rise of Hernández Martínez to power closed the door to popular participation in politics. Convinced that the new regime had no intention of allowing reforms or free elections, Martí and other radical leaders decided on insurrection. Simultaneous uprisings were set to take place in several towns on January 22, 1932. But the authorities got wind of the plot several days in advance, and Martí and two of his aides were seized. Other rebel leaders then tried to call off the revolt, but communications had broken down, and the largely indigenous revolt began without its ladino leadership.

In town after town, these campesinos rose up, often armed only with machetes. Having taken over much of the western area of the country, they attacked the regional center of Sonsonate, where the cacique José Feliciano Ama led a revolt that fused long-standing class, racial, and ethnic grievances. The unequal combat between peasants armed with machetes and the garrison, supported by the Guard and other police units, all armed with modern weapons, ended in total defeat for the insurgents. In a few days the captured towns were retaken. Then the oligarchy began to take its revenge, relentlessly hunting down the "communists," defined as any peasant who was not vouched for by a landowner as not having taken part in the revolt. As many as thirty thousand peasants died in this *matanza* (massacre), which verged on genocide by wiping out indigenous dress, languages, and cultural traditions. Ferocious repression was the coffee oligarchy's way of teaching the peasantry a lesson, of ensuring social stability. The history of El Salvador since 1932 shows how vain that expectation was.

OLIGARCHS AND GENERALS, 1932–1979

The coup that installed Hernández Martínez in the presidency marked a turning point in modern Salvadoran history. Terrified by the peasant uprising of 1932, the oligarchy struck a bargain with the military that allowed the military to hold the reins of government while the oligarchy directed the economic life of the country. A network of corruption that permitted the officer class to share in the oligarchy's wealth cemented the alliance between the two groups. Nevertheless, the persistence of reformist tendencies among junior officers and a growing faction of agro-industrialists involved in the coffee-processing industry periodically produced tensions within the alliance that threatened its existence.

Hernández Martínez, known as *El Brujo* (the Witch Doctor) because of his dabbling in the occult, maintained a tight rule over the country through his control of the army and the National Guard until 1944. In addition, power and access to wealth were concentrated in a clique of Hernández Martínez's cronies. This created discontent among junior officers, who allied with agro-industrialists and urban professionals, inspired by wartime rhetoric about democracy, to overthrow Martínez and demand political reform, women's suffrage, economic modernization, and agricultural diversification. This "Revolution of 1948," championed by Colonel Oscar Osorio, inaugurated a decade of import-substitution industrialization, expanded cotton cultivation, and greater export dependency, all under the watchful eye of the military and its oligarchical allies. Then in 1961, alienated by the civilian-military junta's increasingly progressive program, its mobilization of popular sectors, and its friendly relations with Cuba, Colonel Julio

Alberto Rivera joined with the U.S. embassy to organize an anticommunist coup d'état that restored the military's monopoly of power.

Rivera established a system, patterned on the Mexican idea of a single dominant party that would perpetuate itself in power, that involved holding elections every five years and employing fraud, coercion, and co-optation to maintain control. This allowed a number of opposition parties to exist. The most important were the Christian Democratic Party (PDC), headed by José Napoleon Duarte, mayor of San Salvador from 1964 to 1970; a Social Democratic Party, *Movimiento Nacional Revolucionario* (MNR), led by Guillermo Manuel Ungo; and the *Unión Democrática Nacionalista* (UDN), a front for the Communist Party, which had been illegal since 1932.

As the economic difficulties of the country multiplied during the 1960s and 1970s, however, the strains within the system grew and it became increasingly unworkable. The roots of the problem lay in the monoculture that made the country dependent on a world market over which it had no control and a system of land tenure and use that progressively reduced the land area available to small landowners and staple food production.

Land monopoly and the prevailing system of land use led to population pressure on land, a problem greatly aggravated by the population explosion. Thanks to the eradication of yellow fever and malaria and to the successes of preventive medicine, the population shot up from 1,443,000 in 1930 to 2,500,000 in 1961 and 3,549,000 in 1969. By 1970 the population density was about 400 per square mile. The swelling population put great pressure on wage levels: the average daily wage for a field hand in the early 1960s was about 62¢ a day, for an overseer or *mayordomo*, a little over $1.00 a day. Because labor on coffee plantations was seasonal and a peon was lucky to get 150 days of work a year, the labor of an entire family for that period might yield a total yearly cash income of $300.

With land reform ruled out as a solution for land hunger and population pressure, Rivera attempted another remedy: industrialization and economic integration through the creation of the

Central American Common Market (CACM) in 1961. The underlying reasoning was that the unrestricted flow of goods and capital throughout the area would stimulate an expansion of markets and industrialization, relieving population pressure and unemployment. Unfortunately, this industrial expansion took place without a corresponding growth in employment, for the new industries were capital intensive and required relatively few workers. Also, much of the new industry was foreign owned and geared to exports; much of it was designed to assemble imported components.

The problem of population pressure on the land grew much more acute as a result of a bitter dispute between El Salvador and Honduras that culminated in a war that took several thousand lives and left at least one hundred thousand Salvadorans homeless. Called the Soccer War because it followed a series of hotly contested games between teams representing the two countries in the qualifying rounds of the 1969 World Cup, the conflict had more pragmatic causes. One was a border dispute of long standing. Another was Honduran resentment over the marked imbalance of trade between the two countries as a result of the operations of CACM, to which both countries belonged. Honduras, an extremely underdeveloped country whose economy was largely based on bananas, lumber, and cattle, felt that it was subsidizing the industrial development of El Salvador. The third and decisive cause of the war was the presence in Honduras of some three hundred thousand illegal Salvadoran settlers. Following adoption of an agrarian reform law, Honduras had ordered the expulsion of some eighty thousand settlers. El Salvador retaliated by invading Honduras and destroying most of its air force on the ground. The war was over in five days, largely due to U.S. pressure on El Salvador in the form of threatened economic sanctions. The war, which was very popular in El Salvador, momentarily diverted popular attention from its great problems, but the effects on the country were entirely negative: El Salvador lost the Honduran market for its manufacturers for over a decade, and the return of Salvadorans from Honduras swelled the number of landless and homeless peasants.

These developments contributed to the ever-growing economic and social crises of the 1970s. Population growth continued to outstrip the food supply; among the Latin American countries, only Haiti's people had a lower caloric intake than El Salvador's. By the early 1970s, unemployment was running at 20 percent and underemployment at 40 percent; in 1974 the annual inflation rate reached 60 percent. The proportion of landless peasantry rose from 11.8 percent in 1950 to 41 percent in 1975. The calamitous economic situation gave the opposition parties hope for victory in the presidential election of 1972; in September of that year the Christian Democratic Party, the MNR, and the Communist UDN formed a united front, the *Unión Nacional Opositora* (UNO). Its candidate for president, José Napoleon Duarte, had clearly won the election by some 72,000 votes, but the electoral commission found that the official candidate, Colonel Arturo Molina, had won by about 100,000 votes. The flagrant electoral fraud provoked a revolt by reformist junior military that ultimately failed. Duarte, the candidate of the united opposition, was arrested, tortured, and exiled to Venezuela.

Clearly, the military and the agrarian wing of the coffee oligarchy had become impatient with the agro-industrialists and their modest reform agenda, which, despite their protests to the contrary, never seemed to pacify the nation, but instead merely provided political space for popular sector mobilization. As a result, the Molina regime increasingly relied on repression to preserve order. In 1975, hoping to promote the emerging tourist industry, Molina hosted the 1975 "Miss Universe" pageant and spent about $30 million on the show. In a country with so many unfilled social needs, this impressed many Salvadorans as a scandalous extravagance. Units of the National Guard—without any provocation—fired on students attending a protest rally in San Salvador. At least thirty-seven died and an unknown number of others "disappeared." The massacre was part of a pattern of growing violence—from the right and from the left. With increasing frequency, guerrilla organizations that had sprung up since 1970 kidnapped and held members of the oligarchy for ransom. In the countryside, the National Guard, aided by right-wing paramilitary organizations like ORDEN *(Organización Democrática Nacionalista)*, conducted sweeps against "subversive" peasants, surrounding and destroying villages, killing many villagers, and abducting others who "disappeared."

Although convinced that the familiar pattern of fraud would be repeated in the 1977 presidential election, the UNO decided to run a symbolic candidate, a hero of the Honduran war, Colonel Ernesto Claramount Rozeville. The election was in fact marked by widespread fraud, with rampant stuffing of the ballot boxes for Carlos Romero and armed ORDEN thugs on hand to discourage close scrutiny by the opposition at the polls. The outcome was never in doubt. A massive protest demonstration held on February 15 in the main square of San Salvador and addressed by Claramount and other speakers was attacked by army and police units and by members of ORDEN. More than two hundred people were killed by machine-gun fire. Claramount was exiled, but as he departed for the airport he uttered a prophetic comment: "This is not the end, it is only the beginning."

Ending all hope of reform via the electoral process, the fraudulent election of 1977 and the spiral of violence that followed it marked the opening of a prerevolutionary stage of Salvadoran political development. On the left, the revolutionary organizations that had emerged since 1970 mobilized their forces and attempted to overcome their ideological and tactical differences. They robbed banks, seized radio stations to broadcast propaganda, kidnapped oligarchs for ransom, and assassinated persons identified with official or unofficial repression. There was a rapid growth of labor and peasant unions and other mass movements, known collectively as *Fuerzas Populares* (Popular Forces), and of umbrella organizations, such as FAPU (Front for United Popular Action), which organized many groups for joint action against the government. On the right, meanwhile, there was increased repressive activity by the National Guard, the National Police, and other security forces as well as by the death squads of ORDEN and another terrorist organization, the White Warrior Union.

A major development of this period was the changing posture of the church toward the Salvadoran crisis. Prior to the Second Vatican Council (1962) and the Medellín Bishops' Conference, the church in El Salvador—as elsewhere in Latin America—had supported the regime and the oligarchy. Although most of the hierarchy maintained that position, Archbishop Luis Chávez y González and his successor Oscar Romero, with Vatican II and Medellín as their guides, committed themselves to what Romero called "the preferential option for the poor." One result of this ferment in the church was the formation in a few short years of hundreds of comunidades de base, which combined Bible study with attention to the economic and social problems of their localities. The messages the priests brought to their parishioners was that God is "a God of justice and love who acts on the side of the poor and oppressed" and that the people "have a basic human right to organize in order to begin taking control of their own lives."

Their social activism inevitably marked the priests as targets of right-wing death squads and security forces. The Jesuit Father Rutilio Grande was murdered by a death squad of the White Warrior Union in March 1977, and three other Jesuits who had been working with him were expelled from the country. By May 1977 leaflets urging Salvadorans to "Be a Patriot! Kill a Priest!" were circulating in San Salvador. Altogether, seven priests were killed by death squads or security forces between 1977 and 1979. The death of Father Grande, three weeks after Romero was installed as archbishop, contributed to what the archbishop referred to as his "transformation." From then on, during his three years and one month as archbishop, Romero used his position to denounce the regime's human rights violations and to plead for social justice. His sermons, transmitted via radio to almost every part of the country, "became the single most listened-to program in the nation."

The church also helped organize human rights groups like COMADRES, mothers of the imprisoned, assassinated, or "disappeared." Created in 1977, COMADRES courageously protested against the repression with public demonstrations, hunger strikes, and sit-ins at government buildings. According to a founding member, Alicia, their objectives were symbolized by their attire: a black dress to mourn the dead, a white scarf to celebrate "peace with justice, not . . . impunity," a red carnation to recall the bloody dictatorship, and its green leaves to represent "the hope for life." In response, military and paramilitary forces bombed their offices five times, threatened to "decapitate" them, and kidnapped, tortured, and raped more than forty members.

As the crisis deepened month after month, divisions began to appear within the military. A group of reformist junior military watched with profound anxiety the revolutionary course of events in Nicaragua in July–August 1979; they became convinced that a coup offered the only alternative to a solution of the Nicaraguan type. After regular consultations with Archbishop Romero, representatives of the Christian Democratic Party, and the U.S. embassy, which indicated it would not oppose such an action, the coup took place on October 15 with virtually no resistance from any garrison. Incumbent President Romero meekly accepted exile, and a military-civilian junta was formed. The civilians included two moderate leftists, Román Mayorga Quiroz, rector of the Central American University, and the Social Democrat Guillermo Ungo; the military representatives were the authentically democratic Colonel Adolfo Majano and the rightist Colonel Jaime Abdul Gutiérrez, head of the Military School, who owed his inclusion to U.S. pressure. The junta's program called for dissolution of the terrorist ORDEN organization, respect for human rights, agrarian reform, freedom for the Popular Forces to operate, and improvement of relations with Nicaragua.

Although Gutiérrez gave his nominal approval to the program, he decided, without consulting his colleagues, to change the balance of forces in the government by appointing another conservative, Colonel José Guillermo García, as defense minister in the cabinet that was to assist the junta. It was a fateful decision.

The left and the Popular Forces, meanwhile, regarded the junta with an intense suspicion that time was to justify. On October 28 a demonstration by several organizations demanding to know the fate of the many persons who had "disappeared" was met with gunfire by the National Guard, leaving twenty-five people dead. In fact, the October 15 coup did not end repression by the security forces; more people were killed by them in the three weeks after the coup than had died in any similar period under Romero. Efforts by civilian junta members Mayorga and Ungo to restrain the official violence were totally ineffective, for the armed forces listened to no one but García.

These events led to the resignation of the civilian members of the junta, followed by the formation of a new government, the product of a secret deal between the military and the Christian Democratic Party. Two Christian Democrats replaced Mayorga and Ungo. The military committed itself to a program of agrarian reform and nationalization of the banks; a cessation of all repression; and a dialogue between the armed forces and the Popular Forces. Barely one week after accepting these conditions, the security forces fired on a massive demonstration of the Popular Forces, the largest in Salvadoran history, killing about twenty persons. This and similar repressive acts that demonstrated the bad faith of the military caused a split in the Christian Democratic Party. One of its representatives, Héctor Dada, resigned from the junta and was replaced by José Napoleón Duarte. At least 60 percent of its membership resigned from the party by November 1981. To add to the junta's problems, a rightist coup led by Roberto d'Aubuisson, head of the White Warrior Union, was barely averted by Defense Minister García and other high military officers. The agrarian reform promulgated with dramatic suddenness by the junta in March 1980 resulted from intense pressure by the United States, eager to give a reformist face to its protégé, even as James Cheek, the U.S. chargé d'affaires, advised the junta to conduct a "clean counterinsurgency war." Typical of its strategy of reform and repression, the junta announced a state of siege on the same day that it promulgated the agrarian reform.

The agrarian reform was to be implemented in three stages. Phase I, promulgated in March 1980, nationalized 376 estates of more than 500 hectares, belonging to 244 owners and consisting largely of pasture and cotton land. The owners were to be compensated with thirty-year bonds, and the estates were to be converted into cooperatives with 29,755 peasant members. As of January 1, 1983, only twenty-two cooperatives had received final title, although 130 of the owners had been paid for their farms. Phase II, which would have affected about 200 farms of between 100 and 500 hectares, including most of the coffee fincas, "died before it was born," postponed for an indefinite period.

Phase III, called "Land to the Tiller," promulgated in April 1980, allowed peasants who rented up to forty-two hectares of land to buy it from the owner. As of January 1983, 58,152 applications had been received, roughly half the number that were possible under Phase III provisions. By June 1982 no permanent titles had been issued to applicants; the number rose to 251 in August of that year, and to 1,050 by January 1983. The Salvadoran Peasants' Union charged that the increase resulted from the need to provide the Reagan administration with proof for certifying to the U.S. Congress that El Salvador was making progress in essential economic reform and had therefore fulfilled the requirements for continued economic and military aid.

This curious land reform was accompanied by a wave of repression directed above all against the peasantry. Responsibility for seizure and distribution of land was assigned to the army and the security forces, who used their authority in several ways. Often they distributed land to members of the terrorist ORDEN organization whether or not they were entitled to it. They also used ORDEN members to identify peasants who belonged to the Popular Forces or to the guerrilla movements; these peasants were then killed by the military. Sometimes they collaborated with landowners who evicted tenants from lands they had recently acquired under land reform provisions.

In December 1981 the Peasants' Union reported to junta President José Napoleón Duarte (he had been named president in a leadership reshuffle in November 1980) that the "failure of the agrarian reform is an immediate and imminent danger." The union claimed that at least ninety of its officials and "a large number of beneficiaries" of the agrarian reform had died during 1981 at the hands of ex-landlords and their allies, who often were members of the local security forces. The report also charged that twenty-five thousand former *aparceros*, or sharecroppers, had been evicted from their plots before they could obtain provisional titles. Duarte's inability to carry out the agrarian reform or to check the terror in the countryside proved that the junta was in fact "a rightist military regime with a civilian façade"; it also showed that Duarte himself was an "ornament," in the words of one observer, needed by the United States to maintain the reformist image of the junta, and accepted by the military to pacify the U.S. State Department.

The most prominent victim of the terror that accompanied the promulgation of the agrarian reform was Monsignor Oscar Romero, archbishop of San Salvador. For years his attacks on the military and the security forces for their violations of human rights had been a thorn in the government's side. Increasingly disillusioned with the role of the Christian Democratic Party in the junta, he gradually moved toward supporting armed struggle as the only remaining resort. In a sermon on February 2, 1980, he proclaimed: "When all peaceful means have been exhausted, the church considers insurrection moral and justified." On March 23, responding to the repression that accompanied the land reform, he appealed to soldiers not to turn their guns on unarmed civilians. The next day, as he celebrated mass in a chapel in San Salvador, he was gunned down, probably by a military officer.

The National Guard celebrated his death with a savage attack on his hometown of Ciudad Barrios that left ten dead. According to the judge appointed to investigate his death—who made these revelations after he had fled for his life to Costa Rica—the assassination was planned by General José Alberto Medrano, founder of ORDEN, and Major Roberto d'Aubuisson. Robert White, former U.S. ambassador to El Salvador, informed a congressional committee that there

Many women, like the Salvadoran guerrilla shown here, took part in recent Central American revolutionary struggles, and some held high positions in the guerrilla commands. [Bettmann/Corbis]

was "compelling" evidence that d'Aubuisson was involved in the killing. Romero's martyrdom was to have profound political and military repercussions.

The Salvadoran Revolution, 1980–1992

"If I am killed," Archbishop Romero had prophesied shortly before his death, "I shall rise again in the struggle of the Salvadoran people." His death, in fact, served as a powerful catalyst for the growth of that struggle. In particular, it hastened the breakup of the Christian Democratic Party and the unification of its center and left wings with Social Democratic and Marxist-led groups in opposition to the junta. In April 1980 a broad coalition of political parties, professional associations, trade unions, and revolutionary groups formed the Democratic Revolutionary Front (FDR). In January 1981, the FDR set up a government-in-exile, headed by the Social Democratic leader Guillermo Ungo.

As important as achieving the political unity of the opposition was the unification of the various guerrilla movements. By mid-summer of 1980 the five major guerrilla groups had united in a single command, which was given the name *Frente Farabundo Martí de Liberación Nacional* (FMLN), in honor of the leader of the abortive 1932 revolt. In January 1981 the FMLN launched its first general offensive and achieved significant successes, capturing from U.S.-equipped government soldiers, M16s that virtually became the FMLN's standard weapon. Between June and October 1982 alone the rebels captured six hundred fifty firearms; over twenty guns, mortars, and heavy machine guns; and about eighty thousand rounds of ammunition.

Although the guerrillas invariably evacuated the large population centers captured in their offensives, by the spring of 1983 they had considerably expanded the zones of their control. They dominated areas inhabited by some two hundred thousand people; in these areas, political power was based on a self-governing system called the *Poder Popular Local* (PPL). To combat rebel successes, the military leadership changed and pursued a more aggressive strategy that relied on increased military aid from the Reagan administration, but this required it to improve the image of the regime by holding elections to legitimize it and give it a "democratic" face. The elections, it was assumed, would give victory to the Christian Democratic Party and its leader, José Napoleón Duarte. He would then preside over a modest reform and civic action program that would win "hearts and minds" for the government; Duarte's reforms, combined with expanded military aid, were expected to lead to a speedy pacification of the country.

In compliance with U.S. wishes, elections for a sixty-member Constituent Assembly were held in El Salvador in March 1982. Insisting that fair elections were impossible under existing conditions, the left and the guerrillas boycotted them. Less than a year earlier, the entire leadership of the FDR had been assassinated and, more recently, the army had published a hit list of FDR and FMLN members; if the government could not guarantee the security of political leaders, it certainly could not protect grassroots campaign workers! As a result, these "demonstration elections," organized for the benefit of the U.S. government, upon which the Salvadoran military depended, were dominated by right-wing parties.

In any event, the outcome of the elections did not conform to the expectations of the Reagan administration. With only 35 percent of the vote, Duarte and the Christian Democrats proved unable to form a majority government. The Nationalist Republic Alliance (ARENA) of Roberto D'Aubuisson garnered one-fourth of the vote and pressed for a coalition with other right-wing parties that would leave the Christian Democrats out in the cold. Thus, instead of legitimating Duarte and the Christian Democrats, as projected in the Reagan administration scenario, the elections appeared to legitimate D'Aubuisson and ARENA. Undaunted, however, the United States pressured

all parties to sign a pact for cooperation in the transition to a new constitutional government. As part of the deal, the U.S.-supported "moderate" banker Álvaro Magaña was elected provisional president of the republic and D'Aubuisson president of the Constituent Assembly.

The Reagan administration's policy in El Salvador had one overriding purpose: at all costs to prevent the FMLN-FDR from coming to power. To ensure congressional support for the large infusions of military and economic aid needed to achieve this objective, the Reagan administration strongly supported the 1984 presidential candidacy of Duarte, who was identified by many in El Salvador and the United States with social reform. At the same time that it backed this supposed reformer, Washington demanded a more aggressive strategy in the war against the rebels, with massive use of air power and large-scale sweeps into rebel territory to force out the civilian population and to isolate the insurgents, thereby denying them the material and logistical support they needed to survive. This more aggressive strategy was to be combined with civic action programs designed to win the rural population's support.

Soon it became evident that Duarte lacked the power, the resources, and perhaps the will to carry out his promises. He initiated peace talks with the FMLN in late 1984 but broke them off; the talks were probably intended above all to prove his goodwill regarding peace to his domestic supporters and his congressional backers in Washington. Duarte's promises of social and economic reform proved equally illusory. He presided over a moribund economy that survived due only to the immense largesse of the United States. (Between 1981 and 1987, U.S. government military and economic aid to El Salvador totaled $2.7 billion.)

Duarte faced a dilemma. His promises and election had encouraged the labor movement to organize, call strikes, and engage in political activity; the right responded with repression, including a revival of death-squad killings and disappearances. Even if he had the means, Duarte could not satisfy labor's economic and social demands over the opposition of the oligarchy, the army, and even the Reagan administration. On the other hand, he could not openly support repression without losing his base in the labor movement. Duarte solved the problem by denouncing repression in words, while tolerating and even sanctioning it in practice.

In January 1986 the Duarte government announced an economic austerity program to help pay the costs of the war against the FMLN-FDR; the program included a 100 percent devaluation of the currency and large increases in fuel prices, measures that hit workers the hardest. Thousands of angry workers responded by leaving the trade union federation, controlled by the Christian Democrats, and joining a newly organized leftist federation, the National Union of Salvadoran Workers (UNTS). In October, Duarte introduced another economic austerity package that levied steep taxes on basic goods and services and reduced already minimal social services. The package, described as an act of "political suicide" by a rebel leader, set off a fresh wave of strikes and demonstrations that drew ever-larger numbers of workers. Duarte's labor base virtually collapsed. He could not even count on the support of the business sector. Of great significance, the strikes and demonstrations increasingly linked economic demands to calls for an end to the civil war through negotiations; these calls were strongly supported by the head of the Salvadoran church, Archbishop Arturo Rivera y Damas.

But the Reaganites still sought a military victory, and a massive influx of new U.S. military aid, including gunships and helicopters, and a considerable increase in the size of the Salvadoran army undoubtedly changed the balance of forces in the civil war. U.S. reconnaissance flights from Honduras and the Panama Canal Zone helped pinpoint rebel columns and command posts, using infrared tracking systems. Unable to compete with the army in numbers and firepower, the FMLN developed a new strategy. The large battalion-size units were broken up into small units of classic guerrilla warfare; these moved out of the way of the army's sweeps and returned after the army had left. The rebels, however, were still capable of launching major surprise attacks. Other new FMLN tactics included using mines, which caused perhaps as much as 70 percent of the army's casu-

alties; another was economic sabotage through efforts to destroy the country's electrical grid by downing power lines and blowing up installations and dams, and through the destruction of coffee-processing plants.

Believing a military triumph unlikely, the FMLN now aimed to mobilize trade unions, a growing antiwar movement, and other popular forces to create conditions for a "negotiated peace." But success also required a separation of the two oligarchical factions, the hard-line coffee planters, or "agrarians," and the moderate coffee processors, or "agro-industrialists," whose unstable marriage had contributed to the government's historical oscillation between repression and reform. The FMLN sought to encourage negotiations by making the war too expensive for the agro-industrialists, led by Alfredo Cristiani, a wealthy coffee processor and past president of their trade association, ABECAFE. U.S. sources estimated the 1979–1985 loss through economic sabotage at $1.2 billion.

By 1988 the failure of the U.S. counterinsurgency strategy in El Salvador was apparent to all. The economy was in ruins, with industry operating at 40 percent of capacity. Riddled with corruption, the Duarte administration had proved unable to end the war, implement serious reforms, or check the repression. The results of March congressional and local elections, carried out under the guns of the military, represented a repudiation of both Duarte and his U.S. sponsors. Most of El Salvador's eligible voters stayed away from the polls; a majority of those who voted cast their ballots for D'Aubuisson's ARENA, which gained control of parliament and most of the country's local governments.

One year later, Alfredo Cristiani assumed the presidency. He complied with his campaign promise to initiate talks with the FMLN guerrillas following his inauguration but demanded their virtual surrender by insisting they lay down their arms as a condition for a cease-fire. As a result the peace talks were suspended and fighting resumed, accompanied by an escalation of death-squad killings and torture of civilians. Cristiani's intransigent attitude, it was widely believed, reflected the decisive influence of the so-called *Tandona*, an elite group of extreme right-wing military from the cadet class of 1966 that included the defense minister, the army's chief of staff, and the chiefs of the air force, the national police, and the national guard. This tight-knit group regarded D'Aubuisson as its leader. Nonetheless, Cristiani's apparent moderation was sufficient to convince some liberal U.S. senators like Christopher Dodd and John Kerry to vote more money for El Salvador.

Prospects of peace suffered a shattering blow in 1989, when bombings of the headquarters of the National Federation of Salvadoran Workers (FENESTRAS) killed ten persons and wounded many others. In response to the bombings, the FMLN announced that it would not resume talks with the government as long as "guarantees for the labor movement are not achieved"; then it launched its most powerful offensive since 1981, striking at a number of cities, including San Salvador. Its main objective was to take control of the working-class quarters in the city's densely populated northern outskirts, where it enjoyed considerable political support. The government responded with a ferocious aerial bombing of these working-class barrios, but the FMLN held sections of the city for up to two weeks before withdrawing.

The concentrated bombardment of densely populated working-class barrios caused many civilian casualties and provoked an international outcry. The bombardment was accompanied by a new wave of repression directed against church and labor critics of the government. Six Jesuit priests and professors at San Salvador's Central American University, whom the military regarded as the "brains" of the uprising, together with their housekeeper and her daughter, were shot in cold blood.

The FMLN's offensive was designed to prove to the Cristiani government and to the United States that after nine years of war the FMLN was stronger than ever and could not be defeated militarily, and thereby to bring the ARENA regime to the bargaining table for serious negotiations.

Moved by this demonstration of rebel power, and even more, perhaps, by the threat of a congressional halt to U.S. aid to El Salvador in reaction to the murder of the six Jesuits and other human rights abuses, the Cristiani government agreed to resume negotiations with the FMLN without preconditions, with the United Nations as mediator.

In 1992, President Cristiani and delegates of the ruling ARENA party and the FMLN finally signed peace accords that ended the decade-long civil war. Its provisions required the National Guard and Treasury Police to be disbanded and replaced with a new professionally trained National Civil Police, open to both former national police and FMLN guerrillas. The size of the armed forces would be reduced by about 50 percent, and the U.S.-trained Immediate Reaction Infantry Battalions, charged with the commission of numerous atrocities, were to be disbanded. FMLN military structures were to be dismantled under U.N. supervision and their members integrated into the political and institutional life of the country, but the FMLN could form its own party and set up its own radio and TV facilities.

The accords also dealt with economic and social issues. The government agreed to implement the existing agrarian code and respect the de facto land tenancy in "conflictive zones" (zones under FMLN control during the war) while it sought to purchase land from absentee owners. The FMLN conceded the right of the government to press on with its neoliberal "structural adjustment" policies; the government in turn agreed to take measures to alleviate the social cost of those policies. With the support of the U.N. Development Program, the government agreed to develop a National Reconstruction Plan for the conflictive zones, involving infrastructural development as well as employment, education, housing, and health programs. Finally, the accords provided for the creation of a "Truth Commission," to be composed of three foreigners, that would investigate human rights abuses during the war and could recommend prosecutions or other punishment for the responsible parties.

In 1993 the U.N.-sponsored Truth Commission released its long-awaited report. The report was based on the testimony of two thousand persons who had come forward, under promises of confidentiality, to testify as witnesses about the fate of seven thousand victims and on secondary information about the fate of more than eighteen thousand victims. The report found that 85 percent of the nine thousand human rights abuses investigated, and 95 percent of the killings, were committed by government-supported death squads and the military. Government atrocities included the massacre of nearly one thousand civilians—men, women, and children—in the village of El Mozote and nearby hamlets by the U.S.-trained Atlacatl Battalion; the 1980 assassination of Archbishop Romero; and the 1989 murder of the six Jesuit priests, their housekeeper, and her daughter. The report found that the FMLN had also committed human rights violations, such as the killing of right-wing mayors, but on a much smaller scale. The report implicitly pointed a finger of blame at the United States by noting that the majority of the human rights abuses were directly attributable to graduates of the School of the Americas at Fort Benning, Georgia, where many of El Salvador's death-squad leaders received their training in counterinsurgency methods.

The Truth Commission's report and newly declassified documents lifted a veil of deception practiced by the Reagan and Bush administrations to persuade Congress to provide continued military assistance to the Salvadoran armed forces. In 1981, for example, the CIA called ARENA party leader D'Aubuisson "the principal henchman for wealthy landowners and a coordinator of right-wing death squads that have murdered several thousand suspected leftists and leftist sympathizers" and described him as "egocentric, reckless, and perhaps mentally unstable." The CIA also reported that D'Aubuisson trafficked in drugs, smuggled arms, and directed the meeting that planned Romero's assassination. But William Walker, Bush's special envoy to San Salvador and Reagan's deputy assistant secretary of state for inter-American affairs, confronted with the documents, displayed no compunction and responded: "We had to deal with D'Aubuisson."

THE SALVADORAN REVOLUTION: A RECKONING, 1992–2003

After twelve years of fighting, seventy-five thousand dead, 2 million displaced, an estimated 1 million war refugees, and billions of dollars in economic losses, what was the revolution's legacy? First, it demilitarized Salvadoran society and created space for popular mobilization that had been suppressed since the 1932 matanza. This transformed domestic power relations and produced a new pluralism, reflected in a reorganized national political structure, that contrasted starkly with a political culture that traditionally had limited competition to two factions within the coffee oligarchy: murderous planters and slightly more moderate processors. As a result, an ongoing movement for social justice and national liberation was not only possible, but irrepressible.

Second, it engendered a new male and female consciousness. Women, traditionally consigned to family roles within the household, became active participants in public life, first as defenders of their families in human rights organizations like COMADRES and later in other organized popular movements like the Salvadoran Women's Association (AMES). Her COMADRE activism, for example, taught one woman that "the fight for human rights is all about . . . the rights of workers, the rights of women—before I didn't know this." The war also depleted the male labor force; created new demands for women workers, whose participation in the waged economy increased dramatically to 40 percent by 1992; and expanded women's presence in trade unions.

Lastly, women sought to escape the prison of patriarchy by joining the revolution, where they made up 30 percent of FMLN combatants and 20 percent of the military leadership: "We grew up with a mentality . . . that a woman is no more than a person to look after the house, raise the children," explained María Serrano, a guerrilla mayor. "But with the revolution this stopped; women found that they could do the same things as men." Naturally, this new feminist consciousness also had implications for men; one guerrillero who fought in a predominantly female unit acknowledged the difficult "process of coming to see women as compañeras and not as sex objects." Their shared experiences gave a gendered meaning to the revolution's national liberation struggle, which now included freedom from patriarchal as well as racial, class, and imperialist domination.

These potentially momentous changes, however, while clearly evinced in the peace accords, required a vigilant popular struggle and unflagging international pressure to secure their fullest development. A vigorous participatory democracy was the best guarantor of social justice, without which there could be no enduring peace. But in March 1994, with the infamous Atlacatl Battalion dissolved, a new police force organized, and the FMLN prepared to participate as a political party in its first elections, dark clouds still threatened the fragile peace. On the eve of the elections there was a dramatic escalation of violence against candidates and other leading members of the FMLN. In addition, since the cease-fire there had been some two hundred unresolved cases of former guerrillas who had been killed. Despite these troubling signs, the Clinton administration continued to send both military and economic aid ($140 million a year) to El Salvador and maintained 450 military advisers in the country.

During the early 1990s, ARENA's well-healed political machine elected Armando Calderón Sol to the presidency, and he ruled with an absolute legislative majority. Over spirited FMLN objections, ARENA implemented an IMF-sponsored neoliberal program even as it blocked fulfillment of the peace accord's provisions regarding the transfer of land in the former conflict zones, the development of reinsertion programs for former combatants in the civil war, and the demilitarization of the national police force. By early 1994 only 25 percent of former FMLN fighters had received the land they were promised in the peace accords. The deployment of the new National Police Force (PNC) was behind schedule; more ominous was the infiltration into the PNC, with the government's consent, of many members of the old security services who were known to be torturers and death-squad members.

But 1997 brought a greater flowering of the peace process and seemed to reward the FMLN's determination to continue the civic struggle. Despite rival ARENA's financially well-endowed political patronage machine, a shortage of campaign funds, and the usual electoral fraud (three hundred thousand dead people remained on the voter rolls and four hundred thousand voters did not receive registration cards), the FMLN won a resounding victory in the March legislative and municipal elections. Compared to 1994 its share of the total vote increased from 21 to 33 percent. It elected twenty-seven deputies, one-third of whom were women; captured fifty-three municipalities, including San Salvador; and governed a majority of the population.

Meanwhile, ARENA's vote declined by 35 percent, leaving it with only twenty-eight of eighty-four National Assembly seats. Although ARENA cobbled together a majority coalition, it could no longer ignore the left. More important, the FMLN and its allies had sufficient votes to block legislative approval required of international loan agreements, thereby potentially frustrating ARENA's neoliberal agenda. This had involved privatization of banks and pensions, slashed tariffs, establishment of maquiladora "free-trade zones," and draconian social service budget cuts in areas like education, whose share of the federal budget fell almost a quarter to 13 percent in a nation with a 30 percent illiteracy rate.

In fact the FMLN's success appeared to owe much to its principled opposition to these widely unpopular neoliberal reforms that enriched foreign capital and produced impressive annual per capita economic growth in 1992–1993, before falling thereafter to a dismal 2 percent in 2000 and 2001. But the price for this small growth was high; it deepened external dependency, expanded underemployment, and increased poverty. El Salvador's foreign debt burden increased steadily since 1988, rising to $4 billion in 2001. More troubling still, 48 percent of the population was mired in poverty, 18.5 percent in extreme poverty. Unemployment remained stubbornly high, and real wages fell consistently.

Equally important to the FMLN's electoral success, however, was its strategic decision to nominate women, comprising half of its national candidates, to carry its gendered social justice message, a message that transcended racial and class lines. This reflected the militancy of FMLN feminists and the party's rhetorical commitment to women's rights, but it also showed a keen understanding that ARENA's neoliberal policies had contributed to the "feminization" of poverty; men's participation in the formal economy steadily declined since 1988 from 93 to 83 percent even as women's share of waged employment grew from 38 to 41 percent, but two-thirds of women worked in the "informal economy." Moreover, by the late 1970s, 40 percent of poor Salvadoran households were headed by women, a rate that rose during the war and worsened under the neoliberal regime.

This growing demand for women's labor outside the home, irrespective of class, did not reduce their private household obligations, however, and left them vulnerable to double exploitation—reflected in gendered wage inequalities, unequal access to credit and landownership, and soaring rates of domestic violence. These gender inequalities mirrored injustices produced by domestic class and dependent foreign relations. Under these conditions, the FMLN's campaign theme, *poder femenino* (woman power), resonated with a broad cross-section of Salvadorans and mobilized new, historically ignored voters who thrilled to its slogan: "When a woman enters politics, the woman changes; but . . . when women enter politics, politics changes."

Ten years after the signing of the 1992 peace accords that ended the civil war in El Salvador, the forces struggling for democracy and social justice since the 1970s could point to some major achievements. Their greatest success was the consolidation of Salvadoran democracy. The FMLN, formerly a revolutionary army, was now registered as a political party, competing with some nine other parties for power and influence. It had become the strongest single party in the National Assembly and, having captured fifty-three municipalities, including San Salvador, it now governed a majority of the population. But it was unable to win a national presidential election. In 1999 ARENA's Francisco Flores, promising social reforms that would benefit the entire population and soft-pedaling the neoliberal core of the party's program, was elected.

Once in office, however, Flores, whom critics called the "president of broken promises," displayed an increasingly authoritarian ideology and pushed for adoption of a full-scale neoliberal program that included privatization of health care, education, and other public services. As director of the national police, he appointed someone linked by the Truth Commission to death squad activity. Corruption returned to the reformed police forces. Crime and violence increased, and the per-capita death rate was as high as during the war years.

More hopeful signs came from FMLN-controlled municipalities. According to Sara Stowell, Tecoluca, governed by the FMLN since 1994, "has community roads, potable water for over 85% of the communities, access to education for all its citizens, a woman's health-care clinic, a new market, and flood protection infrastructure. In the wake of the two devastating earthquakes, Tecoluca mayor and council were able to work together with their population to respond rapidly to the need for shelter and food, and have one of the most comprehensive reconstruction plans under way as a result of good planning and excellent mayor-community relations."

Clearly, Tecoluca and other progressive Salvadoran communities had mastered the teaching of the martyred Archbishop Oscar Romero: "Learn about the mechanisms that engender poverty, struggle for a more just world, support the workers and peasants in their demands and in their right to organize, and be very close to the people."

Lands of Bolívar: Venezuela and Colombia in the Twentieth Century

MODERN VENEZUELA AND COLOMBIA have often been cited as oases of democratic and economic stability in a turbulent, poverty-ridden continent. A closer look at their recent history, however, suggests they have not escaped the general crisis of Latin American dependent capitalism. Its effects are clearly evident in the devastating impact of Venezuela's foreign debt on a country whose oil wealth once made it the envy of the continent. In February 1989, after Venezuelan President Carlos Andrés Pérez announced drastic increases in the prices of basic goods and services to satisfy the requirements of the International Monetary Fund (IMF) for loans to his government, the country exploded into riots that were crushed with the loss of hundreds of lives. Between 1981 and 1987 the number of Venezuelans living in poverty had risen from 22 to 54 percent of the population.

Neighboring Colombia presented an even darker picture. Colombia was the home of the Cali drug cartel, which accounted for most of the refined cocaine smuggled into the United States. Under an ostensibly democratic regime, death squads linked to the army, security forces, and the drug mafia operated with impunity against leftists, trade unionists, and human rights activists. Meanwhile, a guerrilla war—the longest continuing insurgency in Latin America, reflecting the vast accumulation of unsolved social problems in

this oligarchical democracy—raged in Colombia's jungles and mountains. As we have seen elsewhere in Latin America, the twentieth-century origins of these problems can be traced to the growth of market forces, external economic dependency, internal social inequality, and an increasingly resolute popular resistance. This pattern began in Venezuela with the rise of Juan Vicente Gómez, a modern dictator in the tradition of Antonio Guzmán Blanco, Manuel Estrada Cabrera, and Porfirio Díaz.

Venezuela in the Early Twentieth Century, 1908–1958

THE TYRANNY OF JUAN VICENTE GÓMEZ, 1908–1935

On taking power, Gómez tried to placate his foreign patrons and promote a flow of investments into Venezuela by nullifying Cipriano Castro's nationalistic policies, restoring foreign companies' concessionary rights, and allowing foreign nationals to circumvent Venezuelan courts with appeals to their own national courts or to international tribunals.

Gómez especially favored foreign oil companies. The explosive growth of the oil industry eventually transformed Venezuelan economy and society, but the process began slowly. This

Juan Vicente Gómez, the early-twentieth-century liberal dictator, relied on a powerful military to implement unpopular policies that favored foreign investors and local elites. [Corbis]

modernization. The agricultural crisis contributed to a wave of rural migration to the oil fields of the Maracaibo Basin and other petroleum areas and to the growing cities.

Committed to progress based on private investment and the exploitation of wage labor, Gómez and the generation of intellectuals who served his dictatorship realized that Venezuela's "salvation" could not rely solely on the nineteenth century's failed racist immigration policy of "whitening." This recognition largely reflected Venezuela's growing export dependency and its demand for abundant, cheap labor, which discouraged potential European immigrants even as it attracted Caribbean blacks and Asians. Increasingly, the Gómez regime celebrated race-mixing to erase indigenous and African traditions by submerging them within a dominant European cultural motif, now labeled the "social race," whose unstable compound justified dictatorship.

In the 1920s nationalist resentment of foreign economic domination and hostility toward Gómez began to pervade the growing middle class. Venezuelan professionals and would-be entrepreneurs chafed at the difficulties of operating in an economic climate dominated by monopoly, nepotism, and corruption. They also resented foreigners' racist discrimination against their multiracial origins. In 1928 a celebration of the "Week of the Student" turned into a protest against the dictatorship, as students joined trade unionists and other anti-Gómez political factions.

The student protest inspired a military revolt in April 1928, led by young officers of the Caracas garrison and cadets of the *Escuela Militar*. Grievances over the favoritism shown in pay and promotions to officers of unquestioned loyalty to Gómez, and awareness that the army had become a repressive force designed to maintain internal order, fueled their discontent. An informer revealed the conspiracy to the military authorities, and government troops easily crushed the revolt before it had well begun. Some students who had collaborated with the rebellion cadets including Rómulo Betancourt, future president of Venezuela, managed to escape and make their way abroad.

economic transformation did not reduce Venezuela's dependence or broaden the base of its economy; the monoculture of coffee and cacao was replaced by the monoculture of "black gold." The oil industry pumped vast wealth into the hands of Gómez, a small native elite linked to the oil industry, and the foreign concessionaires, three of whom—Dutch Shell, Standard Oil, and Gulf—controlled 89 percent of the market. But little of this wealth trickled down to the masses, nor did it generate significant industrial progress. Government subsidies failed to stem the decline of agriculture, a sector that traditionally resisted

Although separated by class and racial status, women also played a powerful role in the emerging coalition that opposed Gómez. The Venezuelan Women's Association (AVM) largely represented elite women, who shunned politics and the equal rights struggle. They limited themselves to social advocacy on behalf of issues central to home and family: charity for the poor, childcare, orphanages, prenatal medical care, and sex education. But even these modest reforms typically envisioned an activist role for the state in the regulation of civil society and, in the words of political scientist Elisabeth Friedman, "proved too challenging to accepted notions of gender relations."

Unlike the AVM, the Women's Cultural Association (ACF), whose founding members included Cecelia Núñez Sucre and Mercedes Fermín, was a predominantly middle-class social movement that aimed to improve Venezuelan women's social condition, establish civil equality, and secure political rights. In addition to calls for greater access to jobs and education for women, they demanded limits on women's work day, increased wages, and pre- and post-maternity leave. But they also called for women's suffrage and reform of the Civil Code, which, according to one contemporaneous observer, gave a "woman no rights whatever against her husband, either personal or financial, even no rights to her own child."

Working-class women like Olga Luzardo, however, typically joined trade unions and actively identified with leftist political parties that, although dominated by men, nonetheless advocated "improvement of the entire exploited sector." Eschewing "feminism" as a middle-class idea incapable "of resolving the problems of working women," Luzardo, a Communist and working-class militant, scorned the bourgeois values of a social movement that limited itself to demands for gender equality and the "freedom" to work outside the home: "What would the women comrades of the soap and perfume factories, the polishers, the seamstresses, say [to the idea] that we ought to pull woman from her idleness and push her into work?" Luzardo asked contemptuously. "Wouldn't they laugh at such an unbalanced way of thinking?"

LIQUIDATING THE GÓMEZ LEGACY, 1936–1945

In 1931, Gómez was at the peak of his power. But in the next few years his health began to decline, and in 1935 the prospect of his early demise led to intense factional maneuvering in his inner circle.

Amid growing signs that Gómez's illness was terminal, his minister of war, Eleazar López Contreras, wove a network of alliances, including the solid support of most army commanders, to ensure his own peaceful coming to power without a civil war or dangerous risings of the masses.

Announcing Gómez's death, López proclaimed two weeks of public mourning, but Venezuelans responded to the announcement with rejoicing; in Caracas angry crowds sacked the palaces of Gómez's most prominent supporters. The jubilation and the demands both for vengeance and for social and political reform provoked by the news of Gómez's death made a mockery of López's eulogy of the dead dictator and foreclosed the possibility of an easy transition to a social order resembling that of the old regime. The entrance of the Venezuelan middle classes and workers onto the political scene opened two decades of complicated struggle, culminating in the victory of a new populist model of capitalist development and its associated political form of representative democracy. Nonetheless, the dead dictator's hand-picked Congress chose López Contreras to replace him.

In an atmosphere of great social and political effervescence, however, many exiles with various ideologies returned home and joined activists emerging from the underground in organizing trade unions, political parties, and professional organizations. López found himself under siege from the right and the left. He sometimes yielded to pressures for reform, then stubbornly resisted demands for change to the undemocratic Gómez political system. For example, he supported a new constitution in 1936 but insisted on retaining a Gómez clause that defined communism and anarchism as treason, effectively outlawing the major opposition parties, the reformist *Partido Democrático Nacional* (PDN) led by Rómulo Betancourt and the Venezuelan Communist Party of Gustavo Machado.

World War II, having created insatiable demand for Venezuela's oil, enabled López's hand-picked successor, General Isaias Medina Angarita, to wrest more favorable terms from the oil companies than had been present in the old inequitable contracts. Moreover, domestic social movements of workers, peasants, women, and industrialists pressured him to support progressive policies like Venezuela's first social security and income-tax legislation. His government also encouraged the formation of trade unions, which gained considerable strength, particularly in the oil industry. Pushed by Mercedes Fermín and the Feminine Cultural Group (ACF), a largely middle-class women's rights organization that had opposed Gómez, Medina viewed favorably a movement toward a more democratic system with enfranchisement of women and direct popular election of the president.

Medina also tackled the country's urgent agrarian problem. Near the end of his administration he asked his minister of agriculture, Angel Biaggini, to draft an agrarian reform bill that would distribute the extensive state landholdings to landless peasants. Congress passed the law, but one month after passage it died stillborn as a result of the overthrow of the Medina administration by a military-civilian revolt headed by two men who would dominate Venezuelan politics for the next two decades, Marcos Pérez Jiménez and Rómulo Betancourt.

Betancourt was the most influential personality among that famous generation of student leaders who in 1928 electrified Caracas by leading a public demonstration against Gómez. Of middle-class background, during his years of exile Betancourt had read widely in the classics of Marxist literature. But the most decisive influence on his thought was a nationalist, reformist ideological current best represented in Latin America by the Peruvian Victor Raúl Haya de la Torre, who argued that in Latin America's specific conditions, characterized by economic backwardness and a small, weak working class, the immediate historical task of social revolutionaries was to complete the unfinished bourgeois revolution.

Betancourt thus appears as the standard-bearer of the Venezuelan bourgeois revolution, which sought to end dependency on oil by diversifying the economy through industrialization, to expand the internal market by improving living standards, and to initiate land reform that would increase the productivity of agriculture. All these goals he hoped to achieve within the framework of parliamentary democracy. Betancourt assigned a decisive role in this process to the state, which should plan, regulate, and assist economic development.

The political instrument Betancourt and his colleagues created to achieve Venezuela's bourgeois, democratic revolution was *Acción Democrática* (AD), a multiclass party and mass organization that enjoyed large growth from 1941 to 1945, gaining a clear superiority in numbers and influence among workers, peasants, women, and the middle class over its closest rival, the Communist Party.

There were four key elements in women's strategy for securing civil and political equality. First, they sought to organize and maintain unity across the seemingly insurmountable dividing lines of class and political party. Reflecting this strategic consensus among middle-class women, Ana Luisa Padra announced in 1941 that "We have different interests, but a common problem: the conquest of our rights for which we ought to [fight] together without rancor or distinctions." Second, rather than seek equality with men, the women's movement in Venezuela sought to mobilize the state's resources to protect children and mothers. Third, women raised the issue of equality without addressing it directly, at least initially by seeking merely to reclaim for married women liberties freely granted to widowed mothers—property rights and custody of their children. Thereafter, they insisted that political rights for women logically should flow directly from the successful attainment of civil equality, rather than vice versa; lacking "voice or vote within the boundaries of her home," a feminist newspaper editorialized, "it would be laughable that [women] would be granted the vote within the boundaries of her country."

This particular strategy also aimed to preserve a gender-based unity, but it fractured later when the women's movement exercised a wartime demand for equal voting rights with men, whose franchise already was limited to literates. This immediately raised issues of class inequality by largely excluding working-class women. Class issues, always lurking in the shadows of the women's movement, took center stage in a 1944 competition to elect the queen of the Amateur Baseball World Series, a cultural event, according to political scientist Friedman, widely viewed as a "primer for universal suffrage." One woman advertised herself as the candidate of the "respectable people," by contrast with her opponent, Yolanda Leal, a poor school teacher, who was "for the common folk." When Leal, "daughter of the people," won overwhelmingly, it created a national furor over the franchise that weakened middle- and upper-class support for universal suffrage.

Even as middle-class women abandoned their working-class counterparts, Acción Democrática, in its populist struggle to fashion a multiclass electoral movement, came to power in 1945 and established universal suffrage two years later. Ironically, after enfranchisement ended women's political segregation and integrated their participation into male-dominated institutions, women's rights organizations lost much of their traditional autonomy, their memberships fragmented, and their political agenda dissipated.

A STRANGE ALLIANCE: BETANCOURT AND THE MILITARY IN POWER, 1945–1948

After the 1945 military-civilian coup that overthrew the Medina regime, a provisional government headed by Betancourt as president seized power. The motives for this coup, born of an alliance between conservative young military officers and the AD's populist leadership, continue to provoke historical debate. The officers, organized in the *Unión Patriótica Militar* (UPM), were disgruntled over promotion, salary, and appointment policies within the military, displayed little interest in governmental affairs, and appeared content to leave government to the AD. Although Medina's progressive record included support for sweeping constitutional reforms, including universal suffrage, his government, composed almost entirely of white elites, had continued to discriminate against nonwhite immigrants and appeared insensitive to the historical links among race, class, and political order that bound together Venezuela's *café con leche* society. Consequently, it had been totally unprepared for the furor over the racist refusal of three posh Caracas hotels to serve the African American singer Robert Todd Duncan. Eager to use race as a powerful organizing tool, the AD had seized upon public outrage to expand and mobilize its political supporters in a bid to control the state.

However dubious the motives that inspired the 1945 coup, it proved a milestone in Venezuelan history. The AD government between 1945 and 1948—a period Venezuelans call the *Trienio*—represented the first serious effort to transform the country's archaic economic and social structures.

Because Acción Democrática was, in effect, the government and had a large nationwide network of party organizations to mobilize the population, it had a distinct advantage over its political rivals. AD control of the distribution of land and agricultural credits under the agrarian reform enabled it to build a clientele of peasant union leaders that gave it a commanding majority of the peasant vote. AD established a similar relationship of influence and leadership over most of the more than five hundred trade unions organized in this period and affiliated with the Venezuelan Confederation of Workers, which included both trade and peasant unions.

The AD also drafted a new constitution that guaranteed many civil and social rights, including labor's right to organize and strike and the principle that land should belong "to him who works it." The constitution established universal, secret voting for all persons over eighteen, with direct election of the president and both houses of Congress.

Among the economic issues with which the AD government had to deal, oil policy was most important, for it involved fundamental questions of dependency, economic sovereignty, and the revenues needed for economic diversification and modernization. In 1946 the government had imposed a supertax of 26 percent on all company profits over 28 million bolívars; the law was aimed primarily at the oil companies. This tax alone increased government income in 1947 by 230 percent over its income in 1938.

In view of the great importance the AD program attached to agrarian reform, the junta's approach was timid. Evidently fearing the political and economic repercussions of a frontal attack on the latifundio, the government preferred to distribute land to the peasants from the extensive state holdings taken over on the death of Gómez, Venezuela's premier latifundist. Out of a landless peasant population estimated at about 330,000, only between 55,000 and 80,000 received land during the Trienio. Because the average peasant received only 2.2 hectares of land to cultivate, "the problem," as Judith Ewell points out, "then changed from *latifundia* to *minifundia*."

The creation of an independent national economy through industrialization was a major government goal. The Venezuelan Development Corporation (CVF) was formed in 1946 to promote this process through loans to private entrepreneurs and direct investment in state corporations. In three years it lent nearly 50 million bolivars to industrial enterprises. But by the Trienio's end, the program of "sowing the petroleum" to diversify and modernize the economy had achieved only modest results. More impressive progress was made in health and education, whose respective budgets for 1948 quadrupled and tripled by comparison to 1945. Important advances were also made in eliminating the country's principal health scourge, malaria, by spraying with DDT the breeding grounds of mosquitos, which carried the disease.

The principal danger to the regime came from the military. The conservative officers, headed by Colonel Marcos Pérez Jiménez, gradually became disenchanted with what they regarded as the radical excesses of their civilian partners. On November 24 the government was overthrown by a virtually bloodless coup, and Minister of Defense Carlos Delgado Chalbaud took power as president of a military junta. Many of the leading members of the AD regime were arrested and imprisoned. Betancourt escaped and took refuge in the Colombian Embassy; later he and other prominent ·AD leaders were permitted to go into exile.

THE MILITARY DICTATORSHIP, 1948–1958

In a proclamation issued on November 25, Delgado Chalbaud, who had personal and political differences with Pérez Jiménez, declared that the junta was a provisional government and did not intend to destroy Venezuelan democracy or prohibit the activities of political parties. But the junta's actions contradicted its claims of democratic intentions. Soon after the coup it dissolved Congress, annulled the 1947 constitution, voided the petroleum law, and abandoned other progressive programs like agrarian reform and school construction. The junta also imposed a strict censorship, forbidding any criticism of the regime. In 1949 the junta launched an offensive against the unions, arresting leaders of the Venezuelan Labor Confederation, forbidding union meetings, and freezing the funds of most of the unions.

Initially resistance to the junta and its repressive policies was largely limited to student protests and the activities of the illegal Communist Party, whose members played a leading role in the organization of the resistance movement. With the Feminine Cultural Group and other women's rights organizations under attack, women activists also quickly joined clandestine opposition movements like the Venezuelan Union of Women and the Communist Women's Organization. In 1949 AD leaders who remained in the country formed an underground organization. Against the objections of the strongly anticommunist Betancourt and other AD leaders in exile, the AD underground cooperated with the Communists and other groups of the resistance movement in the struggle against the dictatorship.

After the assassination of Delgado Chalbaud in 1950, the military regime intensified its repressive activity. By the fall of 1952, the regime, evidently convinced that the repression had intimidated the Venezuelan people into accepting its rule, decided it would be safe to hold elections for a Constituent Assembly.

Despite the repressive conditions and the call issued by the exiled AD leadership to abstain from voting—a position it reversed at the last moment—Venezuelans gave a two-thirds majority of the popular vote to the opposition parties. Furious at this outcome, Pérez Jiménez nullified the election and announced he was taking office as provisional president in the name of the armed forces.

For the next five years (1953–1958) Pérez Jiménez was the absolute ruler of Venezuela. A brutally efficient repression, whose principal instrument was the *Seguridad Nacional*, the secret police, made antigovernment activities very difficult. A resistance movement uniting persons of all political tendencies survived and continued its struggle against the dictatorship, however.

The social and economic policies of the regime generated discontent among ever wider sections of the population. Its limitations on the right to organize and strike contributed to a decline in labor's share of the national income. In place of the AD's focus on education, health, agrarian reform, and balanced economic development, the Pérez Jiménez regime emphasized grand works of infrastructure—highways, urban freeways, and port improvements—and urban constructions, some of little or no social utility, like the Officers Club in Caracas or the many-storied shopping center built on the side of one of Caracas's hills.

Women's roles in Venezuelan society once again changed dramatically in this period. First, as Pérez Jiménez promoted economic growth by offering incentives to private, especially foreign, businesses, there was more demand for low-cost labor, which increased women's participation in the work force, to be sure, mostly concentrated in menial jobs as domestics, laundresses, and waitresses. As a share of the wage-earning work force, women's participation increased from 17 to 22 percent during this period. Second, because the dictator dismissed women as political actors, his brutal repression largely targeted men, the effect of which was to create more opportunities for women in the labor market and in popular resistance movements. One of the more active organizations in the antidictatorial struggle was the Venezuelan Teachers' Federation (FVM), 75 percent of whose membership was female.

Although the movement's public leadership remained overwhelmingly male, women shouldered a large measure of the daily organizational responsibilities, ranging from intelligence collection to communications work. The Women's Committee, arguably the most influential of all the women's groups involved in the resistance, was especially successful at building cross-class alliances and uniting women politically even as it mobilized thousands in their opposition to dictatorship. Women also were effective in organizing cultural foundations, like the Gabriela Mistral Center, that efficiently disguised clandestine political objectives. But once again, when the dictatorship collapsed and a fragile democracy reemerged, the women's movement suffered a decline. In the words of Argelia Laya, a prominent activist, guerrilla leader, and founder of Socialist Women, male domination or machismo "was stronger than a military dictatorship!"

Signs of defection from the regime multiplied in 1957. Especially significant was the increasingly critical attitude of the conservative Catholic hierarchy, which issued statements deploring the government's disregard for the interests of the poor. Disaffection also grew among national capitalists, who complained of the government's neglect. With the end of the oil export boom in the late 1950s, the regime's capacity to generate business activity and employment through public works programs began to run out of steam. Within the armed forces there was growing resentment of Pérez Jiménez's arbitrary ways and his reliance on the secret police to watch over the loyalty of officers.

By mid-1957, an underground organization called the *Junta Patriótica* had been formed to unite the principal political parties. This group became the principal motor of the resistance movement and its preparation for a popular revolt. On January 21, 1958, the Junta Patriótica proclaimed a general strike that was overwhelmingly effective and was accompanied by clashes between the people and the regime's security forces. Barricades appeared in the streets of Caracas. The next day the insurgents seized key strategic points in the capital. The majority of military units refused to obey Pérez Jiménez and fraternized with the rebels. Fearing the radicalism of the popular opposition, a new military junta demanded that Pérez Jiménez resign and shortly thereafter he fled the country for the Dominican Republic.

The military junta became a provisional government: its first decrees proclaimed the restoration of all democratic freedoms, amnesty for all political prisoners and exiles, and legalization of all political parties. Almost ten years of rule by a repressive military dictatorship had ended.

Venezuela's Representative Democracy, 1958–2003

The military-civilian junta presided over the transition to democratic elections, set for December 1958, and invited the return of political exiles like Betancourt. Chastened by experience, Betancourt had become politically more moderate than he had been during the Trienio. Betancourt's efforts to reassure Venezuela's economic elite about his intentions and his decision to choose moderates as his principal political allies reflected his new caution. So too did his decision to join with the nation's other centrist parties to endorse the Pact of Punto Fijo, which provided that whatever the election results, they would form a coalition government to carry out a program of democratic socioeconomic and political reforms.

The Pact of Punto Fijo was important far beyond its impact on the 1958 elections because it created a unique Venezuelan model of representative democracy. The Venezuelan government was consciously tailored to isolate the Marxist left, making it virtually impossible for Marxists to wield political power. Second, although the Pact of Punto Fijo provided for a three-party coalition, the system evolved toward hegemonic control of political life by two parties, the social democratic AD and the social Christian COPEI, whose reformist programs were broadly similar.

A third distinctive feature of the Venezuelan populist model of representative democracy was the major role that it assigned to the state as regulator and arbiter of relations between the classes and interest groups. The massive influx of petroleum revenues over most of the past three decades had strengthened the state and endowed it with the financial resources to perform this role, which required it to balance and mediate the conflicting demands and interests of all the major classes and pressure groups—labor, the peasantry, capitalists, the middle class, the armed forces, the church, the political parties.

Finally, the architect of this model, Rómulo Betancourt, viewed the state as an instrument for the gradual recapture of the nation's natural resources from foreign control, the reform of its socioeconomic structures, and the promotion of a balanced economic development. Betancourt hoped that, in time, economic development would lead to the rise of an autonomous Venezuelan capitalism capable of providing Venezuelans with a high standard of living and culture. Indeed, over the next three decades Venezuela made large advances in such problem areas as health and literacy. But the vast sums expended in "sowing the petroleum" over those decades did not achieve Betancourt's main goals; poverty did not decline but increased, income distribution remained as inequitable as in Mexico and Brazil, and today's Venezuela, burdened with an unpayable foreign debt, is more deeply dependent than it was in the time of Juan Vicente Gómez.

A DECADE OF AD RULE, 1959–1969

Although the three centrist parties had approved a common program of economic, social, and political reform broadly similar to the one carried out during the Trienio, there remained considerable disagreements that were aggravated by the continuing economic crisis and Betancourt's own contentious nature. The victory of the Cuban Revolution in January 1959 and Cuba's gradual turn toward socialism created an especially divisive issue. Younger activists hailed the revolution as a model that Venezuela could well emulate. But Betancourt, virulently anticommunist, regarded the Cuban socialist regime as a direct challenge to his own reformist philosophy and program and fully supported U.S. efforts to isolate Castro's regime economically and politically.

In 1961 Betancourt promulgated a new constitution that proclaimed the government's responsibility for its citizens' social well-being, provided for proportional minority representation in Congress, and prohibited the president from succeeding himself. But it also gave him significant powers to suspend constitutional guarantees of personal and civil liberties. Moreover, although he had campaigned on the need for redistribution-of-land reform, which earned him an overwhelming majority of the peasant vote, the results of his agrarian reform were mixed, at best, and fell far short of solving Venezuela's acute agrarian problem.

By 1969 only some 150,000 out of the 350,000 peasant families without land in 1960 had received plots. Combined with the estimated 200,000 new families formed in those eight years, there remained 400,000 families without land. Government investments in irrigation, roads, and credit and technical assistance primarily benefited large- and medium-sized commercial farms, which produced the lion's share of profitable crops and accounted for most of the 150 percent increase in agricultural production during the years between 1959 and 1968.

More significant, perhaps, were the large advances made in health and public education during the Betancourt administration. Nearly 9 percent of the national budget was assigned to the Ministry of Health and Social Assistance. A concerted attack on the problems of endemic disease, infant mortality, and malnutrition resulted in a decline of infant mortality from 64 per 1,000 live births in the 1955–1959 period to 46.5 in 1966. The Betancourt years also saw a significant growth of public education.

A major objective of the Betancourt regime was to increase its share of oil profits to make more funds available for industrial development. A 1958 law therefore raised the tax rate on oil profits to 65 percent. In fact, industrialization was a cornerstone of the new Venezuela Betancourt wished to build. The slogan "Venezuela must industrialize or die" expressed the militant spirit of the AD's new campaign to industrialize. The AD government transferred large resources generated by oil exports to the industrialization process in the form of loans and direct subsidies.

The campaign for "economic independence," however, had a peculiar outcome; it fastened more firmly the chains of dependence on Venezuela. Confronted with high tariff walls, unwilling to lose the large consumer market created by oil wealth, a growing number of U.S. and other foreign firms chose to establish branches in Venezuela, frequently in association with local capital. The label "made in Venezuela" increasingly came to mean an article made with raw materials and intermediate materials imported from the United States and finished or assembled in Venezuela.

Between 1958 and 1970 the number of plants producing such items as cans, foodstuffs, clothing, automobiles, auto tires, paint, and cigarettes mushroomed. The alliance of foreign and native capital achieved the goal of import substitution, but because the dominant partner in the alliance was foreign capital, most of the profits flowed back to the home offices of foreign firms. By 1971, Venezuela had the largest gross accumulated foreign investment in any Third World country: $5.57 billion. But the export of profits reached an annual average of $672 million. Venezuela, observes one economist, had become a "fiscal paradise of foreign monopoly capital."

The drive for import-substitution industrialization was accompanied by the incorporation of labor as a less-than-equal partner in an alliance with the state and industry. In 1958, labor leaders signed a pact with management that committed the unions to seek conciliation of conflicts with employers. The subordination of labor was completed during the following decade of AD rule.

POPULIST PROBLEMS IN A PETROLEUM REPUBLIC, 1969–1988

Internal division contributed to the loss of the AD candidate in the election of 1968. Responding to growing nationalist sentiment and charges that the foreign oil companies were withholding further investment in Venezuela in reprisal for higher taxes and increased government control, Rafael Caldera of the Social Christian Party promised to pass a law that provided for the reversion to the state of all existing oil concessions beginning in 1983 and was elected president. The law also stipulated that unexploited concessions be ceded to the state petroleum company, CVP, in 1974. In addition, the oil companies were required to post bonds guaranteeing that their plant and machinery would be turned over in good condition. Also enacted in 1971 were bills nationalizing the foreign-owned natural gas industry and giving the government power to control oil-production levels. Finally, during his last months in office, Caldera issued a decree that forbade foreign interest in radio and television stations and electric companies.

Despite the establishment of representative democracy in 1958 and the reforms initiated by Caldera in 1969, a survey of Venezuela's economic and social conditions made in 1973 gave no cause for satisfaction with either of the country's two ruling parties. No basic change in economic structure had occurred; the government remained heavily dependent on oil income. True, import-substitution industrialization had achieved some economic diversification, but it was a dependent industrialization largely based on foreign capital, inputs, and technology. Despite the agrarian reform, agriculture remained the most backward branch of the national economy. In 1971, Venezuela still imported 46 percent of its basic foodstuffs. The failure of the agrarian reform to correct fundamental problems was also reflected in the continuing high concentration of landownership; 1.4 percent of the large estates held 67 percent of all privately owned land in 1973.

Thanks to improved health care and the eradication of such scourges as malaria, the Venezuelan population had grown rapidly, increasing from 7,524,000 in 1958 to 10,722,000 in 1971. But it is doubtful whether the quality of life for the majority of Venezuelans had improved after fifteen years of democratic rule. Although women's share of the labor force had doubled, they still made up a small percentage of wage workers, mostly employed in low-wage service jobs. Prostitutes typically made more money. In 1974, 30 percent of all Venezuelan children suffered from malnutrition; 12 percent of all adults suffered from mental retardation from the same cause, combined with other difficult living conditions. In the early 1960s a United Nations study described Venezuela's income distribution as one of the most unequal in the world. A decade later the situation had not improved.

The AD candidate, Carlos Andrés Pérez, a Betancourt protégé, emerged an easy winner in the 1973 election. The flamboyant Pérez, a master of populist rhetoric, had promised a "war on poverty" and against "privilege." Despite his rhetoric, his program did not differ substantially from those of his predecessors.

Pérez took office under the most favorable auspices: the Arab oil embargo of 1973 had brought a rapid rise in the price of oil, which had gone from $2.01 a barrel in 1970 to $14.26 in January 1974. The resulting vast increase in state revenues appeared to give Venezuela the means to solve all its major social and economic problems. Pérez promised to "manage abundance with the mentality of scarcity," but the flood of oil riches and the irresistible drive to modernize overwhelmed his administration and frustrated his good intentions.

On August 29, 1975, Pérez signed a law nationalizing the Venezuelan oil industry, to take effect January 1, 1976. A state oil company, *Petroven*, was created to control a sector of the economy whose annual sales volume exceeded $10 billion. In addition to a generous compensation of $1 billion to the foreign companies, the nationalization agreement authorized the state to enter into contracts with those companies for the provision of technological assistance and equipment, as well as marketing agreements for the international transshipment of Venezuelan oil exports.

Pérez's populist economic program called for the creation and expansion of heavy industries, especially petrochemicals, steel, and shipbuilding, that would supply the needs of Venezuela's consumer-goods industry. Gradually other projects—a fishery industry, a national rail system, the Caracas metro, and modernized port facilities—were added to this list.

During his campaign Pérez had pledged he would direct "priority attention to the needs of Venezuelan agriculture as the essential motor of economic development." But like his predecessors, Pérez understood those "needs" as the needs of large commercial farmers. Although Pérez claimed in 1975 to have achieved an "agricultural miracle," the reality was very different. Domestic food production increased, but imports of the country's basic foodstuffs rose from 46 percent in 1971 to almost 70 percent by the close of his administration. The rapid growth of the urban population contributed to this increased food dependence.

The immense oil revenues that flowed to the state from 1974 to 1979 proved inadequate to cover the costs of the government's ambitious development program, and Pérez, fearful of alienating business leaders, refused to undertake serious tax reform. Increasingly Pérez had to resort to foreign loans; between 1974 and 1978 Venezuela's foreign debt grew by almost $10 billion.

Pérez cultivated a populist image that did not correspond to his social policies. As a result of the orgy of state spending during his administration, the economy heated up and inflation cut deeply into workers' living standards. For the business, financial, and political elites, however, the boom created vast opportunities for enrichment resulting in an explosion of conspicuous consumption by these classes as the standard of living for peasants and workers deteriorated. The intimate ties among the state, the ruling party, and the economic elites generated corruption on an unheard-of scale.

Finally, the Pérez economic program had clearly failed to solve the dilemma of dependency that continued to plague Venezuela. Measured by the yardsticks of foreign indebtedness and the degree of its reliance for revenue on a single resource—oil—Venezuela was more dependent in 1980 than it had been in 1974.

Pérez's successors in the presidency—the COPEI leader Luis Herrera Campins, elected in 1978, and the AD leader Jaime Lusinchi, elected in 1983—had to struggle with the devastating combined effects of recurrent drops in oil prices and the massive outflow of funds to service the foreign debt. In a New Year's Eve 1989 address to the nation, Lusinchi, proclaiming that debt "is strangling our country's social and economic development and that of the majority of the world's people," announced a payment moratorium on the principal of all debts accumulated with foreign banks before 1983.

NEOLIBERALISM AND THE DILEMMAS OF A PETROLEUM REPUBLIC, 1988–2003

The 1988 election saw the return of Carlos Andrés Pérez to the presidency. Despite a populist campaign that denounced subservience to foreign bankers, once in office Pérez inaugurated an economic austerity program in response to conditions demanded by the IMF in exchange for a $4.5 billion loan over a three-year period. The program included a massive currency devaluation; the lifting of controls and subsidies on a wide range of products and services such as gasoline, bread, and electricity; and a rise in interest rates. The price increases were announced in advance of their application; as a result, goods vanished from the shelves as shopkeepers prepared to take advantage of the higher prices.

In February 1989 a popular explosion rocked Caracas when a significant rise in bus fares was announced. For many Venezuelans, whose wage increases were cut in half by this measure alone, it was the last straw. Tens of thousands of people took to the streets, rioting and looting shops; from Caracas the rioting spread to the poor barrios surrounding the city, then to the nearby port of La Guaira, and later to more distant cities and towns.

The Pérez government responded with a display of force that many observers found excessive; in contrast to the officially admitted death toll of around three hundred, unofficial estimates placed the number of dead at between four hundred and one thousand. The shock waves of the explosion soon reached Washington, where the U.S. Treasury hastened to make a $453 million "bridging loan" to the Pérez government in advance of its signing an IMF economic adjustment program. In another apparent reaction to events in Venezuela, U.S. Treasury Secretary Nicholas Brady announced a plan providing for a partial reduction of the Latin American debt. Pérez continued to insist that his "six-month shock" economic program was correct in its essentials and would in time create "a new Venezuela."

In the meantime, however, this neoliberal program deepened the recession. Prices for many basic foods and household items, transport, and electricity rose between 50 and 100 percent. Real wages fell between 20 and 50 percent.

Pérez faced a dilemma. He was caught between the neoliberal demands of the IMF, World Bank, and foreign bankers that he continue his austerity program as a condition for obtaining the new loans needed to reactivate the economy and the counterdemands of labor and the middle class that he change course and relieve the suffering caused by his economic adjustment program and a deepening recession. He decided to continue with his economic adjustment plan, which included the privatization of a large number of state-owned enterprises. Not the least irony was that it was Pérez himself who had nationalized the iron and steel industries and proclaimed "evolutionary socialism" his long-term goal. Pérez even called his IMF-style austerity program *el gran viraje* (the great turnabout). For many suffering Venezuelans, however, it was "the great betrayal."

Pérez's privatization program caused significant loss of jobs in a country already burdened with high unemployment. It also transferred ownership of those enterprises to foreign multinationals. The first privatizations resulted in the sale of 40 percent of the state-owned telephone company to the U.S. telecommunications giant GTE, the national airline to the Spanish Iberia, and several large hotels to various international private interests. The sales prices also grossly undervalued these assets and led to considerable corruption.

A one-time bonanza of $2 billion in government revenues from the sale of state companies and a boom in the import-led commercial sector as a result of a reduction in import duties helped spur a partial revival of the economy from its deep recession. But the recovery was mainly in the realm of stock market speculation; industry and agriculture continued to stagnate. Some economic and social indicators reflected the failure of neoliberal economic policy to improve the life of most Venezuelans. The real minimum wage in 1991 was only 44 percent of its 1987 value; the number of people living below the poverty line jumped from 15 percent at the end of 1988 to 41 percent in 1991; and inflation reached a record high of 80 percent in 1989.

Mounting anger over Pérez's austerity program, the growing gap between rich and poor, and revelations of corruption in official circles sparked a series of strikes and protests demanding Pérez's resignation. The growing discontent reached into the middle and lower echelons of the military, whose members were unhappy with their own deteriorating living conditions and with Pérez's privatization program; in 1992 a coup attempt, led by Lieutenant Colonel Hugo Chávez Frías, involved 10 percent of the nation's armed forces and came perilously close to overthrowing the regime and seizing power. Its program included putting all those engaged in corruption on trial; a reversal of Pérez's neoliberal policies; an emergency program to combat misery and poverty; and a dissolution of government and election of a constitutional assembly. Although defeated, Chávez became a folk hero overnight among the poor in Caracas's "belt of misery."

The foiled coups combined with the unending wave of strikes, protests, and other expressions of seething unrest to place Pérez and his corrupt practices in the dock of Venezuelan public opinion. Responding to this pressure, the Supreme Court indicted Pérez, charging him with misappropriating $17 million from a secret fund earmarked for national security. Congress then voted to remove him from office.

Meanwhile, more than a thousand small- and medium-size companies closed, causing the loss of fifty-nine thousand jobs. High interest rates, inflation approaching 40 percent, an influx of imports, and weak demand caused by low purchasing power were blamed for the increasingly severe recession. Foreign investment fell by more than 40 percent.

The 1993 presidential election represented a crushing repudiation, not only of Pérez and his neoliberal policies, but also of the two-party rule that had prevailed since the fall of General Marcos Pérez Jiménez in 1958. Rafael Caldera, the seventy-seven-year-old populist who had been rejected by his own COPEI party for his opposition to neoliberal policies was elected president. His victory and the large gains made by left-wing parties testified to the strength of the movement for social and economic change.

Although it provoked alarm among Venezuelan business elites and foreign investors, in reality,

Caldera's reform program was quite modest. It called for a new labor law—strongly opposed by big business—the provisions of which would discourage layoffs in a time of deep recession. Other goals included a monthly minimum wage increase, repeal of an IMF-inspired value-added tax that sharply increased prices on items of popular consumption, new taxes on luxury items, and a reform of the income tax system that would improve tax collection by imposing heavy fines on tax evasion, estimated at 70 percent of all taxpayers.

As his program evolved, however, Caldera's response to the desperate economic crisis deviated more and more from the expectations of many of his supporters, who had thought he would make a sharp break with the discredited neoliberal policies. Soon, reform-minded ministers in his government resigned and were replaced with neoliberals who renewed the drive to privatize practically all state companies and bail out eight private banks.

Caldera's return to economic orthodoxy was hailed by the business sector but damaged his image as a crusading populist president among workers and shantytown dwellers. Apparently fearing uprisings like the failed military coups of 1992 and the food riots of 1989, Caldera suspended constitutional guarantees, including the rights to liberty, personal security, and free travel, and to protection against unreasonable search. Security forces searched the homes of activists, former military officials, and politicians on both the left and right; they rounded up hundreds of persons in Caracas's slums. Human rights activists and church leaders condemned the suspensions of constitutional guarantees. Increasingly, it appeared that the Caldera phenomenon represented another example of the sadly familiar tendency of populist politicians to make promises of sweeping social and political change that they did not intend to keep, simply to keep the neoliberal boat afloat.

In 1996 the Caldera who in 1993 had denounced his electoral rivals as "IMF-package candidates" accepted a package agreement with the IMF that lent his government $3.3 billion, cut federal spending, and eased the rules of foreign investment, opening the way for privatization of the economy's crown jewels—the oil industry and the aluminum, steel, and electrical companies operated by the public Venezuelan Corporation of Guyana (CGV).

The Caldera regime's acceptance of neoliberal orthodoxy and especially its privatization proposals provoked bitter debates. Aware of the immense public opposition to the privatization of oil, the neoliberal politicians chose a more indirect route. In 1997, Congress passed the so-called "oil opening," which invited private capital to participate in the exploration for and exploitation of oil reserves, but it limited the state's participation in the development of potentially rich reserves to between 1 percent and 35 percent of the total capital of each joint venture. Despite the circumlocutions of the "opening," it was clear, as an anonymous eight-page advertisement in *Time* magazine explained, that it represented "the backdoor route to privatization" of the state-owned oil industry. "Undoubtedly," says Steve Ellner, "the arrangement generates substantial public revenue, but the state's relinquishment of its status as a major investor points in the direction of the early days of the industry when Shell and Standard ruled the oilfields." Meanwhile, privatization of the steel and aluminum industries was stalled by continuing opposition and debate over its terms and, in the case of aluminum, because foreign investors refused to pay the price asked by Venezuela.

These debates took place against a background of continuing economic crisis, reflected in high inflation and unemployment rates, a crisis worsened in 1998 by depressed oil prices and a resulting decline of 35 percent in the central government's revenues. Poverty nearly doubled during the 1990s. A 1996 study by Mark Ungar noted that "62% of Venezuelans live below the poverty line, while prices for basic foodstuffs have risen beyond the reach of 75% of the population." The growth of poverty was accompanied by a parallel growth of crime. Since 1990 the murder rate grew by 73 percent, the robbery rate by 26 percent. A profile of the prison population showed that it was overwhelmingly poor and young. Caldera's neoliberal remedies of austerity and other "structural adjustments" sharpened the pain but did not remove its causes; indeed, they contributed to the panorama of social devastation in Venezuela.

As the 1998 presidential elections approached, the price of oil had dropped by a third, the stock market had lost 70 percent of its value, foreign reserves dwindled, and fears of devaluation raised lending rates to around 100 percent a year. This did not favor Venezuela's traditional political parties and their free-market, neoliberal programs of privatization and public-spending restraints. "Their political mood," wrote a *New York Times* reporter, "seems to be swinging in precisely the opposite direction, with an overwhelming majority apparently convinced that the oil wealth should guarantee decent salaries, government services, job protection, and retirement benefits."

Despite a last-ditch effort to stop his populist juggernaut, retired Lieutenant Colonel Hugo Chávez Frías, whose abortive coup of February 1992, with a left-wing program to combat poverty and misery, had become a hero to many poor Venezuelans. He scored a decisive victory in the 1998 elections, described by the *New York Times* as "freighted with a sense of history in the making." His electoral program stressed protection of domestic industry, a two-year moratorium on debt payments, a review of concessions that had been made to foreign oil companies, a halt to privatization of state assets, and reform of the constitution.

Chávez swiftly moved to secure from Congress for six months all the powers he needed to enact by decree a package of economic and financial legislation. Venezuelans also were treated to the unfamiliar sight of army teams entering the poor barrios of their towns to sell food at low fixed prices, repair schools, and engage in other public works. By the year 2000 it had become clear that Chávez, fortified by a series of sweeping electoral victories, contemplated nothing less than an economic and social revolution. A new constitution, adopted in 1999 and ratified by an overwhelming majority of voters, swept away the elitist, corruption-ridden political system established by the 1958 Pact of Punto Fijo and cleared the way for the construction of what Chávez called "Bolivarian Democracy." "The fight for justice, the fight for equality and the fight for

liberty," Chávez told a Spanish interviewer in April 2002, "some call socialism, others Christianity; we call it Bolivarianism."

The ambitious program issued by his government spelled out in careful detail the reforms to be made, down to the number of new hospitals to be constructed and the medical care they would provide. But the Chávez revolution was essentially moderate in its goals; it did not threaten to destroy Venezuelan capitalism, seeking rather to make it more functional and socially responsible by reforms that would correct the enormous imbalance in access to goods and culture between Venezuela's haves and have-nots. An early achievement of the Chávez revolution was the sense of dignity that it gave to the popular masses. Proud of his indigenous, African, and Spanish ancestry, Chávez helped to eradicate the social stigma historically attached to the terms *mulatto*, *mestizo*, and *black*. This new sense of dignity, not just the hope for improvement in economic status, helped explain the fierce loyalty of these mixed-race masses toward their leader.

Because Venezuela still imported half of its food supply, agrarian reform was fundamental. Consequently, Chávez passed a law that limited farm size in some regions to 250 acres and permitted the government to expropriate uncultivated land over 5,000 hectares in size. Traditionally, the vast majority of land was in private hands, and this law was directed above all at vast cattle ranches and the great, frequently uncultivated estates called latifundios. "We have to finish off the latifundios," the president proclaimed in 2001, "the latifundio is the enemy of the country." The agrarian reform proposed to give parcels of land to as many peasants as possible, chiefly from public lands. But the government also planned to redistribute private lands that lacked a clear title. The distribution of land that was not in dispute had already begun, benefiting thousands of peasants. This land reform, combined with the construction of housing for poor families and other programs for the development of small- and medium-size industry, aimed to correct the enormous imbalance between rural and urban populations. In 2002, 80 percent of Venezuelans were urban dwellers, and most lived in shantytowns on the hillsides that surround Caracas and a few other large cities.

Improved access to education for children of the poor was another important goal of the Chávez revolution. The educational reform eliminated the fees that students formerly had to pay. More than 1.5 million children were added to the public school rolls, and all children received breakfast, lunch, and an afternoon snack in their school. A massive vaccination program was launched in poverty-ridden areas, and the infant mortality rate, which had stood at 23 per thousand, declined a few points. A special bank was created to provide micro credit to women who wished to start their own enterprises. A new mass organization, the "Bolivarian Circles," neighborhood groups that met to discuss and seek solutions for local problems, was another important component of the Chávez program. They received modest subsidies from the state to carry out local improvements.

The state oil company, *Petroleos de Venezuela* (PDVSA), was the main source of state revenue on which the success of Chávez's reform program in education, housing, health, and other areas depended. Chávez doubled the royalties paid by foreign oil companies operating in Venezuela. In cooperation with other members of OPEC (the oil-producing countries' organization) and independent producers, he sought to keep oil prices at satisfactory levels by reducing production quotas when necessary. Finally, he insisted that the state oil company have a controlling interest in new mixed enterprises with foreign oil companies. His nationalistic positions led to conflicts with the state oil company's established bureaucracy, traditionally dominated by the Democratic Action machine and more favorable to foreign companies.

Oil played an important role in Chávez's foreign policy to strengthen Venezuela's ties with its Latin American neighbors. In 2000 delegates from Venezuela and ten Central American and Caribbean countries met in Caracas to sign a document that lowered oil prices for signatory countries and eased the terms of payment when the international price of crude became too high. Venezuela also contracted to supply Cuba with up to 53,000 barrels a day; in exchange, Cuba, whose health system was famed for its high quality, agreed to provide Venezuela with medical services.

The warming relations between Venezuela and Cuba were not lost on the United States, which was angered by Chávez' political "errors." Chávez recently quoted Simón Bolívar's celebrated remark that "the United States appeared destined by Providence to plague America with misery in the name of liberty." He also defined neoliberalism as "the road to hell for Latin America," urged stopping in its tracks "the savage and irrational cart of globalization that destroys and excludes millions," and flatly rejected the United States's project for a "Free Trade Area of the Americas." His political sins included visits in defiance of the United States to countries like Iraq, Libya, and Iran; his embrace of Mercosur, the South American common market; and his refusal to endorse President George W. Bush's "war on terrorism," especially U.S. military operations in Afghanistan.

Thus, it seemed inevitable that if an opportunity arose to topple this Venezuelan "troublemaker," Washington would not hesitate to seize it. In early 2002 the United States temporarily withdrew its ambassador to Venezuela, and high-ranking U.S. policymakers like Elliot Abrams, Otto Reich, and John Negroponte, all of whom had been active in the covert Reagan wars against revolution in Central America, met regularly with Chávez's Venezuelan opponents. These included large business interests, labor leaders, dissident officials of the state oil company's bureaucracy, and a few active military officers. This was accompanied by a drumbeat of attacks on Chávez and his program by the press, radio, and television. It was widely reported that, in the previous year, the United States also had channeled hundreds of thousands of dollars to opposition business and labor groups, using as a transmission belt the National Endowment for Democracy, a nonprofit agency created and financed by Congress.

This agitation took place against a background of economic decline, the result of falling international prices for oil, which reduced state revenue and compelled Chávez to make budget cuts in all areas except social programs. Chávez also allowed the overpriced bolívar (the national unit of currency) to float, causing a measure of inflation that was bitterly resented by the large middle class. The economic downturn and inflation also fed the racist hostility of many white members of that class toward Chávez, whom they contemptuously dubbed *el Mono* (the monkey) or *el Negro* (the black).

The long-prepared blow fell on April 11. On that day two large demonstrations, one for, the other against Chávez, milled about in the streets of Caracas and marched on the presidential palace of Miraflores. In the resulting melee shooting began and some fifty people, mostly Chávez supporters, died in four days of revolt and counterrevolt. Meanwhile, a group of military plotters had invaded the palace, tried in vain to make the president sign a letter of resignation, and then spirited him away to an island off the coast of Venezuela. In Caracas, a prominent businessman, Pedro Carmona, was installed as president, "with a cabinet of conservative fanatics," in the words of *The Economist*, a British magazine generally known for its neoliberal sympathies. Carmona promptly decreed the immediate closure of the Supreme Court and the National Assembly, while a hunt began for prominent members of the Chávez government. A classic military coup or "Pinochetazo" seemed to be in the making.

But the oligarchy, its military and clerical collaborators, and its allies in Washington had badly miscalculated. The generals and admirals of elite origins who supported the coup did not represent the middle-level commanders and the rank-and-file troops. After the initial reaction of surprise and bewilderment, the presidential guard and loyalist military, spearheaded by the parachute division of which Chávez was a former commander, swiftly crushed the revolt and arrested its leaders. Meanwhile a torrent of Chávez's humble supporters, furious at the conspiracy to topple their leader, poured into Caracas from the surrounding shantytowns and took command of the streets.

Restored to power, Chávez promised a full investigation of the coup and trials for those who orchestrated it, but he also struck a conciliatory note. Stressing that he was president of all the classes of Venezuelan society—upper, middle, and lower—he admitted that he had made mistakes, replaced a number of officials the opposition had sharply criticized, and regretted the harsh language he had used against his critics. Two weeks after the coup, looking relaxed as if he had not just survived a political hurricane, Chávez informed the country in an interview that his peaceful Bolivarian revolution continued on course, with the aim of transforming an oil-dependent, neoliberal economy and channeling funds into social programs to achieve social equality in a country that had been plundered for centuries by the rich. He made tactful reference to charges that the United States was involved in the recent coup, saying it would be "horrible" if the United States was involved. "What I have said is that I ask God that it turns out to be false."

Despite Chávez's conciliatory attitude and gestures to win over some of his enemies, the diehard opposition, centered in the most reactionary sectors of the economic elite, remained sullen and unrelenting. It organized an unsuccessful two-month general strike that crippled the economy in early 2003 and thereafter promised to try to bring Chávez down by a referendum, possible in 2004 under the Constitution. For the present, therefore, Venezuela remained largely divided into two nations, a majority struggling to emerge from poverty and backwardness and a minority determined to hold on to its power and privileges.

Colombia in the Twentieth Century

THE CONSERVATIVE REPUBLIC, 1903–1930

For Colombia, the twentieth century began inauspiciously with the War of a Thousand Days, which raged for three years at the cost of thousands of lives and untold damage to the nation's economic infrastructure. The savage civil war slowed economic growth and weakened, at least momentarily, the power of the nation-state. Quick to seize on this vulnerability, Panamanian separatists, who had struggled in vain for years to establish their independence from Colombia, now seized the twin opportunities afforded by both the civil war and a renewed U.S. interest in the construction of a trans-isthmian interoceanic canal through Panama. The Colombians had made clear their refusal to approve the Hay-Herran Treaty, which provided for a $40 million payment to a French concessionary company and a mere $10 million for Colombia, in exchange for Colombia's surrender of its sovereignty over the proposed canal zone. Suddenly, the Panamanian nationalists had a new and powerful ally, and with the assistance of President Theodore Roosevelt, they established Panama's official independence in 1903. Needless to say, this dealt a profound psychological shock to Colombians.

At the war's end, Conservative General Rafael Reyes (1904–1909) dissolved Congress and established his personal dictatorship, ruling by decree through a puppet national assembly. Despite his dictatorial methods, Reyes's policies of enforcing peace and order, construction of railroads and highways, encouragement of export agriculture, and protection and subsidies for industry initially attracted much elite support.

Reyes's downfall came when he attempted to conclude a treaty with the United States under which Colombia was to receive an indemnity in return for its recognition of Panama's independence. Colombia's governing class, aware of the growing importance of the North American market for its coffee and hopeful of attracting North American capital, accepted the new relations. But the wound of Panama was still fresh, and news of the treaty aroused a public fury of which Reyes's enemies took advantage to force his resignation.

Conservatives and Liberals now organized a constituent assembly to reform the constitution of 1886. They agreed to weaken the executive, increase the powers of Congress, and ensure minority representation in elective bodies. Other changes included direct election of the president, establishment of elected departmental assemblies, and abolition of the death penalty. These reforms left intact the privileged position of the church, however, as well as property and literacy qualifications for voting that excluded all women and 90 percent of the adult male population from the suffrage.

Although the constitutional reforms made the total hegemony of one party more difficult, control of the electoral process remained in government hands. The constitutional changes also left intact the *gamonal* system under which landowners, public officials, and priests exerted influence on rural voters.

The characteristic blandness of Colombian politics between 1910 and 1930 contrasted sharply with the sometimes stormy developments in economic and social life. These developments, reflecting the rapid overall growth of Colombian capitalism, included the upsurge of coffee exports, centered in Antioquia, with its system of free labor; the accumulation of capital and its transfer from commerce to industry, with the formation of many new companies; a partial shift from the old semiservile forms of rural labor to free, capitalist wage labor, accompanied by a wave of strikes, land invasions, and clashes between landowners and peasants; adoption of racist immigration policies designed to "whiten" Colombia by prohibiting "the entrance of those elements whose organic and racial conditions may be inappropriate for the nation"; and the emergence in cities and plantation areas of the first true trade union movements, left-wing parties, and struggles between workers and employers.

In this period, U.S. capital began to flow into Colombia, facilitated by the 1914 treaty by which the United States paid Colombia for its loss of Panama. The "dance of the millions" began in 1921–1922 and was fueled initially by the first installment of a $25 million U.S. indemnity. Between 1922 and 1928 the U.S. government and private investors poured $280 million into Colombia, most of which was expended for a vast, chaotic program of public construction. The boom lured workers from agriculture into the cities and created low-wage, unskilled employment opportunities for working-class women, who functioned as a "reserve army" for industry. But it reduced food production and raised living costs, leaving workers worse off than before. Naturally, trade unions, energized by the fiery oratory of labor leaders like María Cano, Colombia's "flor de trabajo," grew more militant, culminating in the 1928 United

Fruit "banana" strike whose savage repression claimed thousands of workers' lives.

The golden shower ended in 1929 with the New York stock market crash and the Great Depression, which soon spread to Colombia. Growing unemployment, food shortages, and the government's severe fiscal problems completely discredited a regime weakened by political scandals, public outrage over the massacre of banana workers, and its own internal divisions. Alarmed by an upsurge of peasant and worker unrest, urban strikes, land invasions by peasants organized in leagues and unions,[1] and the rise of new radical ideologies, the nation's oligarchs temporarily closed ranks to avoid revolution and supported Enrique Olaya Herrera, a man of their own kind, in the 1930 election.

THE POPULIST INTERREGNUM: "THE REVOLUTION ON THE MARCH," 1934–1946

Olaya's term was spent waiting for the Depression to end and the infusions of U.S. loans and investments to resume. His failure to respond to popular expectations for change caused growing tension. In departments where the problem of latifundismo and landlessness was particularly severe, such as Cundinamarca, Tolima, and Cauca, clashes between peasants and landowners and police were frequent. This growing social instability strengthened the appeal of the left-wing Liberal Alfonso López, who won the 1934 elections. He promptly announced a program called *La Revolución en Marcha* (The Revolution on the March). In 1936 he obtained the congressional majority needed to implement his policies.

López and other Liberal reformers knew that social justice and national economic interest required land reform. The advance of Colombian capitalism was blocked by the backwardness of agriculture, especially the food-producing sector, which could not even provide enough food for the growing urban population. The 1936 agrarian reform law provided for reversion to the state of lands not rationally exploited by their owners but gave the latifundists ten years to make the transition to efficient land exploitation based on wage labor. The law also prohibited payment of rent in labor or in kind; this had the effect of speeding up the spread of wage labor and the rise of a land market. The law confirmed the property titles of the great landowners, but it also gave peasants "squatters' rights" on unused public and private lands that they had improved. The eviction of squatters thus became more difficult and dropped sharply.

Other legislation adopted during López's administration defined the rights of labor. Congress passed a law that established a minimum wage and paid vacations and holidays, forbade the use of strikebreakers, set up the eight-hour day and the forty-eight-hour week, and created a special tribunal to provide arbitration in labor disputes. With López's support, the number of organized workers quadrupled between 1935 and 1947. Equally important was the formation in 1936 of the Colombian Confederation of Labor (CTC), headed by syndicalists, Communists, and liberals.

One of the most revolutionary innovations of the López reform era was a new progressive tax law. Before 1936 tax laws had been ineffectually enforced. The new tax law, effectively enforced, almost doubled the state's revenue-raising capacity.

Despite the moderate character of these reforms, they came under bitter attack from all reactionary elements, and López began to retreat. In 1936 he announced a "pause" in reform. This "pause," accentuated by López's successor, the moderate Liberal Eduardo Santos (1938–1942), created a bitter division within the Liberal ranks between moderates and reformers, the leading advocate for whom was Jorge Eliécer Gaitán. As mayor of Bogotá, he had been regarded as the best the capital ever had.

Conservatives and many moderate Liberals denounced Gaitán as a demogogue. He was in fact a magnetic speaker of burning sincerity, capable of presenting his economic and social ideas to audi-

---

[1]The land invasions were spurred by a 1926 Supreme Court ruling that the only proof of ownership was the original title stating the government had ceded title to the land. Many peasants knew that the estates on which they worked had no such titles and had been formed through illegal acquisition of public lands.

ences of peasants and workers in a clear way, but there was nothing exotic or extravagant about those ideas. Although he used socialist terminology, the essence of Gaitán's program was the need for state intervention in the economy to democratize capitalism, control the great private monopolies, and ensure that peasants owned the land they cultivated. In 1945 he proposed limiting landownership to a maximum of 1,000 hectares and suggested a minimum size of four hectares for landholdings to avoid the low productivity of minifundios.

In the 1946 presidential elections, however, Conservatives took advantage of this Liberal split to elect Mariano Ospina Pérez with only 42 percent of the vote.

COUNTERREVOLUTION ON THE MARCH, 1946–1958

After his inauguration, in a conciliatory gesture to the Liberal Party, Ospina Pérez invited six Liberals into his cabinet, thus establishing parity in the twelve ministries and implementing his campaign promise to form a National Union government. He made no effort to consult Gaitán. The snubbing of Gaitán suggests a design on the part of Ospina Pérez to isolate him politically, deepen the rift between Liberal moderates and reformists, and form a bipartisan coalition of conservative elements to barricade against Gaitán's program of social and economic change. High inflation, static wages, and growing unemployment in the postwar period added to the anger and frustration of workers as they saw their hopes for change crushed by what they perceived as a conspiracy of the "double oligarchy"—Liberal and Conservative—that controlled government.

The Conservative leadership in 1946 presented two faces. Ospina Pérez represented its conciliatory aspect, the desire for a peaceful coexistence of the two traditional parties and their collaboration in a National Union government of sound conservative views. But this aspect was contradicted by the supreme chief of the Conservative Party, Laureano Gómez, who emerged as the new government's gray eminence, the power behind the throne, and scarcely concealed his scorn for the National Union policy.

Gómez quickly had the Liberal general who commanded the national police force dismissed and then followed with a wholesale purge of Liberal police officers, who were replaced by officers known for their fanatical conservatism. The pace of events quickened in 1947. In an evident effort to gain the advantage in the March congressional elections, armed bands organized by Conservative landowners and officials began to attack and persecute Liberals in many rural areas. The outcome of the elections, however, was a clear victory for the Liberals; equally significant was the predominance of radicals over moderates on the Liberal slate.

Claiming the need to restore law and order, Ospina organized a new security force, the *policía política*, which soon became an extension of the Conservative Party and an additional instrument of terror against Liberals; it was widely known as the "creole Gestapo." Beatings, killings, and outrages of every kind spread throughout the countryside, provoking a growing polarization and armed responses by the Liberal peasantry, middle class, and landowners.

As 1948 opened, the violence in some areas began to assume the proportions of a civil war, with battles taking place between Conservative and Liberal towns. The church, with its immense power, also instigated violence and persecution of Liberals. In March the Liberal convention called on party members to resign from every public office under the Conservative administration. The Conservatives rejoiced; one of their journals exulted: "At last we are alone."

In an atmosphere of growing tension, the government prepared to host the Ninth Inter-American Conference. On April 9, 1948, as Gaitán was on his way to lunch, he was approached by a stranger who fired four bullets into him. Mortally wounded, Gaitán collapsed on the sidewalk. The man regarded by the masses as the sole hope for their liberation, generally expected to run and win the election for president in 1950, died the same day he was shot. The assassin was an obscure figure with a history of mental trouble.

Gaitán's murder unleashed long-suppressed racial, ethnic, and class antagonisms and signaled a formidable popular insurrection that tore Bogotá apart and spread to the provinces before it was put down by the army at the cost of thousands of lives. The spontaneous rising of the masses, accompanied by peasant expropriation of haciendas, establishment of revolutionary committees and workers' control over foreign-owned oil installations, and other radical measures, frightened Conservative and Liberal elites, both of whom blamed the violence on the "genetically imprinted resentments" of blacks and indigenous people. Liberal leaders, faced with the choice of joining the insurrection or accepting Ospina's offer to reconstitute a National Union coalition, chose the latter.

During 1949 the coalition government began to come apart as the official and unofficial violence in the countryside, directed above all at Liberals of all classes, continued and widened; it had become a persistent, widespread phenomenon generically called *la Violencia*.

As the 1950 presidential election drew nearer, the threatening, repressive atmosphere visibly deepened. In the countryside goon squads, backed by the military, compelled Liberal peasants to turn in their voting cards and register as Conservatives. In some areas landowners took revenge for the land invasions of the 1930s, using hired thugs to kill or expel peasant occupants. In this stage of the Violencia, however, the conflict had primarily a political character and was based on the peasants' loyalty to political bosses on each side. Finally, in response to a move by a Liberal congressional majority to impeach him, Ospina issued a series of decrees providing for a state of siege, the dissolution of Congress and all departmental legislatures and municipal councils, the grant of extraordinary powers for the governors, and national censorship of the press and radio. With the suppression of all effective opposition, Laureano Gómez assumed the presidency.

Ideologically, the Gómez regime (1950–1953) appeared "feudal" in its effort to restore the intellectual atmosphere of sixteenth-century Spain. In its economic policies, however, the regime showed itself quite favorable to modern corporate capitalism. In the spirit of economic liberalism, all import and export restrictions were removed and foreign investment was encouraged in all possible ways. But for labor it was the worst of times. Wages lagged behind prices, and the state regularly intervened in labor struggles in favor of employers, permitting the use of strikebreakers and blacklists.

In the Colombian countryside, meanwhile, the Violencia gained in intensity and expanded into new regions. But the conflict now increasingly assumed the nature of a class struggle as peasants resisted the efforts of landowners and their hired thugs to eject them from their parcels and Communist Party activists as well as peasant leaders loyal to the Liberal Party became active in organizing strongholds of self-defense among uprooted peasants. Thus the period between 1949 and 1953, in addition to a growth of landowner and official terrorism and banditry, saw the rise of an extensive, well-organized resistance in guerrilla zones inhabited by peasants and other fugitives from regions marked by anarchy or terror. Some of these zones had an elaborate political, economic, and social organization. These guerrilla enclaves may have held twenty thousand armed men, of whom about half were based in the Llanos region. Each zone had its own commander or commanders, some of whom soon became legends.

The failure of the Conservative dictatorship to achieve a military solution to the guerrilla problem contributed to its gradual weakening and eventual collapse on June 13, 1953, when General Gustavo Rojas Pinilla assumed the presidency with the support of the armed forces and representatives of both parties.

To resolve the social and political crisis, his campaign of "Peace, Justice, Liberty" sought compromise among political elites and peasant radicals. One of his first initiatives was to proclaim an unconditional amnesty to all guerrillas who would return to civilian life.

Several thousand accepted the amnesty, surrendered their weapons, and returned to their old homes, but the leaders of some guerrilla fronts, especially the Communist leadership in southern Tolima and the Sumapaz region of southern Cundinamarca, distrusted Rojas Pinilla's sincerity, recalled his role as army commander in a famous massacre of Liberals in Cali in 1949, and warned their comrades not to "believe the false promises of propaganda thrown from planes of the dictatorship." These guerrilla fronts preferred to maintain an armed truce and await further developments.

Events proved the skeptics right. The honeymoon between Rojas Pinilla and the elites and the nation as a whole began to wane as it became evident that instead of restoring the traditional political arrangements he was moving toward the establishment of a personal dictatorship with some populist features, not unlike Argentina's Peronist system. One of his reformist measures was giving women the vote in 1954.

Despite some reforms, the Rojas Pinilla's policies were essentially reactionary. One sign of this was the revival of the Violencia as the president gave a free hand to notorious *pájaros* (hired assassins), Conservative vigilante gangs, and army-police forces to wreak vengeance on veterans of the guerrilla war who had accepted amnesty. As a result, many former guerrillas left their farms and rejoined the surviving guerrilla fronts. The renewal of the civil war combined with other repressive measures and the effects of a deepening depression to unify all elite elements against Rojas Pinilla, whose military colleagues prevailed on him to resign and surrender power to a five-man caretaker military junta.

In July 1957, Liberal leader Alberto Lleras Camargo and Laureano Gómez met and signed an agreement creating a National Front coalition, which in effect provided for a monopoly of shared power for sixteen years by the two parties. There would be parity in legislative positions on both national and local levels and alternation of the presidency between the two parties. The Colombian experiment in bipartisan rule and "controlled democracy" had begun.

THE NATIONAL FRONT: REFORM AND REPRESSION, 1958–1974

The constitutional pact creating the Colombian National Front in 1958 bears an obvious resemblance to the pact signed between Venezuela's centrist parties the same year. In both cases the intent was the same: to preserve elite rule and to marginalize or isolate political movements that might threaten its property or power. Both may therefore be considered variants of a type of representative democracy that has been called "controlled democracy" or more correctly, "restricted democracy."

The Colombian power-sharing pact, providing for a monopoly of political power for the Conservative and Liberal Parties, excluded the existing Communist and the Christian Democratic Parties as well as new parties that might be formed later. Thus the electorate was denied the opportunity to reject the policies of the National Front coalition or exercise its sovereign right to change the government. The relative absence of issues between the parties promoted voter apathy and alienation, reflected in low turnout rates; participation in congressional elections fell from a high of 68.9 percent in 1958 to a low of 36.4 percent in 1972.

The rules of the political game established by the National Front, designed to prevent the hegemony of either party, tended to immobilize its governments. Their social policies reflected their fundamentally conservative orientation and did nothing to alter the great inequalities in income distribution. Although the unions gained legal recognition, the government repeatedly intervened in labor conflicts on the employers' side.

In 1958 President Lleras Camargo issued an amnesty—to expire in 1959—for all guerrillas who would return to peaceful life. The establishment of the National Front coalition marked the end of the Violencia, a conflict estimated to have taken between 200,000 and 300,000 lives. Between 1958 and 1965 the army and police hunted down the remaining outlaw bands. But the continued existence of the latifundio, an estimated 1 million landless peasants, and landowner and official repression of land-hungry peasants continued to generate violence in the Colombian countryside.

This violence grew so rapidly that, in 1961, evidently fearing that failure to act might produce a Cuban-style revolution, Congress adopted an agrarian reform law that vested apparently limitless power to expropriate and redistribute inefficiently exploited land in a new state agency (INCORA). In Tolima, the site of the first program, however, only 1,115 out of 90,000 landless agricultural workers

The Colombian army's mobilization of paramilitary violence against unarmed civilians increased the popularity of guerrilla movements like the FARC, whose combatants expanded their power and territorial control. [Wide World Photos]

had received titles to land by 1969. Naturally this failed to satisfy the peasants' hunger for land, and the five-hundred-thousand-member National Association of Peasant Unity (ANUC), originally organized to mobilize rural support for the government, quickly became an outspoken critic.

This innocuous agrarian reform coincided with the launching of a large-scale military effort to destroy the guerrilla zones established under Communist Party leadership in eastern and southern Tolima. Like the agrarian law, this offensive seems to have been inspired by the anticommunist strategy of the Kennedy administration's Alliance for Progress, a program combining reform and repression.

The success of this and many other later offensives can be gauged by the fact that twenty years later the few guerrilla bases had grown into a network of thirty guerrilla fronts in the Colombian backcountry, with their own military organization, the Communist-led Revolutionary Armed Forces of Colombia (FARC). In addition to the FARC—the largest of the guerrilla groups, created in 1966, whose members and leaders were primarily peasants—the 1960s and 1970s saw the emergence of other revolutionary organizations, such as the National Liberation Army (ELN), inspired by the Cuban example, and the April 19 Movement (M-19), both largely composed of radical students and other urban elements. The ELN, led briefly by Father Camilo Torres Restrepo, the radical priest whose 1966 death inspired the 1968 Conference of Latin American Bishops at Medellín to endorse a "preferential option for the poor," advocated agrarian reform, nationalization, social justice, and gender equality. Historian Francesca Miller speculates that the endorsement of women's equality reflected the influence of Torres's feminist mother, Isabel Restrepo Gaviria, who was notorious for her public demonstrations "against her sex's inequalities."

In summary, the National Front's political, economic, and social policies produced basically negative results. Its economic policies successfully promoted the accumulation of foreign and domestic capital but neglected the interests of workers and peasants, whose living standards sharply declined. In 1964, 25 percent of the total labor force, 24.6 percent of the urban labor force, and 25.4 percent of the rural labor force lived below the absolute poverty line. By 1973 those percentages had risen to 50.7 percent, 43.4 percent, and 67.5 percent. Clearly, instead of contributing to the solution of grave socioeconomic problems, the sixteen years of National Front rule sharpened them.

DRUG LORDS, GUERRILLAS, AND THE QUEST FOR PEACE, 1974–2003

Beginning with the 1974 elections, Colombia returned to the political system of electoral competition; but there were still vestiges of the power-sharing system. Despite the renewal of competition, the political system remained a restricted, oligarchical democracy designed to limit the level of conflict between elites and to "keep the masses in their place" with a system of electoral mobilization based on machine politics and payoffs, known as *clientelismo*.

In addition to their loss of credibility, post–National Front governments faced economic problems of unprecedented proportions. The quadrupling of oil prices in 1974, coming at a time when Colombia had ceased to be self-sufficient in oil production, dealt a very heavy shock to the economy. By 1982, Colombia had not only severe inflation but also its worst recession in fifty years.

In this time of economic gloom, some relief came from an unexpected quarter: the drug traffic with the United States. Until recently that traffic had been negligible, mostly confined to the export of marijuana. It began to mushroom in the 1970s, most likely as a result of antidrug campaigns in Turkey and the Middle East. Skyrocketing prices resulting from effective antidrug efforts and high transportation costs forced the international drug cartels to seek closer sources of supply for the U.S. market. Colombia, with its access to both U.S. coasts, and cocaine, lower in price than heroin or opium and easier to carry in short plane trips to the Florida coast, provided a solution. An efficient distribution system made the new drug available to the ever-swelling U.S. market. A division of labor and profits emerged between the Colombian producers and exporters, centered in Medellín and Cali, and North American domestic wholesalers, bankers, and money launderers. Contrary to a common misconception, Colombia is not a large grower of coca but rather processes the substance, which comes from Peru, Bolivia, Ecuador, and Brazil. By the mid-1980s, with cocaine prices dropping, a new product—crack—known as *bazuco* in Colombia and packaged in small quantities costing only a fraction of cocaine powder, created a large new class of consumers.

Colombia's Medellín and Cali cartels, it was estimated, made $4 to $6 billion annually in cocaine traffic. Of this amount, according to the economist Salomón Kalmanovitz, between $1 and $1.5 billion entered the Colombian black market. Without this "cushion" for the country's balance of payments, he suggests, an exchange crisis would have broken out in 1983 or 1984 at the latest. This contribution of Colombian narcocapitalism to the country's financial stability and the close ties established between the drug lords and landowners, businessmen, government officials, and members of the police and the armed forces explain the singular immunity that the drug mafias enjoyed until recently.

This situation changed as a result of three developments. First, in 1984, Conservative President Belisario Betancur (1982–1986) negotiated a series of historic truce agreements with three of the four major guerrilla movements that did not require them to surrender their arms. The accord with the FARC, the largest of the insurgent groups, stipulated that the government would adopt an agrarian reform program; legislate improvements in public health, education, and housing; and permit local elections of mayors and city councils to broaden popular participation in government.

Although the armed forces and other factions effectively blocked implementation of the agreement, the peace process survived and made available additional resources to pursue a war on drugs. Second, the U.S. placed increased pressure on the government of Liberal President Virgilio Barco (1986–1990) to wage a more effective war on drug trafficking. This pressure was accompanied by an offer of financial aid that was difficult to refuse.

Finally, there was a growing concern on the part of sectors of the elite that the drug traffickers had gotten out of control and their violence was threatening the monopoly of power the elite had enjoyed since Colombia achieved independence from Spain. For years death squads, 149 of which the government acknowledged, were trained by the drug mafia, in alliance with the police and the armed forces. They had murdered, with complete impunity, thousands of trade-union and peasant leaders, left-wing activists, judges, and others who sought to make Colombia a functioning democracy.

In the course of 1989, however, the mafia went too far and began killing prominent members of the elite, including the governor of Antioquia, the country's attorney general, Medellín's police chief, and presidential candidate Luis Carlos Galán. Within hours after Galán's death the Barco government had already ordered the searches and seizures of dozens of mansions, hundreds of cars, and more than one hundred airplanes and helicopters claimed to belong to the drug traffickers. To give these confiscations a firm legal basis, Barco issued a decree making "illicit enrichment" a crime punishable by five to ten years in prison. He also reinstated, by decree, the extradition of drug traffickers to the United States. This was declared unconstitutional by the Colombian Supreme Court in 1987 and opposed by many Colombians as a surrender of the state's autonomy and an admission of the impotence of its judicial system. By 1989 the government's offensive against the cartels had only made a temporary impact and the basic structure of the paramilitary groups remained intact.

To be sure, without major social and economic reforms in Latin America, the principal supplier of cocaine, and in the United States, its principal consumer, the drug wars could not be won. Without new policies that provided Latin American peasants with a viable alternative to growing coca as a cash crop, its cultivation continued, no matter how many fields were burned or sprayed with defoliants. As laboratories that processed coca were destroyed in one part of the region, they moved to another. In both the United States and Latin America, the cocaine epidemic was growing dangerously, the principal social roots of the drug trade were mass poverty, despair, and frustration. Neither the supply side nor the demand side of the problem, in the last analysis, could be solved by military means alone.

But in a land famous for the illusions of "magical realism," the Colombian war against the drug cartels did provide a perfect cover for the government's thirty-year-old war against the guerrilla insurrection. The drug and guerrilla problems always were indissolubly linked, for it had long been common knowledge that there existed a network linking government agencies, elements of the armed forces and police, landowners, industrialists, and drug lords. The primary target of this alliance was Colombia's left-wing movement—the guerrillas first, but also trade unions, peasant cooperatives, and opposition parties.

The country's greatest writer, Gabriel García Márquez, says: "The Constitution, the laws . . . everything in Colombia is magnificent, everything on paper. It has no connection with reality." Typical of that gap between Colombian form and reality was the new constitution of July 1991. The new charter was designed to open up Colombia's political system, ending the monopoly of power and property long held by a handful of Colombian clans. It provided for the popular election of state governors, limited the president to one term, granted Congress the right to veto cabinet members, established the office of a "people's" defender to investigate human rights abuses, recognized the authority of traditional courts on indigenous *resguardos*, ensured representation for minorities in Congress, and barred the extradition of native-born Colombians. It also recognized the "collective ownership rights" of Afro-Colombians and indigenous peoples in this multiethnic, multicultural nation.

The new constitution provided a splendid façade for a corrupt, arbitrary social order, but it was still a façade. It did away with the "state of siege" in force in Colombia for most of the previous four decades but conveniently replaced it with the *estado de excepción*, utilized to put the country on a war footing and ride roughshod over the rights of workers and others. Popular cynicism concerning the new Colombian democracy was reflected in the voter abstention rate of 70 percent. Colombia's murder rate, with 86 murders per 100,000 inhabitants, probably the highest in the world, exposed the thin democratic veneer that masked a lawless state and society. The militarization of the state under cover of the state of emergency also facilitated the imposition of a neoliberal policy featuring the privatization of state enterprises, elimination of subsidies, and other austerity measures promoted by the IMF and the World Bank. These measures, added to the immense costs of the guerrilla war, sharpened all of Colombia's economic and social problems; more than half of Colombia's 33 million people lived below the poverty line and the official unemployment rate in 1998 was 14.5 percent.

Part of the Colombian "reality" of which García Márquez speaks was that Colombia had been the scene of two wars. One was the drug war. From the official U.S. point of view, this war was waged to stem the tide of cocaine flowing into the United States. For the Colombian elite, however, it was a private quarrel with that section of the "cocaine nouveau riche," centered in Medellín, that sought too aggressively to join it in the seats of power. It is noteworthy that the Cali cartel, which was more discreet in its dealings with the traditional oligarchy, experienced less interference from the government than did the Medellín cartel. "We do not kill politicians," a member of the Cali cartel explained, "we bribe them." Consequently, by the end of 1994 the Medellín cartel was only a shadow of its former self, with most of its leaders dead or in prison, whereas the rival Cali cartel had taken over most of the heroin and cocaine trade to the United States and Europe.

The other Colombian war was the "dirty war" waged by an alliance of the military, the security services, drug lords, great landowners, and businessmen against Colombia's left-wing movement, trade unions, peasant leagues, and ethnic minorities. The military made no secret that it was far more interested in fighting guerrillas than in fighting drugs. It repeatedly thwarted government efforts to achieve a cease-fire with the guerrilla movements and continued its repressive activity—bombardment, disappearances, torture, and murder. The majority of the victims were not guerrillas but peasants, workers, and left-wing activists. Despite official government offers to negotiate, successive administrations accelerated the military's counterinsurgency campaign, with a marked increase in aerial bombardments, by U.S.-supplied planes and helicopters, of rural communities. Ostensibly launched to protect the electoral process from "narcoterrorism," the operation actually targeted rural areas where guerrilla forces were active.

Under the discredited Liberal President Ernesto Samper (1994–1998), the government's military fortunes took a turn for the worse. The FARC, numbering an estimated fifteen thousand fighters, maintained a strong presence in 622 of Colombia's 1,071 municipalities. Its military and political control was strongest in the southern departments of Caquetá, Guaviare, Putumayo, Meta, and the Amazon region, but it expanded its military operations into more densely populated northern and central departments like Antioquia, Santander and North Santander, Cundinamarca, and Bolívar. In 1996 the FARC showed its growing military strength by inflicting a number of humiliating defeats on government forces. In June 1997 the FARC handed over to the military some seventy soldiers captured in these operations, in return for the government's agreement to withdraw the army from 5,000 square miles of territory in southern Colombia.

This expansion of guerrilla power reflected the structural crisis of a corrupt, exclusionary two-party system, or "duopoly," the poor training and morale of government troops, and a continuing economic crisis that brought recruits and support to the guerrillas. In the government's mad rush to expand private commercial development of export-oriented logging, shrimp aquaculture, plantation agriculture, and cattle raising, it trampled on the traditional rights of indigenous people and Afro-Colombians in the northern Pacific coastal department of Chocó, home to 455,000 Afro-Colombians, 49,000 natives, and 36,000 mestizos. By 1997 the previously peaceful region had succumbed to violence with the appearance of the army and popular guerrilla groups like the black "Benkos Biojo" and Revolutionary Indigenous Armed Forces (FARIP).

Guerrilla support also was particularly strong in the long-neglected colonization areas in the southern part of the country, where peasant communities produced coca leaves and poppies as the only alternative to the economic crisis. By compelling "fair" payment by the drug traffickers to the coca growers for their products and by resisting the government's herbicidal spraying of the coca fields, which also destroyed subsistence crops, the guerrillas defended peasants against the government's eradication campaigns and against land-grabbing efforts by the rapacious new narcobourgeoisie. In addition to playing a protective role in the regions under their control, the guerrillas assumed many local-level functions of the state, "maintaining order, officiating at weddings, births, and divorces, organizing education, mediating conflict and administering justice, and marketing agricultural products." To finance their activities, the guerrillas imposed "taxes" on the drug barons, laboratories, roads, and drug shipments.

The FARC and peasant leaders were well aware of the devastating human, social, and environmental effects of drug cultivation and trade. The FARC proposed a program for the eradication of coca, poppy, and marijuana plantations by the substitution of other crops, with government aid to farmers in land, seeds, and equipment. In 1998, according to *The Nation*, FARC spokesmen sounded out U.S. officials with a proposal to sever all drug connections in return for a U.S. crop-substitution plan. But neither the Colombian government nor Washington expressed interest.

The "dirty war" had an unexpected impact on gender balance, family structure, and the labor force. With an average of 79 homicides per 100,000 people, seven times the U.S. rate, some 40 percent of families in the 1990s were headed by women who, in addition to their unpaid household labor, were forced to work outside the home, usually for low wages either in unskilled jobs or as self-employed workers in the "informal sector." Within a generation, the proportion of women in the urban work force rose from approximately 33 percent to 43 percent, but women's wages still lagged 30 percent behind men's. The United States, which generously supplied the Colombian military with arms, bore a heavy responsibility for this carnival of death. In March 1994 an Amnesty International report criticized the United States "for remaining silent when aid destined to combat arms trafficking was diverted to counterinsurgency operations and thence to killing of unarmed peasants." In 1991 the CIA established a new military intelligence network in Colombia, ostensibly to fight drugs. "Instead," says journalist Frank Smyth, "they incorporated illegal paramilitary groups into their ranks and fostered death squads. These death squads killed trade unionists, peasant leaders, human rights monitors, journalists, and other suspected 'subversives.' The evidence, including secret Colombian military documents, suggests that the CIA may be more interested in fighting a leftist resistance movement than in combating drugs."

The killings went on. In February 1998 a death squad murdered another leading human rights activist, Jesús María Valle Jaramillo, who had accused certain politicians and members of the military of sponsoring death squads. In April one of Colombia's leading human rights lawyers, Eduardo Umana Mendoza, was murdered in his office. Before his death he had alerted authorities that state security officers were planning to kill him. Yet there was evidence that the tide in Colombia was turning against the killers and their sponsors. In October 1997, 10 million voters—the largest turnout in Colombian history—approved a mandate for peace that called for a cease-fire, peace talks, and respect for the lives and other human rights of noncombatants. In May 1998, in the first round of the presidential election, Noemi Sanin, seeking to become Colombia's first female president with a platform that stressed the fight against corruption, economic recovery, and the search for peace, jolted the two-party system by getting one-third of the vote, carrying Bogotá and the country's next-largest cities, Cali and Medellín. Although Andres Pastrana won the run-off election, he clearly understood his national mandate and announced that he was ready to begin "the long road toward peace" by meeting with the legendary leader and founder of the FARC, Manuel Marulanda Pérez. The FARC in turn announced that it was ready to resume negotiations.

But many obstacles to peace remained, not the least of which was the uncertain stand of the United States, whose support of or opposition to the Colombian peace process would determine whether these negotiations represented a true turning point in Colombia's tragic modern history. A series of events soon put all doubts to rest. On January 11, 2000, President Bill Clinton announced a $1.3 billion aid package for Colombia to assist "in vital counter-drug efforts aimed at keeping illegal drugs off our shores" and "to help Colombia promote peace and prosperity and deepen its democracy." The measure, which made Colombia the third largest beneficiary of military aid from the United States (after Israel and Egypt), formed part of a $7.3 billion "Plan Colombia" prepared by the two governments; but the hand of Washington showed on every page. Colombia was to contribute $4 billion, though it was unclear where the financially strapped government would find the money; the rest was to come from the United States and countries of the European Union, which showed little enthusiasm for the plan and eventually withdrew from the project, believing that a war against the FARC would only worsen Colombia's social and economic problems. Announced after formal peace talks between the Colombian government and the FARC had begun, it made clear that the United States had chosen war over peace in Colombia.

The ambitious plan had several objectives. Its main goal was the reconquest of the vast area, some 40 percent of the national territory, which

the FARC controlled, mostly in southern Colombia. This reconquest would go hand in hand with a coca eradication campaign, and the former coca growers would be assisted with a crop-substitution program. The plan ignored altogether the narco-traffickers and their paramilitary allies in the North. As Garry Leech points out in the *Colombia Report* (May 14, 2001), the plan wielded a huge stick, while offering a tiny carrot. Approximately 80 percent of the U.S. aid would go to the military and the police, 8 percent to the crop substitution program, 6 percent to human rights programs, 4 percent to displaced farmers, and 1 percent to the continuing peace process.

The plan also had an economic component that required Colombia to further restructure its economy along neoliberal lines, cut government social spending, and privatize state-owned enterprises, including banks, utilities, and the state's coal company. These policies, needed to comply with commitments made to the IMF in return for a $2.7 billion loan in 1999, were certain to increase the current Colombian combined unemployment and underemployment figure of over 60 percent.

Colombia's former attorney general, Gustavo de Greiff, sharply questioned the effectiveness of Plan Colombia. In July 2001 he wrote that to claim success for the plan's strategy of drug eradication, one would have to show that it resulted in (1) a decline in the area of cultivation of the plants from which cocaine, heroin, and marijuana were produced; (2) reduced availability of those drugs in the market; (3) higher prices for these drugs; (4) a decline in the number of consumers, habitual and occasional. Greiff demonstrated with data from national and international organizations that none of those results had been obtained. For Colombia he cited satellite photographs showing that after the fumigation of 60,000 hectares the area cultivated in coca had grown 60 percent in the previous year. Greiff bristled at the "arrogance" of a U.S. State Department official who, confronted with evidence of increased coca production in Colombia, said in a press interview that this meant "we have to do more of what we have been doing, not less."

The other official justification for military aid to Colombia, "to help Colombia promote peace and prosperity and deepen its democracy," must sound equally unrealistic to students of Colombia's recent history, because this aid failed to address the historical causes of the civil war and the general crisis of Colombian society, which lay in the land-grabbing of a selfish elite and in the massacres of peasants and workers by death squads in its service half a century ago. The successors to those death squads were the contemporary brutal paramilitary outfits, closely linked to the Colombian armed forces, which provided them with intelligence, transport, and weapons. The military officer class, corrupt and incompetent, commanded a rank-and-file consisting mostly of demoralized young workers and peasants who lacked the high school degree necessary to exempt them from the draft. Stung by successive defeats at the hands of the guerrillas, the military recently chose to "privatize" or "outsource" the war, leaving most of the fighting to the paramilitaries. These gunmen served a variety of masters: drug traffickers, great landowners, especially cattle raisers, and modern capitalists. They served the interests of the old and new elites by murdering militant peasants, workers, indigenous people, blacks, or anyone they suspected of sympathy with the guerrillas. They threatened, kidnapped, and killed progressive lawyers, human rights activists, and journalists too zealous in the exposure of their crimes. According to Human Rights Watch, the paramilitaries were responsible for 78 percent of the human rights violations in Colombia in 1999.

Early in the twenty-first century, corruption still pervaded the political life of Colombia, dominated by the two historical parties, Conservatives and Liberals. A pervasive cynicism regarding politics and politicians was reflected in traditionally high abstention rates; only 46 percent of eligible voters turned out for the May 2002 presidential election. Moreover, electoral fraud, including the purchase of votes, was common; in some regions, like the Atlantic coast, a vote had one price at 8 A.M. and was eight or ten times higher at 3 P.M. "Congress," observed *The Economist* in a piece on the March 2002 congressional election, "has come to be seen as a center of shady deals." This corruption, public distrust of politicians, and resulting high abstention rates meant that in his 2002 "landslide" victory, newly elected president Alvaro Uribe Velez captured only 5.8 million votes—24 percent of the eligible electorate.

If the official justifications for the military aid program for Colombia appeared too glib and unrealistic to be adequate, were other, more pragmatic motives involved? Answers to this question were implied in the financial details of the aid package and the new heightened importance of Colombian oil to multinational companies and the U.S. government. A major beneficiary of the aid package was United Technologies Corporation, the Connecticut company that was to supply Colombia with some 30 Blackhawk helicopters, each costing $12.8 million. Another was Bell Helicopter Textron, a Texas subsidiary of Textron, which produces the Huey II helicopter. Indeed, one reason for the delay in getting final approval for the aid package was pork barrel wrangling between Texas and Connecticut legislators over apportionment of the aid package.

Occidental Petroleum, which operated the Caño-Limón pipeline in northeast Colombia, stood to gain hugely if the hopes invested in the aid package were fulfilled. In 2002, Colombia was the seventh-largest supplier of oil to the United States, and it controlled the largest untapped pool of petroleum in the Western Hemisphere. But guerrilla attacks between 1982 and 1990 spilled 1.6 billion gallons of Occidental oil along the way. Washington's 1997 decision to reduce its dependence on Middle Eastern oil suggests that its principal interest may not have been drugs but oil. Other companies with stakes in the aid package included DynCorp, a defense contractor with a $600 million contract to spray coca crops in Colombia, and Monsanto, producer of the herbicide currently used. Colombia recently at least temporarily shelved plans to use a more deadly herbicide, a fungus spray that kills coca plants, because of evidence that it was harmful to the environment and to humans.

The Republican victory in the 2000 U.S. presidential election brought to power George W. Bush, member of a dynasty that had many close links with the oil industry. But the dramatic events of September 11, 2001, raised the question of continuity of U.S. policy in Colombia. Would Washington, deeply involved in a global "war on terrorism" in Afghanistan and at home, reverse its steep descent into the Colombian quagmire? Or would Colombia become a new active front in that war? Colombia, after being temporarily forgotten, sprang back into the news. The United States, although still professing neutrality toward the peace talks, intervened to assure an outcome in conformity with the warlike logic of Plan Colombia.

But media claims of virtually unanimous support for the drug war and the campaign of defoliation were contradicted by evidence of overwhelming opposition to both in the south of the country, the provinces that were the main targets of Plan Colombia. Six governors of that region, all elected in October 2000, said the *New York Times*, "have organized into a formidable bloc that has harshly criticized the central government for everything from the handling of finances to the drug war." Rather than war, these governors demanded "regional public projects and agricultural development programs seen as alternatives to defoliation." The *New York Times* also noted that the group had "the most unlikely governor in Colombia, Mr. Tunubala, a Guambiano Indian who won office in a province well known for discrimination and social inequality." His political movement, "composed of Indians, union leaders, poor farmers, intellectuals, and outside the province's circle of power—has already angered some people in the province of Cauca and prompted death threats."

Against this background of regional discontent and resistance to Plan Colombia, the Bush team fueled the Colombian fire with its "Andean Regional Initiative," announced in 2001 and developed in budgetary detail in 2002. The program increased funding for the counter-drug effort by $731 million, but it also represented a major qualitative change from the Clinton aid package. The stress on the war against drugs was now joined to a new stress on the terrorist threat allegedly presented by the FARC. The qualitative change was illustrated by the fact that the new program would finance a brigade to protect Occidental's oil pipeline, which of course had nothing to do with drugs.

Two years into Plan Colombia, its Colombian and U.S. authors had failed to eradicate coca or reconquer southern Colombia from the FARC, now boasting an army eighteen thousand strong. The Bush "Andean Initiative" evidently contemplated a deeper involvement in Colombia, including the prospect of armed confrontation with the FARC and a smaller guerrilla movement, the Army of National Liberation (ELN). A 2001 study by the Rand Corporation, financed by the U.S. Air Force, even suggested that "the U.S. program of military assistance to El Salvador during the Reagan Administration could be a relevant model." Commenting on this suggestion in *The NACLA Report on the Americas*, Adam Isacson urged those who might want to repeat this model in Colombia to recall that "the United States spent $2 billion on El Salvador's military over a 12-year period, during which 70,000 people died and over a million were forced into exile. Colombia is fifty-three times larger than El Salvador."

As President Uribe's term began, two new, unforeseen obstacles to the success of Plan Colombia appeared. In early July 2002 the Colombian finance minister announced that the Argentine "fever," having spread to Uruguay, Brazil, and Venezuela, had reached Colombia. In other words, the minister implied that Colombia now lacked the financial means to pay for the massive military mobilization necessary to defeat the FARC. A second blow to the implementation of Plan Colombia came from the FARC itself. In June 2002 it responded to the government's termination of the truce by sending every mayor, provincial governor, and government official in Colombia's 1,098 municipalities an ultimatum to resign in 72 hours or become military targets. Panic set in among some officials, including one who decided, "I am not going to lay my life on the line for a problem that I didn't cause."

Meanwhile, in some parts of the 40 percent of the national territory that it claimed to control, the FARC had created "pilot communities" that suggested the kind of political organization it envisioned to replace the ousted mayors. In Caqueta province, for example, the FARC established "people's committees" composed of peasant, worker, and business representatives to administer local affairs. This model of self-governance was given the name "participatory democracy." "We are handing power back to the people," said one guerrilla political officer in Caqueta. "We will not recognize political authorities, but only the desires of civic organizations. Town hall officials will simply become administrators, but the people will give the orders."

The Two Americas: United States–Latin American Relations

T WO CONSISTENT THEMES appear when the relations of the United States with Latin America over nearly two centuries are examined. First and foremost, the United States sought to protect and expand its economic and strategic interests in the region. Ever since the administration of James Monroe, the United States attempted to establish and maintain Latin America as an economic appendage. U.S. policymakers displayed resourcefulness and flexibility in pursuit of this goal, adapting their methods to meet the varying domestic political pressures, the changing requirements of U.S. business, and the shifting conditions in Latin America. Thus, U.S. policy never relied exclusively or even primarily on unilateral military conquest and subjugation of Latin America; instead, it sought to establish its hegemony, that is, to "manage" hemispheric events by securing Latin America's consent to a multilateral system of inter-American relations whose "general rules," though expressed in universal, humanitarian terms, nonetheless incorporated its special political, economic, and strategic interests.

Second, U.S. leaders consistently justified U.S. policy by portraying the region as hopelessly backward, desperately in need of beneficent U.S. tutelage to save its people from the ravages of barbarism and promote the development of virtuous, democratic republics modeled on an idealized U.S. experience. In this process, according to

Mark T. Berger, the work of historians and social scientists in Latin American studies was complicit. This "discourse" of a U.S. "civilizing mission," rooted in white supremacist ideas in the nineteenth century and the discursive language of modernization theory in the twentieth, facilitated "the creation and maintenance of the national and international organizations, institutions, interstate relations and politico-economic structures that sustain and extend U.S. hegemony in Latin America and around the world."

U.S. Policy Objectives

U.S. policy toward Latin America changed over time to accommodate its burgeoning economic activities in the region. During the early years of the nineteenth century, U.S. commerce with its southern neighbors demanded little more than policing the Caribbean for marauding pirates. As the United States grew into a commercial, industrial, and, eventually, financial power, its foreign policy broadened in scope. The hunt for new markets brought it into competition with European nations, especially Great Britain. As a result, it became one of the major aims of U.S. policy to check the further penetration of European commerce and capital into Latin America.

By the turn of the century, Latin America had become not only a substantial market for U.S.

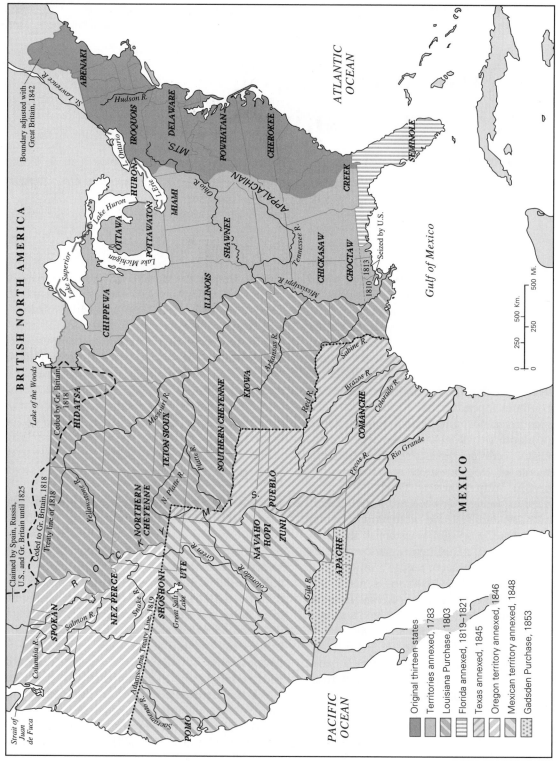

U.S. Territorial Expansion

Original thirteen states
Territories annexed, 1783
Louisiana Purchase, 1803
Florida annexed, 1819–1821
Texas annexed, 1845
Oregon territory annexed, 1846
Mexican territory annexed, 1848
Gadsden Purchase, 1853

ATLANTIC OCEAN

BRITISH NORTH AMERICA

Boundary adjusted with Great Britain, 1842

St. Lawrence R.
ABENAKI
Hudson R.
IROQUOIS
DELAWARE
POWHATAN
CHEROKEE
SEMINOLE
CREEK
Seized by U.S.
APPALACHIAN MTS.
Ohio R.
MIAMI
SHAWNEE
Tennessee R.
CHICKASAW
CHOCTAW
1813
1810
Mississippi R.
Gulf of Mexico

L. Ontario
L. Erie
HURON
OTTAWA
POTTAWATON
Lake Huron
Lake Michigan
Lake Superior
CHIPPEWA
ILLINOIS

Lake of the Woods
Ceded by Gr. Britain, 1818
HIDATSA
Missouri R.
TETON SIOUX
SOUTHERN CHEYENNE
KIOWA
Arkansas R.
Red R.
COMANCHE
Brazos R.
Colorado R.
Sabine R.
Rio Grande
Pecos R.

Ceded to Gr. Britain, 1818
Treaty line of 1818
Claimed by Spain, Russia, U.S., and Gr. Britain until 1825

Yellowstone R.
NORTHERN CHEYENNE
Platte R.
N. Platte R.
PUEBLO
NAVAHO
HOPI
ZUNI
APACHE
Gila R.

MEXICO

Columbia R.
Strait of Juan de Fuca
SPOKAN
Salmon R.
NEZ PERCE
Snake R.
SHOSHONI
UTE
Great Salt Lake
Green R.
Colorado R.
Adams-Onis Treaty Line, 1819
Sacramento R.
POMO

PACIFIC OCEAN

500 Mi.
500 Km.
250
250
0
0

522

products but also an important source of raw materials and a major area for capital investment. Having recently built a powerful navy, the United States assumed the responsibility of protecting its commerce and investment by forcibly maintaining order in the region. Uninvited, it assumed the role of policeman of the Western Hemisphere. In this capacity, the United States focused its attention on the weak and chaotic nations of the Caribbean and Central America, where U.S. economic activity was concentrated.

At mid-century, South America replaced the Caribbean as the focus of U.S. economic expansion. Geography, logistics, and the anti-imperialist temper of the times required the United States to abandon the old policies of military intervention in favor of more subtle and sophisticated ways of achieving its ends; these new methods included the lure of grants and loans, the threat of economic sanctions, and subversion. When these methods failed, however, as they did in Guatemala in 1954, in Cuba in 1959, and in the Dominican Republic in 1965, the United States did not hesitate to resort to the open or covert use of force.

Ideology always figured in U.S. policy toward Latin America. Thus, Theodore Roosevelt vowed to "civilize," Woodrow Wilson to "democratize," and John F. Kennedy to "reform" Latin America. But ideology always was subordinated to the material needs of United States–Latin American policy, and the presidents who made these pious professions were ready to use force in defense of the U.S. empire in Latin America. They were also ready to support the most oppressive regimes in the area as long as they cooperated with the United States. Highlighting this link between high ideals and capitalist class interests, Wilson, for example, argued in 1912 that "if America is not to have free enterprise, then she can have freedom of no sort whatever."

The two Americas, both born in wars of national liberation, followed very different historical paths. In two centuries, the United States rose to become the industrial and financial giant of the capitalist world; despite its many economic and social problems, it provided the majority of its people with a satisfactory material standard of living. Latin America fell far behind the other America in terms of its capacity to meet the economic needs of its citizens.

Many Latin Americans are convinced that these divergent trends are related, that Latin American underdevelopment is the other side of North American development, that Latin American poverty and misery have accumulated as the economic and political power of foreign (chiefly North American) multinational corporations have grown.

Prelude to Empire, 1810–1897

MANIFEST DESTINY, 1810–1865

During the early decades of the nineteenth century, westward expansion and nascent commerce brought the United States into its first contact with its southern neighbors. However, U.S. military and economic weakness, lack of information, and British predominance in the area limited U.S. activities in Latin America. U.S. trade with Latin America began in earnest in 1797, when Spain opened the ports of its New World colonies to foreign trade. By 1811 the Spanish colonies accounted for 16 percent of all U.S. trade. A dozen years later, despite the disruptions of the War of 1812, the figure had increased to 20 percent.

With only a small navy and few funds at its disposal, the U.S. government could offer little aid to the Spanish-American nations during their wars of independence (1810–1826). During the first stage of these wars, the War of 1812 consumed the attention and resources of the United States. From 1817 to 1819, it undertook delicate negotiations with Spain for the purchase of Florida and chose not to jeopardize these dealings by helping the Spanish-American insurgents. However, their victory offered powerful strategic and commercial advantages to the United States. First, with the French retreat from Haiti and the Louisiana territories in 1803 and the British in search of a U.S. alliance in the 1820s, Latin American independence eliminated Spain, the hemisphere's last potential military threat to U.S. security. This enabled the United States to spend less on defense and invest more in the development of its civilian economy.

Second, it meant, in Thomas Jefferson's words, that the United States could absorb "piece by piece" the old Spanish-American empire, "a huge, helpless and profitable whale." Similarly, John Quincy Adams, anticipating U.S. economic relations with a "free" Latin America, expected that the United States would grow wealthy from the region's dependence on it: "As navigators and manufacturers, we are already so far advanced in a career upon which they have yet to enter that we may, for many years after the conclusion of the [independence] war, maintain with them a commercial intercourse, highly beneficial to both parties, as carriers to and for them of numerous articles of manufacture and foreign produce."

When it was clear that the Latin American independence movements had succeeded, the United States accordingly acted to prevent other European nations from acquiring colonies or undue influence in the region, developments that could shut off U.S. access to potentially lucrative markets. In his message to Congress on December 2, 1823, President James Monroe declared that as a matter of principle, "the American continents, by the free and independent condition they have assumed and maintain, are henceforth not to be considered subjects for future colonization by any European powers. . . . We should consider any attempt on their [the European powers'] part to extend their system to any portion of this hemisphere as dangerous to our peace and safety." Monroe went on to say that the United States would not interfere with existing colonies, nor would it meddle in European affairs.

The Monroe Doctrine was ineffective for much of the nineteenth century because the United States had neither the resources nor the inclination to back it up. The doctrine, furthermore, failed to prevent repeated European interventions in Latin America. Following the accepted practice of the time, French and British gunboats regularly bombarded or blockaded Latin American ports to force payment of debts or reparations. The United States, too, adopted this practice, landing troops in the Falkland Islands, Argentina, and Peru during the 1830s, in Argentina, Nicaragua, Uruguay, Panama, Paraguay, and Mexico during the 1850s,

and in Panama, Uruguay, Mexico, and Colombia during the 1860s.

Nineteenth-century westward territorial expansion involved the United States in countless wars against Native Americans and two wars against Mexico. After the purchase of Louisiana (1803) and Florida (1821), the country began to covet Mexico's northern provinces, where U.S. citizens conducted a flourishing commerce. In 1825, President John Quincy Adams authorized the U.S. minister to Mexico to negotiate the purchase of Texas. The Mexican government rejected the proposal. During the early 1830s, U.S. settlers poured into Texas and quickly found themselves at odds with Mexican authorities over the issues of local autonomy and the illegal introduction of slavery into the area. In 1836 the settlers rebelled, defeated Mexico in a short war, and won their independence. Texas remained an independent nation for ten years, for the bitter debate over the extension of slavery prevented its annexation to the United States until 1845.

In 1845 President James Polk sent an emissary, James Slidell, to Mexico to arrange the acquisition of California. Outraged at the annexation of Texas, the Mexicans refused to cede any of their territory. Consequently, Polk trumped up a border incident along the Rio Grande, provoking a military clash that led to the war against Mexico (1846–1848). The victorious United States took the territories of Arizona, New Mexico, and California. Barely some seventy years old, the United States, building upon its conquest of Native American lands, had successfully waged another war of territorial acquisition.

COMMERCE AND THE CANAL

From 1815 to 1860, U.S. foreign commerce increased dramatically; exports grew by nearly 400 percent and imports by 300 percent. The nature of U.S. trade was transformed, for instead of reexporting foreign-made goods, U.S. merchants exported agricultural commodities and manufactured goods produced in the United States. Because of the increased economic activity in the Caribbean, especially Cuba and Central America, the United States began to pay close attention to the region. Cuba became one of the most important U.S. overseas markets, ranking third behind Great Britain and France in total U.S. trade. Throughout the 1850s, there was a strong sentiment, particularly among southern slave owners, to annex the island. President Millard Fillmore tried unsuccessfully to purchase Cuba from Spain in 1852.

Central America became important because of the prospect of a canal through the Central American isthmus. After discussions began in 1825 the United States signed an 1846 agreement with New Granada (Colombia) that guaranteed U.S. access to any canal built in its province of Panama. This concern over a canal and commercial interests in Central America brought the United States into direct confrontation with Great Britain, which had colonies in the region. Each nation sought to keep the other from dominating the area or controlling any canal that would be built. As a result, in 1850 they agreed to the Clayton-Bulwer Treaty, which provided that neither would try to dominate Central America or any part of it or would acquire exclusive rights to a canal. Thus, they eliminated a potential cause of hostilities.

The gold rush to California in 1849 increased the importance of transportation across the isthmus. U.S. entrepreneurs invested heavily in steamships and railroad construction in the region to satisfy the demand for cheap and fast transport across the isthmus to California. Despite the treaty with Britain and these heavy investments in transportation, U.S. interest in a canal continued.

The Awakening Giant, 1865–1887

In the two decades after the Civil War (1861–1865), U.S. policymakers focused their concerns on territorial expansion and increased trade in Latin America, finding little success in either. The major diplomatic triumph of the era came in 1866 when Secretary of State William H. Seward, belatedly invoking the Monroe Doctrine, demanded that France remove its troops from Mexico, where they propped up the rule of the Emperor Maximilian, the Austrian archduke. Emperor Napoleon III of France complied the fol-

lowing year, more because of growing tensions with Prussia in Europe than because of fear of the United States.

A succession of U.S. presidents and secretaries of state attempted to acquire new territories, but they were inevitably thwarted by Congress. There were also major efforts to expand U.S. trade to Latin America through the negotiation of reciprocal trade treaties and establishment of inter-American diplomatic conferences. The United States signed bilateral reciprocal trade agreements with six Latin American nations during the 1880s, but no real benefits accrued. The first Inter-American Conference met in Washington, D.C., in 1889. It resulted in little more than the airing of long-simmering grievances and mistrust.

Adventures in Latin America, 1888–1896

U.S. adventurism in Latin America in the last years of the nineteenth century stemmed from severe domestic economic and social problems, pervasive racism, and from the country's growing stake in commerce and investment in the region. The United States experienced a deep depression from 1893 to 1898, the third such downturn in twenty-five years (the others had occurred in 1873–1878 and 1882–1885). It became evident that the domestic market could not profitably absorb the rapidly growing output of U.S. agriculture and industry. U.S. leaders unanimously agreed that the answer to the problem was to expand foreign markets. The depression of 1893 created deep-seated social unrest as well, resulting in a series of bitter and bloody strikes. Businessmen and politicians alike feared that continued depression would lead to class warfare.

At the same time, U.S. capitalists increased their investment in Latin America. Paradoxically, despite the depression, U.S. banks had surplus funds to invest. Because investments in the United States were unattractive, the bankers turned to potentially more lucrative foreign enterprises. These investors poured millions of dollars into Cuban sugar and Mexican mining and railroads. By 1900 the U.S. stake in Mexico alone had reached $500 million.

U.S. interest, however, was not limited to areas like Mexico and Cuba, where it already had large investments. The United States was willing to go to great lengths, even at the risk of war, both to protect potential markets and to reinforce its political dominance in the region. This was particularly true of the Caribbean, which leaders tended to view as an "American lake." Thus, in 1888 the United States intervened in a civil war in Haiti to secure a favorable commercial agreement and a naval base at Môle St. Nicolas. The U.S. fleet actually broke a blockade to bring about the victory of the faction it favored. Once entrenched in power, however, this group reneged on its promises to the Harrison administration (1887–1893). Then Secretary of State James G. Blaine also tried unsuccessfully to obtain Samaná Bay from Santo Domingo.

Naturally, the same doctrines of white supremacy that sought to justify a domestic racial apartheid, the lynching of thousands of African Americans, disfranchisement of 8 million southern blacks, the "tribalization" of sovereign Native American nations, and the exclusion of Chinese immigrants also shaped U.S. relations with Latin America. U.S. policymakers increasingly came to share the view of Atlanta's Henry Grady, an influential "New South" publisher, who argued that white supremacy reflected "the right of character, intelligence, and property to rule." This, according to diplomatic historian Walter LaFeber, "anticipated some of the arguments Americans later used to justify their new foreign policies."

As the depression of 1893 deepened, U.S. leaders looked southward with growing anxiety. President Grover Cleveland declared in his annual message to Congress in 1893 that unrest and European meddling had threatened U.S. interests in Nicaragua, Guatemala, Costa Rica, Honduras, and Brazil in 1892; the U.S. fleet was finding it difficult to keep up with its "responsibilities." Markets desperately needed by the United States were threatened by disorders and competition from European nations, particularly Britain.

In 1894 the United States became involved in another revolution when it intervened in Brazil to protect a potentially important market and to check British influence there. The United States had signed a reciprocal trade agreement with the newly proclaimed republic of Brazil in 1891, but the rebels who rose up in 1893 opposed the pact. The main strategy of the rebel forces was to blockade the harbor of Rio de Janeiro, the nation's principal city; they hoped to strangle the government by denying it the all-important customs revenue. The United States helped undermine this strategy by refusing to recognize the blockade. U.S. vessels unloaded their cargoes without interference.

Late in 1894, however, with clandestine aid from the British, the rebellion regained momentum. At this time, important mercantile and oil (Rockefeller) interests, fearing the loss of their Brazilian market, brought pressure on the State Department to intervene. The United States responded by sending most of the Atlantic fleet to the harbor of Rio de Janeiro. By maneuvering to prevent rebel bombardment of the capital, the U.S. warships played a crucial part in the defeat of the revolt.

Shortly thereafter, the United States intervened in Nicaragua to protect its rights to an isthmian canal and the substantial holdings of U.S. investors. In 1893 a nationalist government, headed by General José S. Zelaya, took power in Nicaragua; it threatened to cancel a concession granted by a previous administration to the Maritime Canal Company to build a canal through Nicaraguan territory. Later, Zelaya also threatened the prosperous U.S.-run banana plantations in the indigenous Miskito reservation (an area claimed by Nicaragua but controlled by the British) by invading the reservation in 1894. In response, British troops landed and quickly subdued the Nicaraguan force. U.S. interests, with a $2 million stake in the Miskito region, were unwilling to accept either British or Nicaraguan rule. To protect its property, the United States stationed two warships off the coast and in July dispatched marines to restore order. U.S. troops landed three more times, in 1896, 1898, and 1899, to protect U.S. lives and property.

THE TURNING POINT: VENEZUELA, 1895–1896

The Venezuelan crisis of 1895–1896 ended in full British recognition of U.S. hegemony in the Western Hemisphere. The United States intervened in a boundary dispute between Venezuela and Great Britain that had festered for over half a century. The controversy concerned the region at the mouth of the Orinoco River, the major commercial artery for northern South America, which was claimed by both Venezuela and the British colony of Guiana (present-day Guyana). In the 1880s, Britain extended its claims, causing Venezuela to break off diplomatic relations.

During 1893 and 1894, the Venezuelan government, confronted with mounting economic difficulties and political unrest, appealed to the United States to help settle the controversy. President Cleveland's entrance into the dispute reflected his deep concern about the apparent resurgence of European intervention in Latin America. Between 1891 and 1895, the British had actively intervened in Chile, Brazil, and Nicaragua. The French had become involved in a dispute with Brazil over the boundary of their colony of Guiana and had threatened intervention in Santo Domingo to obtain satisfaction for the killing of a French citizen. The simultaneous scramble for territories in Africa magnified the threat; what the European rivals did on one continent, they could do on another. Specifically, President Cleveland feared that British control of the mouth of the Orinoco would exclude U.S. commerce from northern South American markets.

In 1895, in an obvious effort to intensify U.S. support, the Venezuelan government granted a lucrative concession to a U.S. syndicate for the exploitation of rich mineral resources located in the disputed zone. In July 1895 Secretary of State Richard Olney spelled out the U.S. attitude toward European meddling in Latin America. Citing the Monroe Doctrine, he declared that the United States would intervene whenever the actions of a European power in the Western Hemisphere posed a "serious and direct menace to its own integrity and welfare." In effect, Olney claimed hegemony for the United States in Latin America.

The British initially responded to Olney's claims with disdain; the English foreign secretary denied the validity of the Monroe Doctrine in international law and brushed aside the U.S. assertion of supremacy in the Western Hemisphere.

President Cleveland, however, firmly supported Olney's position and made it clear that the United States was willing to go to war to uphold it. Meanwhile, international developments worked to soften the British stand; the threat of a war with Germany and British problems in South Africa took precedence. Accordingly, in late 1896 the British agreed to submit the dispute to arbitration. The government of Venezuela neither participated in nor was informed of this agreement.

The Venezuelan affair marked the end of British military predominance in Latin America. Its attention now focused on the growing German power and the competition for territory in Africa, Britain could no longer commit substantial resources to the region. With the growing threat of a general war in Europe, British leaders also could not afford to alienate the United States, a powerful potential ally. Thus, the British formally recognized U.S. hegemony in Latin America with the signing of the Hay-Pauncefote Treaty of 1901, which allowed the United States unilaterally to build, control, and fortify an isthmian canal. In 1906, Britain withdrew its fleet from the Caribbean. Great Britain retained its predominant economic position in southern South America but was fated to lose that also to the United States after World War I.

An Imperial Power, 1898–1945

By 1898 the United States had emerged as an industrial, financial, and naval power. It surpassed Great Britain as the world's leading manufacturing state. Giant U.S. banks and corporations invested heavily overseas. Increasingly, the nation looked abroad for markets, raw materials, and profits. Recurring economic difficulties and mounting social unrest spurred U.S. leaders to seek solutions in overseas economic expansion and foreign adventures.

THE WAR WITH SPAIN

The war with Spain in 1898 established the United States as a full-fledged imperial power. The primary goal of its Cuban policy during the 1890s was to protect the very large (over $50 million) U.S. investment in the island by stopping the chronic political disorder there. When Spain proved unable to end the turmoil, and it appeared that ungovernable native rebels might take over, the United States intervened. In declaring war against Spain, the U.S. Congress pledged to free Cuba from Spanish tyranny and in the Teller Resolution disavowed any intention to annex the island. But to the dismay of Cuban rebels, the McKinley administration had opposed the Teller Amendment and defeated the Turpie-Foraker bill, which would have recognized the Cuban government-in-exile. The U.S. government proceeded to conduct the war and negotiate the peace without consulting the Cubans.

The United States occupied and ruled the island from 1898 to 1902, departing only after the Cubans agreed to include in their constitution the notorious Platt Amendment, which made the country a virtual U.S. colony. U.S. forces occupied the island three more times—1906 to 1909, 1912, and 1917 to 1922. As noted in Chapter 17, instead of bringing the Cubans liberty and economic progress, U.S. intervention promoted and perpetuated racism, corruption, violence, and economic stagnation.

AN "AMERICAN LAKE": THE "BIG STICK" AND "DOLLAR DIPLOMACY" IN THE CARIBBEAN

From 1898 to 1932 the United States intervened militarily in nine Caribbean nations a total of thirty-four times. Its occupation forces ran the governments of the Dominican Republic, Cuba, Nicaragua, Haiti, and Panama for long periods; Honduras, Mexico, Guatemala, and Costa Rica experienced shorter invasions. Military intervention was not the only method employed by the United States to control the region; other effective means included threats, nonrecognition, and economic sanctions.

The U.S. economic stake in the Caribbean was substantial. Moreover, the nature of this investment, which was concentrated primarily in agricultural commodities, mineral extraction, oil production, and government securities, made it particularly vulnerable to political disorders. From 1887 to 1914, U.S. investment in Cuba and the West Indies rose almost sevenfold, from $50 million to $336 million. Investment in Central America more than quadrupled, from $21 million to $93 million. By 1914, U.S. investment in Mexico had risen to over $1 billion. In 1914, 43 percent of this investment was in mining, 18.7 percent in agriculture, and 10 percent in oil. An additional 13 percent was invested in railroads, which were built to transport export products to market. The owners of these enterprises often had considerable influence on U.S. policy.

The United States justified its actions in the Caribbean by the so-called Roosevelt Corollary (1904) to the Monroe Doctrine, so named because President Theodore Roosevelt maintained that the United States, as a "civilized" nation, had the right to end "chronic wrongdoing" and thus could intervene in the Caribbean to maintain order. The Roosevelt Corollary was a logical outgrowth of the increasingly aggressive policies successively advanced by Seward, Grant, Cleveland, and Olney.

THE PANAMA CANAL

U.S. interest in a canal across Central America to join the Atlantic and Pacific oceans had intensified as the nation filled out its continental boundaries and expanded its commercial activities throughout the Western Hemisphere. But the first to attempt to build a canal was Ferdinand de Lesseps, the Frenchman who had constructed the Suez Canal. He began a project to dig a sea-level canal across Panama in 1878. After eleven years of effort, de Lesseps, thwarted by tropical disease and engineering problems, gave up the project. Throughout this period, the United States pressured France to abandon the undertaking; it asserted its "rightful and long-established claim to priority on the American continent." The growth of a large United States Navy, which had two coasts to defend, added to the urgency of constructing an isthmian passageway.

In the 1880s and 1890s support grew for building a canal through Nicaragua. In 1901 a presidential commission endorsed the Nicaraguan route, despite the more favorable engineering

U.S. Interventions in the Caribbean and Central America, 1898–1945

and logistical characteristics of the Panamanian alternative, because the French company that controlled the canal concession in Panama wanted the fantastic sum of $109 million for its rights. At this point, two extraordinary entrepreneurs, William N. Cromwell, an influential New York attorney, and Philippe Bunau-Varilla, chief engineer of the de Lesseps project and an organizer of the New Panama Canal Company (the French company that had rights to the canal), acted to change the course of U.S. policy. Cromwell, as lawyer for the canal company, bribed the Republican Party to end its support of the Nicaraguan route. He and Bunau-Varilla then convinced the company to

lower the price for its concession to a more reasonable $40 million.

The two men were faced with the problem of convincing the United States to purchase their company's concession before it expired in 1904. In 1902, Bunau-Varilla and Cromwell managed to push through Congress the Spooner Amendment, which authorized President Roosevelt to buy the New Panama Canal Company's rights for the asking price of $40 million if he could negotiate a treaty with Colombia. In 1903, Secretary of State John Hay pressured the Colombian ambassador to the United States to sign a pact that gave the United States a 99-year lease on a strip of land across the

Intersection between lower and middle locks, Gatun, Panama Canal.

The construction of the Panama Canal, as depicted in a postcard from the time.
[The Granger Collection, New York]

isthmus in return for $10 million and an annual payment of $250,000. The Colombian Senate, demanding more money, rejected the proposal.

In the meantime, Bunau-Varilla undertook to exploit the long tradition of Panamanian nationalism and rebelliousness for his own end. From the time that Colombia won its independence from Spain in 1821, it had never been able to establish its rule in Panama. During the nineteenth century, the Panamanians revolted fifty times against their Colombian masters. On two occasions, when the Panamanian rebels seemed near success (1855–1856 and 1885), the United States intervened militarily to protect its interests and end the revolts. After a terrible civil war (1899–1902) had severely weakened Colombia, Panamanian nationalists again prepared to rise in revolt. Working closely with the U.S. State Department and the Panamanians, Bunau-Varilla triggered a successful uprising in early November 1903. With the

help of the United States Navy and bribes paid to the Colombian officers who were supposed to crush the revolt, Panama won its independence.

The Panamanians, to their own undoing, entrusted to Bunau-Varilla the subsequent negotiations with the United States over the canal concession. Feverishly working to complete the arrangements before the New Panama Canal Company's rights expired, he produced a treaty that gave the United States control over a ten-mile-wide canal zone "as if it were a sovereign of the territory." The United States was to have "in perpetuity the use, occupation, and control" of the zone. In return, the United States was to pay Panama $10 million and assume a virtual protectorate over the new nation. The Panamanian government indignantly protested the terms of the agreement but eventually accepted the pact, fearing that the United States might either seize the canal with no compensation or build one in Nicaragua instead.

U.S. Marines were stationed in Panama from late 1903 until 1914 to protect U.S. interests while the canal was built, largely by black workers recruited from the West Indies. During this period, the United States disbanded the Panamanian army and assumed the responsibility of defending Panama against any external threat. The United States established its own postal system, customhouses, and commissaries in the Canal Zone, privileges that seriously undermined the Panamanian economy and badly injured Panamanian pride. The canal was completed in 1914.

THE DOMINICAN REPUBLIC, HAITI, AND NICARAGUA

The United States occupied and administered the governments of the Dominican Republic (1916–1924), Haiti (1915–1934), and Nicaragua (1912–1925 and 1926–1933) to the detriment of these nations' long-range political and economic development.

President Ulysses S. Grant had sought to annex the Dominican Republic (then known as Santo Domingo) in 1869; only rejection of the agreement by the United States Senate, influenced by fears of mingling with "people of the Latin race mixed with the Indian and African blood," prevented him from acquiring the nation, which shares the island of Hispaniola with Haiti. In the decades that followed, a series of venal and brutal dictators, often supported by loans from U.S. banks, produced a debilitating cycle of repression and rebellion. In 1893 the Santo Domingo Improvement Company, a U.S. firm, purchased the country's heavy foreign debt in return for the right to collect its customs revenue. In both 1903 and 1904, the United States dispatched marines to protect the interests of the influential New York financiers who were principals in the company. In 1905 the U.S. government assumed the administration of Dominican customs.

But unrest persisted. In 1916, President Woodrow Wilson sent in Marines after the Dominican government refused to accept broader U.S. control over the nation's internal affairs, and the U.S. Navy maintained a military dictatorship until 1924. The Marines brutally repressed guer-rilla activities that threatened U.S.-owned sugar plantations. In addition, several U.S. officers were subsequently court-martialed for the commission of atrocities.

The U.S. occupation forces attempted administrative and fiscal reforms and built some roads, but these projects were abandoned when the soldiers departed. One institution that remained intact after the occupation ended was the *Guardia Nacional*, the national police force. Rafael Trujillo, with U.S. support, rose through the ranks of the Guardia to become dictator of the Dominican Republic in 1928. His rapacious rule, extending over three decades (he was assassinated in 1961), was the bitter legacy of U.S. intervention.

Events in Haiti followed a similar course. For a century after winning independence from France in 1804, Haiti experienced ruinous political turmoil. Seizing the opportunity presented by the brutal murder of the Haitian president in 1915, Woodrow Wilson sent in Marines, ostensibly to prevent Germany from taking advantage of the chaos to establish a base on the island, which would endanger U.S. commerce and the access routes to the Panama Canal. A treaty signed the next year placed the United States in full control of the country. Although Haitians held public office, they served only at the pleasure of U.S. authorities. Here, too, U.S. troops committed atrocities while engaged in the suppression of rural guerrillas, and civil liberties were ignored. U.S. control lasted until 1934.

The United States also intervened in Nicaragua to protect the interests of U.S. companies operating there. The U.S. investment totaled only $2.5 million, but the largest company, the United States–Nicaraguan Concession, had considerable influence in the Taft administration (1909–1913); Secretary of State Philander C. Knox had been the company's legal counsel. In 1909, General José Zelaya, an old nemesis of the United States, canceled a concession to one U.S. company and threatened the Nicaraguan Concession. The same year, the United States backed a revolution that overthrew Zelaya. In 1912, at the request of the Nicaraguan government, President William Howard Taft sent in Marines to crush a new rebellion; the Marines remained for thirteen years. In

1916 the United States and Nicaragua agreed to the Bryan-Chamorro Treaty, which gave the United States sole rights to build a canal through Nicaragua in return for payment of $3 million.[1] President Calvin Coolidge withdrew U.S. troops for a short period in 1925 but dispatched them again to subdue yet another revolution the following year; the soldiers stayed until 1933.

PUERTO RICO

The United States became a colonial power with the conquest and acquisition of the island of Puerto Rico in 1898 during the Spanish-American-Cuban War. From December 1898 until May 1900, U.S. military governors ruled the island. In 1900 the U.S. Congress passed the Foraker Act, which established a new civilian government for the island with a governor and an executive council appointed by the U.S. president. In 1917 this government was modified by replacing the executive council with an elected Senate. But the president maintained the power to veto legislation passed by the Puerto Rican Congress. The same year the U.S. Congress granted Puerto Ricans U.S. citizenship in time to make them eligible for the military draft for World War I.

U.S. occupation cost Puerto Ricans dearly politically. At the time of the Spanish-American War, the island had won a large degree of autonomy from Spain. The new colonial regime stripped that from them and ruled Puerto Rico with tactless, condescending mainlanders who had no experience in dealing with different cultures. When Puerto Ricans protested against unresponsive government, U.S. authorities reacted harshly. In 1909, for example, members of the Puerto Rican House of Delegates refused to pass the year's appropriation bill because of their objections to the indifference shown in the court system to struggling coffee growers. President Taft angrily demanded that the right of appropriations be taken from the House of Delegates, and the U.S. Congress enacted this legislation in the so-called

Olmstead Amendment. Puerto Rico did not have a native-born governor until 1947 or an elected governor until 1948.

Puerto Rico also underwent drastic economic changes as a result of the U.S. occupation. In 1898 its leading crop, coffee, was exported to Europe. U.S. policies transformed the island into a monocrop sugar economy with landownership concentrated in very few hands, mostly absentee foreign corporations. Puerto Ricans became dependent on the U.S. sugar quota. The decline of sugar prices during the 1920s and their collapse during the Depression of the 1930s brought chronic economic problems. By 1929 near starvation prevailed in many parts of the island. New Deal agencies, such as the Puerto Rican Emergency Relief Administration and the Puerto Rican Reconstruction Administration, poured some $230 million into the island from 1933 to 1941.

During the 1930s and for decades thereafter, the influence of two Puerto Ricans, Pedro Albizu Campos and Luis Muñoz Marín, dominated Puerto Rican politics. Harvard-educated Albizu became the foremost spokesman for independence. He formed the Nationalist Party and took an ardently anti-U.S. stand. He spent many years in prison for supporting violent confrontation with the island's colonial master. Muñoz Marín, whose father had led the Unionists in the early years of U.S. rule, was also educated in the United States. He did not live in Puerto Rico permanently until 1931. During the dark Depression days of the 1930s, Muñoz Marín became the star protégé of the New Deal.

The terrible plight of Puerto Rico during the Depression led to a reevaluation of its status by policymakers in the United States in the late 1930s. It was, as historian Arturo Morales Carrión has said, "a crisis of the whole colonial system." North Americanization had brought the "rise of absentee landownership, the collapse of coffee culture, the migration to growing slums, and shocking poverty in rural areas." U.S. rule had been a "mixture of paternalism and neglect, self-righteousness and condescension." The U.S. administrators of the island reacted harshly to such criticism and to nationalist protests. In March 1937 during a parade

---

[1]This treaty gave the United States control over the two best routes for a canal in Central America.

of the Nationalist Party in San Juan, police killed seventeen protesters in an unprovoked attack. In the crisis that followed in the aftermath of the massacre, old political coalitions realigned and Muñoz Marín emerged as the leading political figure. Based on his grassroots organization in the countryside, Muñoz Marín's Popular Democratic Party (PPD) rose meteorically, sweeping elections from 1944 until 1968. With help from Washington, he was able to lead Puerto Rico into a new era of industrialization and economic expansion.

Characteristic of Puerto Rican development was its dependence on the U.S. economy. North American corporations effectively monopolized the key sectors of banking, transport, tourism, and high-tech industrialization. This discouraged native capital formation. For North American corporations, however, the combination of low wages and tax breaks proved a bonanza, with profits in the range of $10 billion a year.

The combination of economic, political, and legal dependency adversely affected Puerto Rican political culture, breeding a colonial psychology that made dependency appear a natural condition and independence an impossible dream.

Accurately summarizing the island's colonial legal status since 1898, Attorney General Richard Thornburg declared that "The Congress of the United States holds full powers over Puerto Rico, a relationship that Puerto Ricans are incapable of altering. . . ." He went on to say that this relationship remained inalterable until changed by an amendment to the U.S. Constitution.

THE MEXICAN REVOLUTION

We have already discussed some aspects of U.S. policy toward the Mexican Revolution (1910–1920) in Chapter 12. That policy was directed above all at safeguarding the vast U.S. investment below the border and securing the favorable political and economic climate required by U.S. interests in Mexico. The specific policies and tactics employed by the administrations of Presidents Taft and Wilson varied with the shifting conditions in Mexico, political pressures in the United States, and the changing international background. The United States twice resorted to military intervention in Mexico. In 1914, U.S. Marines occupied the gulf ports of Veracruz and Tampico in an effort to bring down General Victoriano Huerta, considered too friendly to British and German investors. The second intervention, General John J. Pershing's incursion into northern Mexico in 1916 in pursuit of Pancho Villa, aimed to pressure the regime of Venustiano Carranza to disavow allegedly radical constitutional constraints on foreign investment.

The United States exerted more decisive influence on the military course of the revolution by regulating the flow of arms and munitions across the United States–Mexican border. Through selective application of its neutrality laws, the U.S. government prevented "undesirable" factions from instigating disruptive activities on the U.S. side of the border. Woodrow Wilson introduced a new tactic in U.S. relations with Mexico by announcing that he would withhold recognition of governments that did not measure up to his standard of "morality." Wilson used this ploy against Huerta, Carranza, and Obregón.

U.S. efforts to control the course of the revolution were diluted by stubborn resistance on the part of nationalist Mexican leaders like Carranza, divisions among U.S. investors in Mexico—some favoring and others opposing military intervention—and finally, growing involvement of the United States in World War I. Its entry into the war in 1917 sharply limited policy alternatives, because the country lacked the military resources to fight in both Mexico and Europe. The threat of a Mexican alliance with Germany—a threat strongly posed by the famous Zimmerman telegram[2]—forced the United States to adopt a more moderate policy toward its neighbor.

[2]In this dispatch the German government, not yet at war with the United States, offered to return to Mexico the southwestern part of the United States (lost during the Mexican War, 1846–1848) if Mexico would invade the United States. This telegram was a major factor in President Woodrow Wilson's decision to go to war in 1917.

QUIET IMPERIALISM: THE GOOD NEIGHBOR IN WORDS AND ACTION, 1921–1945

U.S. investment in Latin America grew rapidly in the period between 1914 and 1929. The world war enabled U.S. entrepreneurs to buy up much of the large British and German investment in the region. Total U.S. investment in Cuba and the West Indies, for example, rose from $336 million in 1914 to $1.2 billion in 1929—nearly a fourfold increase. U.S. capital in Central America more than tripled, while investment in South America increased eightfold. In 1929 total U.S. investment in Latin America had reached the staggering sum of $5.4 billion, or 35 percent of all U.S. foreign investment.

Much of the new investment went into oil: U.S. companies channeled $235 million to Venezuela, $134 million to Colombia, $120 million to Mexico, and $50 million to Peru for oil exploration and production. Another $163 million went to manufacturing enterprises in South America. U.S. companies also invested heavily in Chilean copper and nitrate, Argentine beef, and Cuban sugar.

This period marked the full-fledged involvement of large U.S. corporations, later called multinationals, in Latin America. Such giants as Standard Oil of New Jersey, the American Smelting and Refining Company, International Telephone and Telegraph, American Foreign Power, and Armour established or added to their vast stake in the region.

The basic goal of U.S. policy in Latin America did not change during the postwar period; it remained the protection of U.S. economic interests. But public opinion and realism dictated modifications. U.S. citizens were weary of overseas adventures and crusades. The United States remained dominant in the Caribbean, exerting decisive influence in the affairs of Mexico and Cuba and continuing to occupy the Dominican Republic, Haiti, and Nicaragua during the 1920s, but there was growing opposition to the old-style imperialism.

Makers of foreign policy in the United States also realized that growing popular hostility to U.S. policy in Latin America, primarily a response to U.S. actions in the Caribbean, posed a serious long-

term danger to U.S. economic interests. An early sign of a shift in U.S. policy came in 1921, when the Colombian government threatened to cancel the concessions of U.S. companies to explore and drill for oil. The United States responded by paying Colombia $25 million to compensate for the loss of Panama. This had a dual meaning: it served to protect U.S. economic interests, and it symbolized a less aggressive policy toward Latin America. The shift in U.S. tactics became even clearer when the United States removed its troops from Cuba in 1922, from the Dominican Republic in 1924, and from Nicaragua in 1925. Despite these actions, the United States encountered bitter criticism of its role in the hemisphere at the Pan-American conferences in Santiago in 1923 and Havana in 1928.

The most important indication that the United States had largely abandoned military intervention as a major tactic was its restraint in dealing with Mexico, the biggest trouble spot in the hemisphere during the 1920s. The Mexican constitution of 1917 was a most radical document by contemporary standards. The constitution's provisions on landownership and ownership of subsoil rights seriously endangered U.S. investments. U.S. oil companies, in particular, objected to the new laws, which sought to reclaim statutory control of Mexico's rich natural resources even as they confirmed foreign usufruct rights.

Throughout the 1920s, the United States and Mexico haggled over application of the constitution, but the basic disagreement inflamed relations until World War II. The United States did not intervene militarily to protect the very large U.S. investments in Mexico because three circumstances discouraged such action. First, public opinion opposed further foreign adventures. Second, a military invasion would have been prohibitively costly in terms of both manpower and finances. Finally, U.S. entrepreneurs with interests in Mexico disagreed sharply over the proper course of action. The oil companies, which were most threatened by the constitution, favored intervention. The banks and the mining companies, whose interests would have been in greater danger in the event of war between the United States and Mexico, opposed intervention. The controversy abated during the late 1920s, after the U.S. government conceded that Mexico's nationalist regulations did not threaten the oil companies' right to profit from oil production.

President Herbert Hoover and Secretary of State Henry L. Stimson continued to shift toward moderation and stepped up U.S. efforts to win goodwill in Latin America. Hoover abandoned Wilson's policy of denying recognition to "unworthy" governments. The Clark memorandum, a milestone in Hoover's efforts, declared that the Roosevelt Corollary had no support in the Monroe Doctrine; consequently, the United States would no longer interfere militarily in the internal affairs of Latin American nations under the provisions of the doctrine. But the president carefully refrained from rejecting intervention outright. In 1933 he withdrew U.S. troops from Nicaragua and would have removed them from Haiti as well had the Haitians not objected to the withdrawal terms.

Building on these experiences, Franklin D. Roosevelt assumed the presidency in 1933 and, officially proclaiming the United States to be a "good neighbor" to the rest of the world, he rejected "interference in the internal affairs of other nations." The following year, the United States abrogated the Platt Amendment, thus abandoning its protectorate over Cuba; the same year, it withdrew its occupation troops from Haiti.

The nonintervention policy was soon put to the test in Cuba. In 1933 political unrest there threatened the substantial U.S. investment on the island. Roosevelt dispatched Sumner Welles to Havana to try to arrange an accommodation between dictator Gerardo Machado and his opponents. After several months of unsuccessful negotiations, Machado fled, and power fell into the hands of a disorganized and disunited junta. Eventually, Dr. Ramón Grau San Martín emerged as leader of the government. He quickly fell into disfavor with the United States when he suspended loan repayments to a large New York bank and seized two U.S.-owned sugar mills. As a result, the United States refused to recognize the Grau government. With U.S. warships lingering in Havana harbor, Grau was forced to relinquish his leadership. Supported by the United States, Fulgencio

Batista emerged as the strongman of Cuba. Despite the protestations of the United States to the contrary, it was evident that it had not entirely abandoned the "big stick."

Nonintervention was tested again in Mexico in 1938. The long dispute between the Mexican government and the oil companies culminated in the expropriation of foreign oil holdings when the oil companies defied an order of the Mexican Supreme Court in a labor dispute. While the oil companies clamored for reprisal, Roosevelt tried to settle matters peacefully. In the face of isolationist sentiment in the United States, intervention was unthinkable. Moreover, with war in Europe on the horizon, the United States did not want to endanger an important source of oil. A settlement was eventually reached during the 1940s.

Roosevelt's "good neighbor" policy toward Latin America also involved efforts to achieve reciprocal trade agreements as a means of increasing U.S. trade and influence in the area. Secretary of State Cordell Hull ardently supported such agreements, believing they would help the United States emerge from the Great Depression. From 1934 to 1941, Hull succeeded in signing reciprocal trade treaties with fifteen Latin American nations. Had those treaties succeeded in significantly increasing U.S. trade, which they did not, they would have adversely affected Latin America's nascent industrialization, which was critically dependent on protective tariffs for its survival. In this area, therefore, United States policy was in direct conflict with the goal of Latin American economic development.

In the 1930s the United States grew increasingly concerned over the spread of German economic and political influence in Latin America. In response to this, the United States pushed for closer cooperation among the nations of the Western Hemisphere by promoting a series of meetings to consider common problems. The participants in successive inter-American conferences agreed to consult in the event of war among themselves or outside the hemisphere, approved a joint declaration of neutrality, proclaimed the existence of a safety zone around the hemisphere and warned belligerents not to wage war within it, and agreed to administer French and Dutch colonies in the Western Hemisphere in the event they were in danger of Nazi takeover. They also proclaimed that an attack on any of the conferring nations would be construed as an attack on all. In early 1942, shortly after the Japanese attack on Pearl Harbor, the conferees agreed to cooperate against the Axis; most Latin American nations severed diplomatic relations with the Axis powers. Every Latin American country but Argentina contributed to the Allied war effort.

The war strengthened the economic links between the United States and Latin America. The United States served as the sole market for the region's exports and the only supplier of its requirements of arms, munitions, industrial equipment, and manufactured goods. A growing proportion of U.S. capital went into manufacturing enterprises instead of raw material extraction. By the end of the war, Argentina accounted for 16 percent of U.S. investment in Latin America, Chile 16 percent, Brazil 13 percent, and Peru 4 percent. For the first time, South America accounted for over half the total U.S. investment in Latin America.

Defending the Empire and Capitalism, 1945–1981

In the postwar era, four factors determined United States–Latin American relations: the need for the United States to protect U.S. interests in the region, its broader efforts to construct global markets open to trade and investment, the desire of Latin American nations to industrialize and diversify their economies, and the rivalry between the United States and the Soviet Union.

INVESTMENT AND TRADE

Several important trends characterized U.S. investment in and trade with Latin America after World War II. First, the amount of investment increased enormously. Furthermore, the type of investment changed from mostly extractive industries, such as mining and oil, to manufacturing. Also, this investment became concentrated in the hands of a few large corporations and banks. Last, although the amount of U.S. trade with Latin America grew substantially, the relative importance of this trade to the economies of the United States and individual Latin American nations decreased.

All these trends did not mean that the United States had changed its policies. Its leaders continued to base their decisions on U.S. economic interests in the region, as trade and investment represented huge sums, despite declining importance. Accordingly, the editors of *Fortune*, an influential voice of corporate America, urged postwar U.S. leaders to "to organize the economic resources of the world so as to make possible a return to the system of free enterprise in every country. . . ." Policymakers like then–Assistant Secretary of State Dean Acheson, himself a corporate lawyer, shared this worldview; fearing a replay of the Great Depression, he conceded in 1944 that "it is a problem of markets. The important thing is markets. We have got to see that what the country produces is used and sold under financial arrangements which make its production possible. . . . You must look to foreign markets." Thus, every overt or covert U.S. intervention in Latin America during this period—in Guatemala, Cuba, the Dominican Republic, and Chile, for example—took place in countries where the security of large U.S. investments appeared to have been endangered. Moreover, each of these countries challenged the U.S. vision of a global open-door system.

POST–WORLD WAR II ADJUSTMENTS

Despite the high degree of wartime cooperation, sharp differences between the United States and Latin America surfaced in the immediate postwar years. These disagreements emerged initially at the Chapultepec Conference in February 1945. Latin American leaders felt they should be rewarded for their contributions and sacrifices during the war. The United States, however, regarded European recovery as its first priority. There were also major disagreements over trade, industrialization, the overall direction of Latin American economic development, and the role of the United States in this development. The United States insisted on an open door to Latin American markets and investment opportunities, but it was unwilling to make any concessions that might injure its own producers. Latin Americans, however, feared that such free access to Latin American markets would destroy much of the industrial progress the region had made in the preceding two decades.

U.S. and Latin American interests were clearly opposed. The major Latin American obstacle to U.S. objectives was the region's nationalism: contrary to the open-door philosophy, according to the State Department's Office of Intelligence Research, in Latin America "the idea that the government has direct responsibility for the welfare of the people has resulted in a phenomenal growth of social and economic legislation designed to protect labor, distribute land more widely . . . and increase opportunities for education." Whereas U.S. leaders regarded private capital investment and free trade as the best routes to development, Latin American nations favored a massive government role in industrialization and restrictions on foreign trade and investment as the only means of modernizing and regaining control over their economies.

After the war, Latin America vainly sought help from the United States to finance industrialization and access to U.S.-manufactured goods, especially capital equipment in order to further industrialization. These efforts were hindered further in the next few years as high prices for manufactured products dissipated the dollar reserves Latin American nations had accumulated during the war; declining prices for raw materials eroded Latin America's terms of trade even further.

There was increasing evidence, moreover, that the United States had reverted to its traditional disregard for Latin American sensitivities and to intervention in the internal affairs of nations of the region. In 1946 the United States interfered in the internal political affairs of three South American nations. It meddled disastrously in the Argentine presidential campaign of that year, assuring the election of Juan Perón; it forced the González Videla government in Chile to oust the Communist members of its coalition cabinet; and it helped undermine a revolutionary regime in Bolivia that had been accused of fascist tendencies.

THE COLD WAR

Alarm in the United States over the vast expansion of communist influence in Eastern and Central Europe as a result of World War II, the communist victory in the Chinese civil war, and the gains of Communist parties in Western Europe had the effect of pushing Latin America to the back burner. In this initial stage of the cold war, which lasted into the 1950s, the United States focused its attention on checking the further spread of communism in Western Europe and Asia by aiding the revival of the shattered capitalist economy.

During this first stage of the cold war, U.S. leaders tended to view the world as two camps, one committed to the United States and its free enterprise system, the other loyal to communism. Since it regarded the world in such black and white terms, the United States viewed with implacable hostility governments and movements that disagreed with its policy or attempted to institute structural social and economic reforms. On two occasions, in Guatemala and Iran, the United States helped topple such governments through the subversive activities of the CIA.

A second stage of the cold war began in the mid-1950s, when a "Third World" emerged, made up of the many newly independent states of Africa and Asia, which proclaimed themselves unaligned in the struggle between the blocs led by the Soviet Union and the United States. The two superpowers, faced with the unacceptable consequences of nuclear war, fought out the cold war in the Third World. In this second stage, the United States became intensely concerned with Latin America, especially after the 1959 Cuban Revolution led to the establishment of the first socialist state in the Americas. U.S. preoccupation with the threat of more Cubas in the hemisphere produced the Alliance for Progress as an alternative to the Cuban model.

Equally important, however, was the use of military aid to shape the internal policies of recalcitrant Latin American nations. The Military Defense Assistance Act of 1951 appropriated an initial $38.5 million to finance the build-up of Latin American armies for "country missions," that is, internal security rather than global or regional defense. This expanded under successive U.S. presidential administrations such that immediate postwar U.S. military aid amounted to more than half a billion dollars for the circum-Caribbean area alone and included paying for the training of thousands of Latin American military officers. By 1954 this policy had borne substantial fruit: thirteen of twenty countries were ruled by pro-U.S. military dictatorships.

The third stage of the cold war followed the disastrous U.S. experience in Vietnam and lasted until Ronald Reagan took office as president in 1981. Losing the Vietnam War and its tragic cost brought home to the U.S. government and its people the limitations of U.S. power and the dangers involved in trying to prevent social revolutions. Nonetheless, the United States remained determined to maintain its hegemony in the Western Hemisphere and to achieve its goals adapted its methods to suit new conditions.

A fourth stage of the cold war brought to the late 1980s the renewal of provocative anticommunist rhetoric, the simplistic 1950s division of the world into "them" and "us," the return to using force as a policy tool, and a revival of illegal, covert activities. The collapse of the Stalinist-type communist regimes in eastern and central Europe and the resulting demise of the cold war created a problem for the military-industrial complex that had flourished in the cold war's protective shadow and for U.S. Latin American policy by depriving it of its traditional enemy, "international communism." In the 1990s the drug trafficker replaced that traditional enemy as a convenient pretext for intervention in Latin America. After the September 11, 2001, terrorist attacks on the Pentagon and World Trade Center, the "war on terrorism" replaced drugs.

THE LATIN AMERICAN POLICIES OF TRUMAN AND EISENHOWER

The Truman administration (1945–1953) focused its attention on fighting communism in Europe and the Far East. But, as we have seen, it meddled with mixed success in the political affairs of Chile, Bolivia, and Argentina in 1946. Under Truman,

the movement for hemispheric cooperation continued, at least outwardly. The Rio Treaty of 1947 brought Central and South America into a military alliance with the United States. The ninth International Conference of American States, held in Bogotá the following year, resulted in the formation of the Organization of American States (OAS). The OAS was to provide collective security, with an attack against one member being viewed as an attack on all. The OAS also was to be a mediator in disputes between members. Truman and his chief advisers were primarily concerned with maintaining the status quo in the region.

The Eisenhower presidency (1953–1961) marked a revival of strong corporate influence in U.S. foreign policy. Eisenhower took office in the middle of the Korean war and at the height of the McCarthy "Red Scare." His administration, particularly the fanatical anticommunist secretary of state, John Foster Dulles, divided the world into two categories: nations that supported the United States and those that did not. Any foreign government that restricted the activities of U.S. corporations under its jurisdiction was adjudged to be communist and a threat to the security of the United States. During his two terms, Eisenhower faced four challenges of this kind in Latin America: Bolivia, British Guiana, Guatemala, and Cuba. In each case, his administration reacted according to the scale of the U.S. economic interests involved and the prevailing domestic and international conditions.

In Bolivia in 1952, a successful revolution headed by Victor Paz Estenssoro and the National Revolutionary Movement (MNR) ushered in sweeping economic and political reforms. In its first year, the new government nationalized the nation's tin mines, wiped out the latifundio system, replaced the old army with workers' and peasants' militias, and greatly increased the number of eligible voters. The outgoing Truman administration, anxious over the radicalism of the regime, withheld recognition and aid from Bolivia. The middle-class leadership of the MNR eventually managed to convince the Eisenhower administration that it was not communist; as a result, Bolivia received millions of dollars in grants and loans and substantial technical assistance over the next decade. U.S. aid had a significant moderating influence on the MNR reform program. Indeed, U.S. assistance decisively altered the whole course of Bolivian development; the United States reestablished, equipped, and trained the Bolivian army, which overthrew Paz Estenssoro in 1964, ushering in a period of conservative rule that continued almost uninterruptedly until 1981.

The United States employed different tactics to achieve the same general results, to adjust to the differing conditions of another Latin American country. In 1953, Marxist Cheddi Jagan was elected on a program of structural reform to head the government of the British colony of Guiana, an important source of bauxite and other metals. Several large U.S. companies, including Reynolds Metals and Kennecott Copper, had substantial holdings in the colony. Alarmed at the prospect of nationalization of these holdings by a Marxist regime, the United States urged the British to nullify the election; the British government duly sent troops to Guiana and deposed the new government.

The Eisenhower administration employed yet other tactics in Guatemala in 1954: conspiring to overthrow a democratically elected government whose reforms threatened the interests of a large and influential U.S. corporation. In 1944 a revolution toppled the oppressive regime of Jorge Ubico, who had ruled Guatemala since 1931. The victorious middle-class revolutionaries favored a capitalist course of development and were friendly to the United States. However, the reform programs of Presidents Juan José Arévalo (1945–1951) and Jacobo Arbenz (1951–1954) provoked the hostility of the United Fruit Company (UFCO) and Dulles. UFCO had operated in Guatemala since the 1890s, when it acquired a virtual monopoly on banana production and distribution. It was Guatemala's largest employer, with ten thousand workers, and its largest landowner. The company also controlled the nation's main transportation artery, the International Railways of Central America (IRCA), and major port facilities on the Gulf of Mexico.

The Guatemalan government clashed with UFCO over labor and land reform. Arévalo enacted a new labor code in 1947. The company, charging that it was being discriminated against, protested sharply. The ensuing labor agitation severely hampered banana production for several years. In 1952 the Guatemalan Congress enacted a land reform program, expropriating large tracts of uncultivated land for distribution among landless peasants. Again, UFCO charged the government with discrimination.

Unfortunately for the Guatemalan government, UFCO enjoyed great influence with the U.S. government. It was a client of Dulles's law firm. Also, the company's headquarters were in Boston, which made it a constituent of three of the most powerful men in the United States Congress: Senator Henry Cabot Lodge, Speaker of the House Joseph Martin, and Democratic Party leader John McCormack. What was more, the family of the assistant secretary of state in charge of Guatemalan relations, John Moors Cabot, was a major stockholder in United Fruit.

Seizing on allegations of communist participation in the Arbenz government to justify its actions, the United States trained and outfitted a rebel group under the command of Carlos Castillo Armas. Castillo Armas invaded Guatemala through UFCO property and overthrew Arbenz in June 1954. His repressive regime, which lasted until his assassination in 1957, erased all of the postwar reforms and restored UFCO's privileges.

THE CUBAN REVOLUTION AND UNITED STATES–LATIN AMERICAN RELATIONS

Eisenhower's successful interventions in Bolivia, British Guiana, and Guatemala produced bitter criticism of the United States in Latin America and contributed to the hostile and violent reception accorded Vice President Richard Nixon on his tour of the region in 1958. No major change in policy, however, occurred until the victory of Fidel Castro in Cuba in 1959.

The United States, a steadfast supporter of Batista's cruel dictatorship, consistently had opposed Castro's revolutionary movement and later embarked on a two-pronged program designed to destroy his government. To avert new Cubas, U.S. policymakers simultaneously sought to placate the rest of Latin America with various concessions. Meanwhile, they imposed economic sanctions on Cuba and began clandestinely to train an invasion force of Cuban exiles. To ensure Latin American backing, the United States committed limited funds to a new Social Trust Fund for the region and agreed to support plans for common markets in the area, such as the Latin American Free Trade Association (LAFTA) and the Central American Common Market, proposals which it had long opposed.

Under the new administration of John F. Kennedy, these economic reforms developed into a comprehensive plan for the region, the Alliance for Progress. The United States pledged to spend $10 billion in the region over ten years, to build badly needed transportation facilities and to buy technology and industrial equipment. In return, Latin American governments were to institute programs of social and political reform. The United States proposed to foster democracy and economic justice in Latin America through a program of incentives. To guard against more radical movements like the Castro-led guerrilla movement in Cuba, the U.S. government also undertook to strengthen the military forces of the region with arms and training.

The Alliance for Progress, however, brought neither economic development nor democracy to Latin America. In the first place, the program was not intended to be philanthropic but rather to foster capitalist, private-sector development and to expand U.S. trade and investments. Much aid to the region was in the form of loans that eventually had to be repaid. Moreover, aid money had to be used to buy U.S. products transported on U.S. ships; by eliminating competition, such restrictions reduced the developmental impact of aid. Although the U.S. government and private sources pumped $10 billion into Latin America during the 1960s, more than that amount of capital flowed out from the area. Debt service payments ate up an increasing share of the budgets of Latin American nations, leaving little for social welfare expenditures and economic development. Often, these nations had to obtain new loans just to pay off their old debts. Unfortunately, too, a significant percentage of aid funds was dissipated through corruption and inefficiency.

U.S. support for the Latin American military was the most effective program of the Alliance. Officers from the region received the most modern training in counterinsurgency tactics against both rural and urban guerrillas and were indoctrinated in the U.S. worldview. Sophisticated torture techniques formed part of the curriculum. One indication of the thoroughness of the training was the success of U.S.-trained and equipped Bolivian rangers in hunting down Che Guevara and his comrades. The United States also urged Latin American military leaders to take a more positive role in their nations' development by participating in civic action programs in which military personnel built roads and other public facilities.

It was clear, however, that despite the Kennedy administration's avowed goal of helping Latin America "strike off the remaining bonds of poverty and ignorance," its major concern was to maintain friendly capitalist regimes in the region. Kennedy continued to interfere in the internal affairs of countries in the area, even after the debacle of the Bay of Pigs. In 1961 he attempted to destroy the regime of Cheddi Jagan in British Guiana for a second time by refusing to grant much-needed aid and pressing the British to overturn the democratically elected premier. The CIA also helped subvert the Jagan government. Kennedy was involved in attempts to rid the Dominican Republic of Rafael Trujillo, and there are allegations that the CIA was responsible for the assassination of the dictator in 1961. In his zeal to get rid of Fidel Castro, Kennedy even planned to enlist the aid of the Mafia to liquidate the Cuban leader.

Like its predecessors, the Kennedy administration supported dictatorial regimes in Latin America when U.S. policymakers considered them the only alternative to disorder and possible revolution. In March 1962 the United States made no protest when the Argentine military overthrew the democratically elected President Arturo Frondizi. Four months later, the U.S.-trained and equipped Peruvian army seized power to prevent a democratically elected president from taking office. For a time, the United States withheld recognition and cut off aid, but it soon reached an understanding with the military regime. Like its predecessors, the

Kennedy administration preferred order, even at the expense of democracy.

President Lyndon Johnson carried on Kennedy's Latin American program, although he increasingly shifted the emphasis of U.S. policy from reform to the maintenance of order. Johnson was determined that he, unlike Kennedy, would not "lose" any nation in any part of the world to communism. In the Dominican Republic in 1965, Johnson faced a rebellion against a reactionary military regime that less than two years before had overthrown the nation's first democratically elected president. Johnson claimed that the United States had the right to intervene unilaterally in Latin America to prevent what he feared would be a Castro-like communist takeover. He dispatched the Marines to suppress the rebellion. Johnson was undoubtedly worried about another Cuba in the Dominican Republic, but there is considerable evidence to indicate that his administration's main concern was to assure Dominican sugar production for several important U.S. firms. Not coincidentally, several of Johnson's key foreign policy advisers, including Ellsworth Bunker and W. Averell Harriman, had close links to the sugar industry.

Under Johnson, the United States also played a major role in the military overthrow of the leftward-leaning regime of João Goulart in Brazil in 1964. Disapproving of Goulart's proposed "radical" reforms—which included a mild land reform and the grant of the vote to illiterates—the United States cut aid to Brazil to a minimum in 1963 and began to channel funds instead to pro-U.S. state governors. In April 1964 the Brazilian military toppled Goulart and instituted fifteen years of brutal, repressive dictatorship. The Johnson administration immediately recognized the new government. In the next five years, the United States poured more than $1.5 billion in economic and military aid into Brazil, one-quarter of all U.S. aid to Latin America.

The lavish aid funneled to the Brazilian military helped persuade the Argentine military that they should overthrow the faltering regime of President Arturo Illia in June 1966. The United States gave the military government $135 million in aid during the three years following the coup.

In political as well as socioeconomic terms, the results of the Alliance under Kennedy and Johnson were dismaying. When Kennedy took office, Alfredo Stroessner in Paraguay was the only dictator in power in South America. By 1968 military dictators ruled in Argentina, Brazil, and Peru, as well as in Paraguay. In Bolivia and Ecuador, civilian-elected governments served as figureheads for the military. In Central America, the record was worse. Rightist military coups overthrew democratically elected governments in Honduras, Guatemala, and El Salvador. The Somozas tightened their grip on Nicaragua. In 1968 a military coup ousted the elected president of Panama. More important, by every measure, the Alliance failed to stimulate economic development or rectify the immense economic and social inequalities of Latin America.

THE VIETNAM ERA

From the late 1960s until 1981, the repercussions of the disastrous U.S. experience in Vietnam and related developments produced readjustments in U.S. foreign policy toward its southern neighbors. But the main goal of this policy—to protect and expand North American economic interests and maintain capitalism as the dominant economic system in the region—remained constant.

In the aftermath of Vietnam, U.S. policymakers did not regard overt military intervention as a realistic option. They relied on such indirect methods as economic sanctions and subversion. The United States used these methods in Chile from 1970 to 1973 to undermine and ultimately to topple a democratically elected socialist government.

The story began in 1958, when the Socialist Salvador Allende narrowly missed victory in the Chilean presidential election. For the next fifteen years, the U.S. government poured millions of dollars into Chile, first to prevent Allende from winning subsequent elections, and then, after his election in 1970, to subvert his administration. The United States helped Eduardo Frei, a moderate reformer, win the presidency and thereafter sent an average of $130 million a year in aid to Chile. Despite this enormous effort and the injection of more millions of dollars in the 1970 campaign, Allende was elected president in 1970.

The United States then tried to orchestrate a military coup d'état, but when it failed, Nixon imposed economic sanctions on the Allende government, cutting aid by 90 percent and denying credit. Meanwhile, the CIA cooperated with opposition groups to destabilize the Chilean economy. Amid growing economic difficulties and political turmoil, the Chilean military overthrew Allende in a bloody coup in September 1973. The United States promptly recognized the military junta and resumed aid and credit.

The U.S. economic stake in Chile, as we saw in Chapter 14, was large and concentrated primarily in copper mining. The first act of the Allende government, supported by the unanimous vote of the Chilean Congress, had been to expropriate the holdings of the U.S. copper companies without compensation. Later, it expropriated the International Telephone and Telegraph Company, whose president enjoyed considerable influence in the Nixon administration. The United States intervened both to protect these investments and to teach a salutary lesson to other Latin American nations that might wish to construct a socialist society in the future.

Nixon also collaborated with brutal military regimes in Argentina and Brazil that organized an international terrorist network, later known as Operation Condor, designed to destroy leftist, antidictatorial political movements throughout South America. An early example of this cooperation developed in response to popular support for the *Frente Amplio* (Broad Front), a coalition of Socialists, Communists, and Christian Democrats, in the 1971 Uruguayan presidential elections. Determined to reduce "the threat of a political takeover by the Frente," Nixon systematically cultivated Brazilian and Argentine military leaders and, in the words of a U.S. Embassy strategy paper, encouraged them to "collaborate effectively with the Uruguayan security forces" to harass Frente candidates and otherwise intervene in the election to secure their defeat. According to a declassified document recently published by the National Security Archive, Nixon himself told British Prime Minister Edward Heath that he knew "Brazil helped rig the Uruguayan elections."

Nixon and his National Security Adviser Henry Kissinger especially identified with these dictators. After a series of personal meetings with Brazil's Garrastazu Médici, Nixon described him as a "strong" ruler whom he wished "were running the whole continent." Kissinger made clear his growing reliance on Brazil as a proxy for U.S. interests in the region. "In areas of mutual concern such as the situations in Uruguay and Bolivia," Kissinger confided to Médici, referring to Brazilian involvement in a 1971 Bolivian coup, "close cooperation and parallel approaches can be very helpful for our common objectives." But Kissinger also made clear his understanding that massive intervention in the internal affairs of sovereign nations, such as he and Médici were contemplating, would not endear them to Latin American people. "[A]s Brazil plays a stronger leadership role," Kissinger lectured, "it may find itself in a position similar to that of the U.S.—respected and admired, but not liked."

CARTER'S LATIN AMERICAN POLICY: NATIONALISM, THE CANAL, AND HUMAN RIGHTS

President Jimmy Carter took office in 1977 proclaiming a "new approach" for U.S. foreign policy based on "a high regard for the individuality and sovereignty of each Latin American and Caribbean nation . . . our respect for human rights, . . . [and] our desire to press forward on the great issues which affect the relations between the developed and developing nations." He immediately put these principles into practice in two major initiatives: the reopening of negotiations with Panama over the canal and the beginning of talks with Cuba about normalization of relations.

Periodically since the signing of the original canal treaty, Panamanians violently protested the U.S. presence in the middle of their country; serious anti-U.S. riots erupted in 1931, 1947, 1959, and 1964. These riots occurred in times of economic hardship in Panama and remained a source of tension that Carter and General Omar Torrijos sought to remove. After four years of sometimes bitter negotiations, the United States and Panama agreed to a new treaty that gradually returned control of the Canal Zone to Panama by the year 2000. Although Panamanians were unhappy with a provision that gave the United States the right to intervene to maintain the operation of the canal, it was received with general satisfaction in Panama and throughout Latin America.

Negotiations with Cuba led eventually to the opening of United States and Cuban Interest Sections in Havana and Washington in September 1977. These initiatives were short-lived, however, for the two nations came into conflict early in 1978 over Cuba's extensive military involvement in Africa, particularly in Angola and Ethiopia. The Carter administration strenuously objected to the presence of thirty-five thousand Cuban troops in Africa and broke off further talks as a result. Relations worsened during 1980 as a consequence of the exodus of 125,000 Cuban refugees to the United States.

Carter's pursuit of human rights proved to be the most controversial aspect of his foreign policy. He centered his attention on Chile, Argentina, and Brazil, the harshest practitioners of repression in the region. The United States instituted sanctions against all of these nations, ending or reducing economic and military aid and impeding their ability to obtain credit from international lending agencies. In the last two years of his term, as a result of stepped-up pressure from U.S. business and concern about growing communist influence in Central America, Carter backed off his human rights activism.

Nicaragua proved to be Carter's most difficult and pressing problem in Latin America. The growing insurrection of the Sandinista National Liberation Front, a broad coalition movement against the U.S.-backed dictator Anastasio Somoza, brought Nicaragua to crisis in 1978. Carter, worried about leftist elements in the Sandinista coalition, sought a more moderate alternative, proposing at one point that the Sandinistas include members of the hated National Guard in the postrevolution Nicaraguan government. Following the Sandinista victory in 1979, the United States offered economic aid to rebuild the nation devastated by civil war. After

considerable debate the U.S. Congress approved $75 million, most of which was designed to support private-sector businesses that opposed the Sandinista government.

The Return to "Gunboat Diplomacy," 1981–2003

Ronald Reagan became president in 1981 determined to turn back "communism" in Latin America and reassert U.S. military power. In the process he openly courted repressive right-wing regimes in Argentina and Chile and committed substantial amounts of U.S. money and military advisers to the antiguerrilla war in Central America. During the next two decades, the U.S. decision to intervene militarily or to refrain from intervention revealed traditional U.S. open-door objectives, perhaps most concisely articulated by John Hay in 1898: "a fair field and no favor."

GRENADA

On October 25, 1983, the United States invaded the tiny island nation of Grenada in the southern Caribbean to oust its allegedly communist, pro-Cuban government. The Reagan administration proclaimed the invasion its greatest triumph in Latin American policy.

In March 1979 the New Jewel Movement, led by Maurice Bishop, had overthrown the British and U.S.-backed dictatorship of Eric Gairy, who had dominated Grenadan politics since the early 1950s. Bishop's program included a massive literacy campaign, the institution of free medical care, free secondary education, and extensive rehabilitation of housing. He regulated foreign investment and stressed agricultural independence, reducing Grenadan food imports. Bishop began to expand tourism, mainly by building a modern airport. The Reagan administration threatened repeatedly to intervene against the popular Bishop regime, but finally invaded Grenada after a radical faction of Bishop's own party had assassinated him.

The invasion of Grenada showed clearly that the United States was as willing as ever to use force to protect its perceived interests in the Caribbean.

The action also conveyed the message—as did U.S. policies in Central America—that the United States opposed far-reaching economic and social reform in its "back yard." Moreover, Grenada, like so many other "crises" in the region, was not seen as a nation struggling to overcome impoverishment, but as part of a worldwide communist threat or at the very least as "another Cuba."

Haiti

The United States played a decisive role in the history of Haiti, the poorest country in Latin America and one of the poorest in the world.

During the long U.S. military occupation of Haiti from 1915 to 1934, the Haitian elite's monopoly of property was preserved and its dependence on coffee exports was reinforced. The U.S. also trained a national army "specifically to fight Haitians." This army imposed the rule of the sinister François "Papa Doc" Duvalier on Haiti in 1957. Duvalier in turn used the army to centralize power in his own hands to an unprecedented degree. He could not tolerate the existence of any independent institution; distrusting his own army, he organized two parallel paramilitary organizations, a much-feared militia and the overlapping secret police, the even more dreaded Tontons Macoutes. The United States may not have approved of his methods, but it supported him, and when he died in 1971 U.S. Ambassador Clinton Knox personally supervised the transition to the rule of the dictator's son, eighteen-year-old Jean-Claude Duvalier.

The predatory, repressive rule of the Duvaliers aggravated all of Haiti's economic and social problems. The ruin of Haitian agriculture as a result of long misuse of the land and the exactions of the regime caused many thousands of impoverished peasants to flock into the urban centers, especially the shantytowns of Port-au-Prince and its environs where between 1.2 and 1.8 million people endured unspeakable conditions. Workers' families usually ate only one meal a day, consisting of cornmeal with onions or boiled plantains with beans.

Acting on U.S. advice, Jean-Claude Duvalier tried to promote economic growth by using this vast underclass to establish export-assembly industries, subcontracted to U.S. firms. But this program did not diminish the immense inequalities of Haitian society or the growing anger of the masses. In 1986 an explosion of urban rioting forced Jean-Claude to depart from Haiti; he was whisked away to a luxurious exile in a jet provided by the Reagan administration. The U.S. Agency for International Development (USAID), meanwhile, continued to promote Haiti as a low-wage haven for U.S. firms, expending $100 million in the effort. A delegation of U.S. trade-union leaders, visiting a "model" apparel factory in Haiti's export-assembly sector in 1991, found that the highest-paid workers received the equivalent of $1.47 a day. After paying for transportation and a meager breakfast and lunch they had 71 cents to take home.

Jean-Claude Duvalier's departure created a political vacuum that U.S. policymakers rushed to fill. They supported Marc Bazin, linked to export-assembly industries and agribusinesses, and opposed Jean-Bertrand Aristide, a populist priest influenced by liberation theology. Aristide represented grassroots worker, peasant, and student organizations. He supported a massive literacy campaign, land reform, defense of national industries, and an end to Duvalierist violence and corruption. His program included price controls on basic foodstuffs and raising the minimum hourly wage to fifty cents. Despite U.S. support and a $36 million campaign, Bazin lost to Aristide, who received 67 percent of the vote. But he held power for only eight months; in September 1991 a military coup headed by Lieutenant General Raoul Cédras forced him into exile. The coup unleashed a reign of terror in Haiti, claiming thousands of lives and causing a flood of refugees.

The Bush administration's response to the coup was marked by an ambiguity reflecting the contradictions of U.S. foreign policy. The United States rhetorically claimed to support constitutionally elected civilian regimes like Aristide's, but Aristide's anti-imperialism and opposition to neoliberalism contradicted basic U.S. foreign policy objectives. President Bush denounced the coup and said he wanted Aristide's return to power. But this pro-Aristide rhetoric was contradicted by a policy of limiting sanctions against the coup leaders to a "porous" embargo easily breached by exporters and importers and of permitting open attacks against Aristide by a State Department–driven media campaign and CIA leaks casting doubt on his mental stability. The U.S. government also pressured him to moderate his positions and strike a deal with the coup leaders.

President Clinton continued Bush's Haitian policy, virtually unchanged, when he took office in January 1993. He forced Aristide to negotiate with the coup leaders and sought to impose conditions that would leave Aristide powerless to carry out his program, once returned to power. This was the essence of the 1993 Governors Island Accord, which called for the military rulers to resign, with the promise of amnesty, and for Aristide to return to power under the control of U.N. monitors and "peacekeeping" forces, an arrangement vehemently opposed by Haitian popular organizations. But U.S. and Canadian troops refused to enforce the agreement when about 100 armed anti-Aristide thugs demonstrated at the port and threatened foreign diplomats. The quick pull-back suggested Pentagon and CIA reluctance to be involved in restoring Aristide to power on any terms.

Even after Clinton talked openly of a military intervention to restore Aristide to the presidency, according to *The Nation*, he made it "distressingly clear that Haitian independence is not on their minds, and that if exiled President Jean-Bertrand Aristide is returned at the head of an American expeditionary force, the result will be continued clienthood, not freedom."

In the event, after a barrage of publicity about an impending invasion to oust Haiti's military rulers if they did not leave peacefully, a carefully staged "solution" of the Haitian problem came with startling suddenness. On the evening of September 18, 1994, a U.S. delegation led by ex-president Jimmy Carter and the Haitian military signed an accord that provided "an early and honorable retirement" for "certain military officers," full amnesty for all human rights abuses, the eventual return of President Aristide to serve out his term, which ended in 1996, and new elections in December 1995. The accord envisioned that a U.S. occupation force of some fifteen thousand troops

The role for former president Jimmy Carter, shown here with the Haitian president Jean-Bertrand Aristide, in negotiating the accord with the military junta that restored Aristide to office in October 1994, displeased many Haitians who believed the accord was too favorable to the military and seriously abrogated Aristide's power. [AP/Wide World Photos]

would remain for an indefinite period to retrain the Haitian army and police.

Aristide's return to Haiti in October 1994 was greeted with joyful demonstrations by his adoring followers. It soon became clear, however, that he was not his own man; on issue after issue his U.S. military and political advisers forced him to back down. Aristide wanted to fire the entire army high command and supervise the formation of a new army and police within his government, but the U.S. military vetoed his plan. The new "professionalized" army and police would be "retrained" and "candidates" for "professionalization" would be drawn largely from the old armed forces, many of the officers and specialists of which had been trained at the notorious School of the Americas at Ft. Benning, Georgia.

Aristide's candidate for prime minister, who had served as foreign minister in his previous government, was turned down by the Haitian business sector and U.S. officials, and the president was forced to accept businessman Smarck Michel to head the new twenty-member cabinet. Virtually none of its members represented the grassroots movement that had brought Aristide to power, but the cabinet was full of people who supported and benefited from the coup d'état. U.S. advisers were working in key offices and ministries to advise Haiti in its return to democracy. Critics complained that in addition to pro-coup politicians and U.S. advisers, Aristide's chief allies appeared to be the Haitian business sector (whom he once described as "patriots of the pocketbook") and U.S. Ambassador William Swing, who almost always accompanied him when he left the palace.

Under U.S. pressure, Aristide scrapped his nationalist program for reviving Haiti's state industries and accepted a program of neoliberal "structural readjustment" of the economy, by which those industries would be sold to private capitalists, both Haitian and U.S. As summarized by Allan Nairn, the plan included, among other features, commitments from Haiti "to eliminate the jobs of half of its civil servants, massively privatize public services, 'drastically' slash tariffs and import restrictions, eschew price and foreign exchange controls, grant 'emergency' aid to the export sector, enforce an 'open foreign investment policy' . . . 'limit the scope of state activity' and regulation . . . and diminish the power of Aristide's executive branch in favor of the more conservative Parliament." In return, Haiti would receive $700 million in financial aid, but $80 million of this would immediately go to pay the debt accrued to foreign bankers in the three years since the coup.

Ordinary Haitians were surprised at what had happened to their idol. The Aristide they elected came to power as the representative of a massive grassroots movement, calling itself the *lavalas* (flood), that proposed to attack the country's fundamental social problems and end the traditional monopoly of power by a repressive military allied with a corrupt merchant bourgeoisie and U.S. economic interests. The new Aristide appeared to have

cut a deal with the World Bank and the IMF that sacrificed the popular welfare in exchange for $700 million in aid. Chevannes Jean-Baptiste, leader of Haiti's largest peasant organization, had already warned against premature celebration of Aristide's return in the wake of the U.S. invasion: "Don't celebrate and think that the U.S. army is here to liberate us. Only Haitians can free Haiti!"

CENTRAL AMERICA

Ronald Reagan's campaigns against the leftist Sandinista regime in Nicaragua and the leftist Farabundo Martí National Liberation Front (FMLN) in El Salvador took on all the characteristics of a holy crusade against communist forces in Central America. Reagan opposed the nationalistic efforts of both groups to use state power to regulate private property and foreign trade to benefit the nation's poor peasants and urban workers. He sought to overthrow the Sandinistas, employing tactics that included economic sanctions, a campaign of public misinformation, support of rightist counterrevolutionary armies (the contras), and covert terrorist operations aided by the CIA.

One of Reagan's first official acts in 1981 was to cut off the last $15 million in aid appropriated by Congress at President Carter's request. More severe economic sanctions followed. By the end of 1985, the United States had effectively foreclosed any possibility of the Sandinistas obtaining loans from any of the major international lending agencies, such as the World Bank or the Inter-American Development Bank. The U.S. government closed Nicaragua's consulates and even forbade the Nicaraguan airline from landing in the United States. The misinformation campaign included unproven allegations against the Sandinistas of running arms to El Salvador, smuggling illegal drugs, and training terrorists.

By far the most damaging U.S. policy against the Sandinistas was support of the armed opposition to the Nicaraguan government. Predominantly led by ex-Somocista National Guardsmen, the contras were the 1979 creation of the CIA, which recruited ex-guardsman Enrique Bermúdez as their leader. In Reagan's first year in office, he secretly funneled $40 million to support these counterrevolutionaries. The CIA forged the Nicaraguan Democratic Force in late 1981, temporarily unifying the contra factions.

Frustrated with Reagan's policy, the U.S. Congress passed the so-called Boland Amendment, which forbade the use of funds to overthrow the Sandinistas; this legislation was in effect from December 1982 until December 1983, but the Reagan administration, in violation of the law, continued to provide covert support. In early 1984 the CIA mined Nicaraguan harbors and staged several helicopter attacks inside Nicaragua. Later that year a CIA manual became public that advised the contras to employ terrorist tactics, including assassinations. The ensuing furor led the Congress to cut off aid to the contras. Nonetheless, by 1987 the United States had invested $200 million in support of the contras and had little to show for it. The counterrevolutionaries were corrupt and quarrelsome, their civilian and military leaders hopelessly divided, and they had made no military headway in overthrowing the Nicaraguan government.

Evidently fearing that the Sandinistas would win a free and fair election in Nicaragua, the Reagan and Bush administrations obstructed the peace process initiated by the Guatemala City Accords of August 1987 and continued to provide millions in "humanitarian" aid to the contras until February 25, 1990, the date of the elections. The United States also gave millions of dollars in aid to the anti-Sandinista coalition (UNO). Exhausted by almost ten years of U.S.-supported contra war and the U.S. economic blockade, Nicaraguans by a large majority voted in the UNO candidate for president, Violeta Chamorro.

In the process of taking over the counterinsurgency war in El Salvador, the United States took over the nation's economy and politics as well. The United States consistently interfered in Salvadoran politics, successfully keeping the far right, led by Roberto D'Aubuisson, from taking power in 1984 and shoring up the tottering centrist government of President José Napoleon Duarte.

The United States poured some $4.5 billion from 1979 to 1990 into a futile military effort to defeat the FMLN guerrillas. This included massive military assistance in the form of equipment and training. Between fifty and a hundred U.S. advisers planned the counterinsurgency campaign, sometimes accompanying Salvadoran government troops in antiguerrilla forays. For a time, during 1984 and 1985, the Salvadoran army kept the guerrillas at bay because of its advantages in equipment. By early 1987, however, the FMLN was again striking at government forces and installations in almost every part of the country at will. Under domestic and U.S. pressure, both Duarte and his successors initiated peace talks with the guerrillas that led to peace accords in 1992 providing for reform of the armed forces and security services, dismantling of FMLN military structures, and elections in which leftist parties, for the first time in El Salvador's history, could take part.

THE INVASION OF PANAMA

Upon his election as president in 1988, George Bush vigorously continued Reagan's Latin American policy of maintaining and reinforcing U.S. dominance over the region. The new noninterventionist course pursued by the Soviet Union, which withdrew its troops from Afghanistan and made no effort to prevent the collapse of Stalinist-type regimes in Eastern and central Europe, was interpreted by Washington to mean that its freedom of action was no longer hampered by the possibility of a Soviet response. Most Latin American countries, mired in the greatest depression in the continent's history and heavily indebted to U.S. banks, were unlikely to make more than token protests against U.S. interventionist actions. If the end of the cold war deprived U.S. imperialism of its stock in trade, the bogeyman of "international communism," a new villain, the Latin American *narcotraficante*, the drug trafficker, provided a convenient pretext for an armed intervention that could advance traditional U.S. strategic and economic interests.

Bush justified the December 1989 invasion of Panama by the need to protect U.S. citizens (a U.S. Marine had been killed in a shooting incident), defend democracy, seize dictator Manuel Antonio Noriega on drug charges, and protect the canal.

These arguments convinced few foreign governments; the great majority denounced or deplored the invasion as a violation of the U.N. charter, the Organization of American States, and the Panama Canal Treaty. But they were accepted without questioning by the U.S. press, which "did little more than parrot the Bush administration's transparent legal justifications for the invasion." The press ignored the fact that until he began to display an inconvenient nationalist independence and stopped being "our man in Panama," Noriega was a prized ally of the United States, receiving, by conservative estimates, more than $1.2 million in payoffs from the CIA just during the last ten years of his thirty-year connection with the agency. As regards his drug connections, as recently as February 1987 Noriega had received a letter from the U.S. Drug Enforcement Administration (DEA), expressing its gratitude for his traditional position of support for the DEA and the cooperation of his army. The notion that Bush, the former CIA director, did not know of Noriega's drug links strains one's credulity.

The press overlooked, too, long-standing Republican objections to the Carter-Torrijos canal treaties, which provided that in the year 2000 the canal would become Panamanian territory and the U.S. military bases would be dismantled. A document titled "Santa Fe II: A Strategy for Latin America in the Nineties," issued during the 1988 campaign and reflecting the views of the Republican right, in effect provided a blueprint for the invasion, stressing the need for the replacement of Noriega by a "democratic regime" with which the United States would hold talks concerning "the United States' retention of limited facilities in Panama . . . for proper force projection throughout the Western Hemisphere." These and other recommendations in the Santa Fe document closely conformed to the Bush administration's Panama policies.

The administration proclaimed "Operation Just Cause" a huge success. Panamanian resistance was soon broken by intense bombardment. Twenty-four American soldiers were killed; estimates of the Panamanian death toll ranged from Washington's figure of 516 to the figure given by

an independent commission of inquiry of between 3,000 and 4,000, the great majority being civilians. The areas hardest hit by the invasion were the poorest neighborhoods of Panama City, inhabited primarily by black and mixed-race people. Thousands were made homeless and resettled in refugee camps that often lacked medical care, sanitary facilities, and food. It was estimated that the invasion had cost $2 billion in damages and reduced the country's economic life, already moribund as a result of U.S. economic sanctions, to paralysis.

In the midst of the invasion, a new president and two vice presidents were sworn in, fittingly enough at a military base of the U.S. Southern Command. The new president, Guillermo Endara, represented the traditional oligarchy of very wealthy white families (90 percent of Panama's 2,200,000 population is black, mulatto, or mestizo) who lost their political but not their economic power as a result of a reformist, nationalist 1968 revolution led by Omar Torrijos. This handful of families, linked by intermarriage and corporate boards, controlled some 150 of Panama's principal businesses. Once again, U.S. policy had rescued propertied elites and preserved open markets for trade and investment.

LATIN AMERICA AND THE GULF WAR

Latin America felt the impact of the crisis that began with the Iraqi invasion of Kuwait in August 1990 and erupted into the short but destructive Gulf War in February 1991. For most countries of the region, heavily dependent on oil imports, the economic effects of the dramatic rise in oil prices were profoundly negative. Brazil, the largest oil importer, was particularly hard hit, for it had a barter arrangement with Iraq whereby it paid for oil with manufactured goods, and U.N. sanctions against Iraq forced Brazil to use its limited hard currency to buy oil from other sources at world market prices. The region's oil exporters— Venezuela, Mexico, Ecuador, Colombia, and Trinidad and Tobago—profited by increasing their oil exports to compensate for the loss of Iraqi and Kuwaiti supplies and to take advantage of the sharp rise in crude oil prices. But even they stood to lose in the long run—the unexpectedly quick ending of the war left them with large oil surpluses, forcing prices down to much lower levels.

Although most Latin Americans condemned Iraq's invasion of Kuwait, polls showed that they opposed the war option by equal or even greater majorities. In Argentina, whose government was the only one to give military aid to the coalition led by the United States, 91 percent of those questioned opposed Argentina's participation in the war and demanded the return of the two warships sent to join the multinational force. In general, editorial opinion was strongly critical of President Bush's haste to abandon reliance on sanctions against Iraq in favor of war, his rejection of various peace proposals, and the massive destruction of life and material resources caused by the war. There was widespread skepticism, too, regarding Bush's professions of concern for self-determination by critics who recalled the U.S. invasions of Panama and Grenada and the covert war against Nicaragua. Many regarded Bush's call for a "new world order" as a thin disguise for the vision of a unipolar world dominated by the United States, the only superpower.

Toward a New World Order?

With the collapse of the Soviet Union, U.S. policy in Latin America focused on promoting free trade. The Clinton administration's stand on a series of issues—economic policy toward Latin America, Cuba, human rights, and the drug problem—reflected this essential continuity in foreign policy.

With the IMF and World Bank as "enforcers," U.S. policy used debt as a powerful coercive weapon to impose on Latin America a neoliberal economic system based on free trade and privatization. That system required Latin American countries to nullify past advances toward economic independence, to sell at bargain prices valuable national enterprises, and to enact austerity programs that helped increase the number of people living in poverty by 39 percent in the course of the 1980s. By the late 1990s, even the World Bank's conservative estimates of Latin American poverty had risen from 31.5 percent of the people in 1989 to 38 percent; worse still, this growing poverty was accompanied by modest economic growth.

The imposition of this system prepared the way for the logical next step, the incorporation of the area into a U.S.-dominated Western Hemisphere common market that would aid the United States in its growing competition with Japan and Europe. The continuity of the Reagan-Bush-Clinton policies in this area was illustrated by the North American Free Trade Agreement with Mexico, negotiated by Bush and pushed through Congress by Clinton over the virtually unanimous opposition of the labor movement that had ensured his election. Similar free-trade agreements were projected with other Latin American countries, beginning with Chile.

Given the absence of strong trade-union movements in many Latin American countries, including some, like Mexico, where democracy was little more than a façade, NAFTA-type agreements in effect placed U.S. and Latin American workers in competition to see who would produce goods for the U.S. and Canadian consumer markets for the lowest possible wages. According to Public Citizen's Trade Watch, although the Clinton administration had promised 200,000 new jobs per year in the United States, after five years it was unable to document any new jobs produced by NAFTA even as it certified that nearly 215,000 U.S. workers were casualties of the agreement. While maquiladoras lured to Mexico by NAFTA grew by 37 percent and employment skyrocketed, Mexican workers' wages fell by 29 percent since 1994. As a result of NAFTA, poverty rates in Mexico in 1999 rose to 60 percent from an annual average of 34 percent between 1984 and 1994.

In conjunction with provisions of the Uruguay round of the General Agreement on Tariffs and Trade (GATT), these free-trade agreements also posed a major threat to environmental standards. The agreements with Canada and Mexico, for example, set up unelected trinational boards, made up of trade experts, as secret and final arbiters in all decisions relating to commerce and trade. Any federal, state, or local law or regulation, no matter how democratically arrived at,

NAFTA, originally touted as a boon to Mexico both by U.S. opponents and proponents, actually has bankrupted many peasant farmers and led to increased pollution, lower wages, less safe working conditions, and greater political unrest. [Jack Kurtz/ Impact Visuals]

could be set aside by a NAFTA disputation board that identified it as an impediment to trade. The "side agreements" added to Clinton's version of the NAFTA package made the process of challenging a labor rights or environmental violation so difficult and time-consuming that a Mexican government official could "assure concerned industrialists that they should never worry about repercussions from NAFTA's labor and environmental enforcement boards." In fact, since 1993, complaints filed against corporations like General Electric and SONY were routinely dismissed, but even when the board certified a complaint against Han Young, a Korean subcontractor for Hyundai, it lacked mechanisms to enforce the decision.

The dangers of environmental pollution posed by NAFTA and GATT were of course much greater to Latin America than to the United States or Canada. The Third World had already become what Eduardo Galeano calls "a kingdom of impunity" for environmental polluters. In the absence of strong grassroots opposition, NAFTA and GATT enhanced the trend to make the South "the garbage dump of the North."

Cuba provided another test of Clinton's willingness to rethink old and discredited Reagan-Bush policies. The United Nations Assembly three times voted overwhelmingly to condemn the U.S. embargo against Cuba; two summits of Latin American heads of state unanimously voted the same way; and a growing number of Cuban-Americans opposed a policy that inflicted hardships on their relatives on the island and obstructed further liberalization of the Cuban regime. The United States had long maintained normal relations with one great communist power,

China, and in early 1994, in apparent response to pressure from U.S. business circles, President Clinton lifted economic sanctions against communist Vietnam, with which the United States once had fought a long and bloody war. As regards Cuba, however, Clinton appeared frozen in the most hard-line cold war attitude. In part this reflected his political debt to the most powerful and ultra-right Cuban-American leader, Jorge Mas Canosa, son of a Batista official, who, until his death in 1997, controlled the Miami-based Cuban American National Foundation and numerous political action committees whose sole reason for existence was to bring about Fidel Castro's downfall. In what was called "a shameless piece of pandering for the votes of extremist elements of Florida's Cuban exile community," during the election campaign Clinton threatened "to drop the hammer on Cuba." He lost Florida anyway but reportedly received millions of dollars in campaign contributions from Mas Canosa's foundation.

On the subject of human rights, the Clinton administration displayed the opportunism of its predecessors. Clinton claimed to favor civilian regimes and oppose dictatorships and military coups. In practice, however, that position was applied selectively, pragmatically, taking account of the relationship of the country in question to the United States and its acceptance or rejection of U.S.-sponsored economic policies. Thus, the Clinton administration remained silent when the Mexican army and paramilitary organizations ran amuck in Chiapas, carrying out summary executions, torture of prisoners, and aerial attacks on civilian populations. Indeed, U.S. military sales and assistance to Mexico, at a historically low total of $214 million from 1988 to 1992, suddenly skyrocketed to $78 million in 1994 alone and annually averaged well over $100 million thereafter. The number of Mexican officers trained at the U.S. School of the Americas also increased dramatically, from an annual average of 7 to 10 before 1982 to 149 in 1996 and 305 in 1997. With its passage of NAFTA, Mexico, of course, had become a favored U.S. junior partner. The Clinton administration took the same benign attitude toward Peru's President Fujimori's *autogolpe* ("self-

coup") after he proved his firm loyalty to the neoliberal economic doctrine and program. In general, in the words of the *Washington Report on the Hemisphere*, "the Administration seems prepared to wink at moderate human rights violations provided they occur in a 'good cause,' like fighting leftist guerrillas."

Despite rhetoric to the contrary, Clinton continued to militarize the "war on drugs." He inherited from Bush a vast antidrug operation with a heavy stress on military involvement. Bush's 1990 Andean Initiative pledged $2.2 billion in military, legal, and economic assistance over five years to be used in the antidrug campaign. Much of the military assistance was openly employed by the Colombian and Peruvian governments for counterinsurgency campaigns that killed more peasants than insurgents. The United States offered no objection to this misuse of its aid. By Bush's last year in office, the U.S. Southern Command was involved in dozens of operations throughout Latin America. That "messy and unsuccessful engagement" continued under Clinton and involved thousands of soldiers and police and billions of dollars of U.S. taxpayers' money. In fact, Clinton's drug-war budget grew to $16 billion, then the highest in U.S. history. Yet the war failed to reduce the availability or use of drugs in the United States. In September 1993 a Senate Judiciary Committee report concluded: "Regrettably, America's drug epidemic is worse today than it was three years ago."

In the decade after the disintegration of the Soviet Union and its strategic restraints on the unilateral exercise of U.S. power, influential U.S. intellectuals and policymakers struggled to define the appropriate mix of economic, political, diplomatic, and military instruments necessary to govern a "new world order" based upon neoliberal principles of globalization, privatization, state deregulation, and free trade. In this task, they shared a certain sympathy with their British counterparts like Richard Cooper, foreign policy adviser to Britain's Prime Minister Tony Blair, who boldly declared in 2001 that "When dealing with the more old-fashioned kinds of states outside the postmodern continent of Europe, we need to revert to the rougher methods of an earlier era—force, pre-emptive attack, deception." Perhaps more bluntly than others, Cooper alleged, "The opportunity, perhaps even the need, for colonization is as great as it ever was in the 19th century" and called for the mobilization of "a new kind of imperialism."

In the United States, these same ideas emerged less candidly in discussions of "nation-building"—that is, external intervention in the sovereign affairs of underdeveloped nations to create institutions to facilitate the process of globalization and manage the growing popular opposition that its expansion inevitably seemed to produce. To this end, in 1994, under the direction of former U.S. Secretary of State Cyrus Vance, the Carnegie Corporation created the Commission on Preventing Deadly Conflict, the purpose of which, according to its 1997 report, was to promote nation-building through multilateral initiatives, including the use of external force. To identify those disputes in which such intervention was justified, the Commission stressed the need to develop "legal standards," against which it might measure regime legitimacy—that is, the degree to which "the responsibilities of governments to themselves and to their peoples" were carried out. This approach provided the intellectual foundation for many Clinton-era interventions in Latin America.

Also in 1997, however, a conservative organization, the Project for the New American Century (PNAC), founded by William Kristol and Robert Kagan, a Reagan-era deputy in the State Department's Bureau of Inter-American Affairs, took up a similar task, although it emphasized unilateral interference. Supported by many who would become high-ranking policymakers in the Bush administration (including Vice President Cheney), the PNAC openly called for a reassertion of the aggressive imperialist intervention that had characterized early-twentieth-century U.S. foreign affairs. According to its senior fellow, Thomas Donnelly, "American imperialism can bring with it new hopes of liberty, security, and prosperity; its attractions can soften the fear of overweening U.S. military power."

Although candidate George W. Bush in 2000 had denounced "liberal" exercises in nation-

building such as those contemplated by the Carnegie Commission, as president in 2001, he nonetheless continued to support Clinton's global initiatives. Especially after the September 11 terrorist attacks on the Pentagon and World Trade Center, however, the Bush foreign-policy team more vigorously embraced the PNAC's idea, if not the specific language, of unilateral imperialist intervention to protect and promote U.S. interests. "Sovereignty entails obligations," according to Richard Haass, director of policy planning in the Bush State Department. "If a government fails to meet these obligations, then it forfeits some of the normal advantages of sovereignty, including the right to be left alone inside your own territory. Other governments, including the U.S., gain the right to intervene."

Naturally, the key question was: What were the special "obligations" that the Bush administration expected sovereign nations to satisfy to avoid U.S. intervention? First and foremost, the president expected them to oppose terrorists who targeted the United States, but he also insisted that they promote free-market principles and practices. According to one administration spokesperson, U.S. policy stressed "the importance of ruling justly, the importance of investing in one's own people, and the importance of operating in an economic policy framework that creates openings for enterprise and entrepreneurship." This meant "sound economic policies" including "more open markets, sustainable budget policies, and strong support for individual entrepreneurship." Wherever a government or popular forces threatened these values or resisted market reforms, the Bush administration overtly intervened politically and sometimes threatened more serious economic and military intervention.

In Venezuela, for example, in the months prior to and during an ill-fated April 2002 military coup against the democratically elected populist president, Hugo Chávez, high-ranking U.S. government officials met repeatedly with military and civilian coup leaders, including Pedro Carmona, formerly head of the Venezuelan Chamber of Commerce (*Fedecámaras*), who was appointed to replace Chávez. One Venezuelan who attended some of these meetings told *Newsday* that U.S. officials only mildly objected to the idea of a coup, leading him to the inescapable conclusion that "All the United States really cared about was that it was done neatly, with a resignation letter or something to show for it." As the coup unfolded, this seemingly was confirmed by a State Department official who allegedly told a Venezuelan diplomat that, although the United States, as a signatory to "the Inter-American Democratic Charter, which condemns any violation of constitutional rule," officially opposed a military coup, it was nonetheless "necessary that the transition currently under way in Venezuela, which [the United States] understands and sympathizes with, conserve constitutional structures." For this reason, the United States unsuccessfully had counseled Carmona against his planned dismissal of the National Assembly.

Although the Organization of American States and every single Latin American government immediately denounced the coup and called for the restoration of democracy, the Bush administration further embarrassed itself by greeting news of the coup with some measure of enthusiasm. Instead of condemning the coup, officials initially blamed it on the alleged "dictatorial" policies of Chávez, the elected president. Chávez apparently had angered U.S. policymakers by his populist rhetoric, his principled opposition to the U.S. war in Afghanistan, his friendly relations with Cuba and other regimes that the United States opposed, and his resistance to neoliberal policies promoted by the United States, the World Bank, and the IMF.

Similarly, the United States openly intervened in Bolivia. First, under the rubric of fighting a hemispheric war on drugs, it funded a mercenary army known as the Expeditionary Task Force, which was accused of murdering an unarmed peasant union leader and engaging in torture and theft. "These are soldiers with no clearly defined loyalties, and a foreign power is funding them to run around our country with guns," a Bolivian official complained. "The existence of this force is a violation of the Bolivian constitution." More recently, in the summer of 2002, the United States

interfered in Bolivian democratic presidential elections. On election eve, the U.S. ambassador announced to the Bolivian press that the United States would cut off all economic aid to the impoverished nation if it elected Evo Morales, candidate of the Movement Toward Socialism Party and an Aymara indigenous leader who had fiercely resisted a U.S.-sponsored coca eradication program. Morales incurred Bush's wrath with his populist proposals and candid insistence that "capitalism is humanity's worst enemy." Notwithstanding U.S. hostility and covert financial support for his opponents, Morales surprised all political analysts with a second-place finish in the race, with 20 percent of the vote.

The United States also openly intervened in Nicaragua's 2001 presidential elections. After early polls showed that Daniel Ortega, candidate of the leftist Sandinista National Liberation Front, led his nearest rival by almost 10 percentage points, the United States organized a spirited campaign to secure his defeat. The U.S. ambassador pressured a Conservative candidate to drop out of the race to avoid splitting the anti-Ortega vote, vociferously denounced Ortega, loudly supported Enrique Bolaños, and used the distribution of emergency food aid to promote his candidacy. Even Jeb Bush, the president's brother, was enlisted in the campaign, alleging that Ortega associated with those "who shelter and condone international terrorism." In the aftermath of September 11 and President Bush's declaration of a "war on terrorism," this sent a powerful message to Nicaraguans, who a decade earlier already had endured horrendous privations caused by U.S. economic and military intervention.

Meanwhile, in Colombia and Ecuador, the Bush administration expanded the Clinton government's militarization of U.S. policy. Under the guise of interdicting drug smuggling, Plan Colombia, developed during the Clinton years, had authorized billions of dollars to support the Colombian military's counterrevolutionary war against the FARC, a guerrilla insurgency that claimed a popular base in the rural communities that it controlled. Even U.S. Ambassador Myle Frechette privately acknowledged in a confidential 1996 memorandum that the FARC's reputation as drug traffickers "was put together by the Colombian military, who considered it a way to obtain U.S. assistance in the counterinsurgency." Nonetheless, according to one U.S. Special Forces trainer in Colombia, although his mission was "ostensibly to aid the counternarcotics effort," everyone understood "perfectly well" that they were "giving military forces training in infantry counterinsurgency doctrine" and "that narcotics was a flimsy cover story for beefing up the capacity of armed forces, who had lost the confidence of the population through years of abuse."

But U.S. military forces continued to cooperate with Colombian forces accused of human rights violations, despite congressional restrictions on such assistance. In May 2000, according to confidential memoranda released to the National Security Archive, U.S. Ambassador Curtis Kamman alerted the State Department that the U.S. Army's "Bravo Company" was "bedding down" with, and receiving logistical support from, a Colombian infantry brigade, whose authorization to receive U.S. military support had not been approved because of unresolved complaints about its involvement in human rights abuses. The State Department, although it acknowledged that the United States could not legally assist this brigade, nonetheless reassured Kamman that its participation was critical "for the success of Plan Colombia."

Shortly after September 11, however, the Bush administration abandoned even these cursory efforts and shamelessly used the "new war on terrorism" to circumvent congressional controls originally designed to guarantee that U.S. military aid would not support human rights violations. Calling the FARC "the most dangerous international terrorist group based in the Western Hemisphere" and alleging that it "engaged in a campaign of terror against Colombians and U.S. citizens," President Bush authorized an additional $1.3 billion to support the Colombian military in 2001–2002 and requested another $98 million to fund the training of a special Colombian military unit to defend Occidental Petroleum's Caño Limón oil pipeline. The Bush government also dramatically increased military assistance to neighboring Peru, Bolivia, and Ecuador, whose military base at Manta became an especially key strategic asset for the U.S. military. This "Andean Regional Initiative" widened the arena of conflict and promised additional military aid through the Foreign Military Sales program, whose funding for Latin America almost doubled, to $8.7 million in 2001. This not only encouraged these impoverished nations to waste precious resources on more military equipment; it also clearly strengthened a sector of Latin American society that had been a historical enemy of democracy and human rights.

As the new millennium opened, popular movements throughout the region gradually coalesced in their fierce rejection of the neoliberal policies that the United States had promoted relentlessly for two decades. From *piqueteros* in Argentina to the FARC *guerrilleros* in Colombia, Latin America appeared to be in revolt. Although some sought to portray this as the routine chaos characteristic of the continent, others saw it as a natural, almost inevitable, consequence of unregulated markets that created wealth for a few and misery for the many. To be sure, it was unclear just how well-organized and politically disciplined these popular movements were. Likewise, it was uncertain how successful they might be. But one thing was indisputable: they challenged a U.S. foreign policy that historically had prized property rights and free markets over human rights and democratic freedoms.

Latin American Society in Transition

As Latin America entered a new millennium, it became obvious that conventional neoliberal strategies for promoting the area's development were not working. Little progress had been made toward solving the area's stubborn problems of hunger and poverty. Indeed, it was evident that the remedies prescribed by the International Monetary Fund (IMF) and the World Bank had not only failed to cure the patient, but had aggravated its condition. The figures provided by international agencies spoke for themselves. In 1997 the area's foreign debt stood at $644 billion; by the middle of 2002 it had risen to $818.8 billion, representing 31.2 percent of the total foreign debt of developing countries. The rate of economic growth for Latin America and the Caribbean in 2001 was 1 percent. For 2002 it was not expected to exceed 2 percent, far below the level required to reduce poverty and unemployment. As the third millennium opened, more than 180 million Latin Americans lived in extreme poverty. In a report titled "The State of Food Insecurity 2000," the U.N. Food and Agriculture Organization noted that the number of malnourished Latin Americans stood at 55 million, 11 percent of the total population. It appeared that the 1990s, like the 1980s, had become a "lost" decade. In the absence of bold new policies, Latin America seemed doomed to a permanent, unending crisis.

Economic Problems: A Permanent Latin American Crisis?

The Latin American crisis formed part of a larger crisis of the Third World. According to a report of Amnesty International, in more than eighty countries per capita income was less in 2000 than in 1990, and at least 1.3 billion people were trying to live on less than $1 a day. Growing opposition to the policies of what had become known as the "Washington Consensus" was reflected in massive demonstrations in Seattle, Geneva, Barcelona, and other cities where the World Trade Organization (WTO), the IMF, and other organizations with neoliberal agendas met. The protests were not directed against "globalization" in itself, generally understood to be the inevitable result of technological progress, but against its misuse for antihuman ends. Increasingly, establishment voices echoed the popular protests. At a forum held in Havana in February 2002 and attended by hundreds of economists, 1980 Nobel Peace Prize winner Adolfo Pérez Esquivel and Joseph Stiglitz, one of former President Clinton's economic advisers, co-winner of the 2001 Nobel Prize in Economics, and former chief economist of the World Bank, sharply criticized economic globalization as currently applied. Stiglitz described U.S. financial prescriptions for developing countries as hypocritical and harmful, noting that although the Bush administration urged U.S. citizens to spend their way out of recession, it gave just the opposite advice to developing countries. Rather than follow the recommendations of the IMF for sharp spending and job cuts as "shock treatments" for developing countries, those countries would do better to focus on the satisfaction of social needs. Stiglitz cited the example of China, noting that China had increased its national income 250 percent in the past decade, largely by focusing on job creation and the promotion of literacy as the means of reducing poverty.

THE FOREIGN DEBT AND THE ARGENTINE DEBACLE

The immense, unpayable foreign debt was the chief obstacle to the solution of Latin America's problems of poverty and underdevelopment. It weighed like a nightmare on Latin America, draining resources otherwise available for sustainable development and imposing policies that made social justice and economic progress impossible. Recognition that the debt is unpayable would lead to negotiations between debtors and creditors that result in forgiveness of all or the greater part of the debt and the extension of new credits on easier terms, or perhaps in a new system that would put the United Nations in charge of funding development, as suggested by Fidel Castro.

Liberation from the debt was a prior condition for the solution of the food and ecological crises of the area. Freed from the burdens of the debt and the associated transnational corporate control of economic policy, Latin Americans could adopt a new agricultural strategy based on different priorities: they could produce to satisfy the area's nutritional needs rather than promote the production of exportable industrial crops, livestock feed, and luxury fruits and vegetables that enrich agribusinesses and generate foreign exchange to pay interest to foreign bankers. But such a shift of priorities would have to take place within the context of thorough, democratically controlled agrarian reforms to overcome the other major obstacle to regional development: the new capitalistic, highly mechanized *latifundio.* These sharply limited employment and absorbed by legal or illegal means

many small plots previously devoted to staple food production, forcing many small farmers to move into rugged hillsides, rain forests, or other land of poor agricultural quality or to migrate to the cities or plantations in search of employment.

It would be naïve, however, to expect that most Latin American governments, currently controlled by and representing elite interests, would willingly accept such new policies. In addition, these governments likely would be unwilling or unable to strictly monitor and control the activities of foreign corporations that in the past have practiced "garbage imperialism"—that is, using Latin America as a dumping ground for toxic waste by freely polluting its soil and rivers, as they have done in the Mexican-U.S. border zone. Sound environmental policies must recognize the relation between poverty and environmental degradation.

Central America offered a prime example. More than two-thirds of the region's rain forests were destroyed, resulting in the loss of many valuable plants and animal species. Deforestation and watershed destruction caused massive soil erosion, undermining the basis for continued subsistence farming. According to an environmental group's 1998 report, "State of Environment and Natural Resources in Central America," deforestation and soil erosion also made the region much more vulnerable to flash floods and landslides unleashed by natural disasters like Hurricane Mitch. These conditions, not the hurricane's high winds, the report noted, caused thousands of deaths and untold destruction of economic infrastructure. Again, much of the deforestation taking place in the Amazonian rain forest was the result of the exodus of landless peasants to the region, where they made clearings for planting, firewood, and other uses. That is why agrarian reform must occupy a central place in the solution of both the food and the ecological crises.

Recognition that the foreign debt problem is insoluble under existing conditions should be the point of departure in the search for solutions. The roots of the problem lie in the dynamics of foreign debt that spiraled upward from $426 billion in 1987 to more than $812 billion in 2002. To begin with, there was a structural imbalance between the economies of advanced and underdeveloped countries. The former, possessing immense technological and industrial superiority, sold expensive machinery, computer software, and know-how to underdeveloped countries like those of Latin America, which depended for the bulk of their exports on primary products like oil and coffee, subject to wide fluctuations in price and demand. True, in recent decades there was a considerable growth of Latin American industry (the *maquilas* or *maquiladoras*), especially in Mexico, Central America, and the Caribbean, that produced manufactured goods for export. But its benefits to the host countries were limited. This industry was foreign owned and low paid, employing unskilled workers to assemble parts or components made in different places. Mexico assembled computers, for instance; it did not make them. Consequently, it retained only one of every four dollars obtained by the export of these manufactures. Finally, the maquila was a highly mobile industry, easily lured away by the prospect of lower wages in another country.

The unequal terms of trade imposed on Latin America, combined with the tariff barriers and subsidies maintained by countries like the United States to protect their own industries (even as they demanded that the dependent countries open their markets wide to foreign imports and capital) almost ensured that sooner or later an underdeveloped country would develop a balance of payments problem. The volatility of investment flows into and out of dependent countries aggravated the problem, because lenders, fearing a possible currency devaluation and debt default, could initiate a flight of capital that spiraled into a devastating depression. At this point the debtor country would turn for help to the IMF and the World Bank. If the discussions went well and the debtor accepted the stringent "structural adjustment" conditions laid down by the international finance agencies, a rescue operation could restore the country's credit and a new cycle of borrowing could begin. Mexico experienced such an adjustment and its sequel of severe depression in the 1990s. "There is no indication," says Mexican economist Carlos Marichal, "that either Mexico or

any other Latin American nation will soon break out of the boom and bust cycles which have been accompanied by large fluctuations in the flows of capital in and out of the region." The current Argentine crisis, affecting the third largest economy of the region, was another case in point.

As president of Argentina (1989–1999), Carlos Menem implemented a sweeping neoliberal reconstruction of the Argentine economy that the military dictatorships of the 1970s had been unable to achieve. He was the IMF's star pupil, an admirer of Margaret Thatcher, Augusto Pinochet, and Ronald Reagan; so close were his relations with Washington that he described them as *relaciones carnales* (blood relations). The process included privatization of all state-owned industries, often sold at fire-sale prices in an atmosphere of shady deals, elimination of all laws that protected labor, and a plan that tied the peso to fictitious parity with the dollar. The parity plan brought temporary relief from the chronic problem of inflation, but the overpriced peso caused a sharp decline in Argentine exports. By 1998 the country was in a recession that steadily deepened. Per capita income, which was $7,300 in December 2001, had fallen by June 2002 to $2,167, making Argentina the continent's sixth poorest country after Paraguay, El Salvador, Ecuador, Bolivia, and Nicaragua. The economy had been in recession for fourteen consecutive trimesters.

Seeking to avoid default on foreign debt payments, Menem's successor, President Fernando de la Rua and his finance minister Domingo Cavallo decided to limit the payment of salaries, pensions, and bank cash withdrawals, using the money thus saved for interest payments. But those measures could not avert default on the $142 billion foreign debt. Outside the Casa Rosada, the government house in Buenos Aires, huge crowds, banging on pots and pans, gathered to protest denial of access to their money and a brutal police repression that took the lives of twenty-seven young demonstrators. De la Rua's proclamation of a state of siege only added to the public anger. On December 20, 2001, de la Rua resigned, fleeing from the roof of the Casa Rosada in a military helicopter. Three more presidents came and went before a legislative assembly on January 2, 2002, elected the Peronist Eduardo Duhalde to the office, pending new elections.

Duhalde abandoned one-to-one parity of the peso to the dollar, but under pressure from the IMF and the United States agreed to let the peso float. As a result bank accounts lost more than half their value overnight, and the peso continued to sink; by the end of June 2002 the exchange rate was about four pesos to the dollar. Meanwhile Duhalde appealed to the IMF and the United States for approval of new loans. Despite his submission to the IMF's demands for austerity and zero budget deficits and his efforts to placate the United States by pledging to support President Bush's anti-Cuban stance, the IMF moved with extraordinary slowness and countered Duhalde's surrender on various issues with new demands. Some believed the IMF's intent was to teach other dependent countries a lesson in fiscal discipline. Whatever the intent, Duhalde's austerity program required the firing of several hundred thousand public employees, which only aggravated the Argentine economic and social crisis. Assuming the IMF granted new loans, the government's first priority was the resumption of interest payments on the old debt, so fresh loans would be needed to revive the collapsed Argentine economy.

Some economists and sociologists argued for an independent economic policy, free from IMF demands and constraints. An eminent scholar, the sociologist Torcuato di Tella, declared: "We need to find a solution without the help of the IMF, to mobilize our own resources, including state intervention in the financial system and the market place." Argentina, he said, must look to "regional trade blocks like Mercosur," including Brazil, while rejecting U.S.-dominated projects such as the Free Trade Area of the Americas. This independent path, he warned "will not be pretty and it will mean more violence and a decline in the standard of living at first," but it was the only approach that would lead Argentina out of the abyss.

Alongside the shattered old economy and the old politics, in which most Argentines had lost all faith, new ways of living and managing were taking shape. One new phenomenon was a resistance movement whose radical tactics angered conser-vatives. Unemployed workers, called *piqueteros*, blocked traffic on the country's main roads to enforce their demand for food and work, and sometimes for land so they could set up cooperatives to raise food for their families. Numerous consumer and producer cooperatives arose to fill many unsatisfied needs. Some took over closed factories and restored them to bustling life. Other groups engaged in barter to satisfy their mutual needs in an increasingly moneyless economy. In Buenos Aires and other cities popular ward assemblies regularly met to discuss and search for solutions to local and national problems. By 2002 this movement had not assumed a political form or issued a program, but its distrust of the traditional parties (and of the Duhalde government) was very evident. There was a growing demand for new elections to replace the existing Congress, president, and courts.

The most alarming aspect of the situation was the rapid growth of extreme poverty and its accompaniment of hunger, malnutrition, and disease. The monthly subsidy provided by the government to unemployed heads of families was 150 pesos, or less than $40. This amount did not cover essential needs, estimated to require 400 pesos a month for a family of four. The cost of all basic foodstuffs doubled. According to the most recent official figures, 51.4 percent of the 37 million Argentines now lived below the poverty threshold. More than 66 percent of them were children or adolescents. The majority no longer attended school, for lack of money, but they could not find work to ensure their survival. It is estimated that each month 30,000 "new poor" joined their ranks. In this "new map of misery," writes a *Le Monde* correspondent, what was most significant was the steady rise of "extreme poverty" (indigence). By June 2002, 42 percent of the population fell into that category. Six million suffered from malnutrition. Until recently, poverty had been a marginal problem for Argentina; in 1970 only 5 percent of all households were "poor."

Another problem was the discovery that the police and security services continued to shelter former operatives of the military dictatorships, specialists in torture and the disappearance of radicals and liberals, practices that the return to democracy had supposedly ended. Evidence that these leopards had not changed their spots and continued to enjoy immunity and official position came on June 26, 2002, a day of massive demonstrations by piqueteros and other protestors in Buenos Aires. Press photographers captured images of a police officer's cold-blooded murder of two young piqueteros. President Duhalde initially blamed the demonstrators, but later he expressed anger and promised a cleansing of the security services. Meanwhile, reporters for the Argentine newspaper, *Página 12*, discovered that the police officers implicated in the affair previously had worked in the concentration camps organized by the military dictatorship two decades ago. But the unanswered question remained: How did former operatives of the concentration camps, known and identified as such, obtain and retain their official positions?

The Argentine "fever," meanwhile, was spreading, with varying degrees of severity, to its immediate neighbors—Brazil, Paraguay, and Uruguay, and even Chile and Mexico; the symptoms included currency devaluations, rising interest rates, some inflation, declining foreign investments, and growing social turmoil. "Everyone is looking at Argentina," wrote one analyst, "and crying 'The pox! The pox!' as if it were a medieval city attacked by the Black Death."

THE CHOICES BEFORE LATIN AMERICA: INTEGRATE OR DISINTEGRATE

How to escape from the tentacles of a strangling foreign debt and still find the resources needed for development? This was Latin America's major economic problem in 2003, and it daily grew more acute as a global recession spilled over most of the continent and the demand and prices for its staples declined, while the flow of investment capital into the area dried up. Increasingly, Latin Americans seemed determined to abandon, or at least to modify, the current "free-market" or neoliberal economic system and to regain control of their nations' natural resources and use them for the general good. Venezuela, where a military

populist, Hugo Chávez, won a stunning electoral victory on a program of radical reform and then easily triumphed over a botched coup supported and financed by the United States, was one straw in the wind. Another was the Bolivian presidential and congressional election in June 2002. An Aymaran leader of Bolivia's coca farmers, Evo Morales and his party, Movement Toward Socialism, surged forward from 4 percent to 12 percent in pre-election polls and finished second, a hair's breadth behind veteran político and oligarch, Gonzalo Sánchez de Lozada. "Evo Morales doesn't just represent an image of ethnicity," one analyst said. "He also represents ideas that are in style all over the world—anti-globalization, anti-neoliberalism, anti-imperialism." Although Morelos lost the run-off election in the Bolivian Congress, the massive participation of indigenous peoples had forever changed the nation.

A closely related problem waited in the wings, and provoked intense Latin American debate. In the next few years, Latin America must decide to accept or reject President George Bush's proposed Free Trade Area of the Americas (FTAA), an agreement that the Bush administration would like implemented by 2005. Although a majority of Latin American heads of state approved the project in principle at a meeting in Quebec in April 2001, Cuban leader Fidel Castro denounced it as a project for U.S. annexation of the continent, and it was harshly criticized by President Fernando Henrique Cardoso of Brazil and President Hugo Chávez of Venezuela. The lower house of the Brazilian Congress, angered by U.S. protectionist measures against Brazilian products ranging from orange juice to steel, voted unanimously for a nonbinding resolution calling for withdrawal of Brazil from current FTAA negotiations with the United States. The head of the Workers' Party, known to most Brazilians as "Lula," won the 2002 presidential election and joined Castro in regarding FTAA as a policy designed to annex Latin America's wealth rather than promote free trade.

The FTAA had been called NAFTA "on steroids," and was based on the same principles, but went farther than NAFTA in its insistence on ending controls over foreign investment and on limiting the state's economic role. The Bush administration claimed that the new pact would promote prosperity by encouraging the free flow of goods among member countries. Critics argued that the immense disparity in wealth and resources between the United States and its trading partners would inevitably result in a total conquest of Latin American markets by the superpower, eliminating all competition and reducing the Latin American countries to the condition of vassal states. They noted that the new pact, like NAFTA, would allow corporations to sue individual governments over legislation that might diminish private profits, including laws that protect labor, indigenous communities, or the environment. In fact, citing Chapter 11 of NAFTA, a U.S. company had successfully sued Mexico for trying to protect itself against toxic dumping by blocking the company's expansion plan. The FTAA would also bar attempts to restrict the free movement of foreign investment capital into and out of Latin America or prevent the total takeover of Latin American companies by such capital.

Since the FTAA proposal was essentially a vast expansion of NAFTA, a brief review of the latter's impact on the Mexican economy since its adoption in 1994 may be instructive. Mexican observers unanimously agreed that it had resulted in an increase of Mexican economic dependence on the United States, a dependence that was almost absolute in 2002. Mexico sent the United States 90 percent of its manufactured exports and 80 percent of its oil exports. Mexico received from the United States 80 percent of its food, 60 percent of its tourism, and about $8.5 billion a year in direct investment. NAFTA gave a large stimulus to U.S. takeover of Mexican companies. Weakened by the Mexican crisis of 1994–1995, they were frequently sold for half their value. In addition, some of Mexico's principal banks were acquired by U.S., Spanish, and Canadian capital. Mexico's control over its money reached a nadir with Citigroup's purchase of Banamex, Mexico's largest bank, in 2000. In 1997 a Mexican think tank monitoring developments in the private economic sector warned that the Mexican entrepreneurial class was disappearing.

An important result of Mexico's dependence on the United States was that the two countries tended to share good and bad times. But the impact of the bad times on the two countries was very uneven. When the United States sneezes, as the saying goes, Mexico gets pneumonia. Thus the recession that began in the United States in 2001 had a marked negative effect on the Mexican maquiladora export zones along the U.S. border and in the interior. These factories had almost no links to the Mexican economy; they assembled components for U.S. and other multinationals. During 2001 employment in the maquiladora industry declined 12 percent, or more than 170,000 jobs from its peak. The decline was due not only to the U.S. recession but also to the fact that many factories were leaving Mexico, Central America, and the Caribbean for countries like China with even lower wage levels. A Mexican think tank reported in September 2001 that Chinese competition was likely to cost Mexico 42 percent of the volume of its exports. Despite the export sector's pitifully low wages, it produced one-third of Mexico's hard currency income from abroad; so its loss may contribute to a future currency crisis. But the shrinkage of Mexican industry was general, affecting steel, shoes, tires, apparel, and auto parts. In October 2001 Carlos Slim Helu, Mexico's leading entrepreneur, issued a gloomy prognosis and called on the Mexican government to prepare a contingency plan to revive the internal market, stimulate employment, and encourage economic activity to confront a looming global recession.

Mexican agriculture suffered most from NAFTA's progressive reduction of tariffs, however, soon to reach zero. Mexico, the classic land of corn agriculture, had lost much of its domestic market for corn and other basic grains, because Mexican peasants could not compete with the intensive production methods of U.S. farmers, aided by massive government subsidies. Roughly a quarter of the corn consumed in Mexico was produced in the United States. Mexican efforts to raise the issue of subsidies at the U.N. International Conference on Financing for Development in Monterrey, Mexico, in March 2002 produced no concessions by the United States or any other great power. Many Mexican small farmers, no longer able to eke out a living on the *milpa* (corn patch) joined maquiladora workers who had lost their jobs in the desperate, often risky search for work across the border in the United States. The deserted, forlorn appearance of a growing number of Mexican villages reflected the crisis of Mexican agriculture.

The patent failure of NAFTA to promote Mexican development or raise living standards— the number of Mexicans unable to satisfy their basic food needs rose between 1989 and 1998 from 5.2 million to 9.5 million, according to a report of the World Bank—and the general failure of neoliberal strategies to achieve their goals have multiplied opposition to FTAA and U.S. trade policy in general. Posing the problem in terms of a choice between disintegration and integration— between greater economic, political, and cultural independence for Latin America and loss of its independence to a hegemonic United States— Cuba's Fidel Castro, President Cardoso of Brazil, and President Chávez of Venezuela sought to revive Simón Bolívar's broad vision of a united, prosperous, and peaceful Latin America as a model for our time. Supporters of this alternative to FTAA argued that the movement toward Latin American unity should build on the gradual strengthening and expansion of such beginnings as Mercosur (the common market uniting Argentina, Brazil, Uruguay, and Paraguay), slated for destruction if FTAA came to pass. They also favored commercial treaties with the European Union and other groupings in order to diversify trade relations and promote greater competition. FTAA's opponents urged that no Latin American state should approve it without consulting its own people and making sure that its people understood the meaning of the pact. (President Chávez noted that a poll of middle-class people and intellectuals in Venezuela showed that less than 5 percent of them knew what FTAA was.) As the target date of 2005 set by the Bush administration for the pact to go into effect drew nearer, the struggle for approval or rejection promised to grow steadily more heated.

Social Problems

In August 2001 the London newspaper *The Guardian*, noting that British Prime Minister Tony Blair was taking a much needed holiday in Cancún, Mexico, "a place well endowed with that combination of natural beauty and comfortable surroundings that our leaders favor when they gather to order our lives," suggested that the prime minister might notice that "the benefits of the economic liberalization that most countries of Latin America have pursued over the past fifteen years are less evident to those around him than he might hope." *The Guardian* went on to quote the words of a senior U.N. development official: "For the millions of poor, the slum dwellers, globalization now has the face of cruelty, of unemployment and marginalization." A year later, Mexico's leading novelist, Carlos Fuentes, added his voice to the chorus of celebrities who denounced globalization in its current form and application, comparing its effects to those of the savage, unregulated Industrial Revolution of the early nineteenth century. "That this revolution provokes disruption, pain, and injustice is as certain now as it was in the nineteenth century. That this revolution will not go away because of the demonstrations against it is as true as it was in the nineteenth century. . . . But in the streets of Seattle, Prague, Genoa, there is an impatience that little by little is changing into an understanding that it is not enough to demonize globalization; rather it must be transformed into an instrument of public good, of growing well-being."

What these voices tell us is that the social problems provoked by the neoliberal revolution or globalization had reached gigantic, intolerable proportions early in the twenty-first century. In Latin America, as elsewhere in the Third World, the main causes of the social problems were growing poverty and reductions in social programs (social-sector spending declined by more than 50 percent since 1985). Both developments were linked to the ongoing debt crisis and the "structural-adjustment programs" willingly or unwillingly adopted by most Latin American governments in response to that crisis. At a 2001 summit in Caracas, Social Debt and Latin American Integration, Bernardo

Inspired by Pedro de Alvarado's sacking of Tenochtitlán, a famous scene described in the sixteenth-century Florentine Codex, El Fisgón's cartoon depicts the destruction of rain forests and indigenous communities as the second conquest of Latin America. In the 1990s, the conquistadors include the International Monetary Fund, modern technology, and transnational corporations (symbolized by the Coca-Cola bottle). [El Fisgón/NACLA]

Kliksberg, research director at the Inter-American Development Bank (IDB), offered some figures that revealed the extent of Latin America's social problems. He reported that 60 out of every 100 Latin Americans lived in poverty; one-third of the population had no potable water, one of every five mothers gave birth without medical assistance, and the average Latin American's education stopped at the fifth grade. Kliksberg linked the growth of urban violence to high unemployment and low education levels among youth and the demoralization produced by misery and hopelessness. Moreover, he noted that the distribution of income in Latin America was the most unequal in the world; the richest ten percent received an income eighty-four times greater than the poorest ten percent.

These overall figures rightly caused dismay, but they actually diminished the severity of Latin America's social problems because they concealed the much higher levels of poverty and deprivation in those areas of Mexico, Guatemala, Bolivia, Ecuador, Peru, and Haiti heavily populated by indigenous peoples and descendants of enslaved Africans, who suffered the twin indignities of racism and neoliberalism.

POVERTY, HOUSING, AND HEALTH

The scarcity of safe, secure, affordable housing was one of the area's worst social problems. Much of it lacked proper sanitary facilities and was improvised, ranging from thatched huts and caves to tin and plywood shacks. A few countries like Cuba and, more recently, Venezuela under reformist President Hugo Chávez, attacked the problem with programs of low-cost housing construction. In most countries, however—Mexico being a prime example—access to housing for low-income groups had become more limited and difficult since the adoption of the neoliberal economic model in the 1980s, because there were fewer loans available from government agencies and more stringent conditions for low-income borrowers. The housing problem grew ever more acute because of the vast rural exodus that began in most of the area more than half a century ago as the result of the interplay of two forces: the "pull" of the city, which attracted rural people with the frequently illusory prospect of factory work and a better life, and the "push" of the countryside, where the concentration of landownership and the mechanization of agriculture expelled millions of peasants from their farms and jobs. "Poverty and despair," writes Jorge E. Hardoy, a leading student of urban problems, "are behind many of these massive displacements." Latin America's urban population continued to increase at more than twice the rate of the population as a whole. By the year 2000, Latin America had become the most urbanized region of the world, with 75 percent of its population living in towns or cities.

In Central America the rural exodus was delayed, primarily because of that region's smaller economies and stronger dependence on subsistence agriculture. There the flight to the cities began in earnest during the civil wars of the 1980s, as peasants sought refuge from the fighting and persecution by government forces and paramilitary death squads. Since then a series of natural disasters such as Hurricane Mitch (1998)—which caused floods and landslides that killed thousands—earthquakes, and droughts, combined with plummeting agricultural prices and the inability to wrest a living from their small worn-out plots of land, caused massive peasant migrations. International development groups estimate that by 2010, 55 percent of Central America's population will live in cities.

The border zone between Mexico and the United States offers an example of unplanned internal migration and its social consequences. In the last decade a tidal wave of workers, drawn by the opportunity to work in the rapidly expanding maquiladora industry, washed over the zone. "The overwhelmed Mexican border cities," commented the *New York Times* in February 2001, "lack the means to provide the most basic services. One of the country's powerful drug cartels holds sway here in Juárez and drug-related crime is common. Dozens of women who have come to work in the maquiladoras have been abducted, tortured, raped, and murdered, their bodies tossed like garbage in the desert. . . . All along the border, the land, the water, and the air are thick with industrial and human waste. The National Water Commission reports that the towns and cities, strapped for funds, can adequately treat less than 35 percent of the sewage generated daily. About 12 percent of the people living on the border have no access to clean water. Nearly a third live in homes that are not connected to sewage systems. Only about half the streets are paved." The *Times* reported that the dwellings of families that had worked long enough to save money for conventional building materials were simple structures with walls of concrete blocks and tin roofs. Newer arrivals built homes from crates, old tires, and cardboard. But these Third World conditions were not confined to the Mexican side of the border. "Mirror images of these communities dot parts of

the Texas side of the line." Since this report was published, however, the maquiladora boom ended and, in Ciudad Juárez alone, 40,000 maquiladora workers lost their jobs.

In these areas of improvised housing, the absence of adequate drinking water and sewage services contributed to a high incidence of parasitic and infectious diseases. Latin America's rising health problems were clearly related to the continuing economic crisis, the worst since the Great Depression of the 1930s. Purchasing power declined by 40 percent or more in recent years; in some countries half the work force was unemployed or underemployed. Many Latin American governments sharply reduced health services as part of austerity programs designed to meet interest payments on foreign debt. These cutbacks were related to the deterioration of hospital care, decline in pharmaceutical imports, and reduced government support for medical schools.

The relation between economic policy and public health was dramatically illustrated in Argentina where, as a direct result of the debt crisis and economic depression that struck the nation in 1999, the Argentine public health system, once famed for its excellence, collapsed. A correspondent for *Le Monde* visited the Posadas hospital, the most modern in the province of Buenos Aires, in April 2002. He found that hundreds of the hospital's employees had gone on strike because they had not been paid their wages. The hospital had not received the four million pesos that should have come from the Ministry of Health; as a result there were no antibiotics, no syringes, no filters for dialysis, and no radiological plates. Admission to the hospital was limited to the most serious cases, and surgery had been suspended. The reporter found the same critical situation at the children's hospital, the Garrahan. A young pediatrician could not hide his impotent rage. "Cardiovascular surgery has been suspended for a month; nine children have died." The operations were resumed as a result of the doctors' protests and the noisy concerts given by the children's families, banging on pots and pans. *Le Monde*'s correspondent noted that the children came to the hospital with diseases caused by poverty and malnutrition. A few months later, *The Guardian* reported that half of all Argentine infants suffered from anemia and a quarter of all children were suffering from malnutrition. It then pointed to the irony of this happening "in a country so rich in farmland that it produces enough to feed ten times its own population." Meanwhile at Quilmes, a few kilometers from the presidential palace, schoolteachers discovered that hungry children were cooking and eating toads, frogs, and the flesh of sick horses. The massive incidence of malnutrition in Argentina, a "Western" country that until recently was the wealthiest in Latin America, reflected the general deterioration of economic and social conditions in the area.

Children everywhere were the principal victims of malnutrition, the greatest health problem. Recent UNICEF statistics indicated that in Latin America, three thousand children under the age of five died every day; malnutrition was believed to account for half of these deaths. Commercial infant formulas, aggressively promoted in Latin America by such transnational corporations as Nestlé and Bristol Myers, contributed to infant malnutrition because poor women had been persuaded to substitute bottled formula for breast milk. In areas without clean water, the mothers' frequent practice of watering down the milk to save money on formula made bottle feeding especially dangerous for newborns, resulting in repeated epidemics of diarrhea and a vicious cycle of diarrhea and malnutrition that brought early death.

The problem of malnutrition and the associated problem of intestinal disease were most acute in areas heavily populated with indigenous peoples, who typically endured the most severe poverty. In Mexico, for example, 83.6 percent of deaths among indigenous children were caused by intestinal infections, a rate resembling that for African children. In indigenous areas of Mexico, the malnutrition rate approached 60 percent, and 58.12 percent of dwellings lacked clean drinking water, compared with the national rate of 15.7. But the disparity between national rates of poverty and those experienced by indigenous peoples was still broader: 88.3 percent of their dwellings lacked drainage, compared with the national rate of 25

percent; 53 percent of their houses lacked electricity, compared with the national rate of 6.48 percent; their illiteracy rate was 45 percent, compared to the national rate of 10.46 percent; 75 percent of their children failed to complete elementary school, compared to the national rate of 36 percent. Small wonder that Mexico's indigenous peoples, led by their vanguard, the Zapatista Army of National Liberation in Chiapas, demanded autonomy and control of their natural resources.

By June of 2002, Central America, battered in recent years by a succession of natural and man-made disasters, was now the scene of a major health and food crisis, with Guatemala as its epicenter. Even before the worst drought in decades left thousands of subsistence farmers without harvests or food reserves, Guatemala had the highest level of chronic malnutrition in Central America. By the government's own admission, half of all children were chronically malnourished. According to officials, "Nearly 60,000 children under age five now suffer from acute malnutrition, and many of them could perish any day from infections, parasites, and dehydration." In response to this crisis, the U.N. World Food Program organized an emergency feeding project. But this health and food crisis could not be understood in isolation from Guatemala's unjust economic and social structures, marked by a concentration of land and wealth probably unequaled in Latin America. President Alfonso Portillo, himself a member of the elite, conceded that "80 percent of Guatemalans live in misery." That state of misery, we recall, was assured in 1954 when a military revolt, organized and supported by the United States, overthrew the first and only government in Guatemala's history to attempt a serious reform of its economic and social inequalities.

Like earlier Latin American rural migrations, the Central American migration gave rise to a multitude of shantytowns on the edges of cities, often in situations that exposed dwellers to the dangers from which they had fled. In Honduras, which was struck hard by Hurricane Mitch, the hills around Tegucigalpa, the capital, were covered with settlements in landslide zones. In El Salvador, the migrants lived on riverbanks, with makeshift levees of discarded tires their only protection from surging waters. Typical of the improvised construction of these shantytowns was La Nueva Capital, on the edge of Tegucigalpa; here the houses were "cobbled together from scraps of scavenged wood planks and cinder blocks." A government social fund financed new white latrines that "look sturdier than most homes."

"Slums," reflected a *New York Times* correspondent, "have sprung up following a simple rule: where there is space, take it. As a result, the spread of poor communities in high-risk zones is a hallmark of the region's urban growth." The same correspondent ruefully observed: "Development experts said migration had also been pushed along by national governments that had done little to provide sound support for rural communities, often focusing instead on short-term emergency foreign aid, or on attracting foreign-owned factories that offer low-paying jobs."

A striking aspect of Latin American urbanization was the growth in the number of cities with over 1 million inhabitants. Between 1950 and 1970 the number of such cities rose from six to seventeen, and the sum of their populations increased from 15 to 55 million. By 2000 the cities contained about 220 million inhabitants, or about 37 percent of the total Latin American population at that time. In the same period the number of people living below the poverty line increased from 40 percent in 1985 to 60 percent in 2000. Industrialization and the rural exodus together produced the phenomenon of hyperurbanization—the rise of vast urban agglomerations or zones of urban sprawl. About 80 percent of Brazil's industrial production was located in the metropolitan zones of São Paulo, Rio de Janeiro, and Belo Horizonte. Two-thirds of Argentine production was concentrated in the area between Buenos Aires and Rosario. More than half of the industrial production of Chile and Peru was located in the metropolitan zones of Santiago and Lima-Callao, respectively. Caracas accounted for 40 percent of the industrial production of Venezuela. Between 25 and 50 percent of the populations of Uruguay, Mexico, and Argentina lived in the capitals of those countries.

As these vast urban concentrations increased, life became more and more difficult for their inhabitants. All the urban problems—food, housing, drinking water, and transportation—were immensely aggravated. Mexico City was a case in point. In 2002 it had a population of about 20 million. The pollution caused by toxic agents generated by the city's thirty-five thousand industrial establishments and 3 million cars were denounced by medical specialists as a major danger to health and life; half of all infants had unacceptable toxic levels in their blood, which, specialists warned, could reduce IQ levels by as much as 10 percent. (Recently, as a result of more stringent regulation of car use and other measures, the level of air pollution in Mexico City is said to have declined.) Shantytowns covered almost 40 percent of the urban area and housed approximately 4 million people, a large proportion of whom were unemployed or underemployed. In 2001, according to *New York Times* reporter Tim Weiner, nationally some 12 million Mexicans lacked easy access to potable water. "The Latin American metropolis," writes city planner Thomas Angotti, "is characterized by mass poverty and severe environmental pollution on a scale generally unparalleled in the North."

There were important differences between the process of urbanization in the North and the South, leading to different results. In Europe and North America urbanization, industry, and the demand for labor grew at a fairly even pace, but in Latin America industrial growth and the demand for labor lagged far beyond the explosive growth of the urban population. Much of the new industry, especially in foreign-owned sectors, was highly mechanized and automated; it therefore generated little new employment. In a traditional Latin American industry such as textiles, mechanization actually produced a net loss of jobs. The low purchasing power of the masses also hindered the creation of new jobs, for the market for goods was quickly saturated and industry continually operated below capacity. Finally, many of the rural migrants were illiterate and lacked the skills required by modern industry.

Industry's inability to absorb the supply of labor produced an exaggerated growth of the so-called service or informal sector. The growth of this sector considerably exceeded that of the industrial labor force, which grew from 20 to 24 percent of the labor force from 1960 to 1980, while the service sector rose from 33 to 45 percent during the same period. Since the advent of neoliberal reforms in the early 1990s, however, the International Labor Organization estimated that the informal sector accounted for 60 percent of all new jobs and grew by 3.9 percent per year during the decade, compared to an anemic 2.1 percent growth in formal employment. This informal sector included a great number of poorly paid domestic servants and a mass of individuals who eked out a living as lottery vendors, car watchers and washers, shoe shiners, and street vendors of all kinds.

Cuba alone has made a serious effort to check and reverse the hypertrophy of the city. Almost from the day it took power, the revolutionary government undertook to redress the imbalance by shifting the bulk of its investments to the countryside and by raising rural living standards through the provision of adequate medical, educational, and social services, a more rational distribution of the economic infrastructure, and the creation of planned new cities. Despite these efforts, including restrictions on migration to the capital, Havana's population grew to 2,000,000, and the provision of adequate housing to the population remained one of Cuba's most difficult, unsolved problems.

The enormous concentration of poverty, on the one hand, and of wealth, on the other, made the great Latin American city a study in stark contrasts. The Brazilian city of São Paulo, "a city of 18,000,000, populated by the fantastically wealthy and the severely poor with little in between," was a case in point. The alienation inevitably generated by such contrasts was heightened by the new shielded way of life that the very rich chose in response to a surging rate of homicides and kidnappings. São Paulo's homicide rate more than tripled during the 1990s, to some 60 murders per 100,000 residents, compared with 7.8 in New York. "The surge in abductions," reported a *Washington Post* correspondent, "has produced a cottage industry of plastic surgeons who specialize in treating wealthy victims who

return home from their ordeals with sliced ears, severed fingers, and other missing body parts that were sent to family members as threats for ransom payments."

More recently, hundreds of rich Paulistas, accompanied by bodyguards, chose to fly "over their fears" in helicopters to and from their homes to work, business meetings, even to church. Liftoffs were estimated to average 100 per hour, and the city had 240 helipads, compared with 10 in New York City. Home for these Paulistas was a different world from the ever-growing slums, peopled by millions of migrants from the parched, poverty-ridden Northeast, and often ruled by gangs dealing in drugs, kidnapping, and arms. More and more of the wealthy chose to live in walled, guarded communities, like Alphaville, only seven and a half miles from the city center, and home to 30,000 of São Paulo's wealthiest residents. It had three helipads and four entrances and exits, monitored 24 hours a day. Black-clad security guards watched over all communal areas, and at night residents could view their exiting employees as they were patted down and searched in front of a live video feed. São Paulo had more than 300 such communities.

"The elite have made a decision," says Teresa Caldeira, anthropologist and author of the book *City of Walls: Crime, Segregation, and Citizenship in São Paulo.* "Instead of looking to better Brazilian society in general, they are abandoning it and finding their own personal protection behind guarded walls. The rich are retrenching, restricting their lives in incredible ways and living their lives in an increasingly paranoid fashion."

If we assume no basic future change in the Latin American economic and social order, which generated poverty and the associated disorders as part of its normal operation, São Paulo may offer a surreal vision of future life in other great cities of the area. But can such a "paranoid" way of life, based on fear and alienation, long endure?

CRIME AND PUNISHMENT

Crime in Latin America is above all the child of poverty, and the growth of crime in the area faithfully reflected the ongoing concentration of wealth

The killing of homeless street children by death squads, sometimes hired by businessmen and conservative middle-class groups to "cleanse" the streets, is a fairly common Latin American phenomenon, especially in Brazil and Guatemala. Here a group of Brazilian street children organize their own protest against the killing of some of their number. [Viviane Moos/Corbis]

at one end of the social scale and of poverty at the other. Growing poverty and unemployment drove many young people into crime to survive. Public anxiety abetted an official "get-tough" policy on crime, accompanied by a growth of vigilantism and lynching. There was a frightening indifference on the part of the authorities to the killing of thousands of street urchins by death squads, often composed of off-duty policemen. These "children of chaos" had been forced into the streets to fend for themselves or as street vendors to help out their parents. Some became petty criminals and a source of annoyance to businessmen and conservative middle-class groups, some of whom hired off-duty policemen to assassinate the offending children to "cleanse" the streets. Violence against children was most common in Brazil and Guatemala, but also occurred elsewhere.

The Latin American prison system was marked by vast overcrowding, inhumane conditions, brutal treatment of inmates, and long delays—sometimes four to eight years—before prisoners were brought to trial. Until recently, at least, in Colombia and Peru defendants were often brought before "faceless courts" and anonymous witnesses, ostensibly to protect judges and witnesses against reprisals by narcotraffickers and subversives—with an obvious chilling effect on the defense process. Brazil offered a dramatic example of an area-wide trend. The rate of incarceration tripled from 30 prisoners per 100,000 inhabitants in 1969 to 95 per 100,000 in 1995, and then soared again to almost 135 in 2000—an increase in the rate of incarceration of 41 percent over a period of five years, reflecting not only a growth in the crime rate but an all-too-willing acceptance by the public of the notion that more prison sentences for longer terms would halt the crime wave. As of December 2000, Brazil's prisoner population numbered 212,000 inmates.

As a consequence of overcrowding, conditions in Brazil's prisons routinely violated prisoners' rights and state laws (the federal government did not have its own prison system, and the states had charge of the police and the penitentiary system). Torture to obtain information and summary execution of prisoners were common practices. Riots by prisoners protesting intolerable conditions were also common and were put down with ferocity. In a case that broke with the usual pattern of tolerance for police brutality, however, in June 2001 a jury found a former police commander guilty of presiding over the worst prison massacre in Brazilian history and handed down a symbolic sentence of 612 years (six years for each death), although 30 years was the maximum sentence under Brazilian law. To put down a riot the commander had stormed Latin America's largest prison, a rundown structure in São Paulo containing 7,000 inmates and massacred 102 prisoners with machine guns, rifles, and pistols. Many of the corpses were naked, interpreted by human rights defenders as a sign of an inmate's surrender. These defenders hoped that the case marked a turning point in the fight against immunity for brutal police officers.

In Mexico City, another metropolis where crime had skyrocketed and the police were notoriously corrupt (police and former police were believed responsible for 60 percent of the crime), two successive elected mayors of the left-wing PRD launched a reform program that stressed improved pay for police officers and a crackdown on corruption. Although handicapped by inadequate financial aid from the federal government, the program appeared to have achieved some initial success.

In Latin America, the official and unofficial violence against real or suspected lower-class criminals contrasted with the impunity often enjoyed by powerful individuals charged with white-collar crime and great landowners or their gunmen who murdered trade unionists or labor organizers. As a result, according to Brazilian political scientist Paulo Pinheiro, "in almost all Latin American countries the poor see the law as an instrument of oppression at the service of the wealthy and powerful."

EDUCATION

In recent years Latin American leaders like Brazil's president, Fernando Henrique Cardoso, and Mexico's president, Vicente Fox, pledged to make improvement of public education in quantity and quality their primary goal, and a number of countries launched schemes that promised to make regular welfare payments to poor families who kept their children in school. In Brazil, for example, the governor of the capital, Brasilia, introduced a plan in 1996 that paid a minimum wage to poor families who kept all their children in school. The impact of the plan was said to have been "extraordinary," and it was thereafter introduced into other cities in Brazil. It enabled Brazil to claim that it had achieved "near-universal primary education for the first time in its history." A similar Mexican scheme, Progresa, was said to have been so successful in raising and retaining enrollments that some economists urged its adoption in the United States.

But the figures that supported this educational triumphalism must be viewed with caution. As noted earlier, the average Latin American still ended her education at the fifth grade, and the dropout rate remained very high. Overall figures that seemed to reflect victories actually concealed some dismal facts. In Mexico the illiteracy rate in some rural areas was as high as 21 percent, double the national rate, and as we have seen, it was 45 percent among indigenous peoples. Researcher John Scott points out that although Mexico's richest 10 percent usually spent twelve years in school, the poorest 10 percent had on average just two years of education.

There were several reasons for the very high dropout rate in Latin American public schools. One was the economic crisis caused by neoliberal policies and its accompanied cuts in social spending. Part of the burden of educational costs was shifted to parents in the form of "user fees" and other charges; given that most Latin American families lived below the poverty line, this burden was often impossible to carry. A second reason, also linked to the economic crisis, was the lack of decent jobs. As one mother in a Chilean shantytown remarked, "Why should kids read Neruda or go to the theater if they're just going to end up picking oranges?" Often schoolchildren were alienated by formal subject matter and teaching methods that had little relevance to their interests and needs. Finally, rising poverty and the strains it imposed were perhaps the most urgent reasons for parents to take their children out of school and send them to work, sometimes as "street children" who cleaned windshields, sold Chiclets, shined shoes, or worked in microenterprises (sometimes their own parents'), making shoes or other commodities. Other children, like those on Ecuador's banana plantations, some as young as eight years old, were forced to work twelve-hour days in agriculture, where they were exposed to toxic chemicals and sexual harassment.

But the regional crisis in education was not inevitable; it merely reflected the misplaced priorities of local policymakers and international organizations like the IMF, whose decisions all too frequently shaped educational policies in Latin America. By contrast, revolutionary Cuba, which launched its campaign to abolish illiteracy in 1961 with the aid of thousands of young volunteers, quickly achieved its goal. Despite the economic hard times associated with the collapse of its major trading partners in 1990, a decade later Cuba still led all Latin American nations in the quality of the education it offered its people. In 1998, UNESCO conducted tests on primary school students in thirteen Latin American countries. The best performers were Cuba's fourth-graders, who scored the most points by far, 350. They were followed by Chile, Argentina, and Brazil, in that order. Cuba's most recent new departure in education was the creation of the Latin American School of Medicine, which offers free medical training to qualified applicants from the Americas who will commit themselves to return to practice in areas sorely in need of medical care. The student body recently was joined by a number of young people from the United States.

The New Class Structure

Naturally, Latin America's contemporary class structure was very much a product of its historical evolution. Although the capitalist mode of production, based on free contractual labor, was dominant since about 1880, the area still had not made a clean break with its precapitalist past. This was reflected in the survival of slavery, debt peonage, and other forms of forced labor in various parts of the continent. Such servile or feudal forms of labor were usually associated with primary industries like agriculture, cattle-raising, and logging; these typically were located in politically and socially backward regions dominated by great landowners or powerful companies, where the state was weak and its representatives often corrupt and ready to make deals with the dominant elite.

By the middle decades of the twentieth century, meanwhile, industrialization, urbanization, and the commercialization of agriculture had significantly altered the Latin American social structure and the relative weight of the various classes. These changes included the transformation of the old landed elite into a new latifundista class with a capitalist character, the emergence of a big industrial and financial bourgeoisie with close ties to foreign capital, an enormous growth of the so-called urban middle sectors, and the rise of a small but militant industrial working class.

In the early twenty-first century such quasifeudal conditions still existed in Brazil's "Wild West," its Amazon frontier, where defenders of the rain forest, indigenous peoples, and small farmers were threatened with death and murdered with impunity. Here thousands of peasants, lured from other parts of the country by promises of good jobs, free housing, and plenty of good food, often found themselves reduced to slavery, felling trees and tending cattle deep in the jungle. One who managed to escape said that "particularly troublesome workers, especially those who kept asking for their wages, were sometimes simply killed." Government authorities admitted that "contemporary forms of slavery," in which workers were held in unpaid, coerced labor, continued to flourish. "The reasons range from ranchers in cahoots with corrupt local authorities to ineffective land-reform policies and high unemployment." Slave-like conditions of labor existed in other regions of Brazil, in the sugar cane factories of Bahia, for example.

Child labor, in violation of the law, flourished among the one million Mexican migrants— *jornaleros* (day laborers)—and their families, who abandoned their homes for part of the year to move north with the harvests. They did not leave their homes, observed a sympathetic *New York Times* reporter, because they were looking for better wages; "they are looking for any wages." There were no jobs at home, and their only means of subsistence was the growing of beans and corn on their little milpas. The $1,500 that he and his family hoped to take home at the end of the harvest, one migrant said, was just about all the money they would see for the year. "If the whole family," including his three children aged 8, 10, and 11, "does not work," he explained, "we all starve."

Mexico's President Vicente Fox, who urged the United States to improve the condition of Mexican laborers who crossed the border, appeared to know little of the problem that migrant laborers faced at home. Informed that children as young as 11 worked packing vegetables in the Fox family's plants, he sheepishly surmised that some other person named Fox was involved. When the claim was verified, more than twenty minors were dismissed and the president admitted that the violations were "a sad reality of Mexican life." But this was increasingly prevalent throughout the region, where it was estimated that in 1999 there were 17.5 million working children between the ages of 5 and 14. In a time of growing unemployment and general instability of labor, illegal forced labor and child labor obviously exerted considerable downward pressure on wages, living standards, and efforts to organize unions.

The neoliberal economic policies adopted by most Latin American governments, favoring multinationals and their local allies, also caused a sharp decline in the number and influence of small- and medium-sized national manufacturers; they caused growing impoverishment and unemployment among the middle class and the working class as a result of the privatization or dismantling of many state enterprises, reduction of social services, and a general downsizing of the state as part of "structural adjustment" programs demanded by the IMF and the World Bank. A survey of these and other developments suggests the complexity of modern Latin American class alignments and the possible direction of future social and political change.

THE GREAT LANDOWNERS

Although they had to yield first place economically and politically to the new bourgeoisie, with which they maintained close links, the great landowners, Latin America's oldest ruling class, retained immense power, thanks to their control over the land and water resources of the area. Over the last few decades, as earlier chapters have shown, there was a major expansion of the latifundio, especially of the new agribusiness type, which produced industrial and export crops with the aid of improved technology and wage labor. More recently, the dominant policies of free trade and open doors to foreign investment further spurred the trend toward concentration of landownership and penetration of Latin American agriculture by foreign capital. Chile, whose civilian government made no effort to restore the agrarian reform destroyed by the Pinochet dictatorship, and Mexico, where Congress recently approved an agrarian law that ended land redistribution and legalized the sale or rental of communally owned ejido land, illustrate the shift toward policies favoring the rise of a new latifundio.

The traditional hacendado was a vanishing breed. His successor was often a cosmopolitan, university-trained type who combined agribusiness with industrial and financial interests. But the arbitrary and predatory spirit of the old hacendados survived in the new latifundistas. The great landowners continued to be the most reactionary class in Latin American society.

THE NEW BOURGEOISIE

A native commercial bourgeoisie arose in Latin America after independence and consolidated its position with the rise of the neocolonial order after mid-century. In the second half of the nineteenth century, an industrialist class, largely of immigrant stock, appeared in response to the demand of a growing urban population for consumer goods. World War I further stimulated the movement for export/import-substitution industrialization. But the day of the industrial entrepreneur did not arrive until the great economic crisis of 1930 disrupted the trading patterns of the area. Aided by favorable international and domestic background conditions and massive state intervention, the native industrial bourgeoisie quickly gained strength and in many countries displaced the landed elite as the dominant social and economic force. As a rule, however, the new bourgeoisie avoided frontal collision with the latifundistas, preferring to form bonds of kinship and interest with the landed elite.

Meanwhile, foreign capital, attracted by the potential of the growing Latin American market, began to pour into the area, particularly after 1945. Possessing immensely superior capital and technological resources, foreign firms absorbed many small- and middle-sized national companies and came to dominate key sectors of the economy of the host countries. Aware, however, that the survival of a national bourgeoisie was essential to their own security, foreign capitalists endeavored to form close ties with the largest, most powerful national firms through the formation of mixed companies and other devices. This dependence on and linkage with foreign corporations explains why the Latin American new bourgeoisie often lacked nationalist sentiment.

In its youth, some sections of the Latin American national bourgeoisie supported the efforts of such nationalist, populist chieftains as Cárdenas, Perón, and Vargas to restrict foreign economic influence and accepted, though with misgivings, their concessions to labor. But soon the new bourgeoisie adopted the hostility of its foreign allies to restrictions on foreign capital and independent trade unionism. With rare exceptions, these capital-ists supported repressive military regimes in such countries as Brazil, Argentina, Uruguay, and Chile until, convinced that the policies of those regimes threatened the stability of capitalism itself, they became converts to democracy.

Neoliberal policies during the 1990s gave an immense stimulus to the alliance of foreign multinationals and local capitalists, an alliance in which foreign capital played the dominant role. The process was under way in many countries, but particularly in Brazil, Argentina, Mexico, Chile, and Venezuela. Privatization became a major instrument for denationalizing the Latin American economy through auctions and debt-equity swaps that virtually donated valuable state companies to foreign firms.

Small groups of local capitalists linked to foreign capital and with "crony" connections to the ruling parties also benefited by the privatization process. In Mexico, for example, after the 1992 privatization of the banking system, "a mere 224 investors held effective control of the Mexican banks. . . . This oligarchy controls the fundamental instruments of economic—and indirectly—political power in Mexico today." Typical of these aggressive new entrepreneurs was Carlos Slim Helú, included in the *Forbes* 1994 ranking of the richest men in the world. With a fortune estimated to be more than $6 billion, Slim, in partnership with two associates and two foreign firms, bought the Mexican telephone giant Telmex during the administration of his friend and business associate Carlos Salinas. Paying little cash and using credit advanced by a number of banks, he paid a mere $1.7 billion for a company whose worth was estimated to be close to $12 billion. After the sale, the price of the company stock "went through the roof." Slim also owned the Denny's and Sanborn's restaurant chains and Mexico's most profitable investment firm in 1996, Carso-Imbursa, in addition to having a monopoly on cigarette manufacturing. His cousin Alfredo Harper Helú was one of a group of billionaires who controlled Banamex, one of Mexico's three largest banks.

Narcorevenues produced another crop of Latin American "new rich." For obvious reasons the membership of the group and the extent of its wealth cannot be stated with certainty. (U.N. agencies put the annual revenue generated by the illegal drug industry at $460 billion, roughly the equivalent of 8 percent of total international trade.) What is certain is that its wealth was vast and that its activity—as revealed in May 1998 by a U.S. money-laundering sting that led to the arrests of about two dozen Mexican bankers—often intersected with the legitimate operations of Latin American entrepreneurs. The drug traffic, the neoliberal policies pushed by the IMF, the World Bank, and other agencies, and the drug war pushed by the United States "have all intersected in an explosive way." By imposing austerity and privatization measures, and by dismantling the Latin American state, neoliberalism created massive unemployment that "generates thousands of recruits for the drug trade—coca growers, day laborers, smugglers, enforcers." By "freeing up" financial markets, neoliberalism also made it easier to launder drug profits and invest them in "legitimate" activities. And by making international borders more porous, trade liberalization created insuperable obstacles to effective interdiction. Between 1993 and 1994, the year NAFTA took effect, the number of trucks entering the United States from Mexico increased 50 percent to 2.8 million, making the problem of locating the odd vehicle with a few hundred kilos of cocaine among its other cargo "more and more akin to finding a needle in a haystack with each passing year." In 1996, 3.55 million commercial trucks and railroad boxcars entered the United States from Mexico; perhaps 5 to 10 percent of them were inspected. The kingdom of the cocaine mafia actually expanded in recent years from Peru, Bolivia, and Colombia to Mexico (now a major transshipment point), Brazil, and Venezuela, with Colombia and Peru branching off into poppy production for heroin as well. The rise of coca capitalism was accompanied by the spread of unprecedented violence (Colombia had one of the highest homicide rates on earth) and a corruption that involved Latin American presidents, generals, and bankers.

THE URBAN MIDDLE SECTORS

The urban middle sectors occupied an intermediate position between the new bourgeoisie and the landed elite, on the one hand, and the peasantry and the industrial working class, on the other. The boundaries of this intermediate group with other classes were vague and overlapping. At one end, for example, the group included highly paid business managers whose lifestyles and attitudes identified them with the new bourgeoisie; at the other, it included store clerks and lower-echelon government servants whose incomes were often lower than those of skilled workers.

The longest-established urban middle sector consisted of self-employed artisans, shopkeepers, and owners of innumerable small enterprises. White-collar employees formed another large urban intermediate sector. Urbanization, the growth of commercial capitalism, and the vast expansion of the state in the middle decades of the century contributed to the growth of both public and private bureaucracies. Until recently, public employees made up about one-fifth of the economically active population of the area.

University students composed a sizable urban middle sector. Between 1960 and 1970 their number rose from 250,000 to over 1 million. The great majority came from middle-class backgrounds, and many combined work and study. Student discontent with inadequate curricula and teaching methods and the injustices of the social and political order made the university a focal point of dissidence and protest. But the students were in the end transients, in Latin America as elsewhere; their radical or reformist zeal often subsided after they entered a professional career.

Because of their great size, the ideology of the urban middle sectors and their actual and potential role in social change were issues of crucial importance. Following World War II, many foreign experts on Latin America, especially in the United States, pinned great hopes on the "emerging middle sectors" (to which they assigned the new industrialist class) as agents of progressive social and economic change. The history of the following decades did not confirm these expectations. The urban middle sectors mushroomed, but with the exception of many students and intellectual workers—teachers, writers, scientists—they were not a force for progressive social change.

But the urban middle sectors should not be written off as hopeless reactionaries. By their very intermediate nature, they were capable of strong political oscillations, especially in response to the movement of the economy. The "savage capitalism" implanted in many Latin American countries in recent decades by both military and civilian governments played havoc with middle-class living standards and expectations. In the process it also transformed the traditionally conservative, complacent thought patterns of the urban middle sectors.

A good example of such a transformation was *El Barzón*, a Mexican middle-class debtors' union that took its name from the leather strap that held the oxen to the plow on the great haciendas of prerevolutionary times. With a membership of half a million to a million Mexicans in thirty-one states and the Federal District, El Barzón became the largest, most militant resistance movement formed in the wake of the peso's crash in December 1994, which sent interest rates up over 100 percent and threatened thousands of farmers, small businesses, and assorted members of the middle class with financial ruin. With a combination of direct action that included the public burning of credit cards and the blocking of entrances to bank branches to shut down their operations, El Barzón was able to stop the foreclosures and impose a moratorium on the banks. El Barzón also formed links with domestic and foreign trade unions, the Catholic church, debtors' unions in other Latin American countries, and the Zapatistas of Chiapas. Its national director, Juan José Quirino, became a senator of the left-center Partido Revolucionario Democrático (PRD). "It's not just personal debt that we are talking about now—the foreign debt is the mechanism by which the IMF keeps us chained up," says Quirino. "Latin American debtor nations missed the opportunity to unite after 1982. This time we must be ready to fight for a continental moratorium."

THE PEASANTRY

The term *peasantry* refers here to all small landowners, tenants, and landless rural laborers. As documented in previous chapters, the expansion of the new type of latifundio created an unparalleled crisis for the Latin American peasantry. The increased use of tractors and other kinds of mechanized farm equipment had already displaced millions of farm workers and the process was accelerating. The removal of trade barriers, opening national markets to competition with more efficient foreign grain producers, threatened the existence of small farmers. Meanwhile, the neoliberal trend reversed land reforms; in Mexico, for example, the passage of legislation making communally owned ejido land alienable removed the last obstacles to the concentration of land in a few hands. The result was a growing exodus of impoverished peasants to the overcrowded cities or, in the case of Mexican and Central American campesinos, a sometimes dangerous and unsuccessful effort to make it across the border into an increasingly inhospitable United States. Behind these desperate migrations were sharply declining standards of living. In January 1998, *El Financiero*, Mexico's leading financial newspaper, reported that 67 percent of households in rural zones were "extremely poor"—meaning that they could not satisfy minimal basic requirements.

THE INDUSTRIAL WORKING CLASS

The rapid growth of capitalism in Latin America since about 1930 was accompanied by a parallel growth of the industrial working class. Although miners and factory workers formed the best-organized and most class-conscious detachments of the army of labor, they were a minority of the labor force. Artisans, self-employed or working in shops employing less than five persons, constituted the largest group. The predominance of the artisan shop, whose labor relations were marked by paternalism and individual bargaining, hindered the development of workers' class consciousness and solidarity.

Despite its small size, the industrial working class played a key role in major movements for social and political democracy in Latin America. Armed Bolivian tin miners helped achieve the victory of the 1952 revolution and its program of land reform and nationalization of mines. Cuban workers gave decisive support to the guerrilla struggle against the Batista dictatorship, and their general strike in 1959 helped topple it. The working class of Buenos Aires intervened at a critical moment in 1945 to save Juan Perón from being overthrown by a reactionary coup, and its pressure broadened his reform program. In Chile the working class led the Popular Unity coalition that brought Salvador Allende to the presidency, ushering in a three-year effort (1970–1973) to achieve socialism by peaceful democratic means.

These advances—particularly the Cuban and Chilean revolutions—provoked a counterrevolutionary reaction that until recently was still ascendant. In many countries under personal or military dictatorships, all working-class parties were banned, trade unions were abolished or placed under strict government control, and many labor leaders were murdered or forced into exile.

The gradual restoration of formal democracy in the region, accompanied by the imposition of the neoliberal economic model, did not bring full recognition of labor's right to organize and other basic rights. In Chile, for example, the new civilian government retained many features of the Pinochet labor code. In Mexico, workers could not freely join unions of their choice, and most union members were forced to join unions affiliated with the ruling Partido Revolucionario Institucional (PRI). In the export-processing areas, like Mexico's maquila sector or the Central American and Caribbean free-trade zones, union rights were routinely ignored. In Argentina, with the election of Carlos Menem in 1989, "a vicious labor counterreform was set in motion" that gutted the traditional Labor Contracting Law, with the result that nearly 90 percent of new hires were temporary rather than permanent. The changes in workplace accident legislation also caused health and safety conditions to deteriorate dramatically. The stated objective of the law was to create more jobs, but the result was just the opposite, with

Argentine unemployment and underemployment estimated at 40 percent of the economically active population.

But Latin American workers still continued the struggle for equality and social justice. In Mexico the Mexican Confederation of Labor (CTM), which held wages to levels decreed by the government and collaborated with the security forces to repress independent unionists, was challenged by a new federation, the National Workers' Union, led by Francisco Hernández Suárez, head of the telephone workers' union; it represented 1.5 million members and was growing fast. In Mexico's maquila sector and the Central American garment sweatshop zone, some breakthroughs in trade-union organization and improvement of working conditions occurred as a result of cooperation between independent local unions and unions and labor rights groups in the United States. The struggle for free-trade unionism and labor's rights was often linked to the struggle against the neoliberal economic model, whose downsizing of the state and other "structural adjustment" policies led to the virtual disappearance of some national industries, a rapid expansion of the informal economy, and the massive unemployment and atomization of labor.

THE SERVICE OR INFORMAL SECTOR

This sector, the largest of all,[1] arose as a result of industry's inability to absorb the supply of labor; it included "a great number of poorly paid domestic servants and a mass of individuals who eke out a precarious living as lottery ticket vendors, car watchers and washers, shoeshiners, and street peddlers." But the meaning of "informal sector" was extremely elastic and the list of occupations that fit the category almost endless. Its main defining elements were self-employment and the irregular and precarious nature of the work. " 'Informal

---

[1] According to the International Labor Organization, from 1980 to 1992 informal-sector employment rose from 40.2 percent to 54.4 percent of total employment and grew 3.9 percent per year thereafter.

sector,' " observes sociologist Tessa Cubitt, "implies a dualist interpretation of the urban economy, since it proposes a dichotomy between a formal modern capitalist sector in which big businesses and multinationals flourish, and the mass of the poor who are unable to benefit from participation in this sector."

In fact, many of the activities of the informal sector were integrated into the modern capitalist sector, and the links between them were exploitative. The garbage pickers of Cali, Colombia, collected wastepaper, which they sold to warehouses, which in turn sold it to the giant paper company Cartón de Colombia, whose main shareholder was the Mobil Oil Company. "Why," asks Cubitt, "does Cartón de Colombia not directly employ the garbage pickers? Clearly, it is cheaper for them to operate like this because they do not have regular wage bills to pay. The income the garbage pickers receive for each item is extremely low and reduced even further by the competition between them, which is encouraged by the system that is very much a buyer's market." In effect, the low income of the garbage pickers subsidized the multinational Cartón de Colombia. Similar exploitive relations existed between manufacturers and workers who subcontracted to do work in their own homes and were paid for each completed piece. In all such cases the companies saved on wages and the costs of social security benefits; there was the additional benefit of keeping workers weak and divided, unable to present a common front to employers.

Attitudes and Mentalities: Change and Resistance to Change

Change was in the air of Latin America as it entered the last quarter of the twentieth century. Economic modernization demanded changes in family life, race relations, education, and the whole superstructure of society, but the old attitudes and mentalities struggled hard to survive. As a result, Latin America presented dramatic contrasts between customs and mores that were as new as the Space Age and others that recalled the age of Cortés and Pizarro.

WOMEN'S PLACE

The status of women was a case in point. In some ways that status had improved; the struggle to obtain the vote, for example, began around World War I and ended successfully when Paraguay granted women suffrage in 1961. More and more Latin American women held appointive and electoral offices, and in increasing numbers they entered factories, offices, and the professions. By 1970, in some countries, notably Brazil and Argentina, the percentage of women classified as professionals was higher than that percentage for men, a significant fact because the proportion of economically active women was much lower than that of men. In Brazil, out of every 100 women working in nonagricultural services in 1970, 18 were engaged in professional and technical operations, whereas for men the figure was only 6 out of every 100. The ratios were reversed, however, for positions of higher responsibility, reflecting the persistence of discriminatory attitudes.

The movement for women's rights could claim much less progress in such areas as family patterns, divorce laws, and sexual codes. The traditions of the patriarchal family, of closely supervised courtship and marriage, continued strong among the upper and middle classes. The ideology of machismo, the cult of male superiority with its corollary of a sexual double standard, continued to reign almost everywhere in the continent. "The Mexican family," wrote sociologist Rogelio Díaz-Guerrero, "is founded upon two fundamental propositions: (a) the unquestioned and absolute supremacy of the father and (b) the necessary and absolute self-sacrifice of the mother." The flood of economic, political, and social change of almost three decades weakened the force of this statement, but with some qualifications it still held for most Latin American republics.

Socialist Cuba made great advances in abolishing sexual discrimination in law and practice, however; in 1975 it introduced the Family Code, which gave the force of law to the division of household labor. Working men and women were required to share housework and child care equally, and a recalcitrant spouse could be taken by the other to court. But Vilma Espín, head of the Cuban women's movement, admitted that the law was one thing and the way people lived was another: "Tradition is very strong. But we have advanced. Before, the machismo was terrible. Before, the men on the streets would brag about how their wives took care of them and did all the work at home. They were very proud of that. At least now we have reached the point where they don't dare say that. That's an advance. And now with young people you can see the difference."

Nicaragua was another country where a liberating revolution transformed the lives and roles of many women. Women, both rural and urban, took part in the struggle against the Somoza tyranny and made an immense contribution to its final triumph in July 1979. Women prepared for the final offensive by stockpiling food, gathering medical supplies, and organizing communications networks to send messages to Sandinista fighters and their families. By the time of the final victory, from one-quarter to one-third of the Sandinista People's Army was female—some as young as thirteen. Three women were guerrilla commanders; two served on the general staff of the People's Army. Following the triumph of the revolution, women assumed responsible positions at all levels of the Sandinista government. A similar process of women's liberation took place as part of the revolutionary struggle in neighboring El Salvador.

In the Southern Cone, women took the lead in the struggle against the military dictatorships that arose in Chile (1973), Uruguay (1973), and Argentina (1976). That role was thrust upon them as a result of the repressive policies of the dictatorships, the banning of trade unions and political parties, and the murder or disappearance of thousands of activists. Women paid a price for their sacrifices. Thirteen members of the Argentine human rights movement, including the president of the Mothers of the Plaza de Mayo, who demanded an accounting for their disappeared children, vanished into the death camps.

Despite their services, women in Cuba, Nicaragua, and the countries of the Southern Cone had not achieved full recognition of their equality. Gioconda Belli, a former Nicaraguan

guerrilla leader, complained: "We'd led troops into battle, we'd done all sorts of things, and then as soon as the Sandinistas took office we were displaced from the important posts. We'd had to content ourselves with intermediate-level positions for the most part." Her complaint was echoed by an Uruguayan trade unionist who had taken part in the struggle against the military dictatorship: "When the men came out of prison or returned from exile, they took up all the spaces, sat down in the same chairs, and expected the women to go back home." And Rosa, one of the Chilean working-class women who played key roles in the resistance to the military dictatorship, wryly remembered: "When the democratic government took over, the men around here said, 'It's okay, Rosa, you can leave it to us now.' We thought, 'Have they forgotten everything we did during the dictatorship?'" Consciously or unconsciously, the old prejudices persisted in the thought patterns of men—even radicals and revolutionaries—from one end of the area to the other.

Women responded to the continuing challenge of machismo by forming a multitude of groups that, whether or not they called themselves feminist, had as their essential goal the end of the old unequal relations between the sexes. One *encuentro*, or meeting, in Nicaragua in March 1992 brought together some five hundred Central American women "who talked about the power Central American women have in their 'public' and 'private' lives, the kind of power they would like to have, and how to go about getting that power." But women were divided among themselves by class, and Latin American working-class women often criticized traditional feminist organizations as middle-class and indifferent to their own practical needs. "We have things in common with middle class women, but we also have other problems that middle class women don't have, like the housing shortage, debt problems, unemployment," said one Chilean woman activist, "and we're not going to advance as women if the two things aren't closely linked."

Economic forces, in particular the disastrous impact of neoliberal economic policies on household incomes and living standards, were silently helping transform gender and familial relations in many parts of the area. It was becoming increasingly difficult for one wage to support a family. From sheer necessity, women were entering industry in record numbers. According to the InterAmerican Development Bank, the proportion of women in the labor force rose 50 percent, from almost 18 percent in 1950 to just under 27 percent in 1990.

The results were particularly evident in an area like the Caribbean Basin, where declining traditional exports such as sugar, coffee, and bananas, industries that employed a predominantly male labor force gave way to export manufacturing, typically employing poorly paid woman workers. Similar economic trends, challenging male dominance in the household, were under way in other countries of the region.

As Latin America entered the twenty-first century, however, a growing gulf appeared between women's legal and social equality. A major legal achievement was the passage of national legislation to prevent and punish violence against women, modeled on the United Nations' Convention on the Elimination of All Forms of Discrimination Against Women. Still another was the creation of state bureaucracies to advance women's interests, sometimes linked to larger agencies responsible for the areas of culture, education, or the family. Finally, in country after country during the 1990s, laws were adopted that established quotas for women in each party's list of candidates. During Fujimori's ten-year rule in Peru, for example, Congress required political parties to field women candidates in at least 30 percent of local and congressional races, enacted laws against domestic violence, and authorized both a Ministry of Women and a Public Defender for Women. Indeed, during Fujimori's last, brief, and chaotic administration, Congress was run by a governing council composed entirely of women.

But, as Maruja Barrig points out, the cause of women's legal equality often advanced without improving their deteriorating social and economic conditions. "In the 1990s, for example, 70% of the Bolivian population was considered poor, climbing to 90% in rural areas. In Peru, close to 50% of the population is classified as poor. The literacy rate among the female indigenous population, as a group, is the lowest in Latin America. The 1991 national census in Bolivia found that 50% of rural women could not read. In Peru, according to the 1993 National Census, the figure was 43%." And the health statistics, Barrig notes, "are no less alarming. . . . In Bolivia, there are 300 maternal deaths for every 100,000 births, but in Potosí the number of maternal deaths per 100,000 could reach 600." Noting that, after Haiti, Bolivia and Peru had the highest rates of maternal death in Latin America, the United Nations Population Fund described this as "one of the most dramatic representations of social injustice and the inequality among women."

Meanwhile, Salvadoran lawmakers, responding to pressure from pro-life groups, eliminated the four legal options for abortion from the country's 1997 legal code. In Chile conservative forces defeated a divorce law and retained in the civil code the statutory definition of the husband as the "head" of the family. In response to these defeats and "internal cracks in the institutional structures created for women," Barrig notes that "in the search for the possible, a subtle pragmatism appears to have become lodged in the strategies of feminists playing by the rules proposed by others." The women's movements of Ecuador and Chile, for example, decided to give priority to lobbying and negotiation "over mobilization and denunciation."

RACE PREJUDICE

Notions of the inferiority of blacks and indigenous peoples were everywhere officially disapproved, but race prejudice remained strong, especially among upper- and middle-class people who identified themselves as white. In Brazil, often touted as a model of racial democracy, sociologist Florestan Fernandes found that these people clung to "the *prejudice of having no prejudice*, limiting themselves to treating blacks with tolerance, maintaining the old ceremonial politeness in inter-racial relationships, and excluding from this tolerance any true egalitarian feeling or content." In 2002 Brazilian newspapers carried advertisements from private companies that called for a "good appearance," a code phrase understood to mean that blacks should not apply. In a 2000 census, only 6 percent of the population of 170 million identified themselves as black, a low figure that proponents of reform attributed to discrimination and a poor racial self-image. A DNA study by Brazilian scientists suggested that as many as 80 percent of Brazilians had African ancestry. But only 2.2 percent of Brazil's 1.6 million college students were black, and blacks were almost invisible on television except in menial or exotic roles. In 2003 the Brazilian Congress had before it a measure that would reserve 20 percent of university admissions for blacks and apply the same figure to Civil Service jobs; the plan would also require black or mixed-race actors to compose 25 percent of the cast of any theatrical or television production. The measure stirred up much debate, for and against.

In Brazil, Venezuela, Colombia, and other Latin American countries with large black populations, unlike the situation in the United States, where people were categorized as either white or black, there was a kind of "sliding scale" of prejudice and discrimination against blacks that tended to vary according to the shade of skin color. Mulattos were usually favored over blacks. As a rule the higher occupations such as medicine, law, upper-level governments posts, and the officer and diplomatic corps were closed to both categories. But mulattos could aspire to become schoolteachers, journalists, bank tellers, low-level municipal officials, and the like. The lowest-paid jobs were reserved for dark-skinned people. The virulent opposition attacks on populist President Hugo Chávez of Venezuela, who boasted of his black and indigenous ancestry, had a clear racist component.

Even in black Haiti, a vast economic and social gulf separated an urban mulatto elite from the rural black masses of poor people and the "black ghetto" of downtown Port-au-Prince. In the neighboring Dominican Republic, the late President Joaquín Balaguer had preached an overt racism, claiming that his "white and Christian" country was threatened by the "biological imperialism" of Haitian immigrants. In fact, the Dominican Republic has been described as the only true mulatto country in the world. A pervasive Dominican racism, based on a rejection of African ancestry and darkness and on supposed links with a superior indigenous Spanish racial heritage, led to a pattern of mistreatment of the large Haitian immigrant community and periodic waves of immigrant expulsion, the latest taking place in 1999. Meanwhile, only revolutionary Cuba had largely eliminated racism in both theory and practice; here, blacks held high positions in government, the armed forces, and the professions. But the roots of racism in a country with Cuba's history were deep and strong, and Castro himself recognized that racial, gender, and class prejudices persisted.

The indigenous peoples of Latin America remained the principal victims of racist exploitation and violence. In Brazil, according to one recent estimate, the number of indigenous people had dropped from 1,000,000 to 180,000 since the beginning of the twentieth century. This process of cultural destruction in the interests of economic progress continued unabated. Since 1975 some 1,000 Yanomamis, of the 9,000 living in Brazil and 12,000 in Venezuela, had been murdered, mostly by gold miners. Similar wanton killings were reported in the jungle lowlands of Colombia, and murderers of natives by land-grabbing hacendados or their *pistoleros* (gunmen) occurred in Mexico, Guatemala, and other countries with sizable indigenous populations. In Guatemala military regimes practiced systematic genocide against the Maya and attempted to eradicate their culture.

In some countries the native peasantry was subjected to a many-sided economic, social, and cultural exploitation. "The Indian problem," writes Mexican sociologist Pablo González Casanova, "is essentially one of internal colonialism. The Indian communities are Mexico's internal colonies. . . . Here we find prejudice, discrimination, colonial forms of exploitation, dictatorial forms, and the separation of a different population, with a different race and culture." Some Mexican social scientists claimed that Mexicans had long been blind to their own racism and discrimination. One cited a paragraph written in 1985 by a leading historian,

Enrique Krauze: "Mexico constructed a tradition of natural liberty and equality that was rooted in the culture of the people and freed us very early from slavery, servitude, and racism."

These revisionist scholars assigned much of the blame for this blindness to an indigenous policy that dated from the time of independence, and that gave native peoples (and people of African descent) the option of abandoning their cultures or becoming wax figures in a historical museum. The framers of this integrationist policy, whose good intentions were not questioned, included such illustrious names in scholarship or politics as Manuel Gamio, Gonzalo Aguirre Beltrán, Alfonso Caso, and the revered Lázaro Cárdenas. Adding a touch of humor, the ethnologist Luz María Martínez Montiel declared that the anthropologists themselves had made the important Instituto Nacional Indigenista "the last *encomienda* in Mexico." For Martínez, integration of the indigenous peoples consisted not in despoiling them of their identities and cultures but in assuring their equal rights in the process of production, education, and expression. And it is they, she stressed, who must decide.

In the spring of 2001 the Zapatista Army of National Liberation, led by Subcomandante Marcos, staged an impressive march from Chiapas to Mexico City to demand that President Fox comply with campaign promises to quickly solve indigenous demands for autonomy and control of their resources. On the way north the Zapatista caravan was greeted by thousands of supporters and received petitions and memorials like the Declaration of the Indigenous Peoples of Morelos: "What do we want and demand? To be treated with respect as indigenous peoples. That we should not be jailed for defending our land. That there should be true justice. An end to industrial and commercial megaprojects in communal and ejido land. An end to the destruction of our forests, waters, and natural resources. An end to the neoliberal modernization that is causing the disappearance of the indigenous peoples. That we be taken into account when decisions are made. We want to be part of development, not a simple rung on which others step up for their development."

But in the capital disillusionment awaited the rebels. Congress left the implementation of a list of native "rights" to the state legislatures, effectively leaving matters as they were. The Zapatista reply was swift and decisive: "If this reform deserves any name, it should be 'the Constitutional Recognition of the Rights and Culture of the Latifundists and Racists.'" Returning to Chiapas, the rebels and their communities faced the same problems of military encirclement and harassment by paramilitary bands in the service of great landowners and reactionary politicians. In a struggle that had now lasted more than eight years, the Zapatistas avoided a suicidal armed project to seize power. But they also refused to limit their demands to conditions in Chiapas, focusing instead on principles of indigenous self-determination and national democratic reform. By adroit use of the most modern means of communication and a series of national and international meetings, they made their struggle known and won sympathy throughout the world, achieving a front-line place in the battle against globalization and neoliberalism, and making the name of Subcomandante Marcos as well known as that of Che Guevara.

The indigenous peoples of America were on the march, forming broad coalitions with unions, middle-class groups, and international organizations, and they were winning victories. In 2001, grassroots movements from all over the world came to Cochabamba, the third-largest city in Bolivia. "Cochabamba," writes Sophia Style, "became a key symbol of the struggle against global capitalism, when thousands of local people took to the streets against the privatization of their water supply by the U.S. transnational Bechtel—and won." The victory had its costs. After a mobilization of 30,000 people had shut down the city center for five days, President Hugo Banzer (former dictator of Bolivia) sent in troops, including a sharpshooter trained at the School of the Americas, who gunned down a 17-year-old protestor.

One milestone in the struggle of the indigenous peoples of America against old and new forms of exploitation was the decision of the United Nations to declare 1993 the International

The 1992 awarding of the Nobel Peace Prize to the Maya activist Rigoberta Menchú gave a large boost to the struggle against genocide of indígenas and for indigenous political and social rights in her native Guatemala and throughout Latin America. [Reuters Newmedia Inc./Corbis]

Year of the Indigenous Peoples of the World. Another was the award of the Nobel Peace Prize to the Guatemalan indigenous leader Rigoberta Menchú (October 1992), in recognition of her work on behalf of the native peoples of America. More recently indigenous-rights organizations in Ecuador and Bolivia successfully mobilized their members to challenge neoliberal agendas; in 2001 they unseated an unpopular president in Ecuador, and the following year they became a dominant force in Bolivian electoral politics.

THE CATHOLIC CHURCH

The ideological crisis of Latin America was illustrated by the rifts that emerged in two of the area's oldest and most conservative institutions, the Catholic Church and the armed forces.

The new reformist and revolutionary currents that emerged within the Catholic Church since about 1960 had different sources. One was a more liberal climate of opinion within the church brought about by the Second Vatican Council, convened in 1962 under Pope John XXIII. Another was concern on the part of some elements of the hierarchy that the church's traditional collusion with the elites risked a loss of the masses to Marxism. Still another was a crisis of conscience on the part of some clergy, especially working clergy whose experiences convinced them that the area's desperate dilemmas required drastic solutions.

The new ferment within the Latin American church found dramatic expression in the life and death of the famous Colombian priest and sociologist Camilo Torres. Born into an aristocratic Colombian family, a brilliant scholar and teacher, Torres, who became convinced of the futility of seeking to achieve reform by peaceful means, joined the communist-led guerrilla National Liberation Army. He was killed in a clash with counterinsurgency forces in February 1966.

The proper stand for the church to take in the face of Latin America's structural crisis was hotly debated at the second conference of Latin American bishops, held at Medellín, Colombia, in 1968. The presence of Pope Paul VI at its opening session underlined the meeting's importance. Reflecting the leftward shift of portions of the clergy, the bishops at Medellín affirmed the commitment of the church to the task of liberating the people of Latin America from neocolonialism and "institutionalized violence." This violence, declared the bishops, was inherent in the economic, social, and political structures of the continent, dependent on what Pope Paul called "the international imperialism of money."

Even before Medellín, a group of Latin American bishops had taken a position in favor of socialism. Their leader was Helder Câmara, archbishop of Recife (Brazil). He and seven other Brazilian bishops had signed a pastoral letter issued by seventeen bishops of the Third World that called on the church to avoid identification of religion "with the oppression of the poor and the workers, with feudalism, capitalism, imperialism." Himself rejecting violence as an instrument of revolutionary change, Helder Câmara expressed sympathy and understanding for those who felt that violence was the only effective tactic.

These developments were accompanied by the emergence and growing acceptance by many clergy of the so-called theology of liberation, the product of the study and reflection of leading church scholars in various Latin American countries. This doctrine taught that the church, returning to its roots, must again become a Church of the Poor. It must cease to be an ally of the rich and powerful and commit itself to the struggle for social justice, to raising the consciousness of the masses, to making them aware of the abuses from which they suffered and of the need to unite to change an oppressive economic and political system. Liberation theology rejected Marxism's atheist world view but drew heavily on the Marxist analysis of the causes of the poverty and oppression in the Third World. On the subject of revolution, though deploring all violence, liberation theologians taught that revolution, or counterviolence, was justified as a last resort against the greater violence of tyrants, an orthodox Catholic teaching that went back to St. Thomas Aquinas. It was in this spirit that Archbishop Oscar Arnulfo Romero of San Salvador, in one of the last sermons he gave before he was murdered by a right-wing assassin in March 1980, declared: "When all peaceful means have been exhausted, the Church considers insurrection moral and justified."

To implement the teachings of liberation theology, progressive clergy set about developing a new type of Christian organization, the *comunidad de base*, or Christian grassroots organization. Composed of poor people in the countryside and the barrios of cities, assisted and advised by priests and students, these communities combined religious study and reflection with efforts to define and solve the practical social problems of their localities. The great landowners and the authorities frequently branded their activities as subversive, and both laity and priests were subjected to severe repression. This led to a growing politicization and radicalization of many communities and their involvement in revolutionary movements.

In Nicaragua the Christian communities were integrated into the revolutionary struggle led by the Sandinista Front for National Liberation to a degree not found elsewhere in Latin America. This unity of rank-and-file Catholic clergy and laity with the revolution continued after the Sandinista triumph in July 1979. Five priests held high office in the revolutionary government and defied a 1980 Vatican ruling barring direct priestly involvement in political life. Many priests and nuns enthusiastically supported and participated in the literacy campaign and other reconstruction projects of the new regime.

But conflict between this progressive faction and conservatives in the church hierarchy soon emerged at the third conference of Latin American bishops, convened at Puebla, Mexico, in March 1979. Unlike Medellín, where the progressives had the upper hand, conservatives controlled the agenda and clearly intended to put down the troublesome liberation theology. They prepared a working paper that urged resignation on the part of the poor in the hope of a better hereafter and placed their trust for the solution of Latin America's great social problems in the failed reformist models of the 1960s. This document raised a storm of criticism among progressive bishops and other clergy.

The unknown element in the equation at Puebla was the position of Pope John Paul II, who was to inaugurate the conference. Despite their ambiguity, the pope's statements in general tended to reinforce the position of progressives and moderates at the Puebla conference. Its final document continued the line of Medellín, especially in its expression of overwhelming concern for the poor: "We identify as the most devastating and humiliating scourge, the situation of inhuman poverty in which millions of Latin Americans live, with starvation wages, unemployment and underemployment, malnutrition, infant mortality, lack of adequate housing, health problems, and labor unrest."

Later the pope's opposition to liberation theology and the so-called popular church appeared to harden. He expressed this opposition during his visit to Nicaragua in 1983, a visit that produced an extraordinary confrontation between the pope and the mass of the faithful who came to hear his homily.

Brazil—where many bishops accepted the basic tenets of liberation theology, actively engaged in the struggle for land reform, and enjoyed the support of many thousands of grassroots communities—became another target of the pope's attack on the supposed subversive or heretical teachings of liberation theology. This attack took the form of sanctions against a very popular theologian, Leonardo Boff, and of efforts to weaken the majority of progressive Brazilian bishops by naming more conservative bishops.

The Vatican also joined the Mexican government in efforts to force Bishop Samuel Ruiz of San Cristóbal de las Casas, in Chiapas, to resign. Ruiz, a champion of the poor Maya campesinos of his diocese, was accused of having a Marxist interpretation of the Gospel and "incorrect theological reflection." The effort apparently collapsed when the Salinas administration asked Ruiz to mediate between the government and the indigenous rebels after the outbreak of a revolt in Chiapas in January 1994.

But in the course of a historic January 1999 visit to Cuba, the pontiff seemed to signal some change of course. Although he called on the Castro government to grant greater religious, civil, and political liberties to Cubans, he praised the social achievements of the Cuban Revolution and, in what appeared to be a thinly veiled reference to the United States, urged Cubans to reject the neoliberal capitalist policies of Western nations because such policies led to the creation of a small wealthy upper class and a large impoverished underclass. Most striking of all, he repeatedly criticized the U.S. embargo against Cuba as unjust.

The recent rapid growth in membership and influence of Protestant evangelical or fundamentalist sects posed a major challenge to the religious supremacy of the Catholic Church in Latin America. Between 1981 and 1987 the membership of these sects had doubled to 50 million. In Guatemala they claimed 30 percent of the population; the most recent figures for Chile and Brazil were 15 and 10 percent of the population. The dramatic economic and social changes taking place throughout the continent had much to do with the phenomenal growth of these new churches. Their revivalist preaching and "pie-in-the-sky" message brought color, excitement, and hope to the lives of the uprooted rural immigrants of the shantytowns that ringed every Latin American city. The churches' support networks often provided these "marginal" people with material assistance as well.

Despite the current pope's ambiguous attitude toward progressive Catholic social thought, liberation theology still strongly influenced the theory and practice of Latin American Catholic clergy. Their continuing activism was reflected in a statement issued by four bishops of dioceses on the Colombian-Ecuadorian border, meeting in

Esmeraldas, Ecuador, June 18–22, 2001. These bishops denounced Plan Colombia, the Free Trade Area of the Americas, and President George W. Bush's Andean Initiative as part of an unjust system that would aggravate instead of solve the area's problems of poverty and violence. Poverty, they declared, was the primary evil and the principal cause of violence in the area. The bishops were responding to a request by priests, religious and lay church workers, and representatives of nongovernmental organizations working on the border that they speak out on the effects of Plan Colombia in their dioceses. "What is happening now in Colombia," declared Bishop Arturo Correa of Ipiales, Colombia, "will happen in Ecuador, Peru, Venezuela, Brazil, and all of poor America."

Interestingly, the bishops' statement directly opposed the official Colombian and Ecuadorian governments' support of Plan Colombia, which included permission for the U.S. government to install a military base at the port of Manta to carry out surveillance of drug cultivation and trafficking in Colombia, Peru, Bolivia, and the Caribbean. But the bishops went farther and rejected "the imposition of an unjust economic system that fails to respect human dignity and attacks the most elemental human rights." They viewed Plan Colombia, the FTAA, and the Andean Initiative as part of the neoliberal economic model, reflecting the ambition of wealthy countries for a redistribution of areas of influence. Ecuadorian Bishop Gonzalo López of Sucumbios saw a connection between the militarization of the drug war and these free-trade initiatives. "One is a military attempt to control the region, while the others will be used to ensure open markets and access to our countries' resources." The bishops stressed that they favored the eradication of illicit crops, but demanded "procedures that respect the ecosystem, biodiversity, and especially human life" and called for a different economic plan "based on sustainability and economic solidarity."

THE MILITARY

Within the Latin American armed forces, as within the church, a differentiation was taking place. The phenomenon of the reformist or even social revolutionary military officer was older than is sometimes supposed. In Brazil the tenente revolts of the 1920s paved the way for the triumph of Getúlio Vargas's reformist revolution of 1930. Juan Perón and other members of the Group of United Officers exemplified a similar tendency within the Argentine officer corps in the 1930s. In Guatemala in 1944 a group of progressive officers led by Colonel Jacobo Arbenz overthrew the Ubico dictatorship and installed a government that enacted a sweeping land reform and other democratic changes. Although the military regimes in Peru (1968), Panama (1968), and Ecuador (1972) differed considerably in the scope and depth of their reforms, they demonstrated the existence of a reformist or even revolutionary officer class.

The massive influx of North American capital into Latin America after 1945, accompanied by the growing political influence of the United States in the area, altered the balance of forces between conservatives and progressives within the Latin American military. Many high-ranking officers became fervent converts to the North American system of free enterprise and accepted the inevitability of a mortal struggle between "atheistical communism" and the "free world." By the Treaty of Rio de Janeiro (1947), the Latin American republics committed themselves to join the United States in the defense of the Western Hemisphere. In the context of the cold war, this commitment entailed collaboration with the United States in a global anticommunist strategy, to the extent of justifying military intervention in any country threatened or conquered by "communist penetration." Under the cover of this doctrine, in 1965 Brazilian troops joined U.S. forces in intervening in the Dominican Republic to crush the progressive revolutionary government of Colonel Francisco Caamaño. The integration of Latin American armies into the strategic plans of the Pentagon converted many into appendages of the North American military machine.

This integration was accompanied by the establishment of the technical and ideological tutelage of the Pentagon over the Latin American military, aimed particularly at the destruction of Latin American revolutionary movements. After the victory of the Cuban Revolution in 1959, this program of training and indoctrination was greatly expanded. Thousands of Latin American officers were sent to take courses in counterinsurgency warfare at Fort Bragg, Fort Knox, Fort Monmouth, and other installations in the United States and in the Panama Canal Zone. An especially important role continued to be played by the School of the Americas (SOA), run by the United States Army for the training of Latin American officers. Founded in 1946 in Panama, it was moved in 1984 to Fort Benning, Georgia, when the Panama Canal Zone Treaty forced its removal from Panama. Since its inception more than 56,000 Latin American personnel received training at the SOA in the art of waging a "dirty little war."

Dubbed by *Newsweek* "a school for dictators," SOA's graduates included General Augusto Pinochet, former head of the Chilean fascist junta; Manuel Noriega, dictator of Panama and U.S. protégé until an imprudent display of independence caused his downfall; and the late Roberto D'Aubuisson, organizer of death-squad activities and charged with responsibility for the assassination of Archbishop Oscar Romero in El Salvador. According to the United Nations Truth Commission in El Salvador, SOA graduates directed many of the massacres and atrocities committed by the military in that country; nineteen of the twenty-seven officers implicated in the Jesuit priest killings in 1989 were SOA alumni, as were eight of the twelve officers charged with responsibility for the El Mozote massacre. Among documents recently discovered in Paraguay's so-called Horror Archives was a folder labeled "Confidential" containing a torture manual used at the SOA. The manual taught "interrogators" how to keep electric shock victims alive and responsive by methods that included dousing their heads and bodies with salt water. In 1997 the number of Mexican military personnel trained at the SOA more than doubled, rising to 305. U.S. Congressperson Joseph Kennedy, a harsh critic of the school, claimed that SOA graduates planned the massacre of 45 indígenas at Acteal, Chiapas. More recently, the U.S. military sought to sanitize the SOA by bestowing on it a new name: The Western Hemisphere Institute of Security Cooperation.

The formation of close ties between high-ranking officers and large foreign and domestic firms contributed to the making of a reactionary military mentality. In Argentina in the 1960s, 143 retired officers of the highest ranks held 177 of the leading posts in the country's largest industrial and financial enterprises, mostly foreign-controlled. Latin America thus developed its own military-industrial complex. Through all these means, the United States acquired an enormous influence over the Latin American military.

The CIA's close links with Latin American right-wing military and their counterrevolutionary projects are well known. The CIA's 1954 role in the destruction of the government of Jacobo Arbenz Guzmán, Guatemala's democratically elected reformist president, offers the classic example. Not until May 1997 did the CIA make public the classified records bearing on that intervention. Perhaps the "most chilling document" in the collection, writes Kate Doyle, is an unsigned "Study of Assassination," in which the agency laid out "in excruciating detail" its proposals to murder leading members of the Arbenz government and military. The CIA also compiled hit lists in preparation for the coup. The success of the operation convinced President Eisenhower that such clandestine operations were "a safe, inexpensive substitute for [the use of] armed force." Not until 1995 did the Clinton administration finally cut off CIA counterinsurgency aid to Guatemala after revelations that an "agency asset," Guatemalan Army Colonel Julio Roberto Alpiréz, had been involved in the murders of U.S. citizen Michael DeVine and Efraín Bámaca Velásquez, a guerrilla leader who was married to the Harvard-educated lawyer Jennifer Harbury. But the Clinton administration still provided counter-drug aid to Guatemala, even though most of the major syndicates uncovered by the Drug Enforcement Agency (DEA) had direct links to Guatemalan military officers.

Revolutionary Cuba was next in line after Guatemala; in 1960 President Eisenhower signed a directive authorizing the CIA "to get rid of

Castro." The Bay of Pigs disaster of April 1961 was "a direct descendant" of the Guatemalan operation, based on the assumption that Castro would suffer the same "loss of nerve" that Arbenz had in 1954. When that failed, the agency launched a series of sabotage efforts against Cuba and unsuccessful assassination attempts against Castro. In July 1998 the *New York Times* published two sensational reports based on interviews with the anti-Castro Cuban exile Luis Posada Carriles as well as declassified CIA files. In the interviews, Posada claimed credit for a series of terrorist activities, including a wave of bombings of Cuban hotels and restaurants in 1997 that killed one tourist and alarmed the Cuban government. "The CIA," he said, "taught us everything—everything. They taught us explosives, how to kill, bomb, trained us in sabotage." The CIA, for its part, commended Posada in one document as "of good character, very reliable, security-conscious," and in another said his "performance in all assigned tasks has been excellent." Posada also claimed that he had received considerable financial support for his terrorist activities from the late Jorge Mas Canosa, the millionaire founder of the anti-Castro Cuban American National Foundation and a close political ally of successive U.S. presidents, including President Clinton; his claim was backed by evidence in the intelligence files.

In Chile, after the election of Socialist Salvador Allende as president in 1970, the CIA desperately tried to prevent his inauguration. According to a recently declassified report on the CIA's Chilean Task Force Activities, the agency "focused on provoking a military coup," the principal obstacle to which was the "apolitical, constitutional-oriented inertia of the Chilean military." To overcome this obstacle, President Nixon ordered CIA chief Richard Helms to "make the economy scream" and pursued a two-track policy combining economic destabilization with shipments of arms and money to right-wing army officers. This eventually led to the overthrow and death of Allende and the establishment of a repressive military dictatorship that ruled for two decades and still casts its long shadow over a supposedly "democratic" Chile.

In 2001 the sons of former Chilean Commander-in-Chief René Schneider, killed in 1970 in a failed attempt to kidnap him, filed suit in a U.S. federal court seeking more than $3 million in damages from Henry Kissinger, President Nixon's national security adviser at the time; Richard Helms, former CIA director; and the U.S. government, for "summary execution," assault, and civil-rights violations. Citing recently declassified CIA documents, the suit charged that U.S. authorities conspired to remove Schneider because he stood in the way of their planned military coup to prevent Salvador Allende from taking office as Chile's elected president. Judges in Chile and Argentina unsuccessfully sought to secure Kissinger's testimony regarding his knowledge of Operation Condor, a vast operation organized between 1970 and 1980 by the dictatorships of Latin America's Southern Cone to aid each other in the elimination of their political opponents, without regard for national borders.

In 1981 in Honduras, turned into a base for the secret war against Sandinist Nicaragua with the cooperation of the Honduran army, the CIA helped create a new army intelligence unit called Battalion 316 to counter subversion. Recently declassified documents reveal that the CIA trained the unit in surveillance, interrogation, and torture. The Battalion learned well, torturing hundreds of Honduran citizens and "disappearing" many others.

In March 1998, attempting to refute charges that the CIA knowingly had cooperated with Nicaraguan contras who ran drugs into the United States, CIA Inspector General Frederick R. Hitz admitted in a curiously roundabout way that, at the very least, there had been instances "where the CIA did not, in an expeditious or consistent fashion, cut off relationships with individuals supporting the contra program who were alleged to have engaged in drug trafficking activity, or take action to resolve the allegations."

The Flowering of Latin American Culture

By mid-century, Latin American culture had attained maturity in a number of fields. Art and scholarship drew closer to the people and their problems and at the same time displayed a growing mastery of the refinements of technique. The swelling output of Latin American art and scholarship grew into a torrent; we can only note some major trends in each field, with special attention to literature, a faithful mirror of Latin American history and problems.

THE SOCIAL SCIENCES

Latin American social scientists, continuing the tradition of such nineteenth-century enlighteners as Sarmiento, Alberdi, and Lastarria, have for the most part rejected an impossible neutrality and have openly taken sides in the political and social struggles of the area. In Latin America even history, the most aristocratic of the social sciences, has walked hand in hand with politics. The liberal current, which dominated nineteenth-century historiography, was represented in the twentieth century by such major figures as the Mexican Daniel Cosío Villegas, who directed and took part in the writing of the monumental *Modern History of Mexico*, and the Argentine Ricardo Levene, who founded a historical school stressing archival research, rigorous critical method, and economic factors.

But there also existed a conservative current whose hallmarks were nostalgia for the colonial period and enthusiasm for such right-wing nineteenth-century caudillos as Alamán and Rosas. In Mexico this tendency was typified by José Vasconcelos, who proclaimed that Cortés was the creator of Mexican nationality; in Argentina it was represented by a group of revisionist historians who sought to rehabilitate the federalist caudillo Juan Manuel Rosas and bitterly criticized such fathers of Argentine liberalism as Mitre and Sarmiento.

Less involved in such historical quarrels were younger scholars who applied the new methods of social and quantitative history to the study of history, especially the colonial period. In Mexico this new school was represented by Enrique Florescano, in Chile by Mario Góngora, Alvaro Jara, and Rolando Mellafe. The Marxist historical method also had its able practitioners, such as

Germán Carrera Damas in Venezuela, Caio Prado Júnior in Brazil, and Enrique Semo in Mexico.

The rise of Latin American anthropology was linked to that of nationalist, reformist movements whose programs stressed the redemption of indigenous peoples and their integration in the national society. The triumph of the Mexican Revolution of 1910 gave a large impetus to such indigenismo. With modest official support and in an atmosphere of widespread and sometimes emotional interest in Mexico's indigenous past, Mexican anthropology made large quantitative and qualitative advances after 1920. The long roster of its distinguished names includes Manuel Gamio, Alfonso Caso, Wigberto Jiménez Moreno, and Miguel Covarrubias. In Peru the pro-indigenista propaganda of the Alianza Popular Revolucionaria Americana (APRA) and other reformist or revolutionary movements stimulated a revival of interest in the study of indigenous peoples, past and present; two pioneers of Peruvian anthropology were Julio Tello and Luis Valcárcel. In the same period, Gilberto Freyre and Arturo Ramos in Brazil and Fernando Ortiz in Cuba began to explore the contributions made by blacks and attack racial myths. In recent decades, Latin American anthropology has combined a strong interest in the social, economic, and political structures of the ancient indigenous peoples with much attention to the problems of contemporary indigenous groups.

The first task of modern Latin American sociology was to rid itself of its nineteenth-century Spencerian heritage, which attributed the area's disorder and backwardness to the racial inferiority of indigenous and other nonwhite groups. Since about 1960 there arose a "new sociology" that rejected the "impartial," empirical sociology in vogue in the United States. The new school openly identified itself with the struggle for radical social change. A Marxist perspective illuminated the writings of such scholars as Fals Borda, Rodolfo Stavenhagen, Pablo González Casanova (Mexico), Octavio Ianni, and Florestan Fernandes (Brazil). The new school made contributions to the understanding of such problems as the causes of rural violence, internal colonialism, the social basis of Latin American populism, and race relations in Brazil.

Economics was a relatively young science in Latin America. Its rise was largely connected with the great crisis of 1930 and its disastrous impact on the economy of the area. In the 1940s the U.N.'s Economic Commission for Latin America (ECLA), led by the Argentine economist Raúl Prebisch, advanced a series of propositions, collectively given the name "structuralism," which attempted to explain Latin America's economic stagnation. Prebisch argued that countries of the "periphery," like those of Latin America, were at a permanent disadvantage in their terms of trade with the "center," the industrialized lands of Europe and North America. Two other alleged obstacles to growth were the traditional structure of agriculture, which led to the stagnation of agricultural output, and the excessive concentration of wealth and power in a few hands, which hampered social mobility, capital formation, and industrial development. The theories of the ECLA and of Prebisch gave an important rationale and stimulus to the movement for Latin American industrialization, economic integration, agrarian reform, and social reform in general. A Brazilian economist, Celso Furtado, applied the structuralist thesis to Brazil in his scholarly *Economic Formation of Brazil* (1963).

Prebisch (who died in 1985) and Furtado believed that Latin America could achieve economic independence and balanced development within a capitalist framework. Disappointment with the ECLA reform program and the Latin American economic performance in the 1960s and 1970s, however, produced a progressive radicalization of Latin American economists, whose writings increasingly stressed Latin America's structural dependence on multinational corporations. Pointing to the deformed, dependent character of Latin American capitalist industrialization and the persistence of such problems as the latifundio, Marxist economists like Theotonio dos Santos argued that socialism alone could cure the area's economic ills.

Variants of economic dependency theory flowered in the 1970s. One of the most influential

was advanced by the Brazilian scholar Fernando Henrique Cardoso. Impressed by Brazil's rapid economic growth under a military regime that relied heavily on foreign loans and investment, Cardoso argued that development was not incompatible with foreign monopoly penetration of dependent economies. To this development, based on collaboration among international capital, the national bourgeoisie, and the state, he gave the name "dependent capitalist development" or "associated dependent development." The collapse of the Brazilian "economic miracle" and incontrovertible evidence that foreign debt represented the greatest single obstacle to Latin American development cast serious doubt on the validity of Cardoso's thesis, at least as far as a long-range solution for the problem of underdevelopment was concerned. Whatever the particular variants to which social scientists subscribed, dependency theory remained a potent analytical force for all who wish to understand contemporary Latin America's problems.

THE ARTS

The arts, like the social sciences, combined mastery of modern technical resources with increased use of national subject matter and local folk traditions. National schools of music arose that achieved a synthesis of those traditions with advanced European techniques and styles; examples of such synthesis were the compositions of Heitor Villa-Lobos in Brazil, Carlos Chávez in Mexico, and Alberto Ginastera in Argentina, the first three Latin American composers to achieve world renown. In painting, the Mexican school, led by Diego Rivera, José Clemente Orozco, and David Alfaro Siqueiros, won acclaim with their bold, socially conscious art. Almost equally famous were the monumental murals of the Brazilian Candido Portinari, which portrayed with moving simplicity and sympathy the bleak lives of Brazilian workers and peasants.

In recent decades, however, there has been a movement in the plastic arts toward a more cosmopolitan aesthetic, illustrated by the magical paintings of the Mexican Rufino Tamayo, very different from the art of Rivera, Orozco, and

Frida Kahlo, *Self-Portrait with Changuito*, 1945.
[Frida Kahlo, *Self-Portrait with Changuito*, 1945, Fundação
Dólores Olmedo, Mexico City, D.F., Mexico, © Banco de México
Trust. Schalkwijk/Art Resource, NY]

Siqueiros in theme and technique yet as intensely
Mexican in their own way. The same could be said
of the work of Frida Kahlo, whose paintings
achieved world renown in the 1990s and cata-
pulted her to cult status in the twenty-first century.
According to her husband, Diego Rivera, her work
"exalted the feminine qualities of endurance and
of truth, reality, cruelty, and suffering." But cultural critic, John Berger, associated the growing
popularity of her art with the social trauma produced by a decade of neoliberal globalization:
"under the new world order, the sharing of pain is
one of the essential preconditions for a refinding of
dignity and hope."

The sardonic, biting portrayal of the Latin
American elite by the Colombian painter Fernando
Botero and the tragic vision of Latin America in
the powerful work of the Ecuadorian painter
Oswaldo Guayasamín continued the great tradition of socially conscious, critical art. Modern
Brazilian architecture impressed foreign observers
with its audacity and its skillful solutions of problems of light and air, as evidenced by the work of
the architect Oscar Niemeyer, who planned and
directed the building of the city of Brasilia.

It is in the field of literature, however, that
Latin American culture burned with the most
brilliant flame. It may appear surprising that
poor countries with masses of illiterates and
therefore very small literary markets should produce such a multitude of distinguished poets and
novelists, including five Nobel Prize winners in
literature,[2] but the phenomenon has its reasons.
In the first place, by the early decades of the
twentieth century, the advance of the export-
import economy had created the necessary economic and social conditions for the rise of
literary circles whose members closely followed
European artistic developments, plus a small
reading public. Second, since colonial times literary culture enjoyed much greater prestige in
Latin America than in the United States, illustrated by the fact that many of Latin America's
greatest men of letters were rewarded with
diplomatic posts, which were often sinecures.
Finally, the dramatic contrasts of Latin
American life—the extremes of wealth and
poverty, the barbarous dictatorships, the rich
variety of regional types, the still untamed
nature—stimulated the creative imagination of
Latin American writers to an extent that did not
occur in happier countries. To a very considerable degree, Latin American literature was a literature of protest and struggle. In this, it
continued the tradition established by such great
nineteenth-century romantic writers as
Sarmiento, Echeverría, Martí, and Montalvo.

[2]They are the Chilean poet Gabriela Mistral (1945), the
Guatemalan novelist Miguel Angel Asturias (1967), the
Chilean poet Pablo Neruda (1971), the Colombian novelist
Gabriel García Márquez (1982), and the Mexican poet
Octavio Paz.

LITERATURE AND SOCIETY, 1910–1930: THE SEARCH FOR SELF-EXPRESSION

After 1900 the art-for-art's-sake creed, of which Rubén Darío had given the supreme example, came under growing attack. Latin American intellectuals, increasingly concerned with backwardness, weakness, and disunity of their continent vis-à-vis its powerful neighbor, the United States, began to descend from Parnassus. In 1899, José Enrique Rodó had already argued that Darío, despite his great technical virtuosity, was not "the poet of America." In a famous poem, "Wring the Neck of the Swan" (1910), the Mexican poet Enrique González Martínez (1871–1952) attacked Darío's proud swan, symbol of beauty as an end in itself. This poem foreshadowed the rise of a new spirit of sincerity, realism, and social consciousness in Latin American literature. By this time, Darío himself had turned away from escapism and had begun to write such powerful public poetry as his "To Roosevelt" (1905).

The intellectuals' concern about the destiny of the continent, about the growing gap in economic and political power between Latin America and the Colossus of the North, inspired numerous essays that probed the causes of the area's problems and suggested solutions. Particularly influential—no doubt because it expressed views Latin Americans wanted to hear—was the essay "Ariel" (1900) by José Enrique Rodó. One of its key themes was the opposition between Latin American spirituality and the materialism of the United States. However, contrary to a common misreading of Rodó, he did not wholly condemn North American utilitarianism; instead, he urged a fruitful fusion of Latin American spirituality and the practical, energetic spirit of the United States. Another important work of stocktaking was *Les democraties latines de l'Amérique* (1912) by the Peruvian Francisco García Calderón, published in France to inform Europeans about Latin America. The book deplores Latin American disunity and anticipates a modern complaint of Latin Americans by its statement that the "new continent, politically free, is economically a vassal." In the same period, there appeared a large number of books that analyzed the problems of individual countries and often found the origins of their malaise in the alleged racial inferiority of indigenous peoples or mixed races; typical of such primitive sociological analysis was Alcides Arguedas's study of Bolivia, *A Sick People* (1909).

The essayists sometimes also stressed the need for artistic originality. García Calderón, for example, claimed that originality in art was as important as economic independence. In the 1920s, a time of preliminary skirmishes in some countries between traditional elites and emerging bourgeois groups, Latin American writers began to try to express the essence of their lands in an original and truly native way. Struggle against an untamed nature, the indígenas, the various regional forms of creole life, and the problems of the peon and the worker were among the varied topics of the new literature. Writers received guidance from one of Latin America's most eminent men of letters, Pedro Henríquez-Ureña, who pointed out in his *Seven Essays in Search of Our Expression* (1928) that every formula of literary Americanism could be useful but that there was only one secret of expression: "To work for it profoundly, to seek to purify it, going to the roots of the things we wish to say, to polish, to refine, with a desire for perfection."

Two postmodernist poets, the Peruvian José Santos Chocano (1875–1934) and the Mexican Ramón López Velarde (1888–1921), illustrate the turning away of the new generation of writers from swans, eighteenth-century palaces, and princesses reclining on velvet divans to the reality of their own lands. Santos Chocano used a wide range of subject matter. He had a certain taste for exotic pre-Columbian and colonial themes: one of his finest poems evokes the ancient city of Cartagena de las Indias, dreaming behind her great walls. Pirates disturb her sleep, but she awakes serene, then softly closes her eyes; fanned by her palm trees and rocked in the hammock of the waves, she falls asleep again. But Santos Chocano could also sound a note of social protest:

> Indian who toils without rest
> on the lands that others own,
> Do you not know that they are yours
> by right of your blood and sweat?[3]

[3]"Quién sabe," quoted in Jean Franco, *The Modern Culture of Latin America* (New York: Praeger, 1967), p. 49.

The intensely personal poems of López Velarde celebrated the provincial scenes of his youth in verse free from sentimentality. His most famous poem, however, is "Suave Patria" (1921), a poem in two tender, teasing "acts" in which the poet expresses his love for Mexico with complete freedom from rhetoric. In the "intermezzo" between the acts, the poet invokes the hero Cuauhtemoc, an early illustration of the indigenismo that is a major aspect of twentieth-century Mexican culture. The intermezzo opens: "Young forebear: hear me praise you, the only hero of artistic stature." But there are no heroics: the mood is subdued, tragic, compassionate. Upon the poet's spirit weigh the terrible losses and sufferings of the Mexican Revolution. His Cuauhtemoc is a Man of Sorrows; he is also an instrument for the fusion of Spanish and indigenous elements into a Mexican synthesis.

The Mexican Revolution, which subtly colors "Suave Patria," also pervades the somber novels of Mariano Azuela (1873–1952). Their main theme is the betrayal by middle-class leaders and cynical intellectuals of the peasants and workers whose ignorance and valor they exploit. Azuela's best novel, *The Underdogs* (1916), tells the story of a peasant, Demetrio Macías, who organizes a guerrilla band, rises to the rank of general, and is killed fighting for Villa. He is the victim of blind forces he does not understand and over which he has no control. His simplicity and naiveté contrast with the cunning of the demagogic medical student Luis Cervantes, who carefully keeps out of harm's way and uses looted diamonds to lay the foundation of his future professional career.

The new cultural nationalism also found expression in the novels of the Colombian José Eustasio Rivera (1888–1928) and the Venezuelan Rómulo Gallegos (1884–1969). In Rivera's best work, *The Vortex* (1924), a violent tale of rubber collectors in the Amazonian jungle, the implacable wilderness joins the "rubber lords" in debasing men, in shattering their hopes and bodies. A novel of protest against the barbarism of his country, it is also a truly national novel, the first Colombian novel to depict the difficult lives of the cowboys of the plains and the rubber collectors of the jungle.

The novels of Rómulo Gallegos, an active opponent of long-time dictator Juan Vicente Gómez, depicted the hitherto-neglected life of Venezuela's *llanos* (plains and jungles) and suggested that the country's destructive regional conflicts could be solved by the fusion of the antagonistic elements: whites and blacks, indigenous and European cultures, barbarism and civilization. In *Doña Bárbara* (1929) the mulatta heroine whose name the novel bears embodies the barbaric vigor and lawless spirit of the people of the plains. Santos Luzardo, on whose land she has encroached, is a city-educated lawyer who finds that he himself must resort to violence to defeat her. Their duel is finally ended by Santos Luzardo's marriage to Doña Bárbara's daughter, a child of nature whom he carefully educates, with particular care that she drop the plebeian dialect of the llanos and learn to speak and act like the "exquisite young ladies of Caracas." The patent artificiality of the civilization-barbarism dichotomy, reflecting Gallegos's middle-class liberalism, weakens his works.

A different viewpoint on the quarrel between civilization and barbarism emerged in the gaucho novel *Don Segundo Sombra* (1926) by Ricardo Guiraldes (1886–1927). One of the most perfect Latin American novels, it evokes with incomparable skill a regional type rapidly receding into the past, but the portrait is clearly touched with nostalgia. The gaucho hero emerges as a dignified and rounded individual, perfectly adapted to his milieu; he needs no transformation from without, for he is already a completely civilized human being.

LITERATURE AND SOCIETY, 1930–2003: A SOCIAL CONSCIOUSNESS

In the 1930s, a time of growing economic difficulties accompanied by the sharpening of class struggles in mines, factories, and plantations, the radicalization of Latin American writers gave rise to the novel of social protest, frequently influenced by Marxist ideology. Because the principal victims of capitalist exploitation in Latin America were indígenas, the new novels of social protest were usually "Indianist" novels as well. Leading representatives of this genre were Jorge Icaza (b. 1906) in Ecuador, Ciro Alegría (1909–1967) and José M. Arguedas (1901–1969) in Peru, and Miguel Á. Asturias (1899–1974) in Guatemala.

The early "Indianist" novels, like *Birds Without a Nest* (1889) by Clorinda Matto de Turner or *Race of Bronze* (1919) by Alcides Arguedas, had found the roots of indigenous misery and exploitation in the personal vices or weaknesses of the ruling classes or of the indígenas themselves. In these indígenas novels, the destruction of the indígenas flows inexorably from the operation of blind economic forces, of which the grasping landlord or exploitive foreign company (these novels often explored anti-imperialist themes as well) are mere instruments. These novels also made a more serious effort to enter the indigenous mind and sometimes prepared themselves for their task by living with the indígenas to learn their speech and customs.

Icaza's *Huasipungo* (1934) reports with blazing anger the brutal exploitation of a group of native Ecuadorians, which culminates in an effort to expel them from their parcels of land (*huasipungos*) to make way for the exploitation of the area by foreign oil companies. But the natives are shown as so degraded by their servitude, so brutish even in dealing with one another, that it is difficult to sympathize with them. More successful in this respect is Ciro Alegría's *Broad and Alien Is the World* (1941), which also relates the destruction of an indigenous community by a landowner bent on acquiring its lands. Alegría's idealized portrayal of indigenous life and virtues borders on the sentimental, yet he convincingly portrays a communal society whose driving force is mutual aid, and therefore engages the reader's sympathy with the indígenas.

Land and labor struggles also characterize the novels of José M. Arguedas, who knew Quechua before he knew Spanish and had a profound mastery of native culture and customs. His novels achieve an unusual penetration of the indigenous mentality through his effort to reproduce the rhythm and syntax of Quechua and evoke the religious world view of the native peoples.

The Guatemalan writer Miguel A. Asturias was one of the founders of the school of magical realism, which attempted to depict indigenous life as the indígenas themselves experienced it, in terms of myth. In *Men of Maize* (1949), he records from this mythic perspective the losing struggle of the natives to retain their land and way of life, using a style whose language and rhythms resemble those of the Maya language. The blend of fantasy and reality in Asturias's novels is far removed from the documentary tone of such regional novelists as Rivera, Gallegos, and Icaza.

In Brazil in the 1920s and 1930s there arose a "northeastern school" that portrayed the varied social types and struggles of the drought-ridden sertão and the coastal sugar plantations. This group included Graciliano Ramos (1892–1953), José Lins do Rego (1901–1957), and Jorge Amado (b. 1912). In *Barren Lives* (1938), Ramos deals with the struggle of a cowherder against drought and starvation and his eventual flight to the city. The "sugar-cane cycle" of Lins do Rego (1932–1943) chronicles the decline and fall of the old sugar aristocracy—the rise of the great *usina* (sugar mill) and the impact of economic change on planters, slaves, and their descendants. Partly based on Lins do Rego's own childhood and adult experiences, these novels reconstruct the social history of Brazilian sugar. In his *Cacao* (1933) Amado describes the life of the workers on the cacao plantations south of Bahia; in *The Violent Land* (1943) he records the bloody struggles for economic and political power of the cacao planters.

Cuban novelist Alejo Carpentier applied the method of magical realism to West Indian blacks in *The Kingdom of This World* (1949); set in Haiti in the time of the French Revolution, it presents the rise and fall of the black dictator Henri Christophe and the emergence of a new mulatto ruling class as seen through the eyes of a house slave. Revolution and the corruption of revolutionaries are major themes of Carpentier's *The Age of Enlightenment* (1962), which is also set in the period of the French Revolution but deals with the Caribbean as a whole.

Poetry, like prose, revealed a new social consciousness. At the same time, Latin American poets struggled to free their verse from rhetoric and the tyranny of old forms. The difficult poetry of Peruvian Cesar Vallejo (1892–1938), though concerned from first to last with human anguish, with the inherently tragic human condition, reveals in its later phase a compassion for the victims of war and exploitation, a vision of a possible better life, that reflects his new socialist ideology. For the Chilean poet Pablo Neruda (1904–1973), as for Vallejo, the Spanish Civil War was a turning point; in a poem written at the beginning of the war he declares that henceforth he will unite his "lone wolf's walk" to the "walk of man." At the end of the war, he joined the Communist Party and combined his poetic career with political activism until his death. His major work is *Canto general* (1950), an epic attempt to tell the history of the Latin American continent from the point of view of figures neglected by textbooks—workers, peasants, and fighters for freedom. Another major poet of left-wing tendencies, the Cuban Nicolás Guillén (b. 1902), founded the Afro-Cuban poetry movement, based on the rhythms and images of Cuban black folk poetry. With the passage of time, his poetry acquired strong social revolutionary and anti-imperialist tones.

The period since 1940 saw a continuing revolution in the technique of the novel. This technical revolution was marked by intensive use of such devices as stream of consciousness, flashbacks, symbolism, and fantasy. Some writers, like Argentina's Jorge Luis Borges in his *Ficciones* (1944), employ fantasy and other avant-garde techniques to demonstrate the absurdity and senselessness of life. Others employ them to heighten awareness of an abhorrent social and political order. To one degree or another, these writers continue the Latin American tradition of employing literature as an instrument of social protest and change. Typical of such novelists is Mario Vargas Llosa, author of *Conversations in the Cathedral* (1970), whose structural and verbal disorder appears to reenact the disorder of Peruvian life and geography.

Guatemala's Miguel Asturias also penned powerful social protest novels. His *Mr. President* (1941) deals with a sinister dictator who rules with a vast apparatus of repression. In it dreams, memories, and imaginings replace the truth the characters cannot speak. Fantasy and reality blend in Asturias's anti-imperialist trilogy, *Strong Wind* (1950), *The Green Pope* (1954), and *The Eyes of the Buried* (1960), which deal with the formation of a monopolistic banana company and the struggles of small farmers and workers against it. In *Strong Wind,* when those struggles fail, a hurricane summoned by a native witch doctor destroys the company's plantations.

Fantasy is the means employed by Gabriel García Márquez to attack a monstrous social and political order in *One Hundred Years of Solitude* (1967), which records the history of an imaginary town set in the remote Colombian *ciénaga* (swampland) where García Márquez grew up. The book describes extraordinary people and events in deadpan fashion; in this magical world, miracles occur in the most natural way. Many of the fantastic situations "are absurd but logical exaggerations of real situations." The fantasies are a parody of Colombian history itself. Indeed, no event depicted in the book is as fantastic as history's la Violencia, the civil war unleashed in the Colombian countryside by conservative repression in 1949, a war that took perhaps 300,000 lives in the course of a few years.

Accelerated urbanization and industrialization placed their stamp on the new novel; frequently, it was set in the great city and dealt with the psychological problems of the urban middle class. In the urban novels of the Mexican Carlos Fuentes (b. 1929), a major theme is the betrayal of revolutionary ideals by the men who made the revolution. In *Where the Air Is Clearer* (1958), *The Clear Consciences* (1959), and *The Death of Armemio Cruz* (1962), Fuentes skillfully depicts the life of a cynical, cosmopolitan society. Alienation and the emptiness of middle- and upper-class life are also common themes in the Argentine urban novel; a good example is *A November Party* (1938) by Eduardo Mallea (1903–1982).

A significant recent development is the emergence of a "testimonial literature" that depicts the struggle of lower-class Latin American women and their families to survive under the most difficult, intolerable conditions. In her diary, *Child of the Dark* (1962), Carolina Maria de Jesus, a black *favela* (shantytown) dweller, records the violence and squalor of favela life. Its publication in Brazil brought Carolina immediate fame, and the book was later translated into many languages. In *Let Me Speak! Testimony of Domitila, A Woman of the Bolivian Mines* (1978), Domitila Barrios de Chungara portrays the bleak lives of a Bolivian miner and his family. In *I, Rigoberta Menchú: An Indian Woman in Guatemala* (1982), the Nobel Peace Prize winner and pro-indigenista activist records the cruelties inflicted by the Guatemalan military on her own family and community. These books testify to the intellectual maturity and talent for self-expression of some Latin American peasant and working-class women with little or no formal education.

Although the beginnings of the Latin American film go back to the first decades of this century, its emergence as a major art form dates from the 1960s, when a group of Latin American filmmakers initiated a reaction against the dominant commercial Hollywood model. Revolutionary Cuba took the lead in this process, producing a large number of excellent films in a variety of styles and relatively free from political constraints. Two such works were Tomás Gutiérrez Alea's *Memories of Underdevelopment* (1968) and Humberto Solas's *Lucía* (1968). Working under difficult, sometimes clandestine or semiclandestine conditions, Argentine, Bolivian, Brazilian, and Central American filmmakers have produced first-class films that explore the history and the social and political problems of their nations. A number of recent Latin American films have won international awards and distinctions. Particularly valuable for an understanding of some episodes of Latin American history are the Argentine filmmaker María Luisa Bemberg's *I, The Worst of All* (1991), a sensitive reconstruction of the life of the poetess Sor Juana de la Cruz, and two Mexican films, Nicolás Echevarría's *Cabeza de Vaca* (1991), which captures the essence of the conquistador's pro-indigenous message, and Alfonso Arau's delightful mix of Mexican twentieth-century history and fantasy, *Like Water for Chocolate* (1992), which broke all foreign-film records for popularity in the United States.

Continuing a tradition established by the founders of Latin American culture, modern Latin American scholars, writers, and artists often tended to view their work not only as a means of self-expression but as an act and instrument of social and political protest. To be sure, in Latin America as elsewhere, there were poets who write very private verse, novelists who deal with intensely personal themes, and painters whose abstract or surrealist art conveys no explicit social message. But to a greater extent than elsewhere, perhaps, the Latin American poet, novelist, painter, and filmmaker have also been the voice and the conscience of the people.

GLOSSARY

Adelantado   Commander of a conquering expedition with governing powers in a frontier or newly conquered province.

Alcabala   Spanish sales tax imposed by the crown.

Alcalde   Member of a *cabildo* who in addition to administrative duties served as a judge of first instance.

Alcalde mayor   Royal governor of a district. See *Corregidor.*

Aldeia   An indigenous community in colonial Brazil, governed and controlled by the Catholic church until the Bourbon crown reasserted its authority in the mid-eighteenth century.

Arpilleras   A folk art tradition that engaged mostly women in communal activities to produce embroidered quilts that communicated the everyday, lived experiences of ordinary people and, especially in Chile, their resistance against social injustice and the brutal repression of a military dictatorship.

Audiencia   A colonial high court and council of state under a viceroy or captain general, or the area of its jurisdiction.

Auto-da-fé or **auto-de-fé**   The church's public ceremony of pronouncing judgment during the Inquisition, followed by execution of the sentence by secular authorities.

Ayllu   A kinship and territorial unit of social organization, originally Inca, in the Andean region.

Bandeirante   Brazilian frontiersmen, usually of mixed racial background, who scoured the interior in search of gold, indigenous slaves, and runaway black slaves.

Note: Terms repeatedly defined or glossed in the text are not included in the Glossary.

Barriadas   Slum neighborhoods.

Bohíos   The traditional thatched-roof shacks in which the vast majority of impoverished Cuban rural workers lived before the 1959 Revolution.

Brujería   Witchcraft, especially as practiced by women of African and indigenous American descent, whose knowledge of native cultural traditions offered a refuge from, and served as a source of resistance to, Spanish cultural domination.

Cabildo   A municipal council in the Spanish colonies.

Cacique   (1) An indigenous chief or local ruler. (2) A tyrannical local boss.

Calpulli   A kinship and territorial unit of social organization in ancient and colonial Mexico.

Campesinos   Usually poor, powerless rural residents, including farm workers, peasants, sharecroppers, and small farmers.

Candomblé   Popular among Afro-Brazilians, a religious sect that worships Ogun, the African god of birth and death, and preserves the cultural traditions of Africa's western Yorubaland, home of many Africans enslaved by the Portuguese and sold to Brazilian fazendeiros.

Capitão mor   The commander in chief of the military forces of a province in colonial Brazil.

Capitulación   The contract between the Spanish monarch and the leader of an expedition of conquest or discovery.

Caudillo   A powerful political boss whose authority is unassailable.

Cédula   A royal decree issued by the Spanish crown.

Charanga   A traditional musical instrument similar to a guitar, combining the technologies of Spanish and indigenous peoples, who originally used the shell of an armadillo to construct it.

Chicha   Originally a type of beer made from corn and common among Andean indigenous communities; later became the slang name for a new musical genre pioneered by recent migrants who combined highland indigenous sounds with urban electronic instruments and rock-and-roll rhythms.

Chinampa   A garden or piece of arable land reclaimed from a lake or pond by dredging up soil from the bottom and piling it on a bed of wickerwork (Mexico).

Científico   A policy maker in the government of Mexico's Porfirio Díaz (1876–1911) who believed in the "science" of positivism, racist doctrines of white supremacy, and national economic modernization based on private property and foreign investment.

Cofradía   A religious brotherhood, originally indigenous; sodality.

Colegio   A college or school.

Compadrazco   Spanish cultural institution of godparents, which expanded aristocrats' patriarchal power by establishing dependent kinship relationships with lower-class families.

Compadrio   Portuguese version of *compadrazgo*.

Composición   A settlement legalizing title to usurped land through payment of a fee to the king.

Congregación   Resettlement of scattered indigenous populations to facilitate Christianization and the collection of tribute.

Consulado   A merchant guild and a tribunal of commerce during the colonial period.

Conversos   Converted Spanish Jews or their descendants.

Corregidor   A royal governor of a district. A *corregidor de indios* administered indigenous pueblos.

Cortes   The Spanish parliament.

Côrtes   The Portuguese parliament.

Creole   An American-born Spaniard in the Spanish colonies.

Cumbe   In Spanish America, the name given to communities composed of African peoples who had escaped enslavement and established settlements independent of Spanish royal control.

Cumbia   An influential musical genre born of Colombia's Atlantic Coast, drawing upon the traditional West African *cumbe* dance and combining Spanish melodies with African rhythms and indigenous American harmonies.

Curaca   A hereditary chief or ruler in ancient or colonial Peru.

Ejidatarios   A member of a community that owned lands in common.

Ejido   Commonly owned lands, customarily farmed collectively by indigenous communities.

Encomendero   The holder of an *encomienda*.

Encomienda   An assignment of indígenas who were to serve the Spanish grantee with tribute and labor; also, the area belonging to indigenous people so granted.

Enganchador   Literally "one who hooks or ensnares," referring to individuals who act as labor contractors to recruit desperate workers by coercion or deceit.

Fazenda   A large estate (Brazil).

Fazendeiro   The owner of a *fazenda*.

Fueros   Special privileges granted to military officers, church officials, and others that exempted them from civil legal proceedings.

Guachibales   Indigenous religious brotherhoods that aimed to maintain cultural identities; defend their autonomy; and preserve communal customs, ancestral languages, and religious rituals.

Hacendado   The owner of a *hacienda*.

Hacienda   A large landed estate.

Hidalgo   A member of the lower nobility of Spain.

Indígenas   Individuals whose customs, traditions, dress, or physical features identified them as peoples indigenous to the Americas before the arrival of Europeans.

Inquilino   A Chilean tenant farmer.

Jipitecos   Mexican or foreign youth who identified with "hippie" counterculture, rejected the commercialism associated with modernity, and emulated the traditional lifestyles of impoverished indigenous peoples.

Ladino   Generally, any person who adopts customs and traditions alien to his own cultural birthright. Depending upon the context, this may refer to (1) Hispanicized people of Jewish, indigenous American, or African descent who embraced Christianity; (2) landless free laborers, born of mixed-race parentage, who embraced the cultural traditions of creole aristocrats; or (3) especially in contemporary Central America, mixed-race peoples who identify as "white" to distinguish themselves from indigenous peoples.

Latifundio   The system of large landholdings, feudal in its origins, that has dominated Latin America since the colonial period.

Mambises   Nineteenth-century Cuban guerrilla soldiers who fought for political independence and racial justice in integrated battalions, often under the command of black officers.

Mandamiento   A system of coerced indigenous labor.

Mayeque   A tenant farmer or serf on the estate of a noble family in ancient Mexico.

Mayorazgo   An entailed estate.

Mazombo   A person born of Portuguese parents in the Americas, similar to the Spanish *creole.*

Mestizo   A person of mixed indigenous and Spanish descent.

Minga   A free indigenous miner in colonial Peru.

Mita   In colonial Peru, the periodic conscription of *indígenas* for labor useful to the Spanish community. See *Repartimiento.*

Moderados   Individuals comprising the moderate wing of the Liberal party in nineteenth-century Mexico.

Ñañiguismo   The practice, common among Afro-Cubans, of organizing religious brotherhoods, under church protection, to resist racism and preserve African cultural traditions.

Negrista   An intellectual who participated in the early-twentieth-century philosophical and literary movement that celebrated African cultural contributions to Latin American societies.

Nueva Canción   Literally "New Song," a cultural movement that swept across Latin America in the 1960s, rejected the marketplace values of modernity, and drew inspiration instead from communal traditions linked to folk arts, music, and crafts.

Obraje   A primitive factory or workshop, especially for textile manufacture, often employing convict or debt labor.

Oidor   A judge of an *audiencia.*

Ouvidor   A royal judge who usually combined judicial and administrative duties (Brazil).

Patria   The fatherland.

Patrón   Master.

Patronato real   The right of the Spanish crown to dispose of all ecclesiastical offices.

Peninsular   A person born of Spanish parents in Spain and temporarily residing in the Americas.

Peso   A monetary unit of eight *reales.*

Piqueteros   Unemployed workers in Argentina who joined together to protest against neoliberal policies that produced poverty and social injustice.

Pitucos   The derisive and derogatory term used by ordinary folk to describe wealthy people accustomed to privilege and power.

Porteño   In Argentina, an inhabitant of Buenos Aires.

Pueblos jovenes   Poor "squatter" communities (literally "young towns") constructed on vacant lands by homeless men and women who lacked proprietary rights, but who insisted that their right to survive superseded all other legal claims.

Quilombo   In Brazil, the name given to communities composed of African peoples who had escaped enslavement and established settlements independent of Portuguese royal control.

Quinto   One-fifth; the royal share or tax on all mine production or spoils of a conquest.

Rancheros   People, usually of mixed race, who owned and operated small farms interspersed among indigenous villages and large commercial estates.

Real A monetary unit; one-eighth of a *peso*.

Rectificación The process of searching self-criticism and economic reform designed to make socialism more efficient in Cuba.

Regidor A councilman in a *cabildo*.

Relacão, *pl.* relaçoes A high court in colonial Brazil that combined judicial and administrative functions.

Repartimiento (1) An assignment of indígenas or land to a Spanish settler during the first years of the Conquest. (2) The periodic conscription of indígenas for labor useful to the Spanish community. (3) The mandatory purchase of merchandise by indígenas from royal officials; also *repartimiento de mercancías.*

Repartimiento de mercancías See *Repartimiento* (sense 3).

Residencia A judicial review of a colonial official's conduct at the end of his term of office.

Santería A religion, popular in Cuba and the Caribbean more generally, that combines Spanish Catholic and African traditions and ritual celebrations.

Senado de câmara A municipal council in colonial Brazil.

Seringueiros Independent rubber tappers whose survival depends on the preservation of Brazilian rain forests threatened by commercial ranchers and mining companies.

Sertão Underdeveloped backlands of Brazil, especially in the impoverished northeastern region.

Soldaderas Women who often fought, gathered military intelligence, fed insurgent troops, and provided medical care to those wounded in the Mexican Revolution.

Son First developed among rural Afro-Cuban workers, a musical genre that combined Spanish melodies and the syncopated rhythms of West Africa and that, by the middle of the twentieth century, became the dominant musical form identified with Cuban popular culture.

Tenente A Brazilian army lieutenant, usually associated with junior army officers who sought political, economic, and social reforms in the 1920s.

Tienda de raya A hacienda's company store, which typically exploited its commercial monopoly to coerce a stable labor supply through debt peonage.

Visita A judicial investigation of a colonial official's conduct; a tour of inspection, or other official visit, usually made unannounced.

Visitador An official entrusted by the crown or the viceroy with the conduct of a *visita.*

Yanacona (1) A servant or retainer of the Inca in ancient Peru. (2) An indigenous laborer or tenant farmer of semiservile status attached to a Spanish master or estate in colonial Peru.

Zambos The offspring of sexual liaisons between Africans and indigenous Americans.

SUGGESTIONS FOR FURTHER READING

The indispensable *Handbook of Latin American Studies*, published annually since 1936 and now available online through the Library of Congress Web site (http://lcweb2.loc.gov/hlas), attempts to digest published material on Latin America in the social sciences and humanities. C. C. Griffin, ed., *Latin America: A Guide to the Historical Literature* (1971), "provides a selective scholarly bibliography, covering the entire field of Latin American history."

Students can keep abreast of the most recent writing in the field by consulting the review sections of *The American Historical Review* (1895–), *The Hispanic American Historical Review* (1918–1922, 1926–), *Revista de Historia de America* (1938–), *The Americas: A Quarterly Review of Inter-American Cultural History* (1944–), *The Review of Inter-American Bibliography* (1951–), *Latin American Research Review* (1965–), the British *Journal of Latin American Studies* (1969–), and the *Colonial Latin American Historical Review* (1993–).

The LANIC Web site at the University of Texas (http://www.lanic.utexas.edu) has abundant information, organized by country and subject directories, with extraordinarily useful electronic links to other relevant Web sites. Molly Molloy's *Internet Resources for Latin America* (http://lib.nmsu.edu/subject/bord/laguia) is also a useful tool for locating reliable electronic sources on Latin America.

For well-informed coverage of current events in the area, see *Latinamerica Press* (Lima, Peru, 1969–) and the *Latin American Weekly Report* and the *Latin American Regional Reports*, published by Latin American Newsletters Ltd. (London). For more extended coverage of particular topics and events, see the bimonthly *NACLA Report on the Americas*, published by the North American Congress on Latin America (1967–) and focusing on the political economy of the area. The articles in *Latin American Perspectives* (1973–) offer scholarly Marxist interpretations of past and present problems of the area.

General Works

James Lockhart and S. B. Schwartz, *Early Latin America: A History of Colonial Spanish America and Brazil* (1983). L. N. McAlister, *Spain and Portugal in the New World* (1984). M. A. Burkholder and L. L. Johnson, *Colonial Latin America*, 3rd ed. (1997). S. J. and B. H. Stein, *The Colonial Heritage of Latin America: Essays on Economic Dependence in Perspective* (1966). David Bushnell and Neill Macaulay, *The Emergence of Latin America in the Nineteenth Century* (1988). Leslie Bethell, ed., *The Cambridge History of Latin America*, 8 vols. (1985–1991). Benjamin Keen, ed., *Latin American Civilization: History and Society, 1492 to the Present*, 6th ed. (1995), provides a compact but comprehensive collection of source materials.

Chapter 1
Ancient America

B. M. Fagen, *The Great Journey: The Peopling of Ancient America* (1987). Friedrich Katz, *The Ancient American Civilizations* (1972). G. A. Collier, R. I. Rosaldo, and J. D. Wirth, *The Inca and Aztec States, 1400–1800: Anthropology and History* (1982). K. D. Bruhns, *Ancient South America* (1994).

R. E. W. Adams, *Prehistoric Mesoamerica*, rev. ed. (1991). E. J. Wolf, *Sons of the Shaking Earth* (1959). Ignacio Bernal, *The Olmecs* (1969). Nigel Davies, *The Toltecs Until the Fall of Tula* (1977). Joseph Whitecotton, *The Zapotecs* (1977). John Paddock, ed., *Ancient Oaxaca* (1966).

Frances Berdan, *The Aztecs of Central Mexico, An Imperial Society* (1982). Inga Clendinnen, *Aztecs: An Interpretation* (1991). Ross Hassig, *Trade, Tribute, and Transportation. The Sixteenth Century Political Economy of the Valley of Mexico* (1985). Ross Hassig, *Aztec Warfare: Imperial Expansion and Political Control* (1988). Jacques Soustelle, *The Daily Life of the Aztecs on the Eve of the Conquest,* tr. Patrick O'Brian (1962). Miguel León-Portilla, *Aztec Thought and Culture: A Study of the Ancient Nahuatl Mind* (1963). M. G. Hodge and M. E. Smith, eds., *Economies and Politics in the Aztec Realms* (1994). Benjamin Keen, *The Aztec Image in Western Thought* (1971). Ross Hassig, *Time, History, and Belief in Aztec and Colonial Mexico* (2001).

Sylvanus Morley, *The Ancient Maya,* revised by G. W. Brainerd (1965). Michael Coe, *The Maya* (1956). Norman Hammond, *Ancient Maya Civilization* (1982). Linda Schele and David Freidel, *A Forest of Kings: The Untold Story of the Ancient Maya* (1990). Peter D. Harrison, *The Lords of Tikal: Rulers of an Ancient Maya City* (1999).

E. P. Lanning, *Peru Before the Incas* (1967). R. W. Keatinge, ed., *Peruvian Prehistory: An Overview of Pre-Inca and Inca Society* (1988). M. E. Moseley, *The Incas and Their Ancestors: The Archaeology of Peru* (1992). Garcilaso de la Vega, *Royal Commentaries of the Inca and General History of Peru,* tr. H. V. Livermore (1966). Alfred Metraux, *The History of the Incas* (1969). J. V. Murra, *The Economic Organization of the Inca State* (1980). Irene Silverblatt, *Moon, Sun, and Witches* (1987). Laura Laurencich Minelli, ed., *The Inca World: The Development of Pre-Columbian Peru,* A.D. *1000–1534* (2000).

Woodrow Borah and S. F. Cook, *The Aboriginal Population of Central Mexico on the Eve of the Spanish Conquest* (1963). S. F. Cook and Woodrow Borah, *Essays in Population History, Mexico and the Caribbean,* 3 vols. (1971–1979). W. M. Denevan, ed., *The Native Population of the Americas in 1492* (1976).

Chapter 2
The Hispanic Background

S. G. Payne, *A History of Spain and Portugal,* 2 vols. (1973). D. W. Lomax, *The Reconquest of Spain* (1978). John Elliott, *Imperial Spain, 1469–1716* (1964). John Lynch, *Spain Under the Hapsburgs,* 2 vols. (1984). Henry Kamen, *Spain, 1469–1714: A Society of Conflict* (1983). J. H. Mariejol, *The Spain of Ferdinand and Isabella,* tr. and ed. Benjamin Keen (1961). Henry Kamen, *The Spanish Inquisition* (1965). Ruth Pike, *Aristocrats and Traders: Sevillian Society in the Sixteenth Century* (1972). Bernard F. Reilly, *The Medieval Spains* (1993). Henry Kamen, *Philip II of Spain* (1997).

Chapter 3
The Conquest of America

C. E. Nowell, *The Great Discoveries and the First Colonial Empires* (1954). J. H. Parry, *The Age of Reconnaissance* (1963). John Elliott, *The Old World and the New, 1492–1650* (1970). Fredi Chiapelli, ed., *First Images of America,* 2 vols. (1976). William Brandon, *New Worlds for Old* (1986).

B. W. Diffie, *Prelude to Empire: Portugal Overseas Before Henry the Navigator* (1961). S. E. Morison, *The European Discovery of America: The Southern Voyages, 1492–1619* (1974). S. E. Morison, *Admiral of the Ocean Sea: A Life of the Admiral Christopher Columbus,* 2 vols. (1942). P. E. Taviani, *Christopher Columbus: The Grand Design* (1985). Kirkpatrick Sale, *The Conquest of Paradise* (1990). William Phillips and C. R. Phillips, *The Worlds of Christopher Columbus* (1991). Tzvetan Todorov, *The Conquest of America: The Question of the Other* (1984). Carl Sauer, *The Early Spanish Main* (1966). J. G. Varner and J. J. Varner, *The Dogs of the Conquest* (1983). A. W. Crosby, *The Columbian Exchange: Biological and Cultural Consequences of 1492* (1972). N. D. Cook, *Demographic Collapse: Indian Peru, 1520–1620* (1981). L. A. Newson, *Indian Survival in Colonial Nicaragua* (1987). N. D. Cook and W. G. Lovell, eds., *"Secret Judgments of God": Old World Disease in Colonial Spanish America* (1991).

Miguel León-Portilla, ed., *The Broken Spears: The Aztec Account of the Conquest of Mexico* (1962). Nathan Wachtel, *The Vision of the Vanquished: The Spanish Conquest of Peru Through Indian Eyes, 1530–1570* (1977). Fernando Cortés, *Letters from Mexico,* tr. and ed. A. R. Pagden (1971). Bernal Díaz del Castillo, *The Conquest of New Spain,* tr. J. M. Cohen (1963). Francisco López de Gómara, *Cortés: The Life of the Conqueror by His Secretary,* tr. L. B. Simpson (1966). R. C. Padden, *The Hummingbird and the Hawk: Conquest and Sovereignty in the Valley of Mexico, 1503–1541* (1967). Hugh Thomas, *Conquest: Montezuma, Cortés, and the Fall of Old Mexico* (1994).

John Hemming, *The Conquest of the Incas* (1970). James Lockhart, *The Men of Cajamarca: A Social and Biographical Study of the First Conquerors of Peru* (1972). John Hemming, *The Search for El Dorado* (1978). James Lockhart and Enrique Otte, eds., *Letters and People of the Spanish Indies: Sixteenth Century* (1976). B. P. Bodmer, *The Armature of Conquest: Spanish Accounts of the Discovery of America* (1992).

Stephanie Gail Wood, *Transcending Conquest: Nahua Views of Spanish Colonial Mexico* (2003). Stuart B. Schwartz, ed., *Victors and the Vanquished: Spanish and Nahua Views of the Conquest of Mexico* (2000). Susan E. Ramírez, *The World Upside Down: Cross-Cultural Contact and Conflict in Sixteenth-Century Peru* (1996). Kenneth J. Andrien, *Andean Worlds: Indigenous History, Culture, and Consciousness Under Spanish Rule, 1532–1825* (2001).

Chapter 4
The Economic Foundations of Colonial Life

Lewis Hanke, *The Spanish Struggle for Justice in the Conquest of America* (1949). J. L. Phelan, *The Millennial Kingdom of the Franciscans in the New World* (1956). Juan Friede and Benjamin Keen, eds., *Bartolomé de Las Casas in History* (1971). Gustavo Gutiérrez, *Las Casas. In Search of the Poor of Jesus Christ*, tr. R. R. Barr (1993).

S. J. Stern, *Peru's Native Peoples and the Challenge of Conquest: Huamanga to 1640* (1982). Karen Spalding, *Huarochiri: An Indian Society Under Inca and Spanish Rule* (1984). Nancy Farriss, *Maya Society Under Spanish Rule* (1984). G. D. Jones, *Maya Resistance to Spanish Rule: Time and History on a Colonial Frontier* (1989). Inga Clendinnen, *Ambivalent Conquests: Maya and Spaniard in Yucatan, 1517–1570* (1987). A. M. Wightman, *Indigenous Migration and Social Change: The Forasteros of Cuzco, 1520–1720* (1990). Rolena Adorno, *Guaman Poma: Writing and Resistance in Colonial Peru* (1986).

J. A. and J. E. Villamarin, *Indian Labor in Mainland Colonial Spanish America* (1975). L. N. Simpson, *The Encomienda in New Spain*, rev. ed. (1950). W. L. Sherman, *Forced Native Labor in Sixteenth-Century Central America* (1979). Charles Gibson, *The Aztecs Under Spanish Rule: A History of the Indians of the Valley of Mexico* (1964). François Chevalier, *Land and Society in Colonial Mexico*, tr. L. B. Simpson (1963). W. B. Taylor, *Landlord and Peasant in Colonial Oaxaca* (1972). John Tutino, *From Insurrection to Revolution in Mexico: Social Bases of Agrarian Violence, 1750–1940* (1986). R. G. Keith, *Conquest and Agrarian Change: Emergence of the Hacienda System on the Peruvian Coast* (1976). K. A. Davies, *Landowners in Colonial Peru* (1984). S. E. Ramirez, *Provincial Patriarchs: Land Tenure and the Economics of Power in Colonial Peru* (1986).

L. B. Rout, Jr., *The African Experience in Spanish America: 1502 to the Present Day* (1971). H. S. Klein, *African Slavery in Latin America and the Caribbean* (1986). F. P. Bowser, *The African Slave in Colonial Peru, 1524–1650* (1973). C. L. Palmer, *Slaves of the White God: Blacks in Colonial Mexico, 1570–1650* (1976). Richard Price, ed., *Maroon Societies: Rebel Slave Communities in the Americas* (1979). J. C. Miller, *Way of Death: Merchant Capitalism and the Angolan Slave Trade, 1730–1830* (1988). Robin Blackburn, *The Making of New World Slavery: From the Baroque to the Modern 1492–1800* (1998). Hugh Thomas, *The Story of the Atlantic Slave Trade 1440–1870* (1997). John Thornton, *Africa and Africans in the Making of the Atlantic World, 1400–1800* (1998).

E. G. K. Melville, *A Plague of Sheep, Environmental Consequences of the Conquest of Mexico* (1994). M. J. MacLeod, *Spanish Central America: A Socioeconomic History, 1520–1720* (1973). J. C. Super, *Food, Conquest, and Colonization in Sixteenth-Century Spanish America* (1988).

P. J. Bakewell, *Silver Mining and Society in Colonial Mexico: Zacatecas, 1546–1700* (1971). P. J. Bakewell, *Miners of the Red Mountain: Indian Labor in Potosí, 1545–1650* (1984). J. A. Cole, *The Potosí Mita, 1573–1700, Compulsory Indian Labor in the Andes* (1985). R. M. Salvucci, *Textiles and Capitalism in Mexico: An Economic History of the Obrajes, 1539–1840* (1987). Jeremy Baskes, *Indians, Merchants and Markets: A Reinterpretation of the Repartimiento and Spanish-Indian Economic Relations in Colonial Oaxaca, 1750–1821* (2000). Ida Altman, *Transatlantic Ties in the Spanish Empire: Brihuega, Spain & Puebla, Mexico 1560–1620* (2000). Enrique Tandeter, *Coercion and Market: Silver Mining in Colonial Potosí, 1692–1826* (1993). Oscar Cornblit, *Power and Violence in the Colonial City: Oruro from the Mining Renaissance to the Rebellion of Túpac Amaru, 1740–1782* (1995). Ann Zulawski, *They Eat from Their Labor: Work and Social Changein Colonial Bolivia* (1994). Kathleen J. Higgins, *"Licentious Liberty" in a Brazilian Gold-Mining Region: Slavery, Gender, and Social Control in Eighteenth-Century Sabara, Minas Gerais* (2000).

C. H. Haring, *Trade and Navigation Between Spain and the Indies in the Time of the Hapsburgs* (1918). Ruth Pike, *Enterprise and Adventure: The Genoese at Seville and the Opening of the New World* (1966). K. R. Andrews, *The Spanish Caribbean: Trade and Plunder, 1530–1630* (1978). C. H. Haring, *The Buccaneers in the West Indies in the Seventeenth Century* (1919). Lance Grahn, *The Political Economy of Smuggling: Regional Informal Economics in Early Bourbon New Granada* (1997).

Chapter 5
State, Church, and Society

C. H. Haring, *The Spanish Empire in America* (1947). Mario Gongora, *Studies in the Colonial History of Spanish America* (1975). J. H. Parry, *The Spanish Theory of Empire in the Sixteenth Century* (1940). Peggy Liss, *Mexico Under Spain, 1521–1556* (1975). J. H. Parry, *The Audiencia of New Galicia in the Sixteenth Century* (1948). J. L. Phelan, *The Kingdom of Quito in the Seventeenth Century: Bureaucratic Politics in the Spanish Empire* (1957). R. H. Vigil, *Alonso de Zorita: Royal Judge and Christian Humanist, 1512–1585* (1987). J. I. Israel, *Race, Class, and Politics in Colonial Mexico, 1610–1670* (1975). K. J. Andrien, *Crisis and Decline: The Viceroyalty of Peru in the Seventeenth Century* (1985).

R. E. Greenleaf, ed., *The Roman Catholic Church in Colonial Latin America* (1971). Robert Ricard, *The Spiritual Conquest of Mexico*, tr. L. B. Simpson (1966). L. M. Burkhart, *The Slippery Earth: Nahua-Christian Moral Dialogue in Sixteenth-Century Mexico* (1989). Serge Gruzinski, *Man-Gods in the Mexican Highlands: Indian Power and Colonial Society, 1520–1800* (1989). Nicholas Griffiths, *The Cross and the Serpent: Religious Repression and Resurgence in Colonial Peru* (1996). R. E. Greenleaf, *The Mexican Inquisition in the Seventeenth Century* (1969). Magnus Morner, *The Political and Economic Activities of the Jesuits in the La Plata Region: The Hapsburg Era* (1953). J. F. Schwaller, *Church and Clergy in Sixteenth-Century Mexico* (1987). Alejandro Caneque, *The King's Living Image: The Culture and Politics of Viceregal Power in Colonial Mexico* (2003). Victor Uribe Uran, *State and Society in Spanish America During the Age of Revolution* (2001). David A. Brading, *Church and State in Bourbon Mexico: The Diocese of Michoacán, 1749–1810* (1994).

James Lockhart, *The Nahuas After the Conquest: A Social and Cultural History of the Indians of Central Mexico, Sixteenth Through Eighteenth Centuries* (1992). Robert Heskett, *Indigenous Rulers: An Ethnohistory of Colonial Cuernavaca* (1991). Magnus Morner, *Race Mixture in the History of Latin America* (1967). L. S. Hoberman and S. M. Socolow, *Cities and Society in Colonial Latin America* (1986). D. G. Sweet and G. B. Nash, *Struggle and Survival in Colonial America* (1981). Eugene Genovese and Laura Foner, eds., *Slavery in the New World* (1970). D. W. Cohen and J. P. Greene, *Freemen of African Descent in the Slave Societies of the New World* (1972). Patrick J. Carroll, *Blacks in Colonial Veracruz: Race, Ethnicity, and Regional Development* (2001). R. Douglas Cope, *The Limits of Racial Domination: Plebeian Society in Colonial Mexico City, 1660–1720* (1994). Herman L. Bennett, *Africans in Colonial Mexico: Absolutism, Christianity, and Afro-Creole Consciousness, 1570–1640* (2003). Susan M. Deeds, *Defiance and Deference in Mexico's Colonial North: Indians Under Spanish Rule in Nueva Vizcaya* (2003).

Peter Boyd-Bowman, *Patterns of Spanish Immigration in the New World, 1492–1580* (1973). James Lockhart, *Spanish Peru, 1532–1560* (1968). Asunción Lavrín, ed., *Sexuality and Marriage in Colonial Latin America* (1989). Patricia Seed, *To Love, Honor, and Obey in Colonial Mexico, 1574–1821* (1988). Luís Martín, *Daughters of the Conquistadores* (1983). Della M. Flusche, *Forgotten Females: Women of African and Indian Descent in Colonial Chile, 1535–1800* (1983). Susan Migden Socolow, *The Women of Colonial Latin America* (2000). Ann Twinam, *Public Lives, Private Secrets: Gender, Honor, Sexuality, and Illegitimacy in Colonial Spanish America* (2001).

Chapter 6
Colonial Brazil

Caio Prado Junior, *The Colonial Background of Modern Brazil*, tr. Suzette Macedo (1967). Charles Boxer, *The Dutch in Brazil, 1625–1654* (1957). Charles Boxer, *The Golden Age of Brazil, 1695–1750* (1962). Dauril Alden, ed., *The Colonial Roots of Modern Brazil* (1972). James Lang, *Portuguese Brazil: The King's Plantation* (1979).

S. B. Schwartz, *Sugar Plantations in the Formation of Brazilian Society: Bahia, 1550–1835* (1985). S. B. Schwartz, *Sovereignty and Society in Colonial Brazil: The High Court of Bahia and Its Judges, 1609–1735* (1973). Dauril Alden, *Royal Government in Colonial Brazil* (1968). K. R. Maxwell, *Conflicts and Conspiracies: Brazil and Portugal, 1750–1808* (1973). John Hemming, *Red Gold: The Conquest of the Brazilian Indians, 1500–1760* (1978). Gilberto Freyre, *The Masters and the Slaves*, tr. Samuel Putnam (1946). Charles Boxer, *Race Relations in the Portuguese Colonial Empire, 1415–1825* (1963). Sylviane Anna Diouf, *Servants of Allah: African Muslims Enslaved in the Americas* (1998). João José Reis, *Slave Rebellion in Brazil: The Muslim Uprising of 1835 in Bahia* (1993). Laird W. Bergad, *Slavery and the Demographic and Economic History of Minas Gerais, 1720–1888* (1999).

Chapter 7
The Bourbon Reforms and Spanish America

Richard Herr, *The Eighteenth-Century Revolution in Spain* (1958). John Lynch, *Spanish Colonial Administration, 1792–1819: The Intendant System in the Viceroyalty of the Rio de la Plata* (1958). J. R. Fisher, *Government and Society in Colonial Peru: The Intendant System, 1784–1814* (1970). M. S. Burkholder and D. S. Chandler, *From Impotence to Authority: The Spanish Crown and the American Audiencias, 1687–1808* (1977). S. M. Socolow, *The Bureaucrats of Buenos Aires, 1769–1810* (1988). C. L. Archer, *The Army in Bourbon Mexico, 1760–1810* (1978). L. G. Campbell, *The Military and Society in Colonial Peru, 1750–1810* (1978). J. K. Chance, *Race and Class in Colonial Oaxaca* (1989).

G. G. Walker, *Spanish Politics and Imperial Trade, 1700–1789* (1979). S. M. Socolow, *The Merchants of Buenos Aires, 1778–1810* (1978). Doris Ladd, *The Mexican Nobility at Independence, 1780–1826* (1978). David Brading, *Miners and Merchants in Bourbon Mexico, 1763–1810* (1971). B. R. Hamnett, *Politics and Trade in Southern Mexico, 1750–1821* (1971). R. L. Garner and Spiro E. Stefanou, *Economic Growth and Change in Bourbon Mexico* (1993). J. R. Fisher, *Silver Mines and Silver Miners in Colonial Peru, 1776–1824* (1977). H. S. Klein, *Haciendas and Ayllus: Society in the Bolivian Andes in the Eighteenth and Nineteenth Centuries* (1993). Eric Van Young, *Hacienda and Market in Eighteenth-Century Mexico: The Rural Economy of the Guadalajara Region, 1675–1820* (1981). John Kicza, *Colonial Entrepreneurs: Families and Business in Bourbon Mexico City* (1983). Ann Twinam, *Miners, Merchants, and Farmers of Colonial Colombia* (1982). Jay Kinsbruner, *Petty Capitalism in Spanish America: The Pulperos of Puebla, Mexico City, Caracas, and Buenos Aires* (1987). Doris Ladd, *The Making of a Strike: Mexican Silver Workers' Struggles in Real del Monte, 1766–1775* (1988).

J. T. Lanning, *Academic Culture in the Spanish Colonies* (1940). Mariano Picon Salas, *A Cultural History of Spanish America, from Conquest to Independence*, tr. Irving Leonard (1962). Octavio Paz, *Sor Juana, or the Traps of Faith*, tr. M. S. Peden (1989). Irving Leonard, *Books of the Brave* (1949). Irving Leonard, *Baroque Times in Old Mexico* (1959). George Kubler, *Mexican Architecture of the Sixteenth Century*, 2 vols. (1948). Jacques Lafaye, *Quetzalcoatl and Guadalupe: The Formation of Mexican National Consciousness*, tr. Benjamin Keen (1976). David Brading, *The First America: The Spanish Monarchy, Creole Patriots, and the Liberal State, 1492–1866* (1991). Antonello Gerbi, *The Dispute of the New World: The History of a Polemic, 1750–1900*, tr. Jeremy Moyle (1973).

L. E. Fisher, *The Last Inca Revolt, 1780–1783* (1966). J. L. Phelan, *The People and the King: The Comunero Revolution in Colombia* (1977).

Chapter 8
The Independence of Latin America

John Lynch, *The Spanish-American Revolutions, 1808–1826* (1973). Jay Kinsbruner, *Independence in Spanish America: Civil Wars, Revolutions, and Underdevelopment* (1994). T. A. Anna, *Spain and the Loss of America* (1983). C. L. R. James, *The Black Jacobins: Toussaint L'Ouverture and the Santo Domingo Revolution* (1963). C. E. Fick, *The Making of Haiti: The Saint Domingue Revolution from Below* (1990). Gerhard Masur, *Simon Bolívar*, 2nd ed. (1969). W. S. Robertson, *The Life of Miranda*, 2 vols. (1929). J. C. Metford, *San Martín* (1950). John Street, *Artigas and the Emancipation of Uruguay* (1959). Simon Collier, *Ideas and Politics of Chilean Independence, 1808–1833* (1969). A. J. R. Russell-Wood, *From Colony to Nation: Essays on the Independence of Brazil* (1975).

John Tutino, *From Insurrection to Revolution in Mexico: Social Bases of Agrarian Violence, 1750–1940* (1986). B. R. Hamnett, *Roots of Insurgency: Mexican Regions, 1750–1824* (1986). J. E. Rodriguez, ed., *The Independence of Mexico and the Creation of the New Nation* (1989). H. M. Hamill, *The Hidalgo Revolt: Prelude to Mexican Independence* (1966). W. H. Timmons, *Morelos of Mexico, Priest, Soldier, Statesman* (1963). T. A. Anna, *The Mexican Empire of Iturbide* (1990).

Tulio Halperin-Donghi, *The Aftermath of Revolution in Latin America* (1973). Tulio Halperin-Donghi, *Politics, Economics, and Society in Argentina in the Revolutionary Period* (1975). K. J. Andrien and L. L. Johnson, eds., *The Political Economy of Spanish America in the Age of Revolution, 1750–1850* (1994). Eric Van Young, *The Other Rebellion: Popular Violence, Ideology, and the Mexican Struggle for Independence, 1810–1821* (2001). Christon I. Archer, Colin M. MacLachlan, and William H. Beezley, eds., *The Wars of Independence in Spanish America* (2000).

Chapter 9
Dictators and Revolutions

David Bushnell and Neill Macaulay, *The Emergence of Latin America in the Nineteenth Century* (1992). Tulio Halperin-Donghi, *The Aftermath of Revolution in Latin America* (1973). E. B. Burns, *The Poverty of Progress: Latin America in the Nineteenth Century* (1980). H. M. Hamill, ed., *Caudillos: Dictators in Spanish America* (1992).

C. A. Hale, *Mexican Liberalism in the Age of Mora, 1821–1853* (1968). Barbara Tenenbaum, *The Politics of Penury: Debts and Taxes in Mexico, 1821–1856* (1986). R. N. Sinkin, *The Mexican Reform, 1855–1876: A Study in Liberal Nation-Building* (1979). Jan Bazant, *Alienation of Church Wealth: Social and Economic Aspects of the Liberal Revolution, 1856–1875* (1971). Nelson Reed, *The Caste War of Yucatan* (1964). Florencia Mallon, *Peasant and Nation: The Making of Postcolonial Mexico and Peru* (1994); Peter F. Guardino, *Peasants, Politics, and the Formation of Mexico's National State: Guerrero, 1800–1857* (1996).

Miron Burgin, *The Economic Aspects of Argentine Federalism, 1820–1852* (1946). John Lynch, *Argentine Dictator: Juan Manuel Rosas, 1829–1853* (1981). David Bushnell, *Reform and Reaction in the Platine Provinces* (1983). J. C. Brown, *A Socioeconomic History of Argentina, 1776–1860* (1979). R. A. White, *Paraguay's Autonomous Revolution* (1978). Thomas Whigham, *The Politics of River Trade: Tradition and Development in the Upper Plata* (1994).

Brian Loveman, *Chile: The Legacy of Hispanic Capitalism* (1979). Simon Collier, *Ideas and Politics of Chilean Independence, 1808–1833* (1969). Arnold Bauer, *Chilean Rural Society from the Spanish Conquest to 1930* (1975).

R. S. Schneider, *"Order and Progress": A Political History of Brazil* (1991). Leslie Bethell, *The Abolition of the Brazilian Slave Trade* (1971). Gilberto Freyre, *The Mansions and the Shanties*, tr. Harriet de Onis (1963). Robert Conrad, *The Destruction of Brazilian Slavery, 1850–1888* (1973). Katia M. de Queiros Mattos, *To Be a Slave in Brazil, 1550–1888* (1986). Stanley Stein, *Vassouras: A Brazilian Coffee County* (1957). Harry Bernstein, *Dom Pedro II* (1973). Peter Blanchard, *Slavery and Abolition in Early Republican Peru* (1992).

Chapter 10
The Triumph of Neocolonialism

Celso Furtado, *The Economic Development of Latin America*, tr. Suzette Macedo (1970). Roberto Cortes Conde, *The First Stages of Modernization in Spanish America* (1974). Florencia Mallon, *The Defense of Community in Peru's Central Highlands: Peasant Struggle and Capitalist Transformation, 1860–1910* (1983).

M. C. Meyer and W. L. Sherman, *The Course of Mexican History*, 4th ed. (1990). J. K. Turner, *Barbarous Mexico* (1910). J. M. Hart, *The Coming and Process of the Mexican Revolution* (1987). R. J. Knowlton, *Church Property and the Mexican Reform, 1856–1910* (1976). R. D. Anderson, *Outcasts in Their Own Land: Mexican Industrial Workers, 1906–1911* (1976). L. B. Perry, *Juarez and Diaz, Machine Politics in Porfirian Mexico* (1979). J. H. Coatsworth, *Growth and Development: The Economic Impact of Railroads on Porfirian Mexico* (1981). J. D. Cockcroft, *Intellectual Precursors of the Mexican Revolution, 1900–1913* (1968). Charles Hale, *The Transformation of Liberalism in Late Nineteenth-Century Mexico* (1990). Mark Wasserman, *Capitalists, Caciques, and Revolution: The Native Elite and Foreign Enterprise in Chihuahua, Mexico, 1854–1911* (1984). Allen Wells, *Yucatán's Gilded Age: Haciendas, Henequen, and International Harvester, 1860–1915* (1985).

Nicolas Shumway, *The Invention of Argentina* (1992). Thomas McGann, *Argentina, the United States, and the Inter-American System, 1880–1914* (1957). H. S. Ferns, *Britain and Argentina in the Nineteenth Century* (1960). James Scobie, *Argentina: A City and a Nation* (1971). James Scobie, *Revolution on the Pampas: A Social History of Argentine Wheat* (1964). David Rock, *Politics in Argentina, 1890–1930: The Rise and Fall of Radicalism* (1975).

Brian Loveman, *Chile: The Legacy of Hispanic Capitalism* (1979). A. J. Bauer, *Chilean Rural Society from the Spanish Conquest to 1930* (1979). William Sater, *Chile and the War of the Pacific* (1986). Harold Blakemore, *British Nitrates and Chilean Politics, 1886–1896* (1974). Maurice Zeitlin, *The Civil Wars in Chile (or the Bourgeois Revolutions That Never Were)* (1984).

R. M. Schneider, *"Order and Progress": A Political History of Brazil* (1991). Euclides da Cunha, *Rebellion in the Backlands*, tr. Samuel Putnam (1957). P. L. Eisenberg, *The Sugar Industry in Pernambuco, 1840–1910* (1974). Richard Graham, *Britain and the*

Onset of Industrialization in Brazil, 1850–1914 (1968). Warren Dean, *The Industrialization of São Paulo, 1880–1945* (1969). June Hahner, *Poverty and Politics: The Urban Poor in Brazil, 1870–1920* (1986). Jeffrey D. Needell, *A Tropical Belle Epoque: The Elite Culture of Turn-of-the-Century Rio de Janeiro* (1986). Sandra Lauderdale Graham, *House and Street: Domestic World of Servants and Masters in 19th Century Rio de Janeiro* (1992). María Odila Silva Dias, *Power and Everyday Life: The Lives of Working Women in Nineteenth-Century Brazil* (1995).

Chapter 11
Society and Culture in the Nineteenth Century

Tulio Halperin-Donghi, *The Aftermath of Revolution in Latin America* (1973). Richard Graham, *Britain and the Onset of Modernization in Brazil* (1968). Frank Safford, *The Ideal of the Practical: Colombia's Struggle to Form a Technical Elite* (1976). Silvia Arrom, *The Women of Mexico City, 1790–1857* (1985). June Hahner, *Emancipating the Female Sex: The Struggle for Women's Rights in Brazil, 1850–1940* (1991). Francesca Miller, *Latin American Women and the Search for Social Justice* (1992).

J. L. Mecham, *Church and State in Latin America: A History of Politico-Ecclesiastical Relations*, rev. ed. (1966). Leopoldo Zea, *The Latin American Mind* (1963). Leopoldo Zea, *Positivism in Mexico*, tr. Josephine Schulte (1974). Charles Hale, *The Transformation of Liberalism in Late Nineteenth-Century Mexico* (1990). Richard Graham, ed., *The Idea of Race in Latin America*, (1990). Jean Franco, *An Introduction to Spanish American Literature* (1969). Allen Woll, *A Functional Past: The Uses of History in Nineteenth-Century Chile* (1982).

Chapter 12
The Mexican Revolution— and After

R. E. Ruiz, *The Great Rebellion: Mexico, 1905–1924* (1980). Friedrich Katz, *The Secret War in Mexico: Europe, the United States, and the Mexican Revolution* (1981). Alan Knight, *The Mexican Revolution*, 2 vols. (1986). J. M. Hart, *The Coming and Process of the Mexican Revolution* (1987).

Thomas Benjamin and Mark Wasserman, eds., *The Mexican Revolution: Essays in Regional Mexican History, 1910–1929* (1990). G. M. Joseph, *Revolution from Without: Yucatán, Mexico, and the United States, 1880–1924* (1988). H. F. Salamini, *Agrarian Radicalism in Veracruz, 1920–1938* (1971).

James Cockcroft, *Intellectual Precursors of the Mexican Revolution, 1900–1913* (1968). John Womack, *Zapata and the Mexican Revolution* (1968). M. C. Meyer, *Huerta: A Political Portrait* (1972). Friedrich Katz, ed., *Riot, Rebellion, and Revolution: Rural Social Conflict in Mexico* (1988). Gilbert M. Joseph and Daniel Nugent, eds., *Everyday Forms of State Formation: Revolution and the Negotiation of Rule in Modern Mexico* (1994).

Ana Macias, *Against All Odds: The Feminist Movement in Mexico to 1940* (1982). Maria Patricia Fernández-Kelly, *For We Are Sold, I and My People: Women and Industry in Mexico's Frontier* (1983). Shirlene Soto, *Emergence of the Modern Mexican Woman: Her Participation in Revolution and Struggle for Equality, 1910–1940* (1990). Heather Fowler-Salamini and Mary Kay Vaughan, eds., *Women of the Mexican Countryside, 1850–1990: Creating Spaces, Shaping Transitions* (1994).

William H. Beezley, William E. French, and Cheryl E. Martin, eds., *Rituals of Rule, Rituals of Resistance: Public Celebrations and Popular Culture in Mexico* (1994). Nestor Garcia Canclini, *Transforming Modernity: Popular Culture in Mexico* (1993). Gilbert M. Joseph, Anne Rubenstein, Eric Zolov, Elena Poniatowska, eds., *Fragments of a Golden Age: The Politics of Culture in Mexico Since 1940* (2001). Eric Zolov, *Refried Elvis: The Rise of the Mexican Counterculture* (1999).

J. D. Cockcroft, *Mexico: Class Formation, Capital Accumulation, and the State* (1983). J. M. Cypher, *State and Capital in Mexico: Development Policy Since 1940* (1990). David Barkin, *Distorted Development: Mexico in the World Economy* (1990). Susan Tiano, *Patriarchy on the Line: Labor, Gender, and Ideology in the Mexican Maquila Industry* (1994).

Chapter 13
Argentina: The Failure of Democracy

David Rock, *Argentina, 1516–1982: From Spanish Colonization to the Falklands War* (1985). C. F. Diaz

Alejandro, *Essays on the Economic History of the Argentine Republic* (1970). Laura Randall, *An Economic History of Argentina in the Twentieth Century* (1978).

J. A. Page, *Perón: A Biography* (1983). Roland Crassweller, *Perón and the Enigma of Argentina* (1987). Daniel James, *Resistance and Integration: Peronism and the Argentine Working Class, 1946–1976* (1994). Peter Ranis, *Argentine Workers: Peronism and Contemporary Class Consciousness* (1992).

Asunción Lavrin, *Women, Feminism, and Social Change in Argentina, Chile, and Uruguay, 1890–1940* (1995). Marifran Carlson, *Feminismo!: The Woman's Movement in Argentina from Its Beginnings to Eva Perón* (1988). Nicholas Fraser and Marysa Navarro, *Evita: The Real Life of Eva Peron* (1996). Donna J. Guy, *Sex and Danger in Buenos Aires: Prostitution, Family, and Nation in Argentina* (1991).

David Rock, *Authoritarian Argentina: The Nationalist Movement, Its History and Impact* (1993). D. C. Hodges, *Argentina, 1943–1976: The National Revolution and Resistance* (1976). Carlos Waisman, *Reversal of Development in Argentina* (1987). M. E. Andersen, *Dossier Secreto. Argentina's Desaparecidos and the Myths of the "Dirty War"* (1993). Monica Peralta-Ramos. *The Political Economy of Argentina: Power and Class Since 1930* (1991). Marguerite Guzman Bouvard, *Revolutionizing Motherhood: The Mothers of the Plaza de Mayo* (1994). J. Patrice McSherry, *Incomplete Transition: Military Power and Democracy in Argentina* (1997).

Laura Podalsky, *Specular City: The Transformation of Culture, Consumption, and Space After Perón* (2002). Donald S. Castro, *The Argentine Tango as Social History, 1880–1955: The Soul of the People* (1991). James P. Brennan, *The Labor Wars in Córdoba, 1955–1976: Ideology, Work, and Labor Politics in an Argentine Industrial City* (1995). Luis Alberto Romero, *A History of Argentina in the Twentieth Century* (2002). Donna J. Guy, *White Slavery and Mothers Alive and Dead: The Troubled Meeting of Sex, Gender, Public Health, and Progress in Latin America* (2000).

Chapter 14
The Chilean Way

Brian Loveman, *Chile: The Legacy of Hispanic Capitalism* (1979). M. J. Mamalakis, *The Growth and Structure of the Chilean Economy from Independence to Allende* (1976). Maurice Zeitlin and R. E. Ratcliff, *Landlords and Capitalists: The Dominant Class of Chile* (1988).

Brian Loveman, *Struggle in the Countryside: Politics and Rural Labor in Chile, 1919–1973* (1976). Peter Deshazo, *Urban Workers and Labor Unions in Chile, 1902–1927* (1983). Thomas Miller Klubock, *Contested Communities: Class, Gender, and Politics in Chile's El Teniente Copper Mine, 1904–1948* (1998). Elizabeth Quay Hutchison, *Labors Appropriate to Their Sex: Gender, Labor, and Politics in Urban Chile, 1900–1930* (2001). Heidi Tinsman, *Partners in Conflict: The Politics of Gender, Sexuality, and Labor in the Chilean Agrarian Reform, 1950–1973* (2002). Peter Winn, *Weavers of Revolution: The Yarur Workers and Chile's Road to Socialism* (1989). Edy Kaufman, *Crises in Allende's Chile* (1988). Barbara Stallings, *Class Conflict and Economic Development in Chile, 1958–1973* (1978). James Petras and Morris Morley, *The United States and Chile* (1976). Margaret Power, *Right-Wing Women in Chile: Feminine Power and the Struggle Against Allende, 1964–1973* (2002).

J. S. Valenzuela and Arturo Valenzuela, eds., *Military Rule in Chile: Dictatorship and Oppositions* (1986). J. R. Ramos, *Neo-Conservative Economics in the Southern Cone of Latin America, 1973–1983* (1986). L. H. Oppenheim, *Politics in Chile: Democracy, Authoritarianism, and the Search for Development* (1993). James Petras and F. I. Leiva, with Henry Veltmeyer, *Democracy and Poverty in Chile* (1994). Annie G. Dandavati, *The Women's Movement and the Transition to Democracy in Chile* (1996). Marjorie Agosin, *Tapestries of Hope, Threads of Love: The Arpillera Movement in Chile, 1974–1994* (1996). Joseph Collins et al., *Chile's Free Market Miracle: A Second Look* (1995). Eduardo Silva, *The State and Capital in Chile: Business Elites, Technocrats, and Market Economics* (1996).

Chapter 15
Republican Brazil

R. M. Schneider, *"Order and Progress": A Political History of Brazil* (1991). June E. Hahner, *Emancipating the Female Sex: The Struggle for Women's Rights in Brazil, 1850–1940* (1990). Susan Kent Besse, *Restructuring Patriarchy: The Modernization of Gender Inequality in Brazil, 1914–1940* (1996). George Reid Andrews, *Blacks and Whites in Sao Paulo, Brazil, 1888–1988* (1991). Kim D. Butler, *Freedoms Given, Freedoms Won: Afro-Brazilians in Post-Abolition Sao Paulo and Salvador* (1998). Joel Wolfe, *Working Women, Working Men: Sao Paulo and the Rise of Brazil's Industrial Working Class, 1900–1955* (1993). John D. French, *The Brazilian*

Workers' ABC: Class Conflict and Alliances in Modern Sao Paulo (1992). Barbara Weinstein, *For Social Peace in Brazil: Industrialists and the Remaking of the Working Class in Sao Paulo, 1920–1964* (1996). Teresa A. Meade, *"Civilizing" Rio: Reform and Resistance in a Brazilian City, 1889–1930* (1997).

Cliff Welch, *The Seed Was Planted: The Sao Paulo Roots of Brazil's Rural Labor Movement, 1924–1964* (1999). Biorn Maybury-Lewis, *The Politics of the Possible: The Brazilian Rural Workers' Trade Union Movement, 1964–1985* (1994). Christopher Dunn, *Brutality Garden: Tropicália and the Emergence of a Brazilian Counterculture* (2001). Hermano Vianna, *The Mystery of Samba: Popular Music and National Identity in Brazil* (1999). John Wirth, ed., *State and Society in Brazil: Continuity and Change* (1987). M. E. Keck, *The Workers' Party and Democratization in Brazil* (1992). S. A. M. Sandoval, *Social Change and Labor Unrest in Brazil Since 1945* (1994).

Sonia E. Alvarez, *Engendering Democracy in Brazil: Women's Movements in Transition Politics* (1990). Nancy Scheper-Hughes, *Death Without Weeping: The Violence of Everyday Life in Brazil* (1992). Michael George Hanchard, *Orpheus and Power: The Movimento Negro of Rio De Janeiro and Sao Paulo, Brazil, 1945–1988* (1994). Warren Dean, *With Broadax and Firebrand: The Destruction of the Brazilian Atlantic Forest* (1997).

Chapter 16
Storm over the Andes: The Struggle for Land and Development

C. M. Conaghan and J. S. Malloy, *Unsettling Statecraft: Democracy and Neoliberalism in the Central Andes* (1994). H. S. Klein, *Bolivia: The Evolution of a Multi-Ethnic Society* (1982). James Malloy and Eduardo Gamarra, *Revolution and Reaction: Bolivia, 1964–1985* (1988). June Nash, *We Eat the Mines and the Mines Eat Us: Dependency and Exploitation in Bolivian Tin Mines* (1979). Lesley Gill, *Precarious Dependencies: Gender, Class, and Domestic Service in Bolivia* (1994). W. Q. Morales, *Bolivia, Land of Struggle* (1994).

Anita Isaacs, *Military Rule and Transition in Ecuador* (1994). C. M. Conaghan, *Restructuring Domination: Industrialists and the State in Ecuador* (1988). N. E. Whitten, Jr., *Cultural Transformations and Ethnicity in Ecuador* (1981).

Paul Gootenberg, *Between Silver and Guano: Commercial Policy and the State in Postrevolutionary Peru* (1991). David G. Becker, *The New Bourgeoisie and the Limits of Dependency: Mining, Class, and Power in Revolutionary Peru* (1983). Nils Jacobsen, *Mirages of Transition: The Peruvian Altiplano, 1780–1930* (1994). J. C. Mariategui, *Seven Interpretive Essays on Peruvian Reality* (1971). R. F. Watters, *Poverty and Peasantry in Peru's Southern Andes* (1993).

Thomas Turino, *Moving Away from Silence: Music of the Peruvian Altiplano and the Experience of Urban Migration* (1993). Raul R. Romero, *Debating the Past: Music, Memory, and Identity in the Andes* (2001). Vincent C. Peloso, *Peasants on Plantations: Subaltern Strategies of Labor and Resistance in the Pisco Valley, Peru* (1998). Jorge Parodi Solari, *To Be a Worker: Identity and Politics in Peru* (2000).

Tom Alberts, *Agrarian Reform and Rural Poverty: A Case Study of Peru* (1983). Rosemary Thorp and Geoffrey Bertram, *Peru, 1890–1977: Growth and Policy in an Open Economy* (1978). J. D. Rudolph, *Peru: The Evolution of a Crisis* (1992). Elsa Chaney and Ximena Bunster, *Sellers and Servants: Working Women in Lima, Peru* (1988). Carol Andreas, *When Women Rebel: The Rise of Popular Feminism in Peru* (1986). Susan C. Stokes, *Cultures in Conflict: Social Movements and the State in Peru* (1995). D. S. Palmer, ed., *Shining Path of Peru* (1992).

Chapter 17
The Cuban Revolution

Hugh Thomas, *Cuba: The Pursuit of Freedom* (1971). Ramiro Guerra y Sanchez, *Sugar and Society in the Caribbean* (1964). F. W. Knight, *Slave Society in Nineteenth Century Cuba* (1970). R. J. Scott, *Slave Emancipation in Cuba: The Transition to Free Labor* (1985).

P. S. Foner, *The Spanish-American-Cuban War, 1895–1906* (1972). L. A. Pérez, *Cuba Under the Platt Amendment, 1902–1934* (1984). Louis A. Pérez, *Cuba: Between Reform and Revolution* (1995). K. Lynn Stoner, *From the House to the Streets: The Cuban Woman's Movement for Legal Reform, 1898–1940* (1991). Aline Helg, *Our Rightful Share: The Afro-Cuban Struggle for Equality, 1886–1912* (1995). Robin Moore, *Nationalizing Blackness: Afrocubanismo and Artistic Revolution in Havana, 1920–1940* (1997). Louis A. Pérez, Jr., *On Becoming Cuban: Identity, Nationality, and Culture* (2001). Alejandro de la Fuente, *A Nation for All: Race, Inequality, and Politics in Twentieth-Century Cuba* (2001).

J. R. O'Connor, *The Origins of Socialism in Cuba* (1970). Lee Lockwood, *Castro's Cuba, Cuba's Fidel*, 2nd ed. (1990). S. B. Liss, *Fidel! Castro's Political and Social Thought* (1994). Marifeli Pérez-Stable, *The Cuban Revolution: Origins, Course, and Legacy* (1993). Lois M. Smith, *Sex and Revolution: Women in Socialist Cuba* (1996). Susan Eckstein, *Back from the Future: Cuba Under Castro* (1994). Carollee Bengelsdorf, *The Problem of Democracy in Cuba: Between Vision and Reality* (1994). Mona Rosendahl, *Inside the Revolution: Everyday Life in Socialist Cuba* (1998).

Andrew Zimbalist and Claes Brundenius, *The Cuban Economy: Measurement and Analysis of Socialist Performance* (1989). Sandor Halebsky and J. M. Kirk, eds., *Cuba: Twenty-Five Years of Revolution, 1959–1984* (1985). Jorge Domínguez, *To Make the World Safe for Revolution* (1988). T. C. Dalton, *"Everything Within the Revolution": Cuban Strategies for Development Since 1960* (1993).

Chapter 18
Revolution and Counterrevolution in Central America: Twilight of the Tyrants?

R. L. Woodward, Jr., *Central America: A Nation Divided* (1976). James Dunkerley, *Power in the Isthmus: A Political History of Modern Central America* (1988). F. S. Weaver, *Inside the Volcano. The History and Political Economy of Central America* (1994). William Roseberry, Lowell Gudmundson, and Mario Samper Kutschback, eds., *Coffee, Society, and Power in Latin America* (1995). Jeffrey M. Paige, *Coffee and Power: Revolution and the Rise of Democracy in Central America* (1998). Aldo Lauria-Santiago and Aviva Chomsky, eds., *At the Margins of the Nation State: Identity and Struggle in the Making of the Laboring Peoples of Central America and the Hispanic Caribbean* (1998).

R. L. Woodward, Jr., *Rafael Carrera and the Emergence of the Republic of Guatemala, 1821–1871* (1993). W. H. Clegern, *The Origins of Liberal Dictatorship in Central America. Guatemala, 1865–1973* (1994). Suzanne Jonas, *The Battle for Guatemala: Rebels, Death Squads, and U.S. Power* (1991). P. J. Dosal, *Doing Business with the Dictators: A Political History of United Fruit in Guatemala, 1899–1944* (1993). Deborah J. Yashar, *Demanding Democracy: Reform and Reaction in Costa Rica and Guatemala, 1870s–1950s* (1997). Deborah Levenson-Estrada, *Trade Unionists Against Terror: Guatemala City 1954–1985* (1994). Tracy Bachrach Ehlers, *Silent Looms: Women and Production in a Guatemalan Town* (1990). Robert M. Carmack, *Rebels of Highland Guatemala: The Quiché-Mayas of Momostenango* (1995). C. A. Smith, ed., *Guatemalan Indians and the State* (1990). Ricardo Falla, *Massacre in the Jungle: Ixcan, Guatemala, 1975–1982*, tr. Julia Howland (1994).

E. B. Burns, *Patriarch and Folk: The Emergence of Nicaragua, 1798–1858* (1991). Jeffrey L. Gould, *To Die in This Way: Nicaraguan Indians and the Myth of the Mestizaje, 1880–1960* (1998). Charles R. Hale, *Resistance and Contradiction: Miskitu Indians and the Nicaraguan State, 1894–1987* (1994). T. W. Walker, *Nicaragua: The Land of Sandino*, 3rd ed. (1991). Gregorio Selser, *Sandino*, tr. Cedric Belfrage (1981). D. C. Hodges, *The Intellectual Foundation of the Nicaraguan Revolution* (1986). Gary Prevost and Harry E. Vanden, eds., *The Undermining of the Sandinista Revolution* (1997). Thomas W. Walker, ed., *Nicaragua Without Illusions: Regime Transition and Structural Adjustment in the 1990s* (1997). Laura J. Enríquez, *Agrarian Reform and Class Consciousness in Nicaragua* (1997). Margaret Randall, *Sandino's Daughters Revisited: Feminism in Nicaragua* (1994). Carlos M. Vilas, *State, Class, and Ethnicity in Nicaragua: Capitalist Modernization and Revolutionary Change on the Atlantic Coast* (1989). Hazel Smith, *The Nicaraguan Revolution: Self-Determination and Survival* (1993).

T. P. Anderson, *Matanza: El Salvador's Revolt of 1932* (1971). T. S. Montgomery, *Revolution in El Salvador, Origins and Evolution*, 2nd ed. (1994). Marilyn Thomson, *Women of El Salvador: The Price of Freedom* (1986). Maria Teresa Tula and Lynn Stephen, *Hear My Testimony: The Story of Maria Teresa Tula, Human Rights Activist of El Salvador* (1994). Leigh Binford, *The El Mozote Massacre: Anthropology and Human Rights* (1996). Philip J. Williams and Knut Walter, *In the Shadow of the Barracks: Militarization and Demilitarization in El Salvador's Transition to Democracy* (1998).

Chapter 19
Lands of Bolívar: Venezuela and Colombia in the Twentieth Century

Judith Ewell, *Venezuela, A Century of Change* (1984). D. C. Hellinger, *Venezuela: Tarnished Democracy* (1991). Winthrop R. Wright, *Cafe Con Leche: Race, Class, and National Image in Venezuela* (1993). Judith Ewell, *Venezuela and the United States: From Monroe's Hemisphere to Petroleum's Empire* (1996).

B. S. McBeth, *Juan Vicente Gomez and the Oil Companies in Venezuela* (1983). Douglas Yarrington, *A Coffee Frontier: Land, Society, and Politics in Duaca, Venezuela, 1830–1936* (1997). Steve Ellner, *Organized Labor in Venezuela 1958–1991* (1993). Terry Lynn Karl, *The Paradox of Plenty: Oil Booms and Petro-States* (1997). Jennifer McCoy et al., *Venezuelan Democracy Under Stress* (1995). Elisabeth J. Friedman, *Unfinished Transitions: Women and the Gendered Development of Democracy in Venezuela, 1936–1996* (2000).

David Bushnell, *The Making of Modern Colombia: A Nation in Spite of Itself* (1993). Jonathan Hartlyn, *Politics of Coalition Rule in Colombia* (1988). Jenny Pearce, *Colombia: Inside the Labyrinth* (1990). Michael Taussig, *Shamanism, Colonialism, and the Wild Man: A Study in Terror and Healing* (1991). Peter Wade, *Blackness and Race Mixture: The Dynamics of Racial Identity in Colombia* (1993). Ann Farnsworth-Alvear, *Dulcinea in the Factory: Myths, Morals, Men and Women in Colombia's Industrial Experiment, 1905–1960* (2000). Peter Wade, *Music, Race, and Nation: Música Tropical in Colombia* (2000).

David Sowell, *The Early Colombian Labor Movement: Artisans and Politics in Bogotá, 1832–1919* (1992). Marco Palacios, *Coffee in Colombia, 1850–1870: An Economic, Social, and Political History* (1980). Charles Bergquist, *Coffee and Conflict in Colombia* (1976). James Park, *Rafael Núñez and the Politics of Colombian Regionalism* (1985). Catherine LeGrand, *Frontier Expansion and Peasant Protest in Colombia* (1986). Herbert Braun, *The Assassination of Gaitan: Public Life and Urban Violence in Colombia* (1986). James Henderson, *When Colombia Bled: A History of the Violencia in Tolima* (1985). Charles Bergquist et al., *Violence in Colombia: The Contemporary Crisis in Historical Perspective* (1992).

Chapter 20
The Two Americas: United States—Latin American Relations

Harold Molineu, *U.S. Policy Toward Latin America: From Regionalism to Globalism* (1986). Michael L. Krenn, *Race and U.S. Foreign Policy from the Colonial Period to the Present* (1998). Walter LaFeber, *The Cambridge History of American Foreign Relations: The American Search for Opportunity, 1865–1913* (1993). Michael L. Krenn, *U.S. Policy Toward Economic Nationalism in Latin America, 1917–1929* (1990). Thomas J. McCormick, *America's Half-Century: United States Foreign Policy in the Cold War and After* (1995). Frank Niess, *A Hemisphere to Itself: A History of U.S.-Latin American Relations* (1990). Dean B. Mahin, *Olive Branch and Sword: The United States and Mexico, 1845–1848* (1997). J. W. Park, *Latin American Underdevelopment: A History of Perspectives in the United States, 1870–1965* (1995).

L. D. Langley, *The Banana Wars: An Inner History of American Empire, 1900–1934* (1983). J. R. Benjamin, *The United States and Cuba: Hegemony and Dependent Development, 1880–1934* (1974). J. R. Benjamin, *The United States and the Origins of the Cuban Revolution: An Empire of Liberty in an Age of National Liberation* (1990). Morris Morley, *Imperial State and Revolution: The U.S. and Cuba, 1952–86* (1987). Piero Gleijeses, *Conflicting Missions: Havana, Washington, and Africa, 1959–1976* (2002). Peter Kornbluh, ed., *Bay of Pigs Declassified: The Secret CIA Report on the Invasion of Cuba* (1998).

J. L. Dietz, *The Economic History of Puerto Rico* (1986). A. Morales Carrion, *Puerto Rico: A Political and Cultural History* (1983). Richard Weiskoff, *Factories and Foodstamps: The Puerto Rican Model of Development* (1985). Pedro Cabán, *Constructing a Colonial People: Puerto Rico and the United States, 1898–1932* (2000).

S. L. Baily, *The United States and the Development of South America, 1845–1975* (1976). David Green, *The Containment of Latin America: A History of the Myths and Realities of the Good Neighbor Policy* (1971). Bryce Wood, *The Dismantling of the Good Neighbor Policy* (1985). Cole Blasier, *The Hovering Giant* (1986).

Ruth Leacock, *Requiem for Revolution: The United States and Brazil, 1961–1969* (1990). Ariel C. Armony, *Argentina, the United States, and the Anti-Communist Crusade in Central America, 1977–1984* (1997). Stephen G. Rabe, *The Road to OPEC: United States Relations with Venezuela, 1919–1976* (1982). Stephen J. Randall, *Colombia and the United States: Hegemony and Interdependence* (1992). Sewall H. Menzel, *Fire in the Andes: U.S. Foreign Policy and Cocaine Politics in Bolivia and Peru* (1996). Jon V. Kofas, *Foreign Debt and Underdevelopment: U.S.–Peru Economic Relations, 1930–1970* (1996). G. K. Lewis, *Grenada: The Jewel Despoiled* (1986). Michel-Rolph Trouillot, *Haiti: State Against Nation: The Origin and Legacy of Duvalierism* (1990). Amy Wilentz, *The Rainy Season: Haiti Since Duvalier* (1990). Alex Dupuy, *Haiti in the New World Order: The Limits of the Democratic Revolution* (1997). J. Zoraida Vasquez and Lorenzo Meyer, *The United States and Mexico* (1986).

Walter LaFeber, *Inevitable Revolutions: The United States in Central America* (1993). Walter LaFeber, *The Panama Canal* (1990). Luis E. Murillo, *The Noriega Mess: The Drugs, the Canal, and Why America Invaded* (1995). Piero Gleijeses, *Shattered Hope: The Guatemalan Revolution and the United States, 1944–1954* (1991). Morris H. Morley, *Washington, Somoza, and the Sandinistas: State and Regime in U.S. Policy Toward Nicaragua, 1969–1981* (1994). E. B. Burns, *At War in Nicaragua: The Reagan Doctrine and the Politics of Nostalgia* (1987). W. L. Robinson, *A Faustian Bargain: U.S. Intervention in the Nicaraguan Elections and American Foreign Policy in the Post–Cold War Era* (1992). P. D. Scott and Jonathan Marshall, *Cocaine Politics: Drugs, Armies, and the CIA in Central America* (1991).

Eldon Kenworthy, *America/Americas: Myth in the Making of U.S. Policy Toward Latin America* (1995). Mark T. Berger, *Under Northern Eyes: Latin American Studies and U.S. Hegemony in the Americas, 1898–1990* (1995). Lars Schoultz, *Beneath the United States: A History of U.S. Policy Toward Latin America* (1998). William I. Robinson, *Promoting Polyarchy: Globalization, U.S. Intervention, and Hegemony* (1996). Philip Oxhorn and Graciela Ducatenzeiler, eds., *What Kind of Democracy? What Kind of Market? Latin America in the Age of Neoliberalism* (1998).

Chapter 21
Latin American Society in Transition

Suzanne Jonas and E. J. McCaughan, eds., *Latin America Faces the Twenty-First Century: Reconstructing a Social Justice Agenda* (1994). M. S. Grindle, *State and Countryside: Development Policy and Agrarian Politics in Latin America* (1986). Rachel Garst and Tom Barry, *Feeding the Crisis: U.S. Food and Farm Policy in Central America* (1990). David Goodman and Michael Redclift, *Environment and Development in Latin America: The Politics of Sustainability* (1991). Alan Gilbert and P. M. Ward, *Housing: The State and the Poor: Policy and Practice in Three Latin American Cities* (1984). Alan Gilbert, *The Latin American City* (1994).

F. H. Cardoso and Enzo Faletto, *Dependency and Development in Latin America* (1979). Peter Evans, *Dependent Development: The Alliance of Multinational, State, and Local Capital in Brazil* (1979). Richard Farmer, ed., *Profits, Progress, and Poverty: Case Studies of International Industries in Latin America* (1985). D. C. Betts and D. J. Slottje, *Crisis on the Rio Grande: Poverty, Unemployment, and Economic Development on the Texas-Mexico Border* (1993). Duncan Green, *Silent Revolution: The Rise of Market Economies in Latin America* (1995).

J. J. Johnson, *Political Change in Latin America: The Emergence of the Middle Sectors* (1958). S. M. Lipset and Aldo Solari, eds., *Elites in Latin America* (1967). I. L. Horowitz, ed., *Masses in Latin America* (1970). Andrew Pearse, *The Latin American Peasantry* (1975). Alain de Janvry, *The Agrarian Question and Reformism in Latin America* (1981). H. A. Spalding, *Organized Labor in Latin America: Historical Case Studies of Workers in Dependent Societies* (1977). Charles Bergquist, *Labor in Latin America: Comparative Studies on Chile, Argentina, Venezuela, and Colombia* (1986). S. B. Liss, *Marxist Thought in Latin America* (1984).

J. S. Jaquette, ed., *The Women's Movement in Latin America: Participation and Democracy*, 2nd ed. (1994). H. I. Safa, *The Myth of the Male Breadwinner: Women and Industrialization in the Caribbean* (1994). Florestan Fernandes, *The Negro in Brazilian Society* (1969). G. R. Andrews, *Blacks and Whites in São Paulo, Brazil, 1888–1988* (1991). Francesca Miller, *Latin American Women and the Search for Social Justice* (1991). John D. French, ed., *The Gendered Worlds of Latin American Women Workers* (1997). Peter Wade, *Race and Ethnicity in Latin America* (1997).

Philip Berryman, *The Religious Roots of Rebellion* (1984). Rowan Ireland, *Kingdom Come: Religion and Politics in Brazil* (1992). E. L. and Hannah Stewart-Gambino, *Conflict and Competition: The Latin American Church in a Changing Environment* (1992). F. M. Nunn, *Yesterday's Soldiers: European Military Professionalism in South America, 1890–1940* (1983). J. K. Black, *Sentinels of Empire: The United States and Latin American Militarism* (1986).

Jean Franco, *An Introduction to Spanish-American Literature* (1969). John King, ed., *Modern Latin American Fiction* (1987). Cristobal Kay, *Latin American Theories of Development and Underdevelopment* (1989). William Rowe and Vivian Schelling, *Memory and Modernity: Popular Culture in Latin America* (1992). E. B. Burns, *Latin American Cinema: Film and History* (1978). Julianne Burton, *Cinema and Social Change in Latin America: Conversations with Filmmakers* (1986).

INDEX